Street by Street

MANCH

BOLTON, BURY, OLDHA. ᴕᴄHDALE, SALFORD, STOCKPORT

Altrincham, Ashton-under-Lyne, Bramhall, Hazel Grove, Hyde, Littleborough, Middleton, Prestwich, Ramsbottom, Sale, Stalybridge, Stretford, Wilmslow

2nd edition August 2003
© Automobile Association Developments Limited 2003

Original edition printed May 2001

Ordnance Survey® This product includes map data licensed from Ordnance Survey ® with the permission of the Controller of Her Majesty's Stationery Office. © Crown copyright 2003. All rights reserved. Licence No: 399221.

Published by AA Publishing (a trading name of Automobile Association Developments Limited, whose registered office is Millstream, Maidenhead Road, Windsor, Berkshire SL4 5GD. Registered number 1878835).

Mapping produced by the Cartography Department of The Automobile Association. (A1709)

A CIP Catalogue record for this book is available from the British Library.

Printed by GRAFIASA S.A., Porto, Portugal

The contents of this atlas are believed to be correct at the time of the latest revision. However, the publishers cannot be held responsible for loss occasioned to any person acting or refraining from action as a result of any material in this atlas, nor for any errors, omissions or changes in such material. This does not affect your statutory rights. The publishers would welcome information to correct any errors or omissions and to keep this atlas up to date. Please write to Publishing, The Automobile Association, Fanum House (FH17), Basing View, Basingstoke, Hampshire, RG21 4EA.

Ref: ML043z

Key to map pages	ii-iii
Key to map symbols	iv–1
Enlarged map pages	2-13
Main map pages	14-201
Index – towns & villages	202-203
Index – streets	204-257
Index – featured places	257-264
Acknowledgements	264

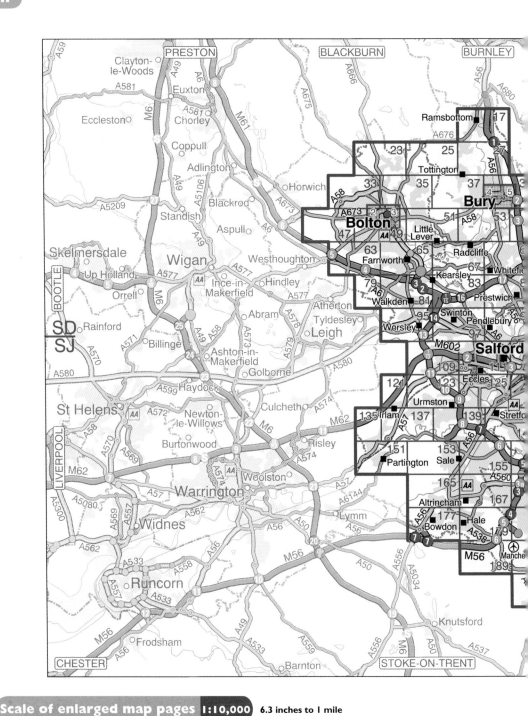

Scale of enlarged map pages 1:10,000   6.3 inches to 1 mile

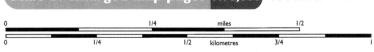

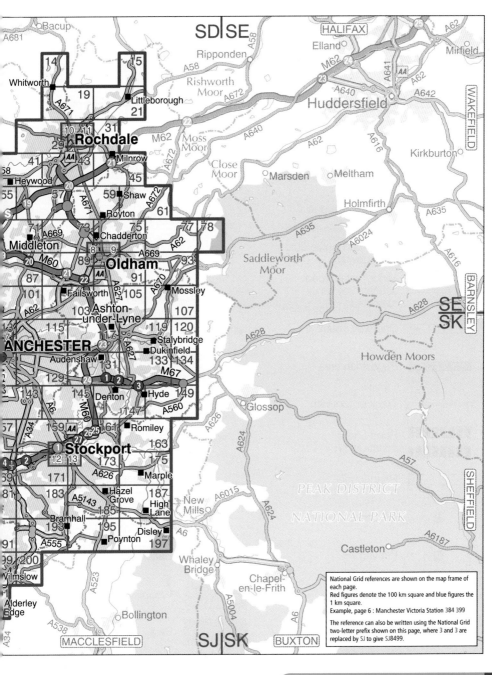

SD | SE

SJ | SK

SE
SK

National Grid references are shown on the map frame of each page.
Red figures denote the 100 km square and blue figures the 1 km square.
Example, page 6 : Manchester Victoria Station 384 399

The reference can also be written using the National Grid two-letter prefix shown on this page, where 3 and 3 are replaced by SJ to give SJ8499.

4.2 inches to 1 mile   **Scale of main map pages**   **1:15,000**

| 0 | 1/4 | miles | 1/2 | 3/4 | 1 |

| 0 | 1/4 | 1/2 | kilometres 3/4 | 1 | 1 1/4 | 1 1/2 |

Junction 9 Motorway & junction

Services Motorway service area

Primary road single/dual carriageway

Services Primary road service area

A road single/dual carriageway

B road single/dual carriageway

Other road single/dual carriageway

Minor/private road, access may be restricted

One-way street

Pedestrian area

Track or footpath

Road under construction

Road tunnel

AA AA Service Centre

P Parking

P+ Park & Ride

Bus/coach station

Railway & main railway station

Railway & minor railway station

Underground station

Light railway & station

Preserved private railway

LC Level crossing

Tramway

Ferry route

Airport runway

County, administrative boundary

Mounds

17 Page continuation 1:15,000

3 Page continuation to enlarged scale 1:10,000

River/canal, lake

Aqueduct, lock, weir

465
▲
Winter Hill Peak (with height in metres)

Beach

Woodland

Park

Cemetery

Built-up area

	Featured building		Abbey, cathedral or priory
	City wall		Castle
A&E	Hospital with 24-hour A&E department		Historic house or building
PO	Post Office	Wakehurst Place NT	National Trust property
	Public library	M	Museum or art gallery
i	Tourist Information Centre		Roman antiquity
i	Seasonal Tourist Information Centre		Ancient site, battlefield or monument
	Petrol station, 24-hour Major suppliers only		Industrial interest
†	Church/chapel		Garden
	Public toilets		Garden Centre Garden Centre Association Member
	Toilet with disabled facilities		Garden Centre Wyevale Garden Centre
PH	Public house AA recommended		Farm or animal centre
	Restaurant AA inspected		Zoological or wildlife collection
Madeira Hotel	Hotel AA inspected		Bird collection
	Theatre or performing arts centre		Nature reserve
	Cinema		Aquarium
	Golf course	V	Visitor or heritage centre
▲	Camping AA inspected		Country park
	Caravan site AA inspected		Cave
	Camping & caravan site AA inspected		Windmill
	Theme park		Distillery, brewery or vineyard

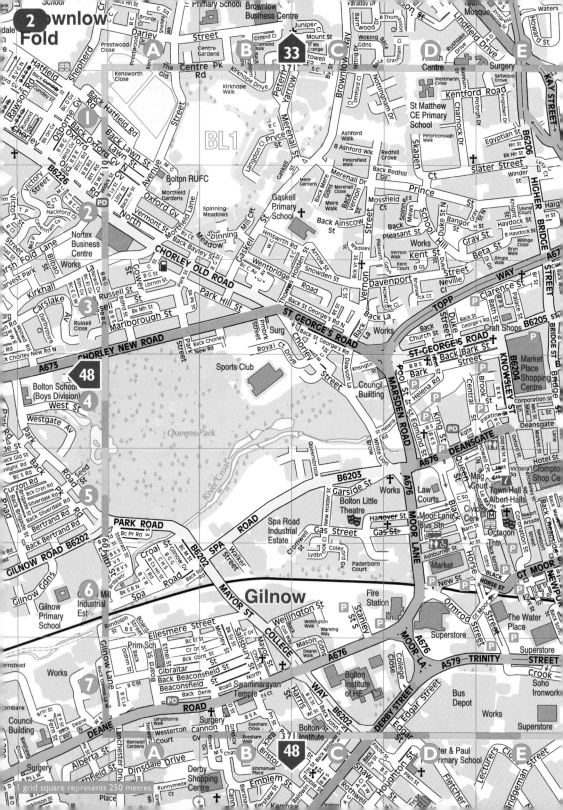

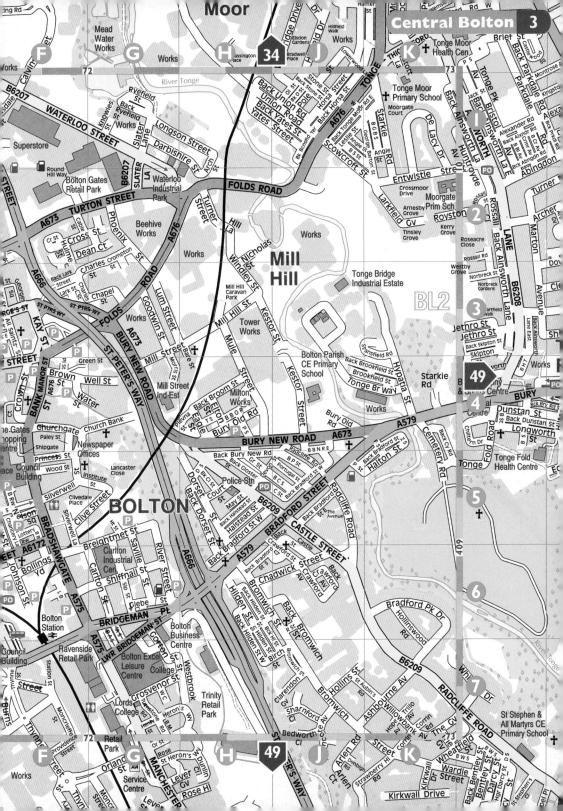

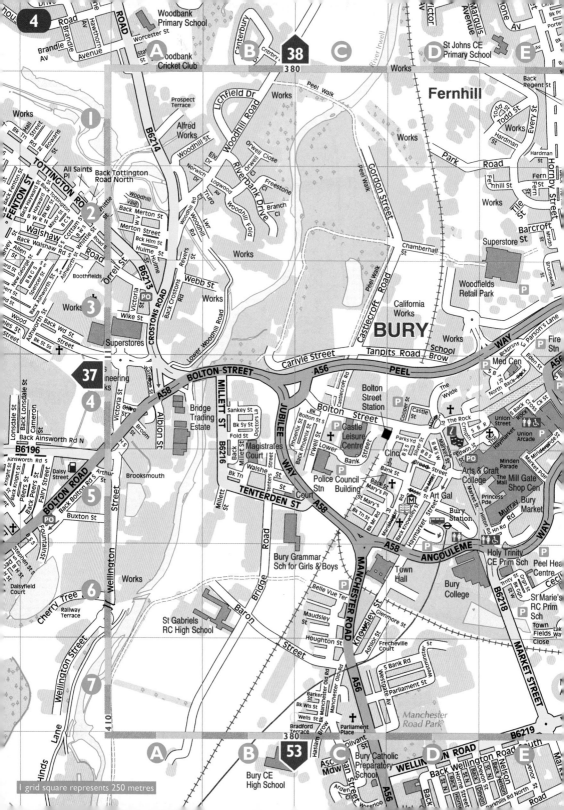

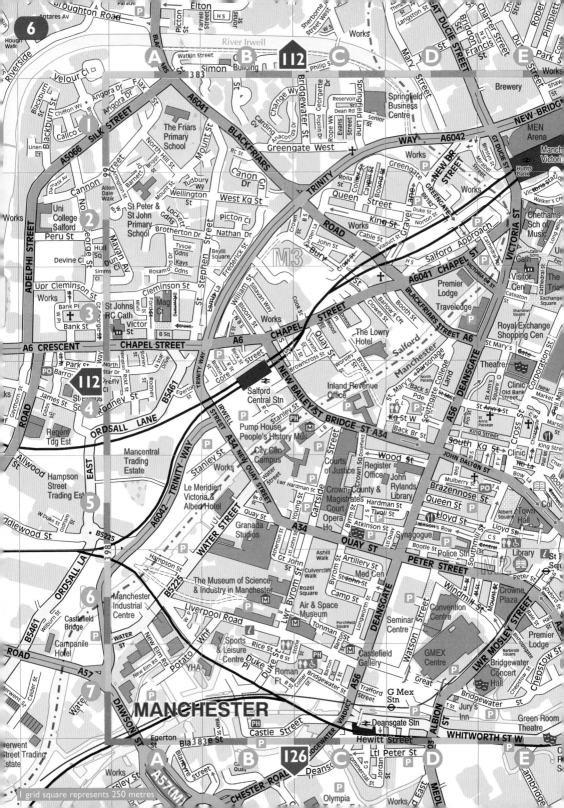

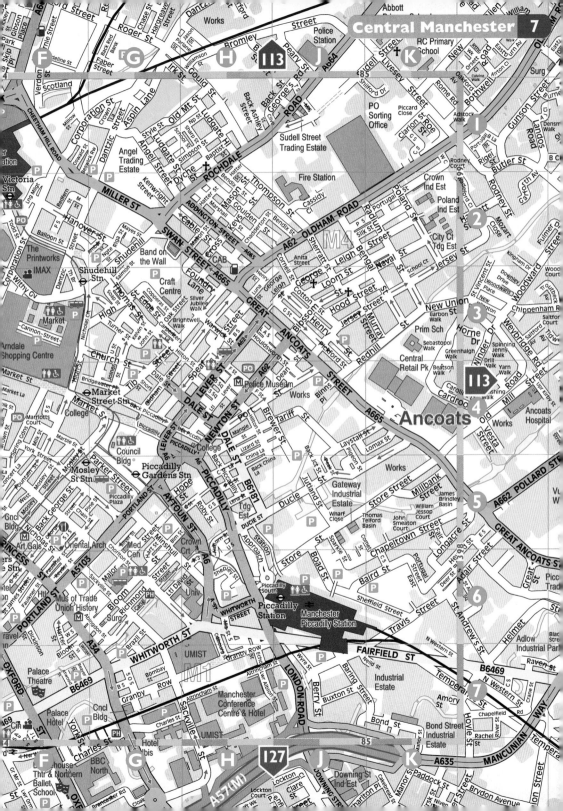

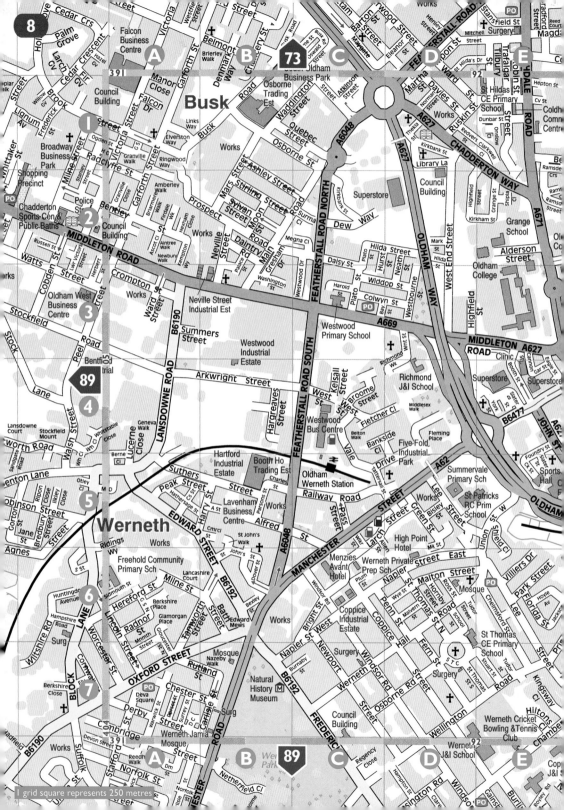

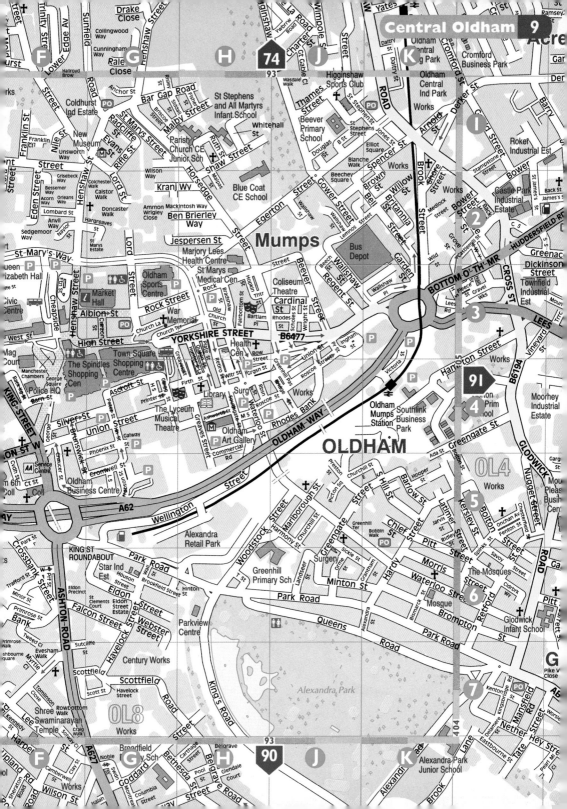

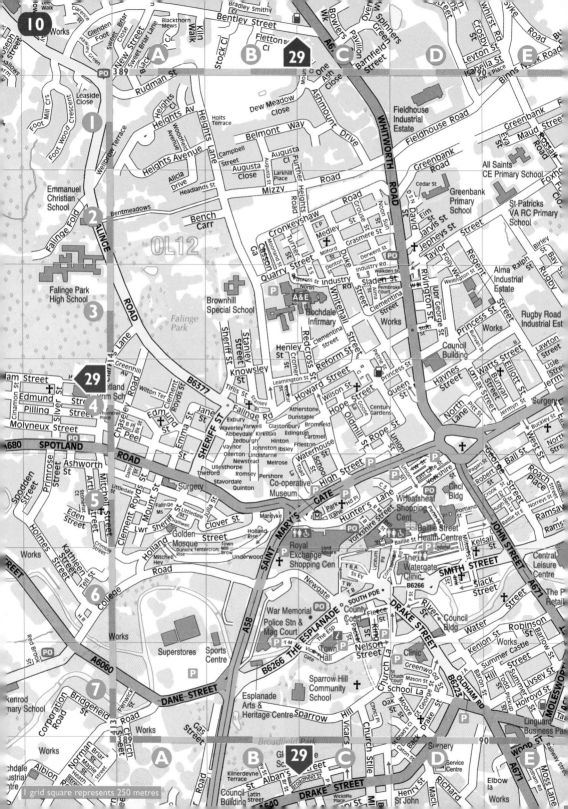

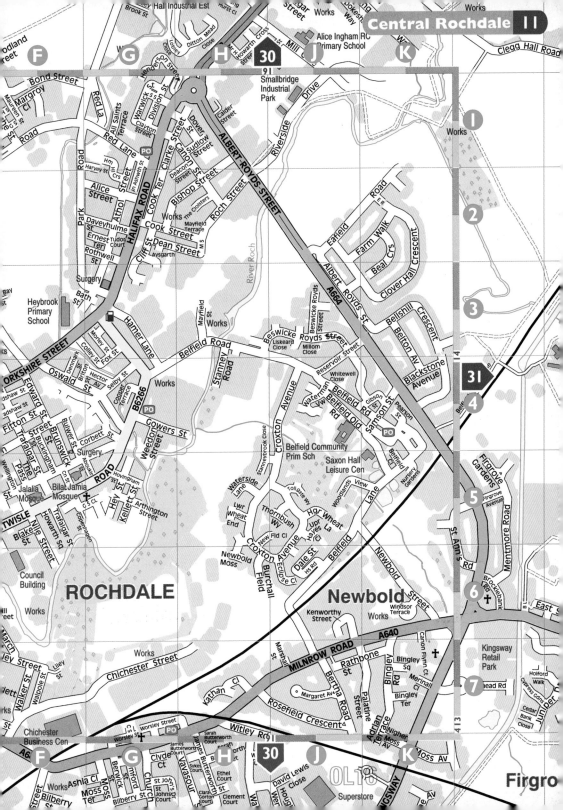

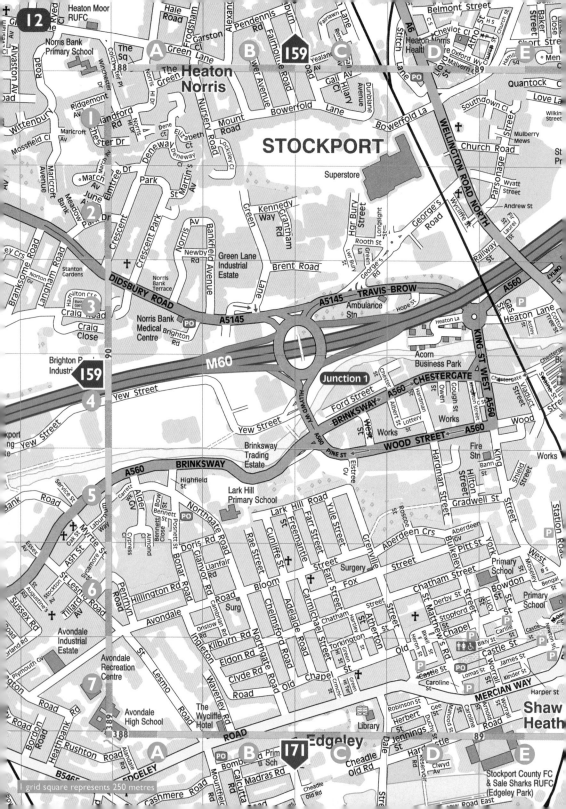

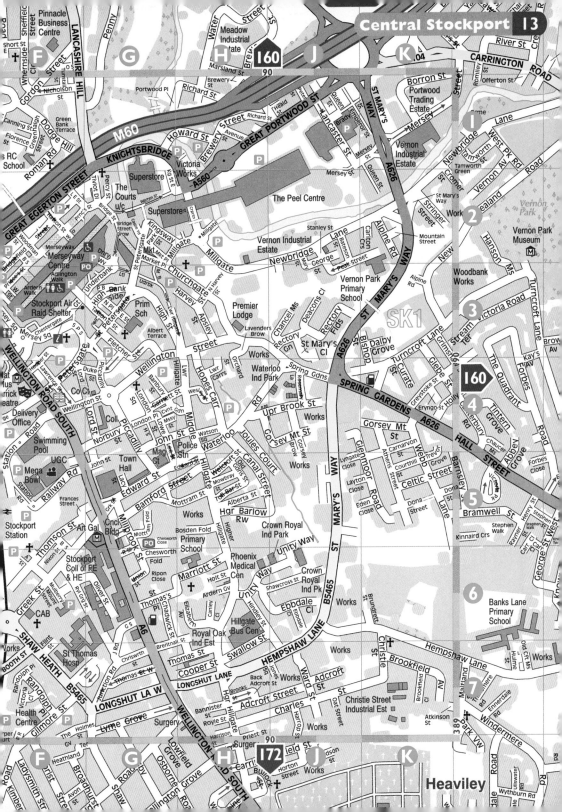

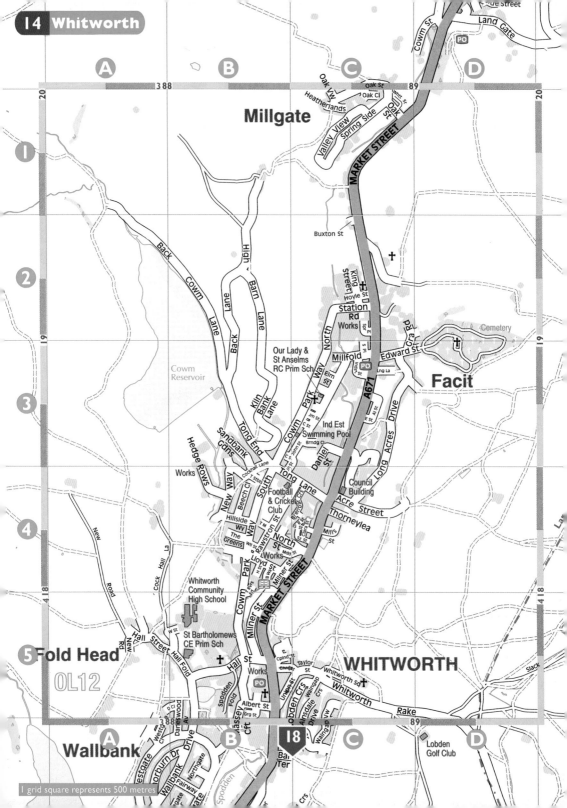

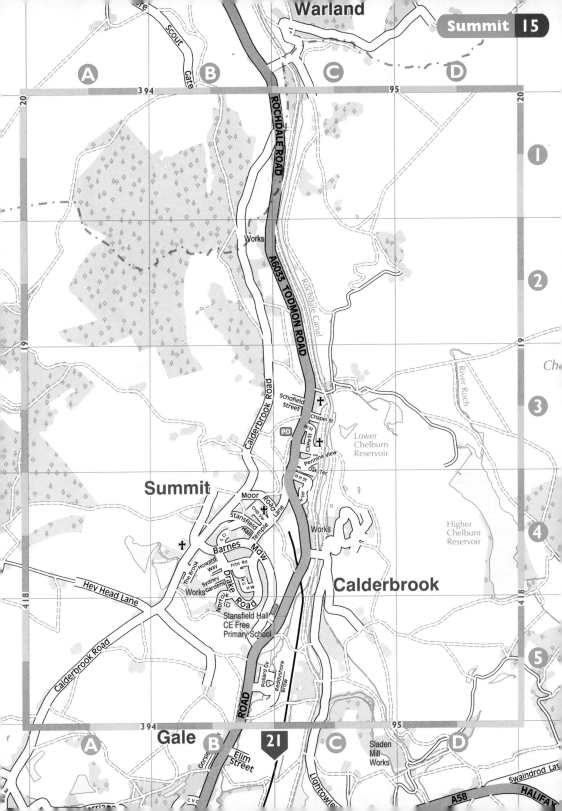

A   B   C   D

20   3 94   95   20

I

2

19   19

3

ROCHDALE ROAD

A6053 TODMON ROAD

Works

Rochdale Canal

River Roch

Ch

Schofield Street

Chapel St

PO

Pennine view

Oak Ter

Lower Chelburn Reservoir

Calderbrook Road

Summit

Moor

Road Lane

Stansfield Hall Temple

Higher Chelburn Reservoir

4

Barnes Mdw

Howard Way

The Brook

Sydney Gardens

Works

Frbs Rd

Drake Road

Nort'k

Works

Calderbrook

418   418

Hey Head Lane

Stansfield Hall CE Free Primary School

Calderbrook Road

5

Pollard Cv

Redpshore

Mdw

ROAD

A   B   21   C   D

20   3 94   95   20

Gale

Elim Street

Gorse

Sladen Mill Works

Swaindrod La

A58   HALIFAX

Lightowle

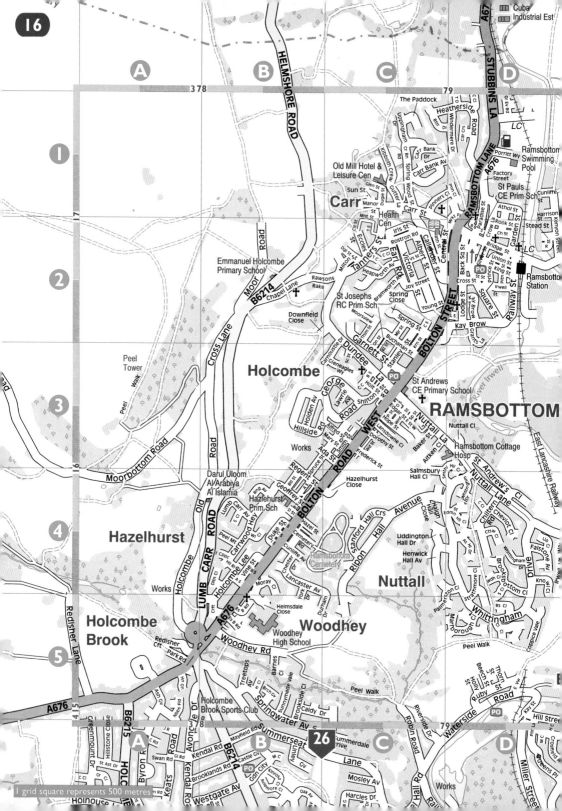

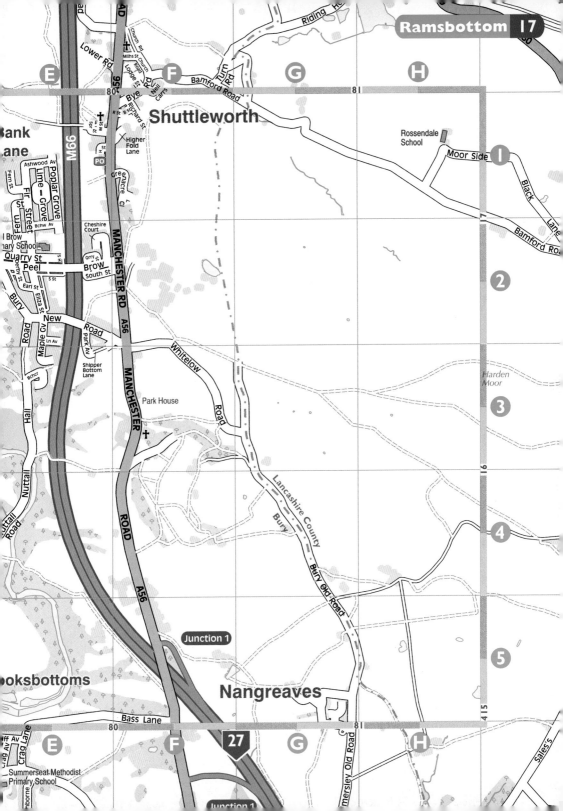

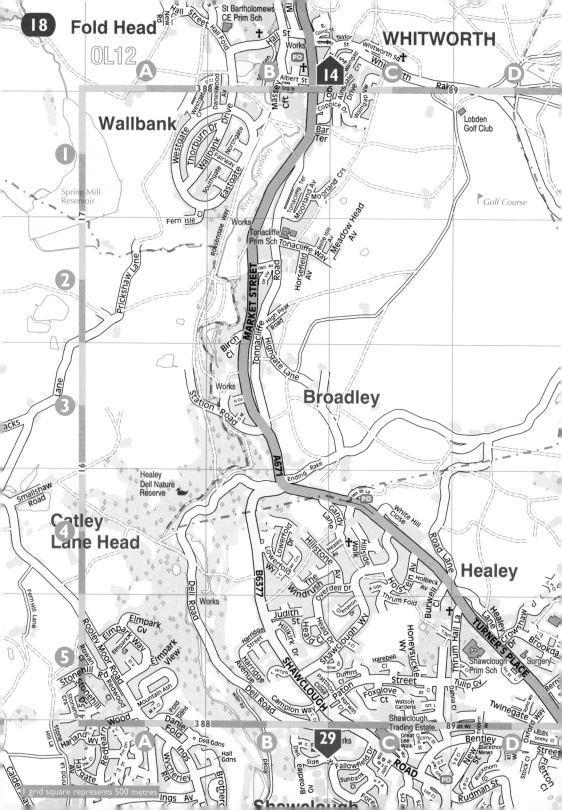

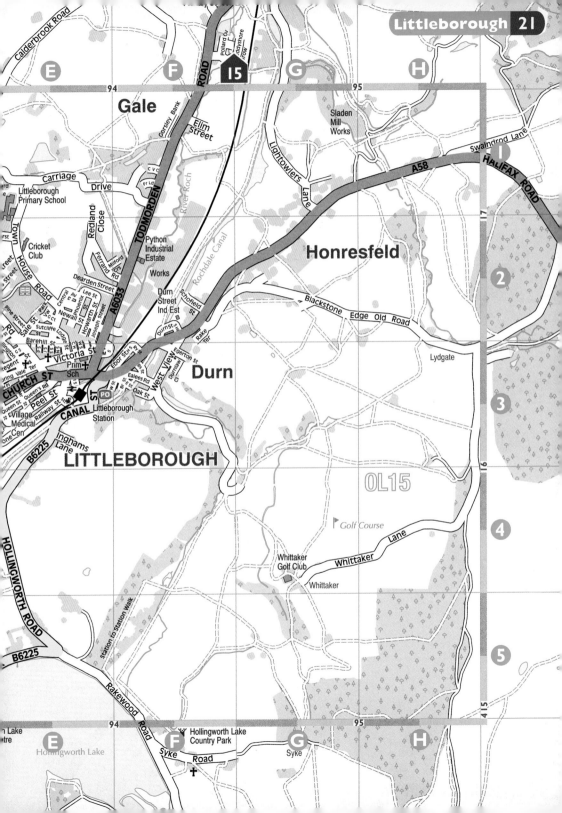

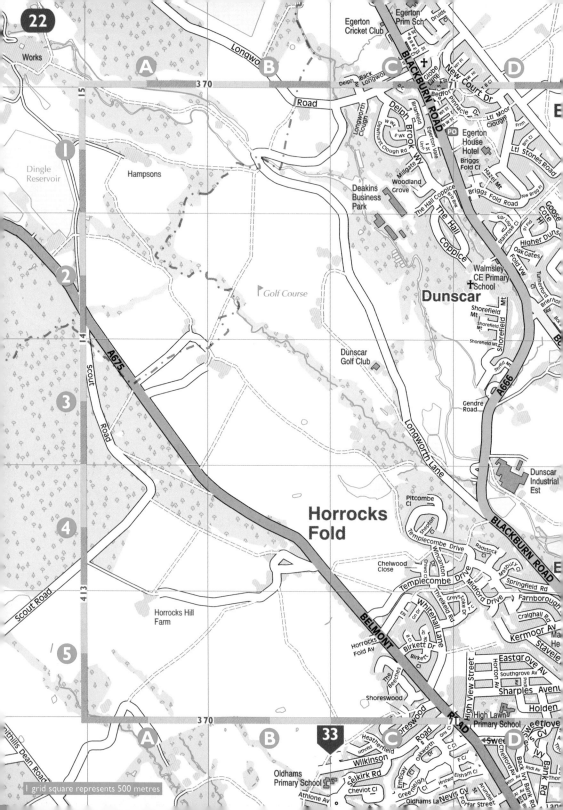

Turton Tower

E   F   G   H

72   73   I5

hittle Hill
arm

ton

1

Turton
Leisure Centre

B6391

The Copse

The Spinney

Horrobin La

Witton Weavers Way

Turton
Golf Club

Jumbles Reservoir

14

2

Jumbles C
Park

Golf Course

Cox Green

The Last
Drop Village

Last Drop
Hotel

CHAPELTOWN

ROAD

Kiln Brow

3

24

Cox Green Road

Rock Ter

Old Quarry La

Lowther
Md

Heath

Haydock Lane

Road

Haydock La

Broadmeadow

Windy Harbour La

Gleavin Way

High Meadow

Woodbrook Dr

Highland Rd

Longridge

Avenue

Jumbles C

Saxby Av

Conningsby

Somersby Dr

Thornby Dr

Institute of Islamic
Higher Education

Hospital

Elm Gv

Boonfields

Horseshoe Lane

Brow

Kibbles Brow

Eagley
Infant School

Crossfields

Hillside

Grange

Road

Bradshaw Brook

BRADSHAW RD

Arnold Road

Hargman's Rd

airfields

Ramwells

Eagley
Junior School

4

DARWEN

Smithy Crs

Stonesteads Wy

Sons Dr

Stonehouse

Montrose Dr

Grange Park Road

Long Meadow

Egerton & Dunscar
Health Cen

St John
RC Prim
Sch

Hardmans

Back Darwen Rd N

Old Barn Pl

Windsor Rd

The Crescent

Lwr House Wk

Rose Hill
Close

Turton
High School

Hgr Shady Lane

Forest Wy

Wood
Fold

Works

Bradshaw
Hall

A676

Bradshaw Meadows

Ridings

Lwr Tong

Hough Lane

Back Hough La

Lord's Stile Lane

Toppings

Bromley Cross Road

Shady

Alder
Gv

printers Lane

Hardcastle
Gdns

5

Bradshaw

School St

Paper Mill Rd

Queen's

Avenue

Birtenshaw Crs

Bromley
Cross Stn

Turton Hts

Beech

Rigby

New
Brook

Eagley
Way

Back Park V

Eagley Brow

Dales Brow

Wrenbury Cl

Bramley Rd

Chetwyn

Guild St

Eagley Brook

Bromley Cross

Turton Hts

Winterburn Av

Redshaw
Av

Seymour Dr

Rainford St

Poplar

Beech Cl

The Coppice

Westcliffe Rd

Andrew Lane

Ashover
Ci

Old Eagley
Ms

Thornham

Lakenheath
Dr

Ranworth

Drive

Hadleigh Dr

Birtenshaw Hall
School

Turton Road

Dell St

adshaw
Cricket
Club

St Maxentius
CE Primary
School

Sharples Hall Dr

The Oaks
Primary School

Barley Brook Meadow

Oulton St

Hugh Lupus St

Langh

Close

72

Aire

Ellerbeck Cl

Hebble Dr

Back Turton Rd E

Dene Bank

Lea

King

E   F   34   G   H

Sharples
Primary
School

Arnot Rd

Cotford Rd

Ashworth

Road

Hill

Bank Top

Ryeburn Dr

Fossgill

Laburnum

ON ROAD

LEE GATE

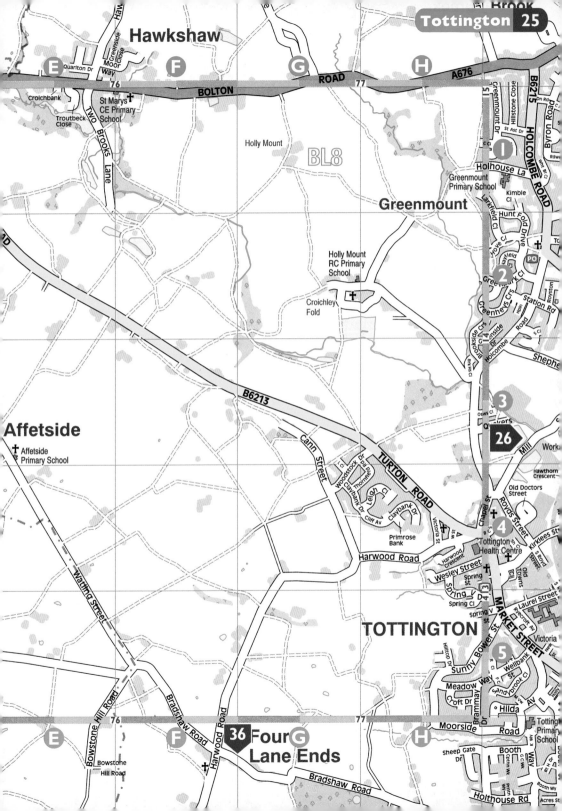

Brook

Hawkshaw

E Quarlton Dr

Croichbank

St Marys CE Primary School

Troutbeck Close

Greenside Moor Way

Hawkshaw

F

BOLTON

76

G

ROAD

77

H

A676

Holcombe La

Greenmount Dr

Hillstone Close

St Ast Dr

Don Rd

Byron Road

B6215

HOLCOMBE ROAD

Rdwfo

I

BL8

Holly Mount

Greenmount

Greenmount Primary School

Kimble Cl

Lankfield Cl

Hoye Cl

Hunt Fold Drive

TC

PO

2

Holly Mount RC Primary School

Croichley Fold

Greenhey's Crs

Lankfield

Station Rd

Royston

Brookside Dr

Brookside Cl

Holcombe

Road

S Cl

Shephe

Two Brooks Lane

Affetside

Affetside Primary School

B6213

Cann Street

Osws Cl

3

Quakers La

26

MILL

Work

Hawthorn Crescent

Old Doctors Street

Watling Street

Woodstock Dr

Clayban Dr

Thornfield

Leigh Cl

Cliff Av

Claybank Dr

Primrose Bank

TURTON ROAD

Victoria St

Chapel St

Royds Street

Kirklees St

S Royd Street

4

Tottington Health Centre

Harwood Road

Harwood Crescent

Wesley Street

Spring St

Old Crowns

TOTTINGTON

Spring Cl

Spring V

D4

3

Spring V

MARKET STREET

Laurel Street

Precroft Av

Victoria

5

Sunny Bower St

Hilltop D

Wellbank

Bramway Way

Sandybrook Cl

Bowstone Hill Road

Bradshaw Road

Meadow Way

Croft Dr

Hilda

AV

Tottington Primary School

E

76

Bowstone Hill Road

F

Harwood Road

36 Four G Lane Ends

Moorside Road

Sheep Gate Dr

H

Booth

Bradshaw Road

77

Holthouse Rd

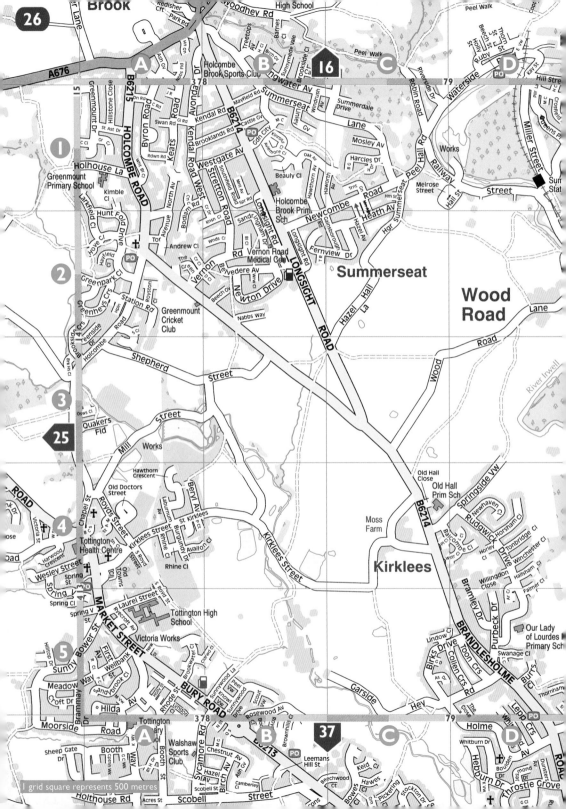

Brooksbottoms

Nangreaves

E F 17 G H

80 Bass Lane 81

I 15

Summerseat-Methodist
Primary School

Junction 1

M66

Baldingstone

2

Falshaw
Dr

WALMERSLEY ROAD

Burnley Rd

Brookfield
Road

Ribble Drive

Walmersley Old Road

Bentley Lane

White Carr Lane

Sales St

14

Golf

Wal
Golf

3

Guiseley
Close

Palatine Drive

Central
Dr

Lumn
St

Works

Peel

Trawden
Dr

Brierfield Dr

Walton Rd

School La

Mill
Road

Trent
Dr

Weaver
Dr

Avon Dr

Calder
Cl

PO

Springside
Road

Springside Road

Humber Dr

Chadwick
Fold

Works

4

Walmersley

Springside County
Primary School

Sabden Cl

Mather

Works

Corn field

Golf Course

Long Lane

Lime Gv

Limefield Brow

Lowes Park
Golf Club

5

Burrs
Country
Park

Peel

Limefield Rd

Southfield Av

Northfield
Rd

Hillside
Crs

Fairlands Rd

Sycamore Drive

Chestnut
Drive

Limefield

Halsall Rd

413

Plumpton
Drive

Burrswood

Eastham
Avenue

Back Walmersley Rd

Milbourne Rd

Hampton Gv

Sefton St

Greymont Rd

Woodman
Drive

Spinney Dr

Potters House
School

Arley Avenue

A56

Lowes Road

Talbot Rd

8

Woodhill Rd

Sleaford Cl

Yates Ter

Stock Street

E F 38 G H

Council
Building

Parkinson St

Mosley Avenue

Linton Av

VALMERSLEY

Chesham
Primary School

Higher
Woodhill

The Drive

Malvern Av

Milner Avenue

The Avenue

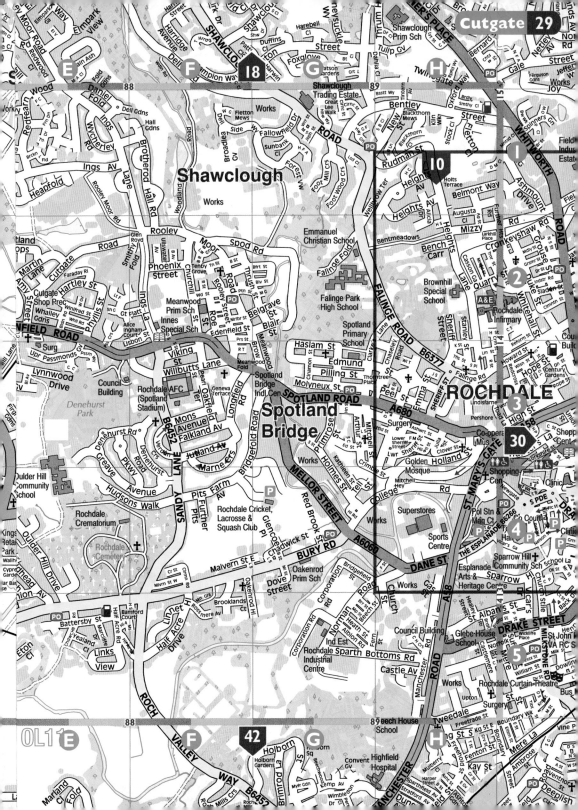

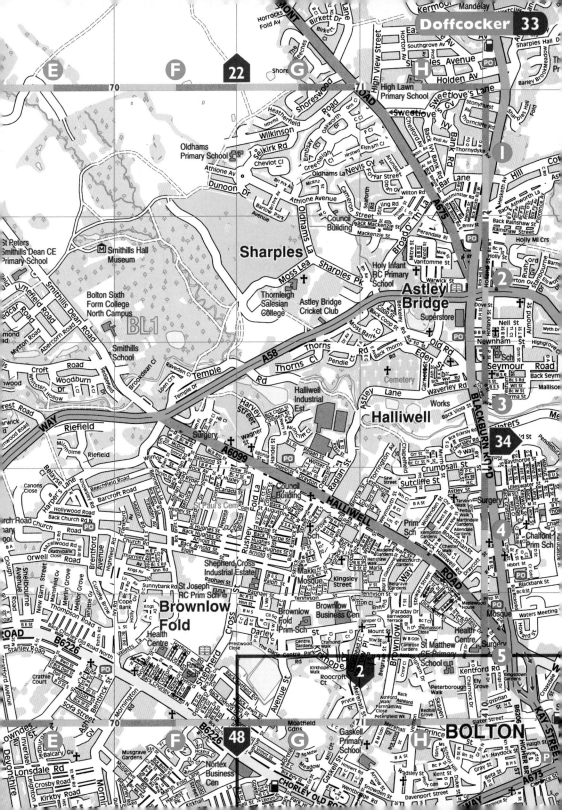

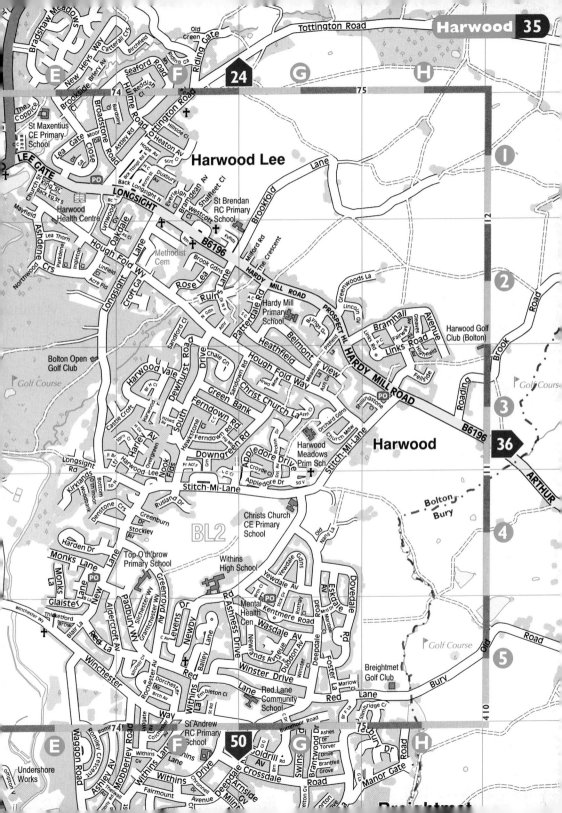

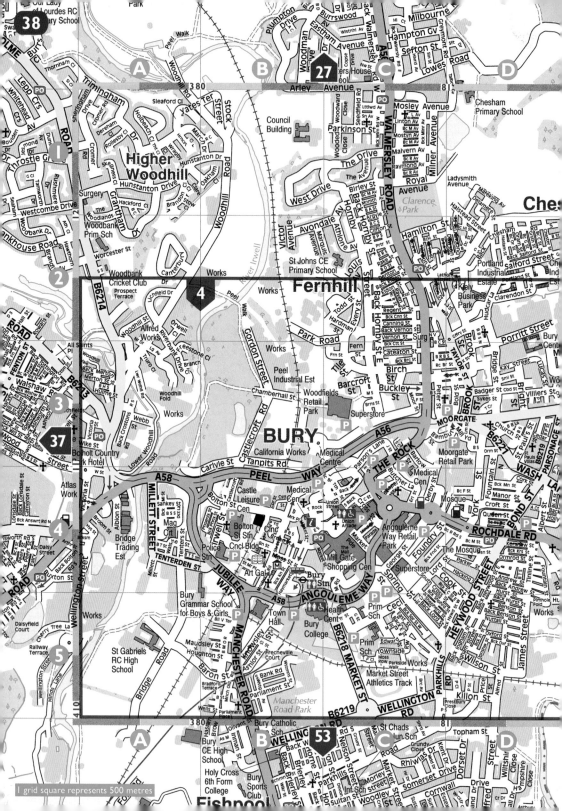

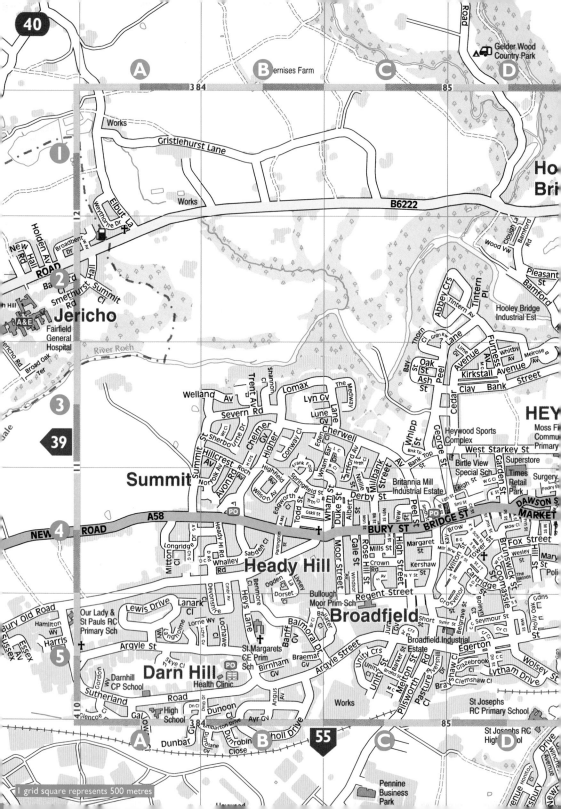

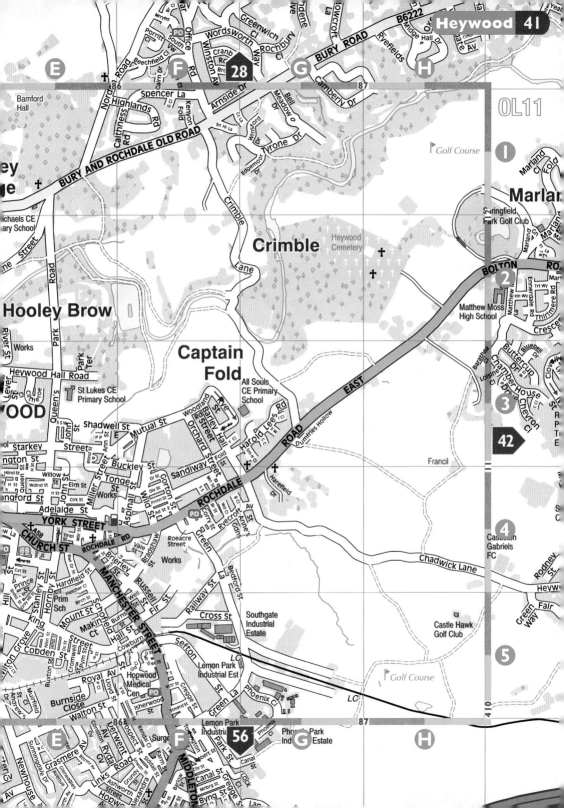

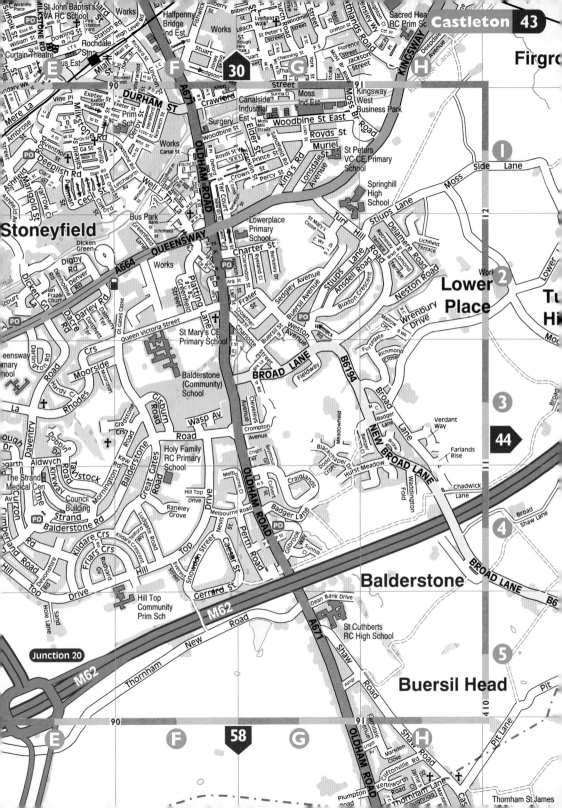

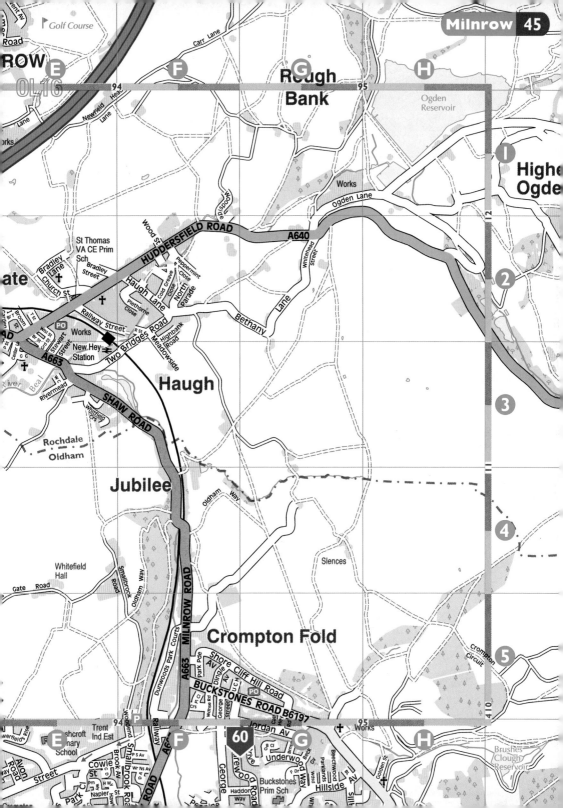

ROW

E   F   **Rough**   G   H
         Bank

OL16

Golf Course

Carr Lane

94   95

Ogden
Reservoir

I

Newfield Head Lane

Lane

Works

Works

Ogden Lane

Highe
Ogde

Wood St

St Thomas
VA CE Prim
Sch

HUDDERSFIELD ROAD   **A640**   2

Bradley
Lane

Bradley
Street

Peppermint
Close

Cold Greave
Close

North Parade

Whitefield
Street

Lane

Church St

Haugh Lane

Piethorne
Close

Bethany   Lane

PO

Railway Street

Broom St

Works

Highbank
Road

Meadowside

Two Bridges Road

Cedar St

Stewart Street

New Hey
Station

Haugh   3

River Beal

A663

Rivermead

SHAW ROAD

Whitfield
Crs

**Rochdale
Oldham**

Jubilee

Oldham   Way

4

Whitefield
Hall

Slences

Gate   Road

Smallbrook Road

Oldham Way

MILNROW ROAD

A663

Crompton Fold

Crompton
Circuit   5

410

Dunwoods Park Courts

Park Pde

Shore Cliff Hill Road

Dingle
Av

BUCKSTONES ROAD B6197

PO

95

E   **60**   F   **60**   Jordan Av   G   Works   H

Ashcroft
nary
School

Trent
Ind Est

P

Railway

A6

Underwood Way

Brushes
Clough
Reservoir

Cowie
St

Brook Av

George
Street

George

Buckstones
Prim Sch

Hillside

Avon
Road

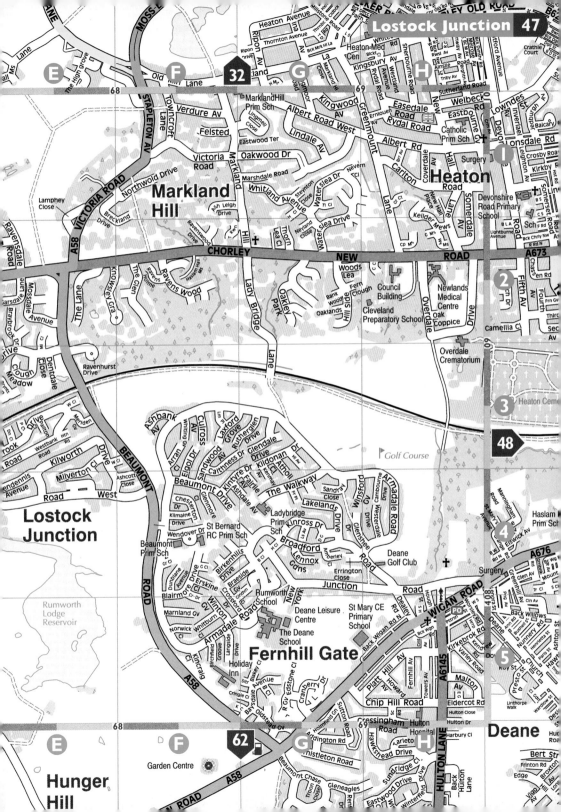

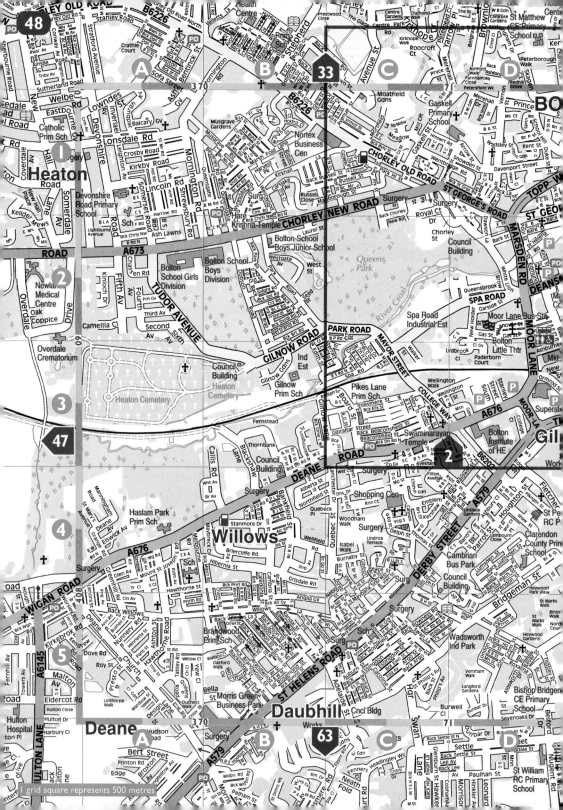

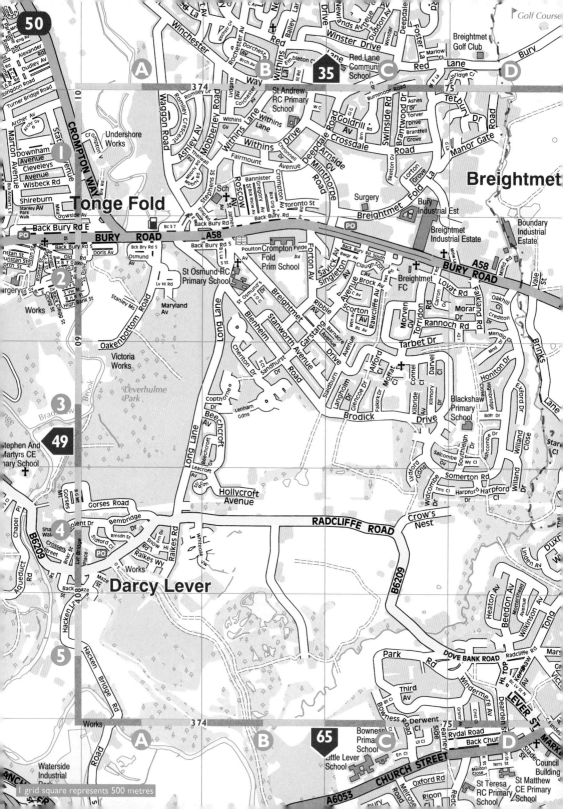

50

35

Breightmet

Tonge Fold

Undershore Works

Tonge Fold

BURY ROAD   A58

St Osmund RC
Primary School

2

Victoria
Works

3

49

Stephen And
Martyrs CE
mary School

Gorses Road

4

Darcy Lever

5

RADCLIFFE ROAD

Crow's
Nest

DOVE BANK ROAD

Breightmet
Industrial Estate

Boundary
Industrial
Estate

Breightmet
Golf Club

Golf Course

Winster Drive

Red Lane
Communi
School

Red   Lane

Bury

St Andrew
RC Primary
School

Blackshaw
Primary
School

CHURCH STREET

65

LEVER ST

Bowness
Primary
School

Little Lever
School

St Teresa
RC Primary
School

St Matthew
CE Primary
School

Council
Building

A6053

BURY   ROAD   A58

Leverhulme
Park

Hacken Bridge Rd

Waterside
Industrial

Works

1 grid square represents 500 metres

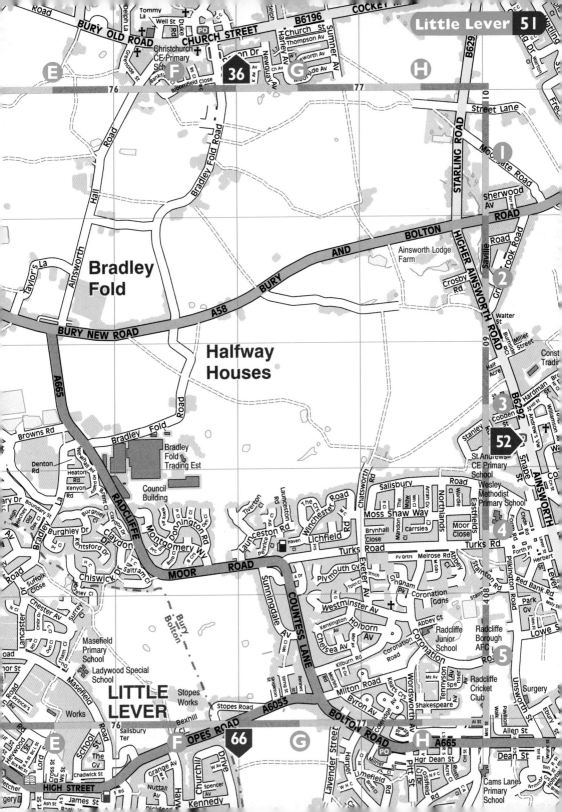

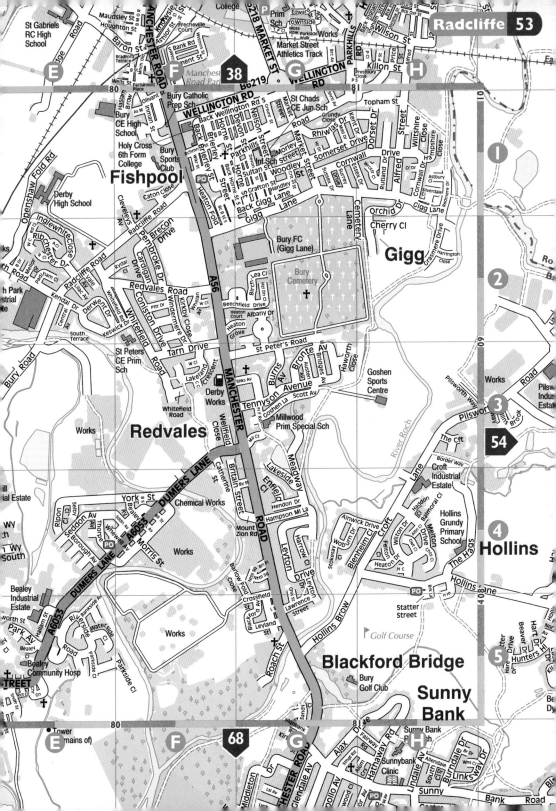

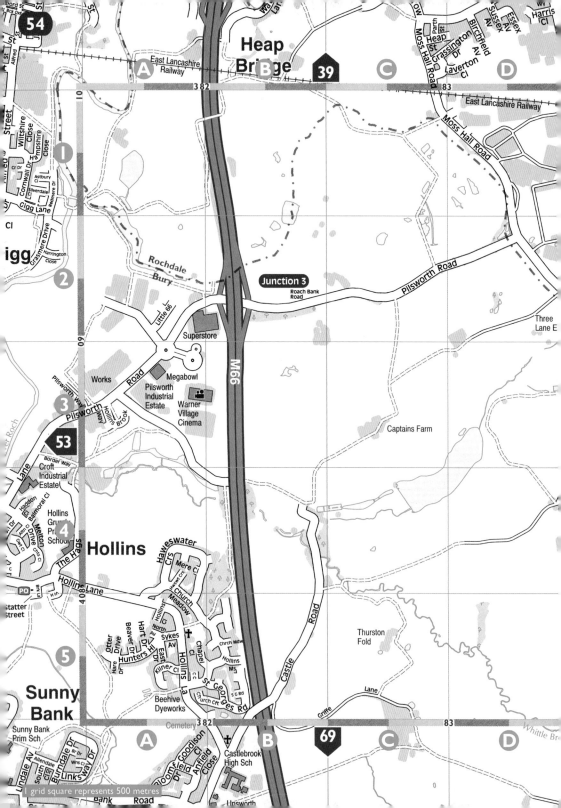

E F 42 G Trows H

St Gabriels RC Prim Sch

Vicarage Rd N
Mount St
Waverley St
Vcrg Rd S
Sherwin Wy
Leander Dr
Gabriel's

Works

88 89

Works

M62

A664

Thornham New Road
Partington Park
Works
Cherrington Drive
Fox Hill Road
Collingwood Street
Earl Street
Lyndhurst Avenue
Croydon Av
Chatburn Av
Chatburn Square

Trub

Saxonholme Road
Chesham Av
Carnforth Av
Carnforth Square
Norton Grange Hotel
Sautridge Close
Garden Centre

I

Thornham La
60

MANCHESTER ROAD

ROCHDALE ROAD

2

Clifton Road
Grange Road
Thornham Cricket Club
St Johns CE Primary School
Church

Rochdale Canal

PO Av
Church
Hillbank St
Thornham Lane

3

Slattocks

Hopwood Cottage

A627(M)

58

A627(M)

Bentley Avenue

Stake Hill

Stakehill Road
Finlan

4

Hopwood Hall College

Whitegates Rd

Whitbrook Way

Finlan Rd
Lane
Hough La
408

5

Stakehill Industrial Estate
Boswell Way

Touchet Road

Cardinal Langley RC High School

Linkway Industrial Estat

88

89

Hall Road

Chadderton Heights

E AD G H
The Close
Stanyclif F 72 Stake G
Acresfield Road
Ashbourne Gv

Higner Boarshaw

Rochdale Oldha

Boarshaw Primary

He

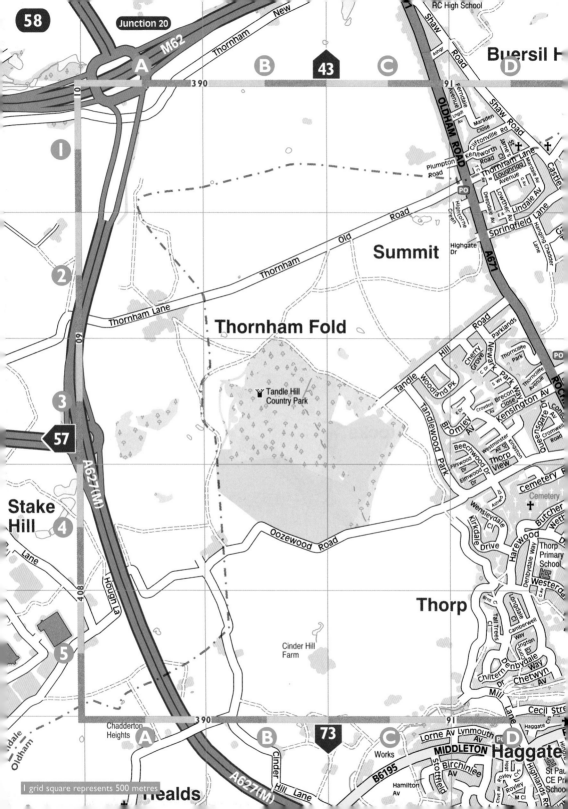

58

Junction 20

M62

A **B** **43** **C** **D**

New Thornham

Thornham

RC High School

Buersil H

Shaw Road

Oldham Road

Ferndale Avenue

Lngdn Av

Marsden Close

Cliftonville Road

Kenilworth Road

James's

St

Thornham Lane

Marple Av

Loughrigg CM

Deepdale Av

Avenue

Lowther Av

Highcroft Green

Lindale Av

Castle

Springfield Lane

Hanging Chadder Lane

A671

Plumpton Road

PO

1

Old Road

Thornham

Summit

Highgate Dr

2

Thornham Lane

Thornham Fold

Road

Parklands

PO

Hill

Cherry Grove

Newark Park Way

Thorncliffe Park

C

Thorncliffe Avenue

ROCH

3

Tandle

Woodland Pk

Breton Close

Croydon Av

Kensington Av

57

Tandle Hill Country Park

Bromley Av

Westminster Av

Kingston

Cromwell Road

Queensgate

A627(M)

Beechwood Dr

Flitswood Dr

Eliwood Dr

Thorp View

Hough La

Cemetery Road

Cemetery

Butcher

Wensleydale Cl

Stake Hill

4

Kirkdale Drive

Harewood

Denbydale Way

Thorp Primary School

Westerdale

Lane

408

Oozewood Road

Thorp

5

Cinder Hill Farm

Longdale Cl

Tall Trees Cl

Camberwell Way

ington Cl

Denbydale Way

Chiltern Dr

Chetwyn Av

Mill Lane

Cecil Stre

Oldale

Oldham

Chadderton Heights

A **B** **73** **C** **D**

Lorne Av

Lynmouth Av

PO

Haggate

Cinder Hill Lane

Works

MIDDLETON

Haggate

B6195

Stotfield

Birchinlee Av

Royley

St Pau CE Pri Schoo

Highlands

A627(M)

Hamilton Av

Healds

1 grid square represents 500 metres

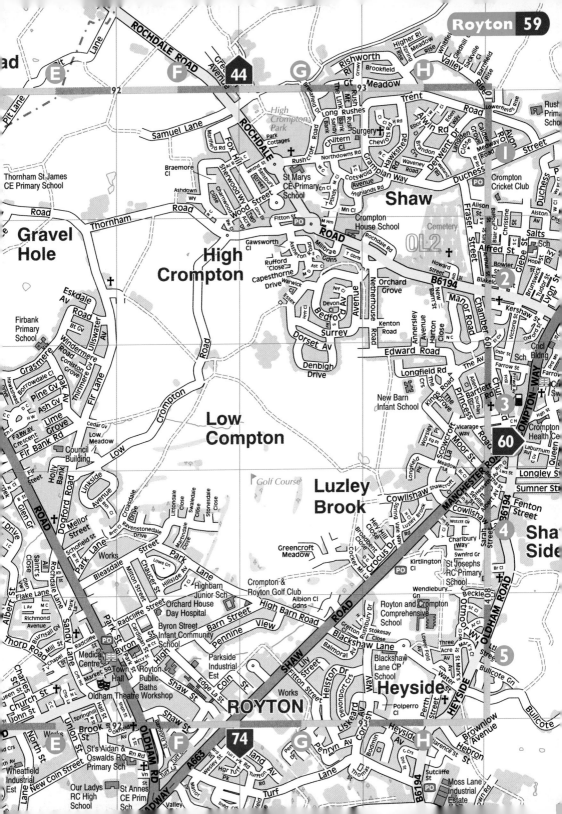

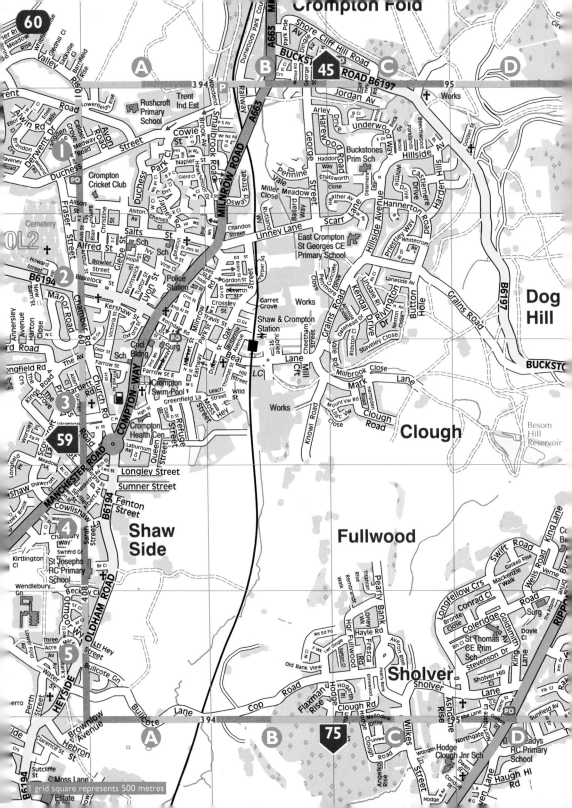

E F G H I

Crompton Moor

View

Wham Lane

Slack Va Lane

Slack Gate

A672 OLDHAM ROAD

A6052

Corbett Way

Brushes Clough Reservoir

Old Tame

A672

Horest Lane

Delph Road

PH

Slackcote Lane

Tame Lane

Lane

2

Mantley Lane

OLDHAM ROAD

Slackcote

Works

A6052

3

ROAD

Slack Lane

Grains Bar

SHIP LANE

Ship Lane

GRAINS ROAD

DENSHAW

4

Li

Medlock Valley Way

Bishop Park

408

B6197

5

Hill Top Lane

Edge Lane

Cherry Way

Spring Hall

Peak Rd

Epsley

Crs

Erica Av

Juniper Cl

Erlesmere Cl

Hill Top Community Special School

Coupland Close

Whitehall La

Hayfield Cl

Broadstone Av

Moorside Av

Arncliffe Rd

Lee Lane

Oakworth Cft

Pit Lane

Medlock Valley Way

High Lane

76

E F G H

Strine Dale

Roebuck

Cabin Lane

97

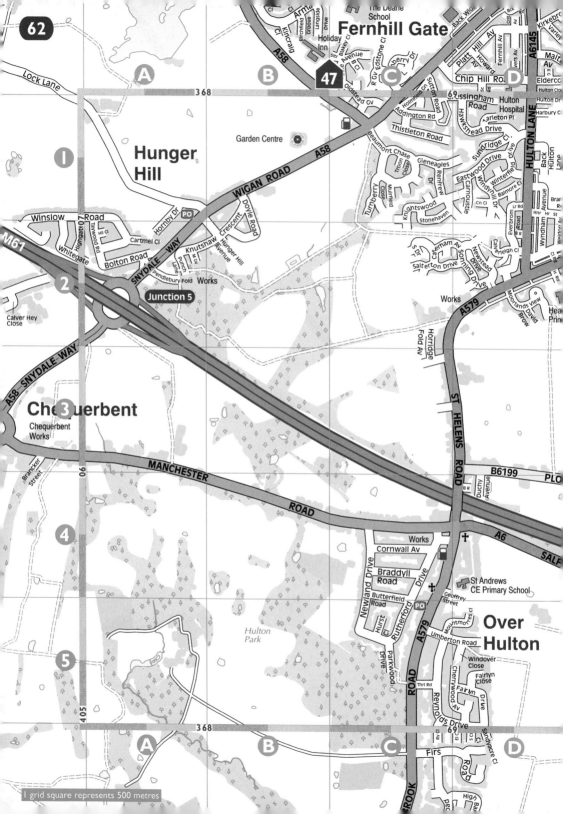

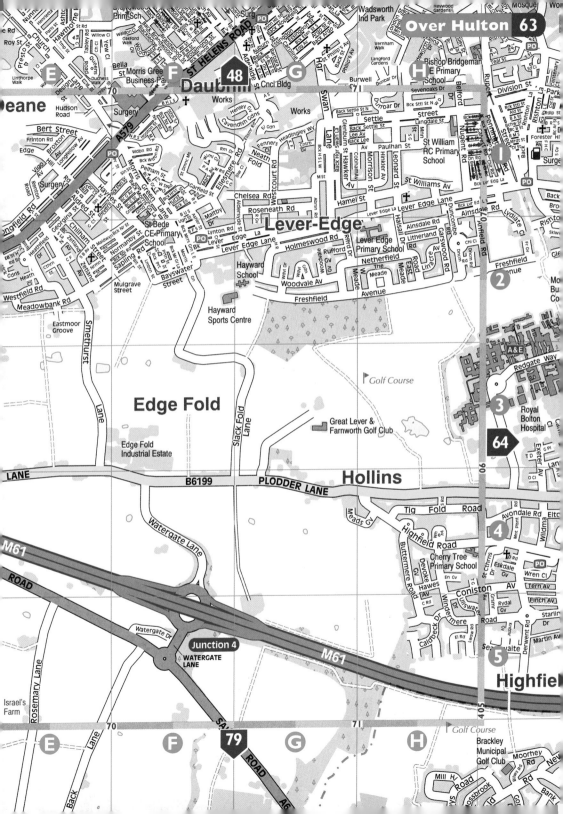

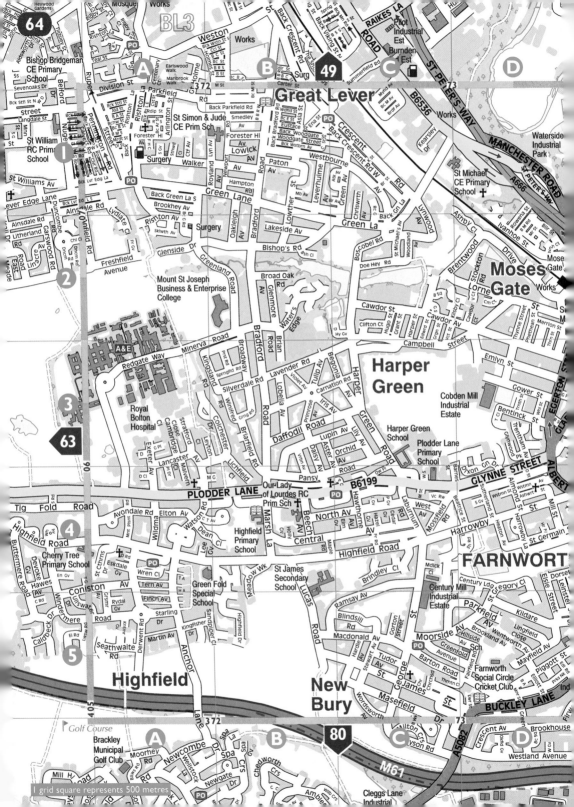

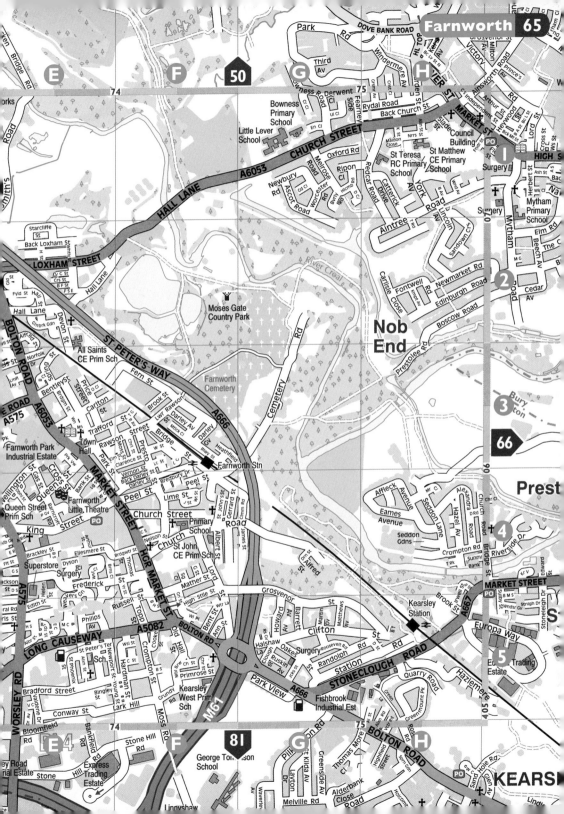

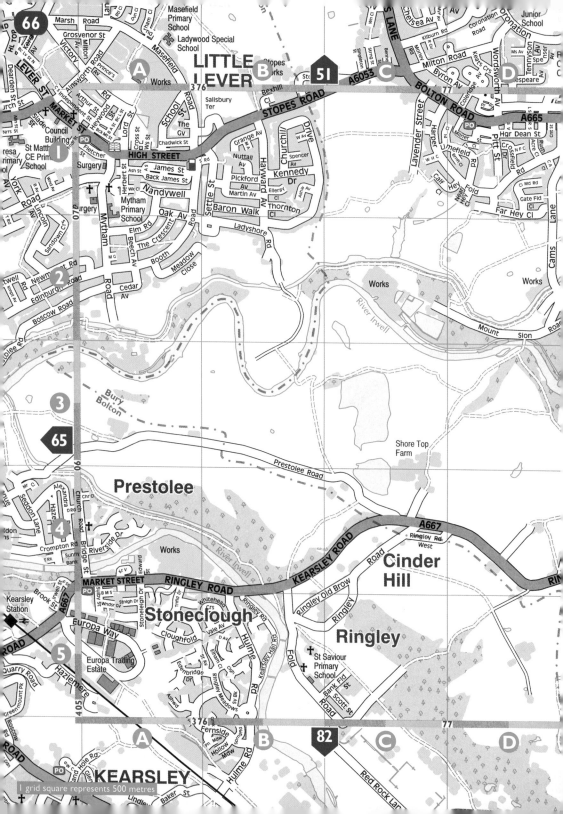

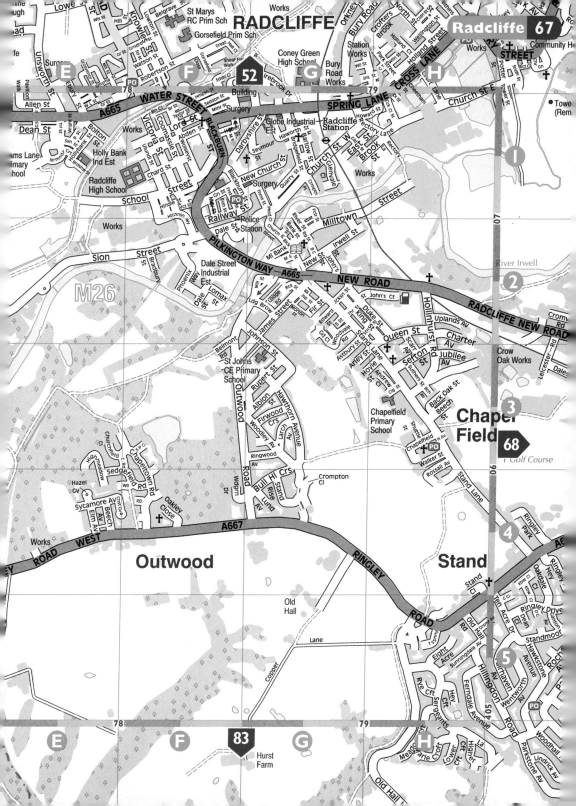

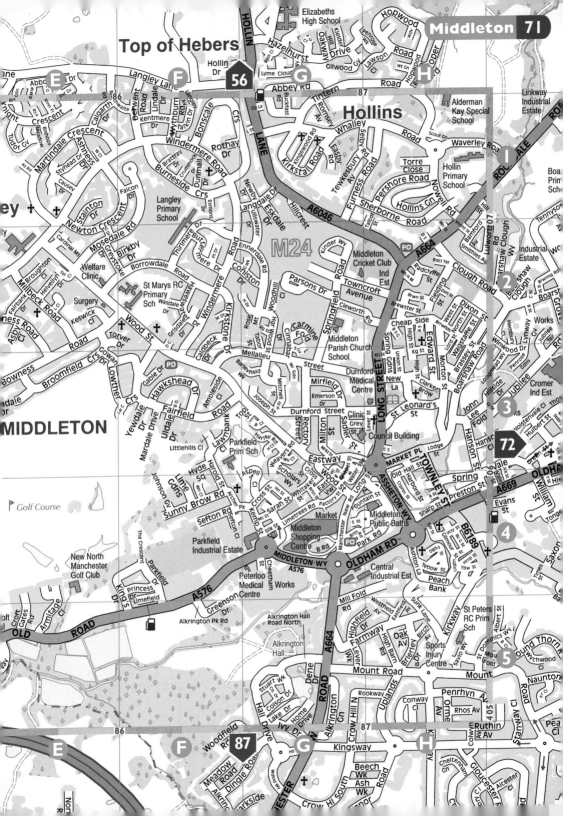

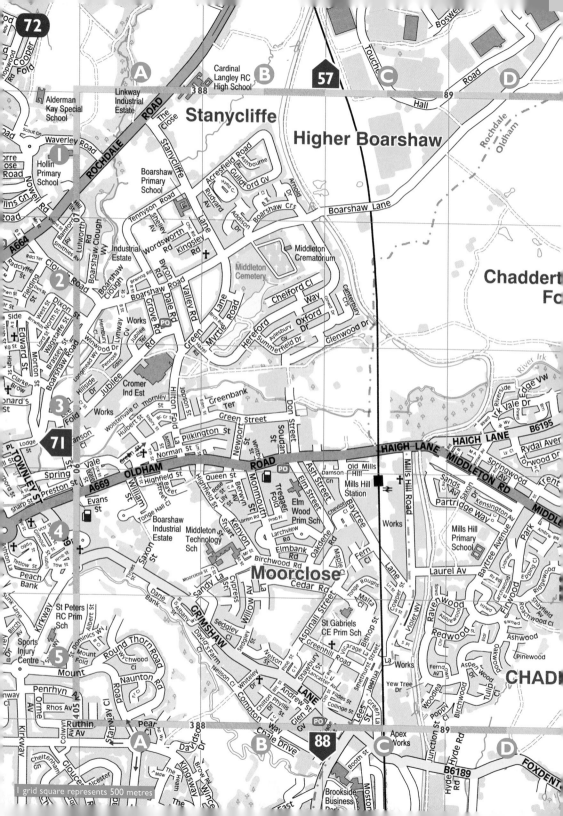

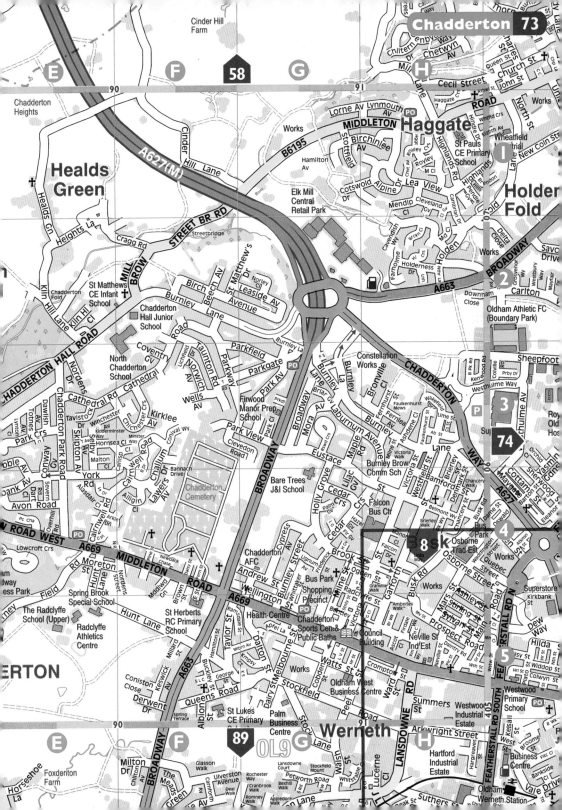

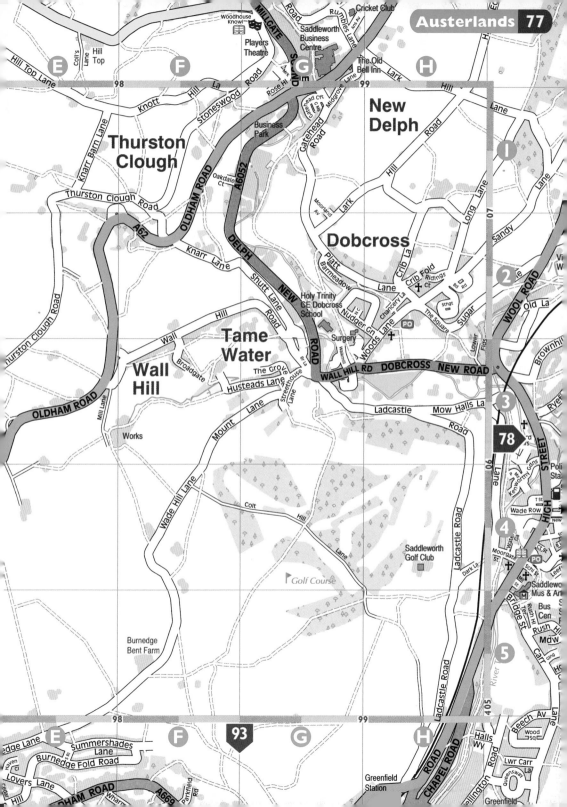

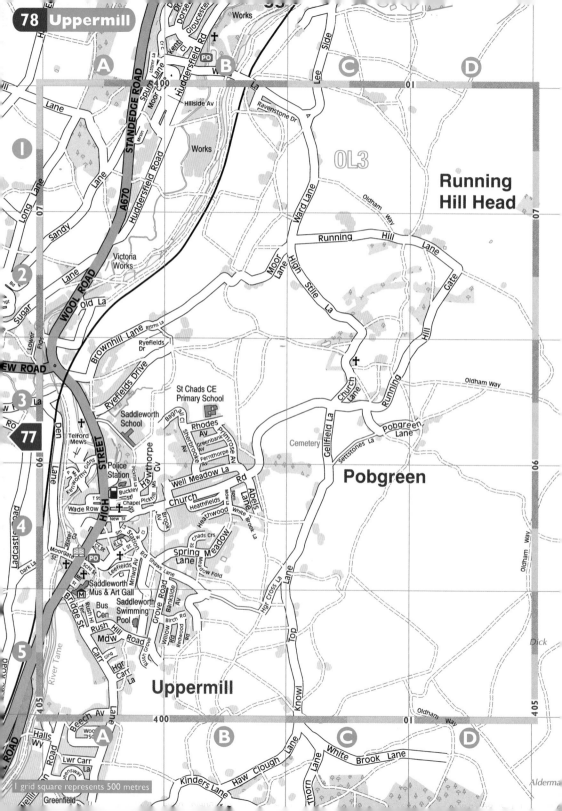

Running
Hill Head

OL3

Pobgreen

Uppermill

St Chads CE
Primary School

Saddleworth
School

Police
Station

Saddleworth
Mus & Art Gall

Saddleworth
Swimming
Pool

Bus
Cen

Cemetery

Victoria
Works

Works

Works

River Tame

Dick

Alderma

Greenfield

1 grid square represents 500 metres

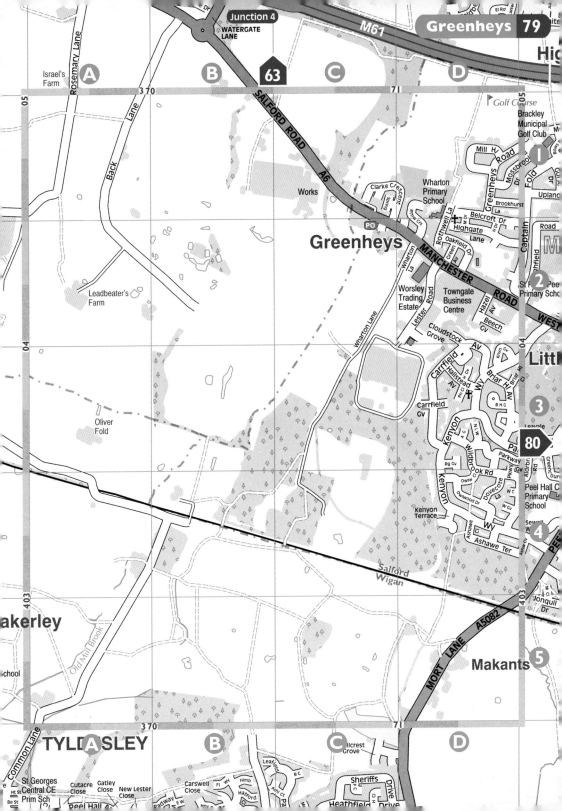

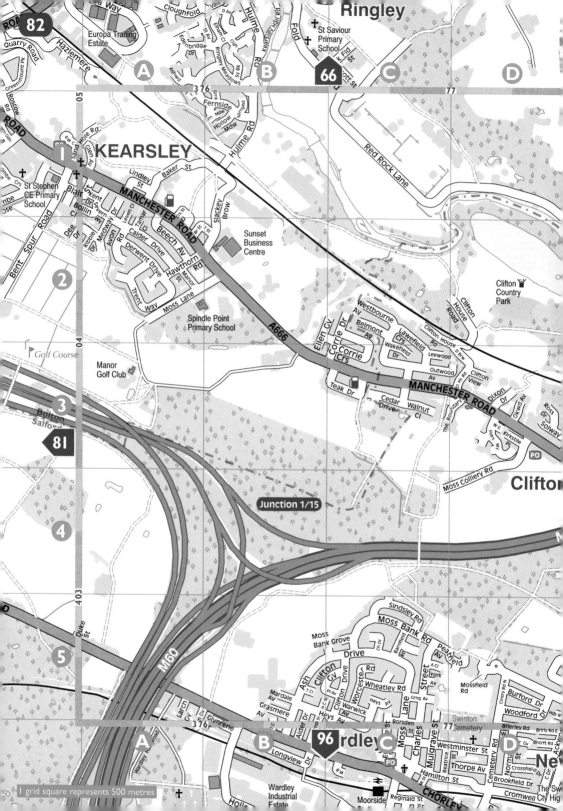

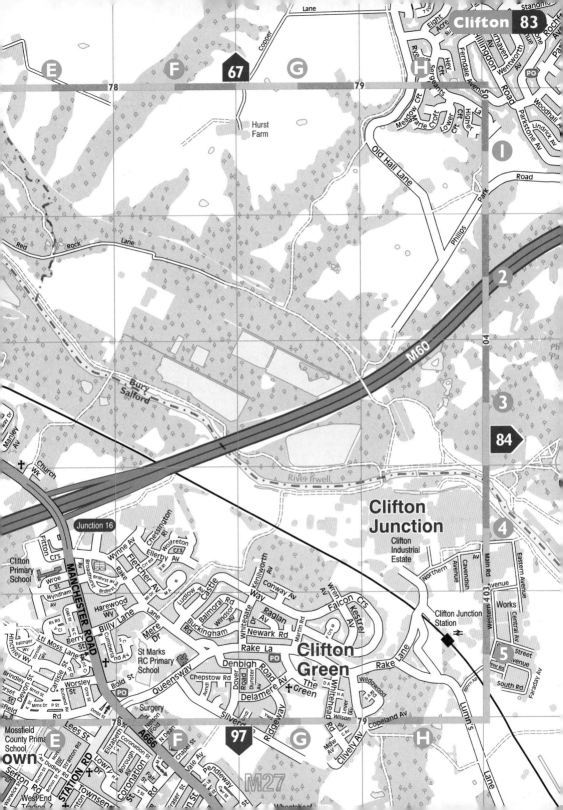

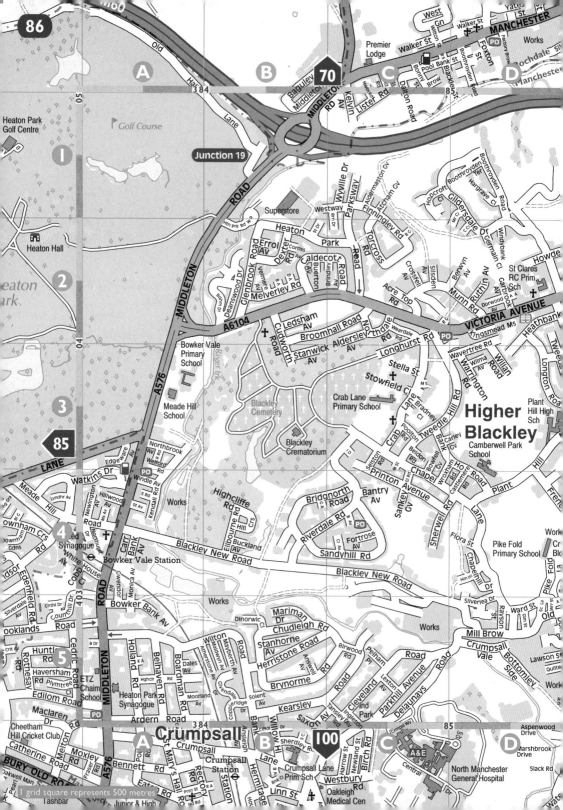

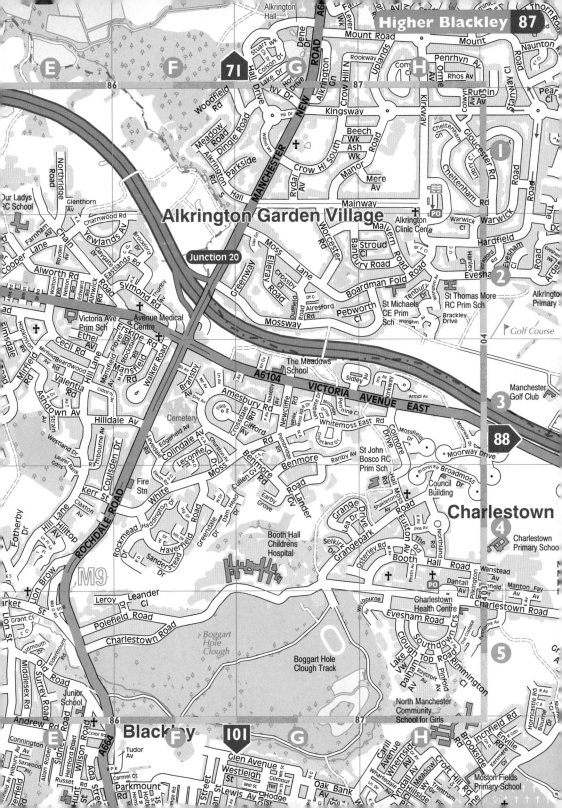

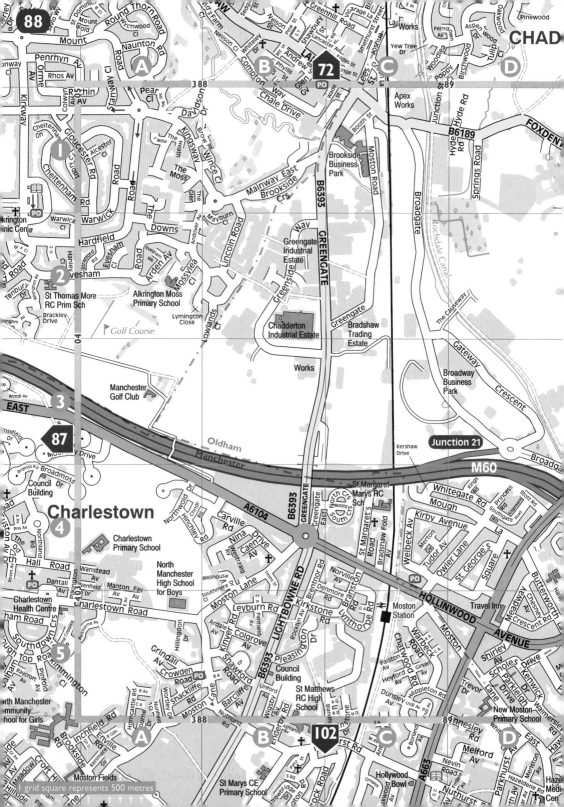

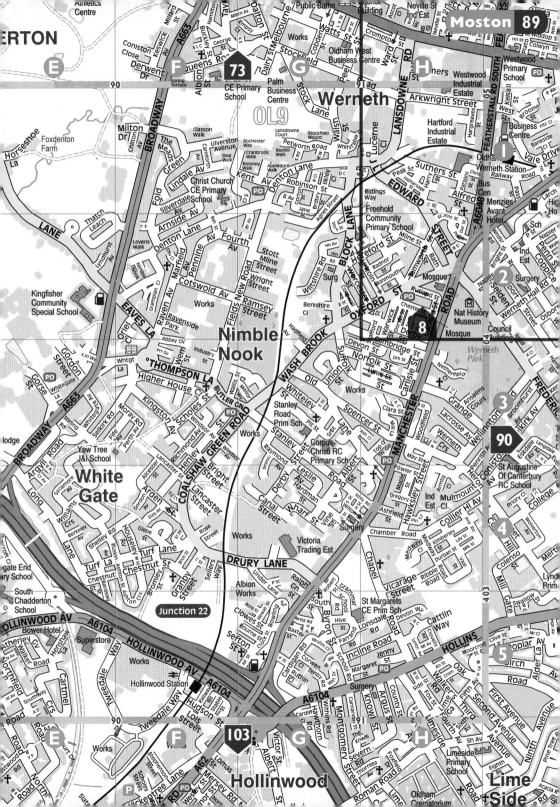

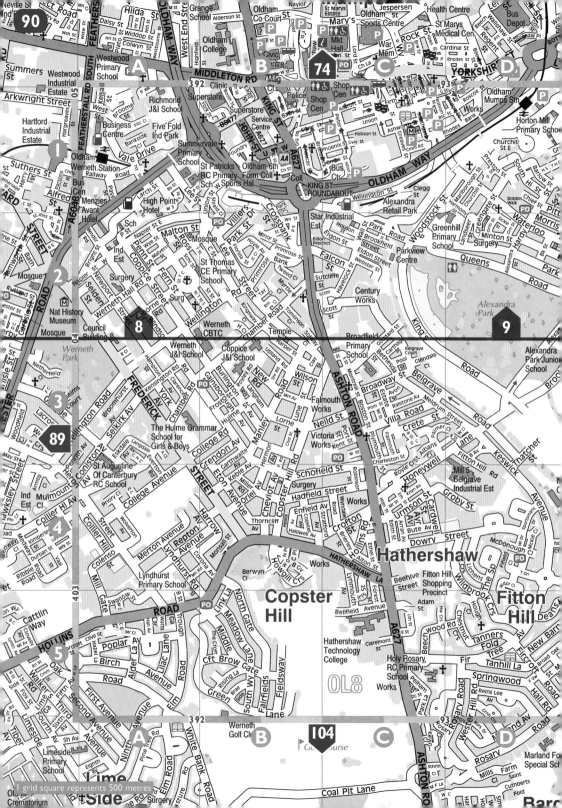

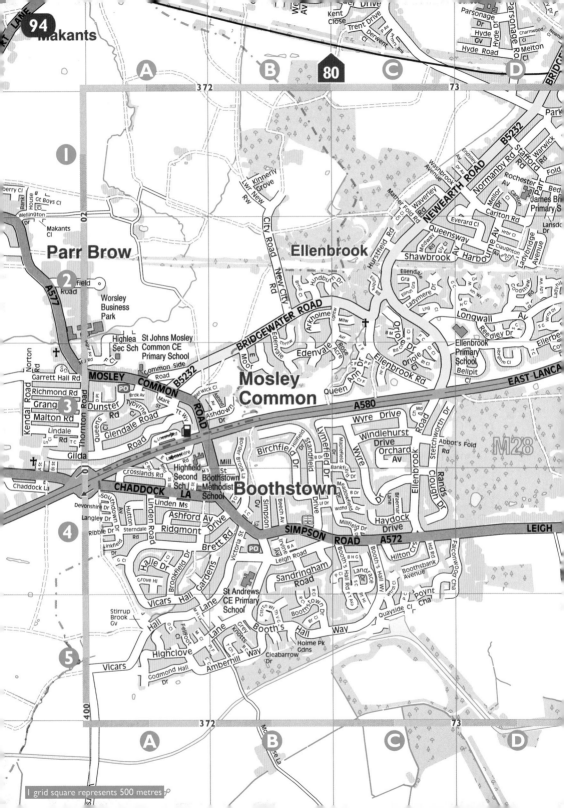

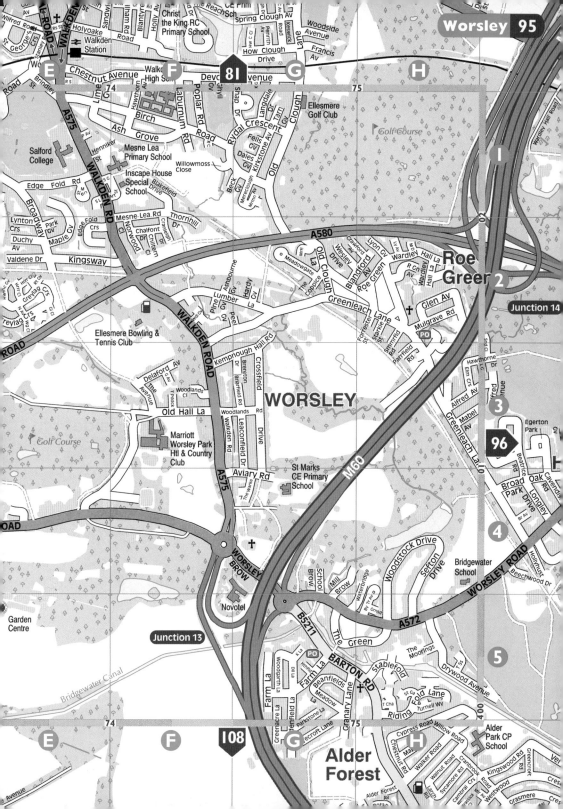

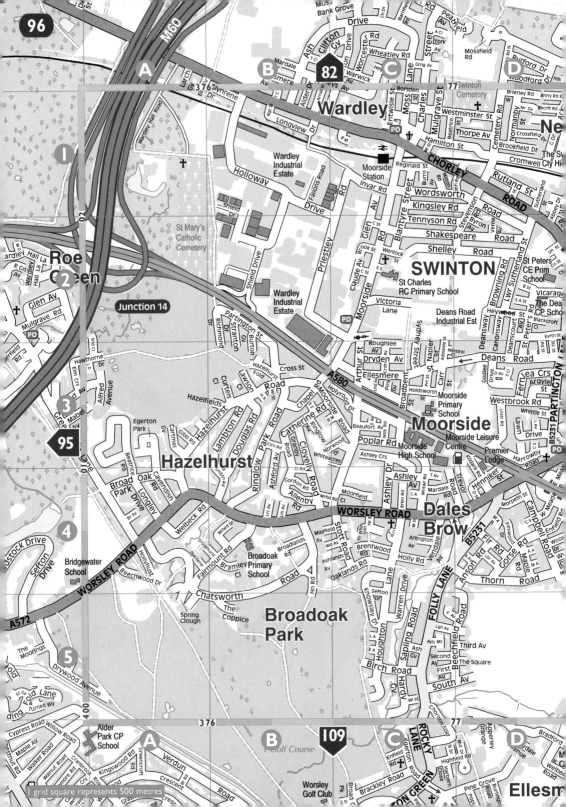

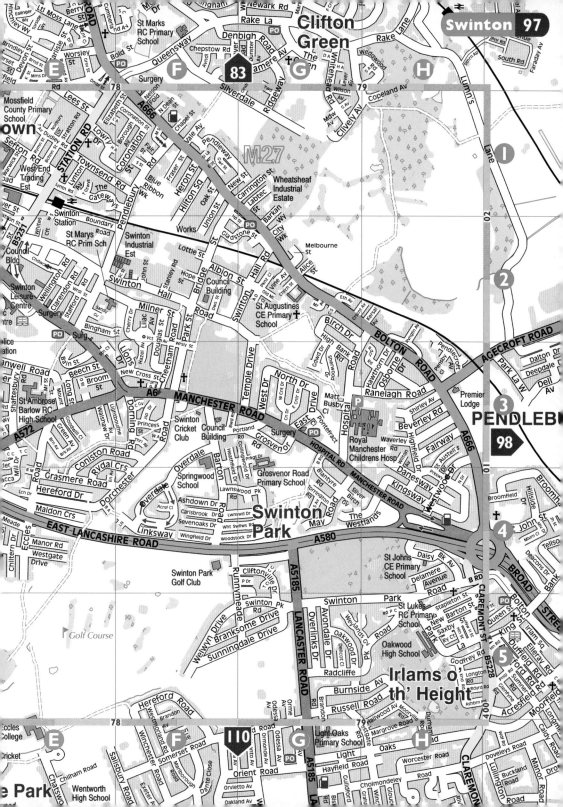

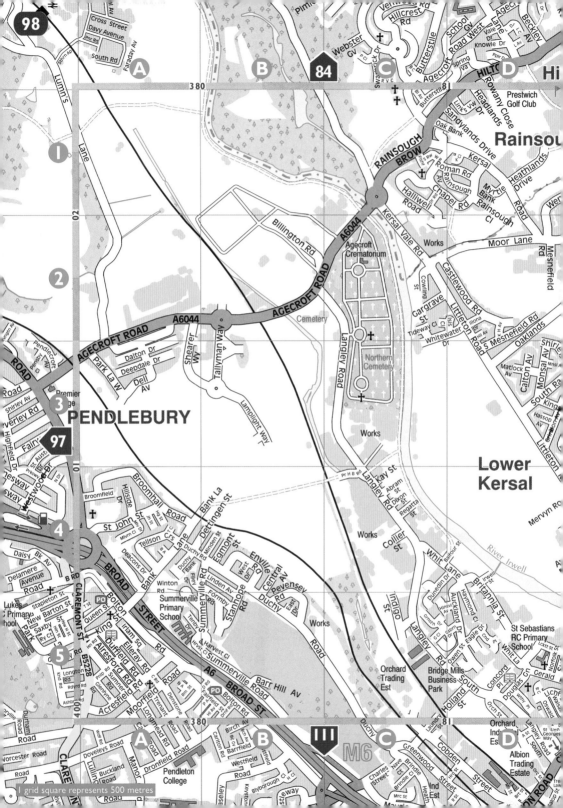

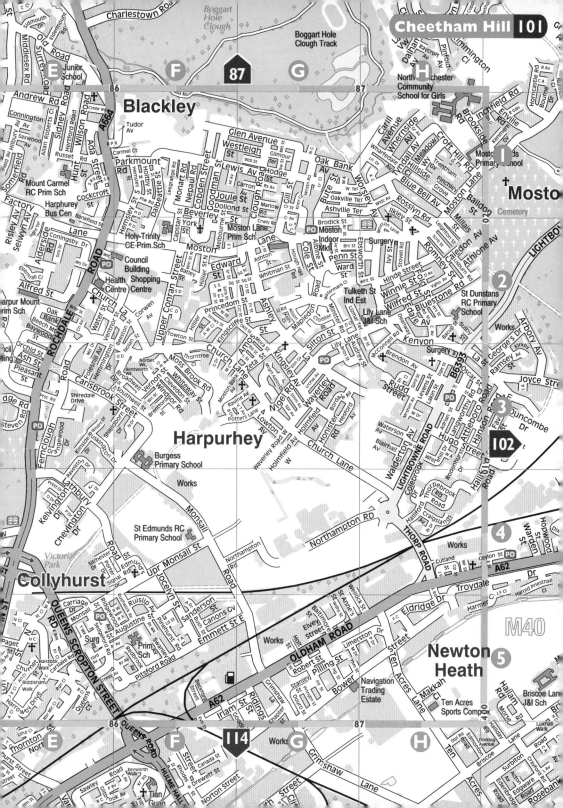

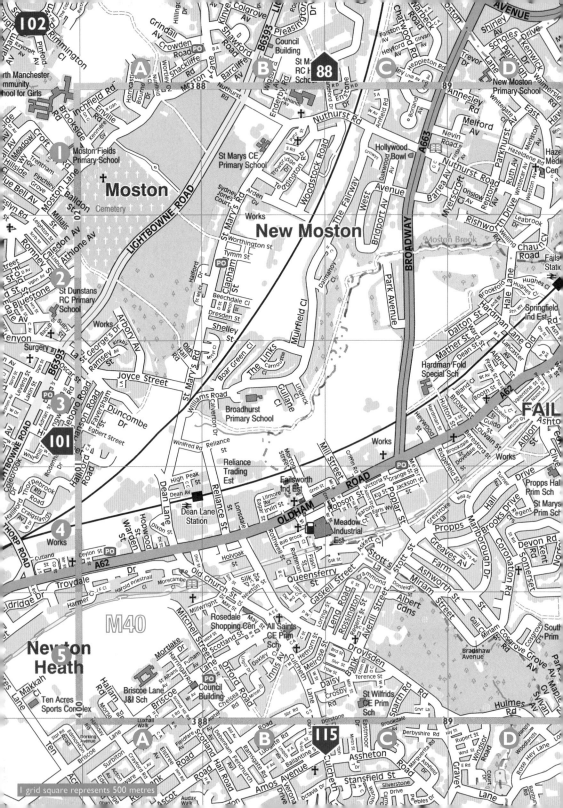

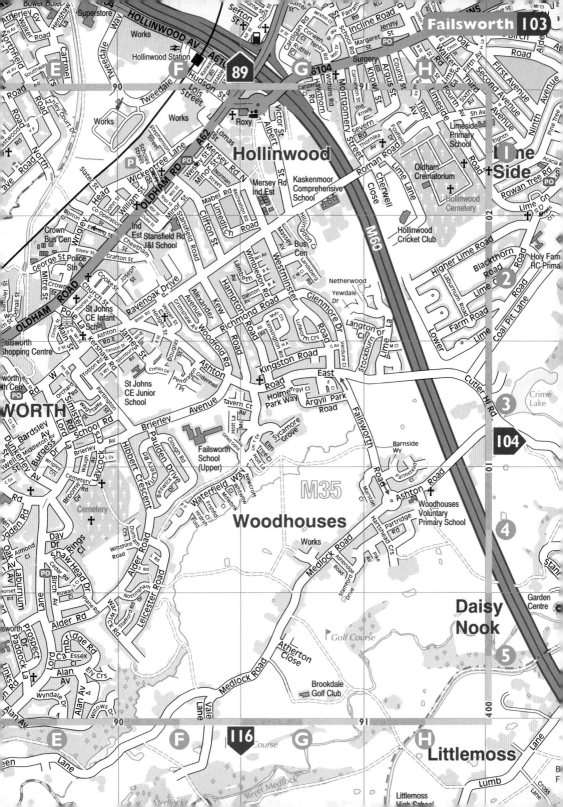

Hollinwood

Line Side

WORTH

Woodhouses

M35

Daisy Nook

Littlemoss

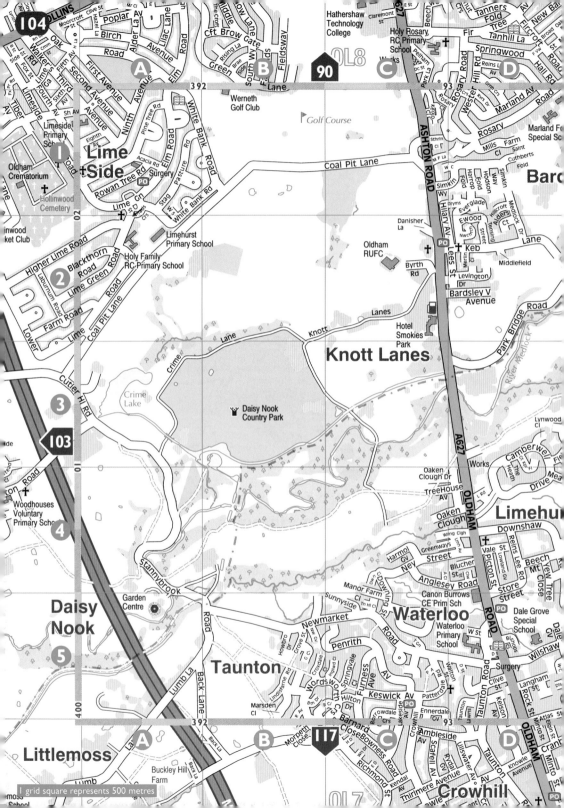

Junction 13

Bridgewater Canal

374

95

A

B

C

D

BARTON RD

PO

Stablefold

The Moorings

Drywoo

Greenacre La

Woodgarth La

Hymers

Farm La

Beanfields

Granary Lane

Meadow

Riding

Turnell WY

Lane

Edenfield

Parkstone La

Ryecroft Lane

75

Cypress Road

Willow Road

Alder Forest

Maple AV

Chestnut Rd

Walker Road

Walnut Road

Sycamore Rd

Cambre

Leaconfield Road

Hastings Road

Botan Rd

Bota AV

Larch

Edgwr Rd

Grange Road

F S

A St

M60

The Nook

Hrt Rd

PO

B5

Grvnr Rd

Brookfield

Bramtre St

Junction 1/12

1

The Avenue

The Avenue

99

2

The Grange

Cleavle

Athletic

Track

3

St Gilber

RC Prim

School

Stannard Road

Salteye Rd

M62

Foxhill Road

Foxhill Road

Chatley Rd

Boddington Road

Brereton Rd

Crdw Rd Cl

PO

4

398

Canon Williamson

CE High School

Northfleet Road

Hiley Road

Brookhouse AV

M60

Barton Hall

Avenue

Schofield

Barton Moss Prim Sch

RCHM Rd

Rd

Senior Road

Moat Hall A

Buckthorn Lane

Lodgepole Close

Robinia Cl

F Cl

Trippier Rd

Verdant Lane

Barton Moss Rd

5

Peel Green

Eccles Crematorium

Junction 11

Shearwater Gdns

Rooke St

Regin

Cemetery

Woodlands AV

Sealand Gdns

LIVERPOOL ROAD

Southlands AV

Newlands AV

Enfield

Wilford Rd

374

122

A

B

C

D

Twelve Yards Road

Argosy

Trent Road

Av Rd

New Hall

AV

M62

Manchester

(Barton) Airfield

1 grid square represents 500 metres

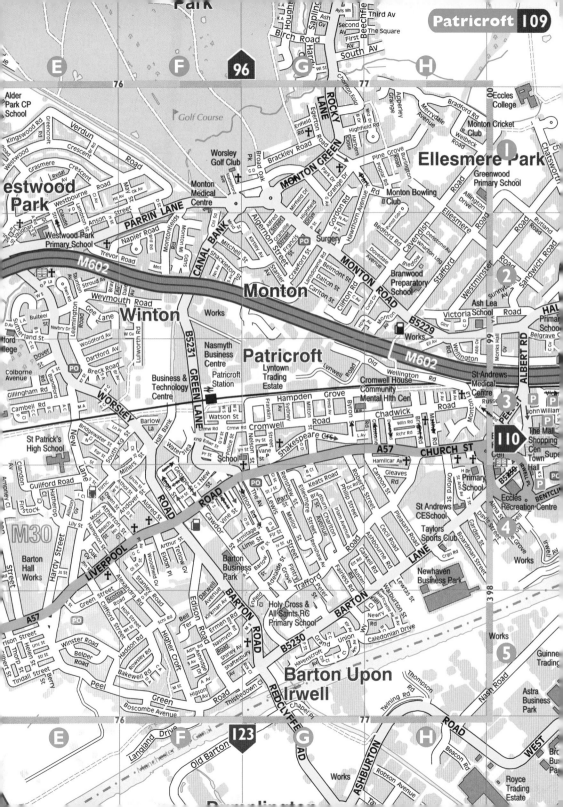

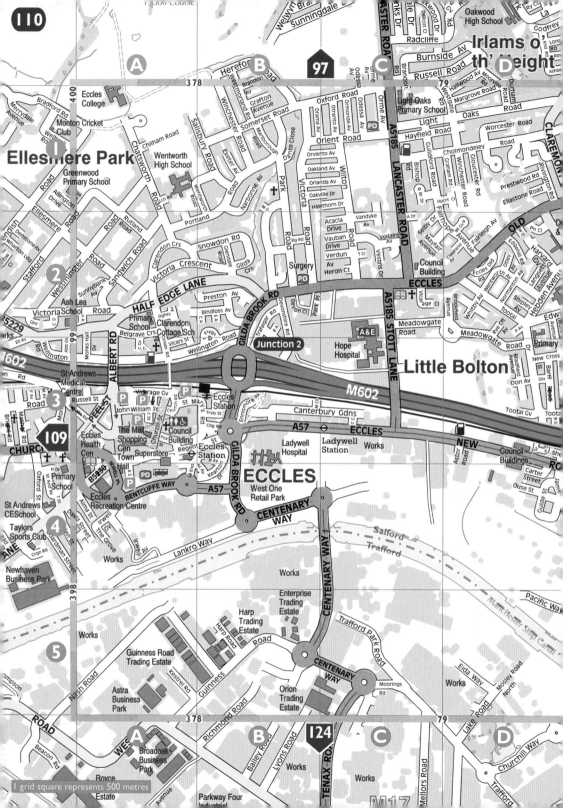

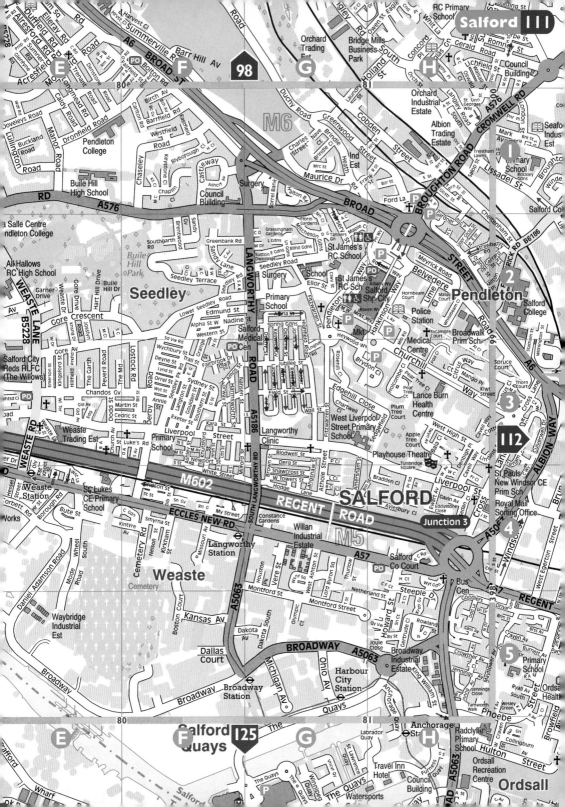

112
99
111
126
6
A
B
C
D
1
2
3
4
5
382
83
398
400
Cromwell Road
A576
A5066
Charlestown
Lower Broughton
Pendleton
Frederick Road
B6186
Broughton Road
Broughton Road East
Seaford Industrial Est
Primary School
Salford University Business Park
Salford Coll
Salford College
Wallness La
River Irwell
University of Salford
Salford Crescent Station
Salford Museum & Art Gallery
Meadow Road
Riverside
Lower Broughton Road
Lower Broughton Health Cen
Great Clowes Street
A5066
Bury New Road
Cambridge Ind Est
Cambridge Industrial Est
Trafalgar Business Park
Broughton Lane
Clarence Street
Silk Street
Blackfriars Road
Adelphi St
Trinity Way
A6041
A6 Chapel St
Chapel Street
Crescent
A6
Police Station
Works
Albion Way
A5063
Albion Trading Estate
Junction
Liverpool St
Windsor St
Regent Road
A57
Red Rose Retail Centre
Oldfield Road
Ordsall La
B5461
East Ordsall La
Trading Estate
Mancentral Trading Estate
Regent Trading Est
Manchester Industrial Cen
Castlefield Bridge
Campanile Hotel
Water St
Irwell New Quay St
A6042
Le Meridien Victoria & Albert Hotel
Granada Studios
Mus of Science & Ind
Air & Space Mus
Liverpool Road
Leisure Cen
Roman Ft
YHA
G-Mex Station
Deansgate Stn
Quay St
A34
Salford Central Stn
City Cen Campus
Courts
Inland Revenue Office
Bridge St
New Bailey St
M3
St Peter & St John Prim Sch
St Philips School
Council Building
Ordsall Health Cen
St Pauls New Windsor CE Prim Sch
Royal Mail Sorting Office
Broadwalk Prim Sch
Bus Cen
Radclyffe Primary School
Ordsall Recreation Centre
Hulton Street
Robert Hall Street
Derwent Street
Dawson St
Cornbrook Estate
Ind Est
Chester Rd
A57(M)
Olympia Trading Est
Castle Quay
1 grid square represents 500 metres

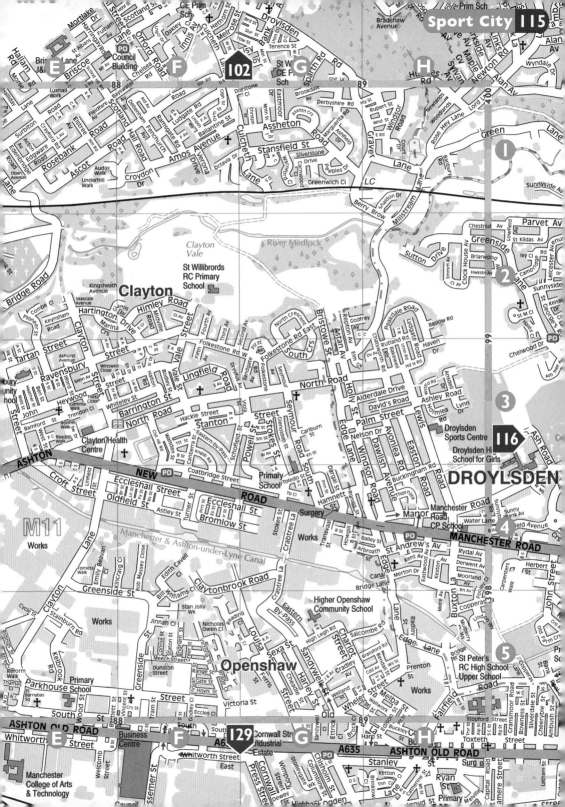

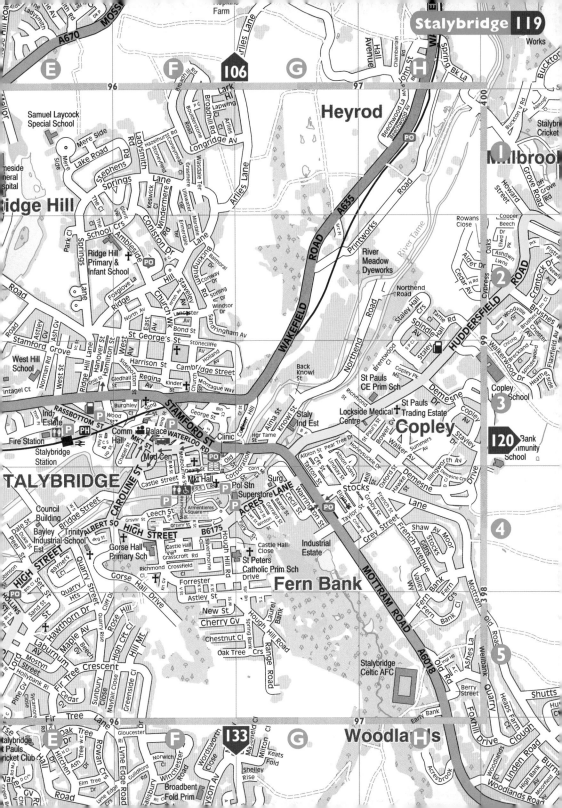

A B C D

I

2

3

122

4

5

M62

LIVERPOOL ROAD

Barton

Birch Farm

Bartonmoss Farm

Twelve Yards Road

Twelve Yards Road

Raspberry Lane

Cutnook Lane

Moss Farm

Raspberry Lane

Barton Grange

Fiddlers Lane

Fields End Fold

Crossfield Rd

Boysnope Whf

Lawfield

Boundary Trading Estate

Flixton FC

Merlin
Road
Morillon Road
McLean Dr
Martin Dr
Neville Dr
Curlew Dr
Keal Dr
Avocet Dr
Swallow
Prim Sch
Robin Dr
Dove Drive
W Dr
Dunlin
Prim Sch
Silver Street
Silverdale Av
Falcon Dr
Leyland Av
Barnley Cl
Lyndhurst Av
Lyndhurst Av
Windsor
Fiddlers Lane
Hartley Grove
Mond Rd
Marlborough Rd
The Crescent
Boundary Rd
Boundary Rd
Princes Av
Addison Road
Mayfield Industrial Park
Woods Primary School
Raven Dr
Kestrel Dr
Heron Av
Hawk Rd
Osprey
Marlow
The Trafford
The De
Trafford
T Pngt
Fiddlers Lane Primary School
Grazing Dr
Pasturegreen Way
Wymbrog
Oleo Rd
Beech
Ter
Sunningdale Dr
Parkstone Av
Quail Dr
Radford
Cutnook Lane
Moorfield Rd
Turner
Windsor
PO
Boat Lane
Exeter Rd
Falmouth
Carr Rd
Sunflower Mdw
Cranford Drive
School
Sandy
Newby
Meadowside Av
Farmdale
Carlisle Rd
Sandiway
Brookfield
Platts Dr
Ratcliffe Av
Balshaw Av
Doodson Av
Queensway
Chapel Rd
Brooklands Cl
Primary School
Chapel Medical Cen
Ferryhill
Boat Lane
Ferry
CADISHEAD WAY

LIVERPOOL ROAD

136

Melton
Tanhouse Rd
Shaftesbury Gdns
Repton
Alton
Valley Rd
Linton Av
Lytham
Lydney
Lydiate Rd
Brecon
Roedean Gdns
Roedean Rd
Ascot Dr
Derby
Denby

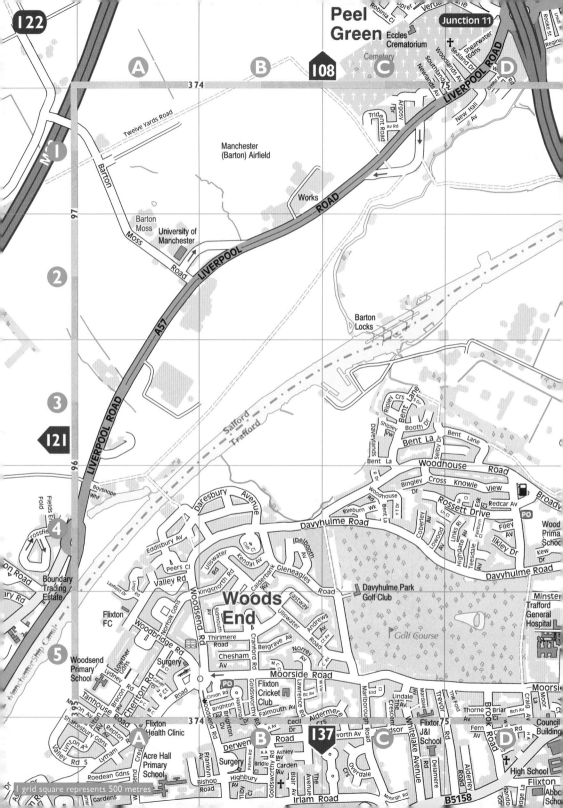

124

110

123

139

Works

Guinness Road
Trading Estate

Nash Road

Astra
Business
Park

A

Kestrel Rd

Guinness

Road

Richmond Road

B

Bailey Road

Lyons Road

Orion Trading
Estate

Centenary
Way

C

Moorings

Elda Way

Mosley Road

Works

D

ROAD

Beacon Rd

WEST

Broadoak
Business
Park

Royce
Trading
Estate

Avenue

Clarence

Parkway Four
Industrial
Estate

Works

Works

TENAX ROAD

Works

M17

Mellors Road

Churchill Way

Trafford

West

1

North Avenue

Superstore

Traders
Avenue

BRIGHT CIRCLE

2

Phoenix Wy

PEEL CIRCLE

Mercury

Cobalt Av

Way

Longbridge Rd

Fourways

Fourways
Trading
Est

Ashbridge

Warren Rd

Longwood Road

Hattons Rd

Westinghouse

Monde
Trading
Estate

Marshall Stevens Wy

VILLAGE WAY (ASHBURTON ROAD EA

Avenue

Eighth

Road

Avenue
Works

P

BARTON DOCK ROAD

PARK WAY

Kratos
Industrial
Estate

Parkway
Trading
Estate

Alba Way

Caledonia Wy

Hibernia Way

Severnside
Trading
Estate

Works

Textilose Road

Praed Road

Southfield
Industrial
Estate

Fifth

Fourth St.

North

3

Mosley Road

A5181

Westinghouse

W. Canteen

West Works Road

East Aisle Road

Main Avenue

123

Junction 9

St Modwen Rd

Clarke
Industrial
Estate

Works

BARTON DOCK ROAD

B5211

Works

South Works Road

Road

South

Works

nsway

Kingsway
Cr

4

Barton Clough
Primary School

Old Hall
Farm

West Road

North Road

South
Road

East Rd

Langham
Court

Works

ROAD

RMSTON

M V Crs

Dalton Avenue

Audley

Avenue

Barton Road

Berkeley Av

Curzon Rd

Sadie Av

Styal

Castleton Rd

Ashbourne Road

Bradwell Av

Edale Rd

Castleton
Avenue

Cromford Av

Trafford
Park Sta

Keswick Road

Park Rd

Hattons Ct

Marple

5

Aylesbury Av

Guildford
Rd

Burford
Rd

Whalley

Welbeck

Wallingford

Abingdon
Road

Moss Vale Road

Ely Av

Lincoln Rd

Norwich Rd

Brompton Rd

Glastonbury
Road

Fountains
Road

Ripon
Road

Selby CI

Chatsworth
Rd

Primary
School

Lostock
College

Selby

Road

Haworth
Dr

Rowsley Rd

Matlock Rd

Bakewell

Buxton

PO

Humphrey
Park Station

Barton Rd

Lostock Rd

Raglan Rd

Melville Rd

Alston
Av

Lyndhurst Rd

PARK

Thirlmere Av

Coniston Rd

ROAD

Surg

Davyhulme Road

Marlborough
Road

ad

Road

Rutland Av

Langley

Willow

LA

Caverdish
Rd

St Ann's
RC High
School

Hilrose Av

Berwick Av

Southbourne
Av

Clevedon
Av

A

Humphrey La

Foxdenton Dr

Abbey Cl

139

Mount

Parkway Rd

Dunmord Av

B

Wood Avenue

Green

Derbyshire

Bradfield

Montrose

West

C

Moss Park
Junior School

Bradfield

Raglan Rd

Westwood

A5181

Larne

Radstock Road

D

Victoria
Park

1 grid square represents 500 metres

378

79

97

395

378

79

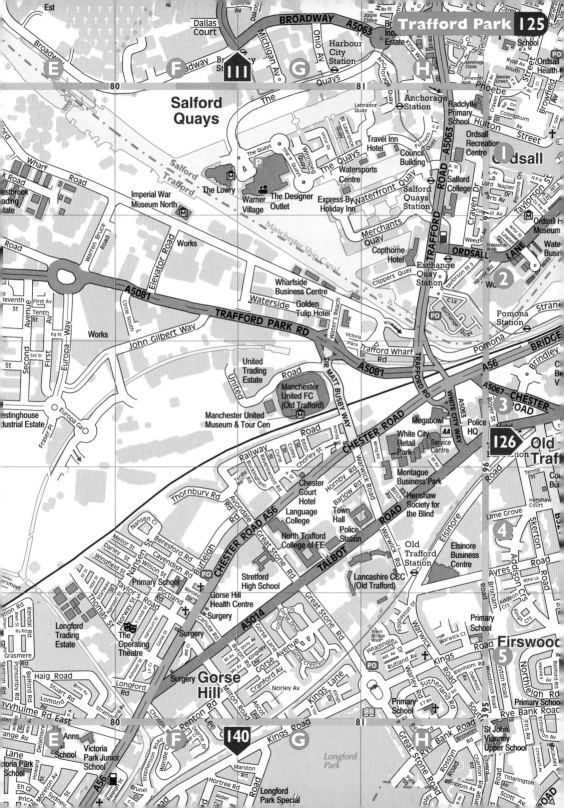

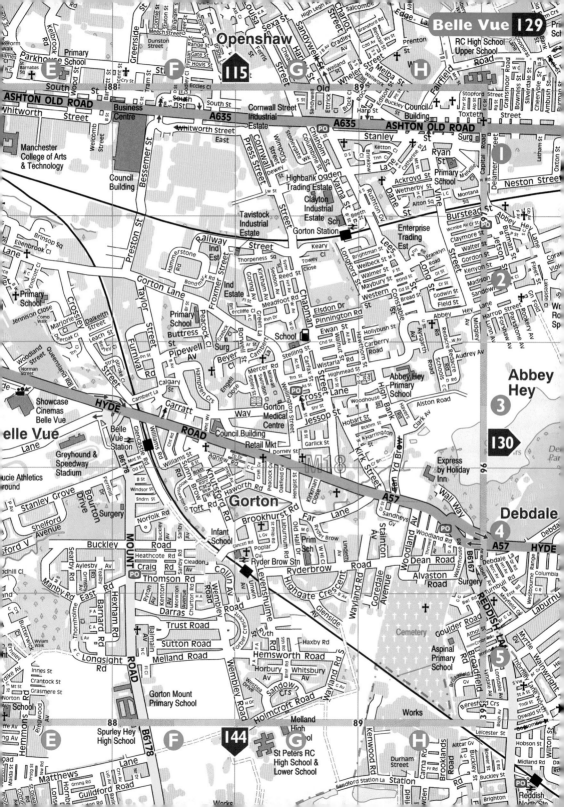

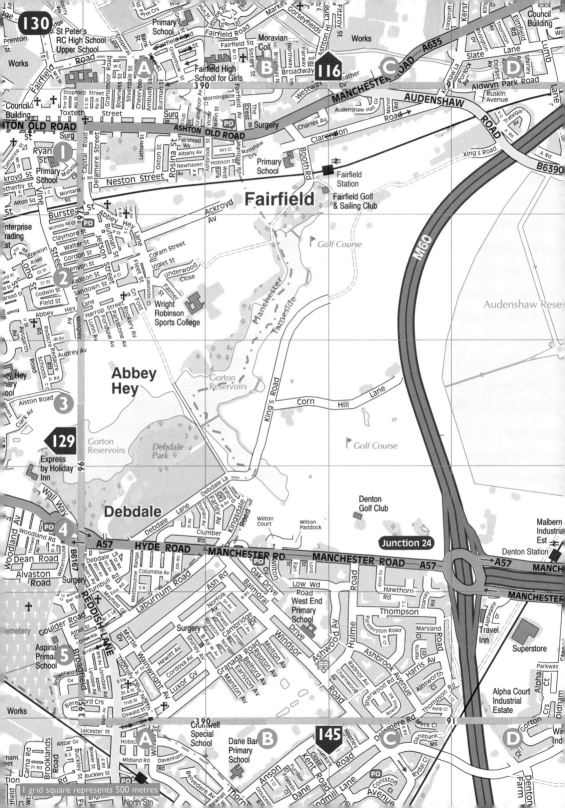

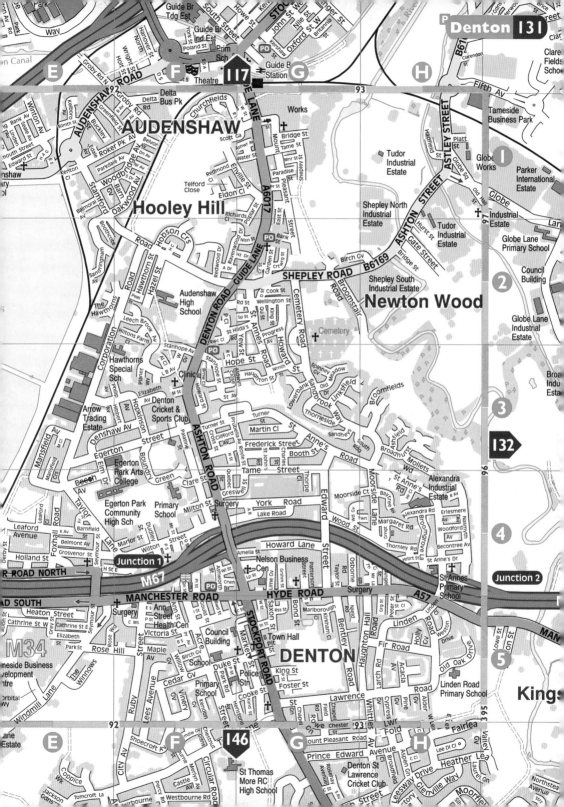

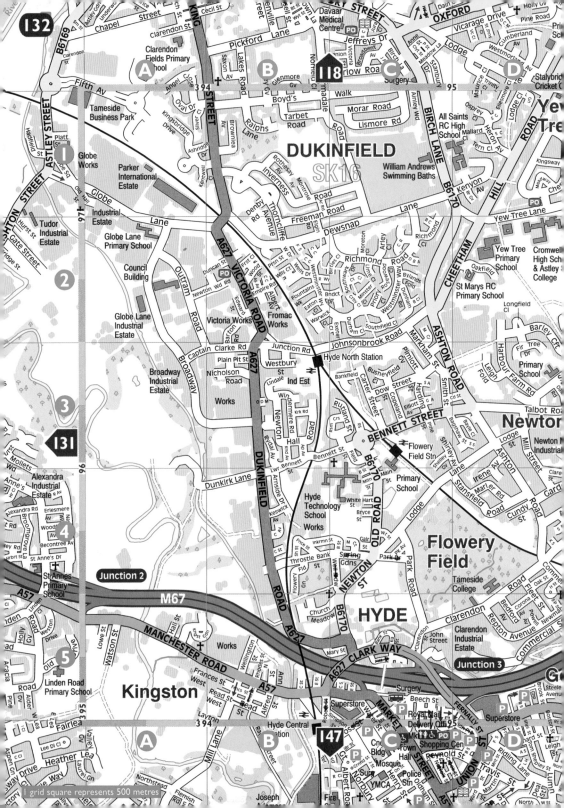

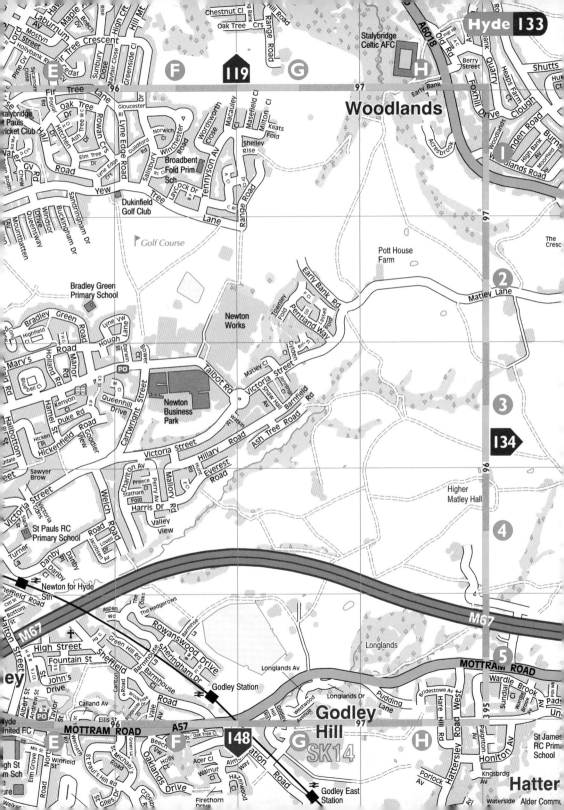

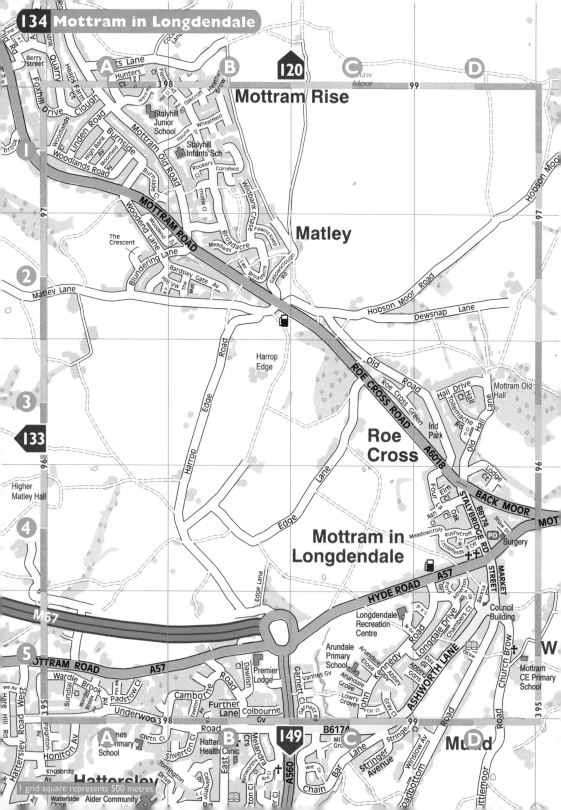

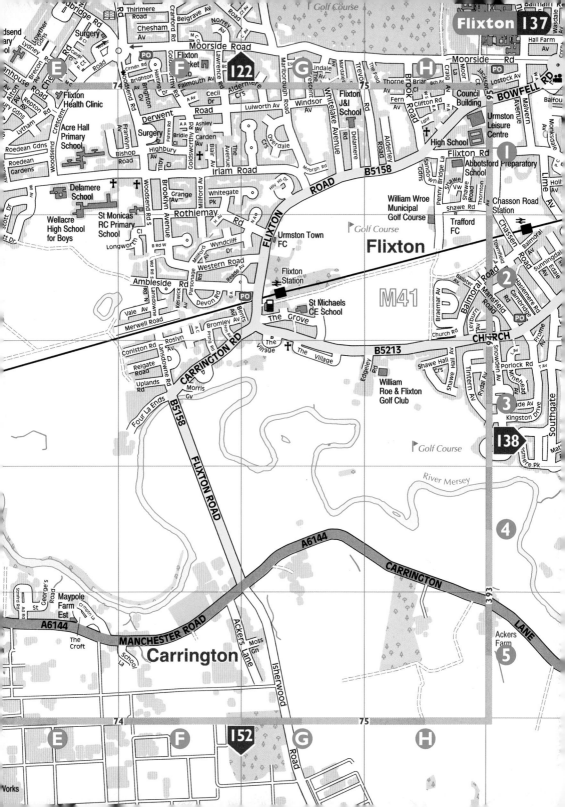

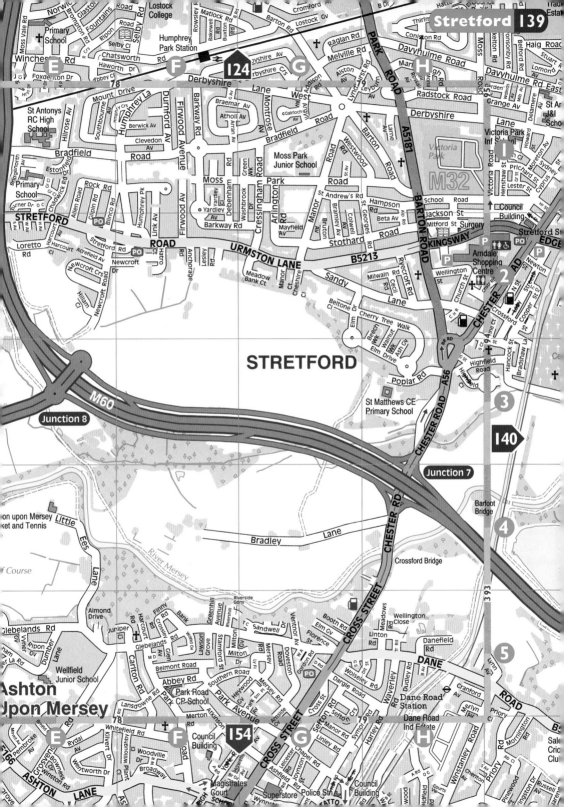

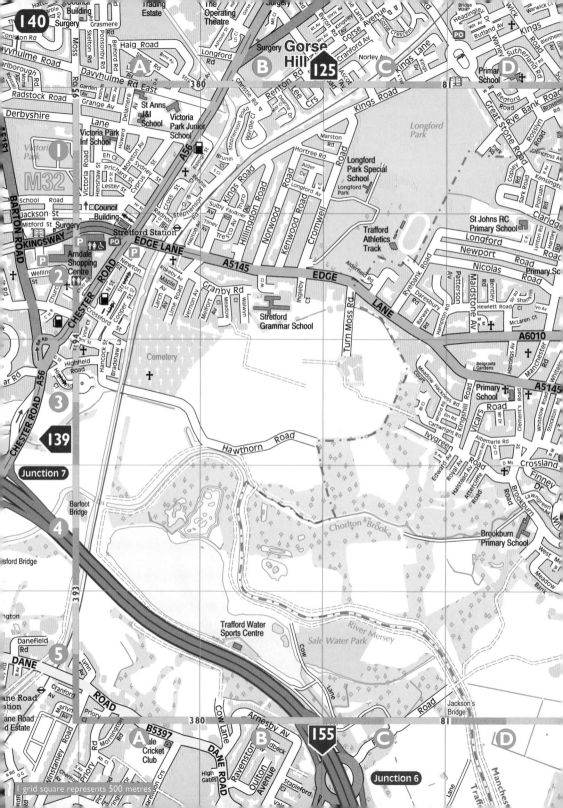

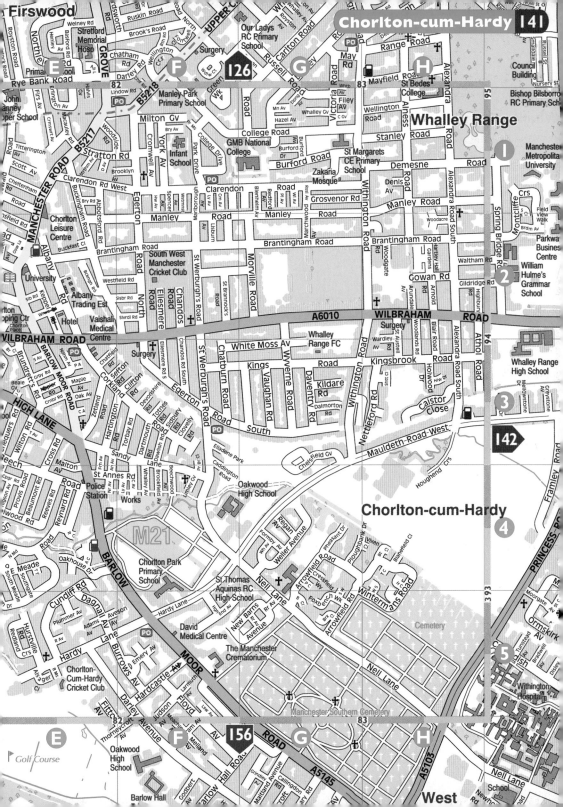

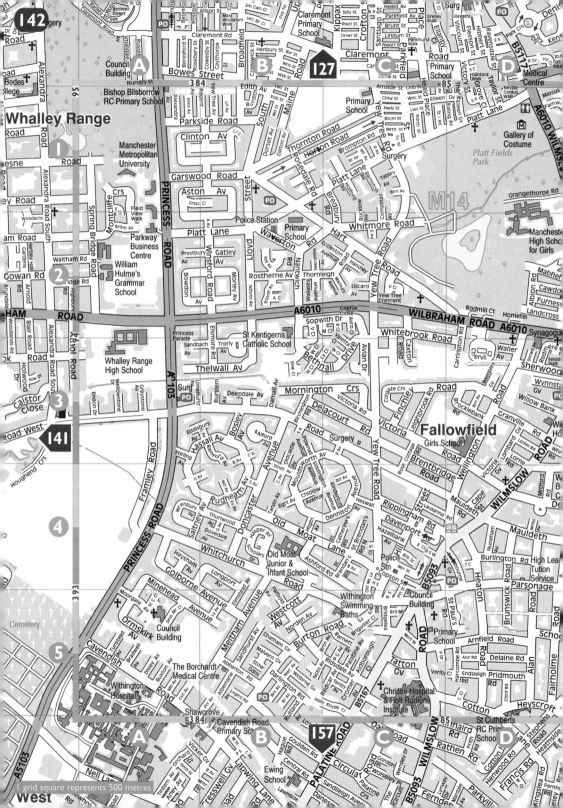

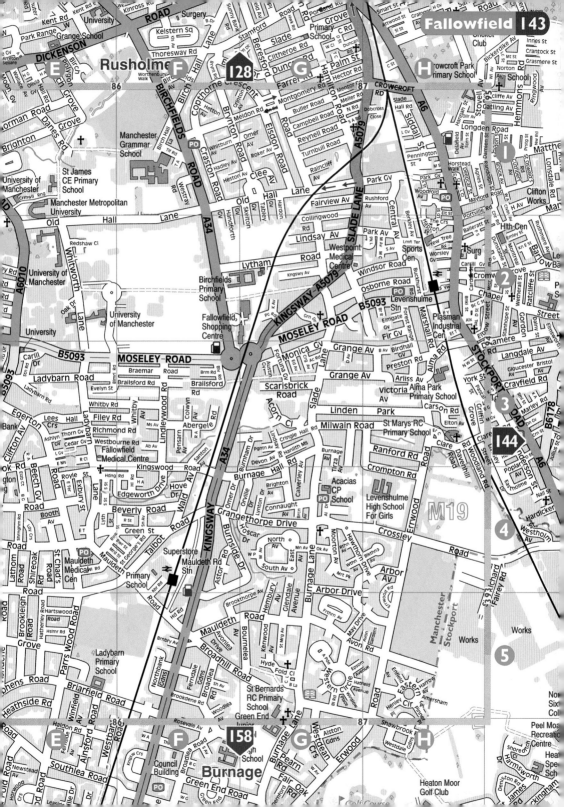

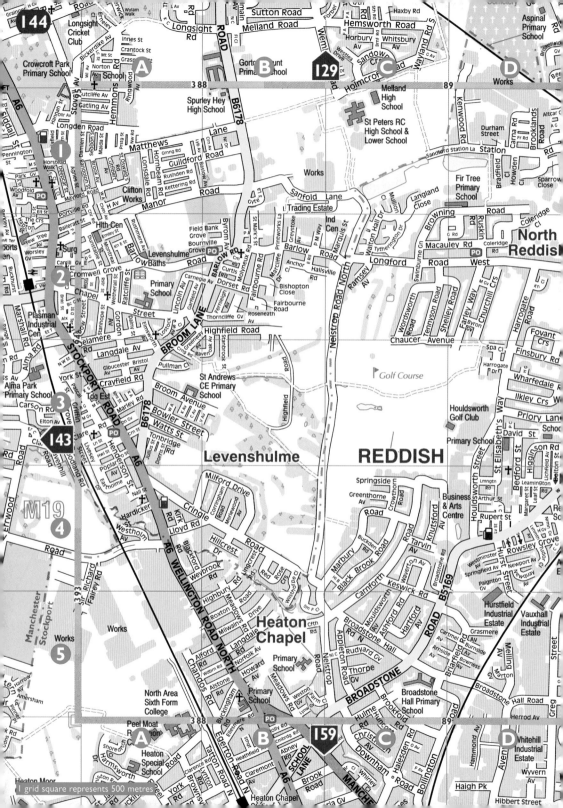

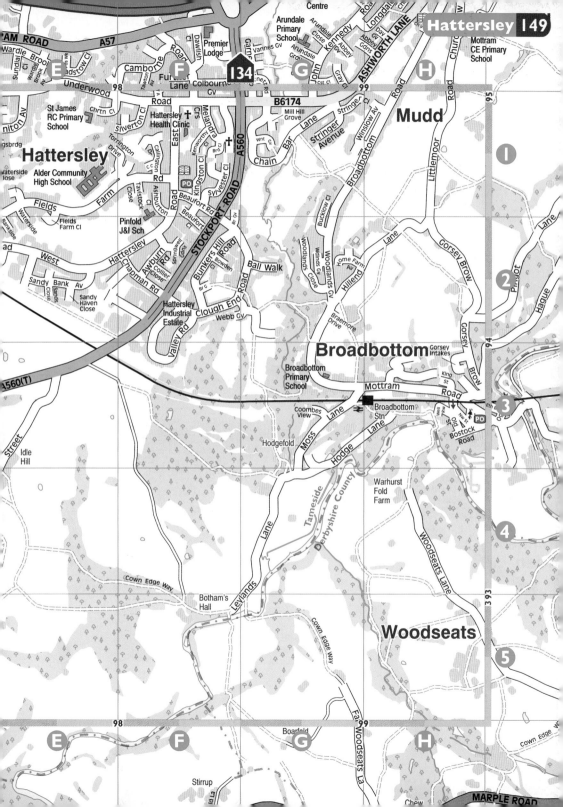

150

Glazebrook

LANE

A

B

Street

135

C

St Mary Primary School

D

Cadishead Junior School

Ashfield G

Northba Industrial Park
Brereton Grove
Nuttall St

Glazebrook Station

Sussex Rd

Berkshire Drive

PO

Purley Dr

Lancaster Road

Dorset Road

MOSS

John St

Anglers Rest

Martens

1

Street Cl

Vetch

Norfolk

Lords

Melville

Kent Rd

Hilton

Fairfield Road

derby Cl

Cumberland Av

York Rd

Warwick Road

Devon Rd

Fir Street

Belgrave Rd

Laburnum

Chestnut Av

Ash Av

Birch Av

Oak Av

Grange

School La

Harriet St

Frances

Green La

Cornwall Rd

Works

Carlton Way

2

Pool Rd

Essex Gdns

Lincoln Av

Cadishead Recreation Centre

Bowness

Hampton Rd

Dudley Road

Lytherton

Manchester Ship Canal

Thirlmere Cl

Penrith Rd

Coniston Road

Grasmere

Cadishead

Rosebank Road

Victory Rd

Hamilton Road

Allenby Av

Byng Av

The Vista

Bob's La

LIVERPOOL

Lock Lane

Our Lady of Lourdes RC Primary School

Buttermere Rd

Langdale

Patt

3

ollinfare

PO

Haig Av

Graham Crs

Kitchener Av

A57

ROAD

Lock Lane

Forest Gdns

Ash Rd

Birch Rd

Wood La

Sycamore

Maple Rd

Gorse Sq

Marine Rd

Grasmere Road

Larch

Cedar Rd

PO

Carmichael Cl

Manchester Road

St Helens CE Prim Sch

Briar Av

Birch Road

Glen Cl

Orchard Br

Forest Gate Community Primary Sch

Walnut Rd

Myrtle Rd

Wood

Plane Tree Road

Willow

Blossom

Redbrook Rd

4

Hollins Green

Works

Warrington Trafford

Red Brook

Chshr Rd

Oak Road

Lane

Kent Rd

Laurel Wk

Cumberland Rd

Lncshr Rd

Rutland

Tulip

Ortenbrook School

ROAD

5

Holly Bank Caravan Park

Warburton

Bridge Road

Manchester Ship Canal

Warburton Park

Heathlands Farm

Moss L

370

390

A

B

Park Road

C

Jack Hey Gate Farm

WARBURTON LANE

D

Toll

1 grid square represents 500 metres

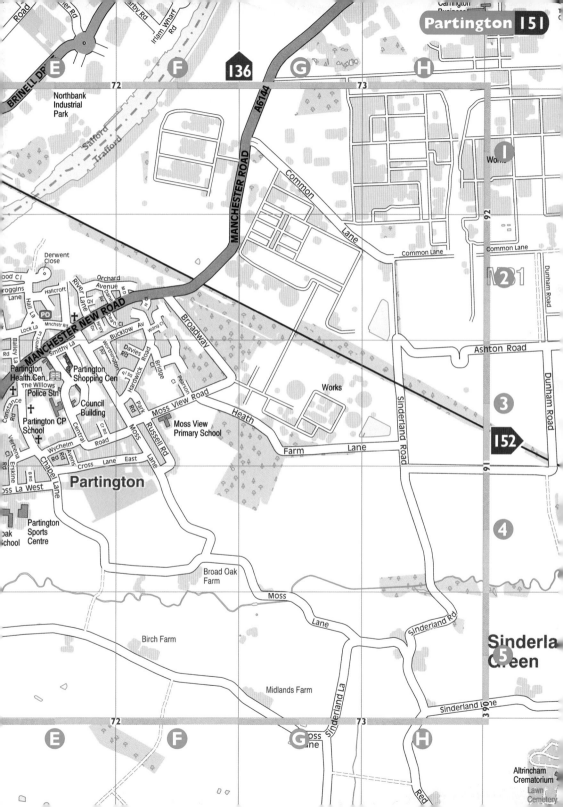

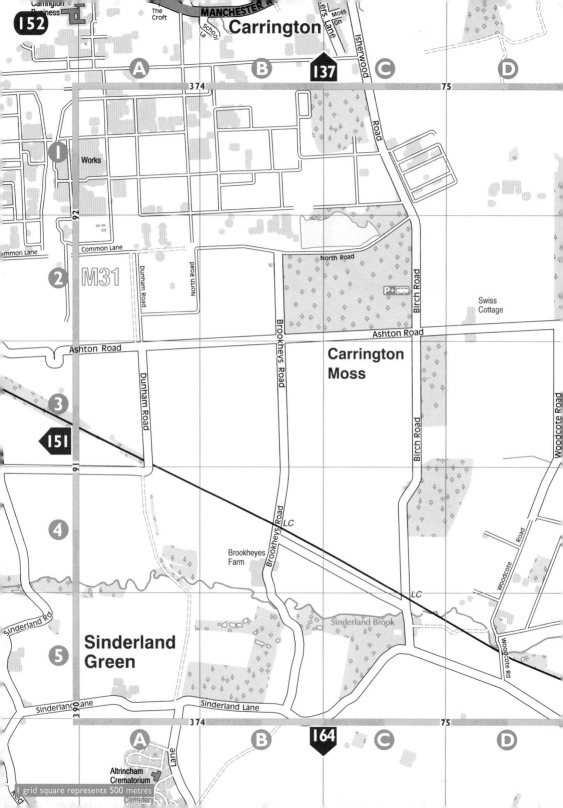

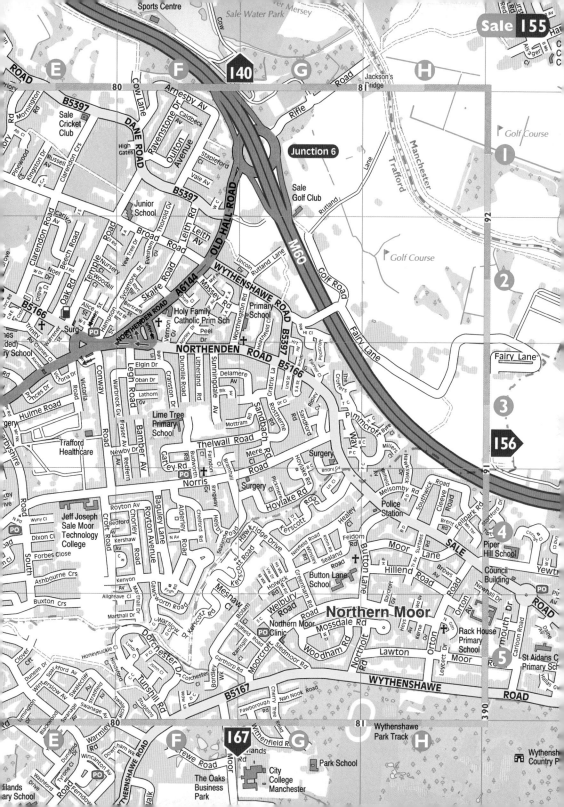

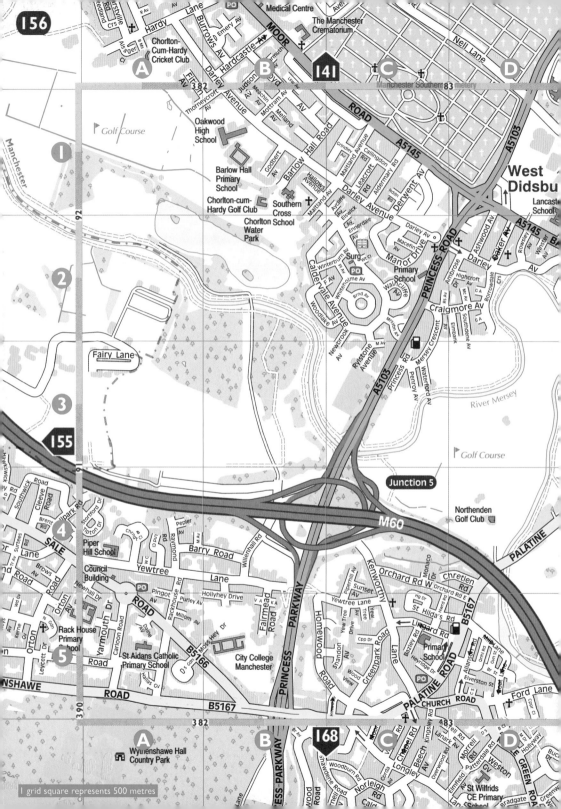

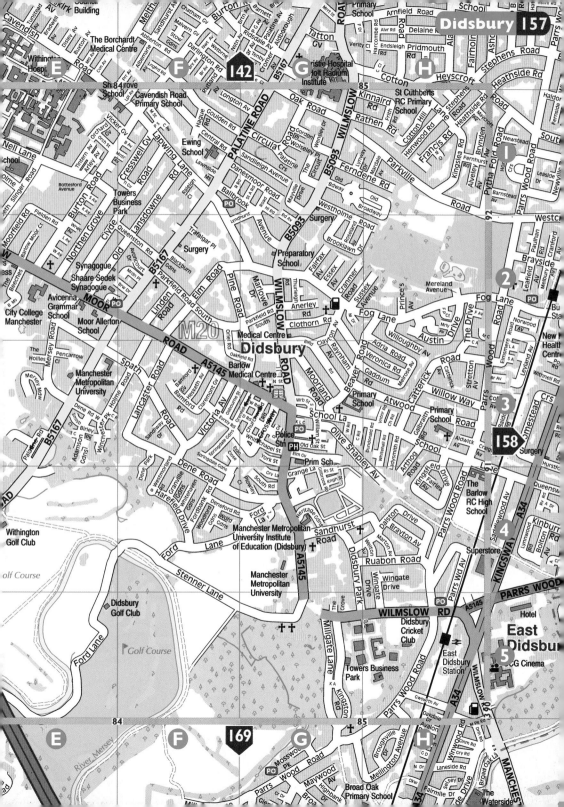

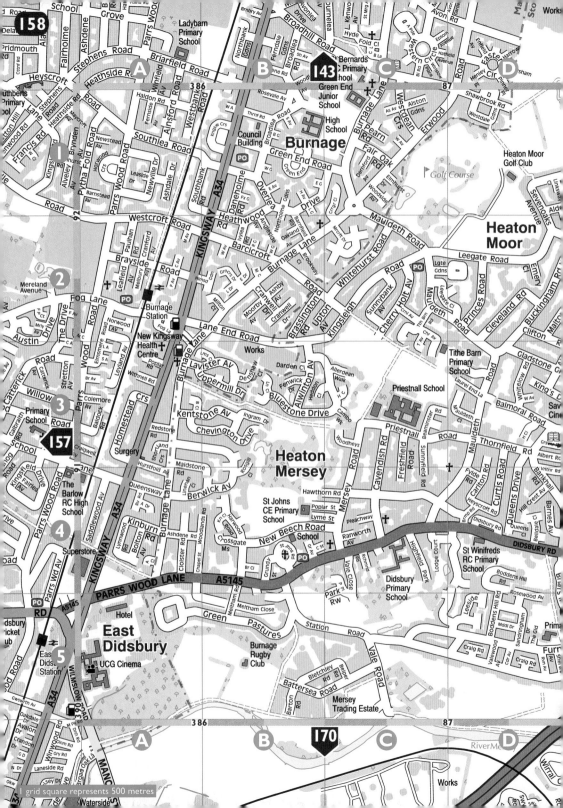

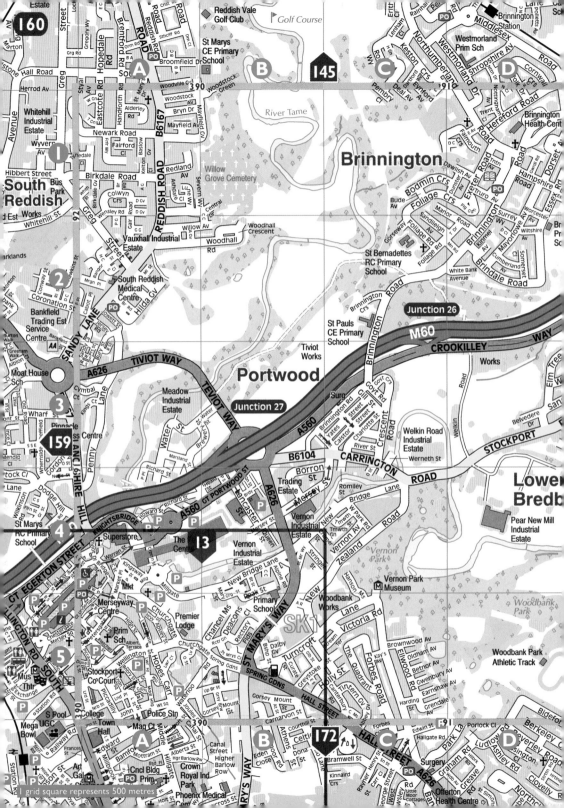

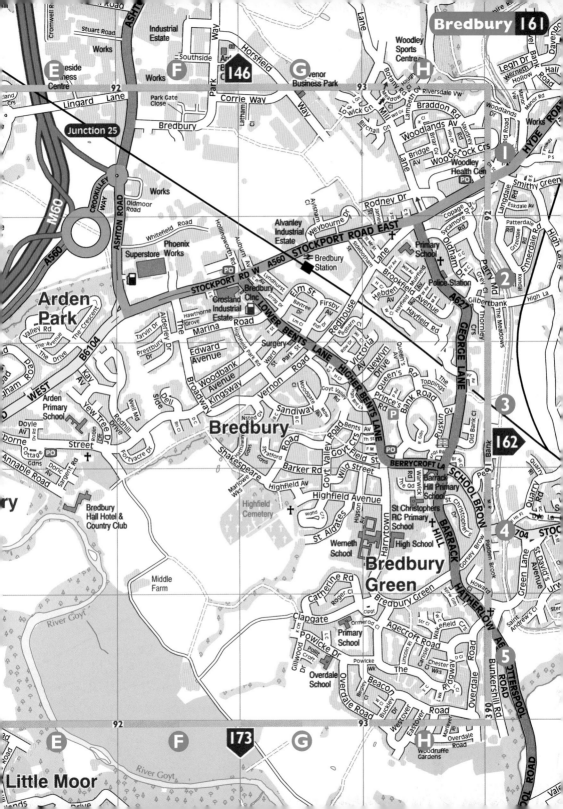

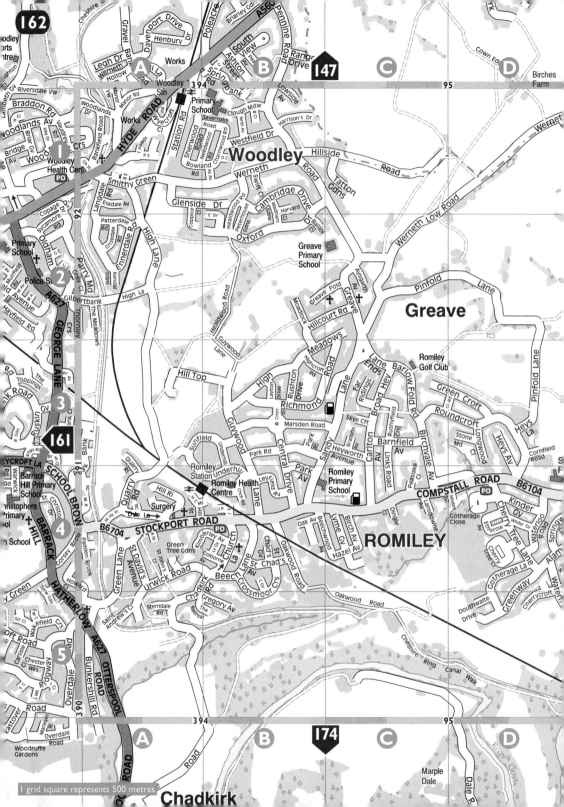

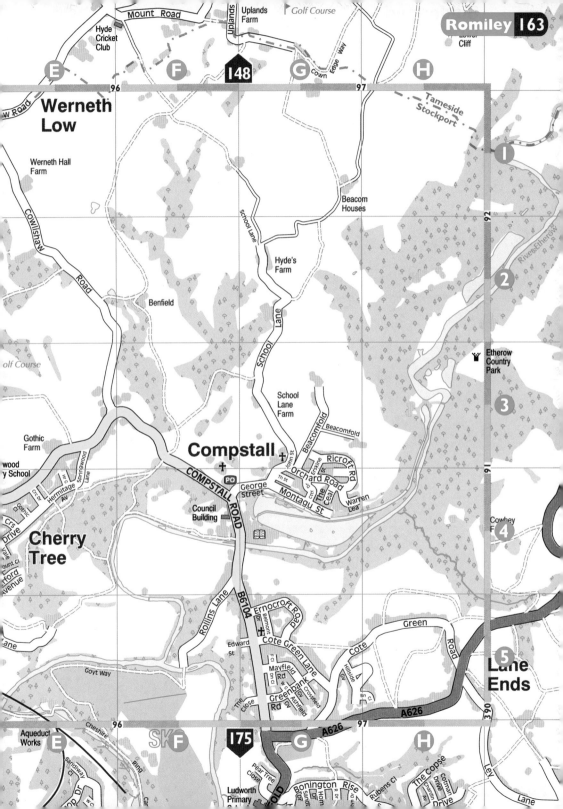

E **F** **148** **G** **H**

96 97

Tameside · Stockport

Werneth Low

Mount Road

Hyde Cricket Club

Uplands

Uplands Farm

Golf Course

Lower Cliff

Edge Way

Gown

I

92

Werneth Hall Farm

Beacom Houses

Rivers Etherow

School Lane

Hyde's Farm

2

Benfield

Etherow Country Park

olf Course

School Lane

School Lane Farm

3

91

Gothic Farm

Beacomfold

Beacomfold

Ricroft Rd

wood y School

Springwood Lane

Hermitage Av

Compstall

COMPSTALL ROAD

PO

John St

Th St

Orchard Road

Erskine St

Warren Lea

The Seal

Cowhey F

4

Crs Drive

Gothic Cl

Mount Cl

Vale

Cherry Tree

George Street

Montagu St

Council Building

tford Avenue

B6104

Rollins Lane

Ernocroft Road

Belmont

Cote Green Lane

Green

Cote

Road

5

Lane Ends

Goyt Way

Edward St

Mayfield Rd

Crossfield

Hillside

Bn Cl

390

Lane

Greenbank Rd

Ashfield

The Close

Cheshire

Ring

E **SKF** **F** **175** **G** A626 **H**

96 97

A626

Aqueduct Works

Sandiway Cl

Pear Tree Close

FOLD

Ludworth Primary

Bonington Rise

Sandt Hom Dr

Rubens Cl

The Copse

Carman Drive Jardin

Lev Lane

Dr Dr

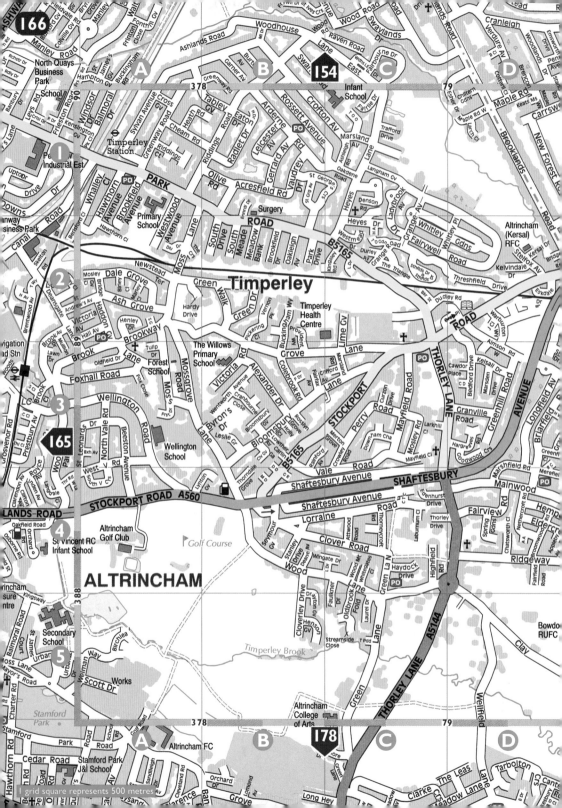

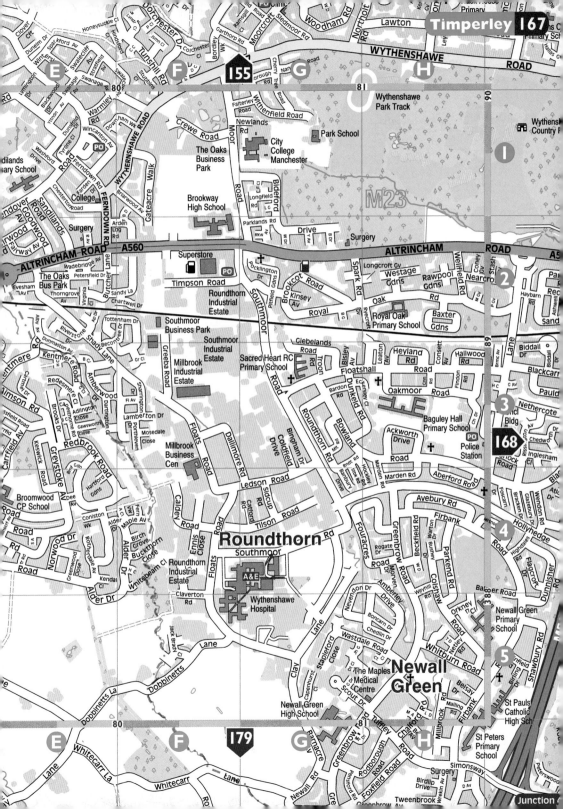

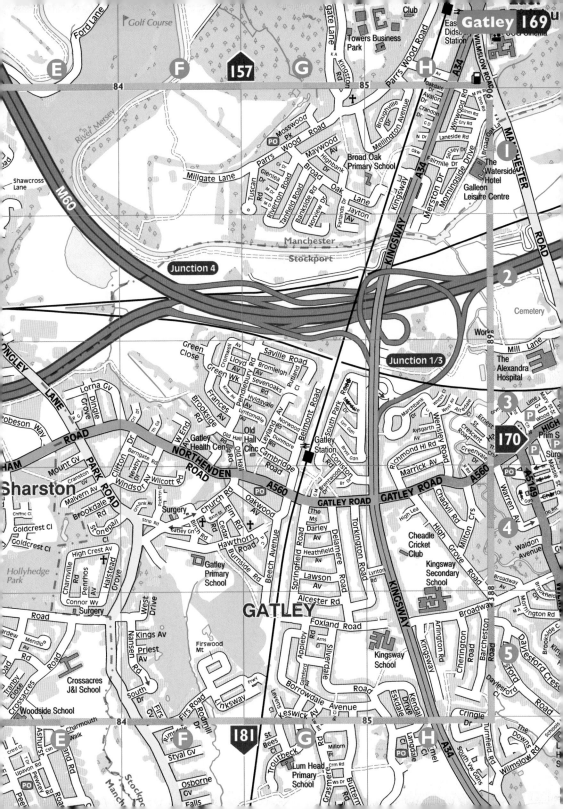

157

E   F   G   H   I

Ford Lane
Golf Course
gate Lane
Club
East Didsbury Station
Towers Business Park
Kingston Rd
Parrs Wood Road
WILMSLOW ROAD
A34
Cinema

River Mersey
M60
Millgate Lane
Shawcross Lane

Mosswood Pk
Wood Road
Maywood
Parrs
Tanfield Road
Bankside Rd
Riverton Road
Tuscan Rd
Glenlea
Highbank
Broad Oak Lane
Broad Oak Primary School
Mellington Avenue
Broughville Dr
Jayton Av
Norlew Dr
Farlands Dr
Crandon Dr
Avalon Dr
Wirwood Rd
Oakdale Dr
Laneside Rd
Fairmile Dr
Morningside Drive
Merston Dr
Kingsway
KINGSWAY
MANCHESTER ROAD
The Waterside Hotel
Galleon Leisure Centre

Junction 4
Manchester
Stockport

2

Cemetery
Works
Mill Lane

Junction 1/3

The Alexandra Hospital

ONGLEY LANE
Green Close
Saville Road
Cornwell Av
Bromleigh Av
Rutland
Lloyd Av
sevenoaks Cl
Green Wk
Frances Av
Hyldavale Av
Lyntonvale Av
Norwood
Dunmore
Belmont Road
South Park Road
Marchbank Dr
Aysgarth Av
Richmond HI Rd
Wensley Road
Crescent Road
Greenvale
Aintree
Ernest
Lime Rd
Wood St
HIGH

170

3

Sharston
NORTHENDEN ROAD
PARK ROAD
Mount Gv
Malvern Av
Brookdale Rd
Clifton
Newby Rd
Windsor Av
Wilcott Av
Gatley Health Cen
Old Hall Clinic
Cambridge Road
Leyland
A560
Gatley Station
Coniston Rd
Marrick Av
GATLEY ROAD
Chadvil Rd
Milton Crs
High Grove Road
Warren Av
PO
4

Goldcrest Cl
Hollyhedge Peel
High Crest Av
Charnville Rd
Penros
Halstead Grove
Connor Wy
Surgery
Church Rd
Elm Rd
Cedar Rd
Hawthorn Road
Burnside Rd
Oakwood Av
Beech Avenue
Springfield Road
The Ms
Darley Av
Heathfield Av
Lawson Av
Alcester Rd
Delamere Road
Torkington Road
Lynton Rd
Cheadle Cricket Club
Kingsway Secondary School
Broadway
Waldon Avenue
5

Gatley Primary School
GATLEY
West Drive
Kings Av
Priest Av
Nansen Rd
Firswood Mt
Foxland Road
Appleby
Silverdale
Gainford
Borrowdale Avenue
Leswick Av
Kingsway School
KINGSWAY
Arlington Rd
Cherington Rd
Barcheston Rd
Cringle Dr
Daviesford Cres
Daviesford Road

Crossacres J&I School
Woodside School
South Dr
Firs Rd
Rodmill
Linksway
St Bees Cl
Troutbeck
Lum Head Primary School
Millom Pl
Grasmere
Buttermere Rd
Langdale
Wilmslow Rd
A34

181

E   F   G   H

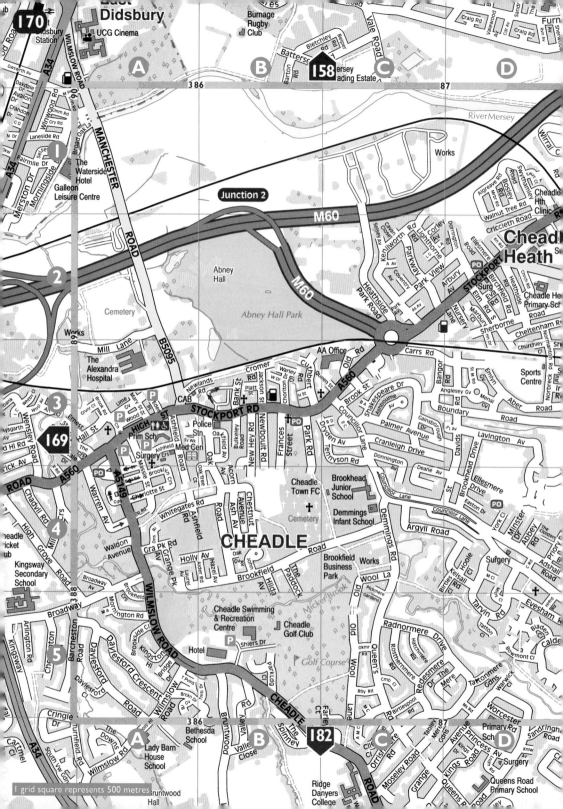

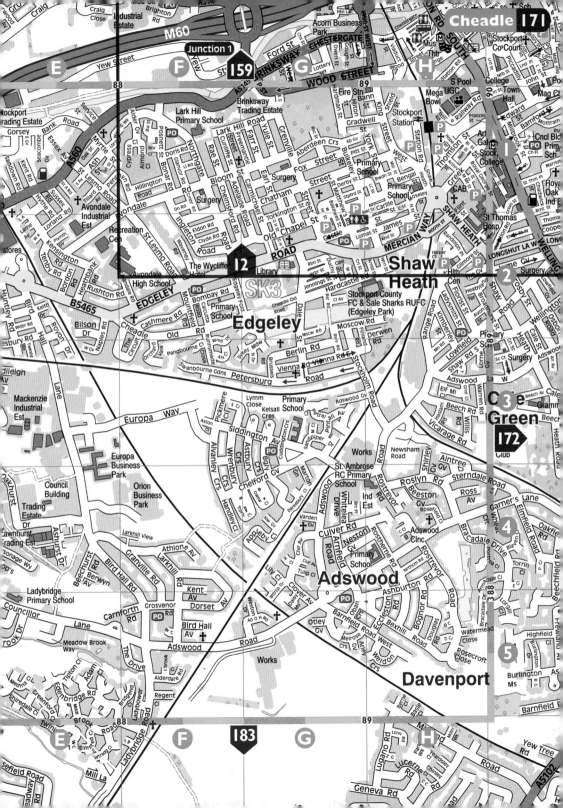

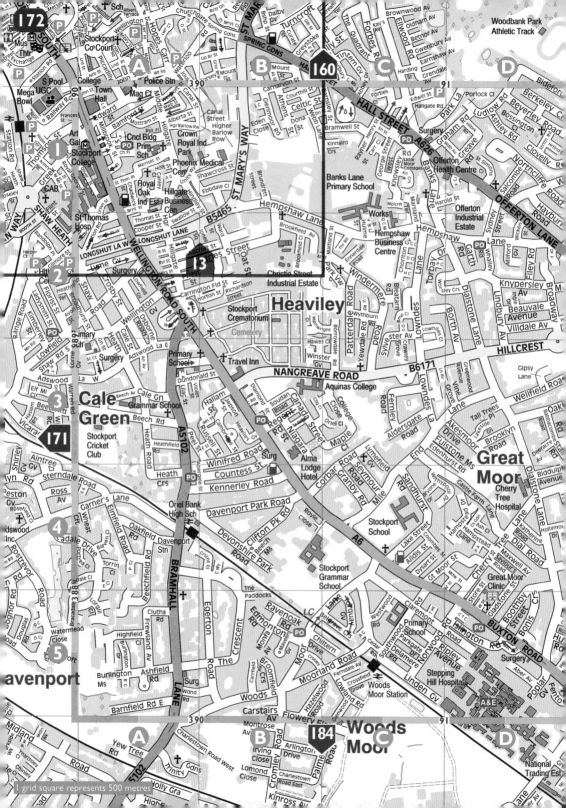

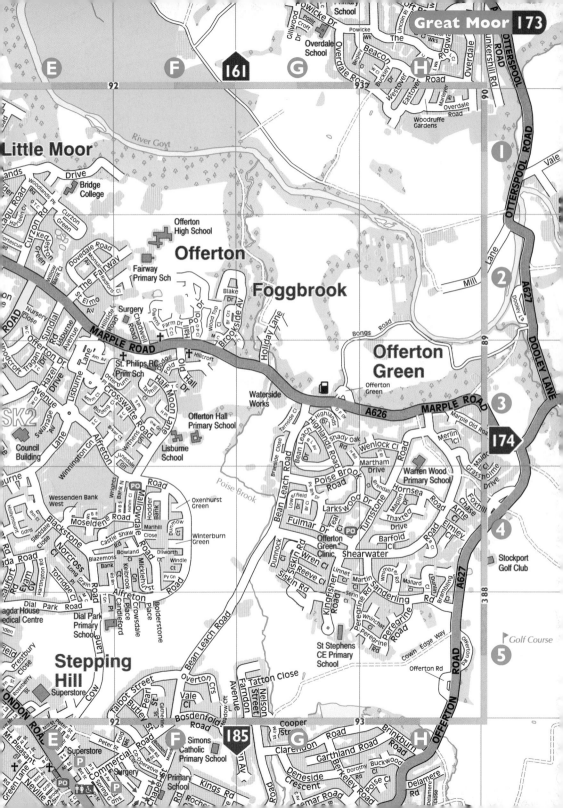

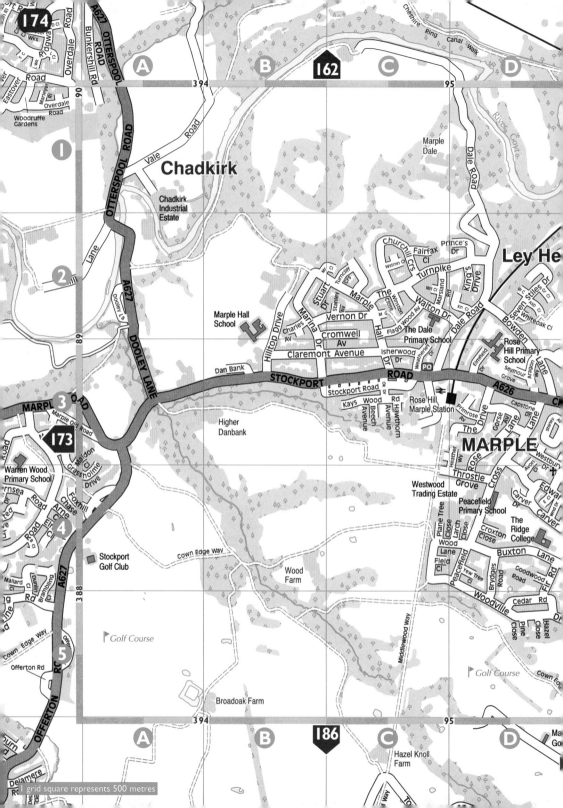

A **B** **C** **D**

I

394 90 95

Eastover Road
Wks
Ridgway
Overdale Road
Bunkershill Rd
OTTERSPOOL ROAD
A627
Woodruffe Gardens
Overdale Road
Merivey Rd

Marple Dale

Vale Road

Chadkirk

Rivers Govt

Dale Road

Chadkirk Industrial Estate

2

Lane

OTTERSPOOL ROAD

DOOLEY LANE

A627

Dooley La

89

Churchill Crs
Prince's Dr
Fairfax Cl
Turnpike
Wstmn Cl
Ley He
Ten Whiteoak Cl
Lew Striles Dr
W.C.
ASP Cl

Marina Dr
Stanley
Marple
The
Winton Close
Walton Dr
Marsland
King's Drive
Bowden Lane
Kn Cl
Stuart Dr
Mri Cl
Rd

Hilltop Drive
Charles Av
Vernon Dr
Cromwell Av
Flagg Wood Av
The Dale Primary School
Rose Hill Primary School
Seymour Grove

Marple Hall School

Claremont Avenue
Isherwood Dr
Weatherley
Elmfield
PO

3 **MARPLE** ROAD
Dan Bank
STOCKPORT ROAD
A626

Marple Old Road
Stockport Road
Rose Hill Marple Station
Primrose Av
Capstone Cl
The Drive

173

Higher Danbank

Kays
Wood
Beech Avenue
Rd
Hawthorn Avenue
Westbury Dr
Avon Dr

Warren Wood Primary School
Maldon Cl
Grassholme
Foxhill
Chase
Grasholme Drive

4

Arne Road
Elm
MARPLE
Throstle Grove
Westwood Trading Estate
Peacefield Primary School
Carver Dr
Edwar
Carver
The Ridge College

Mallard
Brambling Rd
A627

Stockport Golf Club

Cown Edge Way

Wood Farm

Plane Tree
Larch Close
Wood Lane
Field Cl
Peacefield
Yew Tree
Croxton Close
Buxton Lane
Goodwood Road
Fir Rd

388
394 95

5

Golf Course

OFFERTON RD
A627
Cown Edge Way
Offerton Rd

Middlewood Way

Broadoak Farm

Golf Course
Cown Ed

Woodville Road
Cedar Rd
Hazel Close
Pine Close

A **B** **C** **D**

Hazel Knoll Farm
Ma Go

Delamere

1 grid square represents 500 metres

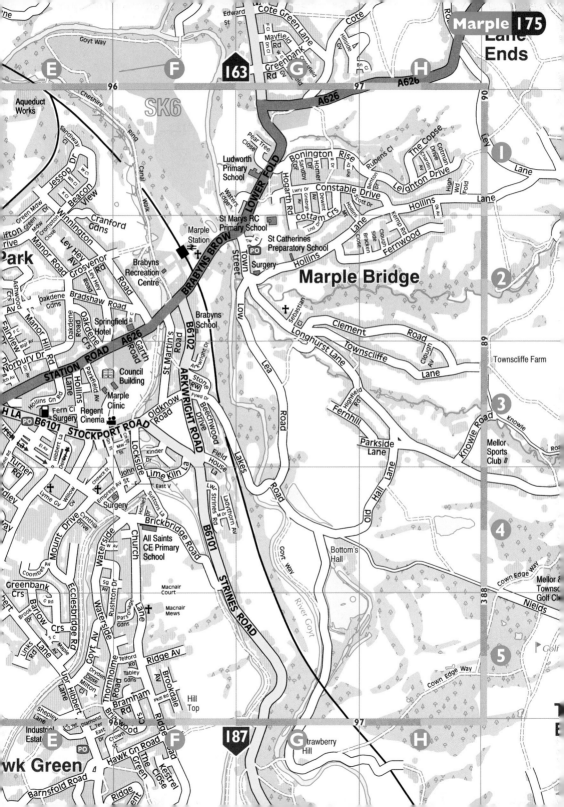

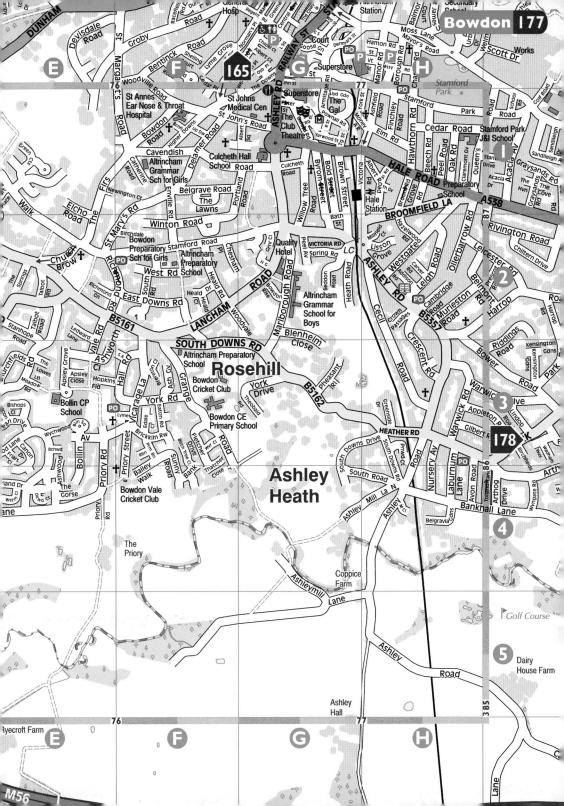

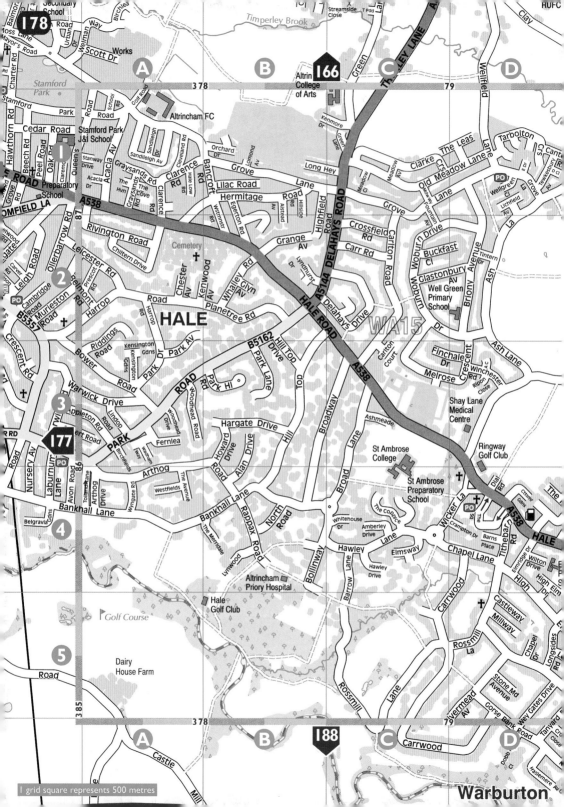

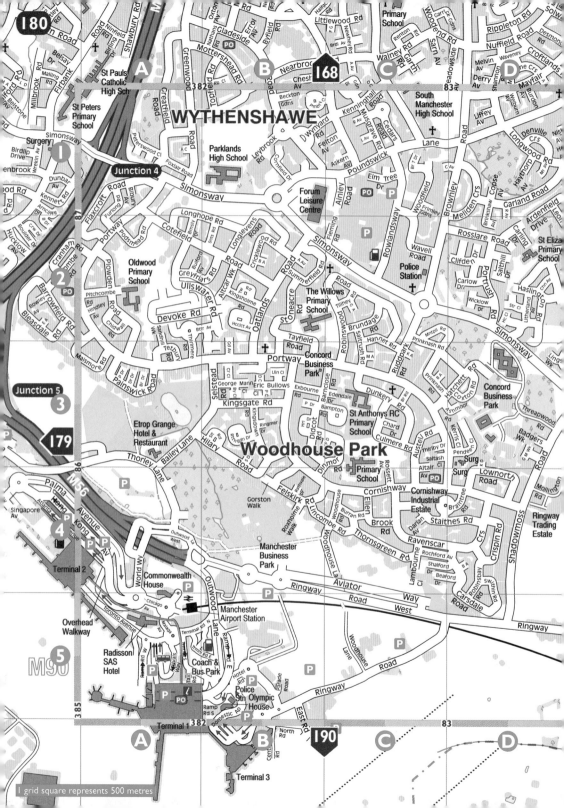

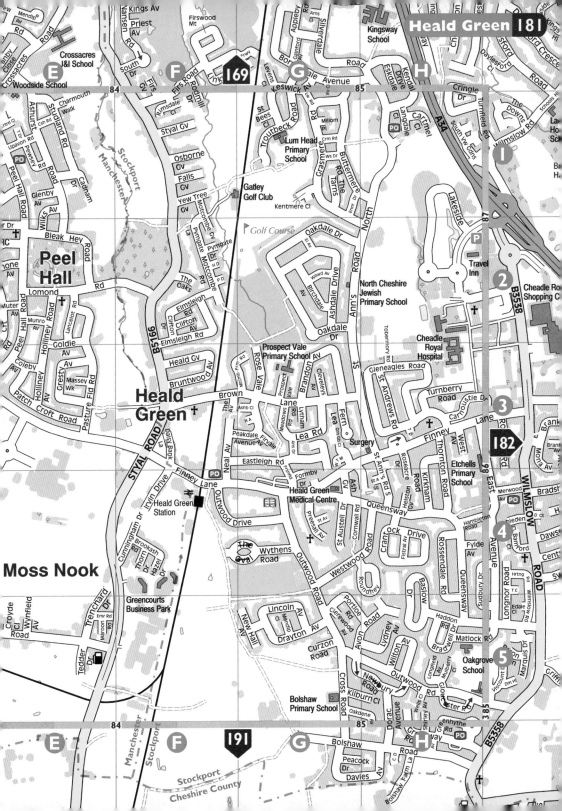

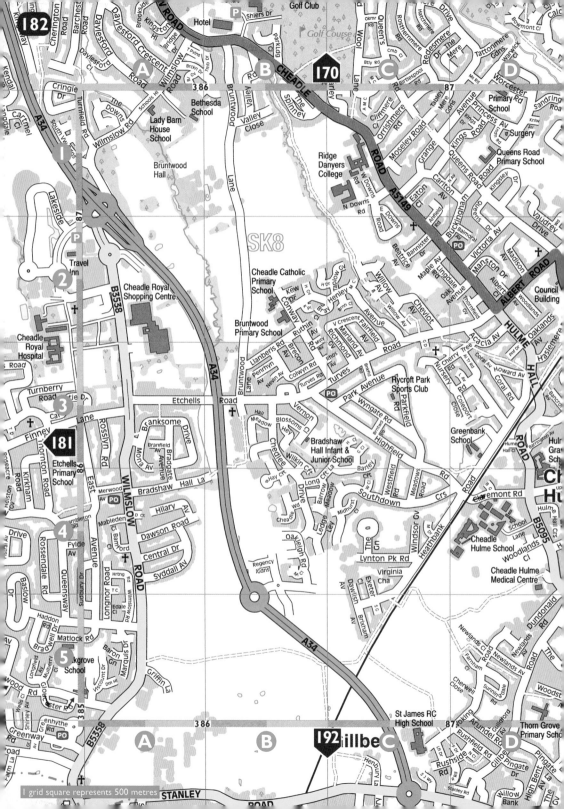

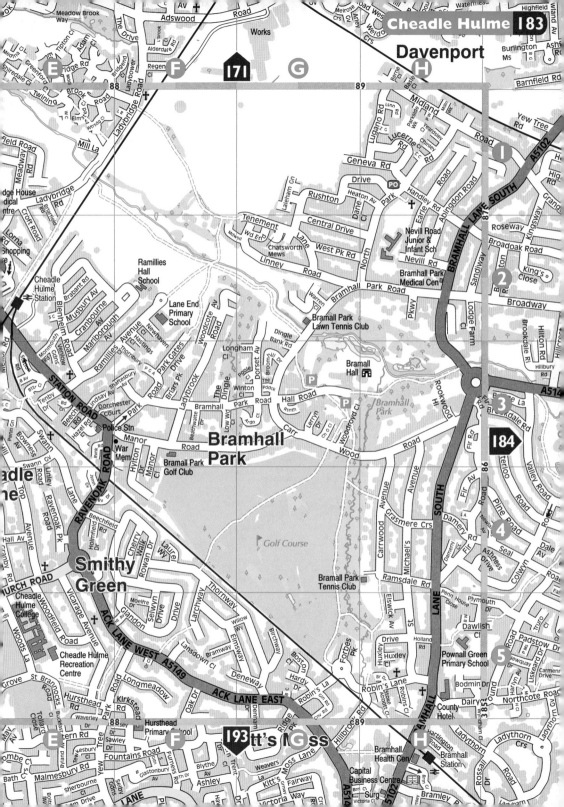

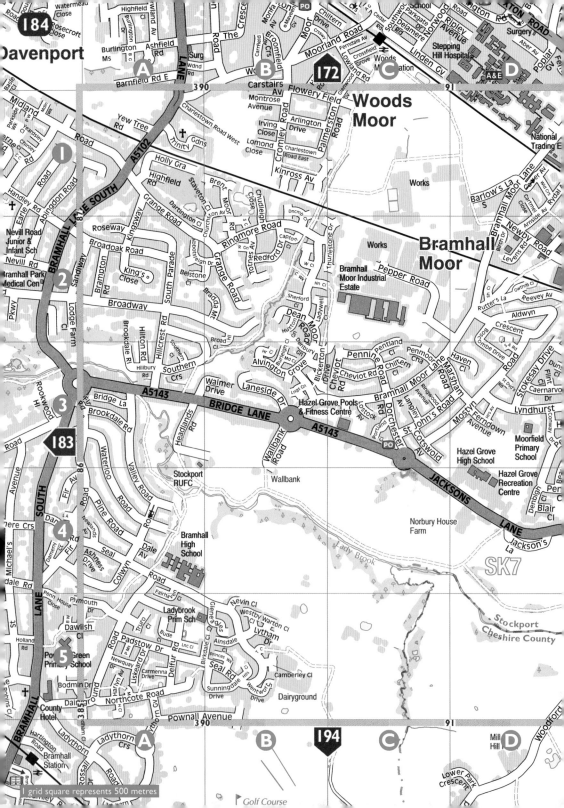

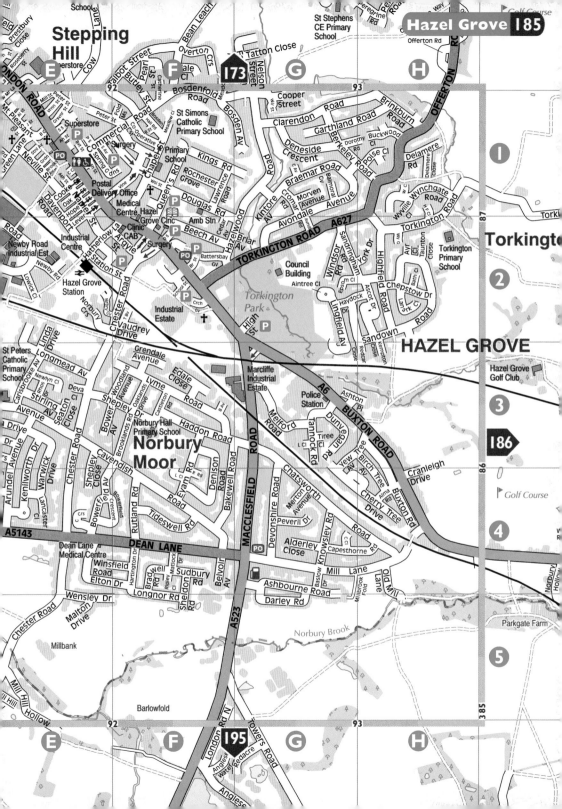

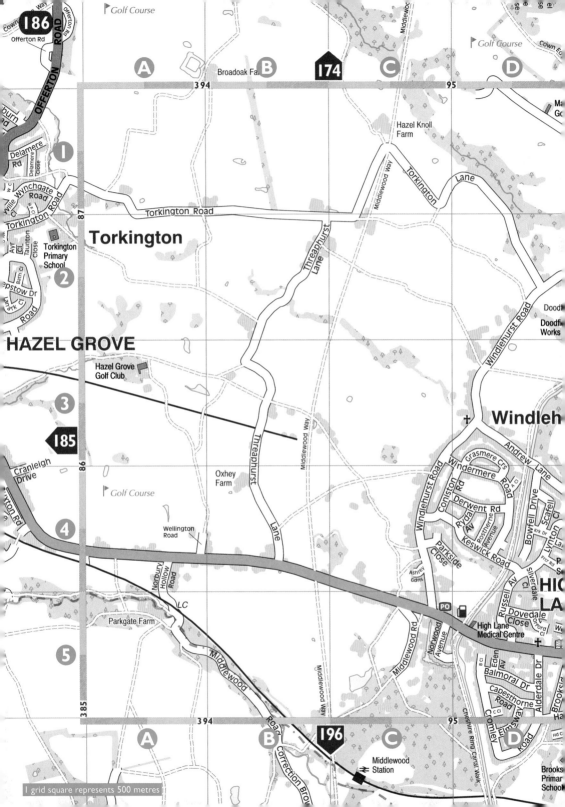

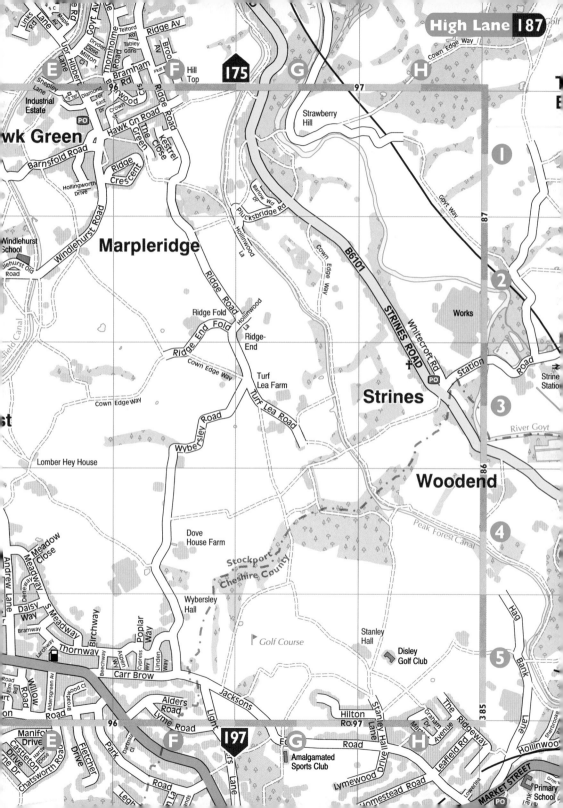

E F **175** G H

I

Links Rd
Goyt Av
Ridge Av
Telford Rd
Tabley Gdns
Cown Edge Way
Golf
Thornholme
Dryden Clo
Maple
Brook Av
Milton
Ridge Road
Hibbert
Bramham Rd
Hill Top
Strawberry Hill

E

Shepley Lane
Jun Ter
Diamond Ter East
Crown Dr
Hawk Gn Road
Kestrel Close
The Green
Goyt Way
Industrial Estate
PO

wk Green

Barnsfold Road
Ridge Crescent
Hollingworth drive

Windlehurst School

Mapleridge

Windlehurst Road

Barrow Way Dr
Plucksbridge Rd
Hollinwood La
Cown Edge Way
B6101
STRINES ROAD
Whitecroft Rd
Works

2

Windlehurst Old Road

Ridge Road
Ridge Fold
Hollinwood La
Ridge-End
Ridge End Fold
Cown Edge Way
PO
Station
Strine Station

3

Cown Edge Way
Turf Lea Farm
Strines
River Goyt

Wybersley Road
Turf Lea Road

Lomber Hey House

Woodend

Peak Forest Canal

Dove House Farm

4

Meadow Close
Meadway
Andrew Lane
Daisy Way
Bramway
S Meadway
Birchway
Thornway
Larchway
Beechway
Aspen
Poplar Way
Cypress
Linden
Carr Brow
Jacksons
Light
Alders Road
Lyme Road
Willow Road
Manifold Drive
Castleton Dr
Chatsworth Drive
Fletcher Drive
Park
Legh
Lyme Road
Darbell
Road

Stockport
Cheshire County

Wybersley Hall

Golf Course
Stanley Hall
Disley Golf Club

5

Hag Bank
The Ridgeway
Hollinwoo

E **197** F G H

Amalgamated Sports Club
Hilton Rd
Ed
Road
Stanley Hall Drive
Stanley Lane
Graham Dr
Avenue
Leafield Rd
Market St
Lowertea
Homestead Road
Lymewood
Lane Bank
Primary School
MARKET STREET
PO

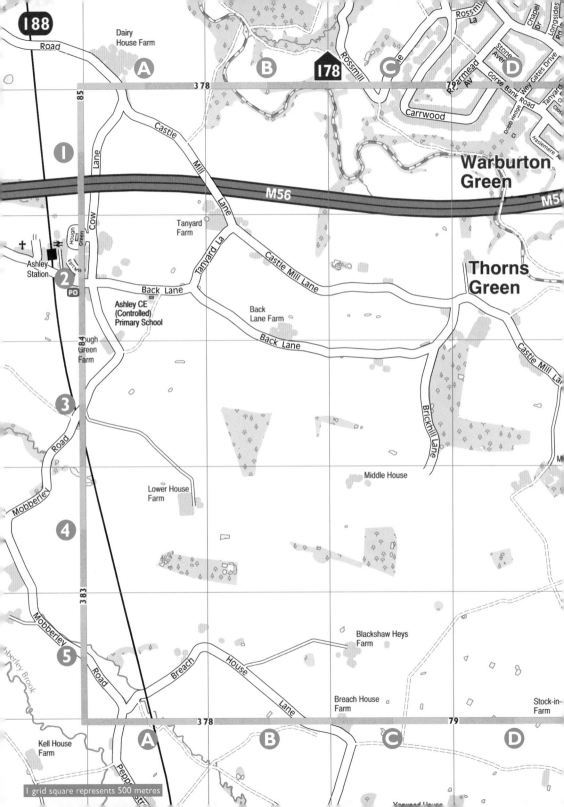

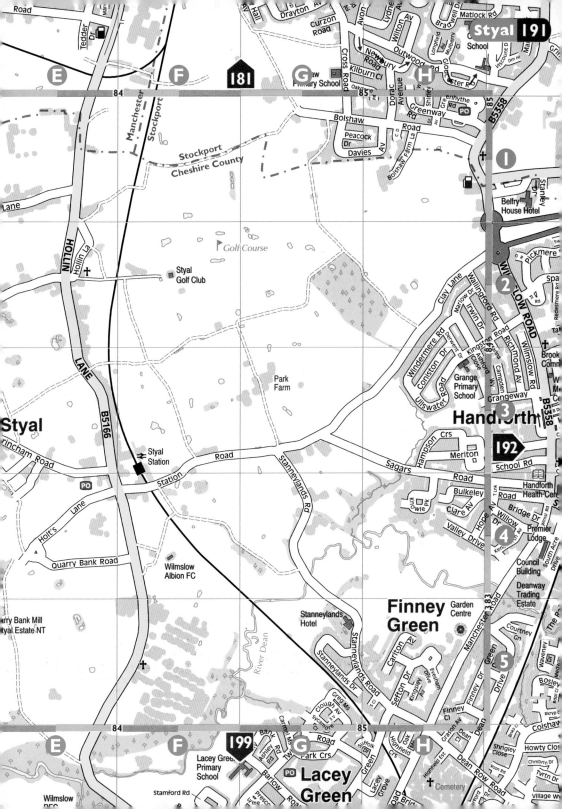

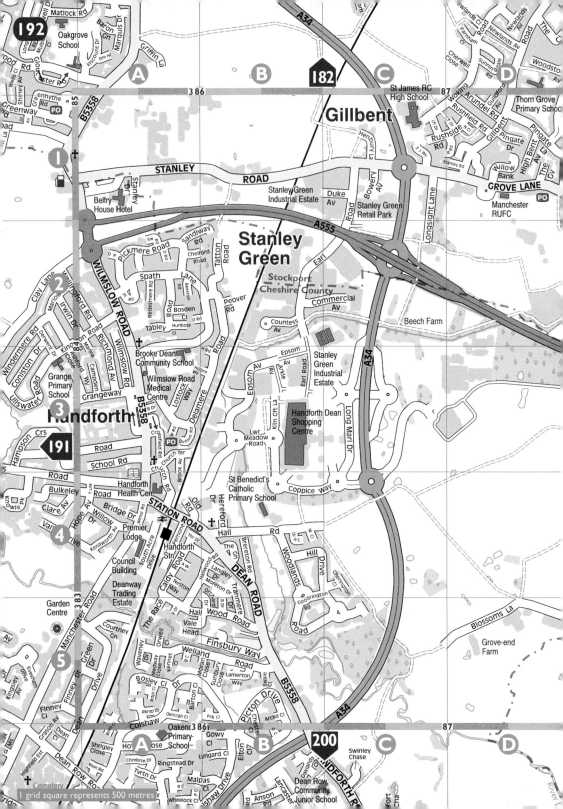

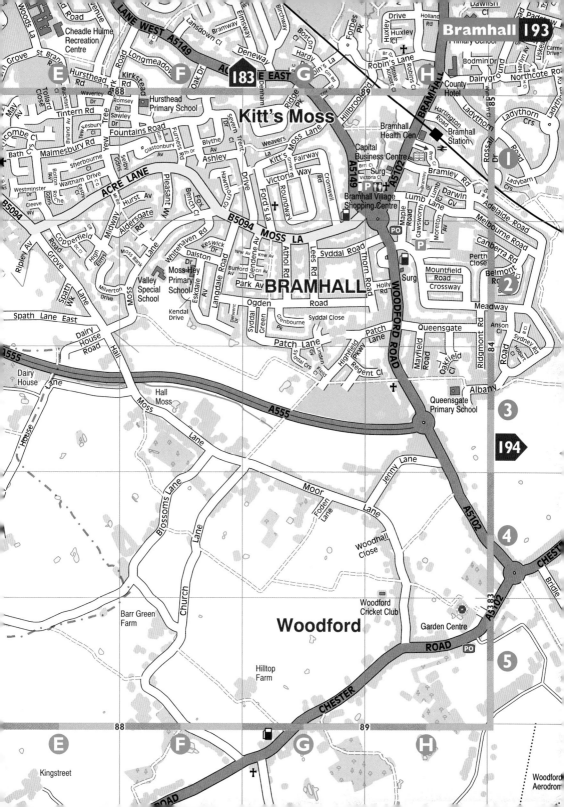

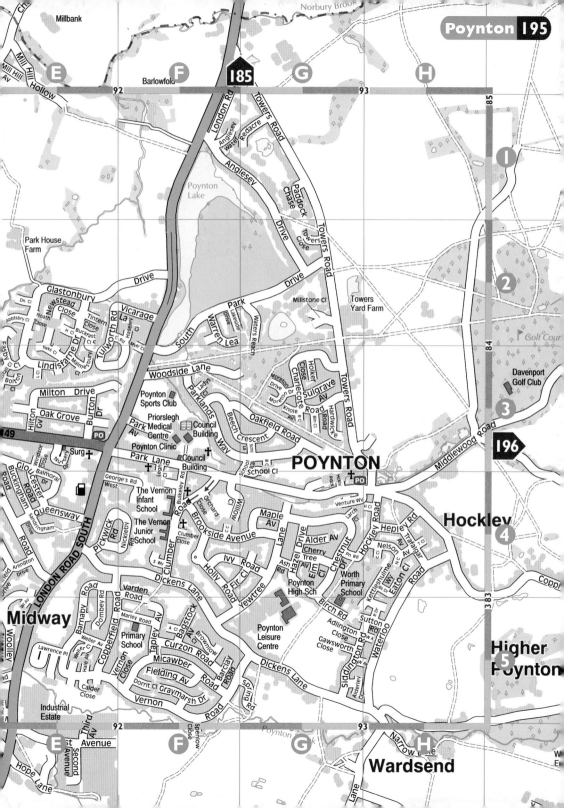

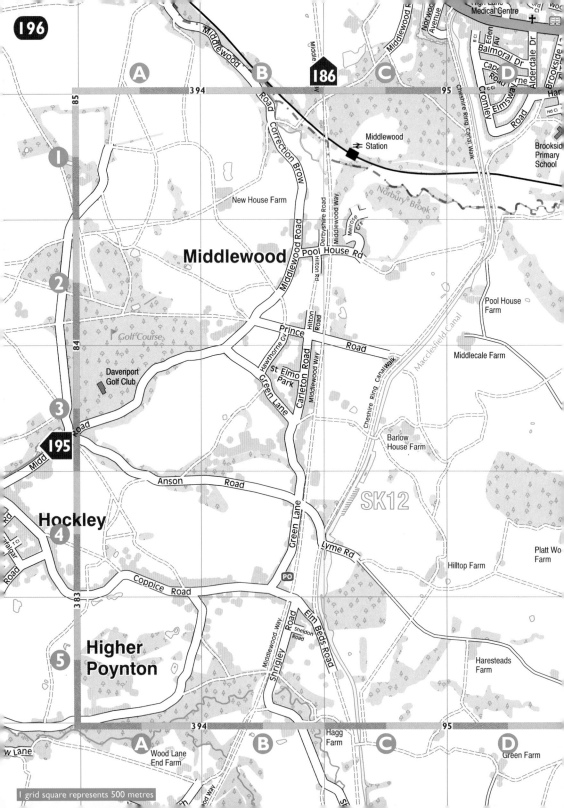

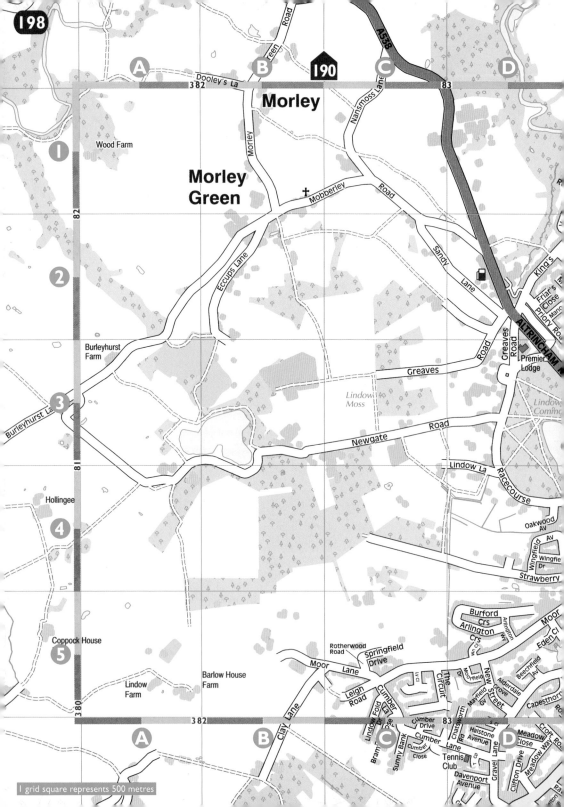

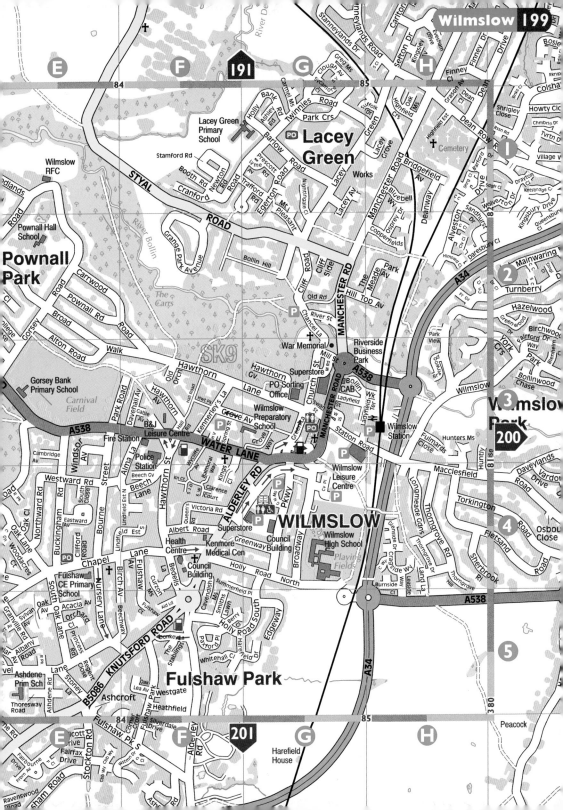

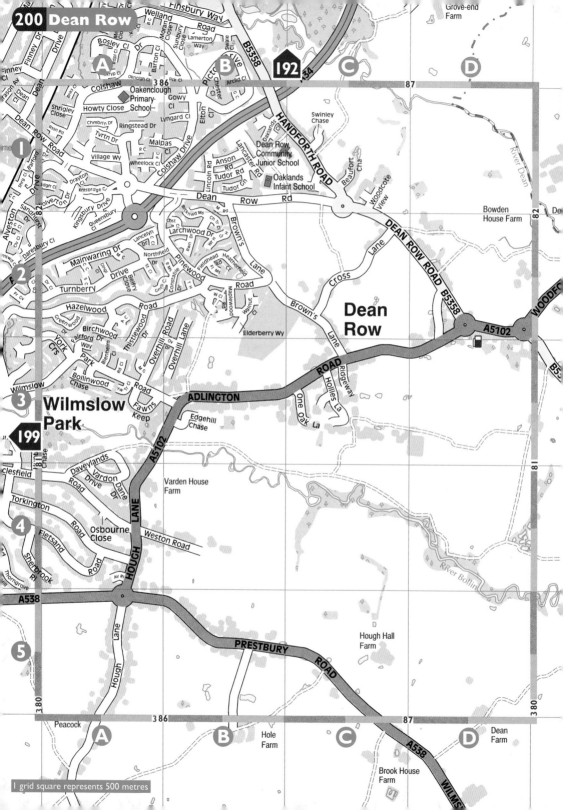

Grove-end Farm

Finsbury Way

Welland Road

Bosley Cl

Finney Dr

Dean Drive

Finney Av

Dean

Dean Drive

A
B
C
D

Colshaw

Oakenclough Primary School

Howty Close

Shrigley Close

Chmbrln Dr

Ringstead Dr

Tvrtn Dr

Malpas

Village Wy

Wheelock Cl

Colshaw Drive

Gowy Cl

Lyngard Cl

Elton Cl

Handforth Road

Swinley Chase

B5358

Dean Row Community Junior School

Anson Rd

Lancaster Rd

Lincoln Rd

Tudor Rd

Tudor Cl

Oaklands Infant School

Beaufort Cha

Woodcote View

Dean Row Road

Bowden House Farm

I

Dean Row Road

Kingsbury Drive

Queensbury Cl

Lancelyn Dr

Larchwood Dr

Northfield Dr

Brown's Lane

Dean

Row

Rd

Cross

Lane

Dean Row Road B5358

A5102

WOODFO

B5

2

Mainwaring Dr

Drive

Turnberry

Hazelwood Road

Birchwood Dr

Fairford Way

Blenheim

Thistlewood Dr

Pinewood Road

Overhill Road

Overhill Lane

Fieldhead

Heatherfield

Maplewood

Walnut

Elderberry Wy

Brown's Lane

Lane

Dean Row

3

Wilmslow Park

York Crs

Green-end

Bollinwood Chase

Fawns Keep

Road

ADLINGTON

Edgehill Chase

ROAD

One Oak La

Hollies La

Ridgeway

A5102

Daveylands

Vardon Drive

Dane Dr

Hough Lane

Weston Road

Varden House Farm

4

Torkington Road

Osbourne Close

Fletsand Road

Sherbrook Rd

Thorngrove R

A538

River Bollin

5

Hough Lane

PRESTBURY ROAD

Hough Hall Farm

3 80

Peacock

A
B
Hole Farm
C
A538
D
Dean Farm

Brook House Farm

WILMS

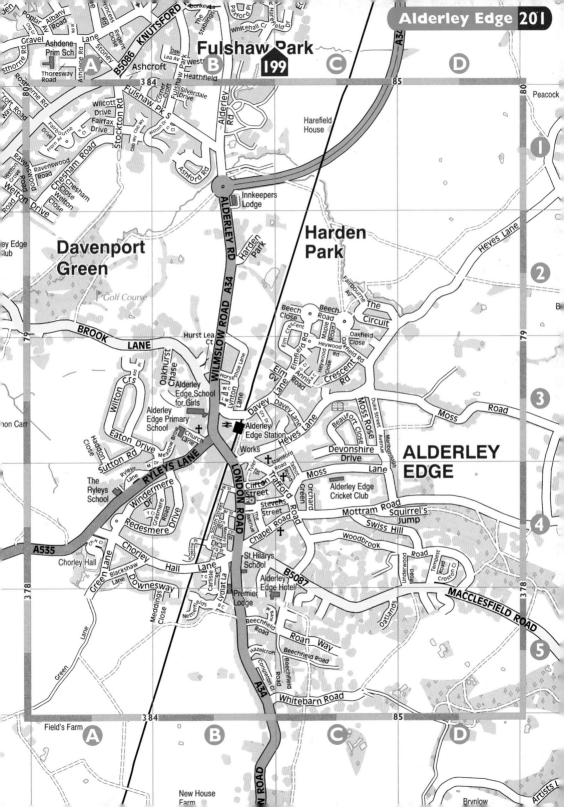

Abbey Hey 130 A3
Acre 75 E3
Adswood 171 G4
Affetside 25 E3
Ainsworth 36 C5
Alder Forest 108 C1
Alderley Edge 201 D3
Alkrington Garden Village 87 F2
Alt 91 G4
Alt Hill 105 F2
Altrincham 166 A4
Ancoats 7 K4
Arden Park 161 E2
Ardwick 127 H1
Ashley Heath 177 G4
Ashton-under-Lyne 117 G2
Ashton Upon Mersey 139 E5
Astley Bridge 33 H2
Audenshaw 131 F1
Austerlands 76 C4
Backbower 147 H3
Bagslate Moor 28 C3
Balderstone 43 G4
Baldingstone 27 F2
Bamford 28 A4
Bank Lane 17 E1
Bank Top 34 B1
Bardsley 104 D1
Barrow Bridge 32 D2
Barton Upon Irwell 109 G5
Belfield 31 E4
Belle Vue 129 E3
Benchill 168 B5
Bentgate 44 D2
Besses o' th' Barn 68 C5
Beswick 114 C4
Birch 55 H5
Blackford Bridge 53 G5
Black Lane 52 A3
Blackley 101 F1
Bolholt 37 F2
Bolton 3 G5
Boothstown 94 B4
Bowdon 176 C3
Bowgreen 176 D3
Bowlee 70 B3
Bradford 114 C3
Bradley Fold 51 E2
Bradshaw 23 H5
Bramhall 193 G2
Bramhall Moor 184 C2
Bramhall Park 183 F3
Bredbury 161 F3
Bredbury Green 161 H4
Breightmet 50 D1
Brinnington 160 C1
Broadbottom 149 G3
Broadfield 40 C5
Broadhalgh 28 C4
Broadheath 165 F2
Broadley 18 B3
Broadoak Park 96 B5
Bromley Cross 23 F5
Brook Bottom 92 B5
Brooklands 154 C4
Brooksbottoms 16 D5
Broughton Park 99 G1
Brownlow Fold 33 F5
Brunswick 127 G2
Brushes 120 B2
Buckley 19 F5
Buckton Vale 107 E4
Buersil Head 43 H5
Burnage 158 B1
Burnden 49 F5
Burnedge 44 B5
Bury 4 C3
Busk 8 A1
Cadishead 150 B2
Calderbrook 15 G4
Caldermoor 20 D2
Cale Green 172 A3
Captain Fold 41 F3
Carr 16 C1
Carrbrook 107 F5
Carrington 137 F5
Carrington Moss 152 C3
Castle Hill 146 B4
Castleton 42 B4
Chadderton 72 D5
Chadderton Fold 72 D2
Chadkirk 174 A1
Chapel Field 67 H3
Charlestown 87 H4
Charlestown 112 A1
Cheadle 170 B4
Cheadle Heath 170 D2
Cheadle Hulme 182 D4
Cheetham Hill 100 C4
Cherry Tree 163 E4
Chesham 38 D1
Chew Moor 46 D5
Chorlton-cum-Hardy 141 G4
Cinder Hill 66 C4
Clarksfield 75 G5
Clayton 115 F2
Clifton 82 D4
Clifton Green 83 G5
Clifton Junction 83 H4
Clough 20 D1
Clough 60 C3
Collyhurst 101 E4
Compstall 163 F3
Copley 119 H3
Copster Hill 90 B5
Cox Green 23 E2
Crimble 41 G2
Crofts Bank 123 F4
Crompton Fold 45 F5
Crowhill 117 G1
Crumpsall 100 A1
Cutgate 28 D3
Daisy Nook 103 H5
Dales Brow 96 C4
Dane Bank 145 G1
Darcy Lever 50 A4
Darn Hill 40 A5
Daubhill 48 B5
Davenport 171 H5
Davenport Green 179 G2
Davenport Green 201 A2
Davyhulme 123 E4
Deane 63 E1
Dean Row 200 C2
Dearnley 20 C4
Debdale 130 A4
Denton 131 G5
Didsbury 157 G3
Disley 197 G1
Dobcross 77 G2
Doffcocker 32 D4
Dog Hill 60 D2
Droylsden 115 H4
Dukinfield 132 B1
Dumplington 123 F1
Dunham Town 164 A5
Dunscar 22 C2
Durn 21 F3
Eagley 22 D4
East Didsbury 158 A5
Eccles 110 B4
Edge Fold 63 F3
Edgeley 171 F2
Egerton 22 D1
Ellenbrook 94 B2
Ellesmere Park 109 H1
Elton 37 G4
Facit 14 D3
Failsworth 102 D3
Fairfield 39 G3
Fairfield 130 B1
Fallowfield 142 C3
Farnworth 64 D4
Fern Bank 119 G4
Fernhill 4 D1
Fernhill Gate 47 G5
Finney Green 191 H5
Firgrove 31 E5
Firswood 126 A5
Firwood Fold 34 D3
Fishpool 53 E1
Fitton Hill 90 D5
Flixton 137 H2
Flowery Field 132 C4
Foggbrook 173 G2
Four Lane Ends 36 C1
Free Town 5 K1
Fullwood 60 C4
Fulshaw Park 199 F5
Gale 21 F1
Gatley 169 F5
Gee Cross 147 H4
Gigg 53 H2
Gillbent 192 C1
Gilnow 2 B6
Glodwick 91 E2
Godley 132 D5
Godley Hill 133 G5
Gorse Hill 125 F5
Gorton 129 F4
Grains Bar 61 F3
Grasscroft 93 E2
Gravel Hole 59 E2
Great Howarth 19 F4
Great Lever 64 B1
Great Moor 172 D3
Greave 162 C2
Greenacres 75 G5
Greenfield 93 H3
Greengate 20 A5
Greenheys 79 C2
Greenmount 25 H1
Greenside 116 C2
Grotton 92 C2
Guide Bridge 117 F4
Haggate 73 H1
Hale 178 A2
Halebarns 179 E4
Halfway Houses 51 F3
Hall i' th' Wood 34 B2
Halliwell 33 H3
Handforth 191 H3
Harden Park 201 C2
Harper Green 64 C3
Harpurhey 101 F3
Hartshead Green 106 C3
Hartshead Pike 106 A1
Harwood 35 H3
Harwood Lee 35 F1
Hathershaw 90 C4
Hattersley 149 E1
Haugh 45 F3
Haughton Green 146 D3
Hawk Green 186 D1
Hazel Grove 185 H3
Hazelhurst 16 A4
Hazelhurst 96 A4
Hazelhurst 106 B5
Heady Hill 40 B4
Heald Green 181 F3
Healds Green 73 E1
Healey 18 D4
Heap Bridge 39 F5
Heaton 47 H1
Heaton Chapel 144 B5
Heaton Mersey 158 B3
Heaton Moor 158 D2
Heaton Norris 12 A1
Heaviley 172 B2
Heyheads 107 E3
Heyrod 119 G1
Heyside 59 H5
Heywood 40 D3
Higginshaw 74 C2
High Crompton 59 F2
Higher Blackley 86 D3
Higher Boarshaw 72 B1
Higher Broughton 99 G4
Higher Poynton 196 A5
Higher Woodhill 38 A1
Highfield 64 A5
High Lane 186 D5
Hill Top 81 E3
Hilton Park 84 D5
Hockley 195 H4
Holcombe 16 B3
Holcombe Brook 16 A5
Holden Fold 74 A1
Hollins 54 A4
Hollins 63 G4
Hollinwood 103 F1
Holts 91 H3
Honresfeld 21 G2
Hooley Bridge 40 D1
Hooley Brow 41 E2
Hooley Hill 131 F1
Horrocks Fold 22 B4
Hulme 126 D2
Hunger Hill 62 A1
Hurst 105 G5
Hurstead 19 H4
Hyde 132 C5
Irlam 136 A2
Irlams o' th' Height 97 H5
Jericho 39 H2
Johnson Fold 32 A3
Jubilee 45 E4
Kearsley 82 A1
Kersal 99 E1
Kingston 132 A5
Kirkhams 85 E1
Kirkholt 42 D3
Kirklees 26 C4
Kitt's Moss 193 G2
Knott Lanes 104 C3
Lacey Green 199 G1
Lady House 44 B2
Langley 70 D1
Lees 91 H1
Levenshulme 144 B3
Lever-Edge 63 G2
Ley Hey Park 174 D2
Limefield 27 G5
Limehurst 104 D4
Lime Side 104 A1
Linnyshaw 81 F4
Little Bolton 110 C3
Littleborough 21 E3
Little Clegg 31 F1
Little Hulton 80 A3
Little Lever 51 E5
Little Moor 173 E1
Littlemoss 116 D1
Long Sight 74 C2
Longsight 128 C3
Lostock Junction 47 E4
Low Compton 59 F3
Lower Bredbury 160 D4
Lower Kersal 98 D4
Lower Place 43 H2
Luzley 106 C4
Luzley Brook 59 G4
Lydgate 92 D2
Makants 79 D5
Manchester 6 A7
Markland Hill 47 F1
Marland 42 A1
Marple 174 D3
Marple Bridge 175 G2
Marpleridge 187 E2
Matley 134 C2
Micklehurst 107 F1
Middleton 71 E3
Middlewood 196 A2
Midway 195 E5
Miles Platting 114 A2
Millbrook 120 A1
Millgate 14 B1
Mill Hill 3 H3
Milnrow 31 H5
Monton 109 G2
Moorclose 72 B4
Moorhey 91 E1
Moorside 75 H1
Moorside 96 C3
Morley 198 B1
Morley Green 198 A1
Moses Gate 64 D2
Mosley Common 94 B3
Mossley 93 E5
Mossley Brow 106 D1
Moss Nook 181 E4
Moss Side 127 E4
Moston 102 A1
Mottram in Longdendale 134 C4
Mottram Rise 134 B1
Mudd 149 H1
Mumps 9 H2
Nangreaves 17 F5
Newall Green 167 H5
Newbold 11 J6
New Bury 64 B5
New Delph 77 H1
Newhey 44 C3
New Moston 102 B2
Newton 132 D3
Newton Heath 101 H5
Newton Wood 131 H2
Newtown 96 D1
Nimble Nook 89 F3
Nob End 65 H2
Norbury Moor 185 F3
Norden 28 A2
Northenden 168 C1
Northern Moor 155 G5
North Reddish 144 D2
Nuttall 16 C4
Oak Bank 68 D5
Offerton 173 F2
Offerton Green 173 H3
Oldfield Brow 165 E4
Oldham 9 J4
Oldham Edge 74 B3
Old Tame 61 G1
Old Trafford 126 A3
Openshaw 115 F5
Ordsall 126 A1
Outwood 67 F4
Over Hulton 62 D5
Park Bridge 91 F5
Partington 151 E4
Patricroft 109 F3
Peel Green 108 C5
Peel Hall 181 E2
Pendlebury 97 H3
Pendleton 111 H2
Pimhole 5 J5
Pitses 91 G4
Pobgreen 78 C4
Portwood 160 B3
Pownall Park 199 E2
Poynton 195 G3
Prestolee 66 A4
Prestwich 84 C3
Quick 92 D3
Quick Edge 92 C4
Radcliffe 52 B5
Rainsough 98 D1
Ramsbottom 16 C3
Reddish 144 C3
Redvales 53 F3
Rhodes 70 C5
Ridge Hill 119 E1
Ringley 66 C5
Roaches 93 E4
Rochdale 11 F6
Roebuck Low 76 B2
Roe Cross 134 C3
Roe Green 95 H2
Romiley 162 C4
Rose Hill 49 F4
Rosehill 177 F3
Roundthorn 167 F4
Royton 59 F5
Running Hill Head 78 D1
Rusholme 128 A5
St George's 126 B2
Sale 153 H3
Salford 111 G4
Salford Quays 125 F1
Scouthead 76 C3
Sedgley Park 85 F5
Seedley 111 F2
Sharples 33 G2
Sharston 169 E4
Shaw 59 H1
Shawclough 29 F1
Shawfield 28 C1
Shaw Heath 12 E7
Shaw Side 60 A4
Sholver 60 C5
Shore 20 C2
Shuttleworth 17 F1
Side of the Moor 24 B5
Simister 69 H4
Sinderland Green 152 A5
Slackcote 61 G2
Slattocks 57 F3
Smallbridge 20 A5
Smallshaw 105 F4
Smithy Bridge 20 D5
Smithy Green 183 E4
South Reddish 159 H1
Spotland Bridge 29 G3
Springhead 92 B1
Spring Hill 75 G3
Stake Hill 57 H4
Stalybridge 118 D4
Stand 67 H4
Stanley Green 192 B2
Stanycliffe 72 A1
Starling 37 F4
Stepping Hill 173 E5
Stockport 12 B1
Stoneclough 66 A5
Stoneyfield 43 E2
Strangeways 113 E1
Stretford 139 G3
Strines 187 H3
Styal 191 E3
Sudden 42 B2
Summerseat 26 C2
Summit 15 A4
Summit 40 A4
Summit 58 C2
Sun Green 120 B1
Sunny Bank 53 H5
Swinton 96 C2
Swinton Park 97 G4
Syke 19 E4
Tame Water 77 F3
Taunton 104 B5
Thornham Fold 58 B2
Thorns Green 188 D2
Thorp 58 C5
Thurston Clough 77 E1
Timperley 166 B2
Tonge Fold 49 H1

Tonge Moor 34 B4
Top of Hebers 56 B5
Top o' th' Meadows 76 A4
Toppings 23 G4
Torkington 186 A2
Tottington 25 H5
Trafford Park 124 B3
Trub 57 F2
Turf Hill 44 A2
Unsworth 69 E2
Uppermill 78 A5
Urmston 123 H4
Walkden 81 E3
Wallbank 18 A1
Wall Hill 77 F3
Walmersley 27 F4
Walshaw 36 D2
Warburton Green 188 D1
Wardle 20 A2
Wardley 96 B1
Waterloo 104 C5
Watersheddings 75 G3
Weaste 111 F4
Well Green 179 E1
Werneth 89 G1
Werneth Low 163 E1
West Didsbury 156 D1
Westwood Park 108 D1
Whalley Range 141 H1
Whitefield 68 B5
White Gate 89 E4
Whitworth 14 C5
Willows 48 B4
Wilmslow 199 G4
Wilmslow Park 200 A3
Windlehurst 186 D3
Winton 109 F2
Woodend 187 H4
Woodford 193 G5
Woodgate Hill 39 G2
Woodhey 16 B5
Woodhouse Park 180 B3
Woodhouses 103 F4
Woodhouses 153 E4
Woodlands 133 G1
Woodley 162 B1
Wood Road 26 D2
Woodseats 149 H5
Woods End 122 B5
Woods Moor 184 C1
Woolfold 37 F2
Worsley 95 G3
Wythenshawe 180 A1
Yew Tree 132 D1

USING THE STREET INDEX

Street names are listed alphabetically. Each street name is followed by its postal town or area locality, the Postcode District, the page number, and the reference to the square in which the name is found.

Standard index entries are shown as follows:

Abberley Dr *NEWH/MOS* M40 ....**88** C5

Street names and selected addresses not shown on the map due to scale restrictions are shown in the index with an asterisk:

Abbeyfield Sq *OP/CLY* * M11 ....**115** E5

GENERAL ABBREVIATIONS

ACC .... ACCESS
ALY .... ALLEY
AP .... APPROACH
AR .... ARCADE
ASS .... ASSOCIATION
AV .... AVENUE
BCH .... BEACH
BLDS .... BUILDINGS
BND .... BEND
BNK .... BANK
BR .... BRIDGE
BRK .... BROOK
BTM .... BOTTOM
BUS .... BUSINESS
BVD .... BOULEVARD
BY .... BYPASS
CATH .... CATHEDRAL
CEM .... CEMETERY
CEN .... CENTRE
CFT .... CROFT
CH .... CHURCH
CHA .... CHASE
CHYD .... CHURCHYARD
CIR .... CIRCLE
CIRC .... CIRCUS
CL .... CLOSE
CLFS .... CLIFFS
CMP .... CAMP
CNR .... CORNER
CO .... COUNTY
COLL .... COLLEGE
COM .... COMMON
COMM .... COMMISSION
CON .... CONVENT
COT .... COTTAGE
COTS .... COTTAGES
CP .... CAPE
CPS .... COPSE
CR .... CREEK
CREM .... CREMATORIUM
CRS .... CRESCENT
CSWY .... CAUSEWAY
CT .... COURT
CTRL .... CENTRAL
CTS .... COURTS
CTYD .... COURTYARD
CUTT .... CUTTINGS
CV .... COVE
CYN .... CANYON
DEPT .... DEPARTMENT
DL .... DALE
DM .... DAM
DR .... DRIVE
DRO .... DROVE
DRY .... DRIVEWAY
DWGS .... DWELLINGS
E .... EAST
EMB .... EMBANKMENT
EMBY .... EMBASSY
ESP .... ESPLANADE
EST .... ESTATE
EX .... EXCHANGE
EXPY .... EXPRESSWAY
EXT .... EXTENSION
F/O .... FLYOVER
FC .... FOOTBALL CLUB
FK .... FORK
FLD .... FIELD
FLDS .... FIELDS
FLS .... FALLS
FLS .... FLATS
FM .... FARM
FT .... FORT
FWY .... FREEWAY
FY .... FERRY
GA .... GATE
GAL .... GALLERY
GDN .... GARDEN
GDNS .... GARDENS
GLD .... GLADE
GLN .... GLEN
GN .... GREEN
GND .... GROUND
GRA .... GRANGE
GRG .... GARAGE
GT .... GREAT
GTWY .... GATEWAY
GV .... GROVE
HGR .... HIGHER
HL .... HILL
HLS .... HILLS
HO .... HOUSE
HOL .... HOLLOW
HOSP .... HOSPITAL
HRB .... HARBOUR
HTH .... HEATH
HTS .... HEIGHTS
HVN .... HAVEN
HWY .... HIGHWAY
IMP .... IMPERIAL
IN .... INLET
IND EST .... INDUSTRIAL ESTATE
INF .... INFIRMARY
INFO .... INFORMATION
INT .... INTERCHANGE
IS .... ISLAND
JCT .... JUNCTION
JTY .... JETTY
KG .... KING
KNL .... KNOLL
L .... LAKE
LA .... LANE
LDG .... LODGE
LGT .... LIGHT
LK .... LOCK
LKS .... LAKES
LNDG .... LANDING
LTL .... LITTLE
LWR .... LOWER
MAG .... MAGISTRATE
MAN .... MANSIONS
MD .... MEAD
MDW .... MEADOWS
MEM .... MEMORIAL
MKT .... MARKET
MKTS .... MARKETS
ML .... MALL
ML .... MILL
MNR .... MANOR
MS .... MEWS
MSN .... MISSION
MT .... MOUNT
MTN .... MOUNTAIN
MTS .... MOUNTAINS
MUS .... MUSEUM
MWY .... MOTORWAY
N .... NORTH
NE .... NORTH EAST
NW .... NORTH WEST
O/P .... OVERPASS
OFF .... OFFICE
ORCH .... ORCHARD
OV .... OVAL
PAL .... PALACE
PAS .... PASSAGE
PAV .... PAVILION
PDE .... PARADE
PH .... PUBLIC HOUSE
PK .... PARK
PKWY .... PARKWAY
PL .... PLACE
PLN .... PLAIN
PLNS .... PLAINS
PLZ .... PLAZA
POL .... POLICE STATION
PR .... PRINCE
PREC .... PRECINCT
PREP .... PREPARATORY
PRIM .... PRIMARY
PROM .... PROMENADE
PRS .... PRINCESS
PRT .... PORT
PT .... POINT
PTH .... PATH
PZ .... PIAZZA
QD .... QUADRANT
QU .... QUEEN
QY .... QUAY
R .... RIVER
RBT .... ROUNDABOUT
RD .... ROAD
RDG .... RIDGE
REP .... REPUBLIC
RES .... RESERVOIR
RFC .... RUGBY FOOTBALL CLUB
RI .... RISE
RP .... RAMP
RW .... ROW
S .... SOUTH
SCH .... SCHOOL
SE .... SOUTH EAST
SER .... SERVICE AREA
SH .... SHORE
SHOP .... SHOPPING
SKWY .... SKYWAY
SMT .... SUMMIT
SOC .... SOCIETY
SP .... SPUR
SPR .... SPRING
SQ .... SQUARE
ST .... STREET
STN .... STATION
STR .... STREAM
STRD .... STRAND
SW .... SOUTH WEST
TDG .... TRADING
TER .... TERRACE
THWY .... THROUGHWAY
TNL .... TUNNEL
TOLL .... TOLLWAY
TPK .... TURNPIKE
TR .... TRACK
TRL .... TRAIL
TWR .... TOWER
U/P .... UNDERPASS
UNI .... UNIVERSITY
UPR .... UPPER
V .... VALE
VA .... VALLEY
VIAD .... VIADUCT
VIL .... VILLA
VIS .... VISTA
VLG .... VILLAGE
VLS .... VILLAS
VW .... VIEW
W .... WEST
WD .... WOOD
WHF .... WHARF
WK .... WALK
WKS .... WALKS
WLS .... WELLS
WY .... WAY
YD .... YARD
YHA .... YOUTH HOSTEL

POSTCODE TOWNS AND AREA ABBREVIATIONS

ALT .... Altrincham
ANC .... Ancoats
AUL .... Ashton-under-Lyne
AULW .... Ashton-under-Lyne west
BKLY .... Blackley
BNG/LEV .... Burnage/Levenshulme
BOL .... Bolton
BOLE .... Bolton east
BOLS/LL .... Bolton south/Little Lever
BRAM/HZG .... Bramhall/Hazel Grove
BRO .... Broughton
BRUN/LGST .... Brunswick/Longsight
BURY .... Bury
CCHDY .... Chorlton-cum-Hardy
CHAD .... Chadderton
CHD/CHDH .... Cheadle (Gtr. Man)/Cheadle Hulme
CHH .... Cheetham Hill
CMANE .... Central Manchester east
CMANW .... Central Manchester west
CSLFD .... Central Salford
DID/WITH .... Didsbury/Withington
DROY .... Droylsden
DTN/ASHW .... Denton/Audenshaw
DUK .... Dukinfield
ECC .... Eccles
EDGW/EG .... Edgeworth/Egerton
EDGY/DAV .... Edgeley/Davenport
FAIL .... Failsworth
FWTH .... Farnworth
GLSP .... Glossop
GOL/RIS/CUL .... Golborne/Risley/Culcheth
GTN .... Gorton
HALE/TIMP .... Hale/Timperley
HEY .... Heywood
HOR/BR .... Horwich/Blackrod
HTNM .... Heaton Moor
HULME .... Hulme
HYDE .... Hyde
IRL .... Irlam
KNUT .... Knutsford
LHULT .... Little Hulton
LIT .... Littleborough
LYMM .... Lymm
MANAIR .... Manchester Airport
MCFLDN .... Macclesfield north
MDTN .... Middleton (Gtr. Man)
MILN .... Milnrow
MOSL .... Mossley
MPL/ROM .... Marple/Romiley
NEWH/MOS .... Newton Heath/Moston
NTHM/RTH .... Northern Moor/Roundthorn
OFTN .... Offerton
OLD .... Oldham
OLDE .... Oldham east
OLDS .... Oldham south
OLDTF/WHR .... Old Trafford/Whalley Range
OP/CLY .... Openshaw/Clayton
ORD .... Ordsall
PART .... Partington
POY/DIS .... Poynton/Disley
PWCH .... Prestwich
RAD .... Radcliffe
RAMS .... Ramsbottom
RDSH .... Reddish
ROCH .... Rochdale
ROY/SHW .... Royton/Shaw
RUSH/FAL .... Rusholme/Fallowfield
SALE .... Sale
SALQ .... Salford Quays
SLFD .... Salford
STKP .... Stockport
STLY .... Stalybridge
STRET .... Stretford
SWIN .... Swinton
TOD .... Todmorden
TOT/BURYW .... Tottington/Bury west
TRPK .... Trafford Park
TYLD .... Tyldesley
UPML .... Uppermill
URM .... Urmston
WALK .... Walkden
WGTN/LGST .... West Gorton/Longsight
WHIT .... Whitworth
WHTF .... Whitefield
WHTN .... Westhoughton
WILM/AE .... Wilmslow/Alderley Edge
WYTH/NTH .... Wythenshawe/Northenden

A

Abberley Dr NEWH/MOS M40 88 C5
Abberton Rd DID/WITH M20 142 B5
Abbey Cl ALT WA14 176 D3
RAD M26 51 H4
STRET M32 124 A5
Abbey Ct RAD M26 51 H5
Abbey Crs HEY OL10 40 C2
Abbeydale WHIT OL12 10 B4
Abbeydale Cl AUL OL6 105 H4
Abbey Dr LIT OL15 20 C5
SWIN M27 96 D2
TOT/BURYW BL8 37 F5
Abbeyfield Sq OP/CLY * M11 115 E5
Abbey Gdns HYDE SK14 134 C5
Abbey Gv CHAD OL9 89 F3
ECC M30 109 H3
HYDE SK14 134 C5
STKP SK1 172 C1
Abbey Hey La GTN M18 129 H2
Abbey Hills Rd OLDS OL8 91 E3
Abbey Lawn OLDTF/WHR M16 126 A5
Abbey Rd CHD/CHDH SK8 170 D4
DROY M43 116 A2
FAIL M35 103 G2
MDTN M24 56 C5
SALE M33 139 F5
Abbeyville Wk HULME * M15 126 D3
Abbeywood Av GTN * M18 129 H4
Abbotsbury Cl POY/DIS SK12 195 E2
Abbots Cl SALE M33 155 E1
Abbotsfield Cl URM * M41 122 A5
Abbot's Fold Rd WALK M28 94 C3
Abbotsford Dr MDTN M24 56 A5
Abbotsford Gv ALT WA14 165 H1
Abbotsford Rd BOL BL1 32 D5
CCHDY M21 141 E1
CHAD * OL9 72 D4
OLD OL1 75 E3
Abbotside Cl OLDTF/WHR M16 126 C5
Abbotsleigh Dr BRAM/HZG SK7 184 A2
Abbott St BOLS/LL BL3 48 D4
ROCH OL11 42 A3
Abden St RAD M26 67 F1
Abels La UPML OL3 78 B4
Aber Av OFTN SK2 172 D5
Abercarn Cl CHH M8 100 B3
Abercorn Rd BOL BL1 33 E3
Abercorn St OLDE * OL4 91 G1
Abercrombie Ct SALE M33 155 E1
Aberdaron Wk
BRUN/LGST * M13 127 G1
Aberdeen Crs EDGY/DAV SK3 12 C6
Aberdeen Gdns WHIT OL12 18 C4
Aberdeen Gv EDGY/DAV SK3 12 D5
Aberdeen St BRUN/LGST M13 127 G3
Aberford Rd NTHM/RTH M23 167 H4
Abergele Rd RUSH/FAL M14 143 F3
Abergele St OFTN SK2 172 A3
Aberley Fold LIT OL15 20 C1
Abernant Cl OP/CLY M11 114 C4
Aber Rd CHD/CHDH SK8 170 D3
Abersoch Av RUSH/FAL M14 143 F3
Abingdon Av WHTF M45 68 C2
Abingdon Cl CHAD * OL9 89 G3
ROCH OL11 42 D2
WHTF M45 68 C2
Abingdon Rd BOLE BL2 49 H1
BRAM/HZG SK7 183 H2
RDSH SK5 145 E4
URM M41 123 H5
Abingdon St AUL OL6 118 C3
CMANE M1 7 F6
Abington Rd SALE M33 154 D3
Abney Gra MOSL OL5 107 F2
Abney Rd HTNM SK4 159 F1
MOSL OL5 106 D2
Aboukir St MILN OL16 11 F5
Abram Cl RUSH/FAL M14 142 B2
Abram St SLFD M6 98 C4
Absalom Dr CHH M8 100 A2
Abson St OLD OL1 73 H3
Acacia Av CHD/CHDH SK8 182 D2
DTN/ASHW M34 131 H5
HALE/TIMP WA15 178 A1
SWIN M27 96 D4
WILM/AE SK9 199 E5
Acacia Dr HALE/TIMP WA15 178 A1
SLFD M6 110 C2
Acacia Gv RDSH SK5 160 A2
Acacia Rd OLDS OL8 104 A1
The Acacias URM * M41 138 D1
Academy Wk HULME * M15 126 D3
Ace Ml CHAD * OL9 89 E3
Acer Cl HYDE SK14 148 B1
ROCH OL11 28 A2
Acheson St GTN M18 129 G3
Ackers La PART M31 137 F5
Ackers St BRUN/LGST M13 127 G3
Ack La East BRAM/HZG SK7 184 A3
BRAM/HZG SK7 193 G1
Ack La West CHD/CHDH SK8 183 E5
Ackroyd Av GTN M18 130 B2
Ackroyd St OP/CLY M11 129 H1
Ackworth Dr NTHM/RTH M23 167 H3
Ackworth Rd SWIN M27 96 D1
Acme Dr SWIN M27 97 G2
Acomb St BRUN/LGST M13 127 G3
Acorn Av CHD/CHDH SK8 170 B3
HYDE SK14 147 H3
Acorn Cl BNG/LEV M19 143 G3
WHTF M45 84 C1
Acorn St OLDE OL4 91 H1
Acorn Wy OLD OL1 9 F2
Acre Barn ROY/SHW OL2 59 F1
Acre Fld BOLE BL2 35 E2
Acrefield SALE M33 154 B3
Acrefield Av HTNM SK4 158 D2
URM M41 139 E2
Acre La CHD/CHDH SK8 193 E1
OLD OL1 74 D3
Acresbrook STLY SK15 133 H1
Acres Ct WYTH/NTH M22 168 C5
Acresdale HOR/BR BL6 46 D3
Acresfield Av DTN/ASHW M34 116 C4
Acresfield Cl SWIN M27 97 F4
Acresfield Rd
HALE/TIMP WA15 166 B1
HYDE SK14 133 E3
LHULT M38 80 C3
MDTN M24 72 B1
SLFD M6 98 A5
Acres La STLY SK15 119 G4
Acres Rd CCHDY M21 140 D3
CHD/CHDH * SK8 169 F4
Acres St TOT/BURYW BL8 37 E1
Acre St CHAD OL9 89 G5
DTN/ASHW M34 131 F5
MPL/ROM SK6 162 A4
RAD M26 66 D1
WHIT OL12 14 C4
Acre Top Rd BKLY M9 86 C2
Acton Av NEWH/MOS M40 115 E1
Acton St OLD OL1 74 D4
WHIT OL12 10 E3
Adair St CMANE M1 113 H5
ROCH OL11 42 A4
Adam Cl CHD/CHDH SK8 171 E5
Adams Av CCHDY M21 141 E5
Adams Cl POY/DIS SK12 195 F5
Adamson Gdns DID/WITH M20 157 E3
Adamson Rd ECC M30 109 F5
Adamson Wk RUSH/FAL * M14 127 G5
Adam St AUL OL6 118 B2
BOLS/LL BL3 49 E4
OLDS OL8 90 C5
Ada St BKLY M9 101 E1
OLDE OL4 9 K5
RAMS BL0 16 B3
WHIT OL12 10 E1
Adcroft St STKP SK1 13 H7
STKP SK1 13 J7
Addenbrook Rd CHH M8 99 H5
Addington Rd BOLS/LL BL3 62 C1
Addington St ANC M4 7 H2
Addison Av AUL OL6 118 C2
Addison Cl BRUN/LGST M13 127 H2
Addison Crs OLDTF/WHR M16 126 A5
Addison Dr MDTN M24 72 B1
Addison Rd HALE/TIMP WA15 177 H2
IRL M44 121 D4
PART M31 137 E5
STRET M32 139 G1
URM M41 138 C2
Adelaide Rd BRAM/HZG SK7 193 H1
EDGY/DAV SK3 12 B6
Adelaide St BOLS/LL BL3 48 C5
CHH M8 100 A5
ECC M30 109 G4
HEY OL10 41 E4
MDTN M24 71 H4
RAMS BL0 16 B4
SWIN M27 96 C3
Adelaide St East HEY OL10 41 F4
Adeline St ANC M4 113 F2
Adelphi Dr LHULT M38 80 C2
Adelphi Gv LHULT M38 80 C2
Adelphi St CSLFD M3 112 C3
RAD M26 52 A4
Aden Cl WGTN/LGST M12 114 A5
Aden St OLDE OL4 91 G2
WHIT * OL12 10 E2
Adisham Dr BOL BL1 34 A5
Adlington Cl HALE/TIMP WA15 167 E3
POY/DIS SK12 195 G5
TOT/BURYW BL8 37 F5
Adlington Dr STRET M32 125 G4
Adlington Rd WILM/AE SK9 200 B3
Adlington St BOLS/LL BL3 63 G1
OLDE OL4 75 G3
Adlington Wk STKP SK1 13 F3
Adrian Rd BOL BL1 33 F4
Adrian St NEWH/MOS M40 101 H3
Adrian Ter MILN OL16 30 D5
Adria Rd DID/WITH M20 157 H3
Adscombe St OLDTF/WHR M16 126 D4
Adshall Rd CHD/CHDH SK8 170 D4
Adshead Cl WYTH/NTH M22 180 A1
Adstock Wk NEWH/MOS M40 7 K1
Adstone Cl ANC M4 114 A4
Adswood Cl OLDE OL4 75 G3
Adswood Gv EDGY/DAV SK3 171 G3
Adswood La East OFTN SK2 172 A3
Adswood La West
EDGY/DAV SK3 171 H3
Adswood Old Hall Rd
CHD/CHDH SK8 171 G5
Adswood Rd CHD/CHDH SK8 171 F5
Adswood St NEWH/MOS M40 114 B3
Adswood Ter EDGY/DAV SK3 171 H3
Aegean Cl BRO M7 99 F5
Aegean Rd ALT WA14 164 D3
Affetside Dr TOT/BURYW BL8 36 D4
Affleck Av RAD M26 65 H4
Afghan St OLD OL1 75 E4
Age Cft OLDS OL8 91 F4
Agecroft Rd MPL/ROM SK6 161 H5
SWIN M27 98 A3
Agecroft Rd East PWCH M25 84 D5
Agecroft Rd West PWCH M25 84 C5
Agincourt St HEY * OL10 40 C4
Agnes Cl CHAD OL9 89 H3
Agnes St BNG/LEV M19 143 H1
BRO M7 100 A3
CHAD OL9 89 G2
Agnew Pl SLFD M6 111 H1
Agnew Rd GTN M18 129 F3
Aigburth Gv RDSH SK5 144 D1
Ailsa Cl NEWH/MOS M40 101 E5
Aimson Rd HALE/TIMP WA15 167 E3
Aimson Rd West
HALE/TIMP WA15 166 D3
Ainley Rd WYTH/NTH M22 180 C1
Ainley Wd DUK SK16 132 C1
Ainscow Av HOR/BR BL6 46 A1
Ainsdale Av PWCH M25 99 G1
TOT/BURYW BL8 37 G4
Ainsdale Cl BRAM/HZG SK7 184 B5
OLDS OL8 90 A3
Ainsdale Crs ROY/SHW OL2 74 B2
Ainsdale Dr CHD/CHDH SK8 181 G3
SALE M33 153 H4
WHIT OL12 18 C1
Ainsdale Gv RDSH SK5 145 E3
Ainsdale Rd BOLS/LL BL3 63 H2
Ainsdale St WGTN/LGST M12 128 C2
Ainsford Rd DID/WITH M20 158 A1
Ainsley Gv WALK M28 81 E5
Ainslie Rd BOL BL1 32 D5
Ainsty Rd RUSH/FAL M14 127 F4
Ainsworth Cl DTN/ASHW M34 130 C5
Ainsworth Ct BOLE BL2 49 H2
Ainsworth Hall Rd BOLE BL2 51 E2
Ainsworth La BOLE BL2 49 H1
Ainsworth Rd BOLS/LL BL3 65 H1
RAD M26 52 A4
TOT/BURYW BL8 37 F4
Ainsworth St BOL BL1 33 F4
MILN OL16 30 B5
Aintree Av SALE M33 153 F3
Aintree Cl BRAM/HZG SK7 185 G2
Aintree Dr ROCH OL11 28 B3
Aintree Gv EDGY/DAV SK3 171 H3
Aintree Rd BOLS/LL BL3 65 H2
Aintree St OP/CLY M11 115 E4
Aintree Wk CHAD OL9 8 A2
Airedale Cl CHD/CHDH SK8 169 H3
Airedale Ct ALT * WA14 165 H4
Aire Dr BOLE BL2 34 C1
Air Hill Ter WHIT * OL12 29 F2
Airton Cl NEWH/MOS M40 113 H2
Aitken Cl RAMS BL0 16 C3
Aitken St BNG/LEV * M19 144 B2
Ajax Dr BURY BL9 68 C1
Ajax St RAMS * BL0 16 C3
ROCH OL11 42 A3
Aked Cl WGTN/LGST M12 128 A2
Akesmoor Dr OFTN SK2 172 D3
Alamein Dr MPL/ROM SK6 162 D4
Alan Av FAIL M35 103 E5
Alanbrooke Wk HULME * M15 126 D3
Alandale Av DTN/ASHW M34 131 F1
Alan Dr HALE/TIMP WA15 178 B4
MPL/ROM SK6 174 D3
Alan Rd DID/WITH M20 142 D5
HTNM SK4 158 D3
Alan St BOL BL1 33 G3
Alan Turing Wy
NEWH/MOS M40 114 B2
Alasdair Cl CHAD OL9 73 E4
Alba Cl ECC M30 109 G4
Alban St BRO M7 99 G5
Albany Av OP/CLY M11 130 A1
Albany Ct URM M41 123 E5
Albany Dr BURY BL9 53 G2
Albany Rd BRAM/HZG SK7 193 H3
CCHDY M21 141 E2
ECC M30 109 E2
WILM/AE SK9 199 E5
Albany St MDTN M24 72 A5
OLDE OL4 75 G3
ROCH OL11 43 F1
Albany Wy SLFD M6 111 H2
Alba Wy STRET M32 124 B3
Albemarle Av DID/WITH M20 142 B5
Albemarle Rd CCHDY M21 140 D3
Albemarle St AUL OL6 118 B2
RUSH/FAL M14 127 F4
Albemarle Ter AUL * OL6 118 B2
Alberbury Av NTHM/RTH M23 167 E2
Albermarle Rd SWIN M27 96 D3
Alberta St BOLS/LL BL3 48 B4
STKP SK1 13 H5
Albert Av DUK SK16 132 B2
GTN M18 129 H4
PWCH M25 99 F1
ROY/SHW OL2 59 H4
URM M41 138 D1
WALK M28 80 D2
Albert Cl CHD/CHDH SK8 182 D2
WHTF M45 68 D4
Albert Ct ALT WA14 165 G5
Albert Gdns NEWH/MOS M40 102 C5
Albert Gv FWTH BL4 65 E4
WGTN/LGST M12 128 D4
Albert Hill St DID/WITH * M20 157 G3
Albert Park Rd BRO M7 99 F5
Albert Pl ALT WA14 165 G4
BRUN/LGST M13 128 C5
Albert Rd BOL BL1 47 H1
CHD/CHDH SK8 182 D2
ECC M30 110 A3
FWTH BL4 64 D3
HALE/TIMP WA15 177 H1
HTNM SK4 158 D3
HYDE SK14 147 G1
SALE M33 154 D2
WHTF M45 68 D4
WILM/AE SK9 199 F4
Albert Rd East
HALE/TIMP WA15 177 H1
Albert Rd West BOL BL1 47 G1
Albert Royds St MILN OL16 11 H1
Albert Sq ALT WA14 177 G1
CMANW M2 6 D5
STLY SK15 119 E4
Albert St BOLS/LL * BL3 66 A1
BRAM/HZG SK7 185 E1
BURY BL9 5 H4
DROY M43 116 C4
DTN/ASHW * M34 131 G5
EDGY/DAV SK3 12 D4
FWTH BL4 65 E5
HEY OL10 40 C4
HYDE SK14 133 E5
IRL M44 135 D5
LIT OL15 20 D3
MDTN M24 72 A5
MILN OL16 44 C1
OLDE OL4 91 H2
OLDS OL8 103 G1
OLDTF/WHR * M16 126 B2
OP/CLY M11 114 C4
PWCH * M25 85 F2
RAMS BL0 16 C2
ROY/SHW OL2 59 E5
ROY/SHW OL2 59 H2
WHIT OL12 14 B5
Albert St West FAIL M35 102 C4
Albert Ter STKP SK1 13 G3
Albine St NEWH/MOS M40 101 G2
Albion Cl HTNM SK4 159 H3
Albion Close Gdns
ROY/SHW OL2 59 G5
Albion Dr DROY M43 116 B3
Albion Fold DROY M43 116 B3
Albion Gdns STLY SK15 119 G3
Albion Gv SALE M33 154 B2
Albion Pl BRAM/HZG * SK7 185 E1
BRO * M7 99 F5
ORD M5 112 B3
PWCH M25 84 D3
Albion Rd ROCH OL11 29 G5
RUSH/FAL M14 142 D2
Albion St AUL OL6 118 B2
BOLS/LL BL3 49 E4
CHAD OL9 89 F1
CMANE M1 6 D7
CMANE M1 127 E1
FAIL M35 102 D3
FWTH BL4 81 H1
LIT OL15 20 D3
OLD OL1 9 F3
OLDTF/WHR M16 126 C4
RAD M26 67 G3
ROCH OL11 42 C5
SALE M33 154 C2
STLY SK15 119 G3
SWIN M27 97 F2
TOT/BURYW BL8 4 A4
Albion Wy ORD M5 112 A4
Albury Dr BNG/LEV M19 158 A4
WHIT OL12 28 C1
Albyns Av CHH M8 100 B3
Alcester Av EDGY/DAV SK3 170 C2
Alcester Cl MDTN M24 88 A1
TOT/BURYW BL8 37 G3
Alcester Rd CHD/CHDH SK8 169 G5
SALE M33 154 C4
Alcester St CHAD OL9 89 F4
Aldborough Cl DID/WITH M20 142 C5
Aldbourne Cl NEWH/MOS M40 101 E5
Aldbury Ter BOL * BL1 33 G5
Aldcroft St GTN * M18 130 A2
Alden Cl WHTF M45 68 D4
Alder Av BURY BL9 39 F3
POY/DIS SK12 195 G4
Alderbank WHIT OL12 19 H1
Alderbank Cl FWTH BL4 81 G1
Alderbrook Rd LHULT M38 80 A4
Alder Cl AUL OL6 105 E3
Alder Ct CHH * M8 100 A1
Aldercroft Av BOLE BL2 35 E5
WYTH/NTH M22 180 B2
Alderdale Dr DROY M43 115 G3
HTNM SK4 158 D1
MPL/ROM SK6 186 D5
Alderdale Gv WILM/AE SK9 198 D5
Alderdale Rd CHD/CHDH SK8 171 F5
Alder Dr HALE/TIMP WA15 167 F4
STLY SK15 119 H2
SWIN M27 96 B1
Alderfield Rd CCHDY M21 140 C2
Alder Forest Av ECC M30 108 D1
Aldergate Gv AUL OL6 106 A5
Alderglen Rd CHH M8 100 A4
Alder Gv BOLE BL2 23 H5
DTN/ASHW M34 131 H5
EDGY/DAV SK3 12 A5
STRET M32 140 B1
Alder La OLDS OL8 90 A5
Alderley Av BOL BL1 33 H1
Alderley Cl BRAM/HZG SK7 185 G4
POY/DIS SK12 195 G5
Alderley Dr MPL/ROM SK6 161 F2
Alderley Ldg WILM/AE SK9 199 F5
Alderley Rd RDSH SK5 160 A1
SALE M33 155 F4
URM M41 137 H1
WILM/AE SK9 199 F4
Alderley St AUL OL6 105 G5
Alderman Foley Dr WHIT OL12 28 D1
Alderman Sq WGTN/LGST M12 114 B5
Aldermary Rd CCHDY M21 156 C1
Aldermaston Gv BKLY M9 86 C1
Alder Meadow Cl WHIT OL12 28 D2
Aldermere Crs URM M41 137 F1
Alderminster Av LHULT M38 80 B2
Aldermoor Cl OP/CLY M11 115 F5
Alder Rd CHD/CHDH SK8 170 A4
FAIL M35 103 E5
MDTN * M24 72 B2
ROCH OL11 42 C4
Alders Av WYTH/NTH M22 168 B4
Alders Ct OLDS OL8 104 D2
Aldersgate Rd CHD/CHDH SK8 193 F2
OFTN SK2 172 C3
Aldersgreen Av MPL/ROM SK6 187 E5
Alderside Rd BKLY M9 101 E2
Aldersley Av BKLY M9 86 C3
Alderson St CHAD OL9 8 E2
SLFD M6 111 H1
Alders Rd POY/DIS SK12 187 F5
WYTH/NTH M22 168 B4
Alder St BOLS/LL BL3 64 A1
ECC M30 108 D1
SLFD M6 111 G3
Aldersyde St BOLS/LL BL3 63 G1
Alderue Av WYTH/NTH M22 168 C3
Alderwood Fold OLDE OL4 92 A3
Aldfield Rd NTHM/RTH M23 155 F5
Aldford Cl DID/WITH * M20 157 H3
Aldford Gv BOLE BL2 51 E4
Aldford Pl WILM/AE SK9 201 A3
Aldham Av NEWH/MOS M40 115 F1
Aldred Cl CHH M8 100 C4
Aldred St BOLS/LL BL3 63 E1
ECC M30 109 F4
FAIL M35 102 D3
ORD M5 112 A3
Aldsworth Dr BOLS/LL BL3 48 D5
NEWH/MOS M40 101 F5
Aldwick Av DID/WITH M20 157 H3
Aldwinians Cl DTN/ASHW M34 131 F3
Aldworth Gv SALE M33 153 G2
Aldwych ROCH OL11 43 E3
Aldwych Av RUSH/FAL M14 127 G5
Aldwyn Cl DTN/ASHW M34 131 F3
Aldwyn Crs BRAM/HZG SK7 184 D2
Aldwyn Park Rd
DTN/ASHW M34 130 D1
Alexander Av FAIL M35 103 F2
Alexander Briant Ct FWTH * BL4 64 D5
Alexander Dr BURY BL9 68 D3
HALE/TIMP WA15 166 B3
MILN OL16 31 F5
Alexander Gdns BRO M7 112 C1
Alexander Rd BOLE BL2 34 D5
Alexander St ROCH OL11 42 A4
SLFD * M6 111 F3
Alexandra Av HYDE SK14 147 F1
RUSH/FAL M14 142 A1
WHTF M45 68 D4
Alexandra Cl EDGY/DAV SK3 171 F3
Alexandra Ct URM M41 137 F2
Alexandra Crs OLD OL1 75 E4
Alexandra Dr BNG/LEV M19 143 G4
Alexandra Gv IRL M44 136 A3
Alexandra Ms OLDS * OL8 9 K7
Alexandra Rd AUL OL6 118 A1
DTN/ASHW M34 131 H4
ECC M30 109 E4
HTNM SK4 159 F3
OLDS OL8 90 D3
OLDTF/WHR M16 126 D4
RAD M26 65 H4
SALE M33 155 E3
WALK M28 80 D2
Alexandra Rd South
OLDTF/WHR M16 126 D5
Alexandra St AUL OL6 118 C1
BOLS/LL * BL3 48 C5
BRO * M7 112 C2
FWTH BL4 65 E5
HEY OL10 56 B1
HYDE SK14 147 F2
OLDS OL8 9 K6
Alexandra Ter BNG/LEV M19 143 H2
OLDE OL4 75 H1
Alford Av DID/WITH M20 142 B3
Alford Cl BOLE BL2 50 C3
Alford Rd HTNM SK4 144 A5
Alford St CHAD OL9 89 G5
Alfred Av WALK M28 95 H3
Alfred James Cl
NEWH/MOS * M40 113 H2
Alfred St AUL * OL6 118 C1
BKLY M9 101 E2
BOLS/LL BL3 49 G4
BURY BL9 53 H1
CHAD OL9 8 B5
ECC M30 109 G2
FWTH BL4 65 E2
FWTH BL4 65 G4
HYDE SK14 132 B5
IRL M44 135 D5
LIT OL15 20 D2
RAMS BL0 16 C3
ROY/SHW OL2 59 H2
WALK M28 81 E4
WHIT OL12 14 C3
Alfreton Av DTN/ASHW M34 146 D3
Alfreton Rd OFTN SK2 173 E3
Alfriston Dr NTHM/RTH M23 155 H4
Alger Ms AUL OL6 118 C1
Algernon Rd WALK M28 80 D3
Algernon St ECC M30 109 G2
SWIN M27 96 C2
Alger St AUL OL6 118 C1
Algreave Rd EDGY/DAV SK3 170 D1
Alice Ingham Ct WHIT OL12 29 E2
Alice St BOLS/LL BL3 48 B4
HYDE SK14 147 H4
SALE M33 155 E2
SWIN M27 97 G2
WHIT OL12 11 G2
Alicia Dr WHIT OL12 10 A2
Alison Kelly Cl BKLY M9 101 G2
Alison St ROY/SHW OL2 59 H1
RUSH/FAL M14 127 E5
Alker Rd NEWH/MOS * M40 114 A2
Alkrington Cl BURY BL9 68 D2
Alkrington Gn MDTN M24 87 G1
Alkrington Hall Rd North
MDTN M24 71 G5
Alkrington Hall Rd South
MDTN M24 87 F1
Alkrington Park Rd MDTN M24 71 F5
Allama Iqbal Rd OLDE OL4 91 F2
Allandale ALT WA14 165 E5
Allandale Dr ROY/SHW OL2 58 D4
Allandale Rd BNG/LEV * M19 143 G2
Allan Roberts Cl BKLY M9 101 E1
Allanson Rd WYTH/NTH M22 156 D5
Alldis Cl WGTN/LGST M12 128 B3
Alldis St OFTN SK2 172 C4
Allen Av HYDE SK14 148 A3
Allenby Rd IRL M44 150 C2
SWIN M27 96 B4
Allenby St ROY/SHW OL2 59 H2
Allen Cl ROY/SHW OL2 59 H3
Allendale Dr BURY BL9 68 D1
Allendale Gdns BOL BL1 33 H4
Allen Dale Wk CSLFD M3 112 C3
Allen Rd URM M41 139 E2
Allen St BOLS/LL BL3 65 H1
MILN OL16 43 F1
OLDS OL8 8 C5
RAD M26 66 D1
TOT/BURYW BL8 37 H3
Allerdean Wk HTNM SK4 158 C3
Allerford St OLDTF/WHR M16 126 D4
Allerton Wk BRUN/LGST * M13 127 G2
Allesley Dr CHH M8 100 A5
Allgreave Cl SALE M33 155 E5
Alligin Cl CHAD OL9 73 F4
Allingham St BRUN/LGST M13 128 B4
Allington ROCH * OL11 29 H5
Allington Dr ECC M30 109 H1
Alliott Wk HULME M15 126 D3
Allison Gv ECC M30 109 E4
Allison St CHH M8 100 A5
Allotment Rd IRL M44 135 C5
All Saint's Cl ROY/SHW OL2 59 E4
All Saints Ct STRET * M32 139 G1
All Saints Pl TOT/BURYW BL8 37 H3
All Saints' Rd HTNM SK4 159 G3
All Saints' St BOL BL1 2 E3
NEWH/MOS M40 102 B5
All Saints Ter WHIT OL12 11 G1
Allsopp St BOL BL1 2 E7
Alma La WILM/AE SK9 199 F4
Alma Rd BNG/LEV M19 143 H3
BRAM/HZG SK7 185 H4
HTNM SK4 159 E1
SALE M33 153 H4
Alma St BOLS/LL BL3 48 B5
BOLS/LL BL3 66 A1
ECC M30 110 A4
FWTH * BL4 82 A2
RAD M26 52 A4
STLY SK15 119 G3
WHIT OL12 10 C3
Alminstone Cl
NEWH/MOS M40 115 G1
Almond Av BURY BL9 39 F3
Almond Cl EDGY/DAV SK3 12 A5
FAIL M35 103 E4
LIT OL15 20 C2
SLFD M6 111 H3
Almond Dr SALE M33 139 E5
Almond Gv BOL * BL1 34 A3
Almond Rd OLDE OL4 75 G3
Almond St BOL BL1 34 A2
FWTH BL4 64 D4
NEWH/MOS * M40 113 G1

Almond Tree Rd
CHD/CHDH SK8 ....182 D3
Almond Wy HYDE SK14 ....148 B1
Alms Hill Rd CHH M8 ....100 B3
Alness Rd OLDTF/WHR M16 ....141 H1
Alnwick Dr BURY BL9 ....53 G4
Alnwick Rd BKLY M9 ....87 E2
Alpha Ct DTN/ASHW M34 ....130 D5
Alphagate Dr DTN/ASHW M34 ....130 D5
Alpha Pl HULME M15 ....126 D1
Alpha Rd STRET M52 ....139 H1
Alpha St OP/CLY M11 ....129 H1
SLFD M6 ....111 G2
Alpha St West SLFD M6 ....111 G2
Alphin Cl MOSL OL5 ....93 F4
Alphingate Cl STLY SK15 ....120 A1
Alphin Sq MOSL OL5 ....107 E1
Alphonsus St OLDTF/WHR M16 ....126 B4
Alpine Dr MILN OL16 ....31 H1
ROY/SHW OL2 ....73 H1
WHIT OL12 ....19 H2
Alpine Rd STKP SK1 ....13 K3
Alpine St OP/CLY M11 ....115 E3
Alport Av OLDTF/WHR * M16 ....141 H1
Alresford Rd MDTN M24 ....87 G2
SLFD M6 ....98 A5
Alsager Cl CCHDY M21 ....141 G5
Alsop Av BRO * M7 ....99 E3
Alstead Av HALE/TIMP WA15 ....178 B1
Alston Av ROY/SHW OL2 ....60 A1
SALE M33 ....154 A3
STRET M52 ....124 D5
Alston Cl BRAM/HZG SK7 ....184 B5
Alstone Dr ALT WA14 ....164 D3
Alstone Rd HTNM SK4 ....144 B5
Alston Gdns BNG/LEV M19 ....158 C1
Alston Rd GTN M18 ....129 H5
Alston St BOLS/LL * BL3 ....63 H1
TOT/BURYW * BL8 ....37 H2
Altair Av WYTH/NTH M22 ....180 C4
Altair Pl BRO M7 ....112 B1
Altcar Gv RDSH SK5 ....144 D1
Altcar Wk WYTH/NTH M22 ....180 B2
Alt Fold Dr OLDS OL8 ....91 G4
Alt Gv AUL OL6 ....105 E2
Altham Cl BURY BL9 ....53 E3
Alt Hill La AUL OL6 ....105 E2
AUL OL6 ....91 F5
Alt La AUL OL6 ....91 F5
OLDS OL8 ....91 F5
Alton Av URM M41 ....137 E1
Alton Cl AUL OL6 ....105 F3
BURY BL9 ....53 H4
Alton Rd WILM/AE SK9 ....199 G2
Alton St OP/CLY M11 ....129 H1
Alton St OLDS OL8 ....8 A7
Altrincham Rd NTHM/RTH M23 ....167 F2
WILM/AE SK9 ....190 B5
Altrincham St CMANE M1 ....7 H7
Alum Crs BURY BL9 ....68 D1
Alvanley Cl SALE M33 ....154 C5
Alvanley Crs EDGY/DAV SK3 ....171 F3
Alvan Sq OP/CLY * M11 ....129 H1
Alva Rd OLDE OL4 ....75 G2
Alvaston Av HTNM SK4 ....159 E3
Alvaston Rd GTN M18 ....129 H4
Alveley Av DID/WITH M20 ....157 H1
Alverstone Rd DID/WITH M20 ....142 D5
Alveston Dr WILM/AE SK9 ....199 H2
Alvington Gv BRAM/HZG SK7 ....184 B3
Alwin Rd ROY/SHW OL2 ....59 H1
Alwinton Av HTNM SK4 ....158 B3
Alworth Rd BKLY M9 ....87 E2
Alwyn Dr BRUN/LGST M13 ....128 B4
Ambassador Pl
HALE/TIMP * WA15 ....165 H4
Amber Gdns DUK * SK16 ....118 A5
Amberhill Wy WALK M28 ....94 A5
Amberley Cl BOLS/LL BL3 ....47 G4
Amberley Dr HALE/TIMP WA15 ....178 C4
IRL M44 ....136 B2
NTHM/RTH M23 ....155 E3
Amberley Rd SALE M33 ....153 H1
Amberley Wk CHAD OL9 ....8 C2
Amber St ANC M4 ....7 G2
Amberwood Dr
NTHM/RTH M23 ....167 E3
Amblecote Dr East LHULT M38 ....80 B1
Amblecote Dr West LHULT M38 ....80 B1
Ambleside STLY SK15 ....119 F2
Ambleside Av AULW OL7 ....105 F4
HALE/TIMP WA15 ....166 D4
MDTN M24 ....71 F1
Ambleside Cl BOLE BL2 ....35 G2
MDTN M24 ....72 D4
Ambleside Rd RDSH SK5 ....145 E5
URM M41 ....138 A1
Ambrose Ct WYTH/NTH * M22 ....156 C5
Ambrose Dr DID/WITH M20 ....156 C5
Ambrose St ROCH OL11 ....43 E1
WGTN/LGST M12 ....128 D1
Ambush St OP/CLY M11 ....115 F4
Amelia St DTN/ASHW M34 ....131 G4
Amersham Cl URM M41 ....123 E5
Amersham Pl BNG/LEV M19 ....143 H5
Amersham St ORD M5 ....111 F4
Amesbury Gv RDSH SK5 ....160 A1
Amesbury Rd BKLY M9 ....87 E3
Amherst Rd DID/WITH M20 ....142 C4
Amlwch Av OFTN SK2 ....173 G5
Ammon Wrigley Cl OLD OL1 ....9 G2
Amory St WGTN/LGST M12 ....7 K7
Amos Av NEWH/MOS M40 ....115 F1
Amos St BKLY M9 ....101 G5
SLFD M6 ....111 G1
Ampney Ct ECC M30 ....109 E4
Amwell St CHH M8 ....100 C3
Amy St MDTN M24 ....72 A3
WHIT OL12 ....29 F1
Anaconda Dr CSLFD M3 ....6 B1
Anchorage Quay SALO M50 ....111 H1
Anchorage Rd URM M41 ....139 F2
Anchor Cl BNG/LEV M19 ....144 B2
Anchor Ct CHH * M8 ....100 C5
Anchor La FWTH BL4 ....64 A5
Anchorside Cl CCHDY M21 ....141 G4
Ancoats Av ANC M4 ....114 A4
Ancoats Gv North ANC M4 ....114 A4
Ancoats Gv ANC M4 ....114 A4
Ancoats St OLDE OL4 ....91 H1
Ancroft St HULME M15 ....127 G2
Anderton Cl TOT/BURYW BL8 ....37 E5
Anderton Gv AUL OL6 ....105 H5

Anderton Wy WILM/AE SK9 ....192 A4
Andoc Av ECC M30 ....110 A4
Andover Av MDTN M24 ....88 A2
Andover St ECC M50 ....109 F4
Andre St OP/CLY * M11 ....115 F3
Andrew Cl RAD M26 ....67 H5
TOT/BURYW BL8 ....26 A2
Andrew La BOL BL1 ....23 E5
Andrew Rd BKLY M9 ....101 E1
Andrews Av URM M41 ....122 B5
Andrew St AUL * OL6 ....105 G5
BURY BL9 ....5 G5
CHAD OL9 ....73 H4
DROY M43 ....116 D1
FAIL M35 ....102 D2
HTNM SK4 ....12 E2
HYDE SK14 ....133 E5
MDTN M24 ....86 D3
MOSL OL5 ....106 D2
Anerley Rd DID/WITH M20 ....157 G2
Anfield Cl BURY BL9 ....69 E1
Anfield Rd BOLS/LL BL3 ....63 H3
CHD/CHDH SK8 ....182 C2
NEWH/MOS M40 ....102 C1
SALE M33 ....154 D1
Angela Av ROY/SHW OL2 ....74 B2
Angela St HULME M15 ....126 C1
Angel Cl DUK SK16 ....132 A1
Angelko Ri OLD OL1 ....75 G1
Angelo St BOL BL1 ....33 G3
Angel Wk HULME M15 ....86 D3
BRAM/HZG SK7 ....185 E1
DTN/ASHW M34 ....131 H4
Anglers Rest IRL M44 ....150 D1
Anglesea Av OFTN SK2 ....172 A5
Anglesey Cl AULW OL7 ....104 C4
Anglesey Dr POY/DIS SK12 ....195 F1
Anglesey Gv CHD/CHDH SK8 ....170 C3
Anglesey Rd AULW OL7 ....104 C4
Anglesey Water POY/DIS SK12 ....195 F1
Angleside Av BNG/LEV M19 ....158 B2
Angle St BOLE BL2 ....3 K1
Anglia Gv BOLS/LL BL3 ....48 B5
Angora Dr CSLFD M3 ....112 C2
Angouleme Wy BURY BL9 ....4 D6
Angus Av HEY OL10 ....40 B5
Anita St ANC M4 ....7 J2
Annable Rd DROY M43 ....116 C4
IRL M44 ....136 A5
MPL/ROM SK6 ....161 E3
Annald Sq DROY M43 ....116 B5
Annan St DTN/ASHW * M34 ....131 G4
Annecy Cl TOT/BURYW BL8 ....37 G2
Anne Nuttall Rd HULME M15 ....126 C1
Annersley Av ROY/SHW OL2 ....59 H3
Annesley Rd NEWH/MOS M40 ....102 C1
Anne St DUK SK16 ....118 C5
Annie St RAMS BL0 ....16 D3
SLFD M6 ....111 F3
Annis Cl WILM/AE SK9 ....201 G3
Annisdale Cl ECC M50 ....109 E5
Annis Rd BOLS/LL BL3 ....48 A5
WILM/AE SK9 ....201 G3
Ann Sq OLDE OL4 ....75 G4
Ann St CHH M8 ....100 C4
DTN/ASHW M34 ....131 H5
FWTH BL4 ....64 A4
HEY OL10 ....41 E3
HYDE SK14 ....132 B5
RDSH SK5 ....159 H2
Anscombe Cl NEWH/MOS M40 ....114 A2
Ansdell Av CCHDY M21 ....141 E4
Ansdell Dr DROY M43 ....115 H3
Ansdell Rd MILN OL16 ....43 G2
RDSH SK5 ....145 H4
Ansell Cl GTN M18 ....128 C2
Anselms Ct OLDS OL8 ....89 H1
Ansleigh Av CHH M8 ....100 D1
Anslow Cl NEWH/MOS M40 ....101 G5
Anson Av SWIN M27 ....96 D4
Anson Cl BRAM/HZG SK7 ....194 A2
Anson Rd DTN/ASHW M34 ....146 B4
POY/DIS SK12 ....195 H4
RUSH/FAL M14 ....128 A3
SWIN M27 ....96 D4
Anson St BOL BL1 ....34 A3
Answell Av CHH M8 ....86 A5
Antares Av BRO M7 ....112 C2
Anthony St MOSL OL5 ....106 C1
Antilles Cl WGTN/LGST M12 ....128 D4
Antrim Cl BNG/LEV M19 ....158 A4
Anvil Wy OLD OL1 ....9 G5
Apethorn La HYDE SK14 ....147 F3
Apfel La CHAD OL9 ....73 G5
Apollo Av BURY BL9 ....68 C3
Apperley Gra ECC M50 ....109 H1
Appian Wy BRO M7 ....99 H5
Appleby Av HALE/TIMP WA15 ....166 D4
HYDE SK14 ....132 B3
Appleby Cl EDGY/DAV SK3 ....171 G4
Appleby Gdns BOLE * BL2 ....3 H1
Appleby Rd CHD/CHDH SK8 ....169 G5
Apple Ct OLDS OL8 ....91 F4
Appledore Dr BOLE BL2 ....35 E4
NTHM/RTH M23 ....167 G2
Appledore Wk CHAD OL9 ....89 G1
Appleford Dr CHH M8 ....100 D4
Apple St HYDE SK14 ....134 D1
Appleton Rd HALE/TIMP WA15 ....176 H1
SALE M33 ....144 C5
Apple Tree Ct ORD M5 ....111 H3
Appleton Wk CHAD OL9 ....72 C5
Applewood CHAD OL9 ....89 F4
April Cl OLDS OL8 ....91 F4
Apsley Cl BOLE BL2 ....35 F2
Apsley Gv BRAM/HZG SK7 ....185 E4
WGTN/LGST M12 ....7 K5
Apsley Rd DTN/ASHW M34 ....131 G4
Apsley St STKP SK1 ....13 H4
Aquarius La SLFD * M6 ....112 A2
Aquarius St HULME M15 ....127 F1
Aqueduct Rd BOLS/LL BL3 ....49 H5
Aragon Dr HEY OL10 ....41 E5
Aragon Wy MPL/ROM SK6 ....174 D3

Arbor Dr BNG/LEV M19 ....143 H4
Arbor Dr BNG/LEV M19 ....143 G4
Arbor Gv DROY M43 ....116 A2
LHULT M58 ....79 D3
Arbory Av NEWH/MOS M40 ....102 A2
Arbour Ct BURY BL9 ....27 F5
SLFD M6 ....111 G2
Arbour La OLDE OL4 ....77 H5
Arbroath St OP/CLY M11 ....115 G4
Arbury Av EDGY/DAV SK3 ....170 C2
The Arcades AUL * OL6 ....118 A2
Arcadia Av SALE M33 ....154 B5
Archer Av BOLE BL2 ....49 H1
Archer Gv BOLE BL2 ....49 H1
Archer Pk MDTN M24 ....116 B4
Archer Pl STRET M52 ....139 E1
Archer St MOSL OL5 ....92 D5
HYDE SK14 ....147 G5
OP/CLY M11 ....114 D3
Archie St ORD M5 ....125 H1
Arch St BOL BL1 ....3 H2
Archway HULME M15 ....127 E3
Arclid Cl WILM/AE SK9 ....192 B5
Arcon Cl MILN OL16 ....31 F5
Arcon Dr OLDTF/WHR M16 ....126 D5
Arcon Pl ALT WA14 ....164 D3
Ardale Av NEWH/MOS M40 ....88 B5
Ardcombe Av BKLY M9 ....86 D2
Ardeen Wk BRUN/LGST * M13 ....127 H2
Arden Av MDTN M24 ....88 A2
Arden Cl AUL OL6 ....106 A4
BURY * BL9 ....27 F5
Arden Ct BRAM/HZG SK7 ....185 G3
Arden St CHAD OL9 ....89 H4
Ardent Wy BRO M7 ....99 E1
Ardenfield DTN/ASHW M34 ....146 D4
Ardenfield Dr WYTH/NTH M22 ....180 D2
Arden Lodge Rd
NTHM/RTH M23 ....167 G2
Arden Rd MPL/ROM SK6 ....146 B4
Ardens Cl SWIN M27 ....82 C5
Arden St CHAD OL9 ....89 H4
Ardern Pl WHM/AE SK9 ....201 B4
Arderne Rd HALE/TIMP WA15 ....166 B1
Ardern Gv STKP SK1 ....13 H6
Ardern Rd CHH M8 ....100 A1
Ardern Wk STKP SK1 ....13 H6
Ardwick Gn North
WGTN/LGST M12 ....127 H1
Ardwick Gn South CMANE M1 ....127 H1
Ardwick Ter WGTN/LGST M12 ....128 A2
Argo St BOLS/LL BL3 ....48 C5
Argosy Dr ECC M30 ....122 C1
MANAIR M90 ....89 H5
Argus St OLDS OL8 ....89 H4
Argyle Av RUSH/FAL M14 ....128 B4
WALK M28 ....80 D2
Argyle Crs HEY OL10 ....40 C5
Argyle Pk RUSH/FAL M14 ....128 B4
DROY M43 ....116 B4
GTM M18 ....129 F3
OLD OL1 ....75 E4
ROCH OL11 ....41 H1
SWIN M27 ....96 D5
Argyle St AUL OL6 ....105 G4
Argyll Cl FAIL M35 ....103 G3
Argyll Park Rd FAIL M35 ....103 G3
Argyll Rd CHD/CHDH SK8 ....182 C3
MOSL OL5 ....106 D1
Argyll St AUL OL6 ....106 D2
Arkendale Cl FAIL * M35 ....103 H3
Arkholme WALK M28 ....94 B2
Arkle Av WILM/AE SK9 ....198 C5
Arkle Dr CHAD OL9 ....73 E4
Arkley Wk BRUN/LGST M13 ....127 G2
Ark St BNG/LEV M19 ....143 H1
Arkwright Cl BOL BL1 ....33 F5
Arkwright Rd MPL/ROM SK6 ....175 F3
Arkwright St CHAD OL9 ....8 A4
Arlen Ct BOLE * BL2 ....3 J5
Arlen Gv OFTN SK2 ....172 D3
Arlen Wy HEY * OL10 ....40 C4
Arley Av BURY BL9 ....38 B1
DID/WITH M20 ....157 E1
Arley Cl ALT WA14 ....165 E4
Arley Dr ROY/SHW OL2 ....60 B1
SALE M33 ....154 B4
Arley Gv EDGY/DAV SK3 ....171 G5
Arley Mere Cl CHD/CHDH SK8 ....182 C1
Arley Moss Wk
BRUN/LGST * M13 ....127 G1
Arley Rd RAD M26 ....67 G3
Arliss Cl STLY SK15 ....119 F4
Arlies Cl STLY SK15 ....119 F4
Arlies St AUL OL6 ....118 C1
Arlington Av DTN/ASHW M34 ....146 D1
PWCH M25 ....85 E5
SWIN M27 ....96 C5
Arlington Crs WILM/AE SK9 ....198 C5
Arlington Dr OFTN SK2 ....172 C5
POY/DIS SK12 ....195 G4
Arlington Rd CHD/CHDH SK8 ....169 G3
STRET M52 ....139 G2
Arlington St AUL OL6 ....118 B2
BOLS/LL BL3 ....64 A1
CHH M8 ....100 A5
CSLFD M3 ....6 A1
Arlington Wy WILM/AE SK9 ....198 C5
Arliss Av BNG/LEV M19 ....143 H5
Armadale Av BKLY M9 ....87 H5
Armadale Cl EDGY/DAV SK3 ....171 H4
Armadale Rd DUK SK16 ....118 B4
HOR/BR * BL6 ....47 F4
Armdale Dr OLDE OL4 ....75 H5
Armentieres STLY SK15 ....119 F4
Armitage Av LHULT M38 ....80 A4
Armitage Cl MDTN M24 ....71 E5
OLDS OL8 ....89 H4
Armitage Gv LHULT M38 ....80 A4
Armitage Rd ALT WA14 ....177 G1
Armitage St ECC M30 ....109 F4
Armit Rd OLDE OL4 ....93 H5
Armour Pl BKLY M9 ....100 C3
Armoury St EDGY/DAV SK3 ....13 G5
Arm Rd WHIT OL12 ....19 G5
Armstrong Hurst Cl WHIT OL12 ....19 G5

Arncliffe Dr NTHM/RTH M23 ....179 H1
Arncliffe Ri OLDE OL4 ....61 F5
Arncott Rd BOL BL1 ....34 A1
Arncott Cl ROY/SHW OL2 ....59 H5
Arne Cl OFTN SK2 ....173 H4
Arnesby Av SALE M33 ....140 D5
Arnesby Gv BOLE BL2 ....3 K2
Arne St CHAD * OL9 ....89 F2
Arnfield Dr WALK M28 ....94 C4
Arnfield Rd DID/WITH M20 ....142 D5
EDGY/DAV SK3 ....171 G4
Arnold Av HEY OL10 ....56 B2
HYDE SK14 ....148 A4
Arnold Cl DUK SK16 ....133 F1
Arnold Dr DROY M43 ....116 B4
MDTN M24 ....72 B1
Arnold Rd EDGW/EG BL7 ....23 E3
HYDE SK14 ....148 A4
OLDTF/WHR M16 ....141 H2
Arnold St AUL OL6 ....118 C1
BOL BL1 ....33 G4
EDGY/DAV SK3 ....13 G7
OLD OL1 ....9 K1
Arncott Crs HULME M15 ....127 E3
Arnside Av CHD/CHDH SK8 ....169 G5
CHAD OL9 ....89 F2
HTNM SK4 ....159 E1
Arnside Cl CHD/CHDH SK8 ....169 G5
MPL/ROM SK6 ....186 D4
ROY/SHW OL2 ....60 C2
Arnside Dr HYDE SK14 ....132 B4
ROCH OL11 ....41 F1
SLFD M6 ....111 H1
Arnside Gv BOLE BL2 ....50 B1
SALE M33 ....155 E3
Arnside St RUSH/FAL M14 ....142 C1
Arran Av OLDS OL8 ....90 C4
SALE M33 ....153 G4
STRET M52 ....139 F1
Arran Cl BOLS/LL BL3 ....47 F3
Arrandale Ct URM * M41 ....123 C5
Arran Gdns URM M41 ....123 C5
Arran Gv RAD M26 ....51 H4
Arran St BRO M7 ....100 C5
NEWH/MOS M40 ....103 G5
Arras Gv RDSH SK5 ....130 A5
Arreton Sq RUSH/FAL M14 ....128 B5
Arrivals Wy MANAIR M90 ....180 A5
Arrowfield Rd CCHDY M21 ....141 F5
Arrowhill Rd RAD M26 ....52 A1
Arrow St BOL BL1 ....2 C2
BRO M7 ....100 B5
Arthington St MILN OL16 ....11 G5
Arthog Dr HALE/TIMP WA15 ....178 A4
Arthog Rd DID/WITH M20 ....157 H2
HALE/TIMP WA15 ....178 A4
Arthur Av WALK M28 ....81 G5
Arthur La BOLE BL2 ....35 H3
Arthur Rd OLDTF/WHR M16 ....140 C4
Arthur St BOLS/LL BL3 ....63 H1
ECC M30 ....109 F4
FWTH BL4 ....66 A3
HEY * OL10 ....56 B2
HYDE SK14 ....147 F2
PWCH M25 ....86 B3
RDSH SK5 ....144 D4
ROY/SHW OL2 ....59 H3
SWIN M27 ....96 A1
TOT/BURYW BL8 ....37 H4
WHIT OL12 ....29 F1
Artillery Pl WYTH/NTH * M22 ....169 E5
Artillery St BOLS/LL BL3 ....49 E4
CSLFD M3 ....6 C6
Arundale CHD/CHDH SK8 ....181 G5
Arundale Av OLDTF/WHR M16 ....141 H2
Arundale Cl HYDE SK14 ....134 C5
Arundale Gv HYDE SK14 ....134 C5
Arundel Av HALE/TIMP WA15 ....178 D3
STLY SK15 ....107 G4
TOT/BURYW BL8 ....26 D5
Arundel Cl BRAM/HZG SK7 ....192 D1
Arundel St AUL OL6 ....118 D2
BOL BL1 ....33 F5
HULME M15 ....126 D3
OLDE OL4 ....92 A4
ROCH OL11 ....42 D2
SWIN M27 ....96 B4
Arundel Wk CHAD OL9 ....72 C5
Ascension Rd BRO M7 ....112 C1
Ascot Av SALE M33 ....153 F4
STRET M52 ....125 G5
Ascot Cl CHAD OL9 ....73 E4
Ascot Dr BRAM/HZG SK7 ....185 H2
NEWH/MOS M40 ....115 E1
URM M41 ....150 D1
Ascot Gv OFTN SK2 ....172 D3
Ascot Pde BNG/LEV M19 ....143 G5
Ascot Rd BOLS/LL BL3 ....63 H3
NEWH/MOS M40 ....115 E1
Ascroft St OLD OL1 ....9 H4
Asgard Dr ORD M5 ....112 B5
Asgard Gv ORD M5 ....112 B5
Ash Av ALT WA14 ....165 G4
CHD/CHDH SK8 ....181 G4
DROY M43 ....116 B5
HALE/TIMP WA15 ....166 A2
LIT OL15 ....20 D3
MILN OL16 ....44 D3
MPL/ROM SK6 ....174 D4
ROY/SHW OL2 ....76 D5
Ashawe Cl LHULT M38 ....79 D4
Ashawe Gv LHULT M38 ....79 D4
Ashawe Ter LHULT M38 ....79 D4
Ashbank Av BOLS/LL BL3 ....47 F3
Ashbee St BOL BL1 ....33 F4
Ashberry Cl WILM/AE SK9 ....200 A2
Ashborne Dr BURY BL9 ....27 E1
Ashbourne Av BOLE BL2 ....51 F3
CHD/CHDH SK8 ....170 B4
DTN/ASHW M34 ....146 B4
URM M41 ....137 E1
Ashbourne Crs SALE M33 ....154 A2
Ashbourne Dr AUL OL6 ....106 A4
BURY BL9 ....27 E1
Ashbourne Gv BRO M7 ....99 F2
WALK M28 ....93 F5
WHTF M45 ....69 E5
Ashbourne Rd BRAM/HZG SK7 ....185 E3
DTN/ASHW M34 ....146 A4
ECC M30 ....109 H3
SLFD M6 ....97 H5

STRET M52 ....124 B4
Ashbourne Sq OLDS OL8 ....9 F7
Ashbourne St ROCH OL11 ....28 B2
Ashbridge TRPK M17 ....124 A2
Ashbridge Rd FAIL M35 ....103 C4
Ashbrook Av DTN/ASHW M34 ....130 C5
Ashbrook Cl CHD/CHDH SK8 ....181 G3
DTN/ASHW M34 ....130 C5
Ashbrook Crs WHIT OL12 ....19 H4
Ashbrook Farm Cl RDSH SK5 ....145 E1
Ashbrook Hey La WHIT OL12 ....19 H4
Ashbrook La RDSH SK5 ....145 E1
Ashbrook St OP/CLY M11 ....130 B1
Ashburn Av BNG/LEV M19 ....2 D6
Ashburn Gv HTNM SK4 ....159 F3
Ashburn Rd HTNM SK4 ....159 F3
Ashburton Cl HYDE SK14 ....149 F1
Ashburton Rd EDGY/DAV SK3 ....171 H5
Ashburton Rd West URM M41 ....123 G1
Ashbury Cl BOLS/LL BL3 ....48 D4
Ashbury Pl NEWH/MOS * M40 ....118 B2
Ashby Av BNG/LEV M19 ....158 B2
Ashby Cl BOLS/LL BL3 ....64 C1
Ashby Gv WHTF M45 ....68 C5
Ash Cl AUL OL6 ....105 G5
DUK SK16 ....134 C4
OFTN SK2 ....172 D4
WHIT OL12 ....19 H4
Ashcombe Br BOLE BL2 ....50 D3
RAD M26 ....51 G4
Ashcroft Av SLFD M6 ....111 F1
Ashcott Cl HOR/BR BL6 ....47 E4
Ashcroft WILM/AE SK9 ....199 E5
Ashcroft Av SLFD M6 ....111 F1
Ashdale Av BOLS/LL BL3 ....160 A1
CHAD OL9 ....73 F4
Ashdale Crs DROY M43 ....116 A4
Ashdale Dr CHD/CHDH SK8 ....181 G2
DID/WITH M20 ....158 A1
Ashdene Cl CHAD OL9 ....73 H3
Ashdene Crs BOLE BL2 ....35 G2
Ashdene Rd OLD OL1 ....60 C5
WILM/AE SK9 ....199 E5
Ashdown Av BKLY M9 ....87 E3
MPL/ROM SK6 ....162 B1
Ashdown Dr BOLE BL2 ....50 D1
SWIN M27 ....97 F4
WALK M28 ....94 A3
Ashdown Lawns STLY SK15 ....120 A2
Ashdown Rd HTNM SK4 ....159 F3
Ashdown Wk CHD/CHDH SK8 ....191 G5
Ashdown Wy ROY/SHW OL2 ....59 F1
Ash Dr SWIN M27 ....82 B5
Ashes St AUL OL6 ....105 H5
Ashes Cl STLY SK15 ....119 H5
Ashes Dr BOLE BL2 ....50 C1
Ashfield DTN/ASHW M34 ....131 H5
Ashfield Av ROCH OL11 ....43 E1
Ashfield Cl OLDE OL4 ....92 A4
Ashfield Crs CHD/CHDH SK8 ....182 B2
OLDE OL4 ....92 A4
Ashfield Dr NEWH/MOS M40 ....115 G1
Ashfield Gv BOL BL1 ....23 F5
GTN M18 ....130 A4
IRL M44 ....135 D5
MPL/ROM SK6 ....163 G5
Ashfield La MILN OL16 ....44 C2
Ashfield Lodge DID/WITH M20 ....158 A1
Ashfield Rd BRUN/LGST M13 ....170 A5
CHD/CHDH SK8 ....170 A5
EDGY/DAV SK3 ....172 A5
HALE/TIMP WA15 ....177 H1
ROCH OL11 ....43 E1
SALE M33 ....138 C1
Ashfield Sq DROY M43 ....116 A4
Ashford SALE M33 ....153 H3
Ashford Av SWIN M27 ....96 B3
WALK M28 ....94 A4
Ashford Cl BOLE BL2 ....35 E1
BRAM/HZG SK7 ....193 F4
NEWH/MOS M40 ....102 B1
Ashford Gn BOL BL1 ....23 E3
Ashford Rd DID/WITH M20 ....144 D4
HTNM SK4 ....159 F4
WILM/AE SK9 ....201 B3
Ashford St HEY OL10 ....40 A4
Ashford Wk BOL BL1 ....2 D3
CHAD OL9 ....89 H1
Ashgate Av WYTH/NTH M22 ....168 D5
Ashgrove MILN OL16 ....31 F5
Ash Gv ALT WA14 ....177 F3
BOLE BL2 ....51 G5
CHD/CHDH SK8 ....181 G4
DROY M43 ....116 B5
HALE/TIMP WA15 ....166 A2
MILN OL16 ....44 D3
MPL/ROM SK6 ....174 D4
PWCH M25 ....85 E3
RAMS BL0 ....16 C1
ROY/SHW OL2 ....59 E3
STLY SK15 ....119 H5
SWIN M27 ....97 E3
TOT/BURYW BL8 ....37 F1
Ashia Cl MILN OL16 ....30 B5
Ashill Wk CSLFD M3 ....6 D3
Ashington Cl BOL BL1 ....33 G3
Ashington Dr TOT/BURYW BL8 ....36 B4
Ashkirk St GTN M18 ....129 G3
Ashlands SALE M33 ....154 A1
Ashlands Av NEWH/MOS M40 ....102 B1
WALK M28 ....96 B4
Ashlands Dr DTN/ASHW M34 ....131 F2
Ashlands Rd HALE/TIMP WA15 ....154 A5

Ash La *HALE/TIMP* WA15 .... **178** D3
Ashlar Dr *WGTN/LGST* M12 .... **114** A5
Ash Lawns *BOL* BL1 .... **48** A2
Ashlea Dl *BKLY* M9 .... **86** D5
Ashlea Gv *OLDE* OL4 .... **92** C1
Ashleigh Cl *ROY/SHW* OL2 .... **74** B2
Ash Leigh Dr *BOL* BL1 .... **47** F1
Ashleigh Rd *HALE/TIMP* WA15 .... **166** C1
Ashley Av *BOLE* BL2 .... **50** A1
OLDTF/WHR M16 .... **126** C4
SWIN M27 .... **96** C4
URM M41 .... **137** F1
Ashley Cl *ROCH* OL11 .... **42** B2
Ashley Court Dr
NEWH/MOS M40 .... **103** E1
Ashley Crs *SWIN* M27 .... **96** C3
Ashley Dr *BRAM/HZG* SK7 .... **193** F1
SALE M33 .... **153** H4
SWIN M27 .... **96** C4
Ashley Gdns *HYDE* SK14 .... **147** H2
MPL/ROM SK6 .... **186** C4
Ashley La *BKLY* M9 .... **101** G2
Ashley Ms *HYDE* SK14 .... **147** H2
WHTF M45 .... **69** E5
Ashleymill La *ALT* WA14 .... **177** G4
Ashley Mill La North *ALT* WA14 .... **177** G4
Ashley Rd *ALT* WA14 .... **177** G1
DROY M43 .... **115** H3
OFTN SK2 .... **172** D1
WILM/AE SK9 .... **199** G1
Ashley St *CHAD* OL9 .... **8** B1
HYDE SK14 .... **132** D4
SLFD M6 .... **111** F3
Ashlor St *BURY* BL9 .... **4** C7
Ashlyn Gv *RUSH/FAL* M14 .... **143** E3
Ashlynne *AUL* OL6 .... **118** B2
Ashmeade *HALE/TIMP* WA15 .... **178** C3
Ashmond Rd *OLDE* OL4 .... **92** A1
Ashmoor Rd *WYTH/NTH* M22 .... **180** C3
Ashmore Av *EDGY/DAV* SK3 .... **170** C2
Ashmount Dr *WHIT* OL12 .... **10** C1
Ashness Dr *BOLE* BL2 .... **35** F5
BRAM/HZG SK7 .... **184** A4
MDTN M24 .... **71** E1
Ashover Av *WGTN/LGST* * M12 .... **128** C2
Ashover Cl *BOL* BL1 .... **23** E5
Ashover St *STRET* M32 .... **125** F5
Ashridge Cl *HOR/BR* BL6 .... **46** D3
Ashridge Dr *DUK* SK16 .... **132** A1
ECC M30 .... **109** F5
Ash Rd *DROY* M43 .... **116** A3
DTN/ASHW M34 .... **130** B4
FWTH BL4 .... **81** G2
PART M31 .... **150** C3
POY/DIS SK12 .... **195** G4
Ash Sq *OLDE* OL4 .... **75** G4
Ashstead Rd *SALE* M33 .... **154** D5
Ash St *BKLY* M9 .... **101** E3
BOLE BL2 .... **3** G6
BRAM/HZG SK7 .... **185** E1
BURY BL9 .... **5** H4
DTN/ASHW M34 .... **131** E1
EDGY/DAV SK3 .... **171** E1
FAIL M35 .... **102** D2
HEY OL10 .... **40** C3
MDTN M24 .... **72** B3
OLDE OL4 .... **91** E1
ROCH OL11 .... **42** B4
SLFD M6 .... **111** G3
Ashton Av *ALT* WA14 .... **165** H3
Ashton Crs *CHAD* OL9 .... **89** F4
Ashton Field Dr *LHULT* M38 .... **80** D3
Ashton Gdns *ROCH* OL11 .... **42** D1
Ashton Hill La *DROY* M43 .... **116** B5
Ashton La *MDTN* M24 .... **71** H4
SALE M33 .... **154** A1
Ashton New Rd *OP/CLY* M11 .... **114** D4
Ashton Old Rd *OP/CLY* M11 .... **114** B5
Ashton Pl *BRAM/HZG* SK7 .... **185** G3
Ashton Rd *BKLY* M9 .... **87** E2
DROY M43 .... **116** B4
DTN/ASHW M34 .... **131** F3
FAIL M35 .... **103** H4
HYDE SK14 .... **132** C2
MPL/ROM SK6 .... **146** B5
OLDS OL8 .... **9** F6
PART M31 .... **151** H3
Ashton Rd East *FAIL* M35 .... **103** E2
Ashton Rd West *FAIL* M35 .... **102** D3
Ashton St *BKLY* M9 .... **101** G2
BOLS/LL BL3 .... **48** A5
BOLS/LL BL3 .... **66** A1
CHAD OL9 .... **89** E4
DUK SK16 .... **131** H2
HEY OL10 .... **40** D4
MPL/ROM SK6 .... **147** F5
ROCH OL11 .... **42** D1
Ash Tree Av *DROY* M43 .... **116** A3
Ash Tree Dr *DUK* SK16 .... **133** E1
Ash Tree Rd *CHH* M8 .... **100** B1
HYDE SK14 .... **133** G3
Ashurst Av *OP/CLY* M11 .... **115** E3
Ashurst Cl *BOLE* BL2 .... **35** G3
HYDE SK14 .... **148** B2
Ashurst Dr *EDGY/DAV* SK3 .... **171** E4
Ashurst Rd *WYTH/NTH* M22 .... **181** E1
Ashville Ter *NEWH/MOS* M40 .... **101** G1
Ash Wk *CHAD* * OL9 .... **73** G4
MDTN M24 .... **87** G1
Ashway *AUL* * OL6 .... **117** H2
Ashway Clough North
OFTN * SK2 .... **173** E4
Ashway Clough South
OFTN * SK2 .... **173** E4
Ashwell Rd *NTHM/RTH* M23 .... **168** A2
Ashwell St *BOLE* * BL2 .... **34** C3
Ashwood *ALT* WA14 .... **177** E4
CHAD OL9 .... **72** D5
RAD M26 .... **66** A5
Ashwood Av *DID/WITH* M20 .... **156** D2
DTN/ASHW M34 .... **130** B5
RAMS BL0 .... **17** E1
SALE M33 .... **153** H3
WALK M28 .... **80** D2
Ashwood Crs *MPL/ROM* SK6 .... **175** E2
Ashwood Dr *LIT* OL15 .... **20** C3
ROY/SHW OL2 .... **58** D4
TOT/BURYW BL8 .... **26** C5
Ashworth Av *BOLS/LL* BL3 .... **66** B1
DTN/ASHW M34 .... **131** F1
URM M41 .... **137** F1
Ashworth Cl *ALT* WA14 .... **177** E3
CHAD OL9 .... **89** G3
LIT OL15 .... **20** D1
Ashworth La *BOL* BL1 .... **34** A1
HYDE SK14 .... **134** C5
Ashworth Ms *HEY* OL10 .... **40** B4
Ashworth St *CHH* M8 .... **99** H5
DTN/ASHW M34 .... **131** F4
FAIL M35 .... **102** C4
FWTH BL4 .... **64** D4
HEY OL10 .... **56** A1
OLD OL1 .... **9** H4
RAD M26 .... **52** D5
TOT/BURYW BL8 .... **37** H3
Asia St *BOLS/LL* BL3 .... **64** B1
Askern Av *WYTH/NTH* M22 .... **180** C1
Askett Cl *NEWH/MOS* M40 .... **102** C4
Aspell Cl *MDTN* M24 .... **71** G4
Aspen Cl *HALE/TIMP* WA15 .... **167** F4
Aspen Gdns *WHIT* * OL12 .... **28** D2
Aspen Gn *DTN/ASHW* M34 .... **146** D1
The Aspens *CHD/CHDH* * SK8 .... **169** F3
Aspen Wy *MPL/ROM* SK6 .... **187** F5
Aspen Wd *HYDE* SK14 .... **133** E5
Aspenwood Cl *MPL/ROM* SK6 .... **174** D2
Aspen Wood Dr *CHAD* OL9 .... **72** D5
Aspenwood Dr *CHH* M8 .... **100** D1
SALE M33 .... **153** F2
Aspinall Cl *WALK* M28 .... **80** A4
Aspinall Crs *WALK* M28 .... **80** A5
Aspinall St *HEY* OL10 .... **41** F4
MDTN M24 .... **72** B5
RUSH/FAL M14 .... **127** H5
Aspin La *ANC* M4 .... **7** G1
Aspland Rd *HYDE* SK14 .... **148** A4
Aspull St *OLDE* OL4 .... **91** F2
Asquith Av *DUK* SK16 .... **132** B2
Asquith St *RDSH* SK5 .... **145** E2
Assheton Av *DTN/ASHW* M34 .... **116** D4
Assheton Cl *AUL* OL6 .... **118** A2
Assheton Crs *NEWH/MOS* M40 .... **115** G1
Assheton Rd *NEWH/MOS* M40 .... **115** G1
ROY/SHW OL2 .... **59** G2
Assheton St *MDTN* M24 .... **71** H3
Assheton Wy *MDTN* M24 .... **71** H4
Assisi Gdns *WGTN/LGST* M12 .... **128** B2
Assumpton Rd *MDTN* M24 .... **71** E1
Astan Av *DROY* M43 .... **115** G2
Astbury Av *DTN/ASHW* M34 .... **117** E4
Astbury Cl *BURY* BL9 .... **53** H1
HALE/TIMP * WA15 .... **165** H3
OLDE OL4 .... **92** A1
Astbury Crs *EDGY/DAV* SK3 .... **171** G3
Astbury St *RAD* M26 .... **67** G3
Aster Av *FWTH* BL4 .... **64** B3
Aster St *OLD* OL1 .... **74** B3
Astley Cl *ROY/SHW* OL2 .... **59** G2
Astley Ct *IRL* M44 .... **135** D3
Astley Gdns *DUK* SK16 .... **118** A5
Astley Gv *STLY* SK15 .... **119** E2
Astley Hall Dr *RAMS* BL0 .... **16** D4
Astley La *BOL* BL1 .... **33** H3
Astley Rd *BOLE* BL2 .... **35** F1
STLY SK15 .... **119** E3
Astley St *BOL* BL1 .... **33** H4
DUK SK16 .... **131** H1
HTNM SK4 .... **12** D3
OP/CLY M11 .... **115** F4
STLY SK15 .... **119** F5
Aston Av *RUSH/FAL* M14 .... **142** A1
Aston Cl *EDGY/DAV* SK3 .... **171** F3
Astor Rd *BNG/LEV* M19 .... **143** F4
SALQ M50 .... **110** D4
Atcham Gv *BKLY* M9 .... **86** C1
Athenian Gdns *BRO* M7 .... **99** F5
Athens Dr *WALK* M28 .... **80** D5
Athens St *STKP* SK1 .... **13** K4
Athens Wy *OLDE* OL4 .... **91** H1
Atherfield *BOLE* BL2 .... **35** F2
Atherley Gv *NEWH/MOS* M40 .... **89** E5
Atherstone *WHIT* OL12 .... **10** B4
Atherstone Av *CHH* M8 .... **86** A5
Atherstone Cl *TOT/BURYW* BL8 .... **37** H2
Atherton Av *HYDE* SK14 .... **134** D5
Atherton Cl *FAIL* M35 .... **103** G5
Atherton Gv *HYDE* SK14 .... **134** D4
Atherton La *IRL* M44 .... **150** D1
Atherton St *CSLFD* M3 .... **6** B6
ECC M30 .... **109** E4
EDGY/DAV SK3 .... **12** C6
OLDE OL4 .... **91** H2
Athlone Av *BOL* BL1 .... **33** G1
BURY BL9 .... **38** C2
CHD/CHDH SK8 .... **171** F4
NEWH/MOS M40 .... **101** H2
Athole St *ORD* M5 .... **111** G4
Atholl Av *STRET* M32 .... **139** F1
Atholl Cl *BOLS/LL* BL3 .... **47** G3
Atholl Dr *HEY* OL10 .... **55** F1
Athol Rd *BRAM/HZG* SK7 .... **193** G2
OLDTF/WHR M16 .... **141** H2
Athol St *AUL* OL6 .... **118** B2
ECC M30 .... **109** E4
GTN M18 .... **129** H5
HTNM SK4 .... **159** G3
RAMS BL0 .... **16** D1
WHIT OL12 .... **11** G2
Atkinson Av *BOLS/LL* BL3 .... **64** C1
Atkinson Rd *URM* M41 .... **138** C1
Atkinson St *CHAD* OL9 .... **8** C1
CSLFD M3 .... **6** C5
OFTN SK2 .... **13** K7
ROCH OL11 .... **42** B4
Atkin St *WALK* M28 .... **81** E5
Atlanta Av *MANAIR* M90 .... **179** H4
Atlantic St *ALT* WA14 .... **164** D3
Atlas Pk *WYTH/NTH* * M22 .... **181** E3
Atlas St *AULW* OL7 .... **117** H1
Atlow Dr *NTHM/RTH* M23 .... **168** A4
Attenburys La *ALT* WA14 .... **165** H1
Attenburys Park Est
ALT * WA14 .... **165** H1
Attercliffe Rd *CCHDY* M21 .... **140** D4
Attewell St *OP/CLY* * M11 .... **114** D5
Attleboro Rd *NEWH/MOS* M40 .... **101** H3
Attlee Wy *WGTN/LGST* M12 .... **114** B4
Attwood Rd *HALE/TIMP* WA15 .... **166** C4
Attwood St *WGTN/LGST* M12 .... **128** D5
Atwood Rd *DID/WITH* M20 .... **157** H3
Atwood St *CMANE* M1 .... **7** F7
Auberson Rd *BOLS/LL* BL3 .... **63** G1
Aubrey Rd *DID/WITH* M20 .... **143** F5
Aubrey St *ORD* M5 .... **125** H1
ROCH OL11 .... **43** E1
Auburn Av *HYDE* SK14 .... **147** H3
MPL/ROM SK6 .... **162** C2
Auburn Dr *URM* M41 .... **138** D2
Auburn Rd *DTN/ASHW* M34 .... **146** A1
OLDTF/WHR M16 .... **126** A4
Auburn St *BOLS/LL* BL3 .... **48** C5
CMANE M1 .... **7** H6
Auckland Dr *SLFD* M6 .... **98** D5
Auckland Rd *BNG/LEV* M19 .... **143** G3
Audax Wk *NEWH/MOS* M40 .... **115** E1
Auden Cl *OP/CLY* M11 .... **115** G4
Audenshaw Hall Gv
DTN/ASHW M34 .... **130** C1
Audenshaw Rd
DTN/ASHW M34 .... **130** D1
Audlem Cl *NEWH/MOS* M40 .... **114** A3
Audley Av *STRET* M32 .... **124** A4
Audley Rd *BNG/LEV* * M19 .... **144** A1
Audley St *AUL* OL6 .... **118** D3
MOSL OL5 .... **107** E2
Audlum Ct *BURY* BL9 .... **5** H4
Audrey Av *GTN* M18 .... **129** H3
Audrey St *BKLY* M9 .... **101** G2
Augusta Cl *WHIT* OL12 .... **10** B2
Augusta St *WHIT* OL12 .... **10** B1
Augustine Webster Cl
BKLY M9 .... **101** F2
Augustus St *BOLS/LL* BL3 .... **49** F5
CSLFD M3 .... **113** F1
Augustus Wy
OLDTF/WHR M16 .... **126** C4
Austell Rd *WYTH/NTH* M22 .... **180** C3
Austen Av *BURY* BL9 .... **53** G3
Austen Rd *ECC* M30 .... **109** G4
Austin Dr *DID/WITH* M20 .... **157** H2
Austin Gv *BNG/LEV* M19 .... **143** G3
Autumn St *BRUN/LGST* M13 .... **127** H4
Avallon Cl *TOT/BURYW* BL8 .... **26** A4
Avalon Dr *DID/WITH* M20 .... **169** H1
Avebury Cl *CHH* M8 .... **100** A4
Avebury Rd *NTHM/RTH* M23 .... **167** H4
Avens Rd *PART* M31 .... **151** E3
The Avenue *BOLE* BL2 .... **3** J5
BRO M7 .... **99** F5
BURY BL9 .... **38** C1
CHD/CHDH SK8 .... **181** F3
ECC M30 .... **109** G4
HALE/TIMP WA15 .... **178** A4
MPL/ROM SK6 .... **161** E3
ROY/SHW OL2 .... **59** H3
SALE M33 .... **153** G3
URM M41 .... **137** F1
WALK M28 .... **95** F3
WALK M28 .... **108** A1
WILM/AE SK9 .... **201** B4
Avenue St *BOL* BL1 .... **2** A2
STKP SK1 .... **13** H1
Averhill *WALK* M28 .... **94** C2
Averill St *NEWH/MOS* M40 .... **102** C5
Averon Ri *OLD* OL1 .... **60** C5
Aveson Av *CCHDY* M21 .... **141** E5
Avian Dr *RUSH/FAL* M14 .... **142** C3
Aviary Rd *WALK* M28 .... **95** F4
Aviator Wy *WYTH/NTH* M22 .... **180** C4
Aviemore Cl *RAMS* BL0 .... **26** B1
Avis St *ROY/SHW* OL2 .... **59** H2
Avocet Dr *ALT* WA14 .... **165** E1
IRL M44 .... **121** B5
Avonbrook Dr *NEWH/MOS* M40 .... **89** E5
Avoncliff Cl *BOL* BL1 .... **33** G3
Avon Cl *MILN* OL16 .... **31** H5
MPL/ROM SK6 .... **174** D4
WALK M28 .... **80** B5
Avoncourt Dr *DID/WITH* M20 .... **157** F2
Avondale *SWIN* M27 .... **83** F5
Avondale Av *BRAM/HZG* SK7 .... **185** G2
BURY BL9 .... **38** B2
Avondale Crs *URM* M41 .... **123** F5
Avondale Dr *RAMS* BL0 .... **26** A1
SLFD M6 .... **97** G5
Avondale Ri *WILM/AE* SK9 .... **200** A4
Avondale Rd *BRAM/HZG* SK7 .... **185** G2
EDGY/DAV SK3 .... **12** A6
FWTH BL4 .... **64** A4
STRET M32 .... **125** F4
WHTF M45 .... **68** B3
Avondale St *BOL* BL1 .... **33** F5
CHH M8 .... **100** B3
Avon Dr *BURY* BL9 .... **27** G3
Avon Gdns *BNG/LEV* M19 .... **143** H5
Avonlea Dr *BNG/LEV* M19 .... **143** F5
Avonlea Rd *DROY* M43 .... **115** H3
SALE M33 .... **153** G5
Avonleigh Gdns *OLD* OL1 .... **75** F3
Avon Rd *BNG/LEV* M19 .... **143** G5
CHAD OL9 .... **73** E4
CHD/CHDH SK8 .... **181** G5
FWTH BL4 .... **82** A2
HALE/TIMP WA15 .... **177** H4
HEY OL10 .... **40** B4
ROY/SHW OL2 .... **60** A1
Avon St *BOL* BL1 .... **33** E5
EDGY/DAV SK3 .... **171** H2
OLDS OL8 .... **90** C3
Avril Cl *RDSH* SK5 .... **145** E3
Avro Cl *RUSH/FAL* M14 .... **142** C2
Avroe Rd *ECC* M30 .... **122** C1
Avro Wy *MANAIR* M90 .... **179** G5
Awburn Rd *HYDE* SK14 .... **149** F2
Axbridge Wk *NEWH/MOS* M40 .... **114** A3
Axford Cl *CHH* M8 .... **100** A4
Axon Sq *OLDTF/WHR* M16 .... **127** E4
Aycliffe Av *CCHDY* M21 .... **156** C1
Aycliffe Gv *BRUN/LGST* M13 .... **128** B5
Aylesbury Av *DTN/ASHW* M34 .... **146** C2
URM M41 .... **123** H4
Aylesbury Cl *ORD* M5 .... **111** H4
Aylesbury Gv *MDTN* M24 .... **72** B2
Aylesby Av *GTN* M18 .... **129** E4
Aylesford Rd *RUSH/FAL* M14 .... **128** A5
Aylesford Wk *BOL* * BL1 .... **2** D1
Aylsham Cl *MPL/ROM* SK6 .... **161** G1
Aylsham Ms *SWIN* M27 .... **96** C5
Aylwin Dr *SALE* M33 .... **154** C3
Ayr Av *OLDS* OL8 .... **90** C4
Ayr Cl *BRAM/HZG* SK7 .... **185** H2
Ayres Rd *OLDTF/WHR* M16 .... **126** B4
Ayr Gv *HEY* OL10 .... **55** F1
Ayrshire Rd *BRO* M7 .... **98** D4
Ayr St *BOLE* BL2 .... **34** C2
Ayrton Gv *LHULT* M38 .... **80** B2
Aysgarth *MILN* OL16 .... **11** G2
Aysgarth Av *CHD/CHDH* SK8 .... **169** H3
GTN M18 .... **129** H2
MPL/ROM SK6 .... **162** C2
Aysgarth Cl *SALE* M33 .... **153** G3
Ayshford Cl *ALT* WA14 .... **165** E3
Ayton Gv *RUSH/FAL* M14 .... **128** B4
Aytoun St *CMANE* M1 .... **7** G5
Azalea Av *GTN* M18 .... **129** G2

B

Babbacombe Gv *BKLY* M9 .... **86** C2
Babbacombe Rd *OFTN* SK2 .... **172** D3
Back Abingdon Rd *BOLE* BL2 .... **34** D5
Back Acton St *CMANE* * M1 .... **7** H6
Back Adcroft St *STKP* SK1 .... **13** H7
Back Adrian Rd *BOL* BL1 .... **33** F4
Back Adrian Rd East *BOL* * BL1 .... **33** F4
Back Ainscow St *BOL* BL1 .... **2** C2
Back Ainsworth La *BOLE* BL2 .... **3** K1
Back Ainsworth La East
BOLE BL2 .... **34** D5
Back Ainsworth Rd North
TOT/BURYW BL8 .... **37** H4
Back Ainsworth Rd South
TOT/BURYW BL8 .... **37** H4
Back Ainsworth St *BOL* * BL1 .... **33** G4
Back Albert St *BURY* BL9 .... **5** H4
Back Albion Pl *BURY* BL9 .... **38** C2
Back Alder St *BOLS/LL* BL3 .... **64** A1
Back Alexander Rd *BOLE* BL2 .... **34** D5
Back Alexandra St *BOLS/LL* BL3 .... **48** B5
Back Alfred St *BOLS/LL* * BL3 .... **49** G5
Back Alice St *BOLS/LL* * BL3 .... **48** B4
BOLS/LL BL3 .... **66** A1
Back Alicia St *BOLS/LL* * BL3 .... **50** A5
Back All Saints' St *BOL* * BL1 .... **3** F3
Back Alston St *BOLS/LL* BL3 .... **63** H1
Back Andrew St *BURY* BL9 .... **5** G5
Back Andrew St North *BURY* BL9 .... **5** H5
Back Anglia Gv *BOLS/LL* BL3 .... **48** B5
Back Annis Rd *BOLS/LL* * BL3 .... **48** A5
Back Anson St *BOL* BL1 .... **34** A3
Back Apple Ter *BOL* * BL1 .... **33** G4
Back Argo St *BOLS/LL* BL3 .... **48** C5
Back Argyle St *BURY* BL9 .... **38** C1
Back Arlington St *BOLS/LL* BL3 .... **64** A1
Back Arnold St *BOL* BL1 .... **33** F4
Back Arnold Ter *BOL* BL1 .... **32** C5
Back Ashbee St *BOL* BL1 .... **33** H3
Back Ashford Wk *BOL* BL1 .... **2** C1
Back Ashley St *ANC* M4 .... **7** H1
Back Ash St *BOLE* BL2 .... **3** G6
BURY * BL9 .... **5** H4
Back Ashton St *BOLS/LL* * BL3 .... **48** A5
Back Ashworth La *BOL* BL1 .... **34** A1
Back Ashworth St
TOT/BURYW BL8 .... **37** H3
Back Astley St *BOL* BL1 .... **33** H3
Back Augustus St *BOLS/LL* * BL3 .... **49** F5
Back Augustus St West
BOLS/LL * BL3 .... **49** F5
Back Avenue St *BOL* BL1 .... **2** A2
Back Avondale St *BOL* * BL1 .... **33** F5
Back Baldwin St *BOLS/LL* * BL3 .... **48** D4
Back Baldwin St North
BOLS/LL BL3 .... **48** D4
Back Balloon St *ANC* * M4 .... **7** F2
Back Banbury St *BOLE* BL2 .... **34** D5
Back Bankfield St *BOLS/LL* BL3 .... **48** B4
Back Bank St *CHH* M8 .... **113** F1
Back Bantry St *BOLS/LL* * BL3 .... **48** D4
Back Barbara St *BOLS/LL* BL3 .... **48** C5
Back Bark St *BOL* BL1 .... **2** D4
Back Bashall St *BOL* BL1 .... **48** B1
Back Battenberg Rd *BOL* * BL1 .... **48** B1
Back Baxendale St *BOL* BL1 .... **33** H2
Back Bayley St *BOL* BL1 .... **2** A2
Back Baythorpe St *BOL* * BL1 .... **34** A4
Back Baythorpe St North
BOL * BL1 .... **34** A3
Back Beaconsfield St
BOLS/LL BL3 .... **2** A7
Back Beaconsfield Ter *BOLE* BL2 .... **3** J1
Back Beatrice Rd *BOL* BL1 .... **33** F5
Back Bedford St *BOL* BL1 .... **2** A3
Back Beech St *BOL* BL1 .... **34** A4
Back Beechwood St
BOLS/LL BL3 .... **64** A1
Back Belbeck St
TOT/BURYW BL8 .... **37** H4
Back Bell La *BURY* BL9 .... **5** G3
Back Belmont Rd *BOL* BL1 .... **33** H1
Back Belmont Rd East *BOL* BL1 .... **33** H1
Back Bennett's La *BOL* BL1 .... **33** F4
Back Bennett's La East *BOL* BL1 .... **33** F4
Back Benson St *BURY* BL9 .... **5** G6
Back Bentinck St *BOL* BL1 .... **33** E5
Back Bentley St *BOLE* BL2 .... **49** H4
Back Bertrand Rd *BOL* BL1 .... **48** B2
Back Beverley Rd *BOL* BL1 .... **48** B1
Back Birch St *BURY* BL9 .... **5** F2
Back Birley St *BOL* BL1 .... **33** H2
Back Blackbank St *BOL* BL1 .... **34** A5
Back Blackburn Rd *BOL* BL1 .... **34** A4
Back Blackburn Rd West
BOL BL1 .... **33** H2
EDGW/EG * BL7 .... **22** D3
Back Blackburn St *BOL* BL1 .... **34** A3
Back Blackwood St *BOLS/LL* BL3 .... **49** F5
Back Bolton Rd North
TOT/BURYW BL8 .... **37** H5
Back Bolton Rd South
TOT/BURYW BL8 .... **37** H5
Back Bolton St *BOL* BL1 .... **34** A4
Back Bolton St South *BURY* BL9 .... **4** C4
Back Bond St West *BURY* BL9 .... **5** H4
Back Boundary St *BOL* BL1 .... **33** G4
Back Bowen St *BOL* * BL1 .... **33** E5
Backbower La *HYDE* SK14 .... **148** A3
Back Bowness Rd *BOLS/LL* BL3 .... **48** C5
Back Bradford Rd *BOLS/LL* BL3 .... **49** F5
BOLS/LL BL3 .... **64** B1
Back Bradford Rd West
BOLS/LL BL3 .... **64** B1
Back Bradford St *BOLE* BL2 .... **3** K5
Back Bradford St East *BOLE* BL2 .... **3** J5
Back Bradford St South *BOLE* BL2 .... **3** H6
Back Bradford St West *BOLE* BL2 .... **3** H6
Back Bradshaw *BOLE* BL2 .... **34** D2
Back Bradshaw Brow West
BOLE * BL2 .... **34** D2
Back Bradshawgate *BOL* BL1 .... **3** F5
Back Bradshaw Rd East
BOLE BL2 .... **35** E1
Back Bradshaw St *MILN* OL16 .... **10** E4
Back Brandon St *BOLS/LL* BL3 .... **48** C5
Back Brandon St North
BOLS/LL BL3 .... **48** C5
Back Brandwood St
BOLS/LL BL3 .... **48** B5
Back Bridgeman St
BOLS/LL BL3 .... **48** C5
Back Bridge St *BOL* BL1 .... **2** E3
CSLFD M3 .... **6** D4
RAMS BL0 .... **16** D2
Back Brierley St *BURY* BL9 .... **53** F1
Back Brierley St South *BURY* BL9 .... **53** F1
Back Brigade St *BOL* BL1 .... **48** B2
Back Brindley St *BOL* BL1 .... **34** A2
Back Brink's Pl *BOL* * BL1 .... **2** C4
Back Bristol Av *BOLE* BL2 .... **34** D5
Back Bristol St *BOLS/LL* BL3 .... **2** B7
Back Broach St *BOLS/LL* BL3 .... **48** D5
Back Broad O' Th' La *BOL* * BL1 .... **33** H2
Back Broad St *BURY* BL9 .... **4** D5
Back Bromwich St *BOLE* BL2 .... **3** J6
Back Brookfield St *BOLE* BL2 .... **3** J4
Back Brook St North *BURY* BL9 .... **5** G1
Back Broom St *BOLE* BL2 .... **3** H4
Back Bryce St *BOLS/LL* BL3 .... **48** D4
Back Burnaby St *BOLS/LL* BL3 .... **48** C4
Back Burnham Av *BOL* BL1 .... **32** D5
Back Bury New Rd *BOLE* BL2 .... **3** H5
Back Bury New Rd East *BOLE* BL2 .... **3** J5
Back Bury Old Rd *BOLE* BL2 .... **3** H4
Back Bury Rd *BOLE* BL2 .... **50** B2
Back Bury Rd East *BOLE* BL2 .... **49** H2
Back Bury Rd South *BOLE* * BL2 .... **3** K4
BOLE BL2 .... **50** A2
Back Bushell St *BOLS/LL* * BL3 .... **48** A5
Back Byrom St *TOT/BURYW* BL8 .... **37** G2
Back Byrom St South
TOT/BURYW * BL8 .... **37** G2
Back Calder Rd *BOLS/LL* BL3 .... **63** H1
Back Caledonia St *BOLS/LL* BL3 .... **48** B4
Back Calvert Rd *BOLS/LL* BL3 .... **64** A1
Back Cambridge St *AULW* * OL7 .... **117** G4
Back Camp St *BRO* * M7 .... **99** G5
Back Canada St *BOL* * BL1 .... **33** F4
Back Canning St *BURY* BL9 .... **4** E1
Back Carter St *BOLS/LL* BL3 .... **49** F5
Back Castle St *BOLE* BL2 .... **3** H5
Back Cateaton St *BURY* BL9 .... **4** E2
Back Cecilia St *BOLS/LL* BL3 .... **49** F5
Back Cecil St *BOLE* BL2 .... **3** J5
Back Cedar St *BURY* BL9 .... **5** J3
Back Cedar St North *BURY* BL9 .... **5** J3
Back Cemetery Rd East
BOLE BL2 .... **3** K4
Back Cestrian St *BOLS/LL* * BL3 .... **64** A1
Back Chalfont St *BOL* BL1 .... **34** A4
Back Chapel St *BNG/LEV* M19 .... **143** H2
BRAM/HZG * SK7 .... **185** F1
TOT/BURYW BL8 .... **26** A4
WHIT * OL12 .... **19** H1
Back Chapman St *BOL* BL1 .... **33** E5
Back Charles Holden St *BOL* BL1 .... **2** A6
Back Chaucer St *BOL* BL1 .... **33** G5
Back Cheapside *BOL* BL1 .... **2** E5
Back Chesham Rd North
BURY * BL9 .... **38** D2
Back Chesham Rd South
BURY BL9 .... **38** D2
BURY * BL9 .... **38** D2
Back Chester St *BURY* BL9 .... **38** D2
Back China La *CMANE* M1 .... **7** H5
Back Chorley New Rd *BOL* BL1 .... **2** A3
Back Chorley New Rd North
BOL BL1 .... **48** B2
Back Chorley Old Rd *BOL* BL1 .... **32** D5
Back Chorley Old Rd North
BOL BL1 .... **32** D5
BOL BL1 .... **33** F5
Back Chorley Old Rd South
BOL BL1 .... **32** D5
BOL * BL1 .... **48** B1
Back Chorley St *BOL* BL1 .... **2** C4
Back Chorley St East *BOL* * BL1 .... **2** C3
Back Church Av *BOLS/LL* BL3 .... **48** B5
Back Church Rd *BOL* BL1 .... **32** D4
Back Church Rd North *BOL* BL1 .... **33** E4
Back Church St *BOL* BL1 .... **2** D3
BOLS/LL BL3 .... **65** H1
Back Clarendon Rd *BOLE* BL2 .... **49** H2
Back Clarke St *BOL* * BL1 .... **48** B1
Back Clay St East
EDGW/EG * BL7 .... **23** F4
Back Clay St West
EDGW/EG * BL7 .... **23** F4
Back Clegg St *BOLE* BL2 .... **49** H2
Back Clifton St *BURY* BL9 .... **38** C2
Back Cloister St *BOL* * BL1 .... **33** F4
Back Clyde St *BOL* BL1 .... **33** H4
Back Cobden St *BOL* BL1 .... **33** G3
Back Colenso Rd *BOLE* * BL2 .... **50** A2
Back College Land *CSLFD* * M3 .... **6** D4
Back College Wy *BOLS/LL* BL3 .... **2** B6
Back Columbia Rd *BOL* * BL1 .... **48** B1
Back Coniston St *BOL* * BL1 .... **34** A3
Back Coop St *BOL* BL1 .... **33** H2
Back Cornall St *TOT/BURYW* BL8 .... **37** H3
Back Corson St *FWTH* BL4 .... **65** E2
Back Cottam St
TOT/BURYW * BL8 .... **37** H3
Back Cotton St *BOL* BL1 .... **33** G4
Back Cowm La *WHIT* OL12 .... **14** A2
Back Cox Green Rd North
EDGW/EG BL7 .... **23** E3
Back Crawford Av *BOLE* BL2 .... **3** J6
Back Crawford St *BOLE* * BL2 .... **3** J6
Back Crescent Av *BOL* BL1 .... **2** B3
Back Crescent Rd *BOLS/LL* BL3 .... **49** F5
Back Crescent Rd West
BOLS/LL BL3 .... **64** B1
Back Croft La *BOLS/LL* BL3 .... **49** G5
Back Cromer Av *BOLE* BL2 .... **34** D5
Back Crostons Rd
TOT/BURYW BL8 .... **4** A3
Back Croston St *BOLS/LL* BL3 .... **48** B5
Back Crumpsall St North
BOL BL1 .... **33** H3
Back Cundey St *BOL* * BL1 .... **33** F5
Back Curzon Rd *BOL* BL1 .... **48** B2
Back Cyril St *BOLS/LL* * BL3 .... **49** F4
Back Daisy St *BOLS/LL* BL3 .... **48** B5
Back Darley St *FWTH* BL4 .... **65** F4
Back Darwen Rd North
EDGW/EG BL7 .... **22** D2
EDGW/EG BL7 .... **23** F3

Back Darwen Rd South
EDGW/EG BL7 23 F4
Back Darwin St BOL * BL1 33 G4
Back Deal St BOLS/LL * BL3 64 A1
BURY BL9 5 J5
Back Deane Church La
BOLS/LL * BL3 48 A5
Back Deane Church La
West BOLS/LL * BL3 48 A5
Back Deane Rd BOLS/LL BL3 48 B4
Back Deane Rd North
BOLS/LL BL3 2 A7
Back Delamere St South
BURY * BL9 38 D1
Back Denton St BURY BL9 38 C2
Back Derby St BOLS/LL BL3 48 D4
BURY BL9 5 F4
Back Design St BOLS/LL * BL3 48 A5
Back Devonshire Rd BOL BL1 32 D5
Back Devon St North
BURY * BL9 53 F1
Back Devon St South
BURY * BL9 53 G1
Back Dijon St BOLS/LL BL3 48 B5
Back Dijon St North BOLS/LL BL3 48 B5
Back Dobie St BOLS/LL * BL3 49 F5
Back Doffcocker Brow BOL BL1 32 C5
Back Dorset St BOLE BL2 3 H5
Back Dougill St BOL BL1 33 E5
Back Dougill St South BOL BL1 33 E5
Back Drake St MILN OL16 30 A5
Back Drummond St BOL * BL1 33 H2
Back Ducie Av BOL BL1 48 B2
Back Duckworth St BURY BL9 38 D2
Back Duncan St BRO M7 99 F3
Back Dunstan St BOLE BL2 49 H2
Back Durham St ROCH OL11 43 F1
Back Duxbury St BOL * BL1 33 G4
Back Earnshaw St BOLS/LL * BL3 63 F1
Back Eastbank St BOL BL1 34 A3
Back East St BURY BL9 5 F6
Back Eckersley Rd BOL BL1 33 H3
Back Edditch Gv BOLE BL2 49 H2
Back Eden St BOL BL1 33 H2
Back Edgmont Av BOLS/LL * BL3 48 C5
Back Eldon St BURY BL9 4 E1
Back Elgin St BOL BL1 33 G4
Back Ellesmere Rd BOLS/LL BL3 63 F1
Back Ellesmere St BOLS/LL BL3 2 A7
Back Elm St BURY BL9 5 J5
Back Elmwood Gv BOL * BL1 48 B1
Back Elmwood Gv West
BOL * BL1 48 B1
Back Elsworth St CSLFD M3 113 F2
Back Empire Rd BOLE BL2 50 A1
Back Empress St BOL BL1 33 E5
Back Ena St BOLS/LL * BL3 64 B1
Back Ernest St BOL BL1 2 A6
Back Eskrick St BOL * BL1 33 G4
Back Eskrick St East BOL * BL1 33 G4
Back Eskrick St South BOL BL1 33 G4
Back Eskrick St West BOL BL1 33 G4
Back Essingdon St BOLS/LL BL3 48 C5
Back Essingdon St South
BOLS/LL BL3 48 C5
Back Eustace St BOLS/LL BL3 64 B1
Back Euxton St BOLS/LL BL3 48 C5
Back Everton St North
BOL * BL1 34 A4
Back Ewart St BOL * BL1 33 H4
Back Fairhaven Rd BOL BL1 34 A3
Back Fair St BOLS/LL BL3 63 F2
Back Fenton St TOT/BURYW BL8 37 H3
Back Fern St East BOLS/LL BL3 48 B3
Back Fir St BURY BL9 5 J4
Back Fletcher St BURY BL9 5 G4
RAD * M26 66 A5
Back Flora St BOLS/LL * BL3 48 D5
Back Florence Av BOL BL1 34 A2
Back Fortune St BOLS/LL BL3 49 G4
Back Foundry St BURY BL9 5 F5
Back Frances St BOL BL1 33 G4
Back Frank St BOL * BL1 33 G5
BURY BL9 5 F6
Back Fylde St FWTH BL4 65 E2
Back Gainsborough Av
BOLS/LL BL3 63 F1
Back Garside Gv BOL * BL1 33 F4
Back Garston St BURY BL9 38 D2
Back Gaskell St BOL BL1 2 B3
Back Gaskell St East BOL * BL1 2 B3
Back Gaythorne St BOL * BL1 34 A3
Back George Barton St BOLE BL2 3 K1
Back George St BOLS/LL BL3 49 F5
CMANE M1 7 F5
Back Georgiana St West
BURY BL9 4 E6
Back Gibraltar St BOLS/LL BL3 2 A7
Back Gibraltar St South
BOLS/LL * BL3 2 A7
Back Gigg La BURY BL9 53 G1
Back Gilmour St MDTN M24 71 H4
Back Gilnow Gv BOL BL1 2 A6
Back Gilnow La BOLS/LL BL3 2 A7
Back Gilnow La West
BOLS/LL BL3 48 B3
Back Gilnow Rd BOL BL1 48 B3
Back Glen Av BOLS/LL * BL3 48 A4
Back Glenboro Av
TOT/BURYW BL8 37 G4
Back Glen Bott St BOL * BL1 33 G4
Back Gloster St BOLE BL2 3 H5
Back Goldsmith St BOLS/LL BL3 48 C5
Back Goodlad St
TOT/BURYW BL8 37 G2
Back Gordon Av BOLS/LL BL3 48 B4
Back Gorses Mt BOLE BL2 49 H4
Back Grafton St BOL BL1 2 A3
Back Grantham Cl BOL * BL1 33 H5
Back Grasmere St BOL BL1 34 A4
Back Greaves St OLD * OL1 9 H4
Back Greenhalgh St
BOLS/LL * BL3 65 H1
Back Greenland Rd BOLS/LL BL3 64 A1
Back Green La BOLS/LL BL3 64 C2
Back Green La South
BOLS/LL BL3 64 A1
Back Green St MDTN M24 72 A3
Back Gregory Av BOLE BL2 50 B1
Back Grendon St BOLS/LL BL3 63 F1
Back Gresham St BOL * BL1 34 A3
Back Grosvenor St STLY SK15 119 F4
Back Grove St BOL BL1 33 G4
Back Hadwin St BOL BL1 2 E1
Back Halliwell La CHH * M8 100 A3
Back Halliwell Rd BOL BL1 33 H4
Back Halliwell Rd South
BOL * BL1 33 G4
Back Halstead St BOLE BL2 3 H5
BURY BL9 38 D2
Back Hamilton St BRO * M7 99 G4
BURY BL9 38 C2
Back Hampson St
NEWH/MOS M40 114 A1
Back Hanson St BURY BL9 38 C2
Back Hargreaves St BOL BL1 33 H4
Back Harper's La South
BOL * BL1 33 E4
Back Hartington Rd BOL * BL1 48 B1
Back Harvey St TOT/BURYW BL8 37 H3
Back Haslam St BURY * BL9 38 D2
Back Haslam Ter BOLE * BL2 49 H2
Back Hatfield Rd BOL BL1 33 F5
Back Hawthorne Rd
BOLS/LL * BL3 48 A5
Back Hawthorne Rd East
BOLS/LL * BL3 48 A4
Back Hawthorn Rd West
BOLS/LL * BL3 48 A4
Back Haydn St BOL BL1 33 G4
Back Haydock St BOL BL1 2 E2
Back Hayward St
TOT/BURYW * BL8 37 H3
Back Hengist St BOLE BL2 49 H2
Back Hennon St BOL BL1 33 G5
Back Henrietta St BOLS/LL * BL3 48 A5
Back Henry Lee St BOLS/LL BL3 63 F1
Back Heywood St East BURY BL9 5 G5
Back Heywood St West BURY BL9 5 G6
Back High Bank St BOLE BL2 49 H2
Back Higher Darcy St
BOLS/LL BL3 49 H4
Back Higher Shady La West
EDGW/EG BL7 23 G4
Back Higher Swan La
BOLS/LL BL3 63 G1
Back Higher Swan La West
BOLS/LL BL3 63 G1
Back High St BOLS/LL BL3 48 C5
Back High St South BOLS/LL BL3 48 D5
Back High St West BOLS/LL * BL3 48 D5
Back Hilden St BOLE BL2 3 H6
Back Hilden St West BOLE BL2 3 H6
Back Hilton St BRO M7 99 G3
BURY * BL9 38 C2
Back Hind St BOLE BL2 49 H2
Back Holland St BOL BL1 34 A2
Back Holland St East BOL * BL1 34 A2
Back Holly Pl BOL BL1 33 H2
Back Holly St BOL BL1 34 A2
BURY BL9 5 H4
Back Holly St South BURY BL9 5 H4
Back Hopefield St BOLS/LL BL3 48 C5
Back Hope St BRO M7 99 G3
OLD OL1 75 E5
Back Horbury St
TOT/BURYW BL8 37 H4
Back Horeb St East
BOLS/LL * BL3 48 C4
Back Hornby St BURY BL9 38 C1
Back Hornby St East BURY BL9 4 E2
Back Hornby St West BURY * BL9 4 E2
Back Horne St North BURY * BL9 53 F1
Back Horne St South BURY BL9 53 F1
Back Horsa St BOLE BL2 3 J1
Back Horsa St North BOLE * BL2 3 J1
Back Hotel St BOL * BL1 2 E4
Back Hough La East
EDGW/EG BL7 23 F4
Back Howarden St BOL * BL1 33 H1
Back Howcroft St BOLS/LL * BL3 48 C5
Back Howe St BRO M7 99 F3
Back Hughes St BOL BL1 33 G4
Back Hulbert St
TOT/BURYW * BL8 37 H5
Back Hulme St ORD M5 112 B4
TOT/BURYW BL8 4 A2
Back Hulton La BOLS/LL * BL3 47 H5
Back Hulton La South
BOLS/LL * BL3 62 D2
Back Hulton La West
BOLS/LL * BL3 47 H5
Back Huntley Mount Rd
BURY BL9 5 J2
Back Hurst St BOLS/LL BL3 63 F1
BURY BL9 5 G6
Back Huxley St BOL BL1 33 F4
Back Ingham St BURY BL9 5 G6
Back Ingham St East BURY BL9 5 G6
Back Irlam St BOL BL1 33 H3
Back Irlam St North BOL * BL1 33 H3
Back Ivy Bank Rd BOL BL1 33 H1
Back Ivy Rd BOL BL1 33 F5
Back Ivy Rd West BOL * BL1 33 F4
Back James St BOLS/LL BL3 66 A1
Back Jauncey St BOLS/LL BL3 48 B4
Back John Brown St BOL * BL1 2 B3
Back John Cross St
BOLS/LL * BL3 48 D5
Back Johnson St BOL * BL1 3 F6
Back John St BOLS/LL BL3 2 C7
Back Junction St CMANE M1 7 J4
Back Keighley St BOL BL1 33 F4
Back Kendal Rd BOL BL1 48 B1
Back Kershaw St BURY BL9 5 H5
Back Kingholm Gdns BOL * BL1 33 G5
Back Kingsley St BOL BL1 33 G4
Back King St BOL BL1 2 D4
CHAD OL9 9 F4
Back King St North
EDGW/EG BL7 23 E3
Back King St South BOLE BL2 35 E1
Back Knight St TOT/BURYW BL8 37 H4
Back Knowl St STLY SK15 119 G3
Back Knowsley Rd BOL * BL1 33 E4
Back Knowsley St BOL BL1 2 E4
BURY BL9 4 D5
Back Kylemore Av BOLS/LL * BL3 48 A4
Back La AUL OL6 92 B5
AULW OL7 104 A5
BOL BL1 2 C3
HALE/TIMP WA15 188 A2
HYDE SK14 134 D5
OLDE OL4 76 D3
WHIT OL12 14 B3
WHTN BL5 79 A1
Back Lark St BOL BL1 3 F3
Back Latham St BOL BL1 34 A4
Back Lathom St BURY BL9 38 D2
Back Laurel St BURY BL9 5 J4
Back Lawn St BOL BL1 33 F5
Back Leachfield St BOL BL1 33 G3
Back Leach St BOLS/LL BL3 48 D4
Back Lee Av BOLS/LL BL3 63 G1
Back Lee St UPML OL3 78 A4
Back Lena St BOL BL1 34 A4
Back Lenora St BOLS/LL * BL3 48 A4
Back Lever Edge La BOLS/LL BL3 63 F2
Back Lever Edge La South
BOLS/LL BL3 63 H1
Back Lever St BOLS/LL BL3 48 D5
Back Lever St North
BOLS/LL BL3 50 D5
Back Lever St South
BOLS/LL * BL3 48 D5
Back Lightburne Av BOL BL1 48 A2
Back Lilly St BOL BL1 2 A2
Back Lincoln Rd BOL * BL1 48 B1
Back Lindley St BOLS/LL * BL3 66 A1
Back Linton Av BURY BL9 38 C1
Back Longden St BOL BL1 48 B1
Back Longfield Rd BOLS/LL * BL3 63 E1
Back Long La BOLE BL2 50 B2
Back Longsight North BOLE BL2 35 F1
Back Longsight South BOLE BL2 35 E1
Back Lonsdale St
TOT/BURYW BL8 37 H4
Back Lord St BOLS/LL BL3 66 A1
BURY BL9 5 F6
Back Loxham St BOLS/LL BL3 65 E2
Back Lumsden St BOLS/LL BL3 48 D4
Back Luton St BOLS/LL BL3 49 F5
Back Lytton St BOL BL1 33 G5
Back Mackenzie St BOL BL1 33 G2
Back Malvern Av BOL BL1 32 D5
BURY BL9 38 C1
Back Manchester Old Rd
BURY BL9 4 C7
Back Manchester Rd BOLE BL2 3 G7
BOLS/LL BL3 64 D2
BURY BL9 4 C5
Back Manchester Rd East
BOLE * BL2 49 F4
Back Manchester Rd South
BOLS/LL BL3 49 F4
Back Manchester Rd West
BOLS/LL BL3 49 G5
Back Manchester St HEY * OL10 41 F5
Back Manor St BURY BL9 5 G4
Back Maple St BOLS/LL * BL3 48 C4
Back Marion St South
BOLS/LL * BL3 64 D2
Back Market St BOLS/LL BL3 66 A1
BURY BL9 4 D5
RAD M26 66 A5
Back Market St West BURY BL9 4 D4
Back Markland Hill La BOL BL1 32 C5
Back Markland Hill La East
BOL * BL1 32 C5
Back Markland Hill La West
BOL * BL1 32 C5
Back Marlborough St BOL BL1 2 A3
Back Marsh Fold La BOL * BL1 48 B1
Back Mary St BOLS/LL * BL3 48 C4
Back Mason St BURY BL9 5 G5
Back Massie St
CHD/CHDH * SK8 170 A3
Back Mawdsley St BOL BL1 2 E5
Back Maxwell St BOL * BL1 33 H2
Back Maybank St BOLS/LL BL3 48 C4
Back Mayfield Av BOLS/LL BL3 64 C1
Back Mayor St BOL BL1 2 A6
TOT/BURYW BL8 37 H3
Back Maze St BOLS/LL BL3 49 H4
Back McDonna St BOL BL1 33 F3
Back McKean St BOLS/LL BL3 49 F5
Back McKean St North
BOLS/LL * BL3 49 F5
Back Melbourne Rd BOLS/LL BL3 48 B4
Back Melbourne St STLY SK15 119 F3
Back Mellor Gv BOL * BL1 33 E5
Back Mellor Gv West BOL * BL1 33 E5
Back Melrose Av BOL BL1 32 D5
Back Melville St BOLS/LL BL3 64 B1
Back Mercia St BOLS/LL BL3 48 B4
Back Meredith St BOLS/LL BL3 64 A1
Back Mere Gdns BOL BL1 2 C2
Back Merlin Gv BOL * BL1 33 E5
Back Merton St TOT/BURYW BL8 4 A2
Back Methwold St BOLS/LL * BL3 48 B5
Back Milford Rd BOLS/LL BL3 63 H1
Back Miller St BOL * BL1 33 H2
Back Millet St BURY BL9 4 B5
Back Mill St North
EDGW/EG * BL7 23 E3
Back Mill St South
EDGW/EG * BL7 23 E3
Back Milner Av BURY BL9 38 C1
Back Minorca St BOLS/LL * BL3 48 D5
Back Monmouth Av BURY BL9 38 C1
Back Moor HYDE SK14 134 D4
Back Moorfield Gv BOLE BL2 34 C5
Back Moorgate BURY BL9 5 F3
Back Mornington Rd East
BOL BL1 48 B1
Back Morris Green La
BOLS/LL BL3 63 F2
Back Morris Green La East
BOLS/LL BL3 63 F2
Back Moss Ter BOL BL1 2 E3
Back Mostyn Av BURY BL9 38 C1
Back Mowbray St BOL * BL1 33 E5
Back Murton Ter BOL BL1 34 A2
Back Musgrave Rd BOL BL1 48 B1
Back Musgrave Rd North
BOL BL1 48 B1
Back Myrtle St BURY BL9 5 J4
Back Myrtle St South BURY BL9 5 J5
Back Nebo St BOLS/LL BL3 48 C5
Back Nelson St North
BURY * BL9 53 G1
Back Nelson St South
BURY * BL9 53 G1
Back Nevada St BOL BL1 33 H5
Back Newbold St
TOT/BURYW BL8 37 H4
Back New George St
TOT/BURYW BL8 37 H3
Back Newhall La BOL BL1 32 D5
Back Newport Rd BOLS/LL * BL3 49 F5
Back Newport St BOL BL1 2 E6
Back Newton St BOL BL1 33 H4
Back Nixon Rd BOLS/LL BL3 63 F1
Back Normanby St BOLS/LL BL3 63 F2
Back Norris St BOLS/LL * BL3 65 H1
Back Northern Gv BOL BL1 33 F5
Back Norwood Gv BOL BL1 48 B1
Back Nunnery Rd BOLS/LL * BL3 48 A5
Back Nut St BOL * BL1 33 G4
Back Oak St RAD M26 67 H3
Back Olaf St BOLE BL2 3 J1
Back Oldham Rd MILN OL16 30 B5
Back Oldham St BOLS/LL BL3 2 A7
Back Olga St BOL BL1 33 G4
Back Olga St North BOL * BL1 33 G4
Back Olive Bank
TOT/BURYW BL8 37 G2
Back Oram St BURY BL9 38 D2
Back Oriel St BOLS/LL BL3 48 B4
Back Ormrod St BURY BL9 5 H5
Back Osborne Gv BOL BL1 33 F5
Back O' Th' Low Rd OLDE OL4 76 A4
Back Oxford Gv North BOL BL1 33 F5
Back Oxford St BURY BL9 5 G6
Back Packer St BOL BL1 33 F4
Back Palace St BOL BL1 2 E3
Back Palm St BOL BL1 33 H3
Back Parkdale Rd BOLE BL2 34 D5
Back Parkfield Rd BOLS/LL BL3 64 B1
Back Parkhills Rd North
BURY * BL9 53 F1
Back Parkinson St BOLS/LL * BL3 48 B4
Back Park Rd BOL BL1 2 A5
Back Park St BOL BL1 2 A3
Back Park Vw EDGW/EG BL7 23 E5
Back Park View Rd
BOLS/LL * BL3 48 B5
Back Parsonage St BURY BL9 5 H3
Backparsons La BURY BL9 4 E4
Back Partington St BOLS/LL BL3 63 F2
Back Patience St WHIT * OL12 29 F2
Back Patterson St BOLS/LL * BL3 47 H5
Back Peabody St BOLS/LL * BL3 48 D5
Back Peace St BOLS/LL BL3 48 C4
Back Pedder St BOL BL1 33 F5
Back Peers St TOT/BURYW BL8 37 H4
Back Penarth Rd BOLS/LL BL3 48 B4
Back Pennington Rd
BOLS/LL BL3 63 H1
Back Percy St BURY BL9 5 J2
Back Peter St BURY BL9 5 G3
Back Peveril St BOLS/LL * BL3 63 E1
Back Phoenix St BURY BL9 4 C5
Back Piccadilly CMANE M1 7 G4
Back Pikes La West BOLS/LL BL3 48 B4
Back Pine St BOL BL1 34 A4
BURY BL9 5 J4
Back Pleasant St BOL BL1 2 D2
Back Pool Fold CMANW * M2 6 E4
Back Poplar Av BOL BL1 34 A2
Back Porter St BURY BL9 38 C2
Back Portland St AUL OL6 117 H3
Back Portugal St BOLE BL2 3 J5
Back Preston St BOLS/LL BL3 49 G5
Back Primrose St BOL * BL1 34 A2
Back Primula St BOL BL1 34 A2
Back Proctor St
TOT/BURYW * BL8 37 H5
Back Progress St BOL * BL1 34 A5
Back Quay St CSLFD M3 6 B5
Back Quebec St BOLS/LL BL3 48 B4
Back Queensgate BOL BL1 48 B1
Back Queen St BOL * BL1 2 D5
Back Radcliffe Rd East
BOLE * BL2 3 J4
Back Raimond St BOL BL1 33 F3
Back Rainshaw St BOL BL1 34 A2
Back Rake St BURY BL9 38 C2
Back Randal St BOLS/LL * BL3 48 B5
Back Range St BOLS/LL * BL3 48 C5
Back Raphael St BOL BL1 33 G5
Back Raven St BURY BL9 5 F1
Back Rawson Rd BOL BL1 33 F5
Back Rawson Rd North BOL BL1 33 F5
Back Raymond Av BURY BL9 38 C1
Back Red Bank ANC M4 113 F2
Back Redhill Gv BOL BL1 2 C2
Back Regent St BURY BL9 4 E1
Back Ribblesdale Rd
BOLS/LL BL3 48 C5
Back Richard Burch St BURY BL9 5 F2
Back Richelieu St BOLS/LL BL3 49 F5
Back Rigby La North BOLE * BL2 23 H5
Back Rigby La South BOLE BL2 23 H5
Back Rishton La BOLS/LL BL3 64 A1
Back Rishton La East
BOLS/LL BL3 64 A1
Back Rochdale Old North Rd
BURY * BL9 39 F3
Back Rochdale Old Rd South
BURY BL9 5 K2
Back Rochdale Old South Rd
BURY BL9 39 F3
Back Rochdale Rd BURY BL9 5 H4
Back Rochdale Rd South
BURY BL9 5 F4
Back Rock Av BOL BL1 33 F3
Back Roland Rd BOLS/LL BL3 48 B4
Back Roman Rd BRO M7 99 H4
Back Romer St BOLE BL2 49 H2
Back Rosamond St BOLS/LL BL3 48 B5
Back Roscow Av BOLE BL2 50 B1
Back Rose Bank BURY * BL9 38 C2
Back Roseberry St BOLS/LL * BL3 48 B5
Back Rossini St BOL * BL1 33 G3
Back Rw WHIT * OL12 18 A2
Back Rowena St BOLS/LL * BL3 64 D2
Back Rowland St BOLS/LL * BL3 63 E1
Back Roxalina St BOLS/LL BL3 48 D5
Back Royal Av BURY BL9 38 C1
Back Royds St MILN OL16 43 F1
Back Rudolph St BOLS/LL BL3 64 A1
Back Rumworth St BOLS/LL BL3 48 C5
Back Rushton Rd BOL * BL1 33 E5
Back Russell Cl BOL * BL1 48 B1
Back Russell St BOL BL1 48 B1
Back Rutland Gv BOL BL1 33 F5
Back Ryefield St BOL BL1 3 G1
Back St Anne's St BURY BL9 38 C2
Back St Ann St BOL BL1 33 H5
Back St Augustine St BOL BL1 33 G4
Back St George's Rd ANC M4 7 H1
BOL BL1 2 D3
Back St George's Rd North
BOL BL1 2 B3
Back St Helens Rd BOLS/LL * BL3 48 C5
Back St Helens Road So
BOLS/LL BL3 63 E2
Back St Helens Rd South
BOLS/LL * BL3 63 E2
BOLS/LL * BL3 63 F1
Back St James's St OLD * OL1 75 E5
Back St Mark's La CHH * M8 100 A2
Back St Mary's Pl BURY BL9 4 C5
Back St Philip's Av BOLS/LL BL3 48 C5
Back St Thomas St East
BOL * BL1 33 G4
Back Salford St BURY BL9 38 D2
Back Salisbury St BOLS/LL BL3 2 B6
Back Salisbury Ter BOLE BL2 50 A2
Back Sandon St West
BOLS/LL * BL3 48 C5
Back Sankey St BURY BL9 4 B4
Back Sapling Rd BOLS/LL BL3 63 F2
Back Sapling Rd South
BOLS/LL * BL3 63 F2
Back Scholes St TOT/BURYW BL8 37 H3
Back Scott St OLDS * OL8 9 F7
Back Scowcroft St BOLE BL2 3 J1
Back Settle St BOLS/LL BL3 63 H1
Back Settle St North
BOLS/LL BL3 63 H1
Back Seymour Rd BOL BL1 34 A3
Back Sharman St BOLS/LL BL3 49 G4
Back Shaw-street BURY BL9 5 J3
Back Shepherd St BURY BL9 5 F5
Back Sherwood St BOL BL1 34 A3
Back Shipton St BOL BL1 33 E5
Back Shuttle St BOLS/LL BL3 2 C7
Back Silverdale Rd BOL BL1 48 B2
Back Silver St BURY BL9 4 D5
Back Skipton St BOLE BL2 49 H1
Back Smethurst La BOLS/LL BL3 63 E2
Back Smethurst La West
BOLS/LL * BL3 63 E2
Back Sofa St BOL BL1 33 E5
Back Soho St BOL BL1 2 E6
Back Somerset Rd BOL BL1 48 A2
Back Somerville St BOL * BL1 33 F3
Back South Cross St East
BURY BL9 5 F5
Back Southfield St BOLS/LL BL3 49 G5
Back South Pde CSLFD M3 6 D4
Back South St BOLS/LL BL3 63 H1
Back South View St BOLE BL2 49 H2
Back Spa Rd BOLS/LL BL3 2 A6
Back Spa Rd North BOL BL1 2 A6
Back Spa Rd West BOL * BL1 2 A6
Back Spear St CMANE * M1 7 H3
Back Springfield St BOLS/LL BL3 49 F5
Back Spring Gdns BOL BL1 2 E6
MDTN M24 71 H2
Back Spring St East BURY BL9 5 F6
Back Spring St West BURY BL9 5 F6
Back Square St RAMS BL0 16 D2
Back Stainsbury St BOLS/LL BL3 48 B5
Back Stanley St RAMS * BL0 16 C3
Back Stephen St
TOT/BURYW BL8 37 H4
Back Stewart St BOL BL1 33 H5
Back Stone St BOLE BL2 3 J1
Back Sunlight Rd BOL BL1 48 B2
Back Sunning Hill St
BOLS/LL * BL3 48 C5
Back Sunnyside Rd BOL BL1 33 F4
Back Swan La BOLS/LL * BL3 48 C5
Back Talbot St BOL BL1 34 A2
Back Tavistock Rd BOL BL1 2 A6
Back Teak St BURY BL9 5 J4
Back Tenterden St BURY BL9 4 C5
Back Tenterdon St BURY BL9 4 B5
Back Thicketford Rd BOLE * BL2 34 D5
Back Thicketford Rd West
BOLE BL2 34 C5
Back Thomasson Cl BOL BL1 33 H5
Back Thomas St ANC * M4 7 G3
Back Thorns Rd BOL BL1 33 H3
Back Thorn St BOL BL1 34 A4
Back Thorpe St BOL BL1 33 G4
Back Thurnham St
BOLS/LL * BL3 63 F1
Back Tinline St BURY BL9 5 H5
Back Tonge Moor Rd BOLE BL2 34 C4
Back Tonge Moor Rd East
BOLE BL2 3 J1
BOLE BL2 34 C4
Back Tonge Old Rd BOLE BL2 49 H2
Back Tottington Rd
TOT/BURYW BL8 37 G2
Back Tottington Rd East
BOLE BL2 35 F1
Back Tottington Rd North
TOT/BURYW * BL8 37 H3
Back Tottington Rd South
TOT/BURYW BL8 37 H3
Back Tudor St BOLS/LL * BL3 48 B5
Back Turner St ANC * M4 7 G3
Back Turton Rd East BOLE BL2 34 D1
Back Turton Rd West BOLE BL2 34 D1
Back Uganda St BOLS/LL BL3 63 F1
Back Ulleswater St BOL BL1 34 A4
Back Union Rd BOLE BL2 3 H1
Back Unsworth St South
BOLS/LL BL3 48 C4
Back Uttley St BOL BL1 33 G4
Back Venice St BOLS/LL BL3 48 B5
Back Vernon St BOL BL1 2 C3
BURY BL9 4 E1
Back Vernon St South BOL * BL1 2 C3
Back Vickerman St BOL BL1 33 G4
Back Victoria Gv BOL BL1 33 F5
Back Victoria Gv North BOL BL1 33 F5
Back Victory St East BOL BL1 48 B1
Back View St BOLS/LL BL3 48 C4
Back Viking St North
BOLS/LL BL3 49 F5
Back Vincent St BOL BL1 2 A6
Back Vine St BOLS/LL * BL3 48 B3
Back Viola St BOL BL1 33 H3
Back Waldeck St BOL BL1 48 B1
Back Walmersley Rd East
BURY BL9 5 F1
BURY BL9 27 G5
Back Walmersley Rd West
BURY BL9 5 F1
BURY * BL9 27 G4
BURY BL9 38 C1
Back Walnut St BOL BL1 34 A3
Back Walshaw Rd North
TOT/BURYW BL8 37 H3

Back Walsham Rd South
TOT/BURYW BL8 ....37 H3
Back Wapping St BOL * BL1 .....33 G4
Back Wardle St BOLE * BL2 ......49 G4
Back Wash La BURY BL9 ....5 H4
Back Wash La South BURY BL9 ...5 H4
Back Water St EDGW/EG BL7 ....22 C1
STKP * SK1 ....13 H1
Back Waverley Rd BOL BL1 ....33 F4
Back Webster St BOLS/LL * BL3 ..49 G5
Back Wellington Rd South
BURY BL9 ....53 F1
Back Wells St BURY BL9 ....4 C7
Back Westbourne Av
BOLS/LL BL5 ....64 B1
Back Weston St North
BOLS/LL BL3 ....49 E5
Back Weston St South
BOLS/LL BL3 ....49 E5
Back Westwood Rd BOLS/LL * BL1 48 B1
Back Wheatfield St BOLE * BL2 ...49 H4
Back Whittle Gv BOL * BL1 ....33 G5
Back Whittle St
TOT/BURYW * BL8 ....37 H3
Back Wigan Av BOL BL1 ....47 H5
Back Wigan Rd North
BOLS/LL * BL3. ....48 A4
Back Wigan Rd South
BOLS/LL BL3. ....48 A5
Back Willows La BOLS/LL BL3. ....48 B5
Back Willows La North
BOLS/LL * BL3. ....48 B5
Back Willows La South
BOLS/LL BL3. ....48 B5
Back Wilmot St BOL * BL1 ....33 F3
Back Wilton St BOL BL1 ....34 A3
Back Windermere St BOL BL1 .....34 A1
Back Windsor Gv BOL * BL1 ....33 F5
Back Wolfenden St BOL * BL1 .....33 G5
Back Woodbine Rd BOLS/LL BL3 ..63 F1
Back Woodfield St
BOLS/LL * BL3. ....64 B1
Back Woodgate St BOLS/LL BL3. ..64 B1
Back Wood St TOT/BURYW BL8 ...37 H5
Back Worcester St BOL BL1 ....33 H5
Back Wordsworth St BOL BL1 .....33 G4
Back Worsel St BOLS/LL BL3. .....48 A5
Back Worsel St North
BOLS/LL * BL3. ....48 B5
Back Wynne St BOL BL1 ....33 H4
Back Yates St BOLE BL2 ....3 H5
Bacon Av DTN/ASHW M34 ....146 D4
Bacup St NEWH/MOS M40 ....107 H2
Badby Cl ANC M4 ....114 A4
Badder St BOL BL1 ....2 E3
Bader Dr HEY OL10 ....56 A2
Badger Cl MILN OL16 ....43 H5
Badger Edge La OLDE OL4 ....76 D1
Badger La MILN OL16 ....43 G4
Badger St BURY BL9 ....5 F3
Badgers Wk WYTH/NTH M22 ....180 D3
Bagnall Cl UPML OL3. ....78 B3
WHIT OL12 ....28 C1
Bagot St OP/CLY M11 ....115 F3
SWIN M27 ....96 B3
Bagshaw St HYDE SK14 ....132 C3
Baguley Moor La ROCH OL11 .....28 C5
Bagslate Moor Rd ROCH OL11 ....28 A4
Bagstock Av POY/DIS SK2 ....195 F5
MDTN M24 ....86 B1
Baguley Dr WHTF M45 ....68 D2
Baguley La SALE M33 ....155 F2
Baguley St DROY M43 ....116 C4
Baildon Rd ROCH OL11 ....29 E2
Baildon St NEWH/MOS M40 .....101 H1
Bailey La BOLE BL2 ....35 F5
MANAIR M90 ....180 A3
PART M31 ....151 E2
Bailey Rd TRPK M17 ....124 B1
Bailey St OLD * OL1 ....9 J3
OP/CLY M11 ....115 G4
PWCH M25 ....85 F2
Bailie St MILN OL16 ....11 H3
Baillie St ALT WA14 ....177 H4
Baillie St East MILN OL16 ....10 E5
The Bails BRO M7 ....99 F4
Bainbridge Cl
WGTN/LGST * M12 ....128 A2
Bainbridge Rd OLDE OL4 ....75 G3
Bainburgh Clough OLDS OL8 ......91 F3
Baines Av IRL M44 ....136 A2
Baines St BOL BL1 ....33 G4
Bain St SWIN M27 ....97 E3
Baird St CMANE M1 ....7 J6
Baker St FWTH BL4 ....82 A1
HALE/TIMP WA15 ....56 B1
HEY OL10 ....56 B1
HTNM SK4 ....159 H3
MDTN M24 ....72 A4
RAMS BL0 ....16 C3
STLY SK15 ....119 G4
Bakewell Av AUL OL6 ....106 A4
DTN/ASHW M34 ....146 D3
Bakewell Rd BRAM/HZG SK7 ....185 H5
DROY M43 ....115 H5
ECC M30 ....109 E5
STRET M32 ....124 B5
Bakewell St WGTN/LGST M12 ....12 D6
GTN M18 ....129 F4
Bala Cl OLD M5 ....111 H3
Balcary Gv BOL BL1 ....33 E4
Balcombe Cl TOT/BURYW BL8 ...26 C4
Balderstone Rd ROCH OL11 ......43 F4
Baldock Rd DID/WITH M20 ....158 A1
Baldwin Rd BNG/LEV M19 ....143 G5
Baldwin St BOLS/LL * BL3. ....48 C5
Bale St CMANW M2 ....6 E6
Balfour Gv RDSH SK5 ....145 E1
Balfour Rd ALT WA14 ....165 G2
URM M41 ....138 A1
WHIT OL12 ....29 F2
Balfour St CHH M8 ....100 B2
OLDE OL4 ....75 G4
ROY/SHW OL2 ....59 G3
SLFD M6 ....98 C4
Balham Wk WGTN/LGST M12 ...115 F1
Balladen St NEWH/MOS M40 ....115 F1
Ballard Cl LIT OL15. ....21 E4
Ballard Wy ROY/SHW OL2 ....60 B2
Ballater Av URM M41 ....137 H2

Ballater Cl HEY OL10 ....40 B5
Ballbrook Av DID/WITH M20 .....157 F1
Balleratt St BNG/LEV M19 ....143 H1
Balliol Cl MPL/ROM SK6 ....162 B2
Balliol St CHH M8. ....100 B3
SWIN M27 ....96 D2
Balloon St ANC M4 ....7 F2
Ball St MILN OL16 ....149 C2
Ball Wk HYDE SK14 ....149 G1
Balmain Av GTN M18 ....129 F5
Balmain Rd URM M41 ....123 E5
Balmer Rd NTHM/RTH M23 ......167 H4
Balmfield St CHH M8 ....100 B5
Balmforth St HULME M15 ....126 C1
Balmoral Av BOLS/LL BL3. ....65 H1
CHD/CHDH SK8 ....182 D2
DTN/ASHW M34 ....131 E1
HYDE SK14 ....147 H3
ROCH OL11 ....30 C2
ROY/SHW OL2 ....59 G5
STRET M32 ....125 E5
URM M41 ....138 A2
WHTF M45 ....68 D5
Balmoral Cl BURY BL9 ....31 H5
MILN OL16 ....31 H5
TOT/BURYW BL8 ....26 B2
Balmoral Dr ALT WA14 ....166 A4
DTN/ASHW M34 ....130 B4
HEY OL10 ....40 B5
MPL/ROM SK6 ....186 D5
POY/DIS SK12 ....195 E4
STLY SK15 ....119 G2
Balmoral Gra PWCH M25 ....85 H4
Balmoral Gv BRAM/HZG SK7 ....185 G1
Balmoral Rd FWTH BL4. ....64 D5
HALE/TIMP WA15 ....165 H5
HTNM SK4 ....158 D5
RUSH/FAL M14 ....143 E3
SWIN M27 ....83 F5
URM M41 ....137 H2
Balmoral St GTN M18 ....129 H3
Balmoral Wy WILM/AE SK9 ......199 F4
Balmore Cl BOLS/LL BL3. ....62 D1
Balm St RAMS BL0 ....16 B4
Balniel Dr BRUN/LGST M13 ......127 H1
Balshaw Av IRL M44 ....136 A1
Balshaw Cl BOLS/LL BL3. ....48 B4
Balshaw St IRL M44 ....136 B1
Baltic Rd ALT WA14 ....164 D5
Baltic St SLFD M6. ....118 B1
Baltimore St NEWH/MOS M40 ...101 G5
Bamber Av SALE M33 ....155 F3
Bamber St BKLY M9 ....87 E2
Bamber Wk BOLS/LL * BL3. ......48 C4
Bamburgh Cl RAD M26. ....51 H4
Bamburgh Dr AULW OL7 ....104 B5
Bambury St BURY BL9 ....5 F5
Bamford Av DTN/ASHW M34 ....146 C3
MDTN M24 ....71 H2
Bamford Cl BURY BL9 ....5 F5
CHD/CHDH SK8 ....182 A4
Bamford Ct ROCH OL11 ....29 E5
Bamford Gdns
HALE/TIMP WA15 ....167 G4
Bamford Gv AUL OL6 ....106 A4
DID/WITH M20 ....157 F3
Bamford Ms ROCH OL11 ....28 B4
Bamford Rd DID/WITH M20 ......157 F3
HEY OL10 ....40 A2
Bamford St CHAD OL9 ....73 H4
LIT OL15. ....20 C3
ROCH OL11 ....115 E3
ROY/SHW OL2 ....59 G1
STKP SK1 ....13 G5
Bamford Wy ROCH OL11 ....28 C5
Bampton Cl OFTN SK2 ....172 C2
Bampton Rd WYTH/NTH M22 ...168 B3
Banbury Dr ALT WA14 ....165 H1
Banbury Ms SWIN M27 ....96 C1
Banbury Rd FAIL M35 ....115 H1
MDTN M24 ....56 C1
NTHM/RTH M23 ....167 G4
Banbury St BOLE BL2 ....54 D5
STKP SK1 ....13 G4
Bancroft Av CHD/CHDH SK8 ....182 D5
Bancroft Cl MPL/ROM SK6 ....161 H4
Bancroft Fold HYDE SK14 ....133 G5
Bancroft Rd HALE/TIMP WA15 ..178 B1
Banff Gv HEY OL10 ....40 B5
Banff Rd RUSH/FAL M14 ....127 H4
Bangor Rd CHD/CHDH SK8 ......170 C3
Bangor St AUL OL6 ....118 D3
BOL BL1. ....2 D1
HULME * M15 ....126 C3
MILN * OL16 ....43 G6
RDSH SK5 ....160 A2
Bank Barn La WHIT OL12 ....20 A1
Bank Bridge Rd OP/CLY M11 ....114 D2
Bank Cl LIT OL15. ....20 D5
Banker St BOLS/LL BL3. ....49 G5
Bankfield HYDE SK14 ....132 C3
Bankfield Av BRUN/LGST M13 ...128 B5
DROY M43 ....116 B3
HTNM SK4 ....159 H1
IRL M44 ....150 C1
Bankfield Cl BOLE BL2 ....36 B5
Bankfield Dr OLDS OL8 ....91 E5
WALK M28 ....94 D4
Bankfield La ROCH OL11 ....28 B3
Bankfield Rd CHD/CHDH SK8 ...182 C3
FWTH BL4. ....65 E5
MPL/ROM SK6 ....143 D5
SALE M33 ....138 D5
Bankfield St BKLY M9 ....101 E1
BOLS/LL BL3. ....48 B5
Bank Field St RAD M26. ....66 C5
Bankfield St RDSH SK5 ....159 H2
Bank Gv LHULT M38 ....67 H3
Bank Hall TOT/BURYW BL8 ......37 H4
Bankhall La HALE/TIMP WA15 ...177 H4
Bank Hey Cl HYDE SK14 ....148 C4
Bankhey St HTNM SK4 ....158 C5
IRL M44 ....150 C1
Bankhirst Cl CHH M8 ....100 B1
Bank House Rd BKLY M9 ....87 H2
Bankhouse Rd TOT/BURYW BL8 .37 H2
Banklands Cl IRL M44 ....150 C1
Bank La LHULT M58. ....80 A1
SLFD M6 ....98 B4
Bankley St BNG/LEV M19 ....143 H2
Bank Mere Cl WALK M28 ....80 C4
Bankmill Cl BRUN/LGST M13 ....127 G1
Bank Pl CSLFD M3 ....112 C3

Bank Rd CHH M8 ....86 B5
MPL/ROM SK6 ....161 H1
STLY SK15 ....107 F5
Banks Crt HEY OL10 ....56 A2
Bankside HALE/TIMP WA15 .....189 E1
HYDE SK14 ....149 E2
Bankside Av RAD M26 ....53 E5
UPML OL3. ....78 B5
Bankside Cl CHAD OL9 ....8 C4
MPL/ROM SK6 ....165 G5
WILM/AE SK9 ....200 A1
Bankside Ct HTNM * SK4 ....158 D4
Bankside Rd DID/WITH M20 .....158 D1
Banks La STKP SK1 ....172 C1
Bank Stanway Av BOLS/LL BL3 ..2 B7
Bank St AULW OL7 ....118 A3
BOL BL1. ....33 H4
BRO M7. ....100 A2
BURY BL9 ....4 C5
CHD/CHDH SK8 ....170 B3
CSLFD M3 ....112 C3
DROY M43 ....116 A5
DTN/ASHW M34 ....147 E3
FWTH BL4. ....65 E4
HEY OL10 ....40 C4
OP/CLY M11 ....114 D3
RAD M26 ....67 G2
RAMS BL0 ....17 F1
ROCH OL11 ....43 F2
SALE M33 ....154 D1
TOT/BURYW BL8 ....37 H5
WHTF M45 ....68 B5
Bank Top AUL OL6 ....118 B3
HEY OL10 ....56 A2
Bank Top Dr BOL BL1 ....34 B1
Bank Top Pk OLDE OL4. ....91 G1
Bank Top St HEY OL10 ....40 C2
Bank Wk MILN OL16 ....47 C2
Banky La SALE M33 ....138 B5
Bannach Dr CHAD OL9 ....73 F4
Bannatyne Cl NEWH/MOS M40 ..102 D2
Banner Dale Cl BRUN/LGST M13 .128 C4
Bannerman Av PWCH M25 ....85 E4
Bannerman Rd DROY M43. ....116 C4
Banner Wk OP/CLY M11 ....114 C4
Bannister Dr CHD/CHDH SK8 ....182 C2
Bannister St BOLE BL2 ....50 B1
OFTN SK2 ....13 H7
Bann St EDGY/DAV SK3 ....12 E5
Bantry Av BKLY M9 ....86 C4
Bantry St BOLS/LL BL3. ....10 E1
WHIT OL12 ....10 E1
Baptist St ANC M4 ....41 H5
Barathea Cl ROCH OL11. ....41 H5
Barbara Rd BOLS/LL BL3. ....62 D2
Barbara St BOLS/LL BL3. ....48 C5
Barbeck Cl NEWH/MOS M40 ....114 B2
Barberry Cl ALT WA14 ....165 E1
Barberry Wk PART M31 ....165 E1
Barber St OP/CLY * M11 ....129 H1
Barbican St DID/WITH M20 ......142 C4
Barbirolli Sq CMANW M2 ....6 C7
Barbon Wk ANC M4. ....7 K5
Barchester Av BOLE BL2 ....35 F5
Barcheston Rd CHD/CHDH SK8 ..169 H5
Barcicroft Rd BNG/LEV M19 .....158 B2
Barclays Av SLFD M6 ....98 A4
Barclyde St ROCH OL11 ....42 D1
Barcombe Cl OLDE OL4. ....75 G2
STRET M32 ....124 A5
Barcroft Rd BOL BL1. ....33 E4
Barcroft St BURY BL9 ....5 K2
Bardell Cl POY/DIS * SK12 ......195 E5
Bardon Cl BOL * BL1 ....33 G5
Bardon Rd NTHM/RTH M23 .....167 G3
Bardsea Av WYTH/NTH M22 ....180 C3
Bardsley Av FAIL M35 ....103 E3
Bardsley Cl BOLE BL2 ....35 E1
Bardsley Gate Av STLY SK15 ....134 B2
Bardsley St CHAD OL9 ....89 E4
HTNM SK4 ....159 G3
MDTN * M24 ....72 A3
NEWH/MOS M40 ....102 C5
OLDE OL4. ....75 G4
Bardsley Vale Av OLDS OL8 .....104 D2
Barehill St LIT OL15. ....20 D5
Bare St BOL BL1. ....3 H5
Barff Rd ORD M5 ....110 D2
Barfold St OFTN SK2 ....173 H4
Barfoot Br SALE M33 ....139 H4
Barford Dr WILM/AE SK9 ....199 H1
Bar Gap Rd OLD OL1 ....9 G1
Baring St CMANE M1 ....7 J7
Barker Rd HYDE SK14 ....148 A4
Barker St BURY BL9 ....4 E1
HEY OL10 ....41 E5
RAD M26 ....67 F3
Barkers La SALE M33 ....154 A1
Barke St LIT OL15. ....20 D3
Barking St NEWH/MOS M40 .....114 B2
Bark St BOL BL1. ....2 D4
Bark St East BOL BL1. ....2 D4
Bark Wk HULME M15 ....127 E2
Barkway Rd STRET M32 ....140 C1
Barkwell La MOSL OL5 ....106 C1
Bar La BOL BL1. ....34 C1
Barlea Av NEWH/MOS M40 .....102 C2
Barley Brook Meadow BOL BL1 ..23 E5
Barleycorn Cl SALE M33 ....153 H1
Barley Cft CHD/CHDH SK8 ......182 C4
Barley Croft Rd WILM/AE SK9 ...199 H1
Barleycroft St OLDTF/WHR M16 .127 F4
Barley Dr BRAM/HZG SK7 ....185 H5
Barleyfield Wk MDTN M24 ....71 E3
Barley Hall St HEY OL10 ....56 B1
Barlow Cl MILN OL16 ....10 C6
Barlow Fold BURY BL9 ....175 G4
Barlow Fold Cl BURY BL9 ....175 G5
Barlow Fold Rd MPL/ROM SK6 ..146 C5
RDSH SK5 ....145 G3
Barlow Hall Rd CCHDY M21 .....156 B5
Barlow La ECC M30 ....109 F3

Barlow Moor Cl WHIT OL12 ....28 B1
Barlow Moor Ct DID/WITH M20 ..157 E2
Barlow Moor Rd CCHDY M21 ....141 E4
DID/WITH M20 ....156 D2
Barlow Park Av BOL BL1 ....33 G1
Barlow Pl BRUN/LGST M13 ......127 H1
Barlow Rd ALT WA14 ....165 E1
DUK SK16 ....119 E2
ORD M5. ....112 B4
STRET M32 ....125 G4
WILM/AE SK9 ....199 G1
Barlow's Cft CSLFD M3 ....6 C3
Barlow's La South
BRAM/HZG SK7 ....184 D1
Barlow St BURY BL9 ....5 F3
ECC M30 ....109 G4
HEY OL10 ....56 A2
MILN OL16 ....10 E6
OLDE OL4. ....76 C2
RAD M26 ....67 G1
WALK M28 ....81 E4
Barlow Wood Dr MPL/ROM SK6 .187 G2
Barmeadow UPML OL3. ....77 G2
Barmhouse Cl HYDE SK14 ....133 F5
Barmhouse La HYDE SK14 ....133 F5
Barmouth St OP/CLY M11 ....114 C5
Barmouth Wk OLDS OL8. ....8 E7
Barnaby Rd POY/DIS SK12 ......195 E5
Barnacre Av BOLE BL2 ....50 C2
Barnard Av HTNM SK4 ....159 E4
WHTF M45 ....69 E5
Barnard Cl AULW OL7 ....117 G1
Barnard Rd GTN M18 ....129 E5
Barnard St BOLE * BL2 ....49 H1
Barnbrook St BURY BL9 ....5 J1
Barnby St WGTN/LGST M12 .....128 D5
Barn Cl URM M41. ....136 D1
Barnclose Rd WYTH/NTH M22 ...180 C3
Barn Ct BOLE * BL2 ....50 D1
Barncroft Gdns
WYTH/NTH * M22 ....168 B4
Barncroft Rd FWTH BL4. ....64 B4
Barnes Av HTNM SK4 ....158 D4
Barnes Cl FWTH BL4. ....65 E4
RAMS BL0 ....16 B4
Barnes Mdw LIT OL15. ....15 E4
Barnes St FWTH BL4. ....65 H2
Barnes Ter FWTH BL4. ....65 E5
Barneswell St NEWH/MOS M40 ..102 B5
Barnet Rd BOL * BL1 ....33 G3
Barnett Av DID/WITH M20 ......142 C5
Barnett Dr CSLFD M3 ....5 G2
Barnfield URM M41. ....138 A3
Barnfield Cl EDGW/EG BL7 ......22 D1
ORD M5. ....66 D1
RAD M26 ....66 D1
Barnfield Crs SALE M33 ....154 A1
Barnfield Dr WALK M28 ....94 C4
Barnfield Rd BNG/LEV M19 ......158 A2
HYDE SK14 ....133 G5
SWIN M27 ....82 C5
Barnfield Rd East
EDGY/DAV SK3. ....171 G5
Barnfield Rd West
EDGY/DAV SK3. ....171 G5
HEY OL10 ....41 F4
Barnfield St DTN/ASHW M34 ....132 A4
HEY OL10 ....41 E4
MILN * OL16 ....44 C1
Barn Fold OLDE OL4. ....91 H2
Barngate Dr MOSL OL5 ....106 D2
Barngate Rd CHD/CHDH SK8 ...181 H1
DTN/ASHW M34 ....131 E1
Barnham Cl BRUN/LGST M13 ...128 A1
Barnhill Av PWCH M25 ....85 E5
Barnhill Dr PWCH M25 ....85 E5
Barnhill Rd PWCH M25 ....85 E5
Barnhill St RUSH/FAL M14 ......142 A5
Barnley Cl IRL M44 ....121 C5
Barnsdale Cl BOLE BL2 ....35 H4
Barnsdale Dr CHH M8 ....100 B4
Barnside Av WALK M28 ....94 C4
Barnsfold Av RUSH/FAL M14 ....142 D3
Barnsfold Rd MPL/ROM SK6 ....187 E5
Barnside Cl BURY BL9 ....27 F3
Barnsley St STKP SK1 ....13 K4
Barns Pl HALE/TIMP WA15 ......178 B1
Barnstable Dr NEWH/MOS M40 ..100 B4
Barnstead Av DID/WITH M20 ....157 H2
Barnston Av RUSH/FAL M14 .....142 A2
Barnston Cl BOL BL1. ....34 A1
Barn St BOL BL1. ....2 D3
OLD OL1. ....9 G4
WHTF M45 ....68 A2
Barnway Wk NEWH/MOS M40 ..102 B5
Barnwell Cl DTN/ASHW M34 ....131 F3
Barnwood Cl BOL * BL1 ....33 H5
Barnwood Dr BOL BL1 ....33 H5
Barnwood Ter BOL * BL1 ....33 H5
Baroness Gv BRO M7 ....112 B1
Baron Fold Crs LHULT M38 ......80 A2
Baron Fold Gv LHULT M38 ......80 A2
Baron Fold Rd LHULT M38 ......80 A2
Baron Gn CHD/CHDH SK8 ....192 D3
Baron Rd HYDE SK14 ....148 A4
Barons Ct FAIL M35 ....103 G3
Baron St BURY BL9 ....4 E4
MILN OL16 ....10 D7
Baron Wk BOLS/LL BL3. ....48 D3
Barrack Hl MPL/ROM SK6 ....161 H4
Barrack Hill Cl MPL/ROM SK6 ...161 H4
Barrack St HULME M15 ....126 C1
Barrass St OP/CLY M11 ....130 A1
Barratt Gdns MDTN M24 ....71 E1
Barrett Av FWTH BL4. ....64 D5
Barrett Ct BURY BL9 ....5 H4
Barrett St OLDE OL4. ....92 A1
Barrfield Rd SLFD M6 ....97 H2
Barr Hill Av SLFD M6. ....98 B5
Barrhill Cl HULME M15 ....126 D2
Barrie Wy BOL BL1 ....23 H5
Barrington Av CHD/CHDH SK8 ..182 D3
DROY M43 ....116 C2
Barrington Cl ALT WA14 ....165 G3
Barrington Rd ALT WA14 ....165 G3
Barrington St OP/CLY M11 ......115 H3
Barrisdale Cl BOLS/LL BL3. ......47 G4

Barrow Bridge Rd BOL BL1. ......32 C2
Barrowfield Rd WYTH/NTH M22 ..179 H2
Barrowfields MDTN M24 ....71 H2
Barrow Hill Rd CHH M8 ....100 A5
Barrow La HALE/TIMP WA15 ....178 C5
Barrow Meadow
CHD/CHDH SK8 ....182 B4
Barrows Ct BOL BL1. ....2 E1
Barrowshaw Cl WALK M28 ......80 D5
Barrow St CSLFD M3 ....112 C4
Barrule Av BRAM/HZG SK7 .....185 F5
Barry Crs WALK M28 ....80 B4
Barry Lawson Cl CHH * M8 .....100 A3
Barry Ri ALT WA14 ....176 D2
Barry Rd NTHM/RTH M23 ....156 A4
RDSH SK5 ....160 A1
Barry St OLD OL1. ....75 E4
Barsham Dr BOLS/LL BL3. ....48 C4
Bar Ter WHIT OL12 ....176 D2
Bartiam Pl OLD OL1. ....9 H5
Bartlemore St OLD OL1. ....74 D3
Bartlett Rd ROY/SHW OL2 ......59 H5
Bartlett St OP/CLY M11 ....114 A3
Bartley Rd WYTH/NTH M22 .....168 B1
Barton Dock Rd URM M41 ....123 G1
Barton Fold HYDE SK14 ....148 C4
Barton Hall Av ECC M30 ....108 D4
Barton Highlevel Br ECC M30 ...123 E1
Barton La ECC M30 ....110 A4
Barton Rd ECC M30. ....109 F5
FWTH BL4. ....64 C5
HYDE SK14 ....158 B3
MDTN M24 ....132 B3
STRET M32 ....139 G1
SWIN M27 ....97 F3
URM M41 ....123 F4
WALK M28 ....95 G5
Barton St CSLFD M3 ....6 E5
OLD OL1. ....74 A4
Barway Rd CCHDY M21 ....140 C2
Barwell Cl RDSH SK5 ....145 E3
Barwell Rd SALE M33 ....153 H1
Barwell Sq FWTH BL4. ....64 C2
Barwick Pl SALE M33 ....154 B2
Basechurch Wk
WGTN/LGST * M12 ....128 C2
Basford Rd OLDTF/WHR M16 ....126 A5
Bashall St BOL * BL1 ....48 B1
Basil Ct MILN * OL16 ....30 C5
Basildon Cl BRUN/LGST M13 ...128 A1
Basil St BOLS/LL BL3. ....48 D4
HTNM SK4 ....159 G3
MILN OL16 ....30 C5
RUSH/FAL M14 ....142 D1
Basle Cl BRAM/HZG SK7 ....183 H1
Baslow Av BNG/LEV M19 ....144 A1
Baslow Dr BRAM/HZG SK7 .....185 G4
CHD/CHDH SK8 ....181 H4
Baslow Gv RDSH SK5 ....160 A1
Baslow Rd DROY M43 ....116 D2
DTN/ASHW M34 ....146 C3
STRET M32 ....124 B5
Baslow St OP/CLY M11 ....114 B4
Basset Av SLFD M6 ....97 H1
Basset Wy WHIT OL12 ....29 H1
Bass La BURY BL9 ....17 F5
Bass St BOLE * BL2 ....49 H2
DUK SK16 ....104 B1
Basten Dr BRO M7 ....99 G4
Batchelor Cl CCHDY M21 ....141 H4
Bates Cl ROCH OL11 ....42 C5
Bateson Dr OLDE OL4. ....92 A1
Bateson St STKP SK1 ....9 G2
Bateson Wy OLDS * OL8 ....9 G6
Bates St BRUN/LGST M13 ......128 C4
DUK SK16 ....118 B5
Bath Cl BRAM/HZG SK7 ....193 E1
Bath Crs CHD/CHDH SK8 ....193 E1
OLDTF/WHR M16 ....126 B3
Bath St ALT WA14. ....177 G2
BOL * BL1 ....2 E3
CHAD OL9. ....8 B6
WHIT OL12 ....11 F3
Batley St BKLY M9 ....101 F2
Battenberg Rd BOL * BL1 ....48 B1
Battersby Ct OFTN * SK2 ....173 F5
Battersby St BURY BL9 ....39 G2
OP/CLY * M11 ....129 H1
ROCH OL11 ....29 E3
Battersea Rd HTNM SK4 ....144 D5
Batty St CHH M8 ....100 D5
The Baum MILN OL16 ....10 C5
Baxendale St BOL BL1 ....33 H2
Baxter Gdns NTHM/RTH M23 ...154 C2
Baxter Rd SALE M33 ....154 D5
Baxter St OLDS OL8 ....89 G5
Baybutt St RAD * M26 ....67 H1
Baycroft Gv NTHM/RTH M23 ....155 H5
Baydon Av CHH M8 ....100 A4
Bayfield Gv NEWH/MOS * M40 ..103 H1
Bayle Cl HYDE SK14 ....132 D3
Bayley St BOL BL1. ....3 H3
Baysdale Av BOLS/LL BL3. ....47 G5
Bayston Wk WGTN/LGST M12 ...128 C2
Bay St CHAD OL9 ....8 C4
Bayswater Av NEWH/MOS M40 ..115 E1
Bayswater St BOLS/LL BL3. ......63 F2
Baythorpe St BOL BL1. ....34 A3
Baytree Av CHAD OL9 ....74 D4
DTN/ASHW M34 ....131 H4
Bay Tree Av WALK M28 ....95 H5
Baytree La MDTN M24 ....72 C4
Baytree Wk WHIT OL12 ....14 B4
Baywood St BKLY M9 ....101 E2
Bazaar St SLFD M9 ....111 H1
Beacomfold MPL/ROM SK6 ......163 G3
Beacon Av NTHM/RTH M23 .....179 H2
Beacon Gv OLD OL1. ....91 F5
Beacon Rd MPL/ROM SK6 ....162 A3
TRPK M17 ....123 H1
Beaconsfield RUSH/FAL * M14 ..142 D4

Beaconsfield Rd *ALT* WA14 165 G2
Beaconsfield St *BOLS/LL* BL3 2 A7
Beaconsfield Ter *STLY* SK15 107 G3
Beacon Vw *MPL/ROM* SK6 175 E1
Beadham Dr *BKLY* M9 86 B2
Beaford Dr *WYTH/NTH* M22 180 C4
Bealbank Cl *MILN* OL16 44 D3
Beal Cl *HTNM* SK4 158 A3
Beal Crs *MILN* OL16 11 K3
Bealcroft Cl *MILN* OL16 31 F4
Beale Gv *CCHDY* M21 141 E3
Bealey Av *RAD* M26 53 F4
Bealey Cl *GTN* M18 129 E2
RAD M26 53 E5
Bealey Dr *BURY* BL9 53 E2
Beal La *ROY/SHW* OL2 60 B3
Beaminster Rd *HTNM* SK4 158 C3
Beaminster Wk
BRUN/LGST * M13 127 H3
Beamish Cl *BRUN/LGST* M13 127 H2
Beamsley Dr *WYTH/NTH* M22 180 A2
Beanfields *WALK* M28 95 G5
Bean Leach Av *OFTN* SK2 173 G3
Bean Leach Dr *OFTN* SK2 173 G3
Bean Leach Rd *BRAM/HZG* SK7 173 F5
Beard Rd *GTN* * M18 129 F4
Beard St *DROY* M43 116 A4
ROY/SHW OL2 74 B1
Beardwood Rd *BKLY* M9 87 E3
Bearswood Cl *HYDE* SK14 148 A2
Beathwaite Dr *BRAM/HZG* SK7 183 F3
Beatrice Av *CHD/CHDH* SK8 182 C2
GTN M18 130 A4
Beatrice Rd *BOL* BL1 48 B1
WALK M28 96 A3
Beatrice St *DTN/ASHW* M34 131 F5
FWTH BL4 64 C4
ROCH OL11 29 G4
SWIN M27 96 C1
Beatrice Wignall St *DROY* * M43 116 B5
Beatson Wk *ANC* M4 7 K4
Beattock Cl *HULME* M15 126 C1
Beattock St *HULME* M15 126 C1
Beauchamp St *AUL* OL6 118 B2
Beaufont Dr *OLDE* OL4 91 F2
Beaufort Av *DID/WITH* M20 157 F1
SALE M33 154 D4
SWIN M27 96 C3
Beaufort Cha *WILM/AE* SK9 200 C1
Beaufort Cl *HYDE* SK14 149 F1
WILM/AE SK9 201 C3
Beaufort Rd *AUL* OL6 118 C2
HYDE SK14 149 F1
OFTN SK2 173 E5
SALE M33 154 D3
Beaufort St *CSLFD* M3 6 B7
ECC M30 109 E2
PWCH M25 85 F3
WHIT OL12 29 G2
Beauly Cl *RAMS* BL0 26 B1
Beaumaris Crs *BRAM/HZG* SK7 184 D4
Beaumonds Wy *ROCH* OL11 28 C5
Beaumont Cha *BOLS/LL* BL3 62 C1
Beaumont Cl *LIT* OL15 20 C3
Beaumont Dr *BOLS/LL* BL3 47 F4
Beaumont Rd *CCHDY* M21 141 E4
HOR/BR BL6 47 F3
Beaumont St *AUL* OL6 118 B2
Beauvale Av *OFTN* SK2 172 D2
Beaver Dr *BURY* BL9 54 A5
Beaver Rd *DID/WITH* M20 157 G3
Beaver St *CMANE* M1 7 F7
Bebbington Cl *SALE* M33 155 G4
Bebbington St *OP/CLY* * M11 115 F4
Beccles Rd *SALE* M33 154 C5
Beckenham Cl *TOT/BURYW* BL8 37 G5
Beckenham Rd *CHH* M8 100 B3
Becket Av *BRO* M7 99 H4
Becket Mdw *OLDE* OL4 91 E1
Beckett St *GTN* M18 129 F4
OLDE OL4 75 H5
Beckfield Rd *NTHM/RTH* M23 167 H4
Beckfoot Dr *BRUN/LGST* M13 128 B5
Beckford St *NEWH/MOS* M40 101 F5
Beck Gv *ROY/SHW* OL2 60 C1
WALK M28 95 F1
Beckhampton Cl
BRUN/LGST M13 127 H3
Beckley Av *PWCH* M25 84 D5
Beckley Cl *ROY/SHW* OL2 59 H5
Beckside *RDSH* SK5 145 F2
Beck St *CSLFD* M3 6 B3
OP/CLY * M11 129 H1
Beckton Gdns *WYTH/NTH* M22 180 B1
Becontree Av *DTN/ASHW* M34 131 H4
Becontree Dr *NTHM/RTH* M23 167 E3
Bedells La *WILM/AE* SK9 199 F4
Bede St *BOL* BL1 33 F4
Bedford Av *HYDE* SK14 132 D5
OLDTF/WHR M16 141 G1
ROY/SHW OL2 59 G2
SALE M33 155 E4
SWIN * M27 96 D3
WALK M28 94 D1
Bedford Dr *HALE/TIMP* WA15 166 D3
Bedford Gn *IRL* M44 135 B5
Bedford Rd *ECC* M30 109 H2
OLDTF/WHR M16 140 D1
URM M41 123 F4
Bedford St *BOL* BL1 2 A3
BURY BL9 38 D2
EDGW/EG BL7 22 C1
HEY OL10 41 F4
PWCH M25 85 F2
RDSH SK5 144 D4
Bedlam Gn *BURY* BL9 4 E4
Bednal Av *NEWH/MOS* M40 114 A1
Bedwell St *OLDTF/WHR* M16 127 E5
Bedworth Cl *BOLE* BL2 49 G4
Beechacre *RAMS* BL0 17 E3
Beech Av *BOLS/LL* BL3 66 A2
BRAM/HZG SK7 185 F2
CHAD OL9 73 F2
CHD/CHDH SK8 169 G4
DROY M43 116 A4
DTN/ASHW M34 131 E4
EDGY/DAV SK3 172 A3
FWTH BL4 64 B4
FWTH BL4 82 A2
IRL M44 121 D5
MPL/ROM SK6 174 C3
OLDE OL4 75 G4
RAD M26 67 E4
SLFD M6 111 F1
URM M41 138 B2
WALK M28 94 B4
WHTF M45 68 C5
WYTH/NTH M22 168 C1
Beech Cl *BOLE* BL2 23 H5
PWCH M25 85 F4
WHIT OL12 14 B4
WILM/AE SK9 201 C2
Beech Cottages *WILM/AE* SK9 201 B5
Beech Ct *WILM/AE* * SK9 200 A4
Beech Crs *POY/DIS* SK12 195 F3
Beechcroft *PWCH* M25 85 F5
Beechcroft Av *BOLE* BL2 50 B3
Beechcroft Cl *NEWH/MOS* M40 113 H2
Beechcroft Gv *BOLE* BL2 50 B3
Beechdale Cl *NEWH/MOS* M40 102 B2
The Beeches *BOL* BL1 22 C5
DID/WITH M20 157 E2
MOSL OL5 93 F5
Beeches Ms *DID/WITH* M20 157 E2
Beechey Sq *OLD* OL1 9 J2
Beechfield *ALT* WA14 177 F1
OLDE OL4 93 E1
SALE M33 154 A4
Beechfield Av *LHULT* M38 80 B2
RAD M26 67 H3
URM M41 122 D5
WILM/AE SK9 198 D5
Beechfield Cl *OLDE* OL4 92 A1
ROCH OL11 28 B5
Beechfield Dr *BURY* BL9 53 F2
Beechfield Ms *HYDE* * SK14 133 F5
Beechfield Rd *BOL* BL1 33 E4
CHD/CHDH SK8 183 E4
EDGY/DAV SK3 172 A5
MILN OL16 44 B1
SWIN M27 96 D5
WILM/AE SK9 201 C5
Beechfield St *CHH* M8 100 B4
Beech Gv *AULW* OL7 117 G4
LHULT M38 79 D2
RUSH/FAL M14 143 E3
SALE M33 154 A2
SLFD M6 111 F1
STLY SK15 119 E5
TOT/BURYW BL8 26 B2
WILM/AE SK9 199 F4
Beech Grove Cl *BURY* BL9 39 E2
Beech Hill Rd *OLDE* OL4 92 D1
Beech Hurst Cl
OLDTF/WHR * M16 141 G1
Beech La *MPL/ROM* SK6 162 B4
OLDE OL4 93 E1
WILM/AE SK9 199 F4
Beech Ms *CCHDY* M21 140 D3
OFTN SK2 172 B4
Beech Mt *AULW* OL7 104 D4
BKLY M9 101 E2
Beechpark Av *WYTH/NTH* M22 168 B2
Beech Rd *CCHDY* M21 141 E3
CHD/CHDH SK8 183 E3
EDGY/DAV SK3 171 H3
HALE/TIMP WA15 177 H1
MPL/ROM SK6 187 E5
SALE M33 155 E2
WILM/AE SK9 201 C2
Beech St *BOL* BL1 34 A4
BURY BL9 5 J4
ECC M30 109 E4
FAIL M35 102 D2
HYDE SK14 132 C5
MDTN * M24 71 G4
MILN OL16 44 D2
OLD OL1 9 J3
RAD M26 67 H3
RAMS BL0 16 D5
ROCH OL11 29 G5
SWIN M27 97 E3
Beechurst Rd *CHD/CHDH* SK8 171 E4
Beech Vw *HYDE* SK14 148 B1
Beech Wk *MDTN* M24 87 G1
STRET M32 139 H3
Beechway *MPL/ROM* SK6 187 E5
WILM/AE SK9 199 E5
Beechwood *ALT* WA14 177 E3
ROCH OL11 42 C1
ROY/SHW OL2 60 C1
Beechwood Av *CCHDY* M21 141 F3
LIT OL15 20 D5
MPL/ROM SK6 162 B4
RAMS BL0 17 E2
STLY SK15 119 H1
URM M41 122 B5
Beechwood Ct *TOT/BURYW* BL8 37 F1
Beechwood Dr *HYDE* SK14 148 A2
MOSL OL5 92 D5
MPL/ROM SK6 175 F3
ROY/SHW OL2 58 D3
SALE M33 153 F2
WALK M28 96 A4
WILM/AE * SK9 200 B2
Beechwood Gv *BKLY* M9 101 F3
CHD/CHDH SK8 182 D4
Beechwood Rd *OLDS* OL8 90 C5
PWCH M25 85 G4
Beechwood St *BOLS/LL* BL3 64 A1
Beede St *OP/CLY* M11 115 E5
Beedon Av *BOLS/LL* BL3 50 D5
Beehive St *OLDS* OL8 90 C4
Beeley St *HYDE* SK14 147 H1
SLFD M6 99 E5
Beenham Cl *SALE* M33 153 F3
Beeston Av *BRO* M7 99 E4
HALE/TIMP WA15 166 A3
Beeston Cl *BOL* BL1 23 F5
Beeston Gv *EDGY/DAV* SK3 171 H4
WHTF M45 69 E5
Beeston Rd *SALE* M33 153 H2
WILM/AE SK9 192 A2
Beeston St *BKLY* M9 101 F3
Beeth St *OP/CLY* M11 129 G2
Beeton Gv *BRUN/LGST* M13 128 B4
Beever St *OLD* OL1 9 J2
OLDTF/WHR M16 126 B3
Begley Cl *MPL/ROM* SK6 161 G5
Begonia Av *FWTH* BL4 64 B3
Belayse Cl *BOL* BL1 33 E3
Belbeck St *TOT/BURYW* BL8 37 H4
Belbeck St South
TOT/BURYW * BL8 37 H4
Belcroft Cl *WYTH/NTH* M22 168 D1
Belcroft Dr *LHULT* M38 79 D1
Belcroft Gv *LHULT* * M38 79 D2
Belding Av *NEWH/MOS* M40 103 E1
Beldon Rd *BKLY* M9 86 C3
Belfairs Cl *AULW* OL7 105 E4
Belfield Cl *MILN* OL16 11 K4
Belfield La *MILN* OL16 11 J6
MILN OL16 31 E4
Belfield Mill La *MILN* OL16 31 E3
Belfield Old Rd *MILN* OL16 11 J4
Belfield Rd *DID/WITH* M20 157 G3
MILN OL16 11 H4
PWCH M25 85 H4
Belford Av *DTN/ASHW* M34 130 B5
Belford Dr *BOLS/LL* BL3 48 D5
Belford Rd *STRET* M32 125 E5
Belfort Dr *ORD* M5 112 A5
Belfry Cl *WILM/AE* SK9 200 A2
Belgate Cl *WGTN/LGST* M12 128 D4
Belgium St *ROCH* OL11 28 B4
Belgrave Av *FAIL* M35 103 G2
MPL/ROM SK6 175 E1
OLDS OL8 90 D3
URM M41 122 B5
Belgrave Ct *OLDS* OL8 90 C3
Belgrave Crs *ECC* M30 110 A2
OFTN SK2 172 B5
Belgrave Dr *RAD* M26 52 B5
Belgrave Gdns *BOL* BL1 33 H4
Belgrave Rd *ALT* WA14 177 F1
IRL M44 150 C1
NEWH/MOS M40 102 D1
OLDS OL8 90 C3
SALE M33 154 B2
Belgrave St *BOL* BL1 33 H4
HEY OL10 40 D5
RAD M26 52 B5
WHIT OL12 29 F2
Belgrave St South *BOL* BL1 2 C1
Belgravia Gdns *CCHDY* M21 140 D3
HALE/TIMP WA15 177 H4
Belgravia Ms *ROY/SHW* OL2 60 B2
Belhaven Rd *CHH* M8 86 A5
Bellairs St *BOLS/LL* BL3 63 F1
Bella St *BOLS/LL* BL3 48 B5
Bell Clough Rd *DROY* M43 116 C2
Bell Crs *OP/CLY* M11 114 C5
Belldale Cl *HTNM* SK4 158 D4
Belle Isle Av *WHIT* OL12 18 B2
Bellerby Cl *WHTF* M45 68 B4
Belleville Av *WYTH/NTH* M22 180 D4
Belle Vue Av *WGTN/LGST* M12 128 C3
Belle Vue St *WGTN/LGST* M12 128 D2
Belle Vue Ter *BURY* BL9 4 C6
Bellew St *OP/CLY* M11 114 B5
Bellfield Av *CHD/CHDH* SK8 183 E3
OLDS OL8 90 C5
Bellhill Gdns *SLFD* M6 111 G2
Bellingham Cl *ROY/SHW* OL2 60 A1
TOT/BURYW BL8 37 E4
Bellis Cl *WGTN/LGST* M12 114 B4
Bell La *BURY* BL9 5 G3
Bell Meadow Dr *ROCH* OL11 41 G1
Bellott St *CHH* M8 100 B4
Bellott Wk *OLD* * OL1 74 B4
Bellpit Cl *WALK* M28 94 D3
Bells Croft Av
NEWH/MOS * M40 102 A3
Bellshill Crs *MILN* OL16 11 K3
Bell St *DROY* M43 116 C3
MILN OL16 10 C5
OLD OL1 9 K2
Bell Ter *ECC* M30 109 F5
Belmont Av *DTN/ASHW* M34 131 E4
FWTH BL4 82 C2
OLDE OL4 76 A5
SLFD M6 110 B2
Belmont Cl *HTNM* SK4 159 H3
Belmont Dr *MPL/ROM* SK6 163 G5
TOT/BURYW BL8 37 F5
Belmont Rd *BOL* BL1 22 C5
BRAM/HZG SK7 193 H2
CHD/CHDH SK8 169 G3
HALE/TIMP WA15 177 H2
RAD M26 67 F3
SALE M33 139 F5
Belmont St *ECC* M30 109 G2
HTNM SK4 159 H3
OLD OL1 8 E1
OLDE OL4 91 H2
ORD M5 111 E4
Belmont Ter *PART* * M31 137 E5
Belmont Vw *BOLE* BL2 35 G2
Belmont Wk
BRUN/LGST * M13 127 H2
Belmont Wy *CHAD* OL9 73 H4
HTNM SK4 159 H3
WHIT OL12 10 B1
Belper Rd *ECC* M30 109 E5
HTNM SK4 158 C5
Belroy Ct *PWCH* * M25 85 E4
Belsay Cl *AULW* OL7 104 B5
Belsay Dr *NTHM/RTH* M23 167 H5
Belsfield Ter *AUL* * OL6 105 F2
Belstone Av *NTHM/RTH* M23 179 H1
Belstone Cl *BRAM/HZG* SK7 184 A2
Belthorne Av *BKLY* M9 87 H5
Belton Av *MILN* OL16 11 K3
Beltone Cl *STRET* M32 139 G2
Belton Wk *CHAD* OL9 8 C4
Belvedere Av *RDSH* SK5 145 E1
TOT/BURYW BL8 26 B2
Belvedere Ct *PWCH* * M25 84 D4
Belvedere Dr *DUK* SK16 118 D5
MPL/ROM SK6 160 D3
Belvedere Ri *OLD* OL1 75 G1
Belvedere Rd *RUSH/FAL* M14 143 F3
SLFD M6 111 H2
Belvedere St *SLFD* * M6 112 A2
Belvoir Av *BNG/LEV* * M19 143 H1
BRAM/HZG SK7 185 F4
Belvoir Mdw *MILN* OL16 20 B4
Belvoir St *BOLE* BL2 49 H2
WHIT OL12 29 G2
Belvor Av *DTN/ASHW* M34 131 F1
Belwood Rd *CCHDY* M21 140 D4
Bembridge Cl *RUSH/FAL* M14 127 H5
Bembridge Dr *BOLS/LL* BL3 50 A4
Bembridge Rd *DTN/ASHW* M34 147 E3
Bempton Cl *OFTN* SK2 173 H4
Bemrose Av *ALT* WA14 165 F3
Bemsley Pl *ORD* * M5 111 H5
Benbecula Wy *URM* M41 123 G3
Benbow Av *WGTN/LGST* M12 128 C3
Benbow St *SALE* M33 154 C1
Ben Brierley Wy *OLD* OL1 9 G2
Bench Carr *WHIT* OL12 10 A2
Benchill Court Rd
WYTH/NTH M22 168 D5
Benchill Dr *WYTH/NTH* M22 168 C4
Benchill Rd *WYTH/NTH* M22 168 B3
Bendall St *OP/CLY* M11 115 H5
Ben Davies Ct *MPL/ROM* * SK6 162 B4
Bendemeer *URM* M41 123 F5
Bendix St *ANC* M4 7 H2
Benedict Cl *BRO* M7 99 F5
Benedict Dr *DUK* SK16 132 B2
Benfield Av *NEWH/MOS* M40 88 B5
Benfield St *HEY* OL10 41 E4
Benfleet Cl *WGTN/LGST* * M12 128 D2
Bengal La *AUL* OL6 118 B1
Bengal St *ANC* M4 7 J2
EDGY/DAV SK3 12 E6
Benmore Cl *HEY* OL10 40 B4
Benmore Rd *BKLY* M9 87 G4
Bennet St *RAD* M26 51 G5
Bennett Cl *EDGY/DAV* SK3 12 A5
Bennett Dr *BRO* M7 99 H4
Bennett Rd *CHH* M8 100 A1
Bennett's La *BOL* BL1 33 F4
Bennett St *AULW* OL7 117 G4
EDGY/DAV SK3 12 A5
HYDE SK14 132 C3
STLY * SK15 119 F4
STRET * M32 139 H2
WGTN/LGST M12 128 B2
Benny La *DROY* M43 117 E2
Benson Cl *BRO* M7 99 H5
Benson St *BURY* BL9 5 G6
Ben St *OP/CLY* M11 115 E3
Bentcliffe Wy *ECC* M30 110 A4
Bentfield Crs *MILN* OL16 44 D2
Bent Fold Dr *BURY* * BL9 68 D3
Bentgate Cl *MILN* OL16 44 D2
Bentgate St *MILN* OL16 44 D3
Bentham Cl *TOT/BURYW* BL8 36 D3
Bent Hill St *BOLS/LL* * BL3 47 H5
Bentinck Cl *ALT* * WA14 165 F5
Bentinck Rd *ALT* WA14 165 F5
Bentinck St *AULW* OL7 118 A3
BOL BL1 33 E5
FWTH BL4 64 D3
HULME M15 126 C1
WHIT OL12 29 F2
Bent La *CHH* M8 100 A3
PWCH M25 85 F3
Bent Lanes *URM* M41 122 C4
Bentley Av *MDTN* M24 57 G4
Bentley Cl *RAD* M26 52 D5
Bentley Ct *FWTH* BL4 65 E3
Bentley Fold *TOT/BURYW* BL8 37 E2
Bentley Fold Cottages
TOT/BURYW * BL8 37 E2
Bentley Hall Rd *TOT/BURYW* BL8 36 C2
Bentley La *BURY* BL9 27 H2
Bentley Ms *WHIT* * OL12 29 H1
Bentley Rd *BRO* M7 99 H2
CCHDY M21 140 D2
DTN/ASHW M34 131 G5
Bentley St *BOLE* * BL2 49 H4
CHAD OL9 73 G5
FWTH BL4 65 E3
OLD OL1 75 E4
WHIT OL12 29 H1
Bentmeadows *WHIT* OL12 10 A2
Benton Dr *MPL/ROM* SK6 175 H1
Benton St *BKLY* M9 101 G3
Bents Av *MPL/ROM* SK6 161 G3
URM M41 137 F2
Bents Farm Cl *LIT* * OL15 20 C3
Bent Spur Rd *FWTH* BL4 81 H2
Bent St *CHH* M8 100 B5
FWTH BL4 65 F5
Bentworth Wk *BKLY* M9 101 F3
Beresford Av *BOLS/LL* BL3 48 B4
Beresford Crs *OLDE* OL4 75 H5
RDSH SK5 129 H5
Beresford Rd *BRUN/LGST* M13 128 C5
STRET M32 125 F4
Beresford St *FAIL* M35 102 D3
MILN OL16 45 E2
OLDE OL4 75 G4
RUSH/FAL M14 127 E5
Berigan Cl *WGTN/LGST* M12 128 B3
Berisford Cl *HALE/TIMP* WA15 165 H2
Berkeley Av *CHAD* OL9 89 E4
RUSH/FAL M14 128 B4
STRET M32 124 B4
Berkeley Cl *HYDE* SK14 147 G2
OFTN SK2 172 D1
Berkeley Crs *HYDE* SK14 147 G2
RAD M26 51 H4
Berkeley Dr *MILN* OL16 43 G2
Berkeley Rd *BOL* BL1 33 H2
BRAM/HZG SK7 185 G1
Berkeley St *AUL* OL6 117 H2
Berkley Av *BNG/LEV* M19 143 H1
Berkley Dr *ROY/SHW* OL2 74 A2
Berkley St *ROY/SHW* OL2 74 B2
Berkley Wk *LIT* OL15 20 C3
Berkshire Cl *CHAD* OL9 89 G2
Berkshire Dr *IRL* M44 150 B1
Berkshire Pl *CHAD* OL9 8 A6
Berkshire Rd *NEWH/MOS* M40 114 A2
Berlin Rd *EDGY/DAV* SK3 171 G3
Berlin St *BOLS/LL* BL3 48 D5
Bermondsay St *ORD* M5 112 A5
Bernard Gv *BOL* BL1 33 G4
Bernard St *BKLY* M9 101 E2
WHIT OL12 18 D5
Berne Cl *BRAM/HZG* SK7 171 H5
CHAD OL9 8 A5
Bernice Av *CHAD* OL9 89 G1
Bernice St *BOL* BL1 33 F4
Berriedale Cl *OLDTF/WHR* * M16 141 G1
Berrie Gv *BNG/LEV* M19 143 H3
Berry Brow *NEWH/MOS* M40 115 G1
Berry Cl *WILM/AE* SK9 199 F5
Berrycroft La *MPL/ROM* SK6 161 H3
Berry St *CMANE* M1 7 J7
ECC M30 109 E5
STLY SK15 119 H5
SWIN M27 83 E5
Bertha Rd *MILN* OL16 11 J7
Bertha St *BOL* BL1 33 G4
OP/CLY M11 129 E1
ROY/SHW OL2 60 A4
Bertie St *ROCH* OL11 42 B2
Bertram St *SALE* M33 155 F2
WGTN/LGST * M12 128 D2
Bertrand Rd *BOL* BL1 48 B2
Bert St *BOLS/LL* BL3 63 E1
Berwick Av *HTNM* SK4 158 A4
URM M41 139 F1
WHTF M45 68 D5
Berwick Cl *HEY* OL10 40 B5
WALK M28 94 A3
Berwick St *MILN* OL16 30 C5
Berwyn Av *BKLY* M9 86 D2
CHD/CHDH SK8 171 E4
MDTN M24 72 B4
Berwyn Cl *OLDS* OL8 90 B4
Beryl Av *TOT/BURYW* BL8 26 A4
Beryl St *BOL* BL1 34 A3
Besom La *STLY* SK15 120 B2
Bessemer Rd *IRL* M44 136 A5
Bessemer St *OP/CLY* M11 129 F1
Bessemer Wy *OLD* OL1 9 F2
Bessybrook Cl *HOR/BR* BL6 46 D3
Beswick Dr *FAIL* M35 103 F4
Beswicke Royds St *MILN* OL16 11 H3
Beswicke St *LIT* OL15 21 F3
WHIT OL12 10 A4
Beswick Rw *ANC* M4 7 F2
Beswick St *ANC* M4 114 A3
DROY M43 116 C4
Beta Av *STRET* M32 139 H2
Beta St *BOL* BL1 2 D2
Bethany La *MILN* OL16 45 F2
Bethel Av *FAIL* M35 102 D3
Bethel Gn *LIT* * OL15 15 B4
Bethel St *HEY* OL10 40 D4
Bethesda St *OLDS* OL8 90 C3
Bethnall Dr *RUSH/FAL* M14 142 B3
Betjeman Pl *ROY/SHW* OL2 60 C2
Betleymere Rd *CHD/CHDH* SK8 170 C5
Betley Rd *RDSH* SK5 145 E2
Betley St *CMANE* M1 7 K6
HEY * OL10 40 D5
RAD M26 52 D5
Betnor Av *STKP* SK1 160 C5
Betony Cl *WHIT* OL12 18 C5
Bettwood Dr *CHH* M8 86 A5
Betula Gv *BRO* M7 99 G4
Betula Ms *ROCH* OL11 28 A2
Bevan Cl *WGTN/LGST* M12 114 B4
Bevendon Sq *BRO* M7 99 H4
Beveridge St *RUSH/FAL* M14 127 F5
Beverley Av *DTN/ASHW* M34 146 D1
URM M41 123 H4
Beverley Cl *WHTF* M45 69 E3
Beverley Pl *MILN* * OL16 10 E5
Beverley Rd *BOL* BL1 48 B1
BOLS/LL BL3 65 G1
OFTN SK2 172 D1
SWIN M27 97 H3
Beverley St *BKLY* M9 101 F1
Beverley Wk *OLDS* * OL8 9 F7
Beverly Cl *AUL* OL6 105 E4
Beverly Rd *RUSH/FAL* M14 143 E4
Beverston *ROCH* * OL11 29 H5
Beverston Dr *BRO* M7 99 H4
Bevill Sq *CSLFD* M3 6 B2
Bevis Gn *BURY* BL9 27 G3
Bewick St *BOLE* BL2 34 C3
Bewley St *OLDS* OL8 90 A5
Bexhill Av *HALE/TIMP* WA15 166 A3
Bexhill Cl *BOLS/LL* BL3 66 B1
Bexhill Dr *BRUN/LGST* M13 128 B5
Bexhill Rd *EDGY/DAV* SK3 171 H5
Bexhill Wk *CHAD* OL9 89 G1
Bexington Rd *OLDTF/WHR* M16 126 C5
Bexley Cl *URM* M41 123 E4
Bexley Dr *LHULT* M38 80 D4
TOT/BURYW BL8 37 G5
Bexley Sq *CSLFD* M3 6 A3
Bexley St *CHAD* OL9 8 B6
Beyer Cl *GTN* M18 129 F3
Bibby La *BNG/LEV* M19 143 G5
Bibby St *BURY* BL9 53 G4
HYDE * SK14 132 C3
Bibury Av *WYTH/NTH* M22 180 A1
Bickerdike Av *WGTN/LGST* M12 129 E5
Bickershaw Dr *WALK* M28 80 D5
Bickerstaffe Cl *ROY/SHW* OL2 59 H4
Bickerton Dr *BRAM/HZG* SK7 184 B3
Bickerton Rd *ALT* WA14 165 E4
Biddall Dr *NTHM/RTH* M23 168 A3
Biddisham Wk *NEWH/MOS* M40 101 E5
Biddulph Av *OFTN* SK2 172 D4
Bideford Dr *BOLE* BL2 50 B3
NTHM/RTH M23 167 G2
Bideford Rd *OFTN* SK2 160 D5
ROCH OL11 42 A3
Bidston Cl *ROY/SHW* OL2 60 C3
TOT/BURYW BL8 37 E4
Bidston Dr *WILM/AE* SK9 192 B5
Bignor St *CHH* M8 100 B4
Bilbao St *BOL* BL1 48 B1
Bilberry St *MILN* OL16 30 B5
Bilbrook St *ANC* M4 113 G2
Billberry Cl *WHTF* M45 69 E4
Billing Av *WGTN/LGST* M12 127 H1
Billinge Cl *BOL* BL1 2 E2
Billington Rd *SWIN* M27 98 B2
Bill Williams Cl *OP/CLY* M11 115 F5
Billy La *SWIN* M27 83 E5
Bilson Dr *EDGY/DAV* SK3 171 E2
Binbrook Wk *BOLS/LL* BL3 48 D5
Bindloss Av *ECC* M30 110 B2
Bingham Dr *NTHM/RTH* M23 167 G3
Bingham St *SWIN* M27 97 E2
Bingley Cl *OP/CLY* M11 114 C5
Bingley Dr *URM* M41 122 C4
Bingley Rd *MILN* OL16 11 K7
Bingley Sq *MILN* OL16 11 K7
Bingley St *FWTH* BL4 65 E5
Bingley Ter *MILN* OL16 11 K7
Binns Nook Rd *WHIT* OL12 10 E1
Binns Pl *CMANE* M1 7 J4
Binns St *STLY* SK15 118 D4
Binsley Cl *IRL* M44 136 B2
Binstead Cl *RUSH/FAL* M14 128 B5
Birchacre Gv *RUSH/FAL* M14 143 E4
Birchall Cl *DUK* SK16 132 C2
Birchall Gn *MPL/ROM* SK6 161 G1
Birchall Wy *HULME* M15 127 E2
Birch Av *FAIL* M35 103 E4
HTNM SK4 159 E2
IRL M44 150 C1
MDTN M24 71 H5
MPL/ROM SK6 162 C4
OLD OL1 73 F2
OLDS OL8 90 A5
OLDTF/WHR M16 125 H4

SALE M33 ...154 C3
SLFD M6 ...111 F1
TOT/BURYW BL8 ...37 F1
WHIT OL12 ...14 B4
WHTF M45 ...84 C1
WILM/AE SK9 ...199 E4
Birch Crs MILN OL16 ...18 B3
Birch Crs MILN OL16 ...44 D3
Birchdale ALT WA14 ...177 F2
Birchdale Av CHD/CHDH SK8 ...181 G2
Birch Dr BRAM/HZG SK7 ...184 D2
OLDE OL4 ...91 H2
SWIN M27 ...97 G2
Birchenall St NEWH/MOS M40 ...101 G2
Birchenlea St CHAD OL9 ...89 F4
The Birches SALE M33 ...153 H1
Birchfield BOLE BL2 ...24 B5
Birchfield Av HEY OL10 ...39 H5
Birchfield Dr ROCH OL11 ...42 B1
WALK M28 ...94 B3
Birchfield Gv BOLS/LL BL3 ...47 F5
Birchfield Ms HYDE * SK14 ...147 G1
Birchfield Rd EDGY/DAV SK3 ...170 D2
Birchfields Cl LHULT M38 ...80 C3
Birchgate Wk BOLS/LL BL3 ...48 D4
Birch Gv DTN/ASHW M34 ...131 F5
DTN/ASHW M54 ...131 G2
HALE/TIMP WA15 ...166 A5
PWCH M25 ...84 D1
RAMS BL0 ...16 B5
RUSH/FAL M14 ...128 A5
Birch Hall Cl OLDE OL4 ...91 H3
Birch Hall La BRUN/LGST M13 ...143 F1
Birch Hey Cl WHIT OL12 ...19 H4
Birch Hill Crs WHIT OL12 ...20 B4
Birch Hill La WHIT OL12 ...20 A4
Birchington Rd DID/WITH M20 ...142 B3
Birchinlee Av ROY/SHW OL2 ...73 G1
Birchin Pl ANC * M4 ...7 G4
Birch La BRUN/LGST M13 ...128 B4
DUK SK16 ...118 C5
Birchlea Cl BURY BL9 ...53 G2
Birchleaf Gv ORD M5 ...110 D5
Birch Mt WHIT OL12 ...19 E4
Birch Polygon RUSH/FAL M14 ...128 A5
Birch Rd CHD/CHDH SK8 ...169 F4
CHH M8 ...100 C1
FWTH BL4 ...81 G1
COL/RIS/CU WA3 ...150 A4
MDTN M24 ...72 B2
PART M31 ...152 C3
POY/DIS SK12 ...195 G5
SWIN M27 ...78 B5
UPML OL3 ...78 B5
WALK M28 ...95 F1
WHIT OL12 ...19 H2
Birch St AULW OL7 ...117 G4
BOLE BL2 ...3 H7
BURY BL9 ...5 G4
DROY * M43 ...116 C5
HEY OL10 ...41 E5
RAD M26 ...53 H4
STLY SK15 ...106 D5
WGTN/LGST M12 ...128 C1
WHIT OL12 ...19 H2
Birch Ter HYDE * SK14 ...147 F1
Birch Tree Av BRAM/HZG SK7 ...185 H3
Birch Tree Cl ALT WA14 ...165 F2
Birch Tree Dr WYTH/NTH M22 ...180 C1
Birchvale Cl HULME M15 ...126 D2
Birchway BRAM/HZG SK7 ...185 H2
MPL/ROM SK6 ...187 E5
Birchwood CHAD OL9 ...73 G5
Birchwood Dr WILM/AE SK9 ...200 A2
Birchwood Rd MDTN M24 ...72 B4
Birchwood Wy DUK * SK16 ...132 C2
Bird Hall Av CHD/CHDH SK8 ...171 F5
Birdhall Gv BNG/LEV M19 ...143 H3
Bird Hall La EDGY/DAV SK3 ...170 D2
Bird Hall Rd CHD/CHDH SK8 ...171 E4
Birdlip Dr NTHM/RTH M23 ...179 H1
Birkby Dr MDTN M24 ...71 F2
Birkdale Av ROY/SHW OL2 ...74 B2
WHTF M45 ...84 C1
Birkdale Cl BRAM/HZG SK7 ...184 A5
HEY OL10 ...56 A1
HYDE SK14 ...132 D3
Birkdale Dr SALE M33 ...153 H4
WHTF M45 ...83 G4
Birkdale Gdns BOLS/LL BL3 ...48 C4
RDSH SK5 ...160 A1
Birkdale Pl SALE * M33 ...139 E5
Birkdale Rd MILN OL16 ...30 C5
RDSH SK5 ...160 A1
Birkdale St CHH M8 ...100 B3
Birkenhills Dr BOLS/LL BL3 ...47 F4
Birkett Cl BOL BL1 ...22 C5
Birkett Dr BOL BL1 ...22 C5
Birkinbrook Cl WHTF M45 ...68 D3
Birks Av OLDE OL4 ...76 A4
Birks Dr TOT/BURYW BL8 ...26 B5
Birkworth Ct OFTN SK2 ...173 E3
Birley Cl HALE/TIMP WA15 ...166 A2
Birley Pk DID/WITH M20 ...157 E3
Birley St BURY BL9 ...38 C1
WHIT OL12 ...10 D1
Birling Dr NTHM/RTH M23 ...168 A5
Birnham Gv HEY OL10 ...40 A5
Birshaw Cl ROY/SHW OL2 ...60 A4
Birtenshaw Crs EDGW/EG BL7 ...23 G4
Birtles Av RDSH SK5 ...130 A5
Birtles Cl CHD/CHDH SK8 ...181 G2
DUK SK16 ...118 B5
Birtlespool Rd CHD/CHDH SK8 ...170 C5
Birtle St NEWH/MOS M40 ...101 G3
Birwood Rd CHH M8 ...86 C5
Biscay Cl OP/CLY M11 ...115 H4
Bishopbridge Cl BOLS/LL BL3 ...49 E5
Bishop Cl OLDTF/WHR M16 ...126 B5
Bishopdale Cl ROY/SHW OL2 ...59 H2
Bishopgate St CHAD OL9 ...89 F2
Bishop Marshall Cl NEWH/MOS M40 ...101 G3
Bishop Marshall Wy MDTN M24 ...56 A1
Bishop Rd SLFD M6 ...110 D1
URM M41 ...137 E1

Bishops Cl ALT WA14 ...177 E3
AULW OL7 ...104 D5
BOLS/LL BL3 ...64 B2
CHD/CHDH SK8 ...170 D4
Bishopsgate CMANW M2 ...6 E6
Bishops Meadow MDTN M24 ...71 E1
Bishops Ms SALE M33 ...138 D5
Bishop's Rd BOLS/LL BL3 ...64 B2
Bishop St MDTN M24 ...72 C5
MILN OL16 ...11 G2
STKP SK1 ...13 G4
Bishopton Cl BNG/LEV M19 ...144 B2
Bisley Av NTHM/RTH M23 ...167 G3
Bisley St OLDS OL8 ...8 D1
Bismarck St OLDS OL8 ...9 K6
Bispham Av BOLE BL2 ...50 C2
RDSH SK5 ...145 E1
Bispham Cl TOT/BURYW BL8 ...37 E5
Bispham Gv BRO M7 ...99 H3
Bispham St BOLE * BL2 ...49 H1
Bittern Cl POY/DIS SK12 ...194 B4
ROCH OL11 ...28 C4
Bittern Dr DROY M43 ...116 D2
Bk Clegg's Bldgs BOL * BL1 ...2 C5
Blackbank St BOL BL1 ...34 A4
Blackberry La RDSH SK5 ...145 G4
Black Brook Rd HTNM SK4 ...144 C4
Blackburn Gdns DID/WITH M20 ...157 F2
Blackburn Pl ORD M5 ...113 G1
Blackburn Rd BOL BL1 ...33 H5
Blackburn St CSLFD M5 ...112 C2
OLDTF/WHR M16 ...126 B3
PWCH M25 ...65 F3
RAD M26 ...67 F1
Blackcap Cl WALK M28 ...94 C3
Blackcarr Rd NTHM/RTH M23 ...168 A4
Blackchapel Dr MILN OL16 ...43 G3
Blackcroft Cl SWIN M27 ...96 B2
Blackdown Gv OLDS OL8 ...90 B4
Blackett St CMANE * M1 ...113 H5
Blackfield La BRO M7 ...99 F2
Blackfields BRO * M7 ...99 F2
Blackford Av BURY BL9 ...53 G5
Blackford Rd BNG/LEV M19 ...144 A4
Blackford Wk NEWH/MOS M40 ...114 A2
Blackfriars Rd CSLFD M5 ...6 D3
Blackfriars St CSLFD M5 ...6 D5
Blackhill Cl BRUN/LGST M13 ...127 G1
Black Horse St BOL BL1 ...2 D5
FWTH BL4 ...65 F5
Blackledge St BOLS/LL BL3 ...48 D5
Blackley Cl BURY BL9 ...38 A4
Blackley New Rd BKLY M9 ...86 A4
Blackley Park Rd BKLY M9 ...101 E1
Blackley St MDTN M24 ...70 C5
OLDTF/WHR M16 ...126 B5
Blacklock St CHH M8 ...113 E1
Black Moss Cl RAD * M26 ...66 C1
Black Moss La ALT M24 ...164 B2
Blackpits Rd ROCH OL11 ...43 H5
Blackpool St OP/CLY M11 ...115 F3
Blackrock STLY SK15 ...106 D4
Blackrock St OP/CLY M11 ...114 C4
Black Sail Wk OLD OL1 ...74 C3
Blackshaw La BOLS/LL BL3 ...48 B5
ROY/SHW OL2 ...59 G5
WILM/AE SK9 ...201 A4
Blackshaw St EDGY/DAV SK3 ...13 F5
Blacksmith La ROCH OL11 ...12 A4
Blackstock Av BRUN/LGST M13 ...127 H4
Blackstone Av MILN OL16 ...11 K4
Blackstone Edge Old Rd LIT OL15 ...21 G2
Blackstone Rd OFTN SK2 ...173 E4
Blackthorn Av BNG/LEV M19 ...143 H4
Blackthorn Cl WHIT OL12 ...29 H1
Blackthorne Cl BOL BL1 ...32 D5
Blackthorne Dr SALE M33 ...153 G4
Blackthorne Rd HYDE SK14 ...147 H5
Blackthorn Ms WHIT OL12 ...29 H1
Blackthorn Rd OLDS OL8 ...105 H2
Blackwin St WGTN/LGST M12 ...128 B1
Blackwood Dr NTHM/RTH M23 ...167 E1
Blackwood St BOLS/LL BL3 ...49 F5
Bladen Cl CHD/CHDH SK8 ...170 D5
Bladon St CMANE * M1 ...7 H5
Blair Av LHULT M38 ...80 C3
URM M41 ...137 F1
Blair Cl BRAM/HZG SK7 ...184 D4
POY/DIS SK12 ...60 A2
SALE M33 ...153 F5
Blairhall Av NEWH/MOS M40 ...101 G5
Blair La BOLE BL2 ...35 E5
Blairmore Dr BOLS/LL BL3 ...47 F5
Blair Rd OLDTF/WHR M16 ...141 H2
Blair St OLDTF/WHR M16 ...23 E3
FWTH BL4 ...81 H1
OLDTF/WHR M16 ...126 B3
WHIT OL12 ...29 G2
Blakedown Wk WGTN/LGST * M12 ...128 B3
Blake Dr OFTN SK2 ...173 F2
Blakefield Dr WALK M28 ...95 F1
Blake Gdns BOL BL1 ...33 G4
Blakelock St ROY/SHW OL2 ...59 H2
Blakemere Av SALE M33 ...155 F3
Blakemore Wk WGTN/LGST * M12 ...114 B4
Blake St BOL BL1 ...33 G4
EDGW/EG BL7 ...23 E4
MILN OL16 ...11 F5
Blakeswell Cl URM M41 ...122 A5
Blakey Cl BOLS/LL BL3 ...48 B5
Blakey St WGTN/LGST M12 ...128 D4
Blanchard St HULME M15 ...126 D3
Blanche St WHIT OL1 ...10 D1
Blanche Wk OLD OL1 ...9 J1
Blandford Av WALK M28 ...95 G2
Blandford Cl TOT/BURYW BL8 ...38 A1
Blandford Ct STLY SK15 ...119 F3
Blandford Dr NEWH/MOS M40 ...88 C5
Blandford Rd ECC M30 ...109 E3
SLFD M6 ...99 G6
Blandford St AUL OL6 ...117 H2
STLY * SK15 ...119 F3
Bland St OLDTF/WHR * M16 ...126 D4
Bland Rd PWCH M25 ...85 E5
Blanefield Cl CCHDY M21 ...141 H4

Blantyre Av WALK M28 ...81 F5
Blantyre Rd SWIN M27 ...97 G4
Blantyre St CSLFD M5 ...6 B7
ECC M30 ...108 D2
HULME M15 ...126 C1
SWIN M27 ...96 C2
Blanwood Dr CHH M8 ...100 C3
Blaven Cl EDGY/DAV SK3 ...173 E4
Blazemoss Bank OFTN SK2 ...173 E4
Bleackley St TOT/BURYW BL8 ...37 H2
Bleak Hey Rd WYTH/NTH M22 ...181 E2
Bleakley St WHTF M45 ...68 B4
Bleak St BOLE BL2 ...34 C4
Bleasby St OLDE OL4 ...75 F5
Bleasdale Cl HOR/BR BL6 ...46 A1
Bleasdale Rd BOL BL1 ...32 C4
WYTH/NTH M22 ...179 H2
Bleasdale St ROY/SHW OL2 ...59 E4
Bleasefell Cha WALK M28 ...94 B5
Bleatarn Rd STKP SK1 ...172 C2
Bledlow Cl ECC M30 ...109 H2
Blenheim Av OLDTF/WHR M16 ...141 G1
Blenheim Cl ALT WA14 ...177 G2
BURY BL9 ...53 G4
HEY OL10 ...41 F4
POY/DIS SK12 ...195 G5
WILM/AE SK9 ...200 A3
Blenheim Rd BOLE BL2 ...34 D5
CHD/CHDH SK8 ...183 E2
OLDTF/WHR M16 ...125 H5
WHIT * OL12 ...29 F2
Blenhiem Av OLDE OL4 ...75 G1
Blenmar Cl RAD M26 ...52 D4
Bletchley Cl BRUN/LGST M13 ...128 A1
Bletchley Rd HTNM SK4 ...158 B5
Blethyn St BOLS/LL BL3 ...63 E2
Blinco Rd URM M41 ...139 E2
Blind La WGTN/LGST M12 ...128 A1
Blindsill Rd FWTH BL4 ...64 C5
Blisworth Av ECC M30 ...109 H5
Blisworth Cl ANC M4 ...114 A4
Block La CHAD OL9 ...89 G2
Blodwell St SLFD M6 ...111 G4
Bloomfield Dr BURY BL9 ...69 E1
WALK M28 ...94 B3
Bloomfield St BOL BL1 ...33 H3
Bloomsbury Gv HALE/TIMP WA15 ...166 B3
Bloomsbury La HALE/TIMP WA15 ...166 B3
Bloom St CMANE M1 ...6 E6
CSLFD M5 ...6 B5
EDGY/DAV SK3 ...12 B6
RAMS BL0 ...16 B4
Blossom St ANC M4 ...7 H3
Blossom St PART M31 ...150 D4
Blossoms Hey CHD/CHDH SK8 ...182 D5
Blossoms La BRAM/HZG SK7 ...192 D5
Blossoms St ANC M4 ...7 H3
Blucher St AULW OL7 ...104 D4
ORD M5 ...112 B4
WGTN/LGST M12 ...128 B2
Blue Bell Av NEWH/MOS M40 ...101 H1
Bluebell Cl HYDE SK14 ...133 E5
Bluebell Dr WHIT OL12 ...29 H1
Bluebell Gv CHD/CHDH SK8 ...170 A5
Blueberry Av WILM/AE SK9 ...199 H1
Blueberry Rd ALT WA14 ...176 D2
Bluefields ROY/SHW OL2 ...60 C1
Blue Ribbon Wk SWIN M27 ...97 F1
Bluestone Dr HTNM SK4 ...158 B2
Bluestone Rd DTN/ASHW M34 ...145 F1
NEWH/MOS M40 ...101 H2
Blundell Cl BURY BL9 ...69 E1
Blundell St HULME M15 ...2 D4
Blundering La STLY SK15 ...134 A2
Blunn St OLDS OL8 ...90 D5
Blyborough Cl SLFD M6 ...111 F1
Blyth Av LIT * OL15 ...20 C5
Blyth Cl HALE/TIMP WA15 ...167 E5
Blythe Av BRAM/HZG SK7 ...184 D4
Blyton St HULME M15 ...127 G3
Boad St CMANE M1 ...7 H5
Boardman Cl BOL BL1 ...33 H4
Boardman Fold Cl MDTN M24 ...87 H2
Boardman Fold Rd MDTN M24 ...87 G2
Boardman La MDTN M24 ...70 C4
Boardman Rd CHH M8 ...86 B5
Boardman St ECC M30 ...108 B3
HYDE SK14 ...147 G1
BOLS/LL BL3 ...2 C7
Boar Green Cl NEWH/MOS M40 ...102 B3
Boarshaw Clough MDTN M24 ...72 B1
Boarshaw Clough Wy MDTN M24 ...72 A2
Boarshaw La MDTN M24 ...72 C1
Boarshaw Rd MDTN M24 ...72 C1
Boat La IRL M44 ...156 D5
WYTH/NTH M22 ...156 D5
Bobbin Wk ANC * M4 ...7 K4
OLDE OL4 ...91 H4
Bob Brook Cl FAIL M35 ...102 A4
Bob Massey Cl OP/CLY M11 ...115 F5
Bob's La IRL M44 ...150 C2
Boddens Hill Rd HTNM SK4 ...158 D5
Boddington Rd ECC M30 ...108 A4
Bodiam Rd TOT/BURYW BL8 ...26 A1
Bodley St OP/CLY M11 ...115 F3
Bodmin Cl ROY/SHW OL2 ...73 F1
Bodmin Crs RDSH SK5 ...145 H2
Bodmin Rd BRAM/HZG SK7 ...183 H5
SALE M33 ...153 G5
Bodney Wk BKLY M9 ...101 G1
Bognor Rd EDGY/DAV SK3 ...171 H5
Bogton Av NTHM/RTH M23 ...155 G5
Boland Dr RUSH/FAL M14 ...143 E3
Bolderod Pl OLD * OL1 ...9 H3
Bolderstone Pl OFTN SK2 ...173 G4
Boldton St AUL * OL6 ...117 H2
BOL BL1 ...33 F5
BURY BL9 ...5 G4
SWIN M27 ...97 H3
Bolesworth Cl CCHDY M21 ...140 C3
Boleyn Ct HEY OL10 ...40 D5

Bolholt Ter TOT/BURYW BL8 ...37 G2
Bolivia St ORD M5 ...110 D3
Bollin Av WA14 ...177 E4
Bollin Cl FWTH BL4 ...81 H1
Bollin Ct HULME M15 ...126 C2
Bollin Dr ALT WA14 ...165 H1
SALE M33 ...154 C4
Bollings Yd BOL BL1 ...3 F5
Bollington Rd HTNM SK4 ...159 G1
NEWH/MOS M40 ...114 A3
Bollington St AULW OL7 ...117 H4
Bollin Hl WILM/AE SK9 ...199 G2
Bollin Sq ALT WA14 ...177 E3
Bollin Wk WHTF M45 ...69 F2
WHTF M45 ...69 G2
Bollinway HALE/TIMP WA15 ...178 B4
Bollinwood Cha WILM/AE SK9 ...200 A3
Bolshaw Farm La CHD/CHDH SK8 ...191 H1
Bolshaw Rd CHD/CHDH SK8 ...191 G1
Bolton Av BNG/LEV M19 ...158 A4
Bolton Cl POY/DIS SK12 ...195 E3
PWCH M25 ...84 C5
Bolton Rd BOLE BL2 ...34 D1
BOLS/LL BL3 ...62 A2
FWTH BL4 ...65 F5
FWTH BL4 ...81 G1
RAD M26 ...51 G5
ROCH OL11 ...41 H2
SLFD M6 ...97 H4
SWIN M27 ...97 F1
TOT/BURYW BL8 ...25 F1
TOT/BURYW BL8 ...52 B1
SWIN M27 ...97 G3
Bolton Rd West RAMS BL0 ...16 B4
Bolton St BURY BL9 ...4 C3
CSLFD M5 ...6 B4
OLDE OL4 ...9 H4
RAD M26 ...67 E1
RAMS BL0 ...16 C2
RDSH SK5 ...144 D4
TOT/BURYW BL8 ...4 A4
Bombay Rd EDGY/DAV SK3 ...171 F2
Bombay St AUL OL6 ...96 C1
CMANE M1 ...7 G7
Bonar Cl EDGY/DAV * SK3 ...12 A6
Bonar Rd EDGY/DAV SK3 ...12 A6
Boncarn Dr NTHM/RTH M23 ...167 H5
Bonchurch Wk WGTN/LGST M12 ...129 E2
Bondmark Rd GTN M18 ...129 F2
Bond Sq BRO * M7 ...99 H4
Bond St DTN/ASHW M34 ...131 G5
STLY SK15 ...119 F2
WHIT OL12 ...11 K7
Bongs Rd OFTN SK2 ...173 G2
Bonhill Wk OP/CLY M11 ...115 E3
Bonington St NTHM/RTH M23 ...175 G1
Bonis Crs OFTN SK2 ...172 D5
Bonny Brow St MDTN M24 ...70 C5
Bonsall St HULME M15 ...127 E2
Bonscale Crs MDTN M24 ...71 F1
Bonville Cha ALT WA14 ...164 D5
Bonville Rd ALT WA14 ...164 D5
Boodle St AUL OL6 ...118 A1
Boond St ANC M4 ...114 A4
CSLFD M5 ...6 C4
Boonfields EDGW/EG BL7 ...23 F1
Booth Av RUSH/FAL M14 ...143 E4
Booth Bridge Cl MDTN M24 ...71 E1
Boothby Rd SWIN M27 ...96 D1
Boothby St OFTN SK2 ...172 D5
Booth Cl STLY SK15 ...119 F2
TOT/BURYW BL8 ...37 F1
Boothcote DTN/ASHW M34 ...131 E4
Booth Ct URM M41 ...122 C4
Boothfield ECC M30 ...108 D2
Boothfield Rd WYTH/NTH M22 ...168 B3
Boothfields TOT/BURYW BL8 ...37 F2
Booth Hall Dr TOT/BURYW BL8 ...37 F1
Booth Hall Rd BKLY M9 ...87 H4
Booth Hill La OLD OL1 ...74 C2
Booth Rd ALT WA14 ...165 F5
BOLS/LL BL3 ...66 A2
DTN/ASHW M34 ...130 D5
OLDTF/WHR M16 ...126 B5
WALK M28 ...95 F4
Booths Hall Gv WALK M28 ...94 A5
Booth's Hall Rd WALK M28 ...94 A5
Booth's Hall Wy WALK M28 ...94 A5
Boothstown Dr WALK M28 ...94 A5
Booth St AUL * OL6 ...118 A1
BOL BL1 ...33 F5
CHAD OL9 ...8 B3
CMANE M1 ...6 E5
DTN/ASHW M34 ...131 E5
EDGY/DAV SK3 ...12 E4
FAIL M35 ...102 D4
HYDE SK14 ...147 G1
MDTN M24 ...71 E4
OLDE OL4 ...91 H1
STLY SK15 ...119 E3
Booth St East BRUN/LGST M13 ...127 F2
Booth St West HULME M15 ...127 E2
Booth Wy TOT/BURYW BL8 ...37 F2
Bootle St CMANW M2 ...6 D5
Bordale Av BKLY M9 ...103 E1
Bordan St OLDTF/WHR M16 ...125 H3
Borden Wk NTHM/RTH M23 ...155 H5
Border Brook La WALK M28 ...94 B3
Bordesley Av LHULT M38 ...80 B1
Bordley Wk NTHM/RTH M23 ...155 F5
Bordon Rd EDGY/DAV SK3 ...171 G1
Boringdon Cl NEWH/MOS * M40 ...102 A4
Borland Av NEWH/MOS M40 ...102 C1
Borron St STKP SK1 ...13 G1
Borrowdale Av BOL BL1 ...33 H2

CHD/CHDH SK8 ...169 G5
Borrowdale Cl ROY/SHW OL2 ...59 E3
Borrowdale Crs AULW OL7 ...117 G5
ROCH OL11 ...42 A2
Borrowdale Rd MDTN M24 ...71 F2
OFTN SK2 ...172 C2
Borsden St SWIN M27 ...96 C1
Borth Av OFTN SK2 ...172 D2
Borwell St GTN M18 ...129 G2
Boscobel Rd BOLS/LL BL3 ...64 C2
Boscombe Av ECC M30 ...109 F5
Boscombe Dr BRAM/HZG SK7 ...184 C2
Boscombe St RDSH SK5 ...145 E1
RUSH/FAL M14 ...142 C1
Boscow Rd BOLS/LL BL3 ...65 H2
Bosden Av BRAM/HZG SK7 ...185 E1
Bosden Cl WILM/AE SK9 ...192 A2
Bosden Fold STKP SK1 ...13 G5
Bosdin Rd East URM * M41 ...137 F2
Bosdin Rd West URM M41 ...137 F2
Bosley Av DID/WITH M20 ...142 B3
Bosley Cl WILM/AE SK9 ...192 A5
Bosley Dr POY/DIS SK12 ...195 H4
Bosley Rd EDGY/DAV SK3 ...170 D1
Bossall Av BKLY M9 ...87 F3
Bossington Cl OFTN SK2 ...172 D1
Bostock Wk BRUN/LGST * M13 ...127 G1
Boston Cl BRAM/HZG SK7 ...185 G5
FAIL M35 ...103 E1
Boston Ct SALQ M50 ...111 F5
Boston St BOL * BL1 ...33 H4
HULME M15 ...127 E5
HYDE SK14 ...132 D5
OLDS OL8 ...90 C3
Boswell Av DTN/ASHW M34 ...117 E4
Boswell Wy MDTN M24 ...72 D5
Bosworth Cl WHTF M45 ...69 F4
Bosworth Sq ROCH * OL11 ...42 C2
Bosworth St OP/CLY M11 ...114 D5
ROCH OL11 ...42 C2
Botanical Av OLDTF/WHR M16 ...125 H3
Botany Cl HEY OL10 ...40 C3
Botany La AUL OL6 ...118 B3
Botany Rd ECC M30 ...108 D1
MPL/ROM SK6 ...163 E1
Botesworth Gv MILN OL16 ...44 D1
Botham Cl HULME M15 ...127 F3
Bothwell Rd NEWH/MOS * M40 ...113 H2
Bottesford Av DID/WITH M20 ...156 D1
Bottomfield Cl OLD OL1 ...74 D1
Bottomley Side BOL BL1 ...98 B5
Bottom O' Th' Moor BOLE BL2 ...35 E4
OLDE OL4 ...9 K3
Boulden Dr TOT/BURYW BL8 ...37 H1
Boulder Dr NTHM/RTH M23 ...179 H2
Boulderstone Rd STLY SK15 ...119 F1
The Boulevard WILM/AE SK9 ...191 G2
The Boundary SWIN M27 ...82 C5
Boundary Cl MPL/ROM SK6 ...161 H2
STLY SK15 ...106 D4
Boundary Dr BOLE BL2 ...50 D4
Boundary Gdns BOL * BL1 ...74 B4
OLD OL1 ...74 B4
Boundary Gv SALE M33 ...155 G4
Boundary La HULME M15 ...127 F2
Boundary Park Rd OLD OL1 ...73 H3
Boundary Rd CHD/CHDH SK8 ...170 D3
IRL M44 ...121 G5
SWIN M27 ...97 E2
Boundary St BOL BL1 ...33 G4
LIT OL15 ...21 D1
ROCH OL11 ...42 D1
Boundary St East BRUN/LGST M13 ...127 F2
Boundary St West HULME M15 ...127 F2
Boundary Ter WYTH/NTH * M22 ...43 E1
Boundry Gn DTN/ASHW M34 ...131 F3
Bourdon St NEWH/MOS M40 ...114 A2
Bourget St BRO M7 ...99 H3
Bournbrook Av LHULT M38 ...80 B1
Bourne Av SWIN M27 ...97 E3
Bourne Dr NEWH/MOS M40 ...102 A1
Bournelea Av BNG/LEV M19 ...143 G5
Bourne Rd ROY/SHW OL2 ...59 G5
Bourne St CHAD OL9 ...89 G5
HTNM SK4 ...159 H2
WILM/AE SK9 ...199 G4
Bournville Av HTNM SK4 ...159 H2
Bournville Dr TOT/BURYW BL8 ...37 G4
Bournville Gv BNG/LEV M19 ...144 A2
Bourton Cl TOT/BURYW BL8 ...37 G5
Bourton Dr GTN M18 ...129 G4
Bowden Cl HYDE SK14 ...149 F2
ROCH OL11 ...57 G1
Bowden La MPL/ROM SK6 ...174 D2
Bowden Rd SWIN M27 ...96 D1
BRAM/HZG SK7 ...185 H1
DTN/ASHW M34 ...131 F5
Bowdon Av RUSH/FAL M14 ...142 A2
Bowdon Rd ALT WA14 ...177 E4
Bowen Cl BRAM/HZG SK7 ...194 A2
Bowen St BOL BL1 ...33 G5
Bower Av HTNM SK4 ...159 F5
HYDE SK14 ...148 A4
Bower Ct HYDE SK14 ...148 A4
Bowerfield Av BRAM/HZG SK7 ...185 F2
Bowerfield Crs BRAM/HZG SK7 ...185 F2
Bowerfield La HTNM SK4 ...12 C1
Bower Gdns STLY SK15 ...120 A5
Bower La CHD/CHDH SK8 ...181 F5
Bower Rd HALE/TIMP WA15 ...166 A4
Bowers Av URM M41 ...123 E5
Bowers St RUSH/FAL M14 ...143 E3
Bower St BRO * M7 ...99 H3
BURY BL9 ...4 D2
NEWH/MOS M40 ...101 G5
OLD OL1 ...75 E4
RDSH SK5 ...145 G2
Bower Ter DROY M43 ...145 E2
Bowery Av CHD/CHDH SK8 ...192 C1
Bowes St RUSH/FAL M14 ...127 H5

Bowfell Dr MPL/ROM SK6 ....186 D4
Bowfell Gv BKLY M9 ....86 C4
Bowfell Rd URM M41 ....138 A1
Bowgreave Av BOLE BL2 ....50 C2
Bow Green Rd ALT WA14 ....176 D3
Bowgreen Wk HULME M15 ......126 C2
Bowker Av DTN/ASHW M54 ......146 D5
Bowker Bank Av CHH M8 ....86 A5
Bowker Cl ROCH OL11 ....28 B2
Bowkers Rw BOL BL1 ....3 F5
Bowker St BRO M7 ....99 G4
   HYDE SK14 ....132 D5
   RAD M26 ....67 F1
   WALK M28 ....80 C4
Bowlacre Rd HYDE SK14 ....147 G5
Bowland Av BOLE BL2 ....130 B4
Bowland Cl AUL OL6 ....105 F5
   OFTN SK2 ....173 F4
   ROY/SHW OL2 ....59 F2
   TOT/BURYW BL8 ....36 D3
Bowland Dr BOL BL1 ....32 B4
Bowland Gv MILN OL16 ....44 B4
Bowland Rd DTN/ASHW M54 .....130 C5
   MPL/ROM SK6 ....162 A1
   NTHM/RTH M23 ....167 G3
Bow Le La ALT WA14 ....176 D4
   CMANW M2 ....6 E5
   HEY OL10 ....40 D4
Bowler Cl WHIT M45 ....68 D3
Bowler St BNG/LEV M19 ....144 A3
   ROY/SHW OL2 ....60 A2
Bowlers Wk WHIT OL12 ....30 A1
Bowley Av WYTH/NTH M22 ......179 H2
Bowling Green St HEY OL10 ......41 E4
   HYDE SK14 ....147 F1
Bowling Green Wy ROCH OL11 ...28 C5
Bowling Rd DTN M18 ....129 H5
Bowling St CHAD OL9 ....89 G5
Bowman Cl WHIT OL12 ....118 C2
Bow Meadow Gra
   WGTN/LGST M12 ....128 C4
Bowmont Cl CHD/CHDH SK8 .....170 D5
Bowness Av CHD/CHDH SK8 .....183 E3
   HTNM SK4 ....144 D5
   IRL M44 ....150 C2
   WHIT OL12 ....29 F2
Bowness Dr SALE M33 ....154 A1
Bowness Rd AULW OL7 ....117 C1
   BOLS/LL BL3 ....53 C5
   BOLS/LL BL3 ....40 A5
   MDTN M24 ....71 E3
Bowness St OP/CLY M11 ....130 A1
   STRET M32 ....125 E5
Bowring Rd BRO * M7 ....99 F5
Bowscale Cl BRUN/LGST M13 ...128 C4
Bowstone Hill Rd BOLE BL2 ......36 A1
Bow St BOL BL1 ....2 E4
   CMANW M2 ....6 D5
   DUK SK16 ....118 B3
   EDGY/DAV SK3 ....12 A5
   OLD OL1 ....9 G4
   ROCH OL11 ....42 C3
Boxgrove Rd SALE M33 ....154 A4
Boxhill Dr NTHM/RTH * M23 .....155 H5
Box St LIT OL15 ....20 D3
   RAMS * BL0
Boxtree Av GTN M18 ....129 C5
Boyd St WGTN/LGST M12 ....128 D2
Boyd's Wk DUK SK16 ....132 B1
Boyer St OLDTF/WHR M16 ....106 A5
Boyle St BOL BL1 ....32 D5
   OLD OL1 ....100 C4
Boysnope Whf ECC M30 ....122 A4
Brabant Rd CHD/CHDH SK8 .....183 E2
Brabham Cl CCHDY M21 ....141 E3
Brabham Ms SWIN M27 ....96 A5
Brabyns Av MPL/ROM SK6 ......162 C3
Brabyns Brow MPL/ROM SK6 ...175 F2
Brabyns Rd HYDE SK14 ....147 H4
Bracadale Dr EDGY/DAV SK3 ...171 H5
Bracewell Cl WGTN/LGST M12 ..128 D3
Bracken Av WALK M28 ....81 F4
Bracken Cl BOL BL1 ....22 C5
   DROY M43 ....116 D5
   HEY OL10 ....56 A1
   MPL/ROM SK6 ....175 H2
   OLDE OL4 ....92 A1
Bracken Dr NTHM/RTH M23 .....168 A4
Brackenhurst Av MOSL OL5 .....107 F1
Bracken Lea Fold WHIT OL12 .....29 E1
Brackenlea Pl EDGY/DAV SK3 ...171 G4
Brackenside RDSH SK5 ....145 F5
Brackenwood Cl ROY/SHW OL2 ...75 H2
Brackenwood Dr
   CHD/CHDH SK8 ....170 A5
Brackenwood Ms WILM/AE SK9 ..193 ?
Brackley Av HULME M15 ....126 C1
   IRL M44 ....135 C5
Brackley Dr MDTN M24 ....87 H2
Brackley Ldg ECC * M30 ....110 C4
Brackley Rd ECC M30 ....110 C4
   HTNM SK4 ....159 G1
   WHTN BL5 ....62 D4
Brackley Sq OLD * OL1 ....9 K1
Brackley St FWTH BL4 ....65 E4
   OLD * OL1 ....9 G1
   WALK M28 ....80 D3
Bracondale Av BOL BL1 ....33 E4
Bradbourne Cl BOLS/LL BL3 .....48 D4
Bradburn Cl ECC M30 ....109 G4
Bradburn Rd IRL M44 ....135 D4
Bradburn St ECC M30 ....109 G4
Bradburn Wk CHH M8 ....M4
Bradbury Av ALT WA14 ....164 D4
Bradbury St AULW * OL7 ....117 H1
   HYDE SK14 ....147 H2
   RAD M26 ....67 F2
Bradda Mt BRAM/HZG SK7 .....184 D5
Braddan Av SALE M33 ....154 D3
Bradden Cl ORD M5 ....111 H4
Braddocks Cl WHIT OL12 ....20 A4
Braddon Av URM M41 ....123 C5
Braddon Rd MPL/ROM SK6 .....161 H1
Braddon St OP/CLY M11 ....115 F2
Braddyll Rd WHTN BL5 ....62 C4
Brade Cl OP/CLY M11 ....115 F5
Bradfield Av SLFD M6 ....110 D3
Bradfield Cl RDSH SK5 ....145 G4
Bradfield Rd URM M41 ....139 E1
Bradford Av BOLS/LL BL3 ....64 C1
Bradford Crs BOLS/LL * BL3 .....49 F5
Bradford Park Dr BOLE BL2 ....3 K6
Bradford Rd BOLS/LL BL3 ....64 B2

ECC M30 ....109 H1
   NEWH/MOS M40 ....114 B2
Bradford St BOLE BL2 ....3 H5
   FWTH BL4 ....65 E5
   OLD OL1 ....74 B4
Bradford Ter BURY BL9 ....4 B7
Bradgate Av CHD/CHDH SK8 ....182 A5
Bradgate Cl WYTH/NTH M22 ....168 D1
Bradgate Rd ALT WA14 ....164 D4
   SALE M33 ....154 C4
Bradgate St AULW OL7 ....117 H4
Bradgreen Rd ECC M30 ....109 F2
Bradley Av BRO M7 ....99 E3
Bradley Cl HALE/TIMP WA15 ....165 H2
Bradley Dr BURY BL9 ....69 E2
Bradley Fold STLY SK15 ....119 G3
Bradley Fold Rd BOLE BL2 ....51 E3
Bradley Green Rd HYDE SK14 ...133 E2
Bradley La BOLS/LL BL3 ....51 E4
   MILN OL16 ....45 E2
   STRET M32 ....139 G4
Bradleys Count CMANE * M1 .....7 H4
Bradley Smithy Cl WHIT OL12 ...29 H1
Bradley St CMANE M1 ....7 H5
   MILN OL16 ....45 E2
Bradley Cl BKLY M9 ....86 C5
Bradnor Rd NTHM/RTH M23 ....168 C2
Bradshaw Av DID/WITH M20 ....142 C4
   NEWH/MOS M40 ....102 D5
   WHTF M45 ....68 C4
Bradshaw Brow BOLE BL2 ....34 C3
   BOLE BL2 ....34 D2
Bradshaw Crs MPL/ROM SK6 ...175 F2
Bradshaw Fold Av
   NEWH/MOS M40 ....88 C4
Bradshawgate BOL BL1 ....3 F5
Bradshaw Hall Fold BOLE BL2 ...23 H5
Bradshaw Hall Fold BOLE * BL2 ..24 A5
Bradshaw Hall La
   CHD/CHDH SK8 ....182 A4
Bradshaw La STRET M32 ....140 A3
Bradshaw Mdw BOLE BL2 ....24 A5
Bradshaw Rd BOLE BL2 ....24 A5
   MPL/ROM SK6 ....175 G2
   TOT/BURYW BL8 ....25 F5
Bradshaw St ANC * M4 ....7 F2
   BRO M7
   FWTH BL4 ....65 E5
   HEY OL10 ....41 F4
   OLD OL1 ....9 H3
   RAD M26 ....67 E1
Bradshaw St North BRO M7 ......7 G1
Bradstock Rd OLDTF/WHR M16 ..126 D5
Bradstone Rd CHH M8 ....100 A5
Bradwell Av DID/WITH M20 .....142 A5
   STRET M32 ....124 D5
Bradwell Dr CHD/CHDH SK8 ....181 H5
Bradwell Fld BOLE BL2 ....34 C5
Bradwell Rd BRAM/HZG SK7 ....185 F4
Bradwen Av CHH M8 ....100 B1
Bradwen Cl DTN/ASHW M54 ....146 D2
Bradwen St STKP SK1 ....13 J1
Braemar Av STRET M32 ....139 F1
   URM M41 ....137 H2
Braemar Dr BURY BL9 ....39 F4
   SALE M33 ....155 F4
Braemar Gv HEY OL10 ....40 B5
Braemar La WALK M28 ....94 C4
Braemar Rd BRAM/HZG SK7 ....185 G1
   RUSH/FAL M14 ....143 F5
Braemore Cl ROY/SHW OL2 ......59 F1
Braemore Dr HYDE SK14 ....149 G2
Brae Side OLDS OL8 ....90 B5
Braeside STRET * M32 ....159 F3
Braeside Cl OFTN SK2 ....173 G4
Braeside Gv BOLS/LL BL3 ....47 F4
Braewood Cl BURY BL9 ....39 F3
Bragenham Gt GTN M18 ....129 F5
Brailsford Rd BOLE BL2 ....34 D3
   RUSH/FAL M14 ....143 F5
Braintree Rd WYTH/NTH M22 ...168 D4
Braithwaite Rd MDTN M24 ......56 A5
Brakehouse Cl MILN OL16 ....31 F5
Brakenhurst Dr BRO * M7 ......100 A4
Brakesmere Gv LHULT M38 ......80 A5
Braley St CMANE * M1 ....7 G4
Bramall Cl BURY BL9 ....69 E2
Bramall St HYDE SK14 ....132 C4
Bramble Av OLDE OL4 ....75 G5
   ORD M5 ....126 B1
Bramble Cl LIT OL15 ....20 D3
Brambling Cl DTN/ASHW M54 ...116 D3
   TOT/BURYW BL8 ....25 H4
Bramcote Av BOLE BL2 ....49 G4
   NTHM/RTH M23 ....168 A3
Bramdean Av BOLE BL2 ....35 F1
Bramfield Wk HULME * M15 ....126 C1
Bramhall Cl BURY BL9 ....27 G5
   HALE/TIMP WA15 ....167 E5
   MILN OL16 ....31 F5
   SALE M33 ....155 F3
Bramhall La South
   BRAM/HZG SK7 ....183 H2
   BRAM/HZG SK7 ....193 H1
   OFTN SK2 ....172 A5
Bramhall Moor La
   BRAM/HZG SK7 ....184 C3
Bramhall Park Rd
   BRAM/HZG SK7 ....183 F3
Bramhall St BOLS/LL BL3 ....64 D5
   GTN * M18 ....129 H3
Bramham Rd MPL/ROM SK6 ....175 E5
Bramley Av BNG/LEV M19 ......144 C3
   STRET M32 ....139 C1
Bramley Cl BRAM/HZG SK7 .....193 H1
   SWIN M27 ....96 B4
Bramley Crs HTNM SK4 ....159 E5
Bramley Dr BRAM/HZG SK7 ....193 H1
   TOT/BURYW BL8 ....26 D3
Bramley Meade BRO M7 ....99 H3
Bramley Rd BRAM/HZG SK7 ....193 H1
   ROCH OL11 ....28 A3
Bramley St BRO M7 ....99 H5
Brammay Dr TOT/BURYW BL8 ...26 D1
Brampton Rd BOLS/LL BL3 ......62 D1
   BRAM/HZG SK7 ....193 H2
Bramway BRAM/HZG SK7 ....183 F5
   MPL/ROM SK6 ....187 G5
Bramwell Dr BRUN/LGST M13 ...127 H2
Bramwell St STKP SK1 ....172 C1
Bramworth Av RAMS BL0 ....16 C2

Brancaster Rd CMANE M1 ......127 F1
Branch Cl TOT/BURYW BL8 ....4 B2
Branch Rd LIT OL15 ....31 F2
Brandish Cl BRUN/LGST M13 ...128 A4
Brandle Av TOT/BURYW BL8 .....37 H2
Brandlehow Dr MDTN M24 ......70 D2
Brandlesholme Rd
   TOT/BURYW BL8 ....26 D5
Brandon Av CHD/CHDH SK8 ....181 G3
   DTN/ASHW M34 ....130 A5
   ECC M30 ....110 B1
   WYTH/NTH M22 ....168 B1
Brandon Brow OLD * OL1 ....74 B4
Brandon Cl TOT/BURYW BL8 ....38 A1
   WILM/AE SK9 ....192 A5
Brandon Crs ROY/SHW OL2 ......59 H1
Brandon Rd SLFD M6 ....97 G5
Brandon St BOLS/LL BL3 ....48 C5
   MILN OL16 ....31 F5
Brandram Rd PWCH * M25 ......111 H5
Brandsby Gdns ORD * M5 ......125 H5
Brandwood Cl WALK M28 ....80 A4
Brandwood St BOLS/LL BL3 .....48 B5
Branfield Av CHD/CHDH SK8 ....182 A3
Branksome Av PWCH M25 ....86 C1
Branksome Dr BKLY M9 ....85 H2
   CHD/CHDH SK8 ....170 C5
   SLFD M6 ....97 F5
Branksome Rd HTNM SK4 ......159 E5
Brannach Dr CHAD OL9 ....73 F4
Bransby Av BKLY M9 ....85 H2
Branscombe Dr SALE M33 ......153 F1
Branscombe Gdns BOLS/LL * BL3 ..50 A4
Bransdale Av ROY/SHW OL2 .....58 D5
Bransdale Cl BOLS/LL BL3 ....47 G5
Bransford Rd OP/CLY M11 ......115 C5
   URM M41 ....123 F5
Branson St NEWH/MOS M40 ....114 A3
Branson Wk HALE/TIMP WA15 ..166 D3
Branson St NEWH/MOS M40 .....88 C5
Brantfell Gv BOLE BL2 ....24 A5
Brantingham Rd CCHDY M21 ...141 E2
Brantwood Cl ROY/SHW OL2 ....58 D5
Brantwood Dr BOLE BL2 ....50 C1
Brantwood Rd BRO M7 ....99 F2
   CHD/CHDH SK8 ....182 C3
   HTNM SK4 ....159 F2
Brantwood Ter BKLY * M9 ......101 G3
Brassey St AUL OL6 ....118 A1
   MDTN M24 ....71 H1
Brassica Cl ECC M30 ....108 D1
Brassington Av CCHDY M21 ....112 A5
Brassington Rd HTNM SK4 ......158 B2
Bratheay Cl BOLE BL2 ....24 A5
Bratton Wk BRUN/LGST * M13 ..128 A2
Brattray Dr MDTN M24 ....71 F1
Braunston Cl ECC M30 ....109 H5
Bray Av ECC M30 ....109 E2
Braybrook Dr BOL BL1 ....47 E2
Bray Cl CHD/CHDH SK8 ....182 B5
Brayford Rd WYTH/NTH M22 ...180 C3
Brayshaw Cl HEY OL10 ....40 C5
Brayside Rd DID/WITH M20 .....143 G2
Braystan Gdns CHD/CHDH SK8 ..169 G3
Brayston Fold MDTN M24 ....70 D4
Brayton Av DID/WITH M20 .....157 H4
   SALE M33 ....153 C1
Brazennose St CSLFD M5 ....5 G5
Brazil St CMANE M1 ....7 G7
Brazley Av BOLS/LL BL3 ....64 B1
Breach House La KNUT WA16 ...188 A5
Bread St GTN M18 ....129 H2
Breckland Cl STLY SK15 ....119 E3
Breckland Dr BOL BL1 ....47 E1
Breckles Pl BOLS/LL * BL3 ....48 C4
Breck Rd ECC M50 ....109 E3
Brecon Av BNG/LEV M19 ......143 G3
   CHD/CHDH SK8 ....182 B5
   DTN/ASHW M34 ....146 C2
   URM M41 ....122 A5
Brecon Cl ROY/DIS SK12 ....195 H5
Brecon Crs AUL OL6 ....105 E4
Brecon Dr BURY BL9 ....39 F4
Brecon Wk OLDS * OL8 ....89 G5
Bredbury Dr FWTH BL4 ....65 H1
Bredbury Gn MPL/ROM SK6 ....161 H5
Bredbury Park Wy
   MPL/ROM SK6 ....161 F1
Bredbury Rd RUSH/FAL M14 ...142 C1
Bredbury St CHAD OL9 ....90 A2
   HYDE * SK14 ....132 C3
Breeze Hill Rd OLDE OL4 ....91 G2
Breeze Mt PWCH M25 ....85 E5
Breightmet Dr BOLE BL2 ....50 B2
Breightmet Fold La BOLE BL2 ...35 G5
Breightmet St BOLE BL2 ....3 J3
Brellafield Dr ROY/SHW OL2 .....44 C5
Brenbar Crs WHIT OL12 ....29 H2
Brenchley Dr NTHM/RTH M23 ..155 H4
Brencon Av SALE M33 ....154 D5
Brendall Cl OFTN SK2 ....173 H4
Brendon Av NEWH/MOS M40 ...101 H5
Brendon Dr DTN/ASHW M34 ....117 E4
Brendon Hills ROY/SHW OL2 ....73 H1
Brennan Cl HULME M15 ....127 F3
Brennan Ct OLDS OL8 ....90 D5
Brennock Cl OP/CLY M11 ......114 A1
Brentbridge Rd RUSH/FAL M14 ..142 C3
Brent Cl BOLE BL2 ....51 E4
   POY/DIS SK12 ....194 D3
Brentfield Av CHH M8 ....100 A3
Brentford Av BOL BL1 ....33 F2
Brentford Rd RDSH SK5 ....145 E5
Brentford St BKLY M9 ....86 C1
Brent Moor Rd BRAM/HZG SK7 ..184 B1
Brentnall St STKP SK1 ....13 G5
Brenton Av SALE M33 ....154 B2
Brent Rd HTNM SK4 ....159 E4
   NTHM/RTH M23 ....155 H4
Brentwood SALE M33 ....154 B4
   SLFD M6 ....111 F2
Brentwood Av ALT WA14 ....165 H2
   IRL M44 ....150 D2
   URM M41 ....138 C1
   WALK M28 ....96 A4
Brentwood Cl HTNM SK4 ....13 G2
   OLDE OL4 ....92 A1
   ROCH OL11 ....28 A5
   STLY SK15 ....119 E4

STLY SK15 ....119 H3
Brentwood Ct PWCH M25 ....84 C4
Brentwood Crs ALT WA14 ......165 H5
Brentwood Dr CHD/CHDH SK8 ..169 G3
   ECC M30 ....109 G1
   FWTH BL4 ....64 A4
Brentwood Rd SWIN M27 ....97 H3
Brereton Cl ALT WA14 ....177 F3
Brereton Dr WALK M28 ....95 G3
Brereton Gv IRL M44 ....135 D5
Brereton Rd ECC M30 ....108 C4
   WILM/AE SK9 ....192 B4
Breslyn St CSLFD M5 ....6 E1
Brethren's Ct DROY M43 ....116 B5
Bretland Gdns HYDE SK14 .....149 F2
Brettargh St SLFD M6 ....111 H1
Brett Rd WALK M28 ....95 F2
Brewer's Gn BRAM/HZG SK7 ...185 E1
Brewer St CMANE M1 ....7 H4
Brewerton Rd OLDE OL4 ....91 F2
Brewery St ALT WA14 ....165 G5
Brewster St BKLY * M9 ....101 G2
   MDTN M24 ....71 H1
Brian Av DROY M43 ....116 B4
Brian Redhead Ct HULME M15 ..126 D1
Brian Rd FWTH BL4 ....64 A3
Brian St ROCH OL11 ....42 A4
Briaracre Ter AUL * OL6 ....105 F2
Briar Av BRAM/HZG SK7 ....185 G2
   GOL/RIS/CU WA3 ....150 A4
   OLDE OL4 ....92 C1
Briar Cl SALE M33 ....153 F2
   URM M41 ....122 D5
   WHIT OL12 ....30 B5
Briar Crs WYTH/NTH M22 ......168 D4
Briardene DTN/ASHW * M54 ....131 H4
Briardene Gdns
   WYTH/NTH M22 ....168 D5
Briarfield EDGW/EG BL7 ....23 E2
Briarfield Rd CHD/CHDH SK8 ...183 E1
   HALE/TIMP WA15 ....166 D3
   HTNM SK4 ....144 D5
   UPML OL3 ....77 H2
   WALK M28 ....95 G3
Briar Gv CHAD OL9 ....89 H5
   MPL/ROM SK6 ....161 H1
Briar Hill Av LHULT M58 ....79 D3
Briar Hill Cl LHULT M58 ....79 D3
Briar Hill Gv LHULT M58 ....79 D3
Briar Hill Wy SLFD * M6 ....111 H2
Briar Hollow HTNM SK4 ....159 E5
Briarlands Av SALE M33 ....153 F2
Briarlands Cl BRAM/HZG SK7 ..193 C1
Briarlea Gdns BNG/LEV M19 ...158 B1
Briarley Gdns MPL/ROM SK6 ...147 F5
Briarmere Wk CHAD OL9 ....8 A2
Briars Mt HTNM SK4 ....158 D4
Briars Pk CHD/CHDH SK8 ......183 F3
Briarstead Cl BRAM/HZG SK7 ..183 H1
Briar St BOLE * BL2 ....29 G5
   ROCH OL11 ....29 C5
Briarwood WILM/AE SK9 ....199 H5
Briarwood Av DROY M43 ....115 H3
   NTHM/RTH M23 ....167 E1
Briarwood Cha CHD/CHDH * SK8 ..183 E3
Briarwood Crs MPL/ROM SK6 ..185 E3
Briarwood Dr HEY OL10 ....40 C5
Brice St DUK SK16 ....118 A5
Brichfield St MILN OL16 ....30 C1
Brickhill La HALE/TIMP WA15 ..188 C4
Brickkiln Rw ALT WA14 ....177 F5
Brickley St CSLFD M3 ....113 F2
Brick St ANC * M4 ....7 H3
   BURY BL9 ....5 F3
Bridcam St CHH M8 ....100 A5
Briddon St CSLFD M5 ....113 H3
Brideoake St OLDE OL4 ....75 H4
Bridestowe Av HYDE SK14 .....133 H5
Bridge Av MPL/ROM SK6 ....161 H1
Bridge Bank Rd LIT OL15 ....20 C5
Bridge Cl PART M31 ....151 F5
   RAD M26 ....67 G2
Bridgecrest Ct CHD/CHDH * SK8 ..182 D2
Bridge Dr CHD/CHDH SK8 ......169 F5
   WILM/AE SK9 ....192 A4
Bridgefield Crs OLDE OL4 ....92 A1
Bridgefield Dr BURY BL9 ....9 F1
Bridgefield St RAD M26 ....67 G1
   ROCH OL11 ....29 G4
   STKP SK1 ....13 F5
Bridgefold Rd ROCH OL11 ....41 H2
Bridgeford St BRUN/LGST M13 ...6 E7
Bridge Gv HALE/TIMP WA15 ...166 A2
Bridge Hall Dr BURY BL9 ....39 F4
Bridge Hall La BURY BL9 ....39 E4
Bridge La BRAM/HZG SK7 ......184 B3
Bridgelea Ms DID/WITH M20 ...142 C5
Bridgelea Rd DID/WITH M20 ...142 C5
Bridgeman St BOLS/LL BL3 .....48 D5
   FWTH BL4 ....65 E5
Bridgemere Cl RAD M26 ....52 D5
Bridgend Cl CHD/CHDH SK8 ....182 B5
   WGTN/LGST M12 ....128 D2
Bridgenorth Av URM M41 ......139 E1
Bridge Rd BURY BL9 ....5 G1
   HALE/TIMP * WA15 ....166 D2
Bridges Av BURY BL9 ....53 G4
Bridges Ct BOL * BL1 ....5 G5
Bridge St BOL BL1 ....2 E4
   BURY BL9 ....5 F4
   DROY M43 ....115 H5
   DUK SK16 ....131 H2
   FWTH BL4 ....65 E4
   HYDE SK14 ....148 A1
   MDTN * M24 ....71 H4
   MILN OL16 ....30 C5
   OLD OL1 ....9 J4
   OLDE OL4 ....92 A1
   RAD M26 ....67 G2
   RAMS BL0 ....16 D2
   ROCH OL11 ....29 F5
   ROY/SHW * OL2 ....60 A2
   STKP SK1 ....13 G2
   STLY SK15 ....119 E4

SWIN M27 ....97 F2
   UPML OL3 ....78 A5
   WHIT * OL12 ....14 B4
   WHIT OL12 ....19 H5
Bridge St Brow STKP SK1 ....13 C1
Bridge St W BOL BL1 ....2 D4
Bridge Ter ROY/SHW OL2 ....75 F4
Bridgeview Cl ECC M30 ....109 C1
Bridgewater Cir TRPK M17 ......123 F2
Bridgewater Pl ANC * M4 ....7 F4
Bridgewater Rd ALT WA14 .....165 G2
   SWIN M27 ....97 G3
   WALK M28 ....94 B3
Bridgewater St BOL BL1 ....2 A6
   CSLFD M5 ....112 D2
   ECC M30 ....109 E3
   FWTH BL4 ....65 E4
   LHULT M58 ....81 C3
   OLD OL1 ....9 J1
   SALE M33 ....154 C1
   STRET * M32 ....140 B3
Bridgewater Vlad
   HULME * M15 ....126 D1
Bridgewater Wy
   OLDTF/WHR M16 ....126 A3
Bridgnorth Rd BKLY M9 ....86 D5
Bridle Cl DROY M43 ....116 D2
   URM M41 ....137 F1
Bridle Fold RAD M26 ....52 B5
Bridle Rd BRAM/HZG SK7 .....194 A4
   PWCH M25 ....84 A5
Bridle Wy BRAM/HZG SK7 .....194 A3
Bridlington Av SLFD * M6 ......110 D2
Bridlington Cl NEWH/MOS M40 ..102 B4
Bridport Av NEWH/MOS M40 ...102 C2
Bridson La BOLE BL2 ....75 F5
   SLFD M6 ....111 F4
Brief St BOLE BL2 ....34 C4
Brien Av ALT WA14 ....165 G5
Briercliffe Cl GTN M18 ....129 F2
Briercliffe Rd BOLS/LL BL3 ......48 B4
Brierfield Dr BURY BL9 ....27 H5
Brierfield Rd BURY BL9 ....27 D2
Brierholme Av EDGW/EG BL7 ...22 D2
Brierley Av FAIL M35 ....103 F3
   WHTF M45 ....68 B2
Brierley Cl DTN/ASHW M34 .....146 B1
Brierley Rd East SWIN M27 ......96 D1
Brierley Rd West SWIN M27 ......96 D1
Brierley St BURY BL9 ....53 F1
   CHAD OL9 ....8 D1
   DUK * SK16 ....10 A4
   HEY OL10 ....41 E4
   OLDS OL8 ....90 C4
   STKP SK1 ....13 H2
Brierton Dr WYTH/NTH M22 ....180 A3
Brierwood Cl WHIT OL12 ....30 A5
Briery Av BOLE BL2 ....24 A5
Brigade St BOL BL1 ....34 D5
Brigadier Cl DID/WITH M20 ....142 C5
Brigantine Cl ORD M5 ....111 H5
Briggs Cl SALE M33 ....153 F5
Briggs Fold Cl EDGW/EG BL7 ...22 D1
Briggs Fold Rd EDGW/EG BL7 ..22 D1
Briggs Rd STRET * M32 ....125 E4
Briggs St CSLFD M3 ....6 A1
Brigham St OP/CLY M11 ....115 F5
Brightman St BOLS/LL BL3 ......48 D5
Brightman St GTN M18 ....129 G2

Brighton Av BNG/LEV M19 ......143 G4
   BOL BL1 ....32 D5
   RDSH SK5 ....145 G2
   URM M41 ....122 B5
Brighton Gv HYDE SK14 ....147 H2
   RUSH/FAL M14 ....143 E1
   SALE M33 ....154 A1
   URM M41 ....122 B5
   URM M41 ....137 F1
Brighton Pl BRUN/LGST M13 ...127 G2
Brighton Range GTN * M18 .....130 A4
Brighton Rd HTNM SK4 ....13 H3
   OLDE OL4 ....76 B3
Brighton St ANC M4 ....113 F2
   BURY BL9 ....5 J2
Bright Rd ECC M30 ....109 E2
Brightstone Wk RUSH/FAL M14 ..128 A4
Bright St AUL OL6 ....118 C3
   BURY BL9 ....5 G4
   CHAD OL9 ....8 C6
   DROY M43 ....116 C4
   MILN OL16 ....11 C6
   OLDS OL8 ....8 C6
   RAD M26 ....52 D5
Brightwell Wk ANC * M4 ....7 G3
Brigstock Av GTN M18 ....129 F3
Briksdal Wy HOR/BR BL6 ....46 D2
Brimelow St MPL/ROM SK6 ....160 D3
Brimrod La ROCH OL11 ....42 C1
Brimscombe Av
   WYTH/NTH M22 ....180 B2
Brindale Rd RDSH SK5 ....160 D2
Brindle Cl SLFD M6 ....111 G1
Brindle Heath Rd SLFD M6 .....111 G1
Brindley Av BKLY M9 ....86 C2
   MPL/ROM SK6 ....175 E4
   WALK M28 ....95 H5
Brindley Cl FWTH BL4 ....64 C4
   OLDS OL8 ....105 G1
Brindley St ECC M30 ....109 E2
   SWIN M27 ....97 H3
   WALK M28 ....94 B3
Brinell Dr IRL M44 ....151 E1
Brink's Row HOR/BR BL6
Brinkburn Rd OP/CLY M11
Brinklow Cl OP/CLY M11 ....130 D1
Brinkshaw Av WYTH/NTH M22 ..180 C3
Brinks La BOLE BL2 ....50 D2
Brinksway BOL BL1 ....47 F2
   EDGY/DAV SK3 ....171 G1
Brinnington Crs RDSH SK5 .....160 C2
Brinnington Rd STKP SK5 ....160 C3
Brinsop Sq GTN M18 ....129 E2
Brinsworth Dr CHH M8 ....100 B4
Brinton Wk BRUN/LGST M13 ...127 G2
Briony Av HALE/TIMP WA15 ....179 F1
Briony Cl ROY/SHW OL2 ....74 D1
Brisbane Cl BRAM/HZG SK7 ....194 A3
Brisbane St HULME M15 ....127 G3
Briscoe La NEWH/MOS M40 ...102 A5
Briscoe St OLD OL1 ....9 G1

Bristle St HULME M15 127 F2
Bristol Av AUL OL6 105 E3
BNG/LEV M19 144 A3
BOLE BL2 34 D5
Bristol St BRO M7 99 H3
Bristowe St OP/CLY M11 115 G2
Britain St BURY BL9 53 F3
Britannia Av ROY/SHW OL2 60 B3
Britannia Cl RAD M26 67 F1
Britannia Rd SALE M33 154 C1
Britannia St AULW OL7 117 G5
HEY OL10 40 C4
OLD OL1 9 K2
SLFD M6 98 D4
Britannia Wy BOL BL1 34 B4
Britnall Av WGTN/LGST M12 128 B3
Briton St MILN OL16 11 F4
ROY/SHW OL2 74 B2
Brixham Av CHD/CHDH SK8 182 C5
Brixham Dr SALE M33 138 C5
Brixham Rd OLDTF/WHR M16 126 A4
Brixham Wk BRAM/HZG SK7 183 H5
BRUN/LGST M13 127 H3
Brixton Av DID/WITH M20 142 B5
Broach St BOLS/LL BL3 48 D5
Broadacre STLY SK15 134 B2
Broad Acre WHIT OL12 28 B1
Broadbent Av AUL OL6 105 F4
DUK SK16 118 C5
Broadbent Cl ROY/SHW OL2 59 G4
STLY SK15 107 F4
Broadbent Dr BURY BL9 39 H2
Broadbent Gv HYDE SK14 149 F2
Broadbent Rd OLD OL1 75 F3
Broadbent St HYDE SK14 132 C4
SWIN M27 96 C3
Broadbottom Rd HYDE SK14 149 G1
Broadcarr La MOSL OL5 106 B1
Broadfield Cl DTN/ASHW M34 146 D1
Broadfield Dr LIT OL15 20 C5
Broadfield Gv RDSH SK5 129 H5
Broadfield Rd GTN M18 129 H5
RUSH/FAL M14 127 F5
Broadfield Stile MILN OL16 29 H5
Broadfield St HEY OL10 40 C5
MILN OL16 29 H5
Broadford Rd BOLS/LL BL3 47 G4
Broadgate MDTN M24 88 C1
UPML OL3 77 F3
Broadgate Meadow SWIN * M27 97 E3
Broadgreen Gdns FWTH * BL4 65 E2
Broadhalgh Av ROCH OL11 28 D4
Broadhalgh Rd ROCH OL11 28 D5
Broad Hey MPL/ROM SK6 162 C3
Broad Hill Cl BRAM/HZG SK7 184 B2
Broadhill Rd BNG/LEV M19 143 F5
STLY SK15 119 F1
Broadhurst DTN/ASHW M34 131 H3
Broadhurst Av SWIN M27 83 E4
Broadhurst Ct BOLS/LL BL3 48 C5
Broadhurst Gv AUL OL6 105 F4
Broadhurst St BOLS/LL * BL3 48 C5
EDGY/DAV SK3 171 H2
Broad Ing WHIT * OL12 29 E2
Broadlands Rd SWIN M27 96 B4
Broad La HALE/TIMP WA15 178 C4
MILN OL16 43 H3
Broad Lea URM M41 123 F5
Broadlea Gv WHIT OL12 29 F1
Broadlea Rd BNG/LEV M19 143 F5
Broadley Av WYTH/NTH M22 168 C5
Broadmeadow EDGW/EG BL7 23 G3
Broadmeadow Av
OLDTF/WHR M16 142 A2
Broadmoss Dr BKLY M9 87 H4
Broadmoss Rd BKLY M9 87 H4
Broadmount Ter CHAD * OL9 89 G3
Broadoak Av WALK M28 94 A3
WYTH/NTH M22 168 B4
Broadoak Crs AUL OL6 105 E5
Broad Oak Crs OLDS OL8 90 D5
Broadoak Dr WYTH/NTH M22 168 C4
Broad Oak La BURY BL9 39 F3
DID/WITH M20 169 H1
Broad Oak Pk ECC M30 109 G1
WALK M28 96 A4
Broad Oak Rd FWTH BL4 64 B2
Broadoak Rd AUL OL6 105 E5
BRAM/HZG SK7 184 A2
ROCH OL11 28 B5
WYTH/NTH M22 168 B5
Broadoaks BURY BL9 39 G3
Broadoaks Rd SALE M33 154 B2
URM M41 138 A2
Broad Oak Ter BURY BL9 39 H3
Broad O' Th' La BOL BL1 33 H2
Broad Rd SALE M33 154 D1
Broad Shaw La MILN OL16 44 A4
Broadstone Av OLDE OL4 61 E5
Broadstone Cl PWCH M25 84 D4
WHIT OL12 28 D2
Broadstone Hall Rd North
HTNM SK4 144 C5
Broadstone Hall Rd South
HTNM SK4 144 D5
Broadstone Rd BOLE BL2 35 E1
HTNM SK4 144 C5
Broad St BURY BL9 4 D5
MDTN M24 70 D5
SWIN M27 98 A4
Broad Wk WILM/AE SK9 199 E2
The Broadway MPL/ROM SK6 161 F2
Broadway BRAM/HZG SK7 184 A2
CHD/CHDH SK8 169 H5
DROY M43 116 B5
FAIL M35 102 C2
FWTH BL4 64 B2
HALE/TIMP WA15 178 B3
HYDE SK14 132 A3
IRL M44 136 B2
OFTN SK2 172 D2
PART M31 151 F2
ROY/SHW OL2 74 A2
SALE M33 154 B1
SALQ M50 111 F5
URM M41 122 D4
WALK M28 95 E1
WILM/AE SK9 199 G4
Broadway Av CHD/CHDH SK8 170 A4
Broadway Cl URM M41 123 F4
Broadway North DROY M43 116 B5
Broadway St OLDS OL8 90 C3
Broadwell Dr BKLY M9 101 F3
Broadwood HOR/BR BL6 46 D2
Broadwood Cl MPL/ROM SK6 187 E5
Brocade Cl CSLFD M3 112 C2
Broche Cl ROCH OL11 42 A3
Brock Av BOLE BL2 50 C2
Brock Cl OP/CLY M11 129 G1
Brock Dr CHD/CHDH SK8 182 D4
Brockenhurst Dr BOLE BL2 35 G3
Brockford Dr BKLY M9 87 F2
Brocklebank Rd MILN OL16 31 E4
RUSH/FAL M14 142 D3
Brocklehurst Av BURY BL9 5 F7
Brocklehurst St BKLY M9 101 H2
Brockley Av RUSH/FAL M14 142 C1
Brock St CMANE * M1 7 J4
Brockway MILN OL16 43 H3
Brodick Dr BOLE BL2 50 C3
Brodick St NEWH/MOS M40 101 G2
Brodie Cl ECC M30 109 E3
Brogan St GTN M18 129 G3
Brogden Dr CHD/CHDH SK8 169 G4
Brogden Gv SALE M33 154 B3
Bromborough Av
DID/WITH M20 142 B3
Bromfield WHIT OL12 10 C4
Bromfield Av BKLY M9 101 E1
Bromleigh Av CHD/CHDH SK8 169 G3
Bromley Av ROY/SHW OL2 58 C3
URM M41 137 F2
Bromley Crs AUL OL6 105 E4
Bromley Cross Rd
EDGW/EG BL7 23 G4
Bromley Rd SALE M33 154 D4
Bromley St ANC M4 113 G2
CHAD OL9 89 F5
DTN/ASHW * M34 131 G5
Bromlow St OP/CLY M11 115 F4
Brompton Av FAIL M35 103 G2
Brompton Rd HTNM SK4 158 D4
RUSH/FAL M14 142 C1
STRET M32 124 A5
Brompton St OLDE OL4 9 K6
Bromsgrove Av ECC M30 109 E3
Bromshill Dr BRO M7 99 H4
Bromwich St BOLE BL2 3 H6
Brondgate Meadow SWIN M27 97 E4
Bronington Cl WYTH/NTH M22 168 D2
Bronte Av BURY BL9 53 G3
Bronte Cl BOL BL1 33 G5
OLD OL1 60 C5
WHIT OL12 28 D1
Bronte St HULME M15 127 F3
Bronville Cl OLD OL1 73 H3
Brookash Rd WYTH/NTH M22 181 F4
The Brook LIT OL15 15 B4
Brook Av BNG/LEV M19 144 A1
DROY * M43 115 H4
HALE/TIMP WA15 163 H5
HTNM SK4 159 G1
ROY/SHW OL2 60 A1
SWIN M27 97 E3
UPML OL3 78 A4
WILM/AE SK9 192 A4
Brook Bank BOLE * BL2 35 E3
Brookbank Cl MDTN M24 72 A5
Brook Bottom Rd RAD M26 52 A3
Brookburn Rd CCHDY M21 140 D4
Brook Cl HALE/TIMP WA15 165 H3
WHTF M45 69 E4
Brookcot Rd NTHM/RTH M23 167 G2
Brookcroft Av WYTH/NTH M22 168 C4
Brookcroft Rd WYTH/NTH M22 168 C4
Brookdale WHIT OL12 18 D5
Brookdale Av DTN/ASHW M34 131 F1
MPL/ROM SK6 175 F5
NEWH/MOS M40 115 G1
Brookdale Cl BOL BL1 34 A4
MPL/ROM SK6 161 G3
Brookdale Pk LHULT * M38 80 C1
Brookdale Ri BRAM/HZG SK7 184 A2
Brookdale Rd BRAM/HZG SK7 184 A3
CHD/CHDH SK8 169 E4
Brookdale St FAIL M35 102 C3
Brookdean Cl BOL BL1 33 F3
Brookdene Rd BNG/LEV M19 143 F5
BURY BL9 68 D3
Brook Dr MPL/ROM SK6 175 E5
WHTF M45 69 E4
Brooke Dr WILM/AE SK9 192 B4
Brookes St MDTN M24 72 A2
Brooke Wy WILM/AE * SK9 192 A3
Brook Farm Cl PART M31 150 D5
Brookfield PWCH M25 85 E3
ROY/SHW OL2 44 D5
Brookfield Av BOLE BL2 36 B5
CCHDY M21 141 F4
HALE/TIMP WA15 166 A2
MPL/ROM SK6 161 H2
POY/DIS SK12 194 D4
ROY/SHW OL2 74 A1
SLFD M6 110 D2
STKP SK1 13 K7
URM M41 137 H1
Brookfield Cl STKP SK1 13 K7
Brookfield Crs CHD/CHDH SK8 170 A4
Brookfield Dr HALE/TIMP WA15 166 B2
LIT OL15 20 B2
SWIN M27 96 D1
WALK M28 94 A4
Brookfield Gdns
WYTH/NTH M22 168 C3
Brookfield Gv AUL OL6 118 C3
Brookfield Rd BURY BL9 27 F3
CHD/CHDH SK8 170 B4
CHH M8 100 B1
ECC M30 109 E1
Brookfield St BOLE BL2 3 J4
OLDS OL8 9 G6
Brookfold FAIL M35 102 D2
Brookfold La BOLE BL2 35 G2
Brookfold Rd HTNM SK4 144 C5
Brook Gdns BOLE BL2 35 F2
HEY OL10 40 D4
Brook Green La GTN M18 130 A5
Brook Gv IRL M44 136 B1
Brookhead Av DID/WITH * M20 142 A4
Brookhead Dr CHD/CHDH SK8 170 D4
Brookhey Av BOLS/LL BL3 64 A1
Brook Hey Cl WHIT OL12 20 A4
Brookheys Rd PART M31 152 B2
Brookhill St NEWH/MOS M40 114 B2
Brookhouse Av ECC M30 108 D4
FWTH BL4 80 D1
Brook House Cl BOLE BL2 35 F3
TOT/BURYW BL8 25 H3
Brookhurst La LHULT M38 79 D1
Brookhurst Rd GTN M18 129 G4
Brookland Av DTN/ASHW M34 146 A1
FWTH BL4 64 D5
Brookland Gv BOL BL1 32 D4
The Brooklands HEY OL10 40 D4
Brooklands Av CHAD OL9 89 G2
DID/WITH M20 142 B5
Brooklands Cl HTNM SK4 159 G1
IRL M44 136 A1
MOSL OL5 92 C5
Brooklands Ct ROCH OL11 29 F5
Brooklands Crs SALE M33 154 C3
Brooklands Dr DROY M43 116 D2
OLDE OL4 92 C1
Brooklands Pde OLDE * OL4 92 C1
Brooklands Rd BRAM/HZG SK7 185 F3
NTHM/RTH M23 166 D1
PWCH M25 85 H5
RAMS BL0 26 A1
RDSH SK5 144 D1
SALE M33 154 C3
SWIN M27 96 C4
Brooklands Station Ap
SALE M33 154 B3
Brooklands St ROY/SHW OL2 59 E4
Brookland St MILN * OL16 43 G3
Brook La BURY BL9 53 H4
HALE/TIMP WA15 165 H3
MILN OL16 43 G3
OLDE OL4 91 H1
OLDS OL8 90 D3
UPML OL3 77 G3
WILM/AE SK9 201 A2
Brooklawn Dr DID/WITH M20 157 G2
PWCH M25 85 F1
Brookleigh Rd DID/WITH M20 143 E5
Brooklet Cl OLDE OL4 92 B2
Brooklyn Av LIT OL15 20 D1
MILN OL16 20 A4
OLDTF/WHR M16 141 E1
URM M41 137 F1
Brooklyn Crs CHD/CHDH SK8 170 A4
Brooklyn Rd CHD/CHDH SK8 170 A4
OFTN SK2 172 D3
Brooklyn St BOL BL1 33 H5
OLD * OL1 75 F3
Brook Rd CHD/CHDH SK8 170 A3
HTNM SK4 159 F1
RUSH/FAL M14 142 D4
URM M41 122 D5
Brooks Av BRAM/HZG SK7 185 E1
HYDE SK14 147 H2
RAD M26 52 A3
Brooksbottom Cl RAMS BL0 16 D4
Brooks Dr FAIL M35 102 D4
HALE/TIMP WA15 167 E3
HALE/TIMP WA15 179 F4
Brooks End ROCH OL11 28 B2
Brookshaw St BURY BL9 5 F1
OP/CLY M11 114 D4
Brookside OLDE OL4 91 G1
Brookside Av DROY M43 116 D2
FWTH BL4 64 D5
OFTN SK2 173 F3
OLDE OL4 92 C1
POY/DIS SK12 195 F4
Brookside Cl BOLE BL2 35 E1
CHD/CHDH SK8 170 A5
HYDE SK14 133 F5
RAMS BL0 16 B5
Brookside Crs MDTN M24 88 B1
TOT/BURYW BL8 26 A3
WALK M28 81 F4
Brookside Dr HYDE SK14 133 F5
PWCH M25 99 G1
Brookside La MPL/ROM SK6 186 D5
Brookside Rd BOLE BL2 50 A1
CHD/CHDH SK8 169 F3
NEWH/MOS M40 101 H1
SALE M33 154 B4
Brooksmouth TOT/BURYW BL8 4 A5
Brook's Pl WHIT OL12 10 A4
Brook's Rd OLDTF/WHR M16 126 B5
Brooks St STKP SK1 13 H7
Brookstone Cl CCHDY M21 141 G5
Brook St BOL BL1 2 E4
BRAM/HZG SK7 185 F2
BURY BL9 5 G1
CHAD OL9 73 G4
CHD/CHDH SK8 170 C3
FAIL M35 102 C4
FWTH BL4 65 F3
HYDE SK14 132 D5
LIT OL15 21 F3
OLD OL1 9 K1
RAD M26 65 H5
RAD M26 67 G1
ROY/SHW OL2 74 A1
SALE M33 154 D1
SLFD M6 112 A1
SWIN M27 96 C2
WHIT OL12 19 H2
Brook St East AUL OL6 117 H3
Brook St West AULW OL7 117 H3
Brookthorn Cl OFTN SK2 173 G4
Brookthorpe Av BNG/LEV M19 143 F5
Brookthorpe Rd
TOT/BURYW BL8 37 F3
Brookwater Cl TOT/BURYW BL8 26 A5
Brookway HALE/TIMP WA15 166 A3
OLDE OL4 91 H2
OLDE OL4 93 F1
Brookway Cl BNG/LEV M19 158 B2
Brookwood Av CHH M8 100 D2
SALE M33 153 H3
Brookwood Cl DTN/ASHW M34 146 D4
Broom Av BNG/LEV M19 144 A3
BRO M7 99 H2
RDSH SK5 145 E5
Broome Gv FAIL M35 103 E4
Broomehouse Av IRL M44 135 D3
Broome St CHAD OL9 8 C4
Broomfield SWIN M27 98 A4
Broomfield Cl BOLE BL2 51 F1
RDSH SK5 145 E5
WILM/AE * SK9 200 B2
Broomfield Crs EDGY/DAV SK3 172 B5
MDTN M24 71 E3
Broomfield Dr CHH M8 100 A3
RDSH SK5 145 E5
Broomfield La
HALE/TIMP WA15 177 H2
Broomfield Rd BOLS/LL BL3 48 B4
HTNM SK4 159 F2
Broomfields DTN/ASHW M34 131 H3
Broomfield Sq ROCH * OL11 43 E1
Broomfield Ter MILN OL16 45 E2
Broomgrove La
DTN/ASHW M34 131 H4
Broomhall Rd BKLY M9 86 B2
SWIN M27 98 A4
Broomhill Dr BRAM/HZG SK7 183 G3
Broomhurst Av OLDS OL8 90 A3
Broom La BNG/LEV M19 144 A3
BRO M7 99 G2
Broom Rd HALE/TIMP WA15 177 H1
PART M31 151 E4
Broomstair Rd DTN/ASHW M34 131 G2
Broom St MILN OL16 45 E2
SWIN M27 97 E3
TOT/BURYW BL8 4 A4
Broomville Av SALE M33 154 C2
Broomwood Rd
HALE/TIMP WA15 166 D4
Broomwood Wk HULME * M15 127 E2
Broseley Av DID/WITH M20 158 A3
Broseley Rd OLDTF/WHR M16 140 D1
Brotherdale Cl ROY/SHW OL2 59 E4
Brotherod Hall Rd WHIT OL12 29 F2
Brotherton Cl HULME M15 126 C1
Brotherton Dr CSLFD M3 6 A2
Brougham St STLY SK15 119 E4
WALK M28 80 D4
Broughton Av LHULT M38 80 B3
Broughton Cl MDTN M24 71 E2
Broughton La BRO M7 99 G5
Broughton Rd RDSH SK5 160 A2
SLFD M6 111 H2
Broughton Rd East SLFD M6 112 A1
Broughton St BOL BL1 33 G4
CHH M8 100 A5
CHH M8 113 F1
Broughville Dr DID/WITH M20 169 H1
Brow Av MDTN M24 88 A1
Brow East BOLE BL2 34 D2
Browfield Av ORD M5 126 A1
Browfield Wy OLD OL1 74 B3
Browmere Dr DID/WITH M20 157 E2
Brownacre St DID/WITH M20 142 C5
Brown Bank Rd LIT OL15 20 C5
Browncross St CSLFD M3 6 B4
Brown Edge Rd OLDE OL4 91 H3
Brownhill Dr OLDE OL4 76 B5
Brownhill La UPML OL3 78 A3
Brownhills Cl TOT/BURYW BL8 37 F1
Brownhills Ct CCHDY * M21 141 E3
Brownhill St OP/CLY * M11 114 D5
Browning Av DROY M43 116 B4
Browning Cl BOL BL1 33 G5
Browning Rd MDTN M24 72 A2
OLD OL1 75 E3
RDSH SK5 144 C2
SWIN M27 96 D2
Browning St CSLFD M3 6 A3
HULME M15 126 C2
Brown La CHD/CHDH SK8 181 F3
Brownlea Av DUK SK16 132 B1
Brownley Court Rd
WYTH/NTH M22 168 C4
Brownley Rd WYTH/NTH M22 168 D4
Brown Lodge St LIT OL15 20 C5
Brownlow Av ROY/SHW OL2 74 D1
Brownlow Cl POY/DIS SK12 195 F5
Brownlow Wy BOL BL1 2 C1
Brownside Cl MILN OL16 19 H5
Brown's La WILM/AE SK9 200 B2
Brownslow Wk
BRUN/LGST * M13 127 G1
Browns Rd BOLE BL2 51 E3
Brown St ALT WA14 177 G1
BOL BL1 3 F4
CHAD OL9 73 F5
CSLFD M3 6 C3
FAIL M35 102 D3
HEY OL10 40 D3
LIT OL15 20 D3
MDTN M24 71 H2
OLD OL1 9 K2
RAD M26 52 A3
RAMS BL0 16 C3
SLFD M6 111 G4
STKP SK1 13 F2
WILM/AE SK9 201 B4
Brownsville Rd HTNM SK4 159 E1
Brownville Gv DUK SK16 132 D1
Brownwood Av STKP SK1 160 C5
Brownwood Cl SALE M33 154 D5
Brows Av NTHM/RTH M23 155 H4
Brow St ROCH OL11 43 F2
Broxton Av BOLS/LL BL3 63 E1
Broxton St NEWH/MOS M40 114 C2
Broxwood Cl GTN * M18 129 G3
Bruce St ROCH OL11 42 B2
Brundage Rd WYTH/NTH M22 180 C2
Brundrett Pl SALE M33 154 A2
Brundrett's Rd CCHDY M21 141 E3
Brundrett St STKP SK1 13 K6
Brunel Av ORD M5 112 A4
Brunel Cl STRET M32 140 B1
Brunel St BOL BL1 33 G3
Brunet Wk WGTN/LGST * M12 128 C2
Brunstead Cl NTHM/RTH M23 167 E3
Brunswick Ct BOL BL1 2 D3
Brunswick Rd ALT WA14 165 G2
DID/WITH M20 142 D5
Brunswick Sq OLD * OL1 9 G4
Brunswick St BRUN/LGST M13 127 H2
BURY BL9 4 E2
DUK SK16 118 B5
HEY OL10 40 D4
MILN OL16 11 F4
MOSL OL5 107 E2
OLD OL1 9 D5
ROY/SHW OL2 60 A2
STRET M32 139 H3
Brunton Rd RDSH SK5 145 E5
Brunt St RUSH/FAL M14 127 G5
Bruntwood Av CHD/CHDH SK8 181 F3
Bruntwood La CHD/CHDH SK8 170 B5
Brushes Av STLY SK15 120 A2
Brushes Rd STLY SK15 120 A2
Brussels Rd EDGY/DAV SK3 171 G3
Bruton Av STRET M32 139 G2
Bryan Rd CCHDY M21 141 E1
Bryan St OLDE OL4 75 F3
Bryant Cl BRUN/LGST M13 127 H3
Bryantsfield BOL BL1 47 E3
Bryce St HYDE SK14 132 C4
Brydges Rd MPL/ROM SK6 174 D4
Brydon Av WGTN/LGST M12 127 H1
Brydon Cl SLFD M6 111 G3
Bryndale Gv SALE M33 154 A5
Brynden Av DID/WITH M20 157 H1
Bryn Dr RDSH SK5 160 A1
Brynford Av BKLY M9 86 B2
Bryngs Dr BOLE BL2 35 G2
Brynhall Cl RAD M26 51 H4
Brynheys Cl LHULT M38 80 B2
Bryn Lea Ter BOL BL1 32 C2
Brynorme Rd CHH M8 86 B5
Brynton Rd BRUN/LGST M13 128 B5
Bryn Wk BOL BL1 2 E2
Bryone Dr OFTN SK2 172 C4
Bryony Cl WYTH/NTH M22 180 B3
Buchanan St RAMS BL0 16 C2
SWIN M27 97 E1
Buchan St OP/CLY M11 115 E3
Buckden Rd HTNM SK4 144 C4
Buckfast Av OLDS OL8 91 F3
Buckfast Cl CCHDY M21 141 E2
CHD/CHDH SK8 183 E5
HALE/TIMP WA15 178 C2
POY/DIS SK12 195 E2
Buckfast Rd MDTN M24 56 C5
SALE M33 138 C5
Buckfield Av ORD M5 126 A1
Buckhurst Rd BNG/LEV M19 143 H2
Buckingham Av ORD M5 111 E3
WHTF M45 68 D5
Buckingham Dr DUK SK16 133 E1
TOT/BURYW BL8 52 C1
Buckingham Park Cl
ROY/SHW OL2 60 A1
Buckingham Rd ALT WA14 154 A5
CCHDY M21 141 E2
CHD/CHDH SK8 182 C2
DROY M43 115 H4
IRL M44 135 B5
POY/DIS SK12 195 E3
PWCH * M25 85 E5
STLY SK15 119 F2
STRET M32 125 G3
SWIN M27 83 F5
WILM/AE SK9 199 E4
Buckingham Rd West
HTNM SK4 158 D2
Buckingham St MILN OL16 11 F4
OFTN * SK2 172 B3
ORD M5 111 G4
Buckingham Wy
HALE/TIMP WA15 166 B3
Buckland Av BKLY M9 86 B4
Buckland Gv HYDE SK14 148 B3
Buckland Rd SLFD M6 111 E1
Buck La SALE M33 138 D5
Buckley Av GTN M18 129 F4
Buckley Brook St WHIT OL12 30 C1
Buckley Cha MILN OL16 44 B1
Buckley Cl HYDE SK14 147 H4
Buckley Dr MPL/ROM SK6 161 H5
Buckley Farm La WHIT OL12 19 G5
Buckley Flds WHIT OL12 30 B1
Buckley Hill La MILN OL16 44 B1
Buckley La FWTH BL4 64 D5
PWCH M25 84 B4
WHIT OL12 19 G5
Buckley Rd GTN M18 129 E4
OLDE OL4 75 G4
Buckley Sq FWTH BL4 80 D1
Buckley St BRO M7 112 C1
BURY BL9 5 F2
CHAD OL9 73 F5
DTN/ASHW M34 131 E1
HEY OL10 41 E3
MILN OL16 10 E4
OLDE OL4 91 H2
OP/CLY M11 129 H1
RDSH SK5 144 D1
ROY/SHW OL2 60 B2
STLY SK15 119 E5
UPML OL3 78 A4
Buckley Vw WHIT OL12 19 G5
Bucklow Av PART M31 151 E2
RUSH/FAL M14 142 C2
Bucklow Cl HYDE SK14 149 G2
OLDE OL4 75 H1
Bucklow Dr WYTH/NTH M22 168 D1
Bucklow Vw ALT WA14 176 D1
Buckstones Rd OLD OL1 60 D3
ROY/SHW OL2 45 F5
Buckthorn Cl CCHDY M21 141 G5
HALE/TIMP WA15 167 F4
Buckthorn La ECC M30 108 C4
Buckton Dr STLY SK15 107 F5
Buckton Vale Ms STLY SK15 107 G3
Buckton Vale Rd STLY SK15 120 A1
Buckwood Cl BRAM/HZG SK7 185 H1
Buddleia Gv BRO M7 99 G4
Bude Av RDSH SK5 160 C1
URM M41 138 A3
Bude Cl BRAM/HZG SK7 184 A5
Budsworth Av DID/WITH M20 142 C4
Budworth Rd SALE M33 155 F3
Buersil Av MILN OL16 43 G2
Buersil St MILN OL16 43 G3
Buerton Av BKLY M9 86 B2
Bugle St CMANE * M1 6 C7
Buile Dr BKLY M9 87 G3
Buile Hill Av LHULT M38 80 C3
Buile Hill Dr ORD M5 111 E2
Buile Hill Gv LHULT M38 80 C2
Buile St BRO M7 99 H3
Bulford Av WYTH/NTH M22 180 A2
Bulkeley Rd CHD/CHDH SK8 170 B3
POY/DIS SK12 195 F4
WILM/AE SK9 191 H4
Bulkeley St EDGY/DAV SK3 12 D5
Bullcote Gn ROY/SHW OL2 59 H5
Bullcote La ROY/SHW OL2 60 A5
Buller Ms TOT/BURYW BL8 37 G5
Buller Rd BRUN/LGST M13 143 G1
Buller St BOLS/LL BL3 64 D2
DROY M43 116 C5
OLDE OL4 75 G4
TOT/BURYW BL8 37 H5
Bullfinch Dr BURY BL9 39 E1
Bull Hill Crs RAD M26 67 G4
Bullock St OFTN SK2 172 A2
Bullows Rd LHULT M38 80 A1
Bulteel St BOLS/LL BL3 63 F2

ECC M30 109 E2
Bulwer St MILN OL16 11 F4
The Bungalows
BRAM/HZG * SK7 173 G5
Bunkers Hl PWCH M25 84 B4
Bunkers Hill Rd HYDE SK14 149 F2
Bunkershill Rd MPL/ROM SK6 162 A5
Bunsen St CMANE * M1 7 H4
Bunting Ms WALK M28 94 C2
Bunyan Cl OLD OL1 60 C5
Bunyan St WHIT OL12 10 D3
Bunyard St CHH M8 100 C4
Burbage Rd NTHM/RTH M23 179 H2
Burbridge Cl OP/CLY M11 114 B5
Burchall Fld MILN OL16 11 H6
Burdale Dr SLFD M6 110 C1
Burder St OLDS OL8 89 H5
Burdett Av ROCH OL11 28 C2
Burdett Wy WGTN/LGST M12 128 B3
Burdith Av RUSH/FAL M14 142 B1
Burdon Av WYTH/NTH M22 168 D5
Burford Av BRAM/HZG SK7 193 F2
OLDTF/WHR M16 141 G1
URM M41 123 H4
Burford Crs WILM/AE SK9 198 D5
Burford Dr BOLS/LL BL3 48 D4
OLDTF/WHR M16 141 G1
SWIN M27 82 D5
Burford Gv SALE M33 153 H5
Burford Rd OLDTF/WHR M16 141 G1
Burgess Av AUL OL6 105 F5
Burgess Dr FAIL M35 103 E3
Burghley Av OLDE OL4 91 G1
Burghley Cl BOLS/LL BL3 51 E4
STLY SK15 119 F3
Burghley Dr BOLS/LL BL3 51 E4
Burgin Wk NEWH/MOS M40 113 H1
Burgundy Dr TOT/BURYW BL8 26 A4
Burke St BOL BL1 33 G4
Burkitt St HYDE SK14 147 H1
Burland Cl BRO M7 99 G5
Burleigh Cl BRAM/HZG SK7 184 B3
Burleigh Ms CCHDY M21 141 E5
Burleigh Rd STRET M32 125 F4
Burleigh St BRUN/LGST M13 127 G3
Burlescombe Cl ALT WA14 165 E3
Burley Ct HTNM * SK4 12 A1
Burlington Av OLDS OL8 90 B3
Burlington Cl HTNM SK4 158 B4
Burlington Dr EDGY/DAV SK3 172 A5
Burlington Gdns EDGY/DAV SK3 172 A5
Burlington Ms EDGY/DAV SK3 172 A5
Burlington Rd ALT WA14 165 G4
DID/WITH M20 142 D4
ECC M30 109 H1
Burlington St AULW OL7 117 G3
HULME M15 127 F3
ROCH OL11 43 F2
Burman St OP/CLY M11 130 A1
Burnaby St BOLS/LL BL3 48 C4
OLDS OL8 8 B7
Burnage Av BNG/LEV M19 143 G3
Burnage Hall Rd BNG/LEV M19 143 F4
Burnage La BNG/LEV M19 158 C1
HTNM SK4 158 A4
Burnage Range BNG/LEV M19 143 H2
Burnbray Av BNG/LEV M19 143 F5
Burndale Dr BURY BL9 68 D1
Burnden Rd BOLS/LL BL3 49 G4
Burnedge Cl WHIT OL12 14 C3
Burnedge Fold Rd OLDE OL4 93 E1
Burnedge La OLDE OL4 92 D1
Burnell Cl NEWH/MOS M40 113 H2
Burneside Crs MDTN M24 71 F1
Burnet Cl MILN OL16 43 H2
Burnett Av ORD M5 112 A5
Burnett Cl NEWH/MOS M40 101 E5
Burnfield Rd GTN M18 129 G5
Burnham Av BOL BL1 32 D5
RDSH SK5 145 E2
Burnham Cl CHD/CHDH SK8 182 C2
Burnham Dr BNG/LEV M19 143 G4
URM M41 123 F5
Burnham Rd DTN/ASHW M34 130 B5
Burnley La CHAD OL9 73 G2
Burnley Rd BURY BL9 27 F3
Burnley St CHAD OL9 73 G5
FAIL M35 103 F3
Burnmoor Rd BOLE BL2 50 C1
Burnsall Av WHTF M45 68 A4
Burnsall Gv ROY/SHW OL2 59 E5
Burns Av BURY BL9 53 G3
CHD/CHDH SK8 170 C3
SWIN M27 96 C1
Burns Cl OLD OL1 60 D4
OP/CLY M11 114 C4
Burns Crs OFTN SK2 173 F2
Burns Fold DUK SK16 133 F1
Burns Gdns PWCH * M25 84 C4
Burns Gv DROY M43 116 B3
Burnside HALE/TIMP WA15 179 F5
ROY/SHW OL2 60 C1
STLY SK15 134 A1
Burnside Av HTNM SK4 144 D5
SLFD M6 97 G5
Burnside Cl HEY OL10 41 E5
MPL/ROM SK6 161 G3
RAD M26 52 A2
STLY SK15 134 A1
WILM/AE SK9 199 H4
Burnside Dr BNG/LEV M19 143 F4
Burnside Rd BOL BL1 33 E4
CHD/CHDH SK8 169 F4
MILN OL16 30 D5
Burns Rd DTN/ASHW M34 146 D4
LHULT M38 80 C2
Burns St BOLS/LL BL3 3 F7
HEY OL10 41 E5
Burnthorp Av BKLY M9 86 C4
Burnthorpe Cl ROCH OL11 28 B5
Burran Rd WYTH/NTH M22 180 C4
Burrows Av CCHDY M21 141 E5
Burrs Cl TOT/BURYW BL8 26 D5
Burrs Lea Cl BURY BL9 27 F5
Burrswood Av BURY BL9 27 F5
Burrswood Dr BURY BL9 27 F5
Burslem Av DID/WITH M20 142 B3
Burstead St GTN M18 129 H2
Burstock St ANC M4 113 G2
Burston St GTN M18 129 F2
Burton Av DID/WITH M20 142 C5
HALE/TIMP WA15 154 B5
TOT/BURYW BL8 37 E2
Burton Dr POY/DIS SK12 195 E3
Burton Gv WALK M28 96 B2
Burton Rd DID/WITH M20 157 E2
Burton St HTNM SK4 159 H3
MDTN M24 71 G4
NEWH/MOS M40 113 G1
OLDE OL4 91 H1
Burton Wk CSLFD M3 6 A2
HTNM SK4 159 H2
Burtonwood Ct MDTN M24 71 G3
Burtree St WGTN/LGST * M12 128 D2
Burwell Cl BOLS/LL BL3 48 C5
WHIT OL12 18 C5
Burwell Gv NTHM/RTH M23 167 G2
Bury & Bolton Rd RAD M26 51 G2
Bury & Rochdale Old Rd
HEY OL10 40 C1
Bury Av OLDTF/WHR M16 141 F1
Bury New Rd BOL BL1 3 G3
BOLE BL2 51 E2
BRO M7 99 G3
HEY OL10 39 G4
PWCH M25 84 D2
RAMS BL0 17 F2
WHTF M45 68 C3
Bury Old Rd BOLE BL2 3 H4
BOLE BL2 35 H5
HEY OL10 39 H5
PWCH M25 84 D1
RAMS BL0 17 G4
Bury Pl OP/CLY M11 115 F3
Bury Rd BOLE BL2 50 A2
RAD M26 52 C5
ROCH OL11 28 C5
TOT/BURYW BL8 26 A5
Bury St CSLFD M3 6 C2
HEY OL10 40 C4
MOSL OL5 106 D2
RAD M26 52 D5
RDSH SK5 160 A3
Bushell St BOLS/LL BL3 48 A5
Bushey Dr NTHM/RTH M23 167 H4
Busheyfield Cl HYDE SK14 132 C3
Bush St NEWH/MOS M40 101 F5
Busk Rd CHAD OL9 8 B1
CHAD OL9 73 H4
Busk Wk CHAD * OL9 73 H4
Butcher La BURY BL9 4 E4
NTHM/RTH M23 167 E2
ROY/SHW OL2 58 D4
Bute Av OLDS OL8 90 C4
Bute St BOL BL1 33 E5
NEWH/MOS M40 101 G1
ORD M5 111 E4
Butler Gn CHAD OL9 89 F3
Butler La NEWH/MOS M40 113 H2
Butler St RAMS BL0 16 B4
Butley St BRAM/HZG SK7 173 F5
Butman St GTN M18 130 A2
Buttercup Av WALK * M28 80 A4
Buttercup Dr EDGY/DAV SK3 171 G5
OLDE OL4 75 H2
ROCH OL11 42 A3
Butterfield Cl CHD/CHDH SK8 183 E3
Butterfield Rd WHTN BL5 62 C4
Butterhouse La UPML OL3 78 A2
Butter La CSLFD * M3 6 D4
Butterley Cl DUK SK16 133 E1
Buttermere Av HEY OL10 56 A1
SWIN M27 97 E4
WYTH/NTH M22 180 A2
Buttermere Cl BOLS/LL BL3 50 C5
STRET M32 124 D5
Buttermere Dr
HALE/TIMP WA15 188 D1
MDTN M24 71 F2
RAMS BL0 16 C1
Buttermere Gv ROY/SHW OL2 59 E2
Buttermere Rd AULW OL7 117 G1
CHD/CHDH SK8 181 G1
FWTH BL4 63 H4
OLDE OL4 75 G4
PART M31 150 D3
Buttermill Cl IRL M44 121 C5
Butterstile Av PWCH M25 98 C1
Butterstile Cl PWCH M25 98 C1
Butterstile La PWCH M25 84 C5
Butterwick Cl WGTN/LGST M12 129 E5
Butterworth Hall MILN OL16 44 D1
Butterworth La CHAD OL9 88 D4
Butterworth St CHAD * OL9 73 G5
LIT OL15 20 D3
MDTN M24 72 B5
OLDE OL4 75 F5
OP/CLY M11 114 D5
Butteryhouse La
HALE/TIMP WA15 179 F2
Butt Hill Av PWCH M25 85 E4
Butt Hill Dr PWCH M25 85 E4
Butt Hill Rd PWCH M25 85 E4
Butt La OLDE OL4 92 C3
Button Hole ROY/SHW OL2 60 C2
Button La NTHM/RTH M23 155 G4
Buttress St GTN M18 129 F2
The Butts MILN OL16 10 C6
The Butts Av MILN OL16 10 C6
Buxted Rd OLD OL1 75 E3
Buxton Av AUL OL6 106 A4
DID/WITH M20 142 A5
Buxton Crs MILN OL16 43 G2
SALE M33 155 E5
Buxton La DROY M43 115 H5
MPL/ROM SK6 174 D4
Buxton Pl OLDS * OL8 9 F7
Buxton Rd BRAM/HZG SK7 185 G3
OFTN SK2 172 C4
STRET M32 124 B5
Buxton St BRAM/HZG SK7 185 E1
CHD/CHDH SK8 169 F4
CMANE M1 7 J7
HEY OL10 41 E5
TOT/BURYW BL8 37 H4
WHIT OL12 14 C2
Bye Rd RAMS BL0 17 F1
Byfield Rd WYTH/NTH M22 168 B5
Byland Av CHD/CHDH SK8 193 E1
OLDE OL4 91 G3
Byland Cl BOL BL1 33 H4
Bylands Cl POY/DIS * SK12 195 E3
Bylands Fold DUK SK16 132 C2
Byng Av IRL M44 150 B2
Byng St FWTH BL4 65 E4
HEY OL10 56 B1
Byrcland Cl WGTN/LGST M12 114 B5
Byre Cl SALE M33 155 H3
Byrom Av BNG/LEV M19 144 B2
Byrom St ALT WA14 177 G1
CSLFD M3 6 C6
OLDTF/WHR M16 126 C4
ORD M5 111 H5
TOT/BURYW BL8 37 G2
Byron Av DROY M43 116 B3
PWCH M25 84 C4
RAD M26 51 G5
SWIN M27 96 D2
Byron Dr CHD/CHDH SK8 170 C3
Byron Gv RDSH SK5 144 D2
Byron Rd DTN/ASHW M34 146 C3
MDTN M24 72 A2
STRET M32 125 F5
TOT/BURYW BL8 26 A1
Byron's Dr HALE/TIMP WA15 166 B3
Byron St ECC M30 109 G3
OLDS OL8 89 G5
ROY/SHW OL2 59 E5
Byron Wk FWTH BL4 80 C1
Byrth Rd OLDS OL8 104 C2

C

Cabin La OLDE OL4 76 B1
Cablestead Wk OP/CLY M11 114 C5
Cable St BOL BL1 3 F2
CSLFD M3 6 C2
Cabot Pl RDSH SK5 160 A2
Cabot St BRUN/LGST * M13 127 G2
Caddington Rd CCHDY M21 141 F3
Cadishead Wy IRL M44 136 B4
Cadnam Dr WYTH/NTH M22 181 E1
Cadogan Pl BRO * M7 99 H1
Cadogan St RUSH/FAL M14 127 F4
Cadum Wk BRUN/LGST M13 127 H2
Caen Av NEWH/MOS M40 88 B4
Caernarvon Cl TOT/BURYW BL8 26 A2
Caernarvon Dr BRAM/HZG SK7 184 D3
Caesar St ROCH OL11 43 F4
Cairn Dr ROCH OL11 41 F1
SLFD M6 99 F5
Cairngorm Dr BOLS/LL BL3 47 F4
Cairns Pl AUL OL6 105 G5
Cairn Wk OP/CLY * M11 114 C4
Cairnwell Rd CHAD OL9 73 F4
Caister Av WHTF M45 68 D5
Caister Cl URM M41 136 D2
Caistor Cl OLDTF/WHR M16 141 H3
Caistor St STKP SK1 160 C3
Caistor Wk OLD OL1 9 G2
Caithness Cl NTHM/RTH M23 167 H5
Caithness Dr BOLS/LL BL3 47 F4
Caithness Rd HEY OL10 41 F1
Cakebread St WGTN/LGST M12 127 H1
Calbourne Crs WGTN/LGST M12 129 E5
Calcutta Rd EDGY/DAV SK3 171 F2
Caldbeck Av BOL BL1 32 C5
SALE M33 155 F1
Caldbeck Dr FWTH BL4 63 H5
MDTN M24 71 F3
Caldecott Rd BKLY M9 86 B2
Calder Av IRL M44 136 A2
LIT OL15 20 D1
WYTH/NTH M22 168 C1
Calderbank Av URM M41 122 B5
Calderbrook Dr CHD/CHDH SK8 170 D5
Calderbrook Rd LIT OL15 15 A5
Calderbrook Wy OLDE OL4 91 E2
Calder Cl BURY BL9 27 H3
POY/DIS SK12 195 E5
RDSH SK5 160 B1
Calder Ct URM M41 122 B4
Calder Crs WHTF M45 69 E2
Calder Dr FWTH BL4 82 A2
SWIN M27 96 D1
WALK M28 80 B5
Calder Gv ROY/SHW OL2 59 H1
Calder Rd BOLS/LL BL3 63 H1
Caldershaw La WHIT OL12 28 D1
Caldershaw Rd WHIT OL12 28 D2
Calder St MILN OL16 11 H1
Caldervale Av CCHDY M21 156 B2
Calderwood Cl TOT/BURYW BL8 26 A5
Caldey Rd NTHM/RTH M23 167 F4
Caldon Cl ECC M30 109 G5
Caldy Dr RAMS BL0 16 B5
Caldy Rd SLFD M6 111 E1
WILM/AE SK9 192 A4
Caledon Av NEWH/MOS M40 101 H2
Caledonian Dr ECC M30 109 H5
Caledonia St BOLS/LL BL3 48 B4
RAD M26 52 D5
Caledonia Wy STRET M32 124 B3
Cale Gn EDGY/DAV SK3 172 A3
Cale St OFTN SK2 172 A2
Caley St BOL BL1 32 C4
CMANE M1 7 F7
Calf Hey LIT OL15 20 C2
Calf Hey Cl RAD M26 66 C1
Calf Hey North ROCH OL11 43 F2
Calf Hey Rd ROY/SHW OL2 60 C1
Calf Hey South ROCH OL11 43 F2
Calf La OLDE OL4 93 F3
Calgarth Dr MDTN M24 71 E1
Calgary St GTN M18 129 F3
Calico Cl CSLFD M3 112 C2
Callaghan Wk HEY OL10 40 D5
Calland Av HYDE SK14 133 E5
Callender St RAMS BL0 16 C2
Calliards Rd MILN OL16 20 B4
Callingdon Rd CCHDY M21 156 C1
Callington Cl HYDE SK14 149 F1
Callington Dr HYDE SK14 149 F1
Callis Rd BOLS/LL BL3 48 B3
Callum Wk BRUN/LGST * M13 127 H2
Calluna Ms DID/WITH * M20 157 F2
Caltha St RAMS BL0 16 C2
Calthorpe Av BKLY M9 100 D3
Calton Av BRO M7 98 D3
Calve Croft Rd WYTH/NTH M22 180 D3
Calver Av ECC M30 109 F5
Calver Cl URM M41 122 A5
Calverleigh Cl BOLS/LL BL3 62 D2
Calverley Av BNG/LEV M19 143 G4
Calverley Cl WILM/AE SK9 199 H2
Calverley Wy WHIT OL12 18 D4
Calverly Rd CHD/CHDH SK8 170 D4
Calverton Dr NEWH/MOS M40 102 B3
Calvert Rd BOLS/LL BL3 63 H1
Calvert St ORD M5 111 E3
Calver Wk NEWH/MOS * M40 113 H2
Calvine Wk NEWH/MOS * M40 113 H2
Calvin St BOL BL1 3 F1
Cambeck Cl WHTF M45 69 E3
Cambell Rd ECC M30 109 E3
Camberley Cl BRAM/HZG SK7 184 B5
TOT/BURYW BL8 37 F1
Camberly Dr ROCH OL11 28 C5
Cambert La GTN M18 129 F3
Camberwell Dr AULW OL7 104 D4
Camberwell St CHH * M8 113 F1
OLDS * OL8 90 B3
Camberwell Wy ROY/SHW OL2 58 D5
Camborne Rd HYDE SK14 134 B5
Camborne St RUSH/FAL M14 142 C1
Cambourne Dr BOLS/LL BL3 47 H4
Cambo Wk HTNM SK4 158 C3
Cambrai Crs ECC M30 108 D1
Cambrian Dr MILN OL16 31 H5
ROY/SHW OL2 73 H1
Cambrian Rd EDGY/DAV SK3 12 B6
Cambrian St NEWH/MOS M40 114 B3
Cambria Sq BOLS/LL * BL3 48 B4
Cambria St BOLS/LL BL3 48 B4
OLDE OL4 75 G5
Cambridge Av OLDTF/WHR M16 141 F1
ROCH OL11 28 D5
WILM/AE SK9 199 E3
Cambridge Cl FWTH BL4 64 A3
SALE M33 153 G3
Cambridge Dr BOLS/LL BL3 51 E5
DTN/ASHW M34 130 B5
MPL/ROM SK6 162 B1
Cambridge Gv ECC M30 110 A3
WHTF M45 68 D4
Cambridge Rd BKLY M9 101 E1
CHD/CHDH SK8 169 G3
FAIL M35 103 E5
HALE/TIMP WA15 177 H2
HOR/BR BL6 46 A1
HTNM SK4 159 F1
URM M41 138 A2
Cambridge St AULW OL7 117 G4
BRO M7 112 D1
CHAD OL9 89 H3
CMANE M1 127 E1
DUK SK16 118 B4
OFTN SK2 172 B3
STLY SK15 119 F3
Camden Av NEWH/MOS M40 115 F1
Camden Cl BOLE BL2 36 B5
Camden St MOSL OL5 93 E4
Camelford Cl HULME * M15 127 F2
Camelia Rd BKLY M9 100 D3
Camellia Cl BOL BL1 48 A2
Cameron Ct ROY/SHW OL2 59 E3
Cameron St BOL BL1 33 G1
CMANE * M1 6 D7
TOT/BURYW BL8 37 H4
Campania St ROY/SHW OL2 74 B2
Campbell Cl TOT/BURYW BL8 36 D2
Campbell Ct FWTH BL4 64 D2
Campbell Rd BOLS/LL BL3 62 D2
BRUN/LGST M13 143 G1
SALE M33 154 A3
SWIN M27 96 D4
Campbell St FWTH BL4 64 C3
RDSH SK5 145 E2
WHIT OL12 10 B1
Campbell Wy WALK M28 80 D4
Campden Wy WILM/AE SK9 192 A3
Campion Wy WHIT OL12 18 B5
Camp St AUL OL6 118 A2
BRO M7 112 B1
CSLFD M3 6 C6
TOT/BURYW BL8 37 H3
Camrose Gdns BOL BL1 33 H5
Camrose Wk BRUN/LGST * M13 128 A3
Cams Acre Cl RAD M26 66 D1
Cams La RAD M26 66 D2
Canada St BOL BL1 33 F4
NEWH/MOS M40 114 B1
OFTN SK2 172 B3
Canal Bank ECC M30 109 F2
Canal Bridge La OP/CLY M11 115 H4
Canal Cottages Yd ANC * M4 113 H4
Canal Rd ALT WA14 165 H2
Canal Side ECC M30 109 F2
Canal St CHAD OL9 89 G4
CMANE M1 7 G6
DROY M43 116 B4
HEY OL10 56 C1
HYDE SK14 132 B5
LIT OL15 21 E3
MPL/ROM SK6 175 F3
ORD * M5 112 B4
ROCH OL11 43 F1
STKP SK1 13 H5
STLY * SK15 119 F4
Canberra Rd BRAM/HZG SK7 193 H2
Canberra St OP/CLY M11 115 F3
Candahar St BOLS/LL BL3 64 B1
Candleford Pl OFTN SK2 173 F5
Candleford Rd DID/WITH * M20 142 C5
Candlestick Ct BURY BL9 39 G2
Candlestick Pk BURY BL9 39 G2
Canisp Cl CHAD OL9 73 F4
Canley Cl STKP SK1 13 H6
Canmore Cl BOLS/LL BL3 62 D1
Cannel Fold WALK M28 94 C3
Canning Dr BOL BL1 33 H4
Canning St BOL * BL1 33 H4
BURY BL9 4 E1
HTNM SK4 13 F1
Cannon Gv BOLS/LL BL3 2 B7
Cannon St ANC M4 7 F3
BOLS/LL BL3 48 C4
CHAD OL9 8 E3
CSLFD M3 112 C3
ECC M30 109 H4
RAD M26 52 A4
RAMS BL0 16 B4
Cannon St North BOLS/LL * BL3 2 B7
Cann St TOT/BURYW BL8 25 G3
Canon Dr ALT WA14 177 E3
Canon Flynn Ct MILN OL16 11 K6
Canon Green Dr CSLFD M3 6 B1
Canons Cl BOL BL1 33 E4
Canons Gv NEWH/MOS M40 101 F5
Canonsleigh Cl CHH M8 99 H5
Canon St BURY BL9 5 G1
MILN OL16 11 G1
Canonsway SWIN M27 96 D3
Canon Tighe Ct CHAD * OL9 73 F5
Canterbury Cl DUK SK16 132 C2
ROCH OL11 28 D4
Canterbury Crs MDTN M24 72 C2
Canterbury Dr PWCH M25 85 F5
TOT/BURYW BL8 38 A2
Canterbury Gdns ORD M5 110 B3
Canterbury Gv BOLS/LL BL3 63 G1
Canterbury Pk DID/WITH M20 157 E3
Canterbury Rd
HALE/TIMP WA15 178 D1
STKP SK1 160 C5
URM M41 123 E5
Canterbury St AUL OL6 118 A1
Canterfield Cl DROY M43 117 E3
Cantrell St OP/CLY M11 115 E4
Canute Rd STRET M32 125 F5
Canute St BOLE BL2 34 D5
RAD M26 66 D1
SLFD * M6 112 A3
Capella Wk BRO M7 112 B1
Capenhurst Cl NTHM/RTH M23 167 G5
Capesthorne Cl BRAM/HZG SK7 185 G4
Capesthorne Dr ROY/SHW OL2 59 G2
Capesthorne Rd
BRAM/HZG SK7 185 G4
DUK SK16 132 C2
HALE/TIMP WA15 167 E3
MPL/ROM SK6 186 D5
WILM/AE SK9 198 D5
Cape St DID/WITH M20 142 D4
Capital Rd OP/CLY M11 130 A1
Capricorn Wy SLFD * M6 112 B1
Capstan St BKLY M9 101 F2
Capstone Dr MPL/ROM SK6 174 D3
Captain Clarke Rd HYDE SK14 132 A3
Captain Fold HEY * OL10 41 F4
Captain Fold Rd LHULT M38 80 A2
Captain's Clough Rd BOL BL1 32 D4
Capton Cl BRAM/HZG SK7 184 B2
Carberry Rd GTN M18 129 H3
Carden Av SWIN M27 96 C3
URM M41 137 F1
Carder Cl SWIN M27 97 E3
Cardew Av WYTH/NTH M22 168 D5
Cardiff Cl OLDS OL8 89 G5
Cardiff St BRO M7 99 H3
Cardigan Dr BURY BL9 53 F2
Cardigan Rd OLDS OL8 89 G5
Cardigan St ROY/SHW OL2 59 F5
SLFD * M6 111 F4
WHIT OL12 18 D5
Cardinal Ms MDTN M24 71 E2
Cardinal St CHH M8 100 C4
OLD OL1 9 J3
Carding Gv CSLFD M3 6 B1
Cardroom Rd ANC M4 7 K4
Cardus St BNG/LEV M19 143 H2
Cardwell Gdns BOL * BL1 33 H4
Cardwell Rd ECC M30 108 D4
Cardwell St OLDS OL8 90 C4
Carey Cl BRO * M7 112 C1
Carey Wk HULME M15 127 E3
Carfax Fold WHIT OL12 29 E1
Carfax St GTN M18 129 G3
Carill Av NEWH/MOS M40 101 H1
Carill Dr RUSH/FAL M14 143 E3
Carina Pl BRO M7 112 B1
Carisbrook Av URM M41 138 B2
WHTF M45 68 D5
Carisbrook Dr SWIN M27 97 F4
Carisbrooke Av BRAM/HZG SK7 185 E3
Carisbrooke Dr BOL BL1 34 A3
Carisbrook St BKLY M9 101 E3
Carlburn St OP/CLY M11 115 G3
Carleton Rd POY/DIS SK12 196 B3
Carley Gv BKLY M9 86 C3
Carlford Gv PWCH M25 84 C4
Carlile St EDGY/DAV SK3 12 E6
Carlin Ga HALE/TIMP WA15 166 B3
Carling Dr WYTH/NTH M22 180 D2
Carlingford Cl EDGY/DAV SK3 171 H4
Carlisle Cl BOLS/LL BL3 65 H2
MPL/ROM SK6 161 H5
WHTF M45 69 E5
Carlisle Crs AUL OL6 105 F3
Carlisle Dr ALT WA14 165 H1
IRL M44 136 B1
Carlisle St EDGW/EG BL7 23 F3
SWIN M27 83 E5
WHIT OL12 18 D5
WILM/AE SK9 201 B5
Carloon Rd NTHM/RTH M23 156 A5
Carlow Dr WYTH/NTH M22 180 D2
Carl St BOL * BL1 33 G4
Carlton Av BOLS/LL BL3 47 H5
BRAM/HZG SK7 193 G2
CHD/CHDH SK8 182 C1
MPL/ROM SK6 162 C3
OLDE OL4 75 G3
PWCH M25 85 H5
WHTF M45 68 A3
WILM/AE SK9 191 H5
Carlton Cl BOLE BL2 35 F3
WALK M28 94 D1
Carlton Ct HALE/TIMP WA15 178 C3
Carlton Crs STKP SK1 13 K2
Carlton Dr CHD/CHDH SK8 169 F3
PWCH M25 85 H5
Carlton Pl BRAM/HZG * SK7 185 G3
FWTH * BL4 65 E3
Carlton Range GTN * M18 130 A4
Carlton Rd AUL OL6 105 F5
BOL BL1 47 H1
HALE/TIMP WA15 178 C2
HTNM SK4 158 D4
HYDE SK14 133 F5
OLDTF/WHR M16 126 C5
SALE M33 139 F5
SLFD M6 111 F1
URM M41 138 B2
WALK M28 94 D1
Carlton St BOLE BL2 3 G6
BURY BL9 53 G1
ECC M30 109 G2
FWTH BL4 65 E3
OLDTF/WHR M16 126 B4
Carlton Wy GOL/RIS/CU WA3 150 B1
ROY/SHW OL2 74 A2
Carlyle Cl CHH M8 100 B4
Carlyle St BURY BL9 4 B4
Carlyn Av SALE M33 155 E1
Carmel Av ORD M5 126 B1
Carmel Cl ORD M5 112 B5

Carmel Ct BKLY M9 101 E1
Carmel Ms WILM/AE SK9 191 G5
Carmenna Dr BRAM/HZG SK7 184 A5
Carmichael Cl PART M31 150 D3
Carmichael St EDGY/DAV SK3 12 C7
Carmine Fold MDTN M24 71 G2
Carmona Dr PWCH M25 84 D3
Carmoor Rd BRUN/LGST M13 127 H3
Carnaby St BKLY M9 101 G1
Carna Rd RDSH SK5 144 D1
Carnarvon St BRO * M7 99 H3
CSLFD M3 113 E2
OLDS OL8 89 G5
STKP SK1 13 K5
Carnation Rd FWTH BL4 64 B3
OLDE OL4 91 H3
Carnegie Av BNG/LEV M19 144 A2
Carnegie Cl SALE M33 153 G3
Carnforth Av CHAD OL9 89 F1
ROCH OL11 57 G2
Carnforth Dr SALE M33 154 B3
TOT/BURYW BL8 26 B1
Carnforth Rd CHD/CHDH SK8 171 E5
HTNM SK4 144 B5
Carnforth Sq ROCH OL11 57 G2
Carnforth St RUSH/FAL M14 127 G5
Carnoustie BOLS/LL BL3 62 D1
Carnoustie Cl NEWH/MOS M40 102 B3
WILM/AE SK9 200 A2
Carnoustie Dr CHD/CHDH SK8 181 H3
RAMS BL0 16 B3
Carnwood Cl NEWH/MOS M40 115 G1
Caroline Dr ANC M4 7 K4
Caroline St AUL OL6 118 B2
BOLS/LL BL3 48 C5
BRO M7 112 D1
EDGY/DAV SK3 12 D7
IRL M44 135 D3
STLY SK15 119 F4
Carpenters La ANC M4 7 G3
Carpenters Wk DROY M43 116 A5
Carpenters Wy MILN OL16 43 G2
Carradale Dr SALE M33 153 F1
Carr Av PWCH M25 84 C5
Carr Bank Av CHH M8 86 A4
RAMS BL0 16 C1
Carr Bank Dr RAMS BL0 16 C1
Carr Bank Rd RAMS BL0 16 C1
Carrbrook Cl STLY SK15 107 F4
Carrbrook Crs STLY SK15 107 G4
Carrbrook Dr OLD OL1 74 B3
Carrbrook Rd STLY SK15 107 G3
Carrbrook Ter RAD M26 52 D5
Carr Brow MPL/ROM SK6 187 F5
Carr Cl STKP SK1 172 C1
Carrfield Av EDGY/DAV SK3 172 B5
HALE/TIMP WA15 167 E4
LHULT M38 79 D3
Carrfield Gv LHULT M38 79 D3
Carr Fold RAMS * BL0 16 C1
Carrgate Rd DTN/ASHW M34 147 E2
Carrgreen Cl BNG/LEV M19 158 C1
Carrhill Quarry Cl MOSL OL5 92 D5
Carrhill Rd MOSL OL5 92 D5
Carrhill Ter MOSL * OL5 92 D5
Carr House Rd OLDE OL4 76 A5
Carriage Dr LIT OL15 21 E1
NEWH/MOS M40 101 E5
The Carriages ALT * WA14 165 F5
Carriage St OLDTF/WHR M16 126 C3
Carrick Gdns MDTN M24 56 C5
Carrie St BOL BL1 48 A1
Carrigart PWCH M25 84 D4
Carrill Gv East BNG/LEV M19 143 H2
Carrington Cl MILN OL16 20 A5
Carrington Dr BOLS/LL BL3 49 E5
Carrington Field St OFTN SK2 172 A2
Carrington La SALE M33 138 C5
Carrington Rd RUSH/FAL M14 142 D3
STKP SK1 160 B3
URM M41 137 F3
Carrington St CHAD OL9 89 G4
SWIN M27 97 G1
Carrington Ter SWIN * M27 97 F1
Carr La STLY SK15 107 G3
UPML OL3 78 A5
Carr Mill Ms WILM/AE * SK9 199 G1
Carron Av BKLY M9 101 F1
Carron Gv BOLE BL2 50 C2
Carr Ri STLY SK15 107 G3
Carr Rd HALE/TIMP WA15 178 C2
IRL M44 136 C1
Carrsfield Rd WYTH/NTH M22 168 D3
Carrslea Cl RAD M26 51 H4
Carrs Rd CHD/CHDH SK8 170 C3
Carr St AUL OL6 105 G5
RAMS BL0 16 C1
SWIN M27 96 C3
Carrsvale Av URM M41 123 E5
Carrswood Rd NTHM/RTH M23 166 D1
Carruthers Cl HEY OL10 41 G3
Carruthers St ANC M4 114 A4
Carrwood HALE/TIMP WA15 178 C5
Carrwood Av BRAM/HZG SK7 183 H4
Carrwood Hey RAMS BL0 16 B4
Carr Wood Rd BRAM/HZG SK7 183 G3
Carrwood Rd WILM/AE SK9 199 E2
Carsdale Rd WYTH/NTH M22 180 D5
Carslake Av BOL BL1 48 B1
Carslake Rd NEWH/MOS M40 101 E5
Carson Rd BNG/LEV M19 143 H3
Carstairs Av EDGY/DAV SK3 172 B5
Carstairs Cl CHH M8 100 A3
Carter Cl DTN/ASHW * M34 146 C1
Carter Pl HYDE * SK14 132 C3
Carter St BOLS/LL BL3 49 F5
BRO * M7 99 G5
FWTH * BL4 65 F5
HYDE SK14 132 C3
MOSL OL5 106 D2
SALQ M50 110 D4
STLY SK15 119 G3
Carthage St OLDS OL8 90 C3
Cartleach Gv WALK M28 80 B5
Cartleach La WALK M28 80 A5
Cartmel WHIT OL12 10 C4
Cartmel Av HTNM SK4 144 C5
MILN OL16 44 C2
Cartmel Cl BOLS/LL BL3 62 A2
BRAM/HZG SK7 184 D1
BURY BL9 68 D1
CHD/CHDH SK8 181 H1
OLDS OL8 90 A4
Cartmel Crs BOLE BL2 34 D4
CHAD OL9 89 E5
Cartmel Dr HALE/TIMP WA15 167 E3
Cartmel Gv WALK M28 96 A3
Cartridge Cl WYTH/NTH M22 181 E1
Cartridge St HEY OL10 40 D4
Cartwright Rd CCHDY M21 140 C3
Cartwright St DTN/ASHW M34 131 G2
HYDE SK14 133 F3
Carver Av PWCH M25 85 F2
Carver Cl OLDTF/WHR M16 126 A3
Carver Dr MPL/ROM SK6 174 D4
Carver Rd HALE/TIMP WA15 177 H2
MPL/ROM SK6 174 D4
Carver St OLDTF/WHR M16 126 A3
Carver Wk HULME * M15 127 E3
Carville Rd BKLY M9 88 B4
Cascade Dr CHH M8 99 H5
Cash Gate Ct OLDS * OL8 90 A4
Cashmere Rd EDGY/DAV SK3 171 F2
Cashmoor Wk WGTN/LGST M12 128 B2
Caspian Rd ALT WA14 164 D3
Cass Av ORD M5 111 H5
Cassidy Cl ANC M4 7 J2
Cassidy Gdns MDTN M24 56 A5
Casson Ga WHIT OL12 10 B2
Casson St FAIL M35 103 E3
Casterton Wy WALK M28 94 B5
Castle Av DTN/ASHW M34 146 B1
ROCH OL11 29 H5
Castlebrook Cl BURY BL9 54 A5
Castle Cl DROY M43 116 C3
Castle Ct AUL OL6 105 E3
Castle Cft BOLE BL2 35 E3
Castlecroft Rd BURY BL9 4 C4
Castledene Av SLFD M6 111 F2
Castle Farm La OFTN SK2 172 D4
Castlefield Av BRO M7 99 H2
Castlefield Br ORD M5 112 C5
Castleford Cl BOL * BL1 2 B2
Castleford St OLD OL1 73 H3
Castle Gv RAMS BL0 26 B1
Castle Hall Cl STLY SK15 119 G4
Castle Hall Ct STLY * SK15 119 F4
Castle Hall Vw STLY SK15 119 F4
Castle Hill Crs ROCH OL11 29 H5
Castle Hill Pk MPL/ROM * SK6 146 C5
Castle Hill Rd BURY BL9 39 G2
PWCH M25 85 G5
Castle Hill St BOLE BL2 34 C4
Castle La MOSL OL5 107 G2
Castlemere Dr ROY/SHW OL2 60 C1
Castlemere Rd BKLY M9 86 D4
Castlemere St ROCH OL11 29 H5
Castlemere Ter ROCH OL11 29 H5
Castle Mill La HALE/TIMP WA15 188 A1
Castlemill St OLD OL1 75 E5
Castlemoor Av BRO M7 99 E2
Castle Quay HULME M15 126 D1
Castlerea Cl ECC M30 109 G5
Castlerigg Dr MDTN M24 70 D2
ROY/SHW OL2 58 D3
Castle Rd BURY BL9 54 B5
Castle Shaw Rd OFTN SK2 173 E4
Castle St BOLE BL2 3 J5
BURY BL9 4 D4
BURY BL9 26 D1
CSLFD M3 6 B7
ECC M30 110 A3
EDGY/DAV SK3 12 E7
FWTH * BL4 65 E5
HYDE SK14 133 E5
MDTN M24 72 C5
STLY SK15 119 F4
Castleton Av STRET M32 124 C5
Castleton Dr MPL/ROM SK6 197 E1
Castleton Gv AUL OL6 106 A4
Castleton Rd BRAM/HZG SK7 185 F3
BRO M7 99 H1
ROY/SHW OL2 58 D1
STRET M32 124 B4
Castleton Rd South ROCH OL11 42 C4
Castleton St ALT WA14 165 F2
BOLE BL2 34 C4
CHAD OL9 8 A5
Castleton Wk OP/CLY * M11 114 C4
Castleway HALE/TIMP WA15 178 D5
ROCH OL11 42 A4
SLFD M6 111 F1
Castle Wy SWIN M27 83 F5
Castlewood Gdns OFTN SK2 172 D4
Castlewood Rd BRO M7 98 C2
Castlewood Sq BOLE BL2 34 D5
Castle Yd STKP SK1 13 G2
Catchdale Cl BKLY M9 86 D2
Catches Cl ROCH OL11 29 E3
Catches La ROCH OL11 29 E2
Cateaton St BURY BL9 4 E2
CSLFD M3 6 E3
Caterham Av BOLS/LL BL3 62 C2
Caterham St ANC M4 114 A4
Catfield Wk HULME * M15 126 C1
Catford Rd NTHM/RTH M23 167 G4
Cathedral Ap CSLFD M3 6 E2
Cathedral Cl DUK SK16 132 C2
Cathedral Gdns CSLFD M3 6 E2
Cathedral Gates CSLFD * M3 6 E3
Cathedral Rd CHAD OL9 73 F3
Cathedral St ANC M4 6 E3
Catherine Houses HTNM * SK4 158 C4
Catherine Rd ALT WA14 177 F1
CHH M8 99 H1
MPL/ROM SK6 161 G5
SWIN M27 96 B3
Catherine St BOLS/LL BL3 63 E2
BRAM/HZG SK7 173 F5
BURY BL9 53 F3
ECC M30 108 D2
HYDE SK14 132 C5
OLDE OL4 91 H1
OP/CLY M11 129 H1
Catherston Cl OLDTF/WHR M16 126 D5
Cathrine St East
DTN/ASHW M34 131 E5
Cathrine St West
DTN/ASHW M34 131 E5
Catlow La ANC * M4 7 G3
Catlow St BRO M7 112 D1
Caton Cl BURY BL9 53 F1
Caton St MILN OL16 30 A5
Cato St RAMS * BL0 16 B4
Catterall Crs BOLE BL2 24 A5
Catterick Av DID/WITH M20 157 H3
SALE M33 153 F4
Catterick Dr BOLS/LL BL3 65 H1
Catterick Rd DID/WITH M20 157 H3
Catterwood Dr MPL/ROM SK6 163 G4
Cattlin Wy OLDS OL8 89 H5
The Causeway ALT WA14 165 G5
CHAD OL9 88 C2
Causewood Cl OLDE OL4 60 D5
Causey Dr MDTN M24 71 E1
Cavanagh Cl BRUN/LGST M13 128 A2
Cavan Cl EDGY/DAV SK3 170 C2
Cavell St CMANE * M1 7 H4
Cavell Wy SLFD M6 111 H4
Cavendish Av DID/WITH M20 142 A5
SWIN M27 83 H4
Cavendish Gdns BOLS/LL BL3 63 F1
Cavendish Gv ECC M30 109 H2
Cavendish Ms WILM/AE SK9 199 F5
Cavendish Pl AUL * OL6 117 H2
Cavendish Rd ALT WA14 177 F1
BRAM/HZG SK7 185 E3
BRO M7 99 G1
DID/WITH M20 142 A5
ECC M30 109 H2
HTNM SK4 158 C4
ROCH OL11 42 D3
STRET M32 125 F4
URM M41 123 H5
WALK M28 96 A4
Cavendish St AUL OL6 117 H2
CHAD OL9 9 F5
HULME M15 127 F2
Cavendish Wy ROY/SHW OL2 73 H2
Cavenham Gv BOL BL1 48 B1
Caversham Dr BKLY M9 101 F2
Cawdor Av FWTH BL4 64 C2
Cawdor Ct FWTH BL4 64 D2
Cawdor Pl HALE/TIMP WA15 166 D3
Cawdor Rd RUSH/FAL M14 142 D2
Cawdor St ECC M30 109 F4
FWTH BL4 64 C2
HULME M15 126 C1
SWIN M27 96 C2
WALK M28 81 F5
Cawley Av PWCH M25 84 C5
Cawley Ter BKLY * M9 86 B2
Cawood Sq RDSH SK5 145 H5
Cawston Wk CHH M8 100 B4
Caxton Rd RUSH/FAL M14 142 C2
Caxton St CSLFD * M3 6 C3
HEY OL10 41 E4
ROCH OL11 42 B4
Caxton Wy ORD M5 112 A4
Caygill St CSLFD M3 6 C2
Cayley St MILN OL16 11 G7
Caythorpe St RUSH/FAL M14 127 F5
Cayton St WGTN/LGST M12 128 D5
The Ceal MPL/ROM SK6 163 G4
Cecil Av SALE M33 153 H3
Cecil Dr URM M41 137 F1
Cecil Gv GTN M18 129 G4
Cecilia St BOLS/LL BL3 49 F5
Cecil Rd BKLY M9 87 E3
ECC M30 109 H4
HALE/TIMP WA15 177 H2
STRET M32 139 H2
Cecil St BOLE BL2 3 J5
BRUN/LGST M13 127 G3
BURY BL9 4 E6
DUK SK16 118 A5
EDGY/DAV * SK3 12 E7
LIT OL15 20 C3
MOSL OL5 106 D2
ROCH OL11 43 E1
ROY/SHW OL2 58 D5
STLY SK15 119 G4
WALK M28 81 E4
Cedar Av ALT WA14 165 F5
AUL OL6 105 G5
BOLS/LL BL3 66 A2
BRAM/HZG SK7 185 F2
HEY OL10 40 D3
STLY SK15 119 H2
WHTF M45 84 C1
Cedar Bank Cl MILN OL16 31 E4
Cedar Cl POY/DIS SK12 195 F4
Cedar Ct HALE/TIMP * WA15 166 C4
Cedar Crs CHAD OL9 73 G4
RAMS BL0 16 D1
Cedar Dr DROY M43 116 C3
SWIN M27 82 C3
URM M41 138 B2
Cedar Gv DTN/ASHW M34 131 F5
DUK SK16 119 E5
FWTH BL4 64 C4
HTNM SK4 159 F1
PWCH M25 84 D1
ROY/SHW OL2 59 E3
ROY/SHW OL2 60 A3
RUSH/FAL M14 143 E3
Cedar La MILN OL16 44 D3
OLDE OL4 93 E1
Cedar Lawn CHD/CHDH * SK8 182 D2
Cedar Ms AULW OL7 104 D5
Cedar Pl BRO M7 112 B1
Cedar Rd CHD/CHDH SK8 169 F4
FAIL M35 103 E4
HALE/TIMP WA15 177 H1
MDTN M24 72 B4
MPL/ROM SK6 174 D5
OFTN SK2 172 C5
PART M31 150 D3
SALE M33 138 C5
Cedars Rd WYTH/NTH M22 180 C1
Cedar St AUL OL6 118 C1
BURY BL9 5 H3
HYDE SK14 132 C3
OLDE OL4 75 F5
WHIT OL12 10 D2
Cedar Vw AUL * OL6 118 C1
Cedarwood Av HTNM SK4 158 D5
Cedar Wood Ct BOL * BL1 47 G1
Cedric Rd CHH M8 85 H5
OLDE OL4 75 F5
Cedric St ORD M5 111 E3
Celandine Cl LIT OL15 20 C2
Celia St CHH M8 100 D2
Cellini Sq BOL BL1 33 G5
Celtic St STKP SK1 13 K5
Cemetery La BURY BL9 53 G1
Cemetery Rd BOLE BL2 3 K4
DROY M43 116 A4
DTN/ASHW M34 131 G2
DTN/ASHW M34 146 C2
FAIL M35 103 E4
FWTH BL4 65 G3
MOSL OL5 107 E3
ORD M5 111 F4
RAD M26 52 A5
RAMS BL0 16 B4
ROY/SHW OL2 58 D4
SWIN M27 96 D1
Cemetery Rd North SWIN M27 82 D5
Cemetery St MDTN M24 71 H3
Cennick Cl OLDE OL4 91 F1
Ceno St OLD OL1 74 D3
Centaur Cl SWIN M27 83 E5
Centenary Ct BOLS/LL BL3 49 E5
Centenary Wy SALQ M50 110 B4
Central Av BNG/LEV M19 143 H1
BURY BL9 53 E2
FWTH BL4 64 B4
LIT OL15 21 E2
SALE M33 153 G5
SLFD M6 98 B4
SWIN M27 84 A5
WALK M28 80 D2
Central Dr BRAM/HZG SK7 183 G2
BURY BL9 27 G3
CHD/CHDH SK8 182 A4
CHH M8 100 C1
MPL/ROM SK6 162 B3
RDSH SK5 160 B1
SWIN M27 97 G3
URM M41 138 C1
Central Park Est TRPK * M17 124 D2
Central Rd DID/WITH M20 157 F1
MANAIR M90 190 B1
PART M31 151 E3
Central St BOL BL1 2 D4
CMANW M2 6 E5
RAMS BL0 16 C2
Central Wy ALT WA14 165 G5
Centre Gdns BOL BL1 33 G5
Centre Park Rd BOL BL1 2 A1
Centre Vale Cl LIT OL15 21 F1
Centurion Gv BRO M7 99 H5
Century Gdns WHIT OL12 10 C4
Century Ldg FWTH BL4 64 D4
Cestrian St BOLS/LL BL3 64 A1
Ceylon St NEWH/MOS M40 101 H4
OLDE OL4 91 G2
Chadderton Dr BURY BL9 68 D2
Chadderton Fold OLD OL1 73 E2
Chadderton Hall Rd CHAD OL9 73 E3
Chadderton Park Rd CHAD OL9 73 E3
Chadderton St ANC M4 7 H2
Chadderton Wy CHAD OL9 8 D1
OLD OL1 73 H3
Chaddesley Wk OP/CLY * M11 114 D5
Chaddock La WALK M28 94 A4
The Chaddock Level WALK M28 94 B5
Chadkirk Rd MPL/ROM SK6 162 A5
Chadvil Rd CHD/CHDH SK8 169 H4
Chadwell Rd OFTN SK2 173 F2
Chadwick Cl MILN OL16 44 D1
RUSH/FAL * M14 127 G5
WILM/AE SK9 199 H1
Chadwick Fold BURY BL9 27 G4
Chadwick Hall Rd ROCH OL11 29 E5
Chadwick La HEY OL10 41 H4
MILN OL16 43 H4
Chadwick Rd ECC M30 109 H3
URM M41 139 E1
Chadwick St AUL OL6 118 D3
BOLE BL2 3 H6
BOLS/LL BL3 66 A1
BURY BL9 39 H2
MILN OL16 31 F4
MPL/ROM SK6 175 E4
ROCH OL11 29 G4
STKP SK1 13 G6
SWIN M27 97 E2
Chaffinch Cl DROY M43 116 D2
OLDE OL4 91 G3
WYTH/NTH M22 169 F4
Chaffinch Dr BURY BL9 39 F2
Chaffinch Gv STLY * SK15 107 F3
Chain Bar La HYDE SK14 149 G1
Chain Rd BKLY M9 87 E2
Chain St CMANE M1 7 F5
Chalcombe Gra
WGTN/LGST * M12 128 C4
Chale Cl NEWH/MOS M40 114 A2
Chale Dr MDTN M24 88 B1
Chale Gn BOLE BL2 35 F3
Chalfont Av URM * M41 138 D1
Chalfont Cl OLDS * OL8 91 E3
Chalfont Dr CHH M8 100 B3
WALK M28 95 F2
Chalfont St BOL BL1 34 A4
Chalford Rd NTHM/RTH M23 179 H1
Challenor Sq WGTN/LGST * M12 128 D2
Challum Dr CHAD OL9 73 F4
Chamber Hall Cl OLDS OL8 90 A3
Chamberhall St BURY BL9 4 D2
Chamber House Dr ROCH OL11 42 A3
Chamberlain Dr WILM/AE SK9 200 A1
Chamberlain Rd STLY SK15 106 D5
Chamberlain St BOLS/LL BL3 2 B7
Chamber Rd OLDS OL8 89 H4
ROY/SHW OL2 59 H2
Chambers Ct HYDE SK14 134 D5
Chambers Field Ct ORD M5 111 H4
Champness Hall MILN * OL16 10 D7
Chancel Av ORD M5 112 B5
Chancel Cl DUK SK16 132 B2
Chancel La WILM/AE SK9 199 G2
Chancellor La WGTN/LGST M12 114 A5
Chancel Ms STKP SK1 13 J3
Chancel Pl CMANE * M1 7 K5
MILN OL16 10 C7
Chancery La BOL BL1 3 F5
CMANW M2 6 E5
ROY/SHW * OL2 60 B2
UPML OL3 77 H2
Chancery St CHAD OL9 74 A4
OLDE OL4 91 F1
Chancery Wk CHAD OL9 73 H4
Chandley St CHD/CHDH * SK8 170 A3
Chandos Gv ORD M5 111 E3
Chandos Rd CCHDY M21 141 F2
HTNM SK4 144 A5
PWCH M25 85 E5
Chandos Rd South
CCHDY M21 141 F2
Chandos St ROY/SHW OL2 60 B2
Change Wy CSLFD M3 6 B1
Channing Ct MILN * OL16 30 C5
Channing Sq MILN OL16 30 C5
Channing St MILN OL16 30 C5
The Chanters WALK M28 94 D3
Chantlers Av TOT/BURYW BL8 37 F5
Chantry Cl RDSH SK5 144 D4
Chapel Aly BOL * BL1 2 E4
Chapel Cl BURY BL9 54 A5
DUK SK16 118 B5
Chapel Ct ALT WA14 165 G5
Chapel Cft ROY/SHW OL2 59 E5
Chapel Dr AUL OL6 105 H5
HALE/TIMP WA15 178 D5
Chapelfield RAD M26 67 H3
Chapelfield Cl STLY SK15 120 A1
Chapelfield Dr WALK M28 80 C4
Chapel Field Rd
DTN/ASHW M34 131 G5
Chapelfield Rd WGTN/LGST M12 113 H5
Chapelfield St BOL BL1 33 H3
Chapel Gdns TOT/BURYW * BL8 25 H2
Chapel Ga MILN OL16 31 G5
Chapel Gn DTN/ASHW M34 131 G5
Chapel Gv URM M41 138 D1
Chapel Hl LIT OL15 21 E2
Chapelhill Dr BKLY M9 86 D4
Chapel La BKLY M9 86 C4
HALE/TIMP WA15 178 C4
PART M31 151 E3
ROY/SHW OL2 59 E5
SALE M33 138 D5
TOT/BURYW BL8 16 B2
WILM/AE SK9 199 E4
Chapel Meadow WALK M28 94 C3
Chapel Pl BOLS/LL BL3 49 H4
URM M41 109 G5
Chapel Rd IRL M44 136 B1
OLDS OL8 89 H4
PWCH M25 98 C1
SALE M33 154 C1
SWIN M27 96 B3
UPML OL3 93 H1
WILM/AE SK9 201 B4
WYTH/NTH M22 168 C1
Chapel St AUL OL6 118 B2
BNG/LEV M19 143 H2
BOL BL1 3 G3
BOLS/LL * BL3 65 H1
BRAM/HZG SK7 185 F1
BURY BL9 4 E4
CHD/CHDH SK8 170 A4
CSLFD M3 6 B3
DROY M43 116 B4
DUK SK16 118 B5
ECC M30 109 F4
FWTH * BL4 65 F4
HEY * OL10 41 E4
HTNM SK4 158 A4
HYDE SK14 147 G2
LIT OL15 15 C3
MDTN * M24 70 D5
MDTN M24 71 G4
MOSL OL5 106 C1
MPL/ROM SK6 162 A1
OLDE OL4 91 H1
PWCH M25 84 D3
ROCH OL11 43 F2
ROY/SHW OL2 59 E5
ROY/SHW * OL2 60 A2
STLY SK15 119 F3
SWIN M27 97 F1
TOT/BURYW BL8 26 A4
UPML OL3 78 A4
WALK M28 94 A4
WHIT OL12 19 H1
WILM/AE SK9 201 B4
Chapeltown Rd EDGW/EG BL7 23 G3
RAD M26 67 F3
Chapeltown St CMANE M1 7 K6
Chapel Vw DUK SK16 118 B5
Chapel Wks CHD/CHDH SK8 192 D1
CMANW M2 6 E4
Chapelway Gdns ROY/SHW OL2 60 E3
Chaplin Cl SLFD M6 111 F1
Chapman Ms GTN * M18 129 G3
Chapman Rd HYDE SK14 149 F2
Chapman St BOL BL1 33 E5
GTN M18 129 G2
Chappell Rd DROY M43 116 B3
Chappeltown Rd RAD M26 67 E3
Chapter St NEWH/MOS M40 114 C1
Charcoal Rd ALT WA14 176 B1
Charcoal Woods ALT WA14 176 D1
Chard Dr WYTH/NTH M22 180 C3
Chardin Av MPL/ROM SK6 175 H1
Chard St RAD M26 67 F1
Charfield St NEWH/MOS M40 102 C5
Charges St AULW OL7 117 G4
Chariot St OP/CLY M11 115 G5
Charlbury Av PWCH M25 85 G4
RDSH SK5 145 E5
Charlbury Wy ROY/SHW OL2 59 H4
Charlecote Rd POY/DIS SK12 195 G3
Charles Av DTN/ASHW M34 130 B1
MPL/ROM SK6 174 B2
Charles Ct BOL * BL1 3 F3
Charles Halle Rd HULME M15 127 F3
Charles Holden St BOL BL1 2 A6
Charles La MILN OL16 44 D1
Charles Ms MILN * OL16 44 D1
Charles Morris Cl FAIL M35 103 G2
Charles Shaw Cl OLDE OL4 75 G3
Charles St AULW OL7 118 A3
BOL BL1 3 F3
BRAM/HZG SK7 185 E1
BURY BL9 5 F2
CHAD OL9 8 B5
CMANE M1 7 G7
DROY * M43 115 H4
DTN/ASHW M34 131 G3
EDGW/EG BL7 22 C1
FWTH BL4 65 F3
HEY OL10 56 B1
IRL M44 135 D5
LIT OL15 20 D3
ROY/SHW OL2 59 E5
SLFD M6 111 G1
STKP SK1 13 J7
SWIN M27 96 C1
WHIT OL12 14 C3
WHTF M45 68 C5
Charleston Cl SALE M33 153 G4
Charleston Sq URM M41 123 E5
Charleston St OLDS OL8 90 C3
Charlestown Rd BKLY M9 87 E5
Charlestown Rd East OFTN SK2 184 B1

Charlestown Rd West
EDGY/DAV SK3 .... 184 A1
Charles Whittaker St WHIT OL12 ... 28 C2
Charlesworth Av BOLS/LL BL3 ... 64 C2
DTN/ASHW M34 .... 146 C3
Charlesworth St OFTN SK2 ... 3 C1
OP/CLY M11 .... 114 C5
Charley Av BRO M7 .... 112 C1
Charlock Sq ALT WA14 .... 165 E1
Charlotte La OLDE OL4 .... 93 H4
Charlotte St BOL BL1 .... 85 G5
CHD/CHDH SK8 .... 170 A4
CMANW * M1 .... 7 F5
RAMS * BL0 .... 16 C3
ROCH OL11 .... 43 F2
STKP SK1 .... 160 C3
Charlton Av ECC M30 .... 109 G4
HYDE SK14 .... 133 H4
PWCH M25 .... 73 H3
Charlton Dr SALE M33 .... 154 D2
SWIN M27 .... 82 B5
Charlton Pl CMANE M1 .... 127 G1
Charlton Rd BNG/LEV M19 .... 144 A1
Charminster Dr CHH M8 .... 100 C2
Charmouth Wk WYTH/NTH M22 .... 181 E1
Charnley Cl NEWH/MOS M40 .... 114 B2
Charnley Rd WHTF M45 .... 68 C4
Charnock Dr BOL BL1 .... 2 C1
Charnville Rd CHD/CHDH SK8 .... 169 E5
Charnwood Av DTN/ASHW M34 .... 130 C5
ROY/SHW OL2 .... 59 F1
WALK M28 .... 80 D5
Charnwood Crs BRAM/HZG SK7 .... 186 E4
Charnwood Rd BKLY M9 .... 87 E2
MPL/ROM SK6 .... 162 B1
Charter Av RAD M26 .... 67 H2
Charter Cl SALE M33 .... 155 C3
Charter Rd HALE/TIMP WA15 .... 165 H3
Charter St CSLFD M3 .... 113 E2
MILN OL16 .... 43 F2
OLDE OL4 .... 71 D4
Chartwell Cl SLFD M6 .... 111 C3
Chartwell Dr NTHM/RTH M23 .... 167 E2
The Chase WALK M28 .... 95 H5
Chase Briar Wd
CHD/CHDH * SK8 .... 183 E3
Chaseley Rd SLFD M6 .... 111 F2
Chasefield ALT WA14 .... 176 D2
WHIT OL12 .... 10 A4
Chassen Av URM * M41 .... 137 H1
Chassen Ct URM * M41 .... 138 A2
Chassen Rd BOL BL1 .... 48 A2
URM M41 .... 138 A2
Chataway Rd CHH M8 .... 100 C2
Chatburn Av ROCH OL11 .... 57 G1
Chatburn Gdns HEY OL10 .... 40 A4
Chatburn Rd BOL BL1 .... 32 C3
CCHDY M21 .... 141 H3
Chatburn Sq ROCH OL11 .... 57 G2
Chatcombe Rd WYTH/NTH M22 .... 179 H2
Chatfield Rd CCHDY M21 .... 141 E3
Chatford Cl BRO M7 .... 112 C1
Chatham Ct DID/WITH * M20 .... 142 B5
Chatham Gdns BOLS/LL BL3 .... 48 C4
Chatham Gv DID/WITH M20 .... 142 B5
Chatham Pl BOLS/LL * BL3 .... 48 C4
OLDTF/WHR M16 .... 126 A3
Chatham St CMANE M1 .... 7 H5
EDGY/DAV SK3 .... 12 C6
HYDE SK14 .... 147 G2
Chatley Rd ECC M30 .... 108 C4
Chatley St CSLFD M3 .... 113 E1
Chatsworth Av PWCH M25 .... 85 E3
Chatsworth Cl BURY BL9 .... 53 H4
DROY M43 .... 115 G2
HALE/TIMP WA15 .... 166 D2
ROY/SHW OL2 .... 60 B1
URM M41 .... 138 D1
Chatsworth Gv
OLDTF/WHR M16 .... 141 G1
Chatsworth Ms BRAM/HZG SK7 .... 185 G1
Chatsworth Rd BRAM/HZG SK7 .... 185 G3
DROY M43 .... 115 H2
ECC M30 .... 110 A3
GTN M18 .... 129 F3
MPL/ROM SK6 .... 197 E1
RAD M26 .... 51 H4
SWIN M27 .... 83 H2
Chatsworth St OLDE OL4 .... 91 F2
WHIT OL12 .... 18 D1
Chatterton Cl DID/WITH M20 .... 142 D5
Chatterton Rd RAMS BL0 .... 16 D2
Chatterton St OLDTF/WHR M16 .... 126 D5
Chatton Cl TOT/BURYW BL8 .... 37 E4
Chatwood Rd NEWH/MOS M40 .... 88 D5
Chaucer Av DROY M43 .... 116 B4
DTN/ASHW M34 .... 146 C4
ROSH SK5 .... 144 C3
Chaucer Ms STKP SK1 .... 160 C5
Chaucer Ri DUK SK16 .... 133 F1
Chaucer St BOL BL1 .... 33 G5
OLD OL1 .... 9 F4
ROCH OL11 .... 43 E4
ROY/SHW OL2 .... 59 F4
Chaucer Wk BRUN/LGST * M13 .... 127 H2
Chauncy Rd NEWH/MOS M40 .... 104 A3
Chaytor Av NEWH/MOS M40 .... 102 A3
Cheadle Av BRO M7 .... 99 G2
Cheadle Old Rd EDGY/DAV SK3 .... 171 G4
Cheadle Pl CHD/CHDH * SK8 .... 171 G4
Cheadle Rd CHD/CHDH SK8 .... 170 D5
Cheadle Sq OP/CLY M11 .... 115 G5
Cheadle Wd CHD/CHDH SK8 .... 182 B4
Cheam Rd HALE/TIMP WA15 .... 166 A1
Cheapside CMANW M2 .... 6 E4
HYDE SK14 .... 132 D5
Cheap Side OLD OL1 .... 71 H2
Cheapside OLD OL1 .... 9 F5
Cheapside Sq BOL * BL1 .... 2 C4
Cheddar St GTN M18 .... 129 G3
Chedlee Dr CHD/CHDH SK8 .... 182 B3
Chedlin Dr NTHM/RTH M23 .... 167 H5
Chedworth Crs LHULT M38 .... 80 B1
Chedworth Dr NTHM/RTH M23 .... 168 A3
Chedworth Gv BOLS/LL * BL3 .... 48 D4
Cheeryble St DROY M43 .... 116 A3
Cheetham Fold Rd HYDE SK14 .... 147 G3

Cheetham Hl ROY/SHW OL2 .... 60 A3
Cheetham Hill Rd ANC M4 .... 7 F1
CHH M8 .... 100 B5
DUK SK16 .... 132 C2
Cheetham Pl MPL/ROM SK6 .... 161 G2
Cheetham Rd SWIN M27 .... 97 F3
Cheetham St FAIL M35 .... 105 F1
MDTN M24 .... 71 G4
MILN OL16 .... 10 C5
NEWH/MOS * M40 .... 115 E1
OLD * OL1 .... 75 E5
RAD M26 .... 52 D5
ROY/SHW OL2 .... 60 B3
Cheetwood Rd CHH M8 .... 100 A5
Cheetwood St CHH M8 .... 112 D1
Chelbourne Dr OLDS * OL8 .... 89 C5
Chelburn Vw LIT OL15 .... 15 B4
Chelford Av BOL BL1 .... 33 H1
Chelford Cl HALE/TIMP WA15 .... 165 H3
MDTN M24 .... 72 B5
Chelford Dr SWIN M27 .... 82 D5
Chelford Gv EDGY/DAV SK3 .... 171 F4
Chelford Rd OLDTF/WHR M16 .... 126 B5
SALE M33 .... 153 H1
WILM/AE SK9 .... 192 A2
Chellow Dene MOSL OL5 .... 106 C1
Chell St WGTN/LGST M12 .... 128 C4
Chelmer Gv HEY OL10 .... 40 B3
Chelmsford Av
NEWH/MOS M40 .... 115 E1
Chelmsford Rd EDGY/DAV SK3 .... 12 B6
Chelmsford St OLDS OL8 .... 8 E6
Chelsea Av RAD M26 .... 51 G5
Chelsea Cl ROY/SHW OL2 .... 60 A2
Chelsea Rd BOLS/LL BL3 .... 63 F1
NEWH/MOS M40 .... 102 B5
Chelsea St BURY BL9 .... 4 C1
ROCH * OL11 .... 42 C1
Chelsfield Gv CCHDY M21 .... 141 G4
Chelston Av NEWH/MOS M40 .... 88 C5
Chelston Dr CHD/CHDH SK8 .... 191 H1
Cheltenham Crs BRO M7 .... 99 H2
Cheltenham Dr SALE M33 .... 154 D2
Cheltenham Gn MDTN M24 .... 87 H1
Cheltenham Rd CCHDY M21 .... 141 E1
EDGY/DAV SK3 .... 12 A6
MDTN M24 .... 87 H1
Cheltenham St OLD OL1 .... 75 E3
ROCH OL11 .... 42 C2
Chelwood Cl BOL BL1 .... 22 C4
Chelwood Dr DROY M45 .... 116 A3
Chelwood Ms HOR/BR * BL6 .... 46 C2
Chendre Rd BKLY M9 .... 88 A4
Cheney Cl OP/CLY * M11 .... 129 E1
Chepstow Av SALE M33 .... 153 F3
Chepstow Dr BRAM/HZG SK7 .... 185 H2
Chepstow Rd CCHDY M21 .... 141 E3
SWIN M27 .... 83 F5
Chepstow St CMANE M1 .... 6 E7
Chepstow St South CMANE M1 .... 6 E7
Cherington Cl NTHM/RTH M23 .... 156 A4
WILM/AE SK9 .... 192 C4
Cherington Rd CHD/CHDH SK8 .... 169 H5
Cheriton Av SALE M33 .... 154 B1
Cheriton Cl HYDE SK14 .... 149 E1
Cheriton Dr BOLE BL2 .... 50 B5
Cheriton Ri OFTN SK2 .... 173 H5
Cheriton Rd URM M41 .... 137 E1
Cherrington Dr ROCH OL11 .... 57 E1
Cherry Av AUL OL6 .... 105 E4
BURY BL9 .... 39 F3
OLDS OL8 .... 91 H4
Cherry Cl BURY BL9 .... 53 F2
OFTN SK2 .... 173 H2
Cherrycroft MPL/ROM SK6 .... 162 D5
Cherry Dr SWIN M27 .... 97 F2
Cherry Gv ROCH OL11 .... 28 D3
ROY/SHW OL2 .... 60 B1
STLY SK15 .... 119 F5
Cherry Hall Dr ROY/SHW * OL2 .... 59 F1
Cherry Hinton OLD * OL1 .... 74 A4
Cherry Holt Av HTNM SK4 .... 158 C2
Cherry La SALE M33 .... 153 F4
Cherry Orchard Cl
BRAM/HZG SK7 .... 185 F2
Cherry St PWCH * M25 .... 85 F2
Cherryton Wk BRUN/LGST M13 .... 127 H2
Cherry Tree Av FWTH BL4 .... 64 A4
POY/DIS SK12 .... 195 G4
Cherry Tree Cl
HALE/TIMP WA15 .... 166 C4
MPL/ROM SK6 .... 162 D4
WILM/AE SK9 .... 200 B2
Cherry Tree Ct OFTN SK2 .... 172 D5
Cherry Tree Dr BRAM/HZG SK7 .... 185 H4
Cherry Tree La MPL/ROM SK6 .... 162 D4
OFTN SK2 .... 172 D4
TOT/BURYW * BL8 .... 37 H5
Cherry Tree Rd
HALE/TIMP WA15 .... 166 C4
Cherry Tree Wk STRET M52 .... 139 G2
Cherry Wk BOLE BL2 .... 34 C2
CHD/CHDH SK8 .... 183 H4
Chertsey Cl GTN M18 .... 129 H3
Cherwell Av OLDS OL8 .... 90 B3
Cherwell Cl CHD/CHDH SK8 .... 182 D5
OLDS OL8 .... 103 H1
WHTF M45 .... 68 D1
Chesham Av BOL BL1 .... 33 H4
ROCH OL11 .... 57 G2
URM M41 .... 122 B5
WYTH/NTH M22 .... 168 B5
Chesham Cl WILM/AE SK9 .... 201 A1
Chesham Crs BURY BL9 .... 5 K1
Chesham Fold Rd BURY BL9 .... 5 K2
Chesham Pl ALT WA14 .... 177 F2
Chesham Rd BURY BL9 .... 5 G1
ECC * M30 .... 109 F5
OLDE OL4 .... 91 F1
WILM/AE SK9 .... 201 A1
Cheshire Cl STRET M52 .... 139 G2
Cheshire Ct RAMS BL0 .... 17 E2

Cheshire Ring Canal Wk
ALT WA14 .... 164 B4
MPL/ROM SK6 .... 147 E5
MPL/ROM SK6 .... 175 E1
Cheshire Rd PART M31 .... 150 C4
STLY SK15 .... 107 E5
The Cheshires MOSL OL5 .... 107 F1
Cheshire Sq STLY SK15 .... 107 F5
Cheshire St MOSL OL5 .... 107 F5
Chesney Av CHAD OL9 .... 88 D5
Cheshyre Av ANC * M4 .... 114 A4
Chessington Ri SWIN M27 .... 83 F4
Chester Av BOLS/LL BL3 .... 51 E5
DUK SK16 .... 132 D1
HALE/TIMP WA15 .... 178 A2
ROCH OL11 .... 43 H5
SALE M33 .... 153 E5
STLY SK15 .... 120 A2
URM M41 .... 123 H5
WHTF M45 .... 68 C5
Chester Cl BOLS/LL BL3 .... 51 E5
IRL M44 .... 150 C1
WILM/AE SK9 .... 192 B5
Chester Dr RAMS BL0 .... 16 B4
Chesterfield Gv AUL OL6 .... 118 C2
Chesterfield St OLDE OL4 .... 91 E1
Chestergate STKP SK1 .... 13 F3
Chester Rd BRAM/HZG SK7 .... 185 E5
OLDTF/WHR M16 .... 126 A3
POY/DIS SK12 .... 194 C3
STRET M52 .... 125 F4
STRET M52 .... 139 H5
Chester St BURY BL9 .... 38 D2
CHAD OL9 .... 8 A7
DTN/ASHW M34 .... 146 C1
EDGY/DAV SK3 .... 12 C4
HULME M15 .... 127 E1
PWCH M25 .... 86 A3
SWIN M27 .... 96 D5
Chesterton Cl BOLS/LL BL3 .... 47 F4
Chesterton Gv DROY M45 .... 116 B3
Chesterton Rd NTHM/RTH M23 .... 167 E1
Chester Wk BOL BL1 .... 33 H1
Chester Wks MPL/ROM SK6 .... 161 H5
Chestnut Av BURY BL9 .... 5 J1
CHD/CHDH SK8 .... 170 B4
DROY M43 .... 115 H5
IRL M44 .... 150 C1
TOT/BURYW BL8 .... 37 F1
WALK M28 .... 81 E4
WHTF M45 .... 68 C5
Chestnut Cl BOLS/LL BL3 .... 48 A5
OLDE OL4 .... 71 G5
STLY SK15 .... 119 F5
WILM/AE SK9 .... 200 B2
Chestnut Crs OLDS OL8 .... 90 D5
Chestnut Dr BURY BL9 .... 27 G4
POY/DIS SK12 .... 195 G4
SALE M33 .... 155 C5
Chestnut Fold RAD M26 .... 52 B5
Chestnut Gdns DTN/ASHW M34 .... 146 B1
HEY OL10 .... 41 H2
Chestnut Gv FAIL M35 .... 103 E4
RAD M26 .... 67 G4
Chestnut Rd ECC M30 .... 109 G4
Chestnut St CHAD OL9 .... 89 F4
Chestnut Wk PART M31 .... 150 D3
Chesworth Cl STKP SK1 .... 13 G5
Chesworth Fold STKP SK1 .... 13 G5
Chetham Cl ORD * M5 .... 126 A1
Chetwyn Av EDGW/EG BL7 .... 22 D1
ROY/SHW OL2 .... 58 D5
Chetwynd Av URM M41 .... 138 B2
Chetwynd Cl SALE M33 .... 153 G3
Chevassut St HULME M15 .... 126 D2
Chevington Dr BKLY M9 .... 101 E4
HTNM SK4 .... 158 A5
Cheviot Av CHD/CHDH SK8 .... 182 C2
OLDS OL8 .... 90 B4
ROY/SHW OL2 .... 73 H1
Cheviot Cl BOL BL1 .... 35 G1
CHAD OL9 .... 73 H4
HTNM SK4 .... 159 G3
MDTN M24 .... 72 C4
RAMS BL0 .... 16 B4
SLFD M6 .... 111 F2
TOT/BURYW BL8 .... 37 F5
Cheviot Cl BKLY M9 .... 101 E2
Cheviot St BRAM/HZG SK7 .... 184 C5
Chevithorne Cl ALT WA14 .... 165 E4
Chevril Cl HULME M15 .... 127 F2
Chevron Cl ROCH OL11 .... 42 B5
SLFD M6 .... 112 A3
Chevron Pl ALT WA14 .... 165 G3
Chew V DUK SK16 .... 133 H1
Chicago Av MANAIR M90 .... 180 A5
Chichester Cl LIT OL15 .... 20 C5
SALE M33 .... 154 D3
Chichester Crs CHAD OL9 .... 73 F5
Chichester Rd HULME M15 .... 126 D5
SLFD M6 .... 111 H5
Chichester Rd South
HULME * M15 .... 126 D5
Chichester St MILN OL16 .... 11 G7
Chidlow Av DID/WITH M20 .... 142 B4
Chidwall Rd WYTH/NTH M22 .... 180 A2
Chief St OLDE OL4 .... 91 E1
Chiffon Wy CSLFD M3 .... 112 C2
Chigwell Cl WYTH/NTH M22 .... 168 D4
Chilcote Av SALE M33 .... 153 E3
Childwall Cl BOLS/LL BL3 .... 63 H2
Chilham Rd ECC M30 .... 110 A1
WALK M28 .... 81 H5
Chilham St BOLS/LL BL3 .... 65 E1
SWIN M27 .... 98 D5
Chilmark Dr NTHM/RTH M23 .... 167 H5
Chiltern Av URM M41 .... 122 C5
Chiltern Cl BRAM/HZG SK7 .... 184 C5
RAMS BL0 .... 16 B4
ROY/SHW OL2 .... 59 G1
WALK M28 .... 95 F2
Chiltern Dr BOLE BL2 .... 50 C2
HALE/TIMP WA15 .... 178 A2
OFTN SK2 .... 173 H4
ROY/SHW OL2 .... 59 G1
SWIN M27 .... 97 E4
TOT/BURYW BL8 .... 37 E1
Chiltern Gdns SALE M33 .... 166 D1
Chiltern Rd RAMS BL0 .... 16 B4
Chilton Av CHAD OL9 .... 89 F1

Chilton Dr MDTN M24 .... 72 B5
Chilworth St RUSH/FAL M14 .... 142 C1
Chime Bank CHH M8 .... 100 C4
China La CMANE M1 .... 7 H5
Chingford Wk
BRUN/LGST * M13 .... 128 C4
Chinley Av NEWH/MOS M40 .... 101 H2
HTNM SK4 .... 124 B4
SALE M33 .... 159 E3
Chinley Cl BRAM/HZG SK7 .... 185 H1
HTNM SK4 .... 159 E3
SALE M33 .... 155 G1
Chinley St SLFD M6 .... 99 F5
Chinwell Vw BNG/LEV M19 .... 143 H2
Chip Hill Rd BOLS/LL BL3 .... 47 H5
Chipping Fold MILN OL16 .... 44 C1
Chipping Rd BOL BL1 .... 32 C4
Chipstead Av WGTN/LGST M12 .... 128 D3
Chirmside St TOT/BURYW BL8 .... 37 G5
Chiselhurst St CHH M8 .... 100 D3
Chisledon Av CHH * M8 .... 100 A4
Chislehurst Av URM M41 .... 138 A2
Chislehurst Cl TOT/BURYW BL8 .... 37 G5
Chiswick Dr BOLS/LL BL3 .... 51 E4
Chiswick Rd DID/WITH M20 .... 157 H5
Chisworth Cl BRAM/HZG SK7 .... 185 H2
Chisworth St BOLE BL2 .... 34 C5
Choir St BRO M7 .... 112 D1
Chokeberry Cl ALT WA14 .... 165 H1
Cholmondeley Av ALT * WA14 .... 165 H1
Cholmondeley Rd SLFD M6 .... 110 C1
Chomlea Mnr SLFD * M6 .... 110 D1
Choral Gv BRO M7 .... 112 D1
Chorley Cl TOT/BURYW BL8 .... 37 E5
Chorley Hall Cl WILM/AE SK9 .... 200 C5
Chorley Hall La WILM/AE SK9 .... 201 A4
Chorley New Rd HOR/BR BL6 .... 46 B1
Chorley Old Rd BOL BL1 .... 33 F2
Chorley Rd SALE M33 .... 155 F4
Chorley St BOL BL1 .... 2 D3
STRET M52 .... 125 G4
Chorley Wood Av
BNG/LEV * M19 .... 143 H3
Chorlton Dr CHD/CHDH SK8 .... 170 B3
Chorlton Fold ECC M30 .... 96 D5
Chorlton Gv STKP SK1 .... 172 C2
Chorlton Pl CCHDY M21 .... 141 E2
Chorlton Rd OLDTF/WHR M16 .... 126 D2
Chorlton St CMANE M1 .... 7 G5
OLDTF/WHR M16 .... 126 D5
Chorlton Ter BRUN/LGST * M13 .... 127 H2
Chretien Rd WYTH/NTH M22 .... 180 A4
Christchurch Av ORD M5 .... 112 A3
Christ Church Cl BOLE * BL2 .... 35 G4
Christ Church La BOLE BL2 .... 35 G4
Christchurch Rd SALE M33 .... 153 F1
Christie Rd STRET M52 .... 125 G5
Christie St STKP SK1 .... 13 K6
Christine St ROY/SHW OL2 .... 60 A2
Christleton Av HTNM SK4 .... 159 G1
Christopher Acre ROCH OL11 .... 57 E1
Christopher St NEWH/MOS M40 .... 114 B1
ORD M5 .... 111 H4
Chronnell Dr BOLE BL2 .... 35 E3
Chudleigh Cl ALT WA14 .... 165 E5
BRAM/HZG SK7 .... 185 H3
Chudleigh Rd CHH M8 .... 86 B5
Chulsey Gate La HOR/BR BL6 .... 46 A3
Chulsey St BOLS/LL BL3 .... 63 E1
Church Av BOLS/LL BL3 .... 48 B5
DTN/ASHW M34 .... 148 A3
MDTN M24 .... 71 H3
NEWH/MOS M40 .... 102 B5
SLFD M6 .... 111 H3
Church Bank BOL BL1 .... 3 F4
Churchbank STLY SK15 .... 120 A3
Church Brow ALT WA14 .... 177 E2
HYDE SK14 .... 134 D5
Church Cl RAD M26 .... 66 A5
Church Ct AUL OL6 .... 119 H3
RAMS BL0 .... 16 C3
Church Ct BURY BL9 .... 5 G5
DUK SK16 .... 118 A4
Church Dr PWCH M25 .... 85 E3
Churchfield CCHDY M21 .... 140 D3
Churchfield Rd SLFD M6 .... 110 C1
Churchfields DTN/ASHW M34 .... 131 F1
SALE M33 .... 153 F1
Churchfield Wk OP/CLY * M11 .... 114 D5
Churchgate BOL BL1 .... 3 F5
STKP SK1 .... 13 J3
URM M41 .... 138 D2
Churchgate Buildings
CMANE * M1 .... 7 K6
Church Gn RAD M26 .... 52 B5
SLFD * M6 .... 111 G2
Church Gv BRAM/HZG SK7 .... 185 F2
Churchill Av BOLS/LL BL3 .... 48 B5
Churchill Cl HEY OL10 .... 40 D4
Churchill Dr BOLS/LL BL3 .... 66 B1
Churchill St BOLE BL2 .... 3 J2
HTNM SK4 .... 159 G1
OLDE OL4 .... 9 K5
WHIT OL12 .... 29 F2
Churchill St East OLDE OL4 .... 9 K5
Churchill Wy SLFD M6 .... 111 H3
TRPK M17 .... 124 B2
Church La BKLY M9 .... 88 D1
BNG/LEV M19 .... 143 H1
BRAM/HZG SK7 .... 185 G2
BRO M7 .... 99 H4
MILN OL16 .... 10 C7
MOSL OL5 .... 107 E1
OLD OL1 .... 9 G3
PWCH M25 .... 85 E3
ROY/SHW OL2 .... 59 G1
SALE M33 .... 153 H2
UPML OL3 .... 78 B4
WHTF M45 .... 68 B4

WILM/AE SK9 .... 201 B3
Churchley Cl EDGY/DAV SK3 .... 170 D5
Churchley Rd EDGY/DAV SK3 .... 170 D2
Church Meadow BURY BL9 .... 54 A4
WILM/AE SK9 .... 132 B5
Church Mdw BOLE BL2 .... 35 G3
Church Ms DTN/ASHW M34 .... 131 H5
Church Rd BOL BL1 .... 33 F4
CHD/CHDH SK8 .... 185 E5
ECC M30 .... 110 A3
FWTH BL4 .... 65 F4
HTNM SK4 .... 12 C1
MDTN M24 .... 72 D1
MILN OL16 .... 30 C5
OLDE OL4 .... 93 F2
RAD M26 .... 65 H4
ROY/SHW OL2 .... 60 A3
SALE M33 .... 155 E2
UPML OL3 .... 78 B4
URM M41 .... 137 H5
WALK M28 .... 81 E4
WILM/AE SK9 .... 192 A4
WYTH/NTH M22 .... 156 C5
Church Rd East SALE M33 .... 155 E2
Church Rd West SALE M33 .... 154 D2
Churchside FWTH BL4 .... 64 C5
Churchside Cl BKLY M9 .... 87 E5
Church Stile MILN OL16 .... 10 C7
Churchston Av BRAM/HZG SK7 .... 184 B2
Church St ALT WA14 .... 165 G4
AUL OL6 .... 118 A3
BOLE BL2 .... 35 E1
BOLS/LL BL3 .... 36 C5
BURY BL9 .... 65 G1
CHD/CHDH SK8 .... 170 A3
DROY M43 .... 116 D4
DTN/ASHW M34 .... 132 D5
ECC M30 .... 109 F5
FAIL M35 .... 105 F3
HEY OL10 .... 41 E4
HYDE SK14 .... 147 G2
LIT OL15 .... 15 H1
MDTN M24 .... 71 H2
MILN OL16 .... 20 C5
MILN OL16 .... 45 E2
MPL/ROM SK6 .... 161 H1
OLDE OL4 .... 67 G2
RAD M26 .... 67 G2
RAMS BL0 .... 10 A7
ROY/SHW OL2 .... 60 A3
STLY SK15 .... 119 F3
STRET M52 .... 139 H2
SWIN M27 .... 96 D2
TOT/BURYW * BL8 .... 37 E1
WHIT OL12 .... 14 B5
WILM/AE SK9 .... 199 G3
Church St East OLDE OL4 .... 75 H4
Church St West RAD M26 .... 67 G1
Church Ter MILN OL16 .... 44 D1
OLD OL1 .... 9 G3
SALE M33 .... 153 H2
WILM/AE SK9 .... 139 F2
Churchtown Av BOL BL2 .... 50 C2
Church Vw HYDE SK14 .... 134 D5
HYDE SK14 .... 147 G2
IRL M44 .... 136 C5
WHIT OL12 .... 28 B1
Church Wk ALT WA14 .... 165 G4
FWTH * BL4 .... 64 D4
SWIN M27 .... 83 E3
Churchwood Rd DID/WITH M20 .... 157 G3
Churnet St NEWH/MOS M40 .... 101 E5
Churston Av BKLY M9 .... 88 A3
Churton Av RUSH/FAL M14 .... 143 E1
Churton Rd GTN M18 .... 129 F5
Churwell Av HTNM SK4 .... 158 C2
Cicero St BKLY M9 .... 101 F2
OLD OL1 .... 9 G3
Cinamon St WHIT OL12 .... 29 G5
Cinder Hill La OLD OL1 .... 73 F1
Cinder St ANC * M4 .... 7 K2
Cinnabar Dr MDTN M24 .... 71 G2
Cipher St ANC M4 .... 7 H2
Circle South TRPK M17 .... 125 F2
The Circuit CHD/CHDH SK8 .... 182 D5
DID/WITH M20 .... 157 E3
EDGY/DAV SK3 .... 171 F3
WILM/AE SK9 .... 201 C2
Circular Rd DID/WITH M20 .... 157 G1
DTN/ASHW M34 .... 146 B2
PWCH M25 .... 85 G5
Circus St CMANE * M1 .... 7 G3
Cirencester Cl LHULT M38 .... 80 B1
Ciss La URM M41 .... 138 D1
Citrus Wy SLFD M6 .... 111 H3
City Av DTN/ASHW M34 .... 146 B4
City Rd DTN/ASHW M34 .... 146 B1
HULME M15 .... 126 C2
WALK M28 .... 94 B2
City Rd East HULME M15 .... 127 E1
City Wk SWIN M27 .... 97 F2
Civic Centre BOL * BL1 .... 33 H4
Clacton Av BRUN/LGST * M13 .... 127 H2
Clague St OP/CLY M11 .... 114 C5
Claife Av NEWH/MOS M40 .... 102 B3
Clammerclough Rd FWTH BL4 .... 65 G4
Clandon Av ECC M30 .... 109 E3
Clapgate MPL/ROM SK6 .... 161 H5
Clapgate Rd ROCH OL11 .... 42 D2
Clara Gorton Ct MILN * OL16 .... 30 D5
Clara St CHAD OL9 .... 89 H3
ROCH OL11 .... 43 E1
WHIT OL12 .... 14 C3
Clare Av WILM/AE SK9 .... 191 H4
Clare Ct TOT/BURYW BL8 .... 38 A1
Claremont Av ALT WA14 .... 165 G1
DID/WITH M20 .... 157 F1
HTNM SK4 .... 158 A5
MPL/ROM SK6 .... 174 B3

Claremont Ct BOL * BL1 ......33 H5
Claremont Dr ALT WA14 .....165 G1
LHULT M38 ......80 C2
Claremont Gdns AUL OL6 ......118 D1
Claremont Gv DID/WITH M20 ..157 F3
HALE/TIMP WA15 ......177 H1
Claremont Range GTN * M18 ..130 A4
Claremont Rd CHD/CHDH SK8 ..182 D4
MILN OL16 ......48 B1
OFTN SK2 ......172 C5
ROCH OL11 ......29 F4
RUSH/FAL M14 ......127 G5
SALE M33 ......154 C1
SLFD M6 ......110 D1
Claremont St AUL OL6 ......118 C1
CHAD * OL9 ......73 H3
FAIL M35 ......103 G2
OLDS OL8 ......90 C5
SLFD M6 ......99 F1
Clarence Av AUL * OL6 ......118 A3
OLDS OL8 ......90 A3
TRPK M17 ......124 A2
WHTF M45 ......68 D5
Clarence Ct BOL * BL1 ......2 C5
WILM/AE SK9 ......199 F4
Clarence Rd AUL OL6 ......118 B1
BRUN/LGST M13 ......128 B5
HALE/TIMP WA15 ......178 A1
HTNM SK4 ......159 E1
SWIN M27 ......96 B3
Clarence St BOL BL1 ......2 E3
BRO M7 ......112 C1
CMANW * M2 ......6 E5
FWTH BL4 ......65 F3
HYDE SK14 ......132 D4
ROY/SHW OL2 ......73 H2
STLY SK15 ......118 D4
WHIT OL12 ......29 C1
Clarendon Av HALE/TIMP WA15 ..165 H4
HTNM SK4 ......159 E3
Clarendon Crs ECC M30 ......110 A2
SALE M33 ......155 E1
Clarendon Gv BOLE BL2 ......3 J7
Clarendon Pl HYDE SK14 ......147 H1
Clarendon Rd BGLY * BL2 ......49 H2
BRAM/HZG SK7 ......185 G1
DTN/ASHW M34 ......131 F3
ECC M30 ......110 A2
HYDE SK14 ......147 E1
MILN OL16 ......43 G2
MOSL OL5 ......107 E2
RDSH * SK5 ......160 A2
WHTF M45 ......68 C4
Clarendon Rd West CCHDY M21 ..141 E1
Clarendon St BOLS/LL BL3 ......48 D5
BURY BL9 ......5 G1
DUK SK16 ......117 H5
HULME M15 ......127 F2
HYDE SK14 ......132 C5
MILN OL16 ......43 G2
MOSL OL5 ......107 E2
RDSH * SK5 ......160 A2
WHTF M45 ......68 C4
Clare Rd BNG/LEV M19 ......143 H5
RDSH * SK5 ......160 A2
Clare St CMANE M1 ......127 G1
DTN/ASHW M34 ......131 F4
OLDS OL8 ......112 B4
Claribel St OP/CLY M11 ......114 B5
Claridge Rd CCHDY M21 ......140 D2
Clarion St ANC M4 ......7 K1
Clark Av GTN M18 ......130 C3
Clarke Av ORD M5 ......126 A1
Clarke Brow MDTN M24 ......71 H1
Clarke Crs HALE/TIMP WA15 ..178 C1
LHULT M38 ......79 C1
Clarkes Cft BURY BL9 ......39 J5
Clarke's La WHIT OL12 ......29 G3
Clarke St AULW * OL7 ......117 G5
BOL BL1 ......48 B1
HEY OL10 ......41 G2
MILN OL16 ......11 G6
Clarksfield Rd OLDE OL4 ......91 F1
Clarksfield St OLDE OL4 ......91 F1
Clark's H PWCH M25 ......86 B3
Clarkson Cl DTN/ASHW M34 ..146 A1
Clark Wy HYDE SK14 ......132 C5
Clarkwell Cl OLD OL1 ......9 H1
Claude Av SWIN M27 ......96 C2
Claude Rd CCHDY M21 ......140 D4
Claude St CHH M8 ......100 B1
ECC M30 ......110 A2
SWIN M27 ......96 C2
Claudia Sq STLY SK15 ......107 F5
Claughton Av BOLE BL2 ......50 C1
WALK M28 ......94 D2
Claughton Rd TOT/BURYW BL8 ..37 E1
Claverton Rd NTHM/RTH M23 ..167 G5
Claxton Av BKLY M9 ......87 E4
Clay Bank DROY M43 ......115 H4
Claybank Dr TOT/BURYW BL8 ..25 H4
Clay Bank St HEY OL10 ......40 D3
Claybar Dr ECC M30 ......108 D3
Claybrook Wk OP/CLY * M11 ..114 D4
Clayburn Rd HULME M15 ......128 D2
Claycourt Av ECC M30 ......109 E1
Claydon Dr BOLS/LL BL3 ......51 E4
Clayfield Dr ROCH OL11 ......28 C3
Claygate Dr BKLY M9 ......87 G2
Clay La HALE/TIMP WA15 ......166 D3
NTHM/RTH M23 ......167 G5
PWCH M25 ......28 B3
WHIT OL12 ......14 D1
Claymore St BOLS/LL * BL3 ......3 K6
GTN M18 ......129 H2
Clay St EDGW/EG BL7 ......23 F4
LIT OL15 ......20 D3
OLDS OL8 ......90 B3
Clayton Av DID/WITH M20 ......157 G3
DID/WITH M20 ......157 G3
Clayton Cl HULME M15 ......128 B3
Clayton Hall Rd OP/CLY M11 ..115 F1
Clayton La OP/CLY M11 ......115 E1
Clayton La South OP/CLY M11 ..128 D1
Claytons Cl OLDE OL4 ......76 A5
Clayton St BOLS/LL BL3 ......4 E3
OLDE OL4 ......89 F4
DTN/ASHW M34 ......146 C5
DUK SK16 ......118 C5
FAIL * M35 ......102 D3

OP/CLY M11 ......115 E2
WHIT OL12 ......11 G1
Cleabarrow Dr WALK M28 ......94 B5
Cleadon Av GTN M18 ......129 F4
Cleadon Dr South
TOT/BURYW BL8 ......37 H1
Cleavley St ECC M30 ......109 E3
Clee Av BRUN/LGST M13 ......143 G1
Cleethorpes Av BKLY M9 ......86 C4
Cleeve Rd NTHM/RTH M23 ....155 H4
OLDE OL4 ......91 F1
Clegg Hall Rd MILN OL16 ......31 E3
Clegg Pl AUL OL6 ......118 C1
Clegg's Buildings BOL * BL1 ......2 C5
Clegg's La LHULT M38 ......80 B2
Clegg St BOLE BL2 ......49 H2
DROY * M43 ......116 A4
LIT OL15 ......20 D3
MILN OL16 ......44 D1
MPL/ROM SK6 ......161 G3
OLD OL1 ......9 G4
OLDE OL4 ......91 H2
WHIT OL12 ......14 B3
WHTF M45 ......68 C5
Cleggswood Av LIT OL15 ......20 D5
Cleland St FWTH BL4 ......65 F5
Clematis St WHIT * OL12 ......10 C3
Clementia Cl MILN OL16 ......10 C3
Clementina St WHIT OL12 ......10 C3
Clement Rd MPL/ROM SK6 ....175 G2
Clement Royds St WHIT OL12 ..10 A3
Clement Scott Cl BKLY M9 ......87 G3
Clement St BRO M7 ......112 C1
HTNM SK4 ......159 H5
Clemison St CSLFD M3 ......6 A3
Clenshaw Cl HEY OL10 ......40 D5
Clerewood Av CHD/CHDH SK8 ..181 G5
Clerke St BURY BL9 ......4 E4
Clevedon Av URM M41 ......139 F1
Clevedon Dr BOLE BL2 ......50 C1
Clevedon Rd CHAD OL9 ......74 D1
Clevedon St BKLY M9 ......101 F3
Cleveland Av BNG/LEV M19 ....144 A1
HYDE * SK14 ......147 F1
SLFD M6 ......110 D2
Cleveland Cl RAMS BL0 ......16 D1
Cleveland Gdns BOLS/LL BL3 ..48 A5
Cleveland Gv ROY/SHW OL2 ....73 H2
Cleveland Rd CHH M8 ......86 A4
HALE/TIMP WA15 ......178 A1
HTNM SK4 ......158 D2
Cleveland St BOLS/LL * BL3 ....48 A5
Cleveleys Av BOLE BL2 ......49 H1
BURY BL9 ......53 F1
CCHDY M21 ......141 H2
CHD/CHDH SK8 ......181 G3
MILN OL16 ......43 G3
Cleveleys Gv BRO M7 ......99 F4
Cleves Ct HEY OL10 ......40 D5
Clevlands Cl ROY/SHW OL2 ......59 H1
Cleworth Rd MDTN M24 ......71 G2
Cleworth St HULME M15 ......126 C1
Cleworth Wk HULME * M15 ....126 C1
Clibran St CHH M8 ......100 C4
Clifden Dr WYTH/NTH M22 ....180 D2
Cliff Av BRO M7 ......99 F4
BRO M7 ......99 G3
TOT/BURYW BL8 ......27 E1
Cliff Circ BRO M7 ......99 G3
Cliff Dl STLY SK15 ......119 E5
Cliffdale Dr CHH M8 ......100 B1
Cliffe St LIT OL15 ......15 C1
Cliff Gv HTNM SK4 ......159 E2
Cliff Hill Rd ROY/SHW OL2 ......45 F5
Cliffmere Cl CHD/CHDH SK8 ..182 C1
Clifford Av DTN/ASHW M34 ....131 H3
HALE/TIMP WA15 ......166 D3
Clifford Rd BOLS/LL * BL3 ......62 D2
POY/DIS SK12 ......194 D3
WILM/AE SK9 ......199 E4
Clifford St ECC M30 ......109 E3
ROCH OL11 ......43 E1
SWIN M27 ......97 G2
Cliff Rd WILM/AE SK9 ......199 G2
Cliff Side WILM/AE SK9 ......199 G2
Cliff St MILN OL16 ......11 G2
Clifton Av CHD/CHDH SK8 ....181 F2
ECC M30 ......109 G2
HALE/TIMP WA15 ......165 H4
OLDE OL4 ......91 G2
RUSH/FAL M14 ......143 E3
Clifton Cl HEY OL10 ......40 D5
OLDE OL4 ......91 G2
OLDTF/WHR M16 ......126 C5
Clifton Crs FWTH BL4 ......65 E5
Clifton Crs ROY/SHW OL2 ......74 D1
Clifton Dr CHD/CHDH SK8 ....169 E4
CHD/CHDH SK8 ......181 F2
MPL/ROM SK6 ......161 G3
SWIN M27 ......82 C5
Clifton Gv OLDTF/WHR M16 ..126 C5
SWIN M27 ......82 B5
Clifton House Rd SWIN M27 ....82 C2
Clifton Park Rd OFTN SK2 ....172 D4
Clifton Pl PWCH * M25 ......84 D2
Clifton Rd CCHDY M21 ......141 F3
ECC M30 ......109 G2
HTNM SK4 ......158 D2
MDTN M24 ......72 A4
PWCH M25 ......84 D3
SALE M33 ......154 C3
URM M41 ......123 F5
Clifton St AUL OL6 ......117 H2
BOL BL1 ......2 C5
BURY BL9 ......38 C2
FAIL M35 ......103 F1
FWTH BL4 ......65 G5
MILN OL16 ......11 G6
NEWH/MOS M40 ......114 C2
OLDTF/WHR M16 ......126 C5
ROCH * OL11 ......43 F1
WILM/AE SK9 ......200 A1
Clifton Vw SWIN M27 ......82 D3
Cliftonville Dr SLFD M6 ......97 G1
Cliftonville Rd MILN OL16 ......58 B1
Clinton Av RUSH/FAL M14 ....142 B1
Clinton Gdns RUSH/FAL M14 ..142 B1
Clinton St AUL * OL6 ......118 C1
Clinton Wk OLDE * OL4 ......3 J5
Clippers Quay SALO M50 ......125 H2
Clipsley Crs OLDE OL4 ......61 E5
Clitton Wk BRAM/HZG SK7 ....184 B2
Clitheroe Cl HEY OL10 ......41 E3

Clitheroe Dr TOT/BURYW BL8 ..37 E4
Clitheroe Rd BRUN/LGST M13 ..128 C5
Clito St BKLY M9 ......101 G2
Clive Av WHTF M45 ......68 B5
Clivedale Pl BOL BL1 ......33 H5
Clively Av SWIN M27 ......97 G1
Clive Rd FAIL M35 ......102 D3
Clive St ANC M4 ......7 H1
AULW OL7 ......117 H5
BOLE BL2 ......3 F5
OLDS OL8 ......90 A5
Clivia Gv BRO * M7 ......99 G4
Cloak St CMANE * M1 ......127 F1
Clock House Av OPEN M43 ....115 H2
Clockhouse Ms DROY * M43 ..115 H2
Clock St CHAD OL9 ......89 G5
Clock Tower Cl HYDE SK14 ....147 H2
WALK M28 ......80 A4
Cloister Cl DUK SK16 ......132 B2
Cloister Rd HTNM SK4 ......158 A4
The Cloisters CHD/CHDH SK8 ..170 D4
MILN OL16 ......11 H2
SALE M33 ......154 B4
Cloister St BKLY M9 ......101 G2
BOL BL1 ......33 F4
Clopton Wk HULME M15 ......126 D2
The Close ALT WA14 ......165 G2
BOLE BL2 ......34 C5
MDTN M24 ......72 A1
MPL/ROM SK6 ......163 F5
STLY SK15 ......119 E2
Colchester Wk OLD OL1 ......9 G1
Closes Farm BOLS/LL * BL3 ......26 D5
Clothorn Rd DID/WITH M20 ..157 G2
Cloudstock Gv LHULT M38 ......79 D2
The Clough BOL * BL1 ......47 F1
RDSH SK5 ......145 E5
Clough Av MPL/ROM SK6 ......175 H5
SALE M33 ......153 G5
WILM/AE SK9 ......191 G5
Clough Bank BKLY * M9 ......87 E5
Cloughbank RAD M26 ......66 B5
Clough Dr PWCH M25 ......84 C3
Clough End Rd HYDE SK14 ....148 A5
Cloughfield Av ORD M5 ......112 A5
Cloughfold RAD M26 ......66 A5
Clough Fold Rd HYDE SK14 ....147 F2
Clough Ga HYDE * SK14 ......65 G5
OLDS OL8 ......90 A5
Clough Gv WHTF M45 ......68 A5
Clough House La WHIT OL12 ....19 C2
Clough La HEY OL10 ......40 C4
OLDE OL4 ......93 F1
Clough Meadow BOL BL1 ......47 E5
MPL/ROM SK6 ......162 B1
Clough Meadow Rd RAD M26 ..66 D1
Clough Park Av OLDE OL4 ......93 F1
Clough Rd BKLY M9 ......87 E5
DROY M43 ......116 C3
FAIL M35 ......103 F3
MDTN M24 ......72 C2
ROY/SHW OL2 ......60 C3
Clough St NEWH/MOS M40 ....102 D5
Clough Side MPL/ROM SK6 ....175 H2
Clough St FWTH BL4 ......65 G5
MDTN M24 ......72 A2
NEWH/MOS M40 ......101 H4
RAD M26 ......67 H3
WHIT OL12 ......19 H2
Clough Ter LIT * OL15 ......21 D1
Clough Top Rd BKLY M9 ......87 H5
Cloughwood Av SWIN M27 ......97 F2
Clovelly Av BOLS/LL BL3 ......64 A1
OFTN SK2 ......172 D1
SWIN M27 ......96 B5
Clovelly Rd CCHDY M21 ......141 E5
OFTN SK2 ......172 D1
SWIN M27 ......96 B5
Clovelly St NEWH/MOS * M40 ..102 C5
ROCH OL11 ......42 A5
Clover Av EDGY/DAV SK3 ......171 G2
Cloverbank Av BNG/LEV M19 ..158 A2
Clover Crs OLDS OL8 ......91 F4
Clover Cft SALE M33 ......155 E5
Cloverdale Sq BOL BL1 ......32 D5
Clover Hall Crs MILN OL16 ......11 K3
Cloverley Dr HALE/TIMP WA15 ..166 B5
Clover Rd HALE/TIMP WA15 ..166 B4
MPL/ROM SK6 ......162 B5
Clover St WHIT OL12 ......10 D5
Clover Vw MILN * OL16 ......11 H5
Clowes St CHAD OL9 ......89 F5
CSLFD M3 ......6 C3
CSLFD M3 ......6 A3
SWIN M27 ......98 C4
WGTN/LGST M12 ......128 D2
Club St OP/CLY M11 ......115 F4
Clumber Cl POY/DIS SK12 ....195 F4
Clumber Rd GTN M18 ......130 A4
POY/DIS SK12 ......195 F4
Clunton Av BOLS/LL BL3 ......48 A5
Clutha Rd EDGY/DAV SK3 ....171 G2
Clwyd Av EDGY/DAV SK3 ......171 G2
Clyde Av WHTF M45 ......68 A5
Clyde Ct MILN OL16 ......11 F3
Clyde Rd DID/WITH M20 ......157 E2
EDGY/DAV SK3 ......12 B7
RAD M26 ......52 A1
Clydesdale St OLDS OL8 ......90 B5
Clyde St AULW OL7 ......117 G4
BOL * BL1 ......33 H4
Clyde Ter RAD * M26 ......52 A1
Clyne St STRET M32 ......125 G3
Coach La ROCH OL11 ......27 E5
Coalbrook Wk WGTN/LGST M12 ..114 A5
Coalburn St WGTN/LGST M12 ..128 D3
Coal Pit La OLDS OL8 ......104 A3
Coalshaw Green Rd CHAD OL9 ..89 F4
Coatbridge St OP/CLY M11 ....115 G4
Cobalt Av URM M41 ......124 A2
Cobb Cl CHH M8 ......86 D5
Cobbett's Wy WILM/AE SK9 ..201 A1
Cobble Bank BKLY M9 ......87 F3
Cobden St AUL * OL6 ......118 C3
BKLY M9 ......101 F1
BOL BL1 ......33 F3
BURY BL9 ......5 G5
CHAD OL9 ......8 A2
EDGW/EG * BL7 ......22 C1
HEY OL10 ......41 G3
OLDE OL4 ......75 G3
RAD M26 ......67 H3
SLFD M6 ......111 G1
Coberley Av URM M41 ......122 C4
Cob Hall Rd STRET M32 ......139 E2
Cobham Av BKLY M9 ......88 B5
NEWH/MOS M40 ......88 B5

Cobourg St CMANE M1 ......7 H6
Coburg Av BRO M7 ......112 C1
Cochrane Av WGTN/LGST M12 ..128 B3
Cochrane St BOLS/LL BL3 ......49 E4
Cock Brow HYDE SK14 ......148 D4
Cock Clod St RAD M26 ......67 H1
Cockcroft St BKLY M9 ......101 E1
Cocker Hl STLY SK15 ......119 G3
Cocker Mill La ROY/SHW OL2 ....3 G6
Cockers La STLY SK15 ......120 A5
Cocker St LHULT M38 ......80 B3
Cockey Moor Rd BOLE BL2 ......36 C5
Cock Hall La WHIT OL12 ......14 A4
Cockhall La WHIT OL12 ......14 B4
Coconut Gv SLFD * M6 ......112 A3
Codale Dr BOLE BL2 ......35 C5
Coddington Av OP/CLY M11 ..115 H5
Coe St BOLS/LL BL3 ......3 G7
Cognian Ct OP/CLY * M11 ......115 E3
Coin St ROY/SHW OL2 ......59 H4
Colborne Av ECC M30 ......109 E3
Colborne Av RDSH SK5 ......160 A4
RDSH * SK5 ......160 A1
Colbourne Av CHH M8 ......100 A1
Colbourne Gv HYDE SK14 ....134 B5
Colchester Av BOLE BL2 ......50 B1
Colchester Dr NTHM/RTH M23 ..155 E5
Colchester Pl HTNM SK4 ......159 E3
Colchester Wk OLD OL1 ......9 G1
Cold Greave Cl MILN OL16 ......31 H4
Coldhurst St OLD OL1 ......74 B4
Coldstream Av BKLY M9 ......87 G3
Colebrook Dr NEWH/MOS M40 ..101 H4
Colebrook Rd HALE/TIMP WA15 ..166 D3
Coleby Av OLDTF/WHR M16 ....126 B5
WYTH/NTH M22 ......181 E3
Coledale Dr MDTN M24 ......72 B1
Coleford Gv BOL BL1 ......2 C6
Colemore Av DID/WITH M20 ..158 A3
Colenso Ct BOLE * BL2 ......3 J2
Colenso Gv HTNM SK4 ......159 E3
Colenso Rd BURY BL9 ......53 G4
Coleport Cl CHD/CHDH SK8 ..182 C3
Coleridge Av MDTN M24 ......72 B1
RAD M26 ......66 D2
Coleridge Rd LIT OL15 ......21 C1
OLD OL1 ......75 G3
RDSH SK5 ......144 D2
WYTH/NTH M22 ......156 D4
Colesbourne CHH M8 ......80 A5
Coleshill St NEWH/MOS M40 ..101 H3
Cole St BKLY M9 ......101 G2
Colgate Crs RUSH/FAL M14 ....142 C4
Colgate La ORD M5 ......125 H2
Colgrove Av NEWH/MOS M40 ..103 G4
Colina Dr CHH M8 ......100 C3
Colindale Av BKLY M9 ......87 F1
Colin Murphy Rd HULME M15 ..126 D1
Colin Rd HTNM SK4 ......159 H2
Colinton Cl BOL BL1 ......33 F1
Colinwood Cl BURY BL9 ......38 B1
Coll Dr URM M41 ......123 F5
College Av OLDS OL8 ......90 C5
College Cl BOLS/LL BL3 ......2 D7
WILM/AE SK9 ......198 D2
Colleen Av BNG/LEV M19 ......158 A2
College Dr OLDTF/WHR M16 ....142 A2
College Rd ECC M30 ......110 A2
OLDS OL8 ......90 C5
OLDTF/WHR M16 ......141 H1
WHIT OL12 ......10 C2
Collett St OLD OL1 ......75 H4
Colley St MILN OL16 ......11 F4
Collie Av SLFD M6 ......99 F5
Collier Av MILN OL16 ......11 F3
Collier Cl BOLS/LL * BL3 ......2 E6
Collier Hl OLDS OL8 ......90 A4
Collier Hill Av OLDS OL8 ......90 A4
Colliers Row Rd BOL BL1 ......32 A1
Collin Av GTN M18 ......129 F4
Collinge Av MDTN M24 ......72 C5
Collinge St BOLE BL2 ......34 B4
HEY OL10 ......41 E4
MDTN M24 ......72 A5
Collingham St CHH M8 ......113 H1
Collington Cl WGTN/LGST M12 ..128 D3
Collingwood Av DROY M43 ....115 H3
Collingwood Cl POY/DIS SK12 ..195 F4
Collingwood Dr SWIN M27 ......97 F3
Collingwood Rd BNG/LEV M19 ..143 H3
Collingwood St ROCH OL11 ....42 D2
Collingwood Wy OLD * OL1 ....74 D4
Collins St TOT/BURYW BL8 ....37 F1
Collop Dr HEY OL10 ......56 B2
Collyhurst Av WALK M28 ......80 D5
Collyhurst Rd NEWH/MOS M40 ..100 D4
Collyhurst St NEWH/MOS M40 ..100 C4
Colman Gdns ORD M5 ......175 (?)
Colmore Dr BKLY M9 ......87 H2
Colmore Gv BOLE BL2 ......34 C4
Colmore St BOLE BL2 ......34 C4
Colne Rd BOLE BL2 ......50 D5
Colonial Rd OFTN SK2 ......172 D4
Colshaw Dr WILM/AE SK9 ......200 A4
Colshaw Rd NTHM/RTH M23 ..167 E2
Colson Dr MDTN M24 ......72 D3
Colsterdale Cl ROY/SHW OL2 ..59 F4
Colt Hill La UPML OL3 ......77 G4
Coltsfoot Dr ALT WA14 ......130 H4
Columbia Av GTN M18 ......130 C3
Columbia Rd BOL BL1 ......33 G3
Columbine Cl WHIT OL12 ......18 B5
Columbine St OPEN M11 ......115 G2
Colville Gv HALE/TIMP WA15 ..166 D5
SALE M33 ......153 H4
Colville Rd OLD OL1 ......74 A3
Colwell Av STRET M32 ......139 G2
Colwick Av ALT WA14 ......165 H3
Colwith Av BOLE BL2 ......35 F5
Colwyn Av MDTN M24 ......87 H1
RUSH/FAL M14 ......143 E3
Colwyn Crs RDSH SK5 ......160 A1
Colwyn Rd BRAM/HZG SK7 ....184 A4
CHD/CHDH SK8 ......182 B3
SWIN M27 ......96 B4
Colwyn St AULW OL7 ......104 D4
CHAD * OL9 ......8 C3
ROCH OL11 ......42 A4
SLFD M6 ......111 G2
Combe Cl OP/CLY M11 ......115 E2
Combermere Av DID/WITH M20 ..142 B4
Combermere Cl CHD/CHDH SK8 ..170 C5
Combermere St DUK SK16 ......118 B4
Comer Ter SALE M33 ......154 B2
Comet St CMANE M1 ......7 H5
Commercial Av CHD/CHDH SK8 ..192 B2
Commercial Brow HYDE SK14 ..132 D4
Commercial Rd BRAM/HZG SK7 ..185 E1
OLD OL1 ......9 H5
Commercial St CHAD OL9 ......8 A1
HULME M15 ......126 D1
HYDE SK14 ......132 D5
Common La PART M31 ......151 G1
PART M31 ......151 G1
Common Side Rd WALK M28 ....94 A3
Como St BOLS/LL * BL3 ......48 B5
Como Wk GTN M18 ......129 E2
Compass St OP/CLY M11 ......115 E1
Compstall Av RUSH/FAL M14 ..142 C2
Compstall Gv GTN * M18 ......129 H2
Compstall Mills Est
MPL/ROM * SK6 ......163 G4
Compstall Rd MPL/ROM SK6 ..162 C4
Compton Cl URM M41 ......136 D2
Compton Dr NTHM/RTH * M23 ..179 H2
Compton St NMDTN M24 ......72 B5
ROY/SHW OL2 ......60 A3
Comus St ORD M5 ......113 B5
Concert La CMANW M2 ......7 F4
Concord Pl SLFD M6 ......98 D3
Condor Cl DROY * M43 ......116 B5
Condor Pl SLFD M6 ......98 D5
Condor Wk BRUN/LGST * M13 ..127 G2
Conduit St AUL OL6 ......118 D3
OLD OL1 ......75 G1
Conewood Wk BRUN/LGST M13 ..127 H2
Coney Gv NTHM/RTH M23 ....167 H2
Coneymead STLY SK15 ......119 F1
Congleton Cl WILM/AE SK9 ....201 B5
Congou St CMANE M1 ......7 H6
Congreave St OLD OL1 ......8 D3
Coningsby Dr BKLY M9 ......101 E2
Conisber Cl EDGW/EG BL7 ......22 D1
Conisborough ROCH * OL11 ....29 H5
Conisborough Pl WHTF M45 ....86 D1
Conisbrough BOL * BL1 ......34 A5
Coniston Av BKLY M9 ......101 E2
FWTH BL4 ......63 H5
LHULT M38 ......132 B4
LHULT M38 ......80 A4
OLDS OL8 ......90 A4
SALE M33 ......154 D4
WHTF M45 ......68 C4
Coniston Cl BOLS/LL BL3 ......50 D5
DTN/ASHW M34 ......145 G1
RAMS BL0 ......16 D1
Coniston Dr BURY BL9 ......53 F2
DUK SK16 ......75 F5
STLY SK15 ......119 F2
WILM/AE SK9 ......191 H3
Coniston Gv AULW OL7 ......117 H1
LHULT M38 ......80 A4
ROY/SHW OL2 ......59 E3
Coniston Rd CHD/CHDH SK8 ..169 G3
MPL/ROM SK6 ......186 C4
PART M31 ......151 E3
RDSH SK5 ......145 E5
STRET M32 ......124 D5
SWIN M27 ......97 E4
URM M41 ......137 F3
Coniston St NEWH/MOS M40 ..102 B5
SLFD M6 ......112 A1
Coniston Wk HALE/TIMP WA15 ..167 E4
Conival Wy CHAD OL9 ......73 H5
Conmere Sq HULME M15 ......127 F1
Connaught Av BNG/LEV M19 ..143 G4
ROCH OL11 ......43 G3
WHIT OL12 ......68 A4
Connaught Cl WILM/AE SK9 ....199 H2
Connaught Sq BOLE BL2 ......34 C4
TOT/BURYW BL8 ......37 G5
Connaught St CHAD OL9 ......73 H5
Connel Cl BOLE BL2 ......50 C3
Connell Rd NTHM/RTH M23 ..167 H5
Connell Wy HEY * OL10 ......40 C1
Connery Crs AUL OL6 ......105 G4
Connie St OP/CLY M11 ......115 F5
Conningsby Cl EDGW/EG BL7 ..22 D2
Connington Av BKLY M9 ......101 E1
Connington Cl ROY/SHW OL2 ....58 D5
Connor Wy CHD/CHDH SK8 ..169 G5
Conrad Cl OLD OL1 ......60 D5
Conran St BKLY M9 ......101 F2
Consett Av NTHM/RTH M23 ..167 H5
Consort Av ROY/SHW OL2 ......58 D3
Consort Cl DUK SK16 ......132 B2
Consort Pl ALT WA14 ......177 E1
Constable Cl BOL BL1 ......33 G1
Constable Dr MPL/ROM SK6 ..175 G1
WILM/AE SK9 ......200 B2
Constable St HULME * M15 ....129 H2
Constance Gdns SLFD M6 ......113 E1
Constance Rd BOLS/LL BL3 ......48 B4
PART M31 ......151 E2
Constance St HULME M15 ......126 D3
LHULT M38 ......80 A4
Constantine St OLDE OL4 ......91 G1
Consul St WYTH/NTH M22 ....156 D5
Convamore Rd BRAM/HZG SK7 ..193 G2
Convent Gv ROCH OL11 ......42 C1
Conway Av BOL BL1 ......32 D5
IRL M44 ......136 A3
SWIN M27 ......83 G4
WHTF M45 ......68 A4
Conway Cl HALE/TIMP WA15 ..166 B3
MDTN M24 ......71 H5

OLDTF/WHR * M16 ....125 H5
RAMS BL0 ....16 C2
Conway Crs RAMS BL0 ....26 A1
Conway Dr BRAM/HZG SK7 ....184 D5
BURY BL9 ....39 G4
HALE/TIMP WA15 ....166 D3
STLY SK15 ....119 F2
Conway Gv CHAD OL9 ....73 E4
Conway Rd CHD/CHDH SK8 ....182 B2
SALE M33 ....155 E5
URM M41 ....123 G4
Conway St FWTH BL4 ....65 E5
Conyngham Rd RUSH/FAL M14 ....128 A4
Cooke St BRAM/HZG SK7 ....185 E1
DTN/ASHW M54 ....131 G5
FAIL M35 ....103 E2
FWTH BL4 ....65 F5
HYDE SK14 ....131 H5
Cook Ter MILN OL16 ....11 G2
Coomassie St HEY OL10 ....40 D4
RAD M26 ....67 F1
SLFD * M6 ....111 G2
Coombes Av HYDE SK14 ....148 A2
MPL/ROM SK6 ....175 E4
Coombes St OFTN SK2 ....172 C4
Coombes Vw HYDE SK14 ....149 G3
Co-operation St FAIL M35 ....103 E1
LHULT * M38 ....79 G2
Co-operative St BRAM/HZG SK7 ....185 F1
OLDE OL4 ....92 A1
ROY/SHW * OL2 ....60 A2
SLFD * M6 ....111 G3
UPML * OL3 ....78 A4
Cooper Fold MDTN M24 ....56 D5
Cooper La BKLY M9 ....87 E2
MDTN M24 ....71 G1
Cooper St BRAM/HZG SK7 ....185 C1
BURY BL9 ....6 E5
CMANW M2 ....6 E5
DROY * M43 ....115 H4
DUK SK16 ....118 A4
OLDE OL4 ....75 F5
STKP SK1 ....13 H7
STRET M32 ....140 A2
WHIT OL12 ....20 A4
Coopers Wk MILN OL16 ....30 D1
Cooper Ter MILN OL16 ....11 G4
Coote St ANC * M4 ....7 G2
BOL BL1 ....33 H2
Copage Dr MPL/ROM SK6 ....161 H2
Cope Bank BOL BL1 ....33 F5
Cope Bank West BOL * BL1 ....33 E4
Cope CI OP/CLY * M11 ....129 H1
Copeland Av SWIN M27 ....97 H1
Copeland CI MDTN M24 ....70 D3
Copeland Ms BOL BL1 ....47 H2
Copeland St HYDE SK14 ....132 C3
Copeman CI BRUN/LGST M13 ....127 H2
Copenhagen Sq MILN * OL16 ....11 F5
Copenhagen St MILN OL16 ....11 F5
NEWH/MOS M40 ....101 H4
Cosgrove Rd CCHDY M21 ....141 E4
Copley Av STLY SK15 ....119 H3
Copley Park Ms STLY SK15 ....119 H5
Copley Rd CCHDY M21 ....140 D2
Copley St STLY SK15 ....119 G2
Copperas La DROY M43 ....115 H3
Copperas St ANC M4 ....7 G3

Copperbeech CI
WYTH/NTH M22 ....156 D5
Copper Beech Dr STLY SK15 ....120 A2
Copperfield Rd CHD/CHDH SK8 ....193 G2
POY/DIS SK12 ....195 E5
Copperfields WHIT M45 ....199 H2
Copper La WHIT M45 ....69 G5
The Coppice BKLY M9 ....87 H5
BOLE BL2 ....35 E1
HALE/TIMP WA15 ....178 D4
PWCH M25 ....84 D3
RAMS BL0 ....16 D2
SWIN M27 ....96 B5
WALK M28 ....95 G2
Coppice Av POY/DIS SK12 ....197 F1
SALE M33 ....153 H2
Coppice CI MPL/ROM SK6 ....162 A2
Coppice Dr WYTH/NTH M22 ....18 B1
WYTH/NTH M22 ....156 C5
Coppice La POY/DIS SK12 ....197 F1
Coppice St BURY BL9 ....39 F3
OLDS OL8 ....90 B3
Coppice V RAMS BL0 ....16 C5
Coppice Wk DTN/ASHW M34 ....146 A4
Copping St WGTN/LGST M12 ....128 C2
Coppleridge Dr CHH M8 ....86 B3
Copplestone Dr SALE M33 ....153 F1
Cop Rd ROY/SHW OL2 ....59 G5
The Copse EDGW/EG BL7 ....23 H1
HALE/TIMP WA15 ....166 A4
Copse Dr BURY BL9 ....27 G5
Copson St DID/WITH M20 ....142 C4
Copster Av OLDS OL8 ....90 B5
Copster Hill Rd OLDS OL8 ....90 B4
Copster PI OLDS OL8 ....90 B5
Copthall La CHH M8 ....86 A2
Copthorne Crs BRUN/LGST M13 ....143 F1
Copthorne Dr BOLE BL2 ....50 B1
Copthorn Wk TOT/BURYW BL8 ....37 E1
Coptrod Head CI WHIT OL12 ....14 B2
Coral Av CHD/CHDH SK8 ....183 G3
Coral Rd CHD/CHDH SK8 ....182 D5
Coral St BRUN/LGST M13 ....128 A2
Coram St GTN M18 ....130 A2
Corbar Rd OFTN SK2 ....172 B4
Corbett St MILN OL16 ....11 H6
OP/CLY11 ....114 D4
Corbrook Rd CHAD OL9 ....73 F2
Corby St WGTN/LGST M12 ....128 C1
Corcoran Dr ALT WA14 ....165 H3
Corda Av WYTH/NTH M22 ....168 C1
Cordingley Av DROY M43 ....116 A3
Cordova Av DTN/ASHW M34 ....130 A5

Corelli St NEWH/MOS M40 ....114 C1
Corfe CI URM M41 ....136 D2
Corfe Crs BRAM/HZG SK7 ....185 E5
Corinthian Av BRO M7 ....99 F5
Corkland CI AUL OL6 ....118 C3
Corkland Rd CCHDY M21 ....141 E3
Corkland St AUL OL6 ....118 D3
Cork St BURY BL9 ....5 H4
WGTN/LGST M12 ....114 A5
Corley Av EDGY/DAV SK3 ....170 C2
Corley Wk OP/CLY * M11 ....114 C4
Cormallen Gv FAIL M35 ....103 F3
Cornall St TOT/BURYW BL8 ....37 H3
Cornbrook Arches HULME M15 ....126 A3
Cornbrook Ct WHIT OL12 ....19 H2
Cornbrook Gv OLDTF/WHR M16 ....126 C3
Cornbrook Park Rd
HULME M15 ....126 B2
Cornbrook St OLDTF/WHR M16 ....126 C3
Corn CI BRUN/LGST M13 ....127 H3
Cornell St ANC M4 ....7 J2
Corner Cft WILM/AE SK9 ....201 B1
Cornet St BRO M7 ....99 G5
Cornfield STLY SK15 ....134 B1
Cornfield CI BURY BL9 ....27 G4
SALE * M33 ....155 G3
Cornfield Dr WYTH/NTH M22 ....180 B1
Cornfield Rd MPL/ROM SK6 ....162 D3
Cornfield St MILN OL16 ....44 C1
Cornhill Av URM M41 ....123 E5
Corn Hill La DTN/ASHW M34 ....130 B3
Cornhill Rd URM M41 ....123 E5
Cornhill St OLD OL1 ....75 F2
Cornish Wy ROY/SHW OL2 ....74 C1
Cornishway WYTH/NTH M22 ....180 C4
Corniea Dr WALK M28 ....94 D5
Corn Mill CI WHIT OL12 ....14 B2
Corn Mill La STLY SK15 ....119 G4
Corn St FAIL M35 ....102 B4
OLDE * OL4 ....9 K3
Cornwall Av BNG/LEV M19 ....144 A3
WHTN BL5 ....62 C4
Cornwall CI MPL/ROM SK6 ....186 D5
Cornwall Crs RDSH SK5 ....145 H5
Cornwall Dr BURY BL9 ....53 H1
Cornwall Rd CHD/CHDH SK8 ....181 G4
DROY M43 ....116 B2
IRL M44 ....150 C1
Cornwall St CHAD OL9 ....89 G2
OP/CLY M11 ....129 G1
Cornwell CI WILM/AE SK9 ....200 A2
Corona Av HYDE SK14 ....132 D5
OLDS OL8 ....90 A4
Coronation Av DUK SK16 ....133 E1
HEY OL10 ....56 B1
Coronation St AUL OL6 ....147 H2
Coronation Gdns RAD M26 ....51 H5
Coronation Rd AUL OL6 ....105 F4
DROY M43 ....116 A2
RDSH * SK5 ....145 H2
RAD M26 ....51 H5
Coronation Sq WGTN/LGST M12 ....113 H5
Coronation St BOL BL1 ....2 C6
DTN/ASHW M34 ....130 D5
OP/CLY * M11 ....115 F5
ORD M5 ....112 A5
RDSH SK5 ....159 H2
SWIN M27 ....97 F1

Cottenham La BRO M7 ....112 D1
Cottenham St BRUN/LGST M13 ....127 G2
Cotterdale CI
OLDTF/WHR * M16 ....126 C5
Cotterill CI SALE M33 ....154 D5
Cotterill St SLFD M6 ....111 H3
Cotter St WGTN/LGST M12 ....127 H1
Cottesmore Dr CHH M8 ....100 D2
Cottesmore Gdns
HALE/TIMP WA15 ....178 D4
Cottingham Dr AUL OL6 ....118 B1
Cottingham Rd
WGTN/LGST M12 ....128 B2
Cottingley CI BOL BL1 ....33 G1
Cotton CI HYDE SK14 ....147 H2
Cottonfield Rd DID/WITH M20 ....142 D5
Cottonfields EDGW/EG BL7 ....23 E4
Cotton Fold MILN OL16 ....30 D5
Cotton Hill DID/WITH M20 ....142 D5
Cotton La DID/WITH M20 ....142 D5
Cotton St ANC M4 ....7 J3
BOL BL1 ....35 E3
Cotton St East AUL OL6 ....117 H3
Cotton St West AUL OL7 ....117 H3
Cotton Tree CI OLDE OL4 ....75 G4
Cotton Tree St HTNM SK4 ....12 D5
Cottonwood Dr SALE M33 ....153 F1
Cottrell Rd HALE/TIMP WA15 ....179 E5
Coucill Sq FWTH BL4 ....4 C5
Coulsden Dr BKLY M9 ....87 E4
Coulthart St AUL OL6 ....118 A4
Councillor La CHD/CHDH SK8 ....170 C4
Councillor St OP/CLY M11 ....114 B4
Countess Av CHD/CHDH SK8 ....192 B2
Countess Gv SWIN M27 ....99 G5
Countess La RAD M26 ....51 G4
Countess PI PWCH M25 ....85 F3
Countess Rd DID/WITH M20 ....157 G3
Countess St AUL OL6 ....118 B3
OFTN SK2 ....172 B4
Counthill Dr CHH M8 ....85 H5
Counthill Rd OLDE OL4 ....75 G3
Count St MILN OL16 ....43 F2
County Av AUL OL6 ....118 D1
County Rd WALK M28 ....80 B3
County St CMANW M2 ....6 E6
OLDS OL8 ....89 H5
Coupland CI OLDE OL4 ....61 E5
Coupland St HULME M15 ....127 F3
WHIT OL12 ....14 B5
Courier St GTN M18 ....129 H2
Course Vw OLDE OL4 ....91 H4
Court Dr NEWH/MOS M40 ....115 H1
Courtfield Av BKLY * M9 ....87 E5
Courthill St STKP SK1 ....13 K5
Courtney Av WILM/AE SK9 ....191 H4
Courtney PI ALT WA14 ....176 D5
Court St BOLE BL2 ....3 J5
UPML OL3 ....78 A4
Courts Vw SALE M33 ....154 D1
The Courtyard BOL * BL1 ....34 A4
HEY * OL10 ....41 G5
Courtyard Dr WALK M28 ....95 H1
Cousin Flds BOLE BL2 ....35 E5
The Cove HALE/TIMP WA15 ....178 A1
Covell Rd POY/DIS SK12 ....195 E2
Covent Gdn STKP SK1 ....15 G4
Coventry Av EDGY/DAV SK3 ....170 C2
Coventry Gv CHAD OL9 ....73 G3
Coventry Rd RAD M26 ....52 A4
Coverdale Av BOL BL1 ....47 H1
ROY/SHW OL2 ....58 D4
Coverdale CI HEY OL10 ....40 D5
Coverdale Crs WGTN/LGST M12 ....128 A2
Coverham Av OLDE OL4 ....92 C2
Coverhill Rd OLDE OL4 ....92 D1
Covert Rd OLDE OL4 ....91 H4
WYTH/NTH M22 ....168 D4
Covington PI WILM/AE SK9 ....199 G4
Cowan St NEWH/MOS M40 ....114 C2
Cowburn St CSLFD M3 ....113 E2
HEY OL10 ....41 F5
Cowdals Rd HOR/BR BL6 ....46 C5
Cowesby St RUSH/FAL M14 ....127 F5
Cowhill La AUL OL6 ....118 B2
Cowie St ROY/SHW OL2 ....60 A1
Cow La BOLS/LL BL3 ....63 E2
BRAM/HZG SK7 ....173 E5
FAIL M35 ....103 D3
HALE/TIMP WA15 ....188 A2
OLDE OL4 ....92 B4
ORD M5 ....112 B4
Cowley St NEWH/MOS M40 ....102 B4
Cowling St BRO M7 ....99 G4
Cowlishaw La ROY/SHW OL2 ....59 H4
Cowlishaw Rd HYDE SK14 ....163 E1
Cowm Park Wy North
WHIT OL12 ....14 B5
Cowm Park Wy South
WHIT OL12 ....14 B5
Cowm Top La ROCH OL11 ....43 F4
Cown Edge Wy HYDE SK14 ....147 G5
HYDE SK14 ....148 A5
MPL/ROM SK6 ....175 H5
OFTN SK2 ....172 D5
Cowper St AUL OL6 ....105 G5
MDTN M24 ....72 C5
Cowper Wk NEWH/MOS M40 ....180 D3
Crabbe St ANC M4 ....113 F2
Crab La BKLY M9 ....87 F2
Crabtree Av HALE/TIMP WA15 ....115 E4
Crabtree La OP/CLY M11 ....115 G4
Crabtree Rd OLDE OL4 ....92 B3
Crabtree St BURY BL9 ....5 K3
Craddock Rd SALE M33 ....154 D4
Craddock St MOSL OL5 ....106 C1
Cradley Av OP/CLY M11 ....115 H5
Crag Av BURY BL9 ....27 E1
Cragg Fold BURY * BL9 ....27 E1
Cragg La BURY BL9 ....27 E1
Cragside Wy WILM/AE SK9 ....199 H4
Craig Av TOT/BURYW BL8 ....37 E1
URM M41 ....122 D5
Craighall Av BNG/LEV M19 ....143 G5
Craighall Rd BOL BL1 ....21 E5
Craiglands MILN OL16 ....43 G4

Craigmore Av DID/WITH M20 ....156 C2
Craignair Ct SWIN * M27 ....97 H2
Craig Rd GTN M18 ....129 F4
HTNM SK4 ....158 D5
Craigslands Av
NEWH/MOS M40 ....101 H4
Craig Wk OLDS OL8 ....9 F7
Craigwell Av DID/WITH M20 ....157 H3
Craigwell Rd PWCH M25 ....85 F5
Cramer St NEWH/MOS M40 ....101 G5
Crammond CI NEWH/MOS M40 ....102 C4
Cramond CI BOL BL1 ....33 G5
Cramond Wk BOL BL1 ....33 G5
Crampton Dr HALE/TIMP WA15 ....178 D4
Crampton La PART M31 ....137 E5
Cranage Rd BNG/LEV M19 ....144 A3
Cranark CI BOL BL1 ....47 H2
Cranberry CI ALT WA14 ....165 E1
Cranberry Dr BOLS/LL BL3 ....47 G5
Cranberry Rd PART M31 ....151 E3
Cranberry St OLDE OL4 ....91 E2
Cranbourne Av CHD/CHDH SK8 ....183 E2
Cranbourne CI
HALE/TIMP WA15 ....166 B3
AULW OL7 ....117 H1
CCHDY M21 ....141 E3
SWIN M27 ....96 A3
Cranbourne Rd AULW OL7 ....105 E5
AULW OL7 ....117 H1
CCHDY M21 ....141 E3
HTNM SK4 ....159 E2
OLDTF/WHR M16 ....126 B4
ROCH OL11 ....28 B5
Cranbourne Ter AUL OL6 ....105 E5
Cranbrook Dr PWCH M25 ....85 F5
Cranbrook Gdns AULW * OL7 ....118 A1
Cranbrook Rd ECC M30 ....108 D1
GTN M18 ....130 A4
Cranbrook St AUL OL6 ....118 A3
CHAD OL9 ....8 A6
OLDE OL4 ....92 A1
RAD M26 ....52 D4
Cranbrook Wk CHAD OL9 ....89 G1
Crandon Dr DID/WITH M20 ....169 H1
Cranesbill CI WYTH/NTH M22 ....180 B5
Crane St BOLS/LL * BL3 ....63 E1
WGTN/LGST M12 ....113 H5
Cranfield CI NEWH/MOS M40 ....114 B1
Cranford Av DID/WITH M20 ....158 A2
SALE M33 ....139 H5
STRET M32 ....125 G5
WHTF M45 ....68 B2
Cranford CI SLFD M6 ....97 H4
Cranford Dr IRL M44 ....121 G5
Cranford Rd URM M41 ....122 B5
WILM/AE SK9 ....199 F1
Cranford St BOLS/LL BL3 ....48 A5
Cranham Cl TOT/BURYW BL8 ....37 G3
Cranham Close Crs LHULT * M38 ....80 B1
Cranham Rd WYTH/NTH M22 ....168 C2
Cranleigh Av HTNM SK4 ....158 C2
Cranleigh CI OLDE OL4 ....77 E5
Cranleigh Dr BRAM/HZG SK7 ....185 H4
CHD/CHDH SK8 ....170 C3
SALE M33 ....154 D5
WALK M28 ....95 F2
Cranlington Dr CHH M8 ....100 D4
Cranmer Ct HEY OL10 ....40 D5
Cranmere Av BNG/LEV M19 ....144 B3
Cranmere Dr SALE M33 ....153 C4
Cranmer Rd DID/WITH M20 ....157 F3
Cranston Dr DID/WITH M20 ....169 C1
Cranswick St RUSH/FAL M14 ....127 F5
Cranworth Av TOT/BURYW BL8 ....37 G3
Cranworth St STLY SK15 ....119 G4
Crathie Ct BOL BL1 ....33 G5
Craven Av ORD M5 ....112 A5
Craven Ct ALT WA14 ....165 F2
ORD M5 ....125 H2
Craven Dr ORD M5 ....125 H2
Craven PI BOL BL1 ....33 F4
OP/CLY M11 ....115 F3
RDSH * SK5 ....145 E5
Craven St AUL * OL6 ....105 G5
BURY BL9 ....5 G3
OLD OL1 ....74 B4
ORD M5 ....112 B4
Craven Ter SALE M33 ....154 D2
Crawford Av BOLE BL2 ....49 H3
WALK M28 ....95 G2
Crawford St AUL OL6 ....118 C3
BOLE BL2 ....49 H3
ECC M30 ....109 G2
NEWH/MOS M40 ....102 B4
WYTH/NTH M22 ....168 D4
Crawley Av OFTN SK2 ....172 D3
The Cray MILN OL16 ....11 G6
Crayfield Rd BNG/LEV M19 ....144 B2
Crayford Rd NEWH/MOS M40 ....115 F1
Cray Wk BRUN/LGST * M13 ....127 G1
Creaton Wy MDTN M24 ....70 C1
Creden Av WYTH/NTH M22 ....180 D1
Credition Cl HULME M15 ....127 E3
Crediton Dr BOLE BL2 ....50 D1
Cresbury St WGTN/LGST M12 ....128 A1
The Crescent ALT WA14 ....177 F2
BNG/LEV M19 ....143 H2
BOLE BL2 ....35 E2
BOLS/LL BL3 ....66 A3
BURY BL9 ....5 K4
CHD/CHDH SK8 ....170 A4
DROY M43 ....116 B3
EDGW/EG BL7 ....22 D2
EDGY/DAV SK3 ....172 A5
HALE/TIMP WA15 ....177 H2
HULME M15 ....127 F1
HYDE SK14 ....147 G1
LHULT M38 ....80 A2
MDTN M24 ....72 A4
ROCH OL11 ....29 H5
SLFD M6 ....111 G2
WHIT OL12 ....19 H5

MPL/ROM SK6 ....161 E2
PWCH M25 ....85 E3
RAD M26 ....51 G4
ROY/SHW OL2 ....59 H3
STLY SK15 ....133 C3
URM M41 ....122 C5
WHIT * OL12 ....14 B5
Crescent ORD M5 ....112 B3
Crescent Av BOL BL1 ....2 B5
CHH * M8 ....80 D1
PWCH M25 ....85 E5
PWCH M25 ....85 E5
SWIN M27 ....97 G2
Crescent Ct DUK SK16 ....118 B4
EDGY/DAV SK3 ....172 B4
Crescent Dr CHH M8 ....100 C2
LHULT M38 ....80 C2
Crescent Pk HTNM SK4 ....158 A1
Crescent Range RUSH/FAL M14 ....127 H5
Crescent Rd ALT WA14 ....118 C3
BOLS/LL BL3 ....64 C1
CHAD OL9 ....88 D5
CHD/CHDH SK8 ....169 H3
CHH M8 ....86 B3
DUK SK16 ....118 B4
HALE/TIMP WA15 ....177 H2
ROCH OL11 ....42 A2
STKP SK1 ....160 C3
WILM/AE SK9 ....201 C3
Crescent Wy EDGY/DAV SK3 ....172 B4
The Crest DROY M43 ....118 B3
Crestfield Av CHH M8 ....100 C2
Crest St CSLFD M6 ....6 E1
Crete St OLDS OL8 ....90 C3
Crewe Rd NTHM/RTH M23 ....167 H3
Crib Fold UPML OL3 ....77 H2
Crib La UPML OL3 ....77 H2
Criccieth Rd EDGY/DAV SK3 ....170 D2
Criccieth St OLDTF/WHR M16 ....127 E4
Cricketfield La WALK M28 ....94 A5
Cricket's La AUL OL6 ....118 B2
Cricket St BOLS/LL BL3 ....48 D4
DTN/ASHW * M34 ....131 H4
Cricket Vw MILN OL16 ....44 C1
Cricklewood Rd
WYTH/NTH M22 ....180 B3
Crimble La HEY OL10 ....41 F1
Crimbles St OLDE OL4 ....75 H4
Crimble St BOL BL1 ....2 E3
Crime La OLDS OL8 ....104 A3
Crimsworth Av
OLDTF/WHR M16 ....141 E1
Crinan Wk NEWH/MOS M40 ....113 H2
Cringlebarrow CI WALK M28 ....94 A5
Cringle CI BOLS/LL BL3 ....47 F5
Cringleford Wk
WGTN/LGST M12 ....128 C2
Cringle Hall Rd BNG/LEV M19 ....143 E3
Cringle Rd BNG/LEV M19 ....144 A4
Cripple Gate La ROCH OL11 ....42 D5
Crispin Rd WYTH/NTH M22 ....180 C1
Critchley CI HYDE SK14 ....148 A2
Criterion St RDSH SK5 ....145 E1
Croal St BOL BL1 ....2 A6
Croasdale Dr ROY/SHW OL2 ....59 F4
Croasdale St BOL BL1 ....3 F2
Crocus Dr ROY/SHW OL2 ....59 H4
The Croft BURY BL9 ....53 H3
HYDE SK14 ....134 D4
OLDS OL8 ....90 D5
PART M31 ....151 E3
Croft Av PWCH M25 ....70 A4
Croft Bank BRO * M7 ....99 F5
GTN M18 ....129 H3
Croft Brow OLDS OL8 ....90 C4
Croft CI HALE/TIMP WA15 ....188 D1
Croft Dr TOT/BURYW BL8 ....36 B4
The Crofters SALE M33 ....155 G3
Crofters Brook RAD M26 ....52 D4
Crofters Gn WILM/AE SK9 ....199 E4
Crofters Wk BOLE BL2 ....23 H5
Croft Ga BOLE BL2 ....35 F2
Croft Gates Rd MDTN M24 ....71 E5
Croft Gv LHULT M38 ....80 C2
Croft Head Dr SALE M33 ....153 G2
Croft Head Rd MILN OL16 ....31 G4
Croft Hill Rd NEWH/MOS M40 ....101 H1
Croftlands RAMS BL0 ....16 D2
Croftlands Rd WYTH/NTH M22 ....168 D5
Croft La BOLS/LL BL3 ....49 H4
BURY BL9 ....53 H3
Croftleigh CI WHTF M45 ....68 B2
Crofton Av HALE/TIMP WA15 ....188 A2
Crofton St OLDS OL8 ....90 C4
OLDTF/WHR M16 ....127 E5
SALE M33 ....155 F4
Crofts Bank Rd URM M41 ....123 G4
Croftside Av WALK M28 ....81 H4
Croftside CI WALK M28 ....81 H4
Croftside Gv WALK M28 ....81 H4
Croftside Wy WILM/AE SK9 ....199 H4
BRO M7 ....99 G5
HALE * M8 ....105 H1
HYDE SK14 ....147 G1
LHULT M38 ....80 A2
STLY SK15 ....120 A2
WHIT OL12 ....19 H5
Croichbank TOT/BURYW BL8 ....
Cromar Rd BRAM/HZG SK7 ....185 G5
Cromarty Av CHAD OL9 ....89 E4
Cromarty Wk OP/CLY M11 ....114 A4
Crombie Av WYTH/NTH M22 ....168 C2
Crombouke Fold WALK M28 ....94 C3
Cromdale Av BOL BL1 ....47 H1
BRAM/HZG SK7 ....185 G5
Cromer Av BOLE BL2 ....34 D5
DID/WITH M20 ....142 C5

DTN/ASHW M34 130 B5
Cromer Rd CHD/CHDH SK8 170 B3
SALE M33 154 D3
TOT/BURYW BL8 38 A1
Cromer St MDTN M24 71 H3
OP/CLY * M11 115 G4
ROY/SHW * OL2 60 A2
STKP SK1 13 K2
WHIT OL12 10 B3
Cromford Av STRET M32 124 C5
Cromford Cl BOL BL1 2 C1
Cromford Gdns BOL BL1 34 A4
Cromford St OLD OL1 74 D4
Cromhurst St CHH M8 100 B1
Cromley Rd MPL/ROM SK6 186 D5
OFTN SK2 184 B1
Crompton Av BOLE BL2 50 B1
ROCH OL11 43 G3
Crompton Cl BOL BL1 34 B2
MPL/ROM SK6 175 E2
RAD M26 67 G4
Crompton Pl BOL * BL1 3 F5
RAD M26 67 G1
Crompton Rd BNG/LEV M19 143 H4
HOR/BR BL6 46 A1
RAD M26 65 H4
Crompton St AUL OL6 118 D1
BOL BL1 3 G3
BURY BL9 4 D4
CHAD OL9 8 A3
FWTH BL4 65 F5
OLD OL1 74 B4
ROY/SHW OL2 60 A2
ROY/SHW * OL2 74 B1
SWIN M27 96 D2
WALK M28 81 G5
Crompton V BOLE BL2 50 A1
Crompton Wy BOLE BL2 49 H1
Cromwell Av CHD/CHDH SK8 169 F3
MPL/ROM SK6 174 B2
OLDTF/WHR M16 141 F1
Cromwell Gv BNG/LEV M19 143 H2
BRO M7 99 F5
Cromwell Range
RUSH/FAL M14 143 E1
Cromwell Rd BRAM/HZG SK7 193 G1
ECC M30 109 F3
IRL M44 135 D4
MPL/ROM SK6 146 A5
PWCH M25 85 F3
ROY/SHW OL2 58 D3
SLFD M6 99 E5
SLFD M6 111 H1
STRET M32 140 B2
SWIN M27 96 D1
WHTF M45 68 A2
Cromwell St BOLS/LL BL3 2 B6
HEY OL10 41 E5
HTNM SK4 159 G3
OLD OL1 9 G5
Crondall St RUSH/FAL M14 127 F5
Cronkeyshaw Rd WHIT OL12 10 B2
Cronshaw St BNG/LEV M19 144 A3
Crookhill Dr CHH M8 100 A3
Crookilley Wy MPL/ROM SK6 161 E1
STKP SK1 160 C3
Crook St BOLS/LL BL3 2 E7
HYDE SK14 147 G1
MILN OL16 10 E5
Crosby Av WALK M28 81 G5
Crosby Rd BOL BL1 48 A1
NEWH/MOS M40 102 C5
RAD M26 51 H2
SLFD * M6 98 A5
Crosby St OFTN SK2 172 A2
WHIT OL12 30 A1
Crosfield Av BURY BL9 26 D1
Crosfield Gv GTN M18 129 G4
The Cross TOT/BURYW * BL8 26 A5
Crossacres Rd WYTH/NTH M22 169 E5
Cross Av PWCH M25 84 D1
Crossbank Av OLDE OL4 76 A5
Crossbank Cl BRUN/LGST M13 128 A3
Crossbank St CHAD OL9 8 E5
OLDS OL8 9 F5
Crossbridge Rd HYDE SK14 148 B1
Crossbrook Wy MILN OL16 44 D1
Crossby Cl MDTN M24 87 G2
Crosscliffe St OLDTF/WHR M16 127 E4
Crossdale Rd BKLY M9 87 F3
BOLE BL2 50 C1
Crossefield Rd CHD/CHDH SK8 182 D1
Crossen St BOLS/LL BL3 49 H4
Crossfell Av BKLY M9 86 C2
Cross Field Cl ROY/SHW OL2 45 F5
Crossfield Cl DTN/ASHW M34 146 D1
STLY SK15 119 F4
WHIT OL12 19 H1
Crossfield Dr RAD M26 66 D1
SWIN M27 96 D1
WALK M28 95 G3
Crossfield Gv MPL/ROM SK6 163 G5
OFTN SK2 172 C5
Crossfield Pl ROCH OL11 43 F1
Crossfield Rd ECC M30 121 D4
HALE/TIMP WA15 178 C2
WHIT OL12 19 H2
WILM/AE SK9 192 A3
Crossfields EDGW/EG BL7 23 G3
Crossfield St BURY BL9 53 G5
Crossford Br SALE M33 139 H4
Crossford Ct SALE * M33 139 G5
Crossford Dr BOLS/LL BL3 47 F4
Crossford St STRET M32 140 A2
Crossgate Av WYTH/NTH M22 168 C3
Crossgate Ms HTNM SK4 158 B4
Crossgates Rd MILN OL16 31 G4
Cross Glebe St AUL * OL6 118 B2
Cross Gv HALE/TIMP WA15 166 A1
Crosshill St OLDTF/WHR M16 127 E4
Cross Keys St ANC M4 7 H2
Cross Knowle Vw URM M41 122 C4
Crossland Rd CCHDY M21 140 D3
DROY M43 116 B3
Crosslands PWCH M25 84 D4
Crosslands Rd WALK M28 94 A4
Cross La DROY M43 117 E1
GTN M18 129 G3
MPL/ROM SK6 174 D4
ORD M5 111 H4
RAD M26 52 D5
TOT/BURYW BL8 16 B3
WILM/AE SK9 200 C2
Cross La East PART M31 151 E4
Cross La West PART M31 150 D4
Cross Lees WHIT OL12 19 F5
Crossley Ct ANC M4 114 A4
Crossley Crs AUL OL6 105 G4
Crossley Rd BNG/LEV M19 143 H4
SALE M33 139 F5
Crossley St BOLS/LL BL3 50 D5
GTN M18 129 E2
MILN OL16 31 F5
ROY/SHW OL2 60 B2
ROY/SHW OL2 74 B2
STLY SK15 119 E3
Crossmead Dr BKLY M9 87 F2
Crossmeadow Cl ROCH OL11 28 D3
Crossmoor Crs MPL/ROM SK6 162 B4
Crossmoor Dr BOLE BL2 3 K2
Crossmoor Gv MPL/ROM SK6 162 B4
Cross Ormrod St BOLS/LL BL3 2 A7
Cross Rd CCHDY M21 141 E4
CHD/CHDH SK8 181 G5
Cross St ALT WA14 165 G5
AUL OL6 105 G5
AUL OL6 117 H3
BOL BL1 3 F2
BOLS/LL BL3 66 A1
BURY BL9 4 E4
CSLFD M3 6 C3
DTN/ASHW M34 131 F3
EDGW/EG BL7 23 E4
FWTH BL4 65 E3
FWTH BL4 82 A2
HEY OL10 41 F5
HYDE SK14 147 G1
MDTN M24 71 G4
MILN OL16 31 E4
MOSL * OL5 92 D5
OLDE OL4 75 E5
OLDE * OL4 91 H1
OLDE OL4 92 B1
OLDTF/WHR M16 126 C3
RAMS BL0 16 D2
ROCH OL11 42 B4
SALE M33 139 G5
STLY SK15 120 A1
STRET M32 140 A1
SWIN M27 84 A5
URM M41 138 B2
WALK M28 96 B3
WHTF M45 68 B3
Crosswaite Rd OFTN SK2 173 E3
Crossway BRAM/HZG SK7 193 H2
DID/WITH M20 157 G3
OFTN SK2 172 B5
Crossways OLDS OL8 104 D1
Croston Cl WILM/AE SK9 201 D4
Crostons Rd TOT/BURYW BL8 4 A3
Croston St BOLS/LL BL3 48 B5
Croston Wk OP/CLY M11 114 B4
Croton St HTNM SK4 158 B4
Croughton Cl OP/CLY * M11 129 G1
Crowborough Wk HULME M15 127 E3
Crowcroft Rd BRUN/LGST M13 128 D5
Crowden Rd NEWH/MOS M40 88 A5
Crow Hl STLY SK15 107 F5
Crow Hl North MDTN M24 87 G1
Crowhill Rd AULW OL7 117 G1
Crow Hl South MDTN M24 87 G1
Crow Hill Vw OLDE OL4 92 A3
Crowland Gdns CHD/CHDH SK8 193 E1
Crowland Rd BOLE BL2 34 D4
NTHM/RTH M23 179 G1
Crow La RAMS BL0 16 D2
Crowley La OLDE OL4 75 G3
Crowley Rd BKLY M9 101 G2
HALE/TIMP WA15 166 C3
Crown Ct BRAM/HZG SK7 185 E1
Crowneast St ROCH OL11 29 F4
Crown Gdns MILN OL16 43 F1
Crowngreen Rd ECC M30 109 H4
Crown Hl MOSL OL5 107 E2
Crownhill Dr DROY M43 116 B3
Crown La ANC M4 7 G1
Crown Passages
HALE/TIMP WA15 177 H2
Crown Point Av
NEWH/MOS * M40 102 B5
Crown Rd HEY OL10 40 C4
Crown Sq CSLFD M3 6 C5
Crown St AUL OL6 118 A3
BOL BL1 3 F4
CSLFD M3 6 C2
DTN/ASHW M34 131 F4
FAIL M35 103 E2
HULME M15 126 D1
MILN OL16 43 G1
MPL/ROM * SK6 161 G2
MPL/ROM SK6 187 E1
NEWH/MOS M40 102 B5
ROY/SHW * OL2 60 A2
Crowsdale Pl OFTN SK2 173 F5
Crowshaw Dr WHIT OL12 18 D5
Crow's Nest BOLS/LL BL3 50 C4
Crowswood Dr STLY SK15 107 E5
Crowther Av ORD M5 111 H5
Crowther St GTN M18 129 G3
LIT OL15 20 B4
MILN OL16 43 F2
Crowthorn Dr NTHM/RTH M23 179 H2
Crowthorn Rd AULW OL7 117 G4
HTNM SK4 144 C4
Crowton Av SALE M33 153 G4
Croxdale Cl AULW OL7 104 B5
Croxton Av MILN OL16 11 H5
Croxton Cl MPL/ROM SK6 174 D4
SALE M33 153 G4
Croyde Cl BOLE BL2 35 G3
WYTH/NTH M22 181 E5
Croydon Av ROCH OL11 57 G2
ROY/SHW OL2 58 D3
Croydon Dr NEWH/MOS M40 115 F1
Croydon Sq ROCH OL11 57 G1
Crummock Cl BOLS/LL BL3 65 G1
Crummock Dr MDTN M24 71 F1
Crummock Rd CHD/CHDH SK8 181 G1
FWTH BL4 63 H5
Crumpsall La CHH M8 100 A1
Crumpsall St BOL BL1 33 H4
Crumpsall V BKLY M9 86 D5
Crumpsall Wy CHH M8 100 C1
Crundale Rd BOL BL1 23 E5
Cruttenden Rd OFTN SK2 172 D5
Cryer St DROY M43 116 D1
Cuba St MDTN M24 72 B4
Cubley Rd BRO M7 99 H2
Cuckoo Gv PWCH M25 85 E1
Cuckoo La BURY BL9 39 F4
PWCH M25 85 E1
Cuddington Av DID/WITH M20 142 B3
Cuddington Crs EDGY/DAV SK3 171 G3
Cudworth Rd BKLY M9 86 B2
Culand St WGTN/LGST M12 128 B2
Culbert Av DID/WITH M20 157 H3
Culchetch Av MPL/ROM SK6 175 E3
Culcheth La NEWH/MOS M40 102 B5
Culcheth Rd ALT WA14 177 G1
Culford Cl WGTN/LGST M12 128 B3
Culham Cl BOL * BL1 33 G4
Cullen Gv BKLY M9 87 F4
Cullercoats Wk
WGTN/LGST * M12 129 E5
Culmere Rd WYTH/NTH M22 180 C3
Culross Av BOLS/LL BL3 47 F3
NEWH/MOS M40 102 D1
Culvercliff Wk CSLFD M3 6 C6
Culver Rd EDGY/DAV SK3 171 G4
Culvert St MILN OL16 43 G4
OLDE OL4 75 H3
Culverwell Dr ORD M5 112 A3
Cumberland Av DUK SK16 118 D5
HEY OL10 40 B4
IRL M44 150 B1
RDSH SK5 160 D2
SWIN M27 83 E5
Cumberland Cl BURY BL9 53 F3
Cumberland Dr ALT WA14 176 D4
OLD OL1 74 A3
Cumberland Gv AULW OL7 118 A1
Cumberland Rd BKLY * M9 101 E1
PART M31 150 C4
ROCH OL11 43 E4
SALE M33 154 D4
URM M41 138 B2
Cumberland St BRO M7 112 C1
STLY SK15 119 E3
Cumber La WILM/AE SK9 198 C5
Cumbrae Gdns ORD M5 111 F4
Cumbrae Rd BNG/LEV M19 144 B2
Cumbrian Cl BRUN/LGST * M13 127 H2
ROY/SHW OL2 59 G1
Cumbria Wk SLFD M6 112 A1
Cummings St OLDS OL8 89 H5
Cunard Cl BRUN/LGST M13 127 H2
Cunliffe Dr ROY/SHW OL2 60 C2
SALE M33 154 D3
Cundey St BOL * BL1 33 F5
Cundiff Rd CCHDY M21 141 E5
Cundy St HYDE SK14 132 D4
Cunliffe Av RAMS BL0 16 B4
Cunliffe Brow BOL BL1 33 E4
Cunliffe St EDGY/DAV SK3 12 B5
HYDE SK14 132 B4
RAMS BL0 16 D1
Cunningham Dr BURY BL9 69 E3
WYTH/NTH M22 181 F4
Cunningham Wy OLD * OL1 74 B4
Curate St STKP SK1 13 K4
Curlew Cl ROCH OL11 28 C4
Curlew Dr IRL M44 121 B4
Curlew Rd OLDE OL4 91 H3
Currier La AUL OL6 118 B3
Curtels Cl WALK M28 96 B3
Curtis Rd BNG/LEV M19 144 B2
HTNM SK4 158 D4
Curtis St BOLS/LL BL3 63 F2
Curzon Av RUSH/FAL M14 128 B4
Curzon Dr HALE/TIMP WA15 166 C3
Curzon Gn OFTN SK2 173 E1
Curzon Ms WILM/AE SK9 199 F4
Curzon Rd AUL OL6 118 C1
BOL BL1 48 B2
BRO M7 99 G3
CHD/CHDH SK8 181 G5
OFTN SK2 173 E2
POY/DIS SK12 195 F5
ROCH OL11 43 E4
SALE M33 154 C1
STRET M32 124 B5
Curzon St MOSL OL5 106 D1
OLD OL1 9 G3
Cutgate Cl NTHM/RTH M23 155 F5
Cutgate Rd WHIT OL12 29 E2
Cuthbert Av BNG/LEV M19 144 A1
Cuthbert Rd CHD/CHDH SK8 170 B3
Cuthbert St BOLS/LL BL3 62 D2
Cutland St NEWH/MOS M40 101 H4
Cutland Wy LIT OL15 20 D4
Cut La WHIT OL12 28 C2
Cutler Hill Rd FAIL M35 103 H3
Cutnook La IRL M44 121 A3
Cutter Cl ORD M5 111 H5
Cycle St OP/CLY M11 115 E5
Cyclone St OP/CLY M11 114 C5
Cygnus Av BRO M7 112 B2
Cymbal Ct RDSH SK5 159 H3
Cynthia Dr MPL/ROM SK6 175 E4
Cypress Av CHAD OL9 73 G4
Cypress Cl EDGY/DAV SK3 12 A5
Cypress Gdns MILN OL16 31 E4
Cypress Gv DTN/ASHW M34 131 H5
FWTH * BL4 65 G5
Cypress Oaks STLY SK15 120 A2
Cypress Rd DROY M43 116 B2
ECC M30 108 D1
OLDE OL4 75 G4
Cypress St MDTN M24 72 B4
Cypress Wy MPL/ROM SK6 187 F5
Cyprus Cl OLDE OL4 91 G2
ORD M5 111 G4
Cyprus St STRET M32 140 A1
Cyril St BOLS/LL BL3 49 F4
ROY/SHW OL2 60 B2
RUSH/FAL M14 127 G5
Cyrus St NEWH/MOS M40 114 A3

D

Daccamill Dr SWIN M27 97 E4
Dacre Av OLDTF/WHR M16 141 E1
Dacre Cl MDTN M24 70 C3
Dacre Rd ROCH OL11 43 E2
Dacres Av UPML OL3 93 G3
Dacres Dr UPML OL3 93 G3
Dacres Rd UPML OL3 93 G3
Daffodil Cl WHIT OL12 18 D5
Daffodil Rd FWTH BL4 64 B3
Daffodil St BOL BL1 34 A1
Dagenham Rd RUSH/FAL * M14 127 H5
Dagmar St WALK M28 80 D3
Dagnall Av CCHDY M21 141 E5
Dahlia Cl WHIT OL12 18 C5
Daimler St CHH M8 100 B4
Dain Cl DUK SK16 118 C5
Daine Av NTHM/RTH M23 156 A5
Dainton St WGTN/LGST M12 128 A1
Daintry Cl HULME M15 127 E2
Daintry Rd CHAD OL9 8 B2
Dairydale Cl IRL M44 121 C5
Dairyground Rd
BRAM/HZG SK7 183 H5
Dairyhouse La ALT WA14 165 E2
Dairy House La BRAM/HZG SK7 193 E4
Dairy House Rd CHD/CHDH SK8 193 E2
Dairy St CHAD OL9 73 G5
Daisy Av BRUN/LGST M13 128 B4
FWTH BL4 64 B3
Daisy Bank NEWH/MOS M40 102 B5
Daisy Bank Av SLFD M6 97 H4
Daisy Bank La WYTH/NTH M22 181 F3
Daisy Bank Rd RUSH/FAL M14 128 A4
Daisyfield Cl WYTH/NTH M22 180 B3
Daisyfield Ct TOT/BURYW BL8 37 H5
Daisyhill Cl SALE M33 155 F2
Daisy Hill Rd MOSL OL5 107 E1
Daisy Ms EDGY/DAV SK3 171 G5
Daisy St BOLS/LL BL3 48 B5
CHAD OL9 8 C2
CHAD OL9 73 F4
OFTN SK2 172 A2
TOT/BURYW BL8 37 H4
WHIT OL12 10 A5
Daisy Wy MPL/ROM SK6 187 E5
Dakerwood Cl NEWH/MOS M40 102 B5
Dakley St OP/CLY M11 129 F1
Dakota Av SALQ M50 111 F5
Dakota South SALQ M50 111 G5
Dalbeattie St BKLY M9 101 F2
Dalberg St WGTN/LGST M12 128 A1
Dalbury Dr NEWH/MOS M40 100 D5
Dalby Av SWIN M27 96 D3
Dalby Gv STKP SK1 13 K3
Dale Av BRAM/HZG SK7 184 A4
ECC M30 109 F2
MOSL OL5 93 F4
Dalebank Ms SWIN * M27 82 C2
Dalebeck Cl WHTF M45 69 E4
Dale Brook Av DUK SK16 132 C2
Dalebrook Ct HTNM * SK4 12 B3
Dalebrook Rd SALE M33 154 D5
Daleford Sq BRUN/LGST * M13 127 G1
Dalegarth Av HOR/BR BL6 46 D2
Dale Gv AULW OL7 104 D5
HALE/TIMP WA15 166 A2
IRL M44 135 D5
Dalehead Dr ROY/SHW OL2 60 C2
Dale Rd MDTN M24 72 A2
MPL/ROM SK6 174 D2
Dales Av CHH M8 86 A5
WHTF M45 68 A3
Dales Brow BOL BL1 23 E5
SWIN * M27 96 C4
Dales Brow Av AULW OL7 104 D5
Dalesfield Crs MOSL OL5 107 F1
Dales Gv WALK M28 95 G1
Dales La WHTF M45 68 B3
Dalesman Cl BKLY M9 101 G2
Dalesman Dr OLD OL1 75 G1
Dalesman Wk HULME * M15 127 E2
Dales Park Dr SWIN * M27 96 C4
Dale St ANC M4 7 G4
EDGY/DAV SK3 171 G2
FWTH * BL4 65 F3
MDTN M24 72 A5
MILN OL16 11 J6
RAD M26 67 F2
ROY/SHW OL2 60 A3
STLY SK15 119 E4
SWIN M27 96 D4
TOT/BURYW BL8 37 H2
Dale St West AULW OL7 117 H3
Daleswood Av WHTF M45 68 A3
Dale Vw DTN/ASHW M34 146 D4
HYDE SK14 147 G3
LIT OL15 31 G1
Dalham Av BKLY M9 87 H5
Dalkeith Gv BOLS/LL BL3 47 G4
Dalkeith Rd RDSH SK5 145 E4
Dalkeith St GTN M18 129 E2
Dallas Ct SALQ M50 111 F5
Dalley Av BRO M7 112 C1
Dallimore Rd NTHM/RTH M23 167 F3
Dalmahoy Cl NEWH/MOS M40 102 B2
Dalmain Cl CHH M8 100 A4
Dalmeny Ter ROCH OL11 43 E2
Dalmorton Rd CCHDY M21 141 G3
Dalny St BNG/LEV M19 144 A2
Dalston Av FAIL M35 103 G2
Dalston Dr BRAM/HZG SK7 193 F2
DID/WITH M20 157 H4
Dalton Av MILN OL16 31 E4
RUSH/FAL M14 142 B1
STRET M32 124 A4
WHTF M45 68 D5
Dalton Cl MILN OL16 31 E4
RAMS BL0 16 B4
Dalton Dr SWIN M27 98 A3
Dalton Gdns URM M41 123 E5
Dalton Gv HTNM SK4 159 F2
Dalton Rd BKLY M9 87 E2
MDTN M24 70 C5
Dalton St ANC M4 113 G2
CHAD OL9 73 G5
ECC M30 109 G2
FAIL M35 102 D2
OLD * OL1 75 E5
SALE M33 139 H5
TOT/BURYW BL8 37 G4
Daltry St OLD OL1 74 D4
Dalveen Av URM M41 123 F4
Dalveen Dr HALE/TIMP WA15 166 A2
Dalymount Cl BOLE BL2 34 C4
Damask Av CSLFD M3 112 C3
Dame Hollow CHD/CHDH SK8 182 A5
Dameny Ct BRAM/HZG SK7 183 H4
Dameral Cl CHH * M8 100 B4
Damery Rd BRAM/HZG SK7 183 H4
Dame St CHAD OL9 74 A4
Dam Head Dr BKLY M9 87 F4
Damien St BNG/LEV M19 144 A1
Damson Gn MDTN M24 72 B4
Dan Bank MPL/ROM SK6 174 B3
Danby Cl HYDE SK14 133 E4
Danby Ct OLD * OL1 74 B4
Danby Pl HYDE SK14 133 E4
Danby Rd BOLS/LL BL3 63 H1
HYDE SK14 133 E4
Dane Av EDGY/DAV * SK3 170 D1
PART M31 151 E2
Dane Bank MDTN M24 72 A4
Danebank Ms DTN/ASHW M34 145 G1
Danebank Wk BRUN/LGST M13 127 G1
Danebridge Cl FWTH * BL4 65 F4
Dane Cl BRAM/HZG SK7 183 G2
Danecroft Cl BRUN/LGST M13 128 A3
Dane Dr WILM/AE SK9 200 A4
Danefield Ct CHD/CHDH SK8 182 A4
Danefield Rd SALE M33 139 H5
Daneholme Rd BNG/LEV M19 158 B1
Dane Ms SALE * M33 139 G5
Dane Rd DTN/ASHW M34 145 F1
SALE M33 139 H5
Danesbury Ri CHD/CHDH SK8 170 A4
Danesbury Rd BOL BL1 34 C2
Daneshill PWCH M25 85 E1
Danesmoor Dr BURY BL9 38 D2
Danesmoor Rd DID/WITH M20 157 F1
Danes Rd RUSH/FAL M14 143 E1
Dane St BOLS/LL * BL3 48 B5
OLDE OL4 75 F5
OP/CLY M11 129 H1
ROCH OL11 10 A7
Danesway PWCH M25 85 G5
SWIN M27 97 H4
Daneswood Av BKLY * M9 87 G3
WHIT OL12 18 B1
Daneswood Cl WHIT OL12 14 A5
Danett Cl WGTN/LGST M12 128 D2
Danforth Gv BNG/LEV M19 144 A3
Daniel Adamson Av PART M31 150 C3
Daniel Adamson Rd SALQ M50 111 E5
Daniel Fold WHIT OL12 29 E1
Daniel's La STKP * SK1 13 G2
Daniel St BRAM/HZG SK7 185 F2
HEY * OL10 40 C4
OLD OL1 75 E4
ROY/SHW OL2 74 D1
WHIT OL12 14 C4
Danisher La OLDS OL8 104 C2
Dannywood Cl HYDE SK14 147 F3
Danson St NEWH/MOS M40 114 B2
Dantall Av BKLY M9 87 H4
Dante Cl SLFD M6 110 B1
Danty St DUK * SK16 118 A4
Dantzic St ANC M4 7 F2
Dantzic St ANC M4 113 G2
Danwood Cl HYDE SK14 147 E2
Darbishire St BOL BL1 3 G1
Darby Rd IRL M44 136 B5
Darbyshire Cl BOL BL1 48 B1
Darbyshire St RAD M26 67 F1
Darcy St BOLE BL2 49 H4
Darden Cl HTNM SK4 158 B3
Darell Wk CHH M8 100 C4
Daresbury Av URM M41 122 A4
Daresbury Cl EDGY/DAV SK3 171 G4
SALE M33 155 G3
WILM/AE SK9 199 H2
Daresbury Rd CCHDY M21 140 C2
Daresbury St CHH M8 100 B2
Dargai St OP/CLY M11 115 G4
Dargle Rd SALE M33 139 G5
Darian Av WYTH/NTH M22 180 C4
Dark La MOSL OL5 93 E5
UPML OL3 77 H4
WGTN/LGST M12 114 A5
Darley Av CCHDY M21 141 F5
CHD/CHDH SK8 169 G4
ECC M30 109 F5
FWTH BL4 65 F3
Darley Gv FWTH BL4 65 F3
Darley Rd BRAM/HZG SK7 185 G5
OLDTF/WHR M16 126 B5
ROCH OL11 43 E2
Darley St BOL BL1 33 G5
FWTH BL4 65 F4
OP/CLY M11 114 B4
SALE M33 154 C2
STRET M32 125 E4
Darley Ter BOL * BL1 33 G5
Darlington Cl TOT/BURYW BL8 37 G2
Darlington Rd DID/WITH M20 142 B5
ROCH OL11 43 E3
Darliston Av BKLY M9 86 B2
Darnall Av DID/WITH M20 142 B3
Darnbrook Dr WYTH/NTH M22 180 A3
Darncombe Cl OLDTF/WHR M16 127 E4
Darnley Av WALK M28 94 D1
Darnley St OLDTF/WHR M16 126 C4
Darnton Gdns AUL OL6 118 D2
Darnton Rd AUL OL6 118 D2
Darras Rd GTN M18 129 F5
Dart Cl CHAD OL9 73 E4
Dartford Av ECC M30 109 E3
RDSH SK5 145 G5
Dartford Cl WGTN/LGST M12 128 A2
Dartford Rd URM M41 138 B2
Dartington Cl BRAM/HZG SK7 184 A1
NTHM/RTH M23 167 E3
Dartmouth Cl OLDS OL8 90 C3
Dartmouth Crs RDSH SK5 160 D1
Dartmouth Rd CCHDY M21 141 F3
WHTF M45 68 D5
Dartnall Cl POY/DIS SK12 197 F1
Darton Av NEWH/MOS M40 114 A2
Darvel Cl BOLE BL2 50 C3
Darwell Av ECC M30 109 F5
Darwen Rd EDGW/EG BL7 23 E3
Darwen St OLDTF/WHR M16 126 B3
Darwin Gv BRAM/HZG SK7 193 H1
Darwin St AULW OL7 117 H3
BOL BL1 33 G4
HYDE SK14 133 F3
OLDE OL4 91 F2
Dashwood Rd PWCH M25 84 C2
Datchett Ter ROCH OL11 43 E2
Dauntesy Av SWIN * M27 98 A3
Davehall Av WILM/AE SK9 199 F3
Davenfield Gv DID/WITH M20 157 G3
Davenfield Rd DID/WITH M20 157 G3
Davenham Rd RDSH SK5 145 E1
SALE M33 138 D5
WILM/AE SK9 192 A3
Davenhill Rd BNG/LEV M19 143 H3
Davenport Av DID/WITH M20 142 C4

Davenport Dr MPL/ROM SK6 ....147 E5
Davenport Fold Rd BOLE * BL2........35 H2
Davenport Gdns BOL BL1 ....2 D3
Davenport Park Rd OFTN SK2........172 B4
Davenport Rd BRAM/HZG SK7 ....185 E1
Davenport St BOL BL1 ....2 C3
DROY * M43 ....115 H4
DTN/ASHW M34 ....117 F5
Daventry Rd CCHDY M21 ....141 G3
ROCH OL11 ....43 E3
Daveyhulme St WHIT OL12 ....11 G2
Daveylands URM M41 ....122 C3
WILM/AE SK9 ....200 A4
Davey La WILM/AE SK9........201 B3
David Brow BOLS/LL BL3 ....62 D2
David Cl DTN/ASHW * M34 ....146 D2
David Lewis Cl MILN OL16 ....30 D5
David's Farm Cl MDTN M24........72 A5
Davids La OLDE OL4 ....76 A5
Davidson Dr MDTN M24........88 A1
David's Rd DROY M43........115 H3
David St DTN/ASHW M34 ....146 D2
RDSH SK5 ....144 D3
TOT/BURYW * BL8 ....37 H2
TOT/BURYW BL8 ....37 H3
WHIT OL12 ....10 D2
David St North WHIT OL12........10 D2
Davies Av CHD/CHDH SK8 ....191 G1
Davies Rd MPL/ROM SK6........161 E3
PART M31 ....151 F3
Davies Sq RUSH/FAL M14........127 F4
Davies St AULW OL7 ....117 G4
FWTH BL4 ....65 H5
OLD OL1 ....8 D1
Davis St ECC M30........109 H4
Davy Av SWIN M27 ....84 A5
Davyhulme Rd STRET M32 ....124 D5
URM M41 ....122 B4
Davyhulme Rd East STRET M32 ....125 E5
Davy St NEWH/MOS * M40 ....113 G1
Dawes St BOL BL1 ....2 E6
Dawlish Av CHAD OL9........73 E3
CHD/CHDH SK8 ....182 C4
DROY M43 ....115 H3
RDSH SK5 ....160 C1
Dawlish Cl BRAM/HZG SK7........183 H5
GOL/RIS/CU WA3........150 A3
HYDE SK14 ....134 B5
Dawlish Rd CCHDY M21 ....141 F3
SALE M33 ....153 H1
Dawnay St OP/CLY * M11 ....129 E1
Dawn St ROY/SHW * OL2 ....60 A3
Dawson La BOL BL1 ....2 C4
Dawson Rd ALT WA14........165 G2
CHD/CHDH SK8 ....182 A4
Dawson St BURY BL9 ....38 D2
CSLFD M3 ....6 A7
CSLFD * M3........6 D2
CSLFD M3 ....112 C5
HEY OL10 ....40 D4
HULME M15 ....126 C1
HYDE SK14 ....147 H2
OLDE * OL4 ....91 G1
OLDE * OL4 ....91 H2
STKP SK1........160 C3
SWIN M27 ....97 F2
Day Dr FAIL M35........103 E4
Day Gv HYDE SK14........134 D5
Daylesford Cl CHD/CHDH SK8 ....169 H5
Daylesford Crs CHD/CHDH SK8........170 A5
Daylesford Rd CHD/CHDH SK8 ....170 A5
Deacon Cl ALT WA14........177 E3
Deacons Cl STKP SK1........13 J3
Deacons Crs TOT/BURYW BL8 ....37 F1
Deacons Dr SLFD M6 ....98 A4
Deacon St MILN OL16 ....11 G2
Deal Av RDSH SK5 ....145 G5
Deal Cl NEWH/MOS M40........102 C5
Dealey Rd BOLS/LL BL3 ....47 H5
Deal St BOLS/LL BL3 ....64 A1
BURY BL9 ....5 J5
CSLFD * M3........6 C3
HYDE SK14 ....147 H1
Deal Wk CHAD OL9 ....89 F1
Dean Av NEWH/MOS M40 ....102 A4
OLDTF/WHR M16........126 A5
Deanbank Av BNG/LEV M19 ....143 G3
Dean Bank Dr MILN OL16........43 G5
Dean Brook Cl
NEWH/MOS * M40........102 A3
Dean Cl FWTH BL4 ....64 A4
PART M31 ....151 E2
WHTF M45 ....68 A5
WILM/AE SK9 ....199 H1
Dean Ct BOL BL1 ....3 F2
HULME * M15........126 C2
Deancourt ROCH OL11 ....42 D2
Dean Dr ALT WA14........177 E3
WILM/AE SK9 ....199 H1
Deane Av BOLS/LL BL3 ....48 A4
CHD/CHDH SK8 ....170 C4
HALE/TIMP WA15 ....166 B4
Deane Church La BOLS/LL BL3 ....48 A5
Deane Rd BOLS/LL BL3........48 B4
Deanery Wy STKP SK1 ....13 G2
Deane Wk BOLS/LL BL3 ....2 C7
Dean Head LIT * OL15 ....15 B2
Dean La BRAM/HZG SK7 ....185 F4
NEWH/MOS M40 ....102 A4
Dean Moor Rd BRAM/HZG SK7 ....184 B2
Dean Rd CSLFD M3 ....6 C1
GTN M18........129 H4
IRL M44........135 D5
WILM/AE SK9........192 B4
Dean Row Rd WILM/AE SK9 ....199 H1
Deanscourt Av SWIN M27 ....96 D3
Deansgate BOL BL1........2 D5
CSLFD M3 ....6 C6
HULME M15 ....126 D1
Deansgate La HALE/TIMP WA15........165 H2
Deanshut Rd OLDS OL8 ....90 D5
Deans Rd SWIN M27 ....96 D3
Dean St AUL OL6 ....117 H2
CMANE M1 ....7 J4
FAIL M35........102 D3
MILN OL16........11 G2
MOSL OL5........106 C1
RAD M26........67 E1
STLY SK15........119 F4
Deansway SWIN M27 ....96 D3
Deanswood Dr BKLY M9 ....86 B2
Deanwater Cl BRUN/LGST M13........127 G1
Deanwater Ct CHD/CHDH * SK8 ....182 A5
STRET * M32........139 H3
Deanway NEWH/MOS M40 ....101 H2
URM M41 ....137 E1
WILM/AE SK9 ....199 H2
Dearden Av LHULT M38 ....80 B2
Dearden Fold TOT/BURYW * BL8 ....37 H5
Deardens St TOT/BURYW BL8 ....37 H5
Dearden St BOLS/LL BL3 ....50 D5
HULME M15 ....126 D2
LIT OL15........21 E2
STLY * SK15........119 F3
Dearmans Pl CSLFD M3 ....6 C3
Dearne Dr STRET M32........140 B1
Dearnley Cl LIT OL15 ....20 C4
Debdale La GTN M18........130 A4
Debenham Av NEWH/MOS M40 ....115 F1
Debenham Ct FWTH * BL4 ....65 E5
Debenham Rd STRET M32........139 F2
Dee Av HALE/TIMP WA15 ....167 E4
Dee Dr FWTH BL4........81 H2
Deepcar St BNG/LEV M19 ....143 H1
Deepdale OLDE OL4 ....91 G1
Deepdale Av DID/WITH M20 ....142 B3
MILN OL16........30 D5
ROY/SHW OL2 ....58 D1
Deepdale Cl RDSH SK5 ....145 E2
Deepdale Dr SWIN M27 ....98 A3
Deepdale Rd BOLE BL2........35 G5
Deeping Av OLDTF/WHR M16 ....141 G1
Deeplish Rd ROCH OL11 ....43 E1
Deeplish St ROCH OL11........43 E1
Deeracre Av OFTN SK2 ....172 D3
Deerfold Cl GTN * M18 ....129 G3
Deerhurst Dr CHH M8........100 A4
Deeroak Cl GTN M18........129 E2
Deerpark Rd OLDTF/WHR M16 ....126 D5
Deer St CMANE M1 ....7 K6
Defence St BOLS/LL BL3........2 B7
Deganwy Gv RDSH SK5 ....160 A1
Delacourt Rd RUSH/FAL M14 ....142 B3
De Lacy Dr BOLE BL2........3 K1
Delafield Av WGTN/LGST M12 ....143 H1
Delaford Av WALK M28 ....95 F3
Delaford Cl EDGY/DAV SK3 ....171 H5
Delahays Dr HALE/TIMP WA15 ....178 B2
Delahays Range GTN M18 ....130 A4
Delahays Rd HALE/TIMP WA15 ....178 C2
Delaine Rd DID/WITH M20 ....142 D5
Delamere Av ROY/SHW OL2 ....60 C1
SALE M33 ....155 F3
SLFD M6 ....97 H4
STRET M32........140 A1
SWIN M27 ....83 G5
WHTF M45 ....68 B4
Delamere Cl BRAM/HZG SK7 ....185 H1
MPL/ROM SK6 ....162 B1
STLY SK15........107 F4
Delamere Rd BNG/LEV M19........143 H3
BRAM/HZG SK7 ....185 H1
CHD/CHDH SK8 ....169 G4
DTN/ASHW M34........145 G1
MILN OL16........43 H2
OFTN SK2 ....172 C5
URM M41 ....137 G1
WILM/AE SK9 ....192 A3
Delamere St AUL OL6 ....118 A3
BURY BL9 ....38 D1
OLDS OL8 ....91 E3
OP/CLY M11 ....130 A1
Delamer Rd ALT WA14 ....177 F1
Delaunays Rd CHH M8 ....86 C5
SALE M33 ....154 A2
Delbooth Av URM M41........122 B4
Delfur Rd BRAM/HZG SK7 ....184 A5
Delhi Rd IRL M44 ....136 A3
Dellar St WHIT OL12........29 F2
Dell Av SWIN M27 ....98 A3
Dell Cl OLDE OL4........92 A2
Dellcot Cl PWCH M25 ....85 G5
SLFD M6 ....97 G5
Dellcot La WALK M28 ....95 G5
Dell Gdns WHIT OL12........29 E1
Dellhide Cl OLDE OL4........92 B1
Dell Meadow WHIT OL12 ....18 B3
Dell Rd WHIT OL12........18 A4
Dell Side MPL/ROM SK6 ....161 F3
Dellside Av WALK M28 ....81 F4
Dell Side Wy WHIT OL12 ....29 F1
Dell St BOLE BL2........34 D1
The Delph WALK * M28........95 G4
Delph Brook Wy EDGW/EG BL7 ....22 C1
Delph Hl BOL BL1........32 B4
Delph Hill Cl BOL BL1........32 B4
Delphi Av WALK M28........81 E5
Delph La BOLE BL2 ....36 B5
Delph New Rd UPML OL3........77 F2
Delph Rd UPML OL3 ....61 H2
Delph St BOLS/LL BL3 ....48 C4
MILN OL16........31 G5
Delside Av NEWH/MOS M40 ....101 H2
Delta Cl ROY/SHW OL2 ....74 A2
Delta Rd DTN/ASHW M34........131 F1
Delvino Wk HULME M15 ....127 F4
Delwood Gdns WYTH/NTH M22 ....168 C5
De-Massey Cl MPL/ROM * SK6 ....147 E5
Demesne Cl STLY SK15 ....119 H4
Demesne Crs STLY SK15........119 H4
Demesne Dr STLY SK15........119 H4
Demesne Rd OLDTF/WHR M16 ....141 H1
Demmings Rd CHD/CHDH SK8 ....170 C4
Dempsey Dr BURY BL9........69 E2
Denbigh Cl BRAM/HZG SK7 ....184 D4
Denbigh Dr ROY/SHW OL2........59 G3
Denbigh Pl SLFD M6 ....111 H4
Denbigh Rd BOLE BL2........49 G4
DTN/ASHW M34........146 C2
SWIN M27 ....83 F5
Denbigh St HTNM SK4 ....159 G3
MOSL OL5 ....107 E2
OLDS * OL8 ....90 C4
Denbigh Wk HULME M15........126 D3
Denbury Dr ALT WA14 ....165 E4
Denbury Gn BRAM/HZG SK7 ....184 B2
Denbydale Wy ROY/SHW OL2........58 D4
Denby La HTNM SK4 ....159 G2
Denby Rd DUK SK16 ....132 B1
Dencombe St BRUN/LGST M13........128 C4
Dene Bank BOLE BL2 ....34 D1
Dene Brow DTN/ASHW M34 ....147 E3
Dene Ct HTNM SK4 ....12 A1
Dene Dr MDTN M24........71 G5
Denefield Cl MPL/ROM SK6........163 G5
Deneford Rd DID/WITH M20 ....157 F4
Dene Hollow RDSH SK5 ....145 F2
Denehurst Rd ROCH OL11 ....29 F3
Denehurst St WGTN/LGST * M12........128 C2
Dene Pk DID/WITH M20 ....157 F4
Dene Rd DID/WITH M20 ....157 F3
Dene Rd West DID/WITH M20........157 E3
Deneside Crs BRAM/HZG SK7 ....185 G1
Dene St BOLE BL2 ....34 D1
Denesway SALE M33........153 H3
Deneway BRAM/HZG SK7 ....183 F5
HTNM SK4........12 A1
MPL/ROM SK6 ....187 E5
Deneway Cl HTNM SK4........12 A1
Deneway Ms HTNM * SK4 ....12 A1
Denewell Cl BRUN/LGST M13 ....128 A3
Denham Cl BOL BL1........34 B1
Denham Dr BRAM/HZG SK7........183 G5
IRL M44 ....136 B2
Denham St BRUN/LGST M13 ....128 A4
Den Hill Dr OLDE OL4 ....92 A1
Denhill Rd HULME M15........127 E4
Denholme Rd ROCH OL11 ....43 E2
Denholm Rd DID/WITH M20 ....169 H1
Denhurst Rd LIT OL15 ....20 D2
Denis Av OLDTF/WHR M16........141 H1
Denison Rd BRAM/HZG SK7........185 F4
RUSH/FAL M14........128 A5
Denison St RUSH/FAL M14........127 H5
Deniston Rd HTNM SK4 ....159 E1
Den La OLDE OL4 ....76 A5
UPML OL3........78 A3
Denmark Rd RUSH/FAL M14 ....127 F4
SALE M33 ....139 G5
Denmark St ALT WA14 ....165 G5
CHAD OL9........73 H4
MILN OL16........11 F4
OLDE * OL4 ....75 E5
Denmark Wy CHAD OL9........8 B1
Denmore Rd NEWH/MOS M40 ....88 B4
Dennington Dr URM M41........123 F4
Dennison Av DID/WITH M20 ....142 C4
Dennison Rd CHD/CHDH SK8........182 D4
Denshaw Av DTN/ASHW M34 ....131 E3
Denshaw Cl BNG/LEV M19........158 B3
Denshaw Rd UPML OL3 ....61 H4
Densmead Wk
NEWH/MOS * M40........113 H2
Densmore St FAIL * M35........102 D3
Denson Rd HALE/TIMP WA15 ....166 C1
Denstone Av ECC M30 ....109 H2
SALE M33 ....153 H3
URM M41 ....123 F5
Denstone Crs BOLE BL2 ....35 E4
Denstone Rd RDSH SK5 ....145 E2
SLFD M6 ....98 A5
URM M41 ....123 F5
Dentdale Cl BOL BL1 ....47 E3
Denton Hall Farm Rd
DTN/ASHW M34........145 H1
Denton La CHAD OL9........89 F2
Denton Rd BOLE BL2 ....51 E3
DTN/ASHW M34........131 F3
Denton St BURY BL9........4 E1
HEY OL10 ....40 D5
WHIT OL12 ....10 C3
Denver Av NEWH/MOS M40 ....114 A2
Denver Dr HALE/TIMP WA15 ....166 B3
Denver Rd ROCH OL11 ....43 E2
Denville Crs WYTH/NTH M22 ....180 D1
Denzell Gdns ALT * WA14........176 D1
Depleach Rd CHD/CHDH SK8........170 A4
Deptford Av NTHM/RTH M23 ....179 H1
De Quincey Rd ALT WA14........153 G5
Deramore Cl AUL OL6 ....118 D2
Deramore St RUSH/FAL M14........127 G5
Derby Av SLFD M6........111 F3
Derby Cl IRL M44 ....150 B1
Derby Ct CHAD OL9 ....8 A7
SALE M33 ....154 D3
Derby Gv BNG/LEV M19 ....144 A2
Derby Range HTNM SK4........159 E2
Derby Rd AUL OL6 ....118 C2
HTNM SK4........159 F2
RAD M26........65 H4
RUSH/FAL M14........142 D4
SALE M33 ....138 D5
SLFD M6 ....111 F3
URM M41 ....123 G5
WHTF M45 ....84 D1
Derbyshire Av STRET M32 ....124 C5
Derbyshire Crs STRET M32 ....124 C5
Derbyshire Gv STRET M32 ....124 B5
Derbyshire La STRET M32 ....139 H1
Derbyshire La West URM M41 ....124 B5
Derbyshire Rd NEWH/MOS M40........115 G1
PART M31........150 C4
POY/DIS SK12........196 C2
SALE M33........154 D2
Derbyshire Rd South SALE M33 ....155 E3
Derbyshire Rw BOL * BL1........33 H3
Derbyshire St OP/CLY M11 ....129 F1
Derby St ALT WA14 ....165 H4
AULW OL7........104 D5
BOLS/LL BL3 ....48 C4
BURY BL9 ....5 F4
CHAD OL9 ....8 A7
CHAD OL9 ....89 G4
CHH M8........99 H5
DTN/ASHW M34........131 E4
EDGY/DAV SK3........12 D6
FAIL * M35........103 F1
HEY OL10 ....40 C4
MOSL * OL5........107 E2
MPL/ROM SK6 ....175 E4
PWCH M25 ....84 D3
RAMS BL0 ....17 E2
ROCH OL11 ....43 F1
Dereham Cl TOT/BURYW BL8 ....38 A1
Derg St SLFD M6 ....111 G3
Derker St OLD OL1........9 K1
Dermot Murphy Cl
DID/WITH M20........142 A5
Dernford Av BNG/LEV M19 ....158 C1
Derry Av WYTH/NTH M22........168 D5
Derwen Rd EDGY/DAV SK3 ....171 H2
Derwent Av AULW OL7........117 H1
CCHDY M21 ....156 C1
DROY M43 ....115 H4
HALE/TIMP * WA15 ....167 E4
HEY OL10 ....56 A1
WHTF M45 ....69 E4
Derwent Cl BOLS/LL BL3 ....65 G1
DTN/ASHW M34........145 G1
PART M31........151 E2
WALK M28........80 C5
WHTF M45 ....69 E5
Derwent Dr BRAM/HZG SK7 ....193 F2
BURY BL9 ....53 E2
CHAD OL9 ....73 F5
FWTH BL4 ....82 A2
LIT OL15........31 G1
ROY/SHW OL2 ....59 H1
SALE M33 ....154 B4
WILM/AE SK9 ....191 H2
Derwent Rd FWTH BL4........64 A5
MDTN M24 ....71 F1
MPL/ROM SK6 ....186 D4
STRET M32 ....125 E5
URM M41 ....137 F1
Derwent St CHH M8 ....100 D4
OP/CLY * M11........115 G4
ORD M5........112 B5
WHIT OL12 ....10 C2
Design St BOLS/LL BL3 ....63 E1
Desmond Rd WYTH/NTH M22........168 D5
The De Traffords IRL M44 ....121 B5
Dettingen St SLFD M6 ....98 B4
Deva Cl BRAM/HZG SK7 ....185 E3
POY/DIS SK12........194 C3
Deva Sq CHAD OL9........8 A7
Devas St HULME M15 ....127 G3
Deverill Av GTN M18 ....130 A4
Devine Cl CSLFD M3 ....112 C3
ROY/SHW OL2 ....59 E3
Devisdale Gra ALT * WA14 ....177 E1
Devisdale Rd ALT WA14 ....165 E5
Devoke Av WALK M28........81 F5
Devoke Gv FWTH BL4 ....63 H4
Devoke Rd WYTH/NTH M22........180 A2
Devon Av BNG/LEV M19........143 G3
WHTF M45 ....68 B3
Devon Cl BOLS/LL BL3........51 E5
RDSH SK5 ....160 D2
ROY/SHW OL2 ....59 G2
SLFD M6 ....110 B2
Devon Dr BOLE BL2........36 B5
Devonport Crs ROY/SHW OL2 ....59 G5
Devon Rd DROY M43 ....116 B2
FAIL M35 ....102 D4
PART M31 ....150 D4
URM M41 ....137 F2
Devonshire Cl HEY OL10........40 B4
URM M41 ....138 D1
Devonshire Dr WILM/AE SK9........201 G3
Devonshire Park Rd OFTN SK2 ....172 B4
Devonshire Pl PWCH M25 ....84 D2
Devonshire Rd ALT WA14........165 F3
BOL BL1........48 A1
BRAM/HZG SK7 ....185 G4
CCHDY M21 ....141 F3
ECC M30........109 H3
HTNM SK4........159 E4
ROCH OL11 ....43 E4
SLFD M6 ....110 B2
WALK M28........80 D1
Devonshire St BRO M7........99 H4
WGTN/LGST M12 ....128 A2
Devonshire St East
NEWH/MOS * M40........102 C5
Devonshire St North
WGTN/LGST M12 ....128 A1
Devonshire St South
BRUN/LGST M13........128 A3
Devon St BOLE BL2........3 H5
BURY BL9 ....53 G1
CHAD OL9 ....89 G3
FWTH BL4 ....65 E2
ROCH OL11 ....30 A5
SWIN M27 ....83 E5
Devon Wy OLDS OL8........89 H5
Dewar Cl OP/CLY M11 ....114 D4
Dewes Av SWIN M27........83 G5
Dewey St OP/CLY M11 ....129 G1
Dewhirst Rd WHIT OL12 ....19 E3
Dewhirst Wy WHIT OL12 ....19 E4
Dewhurst Clough Rd
EDGW/EG BL7 ....22 C1
Dewhurst Rd BOLE BL2 ....35 F3
Dewhurst St CHH M8 ....113 E1
HEY * OL10 ....41 F4
Dewint Av MPL/ROM SK6 ....175 G1
Dew Meadow Cl WHIT OL12 ....10 B1
Dewsnap Cl DUK * SK16 ....132 B2
Dewsnap La DUK SK16 ....132 B2
HYDE SK14 ....134 D2
Dew Wy CHAD OL9 ....8 C2
Dexter Rd BKLY M9........86 B2
Deyne Av PWCH M25 ....85 E3
RUSH/FAL M14........127 H4
Deyne St SLFD M6........111 F3
Dial Ct FWTH * BL4........65 E4
Dial Park Rd OFTN SK2 ....173 E5
Dial Rd HALE/TIMP WA15........178 D4
OFTN SK2 ....172 D4
Dialstone La OFTN SK2 ....172 D2
Diamond St AUL OL6........118 C1
OFTN SK2 ....172 B3
Diamond Ter MPL/ROM SK6 ....187 E1
Dicken Gn ROCH OL11........43 E2
Dicken Green La ROCH OL11 ....43 E2
Dickens Cl CHD/CHDH SK8........193 E2
Dickens La POY/DIS SK12........195 F4
Dickenson Rd RUSH/FAL M14 ....128 A5
Dickens Rd ECC M30........109 G4
Dickens St HEY * OL10 ....40 C4
OLD OL1 ....60 D5
Dickinson Cl BOL * BL1 ....33 H5
Dickinson St BOL BL1 ....33 H5
CMANE M1 ....7 F6
CSLFD M3 ....112 D2
OLDE OL4 ....75 E5
Didcot Rd WYTH/NTH M22........180 B3
Didley Sq WGTN/LGST * M12 ....128 D2
Didsbury Pk DID/WITH M20........157 G4
Didsbury Rd HTNM SK4 ....158 B4
Digby Rd ROCH OL11 ....43 E2
Dig Gate La MILN OL16 ....44 B3
Diggles La ROCH OL11 ....28 B5
Diggle St ROY/SHW OL2 ....60 A3
Dijon St BOLS/LL BL3........48 B5
Dilham Ct BOL BL1........48 B1
Dillmoss Wk HULME * M15 ....126 C2
Dillon Dr WGTN/LGST M12 ....128 B3
Dilston Cl BRUN/LGST M13........127 H2
Dilworth Cl HEY OL10 ....40 A4
Dilworth Ct OFTN SK2........173 F4
Dilworth St HULME M15 ....127 G3
The Dingle BRAM/HZG SK7 ....183 F3
HYDE SK14 ....147 H5
Dingle Av ROY/SHW OL2 ....45 F5
Dingle Bank Rd BRAM/HZG SK7 ....183 G2
Dingle Cl MPL/ROM SK6........162 C4
Dingle Dr DROY M43 ....116 C2
Dingle Gv CHD/CHDH SK8 ....169 E3
Dingle Rd MDTN M24 ....87 F1
Dingle Ter AUL OL6 ....91 E5
Dingle Wk BOL BL1 ....2 E2
Dinmor Rd WYTH/NTH M22........180 B4
Dinnington Dr CHH M8 ....100 A4
Dinorwic Cl CHH M8 ....86 B5
Dinsdale Dr BOLS/LL BL3 ....48 C4
Dinting Av DID/WITH M20 ....142 B4
Dinton St HULME M15 ....126 B1
Dirty La OLDE OL4 ....76 C3
Dirty Leech WHIT OL12 ....19 E2
Discovery Pk HTNM * SK4 ....159 F1
Disley Av DID/WITH M20 ....142 A5
Disley St ROCH OL11 ....42 B2
Distaff Rd POY/DIS SK12........194 C3
Ditton Mead Cl WHIT OL12........30 C1
Division St BOLS/LL BL3 ....64 A1
WHIT OL12 ....11 G1
Dixon Av BRO M7 ....99 G4
Dixon Cl SALE M33........155 E4
Dixon Closes ROCH OL11 ....28 B4
Dixon Dr SWIN M27........82 D3
Dixon Green Dr FWTH BL4........64 D4
Dixon Rd DTN/ASHW M34 ....147 E2
Dixon St AUL OL6........118 C1
IRL M44........135 D3
MDTN M24 ....71 H2
NEWH/MOS M40 ....102 A4
OLDE OL4 ....75 H4
ROCH OL11 ....42 B2
SLFD M6 ....98 C4
Dobb Hedge Cl
HALE/TIMP WA15 ....188 D1
Dobbin Dr ROCH OL11 ....43 E3
Dobbinetts La
HALE/TIMP WA15 ....179 E1
NTHM/RTH M23........167 F5
Dobcross Cl BRUN/LGST M13 ....143 H1
Dobcross New Rd UPML OL3 ....77 H3
Dobhill St FWTH BL4 ....65 E4
Dobroyd St CHH M8 ....100 B2
Dobson Cl BRUN/LGST M13 ....128 A2
Dobson Rd BOL BL1 ....48 B2
Dobson St BOL BL1 ....33 G4
Doctor Fold La HEY OL10........55 G3
Doctor La OLDE OL4 ....76 D3
Doctors La BURY BL9 ....4 B4
Dodd Cft MILN OL16 ....43 G4
Doddington La ORD M5........111 H5
Doddington Wk
DTN/ASHW * M34 ....146 B2
Dodd St ORD M5 ....111 E3
Dodge Fold OFTN SK2........173 F3
Dodge Hl HTNM SK4 ....13 F1
Dodgson St MILN OL16........30 B5
Dodworth Cl HULME M15 ....127 E2
Doe Brow SWIN M27........82 D3
Doefield Av WALK M28........94 D2
Doe Hey Gv FWTH BL4 ....64 C2
Doe Hey Rd BOLS/LL BL3 ....64 C2
Doffcocker Brow BOL BL1........32 C5
Doffcocker La BOL BL1 ....32 C5
Dogford Rd ROY/SHW OL2 ....59 E4
Dolbey St ORD M5........111 F4
Dolefield CSLFD M3........6 C5
D'Olivera Ct MDTN M24 ....71 F2
Dollond St BKLY M9 ....101 F1
Dolphin Pl WGTN/LGST M12........127 H1
Dolphin St WGTN/LGST M12 ....127 H1
Doman St BOLS/LL BL3........49 E4
Dombey Rd POY/DIS SK12........195 E5
The Dome ALT * WA14 ....165 G5
Domestic Ap MANAIR M90........190 B1
Domett St BKLY M9........86 D5
Dominic Cl NTHM/RTH M23........155 F5
Donald Av HYDE SK14........148 A2
Donald St CMANE * M1........7 G7
Dona St STKP SK1 ....13 K5
Don Av SLFD M6 ....110 D3
Doncaster Av DID/WITH M20 ....142 B4
Doncaster Cl BOLS/LL BL3 ....65 G1
Doncaster Wk OLD OL1 ....9 G2
Donhead Wk BRUN/LGST * M13 ....127 H2
Donkey La WILM/AE SK9........199 F5
Donleigh St NEWH/MOS M40 ....102 C4
Donnington ROCH * OL11 ....29 H5
Donnington Av CHD/CHDH SK8 ....170 C4
Donnington Gdns WALK * M28........81 E4
Donnington Rd GTN M18........129 H3
RAD M26........51 F4
Donnison St WGTN/LGST M12 ....128 D2
Donovan Av NEWH/MOS M40........113 H1
Don St BOLS/LL BL3........63 G1
MDTN M24 ....72 B3
Doodson Av IRL M44 ....136 A1
Doodson Sq FWTH BL4........65 E4
Dooley La MPL/ROM SK6 ....174 A2
Dooley's La WILM/AE SK9 ....190 A5
Dorac Av CHD/CHDH SK8........191 H1
Dora St RAMS BL0 ....16 B4
Dorchester Av BOLE BL2 ....35 F5
DTN/ASHW M34........146 C2
PWCH M25 ....85 F5
URM M41 ....124 A5
Dorchester Cl HALE/TIMP WA15........178 D1
WILM/AE SK9 ....200 A2
Dorchester Ct CHD/CHDH SK8 ....183 E3
SALE M33 ....154 C4
Dorchester Dr NTHM/RTH M23 ....155 F5
ROY/SHW OL2 ....74 A2
Dorchester Gv HEY OL10........55 H1
Dorchester Rd BRAM/HZG SK7 ....184 C3
SWIN M27 ....97 E4
Dorclyn Av URM M41 ....138 C1
Dorfield Cl MPL/ROM SK6 ....161 F3
Doric Av MPL/ROM SK6 ....161 E3
Doric Cl OP/CLY M11........114 C4
Doris Av BOLE BL2........50 A2
Doris Rd EDGY/DAV SK3........12 A6
Doris St MDTN M24........71 H2
Dorking Av NEWH/MOS M40........114 D1
Dorking Cl BOL BL1 ....34 A4
STKP SK1........172 C2
Dorlan Av GTN M18........130 A4
Dorland Gv OFTN SK2 ....172 C2
Dorman St OP/CLY M11 ....129 G1
Dormer St BOL BL1........34 A3
Dorney St GTN M18........129 G3
Dorning Rd SWIN M27 ....97 F3
Dorning St ECC M30........109 G4

FWTH BL4 ...65 G4
TOT/BURYW BL8 ...37 G2
Dorothy Rd BRAM/HZG SK7 ...185 G1
Dorothy St BRO M7 ...16 C3
Dorrington Rd EDGY/DAV SK3 ...170 D2
SALE M33 ...153 G2
Dorris St BNG/LEV M19 ...144 A3
BOLS/LL * BL3 ...63 F1
Dorrit Cl ROY/DIS SK12 ...195 F5
Dorset Av BRAM/HZG SK7 ...183 G3
CHD/CHDH SK8 ...171 F5
DTN/ASHW M34 ...116 D5
FWTH BL4 ...4 A3
RDSH SK5 ...160 D1
ROY/SHW OL2 ...59 G2
RUSH/FAL M14 ...142 B1
Dorset Cl FWTH BL4 ...64 D4
HEY OL10 ...40 B5
Dorset Dr BURY BL9 ...53 H1
Dorset Rd ALT WA14 ...165 E5
BNG/LEV M19 ...144 B2
DROY M43 ...116 A2
IRL M44 ...135 C5
Dorset St AUL OL6 ...118 C3
BOLE BL2 ...3 H5
CHAD OL9 ...8 A7
ROCH OL11 ...30 A5
STRET M32 ...140 A2
SWIN M27 ...83 E5
Dorsey St ANC * M4 ...7 H3
Dorstone Cl NEWH/MOS M40 ...115 F1
Dorwood Av BKLY M9 ...86 D2
Dougall Av WGTN/LGST M12 ...128 D2
Doughty Av ECC M30 ...110 A2
Douglas Av GTN M18 ...129 G3
STRET M32 ...125 E5
TOT/BURYW BL8 ...37 G4
Douglas Gdns WHTF M45 ...68 C2
Douglas Gn SLFD M6 ...98 D5
Douglas Rd BRAM/HZG SK7 ...185 F1
EDGY/DAV SK3 ...11 K5
SWIN M27 ...96 B3
Douglas St AUL OL6 ...118 C2
BOL * BL1 ...33 H1
BRO M7 ...101 H4
FAIL M35 ...103 F3
HYDE SK14 ...147 H1
NEWH/MOS M40 ...101 H5
OLD OL1 ...3 J1
RAMS BL0 ...16 C2
SWIN M27 ...96 B3
Doulton St NEWH/MOS M40 ...102 B2
Douro Av DUK SK16 ...109 E2
Douro St NEWH/MOS M40 ...101 G5
Douthwaite Dr MPL/ROM SK6 ...162 D5
Dove Bank Rd BOLS/LL BL3 ...50 C5
Dovebrook Cl STLY SK15 ...107 F3
Dovecote DROY M43 ...117 E2
Dovecote Cl EDGW/EG BL7 ...23 G5
Dovecote La LHULT M38 ...79 D4
Dovecote Ms CCHDY M21 ...140 D3
Dovedale Av DID/WITH M20 ...142 B4
DROY M43 ...115 H5
ECC M30 ...109 H2
PWCH M25 ...85 G4
URM M41 ...138 C1
Dovedale Cl MPL/ROM SK6 ...186 D5
Dovedale Rd BOLE BL2 ...20 A2
OFTN SK2 ...173 G2
Dove Dr BURY BL9 ...5 K1
IRL M44 ...121 B5
Dovehouse Cl WHTF M45 ...68 A4
Doveleys Rd SLFD M6 ...99 H2
Dover Cl TOT/BURYW BL8 ...76 R2
Dovercourt Av HTNM * SK4 ...158 C3
Dover Gv BOLS/LL BL3 ...48 C4
Doveridge Gdns SLFD M6 ...111 C2
Dover Pk URM M41 ...123 G4
Dover Rd SWIN M27 ...96 B3
Dover St BRUN/LGST M13 ...127 C2
CHAD OL9 ...8 B6
ECC M30 ...109 E3
FWTH BL4 ...64 D2
MILN OL16 ...11 H1
RDSH * SK5 ...144 D4
Dovestone Crs DUK SK16 ...133 E1
Dovestone Wk
NEWH/MOS * M40 ...102 D1
Doveston Rd SALE M33 ...139 C5
Dove St BOL BL1 ...33 H2
OLDE OL4 ...9 G4
ROCH OL11 ...29 H4
Dow Fold TOT/BURYW BL8 ...37 E3
Dowland Cl NTHM/RTH M23 ...155 G4
Dow La TOT/BURYW BL8 ...37 E3
Dowling St ROCH OL11 ...30 A5
Downesway AULW/HILW * OL7 ...144 B3
Downfield Cl TOT/BURYW BL8 ...14 B2
Downfields RDSH SK5 ...145 F2
Downgreen Rd BOLE BL2 ...35 F3
Downhall Gn BOL BL1 ...2 D3
Downham Av BOLE BL2 ...49 H1
Downham Cha
HALE/TIMP WA15 ...166 C3
Downham Cl ROY/SHW OL2 ...59 H2
Downham Crs PWCH M25 ...85 H4
Downham Gdns PWCH M25 ...85 H4
Downham Rd HTNM SK4 ...158 D4
HTNM SK4 ...159 C1
Downhill Cl OLD OL1 ...74 B3
Downing Cl AULW OL7 ...104 C4
CMANE M1 ...7 H7
Downley Cl AULW OL7 ...104 C4
Downley Dr ANC M4 ...113 H5
The Downs ALT WA14 ...177 C1
CHD/CHDH SK8 ...182 A1
MDTN M24 ...72 B4
PWCH M25 ...84 D4
Downs Dr ALT WA14 ...165 H1
Downshaw Rd AULW OL7 ...104 D4
Dowry Rd OLDE OL4 ...75 H5
Dowry St OLDS OL8 ...90 C4
Dowson Rd HYDE SK14 ...147 H5
Doyle Av BROM SK6 ...161 E3
Doyle Cl OLD OL1 ...60 D5

Doyle Rd BOLS/LL * BL3 ...62 B1
Drake Av FWTH BL4 ...81 E1
IRL M44 ...135 D5
Drake Cl OLD OL1 ...74 D4
Drake St RDSH SK5 ...159 H2
Drake Rd ALT WA14 ...165 E1
LIT OL15 ...15 B4
Drake St MILN OL16 ...10 C6
ROCH OL11 ...30 A5
Draycott St BOL BL1 ...33 H4
Draycott St East BOL BL1 ...34 A4
Drayfields DROY M43 ...117 E3
Drayford Cl NTHM/RTH M23 ...155 G4
Drayton Av CHD/CHDH SK8 ...181 G5
Drayton Cl BOL BL1 ...33 G4
SALE M33 ...153 G4
WILM/AE SK9 ...200 A1
Drayton Gv HALE/TIMP WA15 ...166 B5
Drayton Wk OLDTF/WHR M16 ...126 B3
Dresden St NEWH/MOS M40 ...102 B2
Drewett St NEWH/MOS M40 ...114 B1
Dreyfus Av OP/CLY M11 ...115 F3
Driffield St ECC M30 ...110 C3
RUSH/FAL M14 ...127 F5
Drill Wk ANC M4 ...113 H4
Drinkwater Rd PWCH M25 ...98 C1
Driscoll St BRUN/LGST M13 ...128 C5
The Drive BRO M7 ...99 F1
BURY BL9 ...38 C1
CHD/CHDH SK8 ...171 F5
DID/WITH M20 ...157 H3
HALE/TIMP WA15 ...179 E4
MPL/ROM SK6 ...174 D3
PWCH M25 ...85 E3
RDSH SK5 ...160 D2
SALE M33 ...153 H5
Droitwich Rd NEWH/MOS M40 ...114 A1
Dronfield Rd SLFD M6 ...111 E1
WYTH/NTH M22 ...168 C1
Droughts La PWCH M25 ...69 E4
Droylsden Rd DTN/ASHW M34 ...116 C4
NEWH/MOS M40 ...102 C5
Drummond St BOL * BL1 ...33 H2
Drury La CHAD OL9 ...89 F4
Drury St BNG/LEV M19 ...143 H2
Dryad Cl SWIN M27 ...96 C1
Drybrook Cl BRUN/LGST M13 ...128 B3
Dryburgh Av BOL BL1 ...33 G3
Dryden Av CHD/CHDH SK8 ...170 B3
SWIN M27 ...96 A5
Dryden Cl DUK SK16 ...133 C1
MPL/ROM SK6 ...175 E5
Dryden Rd OLDTF/WHR M16 ...126 B5
Dryden St BRUN/LGST M13 ...127 F2
Dryhurst Wk HULME M15 ...127 F2
Drymoss OLDS OL8 ...104 C1
Drywood Av WALK M28 ...95 H5
Ducal St ANC M4 ...113 G1
Duchess Park Cl ROY/SHW OL2 ...60 A4
Duchess Rd CHH M8 ...100 C2
Duchess St ROY/SHW OL2 ...59 H1
Duchy Av BOLS/LL BL3 ...48 A5
Duchy Av WALK M28 ...95 E5
WHTN BL5 ...62 D4
Duchy Bank SLFD M6 ...98 A4
Duchy Rd SLFD M6 ...98 A4
Duchy St EDGY/DAV SK3 ...12 D7
SLFD M6 ...111 C2
Ducie Av BOL BL1 ...2 A4
Ducie Gv HULME M15 ...127 C3
Ducie St CMANE M1 ...7 H5
OLDS OL8 ...8 D7
RAD M26 ...52 A4
WHTF M45 ...68 C4
Duckshaw La FWTH BL4 ...64 D4
Duckworth Rd PWCH M25 ...69 F4
Duckworth St BURY BL9 ...38 D2
ROY/SHW OL2 ...60 B1
Duddon Av BOLE BL2 ...35 G5
Duddon Cl WHTF M45 ...69 E4
Dudley Av BOLE BL2 ...34 D5
WHTN BL5 ...62 D4
Dudley Cl HULME M15 ...126 D3
IRL M44 ...150 C2
Dudley Rd OLDTF/WHR M16 ...142 A3
SALE M33 ...139 H5
SWIN M27 ...97 E1
Dudley St CHH M8 ...100 A4
DTN/ASHW M34 ...116 D4
ECC M30 ...109 F4
OLDE OL4 ...91 G1
Dudlow Wk HULME * M15 ...126 C2
Dudwell Cl BOL BL1 ...33 F5
Duerden St BOLS/LL * BL3 ...62 D2
Duffield Cl MDTN * M24 ...87 C2
Duffield Gdns MDTN M24 ...87 C2
Duffield Rd SLFD M6 ...98 C5
Duffins Cl WHIT OL12 ...18 C5
Dugdale Av BKLY M9 ...87 F3
Dugie St RAMS BL0 ...16 C1
Duice Pl ORD M5 ...112 B4
Duke Av CHD/CHDH SK8 ...192 C1
Duke Cl OLDTF/WHR M16 ...126 C4
Dukefield St WYTH/NTH M22 ...168 D1
Duke Pl CSLFD M3 ...6 B7
Duke Rd HYDE SK14 ...133 E5
Dukes Platting AUL OL6 ...106 A5
Duke St AUL * OL6 ...118 A3
BOL BL1 ...2 A3
BRO M7 ...6 D2
CSLFD M3 ...6 D2
DTN/ASHW M34 ...131 F5
FAIL M35 ...105 F1
HEY OL10 ...40 C4
LHULT M38 ...80 B2
LIT OL15 ...20 D5
OLDS OL8 ...107 F1
RAD M26 ...16 B4
ROY/SHW OL2 ...60 B3
STKP SK1 ...13 H5
STLY SK15 ...119 E4
WALK M28 ...81 H5
WHIT OL12 ...10 C2
WILM/AE SK9 ...201 D3
Duke St North BOL BL1 ...2 B2
Dukinfield Rd HYDE SK14 ...132 B3
Dulford Wk BRUN/LGST * M13 ...127 H3
Dulgar St OP/CLY * M11 ...115 E5

Dulverton Gdns BOLS/LL * BL3 ...66 A2
Dulverton St NEWH/MOS M40 ...102 A4
Dulwich Cl SALE M33 ...153 C3
Dulwich St ANC M4 ...113 C2
Dumbarton Cl RDSH SK5 ...145 E5
Dumbarton Dr HEY OL10 ...55 E1
Dumbarton Rd RDSH SK5 ...145 E4
Dumbell St SWIN M27 ...83 E5
Dumber La SALE M33 ...139 F1
Dumers La RAD M26 ...53 E5
Dumfries Hollow HEY OL10 ...41 G3
Dunbar Av NTHM/RTH M23 ...179 H1
Dunbar Dr BOLS/LL BL3 ...65 E1
Dunbar Gv HEY OL10 ...55 E1
Dunbar St OLD OL1 ...8 E1
Dunblane Av BOLS/LL BL3 ...47 F4
HTNM SK4 ...159 E4
Dunblane Gv HEY OL10 ...55 E1
Duncan Rd BRUN/LGST M13 ...128 C5
Duncan St BRO M7 ...99 F4
DUK SK16 ...132 A2
ORD M5 ...126 C2
Dunchurch Cl LHULT M38 ...78 C1
Dunchurch Rd SALE M33 ...153 H2
Dun Cl CSLFD M3 ...6 A2
Duncombe Cl BRAM/HZG SK7 ...184 B1
Duncombe Dr NEWH/MOS M40 ...102 A5
Duncombe Rd BOLS/LL BL3 ...63 H2
Duncombe St BRO M7 ...99 H4
Duncote Gv ROY/SHW OL2 ...59 G4
Dundee Cl HEY OL10 ...40 A5
Dundee La RAMS BL0 ...16 C2
Dundonald Rd CHD/CHDH SK8 ...182 D5
DID/WITH M20 ...157 H3
Dundonald St OFTN SK2 ...172 A3
Dundraw Cl MDTN M24 ...71 E3
Dundrennan Ct ROY/DIS SK12 ...195 E2
Dunecroft DTN/ASHW * M34 ...131 H4
Dunedin Dr SLFD M6 ...98 C5
Dunedin Rd TOT/BURYW BL8 ...37 E4
Dunelm Dr NTHM/RTH M23 ...155 E5
Dunham Lawn ALT WA14 ...165 E5
Dunham Ms ALT * WA14 ...176 C3
Dunham Ri ALT WA14 ...165 F5
Dunham Rd ALT WA14 ...165 F5
ALT WA14 ...176 C2
WILM/AE SK9 ...199 C1
Dunham St HULME M15 ...126 D2
OLDE OL4 ...75 H4
Dunkeld Rd NTHM/RTH M23 ...167 G3
Dunkerley Av FAIL M35 ...103 E3
Dunkerley St AULW OL7 ...104 D5
OLDE OL4 ...75 F4
ROY/SHW OL2 ...59 E5
Dunkery Rd WYTH/NTH M22 ...180 C3
Dunkirk Cl DTN/ASHW M34 ...145 F1
Dunkirk La HYDE SK14 ...132 A4
Dunkirk Ri WHIT OL12 ...10 A6
Dunkirk Rd DROY M43 ...116 C4
Dunkirk St DROY M43 ...116 D4
Dunley Cl WGTN/LGST M12 ...128 D2
Dunlin Cl ROY/SHW OL2 ...59 F4
Dunlin Dr IRL M44 ...121 B5
Dunlop Av ROCH OL11 ...42 D5
Dunlop St CSLFD * M3 ...6 D4
Dunmail Av MDTN M24 ...71 E3
Dunmaston Av HALE/TIMP WA15 ...167 E2
Dunmore Rd CHD/CHDH SK8 ...169 G3
Dunmow Ct OFTN SK2 ...173 F4
Dunnisher Rd NTHM/RTH M23 ...168 A5
Dunnock Cl OFTN SK2 ...173 F4
Dunollie Rd SALE M33 ...155 F3
Dunoon Cl HEY OL10 ...40 B5
Dunoon Rd RDSH SK5 ...145 E4
Dunscar Cl WHTF M45 ...68 A5
Dunsfold Dr NTHM/RTH M23 ...167 E1
Dunsley Av NEWH/MOS M40 ...88 C5
Dunsmore Cl OLDTF/WHR M16 ...126 C4
Dunsop Dr BOL BL1 ...32 C2
Dunstable WHIT OL12 ...10 B4
Dunstable St BNG/LEV M19 ...144 A2
Dunstall Rd WYTH/NTH M22 ...168 D4
Dunstan St BOLE BL2 ...34 C4
Dunstar Av DTN/ASHW M34 ...131 F1
Dunster Av BKLY M9 ...87 F3
RDSH SK5 ...145 D1
ROCH OL11 ...43 D1
SWIN M27 ...95 E5
Dunster Cl BRAM/HZG SK7 ...185 F2
Dunster Dr URM M41 ...136 D2
Dunster Pl WALK M28 ...94 A3
Dunster Rd WALK M28 ...94 A3
Dunsters Av TOT/BURYW BL8 ...37 H1
Dunsterville Ter ROCH OL11 ...42 D1
Dunston St OP/CLY M11 ...115 F5
Dunton Gn RDSH SK5 ...145 G5
Dunvegan Rd BRAM/HZG SK7 ...185 E5
Dunwood Av ROY/SHW OL2 ...43 D5
Dunwood Park Cts
ROY/SHW OL2 ...45 F5
Dunworth St RUSH/FAL M14 ...127 G5
Durant St ANC * M4 ...7 H1
Durban Cl ROY/SHW OL2 ...59 H3
Durban Rd BOL BL1 ...47 H4
Durban St AULW OL7 ...117 F4
OLDS OL8 ...89 H4
ROCH OL11 ...42 B4
Durden Ms ROY/SHW OL2 ...60 B3
Durham Av URM M41 ...123 H5
Durham Cl BOLS/LL BL3 ...64 A1
DUK SK16 ...132 C2
Durham Crs FAIL M35 ...105 F4
Durham Dr AUL OL6 ...105 H4
BURY BL9 ...5 J3
Durham Gv IRL M44 ...150 C2
Durham Rd SLFD M6 ...100 D5
Durham St BKLY * M9 ...101 F3
BOL BL1 ...2 D1
CHAD OL9 ...89 H1
DROY M43 ...116 B5
RAD M26 ...52 B4
RDSH SK5 ...144 D1
ROCH OL11 ...43 F1

Durley Av CHH M8 ...100 C3
HALE/TIMP WA15 ...166 C2
Durling St WGTN/LGST M12 ...127 H1
Durnford Av DTN/ASHW * M34 ...131 F1
Durnford Cl WHIT OL12 ...18 C2
Durnford St MDTN M24 ...71 G3
Durnlaw Cl LIT OL15 ...21 F3
Duty St BOL BL1 ...33 H5
Duxbury Av BOLE BL2 ...35 E5
BOLS/LL BL3 ...50 D4
Duxbury Dr BURY BL9 ...39 F4
Duxbury St BOL BL1 ...33 G4
Dyche St ANC M4 ...7 G2
Dye House La MILN OL16 ...19 H5
Dye La MPL/ROM SK6 ...162 A4
Dyer La OLDE OL4 ...76 A4
Dyer St OP/CLY M11 ...114 D5
ORD M5 ...126 B3
Dyers Ct LIT * OL15 ...20 D2
Dyer St OP/CLY M11 ...114 D5
Dymchurch Av RAD M26 ...66 B5
Dymchurch St NEWH/MOS M40 ...115 F1
Dysarts Cl MOSL OL5 ...93 F4
Dysart St AUL OL6 ...118 C3
OFTN SK2 ...172 C4
Dyserth Gv RDSH SK5 ...160 A1
Dyson Cl FWTH BL4 ...65 E4
Dyson Gv OLDE * OL4 ...76 A4
Dyson St FWTH * BL4 ...65 E4
MOSL * OL5 ...92 C5

E

Eades St SLFD M6 ...111 H2
Eadington St CHH M8 ...100 B1
Eafield Av MILN OL16 ...31 G4
Eafield Cl MILN OL16 ...31 G4
Eafield Rd MILN OL16 ...31 G4
MILN OL16 ...20 E5
Eagar St NEWH/MOS M40 ...102 B4
Eagle Dr SLFD M6 ...98 D5
Eagle St BOLE BL2 ...3 G3
CHAD OL9 ...8 E3
ROCH * OL11 ...10 E7
Eagley Brook Wy BOL BL1 ...34 A3
Eagley Brow BOL BL1 ...23 H5
Eagley Dr TOT/BURYW BL8 ...37 F5
Eagley Wy EDGW/EG BL7 ...23 E5
Eagley Wy SWIN M27 ...83 E5
Eames Av RAD M26 ...65 H4
Earby Gv BKLY M9 ...87 G1
Earle Rd BRAM/HZG SK7 ...183 F2
Earlesfield Cl SALE M33 ...155 E1
Earle St AULW OL7 ...117 G4
Earl Rd CHD/CHDH SK8 ...192 B2
HTNM SK4 ...159 F2
RAMS BL0 ...16 C2
Earlston Av DTN/ASHW M34 ...131 F4
Earl St BRO M7 ...112 C1
BURY BL9 ...5 F4
DTN/ASHW M34 ...131 F4
EDGY/DAV SK3 ...12 A7
HEY OL10 ...40 D4
MOSL OL5 ...94 C1
PWCH M25 ...85 F3
RAMS BL0 ...16 C2
Earls Wy FAIL M35 ...102 C4
Earlswood Wk BOLS/LL BL3 ...48 C5
Early Bank STLY SK15 ...120 D5
Early Bank Rd HYDE SK14 ...133 F2
Earnshaw Av STKP SK1 ...160 C5
WHIT OL12 ...18 C1
Earnshaw Cl AULW * OL7 ...104 C5
Earnshaw St BOLS/LL * BL3 ...63 G3
Easby Cl CHD/CHDH SK8 ...195 E2
POY/DIS SK12 ...195 E2
Easby Rd MDTN M24 ...71 E1
Easdale Cl URM M41 ...122 C5
Easedale Rd BOL BL1 ...33 G2
East Av BNG/LEV M19 ...143 G3
CHD/CHDH SK8 ...
STLY SK15 ...119 F2
WHTF M45 ...68 B4
Eastbank St BOL BL1 ...33 H1
Eastbourne Gv BOL BL1 ...47 H1
Eastbrook Av RAD * M26 ...52 C5
Eastburn Av NEWH/MOS M40 ...102 A5
East Central Dr SWIN M27 ...97 G3
Eastchurch Cl FWTH BL4 ...63 H5
Eastcombe Av BRO M7 ...99 G2
Eastcote Rd RDSH SK5 ...160 A1
Eastdale Pl ALT * WA14 ...165 H2
East Downs Rd ALT WA14 ...177 F2
CHD/CHDH SK8 ...170 D4
East Dr BURY BL9 ...27 H3
MPL/ROM SK6 ...175 H1
SLFD M6 ...98 C4
SWIN M27 ...97 G2
Eastern By-Pass OP/CLY M11 ...115 F3
Eastern Cir BNG/LEV M19 ...143 H5
Eastfield SLFD M6 ...111 H1
Eastfield Av MDTN M24 ...71 H4
NEWH/MOS M40 ...102 B5
Eastfields RAD M26 ...51 H4
Eastford Sq NEWH/MOS M40 ...114 B1
Eastgate WHIT OL12 ...18 D1
Eastgate St AULW OL7 ...117 H4
East Gate St MILN OL16 ...11 K5
East Gra OP/CLY M11 ...115 F2
East Gv BRUN/LGST M13 ...128 A3
Eastgrove Av BOL BL1 ...23 H5
Eastham Av BURY BL9 ...27 F5
RUSH/FAL M14 ...142 D2
Eastham Wy LHULT M38 ...78 C5
Easthaven Av OP/CLY M11 ...115 G3
Eastholme Dr BNG/LEV M19 ...144 A4
Easthope Cl DID/WITH M20 ...142 C4
East Lancashire Rd WALK M28 ...87 B2
Eastlands Rd BKLY M9 ...87 E2
East Lea DTN/ASHW M34 ...131 H5

Eastleigh Av BRO M7 ...99 H2
Eastleigh Dr NEWH/MOS M40 ...114 C1
Eastleigh Rd CHD/CHDH SK8 ...181 G5
PWCH M25 ...85 H4
East Lynn Dr WALK M28 ...95 H1
East Meade BOLS/LL BL3 ...63 H2
CCHDY M21 ...141 E4
PWCH M25 ...85 G5
SWIN M27 ...96 D4
East Moor WALK M28 ...95 H1
Eastmoor Dr NEWH/MOS M40 ...115 C1
Eastmoor Gv WHTN BL5 ...63 E2
East Newton St ANC * M4 ...113 H2
Easton Dr CHD/CHDH SK8 ...170 D4
Easton Rd DROY M43 ...115 H3
East Ordsall La ORD M5 ...6 A5
Eastover MPL/ROM SK6 ...175 H1
East Park Cl BRUN/LGST M13 ...127 H2
Eastpark Cl BRUN/LGST M13 ...127 H2
East Philip St CSLFD M3 ...112 D2
East Rd BOL BL1 ...
MANAIR M90 ...180 B5
STLY SK15 ...107 F4
STRET M32 ...124 C4
WGTN/LGST M12 ...128 D5
Eastry Av RDSH SK5 ...160 C1
East St AUL OL6 ...118 C1
BURY BL9 ...
DTN/ASHW M34 ...131 C2
LIT OL15 ...21 F3
OLDE OL4 ...10 E4
RAD M26 ...67 G1
WHIT OL12 ...19 H2
East V MPL/ROM SK6 ...175 H4
East Vw MDTN M24 ...72 C4
RAMS BL0 ...16 C3
Eastville Gdns BNG/LEV M19 ...158 B5
East Wk EDGW/EG BL7 ...22 C1
Eastward Av WILM/AE SK9 ...199 E4
East Way BOL BL1 ...
Eastway MDTN M24 ...71 G3
ROY/SHW OL2 ...60 A3
SALE M33 ...154 A2
URM M41 ...122 B5
Eastwood Av DROY M43 ...115 H4
NEWH/MOS M40 ...103 E1
URM M41 ...138 C1
WALK M28 ...80 B4
Eastwood Cl BURY BL9 ...5 G5
Eastwood Dr BOLS/LL BL3 ...62 D1
Eastwood Rd NEWH/MOS M40 ...103 E1
Eastwood St DTN/ASHW M34 ...131 E1
LIT OL15 ...47 G1
Eastwood Ter BOL BL1 ...47 G1
Eaton Cl CHD/CHDH SK8 ...182 C1
DUK SK16 ...132 B2
Eaton Dr AULW OL7 ...117 G1
HALE/TIMP WA15 ...166 B3
WILM/AE SK9 ...201 A3
Eaton Rd ALT WA14 ...177 F3
CHH M8 ...101 A3
SALE M33 ...154 B2
Eaves La CHAD OL9 ...89 F2
Ebbdale Cl STKP SK1 ...13 J6
Ebberstone St RUSH/FAL M14 ...142 B1
Ebden St CMANE * M1 ...7 G5
Ebor Cl ROY/SHW OL2 ...59 H1
Ebor Rd WYTH/NTH * M22 ...168 D5
Ebsworth St NEWH/MOS M40 ...101 G2
Ebury St RAD M26 ...52 A5
Ecclesbridge Rd MPL/ROM SK6 ...175 E4
Eccles Cl OP/CLY M11 ...115 F5
Eccleshall St OP/CLY M11 ...115 C5
Eccles New Rd ORD M5 ...110 C5
Eccles Old Rd SLFD M6 ...110 D2
Eccles Rd SWIN M27 ...97 E4
Eccles St RAMS BL0 ...16 C1
Eccleston Av BOLE BL2 ...34 C5
BRUN/LGST M13 ...128 A3
Eccleston Cl TOT/BURYW BL8 ...37 F5
Eccleston Pl BRO M7 ...99 G2
Eccleston Rd EDGY/DAV SK3 ...183 G5
Eccleston St FAIL * M35 ...103 F2
Eccups La WILM/AE SK9 ...198 B2
Echo St CMANE M1 ...7 H7
Eckersley Cl NTHM/RTH M23 ...167 G3
Eckersley Rd BOL BL1 ...33 H1
Eckersley St BOLS/LL BL3 ...48 B5
Eckford St CHH M8 ...100 C4
Eclipse Cl MILN OL16 ...11 J6
Edale Av DTN/ASHW M34 ...146 C3
NEWH/MOS M40 ...101 H2
RDSH SK5 ...145 F2
URM M41 ...138 A2
Edale Cl ALT WA14 ...165 F5
BRAM/HZG SK7 ...185 F3
CHD/CHDH SK8 ...182 A5
IRL M44 ...136 A4
Edale Gv AUL OL6 ...106 B4
SALE M33 ...153 H4
Edale Rd BOLS/LL * BL3 ...47 H5
FWTH BL4 ...64 D5
STKP SK1 ...
Edale St SLFD M6 ...99 E5
Edbrook Wk BRUN/LGST * M13 ...128 A3
Eddie Colman Cl
NEWH/MOS * M40 ...102 A5
Eddisbury Av DID/WITH M20 ...
URM M41 ...122 A4
Edditch Gv BOLE BL2 ...49 H2
Eddystone Cl ORD M5 ...111 H4
Eden Av BOL BL1 ...33 H1
MPL/ROM SK6 ...
Edenbridge Rd CHD/CHDH SK8 ...171 E5
NEWH/MOS M40 ...102 B5
Eden Cl HEY OL10 ...40 B5
HULME M15 ...127 H3
STKP SK1 ...
WILM/AE SK9 ...198 C5
Edendale Dr WYTH/NTH M22 ...180 C3
Edenfield La WALK M28 ...108 D1
Edenfield Rd PWCH M25 ...85 H4
ROCH OL11 ...28 E2
Edenhall Av BNG/LEV M19 ...143 G3
Edenhurst Dr HALE/TIMP WA15 ...166 C4
Edenhurst Rd OFTN SK2 ...172 C3

Eden Pl CHD/CHDH SK8 170 A3
Edensor Dr HALE/TIMP WA15 178 D1
Eden St BOL BL1 33 H3
BURY BL9 4 E3
OLD OL1 9 F2
WHIT OL12 29 G3
Edenvale WALK M28 94 B3
Eden Wy ROY/SHW OL2 59 H1
Edgar St BOLS/LL BL3 2 D7
MILN OL16 30 D1
RAMS BL0 16 C3
Edgar St West RAMS BL0 16 C3
Edgbaston Dr OLDTF/WHR M16 125 H5
Edgedale Av BNG/LEV M19 158 B1
Edgefield Av BKLY M9 87 F3
Edge Fold FWTH * BL4 63 F3
Edge Fold Crs WALK M28 95 E2
Edge Fold Rd WALK M28 95 E1
Edge Gn WALK * M28 94 D2
Edge Hill Av ROY/SHW OL2 74 B2
Edgehill Cha WILM/AE SK9 200 B3
Edgehill Cl SLFD M6 111 G3
Edge Hill Rd BOLS/LL BL3 63 E1
ROY/SHW OL2 74 B1
Edgehill Rd SLFD M6 110 D2
Edgehill St ANC * M4 7 G3
Edge La HYDE SK14 134 B5
OP/CLY M11 115 G3
STRET M32 140 B2
Edge Lane Rd OLD OL1 74 C4
Edge Lane St ROY/SHW OL2 59 F5
Edgeley Fold EDGY/DAV SK3 171 F2
Edgeley Rd EDGY/DAV SK3 171 F2
URM M41 137 H3
Edgemoor ALT WA14 176 D2
Edgemoor Cl OLDE OL4 75 G3
RAD M26 51 H4
Edgemoor Dr ROCH OL11 41 G1
Edge St ANC M4 7 G3
Edge Vw OLD OL1 72 D3
Edgeware Av PWCH M25 86 A3
Edgeware Rd CHAD OL9 88 D4
ECC M30 108 D1
Edgewater ORD M5 111 E3
Edgeway WILM/AE SK9 199 G5
Edgeworth Av BOLE BL2 36 C5
Edgeworth Dr RUSH/FAL M14 143 F4
Edgmont Av BOLS/LL BL3 48 C5
Edgware Rd NEWH/MOS M40 115 E1
Edgworth Cl HEY OL10 40 B4
Edgworth Dr TOT/BURYW BL8 37 F5
Edilom Rd CHH M8 85 H5
Edinburgh Cl CHD/CHDH SK8 170 C3
Edinburgh Dr MPL/ROM SK6 162 B2
Edinburgh Rd BOLS/LL BL3 65 H2
Edinburgh Sq NEWH/MOS M40 114 A1
Edinburgh Wy ROCH OL11 42 C2
Edington WHIT OL12 10 B4
Edison Rd ECC M30 109 F5
Edison St OP/CLY M11 129 H1
Edith Av RUSH/FAL M14 142 B1
Edith Cavell Cl OP/CLY M11 115 F4
Edith St BOL BL1 48 B3
FWTH BL4 65 E5
OLDS OL8 90 C4
Edlin Cl WGTN/LGST M12 128 B3
Edlingham ROCH * OL11 29 H5
Edinburgh Cl SALE M33 153 G3
Edmonds St MDTN M24 72 A3
Edmonton Rd EDGY/DAV SK3 172 B5
NEWH/MOS M40 114 D1
Edmund Cl HTNM SK4 159 H3
Edmunds Ct BOLS/LL BL3 2 B7
Edmunds Fold LIT OL15 20 C2
Edmund St CSLFD * M3 6 B3
DROY M43 116 B5
FAIL * M35 103 E2
RAD * M26 52 D5
ROY/SHW OL2 60 B2
SLFD M6 111 F2
WHIT OL12 10 A4
Edna St HYDE SK14 147 G1
Edson Rd CHH M8 86 A4
Edstone Cl BOLS/LL BL3 47 G5
Edward Av CCHDY M21 140 C4
LIT OL15 20 C5
MPL/ROM SK6 161 F3
SLFD M6 110 D2
Edward Charlton Rd
OLDTF/WHR M16 141 E1
Edward Ct ALT WA14 165 E2
Edward Ms CHAD OL9 8 B6
Edward Rd BKLY M9 87 E2
ROY/SHW OL2 59 H3
Edwards Cl MPL/ROM SK6 174 D4
Edwards Dr WHTF M45 69 E4
Edward St AUL OL6 118 D3
BKLY M9 101 F2
BOLS/LL BL3 48 C4
BRO M7 112 D1
BURY BL9 4 E6
CHAD OL9 8 A5
CHAD OL9 73 F5
DROY * M43 116 B5
DTN/ASHW M34 131 E1
DTN/ASHW M34 131 G4
DUK SK16 132 B2
FWTH BL4 64 C2
HYDE SK14 132 B5
MDTN M24 71 H2
MILN OL16 11 F4
MPL/ROM SK6 163 F5
PWCH M25 84 D2
RAD M26 66 A4
RAD M26 67 G2
SALE M33 155 F2
STKP SK1 13 G5
WHIT OL12 14 C3
WHIT OL12 20 A4
Edwards Wy MPL/ROM SK6 174 D4
Edwin Rd OP/CLY M11 114 B4
Edwin St BURY BL9 4 D5
STKP SK1 172 C1
Eeasbrook URM M41 138 C2
Egbert St NEWH/MOS M40 102 A3
Egerton Ct WALK * M28 95 H2
Egerton Crs DID/WITH * M20 142 C4
Egerton Dr SALE * M33 154 C1
Egerton Gv WALK M28 81 E4
Egerton Ldg EDGW/EG BL7 22 D2
Egerton Ms DROY * M43 116 B5
RUSH/FAL M14 143 E3
Egerton Pk WALK M28 96 A3
Egerton Pl ROY/SHW OL2 59 H3
Egerton Rd ECC M30 109 G1
EDGY/DAV SK3 172 B5
HALE/TIMP WA15 178 B1
RUSH/FAL M14 143 E3
WALK M28 81 E4
WHTF M45 68 C5
WILM/AE SK9 199 G2
Egerton Rd North CCHDY M21 141 F1
HTNM SK4 159 F1
Egerton Rd South CCHDY M21 141 F3
HTNM SK4 159 F1
Egerton St AUL OL6 118 B2
CSLFD M3 6 A4
DROY M43 116 C4
DTN/ASHW M34 131 E3
ECC M30 109 E3
FWTH BL4 64 D3
HEY OL10 40 D5
HULME M15 126 C1
LIT OL15 21 F3
MDTN * M24 70 D5
MOSL OL5 92 D5
OLD OL1 9 H2
PWCH M25 85 F3
Egerton Ter RUSH/FAL M14 143 E4
Egerton V EDGW/EG BL7 22 C1
Eggington St NEWH/MOS M40 100 D5
Egham Ct BOLE * BL2 3 J1
Egmont St CHH M8 100 B2
MOSL OL5 107 E2
SLFD M6 98 B4
Egremont Av DID/WITH M20 142 B4
Egremont Cl WHTF M45 68 D3
Egremont Ct BRO * M7 99 F2
Egremont Gv EDGY/DAV SK3 171 E1
Egremont Rd MILN OL16 44 B2
Egret Dr IRL * M44 121 B5
Egyptian St BOL BL1 2 E1
Egypt La PWCH M25 69 G3
Eida Wy TRPK M17 110 D5
Eight Acre WHTF M45 67 H5
Eighth Av OLDS OL8 104 A1
Eighth St TRPK M17 124 D2
Eileen Gv RUSH/FAL M14 142 D1
Eileen Gv West RUSH/FAL M14 142 C1
Elaine Av BKLY M9 88 A5
Elbe St WGTN/LGST M12 113 H5
Elbow La ROCH OL11 30 B5
Elbow St BNG/LEV M19 143 H2
Elbut La BURY BL9 40 A1
Elcho Ct ALT * WA14 177 E2
Elcho Rd ALT WA14 177 E1
Elcot Cl NEWH/MOS * M40 100 D5
Elderberry Wy WILM/AE SK9 200 B2
Elder Cl OFTN SK2 173 E1
Eldercot Gv BOLS/LL BL3 47 H5
Eldercot Rd BOLS/LL BL3 47 H5
Eldercroft Rd HALE/TIMP WA15 166 D4
Elderfield Dr MPL/ROM SK6 161 G2
Elder Gv NEWH/MOS M40 89 E5
Eldermount Rd BKLY M9 87 E5
Elder Rd OLDE OL4 91 H1
Elder St MILN OL16 43 G1
Elderwood CHAD OL9 72 D5
Eldon Cl DTN/ASHW M34 131 F1
Eldon Pl ECC M30 109 F4
Eldon Prec OLDS OL8 9 F6
Eldon Rd EDGY/DAV SK3 12 B7
IRL M44 136 B1
Eldon St BOLE BL2 34 C5
BURY BL9 4 E1
OLDS OL8 9 G6
Eldon Street Est OLDS OL8 9 G6
Eldridge Dr NEWH/MOS M40 101 H5
Eleanor Rd CCHDY M21 140 C3
ROY/SHW OL2 74 B2
Eleanor St BOL BL1 34 B1
OLD OL1 74 A4
Electo St OP/CLY M11 129 H1
Elevator Rd TRPK M17 125 F2
Eleventh St TRPK M17 125 E2
Elf Mill Cl EDGY/DAV SK3 171 H3
Elford Gv GTN M18 130 B4
Elgar St WGTN/LGST M12 128 D5
Elgin Av DID/WITH * M20 158 A3
Elgin Dr SALE M33 155 F3
Elgin Rd DUK SK16 132 B2
OLDE OL4 91 E1
Elgin St AULW OL7 117 H1
BOL BL1 33 F4
STLY SK15 119 G4
Elgol Cl EDGY/DAV SK3 172 A4
Elgol Dr BOLS/LL BL3 47 F4
Elham Cl RAD M26 66 B5
Elim St LIT OL15 21 F1
Eliot Rd ECC M30 109 G4
Eli St CHAD OL9 89 F4
Eliza Ann St ECC M30 109 F4
NEWH/MOS M40 113 H1
Elizabethan Wy MILN OL16 31 F5
Elizabeth Av CHAD OL9 89 F4
DTN/ASHW M34 131 F3
ROY/SHW OL2 73 H1
STKP SK1 13 H6
Elizabeth Cl STRET M32 140 A1
Elizabeth Ct HTNM SK4 12 A1
RUSH/FAL M14 143 E4
Elizabeth Gv ROY/SHW OL2 60 A3
Elizabeth Rd PART M31 151 E2
Elizabeth Slinger Rd
DID/WITH M20 156 D2
Elizabeth St AUL OL6 118 A1
CHH M8 100 A4
DTN/ASHW M34 131 E5
HEY OL10 40 D4
HYDE SK14 132 C5
RAD M26 67 F1
ROCH OL11 42 B3
SWIN M27 97 E1
WHTF M45 68 C5
Eliza St HULME M15 126 D2
RAMS BL0 17 E2
Elkanagh Gdns SLFD M6 111 G2
Elkstone Av LHULT M38 80 B1
Ellanby Cl RUSH/FAL M14 127 G5
Elland Cl BURY BL9 69 E2
Ellaston Dr URM * M41 138 C1
Ellastone Rd SLFD M6 110 D1
Ellbourne Rd BKLY M9 86 B4
Ellenbrook Cl WGTN/LGST M12 129 E2
Ellenbrook Rd WALK M28 94 C2
Ellen Brook Rd WYTH/NTH M22 180 C4
Ellendale Gra WALK M28 94 C2
Ellen Gv FWTH BL4 82 B3
Ellenhall Cl BKLY M9 101 E2
Ellenroad Ap MILN OL16 44 D2
Ellenroad St MILN OL16 44 D2
Ellenrod Dr WHIT OL12 28 D1
Ellenrod La WHIT OL12 28 D1
Ellenshaw Cl WHIT OL12 28 D1
Ellen St BOL BL1 33 F3
CHAD OL9 74 A4
DROY M43 116 C5
HTNM SK4 159 G3
Ellen Wilkinson Crs
WGTN/LGST M12 128 D3
Elleray Cl BOLS/LL BL3 66 B1
Elleray Rd MDTN M24 87 G2
SLFD M6 98 A5
Ellerbeck Cl BOLE BL2 34 C1
Ellerbeck Crs WALK M28 94 D3
Ellerby Av SWIN M27 83 F4
Ellesmere Av AUL OL6 105 F3
ECC M30 109 H3
MPL/ROM SK6 175 E3
WALK M28 80 D4
Ellesmere Cir URM M41 123 G1
Ellesmere Cl DUK SK16 132 D1
Ellesmere Dr CHD/CHDH SK8 170 D4
Ellesmere Gdns BOLS/LL BL3 63 G1
Ellesmere Rd ALT WA14 165 G3
BOLS/LL BL3 63 G1
CCHDY M21 141 F2
ECC M30 109 H1
EDGY/DAV SK3 170 D2
Ellesmere Rd North HTNM SK4 159 F1
Ellesmere Rd South
CCHDY M21 141 F3
Ellesmere St BOLS/LL BL3 2 A7
ECC M30 109 G4
FAIL M35 103 E2
FWTH BL4 65 E4
HULME M15 126 C1
LHULT M38 80 D4
ROCH OL11 43 E1
SWIN M27 96 C3
SWIN M27 97 F1
Ellesmere Ter RUSH/FAL M14 143 E4
Ellingham Cl OP/CLY M11 114 C4
Elliot Sq OLD OL1 9 K1
Elliot St BOL BL1 33 F3
OLDE OL4 91 H1
Elliott Av HYDE SK14 132 C3
Elliott Dr SALE M33 153 H2
Elliott St FWTH BL4 64 D5
WHIT OL12 10 E4
Ellis Crs WALK M28 80 C4
Ellis Dr CHH M8 100 C1
Ellis Fold WHIT OL12 28 B1
Ellis La MDTN M24 70 C4
Ellis St BOLS/LL BL3 48 C4
BRO M7 112 D1
HULME M15 126 D2
HYDE SK14 148 A1
TOT/BURYW * BL8 37 G4
Elliston Sq WGTN/LGST M12 128 D2
Ellonby Ri HOR/BR BL6 46 D4
Ellor St SLFD M6 111 G2
Ellwood Rd STKP SK1 160 C5
Elly Clough ROY/SHW * OL2 73 H1
Elm Av RAD M26 67 E4
Elmbank Av DID/WITH M20 156 D2
Elmbank Rd MDTN M24 72 B4
Elm Beds Rd POY/DIS SK12 196 B5
Elmbridge Wk BOLS/LL BL3 48 C4
Elm Cl HYDE SK14 134 D4
POY/DIS SK12 195 G4
Elm Crs WALK M28 95 H3
WILM/AE SK9 201 C3
Elmdale Av CHD/CHDH SK8 181 G2
Elmdale Wk HULME * M15 127 F2
Elm Dr DTN/ASHW M34 131 E3
STRET M32 139 G2
Elmfield Av WYTH/NTH M22 168 D1
Elmfield Dr MPL/ROM SK6 174 D3
Elmfield Rd DTN/ASHW M34 116 D5
EDGY/DAV SK3 172 A4
WILM/AE SK9 201 G3
Elmfield St BOL BL1 34 A4
CHH M8 100 B4
Elmgate Gv BNG/LEV M19 143 H2
Elm Gv AUL OL6 105 F5
DID/WITH M20 157 G3
DROY M43 115 G3
EDGW/EG BL7 23 F3
FWTH BL4 64 C4
HYDE SK14 148 A1
MILN OL16 44 D3
OLDE OL4 92 C1
PWCH M25 84 D1
ROCH OL11 42 D1
SALE M33 139 G5
URM M41 138 D1
WALK M28 96 A1
WHIT OL12 19 H3
WILM/AE SK9 201 B3
Elmham Wk NEWH/MOS M40 113 H1
Elmhurst Dr BNG/LEV M19 158 C1
Elmley Cl OFTN SK2 173 H4
Elmore Wd LIT OL15 20 B2
Elmpark Ga WHIT OL12 18 A5
Elmpark Gv WHIT OL12 18 A5
Elmpark V WHIT OL12 18 A5
Elmpark Vw WHIT OL12 18 A5
Elmpark Wy WHIT OL12 18 A5
Elmridge Dr HALE/TIMP WA15 178 D4
Elm Rd BOLS/LL BL3 66 A2
CHD/CHDH SK8 169 F4
DID/WITH M20 157 F2
FWTH BL4 81 G2
HALE/TIMP WA15 177 H1
MPL/ROM SK6 187 E5
OLDS OL8 104 A1
Elm Rd South EDGY/DAV SK3 170 D2
The Elms LIT OL15 20 B4
MOSL * OL5 106 C1
Elms Cl WHTF M45 68 C2
Elmscott Wk BRUN/LGST M13 128 A3
Elmsdale Av BKLY M9 87 E2
Elmsfield Av ROCH OL11 28 B2
Elmsleigh Rd CHD/CHDH SK8 181 F3
Elmsmere Rd DID/WITH M20 158 A3
Elms Rd HTNM SK4 159 E1
STLY SK15 120 A2
WHTF M45 68 C3
Elms St WHTF M45 68 B3
Elmstead Av DID/WITH M20 142 B5
Elmsted Cl CHD/CHDH SK8 183 E1
Elmstone Gv BOL * BL1 2 E1
Elm St BURY BL9 5 J5
ECC M30 109 G4
FAIL M35 103 E2
FWTH BL4 65 E3
HEY OL10 41 E4
MDTN M24 72 B4
MPL/ROM SK6 161 G2
RAMS * BL0 17 E2
SWIN M27 96 D1
WHIT OL12 10 D2
WHIT OL12 14 C3
Elmsway BRAM/HZG SK7 183 F5
HALE/TIMP WA15 178 C4
MPL/ROM SK6 196 D1
Elmswood OLD OL1 60 C5
Elmswood Av RUSH/FAL M14 142 A1
Elmswood Dr HYDE * SK14 133 F5
Elmsworth Av BNG/LEV M19 144 A2
Elmton Rd BKLY M9 87 F4
Elm Tree Cl FAIL M35 103 G3
Elm Tree Dr DUK SK16 133 E1
Elmtree Dr HTNM SK4 159 E4
Elm Tree Dr WYTH/NTH M22 180 C1
Elm Tree Rd MPL/ROM SK6 160 D3
Elmwood SALE M33 153 F2
Elmwood Dr ROY/SHW OL2 58 D4
Elmwood Gv BKLY M9 101 G3
BOL * BL1 48 B1
FWTH BL4 80 D1
Elmwood Pk STLY SK15 120 A2
Elsa Rd BNG/LEV M19 144 B2
Elsdon Dr GTN M18 129 G2
Elsdon Gdns BOLE BL2 34 C5
Elsdon Rd BRUN/LGST M13 143 G1
Elsfield Cl BOL * BL1 33 G4
Elsham Cl BOL BL1 33 H1
Elsham Dr WALK M28 80 C4
Elsham Gdns GTN M18 129 E4
Elsie St BKLY M9 101 F2
FWTH BL4 64 D4
RAMS * BL0 16 B4
Elsinore Av IRL M44 136 A2
Elsinore Cl FAIL M35 103 G3
Elsinore Rd OLDTF/WHR M16 125 H4
Elsinore St BOLE BL2 34 C3
Elsma Rd NEWH/MOS M40 115 H1
Elsmore Rd RUSH/FAL M14 142 B2
Elson St TOT/BURYW BL8 37 G2
Elsted Rd OLDE OL4 93 F2
Elstree Av NEWH/MOS M40 115 E1
Elstree Gv EDGY/DAV SK3 12 C5
Elswick Av BOLS/LL BL3 48 A4
BRAM/HZG SK7 183 H5
CCHDY M21 156 C2
Elsworth Dr BOL BL1 34 A2
Elsworth St CSLFD M3 113 F2
Elterwater Cl TOT/BURYW BL8 37 G2
Elterwater Rd FWTH BL4 63 H5
Eltham Av OFTN * SK2 172 D4
Eltham Dr URM M41 123 F4
Eltham St BNG/LEV M19 143 H1
Elton Av BNG/LEV M19 143 H3
FWTH BL4 64 A4
Elton Brook Cl TOT/BURYW BL8 37 G3
Elton Cl WHTF M45 68 D4
WILM/AE SK9 200 B1
Elton Dr BRAM/HZG SK7 185 E4
Elton Rd SALE M33 153 G4
Elton St BOLE BL2 3 H4
BRO M7 112 C2
ROCH OL11 42 B5
STRET M32 125 G3
Elton's Yd BRO M7 112 C2
Elton Vale Rd TOT/BURYW BL8 37 G4
Elvate Crs CHH M8 99 H5
Elverdon Cl HULME M15 126 D3
Elverston St WYTH/NTH M22 156 D5
Elverston Wy CHAD OL9 8 A1
Elvey St NEWH/MOS M40 101 G5
Elvington Crs WALK M28 94 D2
Elwick Cl OLDTF/WHR M16 127 E5
Elwyn Av WYTH/NTH M22 168 C2
Ely Av STRET M32 124 A5
Ely Cl WALK M28 94 C4
Ely Crs FAIL M35 103 E5
Ely Dr TOT/BURYW BL8 4 B1
Ely Gv BOL * BL1 2 D1
Elysian St OP/CLY M11 115 F5
Ely St CHAD OL9 89 G2
Emaline Gra SLFD M6 111 F3
Ember St OP/CLY * M11 115 G3
Emblem St BOLS/LL BL3 48 C4
Embleton Cl BOLE BL2 35 F5
Embsay Cl BOL BL1 33 G1
Emerald Rd WYTH/NTH M22 181 E5
Emerald St BOL BL1 34 A3
DTN/ASHW M34 131 F5
Emerson Av ECC M30 110 B2
Emerson Dr MDTN M24 71 G3
Emerson St ORD M5 111 E3
Emery Av CCHDY M21 141 F5
Emery Cl ALT WA14 165 G2
HTNM SK4 158 D2
Emily Beavan Cl OP/CLY M11 115 E4
Emily Pl DROY M43 116 A4
Emily St BNG/LEV M19 144 A2
Emlyn Gv CHD/CHDH SK8 170 D3
Emlyn St FWTH BL4 64 D3
SWIN M27 96 C2
WALK M28 81 E4
Emmanuel Cl BOLS/LL * BL3 48 C4
Emmanuel Pl BOLS/LL * BL3 48 C4
Emma St OLDS OL8 90 C4
WHIT OL12 10 A4
Emmett St East
NEWH/MOS M40 101 F5
Emmott Cl HEY OL10 40 D4
Emperor St STKP SK1 13 J1
Empire Rd BOLE BL2 50 A1
DUK SK16 132 B2
Empire St CSLFD M3 113 E1
Empress Av MPL/ROM SK6 175 E4
Empress Dr HTNM SK4 159 G2
Empress St BOL * BL1 33 E5
CHH M8 100 A2
OLDTF/WHR M16 126 B2
Emsworth Dr SALE M33 154 D5
Ena St BOLS/LL BL3 64 B1
OLD OL1 75 F3
Enbridge St ORD * M5 111 H5
Encombe Pl CSLFD * M3 112 C3
Endcott Cl GTN M18 129 E2
Enderby Rd NEWH/MOS M40 102 B1
Ending Rake WHIT OL12 18 B4
Endon Dr OLDTF/WHR M16 142 A3
Endon St BOL BL1 33 E5
Endsleigh Rd DID/WITH M20 142 D5
Endsley Av WALK M28 94 D1
Energy St NEWH/MOS * M40 114 B2
Enfield Av BNG/LEV M19 143 H5
OLDS OL8 90 B4
Enfield Cl BOL BL1 33 H5
BURY BL9 53 G4
ECC M30 109 G5
ROCH OL11 28 B2
Enfield Dr OP/CLY M11 115 F3
Enfield Rd ECC M30 109 G1
Enfield St HYDE * SK14 147 H4
WALK M28 81 E2
Enford Av WYTH/NTH M22 179 H2
Engell Cl GTN M18 129 F3
Engine Fold Rd WALK M28 80 B4
Engine St CHAD OL9 89 G3
Engledene BOL BL1 22 C5
Enid Cl BRO M7 99 G5
Ennerdale Av BOLE BL2 35 G5
CCHDY M21 156 C2
ROY/SHW OL2 58 D2
SWIN M27 97 E4
Ennerdale Cl BOLS/LL BL3 65 G1
Ennerdale Dr BURY BL9 68 D2
CHD/CHDH SK8 181 G1
HALE/TIMP WA15 166 B2
SALE M33 153 H1
Ennerdale Gv AULW OL7 104 C5
FWTH BL4 63 H4
Ennerdale Rd MDTN M24 71 F2
MPL/ROM SK6 162 A2
PART M31 150 D3
ROCH OL11 42 A2
STKP SK1 172 C2
STRET * M32 124 D5
Ennerdale Ter STLY SK15 119 F2
Ennis Cl NTHM/RTH M23 167 F4
Ennismore Av ECC M30 110 B3
Enstone Dr NEWH/MOS M40 102 C1
Enticott Rd IRL M44 150 B1
Entwisle Av URM M41 123 E4
Entwisle Rd MILN OL16 10 E5
Entwisle Rw FWTH BL4 65 E4
Entwisle St FWTH * BL4 65 E3
MILN OL16 31 F5
SWIN M27 96 C1
Entwistle St BOLE BL2 3 K2
Enver Rd CHH M8 100 C2
Enville Rd ALT WA14 177 F1
NEWH/MOS M40 102 A1
SLFD M6 98 B4
Enville St AUL OL6 118 B2
BKLY M9 87 E4
DTN/ASHW M34 131 F1
Epping Cl AUL OL6 105 F3
CHAD OL9 72 D4
Epping Dr SALE M33 153 F1
Epping Rd DTN/ASHW M34 145 G1
Epping St HULME M15 127 E2
Eppleworth Ri SWIN M27 83 F4
Epsley Cl HULME M15 127 F2
Epsom Av BNG/LEV M19 143 G5
CHD/CHDH SK8 192 B3
SALE M33 153 F4
Epsom Cl BRAM/HZG SK7 185 G2
ROCH OL11 28 B3
Epworth St CMANE M1 113 H4
Equitable St MILN OL16 44 C1
OLDE OL4 75 G4
Era St BOLE BL2 50 A2
SALE M33 154 C2
Ercall Av WGTN/LGST M12 128 B2
Erica Av OLDE OL4 61 E5
Erica Cl RDSH SK5 145 E3
Erica Dr BNG/LEV M19 158 B2
Eric Brook Cl RUSH/FAL M14 127 F5
Eric Bullows Cl WYTH/NTH M22 180 B3
Eric St LIT OL15 20 D2
OLDE OL4 91 F1
Erin St OP/CLY * M11 129 H1
Erith Cl RDSH SK5 145 G5
Erith Rd OLDE OL4 91 E1
Erlesmere Av DTN/ASHW M34 131 H4
Erlesmere Cl OLDE OL4 61 E5
Erlington Av OLDTF/WHR M16 126 A5
Ermen Rd ECC M30 109 F5
Ermington Dr CHH M8 100 A4
Erneley Cl WGTN/LGST M12 129 E5
Ernest St BOL BL1 2 A5
CHD/CHDH SK8 169 H3
OFTN SK2 172 B3
PWCH M25 84 C3
Ernest Ter WHIT OL12 11 G2
Ernlouen Av BOL BL1 47 H1
Ernocroft Gv GTN * M18 129 H2
Ernocroft Rd MPL/ROM SK6 163 G5
Erringdon Cl OFTN SK2 173 F3
Errington Cl BOLS/LL BL3 47 G4
Errington Dr BRO M7 112 C1
Errol Av BKLY M9 86 B2
WYTH/NTH M22 168 B5
Errwood Crs BNG/LEV M19 143 H3
Errwood Rd BNG/LEV M19 143 H5
Erskine Cl BOLS/LL BL3 47 F4
Erskine Rd BKLY M9 87 F2
PART M31 151 E3
Erskine St HULME M15 126 C2
MPL/ROM SK6 163 G4
Erwin St NEWH/MOS M40 102 A4
Erwood Rd HTNM SK4 158 C1
Eryngo St STKP SK1 13 K4
Esher Dr SALE M33 166 C1
Esk Cl URM M41 122 D4
Eskdale CHD/CHDH SK8 169 H5
Eskdale Av BOLE BL2 35 G4
BRAM/HZG SK7 193 F2
DID/WITH M20 142 B4
MPL/ROM SK6 162 A1
OLDS OL8 90 A3
ROCH OL11 42 A2
ROY/SHW OL2 59 E2
Eskdale Cl BURY BL9 68 D1
Eskdale Dr HALE/TIMP WA15 166 D2
MDTN M24 71 G1
Eskdale Gv FWTH BL4 64 A4
Eskrick St BOL BL1 33 G4
Eskrigge Cl BRO M7 100 A2
Esmond Rd CHH M8 100 B3
Esmont Dr MDTN M24 71 F1
The Esplanade MILN OL16 10 B7

Essex Av DID/WITH M20 157 G2
DROY M43 116 B2
EDGY/DAV SK3 171 E1
HEY OL10 39 H5
Essex Cl FAIL M35 103 E5
ROY/SHW OL2 59 G2
Essex Dr BURY BL9 53 G1
Essex Gdns IRL M44 150 B2
Essex Rd GTN M18 130 A5
RDSH SK5 160 D1
Essex St CMANW M2 6 E5
ROCH OL11 30 A5
Essex Wy HULME M15 126 C3
Essingdon St BOLS/LL BL3 48 C5
Estate St OLDS OL8 90 C3
Estate St South OLDS * OL8 90 C3
Est Bank Rd RAMS BL0 16 B5
Esther St OLDE OL4 75 F5
Estonfield Dr URM M41 139 E1
Eston St BRUN/LGST M13 128 A4
Eswick St OP/CLY M11 115 F4
Etchells Rd CHD/CHDH SK8 182 A3
Etchells St STKP SK1 13 G3
Etchell St NEWH/MOS * M40 100 D5
Ethel Av BKLY M9 87 E2
SWIN M27 97 G2
Ethel Ct MILN * OL16 30 C5
Ethel St BOLS/LL BL3 2 A7
OLDS OL8 90 C4
WHIT OL12 14 C3
Ethel Ter BNG/LEV M19 143 H2
Etherley Cl IRL M44 136 B1
Etherow Av MPL/ROM SK6 162 D4
NEWH/MOS * M40 89 E5
Etherstone St CHH M8 100 D2
Eton Av OLDS OL8 90 B4
Eton Cl OLDTF/WHR M16 126 C3
ROCH OL11 29 E5
Eton Ct OLDTF/WHR * M16 126 C3
Eton Hill Rd RAD M26 52 D4
Eton Wy North RAD M26 52 D4
Eton Wy South RAD M26 52 D4
Etruria Cl BRUN/LGST M13 128 B3
Ettington Cl TOT/BURYW BL8 37 F3
Ettrick Cl OP/CLY M11 129 G1
Euclid Cl OP/CLY M11 114 B4
Europa Ga TRPK M17 125 E3
Europa Wy CHD/CHDH SK8 171 F3
RAD M26 65 H5
TRPK M17 125 E3
Eustace St BOLS/LL BL3 64 B1
CHAD OL9 73 G3
Euston Av BKLY M9 87 H4
Euxton Cl TOT/BURYW BL8 37 F5
Evan Cl DID/WITH M20 157 F3
Evans Cl DID/WITH M20 157 F3
Evans Rd ECC M30 108 D4
Evans St AUL OL6 118 C1
CSLFD M3 6 C1
MDTN M24 72 A4
OLD OL1 9 G1
Evan St NEWH/MOS M40 101 F5
Eva Rd EDGY/DAV SK3 170 D2
Eva St RUSH/FAL M14 127 H5
WHIT OL12 10 E1
Evelyn St OLD OL1 75 E3
RUSH/FAL M14 143 E3
Evening St FAIL M35 103 E2
Evenley Cl GTN * M18 129 H2
Everard Cl WALK M28 94 C2
Everard St ORD M5 126 B1
Everbrom Rd BOLS/LL BL3 62 D2
Everest Av AULW OL7 105 E5
Everest Cl HYDE SK14 133 F4
Everest Rd HYDE SK14 133 F4
Everest St ROCH OL11 43 F4
Everglade OLDS OL8 104 D1
Everleigh Cl BOLE BL2 35 F1
Everleigh Dr CHH M8 100 A4
Eversden Ct BRO * M7 112 D1
Eversley Rd DID/WITH M20 157 F3
Everton Rd OLDS OL8 90 A3
RDSH SK5 145 E1
Everton St SWIN M27 96 D2
Every St ANC M4 114 A4
BURY BL9 4 E1
RAMS * BL0 17 E2
Evesham Av HTNM SK4 159 E3
NTHM/RTH M23 167 E2
Evesham Cl BOLS/LL BL3 2 B7
MDTN M24 88 A2
Evesham Dr FWTH * BL4 64 C2
Evesham Drive WILM/AE SK9 191 H5
Evesham Gdns MDTN * M24 87 H2
Evesham Gv AUL OL6 105 F3
SALE M33 155 F2
Evesham Rd BKLY M9 87 H5
CHD/CHDH SK8 170 D5
MDTN M24 87 H2
Evesham Wk BOLS/LL * BL3 48 C4
MDTN M24 88 A2
OLDS OL8 9 F7
Eveside Cl CHD/CHDH * SK8 171 E5
Eve St OLDS OL8 90 C5
Ewan St GTN M18 129 G2
Ewart Av ORD M5 111 H4
Ewart St BOL BL1 33 H4
Ewhurst Av SWIN M27 96 C4
Ewing Cl CHH M8 100 B1
Ewood OLDS OL8 104 D2
Ewood Dr TOT/BURYW BL8 52 B1
Exbourne Rd WYTH/NTH M22 180 B3
Exbury WHIT OL12 10 B4
Exbury St RUSH/FAL M14 143 E4
Excalibur Wy IRL M44 136 A4
Excelsior Ter MILN OL16 20 C5
Exchange Quay ORD M5 125 H2
Exchange Sq CSLFD M3 6 E3
Exchange St BOL * BL1 2 E5
CMANW * M2 6 E4
EDGY/DAV SK3 12 E4
OLDE * OL4 75 E5
Exeter Av BOLE BL2 34 C4
DTN/ASHW M34 146 C2
ECC M30 110 B1
FWTH BL4 64 A3
RAD M26 51 G4
Exeter Cl CHD/CHDH SK8 182 C4
DUK SK16 132 C2
Exeter Dr AUL OL6 105 G3
IRL M44 136 C1
Exeter Gv ROCH OL11 43 E1
Exeter Rd RDSH SK5 160 D1
URM M41 123 G4
Exeter St ROCH OL11 43 E1
SLFD M6 111 F3
Exford Cl NEWH/MOS M40 114 A2
RDSH SK5 145 E5
Exford Dr BOLE BL2 50 D3
Exit Rd West MANAIR * M90 180 A5
Exmoor Cl AUL OL6 105 F3
Exmouth Av RDSH SK5 160 D1
Exmouth Pl ROCH OL11 43 F3
Exmouth Rd SALE M33 153 G1
Exmouth Sq ROCH * OL11 43 F2
Exmouth St ROCH OL11 43 F3
Exmouth Wk OLDTF/WHR M16 126 D5
Eyam Gv OFTN SK2 173 E5
Eyam Rd BRAM/HZG SK7 185 F4
Eyebrook Rd ALT WA14 176 D3
Eynford Av RDSH SK5 145 G5
Eyre St HULME M15 127 F3

F

Faber St ANC M4 113 F2
Factory Brow MDTN M24 70 D5
Factory La BKLY M9 101 E1
ORD * M5 112 C4
Factory St MDTN M24 71 G4
RAD M26 67 G1
RAMS BL0 16 D1
Failsworth Rd FAIL M35 103 G3
Fair Acres BOLE BL2 35 F3
Fairacres Rd MPL/ROM SK6 186 D4
Fairbank Dr MDTN M24 71 E2
Fairbottom St OLD OL1 9 H3
Fairbourne Av WILM/AE SK9 201 A1
Fairbourne Cl WILM/AE SK9 201 A1
Fairbourne Dr
HALE/TIMP WA15 154 C5
WILM/AE SK9 201 A1
Fairbourne Rd BNG/LEV M19 144 B2
DTN/ASHW M34 146 B1
Fairbrook Dr SLFD M6 111 F3
Fairbrother St ORD M5 126 B1
Fairburn Cl URM M41 122 D4
Fairclough St BOLS/LL BL3 49 E5
OP/CLY M11 114 D3
Fairfax Av DID/WITH M20 157 G2
HALE/TIMP WA15 166 B3
Fairfax Cl MPL/ROM SK6 174 C2
Fairfax Dr LIT OL15 20 C5
WILM/AE SK9 201 A1
Fairfax Rd PWCH M25 84 D2
Fairfield Av CHD/CHDH SK8 182 C2
DROY M43 116 B5
MPL/ROM SK6 161 H2
Fairfield Dr BURY BL9 39 G3
Fairfield Rd DROY M43 116 B5
FWTH BL4 64 D5
HALE/TIMP WA15 166 D4
IRL M44 150 B1
MDTN M24 71 F3
OP/CLY M11 129 H1
Fairfields EDGW/EG BL7 23 E3
OLDS OL8 90 B5
Fairfield Sq DROY M43 116 B5
Fairfield St CMANE M1 7 J7
SLFD M6 98 A5
Fairford Cl RDSH SK5 160 A1
Fairford Dr BOLS/LL BL3 48 D4
Fairford Wy RDSH SK5 160 A1
WILM/AE SK9 200 A3
Fairhaven Av CCHDY M21 141 E4
WHTF M45 68 A5
Fairhaven Cl BRAM/HZG SK7 184 A4
Fairhaven Rd BOL BL1 34 A3
Fairhaven St WGTN/LGST M12 128 C2
Fairhills Rd IRL M44 136 B3
Fairholme Av URM M41 138 B1
Fairholme Rd DID/WITH M20 142 D5
HTNM SK4 159 F3
Fairhope Av SLFD M6 110 C1
Fairhurst Dr WALK M28 80 A5
Fairisle Cl OP/CLY M11 114 C4
Fairlands Rd BURY BL9 27 G4
SALE M33 154 A4
Fairlands St ROCH OL11 43 G4
Fairlawn HTNM SK4 159 G3
Fairlawn Cl RUSH/FAL M14 127 F4
Fairlea DTN/ASHW M34 146 D1
Fairlea Av DID/WITH M20 157 H4
Fairlee Av DTN/ASHW M34 116 D4
Fairleigh Av SLFD M6 110 D2
Fairless Rd ECC M30 109 G4
Fairlie Av BOLS/LL BL3 47 G4
Fairlie Dr HALE/TIMP WA15 166 C1
Fairlyn Cl WHTN BL5 62 D5
Fairlyn Dr WHTN BL5 62 D5
Fairman St OLDTF/WHR M16 127 E5
Fairmead Rd NTHM/RTH M23 156 B5
Fairmile Dr DID/WITH M20 169 H1
Fairmount Av BOLE BL2 50 B1
Fairmount Rd SWIN M27 96 A4
Fairoak Ct BOLS/LL BL3 48 C4
Fair Oak Rd BNG/LEV M19 158 C1
Fairstead Wk OP/CLY M11 130 A1
Fair St BOLS/LL * BL3 63 F2
CMANE M1 7 K5
SWIN M27 97 F1
Fairview Av BNG/LEV M19 143 G1
DTN/ASHW M34 145 F2
Fairview Cl CHAD OL9 72 D4
MPL/ROM SK6 175 E2
Fairview Dr MPL/ROM SK6 175 E2
Fairview Rd DTN/ASHW M34 145 F1
HALE/TIMP WA15 166 D4
The Fairway NEWH/MOS M40 102 C2
OFTN SK2 173 E2
Fair Wy ROCH OL11 42 A5
Fairway BRAM/HZG SK7 193 G1
CHD/CHDH SK8 169 G5
DROY M43 116 B5
PWCH M25 85 G5
SWIN M27 97 H3
WHIT OL12 18 B1
Fairway Av BOLE BL2 35 H2
NTHM/RTH M23 167 E2
Fairway Crs ROY/SHW OL2 59 E3
Fairway Dr SALE M33 153 H4
Fairway Rd BURY BL9 68 D1
OLDE OL4 91 H3
The Fairways WHTF M45 84 C1
Fairwood Rd NTHM/RTH M23 167 E2
Fairy La CHH M8 99 H5
SALE M33 155 G2
Fairy St TOT/BURYW BL8 37 H4
Fairywell Cl WILM/AE SK9 200 A1
Fairywell Dr SALE M33 154 B5
Fairywell Rd HALE/TIMP WA15 166 C2
Faith St BOL BL1 32 C5
Falcon Av URM M41 138 D1
Falcon Cl BURY BL9 5 H1
WHIT OL12 28 A1
Falcon Crs SWIN M27 83 G5
Falcon Dr CHAD OL9 8 A1
IRL M44 121 C4
LHULT M38 80 B2
MDTN M24 71 F1
Falcon St OLDS OL8 9 F6
Falconwood Cha WALK M28 94 C4
Falfield Dr CHH M8 100 C5
Falinge Fold WHIT OL12 29 G2
Falinge Ms WHIT OL12 10 A5
Falinge Rd WHIT OL12 10 B4
Falkirk Dr BOLE BL2 50 C3
Falkirk St OLDE OL4 75 F5
Falkland Av NEWH/MOS M40 114 A1
ROCH OL11 29 F3
Falkland Cl OLDE OL4 60 D5
Falkland Rd BOLE BL2 50 D2
Fall Birch Rd HOR/BR BL6 46 A1
Fallons Rd WALK M28 96 B1
Fallowfield Av ORD M5 112 A5
Fallowfield Dr WHIT OL12 29 G1
Fallow Fields Dr RDSH SK5 145 F2
The Fallows CHAD OL9 89 F2
Falls Gv CHD/CHDH SK8 181 F1
Falmer Cl TOT/BURYW BL8 26 D5
Falmer Dr WYTH/NTH M22 180 C3
Falmer St GTN M18 130 A2
Falmouth Av SALE M33 153 G1
URM M41 122 B5
Falmouth Crs RDSH SK5 160 D1
Falmouth Rd IRL M44 136 C1
Falmouth St NEWH/MOS M40 114 C1
OLDS OL8 90 C3
ROCH OL11 43 F1
Falsgrave Cl NEWH/MOS M40 101 H5
Falshaw Dr BURY BL9 27 F2
Falstaff Ms MPL/ROM SK6 161 H3
Falston Av NEWH/MOS M40 88 C5
Falstone Av RAMS BL0 16 D4
Falterley Rd NTHM/RTH M23 167 F1
Fancroft Rd WYTH/NTH M22 168 B4
Faraday Av CHH M8 100 B4
SWIN M27 84 A5
Faraday Dr BOL BL1 33 H5
Faraday Ri WHIT OL12 29 E2
Faraday St CMANE M1 7 H4
Farcroft Av RAD M26 52 D4
Farcroft Cl NTHM/RTH M23 167 G1
Far Cromwell Rd MPL/ROM SK6 146 A5
Fardale ROY/SHW OL2 60 A3
Farden Dr NTHM/RTH M23 167 E1
Farewell Cl ROCH OL11 42 B4
Far Hey Cl RAD M26 66 D1
Farholme ROY/SHW OL2 73 H2
Faringdon ROCH * OL11 29 H5
Faringdon Wk BOLS/LL * BL3 48 D4
Farland Pl BOLS/LL BL3 47 G4
Farlands Dr DID/WITH M20 169 G2
Farlands Ri MILN OL16 43 H3
Far La GTN M18 129 G4
Farley Av GTN M18 130 B4
Farley Ct CHD/CHDH SK8 170 C5
Farley Rd SALE M33 154 D4
Farley Wy RDSH SK5 144 D2
Farman St BOLS/LL * BL3 63 G1
Farm Av STRET M32 124 B4
Farm Cl HTNM SK4 144 B5
TOT/BURYW BL8 26 A5
Farmers Cl NTHM/RTH M23 155 H4
Farmer St HTNM SK4 159 G3
Farmfield SALE M33 138 D5
Farm Hl PWCH * M25 84 D2
Farmlands Wk OLD OL1 60 B5
Farm La HYDE SK14 147 G3
POY/DIS SK12 197 F1
PWCH M25 69 H4
WALK M28 95 G5
Farm Rd OLDS OL8 103 H2
Farmside Av IRL M44 121 B5
Farmstead Cl FAIL M35 103 H4
Farm St CHAD OL9 73 G3
FAIL M35 102 C4
HEY OL10 56 B1
Farm Wk ALT WA14 176 B2
LIT OL15 20 C3
MILN OL16 11 J2
Farmway MDTN M24 71 G5
Farm Yd BNG/LEV M19 143 H2
Farn Av RDSH SK5 144 D1
Farnborough Av OLDE OL4 91 G1
Farnborough Rd BOL BL1 22 D5
NEWH/MOS M40 114 A2
Farndale Sq LHULT M38 80 D4
Farndon Av BRAM/HZG SK7 173 G5
Farndon Cl SALE M33 155 F3
Farndon Dr HALE/TIMP WA15 166 B3
Farndon Rd RDSH SK5 144 D1
Farnham Av BKLY M9 87 E2
Farnham Cl BOL * BL1 2 C1
CHD/CHDH SK8 182 D5
Farnham Dr IRL M44 136 B2
Farnley Cl WHIT OL12 28 C1
Farnley St WGTN/LGST * M12 128 D2
Farnsworth Cl AULW OL7 105 E5
Farnworth Dr RUSH/FAL M14 142 D1
Farnworth St BOLS/LL * BL3 48 B5
HEY OL10 40 D4
Farrand Rd OLDS OL8 89 G5
Farrant Rd WGTN/LGST M12 128 D5
Farrar Rd DROY M43 116 A5
Farrell St CSLFD M3 112 D2
Farrer Rd BRUN/LGST M13 143 G1
Far Ridings MPL/ROM SK6 162 C3
Farrier Cl SALE M33 155 G3
Farriers La ROCH OL11 42 A2
Farringdon St SLFD * M6 111 F2
Farrowdale Av ROY/SHW OL2 60 A3
Farrow St ROY/SHW OL2 60 A3
Farrow St East ROY/SHW OL2 60 A3
Farr St EDGY/DAV SK3 12 C5
Farwood Cl OLDTF/WHR M16 126 B3
Far Woodseats La GLSP SK13 149 G5
Fastnet St OP/CLY M11 114 D5
Faulkenhurst Ms OLD OL1 73 H3
Faulkenhurst St CHAD OL9 73 H3
Faulkner Dr HALE/TIMP WA15 166 C5
Faulkner Rd STRET M32 140 B1
Faulkner St BOLS/LL BL3 48 D4
CMANE M1 7 F6
MILN OL16 10 D6
Faversham Brow OLD * OL1 74 B4
Faversham St NEWH/MOS M40 102 A3
Fawborough Rd
NTHM/RTH M23 155 G5
Fawcett St BOLE BL2 3 K4
Fawley Av HYDE SK14 147 G2
Fawley Gv WYTH/NTH M22 168 C5
Fawns Keep STLY SK15 134 B2
WILM/AE SK9 200 A3
Fay Av BKLY M9 88 A5
Faywood Dr MPL/ROM SK6 175 F3
Fearney Side BOLS/LL BL3 65 G1
Fearnhead St BOLS/LL BL3 48 B5
Fearn St HEY OL10 40 D4
Featherstall Brook Vie LIT OL15 20 D3
Featherstall Rd LIT OL15 20 C3
Featherstall Rd North CHAD OL9 8 C3
Featherstall Rd South CHAD OL9 8 C5
Federation St ANC M4 7 F2
PWCH M25 84 C2
Feldom Rd NTHM/RTH M23 155 G4
Fellbrigg Cl GTN M18 129 F5
Fellfoot Cl WALK M28 94 A5
Fellpark Rd NTHM/RTH M23 155 H4
Fells Gv WALK M28 95 G1
Fellside BOLE BL2 35 H3
Fellside Cl TOT/BURYW * BL8 26 A2
Fellside Gdns LIT OL15 20 C1
Fellside Gn STLY SK15 119 F2
Fell St TOT/BURYW BL8 37 H4
Felltop Dr RDSH SK5 145 F3
Felskirk Rd WYTH/NTH M22 180 B4
Felsted BOL BL1 47 F1
Felt Ct DTN/ASHW M34 145 H1
Felthorpe Dr CHH M8 100 A4
Felton Av WYTH/NTH M22 180 B1
Felton Cl BURY BL9 53 H4
Felton Wk BOL BL1 33 H4
Fencegate Av HTNM SK4 159 G1
Fence St OFTN SK2 173 E5
Fenchurch Av NEWH/MOS M40 115 F1
Fencot Dr WGTN/LGST M12 128 D4
Fenella St BRUN/LGST M13 128 B4
Fenham Cl NEWH/MOS * M40 100 D5
Fenmore Av GTN M18 129 E5
Fennel St ANC M4 6 E2
Fenners Cl BOLS/LL BL3 63 G1
Fenney St BRO M7 99 G5
Fenney St East BRO M7 99 H4
Fenn St HULME M15 126 D2
Fenside Rd WYTH/NTH M22 168 D4
Fenton Av OFTN SK2 172 D5
Fenton Ms ROCH * OL11 42 D1
Fenton St OLDE OL4 91 E1
ROCH OL11 42 D1
ROY/SHW OL2 60 A4
TOT/BURYW BL8 37 H3
Fenwick Dr HTNM SK4 158 B3
Fenwick St HULME M15 127 F2
ROCH OL11 10 A7
Ferdinand St NEWH/MOS * M40 114 A1
Fereday St WALK M28 80 D3
Ferguson Gdns WHIT OL12 19 E5
Ferguson Wy OLDE OL4 75 G3
Fernacre SALE M33 154 D1
Fernally St HYDE SK14 132 D5
Fern Av URM M41 137 H1
Fern Bank NEWH/MOS * M40 102 B3
STLY SK15 119 H5
Fernbank RAD * M26 67 F4
Fern Bank Cl STLY SK15 119 H5
Fern Bank Dr NTHM/RTH M23 167 F2
Fern Bank St HYDE SK14 147 H3
Fernbray Av BNG/LEV M19 158 A2
Fernbrook Cl BRUN/LGST M13 128 A3
Fern Cl MDTN M24 72 C4
MPL/ROM SK6 175 E3
OLDE OL4 92 A1
Fern Clough BOL BL1 47 G2
Fernclough Rd BKLY M9 101 E4
Fern Crs STLY SK15 119 H5
Ferndale Av MILN OL16 43 H5
OFTN SK2 172 C5
WHTF M45 67 H5
Ferndale Cl OLDE OL4 91 G3
Ferndale Gdns BNG/LEV M19 143 F5
Ferndale Rd SALE M33 154 C4
Fern Dene WHIT OL12 29 E1
Ferndene Rd DID/WITH M20 157 G1
WHTF M45 69 F5
Ferndown Av BRAM/HZG SK7 184 D3
CHAD OL9 72 C5
Ferndown Dr IRL M44 121 B5
Ferndown Rd BOLE BL2 35 F3
NTHM/RTH M23 167 E1
Ferney Field Rd CHAD OL9 73 E5
Ferngate Dr DID/WITH M20 142 C5
Ferngrove BURY BL9 39 E2
Fernhill MPL/ROM SK6 175 G3
Fernhill Av BOLS/LL BL3 47 H5
Fernhill Dr GTN M18 129 E4
Fernhills EDGW/EG BL7 22 D1
Fernhill St BURY BL9 4 E2
Fernholme Ct OLDS OL8 89 H3
Fernhurst Rd DID/WITH M20 157 H1
Fernhurst St CHAD OL9 73 H3
Fernie St ANC * M4 113 F2
Fern Isle Cl WHIT OL12 18 A2
Fern Lea CHD/CHDH SK8 181 G3
Fernlea HALE/TIMP WA15 178 A3
Fernlea Av OLD OL1 73 H3
Fernlea Cl WHIT OL12 29 E1
Fernlea Crs SWIN M27 96 D3
Fern Lea Gv LHULT M38 80 A3
Fernleigh Av BNG/LEV M19 144 B2
Fernleigh Dr OLDTF/WHR * M16 126 B3
Fernley Av DTN/ASHW M34 146 D1
Fernley Rd OFTN SK2 172 C3
Fernone WILM/AE SK9 192 A4
Ferns Gv BOL BL1 48 A2
Fernside RAD M26 82 A1
Fernside Av DID/WITH M20 158 A1
Fernside Gv WALK * M28 81 F3
Fernside Wy WHIT OL12 28 D2
Fernstead BOLS/LL BL3 48 B3
Fern St BOLS/LL BL3 48 B3
BURY BL9 4 E2
CHAD OL9 73 F4
CHH M8 113 F1
FWTH BL4 65 F3
OLDS OL8 8 D6
RAMS BL0 17 E2
ROCH OL11 29 G5
WHIT OL12 19 H2
Fernthorpe Av UPML OL3 78 B3
Fern Vw HALE/TIMP WA15 167 F4
Fernview Dr RAMS BL0 26 B2
Fernwood MPL/ROM SK6 175 H2
Fernwood Av GTN M18 129 G5
Fernwood Gv WILM/AE SK9 199 H2
Ferrand Ldg LIT OL15 21 F1
Ferrand Rd LIT OL15 21 E2
Ferring Wk CHAD * OL9 89 G1
Ferris St OP/CLY M11 115 G5
Ferrous Wy IRL M44 136 A5
Ferryhill Rd IRL M44 136 B1
Ferry Rd IRL M44 136 C1
Ferry St OP/CLY M11 114 B5
Fettler Cl SWIN M27 96 D3
Fewston Cl BOL BL1 33 H1
Fiddlers La IRL M44 121 C5
Field Bank Gv BNG/LEV M19 144 A2
Field Cl BRAM/HZG SK7 193 G3
MPL/ROM SK6 174 C4
Fieldcroft ROCH OL11 29 E4
Fielden Av CCHDY M21 141 E2
Fielden Rd DID/WITH M20 157 E1
Fielders Wy SWIN M27 82 D3
Fieldfare Av NEWH/MOS M40 115 E1
Fieldfare Wy AULW OL7 104 D3
Fieldhead Av ROCH OL11 28 D4
TOT/BURYW BL8 37 F5
Fieldhead Ms WILM/AE SK9 200 B2
Fieldhead Rd WILM/AE SK9 200 B2
Field House La MPL/ROM SK6 175 F3
Fieldhouse Rd WHIT OL12 10 D1
Fielding Av POY/DIS SK12 195 F5
Fielding St ECC M30 109 F4
MDTN M24 71 H2
Field La AUL OL6 105 G5
Field Pl DID/WITH * M20 157 G3
Field Rd MILN OL16 31 E4
SALE M33 138 D5
Fieldsend Cl STLY SK15 120 A5
Fields End Fold ECC M30 121 D4
Fields Farm Cl HYDE SK14 149 E2
Fields Farm Rd HYDE SK14 149 E1
Fields New Rd CHAD OL9 89 F2
Field St DROY M43 116 A5
FAIL M35 102 D3
GTN M18 129 H2
HYDE SK14 132 C3
MPL/ROM SK6 161 G3
ROCH OL11 43 F2
SLFD M6 111 G3
Fieldsway OLDS OL8 90 B5
Field Vale Dr RDSH SK5 145 F2
Fieldvale Rd SALE M33 153 H5
Field View Wk OLDTF/WHR M16 142 A1
Field Wk HALE/TIMP * WA15 178 C1
Fieldway MILN OL16 43 G3
Fife Av CHAD OL9 89 E3
Fifield Cl OLDS OL8 90 D4
Fifth Av BOL BL1 48 A2
BURY BL9 39 G2
DUK SK16 117 H5
OLDS OL8 89 H5
OP/CLY M11 115 F3
TRPK M17 124 D3
Fifth St BOL BL1 32 C2
TRPK M17 124 D3
Filbert St OLD OL1 75 F3
Filby Wk NEWH/MOS M40 114 B1
Fildes St MDTN M24 72 C5
Filey Av OLDTF/WHR M16 141 G1
URM M41 122 D4
Filey Dr SLFD M6 98 A4
Filey Rd OFTN SK2 172 D2
RUSH/FAL M14 143 E3
Filey St MILN OL16 30 D1
Filton Av BOLS/LL BL3 48 C4
Finance St LIT OL15 20 B3
Finborough Cl
OLDTF/WHR M16 126 D4
Finchale Dr HALE/TIMP WA15 178 C3
Finch Av FWTH BL4 64 A5
Finchley Av NEWH/MOS M40 115 F1
Finchley Cl TOT/BURYW BL8 37 G5
Finchley Gv NEWH/MOS M40 101 H1
Finchley Rd HALE/TIMP WA15 177 H1
RUSH/FAL M14 142 C3
Finchwood Rd WYTH/NTH M22 168 D4
Findon Rd NTHM/RTH M23 167 H3
Finghall Rd URM M41 138 A1
Finishing Wk ANC * M4 113 H4
Finland Rd EDGY/DAV SK3 171 G2
Finlan Rd MDTN M24 57 H4
Finlay St FWTH * BL4 65 E4
Finney Cl WILM/AE SK9 191 H5
Finney Dr CCHDY M21 140 D4
WILM/AE SK9 191 H5
Finney La WYTH/NTH M22 181 F4
Finney St BOLS/LL * BL3 49 E5
Finningley Rd BKLY M9 86 C1
Finny Bank Rd SALE M33 139 F5
Finsbury Av NEWH/MOS M40 115 F1
Finsbury Rd RDSH SK5 144 D3
Finsbury St ROCH OL11 42 C1
Finsbury Wy WILM/AE SK9 192 B5
Finstock Cl ECC M30 109 E4
Fintry Gv ECC M30 109 G4
Fir Av BRAM/HZG SK7 183 H4
Firbank Rd NTHM/RTH M23 179 H1
Fir Bank Rd ROY/SHW OL2 59 E3
Firbarn Cl MILN OL16 31 E4
Firbeck Dr ANC M4 114 A3
Fir Cl POY/DIS SK12 195 F4
Fircroft Rd OLDS OL8 90 D5
Firdale Av NEWH/MOS M40 102 D1
Firdale Wk CHAD OL9 8 A2
Firecrest Cl WALK M28 94 C2
Firefly Cl CSLFD M3 112 C4
Fire Station Sq ORD * M5 112 B3
Fire Station Yd ROCH OL11 30 A5
Firethorn Av BNG/LEV M19 143 G5
Firethorn Dr HYDE SK14 148 B1
Firfield Gv WALK M28 81 G4
Fir Gv BNG/LEV M19 143 H2
CHAD OL9 73 G4
Firgrove Av MILN OL16 31 E3
Firgrove Gdns MILN OL16 31 E3
Fir La ROY/SHW OL2 59 E3

Fir Rd BRAM/HZG SK7 ....183 H4
DTN/ASHW M34 ....131 H5
FWTH BL4 ....64 C4
MPL/ROM SK6 ....174 D1
SWIN M27 ....96 D4
Firs AV AUL OL6 ....118 A1
OLDTF/WHR M16 ....141 E1
The Firs ALT WA14 ....177 E2
Firsby Av MPL/ROM SK6 ...161 G2
Firsby St BNG/LEV M19 .....143 H2
Firs Gv CHD/CHDH SK8 .....169 F5
Firs Rd CHD/CHDH SK8 .....181 F1
SALE M33 ....153 G2
First AV OLDS OL8 ....90 A5
OP/CLY M11 ....115 G3
STLY SK15 ....107 F5
SWIN M27 ....96 C5
TOT/BURYW BL8 ....26 A5
TRPK M17 ....125 E5
First St BOL BL1 ....32 C2
Firs Wy SALE M33 ....153 F5
Firswood Dr HYDE SK14 ....133 F5
ROY/SHW OL2 ....58 D4
SWIN M27 ....96 F5
Firswood Mt CHD/CHDH SK8..169 F5
Firth St DUK OL1 ....9 H4
Fir Tree AV OLDS OL8 ....90 D5
SALE M33 ....153 F2
WALK M28 ....94 C4
Fir Tree CI DUK SK16 ....133 E1
Fir Tree Crs OLDE OL4 ....119 E5
Fir Tree Dr HYDE SK14 ......132 D5
Fir Tree La DUK SK16 ....133 E1
Firvale AV CHD/CHDH SK8 .181 G3
Firwood AV FWTH BL4 ....80 D1
URM M41 ....139 F2
Firwood CI OFTN SK2 ....172 D1
Firwood Crs RAD M26 ....67 G5
Firwood Gv BOLE BL2 ....34 C3
Firwood La BOLE BL2 ....34 C3
Firwood Pk OLDE OL4 ....72 D5
Fishbourne Sq RUSH/FAL * M14..127 H5
Fisherfield WHIT OL12 ....28 C2
Fishermore Rd URM M41 ....137 F1
Fisher St OLD OL1 ....9 H1
Fishwick St MILN OL16 ....10 C5
Fistral AV CHD/CHDH SK8 ...181 H4
Fistral Crs STLY SK15 ....120 A2
Fitton AV CHDY M21 ....141 E5
Fitton Crs SWIN M27 ....83 E4
Fitton Hill Rd OLDS OL8 ....90 D3
Fitton St CHAD OL9 ....9 H1
ROY/SHW OL2 ....59 G2
Fitzgeorge St NEWH/MOS M40..100 C5
Fitzgerald CI PWCH M25 ....84 C5
Fitzgerald Wy SLFD * M6 ....111 E1
Fitzhugh St BOL * BL1 ....34 B1
Fitzroy St AULW OL7 ....117 G4
DROY M43 ....116 C4
STLY SK15 ....120 A2
Fitzwarren St SLFD M6 ......111 G3
Fitzwilliam St BRO M7 ....112 C1
Five Quarters RAD M26 ....51 H4
Flagcroft Dr NTHM/RTH M23..168 A4
Flagg Wood AV MPL/ROM SK6..174 C2
Flag Rw ANC * M4 ....113 G2
Flagship AV ORD * M5 ....112 A5
Flake La ROY/SHW OL2 ....59 E5
Flamborough Wk
RUSH/FAL * M14 ....127 G5
Flamingo CI WGTN/LGST M12..128 D2
Flamstead AV NTHM/RTH M23..167 F3
Flannel St WHIT OL12 ....10 E4
Flashfields PWCH M25 ....98 C1
Flash St NEWH/MOS M40 ...102 B4
Flatley CI HULME M15 ....127 G5
Flavian Wk OP/CLY * M11 ...115 G5
Flaxcroft Rd WYTH/NTH M22..180 A2
Flaxfield AV STLY SK15 ......120 A3
Flaxman Ri OLD OL1 ....60 B5
Flaxpool CI OLDTF/WHR M16..126 A4
Flax St CSLFD M3 ....6 A1
RAMS * BL0 ....16 B4
Fleece St MILN OL16 ....10 C5
OLDE * OL4 ....9 G4
Fleeson St RUSH/FAL M14 .127 H5
Fleet St AUL OL6 ....117 H3
CTN M18 ....130 A2
HYDE SK14 ....132 D4
OLDE OL4 ....9 G4
Fleetwood Rd WALK M28 ......80 B4
Fleming PI CHAD OL9 ....9 E4
Fleming Rd WYTH/NTH M22 .180 C2
Flemish Rd HYDE SK14 ....147 E1
Fletcher AV SWIN M27 ....83 F4
Fletcher CI CHAD OL9 ....9 E4
Fletcher Dr ALT WA14 ....177 F5
POY/DIS SK12 ....197 E1
Fletcher Fold Rd BURY BL9 ...53 G3
Fletcher St BOLS/LL BL3 ....66 A1
BOLS/LL BL3 ....66 A1
BURY BL9 ....5 G4
FWTH BL4 ....65 E1
NEWH/MOS M40 ....101 G5
RAD M26 ....52 D5
STKP SK1 ....13 G3
Fletsand Rd WILM/AE SK9 ..199 H4
Fletton CI WHIT OL12 ....29 F1
Fletton Ms WHIT OL12 ....29 F1
Flint CI BRAM/HZG SK7 ....184 D1
OP/CLY * M11 ....115 G3
Flint Lea OLDE OL4 ....60 B1
Flint St DROY M43 ....116 C3
EDGY/DAV SK3 ....13 F7
OLDE * OL4 ....9 G4
Flitcroft Ct BOLS/LL * BL3 .....49 E5
Flixton Rd PART M31 ....137 F3

URM M41 ....137 H1
Floatshall Rd NTHM/RTH M23..167 G4
Floats Rd NTHM/RTH M23 ..167 G4
Flora St BKLY M9 ....86 D4
OLD OL1 ....9 F2
Florence Ct EDGY/DAV * SK3..171 E2
Florence Park Ct
DID/WITH M20 ....157 H2
Florence Steet MILN OL16 ....30 C5
Florence St BOLS/LL * BL3 ...48 C5
DROY M43 ....116 C4
ECC M30 ....109 E4
FAIL M35 ....103 E2
HTNM SK4 ....13 F1
SALE M33 ....139 G5
Florida St BOLS/LL BL3 ....8 E6
Florin Gdns SLFD M6 ....111 G2
Florist St EDGY/DAV SK3 ....171 H2
Flowery Bank OLDS OL8 ....91 E5
Flowery Fld OFTN SK2 ....184 B1
Flowery Field Gn HYDE SK14 .132 B4
Floyd AV CCHDY M21 ....141 F5
Floyer Rd BKLY M9 ....87 F5
Foden La BRAM/HZG SK7 ....169 E5
Fog La BNG/LEV M19 ....158 A2
The Fold BKLY M9 ....87 E4
URM M41 ....122 D5
Fold AV DROY M43 ....116 C3
Fold Crs STLY SK15 ....107 G4
Fold Gdns WHIT OL12 ....18 A5
Fold Gn CHAD OL9 ....89 F1
Fold Ms BRAM/HZG SK7 .....185 F1
Fold Rd RAD M26 ....66 B5
Folds Rd BOL BL1 ....3 G2
Fold St BOL * BL1 ....3 F5
BURY BL9 ....4 B4
HEY OL10 ....41 F5
NEWH/MOS M40 ....101 H2
OLDS OL8 ....90 D5
Foleshill AV BKLY M9 ....101 E5
Foley Gdns HEY OL10 ....54 B5
Foliage Crs RDSH SK5 ....160 C5
Foliage Gdns RDSH SK5 .....160 C5
Foliage Rd RDSH SK5 ....160 C5
Folkestone Rd OP/CLY M11 .115 G3
Folkestone Rd East
OP/CLY M11 ....115 G3
Folkestone Rd West
OP/CLY M11 ....115 F3
Follows St GTN M18 ....129 F2
Folly La SWIN M27 ....96 C5
Folly Wk WHIT OL12 ....10 D2
Fonthill Gv SALE M33 ....154 A3
Fontwell La OLD OL1 ....74 D4
Fontwell Rd BOLS/LL BL3 ......65 H4
Fooley CI DROY M43 ....115 H5
Foot Mill Crs WHIT OL12 ......29 G1
Foot Wood Crs WHIT OL12 ...29 G1
Forber Crs GTN M18 ....129 F5
Forbes CI SALE M33 ....172 C1
STKP SK1 ....13 J5
Forbes Pk BRAM/HZG SK7 .183 G5
Forbes Rd STLY SK15 ....160 C5
Forbes St MPL/ROM SK6 ....161 G2
Fordham Gv BOL BL1 ....40 A3
Ford La SLFD M6 ....111 H1
WYTH/NTH M22 ....156 D5
Ford Ldg OLDTF/WHR M16 ...28 A4
Ford's La BRAM/HZG SK7 ...193 G1
Ford St CSLFD M3 ....6 D3
DUK SK16 ....132 B2
EDGY/DAV SK3 ....12 C4
RAD M26 ....65 H4
WGTN/LGST M12 ....129 E1
Foreland CI NEWH/MOS M40..101 E5
Forest CI DUK SK16 ....133 H2
Forest Ct URM M41 ....122 A5
Forest Dr HALE/TIMP WA15 .166 A3
SALE M33 ....153 H4
Forester Hill AV BOLS/LL BL3..48 A4
Forester Hill CI BOLS/LL BL3..48 A4
Forest Gdns PART M31 ....150 C3
Forest Range BNG/LEV M19 .143 H2
Forest Rd BOL BL1 ....33 H4
Forest St AUL OL6 ....118 B1
ECC M30 ....108 D1
OLDS OL8 ....90 C4
Forest Vw WHIT OL12 ....29 G1
Forest Wy BOLE BL2 ....23 H5
Forfar St BOL BL1 ....33 H1
Forge La OP/CLY M11 ....114 C3
Forge Rd STLY SK15 ....107 G4
Formby AV CCHDY M21 ....141 G4
Formby Dr CHD/CHDH SK8 .181 G4
Formby Rd SLFD M6 ....98 B5
Forrester Dr ROY/SHW OL2 ...59 E5
Forrester St WALK M28 ....95 H2
Forrest Rd DTN/ASHW M34 .147 E2
Forshaw AV GTN M18 ....130 A2
Forshaw St DTN/ASHW M34 131 H4
Forsyth St WHIT OL12 ....9 G1
Fortescue Rd OFTN SK2 ......173 E2
Forth PI RAD M26 ....52 A4
Forton AV BOLE BL2 ....50 B2
Fortran CI SLFD M6 ....111 H4
Fort Rd PWCH M25 ....85 G5
Fortrose AV BKLY M9 ....87 H3
Fortuna Gv BNG/LEV M19 ...143 G3
Fortune St BOLS/LL BL3 ....8 E7
Fortyacre Dr MPL/ROM SK6 .161 F5
Forum Gv BRO M7 ....99 H5
Fosbrook AV DID/WITH M20 .157 F2
Foscarn Dr NTHM/RTH M23 .156 A4
Fossgill AV BOLE BL2 ....34 D1
Foster Ct BURY * BL9 ....39 G2
Foster La BOLE BL2 ....34 C2
Foster St DTN/ASHW M34 ...131 H4
OLDE OL4 ....60 A5
RAD M26 ....67 H1
Fotherby Dr BKLY M9 ....87 F4
Foulds AV TOT/BURYW BL8 ...37 H4
Foundry La ANC M4 ....7 G3
Foundry St BOLS/LL BL3 ....65 H4
BOLS/LL BL3 ....65 H4
BURY BL9 ....5 J5
CHAD OL9 ....8 E5
DUK SK16 ....118 B5

HEY OL10 ....40 D4
RAD M26 ....67 H1
Fountain AV HALE/TIMP WA15..178 C1
Fountain PI WHTF M45 ....68 C5
Fountains AV BOLE BL2 ....34 D5
Fountains Rd CHD/CHDH SK8..193 E1
STRET M32 ....124 A5
Fountain St AUL OL6 ....118 B1
BURY BL9 ....5 H5
CMANW M2 ....7 F5
CMANW M2 ....7 F5
HYDE SK14 ....133 E5
MDTN M24 ....71 G4
OLD OL1 ....9 F3
TOT/BURYW BL8 ....37 H4
Fourth AV BURY BL9 ....27 G4
BURY BL9 ....39 F2
CHAD OL9 ....89 H5
OLDS OL8 ....89 H5
OP/CLY M11 ....115 F2
STLY SK15 ....107 F4
TRPK M17 ....124 D5
Fourways TRPK M17 ....124 B2
Four Yards CMANW M2 ....6 E5
Fovant Crs RDSH SK5 ....160 A4
Fowler AV GTN M18 ....130 A1
Fowler St OLDS OL8 ....89 H4
Fownhope AV SALE M33 ......154 A3
Fownhope Rd SALE M33 ....154 A3
Foxall CI MDTN M24 ....70 D5
Foxall St MDTN M24 ....70 D5
Foxbank St BRUN/LGST M13..128 B4
Fox Bench CI CHD/CHDH SK8..193 F1
Foxcroft Wk CHDY M21 ....166 A5
Foxcroft St LIT OL15 ....20 C3
Foxdale St OP/CLY M11 ....115 F4
Foxdenton Dr STRET M32 ....124 A5
Foxdenton La MDTN M24 ....88 D1
Foxendale Wk BOLS/LL * BL3..48 D4
Foxfield CI OLDS OL8 ....103 H1
Foxfield Rd NTHM/RTH M23 .155 H5
Foxfield CI WALK M28 ....94 A3
Foxglove CI WHIT OL12 ....18 C5
Foxglove Dr ALT WA14 ....165 F1
Foxglove La STLY SK15 ....119 G3
Foxhall Rd DTN/ASHW M34 ..131 E4
HALE/TIMP WA15 ....165 H3
Foxham CI OLDS * OL8 ....48 D4
Fox Hi RI ROY/SHW OL2 ....59 F1
Foxhill Cha OFTN SK2 ....173 H4
Foxhill Dr STLY SK15 ....119 H5
Foxhill Rd ECC M30 ....108 C4
Fox Hill Rd ROCH OL11 ....57 G1
Foxholes CI WHIT OL12 ....10 E2
Foxholes Rd HYDE SK14 ......147 G3
WHIT OL12 ....10 E2
Foxlair Rd WYTH/NTH M22 ..156 A4
Foxland Rd CHD/CHDH SK8 .169 G5
Foxley Gv BOLS/LL BL3 ....2 B6
Fox Park Rd OLDS OL8 ....103 H1
Fox Platt Rd MOSL OL5 ....106 C1
Fox Platt Ter MOSL OL5 ....106 C2
Fox St BURY BL9 ....5 F5
ECC M30 ....110 A3
EDGY/DAV SK3 ....12 C6
HEY OL10 ....40 B1
MILN OL16 ....11 G4
OLDE OL4 ....91 H5
OLDS OL8 ....89 H5
Foxton St MDTN M24 ....70 D5
Foxwood Dr MOSL OL5 ....106 C1
Foxwood Gdns BNG/LEV M19..158 B1
Foynes CI NEWH/MOS * M40..101 E5
Framingham Rd SALE M33 ...154 C4
Framley Rd CCHDY M21 ......142 A4
Frampton CI MDTN M24 ....72 A4
Fram St BKLY M9 ....101 G2
SLFD * M6 ....111 F3
Frances AV CHD/CHDH SK8 .169 F3
Frances St BOL BL1 ....33 G5
BRUN/LGST M13 ....127 G2
CHD/CHDH SK8 ....170 B3
DTN/ASHW M34 ....147 E3
EDGY/DAV SK3 ....13 F5
HYDE SK14 ....132 D5
LIT OL15 ....20 A5
MILN OL16 ....150 D1
OLD OL1 ....9 J2
OLD OL1 ....9 J2
Frances St West SK14 ....109 H5
Francis AV ECC M30 ....109 H5
WALK M28 ....81 G5
Francis St CSLFD M3 ....6 C1
ECC M30 ....109 G2
FAIL M35 ....103 G3
FWTH BL4 ....64 D3
Frankby CI SWIN * M27 ....97 H5
Frank Fold HEY OL10 ....40 C3
Frankford AV BOL BL1 ....33 F4
Frankford Sq BOL * BL1 ....33 F4
Frankland CI OP/CLY M11 ....115 G4
Franklin CI DTN/ASHW M34 .145 E1
OLD OL1 ....9 J2
Franklin St ECC M30 ....116 B4
OLD OL1 ....9 J2
Franklyn AV URM M41 ....137 F1
Franklyn Rd GTN M18 ....129 H2
Frank Perkins Wy IRL M44 ...136 A4
Frank St BOL BL1 ....33 G5
BURY BL9 ....5 G4
HYDE SK14 ....147 G1
MDTN M24 ....54 D5
RUSH/FAL M14 ....142 C1
URM M41 ....123 G5
Franton Rd OP/CLY M11 ......115 G3
Fraser AV SALE M33 ....155 F3
Fraser PI TRPK M17 ....125 E3
Fraser Rd CHH M8 ....100 A1

Fraser St AUL OL6 ....118 B2
MILN OL16 ....43 G2
ROY/SHW OL2 ....59 H1
SWIN M27 ....97 F1
Frecheville Ct BURY BL9 ....4 C7
Freckleton AV CCHDY M21 ..156 B2
Freckleton Dr TOT/BURYW BL8..52 A1
Frederick AV ROY/SHW * OL2..59 G4
Frederick Rd SLFD M6 ....112 A2
Frederick St AUL OL6 ....118 D3
CHAD OL9 ....73 G4
CSLFD M3 ....6 B5
DTN/ASHW M34 ....131 G3
FWTH BL4 ....64 A1
LIT OL15 ....20 D2
OLD OL1 ....9 H3
RAMS BL0 ....16 C5
Frederick Ter BKLY * M9 .....101 E1
Fred Tilson CI RUSH/FAL M14..127 F5
Freehold St ROCH OL11 ....42 D5
Freeman AV AUL OL6 ....118 C3
Freeman Rd DUK SK16 ....132 B4
Freeman Sq HULME * M15 ..127 F2
Freemantle St EDGY/DAV SK3..12 B5
Freesia AV WALK M28 ....80 A4
Freestone CI TOT/BURYW BL8..4 A2
Freetown CI RUSH/FAL M14 .127 F4
Freetrade St ROCH OL11 ....42 D1
Fremantle AV GTN M18 ....129 G5
French AV OLD OL1 ....75 H4
STLY SK15 ....119 H4
French Barn La BKLY M9 ....86 D4
French Gv BOLS/LL BL3 ....50 A4
FWTH BL4 ....65 E2
STLY SK15 ....119 H4
Fresca Rd OLD OL1 ....60 C5
Freshfield CHD/CHDH SK8 ..181 G3
Freshfield AV BOLS/LL BL3 ....63 G2
HYDE SK14 ....147 F2
PWCH M25 ....85 F4
Freshfield CI FAIL M35 ....103 F4
MPL/ROM SK6 ....163 G5
Freshfield Gv BOLS/LL BL3 ....64 A2
Freshfield Rd HTNM SK4 .....158 C4
Freshfields RAD M26 ....51 G4
Freshpool Wy WYTH/NTH M22..168 D3
Freshville St CMANE * M1 ....7 J6
Freshwater Dr DTN/ASHW M34..147 E3
Freshwater St GTN M18 ......129 H2
Fresnel CI HYDE SK14 ....133 H2
Frewland AV EDGY/DAV SK3..172 A5
Freya Gv ORD M5 ....112 B5
Friars CI ALT WA14 ....177 E5
WILM/AE SK9 ....198 D2
Friars Crs ROCH OL11 ....42 B5
Friar's Rd SALE M33 ....154 C2
Friendship AV GTN * M18 .....130 B1
Frieston WHIT OL12 ....28 C2
Frieston Rd ALT WA14 ....153 H5
Friezland La UPML OL3 ....93 H5
Frimley Gdns WYTH/NTH M22..180 C1
Frinton AV NEWH/MOS * M40..88 D2
Frinton CI SALE M33 ....154 A5
Frinton Rd BOLS/LL BL3 ....49 E5
Frith AV DID/WITH M20 ....157 H1
Frobisher CI BRUN/LGST M13..128 A3
Frobisher PI RDSH SK5 ....159 H2
Frodesley Wk
WGTN/LGST * M12 ....129 E1
Frodsham AV HTNM SK4 .....159 F5
Frodsham St RUSH/FAL M14 .127 G5
Frodsham Wy WILM/AE SK9 .199 F5
Frogley St BOL * BL1 ....34 B1
Frogmore AV HYDE SK14 ....147 G2
Frome AV OFTN SK2 ....172 D4
URM M41 ....138 A1
Frome Dr CHH M8 ....100 C3
Frome St OLDE OL4 ....91 F1
Frostlands St OLDTF/WHR M16..126 D4
Frostlands St
OLDTF/WHR * M16 ....126 D5
Frost St ANC * M4 ....114 A4
OLDS OL8 ....90 B5
Froxmer St GTN M18 ....129 F2
Fulbrook Dr CHD/CHDH SK8 .192 D1
Fulford St OLDTF/WHR M16 .126 B4
Fulham AV NEWH/MOS M40 ..101 H1
Fullerton Rd HTNM SK4 ....159 E4
Full Pot La ROCH OL11 ....28 A2
Fulmar AV CI POY/DIS SK12 .194 B5
Fulmar Dr OFTN SK2 ....173 G4
SALE M33 ....153 H1
Fulmard CI WILM/AE SK9 ....199 H3
Fulmer Gdns NEWH/MOS M40..111 H1
Fulmere Ct SWIN M27 ....96 C3
Fulneck Sq DROY M43 ....116 D5
Fulshaw AV WILM/AE SK9 ..199 G5
Fulshaw Ct WILM/AE SK9 ...199 G5
Fulshaw Pk WILM/AE SK9
....201 A1
Fulshaw Pk South
WILM/AE SK9 ....201 A1
Fulstone Ms OFTN SK2 ....172 C3
Fulwell AV OLDTF/WHR M16 .126 A4
Fulwood CI TOT/BURYW BL8 ..37 G5
Fulwood Rd BKLY M9 ....87 F3
Furbarn La ROCH OL11 ....28 A3
Furbarn Rd ROCH OL11 ....28 A3
Furlong CI WYTH/NTH M22 ..180 A1
Furlong Rd WYTH/NTH M22 .180 A1
Furnace St DUK SK16 ....118 A4
HYDE SK14 ....133 G5
Furness AV AULW OL7 ....105 G5
BOLE BL2 ....34 C4
HEY OL10 ....40 A4
LIT OL15 ....21 F4
OLDS OL8 ....91 F3
WHTF M45 ....69 F3
Furness Gv HTNM SK4 ....158 D5
Furness Quay SALQ M50 .....125 H1
Furness Rd BOL BL1 ....33 F4
MDTN M24 ....71 H4
RUSH/FAL M14 ....142 B2
URM M41 ....123 G5
Furnival CI DTN/ASHW M34 .145 E1
Furnival Rd GTN M18 ....130 A1
Furnival St ROCH OL11 ....43 E2
RDSH SK5 ....159 H3
Furrow Dr ECC M30 ....109 E1
Further Fld ROCH OL11 ....28 A2

Further Heights Rd WHIT OL12..10 B1
Further Hey CI OLDE OL4 ....75 H5
Further Pits ROCH OL11 ....29 F4
Furzegate MILN OL16 ....43 H3
Furze La OLDE OL4 ....75 G3
Fushia Gv BRO * M7 ....99 G4
Furze La OLDE OL4 ....75 G3
CHD/CHDH SK8 ....181 H4
Fylde AV BOLE BL2 ....50 C2
Fylde Av HTNM SK4 ....158 D4
Fylde St FWTH BL4 ....65 E2
Fylde St East FWTH BL4 ....65 E2

G

Gable AV WILM/AE SK9 ....199 F3
Gable Dr MDTN M24 ....71 F3
The Gables SALE M33 ....154 C3
Gable St BOLE * BL2 ....35 F3
OP/CLY M11 ....114 C5
The Gabriels ROY/SHW OL2 ..59 G2
Gabriels Ter MDTN M24 ....72 B5
Gaddum Rd ALT WA14 ....176 C4
DID/WITH M20 ....157 H5
Cadwall CI WALK M28 ....95 E2
Gail Av HTNM SK4 ....12 C1
Gail CI FAIL M35 ....102 D5
Gainford AV CHD/CHDH SK8 .182 A3
Gainford Gdns NEWH/MOS M40..102 A1
Gainford Rd RDSH SK5 ....145 E2
Gainford Wk BOLS/LL * BL3 ...48 D5
Gainsborough AV BOLS/LL BL3..65 F1
DID/WITH * M20 ....157 H1
MPL/ROM SK6 ....175 G1
OLDS OL8 ....90 B2
STRET * M32 ....125 G5
Gainsborough CI WILM/AE SK9..200 A2
Gainsborough Dr
CHD/CHDH SK8 ....170 C3
Gainsborough Rd CHAD OL9 ..72 D4
DTN/ASHW M34 ....117 E4
RAMS BL0 ....26 B2
Gainsborough St BRO M7 ....99 H3
Gairloch AV STRET M32 ....139 F1
Gair Rd RDSH SK5 ....160 A2
Gair St HYDE SK14 ....132 C4
Gaitskell CI WGTN/LGST M12..114 B4
Galbraith Rd DID/WITH M20 .157 H5
Galbraith St CMANE * M1 ....7 G7
Gale Dr MDTN M24 ....71 E2
Gale Rd PWCH M25 ....84 C4
Gales Ter ROCH OL11 ....42 D1
Gale St HEY OL10 ....40 B2
MILN OL16 ....19 E5
Galgate CI HULME M15 ....126 D1
TOT/BURYW BL8 ....37 F5
Galindo St BOLE BL2 ....34 D5
Galland St OLDE OL4 ....75 G3
Galloway CI BOLS/LL BL3 ....47 F4
HEY OL10 ....40 A3
Galloway Dr SWIN M27 ....83 E5
Galloway Rd SWIN M27 ....111 E1
Gallowsclough Rd STLY SK15 .134 A3
Galston St OP/CLY M11 ....114 D5
Galsworthy AV CHH M8 ....100 B5
Galton Gv BKLY M9 ....99 F1
Galway St OLD OL1 ....9 G5
Gambleside CI WALK M28 ....94 C2
Gambrel Bank Rd AUL OL6 ...105 G4
Gambrel Gv AUL OL6 ....105 G4
Gamma Wk OP/CLY M11 ......115 G3
Gantock Wk RUSH/FAL M14 .127 H5
Ganton AV WHTF M45 ....68 D2
Garbrook AV BKLY M9 ....86 D2
Garden AV DROY M43 ....116 C3
STRET M32 ....140 A1
Garden City RAMS BL0 ....26 A3
Garden CI LIT OL15 ....31 G1
Garden La ALT WA14 ....165 G4
CSLFD M3 ....6 C2
SLFD M3 ....6 A4
WALK M28 ....94 B4
Garden Ms AUL * OL6 ....118 C3
Garden Rw HEY OL10 ....40 C2
The Gardens BOL BL1 ....33 H3
Garden St DTN/ASHW M34 ...131 G2
ECC M30 ....109 H4
FWTH BL4 ....65 F4
HEY OL10 ....40 C2
HYDE SK14 ....132 D4
MILN OL16 ....45 E2
OFTN * SK2 ....172 C4
OLD OL1 ....9 K2
RAMS BL0 ....16 C4
Garden Ter ROY/SHW OL2 .....59 D2
Garden Wk AUL OL6 ....118 C3
Garden Wall CI ORD M5 ....112 A5
Garden Wy LIT OL15 ....31 G1
Gardner Rd PWCH M25 ....84 C3
Gardner St SLFD M6 ....111 H4
WGTN/LGST M12 ....129 E2
Garfield AV BNG/LEV M19 ....144 A2
Garfield CI BOLS/LL BL3 ....2 B7
Garfield Gv BOLS/LL BL3 ....2 B7
STKP * SK1 ....13 J1
Garfield St BOL BL1 ....113 H3
Garforth St CHAD OL9 ....90 B2
Gargrave AV BOL BL1 ....32 C4
Gargrave St BRO M7 ....99 H1
OLDE OL4 ....91 E1
Garland Rd WYTH/NTH M22 .180 D1
Garlick St CHAD OL9 ....74 C4
GTN M18 ....129 G3
Garnant CI BKLY M9 ....101 G2
Garner AV HALE/TIMP WA15 .166 A4
Garner CI ALT WA14 ....177 G2
Garner Dr ECC * M30 ....109 F2
SLFD M6 ....111 E2
Garner's La EDGY/DAV SK3 ..172 A4
Garnet St BOL BL1 ....33 H5
Garnett Rd HYDE SK14 ....134 C5
Garnett St BOL BL1 ....33 H5

RAMS BL0 ... 16 C2
STKP SK1 ... 13 G4
Garratt Wy GTN M18 ... 129 F3
Garret Gv ROY/SHW OL2 ... 60 B2
Garrett Wk EDGY/DAV SK3 ... 12 A5
Garrick Gdns WYTH/NTH M22 ... 168 C5
Garsdale La BOL BL1 ... 47 E2
Garside Gv BOL BL1 ... 33 F4
Garside Hey Rd TOT/BURYW BL8 ... 26 C5
Garside Dr BOL BL1 ... 2 C5
  DTN/ASHW * M34 ... 146 C1
  HYDE SK14 ... 147 H2
Garstang Av BOLE BL2 ... 50 C1
Garstang Dr TOT/BURYW BL8 ... 37 E5
Garston Cl HTNM SK4 ... 159 F3
Garston St BURY ... 38 D2
Garswood Dr TOT/BURYW BL8 ... 26 C5
Garswood Rd BOLS/LL BL3 ... 63 H2
  RUSH/FAL M14 ... 142 A1
Garth Av HALE/TIMP WA15 ... 165 H3
Garthland Rd BRAM/HZG SK7 ... 185 E1
Garthorne Cl OLDTF/WHR M16 ... 126 C4
Garthorp Rd NTHM/RTH M23 ... 155 F5
The Garth ORD M5 ... 111 E3
Garth Rd MPL/ROM SK6 ... 175 F5
  GTN M18 ...
  WYTH/NTH M22 ... 168 C5
Garthwaite Av OLDS OL8 ... 90 B4
Gartside St AULW * OL7 ... 117 F4
  CSLFD M5 ... 6 C5
  OLDE OL4 ... 91 E2
Garwick Rd BOL BL1 ... 33 E3
Gascoyne St RUSH/FAL M14 ... 127 H5
Gascare Wk NTHM/RTH M23 ... 167 F2
Gate Field Cl RAD M26 ... 66 D1
Gatehead Cft UPML OL3 ... 77 G1
Gatehead Ms UPML OL3 ... 77 G1
Gatehouse LIT * OL15 ... 21 G2
Gatehouse Rd WALK M28 ... 80 B3
Gate Keeper Fold AULW OL7 ... 104 D3
Gatesgarth Rd MDTN M24 ... 71 H3
Gateshead Cl RUSH/FAL M14 ... 127 G4
Gate St DUK SK16 ... 131 H2
  OP/CLY M11 ... 115 F5
Gateway Crs OLD OL9 ... 88 D3
Gateway Rd GTN * M18 ... 129 F2
The Gateways SWIN M27 ... 97 E1
Gathill Cl CHD/CHDH SK8 ... 182 C3
Gathurst St OP/CLY M11 ...
Gatley Av RUSH/FAL M14 ... 142 B2
Gatley Brow OLD * OL1 ... 74 B4
Gatley Gn CHD/CHDH SK8 ... 169 F4
Gatley Rd CHD/CHDH SK8 ... 169 E3
  SALE M33 ... 155 F5
Gatling Av WGTN/LGST M12 ... 143 H1
Gatwick Av NTHM/RTH M23 ... 168 A3
Gavin Av ORD M5 ... 112 D5
Gawsworth Av DID/WITH M20 ... 157 H5
Gawsworth Cl BRAM/HZG SK7 ... 193 H5
  EDGY/DAV SK3 ... 171 G4
  HALL/TIMP WA15 ... 167 F4
  ROY/SHW OL2 ... 59 G2
Gawsworth Ms CHD/CHDH SK8 ... 169 G4
Gawsworth Rd SALE M33 ... 155 F4
Gawthorpe Cl BURY BL9 ... 53 G2
Gaydon Rd SALE M33 ... 153 G2
Gaythorne St BOL BL1 ... 34 A3
Gee Cross Fold HYDE SK14 ... 147 H4
Gee La ECC M30 ... 109 E2
Gee St EDGY/DAV SK3 ... 12 C5
Geinsbury Cl OLDS OL8 ... 91 E3
Gellfield La UPML OL3 ... 78 C5
Gemini Rd SALE M33 ... 153 H2
Gencoyne Dr BOL BL1 ... 22 C5
Gendre Rd EDCW/EG BL7 ... 22 D5
Geneva Rd BRAM/HZG SK7 ... 183 G1
Geneva Ter ROCH OL11 ... 29 F3
Geneva Wk CHAD OL9 ... 8 A4
Genista Gv BRO * M7 ... 99 G4
Geoffrey St BURY BL9 ... 5 G1
  RAMS BL0 ... 16 B4
  WHTN BL5 ... 62 C4
George Barton St BOLE BL2 ... 3 J1
George La MPL/ROM SK6 ... 161 H2
George Leigh St ANC M4 ... 7 J3
George Mann Cl
  WYTH/NTH M22 ... 180 B3
George Richards Wy ALT WA14 ... 165 E2
George Rd RAMS BL0 ... 16 D3
George Sq OLD OL1 ... 9 F4
George's Rd HTNM SK4 ... 12 C3
  SALE M33 ... 154 C3
George's Rd West
  POY/DIS SK12 ... 195 E4
George St AUL OL6 ... 118 B2
  BURY BL9 ... 5 F5
  CHAD OL9 ... 73 J3
  CMANE M1 ... 7 F6
  DTN/ASHW M34 ... 131 H5
  ECC M30 ... 109 F4
  FAIL M35 ... 103 G2
  FWTH BL4 ... 65 H1
  HEY OL10 ... 40 D3
  IRL M44 ... 121 G5
  LIT * OL15 ... 21 G3
  MILN OL16 ... 10 E4
  MILN OL16 ... 44 A3
  MOSL OL5 ... 106 D1
  MPL/ROM SK6 ... 163 G4
  OLD OL1 ... 9 F1
  PWCH M25 ... 99 E1
  RAD M26 ... 52 C5
  ROY/SHW OL2 ... 45 F5
  STKP SK1 ... 13 J5

STLY SK15 ... 119 F3
URM M41 ... 138 D1
WHIT OL12 ... 11 B5
WHTF M45 ... 68 B3
WILM/AE SK9 ... 201 B4
George St East STKP SK1 ... 172 C1
George St North BRO M7 ... 100 A2
George St South BRO M7 ... 99 H2
George St West STKP SK1 ... 172 C1
Georgette Dr CSLFD M5 ... 6 C1
Georgiana St BURY BL9 ... 4 E6
  FWTH BL4 ... 64 C3
Georgina Ct BOLS/LL BL3 ... 63 E2
Georgina St BOLS/LL BL3 ... 63 E2
Gerald Av CHH M8 ... 100 B2
Gerald Rd SLFD M6 ... 98 D5
Germain Cl BRO M7 ... 86 D2
Gerrard Av HALE/TIMP WA15 ... 166 B1
Gerrards Cl IRL M44 ... 136 B1
Gerrards Gdns HYDE SK14 ... 147 H4
Gerrards Hollow HYDE SK14 ... 147 G4
Gerrard St FWTH BL4 ... 65 F4
  ROCH OL11 ... 43 F5
  SLFD M6 ... 111 H2
  STLY SK15 ... 119 G4
Gerrards Wd HYDE SK14 ... 147 G4
Gertrude Cl ORD M5 ... 111 E5
Gervis Cl NEWH/MOS * M40 ... 101 E5
Ghyll Gv WALK M28 ... 81 F5
Gibbon Av WYTH/NTH M22 ... 180 C2
Gibbon St BOLS/LL BL3 ... 48 C4
  OP/CLY M11 ... 114 D3
Gibb Rd WALK M28 ... 96 A3
Gibbs St CSLFD M5 ... 112 C4
Gib La NTHM/RTH M23 ... 168 A2
Gibraltar La DTN/ASHW M34 ... 147 E5
Gibraltar St BOLS/LL BL3 ... 2 E7
  OLDE OL4 ... 91 G2
Gibsmere Cl HALE/TIMP WA15 ... 167 E5
Gibson Av GTN M18 ... 130 A1
Gibson Gv WALK M28 ... 80 B4
Gibson La WALK M28 ... 80 B4
Gibson Pl ANC M4 ... 113 F2
Gibson Rd HTNM SK4 ... 159 E2
Gibson St BOLE BL2 ... 34 D5
  MILN OL16 ... 11 K4
  OLDE * OL4 ... 91 F1
Gibson Wy ALT WA14 ... 165 F1
Giewood Rd WYTH/NTH M22 ... 168 B1
Gidlow St GTN M18 ... 129 H2
Gifford Av BKLY M9 ... 87 G3
Gigg La BURY BL9 ... 53 G2
Gilbertbank MPL/ROM SK6 ... 161 H2
Gilbert Rd HALE/TIMP WA15 ... 177 H5
Gilbert St ECC M30 ... 110 B2
  HULME M15 ... 126 D1
  ORD * M5 ... 112 B4
  WALK M28 ... 94 D1
Gilbrook Wy MILN OL16 ... 43 G4
Gilchrist Rd IRL M44 ... 136 B1
Gilda Brook Rd ECC M30 ... 110 B3
Gilda Crs Rd ECC M30 ... 110 B3
Gildenhall FAIL M35 ... 103 F3
Gilderdale Cl ROY/SHW OL2 ... 60 A1
Gilderdale St BOLS/LL BL3 ... 49 F4
Gildersdale Dr BKLY M9 ... 86 C1
Gildridge Rd OLDTF/WHR M16 ... 141 H2
Giesgate RUSH/FAL M14 ... 127 H5
Giles St WGTN/LGST M12 ... 128 D4
Gillbent Rd CHD/CHDH SK8 ... 192 D1
Gillbrook Rd DID/WITH M20 ... 157 G4
Gillemere Gv ROY/SHW OL2 ... 60 A2
Gillers Gn WALK M28 ... 80 D5
Gilliford Av BKLY M9 ... 101 G2
Gillingham Rd ECC M30 ... 109 E3
Gillingham Sq OP/CLY M11 ... 114 C5
Gilt St BKLY M9 ... 101 G2
  STKP SK1 ...
Gillwood Dr MPL/ROM SK6 ... 161 G5
Gilman Cl BKLY * M9 ... 86 D5
Gilman St BKLY M9 ... 86 D5
Gilmerton Dr NEWH/MOS * M40 ... 102 B5
Gilmore Dr PWCH M25 ... 85 E2
Gilmore St EDGY/DAV SK3 ... 13 F7
Gilmour St MDTN M24 ... 71 H3
Gilnow Gdns URM M41 ... 137 G4
Gilnow Gv BOL BL1 ... 2 A6
Gilnow La BOLS/LL BL3 ... 48 A5
Gilnow Rd BOL BL1 ... 2 A6
Gilpin Rd URM M41 ... 139 E2
Giltbrook Av NEWH/MOS M40 ... 114 A1
Gilwell Dr NTHM/RTH M23 ... 167 H5
Gilwood Gv MDTN M24 ... 56 C5
Gingham Pk RAD M26 ... 51 H4
Gipsy La OFTN SK2 ... 172 D3
Girton St BRO M7 ... 112 D1
Girvan Av NEWH/MOS M40 ... 88 B5
Girvan Cl BOLS/LL BL3 ... 63 F1
Gisborn Dr SLFD M6 ... 98 C5
Gisburn Av BOL BL1 ... 32 B4
Gisburn Dr TOT/BURYW BL8 ... 26 B3
Gisburne Av NEWH/MOS M40 ... 88 D1
Gisburn Rd BOLS/LL BL3 ... 63 H1
Givendale Dr CHH M8 ... 86 B5
Givvons Fold OLDE OL4 ... 75 G3
Glabyn Av HOR/BR BL6 ... 46 A1
The Glade BOL BL1 ... 33 G5
Glade Brow OLDE * OL4 ... 92 B1
Gladeside Rd WYTH/NTH M22 ... 168 B5
Gladewood Cl WILM/AE SK9 ... 199 H2
Gladstone Cl BOL * BL1 ... 33 H4
Gladstone Ct HULME M15 ... 126 D4
Gladstone Crs ROCH OL11 ... 43 E5
Gladstone Gv HTNM SK4 ... 158 D3
Gladstone Ms HTNM * SK4 ... 159 H4
Gladstone Pl FWTH BL4 ... 65 E2
Gladstone Rd ALT WA14 ... 165 E2
  ECC M30 ... 109 E3
  FWTH BL4 ... 65 E1
  URM M41 ... 138 D1
Gladstone St BOL BL1 ... 33 H4
  BURY BL9 ... 4 C2
  OFTN SK2 ... 172 D5
  OLDE OL4 ... 91 E1
  SWIN M27 ... 97 F2
Gladstone Terrace Rd UPML OL3 ... 93 H5
Gladwyn Av DID/WITH M20 ... 156 D3
Gladys St FWTH BL4 ... 65 G3
Glaisdale OLDE OL4 ... 91 G1
Glaisdale Cl BOLE BL2 ... 34 C4
Glaisdale St BOLE BL2 ... 34 C4

Glaister La BOLE BL2 ... 35 E5
Glamis Av HEY OL10 ... 56 B2
  STRET M32 ... 139 F1
Glamorgan Pl CHAD OL9 ... 8 A1
Glandon Dr CHD/CHDH SK8 ... 183 F5
Glanford Av BKLY M9 ... 86 B4
Glanvor Rd EDGY/DAV SK3 ... 12 A6
Glasshouse St ANC M4 ... 7 K1
Glass St FWTH * BL4 ... 65 F5
Glastonbury WHIT OL12 ...
Glastonbury Av CHD/CHDH SK8 ... 193 F1
  HALE/TIMP WA15 ... 178 C2
Glastonbury Dr POY/DIS SK12 ... 195 G2
Glastonbury Rd STRET M32 ... 124 A5
Glaswen Gv OFTN SK2 ... 160 A2
Glazebrook Cl HEY OL10 ... 56 B5
Glazebury Dr NTHM/RTH M23 ... 168 A4
Glazedale Av ROY/SHW OL2 ... 58 D5
Glaze Wk WHTF M45 ... 85 E1
Gleaves Av BOLE BL2 ... 35 H2
Gleaves Rd ECC M30 ... 109 H4
Gleave St BOL * BL1 ... 3 G3
  SALE M33 ... 139 F5
Glebecourt Dr WHIT OL12 ...
Glebelands Rd NTHM/RTH M23 ... 167 G2
  PWCH M25 ... 84 D2
  SALE M33 ... 139 F5
Glebe La OLD OL1 ... 75 H1
Glebe Rd URM M41 ... 138 C1
Glebe St BOLE BL2 ... 3 G6
  CHAD OL9 ... 8 D1
  RAD M26 ... 67 G1
  ROY/SHW OL2 ... 60 A2
  WHTF M45 ... 68 D3
Gleden St NEWH/MOS M40 ... 114 B3
Gledhall St STLY SK15 ... 119 E3
Gledhill Av ORD M5 ... 125 H1
Gledhill Cl ROY/SHW OL2 ... 44 D5
Gledhill St DID/WITH M20 ... 142 C4
Gledhill Wy EDGW/EG BL7 ... 23 F2
Glemsford Cl NEWH/MOS * M40 ... 102 A4
The Glen BOL BL1 ... 47 E2
  MDTN M24 ...
Glenacre Gdns GTN M18 ... 129 H5
Glenart ECC M30 ... 110 D1
Glen Av BKLY M9 ... 101 F1
  BOLS/LL BL3 ... 48 A4
  FWTH BL4 ... 64 A5
  SWIN M27 ... 96 C2
  WALK M28 ... 95 H2
Glenavon Dr ROY/SHW OL2 ... 59 G1
  WHIT OL12 ... 18 C5
Glenbarry Cl BRUN/LGST M13 ... 127 G2
Glenbarry St WGTN/LGST M12 ... 114 A5
Glenbeck Rd WHTF M45 ... 68 B3
Glenbourne Pk BRAM/HZG SK7 ... 193 G2
Glenbrook Gdns FWTH BL4 ... 65 H2
Glenbrook Rd BKLY M9 ... 86 B3
Glenburn St BOLS/LL BL3 ... 63 G1
Glenby Av WYTH/NTH M22 ... 181 E1
Glencastle Rd GTN M18 ... 129 F3
Glen Cl GOL/RIS/CU WA3 ... 150 A4
Glencoe BOLS/LL BL3 ... 66 C1
Glencoe Dr BOLE BL2 ... 35 H5
  SALE M33 ... 153 F4
Glencoe Pl ROCH OL11 ... 43 E4
Glencoe St OLDS * OL8 ... 90 B5
Glen Cottages BOL * BL1 ... 32 B3
Glencross Av CCHDY M21 ... 140 D1
Glendale SWIN M27 ... 96 B2
Glendale Av GTN M18 ... 143 G5
Glendale Cl HEY OL10 ...
Glendale Ct OLDS OL8 ... 90 C5
Glendale Dr BOLS/LL BL3 ... 47 G5
Glendale Rd ECC M30 ... 110 B2
  WALK M28 ... 94 A3
Glendevon Cl BOLS/LL BL3 ... 47 H5
  WHTN BL5 ... 62 B5
Glendinning St SLFD M6 ... 111 F3
Glendon Ct OLD OL1 ... 9 J2
Glendon Crs AUL OL6 ... 105 E3
Glendore ORD M5 ... 110 D3
Glendower Dr NEWH/MOS M40 ... 115 H1
Gleneagles BOLS/LL BL3 ... 62 C1
Gleneagles Av OP/CLY M11 ... 116 A2
Gleneagles Cl BRAM/HZG SK7 ... 184 B5
  WILM/AE SK9 ... 200 A2
Gleneagles Rd CHD/CHDH SK8 ... 181 H5
  URM M41 ... 136 A5
Glenfield ALT WA14 ... 165 E5
Glenfield Dr POY/DIS SK12 ... 195 G4
Glenfield Rd HTNM SK4 ... 159 G2
Glenfield Sq FWTH BL4 ... 64 D4
Glenfyne Rd SLFD M6 ... 98 B4
Glengarth Dr BOLS/LL BL3 ... 47 F5
  WHTN BL5 ... 62 B5
Glengarth ROCH OL11 ... 19 H5
Glenham Ct OLDS OL8 ... 90 C5
Glenhaven Av URM M41 ... 138 C1
Glenholme Rd BRAM/HZG SK7 ... 183 G5
Glenhurst Rd BNG/LEV * M19 ... 158 B3
Glenilla Av WALK M28 ... 95 H1
Glenluce Dr BOLS/LL BL3 ... 64 A2
Glenmaye Gv WHTF M45 ...
Glenmere Cl PWCH M25 ... 84 C1
Glenmere Rd DID/WITH M20 ... 157 H4
Glenmoor Rd STKP SK1 ... 13 K4
Glenmore Av FWTH BL4 ... 64 A5
Glenmore Cl BOLS/LL BL3 ... 47 F4
  ROCH OL11 ... 18 D5
Glenmore Dr CHH M8 ... 100 C3
  FAIL M35 ... 103 H4
Glenmore Gv DUK SK16 ... 118 D5
Glenmore Rd RAMS BL0 ... 26 A3
Glenmore St BURY BL9 ... 5 H3
Glennidge St OP/CLY M11 ... 114 D3
Glenridding Cl OLD OL1 ... 74 D3
Glenridge Cl BOL BL1 ... 33 H3
Glen Ri HALE/TIMP WA15 ... 166 B4
Glen Rd OLDE OL4 ... 92 C1
Glen Royd WHIT OL12 ...
Glensdale Dr NEWH/MOS M40 ... 102 D1
Glenshee Dr BOLS/LL BL3 ... 63 H2
Glenside Av GTN M18 ... 129 G3
Glenside Dr BOLS/LL BL3 ... 64 A2

MPL/ROM SK6 ... 162 A1
WILM/AE SK9 ... 199 H4
Glenside Gdns FAIL M35 ... 103 F3
Glenside Gv WALK M28 ... 81 F5
Glen St RAMS BL0 ... 16 C1
  SALQ M50 ... 125 H1
Glenthorn Av BKLY M9 ... 87 E1
Glenthorne St BOL BL1 ... 33 H3
Glenthorn Gv SALE M33 ... 154 C3
Glentrool Ms BOL BL1 ... 47 H2
Glent Vw STLY SK15 ... 119 F1
Glenvale Ct RAD M26 ... 67 G1
Glen Vw ROY/SHW OL2 ... 59 E4
Glenville Wy DTN/ASHW M34 ... 146 D1
Glenwood Cl BOLS/LL BL3 ... 65 G2
Glenwood Dr BKLY M9 ... 101 F5
  MDTN M24 ... 72 C2
Glenwood Gv OFTN SK2 ... 184 C1
Glenwyn Av BKLY M9 ... 87 F3
Globe Cl OLDTF/WHR M16 ... 125 G5
Globe La DUK SK16 ... 132 A1
Globe Sq DUK SK16 ... 131 H1
Glodwick Rd OLDE OL4 ... 91 E2
Glossop Rd MPL/ROM SK6 ... 163 H5
Gloster St BOLE BL2 ... 3 H5
Gloucester Av BNG/LEV M19 ... 144 A3
  HEY OL10 ... 55 H2
  MPL/ROM SK6 ... 175 E3
  OLDE OL4 ... 20 A4
  WHTF M45 ... 68 A2
Gloucester Cl AUL OL6 ... 105 G2
Gloucester Dr SALE M33 ... 153 G2
Gloucester Pl DUK SK16 ... 133 F1
Gloucester Rd CHD/CHDH SK8 ... 181 H5
  DROY M43 ... 116 B2
  DTN/ASHW M34 ... 145 F1
  MDTN M24 ... 87 H1
  POY/DIS SK12 ... 195 E3
  SLFD M6 ... 110 D1
  URM M41 ... 138 A3
Gloucester St CMANE * M1 ... 127 E1
  ORD M5 ... 112 B5
  SLFD M6 ... 111 H1
Gloucester St North CHAD ... 8 A6
Glover Centre MOSL * OL5 ... 107 E2
Glover Ct BURY BL9 ...
Glyn Av HALE/TIMP WA15 ... 178 B2
Glynne St FWTH BL4 ... 64 D4
Glynrene Dr SWIN M27 ... 97 E4
Glynwood Pk FWTH BL4 ... 64 D4
Goats Gate Ter WHTF * M45 ... 68 A2
Godbert Av CCHDY M21 ... 156 B1
Goddard St OLDS OL8 ... 90 C3
Godfrey Av DROY M43 ... 117 H2
Godfrey Range GTN M18 ... 130 A4
Godfrey Rd SLFD M6 ... 97 H5
Godlee Dr SWIN M27 ... 96 D3
Godley Cl OP/CLY M11 ... 129 F1
Godley St HYDE SK14 ... 133 E4
Godmond Hall Dr WALK M28 ... 94 A5
Godson St OLD OL1 ... 74 B5
Godward Rd MPL/ROM SK6 ... 175 G3
Godwin St GTN M18 ... 129 H2
Golborne Av DID/WITH M20 ... 142 C4
Goldbourne Dr ROY/SHW OL2 ... 60 A1
Goldbrook Cl HEY OL10 ... 41 F5
Goldcrest Cl WALK M28 ... 95 F1
  WYTH/NTH M22 ... 169 E4
Goldenhill Av OP/CLY M11 ... 115 G3
Golden St ECC M30 ...
  ROY/SHW OL2 ... 60 D1
Goldfinch Dr BURY BL9 ... 53 E5
Goldfinch Wy DROY M43 ... 118 C3
Goldie Av WYTH/NTH M22 ... 181 E3
Goldrill Av BOLE BL2 ... 50 C1
Goldrill Gdns BOLE BL2 ... 50 C1
Goldsmith Av OLDS OL8 ... 90 C5
Goldsmith Rd RDSH SK5 ... 144 C2
Goldsmith St BOLS/LL BL3 ... 48 C5
Goldsmith Wy DTN/ASHW M34 ... 137 F1
Goldsworthy Rd URM M41 ... 122 B5
Golf Rd HALE/TIMP WA15 ... 178 A1
  SALE M33 ... 155 G2
Golfview Dr ECC M30 ... 133 G2

GTN M18 ... 129 H2
HTNM SK4 ... 13 F1
HYDE SK14 ... 147 H1
MILN OL16 ... 45 E3
OLDE OL4 ... 92 B1
OLDTF/WHR M16 ... 126 C4
ROCH OL11 ...
ROY/SHW OL2 ... 60 B2
STLY SK15 ... 119 G4
Gordon Ter BKLY * M9 ... 101 F2
Gordon Wy HEY OL10 ... 40 A5
Gore Av FAIL M35 ... 105 G3
  ORD M5 ... 111 E3
Gorebrook Ct WGTN/LGST M12 ... 128 D4
Gore Cl BURY BL9 ... 39 F5
Gore Crs ORD M5 ... 111 E2
Goredale Av GTN M18 ... 129 H5
Gore Dr SLFD M6 ... 111 E2
Gorelan Rd GTN * M18 ... 129 G2
Gore St CMANE M1 ... 7 H5
  CSLFD M5 ... 6 D5
  SLFD M6 ... 111 H1
Goring Av GTN M18 ... 129 G2
Gorrells Wy ROCH OL11 ... 42 C3
Gorrels Cl ROCH OL11 ... 42 C3
Gorrel St ROCH * OL11 ... 43 F1
The Gorse ALT WA14 ... 177 E4
Gorse Av DROY M43 ... 116 D3
  MOSL OL5 ... 107 F1
  MPL/ROM SK6 ... 174 D3
  OLDS OL8 ... 91 F4
  STRET M32 ... 125 G5
Gorse Bank BURY BL9 ... 39 F3
Gorse Bank Rd
  HALE/TIMP WA15 ... 178 D5
Gorse Crs STRET M32 ... 125 G5
Gorse Dr LHULT M38 ... 80 A1
  STRET M32 ... 125 G5
Gorsefield Dr SWIN M27 ... 97 F3
Gorsefield Hey WILM/AE SK9 ... 200 B2
Gorse Hall Cl DUK * SK16 ... 133 E1
Gorse Hall Dr STLY SK15 ... 119 E4
Gorse Hall Rd DUK SK16 ... 132 D1
Gorselands CHD/CHDH SK8 ... 192 C5
Gorse La STRET M32 ... 125 G5
Gorse Rd MILN OL16 ...
  SWIN M27 ... 97 F3
  WALK M28 ... 81 F5
Gorses Mt BOLE BL2 ... 49 H4
Gorse Sq PART M31 ... 150 C3
Gorse St BOLS/LL BL3 ... 50 A4
  CHAD OL9 ... 89 E3
  STRET M32 ... 125 G5
Gorseway RDSH SK5 ... 160 C2
Gorsey Av WYTH/NTH M22 ... 168 B5
Gorsey Bank Rd EDGY/DAV SK3 ... 171 E1
Gorsey Brow MPL/ROM SK6 ... 161 H4
  STKP SK1 ... 13 J4
Gorsey Clough Wk
  TOT/BURYW BL8 ... 37 E1
Gorseyfields DROY M43 ... 116 B5
Gorsey Hill St HEY OL10 ... 41 E5
Gorsey Intakes HYDE SK14 ... 149 H3
Gorsey La AUL OL6 ... 104 A4
  AULW OL7 ...
  STKP SK1 ... 13 K4
Gorsey Mount St STKP SK1 ... 13 K4
Gorsey Rd WILM/AE SK9 ... 199 E3
  WYTH/NTH M22 ...
Gorsey Wy AUL OL6 ... 105 H4
Gorsley Bank LIT OL15 ... 21 F1
Gorston Wk WYTH/NTH M22 ... 180 B4
Gorton Crs DTN/ASHW M34 ... 145 H1
Gorton Gv WALK M28 ... 80 D2
Gorton La WGTN/LGST M12 ... 128 C1
Gorton Rd OP/CLY M11 ... 128 C1
  RDSH SK5 ...
Gorton St AULW OL7 ... 117 G4
  BOLE BL2 ... 3 G6
  CHAD OL9 ... 89 G1
  CSLFD * M5 ... 6 D2
  ECC M30 ... 109 H3
  FWTH BL4 ...
  HEY OL10 ... 41 F4
Gortonvilla Wk
  WGTN/LGST M12 ... 128 C2
Gosforth Cl OLD OL1 ... 74 D3
  TOT/BURYW BL8 ...
Goshen La BURY BL9 ... 53 G3
Gosport Sq BRO M7 ...
Goss Hall St OLDE * OL4 ... 91 F1
Gotha Wk BRUN/LGST * M13 ... 127 H2
Gotherage Cl MPL/ROM SK6 ... 162 D4
Gotherage La MPL/ROM SK6 ... 162 D4
Gothic Cl MPL/ROM SK6 ... 163 E4
Gough St HTNM * SK4 ...
  HEY OL10 ...
Goulden Rd DID/WITH M20 ... 157 F1
Goulden St ANC M4 ...
  SLFD M6 ...
Goulder Rd GTN M18 ... 129 H5
Gould St ANC M4 ... 115 G2
  DTN/ASHW M34 ... 131 G5
  OLD OL1 ... 75 E4
Gourham Dr CHD/CHDH SK8 ...
Govan St WYTH/NTH M22 ... 156 D5
Gowan Dr MDTN M24 ... 71 G1
Gowanlock's St BOL BL1 ... 33 H4
Gowan Rd OLDTF/WHR M16 ... 140 B1
Gower Av BRAM/HZG SK7 ... 185 G5
Gowerdale Rd RDSH SK5 ... 160 D1
Gower Hey Gdns HYDE SK14 ... 147 G2
Gowers St MILN OL16 ... 11 J3
Gower St AUL * OL6 ... 118 B2
  BOL BL1 ...
  FWTH BL4 ... 64 D3
  HEY OL10 ...
  PWCH M25 ... 99 G2
Gowran Pk OLDE OL4 ... 92 B1
Gowy Cl WILM/AE SK9 ... 200 B1
Goya Rd MPL/ROM SK6 ...
Goyt Av MPL/ROM SK6 ... 175 F5
Goyt Crs MPL/ROM SK6 ... 163 E5
Goyt Hall MPL/ROM SK6 ... 161 H3
  STKP SK1 ... 13 G6
Goyt Rd MPL/ROM SK6 ... 175 G4
Goyt St MPL/ROM SK6 ... 175 G3
  MPL/ROM SK6 ... 175 G4
Goyt Valley Rd MPL/ROM SK6 ... 161 G4
Goyt Wy MPL/ROM SK6 ... 175 G4
  MPL/ROM SK6 ... 175 G4
Grace St WHIT OL12 ... 11 H1

Grace Wk ANC M4 114 A4
Gracie Av OLD OL1 75 E3
Gradwell St EDGY/DAV SK3 12 D5
Grafton Av ECC M30 110 B1
Grafton Ct MILN * OL16 30 C5
The Graftons ALT * WA14 165 G5
Grafton St ALT WA14 165 G5
AUL OL6 118 C3
BOL BL1 2 A3
BRUN/LGST M13 127 G3
BURY BL9 53 G1
FAIL M35 103 E2
HTNM SK4 159 H3
MILN OL16 30 C5
OLD OL1 60 D5
STLY SK15 120 A2
Graham Crs IRL M44 150 B2
Graham Dr POY/DIS SK12 187 H5
Graham Rd SLFD M6 110 D1
STKP SK1 172 C1
Graham St AULW OL7 117 G4
BOL * BL1 2 E2
OP/CLY M11 114 D5
Grainger Av WGTN/LGST M12 128 D5
Grains Rd ROY/SHW OL2 60 B2
UPML OL3 61 G4
Grain Vw ORD * M5 111 H5
Gralam Cl SALE M33 155 F5
Grammar School Rd OLDS OL8 89 G4
Grampian Cl CHAD OL9 89 F2
Grampian Wy ROY/SHW OL2 59 H1
Granada Ms OLDTF/WHR * M16 141 H2
Granada Rd DTN/ASHW M34 130 B5
Granary La WALK M28 108 C1
Granary Wy SALE M33 154 A4
Granby Rd CHD/CHDH SK8 183 E4
HALE/TIMP WA15 154 B5
OFTN SK2 172 C4
STRET M32 140 B2
SWIN M27 96 B3
Granby Rw CMANE M1 7 H7
Granby St CHAD OL9 89 F5
TOT/BURYW BL8 37 E2
Grandale St RUSH/FAL * M14 127 H5
Grand Central Sq
EDGY/DAV * SK3 13 F5
Grandidge St ROCH OL11 42 D1
Grand Union Wy ECC M30 109 G5
Granford Cl ALT * WA14 165 G2
The Grange HYDE SK14 148 A2
OLD * OL1 75 E4
RUSH/FAL M14 127 H5
Grange Av BNG/LEV M19 143 G3
BOLS/LL BL3 66 B1
CHD/CHDH SK8 182 C1
ECC M30 109 G1
HALE/TIMP WA15 166 C2
HALE/TIMP WA15 178 B2
HTNM SK4 159 F1
MILN OL16 44 C2
OLDS OL8 89 H3
STRET M32 140 A1
SWIN M27 82 C5
URM M41 137 F1
Grange Cl HYDE SK14 148 A2
Grange Ct OLDS * OL8 89 H3
Grange Crs URM M41 138 B2
Grange Dr BKLY M9 87 G4
ECC M30 109 G1
Grangeforth Rd CHH M8 100 A2
Grange Gv WHTF M45 68 C4
Grange La DID/WITH M20 157 G4
Grange Park Av AUL OL6 106 A4
CHD/CHDH SK8 170 A4
WILM/AE SK9 199 F2
Grangepark Rd BKLY M9 87 G4
Grange Park Rd BOLE BL2 23 H5
CHD/CHDH SK8 170 A4
Grange Pl IRL M44 150 C1
Grange Rd ALT WA14 177 F3
BOLE BL2 23 H4
BOLS/LL BL3 48 A4
BRAM/HZG SK7 184 A1
CCHDY M21 140 D1
ECC M30 108 C1
FWTH BL4 64 B3
HALE/TIMP WA15 166 C2
HYDE SK14 148 A2
MDTN M24 57 G3
SALE M33 154 A2
TOT/BURYW BL8 37 G4
URM M41 138 B2
WHIT OL12 14 C3
Grange Rd North HYDE SK14 148 A1
Grange Rd South HYDE SK14 148 A2
Grange St CHAD OL9 8 E2
FAIL M35 102 C4
SLFD M6 111 F3
Grangethorpe Dr BNG/LEV M19 143 F4
Grangethorpe Rd
RUSH/FAL M14 142 D1
URM M41 138 B2
Grangeway WILM/AE SK9 192 A3
Grangewood BOLE BL2 23 H4
Grangewood Dr BKLY M9 101 E3
Granite St OLD OL1 75 E4
Gransden Dr CHH M8 100 D4
Granshaw St NEWH/MOS M40 114 B2
Gransmoor Av OP/CLY M11 130 A1
Gransmoor Rd OP/CLY M11 130 A1
Grantchester Pl FWTH BL4 64 A3
Grantchester Wy BOLE BL2 35 F5
Grant Cl BKLY M9 87 E5
Grantham Cl BOL * BL1 33 H5
Grantham Dr TOT/BURYW BL8 38 A1
Grantham Rd HTNM SK4 12 B2
Grantham St OLDE OL4 9 K6
Grants La RAMS BL0 16 D2
Grant St FWTH BL4 64 C2
ROCH OL11 42 C4
Granville Av BRO M7 99 H2
Granville Cl CHAD OL9 8 A2
Granville Ct MILN OL16 45 E3
Granville Gdns DID/WITH M20 157 F4
Granville Rd BOLS/LL BL3 63 F1
CHD/CHDH SK8 171 F4
DTN/ASHW M34 116 C4
HALE/TIMP WA15 166 D3
RUSH/FAL M14 142 D3
URM M41 123 H5
WILM/AE SK9 199 E5
Granville St AUL OL6 118 C3
CHAD OL9 8 A1
ECC M30 109 G2
FWTH BL4 65 E3
OLD OL1 74 B3
WALK M28 80 D4
Granville Wk CHAD OL9 8 A1
Grasmere Av BOLS/LL BL3 50 D5
FWTH BL4 64 A5
HEY OL10 56 A1
HTNM SK4 144 D5
SWIN M27 82 B5
URM M41 137 F2
WHTF M45 67 H5
Grasmere Cl STLY SK15 119 F1
Grasmere Crs BRAM/HZG SK7 183 H4
ECC M30 109 E1
MPL/ROM SK6 186 D3
Grasmere Dr BURY BL9 53 H2
Grasmere Gv AULW OL7 117 G1
Grasmere Rd CHD/CHDH SK8 181 G1
HALE/TIMP WA15 166 D3
OLDE OL4 91 F1
PART M31 150 D3
ROY/SHW OL2 59 E3
SALE M33 154 D4
STRET M32 125 E5
SWIN M27 97 E4
WILM/AE SK9 201 B4
Grasmere St BOL BL1 34 A4
WGTN/LGST M12 129 E5
WHIT OL12 10 C2
Grasmere Wk MDTN M24 71 G2
Grason Av WILM/AE SK9 199 H1
Grasscroft RDSH SK5 145 H5
Grasscroft Cl RUSH/FAL M14 142 A1
Grasscroft Rd STLY SK15 119 F4
Grassfield Av BRO M7 99 F4
Grassholme Dr OFTN SK2 173 H4
Grassingham Gdns SLFD M6 111 G2
Grassington Av
NEWH/MOS M40 101 H1
Grassington Ct TOT/BURYW BL8 36 D2
Grassington Dr HEY OL10 39 G5
Grassington Pl BOL BL1 34 B5
Grass Md DTN/ASHW M34 146 D3
Gratrix Av ORD M5 126 A1
Gratrix La SALE M33 155 G3
Gratrix St GTN M18 129 H4
Gratten Ct WALK M28 80 D3
Gravel Bank Rd MPL/ROM SK6 147 E5
Gravel La CSLFD M3 6 D2
WILM/AE SK9 198 D5
Gravel Wks OLDE OL4 75 E5
Gravenmoor Dr BRO M7 99 H4
Graver La NEWH/MOS M40 102 C5
Gray Cl HYDE SK14 134 C5
Graymar Rd LHULT M38 80 B3
Graymarsh Dr POY/DIS SK12 195 F5
Graysands Rd HALE/TIMP WA15 178 A1
Grayson Av WHTF M45 68 D5
Grayson Rd LHULT M38 80 C3
Gray St BOL BL1 2 D2
Gray St North BOL BL1 2 D2
Graythorpe Wk ORD * M5 111 H4
Graythorp Wk RUSH/FAL M14 127 G5
Graythwaite Rd BOL BL1 32 C4
Grazing Dr IRL M44 121 C5
Greame St OLDTF/WHR M16 127 E5
Great Ancoats St ANC M4 7 H3
Great Bent Cl WHIT OL12 20 A4
Great Bridgewater St CMANW M2 6 D7
Great Cheetham St East BRO M7 99 H4
Great Cheetham St
West BRO M7 99 F5
Great Clowes St BRO M7 99 F4
Great Ducie St CHH M8 113 E1
CSLFD M3 6 E1
Great Eaves Rd RAMS BL0 16 D1
Great Egerton St STKP SK1 13 F2
Greatfield Rd WYTH/NTH M22 168 A5
Great Flatt WHIT OL12 29 E2
Great Gable Cl OLD OL1 74 D4
Great Gates Cl ROCH OL11 43 F2
Great Gates Rd ROCH OL11 43 F4
Great George St CSLFD M3 112 C3
MILN OL16 10 D7
Great Heaton Cl MDTN * M24 70 D5
Great Holme BOLS/LL BL3 64 A1
Great Howarth WHIT OL12 19 G4
Great Jackson St HULME M15 126 D1
Great John St CSLFD M3 6 B6
Great Jones St WGTN/LGST M12 128 D2
Great Lee WHIT OL12 18 C5
Great Lee Wk WHIT OL12 29 G1
Great Marlborough St
CMANE M1 6 E7
Great Marld Cl BOL BL1 32 C4
Great Meadow ROY/SHW OL2 44 C5
Great Moor St BOL BL1 2 E6
OFTN SK2 172 C4
Great Newton St
NEWH/MOS M40 102 B5
Great Norbury St HYDE SK14 147 G1
Great Portwood St STKP SK1 13 H1
Great Southern St
RUSH/FAL M14 127 G5
Great Stone Cl RAD * M26 66 C1
Great Stone Rd STRET M32 125 G4
Great Stones Cl EDGW/EG BL7 22 D1
Great St CMANE M1 113 H5
Great Underbank STKP SK1 13 F3
Great Western St
OLDTF/WHR M16 126 D4
Greave MPL/ROM SK6 162 C2
Greave Av ROCH OL11 29 E3
Greave Fold MPL/ROM SK6 162 B2
Greave Rd STKP SK1 172 D1
Greaves Av FAIL M35 102 D4
Greaves Rd WILM/AE SK9 198 D3
Greaves St MOSL OL5 92 C5
OLD OL1 9 G3
OLDE OL4 92 A1
ROY/SHW * OL2 60 B2
Greave St ROY/SHW OL2 60 B2
Grebe Cl POY/DIS SK12 194 C3
Grecian Crs BOLS/LL BL3 49 E5
Grecian St BRO M7 99 F5
Grecian St North BRO M7 99 F4
Grecian Ter BRO * M7 99 F5
Gredle Cl URM M41 139 E1
Greeba Rd NTHM/RTH M23 167 F3
Greek St CMANE * M1 127 G1
EDGY/DAV SK3 13 F6
The Green CHD/CHDH SK8 182 C4
HTNM SK4 12 A1
MPL/ROM SK6 187 F1
OLDS OL8 90 D4
ROCH OL11 42 B3
SWIN M27 83 G5
TOT/BURYW BL8 26 A2
WALK M28 95 G5
WILM/AE SK9 192 B4
Greenacre Cl RAMS BL0 17 F1
Greenacre La WALK M28 108 C1
Green Acre Pk BOL * BL1 34 A5
Greenacres Dr BNG/LEV M19 158 B2
Greenacres Rd OLDE OL4 75 F5
Green Av BOLS/LL BL3 64 C1
LHULT M38 79 D2
SWIN M27 97 E3
Green Bank BOLE BL2 35 F3
Greenbank Av CHD/CHDH SK8 169 F4
HTNM SK4 158 B4
SWIN * M27 96 C4
UPML OL3 78 B3
Greenbank Crs MPL/ROM SK6 175 E4
Greenbank Dr LIT OL15 20 C5
Greenbank Rd BOLS/LL BL3 48 A4
CHD/CHDH * SK8 169 F3
MPL/ROM SK6 163 G5
RAD M26 52 A4
SALE M33 153 H1
SLFD M6 111 F2
WHIT OL12 10 D2
Green Bank Ter HTNM SK4 13 F1
Greenbank Ter MDTN M24 72 B3
Greenbeech Cl MPL/ROM SK6 174 D2
Green Booth Cl DUK SK16 133 E1
Green Bridge Cl ROCH * OL11 43 E2
Greenbridge La UPML OL3 93 H2
Green Brook Cl BURY BL9 38 D2
Greenbrook St BURY BL9 38 D2
Greenbrow Rd NTHM/RTH M23 179 G1
Greenburn Dr BOLE BL2 35 F4
Green Cl CHD/CHDH SK8 169 F3
Greencourt Dr LHULT M38 80 A3
Green Cts ALT WA14 177 E1
Green Cft MPL/ROM SK6 162 C3
Greencroft Meadow
ROY/SHW OL2 59 G4
Greencroft Rd ECC M30 109 E1
Greendale Dr BKLY M9 87 F4
Greendale Gv DTN/ASHW M34 147 E3
Green Dr BNG/LEV M19 143 G2
HALE/TIMP WA15 166 B2
HOR/BR BL6 46 D2
WILM/AE SK9 192 A5
Green End BNG/LEV M19 158 B1
DTN/ASHW M34 147 E3
Green End Rd BNG/LEV M19 158 B1
Greenfield Av ECC M30 122 D1
URM M41 138 C1
Greenfield Cl EDGY/DAV SK3 171 H3
HALE/TIMP WA15 166 D3
TOT/BURYW BL8 37 F5
Greenfield Ct HEY OL10 41 E5
Greenfield La MILN OL16 20 A5
ROCH OL11 43 F2
ROY/SHW OL2 60 A3
Greenfield St DTN/ASHW M34 131 E1
HYDE SK14 147 G1
ROCH OL11 43 F2
Green Fold GTN M18 130 A2
Greenfold Av FWTH BL4 64 C5
Greenford Cl CHD/CHDH SK8 171 E5
Greenford Rd CHH M8 100 B3
Green Gables Cl CHD/CHDH SK8 181 G3
Greengate CSLFD M3 6 D2
HALE/TIMP WA15 179 E5
HYDE SK14 147 G3
MDTN M24 88 B2
Greengate Cl WHIT OL12 20 A4
Greengate East NEWH/MOS M40 88 B4
Greengate La BOLE BL2 50 C1
PWCH M25 84 D3
Greengate Rd DTN/ASHW M34 131 H4
Greengate St OLDE OL4 9 J6
Greengate West CSLFD M3 6 B1
Green Grove Bank MILN OL16 19 H5
Greenhalgh Moss La
TOT/BURYW BL8 37 G1
Greenhalgh St FAIL M35 102 B4
HTNM SK4 13 F1
Greenhalgh Wk ANC M4 7 K3
Green Hall Ms WILM/AE SK9 199 G4
Greenham Rd NTHM/RTH M23 155 G4
Greenhaven Cl WALK M28 81 G4
Greenheys BOLE BL2 35 F3
DROY M43 116 B3
Greenheys Crs TOT/BURYW BL8 25 H2
Greenheys La HULME M15 127 E3
Greenheys La West
HULME M15 127 E3
Greenheys Rd LHULT M38 79 D1
Greenhill PWCH M25 84 D3
Greenhill Av BOLS/LL BL3 48 A4
FWTH BL4 64 D5
ROY/SHW OL2 44 B5
SALE M33 139 F5
WHIT OL12 10 A4
Greenhill Pas OLD OL1 9 J3
Green Hill Rd HYDE SK14 133 E5
Greenhill Rd CHH M8 100 B3
HALE/TIMP WA15 166 D3
MDTN M24 72 B5
TOT/BURYW BL8 37 F5
Green Hill St EDGY/DAV SK3 12 C7
Green Hill Ter EDGY/DAV SK3 12 C7
Greenhill Ter OLDE OL4 9 J5
Green Hollow STLY SK15 120 A1
Greenholm Cl NEWH/MOS M40 102 C1
Greenhow St DROY M43 116 A5
Greenhurst Crs OLDS OL8 90 D5
Greenhurst La AUL OL6 105 H4
Greenhurst Rd AUL OL6 105 G3
Greenhythe Rd CHD/CHDH SK8 191 H1
Greening Rd BNG/LEV M19 144 A1
Greenland Rd BOLS/LL BL3 64 A2
Greenland St CHH M8 100 A3
SLFD * M6 111 F3
Green La AUL OL6 105 E5
BOLS/LL BL3 64 A1
BRAM/HZG SK7 185 E1
ECC M30 109 F3
FAIL M35 115 H1
FWTH BL4 65 H5
GTN M18 129 G2
HALE/TIMP WA15 166 C5
HEY OL10 41 F4
HEY * OL10 56 B1
HTNM SK4 12 C2
HYDE SK14 148 B2
IRL M44 150 C1
MDTN M24 72 A3
MDTN M24 72 C5
MPL/ROM SK6 162 A5
OLDE OL4 76 B2
OLDS OL8 90 B5
POY/DIS SK12 196 B3
SALE M33 138 D5
WHIT * OL12 10 B4
WHTF M45 68 C3
WILM/AE SK9 199 G3
WILM/AE SK9 201 A5
Green La North
HALE/TIMP WA15 166 C5
Greenlea Av GTN M18 129 G5
Greenleach La WALK M28 95 G2
Greenleaf Cl WALK M28 94 A4
Greenleas HOR/BR BL6 46 D3
Greenlees St WHIT OL12 10 C4
Greenleigh Cl BOL BL1 33 G1
Green Meadow WHIT OL12 20 A4
Green Mdw MPL/ROM SK6 175 E2
Green Meadows Dr
MPL/ROM SK6 175 E2
Green Meadows Wk
WYTH/NTH M22 180 D3
Greenmount Cl TOT/BURYW BL8 26 A1
Greenmount Ct BOL BL1 47 H1
Greenmount Dr HEY OL10 56 C2
TOT/BURYW BL8 16 A5
Greenmount La BOL BL1 47 G1
Greenmount Pk FWTH BL4 81 H1
Greenoak RAD M26 66 B5
Greenoak Dr SALE M33 154 D5
WALK M28 80 D2
Greenock Cl BOLS/LL BL3 47 F4
Greenpark Cl TOT/BURYW BL8 25 H2
Greenpark Rd WYTH/NTH M22 156 C5
Green Park Vw OLD * OL1 75 E4
OLD OL1 75 G2
Green Pastures HTNM SK4 158 B5
Green Rd PART M31 150 D3
Greenroyd Av BOLE BL2 35 F4
Greenroyde ROCH * OL11 42 D1
The Greens WHIT OL12 14 B4
Greenshank Cl ROCH * OL11 28 C4
Greenside WALK M28 95 H5
Greenside Av FWTH BL4 81 G1
OLDE OL4 75 G2
Greenside Cl DUK SK16 119 F5
Greenside Crs DROY M43 116 A2
Greenside Dr HALE/TIMP WA15 177 H3
IRL M44 136 A2
TOT/BURYW BL8 25 H3
Greenside La DROY M43 115 H2
Greenside Pl DTN/ASHW * M34 146 D3
Greenside St BOLE BL2 36 B5
OP/CLY M11 115 E4
Greenside Wy MDTN M24 88 B2
Green & Slater Homes
HTNM * SK4 158 D3
Greenson Dr MDTN M24 71 F5
Greenstead Av CHH M8 100 B2
Greenstone Dr SLFD M6 98 C5
Green St BOL BL1 3 F4
ECC M30 109 E5
EDGY/DAV SK3 172 A3
FWTH BL4 64 D3
HYDE SK14 147 H2
OLDS OL8 8 D5
RAD M26 67 F1
RUSH/FAL M14 143 F4
STRET M32 139 H3
TOT/BURYW BL8 37 E2
WILM/AE SK9 201 B4
Greenthorne Av HTNM SK4 144 C4
Green Tree Gdns MPL/ROM SK6 162 A4
Greenvale ROCH OL11 28 A3
Greenvale Dr CHD/CHDH SK8 169 H3
Greenview Dr DID/WITH M20 169 H1
ROCH OL11 28 C3
Green Wk ALT WA14 176 D1
CHD/CHDH SK8 169 F3
HALE/TIMP WA15 166 A2
OLDTF/WHR M16 141 F1
STRET M32 139 G1
Green Wks PWCH M25 85 F4
Greenwatch Cl ECC M30 109 F4
Green Wy BOL BL1 34 C3
ROCH OL11 42 A5
Greenway ALT WA14 164 D4
BRAM/HZG SK7 193 G1
HYDE SK14 147 G2
MDTN M24 87 F2
MPL/ROM SK6 162 D5
ROY/SHW OL2 44 C5
WILM/AE SK9 199 F4
WYTH/NTH M22 168 D1
Greenway Av BNG/LEV M19 144 A3
Green Way Cl BOL BL1 34 B2
Greenway Cl SALE M33 153 G3
TOT/BURYW BL8 37 G3
Greenway Dr MOSL OL5 92 D5
Greenway Rd CHD/CHDH SK8 191 H1
HALE/TIMP WA15 166 A1
Greenways AULW OL7 104 C4
NEWH/MOS M40 102 C1
Greenwich Cl NEWH/MOS M40 115 G1
ROCH OL11 28 C5
Greenwood Av AUL OL6 105 F4
LHULT M38 80 D4
OFTN SK2 172 D3
SWIN M27 97 G1
Greenwood Cl
HALE/TIMP WA15 167 E4
Greenwood Dr WILM/AE SK9 200 A2
Greenwood Rd WYTH/NTH M22 168 A5
Greenwoods La BOLE BL2 35 G2
Greenwood St ALT WA14 165 G5
FWTH BL4 65 E4
LIT OL15 21 E3
MILN OL16 10 D7
OLDE OL4 75 F4
OLDS * OL8 104 C1
SLFD M6 111 G1
Greenwood V BOL BL1 33 H3
Greenwood V South BOL * BL1 34 A3
Greer St OP/CLY M11 115 F5
Greetland Dr BKLY M9 87 G3
Gregge St HEY OL10 41 F5
Greg Ms WILM/AE SK9 191 G5
Gregory Av BOLE BL2 50 B1
MPL/ROM SK6 162 A5
Gregory St OLDS OL8 89 H4
WGTN/LGST M12 128 C2
Gregory Wy RDSH SK5 145 E5
Gregson Fld BOLS/LL BL3 48 D5
Gregson Rd RDSH SK5 144 D5
Gregson St OLD OL1 9 H4
Greg St RDSH SK5 144 D5
Grelley Wk RUSH/FAL M14 127 G5
Grendale Av BRAM/HZG SK7 185 F3
STKP SK1 160 C5
Grendon Av OLDS OL8 90 B4
Grendon St BOLS/LL BL3 63 F1
Grendon Wk WGTN/LGST M12 128 D2
Grenfell Rd DID/WITH M20 157 F3
Grenham Av HULME M15 126 C2
Grenville Rd BRAM/HZG SK7 184 D1
Grenville St DUK SK16 118 B5
EDGY/DAV SK3 12 C5
STLY SK15 120 A1
Gresford Cl CCHDY M21 140 D3
Gresham Cl WHTF M45 68 A5
Gresham Dr CHAD OL9 8 B3
Gresham St BOL BL1 34 A3
DTN/ASHW M34 131 G4
Gresham Wk HTNM SK4 159 H3
Gresty Av WYTH/NTH M22 181 E3
Greswell St DTN/ASHW M34 131 F4
Greta Av CHD/CHDH SK8 191 H1
Greton Cl BRUN/LGST M13 128 B4
Gretton Cl ROY/SHW OL2 59 G5
Greville St BRUN/LGST M13 128 B5
Grey Cl MPL/ROM SK6 161 H2
Greyfriars Rd WYTH/NTH M22 180 A2
Greyhound Dr SLFD M6 99 E5
Grey Knotts WALK M28 94 B5
Greylag Crs WALK M28 95 E2
Greylands Cl SALE M33 153 H2
Greylands Rd DID/WITH M20 169 H1
Grey Mare La OP/CLY M11 114 D4
Greymont Rd BURY BL9 27 G5
Grey Rd ALT WA14 165 F4
Greystoke Av BNG/LEV M19 144 B2
HALE/TIMP WA15 167 E3
SALE M33 154 C3
Greystoke Crs WHTF M45 68 B2
Greystoke Dr BOL BL1 22 C5
MDTN M24 71 E2
WILM/AE SK9 201 B3
Greystoke La FAIL M35 102 C4
Greystoke St STKP SK1 13 K4
Greystone Av OLDTF/WHR M16 142 A3
Grey St AUL OL6 118 B3
DTN/ASHW M34 131 E5
MDTN M24 71 G3
PWCH M25 85 F3
STLY SK15 119 H4
WGTN/LGST M12 128 B2
Greyswood Av CHH M8 100 A4
Greytown Cl SLFD M6 98 C5
Greywood Av BURY BL9 5 K4
Grierson St BOL BL1 33 H3
OLDTF/WHR M16 126 D4
Griffe La BURY BL9 54 B5
Griffin Cl BURY BL9 5 H1
Griffin Ct CSLFD * M3 6 B3
Griffin Gv BNG/LEV M19 143 H3
Griffin La CHD/CHDH SK8 182 A5
Griffin Rd FAIL M35 102 C3
Griffin St BRO M7 99 F4
Griffiths Cl BRO * M7 112 C1
Griffiths St NEWH/MOS M40 102 B5
Grimes St WHIT OL12 28 C2
Grime St RAMS BL0 16 B4
Grimscott Cl BKLY * M9 101 G1
Grimshaw Av FAIL M35 103 F2
Grimshaw Cl MPL/ROM SK6 161 H2
Grimshaw La MDTN M24 72 A5
NEWH/MOS M40 101 G5
Grimshaw St FAIL * M35 102 D2
STKP SK1 13 K3
Grimstead Cl NTHM/RTH M23 167 F3
Grindall Av BKLY M9 88 A5
Grindley Av CCHDY M21 156 C1
Grindlow St BRUN/LGST M13 128 B3
Grindon Av BRO M7 98 D3
Grindrod St RAD M26 52 B5
Grindsbrook Rd RAD M26 52 A2
Grinton Av BRUN/LGST M13 143 F1
Grisdale Dr MDTN M24 71 F2
Grisdale Rd BOLS/LL BL3 48 B4
Grisebeck Wy OLD OL1 9 F2
Grisedale Av ROY/SHW OL2 58 D1
Grisedale Rd ROCH OL11 42 A2
Gristlehurst La BURY BL9 40 A1
Grizebeck Cl GTN M18 129 F2
Grizedale Cl BOL BL1 32 C4
STLY SK15 107 F3
Grizedale Rd MPL/ROM SK6 162 A2
Groby Rd ALT WA14 165 F5
CCHDY M21 141 E3
DTN/ASHW M34 131 F1
Groby Rd North
DTN/ASHW M34 117 E5
Groby St OLDS OL8 90 C4
STLY SK15 119 H4
Groom St CMANE M1 127 G1
The Grove ALT * WA14 165 G4
BOLE BL2 49 G4
BOLS/LL BL3 66 A1
CHD/CHDH SK8 192 D1
DID/WITH M20 157 G5
ECC M30 110 A4
EDGY/DAV SK3 171 H2
ROY/SHW OL2 59 H3
SALE M33 154 C3
UPML OL3 77 G3
URM M41 137 G2
Grosvenor Av WHTF M45 68 B4
Grosvenor Cl WALK M28 80 D2
WILM/AE SK9 201 B1
Grosvenor Ct AULW OL7 117 H4
CHD/CHDH SK8 170 A3
Grosvenor Crs HYDE SK14 147 F2
Grosvenor Dr POY/DIS SK12 194 D4
WALK M28 80 D2
Grosvenor Gdns BRO M7 112 C1
STLY * SK15 119 F4
WYTH/NTH M22 168 D3
Grosvenor Pl AULW * OL7 117 H4
Grosvenor Rd ALT WA14 165 H3
CHD/CHDH SK8 171 F5
ECC M30 108 D2
HTNM SK4 158 D3

HYDE SK14 ...147 G2
MPL/ROM SK6 ...175 E2
OLDTF/WHR M16 ...141 C1
SALE M33 ...154 A1
SWIN M27 ...97 G3
URM M41 ...138 B1
WALK M28 ...80 D2
WHTF M45 ...68 B5
Grosvenor Sq BRO M7 ...112 C1
SALE M33 ...154 A2
Grosvenor St AULW OL7 ...117 H4
BOLE BL2 ...
BOLS/LL BL3 ...50 D5
BRAM/HZG SK7 ...185 E1
BURY BL9 ...53 C1
CMANE M1 ...127 G1
DTN/ASHW M34 ...131 E4
FWTH BL4 ...65 G4
HEY OL10 ...40 C5
PWCH M25 ...85 F1
RAD M26 ...52 A5
ROCH OL11 ...42 B5
STKP SK1 ...13 G6
STLY SK15 ...119 F4
STRET M32 ...140 A1
SWIN M27 ...83 E5
Grosvenor Wy ROY/SHW OL2 ...74 A2
Grotton Hollow OLDE OL4 ...92 C1
Grotton Mdw OLDE OL4 ...92 C1
Grouse St WHIT OL12 ...10 C2
Grove Av FAIL M35 ...102 D5
WILM/AE SK9 ...199 F3
Grove CI RUSH/FAL M14 ...127 H5
Grove Ct BRAM/HZG * SK7 ...185 E2
SALE M33 ...155 E2
Grove HI WALK M28 ...94 A4
Grovehurst SWIN M27 ...96 A4
Grove La CHD/CHDH SK8 ...192 D7
DID/WITH M20 ...157 C4
HALE/TIMP WA15 ...166 B3
HALE/TIMP WA15 ...178 B1
Grove Ms WALK * M28 ...81 G4
Grove Rd HALE/TIMP WA15 ...177 H1
MDTN M24 ...72 A2
STLY SK15 ...120 A1
UPML OL3 ...78 A5
Grove Spring WHTF M45 ...68 B2
Grove St AULW OL7 ...104 B5
BOL BL1 ...33 G4
BRAM/HZG * SK7 ...185 F1
BRO M7 ...99 H6
DROY M43 ...116 A5
DUK SK16 ...118 C4
FWTH BL4 ...65 F4
HEY OL10 ...41 F4
OLD OL1 ...9 E2
ROCH OL11 ...42 D3
WILM/AE * SK9 ...199 G3
Grove Wy WILM/AE SK9 ...199 G3
Grovewood CI ANC M4 ...
Grundy Av PWCH M25 ...84 B5
Grundy CI BURY * BL9 ...53 F1
Grundy Rd FWTH BL4 ...
Grundy St BOLS/LL BL3 ...48 C5
HEY OL10 ...56 B1
HTNM SK4 ...158 B4
WALK M28 ...81 G4
Guardian Av NTHM/RTH * M23 ...154 D5
Guernsey CI BNG/LEV * M19 ...143 H5
Guest Rd PWCH M25 ...84 D1
Guide La DTN/ASHW M34 ...117 F5
Guide Post Sq
BRUN/LGST * M13 ...128 A2
Guide Post St BRUN/LGST M13 ...128 A2
Guide St BOL BL1 ...33 G4
M ...32 ...
FAIL M35 ...
Guild Av WALK M28 ...81 E5
Guildford Av CHD/CHDH SK8 ...192 D1
Guildford Cl STKP SK1 ...172 C2
Guildford Dr AUL OL6 ...105 E3
Guildford Gv MDTN M24 ...72 B1
Guildford Rd BNG/LEV M19 ...144 A1
BOL BL1 ...33 E4
DUK SK16 ...133 F1
OLD OL1 ...
URM M41 ...123 H4
Guildford St MILN * M15 ...10 E7
Guildhall Cl HULME M15 ...127 F3
Guild St EDGW/EG BL7 ...23 C5
Guilford Rd ECC M30 ...109 E4
Guinness Rd TRPK M17 ...110 B5
Guiseley Cl BURY BL9 ...27 F3
Gullane Cl NEWH/MOS M40 ...102 B3
Gull Cl POY/DIS SK12 ...194 C4
Gulvain Pl CHAD OL9 ...73 E4
Gunson St NEWH/MOS M40 ...113 H2
Gun St ANC M4 ...7 J3
Gurner Av ORD M5 ...126 A4
Gurney St ANC M4 ...114 A4
Gutter La RAMS BL0 ...16 C1
Guy Fawkes St ORD M5 ...126 A1
Guy St BRO M7 ...100 A3
Guywood La MPL/ROM SK6 ...162 B3
Gwelo St OP/CLY M11 ...114 D3
Gwenbury Av STKP SK1 ...160 C5
Gwendor Av CHH M8 ...86 A4
Gwladys St STLY SK15 ...107 F4
Gvlden Cl PYCH OL16 ...11 ...
Gypsy La OFTN SK2 ...173 E3
ROCH OL11 ...42 B3
Gyte's La BNG/LEV M19 ...144 B1

H

Habergham Cl WALK M28 ...94 D3
Hackberry Cl ALT WA14 ...165 E1
Hacken Bridge Rd BOLS/LL BL3 ...50 A5
Hacken La BOLS/LL BL3 ...49 H5
Hackford Cl BOL BL1 ...48 A1
TOT/BURYW BL8 ...38 A1
Hacking St BRO M7 ...99 H4
BURY BL9 ...5 G5
Hackle St OP/CLY M11 ...115 F5
Hackleton Cl ANC M4 ...114 A4
Hackness Rd OP/CLY M11 ...130 C5
Hackney Av NEWH/MOS M40 ...115 F1
Hackney Cl RAD M26 ...52 B4

Haddington Dr BKLY M9 ...87 F4
Haddon Av NEWH/MOS M40 ...102 D1
Haddon Cl BURY BL9 ...53 H4
MPL/ROM SK6 ...196 D1
WILM/AE SK9 ...201 H3
Haddon Gv HALE/TIMP WA15 ...166 A4
RDSH SK5 ...144 D4
SALE M33 ...154 B3
Haddon Hall Rd DROY M43 ...115 H3
Haddon Rd BRAM/HZG SK7 ...185 F3
CCHDY M21 ...156 C1
CHD/CHDH SK8 ...181 H5
ECC M30 ...109 F5
SWIN M27 ...96 B5
Haddon St ROCH OL11 ...42 D1
SLFD M6 ...
STRET M32 ...
Hadleigh Cl BOL BL1 ...23 F5
Hadley Av BRUN/LGST M13 ...143 F1
Hadley Cl CHD/CHDH SK8 ...182 C5
Hadley St SLFD M6 ...99 E5
Hadlow Wk NEWH/MOS * M40 ...114 B2
Hadwin St BOL BL1 ...2 E1
Hafton Rd BRO M7 ...99 E4
Haggate ROY/SHW OL2 ...73 H1
Haggate Rd OLDE OL4 ...73 H1
Hagley Rd ORD M5 ...
The Hags BURY BL9 ...53 H4
Hague Rd DID/WITH M20 ...157 F1
Hague St AUL OL6 ...118 B1
NEWH/MOS M40 ...101 G5
OLDE OL4 ...75 H4
Haig Av IRL M44 ...150 B2
Haig Ct TOT/BURYW BL8 ...37 G5
Haigh Av HTNM SK4 ...159 H1
Haigh Hall Cl RAMS BL0 ...16 C4
Haigh La CHAD OL1 ...70 B2
Haigh Pk HTNM SK4 ...159 H1
Haigh St BOL BL1 ...2 E2
ROCH OL11 ...30 B5
Haig Rd STRET M32 ...125 E5
TOT/BURYW BL8 ...37 G4
Haile Dr WALK M28 ...94 A4
Hailsham Cl TOT/BURYW BL8 ...26 A4
Hall St RAMS * BL0 ...16 C4
Halbury Wk BOL * BL1 ...34 A4
Haldon Rd DID/WITH M20 ...158 A1
Hale Av POY/DIS SK12 ...195 E5
Hale La FAIL M35 ...102 D2
Hale Low Rd HALE/TIMP WA15 ...178 A1
Hale Rd HALE/TIMP WA15 ...177 H1
HTNM SK4 ...159 F5
Hales Cl DROY M43 ...116 A2
Halesden Rd HTNM SK4 ...159 G1
Halesworth Wk
NEWH/MOS * M40 ...113 H4
Hale Vw ALT * WA14 ...177 G2
Haley Cl RDSH SK5 ...145 H3
Haley St CHH M8 ...100 B3
Half Acre Dr ROCH OL11 ...29 E5
Half Acre La ROCH OL11 ...29 E5
Half Acre Ms ROCH OL11 ...29 E5
Halfacre Rd WYTH/NTH M22 ...168 B5
Half Edge La ECC M30 ...110 A2
Half Moon La OFTN SK2 ...173 F5
Halford St NEWH/MOS M40 ...113 H4
Halifax Rd MILN OL16 ...11 G2
MILN OL16 ...20 A5
Halifax St AUL OL6 ...118 A1
Hallas Gv NTHM/RTH M23 ...156 A5
Hall Av HALE/TIMP WA15 ...166 A2
RUSH/FAL M14 ...128 B5
SALE M33 ...138 D5
STLY SK15 ...106 D5
Hall Bank ECC M30 ...109 F3
Hallbottom St HYDE SK14 ...133 E5
Hall Cl HYDE SK14 ...134 D3
The Hall Coppice EDGW/EG BL7 ...22 C2
Hallcroft PART M31 ...151 E2
Hallcroft Gdns MILN OL16 ...31 F5
Hall Dr HYDE SK14 ...147 H1
MDTN M24 ...71 G5
Hall Farm Av URM M41 ...123 H4
Hall Farm Cl BRAM/HZG SK7 ...185 H1
Hall Fold WHIT OL12 ...14 B1
Hall Gdns WHIT OL12 ...29 F1
Hallgate Dr CHD/CHDH SK8 ...181 F2
Hallgate Rd STKP SK1 ...172 C1
Hall Green Cl DUK * SK16 ...118 B4
Hall Green Rd DUK SK16 ...118 B4
Hall Gv RUSH/FAL M14 ...142 B1
Halliday Rd NEWH/MOS M40 ...115 E1
Halliford Rd NEWH/MOS M40 ...114 B5
Hallington Cl BOLS/LL BL3 ...49 E5
Hall i' Th' Wood La BOL BL1 ...34 B2
Halliwell Av OLDS OL8 ...91 H4
Halliwell La CHH M8 ...100 A3
Halliwell Rd BOL BL1 ...33 G4
OLDS OL8 ...91 H4
Halliwell St BOL * BL1 ...33 G4
CHAD * OL9 ...
MILN OL16 ...31 F4
Halliwell St West CHH * M8 ...100 A4
Hall La FWTH BL4 ...65 E2
MPL/ROM SK6 ...147 E5
NTHM/RTH M23 ...168 A3
PART M31 ...151 E4
Hall Meadow CHD/CHDH SK8 ...182 B3
Hall Moss La BRAM/HZG SK7 ...193 E3
Hall Moss Rd BKLY M9 ...87 H1
Hallows Av CCHDY M21 ...156 B1
Hallows Farm Av WHIT OL12 ...29 G1
Hall Pool Dr OFTN SK2 ...173 F2
Hall Rd ALT WA14 ...177 F3
AUL OL6 ...107 H5
BRAM/HZG SK7 ...183 G5
RUSH/FAL M14 ...128 A5

WILM/AE SK9 ...192 B4
WILM/AE SK9 ...199 F3
Hallroyd Brow OLD * OL1 ...74 A4
Hallstead Av LHULT M38 ...79 D3
Hallstead Gv LHULT M38 ...79 D3
Halls St AUL OL6 ...118 C3
BURY BL9 ...26 C1
CHD/CHDH SK8 ...170 A3
CMANW M2 ...6 E6
FAIL M35 ...102 C4
FWTH BL4 ...65 E2
HEY OL10 ...41 E5
HYDE SK14 ...132 A5
MDTN * M24 ...71 H4
OLDE OL4 ...76 A6
RAD M26 ...52 A3
ROY/SHW OL2 ...59 H3
SWIN M27 ...83 E5
TOT/BURYW BL8 ...36 D1
TOT/BURYW BL8 ...37 H2
WHIT OL12 ...14 B5
Hallsville Rd BNG/LEV M19 ...144 B2
Halls Wy UPML OL3 ...95 H1
Hallsworth Rd ECC M30 ...108 D4
Hallwood Av SLFD M6 ...99 H1
Hallwood Rd NTHM/RTH M23 ...167 H5
Hall Wood Rd WILM/AE SK9 ...192 A5
Hallworth Av DTN/ASHW M34 ...118 A5
Hallworth Rd CHH M8 ...100 C2
Halmore Rd NEWH/MOS M40 ...114 A3
Halsall Cl BURY * BL9 ...27 G5
Halsall Dr BOLS/LL BL3 ...63 H3
Halsbury Cl WGTN/LGST M12 ...128 B2
Halsey Cl CHAD OL9 ...88 D4
Halshaw La FWTH BL4 ...65 G5
Halsmere Dr BKLY M9 ...87 F4
Halstead Av CCHDY M21 ...141 H4
SLFD M6 ...98 B5
Halstead Dr IRL M44 ...136 C1
Halstead Gv CHD/CHDH SK8 ...169 E4
Halstead St BOLE BL2 ...3 H5
BURY BL9 ...38 D1
Halstead Wk BURY * BL9 ...38 D1
Halstock Wk NEWH/MOS M40 ...101 G5
Halston Cl RDSH SK5 ...160 A2
Halston St HULME M15 ...126 D2
Halton Bank SLFD M6 ...111 C1
Halton Dr HALE/TIMP WA15 ...154 C5
Halton Rd OP/CLY M11 ...115 F3
Halton St BOLE BL2 ...3 K6
Halvard Av BURY BL9 ...27 G5
Halvard Ct BURY BL9 ...27 G5
Halvin Gv OLDTF/WHR M16 ...126 A5
Hambledon Cl BOLS/LL BL3 ...47 E5
Hambleton Cl TOT/BURYW BL8 ...37 E5
Hambleton Dr SALE M33 ...153 G1
Hambleton Rd CHD/CHDH SK8 ...181 H4
Hambridge Cl CHH M8 ...100 B3
Hamel St BOLS/LL BL3 ...64 A1
HYDE SK14 ...133 E5
Hamer Dr OLDTF/WHR M16 ...126 A3
Hamer Hall Crs WHIT OL12 ...11 H1
Hamer Hl BKLY M9 ...86 D4
Hamer La MILN OL16 ...11 G1
Hamer St BOLE BL2 ...34 C5
HEY OL10 ...40 C4
NEWH/MOS M40 ...113 H2
RAMS BL0 ...17 G2
Hamerton Rd NEWH/MOS M40 ...113 H1
Hamilcar Av ECC M30 ...109 H5
Hamilton Av IRL M44 ...150 C2
ROY/SHW OL2 ...59 E4
Hamilton Cl PWCH M25 ...84 D4
Hamilton Crs HTNM SK4 ...159 E5
Hamilton Gv OLDTF/WHR M16 ...126 D3
Hamilton Ms FCC * M30 ...109 E2
PWCH * M25 ...84 D4
Hamilton Rd BRUN/LGST M13 ...128 C5
NEWH/MOS M40 ...114 A1
PART M31 ...150 D4
WHTF M45 ...68 B4
Hamilton Sq HTNM SK4 ...159 H5
Hamilton St AULW OL7 ...117 G4
BOL BL1 ...33 H2
BRO * M7 ...99 H6
BURY BL9 ...38 C2
CHAD OL9 ...73 F5
ECC M30 ...109 E2
OLDTF/WHR M16 ...126 C3
STLY SK15 ...119 E3
SWIN M27 ...96 C1
Hamilton Wy HEY OL10 ...39 H5
Hamlet Dr SALE M33 ...153 E3
Hammerstone Rd GTN M18 ...129 F2
Hammett Rd CCHDY M21 ...140 D3
Hammond Av HTNM SK4 ...159 H1
Hamnate Dr BKLY M9 ...86 C3
Hamnett St HYDE * SK14 ...147 G1
OP/CLY M11 ...115 G4
Hamon Rd HALE/TIMP WA15 ...165 H5
Hampden Crs GTN M18 ...129 F3
Hampden Gv ECC M30 ...109 H3
Hampden PI PWCH M25 ...
Hampden Rd PWCH M25 ...84 D4
ROY/SHW OL2 ...60 C5
SALE M33 ...154 B3
Hampshire St HEY OL10 ...41 E5
Hampshire Cl BURY BL9 ...53 H1
Hampshire Rd CHAD OL9 ...116 B2
DROY M43 ...150 C4
PART M31 ...150 C4
RDSH SK5 ...160 C1
Hampshire St BRO M7 ...100 A5
Hampson Cl ECC M30 ...109 E4
Hampson Crs WILM/AE SK9 ...191 G5
Hampson Fold RAD M26 ...52 A5
Hampson Mill La BURY BL9 ...53 G5
Hampson Rd AUL OL6 ...105 H4
STRET M32 ...139 H1
Hampson St DROY M43 ...116 B3
ECC M30 ...109 G4
NEWH/MOS * M40 ...
ORD M5 ...
RAD M26 ...67 F1
SALE M33 ...155 C2
SWIN M27 ...98 C1
SWIN M27 ...83 E5
Hampstead Av URM M41 ...137 G2
Hampstead Dr OFTN SK2 ...172 D4
Hampstead La OFTN SK2 ...172 D4
Hampton Gv ALT WA14 ...153 H5

BURY BL9 ...27 G5
CHD/CHDH SK8 ...182 B2
Hampton Rd BOLS/LL BL3 ...64 B1
CCHDY M21 ...140 C2
FAIL M35 ...103 F2
IRL M44 ...149 E2
URM M41 ...138 C2
Hampton St OLDS OL8 ...90 A3
Hamsell Rd BRUN/LGST M13 ...127 H1
Hancock Cl RUSH/FAL M14 ...127 G5
Hancock St STRET M32 ...140 A3
Handel Av URM M41 ...137 H1
Handel Ms SALE M33 ...154 D2
Handel St BOL BL1 ...33 G3
Handforth Gv BRUN/LGST M13 ...143 G1
Handforth Rd BRAM/HZG SK5 ...160 A1
WILM/AE SK9 ...200 B1
Handley Av RUSH/FAL M14 ...142 C2
Handley CI EDGY/DAV SK3 ...171 F4
Handley Rd BRAM/HZG SK7 ...185 E1
Handley St BURY BL9 ...53 C1
WHIT OL12 ...29 G3
Hands worth St
WGTN/LGST M12 ...128 A1
Hanging Chadder La
ROY/SHW OL2 ...58 D2
Hankinson Cl PART M31 ...150 D4
Hankinson Wy SLFD M6 ...111 H2
Hanley Cl MDTN M24 ...87 H2
Hanlith Ms BNG/LEV M19 ...143 G3
Hanlon St CHH M8 ...100 A2
Hannah Baldwin Cl
OP/CLY M11 ...114 C5
Hannah St WGTN/LGST M12 ...143 H1
Hannerton Rd ROY/SHW OL2 ...60 C1
Hannesburg Gdns
NTHM/RTH * M23 ...167 G5
Hannet Rd WYTH/NTH M22 ...180 C5
Hanover Ct BRO M7 ...99 G3
WALK * M28 ...96 A4
Hanover Crs RUSH/FAL M14 ...128 A4
Hanover Gdns BRO M7 ...99 H2
Hanover Rd ALT WA14 ...165 E2
Hanover St ANC M4 ...7 F2
BOL BL1 ...2 C5
LIT OL15 ...20 D6
MOSL OL5 ...92 D5
ROCH OL11 ...42 B4
STLY SK15 ...119 E3
Hanover St North
DTN/ASHW M34 ...117 F5
Hanover St South
DTN/ASHW M34 ...117 F5
Hansdon CI CHH M8 ...100 B4
Hanson Cl MDTN M24 ...71 H5
Hanson Ms STRET M32 ...160 C4
Hanson Pk MDTN * M24 ...72 B4
Hanson Rd NEWH/MOS M40 ...101 H5
Hanson St BURY BL9 ...38 C2
MDTN M24 ...72 B4
OLDE OL4 ...75 F5
Hanworth CI BRUN/LGST M13 ...127 G1
Hapton Av STRET M32 ...138 A2
Hapton PI HTNM * SK4 ...159 H4
Hapton St BNG/LEV M19 ...143 H2
Harbern Cl ECC M30 ...109 C1
Harbord St BRUN/LGST M13 ...127 H1
Harboro Gv SALE M33 ...154 A2
Harboro Rd SALE M33 ...154 A2
Harboro Wy SALE * M33 ...154 A2
Harbour Farm Rd HYDE SK14 ...132 D3
Harbour La North MILN OL16 ...31 G5
Harbourne Av WALK M28 ...94 D2
Harbourne Cl WALK M28 ...94 D2
Harbury Cl BOLS/LL BL3 ...62 D1
Harbury Crs WYTH/NTH M22 ...168 B4
Harcles Dr RAMS BL0 ...26 C1
Harcombe Rd DID/WITH M20 ...142 D5
Harcourt Av URM M41 ...139 E2
Harcourt Cl URM M41 ...139 E2
Harcourt Rd ALT WA14 ...165 G5
SALE M33 ...139 F5
Harcourt St OLD OL1 ...75 E4
RDSH SK5 ...145 E3
STRET M32 ...125 F5
WALK M28 ...81 H4
Hardberry PI OFTN SK2 ...173 E5
Hardcastle Cl BOLE BL2 ...23 H5
Hardcastle Gdns BOLE BL2 ...
Hardcastle Rd EDGY/DAV SK3 ...171 G2
Hardcastle St BOL BL1 ...34 A4
Harden Dr BOLE BL2 ...34 C2
Harden Hills ROY/SHW OL2 ...60 C1
Hardfield Rd MDTN M24 ...87 H2
Hardfield St HEY OL10 ...41 E4
Hardicker St BNG/LEV M19 ...144 A4
Hardie Av FWTH BL4 ...65 E3
Harding St ANC M4 ...114 A4
SLFD M6 ...111 H1
SLFD M6 ...111 H1
STKP SK1 ...172 D3
Hardman Av MPL/ROM SK6 ...161 H5
PWCH M25 ...85 G5
Hardman Cl RAD M26 ...52 A5
Hardman La FAIL M35 ...102 D3
Hardmans BOLE BL2 ...23 H5
Hardmans Rd WHTF M45 ...84 C1
Hardman's Rd WHTF M45 ...68 C4
Hardman St BURY BL9 ...4 E3
CHAD OL9 ...89 G4
CSLFD M3 ...6 A3
EDGY/DAV SK3 ...12 C5
FAIL M35 ...102 D3
FWTH BL4 ...66 A5
HEY OL10 ...41 E4
MOSL OL5 ...94 C1
Hardon Gv BRUN/LGST M13 ...143 G1
Hardrush Fold FAIL M35 ...103 F4
Hardshaw Cl BRUN/LGST * M13 ...127 G2
Hardwick Cl BOLS/LL BL3 ...51 E4
MPL/ROM SK6 ...161 H4
Hardwick Rd POY/DIS SK12 ...195 G3
Hardwicke Rd POY/DIS SK12 ...195 G3
Hardwick St ROCH OL11 ...43 C2
Hardwood Cl CHH M8 ...101 H3
Hardy Av CCHDY M21 ...140 D3
Hardy Cl ROCH OL11 ...43 E3

Hardy Dr BRAM/HZG SK7 ...183 G5
HALE/TIMP WA15 ...166 A2
Hardy Gv SWIN M27 ...96 C5
WALK M28 ...
Hardy La CCHDY M21 ...141 F5
Hardy Mill Rd BOLE BL2 ...35 G3
Hardy St ECC M30 ...109 E4
OLDE OL4 ...9 C6
Hardywood Rd DTN/ASHW M34 ...146 D4
Harebell Av WALK * M28 ...80 A4
Harebell Cl WHIT OL12 ...18 C5
Haredale Dr CHH M8 ...100 C4
Hare Dr BURY BL9 ...54 A5
Harefield Av ROCH OL11 ...43 E1
Harefield Dr DID/WITH M20 ...157 F4
HEY OL10 ...41 G4
WILM/AE SK9 ...199 F5
Harefield Rd WILM/AE SK9 ...192 B3
Harehill Cl BRUN/LGST M13 ...127 G1
Hare Hill Rd HYDE SK14 ...133 H5
LIT OL15 ...20 D2
Hareshill Rd HEY OL10 ...55 F2
Hare St ANC * M4 ...7 G3
ROCH OL11 ...30 B5
Harewood Av ROCH OL11 ...28 A1
SALE M33 ...153 G2
Harewood Dr ROY/SHW OL2 ...58 D3
RDSH SK5 ...144 D3
Harewood Gv RDSH SK5 ...144 D3
ROY/SHW OL2 ...60 B1
Harewood Wy SWIN M27 ...83 E5
Harford Cl BRAM/HZG SK7 ...184 D3
Hargate Av ROCH OL11 ...28 D1
Hargate Cl BURY BL9 ...12 ...
Hargate Dr HALE/TIMP WA15 ...178 D3
IRL M44 ...121 B5
Hargrave Cl BKLY M9 ...86 D1
Hargreaves Rd
HALE/TIMP WA15 ...166 D3
Hargreave's St ANC M4 ...113 F2
BOL * BL1 ...33 H4
CHAD OL9 ...9 F2
OLD OL1 ...9 F2
ROCH OL11 ...42 D2
Harkness St WGTN/LGST M12 ...127 H1
Harland Dr CHH M8 ...100 C3
Harland Wy WHIT OL12 ...28 D1
Harlech Av WHTF M45 ...85 E1
Harlech Dr BRAM/HZG SK7 ...184 D3
Harleen Gv OFTN SK2 ...172 D3
Harlesden Crs BOLS/LL * BL3 ...48 A4
Harley Av BOLE BL2 ...
BOLE BL2 ...35 G1
RUSH/FAL M14 ...128 B5
Harley Cl MDTN M24 ...87 H2
Harley Rd MDTN M24 ...87 H2
SALE M33 ...154 D1
Harley St AUL * OL6 ...118 A2
OP/CLY M11 ...115 G5
Harling Rd WYTH/NTH M22 ...168 C2
Harlow Dr GTN M18 ...129 G5
Harmer Cl NEWH/MOS M40 ...103 C4
Harmol Gv AULW OL7 ...104 C4
Harmony St OLDE OL4 ...9 J5
Harmsworth Dr HTNM SK4 ...158 C5
Harmsworth St SLFD M6 ...111 F3
Harold Av DUK SK16 ...130 A4
GTN M18 ...130 A4
Haroldene St BOLE BL2 ...34 C2
Harold Lees Rd HEY OL10 ...41 G3
Harold Priestnall Cl
NEWH/MOS M40 ...114 A1
Harold St BOL BL1 ...33 G4
CHAD OL9 ...
FAIL * M35 ...102 D3
MDTN M24 ...71 F3
MILN OL16 ...11 G6
OLDTF/WHR M16 ...126 B2
PWCH M25 ...
STKP SK1 ...172 C1
Harper Ct EDGY/DAV SK3 ...13 F7
Harper Fold Rd RAD M26 ...66 C1
Harper Gn Rd FWTH BL4 ...64 C3
Harper PI AUL OL6 ...118 B2
Harper Rd WYTH/NTH M22 ...180 A2
Harper's La BOL BL1 ...33 G4
Harper St EDGY/DAV SK3 ...12 E7
FWTH BL4 ...64 C2
OLDS OL8 ...91 F5
ROCH OL11 ...42 D1
Harpford Cl BOLE BL2 ...35 C5
Harpford Dr BOLE BL2 ...35 C5
Harp Rd TRPK M17 ...110 B5
Harp St OP/CLY M11 ...130 A2
Harpurhey Rd CHH M8 ...100 D2
The Harridge WHIT OL12 ...18 A5
Harridge Av STLY SK15 ...107 H4
WHIT OL12 ...18 A5
Harridge St WHIT OL12 ...18 A4
Harrier Cl WALK M28 ...95 E2
WYTH/NTH M22 ...168 D4
Harriet St IRL M44 ...136 A1
WALK M28 ...81 E5
Harriett St ANC M4 ...114 A3
MILN OL16 ...10 E7
Harringay Rd NEWH/MOS M40 ...115 H1
Harrington Cl BURY BL9 ...53 G1
Harrington Rd ALT WA14 ...165 E4
Harrington St GTN M18 ...143 H1
Harris Av DTN/ASHW M34 ...118 C5
URM M41 ...123 G3
Harris Cl DTN/ASHW M34 ...117 G5
HEY OL10 ...39 H5
Harris Dr BURY BL9 ...53 C4
HYDE SK14 ...133 H4
Harris St BOLS/LL BL3 ...48 D5
CHH M8 ...112 D1
Harrogate Av PWCH M25 ...85 G5
Harrogate Cl OP/CLY M11 ...129 H1
Harrogate Dr RDSH SK5 ...144 D3

Harrogate Rd RDSH SK5 144 D2
Harrop Edge Rd HYDE SK14 134 B4
Harrop Fold OLDS OL8 104 D1
Harrop Rd HALE/TIMP WA15 178 A2
Harrop St BOLS/LL BL3 47 H5
GTN M18 130 A2
STKP SK1 13 J7
STLY SK15 119 E3
WALK M28 80 C4
Harrow Av BNG/LEV M19 143 H5
OLDS OL8 90 A4
ROCH OL11 28 D5
Harrowby Dr NEWH/MOS M40 101 E5
Harrowby Fold FWTH BL4 64 D4
Harrowby La FWTH BL4 64 D4
Harrowby Rd BOL BL1 32 C4
BOLS/LL * BL3 62 D1
SWIN M27 96 D3
Harrowby St FWTH BL4 64 C4
Harrow Cl BURY BL9 53 G4
Harrow Dr SALE M33 154 B4
Harrow Ms ROY/SHW OL2 60 A2
Harrow Rd BOL BL1 48 A2
SALE M33 154 B4
Harrow St CHH M8 100 C1
ROCH * OL11 43 G4
Harrycroft Rd MPL/ROM SK6 162 A1
Harry Hall Gdns BRO * M7 112 B1
Harry Rd RDSH SK5 145 E3
Harry Rowley Cl
WYTH/NTH * M22 180 B2
Harry St CHAD OL9 8 B5
ROCH OL11 42 A3
ROY/SHW OL2 74 B2
Harry Thorneycroft Wk
OP/CLY M11 114 B5
Harrytown MPL/ROM SK6 161 H4
Hart Av DROY M43 116 C4
SALE M33 155 G3
Hart Ct MOSL OL5 92 C5
Hart Dr BURY BL9 54 A5
Harter St CMANE M1 7 F6
Hartfield Cl BRUN/LGST M13 127 H2
Hartfield Wk BOLE * BL2 49 H1
Hartford Av HEY OL10 40 C4
HTNM SK4 144 C5
WILM/AE SK9 199 E5
Hartford Cl HEY OL10 40 C3
Hartford Gdns
HALE/TIMP WA15 167 E4
Hartford Rd SALE M33 153 G5
URM M41 123 H4
Hartford Sq CHAD * OL9 8 B5
Hartford St DTN/ASHW * M34 131 F3
Hart Hill Dr ORD M5 111 E2
Harthill St CHH M8 100 A5
Hartington Cl URM M41 138 D1
Hartington Dr BRAM/HZG SK7 185 F4
OP/CLY M11 115 E2
Hartington Rd ALT WA14 165 G2
BOL BL1 48 B1
BRAM/HZG SK7 193 H1
CCHDY M21 141 E3
CHD/CHDH SK8 182 A4
ECC M30 108 D2
MPL/ROM SK6 196 D1
OFTN SK2 173 E5
Hartington St RUSH/FAL M14 127 E5
Hartis Av BRO M7 99 H4
Hartland Cl OFTN SK2 172 D1
POY/DIS SK12 195 E2
Hartland St HEY OL10 41 E4
Hartlebury ROCH * OL11 29 H5
Hartlepool Cl RUSH/FAL M14 127 G5
Hartley Av PWCH M25 85 F4
Hartley Gv IRL M44 121 C4
Hartley Hall Gdns
OLDTF/WHR M16 141 H2
Hartley La ROCH OL11 42 D3
Hartley Rd ALT WA14 165 F4
CCHDY M21 140 D2
Hartley St EDGY/DAV SK3 12 C6
HEY OL10 41 E4
LIT OL15 20 D3
MILN * OL16 31 E4
NEWH/MOS M40 101 G2
STLY * SK15 120 A2
WHIT OL12 19 H2
WHIT OL12 29 E2
Hart Mill Cl MOSL OL5 92 C5
Harton Av GTN M18 129 F5
Harton Cl ROY/SHW OL2 59 H3
Hart Rd RUSH/FAL M14 142 C2
Hartshead Av AUL OL6 105 F4
STLY SK15 119 F2
Hartshead Cl OP/CLY M11 130 B1
Hartshead Crs FAIL M35 103 H4
Hartshead Rd AUL * OL6 105 F4
Hartshead St OLDE OL4 92 A2
Hartshead Vw HYDE SK14 148 A2
Hartsop Dr MDTN M24 70 D2
Hart St ALT WA14 165 G4
CMANE M1 7 G6
DROY M43 116 B3
Hartswood Cl DTN/ASHW M34 131 H4
Hartswood Rd DID/WITH M20 143 E5
Hartwell Cl BOLE BL2 34 D4
OP/CLY M11 114 C5
Harvard Cl MPL/ROM SK6 162 B1
Harvard Gv SLFD M6 110 D2
Harvard St ROCH OL11 43 F2
Harvest Cl SALE M33 155 H3
SLFD M6 98 B5
Harvest Pk BOL BL1 48 B1
Harvey St BOL BL1 33 G3
STKP SK1 13 G3
TOT/BURYW BL8 37 H3
WHIT OL12 11 G1
Harvin Gv DTN/ASHW M34 146 D1
Harwich Cl BNG/LEV * M19 143 H2
RDSH SK5 145 H5
Harwin Cl WHIT OL12 18 C5
Harwood Ct SLFD M6 112 A1
Harwood Crs TOT/BURYW BL8 25 H4
Harwood Dr TOT/BURYW BL8 37 F5
Harwood Gv BOLE * BL2 34 C5
Harwood Meadow BOLE BL2 35 G3
Harwood Rd BNG/LEV M19 143 F5
BOLE BL2 36 A2
HTNM SK4 158 B4
Harwood St HTNM SK4 159 H3
LIT OL15 20 C3
Harwood V BOLE BL2 35 F3
Haseley Cl BOLS/LL BL3 51 E4
POY/DIS SK12 195 F2
Haselhurst Wk NTHM/RTH M23 155 G4
Hasguard Cl BOL BL1 47 G2
Haslam Brow BURY BL9 53 F1
Haslam Hall Ms BOL BL1 47 F2
Haslam Hey Cl BOLE * BL2 36 B5
TOT/BURYW BL8 37 E4
Haslam Rd EDGY/DAV SK3 171 H3
Haslam St BOLS/LL BL3 48 C4
BURY BL9 38 D2
MDTN * M24 72 B5
WHIT OL12 29 G3
Haslemere Av HALE/TIMP WA15 188 D1
Haslemere Dr CHD/CHDH SK8 182 D3
Haslemere Rd DID/WITH M20 143 E5
URM M41 138 A2
Haslington Rd WYTH/NTH M22 180 D2
Hasper Av DID/WITH M20 142 B4
Hassall Av DID/WITH M20 142 A3
Hassall St STLY * SK15 119 G4
Hassop Av BRO M7 98 D3
Hassop Cl OP/CLY M11 114 B4
Hassop Rd RDSH SK5 145 F2
Hastings Av CCHDY M21 140 D3
WHTF M45 69 E5
Hastings Cl CHD/CHDH SK8 183 F2
STKP SK1 172 C2
WHTF M45 69 E5
Hastings Dr URM M41 122 B5
Hastings Rd BOL BL1 48 A1
ECC M30 108 D1
PWCH M25 85 F2
Hastings St ROCH OL11 43 E1
Hasty La HALE/TIMP WA15 179 G5
Hatchett Rd WYTH/NTH M22 180 D3
Hatchmere Cl HALE/TIMP WA15 167 E3
Hatchmere Rd CHD/CHDH SK8 170 C5
Hatfield Av BNG/LEV M19 143 G5
Hatfield Rd BOL BL1 33 F5
Hathaway Dr BOL BL1 34 B1
Hathaway Gdns MPL/ROM SK6 161 F3
Hathaway Rd BURY BL9 68 D1
Hatherley Rd DID/WITH M20 143 E5
Hatherlow MPL/ROM SK6 161 H4
Hatherlow La BRAM/HZG SK7 185 E2
Hatherop Cl ECC M30 109 E4
Hathersage Rd
BRUN/LGST M13 127 H4
Hathersage St CHAD OL9 8 A5
Hathershaw La OLDS OL8 90 C4
Hatro Ct URM M41 139 F2
Hattersley Rd East HYDE SK14 149 E2
Hattersley Rd West HYDE SK14 148 D1
Hatter St ANC M4 7 H2
Hatton Av BRO M7 112 C2
Hatton Gv BOL BL1 34 B1
Hattons Ct STRET M32 124 D5
Hattons Rd TRPK M17 124 C2
Hatton St STKP SK1 13 F2
Haugh Hill Rd OLDE OL4 75 H1
Haugh La MILN OL16 45 F2
Haughton Cl MPL/ROM SK6 146 D5
Haughton Dr WYTH/NTH M22 156 C5
Haughton Green Rd
DTN/ASHW M34 146 D3
Haughton Hall Rd
DTN/ASHW M34 131 H5
Haughton St DTN/ASHW M34 131 G3
HYDE SK14 147 H2
Havana Cl OP/CLY M11 114 C4
Haveley Rd WYTH/NTH M22 168 B4
Havelock Dr BRO M7 112 C1
Havelock St OLDS OL8 9 G7
The Haven HALE/TIMP WA15 178 A1
Havenbrook Gv RAMS * BL0 16 B5
Haven Cl BRAM/HZG SK7 184 D3
OLDE OL4 93 E1
RAD M26 51 G4
Haven Dr DROY M43 115 H3
Haven La OLDE OL4 75 H1
Havenscroft Av ECC M30 109 G5
Haven St SLFD M6 111 F4
Haverfield Rd BKLY M9 87 F4
Haverford St WGTN/LGST M12 128 C2
Haverhill Gv BOLE BL2 34 C4
Haversham Rd CHH M8 85 H5
Havers Rd GTN M18 129 H3
Havisham Cl HOR/BR BL6 46 C5
Hawarden Av OLDTF/WHR M16 141 F1
Hawarden Rd ALT WA14 165 G3
Hawarden St BOL BL1 33 H2
Hawdraw Gn OFTN SK2 173 F3
Hawes Av FWTH BL4 63 H4
RUSH/FAL M14 143 F4
SWIN * M27 97 E4
Hawes Cl OFTN SK2 172 B3
TOT/BURYW BL8 37 G1
Haweswater Cl DTN/ASHW M34 145 F1
Haweswater Crs BURY BL9 54 A4
Haweswater Dr MDTN M24 71 F2
Hawfinch Gv WALK M28 95 E2
Hawk Cl BURY BL9 5 J1
Hawker Av BOLS/LL BL3 63 G1
Hawkeshead Rd CHH M8 100 C4
Hawke St STLY SK15 119 H4
Hawk Green Rd MPL/ROM SK6 187 E1
Hawkhurst Rd BRUN/LGST M13 128 C5
Hawkins St RDSH SK5 159 H2
Hawkins Wy LIT OL15 15 B4
Hawkridge Dr NTHM/RTH M23 155 G4
Hawk Rd IRL M44 121 B5
Hawkshaw Ct ORD M5 111 H4
Hawkshead Dr BOLS/LL BL3 62 D1
MDTN M24 71 F3
ROY/SHW OL2 59 E3
Hawkshead Rd ROY/SHW OL2 59 H1
Hawksheath Cl EDGW/EG BL7 22 D2
Hawksley St OLDS OL8 89 H4
Hawksmoor Dr ROY/SHW OL2 60 A1
Hawkstone Av DROY M43 115 H2
WHTF M45 68 A5
Hawkstone Cl BOLE BL2 35 F3
Hawkswick Dr NTHM/RTH M23 155 H3
Hawley Dr HALE/TIMP WA15 178 C4
Hawley Gn WHIT OL12 29 G1
Hawley La HALE/TIMP WA15 178 C4
Hawley St BNG/LEV M19 144 A3
Haworth Av RAMS BL0 26 C1
Haworth Cl BURY BL9 53 G3
Haworth Dr STRET M32 124 A5
Haworth Rd GTN M18 129 F4
Haworth St OLD OL1 74 B3
RAD M26 67 G1
TOT/BURYW BL8 36 D2
Hawthorn Av ECC M30 109 G2
HALE/TIMP WA15 166 A2
MPL/ROM SK6 174 C5
RAD M26 67 G3
RAMS BL0 26 B1
TOT/BURYW BL8 37 H2
URM M41 139 E2
WALK M28 95 F1
WILM/AE SK9 199 F3
Hawthorn Cl HALE/TIMP WA15 166 A2
Hawthorn Crs ROY/SHW * OL2 60 A3
TOT/BURYW BL8 26 A4
Hawthorn Dr BNG/LEV M19 143 G4
IRL M44 150 C1
SLFD M6 110 B1
STLY SK15 119 E5
SWIN M27 97 H3
Hawthorne Av FWTH BL4 64 C4
Hawthorne Crs OLDS OL8 90 C5
Hawthorne Dr WALK M28 95 H3
Hawthorne Gv AULW OL7 117 G4
CHAD OL9 73 G4
MPL/ROM SK6 161 F2
POY/DIS SK12 196 B3
Hawthorne La MILN OL16 44 D2
Hawthorne Rd BOLS/LL BL3 48 A5
Hawthorne St BOLS/LL BL3 48 A5
Hawthorn Gv BRAM/HZG SK7 193 F1
HTNM SK4 159 E3
HYDE SK14 147 G2
WILM/AE SK9 199 G3
Hawthorn La CCHDY * M21 140 C3
SALE M33 138 C5
WILM/AE SK9 199 F3
Hawthorn Pk WILM/AE SK9 199 F3
Hawthorn Rd CHD/CHDH SK8 169 F4
DROY M43 116 D3
DTN/ASHW M34 130 C4
FWTH BL4 82 A2
HALE/TIMP WA15 177 H1
HTNM SK4 158 B4
NEWH/MOS M40 102 D1
OLDS OL8 89 G5
ROCH OL11 28 B5
STRET M32 140 B1
Hawthorn Rd South DROY M43 116 D3
The Hawthorns
DTN/ASHW M34 131 E2
Hawthorn St DTN/ASHW M34 131 F2
GTN M18 129 G2
WILM/AE SK9 199 F4
Hawthorn Ter HTNM * SK4 159 E3
Hawthorn Vw WILM/AE SK9 199 F3
Hawthorn Wk LIT OL15 20 C3
WILM/AE * SK9 199 F3
Hawthorpe Gv UPML OL3 78 A4
Haxby Rd GTN M18 129 G3
Haybarn Rd NTHM/RTH M23 168 A2
Hayburn Rd OFTN SK2 172 D1
Haycock Cl STLY SK15 134 B1
Hay Cft CHD/CHDH SK8 182 B4
Haydn Av RUSH/FAL M14 127 G4
Haydock Av SALE M33 153 F4
Haydock Dr BRAM/HZG SK7 185 G2
HALE/TIMP WA15 166 C4
WALK M28 94 C4
Haydock La EDGW/EG BL7 23 G3
Haydock St BOL BL1 2 E2
Haye's Rd IRL M44 150 D1
Hayeswater Rd URM M41 123 F5
Hayfield Av MPL/ROM SK6 161 H2
Hayfield Cl MDTN M24 72 B1
OLDE OL4 61 E5
TOT/BURYW BL8 26 A2
WGTN/LGST M12 128 B2
Hayfield Rd MPL/ROM SK6 161 H2
SLFD M6 110 C1
Hayfield St SALE M33 154 B2
Hayfield Wk HALE/TIMP WA15 166 D3
Hayle Rd OLD OL1 60 C5
Hayley St BRUN/LGST * M13 128 B4
Hayling Rd SALE M33 153 H1
Haymaker Ri WHIT OL12 19 H2
Haymans Wk BRUN/LGST M13 127 G1
The Haymarket BURY BL9 4 E4
Haymarket Cl BRUN/LGST M13 127 H3
Haymarket St BURY BL9 4 D6
Haymill Av LHULT M38 80 B1
Haymond Cl SLFD M6 98 D4
Haynes St BOLS/LL BL3 63 E1
WHIT OL12 10 D4
Haysbrook Av LHULT M38 80 A3
Haysbrook Cl AULW OL7 104 D3
Haythorp Av WYTH/NTH M22 180 D1
Hayward Av BOLS/LL BL3 66 B1
Hayward St TOT/BURYW BL8 37 H3
Hazel Av AUL OL6 105 H4
BURY BL9 5 K4
CHD/CHDH SK8 170 B4
LHULT M38 79 D2
MILN OL16 44 D3
MPL/ROM SK6 162 C4
OLDTF/WHR M16 141 G1
RAD M26 65 H4
RAMS BL0 26 C2
SALE M33 154 C3
SWIN M27 96 C3
TOT/BURYW BL8 37 E1
Hazelbadge Cl POY/DIS SK12 194 D3
Hazelbadge Rd POY/DIS SK12 194 D3
Hazelbank Av DID/WITH M20 142 C4
Hazelbottom Rd CHH M8 100 C3
Hazel Cl DROY M43 116 D3
MPL/ROM SK6 174 D5
Hazelcroft WILM/AE SK9 201 B5
Hazel-dene Cl BURY BL9 53 G2
Hazeldene Rd NEWH/MOS M40 102 D1
Hazel Dr OFTN SK2 173 E3
POY/DIS SK12 195 G4
WYTH/NTH M22 181 F4
Hazelfields WALK M28 96 A3
Hazel Gv CHAD OL9 73 G4
FWTH BL4 64 C4
ORD M5 110 D3
RAD M26 67 E4
URM M41 138 D1
Hazel Hall La RAMS BL0 26 C2
Hazelhurst Cl BOL BL1 33 H4
RAMS BL0 16 C4
Hazelhurst Dr MDTN M24 56 C5
Hazelhurst Fold WALK M28 96 B3
Hazelhurst Rd AUL OL6 106 A4
STLY SK15 119 F1
WALK M28 96 A3
Hazel La OLDS OL8 90 A5
Hazelmere Av ECC M30 109 E1
Hazelmere Cl ECC M30 109 H5
Hazel Mt EDGW/EG BL7 22 D1
Hazel Rd ALT WA14 165 G4
CHD/CHDH SK8 183 E3
MDTN M24 72 A2
STLY SK15 119 H2
WHTF M45 69 E4
Hazel St BRAM/HZG * SK7 185 F1
DTN/ASHW M34 131 F2
RAMS BL0 16 B4
Hazel Ter BKLY * M9 87 E3
Hazelwell SALE M33 154 C3
Hazelwood CHAD OL9 72 D5
Hazelwood Av BOLE BL2 35 F3
Hazelwood Cl HYDE SK14 148 B1
Hazelwood Dr BURY BL9 27 G4
DTN/ASHW M34 131 F2
Hazelwood Rd BOL BL1 33 E4
BRAM/HZG SK7 185 F2
HALE/TIMP WA15 177 H2
OFTN SK2 172 B5
WILM/AE SK9 200 A2
Hazlemere FWTH BL4 65 H5
Headingley Dr
OLDTF/WHR M16 125 H5
Headingley Rd RUSH/FAL M14 143 E4
Headingley Wy BOLS/LL BL3 63 G1
Headlands Dr PWCH M25 98 D1
Headlands Rd BRAM/HZG SK7 184 A3
Headlands St WHIT OL12 10 A2
Heady Hill Rd HEY OL10 40 B4
Heald Av RUSH/FAL M14 127 G5
Heald Cl ALT WA14 177 F2
LIT OL15 20 D5
WHIT OL12 18 B5
Heald Dr ALT WA14 177 F2
WHIT OL12 18 B5
Heald Gv CHD/CHDH SK8 181 F3
RUSH/FAL M14 127 G4
Heald Pl RUSH/FAL M14 127 G5
Heald Rd ALT WA14 177 F2
Healds Gn OLD OL1 73 E1
Heald St STKP SK1 13 J1
Healdwood Rd MPL/ROM SK6 162 B2
Healey Av HEY OL10 41 F3
WHIT OL12 18 C4
Healey Cl BRO M7 99 F2
NTHM/RTH M23 155 G4
Healey Gv WHIT OL12 18 B3
Healey La WHIT OL12 18 D5
Healey St MILN OL16 29 H5
Healing St ROCH OL11 43 F1
Heanor Av DTN/ASHW M34 146 D3
Heap Br BURY BL9 39 F4
Heap Brow BURY BL9 39 G5
Heape St ROCH OL11 42 B5
Heapfold WHIT OL12 29 E1
Heaplands TOT/BURYW BL8 26 A2
Heaps Farm Ct STLY SK15 120 A5
Heap St BOLS/LL BL3 48 D5
HEY OL10 39 G5
OLDE OL4 75 F5
WHTF * M45 68 C5
Heapworth Av RAMS BL0 16 C2
Heapy Cl TOT/BURYW BL8 37 E4
The Heath AULW OL7 104 D3
MDTN M24 88 A1
Heath Av BRO M7 112 B1
RAMS BL0 26 C2
Heathbank Rd BKLY M9 86 D2
CHD/CHDH SK8 182 C4
EDGY/DAV SK3 171 E2
Heathcliffe Wk
BRUN/LGST M13 127 H3
Heath Cl BOLS/LL BL3 63 E2
Heathcote Av HTNM SK4 159 F3
Heathcote Rd GTN M18 129 F4
Heath Crs EDGY/DAV SK3 172 A4
Heather Av DROY M43 116 D3
IRL M44 135 C5
ROY/SHW OL2 60 C1
Heather Bank LIT * OL15 21 G2
TOT/BURYW * BL8 25 H4
Heather Brow STLY SK15 134 B1
Heather Cl OLDE OL4 75 H3
Heatherdale Dr CHH M8 100 B4
Heatherfield BOL BL1 33 G1
Heatherfield Ct WILM/AE SK9 200 B2
Heather Gv DROY M43 116 C5
Heatherlands WHIT OL12 14 C1
Heather Lea DTN/ASHW M34 146 D1
Heather Rd ALT WA14 177 H3
The Heathers OFTN SK2 172 C5
Heatherside RDSH SK5 145 F2
STLY SK15 120 A3
Heatherside Av MOSL OL5 107 F1
Heatherside Rd RAMS BL0 16 C1
Heather St OP/CLY M11 115 E3
Heather Wy MPL/ROM SK6 174 D4
Heatherway SALE M33 153 G1
Heath Farm La PART M31 151 F3
Heathfield BOLE BL2 35 G2
FWTH BL4 65 F3
WALK M28 95 G5
WILM/AE SK9 199 F5
Heathfield Av CHD/CHDH SK8 169 G4
DTN/ASHW M34 146 A1
HTNM SK4 159 F1
Heathfield Cl SALE M33 155 G3
Heathfield Dr BOLS/LL BL3 63 E2
SWIN M27 97 F3
Heathfield Rd BURY BL9 68 C1
OFTN SK2 172 A3
Heathfields UPML OL3 78 B4
Heathfield St NEWH/MOS M40 102 B5
Heathland Rd BRO M7 99 E2
Heathlands Dr PWCH M25 98 D1
Heathland Ter EDGY/DAV SK3 171 H2
Heath Rd ALT WA14 177 G2
EDGY/DAV SK3 172 A3
HALE/TIMP WA15 166 A1
WHIT OL12 19 H2
Heathside Gv WALK M28 81 E4
Heathside Park Rd
EDGY/DAV SK3 170 C2
Heathside Rd DID/WITH M20 157 H1
EDGY/DAV SK3 170 D2
Heath St CHH M8 100 A3
ROCH OL11 29 G5
Heathwood UPML OL3 78 B4
Heathwood Rd BNG/LEV M19 158 B2
Heatley Cl DTN/ASHW M34 145 G1
Heatley Rd MILN OL16 31 E5
Heaton Av BOL BL1 32 C5
BOLE BL2 35 F1
BOLS/LL BL3 50 D5
BRAM/HZG SK7 183 G1
FWTH BL4 64 D4
Heaton Cl BURY BL9 53 H4
HTNM SK4 158 D3
Heaton Ct BURY BL9 53 F2
Heaton Dr BURY BL9 53 H4
Heaton Fold BURY BL9 53 F1
Heaton Grange Dr BOL * BL1 47 H2
Heaton Gv BURY BL9 53 F2
Heaton La HTNM SK4 12 E3
Heaton Moor Rd HTNM SK4 159 E3
Heaton Mt BOL BL1 32 C5
Heaton Park Rd BKLY M9 86 B2
Heaton Park Rd West BKLY M9 86 B2
Heaton Rd BOLE BL2 51 E4
DID/WITH M20 142 D4
HOR/BR BL6 46 D4
HTNM SK4 159 G3
Heaton St BRO M7 99 H3
DTN/ASHW M34 131 E5
MILN OL16 44 D1
PWCH M25 85 F3
Heaviley Gv OFTN SK2 172 B3
Hebble Butt Cl MILN * OL16 31 F5
Hebble Cl BOLE BL2 34 C1
Hebburn Dr TOT/BURYW BL8 37 H1
Hebburn Wk RUSH/FAL M14 127 G4
Hebden Av MPL/ROM SK6 161 H2
SLFD M6 110 D2
Hebden Wk HULME M15 127 E3
Heber Pl LIT OL15 21 E3
Heber St RAD M26 67 F1
Hebron St ROY/SHW OL2 74 D1
Hector Av MILN OL16 11 G4
Hector Rd BRUN/LGST M13 128 C5
Heddon Cl HTNM SK4 158 B3
The Hedgerows HYDE SK14 133 F5
Hedge Rows WHIT OL12 14 B3
Hedges St FAIL M35 103 F2
Hedley St BOL BL1 33 F4
Heginbottom Crs AUL OL6 105 F5
Heights Av WHIT OL12 10 A2
Heights Cl WHIT OL12 10 A1
Heights La OLD OL1 73 E2
WHIT OL12 10 A1
Helena St SLFD M6 97 H5
Helen St BRO M7 99 F5
ECC M30 109 E5
FWTH BL4 65 E4
Helensville Av SLFD M6 98 C5
Helga St NEWH/MOS M40 114 A1
Helias Cl LHULT M38 80 A4
Helmclough Wy WALK M28 94 D2
Helmet St CMANE M1 113 H5
Helmsdale WALK M28 80 D5
Helmsdale Av BOLS/LL BL3 47 G3
Helmsdale Cl RAMS BL0 16 B5
Helmshore Av OLDE OL4 75 G1
Helmshore Wk
BRUN/LGST * M13 127 G1
Helmshore Wy ROY/SHW OL2 60 A1
Helsby Cl OLDE OL4 92 B1
Helsby Gdns BOL BL1 34 A2
Helsby Rd SALE M33 155 F4
Helsby Wk WGTN/LGST M12 114 B5
Helston Cl BRAM/HZG SK7 184 A5
IRL M44 136 C1
Helston Dr ROY/SHW OL2 59 G5
Helston Gv CHD/CHDH SK8 181 H4
Helston St NEWH/MOS M40 114 C1
Helvellyn Dr MDTN M24 71 E2
Helvellyn Wk OLD * OL1 74 C3
Hembury Av BNG/LEV M19 143 G5
Hembury Cl MDTN M24 72 A2
Hemlock Av OLDS OL8 90 B4
Hemming Dr ECC M30 109 H4
Hemmington Dr BKLY M9 101 E3
Hemmons Rd WGTN/LGST M12 144 A1
Hempcroft Rd
HALE/TIMP WA15 166 D4
Hempshaw La STKP SK1 13 H7
Hemsley St BKLY M9 101 F1
Hemsley St South BKLY M9 101 F2
Hemswell Cl SLFD M6 111 F1
Hemsworth Rd BOL BL1 2 B2
GTN M18 129 G5
Henbury Dr MPL/ROM SK6 147 E5
Henbury La CHD/CHDH SK8 192 C1
Henbury Rd WILM/AE * SK9 192 A3
Henbury St OFTN SK2 172 D5
RUSH/FAL M14 127 F5
Henderson Av SWIN M27 97 E1
Henderson St BNG/LEV M19 144 A3
LIT OL15 20 D3
WHIT OL12 11 G1
Henderville St LIT OL15 20 D2
Hendham Cl BRAM/HZG SK7 184 B2
Hendham Dr ALT WA14 165 E3
Hendham V BKLY M9 100 D3
Hendon Dr BURY BL9 53 G4
EDGY/DAV SK3 170 D2
Hendon Rd BKLY M9 86 D3
Hendriff Pl WHIT * OL12 10 B2
Hengist St BOLE BL2 49 H2
GTN M18 129 G4
Henley Av CHD/CHDH SK8 182 C2
IRL M44 135 D5
OLDTF/WHR M16 126 A5
Henley Cl TOT/BURYW BL8 52 C1
Henley Dr AULW OL7 117 G1
HALE/TIMP WA15 166 A2
Henley Gv BOLS/LL BL3 63 F1
Henley Pl BNG/LEV M19 143 H5
Henley St CHAD OL9 89 F4
OLD OL1 74 A4
WHIT OL12 10 B3
Henley Ter ROCH OL11 42 D1
Henniker Rd BOLS/LL BL3 62 D2
Henniker St SWIN M27 96 D4
WALK M28 95 E1
Hennon St BOL BL1 33 G5
Henrietta St AUL OL6 105 E5
BOLS/LL BL3 48 A5
OLDTF/WHR M16 126 B3
Henry Herman St BOLS/LL BL3 62 D1
Henry Lee St BOLS/LL * BL3 63 F1
Henry St ANC M4 7 J3
BOLS/LL BL3 3 G7
DROY M43 116 B4
DTN/ASHW * M34 147 E3

ECC M30 109 F4
FAIL M35 103 E3
HYDE SK14 147 G1
LIT OL15 20 C5
MDTN M24 71 G4
OLDTF/WHR M16 126 B3
PWCH M25 85 F2
RAMS BL0 17 E1
ROCH OL11 30 A5
STKP SK1 172 C1
Henshaw Ct OLDTF/WHR M16 126 A4
Henshaw La CHAD OL9 89 E5
Henshaw St OLD OL1 9 F3
STRET M32 140 A1
Henshaw Wk BOL BL1 33 H4
Henson Gv HALE/TIMP WA15 166 B5
Henthorn St ROY/SHW OL2 60 A3
Henton Wk NEWH/MOS M40 113 H1
Henwick Hall Av RAMS BL0 16 C4
Henwood Rd DID/WITH M20 157 H1
Hepley Rd POY/DIS SK12 195 H4
Hepple Cl HTNM SK4 158 C3
Heppleton Rd NEWH/MOS M40 88 C5
Hepple Wk AULW * OL7 104 B5
Hepton St OLD OL1 8 E1
Hepworth St HYDE SK14 147 H4
Herbert St BOLS/LL BL3 66 A1
CHAD OL9 73 G5
CHH * M8 100 A5
DROY M43 116 A4
DTN/ASHW M34 131 H4
EDGY/DAV SK3 12 D7
OLDE OL4 75 F3
PWCH M25 84 C3
RAD M26 52 A4
STRET M32 140 A1
Hereford Cl AUL OL6 105 G3
ROY/SHW OL2 59 G2
Hereford Dr BURY BL9 53 G1
PWCH M25 85 F5
SWIN M27 97 E4
WILM/AE SK9 192 B4
Hereford Gv URM M41 138 B1
Hereford Rd BOL BL1 48 A1
CHD/CHDH SK8 170 D5
ECC M30 97 F5
RDSH SK5 160 D1
Hereford St BOL BL1 34 A4
CHAD OL9 8 A6
ROCH OL11 43 F1
SALE M33 154 C2
Hereford Wy MDTN M24 72 B3
STLY SK15 134 A1
Herevale Gra WALK M28 94 C3
Herevale Hall Dr RAMS * BL0 16 C4
Heristone Av DTN/ASHW M34 131 F5
Heritage Gdns DID/WITH M20 157 G4
Herle Dr WYTH/NTH M22 180 B3
Hermitage Av MPL/ROM SK6 163 E4
Hermitage Gdns MPL/ROM SK6 163 E4
Hermitage Rd CHH M8 100 B1
HALE/TIMP WA15 178 B1
Hermon Av OLDS OL8 90 B4
Herne St OP/CLY M11 114 D5
Heron Av DUK SK16 132 D1
FWTH BL4 64 A5
Heron Ct SLFD M6 110 C2
Herondale Cl NEWH/MOS M40 102 A5
Heron Dr DTN/ASHW M34 116 D4
IRL M44 121 B5
POY/DIS SK12 194 B4
Heron Ml OLDS * OL8 90 A4
Heron St EDGY/DAV SK3 12 D6
HULME M15 126 D3
OLDS OL8 89 H4
SWIN M27 97 F1
Heron's Wy BOLE BL2 3 G7
Herries St AUL OL6 118 C1
Herristone Rd CHH M8 86 B5
Herrod Av HTNM SK4 150 H1
Herschel St NEWH/MOS M40 101 H2
Hersey St SLFD * M6 111 F3
Hertford Gv IRL M44 135 B5
Hertford Rd BKLY M9 101 E1
Hertfordshire Park Cl
ROY/SHW * OL2 60 A1
Hertford St AULW OL7 117 H4
Hesford Av BKLY M9 101 G3
Hesketh Av BOL BL1 34 A1
DID/WITH M20 157 F3
ROY/SHW OL2 59 H4
Hesketh Rd MILN OL16 11 J6
SALE M33 154 A3
Hesketh St HTNM SK4 159 H2
Hessel St SALQ M50 111 E4
Hester Wk HULME * M15 127 E2
Heston Av BRUN/LGST M13 143 F1
Heston Dr URM M41 123 F5
Heswall Av DID/WITH M20 142 C4
Heswall Dr TOT/BURYW BL8 36 D1
Heswall Rd RDSH SK5 145 E2
Hetherington Wk
WGTN/LGST M12 128 C4
Hethorn St NEWH/MOS M40 102 B5
Hetton Av BRUN/LGST M13 143 F1
Heversham Av ROY/SHW OL2 60 C2
Hewart Cl NEWH/MOS M40 113 H1
Hewart Dr BURY BL9 39 F4
Hewitt Av DTN/ASHW M34 130 A5
Hewitt St CSLFD M3 6 C7
Hewlett Rd CCHDY M21 140 D2
Hewlett St BOLE BL2 3 G5
Hexham Av BOL BL1 32 C5
Hexham Cl CHAD OL9 8 A2
OFTN SK2 173 F4
Hexham Rd GTN M18 129 E4
Hexon Cl SLFD M6 111 F2
The Hey ROY/SHW * OL2 45 H5
Hey Bottom La WHIT OL12 19 F2
Heybrook Cl WHTF M45 69 F4
Heybrook Rd NTHM/RTH M23 168 A4
Heybrook St MILN * OL16 11 G3
Heybury Cl OP/CLY M11 114 C5
Hey Crs OLDE OL4 76 A5
Hey Cft WHTF M45 67 H5
Heyes Av HALE/TIMP WA15 166 C2
Heyes Dr HALE/TIMP WA15 166 C2
Heyes La HALE/TIMP WA15 166 C1
WILM/AE SK9 201 C3
Heyes Leigh HALE/TIMP * WA15 166 C2
Heyes Ter HALE/TIMP * WA15 166 C1
Heyford Av NEWH/MOS M40 88 C5
Hey Head La LIT OL15 15 A4
Heyheads New Rd MOSL OL5 107 F3
Hey Hill Cl ROY/SHW OL2 59 H4
Heyland Rd NTHM/RTH M23 167 H3
Heyridge Dr WYTH/NTH M22 156 C5
Heyrod St CMANE M1 7 K6
STLY SK15 107 E5
Heyrose Wk HULME M15 126 C2
The Heys PWCH M25 85 E2
RDSH SK5 145 F2
Heys Av MPL/ROM SK6 162 D3
NTHM/RTH M23 155 H5
SWIN M27 82 B5
Heys Cl North SWIN M27 82 B5
Heyscroft Rd DID/WITH M20 142 D5
HTNM SK4 158 D4
Heysham Av DID/WITH M20 142 A4
Heyside ROY/SHW OL2 59 H5
Heyside Av ROY/SHW OL2 74 D1
Heyside Cl STLY SK15 107 F4
Heyside Wy BURY BL9 5 F6
Heys La HEY OL10 40 B4
MPL/ROM SK6 162 D3
Heys Rd AUL OL6 118 C2
PWCH M25 85 E2
Heys St TOT/BURYW BL8 4 A4
Hey St MILN OL16 11 G5
Heys Vw PWCH M25 85 E3
Hey Willow BOLE BL2 23 H4
Heywood Av OLDE OL4 76 B4
SWIN M27 83 G5
Heywood Cl WILM/AE SK9 201 C3
Heywood Fold Rd OLDE OL4 76 A5
Heywood Gdns BOLS/LL BL3 48 D5
PWCH M25 85 E3
Heywood Gv SALE M33 139 F5
Heywood Hall Rd HEY OL10 41 E3
Heywood La OLDE OL4 76 B5
Heywood Old Rd MDTN M24 70 B4
Heywood Park Vw BOLS/LL BL3 48 D4
Heywood Rd PWCH M25 85 E1
ROCH OL11 42 A4
SALE M33 154 C3
WILM/AE SK9 201 C3
Heywood's Hollow BOL BL1 34 A3
Heywood St BOL BL1 2 E2
BOLS/LL BL3 66 A1
BURY BL9 5 G6
CHH M8 100 B4
FAIL M35 102 C3
OLDE OL4 75 H4
SWIN M27 96 D2
Heywood Wy SLFD M6 111 G2
Heyworth Av MPL/ROM SK6 162 C3
Heyworth St ORD * M5 111 F4
Hibbert Av DTN/ASHW M34 131 E3
HYDE SK14 147 H2
Hibbert Crs FAIL M35 103 F3
Hibbert La MPL/ROM SK6 175 E4
Hibbert St BOL BL1 34 A4
HTNM SK4 159 H1
OLDE OL4 76 A5
RUSH/FAL M14 127 H5
Hibernia St BOLS/LL BL3 48 B4
Hibernia Wy STRET M32 124 B3
Hibson Av WHIT OL12 28 B1
Hibson Cl WHIT OL12 19 H2
Hickenfield Rd HYDE SK14 133 E3
Hicken Pl HYDE SK14 133 E3
Hickton Dr ALT WA14 165 E3
Higgingshaw Rd OLD OL1 74 C3
Higginshaw La OLD OL1 74 D2
Higginshaw Rd OLD OL1 74 C4
Higginson Rd RDSH SK5 144 D4
Higgs Cl OLDE OL4 75 G5
Higham Cl ROY/SHW OL2 59 H4
Higham La HYDE SK14 148 A3
Higham Vw SLFD M6 111 H2
High Ash Gv DTN/ASHW M34 131 E1
High Av BOLE * BL2 50 B2
High Bank ALT WA14 165 G4
EDGW/EG BL7 23 F4
GTN M18 129 H3
High Bank Av STLY SK15 134 A1
High Bank Cl IRL M44 135 C5
Highbank Crs OLDE OL4 93 F2
High Bank Crs PWCH M25 85 F4
Highbank Dr DID/WITH M20 169 G1
High Bank Gv PWCH M25 85 F4
High Bank La HOR/BR BL6 46 C2
High Bank Rd DROY M43 116 A5
HYDE SK14 133 E5
SWIN M27 97 G2
Highbank Rd BURY BL9 68 C1
MILN OL16 45 F3
High Bank Side STKP SK1 13 G3
High Bank St BOLE BL2 49 H2
High Barn Cl ROCH OL11 42 D1
High Barn La WHIT OL12 14 B2
High Barn Rd MDTN M24 71 H5
ROY/SHW OL2 59 G5
High Barn St ROY/SHW OL2 59 F5
High Beeches BOLE BL2 51 E4
High Bent Av CHD/CHDH SK8 192 D1
Highbridge Cl BOLE BL2 50 D3
Highbury Av IRL M44 136 B2
URM M41 137 F1
Highbury Rd HTNM SK4 144 B5
OLDTF/WHR M16 141 H2
Highbury Wy ROY/SHW OL2 59 E3
Highclere Av CHH M8 100 A4
Highclere Rd CHH M8 86 A5
Highcliffe Rd BKLY M9 86 B4
Highclove La WALK M28 94 A5
High Crest Av CHD/CHDH SK8 169 E4
Highcroft HYDE SK14 147 H4
Highcroft Av DID/WITH M20 156 D2
High Croft Cl DUK SK16 119 F5
Highcroft Rd MPL/ROM SK6 162 B3
Highcroft Wy WHIT OL12 19 E4
Highdales Rd NTHM/RTH M23 168 A4
High Elm Dr HALE/TIMP WA15 178 D4
High Elm Rd HALE/TIMP WA15 178 D4
High Elms CHD/CHDH SK8 193 E2
Higher Ainsworth Rd RAD M26 51 H2
Higher Ardwick
WGTN/LGST M12 127 H1
Higher Bank Rd LIT OL15 20 D5
Higher Barlow Rw STKP SK1 13 H5
Higher Bents La MPL/ROM SK6 161 G3
Higher Bridge St BOL BL1 2 E2
Higher Bury St HTNM SK4 12 C2
Higher Cambridge St
HULME M15 127 F2
Higher Carr La UPML OL3 78 A5
Higher Chatham St
HULME * M15 127 F2
Higher Cleggswood Av
LIT OL15 20 D5
Higher Cft ECC M30 109 F5
WHTF M45 83 H1
Higher Crossbank OLDE OL4 76 A4
Higher Cross La UPML OL3 78 B5
Higher Darcy St BOLS/LL BL3 49 H4
Higher Dean St RAD M26 66 D1
Higher Downs ALT WA14 177 F1
Higher Dunscar EDGW/EG BL7 22 D2
Higher Fold Farm
MPL/ROM * SK6 186 D3
Higher Fold La RAMS BL0 17 F1
Higher Fullwood OLD OL1 60 C5
Higher Henry St HYDE SK14 147 G2
Higher Hillgate STKP SK1 13 H5
Higher House Cl CHAD OL9 89 F3
Higher La WHTF M45 68 B4
Higher Lime Rd OLDS OL8 103 H2
Higher Lomax La HEY OL10 40 B3
Higher Lydgate Pk OLDE OL4 92 D1
Higher Market St FWTH BL4 65 F4
Higher Ormond St
HULME * M15 127 F2
Higher Ridings EDGW/EG BL7 22 D3
Higher Ri ROY/SHW OL2 44 D5
Higher Rd URM M41 138 C1
Higher Rw BURY BL9 5 J2
Higher Shady La EDGW/EG BL7 23 H4
Higher Shore Rd WHIT OL12 20 B1
Higher Summerseat RAMS BL0 26 C2
Higher Swan La BOLS/LL BL3 48 C5
Higher Tame St STLY SK15 119 G3
Higher Turf La OLDE OL4 76 C4
Higher Turf Pk ROY/SHW OL2 74 B1
Higher Wharf St AULW OL7 118 A3
Higher Wheat La MILN OL16 11 J5
Higher Wood St MDTN M24 71 G2
Highfield SALE M33 154 D3
Highfield Av BOLE BL2 35 H3
HEY OL10 40 B4
MPL/ROM SK6 161 G4
RAD M26 67 H3
Highfield Cl EDGY/DAV SK3 172 A5
HYDE SK14 133 E2
STRET M32 139 H3
Highfield Crs WILM/AE SK9 199 H1
Highfield Dr ECC M30 109 G2
FWTH BL4 64 B5
MDTN M24 71 G5
MOSL OL5 106 D2
ROY/SHW OL2 74 B2
SWIN M27 97 H3
URM M41 123 F5
Highfield Est WILM/AE SK9 199 H1
Highfield Gdns HYDE SK14 133 E5
Highfield Gln AUL OL6 106 A5
Highfield La WHTF M45 68 C2
Highfield Pk HTNM SK4 158 C4
Highfield Park Rd
MPL/ROM SK6 161 F2
Highfield Pkwy BRAM/HZG SK7 193 G3
Highfield Pl GTN * M18 130 A4
Highfield Range GTN * M18 130 A4
Highfield Rd BNG/LEV M19 144 B2
BOL BL1 33 E4
BRAM/HZG SK7 184 A1
BRAM/HZG SK7 185 H2
CHD/CHDH SK8 182 C3
ECC M30 109 G1
FWTH BL4 63 H4
HALE/TIMP WA15 166 C4
HALE/TIMP WA15 178 B2
HTNM SK4 144 B3
LHULT M38 80 A2
MILN OL16 31 H5
MPL/ROM SK6 175 E4
POY/DIS * SK12 194 B3
PWCH M25 84 D1
ROCH OL11 28 B2
SLFD M6 111 G2
STRET M32 139 H3
Highfield St BRO M7 100 A3
CHAD OL9 8 D3
DTN/ASHW M34 131 F3
DUK SK16 118 A4
EDGY/DAV SK3 12 A5
FWTH BL4 81 H1
MDTN M24 72 A4
Highfield Ter BKLY M9 101 E2
OLDE OL4 75 G2
Highgate Av URM M41 122 D4
Highgate Crs GTN M18 129 G4
Highgate Dr LHULT M38 79 D2
ROY/SHW OL2 58 D2
Highgate La LHULT M38 79 D2
WHIT OL12 18 B2
Highgate Rd ALT WA14 165 E5
High Gates SALE M33 155 F1
The Highgrove BOL BL1 32 A5
Highgrove Cl BOL BL1 34 A3
High Grove La OLDE OL4 93 F2
High Grove Rd CHD/CHDH SK8 169 H4
High Houses BOL * BL1 22 C5
High Hurst Cl MDTN * M24 70 D5
Highland Rd EDGW/EG BL7 23 G3
The Highlands MOSL * OL5 106 C1
Highlands LIT OL15 20 D5
ROY/SHW OL2 73 H1
Highlands Dr OFTN SK2 173 G3
Highlands Rd HEY OL10 41 E1
OFTN SK2 173 G3
ROY/SHW OL2 59 G1
ROY/SHW OL2 73 H1
High La CCHDY M21 141 E3
MPL/ROM SK6 162 A2
High Lea CHD/CHDH SK8 169 H4
High Lee La OLDE OL4 76 C1
High Legh Rd OP/CLY M11 115 G5
High Level Rd ROCH OL11 30 B5
High Meadow CHD/CHDH * SK8 182 B4
Highmeadow RAD M26 67 E3
High Mdw EDGW/EG BL7 23 G3
MPL/ROM SK6 162 B3
Highmead St GTN M18 129 G3
Highmead Wk OLDTF/WHR M16 126 C3
High Moor Crs OLDE OL4 75 H3
Highmore Dr BKLY M9 87 F4
High Mt BOLE BL2 35 F3
High Peak Rd AUL OL6 106 A4
WHIT OL12 18 B2
High Peak St NEWH/MOS M40 102 A4
Highshore Dr CHH M8 100 A3
High Stile La UPML OL3 78 C2
High Stile St FWTH BL4 65 F5
Highstone Dr CHH M8 100 D4
High St ALT WA14 165 G5
ANC M4 7 F4
BOLS/LL BL3 48 D5
BOLS/LL BL3 66 A1
BRAM/HZG SK7 185 G2
CHD/CHDH SK8 170 A3
DROY M43 116 B4
HEY OL10 40 C4
HYDE SK14 133 E5
LIT OL15 20 C3
MDTN M24 71 H3
MOSL * OL5 93 E5
OLD OL1 9 F3
OLDE OL4 91 H1
ROY/SHW * OL2 59 E5
ROY/SHW OL2 60 A3
STKP SK1 13 G3
STLY SK15 119 F4
TOT/BURYW BL8 37 E3
UPML OL3 78 A4
WALK M28 80 D4
WHIT OL12 10 C5
Highthorne Gn ROY/SHW OL2 58 D1
High View St BOL BL1 33 H1
BOLS/LL * BL3 48 B5
Highwood ROCH OL11 28 B2
Highwood Cl BOLE * BL2 35 G5
High Wood Fold MPL/ROM SK6 175 H1
Highworth Cl BOLS/LL * BL3 48 D4
Highworth Dr NEWH/MOS M40 88 C5
Higifield Av SALE M33 154 D3
Higson Av CCHDY M21 141 E4
ECC M30 109 F5
MPL/ROM SK6 161 G4
Hilary Av CHD/CHDH SK8 182 A4
OLDS OL8 104 C1
Hilary Cl HTNM SK4 12 C1
Hilary Gv FWTH BL4 64 D5
Hilary Rd WYTH/NTH M22 180 A3
Hilary St ROCH * OL11 42 C5
Hilbre Av ROY/SHW OL2 74 A2
Hilbury Av BKLY M9 101 E1
Hilda Av CHD/CHDH SK8 170 B4
TOT/BURYW BL8 26 A5
Hilda Gv RDSH SK5 160 A2
Hilda Rd HYDE SK14 147 G4
Hilda St BOLS/LL BL3 49 F5
CHAD OL9 8 D2
HEY OL10 41 E4
Hilden Ct OLDTF/WHR M16 126 C4
Hilden St BOLE BL2 3 H6
Hilditch Cl NTHM/RTH M23 168 A3
Hiley Rd ECC M30 108 C5
Hillam Cl URM M41 139 E2
Hillary Av AULW OL7 105 E5
Hillary Rd HYDE SK14 133 F3
Hillbank Cl BOL BL1 33 F3
Hillbank St MDTN M24 57 G3
Hillbre Wy WILM/AE SK9 192 A3
Hillbrook Av NEWH/MOS * M40 88 A5
Hillbrook Rd BRAM/HZG SK7 193 G1
STKP SK1 172 D1
Hillbury Rd BRAM/HZG SK7 184 A3
Hillcote Wk GTN * M18 129 E2
Hill Cot Rd BOL BL1 34 A1
Hill Court Ms MPL/ROM SK6 162 A4
Hillcourt Rd MPL/ROM SK6 162 B2
MPL/ROM SK6 186 D5
Hillcourt St CMANE M1 127 F1
Hill Crs BKLY M9 86 B4
Hillcrest HYDE SK14 148 A4
MDTN M24 71 G1
SLFD * M6 110 B2
Hillcrest Av HEY OL10 40 B3
Hill Crest Av HTNM SK4 158 D4
Hillcrest Crs HEY OL10 40 B3
Hillcrest Dr BNG/LEV M19 144 B4
DTN/ASHW M34 147 E2
Hillcrest Rd BRAM/HZG SK7 184 A3
OFTN SK2 172 D3
PWCH M25 84 C5
ROCH OL11 42 C4
Hillcroft OFTN SK2 173 F3
OLDS OL8 104 D2
Hillcroft Cl CHH M8 100 B2
Hillcroft Rd ALT WA14 164 D4
Hilldale Av BKLY M9 87 E3
Hill Dr WILM/AE SK9 192 B4
Hill End MPL/ROM * SK6 162 C2
Hillend La HYDE SK14 149 G2
Hillend Pl NTHM/RTH M23 155 H4
Hillend Rd NTHM/RTH M23 155 H4
Hill Farm Cl OLDS OL8 91 E4
Hillfield ORD M5 111 E3
Hillfield Cl BRUN/LGST M13 128 A3
Hillfield Dr BOLE BL2 34 C5
WALK M28 94 B3
Hillfield Wk BOLE BL2 34 C5
Hillfoot Wk HULME * M15 126 C2
Hillgate Av ORD M5 126 A1
Hillgate St AUL OL6 118 B1
Hillier St BKLY M9 101 F2
Hillier St North BKLY M9 101 F2
Hillingdon Cl OLDS OL8 103 G1
Hillingdon Dr NEWH/MOS M40 88 A5
Hillingdon Rd STRET M32 140 B2
WHTF M45 67 H5
Hillington Rd EDGY/DAV SK3 12 A6
SALE M33 153 H2
Hillkirk Dr WHIT OL12 18 B5
Hillkirk St OP/CLY M11 114 B4
Hill La BKLY M9 87 E4
BOLE BL2 3 H2
Hillman Cl NEWH/MOS M40 101 E5
Hill Mt DUK SK16 119 F5
Hill Ri ALT WA14 164 D4
MPL/ROM SK6 162 A4
RAMS BL0 16 B4
Hillsborough Dr BURY BL9 69 E2
Hill's Ct TOT/BURYW BL8 37 G2
Hillsdale Gv BOLE BL2 35 F3
Hill Side BOL BL1 47 G2
Hillside Av BRO M7 98 D2
EDGW/EG BL7 23 G4
FWTH BL4 64 D5
HYDE SK14 148 A5
OLDE OL4 75 F5
OLDE OL4 92 B2
ROY/SHW OL2 59 F4
ROY/SHW OL2 60 C2
STLY SK15 107 G4
UPML OL3 78 B1
WALK M28 80 D3
WHTF M45 68 B2
Hillside Cl BOLE BL2 35 F1
BOLS/LL BL3 62 A2
BRAM/HZG SK7 184 B5
NEWH/MOS M40 101 H1
Hillside Crs AUL OL6 106 A5
BURY BL9 27 G5
Hillside Dr MDTN M24 71 H3
SWIN M27 98 A4
Hillside Gv MPL/ROM SK6 163 G5
Hillside Rd HALE/TIMP WA15 178 B1
MPL/ROM SK6 162 B1
OFTN SK2 173 E2
RAMS BL0 16 B3
Hillside St BOLS/LL BL3 48 C4
Hillside Vw DTN/ASHW M34 146 D4
Hillside Wk WHIT OL12 18 C4
Hillside Wy WHIT OL12 14 B4
Hills La BURY BL9 69 F2
Hillspring Rd OLDE OL4 92 B1
Hillstone Av WHIT OL12 18 B4
Hillstone Cl TOT/BURYW BL8 26 A1
Hill St AULW OL7 117 H3
BRO M7 99 G4
BURY BL9 16 D5
DID/WITH M20 142 C4
HEY OL10 40 D4
MDTN M24 71 H1
MILN OL16 10 E7
MPL/ROM SK6 162 A4
OLDE OL4 75 E5
RAD M26 52 A5
ROY/SHW OL2 60 B3
TOT/BURYW * BL8 37 E2
Hill Top BOLS/LL BL3 50 D5
HALE/TIMP WA15 178 B3
MPL/ROM SK6 162 A3
Hill Top Av CHD/CHDH SK8 183 E3
PWCH M25 85 E3
Hilltop Av BKLY M9 87 E4
WHTF M45 69 E4
Hill Top Av WILM/AE SK9 199 G2
Hill Top Ct CHD/CHDH SK8 183 E3
Hill Top Dr HALE/TIMP WA15 178 B2
ROCH OL11 43 F4
Hilltop Dr MPL/ROM SK6 174 B3
ROY/SHW OL2 74 B2
TOT/BURYW BL8 25 H5
Hilltop Gv WHTF M45 69 E4
Hill Top Rd WALK M28 81 E3
Hill Vw STLY SK15 134 A2
Hill View Cl OLD OL1 75 F2
Hillview Rd BOL * BL1 33 H2
DTN/ASHW M34 145 F2
Hillwood Av CHH M8 86 A4
Hillyard St TOT/BURYW BL8 37 H3
Hilly Cft EDGW/EG BL7 23 E3
Hilmarton Cl BOLE BL2 35 F1
Hilrose Av URM M41 139 E1
Hilton Av URM M41 138 C1
Hilton Ct EDGY/DAV * SK3 12 E5
Hilton Crs AUL OL6 105 F5
WALK M28 94 C4
Hilton Dr AULW OL7 104 C5
IRL M44 150 B1
PWCH M25 85 E5
Hilton Fold La MDTN M24 72 A3
Hilton Gv POY/DIS SK12 195 E3
WALK M28 80 C4
Hilton La PWCH M25 84 D5
WALK M28 80 C5
Hilton Rd BRAM/HZG SK7 184 A2
BURY BL9 4 E5
POY/DIS SK12 187 G5
POY/DIS SK12 196 B2
WYTH/NTH M22 168 D4
Hiltons Cl OLDS OL8 8 E7
Hiltons Farm Cl DTN/ASHW M34 131 F2
Hilton Sq SWIN M27 97 F1
Hilton St ANC M4 7 G3
BOLE BL2 49 H2
BRO M7 99 G4
BURY BL9 5 F1
EDGY/DAV SK3 12 D5
HYDE * SK14 133 E3
LHULT M38 80 B3
Hilton St North BRO M7 99 G4
Hilton Wk MDTN M24 70 D4
Himley Rd OP/CLY M11 115 F2
Hinchcombe Cl LHULT * M38 80 B1
Hinchley Rd BKLY M9 88 A4
Hinchley Wy SWIN M27 83 E5
Hinckley St OP/CLY M11 114 C5
Hindburn Cl WHTF M45 69 E4
Hindburn Dr WALK M28 94 B2
Hinde St NEWH/MOS M40 101 H2
Hind Hill St HEY OL10 41 E5
Hindle Dr ROY/SHW OL2 73 H1
Hindle St RAD M26 67 F1
Hindley Av WYTH/NTH M22 180 A2
Hindley St AULW OL7 117 G4
STKP SK1 13 H6
Hindsford Cl NTHM/RTH M23 155 E5
Hinds La RAD M26 52 D2
TOT/BURYW BL8 37 H5
Hind St BOLE BL2 50 A2
Hinkler Av BOLS/LL BL3 63 H1
Hinton WHIT OL12 10 B4
Hinton Cl ROCH OL11 28 B5
Hinton Gv HYDE SK14 148 B3
Hinton St ANC * M4 7 J1
OLDS OL8 9 H6
Hipley Cl MPL/ROM SK6 161 H1
Hirons La OLDE OL4 92 B2
Hirst Av WALK M28 80 D2
Hitchen Cl DUK SK16 133 E1
Hitchen Dr DUK SK16 133 E1
Hitchen Wk BRUN/LGST M13 127 H3
Hive St OLDS OL8 89 G5
Hobart Cl BRAM/HZG SK7 194 A2
Hobart St BOL BL1 33 G4
GTN M18 129 G3
Hobson Ct DTN/ASHW M34 131 F2
Hobson Crs DTN/ASHW M34 131 F2
Hobson Moor Rd HYDE SK14 134 C2
Hobson St FAIL M35 102 C4
OLD OL1 9 G5
OP/CLY M11 130 B1
RDSH SK5 145 E1
Hockenhull Cl WYTH/NTH M22 180 D2
Hockley Cl POY/DIS SK12 195 G4

Hockley Paddock
POY/DIS SK12 195 G4
Hockley Rd NTHM/RTH M23 167 G3
POY/DIS SK12 195 G4
Hodder Av LIT OL15 20 C2
Hodder Bank OFTN SK2 173 F4
Hodder Wy WHTF M45 69 F4
Hoddesdon St CHH M8 100 C3
Hodge Clough Rd OLD OL1 60 C5
Hodge La HYDE SK14 149 G3
SLFD M6 111 G4
Hodge Rd OLD OL1 75 G1
WALK M28 81 E5
Hodge St BKLY M9 101 G1
Hodgson Dr HALE/TIMP WA15 166 B1
Hodgson St AUL OL6 117 H3
CHH M8 100 A5
Hodnett Av URM M41 137 F2
Hodson Fold OLDS OL8 104 D1
Hodson Rd SWIN M27 82 D5
Hogarth Ri OLD OL1 60 C5
Hogarth Rd MPL/ROM SK6 175 G1
ROCH OL11 43 E4
Holbeach Cl TOT/BURYW BL8 38 A1
Holbeck Av WHIT OL12 18 C4
Holbeck Gv RUSH/FAL M14 128 B4
Holbeton Cl CHH M8 99 H5
Holborn Av FAIL M35 103 G3
RAD M26 51 G5
Holborn Dr CHH M8 100 C5
Holborn Gdns ROCH OL11 42 C1
Holborn Sq ROCH OL11 42 C1
Holborn St ROCH OL11 42 C1
STKP SK1 13 G4
Holbrook Av LHULT M38 80 B1
Holbrook St CMANE * M1 7 G7
Holcombe Av TOT/BURYW BL8 37 G4
Holcombe Cl ALT WA14 165 E3
FWTH BL4 81 H1
OLDE OL4 76 B5
SLFD M6 111 H3
Holcombe Ct RAMS * BL0 26 A1
Holcombe Crs FWTH BL4 81 H1
Holcombe Lee RAMS BL0 16 B5
Holcombe Old Rd
TOT/BURYW BL8 16 A5
Holcombe Rd BOLS/LL BL3 65 G1
RUSH/FAL M14 143 F4
TOT/BURYW BL8 16 A5
Holcombe View Cl OLDE OL4 75 G2
Holden Av BOL BL1 22 D5
BURY BL9 39 H2
RAMS BL0 16 B3
Holden Clough Dr AULW OL7 104 D3
Holden Fold La ROY/SHW OL2 73 H2
Holden Rd BRO M7 99 G1
Holden St AUL OL6 118 B1
OLDS OL8 90 C4
WHIT OL12 11 F1
Holder Av BOLS/LL BL3 51 E4
Holderness Dr ROY/SHW OL2 73 H2
Holdgate Cl HULME M15 126 D3
Holdsworth St SWIN M27 96 C3
Holebottom AUL OL6 105 F4
Hole House Fold MPL/ROM SK6 162 A4
Holford Av RUSH/FAL M14 142 C1
Holford St SLFD M6 112 B1
Holford Wk MILN OL16 31 E4
Holgate St OLDE OL4 75 H3
Holhouse La TOT/BURYW BL8 25 H1
Holiday La OFTN SK2 173 G3
Holker Cl BRUN/LGST M13 128 A3
POY/DIS SK12 195 G3
Holkham Cl ANC * M4 113 H3
Holland Av STLY SK15 119 F3
Holland Ct RAD M26 52 D5
Holland Gv AUL OL6 105 E4
Holland Ri WHIT OL12 10 B5
Holland Rd BRAM/HZG SK7 183 H5
CHH M8 86 A5
HYDE SK14 133 E3
Holland St BOL BL1 34 A2
DTN/ASHW M34 131 E4
HEY OL10 41 E4
MILN OL16 20 A4
NEWH/MOS M40 114 A3
RAD M26 52 D5
SLFD M6 98 D5
WHIT OL12 10 A6
Holland St East DTN/ASHW M34 131 E4
Holland St West
DTN/ASHW M34 130 D4
The Hollies CHD/CHDH * SK8 169 G4
DID/WITH M20 157 E3
Hollies Dr MPL/ROM SK6 175 F4
Hollies La WILM/AE SK9 200 C3
Hollin Bank HTNM SK4 144 C4
Hollin Crs OLDE OL4 93 F3
Hollin Dr MDTN M24 56 B5
Holliney Av WYTH/NTH M22 181 E3
Holliney Rd WYTH/NTH M22 181 E3
Hollingworth Av
NEWH/MOS M40 89 E5
Hollingworth Cl STKP * SK1 13 G5
Hollingworth Dr MPL/ROM SK6 187 E1
Hollingworth Rd LIT OL15 21 E4
MPL/ROM SK6 161 F2
Hollingworth St CHAD OL9 89 G4
Hollinhall St OLDE OL4 75 F5
Hollin Hey Rd BOL BL1 32 B3
Hollinhurst Dr HOR/BR BL6 46 D2
Hollinhurst Rd RAD M26 67 H2
Hollin La MDTN M24 56 C5
ROCH OL11 28 B5
WILM/AE SK9 191 E2
Hollins FWTH * BL4 63 G4
Hollins Av HYDE SK14 147 H4
OLDE OL4 76 A4
Hollins Brook Cl BURY * BL9 54 A4
Hollins Brook Wy BURY BL9 54 A3
Hollins Brow BURY BL9 53 G5
Hollins Cl BURY BL9 54 A5
Hollinsclough Cl
WYTH/NTH M22 168 D4
Hollinscroft Av
HALE/TIMP WA15 167 E4
Hollins Gn MDTN M24 71 H1
Hollins Green Rd MPL/ROM SK6 175 F3
Hollins Gv SALE M33 154 B2
WGTN/LGST M12 128 D5
Hollins La BURY BL9 53 H4
MOSL OL5 107 E1
MPL/ROM SK6 175 E3
MPL/ROM SK6 175 H1
Hollins Ms BURY BL9 54 B5
Hollins Mt MPL/ROM SK6 175 G1
Hollins Rd OLDE OL4 76 A4
OLDS OL8 89 H5
Hollins St BOLE BL2 3 J7
OLDE OL4 92 A1
STLY SK15 119 E5
Hollinswood Rd BOLE BL2 3 K6
WALK M28 94 C4
Hollinwood Av CHAD OL9 89 F5
NEWH/MOS M40 88 C5
Hollinwood La MPL/ROM SK6 187 G2
Holloway Dr WALK M28 96 B1
Hollowbrook Wy WHIT OL12 29 G1
Hollow End RDSH SK5 145 G4
Hollowfield ROCH OL11 28 A2
Hollow Mdw RAD M26 82 B1
The Hollows CHD/CHDH * SK8 181 H3
Hollowspell WHIT OL12 19 H5
Hollow Vale Dr RDSH SK5 145 F2
Holly Av CHD/CHDH SK8 170 A4
URM M41 138 A1
WALK M28 81 F5
Holly Bank NEWH/MOS * M40 102 B3
ROY/SHW OL2 59 E4
SALE M33 154 D3
Hollybank Ri DUK SK16 119 E5
Holly Bank Rd WILM/AE SK9 199 G1
Hollybank St RAD M26 67 E1
Hollybrook Dene
MPL/ROM SK6 162 D4
Hollybush St GTN M18 129 H2
Holly Cl HALE/TIMP WA15 166 B3
Holly Ct HYDE SK14 148 B1
Hollycroft Av BOLE BL2 50 B4
WYTH/NTH M22 168 C3
Holly Dene Dr HOR/BR BL6 46 C2
Holly Dr SALE M33 154 B2
Hollyedge Dr PWCH M25 84 D5
Holly Fold WHTF M45 68 C3
Holly Gra ALT WA14 177 G2
BRAM/HZG SK7 184 A1
Holly Gv BOL BL1 33 F5
CHAD OL9 73 G4
DTN/ASHW M34 131 H5
DUK SK16 118 D5
FWTH BL4 64 B4
OLDE OL4 75 H4
SALE M33 155 E2
Hollyhedge Av WYTH/NTH M22 168 C4
Hollyhedge Court Rd
WYTH/NTH M22 168 D4
Hollyhedge Rd NTHM/RTH M23 168 A4
Hollyhey Dr NTHM/RTH M23 156 A5
Hollyhouse Dr MPL/ROM SK6 161 H1
Holly House Dr URM M41 137 G1
Hollyhurst WALK M28 96 A4
Holly La OLDS OL8 89 H5
WILM/AE SK9 190 D2
Holly Mill Crs BOL BL1 34 A2
Hollymount Av OFTN SK2 172 D4
Hollymount Dr OFTN SK2 172 D4
OLDE OL4 75 H1
Hollymount Gdns OFTN SK2 173 E4
Hollymount Rd OFTN SK2 172 D4
Holly Oak Gdns HEY OL10 40 D5
Holly Rd BRAM/HZG SK7 193 H2
HTNM SK4 159 F1
MPL/ROM SK6 186 D5
POY/DIS SK12 195 F4
SWIN M27 96 C4
Holly Rd North WILM/AE SK9 199 F4
Holly Rd South WILM/AE SK9 199 F5
Holly Royde Cl DID/WITH M20 142 B5
Holly St BOL BL1 34 A2
BURY BL9 5 H4
DROY M43 115 G3
OP/CLY M11 114 B5
RAMS BL0 16 D5
STKP SK1 13 K4
TOT/BURYW BL8 26 A5
WHIT OL12 19 H2
Hollythorn Av CHD/CHDH SK8 183 F5
Hollyway WYTH/NTH M22 168 D1
Hollywood Rd BOL BL1 33 E4
Hollywood Wy HTNM SK4 12 C4
Holmbrook Wk CHH M8 100 B4
Holm Ct SLFD * M6 111 H2
Holmcroft Rd GTN M18 144 C1
Holmdale Av BNG/LEV M19 158 B1
Holme Av TOT/BURYW BL8 37 H1
Holme Beech Gv OFTN * SK2 172 D1
Holme Crs ROY/SHW OL2 73 H2
Holmefield SALE M33 154 C2
Holme House St LIT OL15 15 C4
Holme Park Gdns WALK M28 94 B5
Holme Park Wy FAIL M35 103 G3
Holme Rd DID/WITH M20 157 E3
Holmes Cottages BOL * BL1 33 F3
Holmes Rd WHIT OL12 29 G4
Holmes St BOLS/LL BL3 49 E5
CHD/CHDH SK8 170 B3
EDGY/DAV SK3 13 F7
WHIT OL12 19 H3
WHIT OL12 29 G3
Holme St HYDE SK14 147 G1
Holmeswood Cl WILM/AE SK9 199 H2
Holmeswood Rd BOLS/LL BL3 63 G2
Holme Ter LIT OL15 15 C4
Holmfield Av BKLY M9 101 G3
PWCH M25 85 F4
Holmfield Av West
NEWH/MOS M40 101 G4
Holmfield Cl HTNM SK4 159 G3
Holmfield Dr CHD/CHDH SK8 183 E4
Holmfield Gn BOLS/LL BL3 62 C1
Holmfirth St BRUN/LGST M13 128 C4
Holmlea Rd DROY M43 115 H3
Holmleigh Av BKLY M9 101 F1
Holmpark Rd OP/CLY M11 129 H1
Holmside Gdns BNG/LEV M19 158 A2
Holmwood ALT WA14 176 D1
Holmwood Rd DID/WITH M20 157 G1
Holroyd St MILN OL16 11 F4
OP/CLY * M11 114 D5
Holset Dr ALT WA14 165 E4
Holst Av CHH M8 100 B4
Holstein Av WHIT OL12 18 C4
Holtby St BKLY M9 101 F1
Holthouse Rd TOT/BURYW BL8 36 D1
Holt La FAIL M35 103 G3
Holt Lane Ms FAIL M35 103 F3
Holts La OLDE OL4 91 G3
WILM/AE SK9 191 E4
Holts Ter WHIT OL12 10 B1
Holt St ALT WA14 165 F2
BOLS/LL BL3 48 C4
DTN/ASHW M34 117 F5
ECC M30 109 F5
LIT OL15 15 C3
MILN * OL16 44 D1
NEWH/MOS M40 101 G5
OLDE OL4 75 F4
RAMS BL0 17 E2
STKP SK1 13 H6
SWIN M27 96 D3
WHIT OL12 14 B4
Holt St West RAMS BL0 16 C3
Holt Town NEWH/MOS M40 114 B3
Holwick Rd NTHM/RTH M23 155 G4
Holwood Dr OLDTF/WHR M16 141 H3
Holy Harbour St BOL * BL1 33 F4
Holyhurst Wk BOL * BL1 33 H4
Holyoake Rd WALK M28 81 E5
Holyoake St DROY M43 116 D3
Holyoak St NEWH/MOS M40 102 B4
Holyrood Cl PWCH M25 85 F1
Holyrood Dr PWCH M25 85 F1
SWIN M27 96 B3
Holyrood Gv PWCH M25 85 E1
Holyrood Rd PWCH M25 85 F2
Holyrood St NEWH/MOS M40 115 G1
OLD OL1 74 D3
Holy St ROCH OL11 43 G4
Holywood St RUSH/FAL M14 127 G5
Homebury Dr OP/CLY * M11 115 E3
Home Dr MDTN M24 71 G5
Home Farm Av HYDE SK14 149 G2
Homelands Cl SALE M33 154 A4
Homelands Rd SALE M33 154 A4
Homer Dr MPL/ROM SK6 175 G1
Homerton Rd NEWH/MOS M40 115 E1
Homestead Cl PART M31 151 F2
Homestead Crs BNG/LEV M19 158 A3
Homestead Gdns WHIT OL12 20 A3
Homestead Rd POY/DIS SK12 197 H1
Hometel RUSH/FAL M14 142 D2
Homewood Av WYTH/NTH M22 156 C5
Homewood Rd WYTH/NTH M22 156 B5
Honduras St OLDE OL4 9 K3
Hondwith Cl BOLE BL2 34 C1
Honeycombe Cottages
CHD/CHDH * SK8 170 B4
Honey St CHH M8 113 F1
Honeysuckle Cl MPL/ROM SK6 161 H1
NTHM/RTH M23 155 E5
Honeysuckle Dr STLY SK15 119 G3
Honeysuckle Wy WHIT OL12 18 C5
Honeywell La OLDS OL8 90 C4
Honeywood Cl RAMS BL0 16 B5
Honford Rd WYTH/NTH M22 168 A5
Hong Kong Av MANAIR M90 179 H4
Honister Dr MDTN M24 71 G2
Honister Rd BKLY M9 101 G3
Honister Wy ROCH OL11 42 A2
Honiton Av HYDE SK14 148 D1
Honiton Cl CHAD OL9 73 G3
HEY OL10 55 H1
Honiton Dr BOLE BL2 50 D3
Honiton Gv RAD M26 51 G4
Honiton Wy ALT WA14 164 D3
Honor St BRUN/LGST M13 128 B5
Hood Sq OLDE OL4 92 B2
Hood St ANC M4 7 J3
Hoole Cl CHD/CHDH SK8 170 D4
Hooley Range HTNM SK4 159 E3
Hooper St OLDE OL4 9 K5
STKP SK1 13 F4
WGTN/LGST M12 114 A5
Hooton St BOLS/LL BL3 63 F1
NEWH/MOS M40 114 B2
Hopcroft Cl BKLY M9 86 C1
Hope Av BOLE BL2 3 K7
BOLE BL2 35 F1
LHULT M38 80 C3
STRET M32 124 C5
WILM/AE SK9 191 H4
Hopecourt Cl SLFD M6 110 C1
Hopedale Rd RDSH SK5 145 E5
Hopefield St BOLS/LL BL3 48 C5
Hopefold Dr WALK M28 81 F5
Hope Green Wy POY/DIS SK12 195 E5
Hope Hey La LHULT M38 80 A2
Hopelea St DID/WITH M20 142 C4
Hope Park Cl PWCH M25 85 E4
Hope Park Rd PWCH M25 85 E4
Hope Pl ROCH * OL11 42 B5
Hope Rd PWCH M25 84 D5
RUSH/FAL M14 128 A4
Hopes Carr STKP SK1 13 H4
Hope St AUL OL6 105 G5
BRAM/HZG SK7 185 E2
BRO M7 99 G3
CMANE M1 7 G5
DTN/ASHW M34 131 F3
DUK SK16 118 B5
HEY OL10 56 C1
HTNM SK4 12 D3
LHULT M38 80 B3
OLD OL1 8 D3
ORD M5 112 B4
RAMS BL0 16 C3
ROY/SHW OL2 60 A2
SWIN M27 97 F2
WHIT OL12 10 C4
Hope Ter DUK * SK16 118 A5
EDGY/DAV * SK3 13 F6
Hopkin Av OLD OL1 75 E4
Hopkins Fld ALT WA14 177 E3
Hopkinson Av DTN/ASHW M34 131 F3
Hopkinson Cl UPML * OL3 78 A4
Hopkinson Rd BKLY M9 87 E2
Hopkins St HYDE SK14 132 D4
Hopkin St OLD OL1 9 H3
Hoppet La DROY M43 116 D3
Hopton Av WYTH/NTH M22 180 D1
Hopwood Av ECC M30 109 G2
HEY OL10 56 A1
Hopwood Cl BURY BL9 68 C1
Hopwood Rd MDTN M24 56 D5
Hopwood St CSLFD * M3 6 C2
NEWH/MOS M40 102 A4
SWIN M27 97 F2
Horace Barnes Cl
RUSH/FAL M14 127 F5
Horace Gv HTNM SK4 159 H2
Horace St BOL BL1 33 G4
Horatio St GTN * M18 130 A2
Horbury Av GTN M18 129 G5
Horbury Dr TOT/BURYW BL8 37 H4
Horeb St BOLS/LL BL3 48 C4
Horest La UPML OL3 61 G1
Horley Cl TOT/BURYW BL8 26 D4
Hornbeam Cl HALE/TIMP WA15 167 F4
SALE M33 153 F1
Hornbeam Ct SLFD M6 111 H2
Hornbeam Rd BNG/LEV M19 144 A1
Hornby Av BKLY M9 87 F2
Hornby Dr BOLS/LL BL3 62 A2
Hornby Rd STRET M32 125 G4
Hornby St BURY BL9 38 C1
CHH M8 113 E1
HEY OL10 41 E5
MDTN M24 71 H4
OLDS OL8 8 D6
Horncastle Cl TOT/BURYW BL8 38 A1
Horncastle Rd NEWH/MOS M40 102 A1
Hornchurch St HULME M15 126 D2
Horne Dr ANC M4 7 K3
Horne St BURY BL9 53 F1
Hornsea Cl CHAD OL9 73 E3
TOT/BURYW BL8 37 E4
Hornsea Rd OFTN SK2 173 H4
Hornsea Wk OP/CLY * M11 114 D4
Horridge Fold Av WHTN BL5 62 C2
Horridge St TOT/BURYW BL8 37 G2
Horrobin Fold EDGW/EG * BL7 23 H1
Horrobin La EDGW/EG BL7 23 H1
Horrocks Fold Av BOL BL1 22 C5
Horrocks St RAD * M26 52 D5
Horsa St BOLE BL2 3 J1
Horsedge St OLD OL1 9 H1
Horsefield Av WHIT OL12 18 B2
Horsefield Cl CCHDY M21 141 H4
Horseforth La UPML OL3 93 H3
Horseshoe La CHAD OL9 89 E1
EDGW/EG BL7 23 F3
WILM/AE SK9 201 B3
Horsfield St BOLS/LL BL3 47 H5
Horsfield Wy MPL/ROM SK6 146 C5
Horsham Av BRAM/HZG SK7 184 D3
Horsham Cl TOT/BURYW BL8 26 D4
Horsham St SLFD M6 111 F3
Horstead Wk BNG/LEV M19 143 H1
Horton Av BOL BL1 22 D5
Horton Rd RUSH/FAL M14 142 B1
Horton St OFTN SK2 172 A2
Hortree Rd STRET M32 140 B1
Horwood Crs DID/WITH M20 158 A1
Hoscar Dr BNG/LEV M19 143 F4
Hoskins Cl WGTN/LGST M12 128 D3
Hospital Rd EDGW/EG BL7 23 F3
SWIN M27 97 G3
Hotel Rd MANAIR M90 180 B5
Hotel St BOL BL1 2 E5
Hothersall Rd RDSH SK5 145 E4
Hothersall St BRO M7 112 D2
Hotspur Cl DID/WITH M20 142 B3
Hough Cl OLDS OL8 90 D5
Hough End Av CCHDY M21 141 F5
Houghend Crs CCHDY M21 141 H4
Hough Fold Wy BOLE BL2 35 E2
Hough Hall Rd NEWH/MOS M40 101 G2
Hough Hill Rd STLY SK15 119 F4
Hough La EDGW/EG BL7 23 E4
HYDE SK14 133 E3
MDTN M24 58 A4
WILM/AE SK9 200 A5
Hough St BOLS/LL BL3 47 H5
Houghton Av OLDS OL8 90 A5
Houghton Cl MILN OL16 30 D5
Houghton La SWIN M27 96 C5
Houghton Rd CHH M8 100 B1
Houghton St BOLS/LL BL3 48 D4
BURY BL9 4 C7
ROY/SHW OL2 74 B2
SWIN M27 98 A4
Hough Wk BRO M7 112 B2
Houldsworth Av ALT WA14 165 H2
Houldsworth Ms RDSH * SK5 144 D4
Houldsworth St CMANE M1 7 H3
RAD M26 52 A4
RDSH SK5 144 D4
Houseley Av CHAD OL9 89 F4
Houson St OLDS OL8 9 G6
Houston Pk SALQ M50 111 G4
Hove Cl TOT/BURYW BL8 26 A2
Hoveden St CHH M8 113 E1
Hove Dr RUSH/FAL M14 143 F4
Hove St BOLS/LL BL3 48 B4
Hove St North BOLS/LL * BL3 48 B4
Hovey Cl CHH * M8 100 A3
Hovingham St MILN OL16 11 G5
Hovis St OP/CLY M11 115 F5
Howard Av BOLS/LL BL3 47 H5
CHD/CHDH SK8 182 D3
ECC M30 109 G2
FWTH BL4 65 G5
HTNM SK4 144 B5
Howard Cl MPL/ROM SK6 161 H4
Howard Ct AUL OL6 118 A2
HALE/TIMP * WA15 166 C3
Howard Dr HALE/TIMP WA15 178 B3
Howard Hl BURY BL9 53 H5
Howard La DTN/ASHW M34 131 G4
Howard Pl MILN OL16 10 C5
Howard Rd WYTH/NTH M22 156 C5
Howard's La MOSL OL5 107 G1
Howard St AULW OL7 117 H1
BOL BL1 34 A5
CHH M8 112 D1
DTN/ASHW M34 131 F3
OLDE OL4 75 H4
ORD M5 111 H5
RAD M26 67 G1
ROY/SHW OL2 59 H2
STKP SK1 13 G1
STLY SK15 120 A1
STRET M32 140 A1
WHIT OL12 10 B4
Howard Wy LIT OL15 15 B4
Howarth Av WALK M28 96 B3
Howarth Cross St MILN OL16 30 C1
Howarth Dr IRL M44 136 A2
Howarth Farm Wy WHIT OL12 19 H5
Howarth Sq MILN OL16 11 F5
Howarth St FWTH BL4 65 E5
LIT OL15 21 E2
OLDTF/WHR M16 126 B4
Howbridge Cl WALK M28 94 D2
Howbro Dr AULW OL7 104 B5
How Clough Cl WALK M28 81 G5
How Clough Dr WALK M28 81 G5
Howcroft Cl BOL BL1 2 C3
Howcroft St BOLS/LL BL3 48 C4
Howden Cl RDSH SK5 144 D1
Howden Rd BKLY M9 86 D2
Howe Dr RAMS BL0 26 C1
Howell Cft North BOL BL1 2 E4
Howell Cft South BOL * BL1 2 E5
Howells Av SALE M33 154 B1
Howe St AULW OL7 117 F5
BRO M7 99 F3
Howgill Crs OLDS OL8 90 B4
Howgill St OP/CLY M11 115 G4
How Lea Dr BURY BL9 27 G5
Howsin Av BOLE BL2 34 C2
Howton Cl WGTN/LGST M12 128 D4
Howty Cl WILM/AE SK9 200 A1
Hoxton Cl MPL/ROM SK6 161 H2
Hoy Dr URM M41 123 G3
Hoylake Cl NEWH/MOS M40 102 C2
Hoylake Rd EDGY/DAV SK3 170 D1
SALE M33 155 G4
Hoyland Cl WGTN/LGST M12 128 C2
Hoyle Av OLDS OL8 8 E6
Hoyles Ct RAD * M26 52 D5
Hoyle's Ter MILN * OL16 31 F5
Hoyle St RAD M26 67 G3
WGTN/LGST M12 113 H5
WHIT OL12 14 C2
Hoyle Wk BRUN/LGST * M13 127 G2
Hucclecote Av WYTH/NTH M22 180 B2
Hucklow Av NTHM/RTH M23 179 H2
Hudcar La BURY BL9 5 G1
Huddart Cl ORD M5 112 A5
Huddersfield Rd MILN OL16 45 F2
OLDE OL4 75 H4
STLY SK15 107 F4
STLY SK15 119 H3
UPML OL3 78 A2
Hudson Rd BOLS/LL BL3 63 E1
HYDE SK14 147 H4
Hudson St CHAD OL9 89 F5
Hudsons Wk ROCH OL11 29 E4
Hudswell Cl WHTF M45 68 B4
Hughenden Ct
TOT/BURYW * BL8 26 A4
Hughes Cl FAIL M35 102 D2
Hughes St BOL BL1 33 G4
OP/CLY M11 114 B5
Hughley Cl ROY/SHW OL2 59 G5
Hugh Lupus St BOL BL1 34 B1
Hugh Oldham Dr BRO M7 99 F4
Hugh St MILN OL16 10 E5
Hughtrede St MILN * OL16 43 G3
Hugo St FWTH BL4 64 C2
NEWH/MOS M40 101 H3
ROCH OL11 42 C4
Hulbert St MDTN M24 72 A3
TOT/BURYW BL8 37 H5
Hull Sq CSLFD M3 112 C3
Hully St STLY SK15 119 E3
Hulme Hall Av CHD/CHDH SK8 182 D4
Hulme Hall Cl CHD/CHDH SK8 182 D3
Hulme Hall Crs CHD/CHDH SK8 182 D4
Hulme Hall La NEWH/MOS M40 114 B1
Hulme Hall Rd CHD/CHDH SK8 182 D2
HULME M15 126 C1
Hulme Pl ORD * M5 112 B4
Hulme Rd BOLE BL2 24 B5
DTN/ASHW M34 130 C5
FWTH BL4 82 B1
HTNM SK4 159 G1
RAD M26 66 B5
SALE M33 155 E3
Hulmes Rd NEWH/MOS M40 102 D5
Hulme St AUL OL6 118 C1
BOL BL1 3 F2
HULME M15 126 D1
OLDS OL8 90 B3
STKP SK1 172 C2
TOT/BURYW BL8 4 A2
Hulton Av WALK M28 80 C4
Hulton Cl BOLS/LL BL3 47 H5
Hulton Dr BOLS/LL BL3 62 D1
OLDTF/WHR M16 126 D4
Hulton La BOLS/LL BL3 47 H5
Hulton St FAIL M35 102 C3
ORD M5 125 H1
Humber Dr BURY BL9 27 G3
Humber Rd MILN OL16 31 H5
Humberstone Av HULME M15 126 D1
Humber St CHH M8 100 B3
SALQ M50 111 E4
Hume St BNG/LEV * M19 144 A3
MILN OL16 43 F1
Humphrey Crs URM M41 139 F1
Humphrey La URM M41 139 F1
Humphrey Pk URM M41 139 F2
Humphrey Rd OLDTF/WHR M16 126 A3
Humphrey St CHH M8 100 A2
Huncoat Av HTNM SK4 144 C5
Huncote Dr BKLY M9 101 F1
Hunger Hill Av BOLS/LL BL3 62 B2
Hunstanton Dr TOT/BURYW BL8 38 A1
Hunston Rd SALE M33 154 A3
Hunt Av AULW OL7 105 E5
Hunter Dr RAD M26 52 B4
Hunters Cl MPL/ROM SK6 161 G3
WILM/AE * SK9 200 C1
Hunters Ct STLY SK15 120 A5
Hunters Gn RAMS BL0 16 A5
Hunters Hl BURY BL9 54 A5
Hunter's La MILN OL16 10 C5
OLD OL1 9 H3
Hunters Ms SALE M33 154 B2
WILM/AE SK9 199 H3
Hunterston Av ECC M30 110 B3
Hunt Fold Dr TOT/BURYW BL8 26 A2
Huntingdon Av CHAD OL9 89 G2
Huntingdon Crs RDSH * SK5 160 D1
Huntingdon Wk BOL * BL1 33 H4
Huntington Av DID/WITH M20 142 B4
Hunt La CHAD OL9 73 E4
Huntley Mount Rd BURY BL9 5 J1
Huntley Rd CHH M8 85 H5
EDGY/DAV SK3 171 E2
Huntley St BURY BL9 5 K2
Huntly Cha WILM/AE SK9 199 H4
Hunt Rd HYDE SK14 133 F3
Huntroyde Av BOLE BL2 49 H1
Hunts Bank CSLFD M3 6 E1
Huntsham Cl ALT WA14 165 E3
Huntsman Dr IRL M44 136 A4
Hunts Rd SLFD M6 98 A5

Hunt St BKLY M9 101 E1
Hurdlow Av BRO M7 98 D3
Hurdsfield Rd OFTN SK2 172 D5
Hurford Av GTN M18 129 G2
Hurlbote Cl WILM/AE SK9 192 A2
Hurley Dr CHD/CHDH SK8 182 B2
Hurlston Rd BOLS/LL BL3 63 G2
Hurst Av CHD/CHDH SK8 193 F1
SALE M33 153 F3
Hurstbank Av BNG/LEV * M19 158 A2
Hurst Bank Rd AUL OL6 118 D1
Hurstbourne Av OP/CLY M11 115 E2
Hurst Brook Cl AUL OL6 118 B1
Hurstbrook Dr STRET M32 139 E1
Hurst Cl WHTN BL5 62 C5
Hurstead Gn WHIT * OL12 20 A4
Hurstead Rd MILN OL16 31 G5
Hurstfield Rd WALK M28 94 C2
Hurstfold Av BNG/LEV M19 158 A3
Hurst Green Cl RAD M26 52 A1
Hurst Gv AUL OL6 105 H5
Hurst Hall Dr AUL OL6 105 G5
Hursthead Rd CHD/CHDH SK8 183 E5
Hursthead Wk BRUN/LGST M13 127 G1
Hurst Hill Crs AUL OL6 118 C1
Hurst Meadow MILN OL16 43 G4
Hurst St BOLS/LL BL3 63 F1
BURY BL9 5 G5
CHAD OL9 8 C3
DUK SK16 131 H2
RDSH SK5 144 D4
ROCH OL11 43 F1
WALK M28 80 D1
Hurstvale Av CHD/CHDH SK8 181 G3
Hurstville Rd CCHDY M21 141 E5
Hurstway Dr BKLY M9 87 F4
Hurstwood BOL BL1 33 G1
Hurstwood Cl OLDS OL8 91 F3
Hurstwood Ct BOLS/LL BL3 49 G5
Hurstwood Rd OFTN SK2 173 G3
Hus St DROY M43 116 A5
Husteads La UPML OL3 77 F3
Hutchins La OLDE OL4 75 G3
Hutchinson Rd ROCH OL11 28 A2
Hutchinson St ROCH OL11 29 E5
Hutchinson Wy RAD M26 67 F2
Hutton Av AUL OL6 118 D3
WALK M28 94 A4
Huxley Av CHH M8 100 B4
Huxley Cl BRAM/HZG SK7 183 H5
Huxley Dr BRAM/HZG SK7 183 H5
Huxley St ALT WA14 165 G2
BOL BL1 33 F4
OLDE OL4 91 F2
Huxley Ter ALT * WA14 177 F3
Huxton Gn BRAM/HZG SK7 184 B2
Hyacinth Cl EDGY/DAV SK3 171 G4
Hyde Dr WALK M28 80 D5
Hyde Fold Cl BNG/LEV M19 143 G5
Hyde Gv BRUN/LGST M13 127 H3
SALE M33 154 C2
WALK M28 80 D5
Hyde Pl BRUN/LGST M13 127 H3
Hyde Rd DTN/ASHW M34 131 G5
GTN M18 130 A4
HYDE SK14 134 C5
MDTN M24 88 D1
MPL/ROM SK6 162 A1
WALK M28 80 D5
WGTN/LGST M12 129 E3
Hyde Sq MDTN M24 71 F4
Hyde St BOLS/LL * BL3 63 F1
DROY M43 116 D1
DUK SK16 118 C5
HULME M15 126 C3
Hydon Brook Wk ROCH OL11 42 B2
Hydrangea Cl SALE M33 153 F1
Hyldavale Av CHD/CHDH SK8 169 G3
Hylton Dr CHD/CHDH SK8 181 F4
Hypatia St BOLE BL2 3 K4
Hythe Cl RUSH/FAL M14 127 H5
Hythe Rd EDGY/DAV SK3 171 E1
Hythe St BOLS/LL * BL3 47 H5
Hythe Wk CHAD * OL9 89 G1

I

Ian Frazer Ct ROCH OL11 43 E2
Ibsley WHIT OL12 10 B4
Ice House Cl WALK M28 80 A4
Iceland St SLFD M6 111 F3
Idonia St BOL BL1 33 G3
Ilex Gv BRO M7 99 G4
Ilford St OP/CLY M11 115 E3
Ilfracombe Rd OFTN SK2 173 E1
Ilfracombe St NEWH/MOS M40 102 C4
Ilkley Cl BOLE BL2 49 H2
CHAD OL9 89 G1
Ilkley Crs RDSH SK5 144 D3
Ilkley Dr URM M41 122 D4
Ilkley St NEWH/MOS M40 101 H1
Ilk St OP/CLY M11 115 E3
Illingworth Av STLY SK15 119 H4
Illona Dr BRO M7 98 D2
Ilminster ROCH * OL11 29 H5
Imperial Ter SALE * M33 139 F5
Ina Av BOL BL1 32 C5
Ince Cl DID/WITH M20 142 C4
HTNM SK4 159 H3
Ince St HTNM SK4 159 H3
Inchcape Dr BKLY M9 86 C3
Inchfield Cl ROCH OL11 28 B2
Inchfield Rd NEWH/MOS M40 101 H1
Inchley Rd BRUN/LGST M13 127 G1
Inchwood Ms OLDE OL4 60 D5
Incline Rd OLDS OL8 89 G5
Independent St BOLS/LL BL3 65 H1
Indigo St SLFD M6 98 C5
Industry Rd WHIT OL12 10 C3
Industry St CHAD OL9 89 F3
LIT OL15 21 E3
ROCH OL11 28 B2
WHIT OL12 14 C3
Infant St PWCH * M25 85 F3
Infirmary St BOL BL1 3 F5
Ingham Rd ALT WA14 153 G5
Inghams La LIT OL15 21 E3
Ingham St BURY BL9 5 G6
NEWH/MOS * M40 115 H1
OLD OL1 9 J3
Inghamwood Cl BRO M7 100 A3
Ingleby Av BKLY M9 87 G3
Ingleby Cl ROY/SHW OL2 59 H1
Ingleby Ct STRET M32 140 B2
Ingleby Wy ROY/SHW OL2 59 H1
Ingledene Av BRO M7 99 H1
Ingledene Gv BOL * BL1 32 D4
Ingle Dr OFTN SK2 172 D2
Inglefield ROCH OL11 28 B2
Inglehead Cl DTN/ASHW M34 146 D1
Ingle Rd CHD/CHDH SK8 170 D3
Ingles Fold WALK M28 94 C3
Inglesham Cl NTHM/RTH M23 168 A3
Ingleton Av CHH M8 86 C5
Ingleton Cl BOLE BL2 35 E4
CHD/CHDH SK8 169 H3
ROY/SHW OL2 59 E4
Ingleton Ms TOT/BURYW BL8 37 G2
Ingleton Rd EDGY/DAV SK3 12 A6
Inglewhite Cl BURY BL9 53 E2
Inglewood Cl AULW OL7 104 C5
BURY BL9 39 F2
PART M31 150 D2
Inglewood Hollow STLY SK15 119 H5
Inglewood Rd CHAD OL9 72 D3
Inglewood Wk
BRUN/LGST * M13 127 H2
Inglis St LIT OL15 21 E2
Ingoe Cl HEY OL10 41 G3
Ingoldsby Av BRUN/LGST M13 128 A4
Ingram Dr HTNM SK4 158 B3
Ings Av WHIT OL12 29 E1
Ings La WHIT OL12 29 E1
Inkerman St HYDE SK14 132 B4
NEWH/MOS M40 101 E5
WHIT * OL12 10 C3
Ink St MILN OL16 10 D6
Inman St BURY BL9 53 F1
DTN/ASHW M34 131 G5
Innes St WGTN/LGST M12 129 E5
Innis Av NEWH/MOS M40 102 B5
Institute St BOL BL1 3 F5
Instow Cl BRUN/LGST M13 128 A3
CHAD OL9 73 E3
Intake Rd UPML OL3 93 H4
International Ap MANAIR * M90 180 A5
Invar Rd WALK M28 96 C1
Inverbeg Dr BOLE BL2 50 D2
Inverlael Av BOL BL1 48 A1
Inverness Av BKLY M9 87 H3
Inverness Rd DUK SK16 132 B1
Inwood Wk CHH M8 100 D4
Iona Pl BOLE BL2 34 D4
Iona Wy URM M41 123 G3
Ionian Gdns BRO M7 99 F5
Ipswich St ROCH OL11 43 E1
Iqbal Cl WGTN/LGST M12 128 D3
Ireby Cl MDTN M24 70 D2
Iredine St OP/CLY M11 115 F4
Irene Av HYDE SK14 132 D4
Iris Av FWTH BL4 64 B3
FWTH BL4 81 G2
Iris St OLDS OL8 90 C5
RAMS BL0 16 C2
Irkdale St CHH M8 100 D4
Irk St ANC M4 113 F2
Irk Vale Dr OLD OL1 72 D3
Irlam Av ECC M30 109 G4
Irlam Rd SALE M33 154 D1
URM M41 137 F1
Irlam Sq SLFD M6 98 A5
Irlam St BOL BL1 33 H3
NEWH/MOS M40 101 F5
Irlam Wharf Rd IRL M44 136 B5
Irma St BOL BL1 34 A3
Iron St DTN/ASHW * M34 131 G5
NEWH/MOS M40 114 B2
Irvin Dr WYTH/NTH M22 181 F4
Irvine Av WALK M28 94 B4
Irving Cl OFTN SK2 184 B1
Irving St BOL BL1 33 H4
OLDS OL8 89 G5
Irvin St NEWH/MOS M40 102 B4
Irwell Av ECC M30 110 A4
LHULT M38 80 C3
Irwell Gv ECC M30 110 A4
Irwell Pl ECC M30 110 A3
ORD M5 112 B4
Irwell St BURY BL9 4 C5
CHH M8 112 D1
CSLFD M3 6 B4
RAD M26 65 H5
RAD M26 67 G2
RAMS BL0 16 D2
SLFD M6 98 D4
Irwell Valley Wy RAMS BL0 16 D4
Irwin Dr WILM/AE SK9 191 H2
Irwin Rd ALT WA14 165 F1
Irwin St DTN/ASHW M34 131 F5
Isaac Cl ORD M5 111 H5
Isaac St BOL BL1 48 B1
Isabella Cl OLDTF/WHR M16 126 B4
Isabella St WHIT OL12 10 D1
Isabel Wk BOLS/LL BL3 48 D4
Isaiah St OLDS * OL8 90 C3
Isa St RAMS BL0 16 B4
Isca St OP/CLY M11 114 C4
Isherwood Dr MPL/ROM SK6 174 C3
Isherwood Rd PART M31 137 G5
Isherwood St HEY OL10 41 F5
ROCH OL11 43 F1
Isis Cl BRO M7 98 D2
Islington Rd OFTN SK2 172 D5
Islington St CSLFD M3 6 A3
Islington Wy CSLFD M3 112 C4
Isobel Cl ECC M30 109 E4
OLDTF/WHR M16 127 E4
Ivanhoe Ct FWTH BL4 64 D2
Ivanhoe St BOLS/LL BL3 64 D2
OLD OL1 75 F3
Iveagh Ct MILN * OL16 30 C5
Ivor St ROCH OL11 42 A3
Ivy Bank Rd BOL BL1 33 H1
Ivybridge Cl BRUN/LGST M13 128 A3
Ivy Cl DROY M43 116 A2
ROY/SHW OL2 42 E4
Ivy Cottages WHIT * OL12 29 F2
Ivy Dr MDTN M24 87 G1
Ivygreen Dr OLDE OL4 92 A1
Ivygreen Rd CCHDY M21 140 C3
Ivy Gv FWTH BL4 64 C4
FWTH * BL4 65 G5
LHULT M38 80 A3
Ivyleaf Sq BRO M7 99 H4
Ivylea Rd BNG/LEV M19 158 B2
Ivy Rd BOL BL1 33 F5
POY/DIS SK12 195 F4
TOT/BURYW BL8 37 G4
Ivy St BOLS/LL BL3 48 B5
ECC M30 109 G4
NEWH/MOS M40 101 H2

J

Jack Brady Cl NTHM/RTH M23 167 F5
Jackdaw Rd RAMS BL0 26 A1
Jack La DROY M43 116 D3
URM M41 138 D1
Jackman Av HEY OL10 56 A2
Jackroom Dr ANC * M4 7 K4
Jackson Av DUK SK16 118 C5
Jackson Cl HALE/TIMP WA15 166 D2
OLDS OL8 8 E6
Jackson Ct URM M41 122 D5
Jackson Crs HULME M15 126 D2
Jackson Gdns DTN/ASHW M34 146 A1
Jackson Ms OLDE OL4 75 G3
Jacksons Edge Rd
POY/DIS SK12 187 F5
Jackson's La BRAM/HZG SK7 184 D4
Jackson's Rw CSLFD M3 6 D5
Jackson St AUL OL6 118 A1
CHD/CHDH SK8 170 B3
FAIL M35 102 C4
FWTH BL4 65 E4
FWTH BL4 65 G5
HYDE * SK14 134 D5
HYDE SK14 147 G1
MDTN M24 72 A3
MILN OL16 30 C5
OLDE OL4 75 G3
OLDE * OL4 92 A1
RAD M26 67 G2
SALE M33 155 E1
STRET M32 139 H2
WALK M28 80 D3
WHIT OL12 19 H2
WHTF M45 68 C5
Jack St BOLE BL2 34 D2
Jack Taylor Ct WHIT * OL12 11 G3
Jacobite Cl BRO M7 99 F1
Jacobsen Av HYDE SK14 133 E4
James Andrew St MDTN * M24 72 A3
James Brindley Basin CMANE M1 7 K5
James Butterworth Ct
MILN * OL16 30 C5
James Butterworth St
MILN OL16 30 C5
James Cl DUK SK16 118 D5
James Corbett Rd SALQ M50 110 D4
James Dr HYDE SK14 147 H1
James Henry Av ORD M5 112 A5
James Hill St LIT * OL15 21 E3
James Leigh St CMANE M1 7 F7
Jameson St ROCH OL11 42 A4
James Rd ROY/SHW OL2 60 A1
James's St OLDE OL4 75 G3
James St BOLS/LL BL3 66 A1
BURY BL9 5 H6
DROY M43 116 C3
DTN/ASHW * M34 131 H5
EDGY/DAV SK3 12 E7
FAIL M35 103 F2
FWTH BL4 65 G4
HEY * OL10 41 E4
LIT OL15 20 C3
MPL/ROM SK6 161 H1
NEWH/MOS M40 114 A2
ORD M5 112 C4
PWCH M25 84 D2
RAD M26 67 G2
ROY/SHW OL2 59 H4
SALE M33 155 E2
STLY * SK15 118 D5
WHIT * OL12 10 C3
WHIT OL12 14 C3
James St South CHAD * OL9 73 F5
Jane St CHAD OL9 89 G1
WHIT OL12 10 A4
Japan St BRO M7 100 A3
Jardine Wy CHAD OL9 89 E3
Jarvis St OLDE OL4 9 K5
WHIT OL12 10 D2
Jasmine Av DROY M43 116 D3
Jasmine Cl NTHM/RTH M23 155 F5
Jason St ANC M4 113 G2
Jauncey St BOLS/LL BL3 48 B4
Jayton Av DID/WITH M20 169 G1
Jean Cl BNG/LEV M19 143 H1
Jedburgh Av BOL BL1 48 A1
Jefferson Wy WHIT OL12 19 E5
Jeffreys Dr DUK SK16 118 C5
Jehlum Cl CHH M8 100 C3
Jellicoe Av IRL M44 135 D5
Jenner Cl HULME M15 126 D2
Jennings Av ORD M5 111 H5
Jennings Cl HYDE SK14 133 G3
ORD M5 111 H5
Jennings St EDGY/DAV SK3 171 G2
Jennison Cl WGTN/LGST M12 129 E2
Jenny La BRAM/HZG SK7 193 H4
Jenny St OLDS OL8 89 H5
Jepheys Pl WHIT * OL12 10 C2
Jepheys St WHIT OL12 10 D2
Jepson St OFTN SK2 172 B3
Jericho Rd BURY BL9 39 H3
Jermyn St WHIT OL12 10 E4
Jerrold St LIT OL15 21 E3
Jersey Rd RDSH SK5 160 A2
Jersey St ANC M4 7 J3
AUL OL6 118 A1
Jerusalem Pl CMANW * M2 6 D6
Jesmond Av PWCH M25 85 E5
Jesmond Dr TOT/BURYW BL8 37 H1
Jesmond Gv CHD/CHDH SK8 183 E4
Jesmond Rd BOL BL1 33 E2
Jespersen St OLD OL1 9 G2
Jessamine Av BRO M7 112 C1
Jessel Cl BRUN/LGST M13 127 H2
Jessie St BOLS/LL BL3 48 B4
NEWH/MOS M40 101 H4
Jessop Dr MPL/ROM SK6 175 E1
Jessop St GTN M18 129 G3
Jethro St BOLE BL2 3 K3
BOLE BL2 34 D2
Jetson St GTN M18 130 A2
Jimmy McMullen Wk
RUSH/FAL * M14 127 F5
Jinnah Cl OLDE OL4 91 F2
OP/CLY M11 115 F5
J J Thomson Ms
RUSH/FAL * M14 142 D2
Joan St NEWH/MOS M40 101 H3
Jobling St OP/CLY M11 114 C5
Jocelyn St NEWH/MOS M40 101 F4
Joddrell St CSLFD M3 6 C5
Joel La HYDE SK14 148 A4
Johannesburg Gdns
NTHM/RTH M23 167 G5
John Ashworth St WHIT OL12 11 G2
John Atkinson Ct ORD * M5 111 E3
John Av CHD/CHDH SK8 170 B4
John Beeley Av OP/CLY M11 115 G5
John Booth St OLDE OL4 92 A2
John Brown St BOL * BL1 2 C3
John Clynes Av
NEWH/MOS * M40 113 H2
John Cross St BOLS/LL BL3 48 D5
John Dalton St CMANW M2 6 D5
John Foran Cl NEWH/MOS M40 102 A4
John Gilbert Wy TRPK M17 125 F3
John Heywood St OP/CLY M11 115 E3
John Kennedy Gdn HYDE SK14 134 D5
John Kennedy Rd HYDE SK14 134 C5
John Knott St OLDE OL4 92 A1
John Lee Fold MDTN M24 71 H3
John Nash Crs HULME M15 126 D2
Johnny King Cl
NEWH/MOS M40 101 E5
John Roberts Cl ROCH * OL11 42 D1
Johns Cl CCHDY M21 141 E3
John Shepley St HYDE SK14 147 H1
John Smeaton Ct CMANE M1 7 K5
Johnsonbrook Rd DUK SK16 132 C3
Johnson Fold Av BOL BL1 32 B4
Johnson Gv MDTN M24 71 F3
Johnson's Sq NEWH/MOS M40 114 A1
Johnson St BOL BL1 3 F6
CSLFD M3 6 C3
RAD M26 67 G2
SWIN M27 98 A4
John's Pl MPL/ROM SK6 162 B4
John Steet MPL/ROM SK6 162 B4
Johnston WHIT OL12 10 B4
Johnston Av LIT * OL15 20 C5
John St ALT WA14 165 G5
ANC M4 7 G3
BOLS/LL * BL3 66 A1
BRAM/HZG SK7 185 E1
BRO M7 112 C1
BURY BL9 4 E3
CHAD OL9 8 E4
CSLFD M3 6 C2
DROY M43 116 A5
DTN/ASHW * M34 131 G4
ECC M30 109 E4
EDGW/EG BL7 23 F4
FAIL M35 103 E1
FWTH BL4 65 F4
HEY OL10 41 E4
HYDE SK14 132 C5
HYDE * SK14 147 G1
IRL M44 150 D1
LIT OL15 20 D3
MILN OL16 10 E6
MILN OL16 19 H5
MPL/ROM SK6 161 H1
MPL/ROM SK6 163 G4
MPL/ROM SK6 175 F4
PWCH M25 69 H4
ROY/SHW OL2 59 E5
ROY/SHW OL2 59 H4
SALE M33 154 C1
STKP SK1 13 G5
STLY SK15 106 D5
SWIN M27 97 F2
WALK M28 81 E3
WHIT OL12 14 C3
John St East AULW OL7 117 H4
John St West AULW OL7 117 G5
John William St ECC M30 110 A3
OP/CLY * M11 115 F4
Joiner St ANC M4 7 G4
ORD M5 112 B4
Join Rd SALE M33 155 E2
Jolly Brows BOLE BL2 35 E3
Jonas St BKLY M9 101 F2
BRO M7 112 D2
Jones Sq STKP SK1 13 H7
Jones St MILN OL16 30 B5
OLD OL1 9 K1
RAD M26 52 C5
ROY/SHW OL2 74 A2
SLFD M6 111 G2
Jonquil Dr LHULT M38 80 A5
Jopson St MDTN M24 72 A3
Jordan Av ROY/SHW * OL2 45 F5
Jordan St HULME M15 126 D1
Josephine Dr SWIN M27 97 F3
Joseph Johnson Ms
WYTH/NTH * M22 156 D5
Joseph St ECC M30 109 E4
FAIL M35 103 F2
FWTH BL4 65 E3
LIT OL15 21 E2
MDTN M24 71 G3
MPL/ROM * SK6 175 F3
RAD M26 67 G2
WHIT OL12 29 G1
Joshua La MDTN M24 72 C5
Josslyn Rd ORD M5 111 E2
Jo St ORD M5 111 H4
Joule Cl ORD M5 111 H5
Joules Ct STKP SK1 13 H4
Joule St BKLY M9 101 F1
Jowett St OLD OL1 75 F3
RDSH SK5 160 A2
Jowett's Wk AULW OL7 117 G3
Jowkin La ROCH OL11 28 A4
Joyce St NEWH/MOS M40 102 A3
Joynson Av BRO M7 112 C1
Joynson St SALE M33 154 C1
Joy St RAMS BL0 16 C2
WHIT OL12 30 A1
Jubilee Av DUK SK16 118 D4
RAD M26 67 H3
Jubilee Houses WALK * M28 80 D4
Jubilee Rd MDTN M24 72 A3
Jubilee St ROY/SHW OL2 60 B2
SLFD M6 111 G3
Jubilee Ter MDTN M24 72 A2
Jubilee Wy BURY BL9 4 B4
Judith St WHIT OL12 18 B5
Judson Av CCHDY M21 156 B1
Judy St BKLY M9 101 G2
Julia St CSLFD M3 113 E2
WHIT OL12 10 B5
Julius St BNG/LEV M19 144 A3
Junction Aly MILN OL16 10 D7
Junction Rd BOLS/LL BL3 47 G4
HYDE SK14 132 B3
OFTN SK2 13 G7
Junction Rd West HOR/BR BL6 46 D4
Junction St MDTN M24 88 C1
OLDS * OL8 90 B3
June Av HTNM * SK4 159 E4
Juniper Bank RDSH SK5 145 F3
Juniper Cl BOL BL1 33 H5
OLDE OL4 61 E5
SALE M33 139 E5
Juniper Dr MILN OL16 31 E5
Juno St OLD OL1 74 D3
Jura Cl DUK SK16 118 C5
Jura Dr URM M41 123 H3
Jura Gv HEY OL10 40 C5
Jurby Av BKLY M9 86 D3
Jury St CHH M8 113 E1
Justin Cl BRUN/LGST M13 127 G1
Jutland Av ROCH OL11 29 F3
Jutland St CMANE M1 7 J5

K

Kale St BRUN/LGST M13 127 G1
Kalima Gv BRO M7 99 G4
Kansas Av SALQ M50 111 F5
Kara St SLFD M6 111 F3
Kate St RAMS * BL0 16 C2
Kathan Cl MILN OL16 11 H7
Katherine Rd OFTN SK2 172 D4
Katherine St AUL OL6 118 A2
AULW OL7 117 G3
Kathleen Gv RUSH/FAL M14 142 D1
Kathleen St WHIT OL12 29 G3
Kay Av MPL/ROM SK6 161 E3
Kay Brow HEY OL10 40 D4
RAMS BL0 16 D2
Kayfields BOLE BL2 35 F2
Kay's Av STKP SK1 160 C5
Kays Gdns CSLFD M3 6 A2
Kay St BOL BL1 2 E1
BOLS/LL BL3 65 H1
BURY BL9 5 H2
BURY BL9 16 D5
HEY OL10 40 D4
OP/CLY M11 128 C1
ROCH OL11 42 D1
SLFD M6 98 C4
STLY SK15 119 F4
Kays Wood Rd MPL/ROM SK6 174 C3
Keadby Cl ECC M30 109 G5
Keal Dr IRL M44 121 B4
Kearsley Dr BOLS/LL BL3 64 C1
Kearsley Hall Rd RAD M26 66 B5
Kearsley Rd CHH M8 86 B5
RAD M26 66 B4
Kearsley St ECC M30 109 E3
Kearsley V RAD M26 66 A4
Kearton Dr ECC M30 110 B4
Keary Cl GTN M18 129 G2
Keaton Cl SLFD M6 111 F1
Keats Av DROY M43 116 B3
DTN/ASHW M34 146 D3
WHIT OL12 28 D2
Keats Crs RAD M26 51 H5
Keats Fold DUK SK16 133 G1
Keats Ms NTHM/RTH M23 166 D1
Keats Rd ECC M30 109 G4
OLD * OL1 75 E3
RAMS BL0 26 A1
Keb La OLDS OL8 104 D2
Keble Av OLDS OL8 90 B4
Kedleston Av RUSH/FAL M14 128 B4
Kedleston Gn OFTN SK2 173 E2
Keele Cl NEWH/MOS M40 113 H2
Keele Wk NEWH/MOS M40 113 H2
Keepers Dr WHIT OL12 28 B1
Keighley Av DROY M43 116 B2
Keighley Cl TOT/BURYW BL8 37 E4
Keighley St BOL BL1 33 F4
Keilder Ms BOL BL1 47 H1
Keith Dr EDGY/DAV SK3 171 E2
Keith Wk NEWH/MOS M40 114 A2
Kelboro Av DTN/ASHW M34 131 E1
Kelbrook Ct OFTN SK2 173 F4
Kelbrook Rd OP/CLY M11 115 E5
Kelby Av NTHM/RTH M23 168 A2
Keld Cl TOT/BURYW BL8 37 G1
Kelfield Av NTHM/RTH M23 155 H4
Kellbrook Crs BRO * M7 98 D2
Kellets Rw WALK * M28 81 E2
Kellett St BOL BL1 23 E5
MILN OL16 11 G5
Kelling Wk HULME * M15 126 C1
Kelmarsh Cl OP/CLY * M11 129 G1
Kelsall Crs EDGY/DAV SK3 171 G3
Kelsall Dr DROY M43 116 A2
HALE/TIMP WA15 166 D3
Kelsall Rd CHD/CHDH SK8 170 D4
Kelsall St CHAD OL9 8 C4
MILN OL16 10 D5
SALE M33 154 B2
WGTN/LGST M12 128 C2
Kelso Cl OLDS OL8 104 C1
Kelson Av AULW OL7 104 D5
Kelstern Av BRUN/LGST M13 128 B5
Kelstern Sq BRUN/LGST M13 128 B5
Kelton Cl RDSH SK5 160 A1
Kelverlow St OLDE OL4 91 F1
Kelvin Av MDTN M24 70 C5
SALE M33 154 C2
Kelvindale Dr HALE/TIMP WA15 166 D2
Kelvin Gv CHH M8 100 B4
Kelvington Dr BKLY M9 101 E4
Kelvin St ANC M4 7 G3
AULW OL7 117 G5
Kemble Av NTHM/RTH M23 156 B5
Kemmel Av WYTH/NTH M22 168 D4
Kemp Av ROCH OL11 42 C1
Kempnough Hall Rd WALK M28 95 F3
Kemp Rd MPL/ROM SK6 175 H1

Kempsey Ct CHAD OL9 ......73 F5
Kempsey St CHAD OL9 ......73 G5
Kempsford Cl NTHM/RTH M23 ..168 A3
Kempster St BRO M7 ......132 B1
Kempston Gdns BOL BL1 ......33 H4
Kemp St HYDE SK14 ......132 D4
  MDTN M24 ......71 G4
Kempton Av BOLS/LL BL3 ......65 H2
  SALE M33 ......154 C1
Kempton Wy CHAD OL9 ......8 B4
Kempton Cl BRAM/HZG SK7 ..185 G2
  DROY M43 ......116 D3
Kemsing Wk ORD * M5 ......111 H3
Kenchester Av OP/CLY M11 ..115 G1
Kendal Av AULW M34 ......117 G1
  DTN/ASHW M34 ......146 D2
  HYDE SK14 ......148 B3
  SALE M33 ......154 D3
  URM M41 ......122 B4
  WHIT OL12 ......28 B1
Kendal Cl HALE/TIMP WA15 ..167 E4
  HEY OL10 ......56 B1
Kendal Dr BRAM/HZG SK7 ..193 F2
  BURY BL9 ......53 E2
  CHD/CHDH SK8 ......169 H5
  ROY/SHW OL2 ......60 C2
Kendal Gdns MPL/ROM SK6 ..162 A2
  WHTF M45 ......68 C4
Kendal Rd BOL BL1 ......48 B1
  RAMS BL0 ......26 A1
  SLFD M6 ......97 H5
  STRET M32 ......125 E5
Kendal Rd West RAMS BL0 ..26 A1
Kendon Gv DTN/ASHW M34 ..131 F5
Kendrew Rd BOLS/LL BL3 ......47 H5
Kenilworth Av CHAD OL9 ......29 H1
  CHD OL9 ......72 D3
  CHD/CHDH SK8 ......182 D1
  DID/WITH M20 ......157 E1
  SWIN M27 ......83 G4
  WHTF M45 ......84 D1
Kenilworth Cl MPL/ROM SK6 ..175 F1
  RAD M26 ......92 A2
Kenilworth Dr BRAM/HZG SK7 ..185 E4
  MILN OL16 ......58 D1
  SALE M33 ......153 H2
  URM M41 ......138 D2
Kenilworth Sq BOL BL1 ......33 E5
Kenion Rd BOL BL1 .... E5
Kenion St MILN OL16 ......10 D7
Kenley Ldg BRAM/HZG * SK7 ..185 G5
Kenmay Av BOLS/LL BL3 64
Kenmere Gv NEWH/MOS M40 ..102 A1
Kenmor Av TOT/BURYW BL8 ..52 A1
Kenmore Av IRL M44 120
Kenmore Cl SALE M33 ......153 F5
  WHTF M45 ......69 E4
Kenmore Gv IRL M44 ......120 B3
Kenmore Rd NTHM/RTH M23 ..168 B2
  SALE M33 ......153 F5
  WHTF M45 ......69 E4
Kenmore Wy WHTF M45 ......69 E4
Kennard Cl BKLY M9 101
Kennedy Dr BOLS/LL BL3 ......66 B1
  BURY BL9 ......69 E2
Kennedy Rd ORD M5 ......110 D4
Kennedy St CMANW M2 6
  OLDS OL8 9
Kennedy Wy DTN/ASHW M34 ..146 A1
Kennerley Rd OFTN SK2 ......172 B4
Kennerley's La WILM/AE SK9 ..199 F3
Kennet Cl WILM/AE SK9 ......192 A5
Kenneth Sq BRO M7 ......99 H4
Kennett Av NTHM/RTH M23 ..179 H1
Kenninghall Rd WYTH/NTH M22 ..180 C1
Kennington Av
  NEWH/MOS M40 ......103 G5
Kennington Fold BOLS/LL BL3 ..65
Kenny Cl OLDE OL4 ......91 G2
Kensington Av AUL OL6 ......118 D1
  CHAD OL9 ......72 D4
  HYDE * SK14 ......147 H2
  RAD M26 ......51 G5
  ROY/SHW OL2 ......60 C1
  RUSH/FAL M14 ......128 A4
Kensington Cl MILN OL16 ......31 H5
  TOT/BURYW BL8 ......26 B2
Kensington Ct BOL * BL1 ......2 B3
  HYDE SK14 ......147 H2
  WILM/AE SK9 ......199 F4
Kensington Dr ORD M5 ......111 E2
  TOT/BURYW BL8 ......52 B1
Kensington Gdns
  HALE/TIMP WA15 ......178 A3
Kensington Gv ALT WA14 ......165 H1
  DTN/ASHW M34 131
  HYDE SK14 ......119 F4
Kensington Rd CCHDY M21 ..140 D1
  EDGY/DAV SK3 ......171 E2
  FAIL M35 ......103 G2
Kensington St BOL BL1 ......2 A5
  HYDE SK14 ......147 H2
  ROCH OL11 ......42 D2
  RUSH/FAL M14 ......127 F5
Kensworth Cl BOL BL1 ......33 G5
Kensworth Dr BOL BL1 33
Kent Av CHAD OL9 ......89 F1
  CHD/CHDH SK8 181
  DROY M43 ......115 H4
Kent Cl WALK M28 ......80 B5
Kent Ct BOL BL1 ......34 A4
Kent Dr BURY BL9 ......53 G1
  FWTH BL4 ......65 F1
Kentford Dr NEWH/MOS M40 ..113 H1
Kentford Rd BOL BL1 ......33 G5
Kentmere Av WHIT OL12 ......14 C3
Kentmere Cl CHD/CHDH SK8 ..181 G1
Kentmere Dr MDTN M24 ......71 E1
Kentmere Gv FWTH BL4 ......64 C5
Kentmere Rd BOLE BL2 ......35 G4
  HALE/TIMP WA15 ......167 G3
Kentmere Rd East
  BRAM/HZG SK7 ......193 F2
Kenton Av GTN M18 ......129 H3
  DTN/ASHW M34 ......131 G1
Kenton Rd ROY/SHW OL2 ......59 H2

Kenton St OLDS OL8 ......91 E2
  EDGY/DAV SK3 ......171 E1
  HEY OL10 102
  IRL M44 ......150 D1
  PART M31 ......150 D4
Kent Rd East RUSH/FAL M14 ..128 A5
Kent Rd West RUSH/FAL M14 ..127 H5
Kentsford Dr BOLS/LL BL3 ......51 E4
Kentstone Av HTNM SK4 ......158 A3
Kent St BOL BL1 2
  BRO M7 6
  CMANW * M2 ......6 E4
  OLDS OL8 ......90 C3
  ROCH OL11 ......30 A5
  SWIN M27 ......83 E5
Kentucky St OLDE OL4 ......91 F1
Kentwell Cl DUK SK16 ......132 A1
Kenwick Dr NEWH/MOS M40 ..88 D5
Kenwood Av BNG/LEV M19 ..143 H3
  BRAM/HZG SK7 ......193 G2
  CHD/CHDH SK8 ......169 F5
  HALE/TIMP WA15 ......178 B2
Kenwood Cl STRET M32 ......140 B1
Kenwood La WALK M28 ......95 G5
Kenwood Rd BOL BL1 ......33 E4
  RDSH SK5 ......144 D1
  STRET M32 ......140 B2
Kenworthy Av AUL OL6 ......105 G5
Kenworthy Cl HYDE SK14 ......14 (?)
Kenworthy Fold ROCH OL11 ..41 F1
Kenworthy Gv LHULT M38 ......78 A4
Kenworthy La MDTN M24 ......156 C4
Kenworthy St MILN OL16 ......11 J6
  STLY SK15 ......119 F4
Kenwright St ANC M4 .... (?)
Kenwyn St NEWH/MOS M40 ..114 B2
Kenyon Av DUK SK16 ......132 C1
  OLDS OL8 ......90 C5
  SALE M33 ......155 F4
Kenyon Cl HYDE SK14 ......133 E3
Kenyon Fold ROCH OL11 ......41 F1
Kenyon Gv LHULT M38 ......79 D3
Kenyon La MDTN M24 ......72 A4
  NEWH/MOS M40 ......101 H2
  PWCH M25 ......85 F3
Kenyon Rd BOLE BL2 ......51 E4
Kenyon St AUL OL6 .... (?)
  BURY BL9 ......5 G2
  DUK SK16 ......118 A5
  GTN M18 ......129 H2
  HEY OL10 ......40 D4
  RAMS BL0 ......16 D1
Kenyon Ter TYLD M29 ......79 D3
Kenyon Wy LHULT M38 ......79 D4
  TOT/BURYW BL8 ......37 E1
Keppel Rd CCHDY M21 ......141 E2
Keppel St AUL OL6 ......118 B2
Kepwick Dr WYTH/NTH M22 ..168 D1
Kerenhappuch St RAMS BL0 ..16 C3
Kerfoot Cl WYTH/NTH M22 ..168 D1
Kermoor Av BOL BL1 ......22 C5
Kerne Gv NTHM/RTH M23 ......155 H5
Kerrera Dr ORD * M5 ......111 E4
Kerridge Dr MPL/ROM SK6 ..161 G2
Kerris Cl WYTH/NTH M22 ......180 C3
Kerr St BKLY M9 ......87 E4
Kerry Gv BOLE BL2 ......3 K2
Kersal Av BRO M7 .... (?)
  SWIN M27 ......97 H2
Kersal Crag BRO M7 ......99 F1
Kersal Dr HALE/TIMP WA15 ..166 D2
Kersal Hall Av BRO M7 ......98 D2
Kersal Rd PWCH M25 ......98 D3
Kersal Vale Rd SWIN M27 ......98 C1
Kersal Wy BRO M7 ......99 E3
Kerscott Rd NTHM/RTH M23 ..155 H5
Kershaw Av BOLS/LL BL3 ......50 D5
  PWCH M25 ......84 C5
  SALE M33 ......155 E4
Kershaw Dr MDTN M24 ......88 C3
Kershaw Gv DTN/ASHW M34 ..146 C1
Kershaw La AULW M34 ......130 C1
Kershaw Rd FAIL M35 ......103 E2
Kershaw St AULW OL7 ......117 G5
  BOLE BL2 ......34 D1
  BOLS/LL BL3 ......3 J7
  BURY BL9 ......5 G5
  DROY M43 ......116 A4
  HEY OL10 ......40 C4
  ROY/SHW OL2 ......59 E4
  ROY/SHW OL2 ......60 A2
  WHIT * OL12 ......10 C4
Kershaw St East ROY/SHW OL2 ..60 A2
Kershope Gv ORD M5 ......111 H5
Kersley St OLDE OL4 ......91 E1
Kerwin Wk OP/CLY * M11 ......114 C5
Kerwood Dr ROY/SHW OL2 ......74 B1
Kesteven Rd BKLY M9 ......101 H1
Keston Av BKLY M9 ......87 H4
  DROY M43 ......115 H4
Keston Crs RDSH SK5 ......145 G5
Keston Rd OLD OL1 ......75 F3
Kestor St BOLE BL2 ......3 K2
Kestrel Av DTN/ASHW M34 ..116 D4
  FWTH BL4 ......64 A5
  LHULT M38 ......80 B2
  OLDE OL4 ......91 G2
  SWIN M27 ......83 G5
Kestrel Cl MPL/ROM SK6 ......187 F1
  PWCH M25 ......84 D1
Kestrel Dr BURY BL9 .... (?)
  IRL M44 121
Kestrel Rd TRPK M17 ......110 A5
Kestrel St BOL * BL1 3
Kestrel Wk WGTN/LGST M12 ..128 D2
Keswick Av AULW OL7 ......106 A5
  CHD/CHDH SK8 ......181 G1
  DTN/ASHW M34 ......131 E4
  HYDE SK14 ......133 G3
  OLDS OL8 ......90 D5
  URM M41 ......137 F2
Keswick Cl BRUN/LGST M13 ..128 A4
  IRL M44 ......150 C2
  MDTN M24 ......71 F2
  STLY SK15 ......119 F1
Keswick Dr BRAM/HZG SK7 ..193 F2
  BURY BL9 ......53 E2
Keswick Gv SLFD M6 ......111 G2

GTN M18 ......130 A2
  PWCH M25 ......85 F2
  WILM/AE SK9 ......199 F4
Kings Ct RDSH SK5 ......160 A3
Kingscourt Av BOL BL1 ......33 F4
Kingsdale Rd DTN/ASHW M34 ..130 B4
Kingsdown Crs OLDTF/WHR M16 ..126 D2
Kingsdown Dr WYTH/NTH M22 ..180 B3
Kings Dr CHD/CHDH SK8 ......182 D1
  HTNM SK4 ......71 F4
  MPL/ROM SK6 ......162 D4
Kingsfield Dr DID/WITH M20 ..157 H4
Kingsfold Av NEWH/MOS * M40 ..113 H1
Kingsford St ORD M5 ......111 E3
Kingsgate BOL BL1 ......2 A4
Kingsgate Rd WYTH/NTH M22 ..125 D3
Kings Gv STRET M32 ......125 G5
Kingshill Ct WHIT OL12 .... (?)
Kingsheath Av OP/CLY M11 ..115 G3
Kingshill Rd CCHDY M21 ......140 D3
Kingsholme Rd WYTH/NTH M22 ..180 A3
Kingsland Cl NEWH/MOS M40 ..114 A2
Kingsland Rd EDGY/DAV SK3 ..170 D4
  FWTH BL4 ......64 A4
  ROCH OL11 ......42 A3
Kings La STRET M32 ......125 G5
Kingslea Rd DID/WITH M20 ..157 H1
Kingsleigh Rd HTNM SK4 ......158 A1
Kingsley Av BKLY M9 ......101 G3
  BRO M7 ......98 D3
  HTNM SK4 ......159 H2
  URM * M41 ......138 A1
  WHTF M45 ......68 C5
  WILM/AE SK9 ......191 H5
Kingsley Cl AUL OL6 ......106 D5
  DTN/ASHW M34 ......146 C4
Kingsley Dr CHD/CHDH SK8 ..182 D1
  OLDE OL4 ......76 D2
Kingsley Gv DTN/ASHW M34 ..116 D5
Kingsley Rd HALE/TIMP WA15 ..178 A1
  MDTN M24 ......71 G2
  OLDE OL4 ......91 G2
  SWIN M27 ......96 C1
  WALK M28 ......80 D5
  WYTH/NTH M22 ......180 D2
Kingsley St BOL BL1 ......33 F5
  TOT/BURYW BL8 ......37 G4
King's Lynn Cl DID/WITH M20 ..157 G2
Kingsmead Ms BKLY M9 .... (?)
Kingsmere Av BNG/LEV M19 ..143 G2
Kingsmill Av BNG/LEV M19 ..144 A2
Kingsnorth Rd URM M41 ......122 A5
King's Rd AUL OL6 ......106 D5
  BRAM/HZG SK7 .... (?)
  CCHDY M21 ......141 G5
  CHAD OL9 .... (?)
  DTN/ASHW M34 ......146 B5
  IRL M44 ......136 A2
  MILN OL16 ......43 G1
  MPL/ROM SK6 ......174 A4
  OLDS OL8 ......9 H7
  ROY/SHW OL2 ......59 H1
  SALE M33 ......154 A2
  STRET M32 ......140 A1
  URM M41 ......138 A1
Kings Ter STRET M32 ......125 G5
Kingston Av BOLE BL2 ......35 E3
  CHAD OL9 ......89 F3
  DID/WITH M20 ......142 A5
  OLDS OL8 .... (?)
Kingston Cl BRO M7 ......101 F1
  CCHDY M21 ......141 G5
  CHAD OL9 .... (?)
  DTN/ASHW M34 ......132 B5
  IRL M44 136
  MILN OL16 43
Kingston Dr ROY/SHW OL2 ..58 D3
  SALE M33 ......154 A2
  URM M41 ......138 A1
Kingston Gdns HYDE SK14 ..119 G5
Kingston Gv BKLY M9 ......87 G3
Kingston Hl CHD/CHDH SK8 ..170 A5
Kingston MI EDGY/DAV * SK3 ..12 A6
Kingston Pl CHD/CHDH SK8 ..182 B2
Kingston Rd DID/WITH M20 ..142 B4
  FAIL M35 ......103 F2
  RAD M26 ......52 D3
  WILM/AE SK9 ......191 H5
Kingston St EDGY/DAV SK3 ..12 D4
Kings St BOL BL1 .... (?)
  BOLE BL2 3
  BRO M7 ......99 H5
  CMANW M2 .... (?)
  CSLFD M3 6
  DROY M43 ......116 B4
  DTN/ASHW M34 ......131 G2
  DUK SK16 ......118 A5
  ECC M30 ......110 A4
  EDGW/EG BL7 ......22 D1
  FAIL M35 103
  HEY OL10 ......40 D4
  HYDE SK14 ......132 D5
  MDTN M24 ......71 G5
  MILN OL16 ......10 C6
  MOSL OL5 ......108 D2
  RAD M26 ......67 G2
  RAMS BL0 16
  SLFD M6 .... (?)
  STLY SK15 .... (?)
King St East ROCH OL11 ......10 D7
King St South ROCH OL11 ..42 D1
King St West CSLFD M3 ......6 C3

MDTN M24 ......87 G1
  MILN OL16 ......30 D5
  MPL/ROM SK6 ......161 F3
  STKP SK1 .... (?)
  STRET M32 ......139 H2
  SWIN M27 ......97 H4
  WALK M28 ......95 E2
Kingsway Av BNG/LEV M19 ..143 G2
Kingsway Cl OLDS OL8 .... (?)
Kingsway Crs BNG/LEV M19 ..158 B1
Kingsway Pk URM M41 ......123 G4
Kingswear Dr BOL BL1 ......33 F5
Kingswood Gv RDSH SK5 .... (?)
Kingswood Rd ECC M30 ......109 E1
  MDTN M24 ......71 G1
  PWCH M25 ......84 C2
Kingthorpe Gdns BOLS/LL * BL3 ..48 C2
  ORD M5 ......111 H5
Kingwood Av BOL BL1 ......47 G1
Kinlet Wy OLDTF/WHR * M16 ..... (?)
Kinloch Dr BOL BL1 ......48 A2
  OP/CLY M11 ......114 D3
Kinmel Av RDSH SK5 .... (?)
Kinnaird Crs STKP SK1 ......172 C1
Kinnaird Rd DID/WITH M20 ..157 G1
Kinnerly Gv WALK M28 ......94 B1
Kinross Av OFTN SK2 ......184 B1
Kinross Cl OLDS OL8 26
Kinross Dr BOLS/LL BL3 ......47 G4
Kinross Rd RUSH/FAL M14 ..128 B3
Kinsey Av NTHM/RTH M23 ..167 G2
Kinsley Dr WALK M28 ......80 D5
Kintore Av BRAM/HZG SK7 ..193 G2
Kintyre Av ORD M5 ......111 E4
Kintyre Cl OP/CLY * M11 ......115 G4
Kintyre Dr BOLS/LL BL3 ......47 F4
Kinver Rd NEWH/MOS M40 ..88 B5
Kipling Av DROY M43 ......116 B2
  DTN/ASHW M34 ......146 D4
Kipling Cl BURY BL9 .... (?)
Kipling Rd CHAD OL1 ......75 C2
Kipling St BRO M7 .... (?)
Kippax St RUSH/FAL M14 ......127 G5
Kirby Av CHAD OL9 ......88 C4
  SWIN M27 ......96 C5
Kirkbank St OLD OL1 .... (?)
Kirkburn Vw TOT/BURYW BL8 ..37 H1
Kirkby Av NEWH/MOS M40 ..102 A3
  SALE M33 ......154 D3
Kirkby Cl BURY BL9 ......53 F2
Kirkby Rd BOL BL1 ......48 A1
Kirkdale Av NEWH/MOS M40 ..88 C4
Kirkdale Dr ROY/SHW OL2 ......58 D4
Kirkebrok Rd BOLS/LL BL3 ......47 H5
Kirkfell Dr MPL/ROM SK6 ..161 H4
Kirkfell Wk OLD * OL1 ......74 C2
Kirkgate Cl NEWH/MOS * M40 ..113 H1
Kirkhall La BOL BL1 ......48 B1
Kirkham Av GTN M18 ......129 G2
Kirkham Cl DTN/ASHW M34 ..... (?)
Kirkham Rd CHD/CHDH SK8 ..181 H4
Kirkham St BOLE BL2 ......34 D5
  OLDS OL8 9
  LHULT M38 ......80 B2
  ORD M5 ......111 F4
Kirkhaven Sq NEWH/MOS M40 ..114 B1
Kirkhope Dr BOL BL1 ......33 G5
Kirkhope Wk BOL BL1 ......33 G5
Kirklands BOLE BL2 ......35 E4
  SALE M33 ......154 B1
Kirklee Av CHAD OL9 ......73 F3
Kirklee Rd ROCH OL11 ......42 A4
Kirklees St TOT/BURYW BL8 ..26 B4
Kirkley St HYDE SK14 ......147 G2
Kirklinton Dr BKLY M9 ......101 E4
Kirkman Av ECC M30 ......109 E1
Kirkman Cl GTN M18 ......129 G4
Kirkmanshulme La
  WGTN/LGST M12 ......128 D2
Kirkman St BURY BL9 ......68 C1
Kirk Rd BNG/LEV M19 ......144 B3
Kirkstall Av HEY OL10 ......40 B4
Kirkstall Cl POY/DIS SK12 ..195 E3
Kirkstall Rd MDTN M24 ......71 H3
  URM M41 ......123 H5
Kirkstall Sq BRUN/LGST M13 ..127 H2
Kirkstead Cl OP/CLY M11 ......114 D5
Kirkstead Rd CHD/CHDH SK8 ..183 F3
Kirkstile Pl SWIN M27 ......82 D5
Kirkstone Av WALK M28 ......95 G1
Kirkstone Cl OLD OL1 ......74 C3
Kirkstone Dr MDTN M24 ......71 H1
  OLD OL1 ......74 C3
  ROY/SHW OL2 ......58 D3
Kirk St GTN M18 ......129 G4
Kirkwall Dr BOLE BL2 ......3 K3
Kirkway MDTN M24 ......87 H1
  BKLY M9 ......101 E4
Kirkwood Dr NEWH/MOS M40 ..113 H1
Kirtley Av ECC M30 ......109 G2
Kirtlington Cl ROY/SHW OL2 ..58 D3
Kitchener Av URM M41 ......150 D2
Kitchener St BOLS/LL BL3 ......64 C1
  TOT/BURYW BL8 .... (?)
Kitchen St MILN OL16 ......10 E5
Kitepool St ECC * M30 ......108 D2
Kitter St WHIT OL12 .... (?)
Kitt's Moss La BRAM/HZG SK7 ..193 G4
Kitty Wheeldon Gdns
  SALE * M33 ......154 B1
Kiveton Cl WALK M28 ......80 D5
Kiwi St SLFD M6 ......111 H1
Knaresborough Cl RDSH SK5 ..144 D2
Knarr Barn La UPML OL3 .... (?)
Knarr La UPML OL3 ......77 F2
Knight Crs MDTN M24 ......71 E1
Knightley Wk NEWH/MOS M40 ..101 E5
Knightsbridge STKP SK1 .... (?)
  WILM/AE SK9 ......200 A1
Knightsbridge Cl PWCH M25 ..85 E2
Knight St AULW OL7 ......117 G3
  BOL BL1 .... (?)
  DID/WITH M20 ......157 G4
  HYDE SK14 ......147 H2
  TOT/BURYW * BL8 ......37 H4
Knightswood BOLS/LL BL3 ..62 C1

Kniveton Cl WGTN/LGST M12 128 C2
Kniveton Rd WGTN/LGST M12 128 C2
Knivton St HYDE * SK14 133 E5
Knole Av POY/DIS SK12 195 G3
The Knoll MOSL OL5 106 C1
ROY/SHW * OL2 60 B3
Knoll St BRO M7 99 G3
ROCH OL11 42 A3
Knott Fold HYDE SK14 147 G3
Knott Hill La UPML OL3 77 F1
Knott La BOL BL1 32 C4
HYDE SK14 147 G3
Knott Lanes OLDS OL8 104 B2
Knott St ORD M5 111 E4
Knowe Av WYTH/NTH M22 180 C3
Knowl Cl DTN/ASHW M34 145 F1
RAMS BL0 16 D4
Knowldale Wy WGTN/LGST M12 128 B3
Knowle Av AULW OL7 117 H1
Knowle Dr PWCH M25 84 D5
Knowle Pk WILM/AE SK9 191 H4
Knowle Rd MPL/ROM SK6 175 H3
The Knowles OLDS OL8 103 G1
Knowles Edge St BOL BL1 33 F4
Knowles St BOL BL1 3 G1
RAD M26 52 B5
Knowl Hill Dr WHIT OL12 28 B1
Knowl Rd MILN OL16 31 E5
ROY/SHW OL2 60 B3
Knowls La OLDE OL4 92 A2
Knowl St OLDS OL8 89 H5
STLY SK15 119 G3
Knowl Syke St WHIT OL12 19 H1
Knowl Top La UPML OL3 78 C5
Knowl Vw LIT OL15 31 G1
TOT/BURYW BL8 26 B5
Knowsley Av OLDE OL4 76 B5
ORD M5 112 A5
URM M41 123 F4
Knowsley Crs STKP SK1 172 C1
Knowsley Dr OLDE OL4 76 B5
SWIN M27 96 C4
Knowsley Gra BOL BL1 47 E2
Knowsley Gn OLDE OL4 76 B5
ORD * M5 112 A5
Knowsley Rd BOL BL1 33 E4
BOLE BL2 36 B5
BRAM/HZG SK7 185 G4
STKP SK1 172 C1
WHTF M45 68 C4
Knowsley St BOL BL1 2 E3
BURY BL9 4 C7
CHH M8 113 F1
WHIT OL12 10 B4
Knowsley Ter OLDE * OL4 76 B5
STKP * SK1 172 C1
Knutsford Av HTNM SK4 144 C4
SALE M33 155 F2
Knutsford Rd GTN M18 129 F4
WILM/AE SK9 199 E5
Knutsford St SLFD M6 111 F3
Knutshaw Crs BOLS/LL BL3 62 A2
Knypersley Av OFTN SK2 172 D2
Kranj Wy OLD OL1 9 G2
Krokus Sq CHAD * OL9 73 F5
Kylemore Av BOLS/LL BL3 48 A4
Kyle Rd BRAM/HZG * SK7 185 G3
Kynder St DTN/ASHW M34 131 G5

L

Labrador Quay SALQ M50 125 G1
Labtec St SWIN M27 97 G1
Laburnum Av AUL OL6 105 F4
CHAD OL9 73 G3
DTN/ASHW M34 116 D4
ECC M30 108 D5
FAIL M35 103 E4
HYDE SK14 147 G3
ROY/SHW OL2 60 A3
STLY SK15 119 E5
SWIN M27 96 D4
TOT/BURYW BL8 26 A4
WHTF * M45 84 C1
Laburnum Cl HALE/TIMP WA15 166 C4
Laburnum Dr WHTF M45 68 D3
Laburnum Gv PWCH M25 84 D2
Laburnum La HALE/TIMP WA15 177 H4
MILN OL16 44 D3
Laburnum Pk BOLE BL2 34 C1
Laburnum Rd DTN/ASHW M34 130 A5
FWTH BL4 64 C4
GTN M18 129 G4
IRL M44 150 C1
MDTN M24 72 B4
OLDS OL8 103 H2
URM M41 123 E4
WALK M28 81 F5
Laburnum St BOL BL1 2 A3
SLFD M6 111 G3
Laburnum Ter ROCH OL11 42 D2
Laburnum Wy EDGY/DAV SK3 171 E1
LIT OL15 20 C3
Lacey Av WILM/AE SK9 199 G2
Lacey Gn WILM/AE SK9 199 G1
Lacey Gv WILM/AE SK9 199 H1
Lackford Dr NEWH/MOS M40 113 H1
Lacrosse Av OLDS OL8 89 H3
Lacy Gv STRET M32 140 A2
Lacy St STKP SK1 13 G5
STRET M32 140 A2
Lacy Wk WGTN/LGST M12 114 A5
Ladbrooke Cl AUL OL6 118 B1
Ladbrooke Rd AUL OL6 105 F5
Ladcastle Rd UPML OL3 77 H3
UPML OL3 93 H1
Ladybarn Crs BRAM/HZG SK7 194 A1
RUSH/FAL M14 143 E4
Ladybarn La RUSH/FAL M14 143 E3
Ladybarn Rd RUSH/FAL M14 143 E3
Ladybower CHD/CHDH SK8 183 F1
Ladybridge Av WALK M28 94 D2
Lady Bridge La BOL BL1 47 G2
Ladybridge Ri CHD/CHDH SK8 183 F1
Ladybridge Rd CHD/CHDH SK8 183 F1
Ladybrook Av
HALE/TIMP WA15 166 C2
Ladybrook Rd BRAM/HZG SK7 183 F3
Ladyfield St WILM/AE SK9 199 G3
Ladyfield Ter WILM/AE SK9 199 G3
Ladyhill Vw WALK M28 94 D2
Ladyhouse Cl MILN OL16 44 D2
Ladyhouse La MILN OL16 44 C1
Ladymere Dr WALK M28 94 C2
Lady Rd OLDE OL4 91 H1
Ladys Cl POY/DIS SK12 195 F3
Ladyshore Cl ORD M5 111 G4
Ladyshore Rd BOLS/LL BL3 66 B2
The Ladysmith AUL OL6 106 A5
Ladysmith Av BURY BL9 38 D1
Ladysmith Dr AUL OL6 106 A5
Ladysmith Rd AUL OL6 106 A5
DID/WITH M20 157 H4
STLY SK15 119 F1
Ladysmith St EDGY/DAV SK3 171 H2
OLDS OL8 89 H4
Ladythorn Av MPL/ROM SK6 175 F4
Ladythorn Ct PWCH M25 84 D5
Ladythorn Crs BRAM/HZG SK7 194 A1
Ladythorne Av PWCH M25 84 D5
Ladythorne Dr PWCH M25 84 D5
Ladythorn Gv BRAM/HZG SK7 194 A1
Ladythorn Rd BRAM/HZG SK7 193 H1
Ladywell Av LHULT M38 80 B3
Ladywell Cl BRAM/HZG SK7 184 B2
Ladywell Gv LHULT M38 80 B2
Lagos Cl RUSH/FAL M14 127 F4
Laindon Rd RUSH/FAL M14 128 B5
Lake Bank LIT OL15 20 D5
Lake Dr MDTN M24 71 G5
Lakeland Crs BURY BL9 53 F3
Lakeland Dr ROY/SHW * OL2 58 D1
Lakelands Dr BOLS/LL BL3 47 G4
Lakenheath Cl BOL BL1 23 E5
Lakenheath Dr BOL BL1 23 E5
Lake Rd DTN/ASHW M34 131 G4
STLY SK15 119 E1
TRPK M17 124 D1
Lakeside BURY BL9 53 G3
CHD/CHDH SK8 181 H1
Lake Side LIT OL15 31 H1
Lakeside Av AULW OL7 117 G1
BOLS/LL BL3 64 B2
WALK M28 81 E2
Lakeside Cl GTN M18 130 A2
Lakeside Dr POY/DIS SK12 195 F2
Lakeside Gn OFTN SK2 172 D3
Lakeside Wy BURY BL9 4 E6
Lakes Rd DUK SK16 118 B5
MPL/ROM SK6 175 F3
Lake St BOLS/LL * BL3 49 E4
OFTN SK2 172 C4
Lakewood DUK * SK16 118 A5
Lake Vw BKLY M9 87 H5
Lakin St NEWH/MOS M40 101 H3
Laleham Gn BRAM/HZG SK7 183 G1
Lamb Cl WGTN/LGST * M12 128 C3
Lamb Ct CSLFD * M3 6 B3
Lambert Dr SALE M33 138 C5
Lamberton Dr NTHM/RTH M23 167 F3
Lambert St AULW OL7 117 G4
Lambeth Av FAIL M35 103 F2
Lambeth Gv MPL/ROM SK6 161 H1
Lambeth Rd NEWH/MOS M40 115 F1
RDSH SK5 145 E4
Lambeth Ter ROCH OL11 42 C1
Lamb La CSLFD M3 6 B3
Lambourn Cl BOLS/LL BL3 48 D4
POY/DIS SK12 195 E3
Lambourne Cl WYTH/NTH M22 180 C4
Lambourne Gv MILN OL16 44 C1
Lambourn Rd URM M41 122 A4
Lambs Fold HTNM SK4 159 G1
Lambton Rd WALK M28 96 B4
Lambton St BOLS/LL BL3 63 F2
ECC M30 109 E1
Lamburn Av NEWH/MOS * M40 88 C5
Lamerton Wy WILM/AE SK9 192 B5
Lamorna Cl BRO M7 99 E2
Lamphey Cl BOL BL1 47 F1
Lamplight Wy SWIN M27 98 B3
Lamport Cl CMANE M1 127 G1
Lamport Ct CMANE M1 127 G1
Lampson St CHH M8 112 D1
Lampton Cl ALT WA14 165 G2
Lamsholme Cl BNG/LEV M19 143 H1
Lanark Av WYTH/NTH M22 168 C1
Lanark Cl BRAM/HZG SK7 185 H2
HEY OL10 40 A5
Lanbury Dr CHH M8 100 A3
Lancashire Ct CHAD OL9 8 A6
Lancashire Hl RDSH SK5 159 H3
Lancashire Rd PART M31 150 D4
Lancashire St NEWH/MOS M40 101 G5
Lancaster Av FAIL M35 102 D3
FWTH BL4 64 A4
MDTN M24 72 B5
RAMS BL0 16 B4
STLY SK15 119 F2
URM M41 123 H5
WHTF M45 68 D5
Lancaster Cl BOL BL1 3 G5
BRAM/HZG SK7 185 E4
MPL/ROM SK6 161 H5
Lancaster Dr BOLS/LL BL3 51 E5
BURY BL9 27 G3
PWCH M25 85 F5
Lancaster Rd DID/WITH M20 157 F3
DROY M43 116 A2
DTN/ASHW M34 146 C2
IRL M44 150 B1
SLFD M6 97 G5
WILM/AE SK9 200 B1
Lancaster St CHAD OL9 89 F4
MOSL * OL5 106 C1
RAD * M26 66 D1
STKP SK1 13 J1
Lancaster Wk BOL * BL1 33 H4
Lancelot Rd WYTH/NTH M22 181 E2
Lancelyn Dr WILM/AE SK9 200 A2
Lanchester Dr BOLS/LL BL3 2 A7
Lanchester St NEWH/MOS M40 114 B2
Lancing Av DID/WITH M20 158 A3
Lancing Wk CHAD * OL9 89 F1
Landcross Rd RUSH/FAL M14 142 D2
Lander Gv BKLY M9 87 G4
Landkey Cl NTHM/RTH M23 155 G4
Land La WILM/AE SK9 199 H4
Landos Rd NEWH/MOS M40 113 H2
Landrace Dr WALK M28 94 C4
Landsberg Rd FAIL M35 103 G2
Landseer Dr MPL/ROM SK6 175 G2
Landseer St OLDE OL4 9 J6
Lands End Rd MDTN M24 70 C5
The Lane BOL BL1 47 E2
Lane Brow OLDE OL4 92 C2
Lane Dr OLDE OL4 92 C2
Lane End ECC M30 110 A4
HEY OL10 56 C1
Lane End Rd BNG/LEV M19 158 A2
Lane Ends MPL/ROM SK6 162 C3
Lanegate HYDE SK14 147 G3
Lane Head Rd OLDE OL4 92 B4
Lane North BOLS/LL * BL3 48 A5
Laneside Av ROY/SHW OL2 60 C2
Laneside Cl LIT OL15 20 D2
Laneside Dr BRAM/HZG SK7 184 B3
Laneside Rd DID/WITH M20 169 H1
Lanfield Dr CHH M8 100 A3
Langcroft Dr NEWH/MOS M40 102 B5
Langdale Av BNG/LEV M19 144 A3
MILN OL16 58 D1
OLDS OL8 90 A3
Langdale Cl CHD/CHDH SK8 181 H1
DTN/ASHW M34 146 B2
HALE/TIMP WA15 165 H4
MPL/ROM SK6 186 D4
Langdale Dr BURY BL9 68 D1
MDTN M24 71 F1
WALK M28 95 G1
Langdale Rd BRAM/HZG SK7 193 F2
HTNM SK4 144 B5
MPL/ROM SK6 162 A1
PART M31 150 D3
RUSH/FAL M14 128 A4
SALE M33 153 H5
STRET * M32 124 D5
Langdale St BOLS/LL BL3 63 H1
FWTH BL4 64 D5
Langden Cl ROY/SHW OL2 59 H1
Langdon Cl BOL BL1 2 B2
Langfield Av OLDTF/WHR M16 126 C5
Langfield Crs DROY * M43 116 D3
Langford Dr IRL M44 136 B2
Langford Gdns BOLS/LL BL3 48 D5
Langford Rd DID/WITH M20 142 B5
HTNM SK4 159 F2
Langford St DTN/ASHW * M34 131 G5
Langham Cl BOL BL1 23 F5
Langham Ct STRET M32 124 B4
Langham Gv HALE/TIMP WA15 166 C1
Langham Rd ALT WA14 177 F2
HTNM SK4 159 E5
OLDS OL8 90 B3
SLFD M6 111 G3
Langham St AULW OL7 104 D5
Langholm Dr BOLE BL2 50 C3
Langholme Cl HULME * M15 126 C4
Langholme Pl ECC M30 109 E3
Langholme Wy HEY OL10 40 A5
Langland Cl RDSH SK5 144 C1
Langland Dr ECC M30 123 F1
Langley Av BRAM/HZG SK7 184 C3
MDTN M24 56 B5
OLDE OL4 92 C2
PWCH M25 85 E2
Langley Cl URM M41 138 D1
Langley Dr WILM/AE SK9 192 B4
Langley Hall Rd PWCH M25 85 E1
Langley La MDTN M24 55 H5
Langley Rd PWCH M25 84 D2
RUSH/FAL M14 142 D2
SALE M33 153 H2
SWIN M27 98 C2
Langley Rd South SLFD M6 98 C5
Langness St OP/CLY M11 115 F4
Lango St OLDTF/WHR * M16 126 B3
Langport Av WGTN/LGST M12 128 B3
Langsett Av SLFD M6 110 D2
Langshaw Rd BOLS/LL BL3 48 B4
Langshaw St ORD M5 111 G4
Langshaw Wk BOLS/LL * BL3 48 B4
Langside Av BKLY M9 87 E5
Langside Dr BOLS/LL BL3 47 F5
Langston Gn BRAM/HZG SK7 184 B3
Langston St CSLFD * M3 113 E2
Langthorne St BNG/LEV M19 144 A3
Langthorne Wk BOLS/LL BL3 2 A7
Langton Cl FAIL M35 103 G2
Langton St HEY OL10 40 D3
MDTN M24 71 H4
SLFD M6 111 F3
Langton Ter ROCH OL11 42 D2
Langtree Cl WALK M28 94 C2
Langworthy Av LHULT M38 80 C3
Langworthy Rd
NEWH/MOS M40 101 H3
SLFD M6 111 G2
Lanhill Dr CHH M8 100 D4
Lankro Wy ECC M30 110 A4
Lansdale Gdns BNG/LEV M19 158 B1
Lansdale St ECC M30 108 D5
Lansdown Cl BRAM/HZG SK7 183 F5
Lansdowne Av DTN/ASHW M34 116 D4
MPL/ROM SK6 162 C4
Lansdowne Cl BOLE * BL2 34 C5
RAMS BL0 16 C3
Lansdowne Ct CHAD OL9 89 G1
Lansdowne Dr WALK M28 94 D2
Lansdowne Rd ALT WA14 165 G3
BOLE BL2 34 C4
CHAD OL9 8 A4
CHH M8 100 B2
ECC M30 109 G2
SALE M33 139 F5
URM M41 137 F3
Lansdowne Rd North URM M41 137 F2
Lansdowne St ROCH OL11 29 F4
Lanstead Dr NEWH/MOS M40 114 B3
Lapwing Cl ROCH OL11 28 B4
STLY SK15 119 F1
Lapwing La DID/WITH M20 157 F1
RDSH SK5 145 H5
Larch Av CHD/CHDH SK8 182 D3
RAD M26 67 G3
STRET M32 140 A2
SWIN M27 96 B4
Larch Cl FAIL M35 103 E4
MPL/ROM SK6 174 D4
NTHM/RTH M23 166 D1
POY/DIS SK12 195 G4
The Larches MOSL OL5 107 E1
Larch Gv CHAD OL9 73 G4
SWIN M27 82 A5
Larch Rd DTN/ASHW M34 131 H5
ECC M30 108 D1
PART M31 150 D3
Larch St BURY BL9 5 K4
OLDS OL8 8 C5
Larchview Rd MDTN M24 72 B4
Larchway BRAM/HZG SK7 183 F5
MILN OL16 31 E4
MPL/ROM SK6 187 E5
Larchwood CHAD OL9 72 D5
Larchwood Av BKLY M9 101 G3
Larchwood Cl SALE M33 153 F2
Larchwood Dr WILM/AE SK9 200 B2
Larchwood St BOL BL1 34 A4
Larkfield Av LHULT M38 80 A2
Larkfield Cl AULW OL7 105 E3
TOT/BURYW BL8 25 H1
Larkfield Gv BOLE BL2 3 K2
Larkhall Ri WYTH/NTH M22 168 D4
Lark Hl FWTH BL4 65 E5
STLY SK15 119 F1
Larkhill Cl HALE/TIMP WA15 166 C3
Larkhill Pl WHIT OL12 10 B2
Larkhill Rd CHD/CHDH SK8 171 F4
Lark Hill Rd EDGY/DAV SK3 12 B5
UPML OL3 77 G2
Larkhill Vw EDGY/DAV SK3 171 F4
Larkhill Wk CHH M8 100 C4
Larkside Av WALK M28 81 E4
Larks Ri DROY M43 117 E2
Lark St BOL BL1 3 F3
FWTH * BL4 65 E5
OLD * OL1 75 G1
Larkswood Dr OFTN SK2 173 G4
Larkwood Cl MOSL OL5 107 F3
Larmuth Av CCHDY M21 141 F5
Larne Av EDGY/DAV SK3 171 G1
STRET M32 139 H1
Larne St OP/CLY M11 114 D5
Larwood Av HTNM SK4 158 D5
Lascar Av ORD M5 111 H5
Lashbrook Cl NEWH/MOS M40 114 A1
Lassell Fold HYDE SK14 133 G2
Lassell St OP/CLY * M11 130 A1
Lastingham St NEWH/MOS M40 102 B4
Latchford St AULW OL7 117 H1
Latchmere Rd RUSH/FAL M14 142 D3
Latham Cl MPL/ROM SK6 161 G1
Latham St BOL BL1 34 A4
OP/CLY M11 130 A1
Lathbury Rd BKLY M9 101 E4
Lathom Gv SALE M33 155 F3
Lathom Hall Av OLDE * OL4 76 B5
Lathom Rd DID/WITH M20 143 E4
IRL M44 136 A3
Lathom St BURY BL9 5 F1
Latimer St OLDE OL4 9 K5
Latin St MILN * OL16 43 E5
Latrigg Crs MDTN M24 70 D2
Latrobe St DROY M43 116 B5
Lauderdale Crs
BRUN/LGST M13 127 H2
Launceston Cl BRAM/HZG SK7 184 A5
OLDS OL8 91 F3
Launceston Rd RAD M26 51 G4
Laundry St SLFD M6 111 G1
Laureate Wy DTN/ASHW M34 146 D4
Laurel Av CHAD OL9 72 C4
CHD/CHDH SK8 170 A4
RUSH/FAL M14 142 B1
Laurel Bank HYDE SK14 147 F3
STLY SK15 119 G5
Laurel Bank Gdns BKLY M9 87 E3
Laurel Ct BOL BL1 2 E2
MILN * OL16 30 C5
Laurel Dr HALE/TIMP WA15 166 C5
LHULT M38 80 B3
Laurel End La HTNM SK4 158 D3
Laurel Gn DTN/ASHW M34 146 D1
Laurel Gv ORD * M5 110 D3
Laurel Rd HTNM SK4 159 E2
The Laurels MOSL OL5 107 E1
Laurels Dr LIT OL15 31 G1
Laurel St BOL BL1 48 B2
BURY BL9 5 J4
HTNM SK4 12 E2
MDTN M24 72 C4
TOT/BURYW BL8 26 A5
Laurel Wk PART M31 150 D4
Laurel Wy CHD/CHDH SK8 183 F4
Laurence Cl WGTN/LGST M12 128 D2
Lauria Ter BOLE BL2 36 C5
Laurie Pl WHIT OL12 10 C2
Lausanne Rd BRAM/HZG SK7 183 H1
DID/WITH M20 142 C4
Lavender Cl NTHM/RTH M23 155 F5
SALE M33 153 F1
Lavender Rd FWTH BL4 64 C2
OLDE OL4 91 H3
Lavenders Brow STKP SK1 13 H3
Lavender St RAD M26 66 C1
Lavenham Av OP/CLY M11 115 G4
Lavenham Cl BRAM/HZG SK7 185 F4
BURY BL9 68 C1
Laverton Cl HEY OL10 39 G5
Lavington Av CHD/CHDH SK8 170 D3
Lavington Gv GTN M18 129 G4
Lavinia St ECC M30 109 E3
Lavister Av BNG/LEV M19 158 B2
Lawefield Crs SWIN M27 82 C2
Lawers Av CHAD OL9 73 F4
Lawflat WHIT OL12 19 H3
Lawler Av ORD M5 126 A2
Lawnbank Cl MDTN M24 71 F3
Lawn Cl OLDS OL8 91 F4
Lawn Dr HALE/TIMP WA15 165 H3
SWIN M27 96 D3
Lawngreen Av CCHDY M21 140 D4
The Lawns ALT WA14 177 F1
Lawnside Ms DID/WITH M20 157 F1
Lawn St BOL BL1 2 A1
Lawnswood ROCH OL11 42 B2
Lawnswood Dr SWIN M27 97 F4
Lawnswood Park Rd SWIN M27 97 F4
Lawrence Cl WHIT OL12 28 D2
Lawrence Pl POY/DIS SK12 195 E5
Lawrence Rd ALT WA14 165 F3
BRAM/HZG SK7 185 F1
URM M41 122 B5
Lawrence St BURY BL9 55 G4
STKP SK1 13 F4
Lawrie Av RAMS BL0 16 C3
Lawson Av CHD/CHDH SK8 169 G4
Lawson Cl MDTN M24 56 D5
WALK M28 96 B3
Lawson Gv SALE M33 139 F5
Lawson Rd BOL BL1 33 E4
Lawson St BKLY M9 86 D5
BOL BL1 33 H2
Law St ROCH OL11 42 B1
Lawton Av BRAM/HZG SK7 183 H4
Lawton Cl MPL/ROM SK6 161 G5
Lawton Moor Rd
NTHM/RTH M23 155 H5
Lawton Rd HTNM SK4 159 F2
Lawton St DROY M43 116 C3
OP/CLY M11 129 G1
STLY SK15 119 G4
WHIT OL12 10 E3
Laxey St NEWH/MOS * M40 102 A3
Laxfield Dr URM M41 122 A4
Laxford Gv BOLS/LL BL3 47 F3
Layard St AUL OL6 117 H2
Laycock Av BOLE BL2 34 C3
STLY SK15 120 B1
Laycock Crs FAIL M35 103 E4
Laycock Dr DUK SK16 133 F1
Laycock Gv FAIL M35 103 E3
Laycock St MILN OL16 20 A5
Layfield Cl TOT/BURYW BL8 25 G3
Laystall St CMANE M1 7 J4
Laythe Barn Cl MILN OL16 31 F5
Layton Av HYDE SK14 132 A5
Layton Cl STKP SK1 13 J5
Layton Dr FWTH BL4 81 G1
MPL/ROM SK6 162 B3
Layton St NEWH/MOS M40 114 A3
Leabank St BNG/LEV M19 143 H2
Leabrook Dr NEWH/MOS M40 102 D2
Leaburn Dr BNG/LEV M19 158 B2
Leach Cl MILN OL16 30 D1
Leach St BOLS/LL BL3 48 D4
FWTH BL4 65 F3
GTN M18 129 E3
MILN OL16 30 C5
MILN OL16 44 C1
PWCH M25 84 C3
ROY/SHW OL2 60 B3
Leach Wk OLDE OL4 75 H4
Leaconfield Dr WALK M28 95 G3
Lea Ct FAIL M35 102 D3
Leacroft Av BOLE BL2 50 A4
Leacroft Rd CCHDY M21 156 C1
Leadale Ri OLDE * OL4 92 B1
Leader Williams Rd IRL M44 136 A2
Lea Dr BKLY M9 87 G4
Leafield Av DID/WITH M20 158 A2
Leafield Cl RAD M26 66 D1
Leafield Dr CHD/CHDH SK8 192 C1
WALK M28 94 B4
Leafield Rd POY/DIS SK12 197 H1
Leaford Av DTN/ASHW M34 131 E4
Leaford Cl DTN/ASHW M34 131 E4
Leaf St BOLS/LL BL3 49 H4
HULME M15 127 E2
RDSH SK5 144 D4
Leagate URM M41 138 D2
Lea Gate Cl BOLE BL2 35 E1
Leaholme Cl NEWH/MOS M40 102 C5
Leah St LIT * OL15 21 E3
Leak St OLDTF/WHR M16 126 B2
Leamington Av BURY BL9 27 F3
DID/WITH M20 157 E2
Leamington Rd ECC M30 109 E2
RDSH SK5 144 D4
URM M41 123 E5
Leamington St OLDE OL4 75 F4
OP/CLY M11 129 G1
WHIT OL12 10 B4
Lea Mount Dr BURY BL9 39 G2
Leam St AUL OL6 118 C1
Leander Cl BKLY M9 87 F5
Leander Dr ROCH OL11 42 C5
Lea Rd CHD/CHDH SK8 181 G3
HTNM SK4 159 E2
The Leas HALE/TIMP WA15 178 C1
Leaside Av OLD OL1 73 F2
Leaside Cl WHIT OL12 29 G1
Leaside Dr DID/WITH M20 158 A1
Leaside Gv WALK M28 81 F4
Leaside Wy WILM/AE SK9 199 H4
Lea Thorn BOLE BL2 35 E2
Leaton Av NTHM/RTH M23 167 H3
Leavale Cl LHULT M38 80 A3
Lea Vw ROY/SHW OL2 73 H1
Leaway WHIT OL12 19 H2
Lecester Rd CHH M8 100 C4
Leckenby Cl WALK M28 94 B4
Leconfield Dr BKLY M9 87 F4
Leconfield Rd ECC M30 108 C1
Lecturers Cl BOLS/LL BL3 49 E4
Ledbrooke Cl ORD M5 126 A1
Ledburn Cl HULME M15 126 C2
Ledbury Av URM M41 123 F5
Ledbury Cl MDTN M24 87 H1
Ledbury Rd FAIL * M35 115 H1
Ledge Ley CHD/CHDH SK8 182 B4
Ledsham Av BKLY M9 86 B2
Ledson Rd NTHM/RTH M23 167 G4
Ledward La ALT WA14 177 E2
Lee Av ALT WA14 165 F2
BOLS/LL BL3 63 G1
Leech Av AUL OL6 105 H5
Leech Brook Av
DTN/ASHW M34 131 F3
Leech St HYDE SK14 148 A1
STLY SK15 119 F4
Lee Cl IRL M44 136 A2
Lee Ct WYTH/NTH * M22 168 D1
Lee Crs STRET M32 140 B1
Lee Dale Cl DTN/ASHW M34 146 D1
Leeds Cl BURY BL9 69 E1
Leefields Cl UPML OL3 78 A4
Lee Ga BOLE BL2 35 E1
Leegate Cl HTNM SK4 158 C2
Leegate Dr BKLY M9 87 G3
Leegate Gdns HTNM SK4 158 C2
Leegate Rd HTNM SK4 158 D2
Leegrange Rd BKLY M9 101 F1
Lee Gv FWTH BL4 64 A4
Leek St RAD M26 66 D1
Leemans Hill St TOT/BURYW BL8 37 F1
Lees Av DTN/ASHW M34 146 B1
Lees Brook Pk OLDE OL4 91 G1
Lees Gv OLDE OL4 91 G2
Lees Hall Crs RUSH/FAL M14 143 E3
Leeside HTNM SK4 158 D5
Lees New Rd AUL OL6 105 G1
OLDE OL4 92 A3
Lees Park Av DROY M43 116 D3
Lees Rd AUL OL6 105 G3
BRAM/HZG SK7 193 G2
OLDE OL4 9 K3

OLDE OL4 .....92 C4
Lees St AUL OL6 .....118 A1
DROY M43 .....19 H4
GTN M18 .....129 H2
MDTN M24 .....72 C5
MOSL * OL5 .....92 D5
OLDS OL8 .....104 C2
STLY SK15 .....119 F3
Lees St East ROY/SHW OL2 .....60 A2
Leestone Rd WYTH/NTH M22 .....168 D3
Lee St BURY BL9 .....27 G3
LIT OL15 .....21 F1
MDTN M24 .....71 G1
OLDS OL8 .....8 D5
STKP SK1 .....13 G4
UPML OL3 .....51 G4
Leesway OLDE OL4 .....91 H2
Leesway Dr DTN/ASHW M34 .....146 D1
Leeswood Av CCHDY M21 .....141 F5
Leewood SWIN M27 .....82 C3
Left Bank CSLFD M5 .....6 C6
Le Gendre St BOLE BL2 .....34 C4
Legh Cl POY/DIS SK12 .....195 F4
Legh Dr DTN/ASHW M34 .....116 C4
MPL/ROM SK6 .....147 E5
Legh Rd BRO M7 .....99 G2
POY/DIS SK12 .....197 F1
SALE M33 .....155 F3
Legh St BRO M7 .....99 G2
ECC M30 .....109 H4
Legion Gv BRO M7 .....99 H4
Legwood Ct URM M41 .....138 D1
Leicester Av BRO * M7 .....100 A2
DROY M43 .....146 C2
DTN/ASHW M34 .....146 C2
HALE/TIMP M45 .....166 B1
Leicester Rd BRO M7 .....99 H5
SALE M33 .....154 C1
HALE/TIMP WA15 .....177 H2
WHTF M45 .....68 A3
Leicester St AULW OL7 .....118 A1
OLDE OL4 .....91 E1
RDSH SK5 .....144 D1
ROCH OL11 .....43 F1
Leigh Av MPL/ROM SK6 .....174 D5
SWIN M27 .....96 C5
Leighbrook Rd RUSH/FAL M14 .....142 C5
Leigh Cl TOT/BURYW BL8 .....25 H4
Leigh Fold HYDE SK14 .....132 D3
Leigh La TOT/BURYW BL8 .....37 F3
Leigh Rd HALE/TIMP WA15 .....177 F3
WALK M28 .....94 B3
WILM/AE SK9 .....198 C5
Leigh St BRO M7 .....99 G5
FWTH BL4 .....65 E4
HEY OL10 .....41 E4
HYDE SK14 .....147 H1
MILN OL16 .....31 E4
TOT/BURYW BL8 .....37 E2
Leighton Av BOL BL1 .....48 A1
LIT OL15 .....31 G1
Leighton Dr MPL/ROM SK6 .....175 H1
Leighton St NEWH/MOS M40 .....101 G5
Leinster Rd SWIN M27 .....96 D5
Leinster St FWTH BL4 .....65 E4
Leith Av SALE M33 .....155 F2
Leith Rd SALE M33 .....155 F2
Le Mans Crs BOL BL1 .....2 C5
Lemnos St OLD OL1 .....9 J2
CMANE M1 .....7 H5
Lena St BOL BL1 .....34 A4
CMANE M1 .....7 H5
Len Cox Wk ANC * M4 .....7 H4
Leng Rd NEWH/MOS M40 .....102 C5
Lenham Ct RDSH SK5 .....145 G5
Lenham Gdns BOLE BL2 .....50 B3
Lennox Av OLDS OL8 .....104 A1
Lennox St AUL OL6 .....118 B2
Lenora St BOLS/LL BL3 .....48 A4
Lenten Gv HEY OL10 .....56 B2
Lentmead Dr NEWH/MOS M40 .....101 H4
Lenton Gdns WYTH/NTH M22 .....180 D1
Leominster Dr WYTH/NTH M22 .....180 D1
Leominster Rd MDTN * M24 .....88 A1
Leonardin Cl ROY/SHW OL2 .....59 G1
Leonard St BOLS/LL BL3 .....63 H1
RAD M26 .....52 A4
Leopold Av DID/WITH M20 .....157 F1
Leopold St ROCH OL11 .....29 G4
Lepp Crs TOT/BURYW BL8 .....26 D5
Leroy Dr BKLY M9 .....101 E1
Lerryn Dr BRAM/HZG SK7 .....183 G5
Lesley Av BURY BL9 .....139 F2
CHAD OL9 .....89 G4
Leslie Av HALE/TIMP WA15 .....166 C1
Leslie Hough Wy SLFD M6 .....112 A1
Leslie St BOLE BL2 .....3 J1
RUSH/FAL M14 .....127 G5
Lester Rd LHULT M38 .....78 D1
Lester St STRET M32 .....140 A1
Letchworth Av ROCH OL11 .....43 F1
Letchworth St RUSH/FAL M14 .....127 G5
Letham St OLDS OL8 .....90 C5
Levedale Rd BKLY M9 .....87 F3
Leven Cl FWTH BL4 .....64 B4
Levenhurst Rd SLFD M6 .....100 A3
Levens Cl CHD/CHDH SK8 .....169 G5
Levens Dr BURY BL9 .....35 F5
Levenshulme Rd GTN M18 .....129 G4
Levenshulme Ter BNG/LEV * M19 .....143 H2
Levens Rd BRAM/HZG SK7 .....184 D2
Levens St NEWH/MOS M40 .....101 H5
SLFD M6 .....99 E5
Lever Av SWIN M27 .....83 G5
Lever Bridge Pl BOLS/LL BL3 .....49 E4
Lever Dr BOLS/LL BL3 .....48 D4
Lever Edge La BOLS/LL BL3 .....63 H2
Leverett Cl ALT WA14 .....164 D4
Lever Gv BOL BL1 .....49 G1
Lever Hall Rd BOLE BL2 .....49 H2
Leverhulme Av BOLS/LL BL3 .....64 B1
BOLS/LL BL3 .....50 D5
BRAM/HZG SK7 .....185 G1
CMANE M1 .....7 J4
HEY OL10 .....41 E3
RAD M26 .....52 A4
RAMS BL0 .....16 D2

Lever Wk MDTN M24 .....71 G5
Levington Dr OLDS OL8 .....104 D2
Levi St BOL BL1 .....32 C5
Lewes Av DTN/ASHW M34 .....146 C2
Lewis Av BKLY M9 .....101 F1
URM M41 .....123 G3
Lewis Dr HEY OL10 .....40 A5
Lewisham Av NEWH/MOS M40 .....115 E1
Lewisham St HYDE * OL2 .....58 D3
Leyburn Av ROY/SHW OL2 .....59 E5
RDSH SK5 .....145 E2
Lewis St ECC M50 .....109 G4
HEY * OL10 .....41 F3
NEWH/MOS M40 .....114 A2
ROY/SHW OL2 .....60 A4
Lexton Av CHH M8 .....86 C5
Leybourne Av BNG/LEV M19 .....144 A1
Leybourne St BOL BL1 .....33 H4
Leybrook Rd WYTH/NTH M22 .....180 B1
Leyburn Av ROY/SHW OL2 .....59 E5
STRET M32 .....139 G1
URM M41 .....137 H2
Leyburn Cl WHTF M45 .....68 B4
Leyburn Gv OFTN SK2 .....172 D5
Leyburn Rd ROY/SHW OL2 .....172 E2
Leyburn Rd HALE/TIMP M45 .....88 B5
Leycett Dr NTHM/RTH M23 .....155 H5
Leycroft St CMANE * M1 .....7 J6
Ley Dr HEY OL10 .....56 B2
Leyfield Av MPL/ROM SK6 .....162 B4
Leyfield Rd MILN OL16 .....31 E5
Ley Hey Av MPL/ROM SK6 .....175 E2
Ley Hey Rd MPL/ROM SK6 .....175 E2
Leyland Av CHD/CHDH SK8 .....169 G3
DID/WITH M20 .....158 A5
IRL M44 .....121 C4
Leylands La HYDE SK14 .....149 F5
Leyland St BURY BL9 .....5 H4
HTNM SK4 .....12 E3
Leys Rd ALT WA14 .....165 H1
Leyton Av NEWH/MOS M40 .....102 A3
Leyton Cl FWTH BL4 .....64 B4
Leyton Dr BURY BL9 .....53 G4
Leyton St WHIT OL12 .....30 A1
Leywell Dr OLD OL1 .....75 H2
Leywell Rd BKLY M9 .....101 G2
Library La CHAD OL9 .....8 D1
Libra St BOL BL1 .....33 G4
Lichens Crs OLDS OL8 .....90 D4
Lichfield Av AUL OL6 .....105 G5
BOLE BL2 .....34 C4
HALE/TIMP WA15 .....178 D1
RDSH SK5 .....144 D4
Lichfield Cl FWTH BL4 .....64 B5
Lichfield Dr CHAD OL9 .....73 H3
CHH M8 .....100 C1
PWCH M25 .....85 F5
SWIN M27 .....97 E4
TOT/BURYW BL8 .....4 B1
Lichfield Rd ECC M30 .....48 A1
RAD M26 .....51 G4
URM M41 .....123 G4
Lichfield St SLFD M6 .....98 D5
Lichfield Ter MILN OL16 .....43 H2
Lidbrook Wk MPL/ROM SK6 .....161 E3
Liddington Hall Dr RAMS BL0 .....16 C4
Lidgett Cl WALK M28 .....80 D2
Lidiard St CHH M8 .....100 B1
Liffey Av WYTH/NTH M22 .....180 D1
Lifton Av NEWH/MOS M40 .....114 B1
Light Alders La POY/DIS SK12 .....187 F5
Lightbourne Rd SALE M33 .....153 G2
Lightbounds Rd BOL BL1 .....32 C3
Lightbourne Av SWIN M27 .....97 E3
Lightbowne Rd
NEWH/MOS M40 .....101 H4
Lightburn Av LIT OL15 .....20 D3
Lightburne Av BOL BL1 .....48 A2
Lighthorne Av EDGY/DAV SK3 .....170 C2
Lighthorne Gv EDGY/DAV SK3 .....170 C2
Lighthorne Rd EDGY/DAV SK3 .....170 C2
Light Oaks Rd SLFD M6 .....96 D3
Lightowlers La LIT OL15 .....21 G1
Lightwood WALK M28 .....94 C2
Lightwood Cl FWTH BL4 .....65 F3
Lignum Av CHAD OL9 .....73 G4
Lilac Av BURY BL9 .....53 E2
MILN OL16 .....31 G4
HYDE SK14 .....147 G5
MILN OL16 .....44 D3
SWIN M27 .....97 F2
Lilac Ct SLFD M6 .....111 G3
Lilac Gv CHAD OL9 .....73 G4
NEWH/MOS M40 .....101 H4
PWCH M25 .....84 D1
Lilac La OLDS OL8 .....91 G4
Lilac Rd HALE/TIMP WA15 .....178 B1
ROCH OL11 .....43 E4
Lila St OFTN SK3 .....172 A3
Lilac View Cl ROY/SHW OL2 .....60 C5
Lila St BKLY M9 .....101 G3
Lilburn Cl RAMS BL0 .....16 D4
Liley St MILN OL16 .....11 F7
Lilford Cl WGTN/LGST M12 .....128 D2
Lilian Gv RDSH SK5 .....145 E3
Lillian St OLDTF/WHR M16 .....126 B4
Lilly St BOL BL1 .....2 A4
HYDE SK14 .....148 A3
Lilmore Av NEWH/MOS M40 .....102 B4
Lily Av FWTH BL4 .....64 B4
Lily Cl EDGY/DAV SK3 .....171 G4
Lily Hill St WHTF M45 .....68 B2
Lily La BKLY M9 .....101 G3
Lily St ECC M30 .....109 E4
MDTN M24 .....72 B4
MILN OL16 .....31 G5
OLD OL1 .....74 B3
ROY/SHW OL2 .....59 H4
Lima St BURY BL9 .....5 K2
Limbert Cir CHH M8 .....101 F1
Lime Av SWIN M27 .....96 B4
URM M41 .....138 A1
WHTF M45 .....68 C5
Lime Bank St WGTN/LGST M12 .....114 A5
Limebrook Cl OP/CLY M11 .....129 H1
Lime Cl DUK SK16 .....132 C2
SLFD M6 .....111 H2
Lime Ct SLFD * M6 .....111 H2
Lime Crs OLDTF/WHR M16 .....126 D4
Limeditch Rd FAIL M35 .....103 F1
Limefield MDTN M24 .....71 F5

Lime Fld MILN OL16 .....31 F4
Limefield MOSL OL5 .....92 C5
Limefield Av FWTH BL4 .....65 F5
Limefield Brow BURY BL9 .....37 H1
Limefield Cl BOL BL1 .....32 D2
Limefield Rd BOL BL1 .....33 E2
BRO M7 .....99 G1
BURY BL9 .....37 H1
RAD M26 .....66 C1
Limefield Ter BNG/LEV M19 .....143 H2
Lime Gdns DUK SK16 .....118 A5
MDTN M24 .....71 F4
Lime Ga OLDS OL8 .....89 H5
Lime Gn OLDS OL8 .....104 A1
Lime Green Rd OLDS OL8 .....103 H2
Lime Gv AUL OL6 .....105 F5
BURY BL9 .....27 G2
CHD/CHDH SK8 .....170 A3
DTN/ASHW M34 .....131 G4
HALE/TIMP WA15 .....166 C3
HEY OL10 .....40 D3
LIT OL15 .....20 D5
OLDTF/WHR M16 .....126 A4
PWCH M25 .....85 H2
RAMS BL0 .....17 E1
ROY/SHW OL2 .....59 H5
STLY SK15 .....118 D5
WALK M28 .....95 E1
Lime Gv AUL OL6 .....104 D4
DID/WITH M20 .....142 A3
Limehurst Av AULW OL7 .....104 D4
Limehurst Rd AULW OL7 .....104 D4
Lime Kiln La MPL/ROM SK6 .....161 E1
Limekiln La WGTN/LGST M12 .....114 A5
Lime La OLDS OL8 .....103 H1
Lime Rd STRET M32 .....140 A2
Limers Ga WHIT OL12 .....19 E3
Limerston Dr NEWH/MOS M40 .....105 C1
The Limes MOSL OL5 .....107 F1
Limesdale Cl BOLE BL2 .....51 E4
Limeside Rd OLDS OL8 .....89 H5
Limestead Av CHH M8 .....100 B2
Lime St BURY BL9 .....27 G5
DUK SK16 .....118 A5
ECC M30 .....109 G4
FWTH BL4 .....64 C5
MPL/ROM SK6 .....161 F2
NEWH/MOS M40 .....101 G3
OLD OL1 .....75 H3
ROCH OL11 .....42 D1
Lime Tree Cl URM M41 .....138 D2
Lime Tree Gv FAIL M35 .....103 G5
Limetrees Rd MDTN M24 .....71 G4
Limley Gv CCHDY M21 .....141 F4
Linacre Av BOLS/LL BL3 .....63 H2
Linby St HULME M15 .....126 D1
Lincoln Av BNG/LEV M19 .....144 A2
BOLS/LL BL3 .....65 H1
CHD/CHDH SK8 .....181 G5
DROY M43 .....117 H4
DTN/ASHW M34 .....146 C2
FAIL M35 .....105 H2
MDTN M24 .....88 B2
WILM/AE SK9 .....200 D1
Lincoln St BRUN/LGST M13 .....128 C4
CHAD OL9 .....89 G2
ECC M30 .....109 G5
ROCH OL11 .....30 D5
Lincombe Rd WYTH/NTH M22 .....180 B4
Linda Dr BRAM/HZG SK7 .....183 E3
Lindale Av BOL BL1 .....34 B3
CHAD OL9 .....73 G1
NEWH/MOS M40 .....88 D5
ROY/SHW OL2 .....58 D2
URM M41 .....123 F4
Lindale Dr MDTN M24 .....71 G5
Lindale Rd ROY/SHW OL2 .....60 C2
Lindbury Av OFTN SK2 .....172 D2
Linden Av BOLS/LL BL3 .....50 D4
DTN/ASHW M34 .....131 F1
HALE/TIMP WA15 .....166 C3
OLDE OL4 .....75 G4
RAD M26 .....53 F4
SALE M33 .....154 A2
SWIN M27 .....83 G3
Linden Cl DTN/ASHW M34 .....131 H5
RAMS BL0 .....17 G1
Linden Dr ORD M5 .....112 A4
Linden Gv BNG/LEV M19 .....143 G5
BRAM/HZG SK7 .....183 G3
Linn St CHH M8 .....100 B1
Linnyshaw Cl BOLS/LL BL3 .....48 D5
Linnyshaw Moss Rd WALK M28 .....79 F1
Linslade Gdns BOLS/LL BL3 .....48 A3
Linslade St SLFD * M6 .....98 D5
SALE M33 .....154 C1
Linstead Dr CHH M8 .....100 A4
Linthorpe Wk BOLS/LL BL3 .....48 B5
Linton Av BURY BL9 .....38 C5
DTN/ASHW M34 .....130 B5
Linton Cl ANC M4 .....114 A5
Linton Rd SALE M33 .....154 A1
Linwood Gv WGTN/LGST M12 .....143 H1
Linwood St FAIL M35 .....102 B4
Lion Brow BKLY M9 .....87 F5
Lion Fold La BKLY M9 .....87 F5
Lions Dr SWIN M27 .....97 H1
Lion St BKLY M9 .....87 F5
Lisbon St ROCH OL11 .....29 E5
Lisburn Av CCHDY M21 .....141 E2
SALE M33 .....154 B3
Lisburne Av OFTN SK2 .....173 F3
Lisburne Cl OFTN SK2 .....173 F3
Lisburne La OFTN SK2 .....172 D4
Liscard Av RUSH/FAL M14 .....142 D2
Lisetta Av OLDE OL4 .....91 E2
Liskeard Av ROY/SHW OL2 .....60 B1
Liskeard Cl MILN OL16 .....44 C4
Liskeard Dr BRAM/HZG SK7 .....184 A5
Lisle St WHIT OL12 .....28 B1
Lismore Av BOLS/LL BL3 .....47 G4
SALE M33 .....154 B3
Lismore Wy URM M41 .....123 G3
Lissadel St SLFD M6 .....111 H1
Lisson Gv HALE/TIMP WA15 .....177 H2
Lister Rd MDTN M24 .....87 F1
Litcham Cl CMANE M1 .....7 H5
Litchfield Gv WALK M28 .....96 A1
Litherland Av WYTH/NTH M22 .....180 D3
Litherland Rd BOLS/LL BL3 .....47 H4
SALE M33 .....155 F3
Little 66 BURY BL9 .....54 A2

Little Ancoats St CMANE M1 .....7 H3
Little Bank St OLDE OL4 .....91 E1
Littlebourne Wk BOL BL1 .....23 F5
Little Brook CI CHD/CHDH SK8 .....169 E3
Little Brook Rd SALE M33 .....155 E5
Little Brow EDGW/EG BL7 .....23 F4
Little Clegg Rd LIT OL15 .....31 G1
Little D St HYDE SK14 .....147 G5
Little David St CMANE M1 .....7 G6
Littledale St WHIT OL12 .....14 C5
Little Egerton St STKP SK1 .....13 F2
Little Ees La SALE M33 .....139 E4
Little Egerton St STKP SK1 .....13 F2
Littlefields HYDE SK14 .....134 C4
Little Flatt WHIT OL12 .....14 A2
Little Gn MDTN * M24 .....72 A3
Littlegreen Gdns SLFD M6 .....111 G2
Little Harwood Lee BOLE BL2 .....35 E3
Littlehaven Cl WGTN/LGST M12 .....128 B3
Little Heath La ALT WA14 .....164 A5
Little Hey St ROY/SHW OL2 .....60 A5
Littlehills Cl MDTN M24 .....71 F3
Little Holme Wk BOLS/LL * BL3 .....48 A5
Little Howarth Wy WHIT * OL12 .....19 H4
Little John St CSLFD M3 .....6 B6
Little Lever St CMANE M1 .....7 H4
Little Meadow Rd ALT WA14 .....177 E3
Little Moor Clough EDGW/EG BL7 .....22 D1
Little Moor Cottages STKP SK1 .....172 C1
Little Moor La OLDE OL4 .....75 F4
Littlemoor Rd HYDE SK14 .....149 F5
Little Moss La SWIN M27 .....83 G5
Littlemoss Rd DROY M43 .....116 D2
Little Nelson St ANC * M4 .....7 G1
Little Oak Cl OLDE OL4 .....91 H1
Little Peter St HULME M15 .....127 F1
Little Pitt St CMANE * M1 .....7 J4
Little Quay St CSLFD M3 .....6 D5
Little Stones Rd EDGW/EG BL7 .....22 D1
Littleton Rd BRO M7 .....99 E1
Little Underbank STKP SK1 .....13 G3
Liverstudd Av RDSH SK5 .....145 E1
Liverton Ct BKLY M9 .....87 G2
Liverpool CI RDSH SK5 .....144 D4
Liverpool Cl RDSH SK5 .....144 D4
ECC M50 .....109 A6
IRL M44 .....136 A3
IRL M44 .....150 C3
Liverpool St RDSH SK5 .....145 E1
SLFD M6 .....111 F3
Liverstudd Av RDSH SK5 .....145 E1
Livesey St ANC M4 .....113 H2
BNG/LEV M19 .....144 A3
OLD OL1 .....75 H4
Livingstone Av MOSL OL5 .....94 B4
Livingstone St OLDE OL4 .....91 H2
Livsey Ct BOL BL1 .....2 E1
Livsey La HEY OL10 .....40 B4
Livsey St BURY BL9 .....5 J3
MILN OL16 .....10 E7
WHIT OL12 .....29 G5
Lizard St CMANE M1 .....7 H4
Lizmar Ter BKLY M9 .....101 G3
Llanberis Rd CHD/CHDH SK8 .....182 B3
Llanfair Rd EDGY/DAV SK3 .....171 G4
Lloyd Av CHD/CHDH SK8 .....169 F3
Lloyd Gdns HALE/TIMP WA15 .....177 G1
Lloyd Rd BNG/LEV M19 .....144 A4
Lloyd Sq ALT WA14 .....165 G5
CMANW M2 .....6 E5
HEY OL10 .....41 E5
HTNM SK4 .....12 D1
ROCH OL11 .....42 C2
WHIT OL12 .....14 B4
Lloyd St South RUSH/FAL M14 .....142 D3
Lobden Crs WHIT OL12 .....18 C1
Lobelia Av FWTH BL4 .....65 G3
Lobley Cl WHIT OL12 .....30 C1
Lochawe Cl HEY OL10 .....40 B5
Lochinver Gv HEY OL10 .....40 B5
Lochmaddy Cl BRAM/HZG SK7 .....185 G5
Lock Cl HEY OL10 .....41 E5
Lockett Gdns CSLFD M3 .....6 A2
Lockett St CHH M8 .....112 D1
SLFD M6 .....100 D5
Lockhart Cl WGTN/LGST M12 .....128 C3
Lockhart St ROCH OL11 .....43 G1
Lockingate St AUL OL6 .....105 G4
Locking Gate Ri OLDE OL4 .....75 H3
Locklands La IRL M44 .....136 D1
Lock La MDTN M24 .....71 F1
Lock Rd ALT WA14 .....165 F3
Lockside MPL/ROM SK6 .....175 F3
Locksley Cl HTNM SK4 .....12 D1
Lockton Cl BRUN/LGST M13 .....128 B1
RDSH SK5 .....144 D5
Lockton Ct CMANE M1 .....7 G6
Lockwood St WGTN/LGST M12 .....130 D1
Lodge Av URM M41 .....138 D1
Lodge Bank Rd LIT OL15 .....20 C5
Lodge Brow RAD M26 .....67 G2
Lodge Cl DUK SK16 .....132 D3
Lodge Ct HTNM SK4 .....158 D2
HYDE SK14 .....134 A1
Lodge Farm Cl BRAM/HZG SK7 .....183 H2
Lodge Fold DROY M43 .....116 D4
Lodge Gn DUK SK16 .....118 C5
Lodge La DUK SK16 .....118 C5
HYDE SK14 .....132 D4
Lodgepole Cl ECC M30 .....108 C2
Lodgeside Cl DROY M43 .....116 D3
Lodge St AULW OL7 .....117 G5
HYDE SK14 .....134 A1
LIT OL15 .....20 C5
MDTN M24 .....71 G5
NEWH/MOS M40 .....101 H5
RAMS BL0 .....16 D2
WHIT OL12 .....19 H2
Lodge St DROY M43 .....116 C5
Loen Crs BOL BL1 .....23 H5
Loganberry Av SLFD M6 .....111 H2
Logan St BOL BL1 .....23 G5
Logwood Av TOT/BURYW BL8 .....37 F4
Loisine Cl ROCH OL11 .....42 A2
Lois St BKLY M9 .....101 F5
Lomas CI BNG/LEV M19 .....158 A3
Lomas St EDGY/DAV SK3 .....12 D7

FAIL M35 103 F1
MDTN M24 72 A3
Lomax's Buildings BOL BL1 3 F6
Lomax St BOL BL1 33 H4
BURY BL9 5 G3
CMANE M1 7 K4
RAD M26 67 F2
WHIT OL12 10 D4
WHTF * M45 68 B2
Lombard Cl MPL/ROM SK6 161 G2
Lombard Gv RUSH/FAL M14 142 D3
Lombard St OLD OL1 9 F2
WHIT OL12 29 G3
Lombardy Ct SLFD * M6 111 H2
Lomond Av HALE/TIMP WA15 178 B1
STRET M32 125 E5
Lomond Cl OFTN SK2 184 B1
Lomond Dr TOT/BURYW BL8 37 G2
Lomond Pl BOLS/LL BL3 47 F3
Lomond Rd WYTH/NTH M22 181 E2
Lomond Ter MILN OL16 43 H2
London Pl STKP SK1 13 G4
London Rd CMANE M1 7 J7
OFTN SK2 173 E5
OLD OL1 75 E3
WILM/AE SK9 201 B4
London Rd North POY/DIS SK12 195 F1
London Rd South POY/DIS SK12 195 E5
London Sq STKP SK1 13 G4
London St BOLS/LL BL3 48 D5
SLFD M6 112 A1
WHTF M45 68 C5
Long Acres Dr WHIT OL12 14 C4
Longacres La WHIT OL12 14 C3
Longacres Rd HALE/TIMP WA15 178 D5
Longacre St CMANE M1 7 K6
Longbow Ct BRO * M7 112 C1
Longbridge Rd TRPK M17 124 B2
Long Cswy FWTH BL4 65 F5
Longcliffe Wk BOL * BL1 34 A4
Longcrag Wk HULME * M15 127 E3
Longcroft Dr ALT WA14 165 E5
Longcroft Gv DTN/ASHW M34 116 C5
NTHM/RTH M23 167 H2
Long Croft La CHD/CHDH SK8 182 B4
Longdale Cl ROY/SHW OL2 58 D5
Longdale Dr HYDE SK14 134 D5
Longden Av OLDE OL4 75 H1
Longden Rd WGTN/LGST M12 143 H1
Longden St BOL BL1 48 B1
Longfellow Av BOLS/LL BL3 63 E1
Longfellow Crs OLD OL1 60 C5
Longfellow St SLFD M6 112 B1
Longfield BURY * BL9 38 D2
Longfield Av CHD/CHDH SK8 181 H5
HALE/TIMP WA15 166 D3
URM M41 138 A1
Longfield Cl HYDE SK14 132 D2
Longfield Crs OLDE OL4 75 F3
Longfield Dr URM M41 138 A1
Longfield La OLDE OL4 75 G3
Longfield Pk ROY/SHW OL2 59 H4
Longfield Rd BOLS/LL BL3 63 E2
NTHM/RTH M23 167 G1
ROCH OL11 29 F3
ROY/SHW OL2 59 H3
Longford Av BOL BL1 33 F4
STRET M32 140 B1
Longford Cl STRET M32 125 F5
Longford Pk STRET M32 140 C1
Longford Pl RUSH/FAL M14 128 B4
Longford Rd CCHDY M21 140 D2
RDSH SK5 145 E2
STRET M32 125 F5
Longford Rd West RDSH SK5 144 C2
Longford St GTN M18 129 G2
HEY OL10 40 D4
Long Grain Pl OFTN SK2 173 E4
Longham Cl BRAM/HZG SK7 183 F3
OP/CLY M11 114 B4
Long Hey HALE/TIMP WA15 178 B1
Longhey Rd WYTH/NTH M22 168 C4
Long Hl ROCH OL11 42 C2
Longhirst Cl BOL BL1 33 E3
Longhope Rd WYTH/NTH M22 180 A1
Longhurst La MPL/ROM SK6 175 G2
Longhurst Rd BKLY M9 86 C3
Longlands Av HYDE SK14 133 G5
Longlands Dr HYDE SK14 133 G5
Long La BOLE BL2 50 A4
BURY BL9 27 F4
CHAD OL9 89 E4
UPML OL3 77 H2
Longlevens Rd WYTH/NTH M22 180 B2
Longley Dr WALK M28 96 A4
Longley La WYTH/NTH M22 168 C1
Longley St OLD OL1 9 G5
ROY/SHW OL2 60 A4
WALK M28 81 E5
Long Marl Dr WILM/AE SK9 192 C3
Longmead Av BRAM/HZG SK7 185 E3
Longmeade Gdns WILM/AE SK9 199 H4
Long Meadow BOLE BL2 23 H4
HYDE SK14 133 E2
Longmeadow CHD/CHDH SK8 183 F5
Longmeadow Gv
DTN/ASHW M34 146 B1
Long Meadow Pas HYDE * SK14 132 C5
Longmead Rd SLFD M6 98 A5
Longmead Wy MDTN M24 71 H3
Longmere Av WYTH/NTH M22 180 C1
Long Millgate ANC M4 6 E2
Longnor Rd BRAM/HZG SK7 185 F5
CHD/CHDH SK8 182 A5
Longport Av DID/WITH M20 142 B4
Longridge EDGW/EG BL7 23 H3
Longridge Av STLY SK15 119 F1
Longridge Crs BOL BL1 32 C4
Longridge Dr HEY OL10 40 A4
TOT/BURYW BL8 52 A1
Long Rw STLY SK15 107 G3
Long Rushes ROY/SHW OL2 59 G1
Longshaw Av SWIN M27 97 E1
Longshaw Dr WALK M28 80 B3
Longshaw Ford Rd BOL BL1 32 C1
Longshut La STKP SK1 13 G7
Longshut La West OFTN SK2 13 G7
Longsides Rd HALE/TIMP WA15 178 D5
Longsight BOLE BL2 35 E1
Longsight La BOLE BL2 35 E2
CHD/CHDH SK8 192 C2
Longsight Rd BOLE BL2 35 E3
GTN M18 129 E5
RAMS BL0 26 B2
Longsight St HTNM SK4 12 C2
Longson St BOL BL1 3 G1
Long St GTN M18 129 H2
MDTN M24 71 G4
SWIN M27 97 E3
Longton Av DID/WITH M20 157 F1
Longton Rd BKLY M9 86 D3
SLFD M6 97 H5
Longton St BURY BL9 53 G5
Longtown Gdns BOL * BL1 33 H4
Longview Dr SWIN M27 96 B1
Longwall Av WALK M28 94 D2
Longwood Av OFTN SK2 172 C3
Longwood Cl MPL/ROM SK6 162 D3
Longwood Rd TRPK M17 124 C2
WYTH/NTH M22 180 D1
Longworth Cl URM M41 137 E2
Longworth Clough
EDGW/EG BL7 22 C1
Longworth La BOL BL1 22 C3
Longworth St BOLE BL2 49 H2
CSLFD M3 6 C6
Lonsdale Av MILN OL16 43 G1
RDSH SK5 130 A5
SWIN M27 96 C5
URM M41 123 E4
Lonsdale Rd BNG/LEV M19 144 A1
BOL BL1 48 A1
OLDS OL8 89 G5
Lonsdale St NEWH/MOS M40 102 B4
TOT/BURYW BL8 37 H4
Loom St ANC M4 7 J3
Loonies Ct STKP * SK1 13 G5
Lord Byron Sq SALQ M50 111 G5
Lord Derby Rd HYDE SK14 147 H5
Lord La FAIL M35 115 H1
Lord Napier Dr ORD M5 125 H1
Lord North St NEWH/MOS M40 114 B1
Lord's Av ORD * M5 111 E3
Lordsfields Av AULW OL7 118 A1
Lords Fold BOL * BL1 32 C4
Lordship Cl BKLY M9 101 G1
Lordsmead St HULME M15 126 C1
Lord Sq MILN OL16 10 C6
Lord's Stile La EDGW/EG BL7 23 G4
Lord's St IRL M44 150 B1
Lord St AUL OL6 118 A1
BOLS/LL BL3 66 A1
BURY BL9 5 F5
CSLFD M3 113 E1
DTN/ASHW M34 130 B4
DUK SK16 119 E5
FWTH BL4 65 F4
MDTN M24 71 H3
OLD OL1 9 G2
RAD M26 67 F1
STKP SK1 13 G4
Loretto Rd URM M41 139 E2
Lorgill Cl EDGY/DAV SK3 172 A5
Loring St NEWH/MOS M40 102 B5
Lorland Rd EDGY/DAV SK3 171 E2
Lorna Gv CHD/CHDH SK8 169 E3
Lorna Rd CHD/CHDH SK8 183 E2
Lorne Av ROY/SHW OL2 73 G1
Lorne Gv EDGY/DAV SK3 171 H3
URM M41 138 D1
Lorne Rd RUSH/FAL M14 142 D3
Lorne St BOL BL1 2 E4
BRUN/LGST M13 127 H3
ECC M30 109 E5
FWTH BL4 64 D2
HEY OL10 41 E5
MOSL OL5 106 D1
OLDS OL8 90 B3
WHIT OL12 19 G5
Lorne Wy HEY OL10 40 A5
Lorraine Cl HEY OL10 56 B1
Lorraine Rd HALE/TIMP WA15 166 B4
Lorton Cl MDTN M24 70 D2
WALK M28 94 A4
Lorton Gv BOLE BL2 50 C1
Lostock Av BNG/LEV M19 144 A2
BRAM/HZG SK7 184 C3
POY/DIS SK12 194 C3
SALE M33 155 F2
URM M41 123 E5
Lostock Cl HEY OL10 40 C3
Lostock Dr BURY BL9 27 G5
Lostock Gv STRET M32 124 C5
Lostock Hall Rd POY/DIS SK12 194 C4
Lostock Junction La
HOR/BR BL6 46 D3
Lostock Park Dr HOR/BR BL6 46 B2
Lostock Rd ORD M5 111 F3
POY/DIS SK12 194 D5
URM M41 123 G4
Lostock St NEWH/MOS M40 114 A2
Lostock Wy WILM/AE SK9 192 A3
Lothian Av ECC M30 109 E2
Lottery Rw BOL BL1 3 F5
Lottery St EDGY/DAV SK3 12 D4
Lottie St SWIN M27 97 F2
Loughborough Cl SALE M33 153 G3
Loughfield URM M41 137 H1
Loughrigg Av ROY/SHW OL2 58 D1
Louisa St BOL BL1 33 G4
OP/CLY M11 115 G5
WALK M28 81 E3
Louis Av BURY BL9 38 C2
Louise Cl WHIT OL12 19 H5
Louise Gdns WHIT OL12 19 G5
Louise St WHIT OL12 19 G5
Louvaine Av BOL BL1 32 C2
Louvain St FAIL M35 102 D3
Lovalle St BOL BL1 33 F5
Lovat Rd BOLE BL2 50 C2
Love La HTNM SK4 12 E1
Lovell Dr HYDE SK14 133 E4
Lovers La OLDE OL4 92 D1
Lowcock St BRO M7 112 D1
Lowcroft Crs CHAD OL9 73 E4
Low Crompton Rd
ROY/SHW OL2 59 E3
Lowcross Rd NEWH/MOS M40 101 H4
Lowe Gn ROY/SHW OL2 59 F4
Lower Albion St CMANE M1 7 H7
Lower Alma St AULW OL7 118 A4
Lowerbank DTN/ASHW M34 131 G3
Lower Bank St BURY BL9 4 C4
Lower Beechwood ROCH * OL11 42 C1
Lower Bennett St HYDE SK14 132 B4
Lower Bents La MPL/ROM SK6 161 G2
Lower Birches OLDE OL4 92 A3
Lower Bridgeman St BOLS/LL BL3 3 G7
Lower Broadacre STLY SK15 134 B2
Lower Brook La WALK * M28 95 H5
Lower Brook St CMANE * M1 7 H6
Lower Broughton Rd BRO M7 99 F5
BRO M7 112 B1
Lower Bury St HTNM SK4 12 C2
Lower Byrom St CSLFD M3 6 B6
Lower Carrs STKP SK1 13 H4
Lower Chatham St HULME M15 127 F1
Lower Cft WHTF M45 83 H1
Lowercroft Rd TOT/BURYW BL8 37 E4
Lower Crossbank OLDE OL4 76 A4
Lower Darcy St BOLS/LL BL3 49 H4
Lower Dingle OLD OL1 60 B5
Lower Edge Av OLD OL1 74 B4
Lowerfield Dr OFTN SK2 173 G4
Lowerfields OLDS OL8 91 E3
Lower Flds UPML OL3 77 H3
Lowerfields Ri ROY/SHW OL2 60 A1
Lower Fold DTN/ASHW M34 146 D1
MPL/ROM SK6 175 G1
Lower Fold Av ROY/SHW OL2 59 H5
Lowerfold Cl WHIT OL12 18 B4
Lowerfold Crs WHIT OL12 18 B4
Lowerfold Dr WHIT OL12 18 B4
Lowerfold Wy WHIT OL12 18 B4
Lower Frenches Dr UPML OL3 93 H1
Lower Goodwin Cl BOLE BL2 35 F4
Lower Gn AUL OL6 118 B1
MDTN M24 87 G2
WHIT OL12 29 F2
Lower Hardman St CSLFD M3 6 B5
Lower Hey La MOSL OL5 93 F4
Lower Hillgate STKP SK1 13 G3
Lower House Dr HOR/BR BL6 46 D2
Lower House La WHIT OL12 19 G1
Lower House St OLD OL1 75 E4
Lower House Wk EDGW/EG BL7 23 F3
Lower Jowkin La ROCH OL11 28 A4
Lower La MILN OL16 44 A2
Lowerlea POY/DIS SK12 197 H1
Lower Lime Rd OLDS OL8 103 H2
Lower Marlands EDGW/EG BL7 23 E3
Lower Md EDGW/EG BL7 23 E2
Lower Meadow Rd
WILM/AE SK9 192 B3
Lower Moat Cl HTNM SK4 159 H3
Lower Monton Rd ECC M30 109 H3
Lower Mosley St CMANW M2 6 D7
Lower Moss La HULME M15 126 C1
WHTF M45 68 C4
Lower New Rw WALK M28 94 B1
Lower Ormond St HULME M15 127 F1
Lower Park Crs POY/DIS SK12 194 C1
Lower Park Rd POY/DIS SK12 194 C2
RUSH/FAL M14 127 H4
Lower Rawson St FWTH BL4 65 F3
Lower Seedley Rd SLFD M6 111 F2
Lower Sheriff St WHIT OL12 10 A5
Lower St FWTH BL4 64 D5
ROCH OL11 43 F2
Lower Strines Rd
MPL/ROM SK6 175 F4
Lower Sutherland St SWIN M27 96 D2
Lower Tenterfield ROCH OL11 28 A1
Lower Tong EDGW/EG BL7 23 E4
Lower Turf La OLDE OL4 76 B5
Lower Tweedale St ROCH OL11 30 A5
Lower Vickers St
NEWH/MOS M40 114 A2
Lower Victoria St CHAD OL9 73 G5
Lower Wharf St AUL OL6 118 A3
Lower Wheat End MILN OL16 11 H5
Lower Woodhill Rd
TOT/BURYW BL8 4 A4
Lowerwood La BOLE BL2 34 C5
The Lowes ALT WA14 177 E3
Lowes Rd BURY BL9 27 G5
Lowestead Rd OP/CLY M11 115 F3
Lowestoft St RUSH/FAL M14 142 C1
Lowe St DTN/ASHW M34 132 A5
RAD M26 52 A5
STKP SK1 13 G4
Loweswater Rd CHD/CHDH SK8 181 G1
FWTH BL4 63 H5
Lowfield Av AUL OL6 106 A5
DROY M43 116 A2
Lowfield Gv OFTN SK2 172 A2
Lowfield Rd EDGY/DAV SK3 171 H3
Low Grove La OLDE * OL4 93 F2
Low Hl WHIT OL12 19 H5
Lowhouse Cl MILN OL16 31 H4
Lowick Av BOLS/LL BL3 64 B1
Lowick Cl BRAM/HZG SK7 185 E2
Lowick Gn MPL/ROM SK6 161 G1
Lowland Gv AULW OL7 104 D4
Lowland Rd OFTN SK2 172 C5
Lowlands Cl MDTN M24 88 B3
Low Lea Rd MPL/ROM SK6 175 G2
Low Mdw ROY/SHW OL2 59 E3
Lowndes Cl OFTN SK2 172 C2
Lowndes La OFTN SK2 172 C2
Lowndes St BOL BL1 48 A1
Lowndes Wk BRUN/LGST * M13 127 H2
Lownorth Rd WYTH/NTH M22 180 D4
Lowood Av URM M41 122 C4
Lowry Ct WHTF * M45 68 A2
Lowry Dr MPL/ROM SK6 175 G1
SWIN M27 97 E1
Lowry Gv HYDE SK14 134 C5
Lowry Houses ECC * M30 109 H3
Lowry Wk BOL BL1 33 G5
The Lows OLDE OL4 91 E2
Lowside Av HOR/BR BL6 46 D3
MPL/ROM SK6 147 F5
Lowside Dr OLDE OL4 91 E2
Low's Pl WHIT OL12 10 D1
Lowstern Cl EDGW/EG BL7 22 D2
Lowther Av GTN M18 129 E5
HALE/TIMP WA15 166 B3
ROY/SHW OL2 58 D1
Lowther Cl PWCH M25 84 D4
Lowther Crs MDTN M24 71 F3
Lowther Gdns URM M41 122 A5
Lowther Rd CHH M8 100 B1
PWCH M25 84 D4
ROCH OL11 42 D2
Lowther St BOLS/LL BL3 64 B2
Lowthorpe St RUSH/FAL M14 142 B1
Lowton Av BKLY M9 101 G3
Lowton Rd SALE M33 153 G4
Lowton St RAD M26 52 B5
Low Wood Cl BRAM/HZG SK7 183 F3
Low Wood Rd DTN/ASHW M34 130 B4
Loxford Ct HULME M15 127 E1
Loxford St HULME M15 127 E2
Loxham St FWTH BL4 65 E2
Lubeck St BKLY M9 101 F2
Lucas Rd FWTH BL4 64 B4
Lucas St BURY BL9 5 H2
OLDE OL4 75 E5
Lucas Wk OP/CLY M11 114 C5
Lucerne Cl CHAD OL9 8 A5
Lucerne Rd BRAM/HZG SK7 183 H1
Lucien Cl WGTN/LGST M12 128 B3
Lucknow St ROCH OL11 43 E1
Lucy St BOL BL1 32 D5
BRO M7 99 G5
EDGY/DAV SK3 12 E6
HULME M15 126 C2
Ludford Gv SALE M33 154 A4
Ludgate Hl ANC M4 7 H1
Ludgate Rd NEWH/MOS M40 115 F1
ROCH OL11 43 F4
Ludgate St ANC M4 7 G1
Ludlow Av SWIN M27 83 F5
WHTF M45 85 E1
Ludlow Pk OLDE OL4 91 G1
Ludlow Rd STKP SK1 172 D1
Lugano Rd BRAM/HZG SK7 183 H1
Luke Rd DROY M43 116 C4
Lullington Cl WYTH/NTH M22 180 B3
Lullington Rd SLFD M6 111 E1
Lulworth Av URM M41 137 G1
Lulworth Cl TOT/BURYW BL8 26 D5
Lulworth Crs FAIL M35 103 G2
Lulworth Gdns NTHM/RTH M23 167 G1
Lulworth Rd BOLS/LL BL3 62 D1
ECC M30 109 F3
MDTN M24 72 A2
Lumb Carr Av RAMS BL0 16 B4
Lumb Carr Rd RAMS BL0 16 B5
Lumb Cl BRAM/HZG SK7 193 H1
Lumber La WALK M28 95 F2
Lumb La BRAM/HZG SK7 193 H1
DROY M43 104 A5
DROY M43 116 D1
DTN/ASHW M34 116 D5
Lumley Cl RUSH/FAL M14 127 G4
Lumn Hollow HYDE SK14 147 H1
Lumn Rd HYDE SK14 147 H1
Lumn's La SWIN M27 83 H5
Lumn St BURY BL9 27 G3
Lumsden St BOLS/LL BL3 48 D4
Lum St BOL BL1 3 G3
Lumwood BOL BL1 33 E3
Luna St ANC M4 7 H3
Lund Av RAD M26 67 G4
Lund St OLDTF/WHR M16 126 B2
Lune Cl WHTF M45 68 D4
Lunedale Gn OFTN SK2 173 F3
Lune Dr WHTF M45 68 D4
Lune Gv HEY OL10 40 B3
Lune St OLDS OL8 90 B3
Lune Wy RDSH SK5 160 A1
Lunn Av GTN M18 130 A2
Lupin Av FWTH BL4 64 B3
Lupton St CSLFD * M3 6 A3
DTN/ASHW M34 131 G4
Lurden Wk CHAD * OL9 89 F3
Lurgan Av SALE M33 154 D3
Lutener Av ALT WA14 165 F1
Luton Dr NTHM/RTH M23 167 H5
Luton Rd RDSH SK5 145 E3
Luton St BOLS/LL * BL3 49 F5
TOT/BURYW BL8 37 G5
Luxhall Wk NEWH/MOS M40 102 A5
Luxor Gv DTN/ASHW M34 130 A5
Luzley Brook Rd ROY/SHW OL2 59 H4
Luzley Rd AUL OL6 106 B4
Lyceum Pas MILN OL16 10 C6
Lyceum Pl HULME M15 127 F1
Lychgate Ct OLDE OL4 91 H4
Lychgate Ms HTNM * SK4 158 B4
Lydbrook Cl BOLE BL2 2 C6
Lydden Av OP/CLY * M11 115 G2
Lydford ROCH * OL11 29 H5
Lydford Gdns BOLE BL2 50 C4
Lydford St SLFD M6 112 A1
Lydford Wk BRUN/LGST * M13 127 H2
Lydgate Av BOLE BL2 50 B1
Lydgate Cl DTN/ASHW M34 147 E2
STLY SK15 107 F4
WHTF M45 68 D4
Lydgate Dr OLDE OL4 91 F2
Lydgate Rd DROY M43 115 H2
SALE M33 154 D4
Lydiate Cl BOLS/LL BL3 64 A1
Lydiat La WILM/AE SK9 201 B5
Lydney Av CHD/CHDH SK8 181 H5
Lydney Rd URM M41 122 A5
Lyefield Wk MILN OL16 30 C5
Lyme Av WILM/AE SK9 199 G1
Lyme Clough Wy MDTN M24 56 C5
Lymefield Dr WALK M28 94 B3
Lymefield Gv OFTN SK2 172 C3
Lyme Gv ALT WA14 165 F5
DROY M43 116 A5
MPL/ROM SK6 162 C4
MPL/ROM SK6 175 E4
OFTN SK2 13 G7
Lyme Rd BRAM/HZG SK7 185 F3
POY/DIS SK12 187 F5
POY/DIS SK12 196 B4
Lymes ALT WA14 177 F3
Lyme St BRAM/HZG * SK7 185 E1
HTNM SK4 158 B4
Lymewood Dr POY/DIS SK12 197 G1
WILM/AE * SK9 200 B2
Lymington Cl MDTN M24 88 A2
Lymington Dr NTHM/RTH M23 167 E1
Lymm Cl EDGY/DAV SK3 171 G3
WALK M28 80 B4
Lyncombe Cl CHD/CHDH SK8 193 E1
Lyndale Av RDSH SK5 130 A5
SWIN M27 96 C4
Lyndale Dr LIT OL15 20 D2
Lyndene Av WALK M28 95 H2
Lyndene Gdns CHD/CHDH SK8 169 G3
Lyndene Rd WYTH/NTH M22 168 C4
Lyndhurst Av AUL OL6 105 E5
BRAM/HZG SK7 184 D3
CHAD OL9 89 E2
DTN/ASHW * M34 131 F5
IRL M44 121 C5
MPL/ROM SK6 161 G2
PWCH M25 85 H4
ROCH OL11 57 G1
SALE M33 154 A3
URM M41 123 F4
Lyndhurst Cl WILM/AE SK9 198 C5
Lyndhurst Dr HALE/TIMP WA15 178 B2
Lyndhurst Rd DID/WITH M20 157 F2
OLDS OL8 90 A4
RDSH * SK5 144 D1
STRET M32 139 G1
Lyndhurst St SLFD M6 111 F3
Lyndhurst Vw DUK * SK16 118 B4
Lyndon Cl OLDE OL4 76 C4
TOT/BURYW BL8 26 A5
Lyndon Rd IRL M44 136 A2
Lyne Edge Crs DUK SK16 133 E1
Lyne Edge Rd DUK SK16 133 F1
Lyne Vw HYDE SK14 133 E2
Lyngard Cl WILM/AE SK9 200 A1
Lyngate Cl STKP SK1 13 J5
Lyn Gv HEY OL10 40 B3
Lynham Dr HEY OL10 56 A1
Lynmouth Av DID/WITH M20 142 B5
OLDS OL8 90 C4
RDSH SK5 144 D4
ROY/SHW OL2 73 H1
URM M41 138 A3
Lynmouth Cl CHAD OL9 72 D3
RAD M26 52 D5
Lynmouth Gv PWCH M25 84 C4
Lynn Av SALE M33 140 A5
Lynndene Ct HEY * OL10 40 D3
Lynn Dr DROY M43 115 H3
Lynn St CHAD OL9 89 H3
Lynnwood Dr ROCH OL11 29 E3
Lynnwood Rd BNG/LEV M19 158 A4
Lynroyle Wy ROCH OL11 42 C3
Lynsted Av BOLS/LL BL3 64 B1
Lynthorpe Av IRL M44 135 C5
Lynthorpe Rd NEWH/MOS M40 88 C5
Lynton Av HYDE SK14 148 D1
IRL M44 135 D5
OLDS OL8 89 H5
ROCH OL11 42 A3
SWIN M27 97 E1
URM M41 136 D1
Lynton Cl CHAD OL9 73 E3
Lynton Crs WALK M28 95 E2
Lynton Dr BNG/LEV M19 143 G4
MPL/ROM SK6 186 D4
PWCH M25 85 F1
Lynton Gv HALE/TIMP WA15 166 B4
Lynton La WILM/AE SK9 201 B3
Lynton Lea RAD M26 52 D5
Lynton Ms WILM/AE SK9 201 B3
Lynton Park Rd CHD/CHDH SK8 182 C4
Lynton Rd BOLS/LL BL3 63 F2
CCHDY M21 140 D2
CHD/CHDH SK8 169 H4
HTNM SK4 159 E1
SWIN M27 97 E1
Lynton St RUSH/FAL * M14 142 C1
Lyntonvale Av CHD/CHDH SK8 169 F3
Lynway Dr DID/WITH M20 157 G1
Lynway Gv MDTN M24 72 A2
Lynwell Rd ECC M30 109 G3
Lynwood HALE/TIMP WA15 178 B4
Lynwood Av BOLS/LL BL3 64 C1
ECC M30 109 G3
OLDTF/WHR M16 141 F1
Lynwood Cl AULW OL7 104 D3
Lynwood Dr OLDE OL4 75 H4
Lynwood Gv BOLE BL2 35 E2
DTN/ASHW M34 116 D4
HTNM SK4 144 B5
SALE M33 154 D1
Lyon Gv WALK M28 95 H2
Lyon Rd ALT WA14 165 F2
FWTH BL4 81 F2
Lyons Dr TOT/BURYW BL8 37 F5
Lyons Fold SALE M33 139 G5
Lyons Rd TRPK M17 124 B1
Lyon St ROY/SHW OL2 60 A2
SWIN M27 96 D3
Lysander Cl RUSH/FAL M14 142 B3
Lytham Av CCHDY M21 141 F4
Lytham Cl AUL OL6 105 H4
Lytham Dr BRAM/HZG SK7 184 B5
HEY OL10 40 D5
Lytham Rd CHD/CHDH SK8 181 G3
RUSH/FAL M14 143 G2
URM M41 136 D1
Lytham St EDGY/DAV SK3 172 A3
WHIT OL12 18 D5
Lytherton Av IRL M44 150 C2
Lyth St RUSH/FAL M14 143 E4
Lytton Av CHH M8 100 B4
Lytton Rd DROY M43 116 B3
Lytton St BOL BL1 33 G4

M

Mabel Av BOLS/LL BL3 64 B1
WALK M28 95 H3
Mabel Rd FAIL M35 103 F1
Mabel's Brow FWTH BL4 65 F5
Mabel St BOL BL1 48 B1
NEWH/MOS M40 102 C5
WHIT OL12 29 G1
Mabfield Rd RUSH/FAL M14 142 D2
Mableden Cl CHD/CHDH SK8 182 A4
Mabs Ct AUL OL6 118 C3
Macaulay St ROCH OL11 42 B5
ROY/SHW OL2 59 F5
Macauley Cl DUK SK16 133 F1
Macauley Rd OLDTF/WHR M16 141 E1
RDSH SK5 144 C2
Macclesfield Rd BRAM/HZG SK7 185 G4
WILM/AE SK9 199 H4
WILM/AE SK9 201 D5
Macdonald Av FWTH BL4 64 B5
Macdonald Rd IRL M44 135 D4
Macdonald St OLDS OL8 90 C3
Macefin Av CCHDY M21 156 C2
Mackenzie Gv BOL BL1 33 G2
Mackenzie Rd BRO M7 99 E4
Mackenzie St BOL BL1 33 G2
WGTN/LGST M12 128 D5
Mackenzie Wk OLD OL1 60 D4
Mackeson Dr AUL OL6 118 D1
Mackeson Rd AUL OL6 118 D1
Mackintosh Wy OLD OL1 9 G2
Maclaren Dr CHH M8 85 H5

Maclure Rd ROCH OL11 .....30 A5
Macnair Ms MPL/ROM * SK6 ...175 E3
Madams Wood Rd WALK M28....80 A4
Maddison Rd DROY M43 .....116 A4
Madeley Cl ALT WA14 .....177 H4
Madeley Dr CHAD OL9 .....89 G1
Madeley Gdns BOL BL1 .....33 G4
...WHIT OL12 .....29 C2
Maden's Sq LIT OL15 .....21 E3
Maden Wk CHAD * OL9 .....73 G4
Madison Av CHD/CHDH SK8..182 D2
...DTN/ASHW M34 .....116 D5
Madison St GTN M18 .....129 H2
Madras Rd EDGY/DAV * SK3...171 F2
Mafeking Av BURY BL9 .....38 D1
Mafeking Rd BOLE * BL2 .....50 D2
Mafeking St OLDS OL8 .....89 H4
Magdala St HEY * OL10 .....56 B1
...OLD OL1 .....74 B4
Magda Rd OFTN SK2 .....172 D4
Magenta Av IRL M44 .....135 G5
Magnolia Cl SALE M33 .....153 F1
Magnolia Dr CHH * M8 .....100 B4
Magpie Cl DROY M43 .....116 D2
Magpie La OLDE OL4 .....91 G3
Magpie Wk OP/CLY * M11 .....114 C4
Maher Gdns HULME M15 .....126 D4
Mahood St EDGY/DAV SK3 .....12 D7
Maida St BNG/LEV M19 .....144 A1
Maidford Cl ANC * M4 .....114 A4
...STRET M32 .....140 B1
Maidstone Av CCHDY M21 .....140 D2
Maidstone Cl CCHDY M21 .....140 D2
Maidstone Rd HTNM SK4 .....158 A3
Main Av BNG/LEV M19 .....143 G4
...TRPK M17 .....124 D4
Maine Rd RUSH/FAL M14 .....127 F5
Mainprice Cl SLFD M6 .....111 G1
Main St FAIL M35 .....103 E2
...HYDE SK14 .....132 C4
Mainwaring Dr WILM/AE SK9 .200 A2
Mainwaring Ter
...NTHM/RTH M23 .....155 H4
Mainway MDTN M24 .....87 G1
Mainway East MDTN M24 .....88 B1
Mainwood Rd
...HALE/TIMP WA15 .....166 D4
Maismore Rd WYTH/NTH M22 .179 F3
Maitland Av CCHDY M21 .....156 D2
Maitland Cl FWTH WA14 .....19 H5
Maitland St STKP SK1 .....172 C2
Maitland Wk CHAD * OL9 .....73 G4
Major St CMANE M1 .....7 G6
...MILN OL16 .....31 C5
...RAMS BL0 .....16 C2
Makin Cl HEY OL10 .....41 E5
Makin St CMANE * M1 .....7 G7
Makkah Cl NEWH/MOS M40 ...101 H5
Malaga Av MANAIR M90 .....180 A6
Malakoff St STLY SK15 .....118 D5
Malbrook Wk BRUN/LGST * M13..127 H2
Malby St OLD OL1 .....9 H1
Malcolm Av SWIN M27 .....83 F5
Malcolm Dr SWIN M27 .....83 F5
Malcolm St ROCH OL11 .....42 C5
Malden Gv NTHM/RTH M23 ...167 H1
Maldon Cl BOLS/LL BL3 .....65 H1
...OFTN SK2 .....173 H4
Maldon Crs SWIN M27 .....97 E4
Maldon St ROCH OL11 .....109 H1
Maldon St ROCH OL11 .....43 E1
Maldwyn Av BOLS/LL BL3 .....63 E2
...CHH M8 .....86 B5
Maleham St BRO * M7 .....99 H4
Malgam Dr DID/WITH M20.....169 G1
Malham Cl ROY/SHW OL2 .....59 E5
Malham Ct OFTN SK2 .....173 E3
Malham Dr WHTF M45 .....68 D4
The Mall BURY BL9 .....4 C4
...STLY SK15 .....134 B2
Mallard Cl DUK SK16 .....132 D2
...OFTN SK2 .....173 H4
...OLDS OL8 .....90 A5
Mallard Crs POY/DIS SK12 ...194 B3
Mallard Dr ALT WA14 .....165 E1
Mallards Reach MPL/ROM SK6 ..162 A4
Mallard St CMANE M1 .....7 F7
Mallet Crs BOL BL1 .....32 C4
Malling Rd NTHM/RTH M23 ..167 H5
Mallison St BOL BL1 .....34 A3
Mallory Av AULW OL7 .....105 G5
Mallory Rd HYDE SK14 .....133 F4
Mallow Cft MILN OL16 .....43 H2
Mallowdale WALK M28 .....94 C2
Mallowdale Rd OFTN SK2 .....173 G4
Mallow St HULME M15 .....126 D2
Mally Gdns MOSL OL5 .....107 E2
Malmesbury Cl POY/DIS SK12....195 E3
Malmesbury Rd CHD/CHDH SK8..193 E1
Malpas Cl CHD/CHDH SK8....193 H4
...WILM/AE SK9 .....200 A1
Malpas St OLD OL1 .....9 H2
...WGTN/LGST M12 .....128 C2
Malpas Wk OLDTF/WHR * M16 ..126 C3
Malrae HALE/TIMP * WA15....166 B2
Malsham Rd NTHM/RTH M23 ..155 H4
Malta Cl MDTN M24 .....72 C4
Malta St ANC M4 .....114 A4
...OLDE OL4 .....91 G1
Maltby Ct OLDE OL4 .....92 A2
Maltby Dr BOLS/LL BL3 .....63 F2
Maltby Rd NTHM/RTH M23 ...167 G5
Malton Av BOLS/LL BL3 .....63 H1
...CCHDY M21 .....141 E3
...WHTF M45 .....68 C2
Malton Cl CHAD OL9 .....73 G4
Malton Dr ALT WA14 .....164 D5
...BRAM/HZG SK7 .....185 G5
Malton Rd HTNM SK4 .....158 D2
Malton St OLDS OL8 .....9 H6
Malus Ct SLFD M6 .....111 H2
Malvern Av AUL OL6 .....105 F3
...BOL BL1 .....32 D5
...BURY BL9 .....38 C1
...CHD/CHDH SK8 .....169 H6
...URM M41 .....138 A1
Malvern Cl FWTH BL4 .....64 A3
...HTNM SK4 .....159 G3
...MILN OL16 .....31 H4

PWCH M25 .....85 F2
Malvern Dr ALT WA14 .....165 E4
...SWIN M27 .....98 A4
Malvern Gv DID/WITH M20 ...142 B5
...SLFD M6 .....110 D2
...WALK M28 .....81 E4
Malvern Rd MDTN M24 .....87 H2
Malvern Rw HULME * M15 .....126 B2
Malvern St OLDS OL8 .....8 D6
Malvern St East ROCH OL11 .....29 F4
Malvern St West ROCH OL11 .....29 F4
Manby Rd GTN M18 .....129 E3
Manby Sq GTN M18 .....129 E4
Manchester Chambers OLD OL1....9 F4
...PART M31 .....151 E3
Manchester Old Rd BURY BL9....4 C7
...MDTN M24 .....70 D5
Manchester Rd ALT WA14 .....165 G3
...BOLS/LL BL3 .....3 G6
...BURY BL9 .....4 D3
...CCHDY M21 .....140 D5
...CHD/CHDH SK8 .....170 A1
...DTN/ASHW M34 .....130 B4
...FWTH BL4 .....82 A1
...GOL/RIS/CU WA3 .....150 A4
...HEY OL10 .....56 A3
...HTNM SK4 .....159 G1
...HYDE SK14 .....132 A5
...MDTN M24 .....71 E1
...MOSL OL5 .....106 D3
...OLDS OL8 .....89 H5
...PART M31 .....151 F2
...RAMS BL0 .....16 C2
...ROCH OL11 .....42 B5
...ROY/SHW OL2 .....59 H4
...SWIN M27 .....83 E4
...WALK M28 .....81 C5
...WILM/AE SK9 .....199 H2
Manchester Rd East WALK M28 ...80 C3
Manchester Rd North
...DTN/ASHW M34 .....130 D4
Manchester Rd South
...DTN/ASHW M34 .....130 D5
Manchester Rd West
...LHULT M38 .....79 D2
Manchester St HEY OL10 .....41 E4
...MDTN M24 .....98 A4
...OLD/WHR M16 .....126 B5
Manchet St ROCH OL11 .....42 A5
Mancroft Av BOLS/LL * BL3 .....48 C5
Mancroft Ter BOLS/LL * BL3 .....48 C5
Mancroft Wk DTN/ASHW M34 ..146 D3
Mancunian Wy
...WGTN/LGST M12 .....127 H1
Mandalay Gdns MPL/ROM SK6 ..174 C2
Mandarin Gn ALT WA14 .....165 E1
Mandarin Wk SLFD * M6 .....111 H2
Mandeville St BNG/LEV M19 ...144 A3
Mandley Av NEWH/MOS * M40 ..102 B5
Mandley Cl BOLS/LL BL3 .....50 D4
Mandley Park Av BRO M7 .....99 H3
Mandon Cl RAD M26 .....51 H4
Manesty Cl MDTN M24 .....70 D2
Manette Cl BRO M7 .....99 E2
Mangle St CMANE M1 .....7 H4
Mango Pl SLFD M6 .....111 H3
Manifold St MPL/ROM SK6 .....197 E5
Manifold St SLFD M6 .....99 E5
Manilla Wk OP/CLY M11 .....114 C5
Manipur St OP/CLY M11 .....114 C5
Mandeville St SLFD * M6 .....111 H2
Manley Av SWIN M27 .....83 E5
Manley Cl BURY BL9 .....26 D1
Manley Gv BRAM/HZG SK7 .....194 A5
...HYDE SK14 .....134 C5
Manley Rd CCHDY M21 .....141 F2
...OLDS OL8 .....90 B3
...ROCH OL11 .....29 E4
...SALE M33 .....153 H5
Manley St BRO M7 .....99 G4
Manley Ter BOL * BL1 .....33 H2
Manningham Rd BOLS/LL BL3 ...48 A4
Manning Av BOLS/LL * BL3 .....63 H2
Mannington Dr CHH M8 .....100 D4
Mannock St OLDS OL8 .....90 B4
Manns Av BOLS/LL BL3 .....66 B1
...OLDTF/WHR M16 .....141 G1
...SALE M33 .....153 G2
Manor Cl CHAD OL9 .....8 A1
...CHD/CHDH SK8 .....183 F4
...DTN/ASHW M34 .....147 E1
...OLDE OL4 .....91 H3
...WILM/AE SK9 .....198 D2
Manor Ct STRET M32 .....139 G2
Manor Dr CCHDY M21 .....156 C2
...OLDE OL4 .....74 B1
Manor Farm Cl AULW OL7 .....104 C4
Manor Farm Ri OLDE OL4 .....75 G5
Manorfield Cl BOL BL1 .....32 D5
Manor Gdns WILM/AE SK9 .....200 A3
Manor Gate Rd BOLE BL2 .....51 E2
Manor Hill Rd MPL/ROM SK6 ...175 E2
Manorial Dr LHULT M38 .....79 D2
Manor Ms CHAD * OL9 .....8 C4
Manor Pk URM * M41 .....138 C2
Manor Rd BNG/LEV M19 .....144 A1
...BRAM/HZG SK7 .....175 E5
...CHD/CHDH SK8 .....183 F3
...DROY M43 .....115 H4
...DTN/ASHW M34 .....130 C1
...HALE/TIMP WA15 .....165 H5
...HYDE SK14 .....133 E5
...MDTN M24 .....87 G1
...MPL/ROM SK6 .....175 E2
...RDSH SK5 .....160 C5
...ROY/SHW OL2 .....59 H2
...SALE M33 .....138 B4
...SLFD M6 .....111 E1
...STRET M32 .....139 G2
...SWIN M27 .....97 E4
...WALK M28 .....98 D2
Manor St BOL BL1 .....3 F4
...BURY BL9 .....5 F4
...DTN/ASHW M34 .....131 G1
...FWTH BL4 .....64 D5
...OLDE OL4 .....82 A2

MDTN M24 .....71 H2
MOSL OL5 .....92 D5
OLD OL1 .....74 D2
RAMS BL0 .....16 C1
WGTN/LGST M12 .....127 H1
Manor Vw MPL/ROM SK6 .....147 E5
The Manse MOSL OL5 .....106 D2
Mansfield Av BKLY M9 .....87 H3
...DTN/ASHW M34 .....131 E3
...RAMS BL0 .....26 C1
Mansfield Cl AULW OL7 .....117 G4
...DTN/ASHW M34 .....131 E3
Mansfield Crs DTN/ASHW M34 ..131 E4
Mansfield Dr BKLY M9 .....87 F3
Mansfield Gra ROCH OL11 .....29 F5
Mansfield Rd BOLS/LL BL3 .....33 E5
Mansfield Rd BKLY M9 .....147 H2
...HYDE SK14 .....147 H2
...MOSL OL5 .....107 F1
...OLDS OL8 .....91 E3
...ROCH OL11 .....28 D4
...URM M41 .....137 H2
Mansfield St AULW OL7 .....117 F5
Manshaw Crs OP/CLY M11 .....130 B1
Manshaw Rd OP/CLY M11 .....130 B1
Mansion Av WHTF M45 .....68 B1
Manson Av HULME M15 .....126 C1
Manstead Wk
...NEWH/MOS * M40 .....114 B3
Manston Dr CHD/CHDH SK8 ...182 D2
Manswood Dr CHH M8 .....100 B3
Mantley La ROY/SHW OL2 .....59 F2
Manton Av BKLY M9 .....88 A4
...DTN/ASHW M34 .....130 D5
Manton Cl CHH M8 .....100 A4
Manvers St RDSH SK5 .....159 H3
Manwaring St FAIL M35 .....103 D2
Maple Av BOL * BL1 .....5 K4
...BURY BL9 .....5 K4
...CCHDY M21 .....141 E3
...CHD/CHDH SK8 .....182 C2
...DTN/ASHW M34 .....116 C4
...DTN/ASHW M34 .....131 F5
...ECC M30 .....108 D1
...HALE/TIMP WA15 .....167 F4
...HYDE SK14 .....132 C5
...HYDE SK14 .....132 C5
...MDTN M24 .....71 G5
...OLDS OL8 .....106 D1
...RAD M26 .....65 H5
...ROY/SHW OL2 .....74 B1
...SWIN M27 .....97 F1
...TOT/BURYW BL8 .....26 A5
...WHIT OL12 .....19 F3
Maple St SALE * M33 .....154 C2
Market Wk SALE M33 .....154 C2
Market Wy SLFD M6 .....111 G2
Markfield Av BRUN/LGST M13...128 A3
Markham Cl WGTN/LGST M12...114 A5
Markham St HYDE SK14 .....132 C4
Markington St RUSH/FAL M14 ..127 F5
Markland Hill BOL BL1 .....47 F1
Markland Hill Cl BOL BL1 .....32 C5
Markland Hill La BOL BL1 .....32 B5
Markland St BOL BL1 .....3 G6
...HYDE SK14 .....147 H2
...RAMS * BL0 .....16 D2
Mark La ROY/SHW OL2 .....60 C3
Mark St ANC M4 .....7 H1
Mark St CHAD OL9 .....89 F4
...WALK M28 .....94 A3
...WHIT * OL12 .....11 F2
Marland Av CHD/CHDH SK8 ...182 C2
Marland Cl ROCH OL11 .....42 A2
Marland Crs RDSH SK5 .....145 E3
Marland Fold ROCH OL11 .....42 A1
Marland Fold La OLDS OL8 .....104 C1
Marland Gn ROCH OL11 .....42 A2
Marland Hill Rd ROCH OL11 .....42 B1
Marland Old Rd ROCH OL11 .....42 A2
Marland St CHAD OL9 .....89 F4
Marlborough Av CCHDY M21 .....141 F2
...CHD/CHDH SK8 .....183 E3
...WILM/AE SK9 .....201 C3
Marlborough Cl AULW OL7 .....117 H5
...DTN/ASHW M34 .....131 G5
...MPL/ROM SK6 .....174 C2
...RAMS BL0 .....16 D5
Marlborough Dr FAIL * BL4 .....102 D4
Marlborough Gdns FWTH BL4 ...64 A4
Marlborough Rd ALT WA14 .....177 G2
...BRO M7 .....100 A4
...DTN/ASHW M34 .....130 D1
...HYDE SK14 .....147 H5
...IRL M44 .....121 G5
...SALE M33 .....154 C2
...STRET M32 .....139 H5
...URM M41 .....122 C5
Marlborough St AULW M34 .....117 G4
...BOL BL1 .....2 A3
...OLDE OL4 .....91 H1
...WHIT OL12 .....29 F2
Marlbrook Wk BOLS/LL BL3 .....49 E5
Marlcroft Av HTNM SK4 .....159 E4
Marl Crs BOL BL1 .....32 C4
Marle Av MOSL OL5 .....107 F1
Marle Cft WHTF M45 .....83 H1
Marle Ri MOSL OL5 .....107 E1
Marler Cl HYDE SK14 .....152 D4
Marler Cl HALE/TIMP WA15 .....166 A3
Marley Dr SALE M33 .....154 B3
Marleyer Cl NEWH/MOS M40 ...102 B3
Marleyer Ri MPL/ROM SK6 .....175 H1
Marley Rd BNG/LEV M19 .....195 F5
...POY/DIS SK12 .....144 A2
Marlfield Rd HALE/TIMP WA15 ...179 G5
...ROY/SHW OL2 .....59 F5
Marlfield St BKLY M9 .....99 H1
Marlhill Cl OFTN SK2 .....172 D4
Marlinford Dr NEWH/MOS M40..102 B3
Marlor St DTN/ASHW M34 .....131 F4
Marlow Cl BOLE BL2 .....35 G5
...URM M41 .....123 G4
Marlow Dr ALT WA14 .....176 C2
...IRL M44 .....121 B5
...SWIN M27 .....96 D4
...WILM/AE SK9 .....191 H2

Marlowe Dr DID/WITH M20 .....157 G2
Marlowe Wks MPL/ROM SK6 ...161 F4
Marlow Rd BKLY M9 .....101 G1
Marlwood Rd BOL BL1 .....32 C4
Marmion Dr CCHDY M21 .....140 D3
Marne Av AUL OL6 .....106 A5
...WYTH/NTH M22 .....168 D4
Marne Crs ROCH OL11 .....29 F4
Marnland Gv BOLS/LL BL3 .....47 F5
Maroon Rd WYTH/NTH M22 ...181 E5
Marple St HULME * M15 .....34 B2
Marple Cl OLDS OL8 .....90 A5
Marple Gv STRET M32 .....124 D5
Marple Hall Dr MPL/ROM SK6 ..174 C2
Marple Old Rd OFTN SK2 .....173 H5
Marple Rd OFTN SK2 .....173 E2
Marple St HULME M15 .....126 C3
Marquis St BNG/LEV M19 .....144 B2
Marquis Dr CHD/CHDH SK8 ...182 A5
Marquis St BNG/LEV M19 .....144 B2
Marrick Av CHD/CHDH SK8 .....169 H4
Marriotts Ct CMANE M2 .....7 F2
Marriott St DID/WITH M20 .....142 C5
...STKP SK1 .....13 H6
Marron Pl CMANW * M2 .....6 D6
Mars Av BOLS/LL BL3 .....63 F1
Marsden Cl AULW OL7 .....104 B5
...MILN OL16 .....58 D1
Marsden Dr HALE/TIMP WA15 ..166 D3
Marsden Rd BOL BL1 .....2 D4
...MPL/ROM SK6 .....162 D3
Marsden St BURY BL9 .....6 E4
...CMANW M2 .....6 E4
...ECC M30 .....108 D2
...WALK M28 .....96 D4
Marsett Cl WHIT OL12 .....28 C2
Marshall Ct AUL OL6 .....118 C3
Marshall Rd BNG/LEV M19 .....143 H2
Marshall Stevens Wy TRPK M17 ..124 C3
Marshall St ANC M4 .....7 H2
...DTN/ASHW M34 .....131 F4
...MILN OL16 .....11 J7
...WGTN/LGST M12 .....127 H2
Marsham Cl BRUN/LGST M13 ...128 B4
...OLDE OL4 .....92 C2
Marsham Dr MPL/ROM SK6 .....175 H5
Marsham Rd BRAM/HZG SK7 ...184 C3
Marshbrook Dr CHH M8 .....100 D1
Marshbrook Rd URM M41 .....123 F5
Marsh Cl EDGY/DAV SK3 .....171 G3
Marshdale Rd BOL BL1 .....47 G1
Marshfield Rd
...HALE/TIMP WA15 .....166 D4
Marshfield Wk BRUN/LGST M13..127 H2
Marsh Fold La BOL BL1 .....48 B1
Marsh La FWTH BL4 .....64 A5
Marsh Rd BOLS/LL BL3 .....50 C5
...LHULT M38 .....80 C3
Marsh St ANC M4 .....7 H2
...HALE/TIMP WA15 .....166 C1
Marsland Av HALE/TIMP WA15 ..166 C1
Marsland Cl DTN/ASHW M34 ...130 C5
Marsland Rd HALE/TIMP WA15 ..166 C1
...MPL/ROM SK6 .....174 C2
...SALE M33 .....153 H5
Marslands UPML OL3 .....78 A1
Marsland St BRAM/HZG * SK7 ...185 E2
...STKP SK1 .....13 J3
Marsland St North BRO M7 .....99 H3
Marsland St South BRO M7 .....100 A3
Marsland Ter STKP SK1 .....172 C1
Mars St CHAD OL9 .....8 B2
Marston Cl FAIL M35 .....103 G4
...HOR/BR BL6 .....46 A1
Marston Dr IRL M44 .....136 C1
Marston Rd BRO M7 .....99 H2
...STRET M32 .....125 H4
Marsworth Dr ANC M4 .....113 H5
Martens Rd IRL M44 .....150 D1
Marthall Dr SALE M33 .....155 E2
Martham Dr OFTN SK2 .....173 H3
Martha's Ter MILN OL16 .....11 K4
Martha St BOLS/LL * BL3 .....48 C5
...CHAD OL9 .....8 B1
Martin Av BOLS/LL BL3 .....64 A5
...FWTH BL4 .....64 A5
...OLDE OL4 .....91 F1
Martin Cl DTN/ASHW M34 .....131 G3
...OFTN SK2 .....173 G4
Martindale Cl ROY/SHW OL2 .....59 F4
...WGTN/LGST M12 .....128 C3
Martindale Gdns BOL BL1 .....33 H4
Martin Dr IRL M44 .....121 B4
Martingale Cl RAD M26 .....52 B4
Martingale Wy DROY M43 .....117 E2
Martin Gv FWTH BL4 .....65 E5
Martin La WHIT OL12 .....29 E2
Martin Rd SWIN M27 .....83 G5
Martinscough HOR/BR BL6 .....46 D4
Martinscroft Rd
...NTHM/RTH M23 .....167 H4
Martins Fld WHIT OL12 .....19 F2
Martin St BURY 39 G3
...DTN/ASHW M34 .....131 G1
...HYDE SK14 .....147 H1
...OLD M1 .....111 E3
Martlesham Wk ANC * M4 .....7 G3
Martlet Av POY/DIS SK12 .....197 H1
...ROCH OL11 .....28 C5
Martlet Cl RUSH/FAL M14 .....142 C2
Martock Av WYTH/NTH M22 ...180 D1
Marton Av BOLE BL2 .....49 G2
...DID/WITH M20 .....157 H4
Marton Gra PWCH M25 .....85 G3
Marton Gn EDGY/DAV SK3 .....171 G4
Marton Pl SALE M33 .....154 D2
Marwood Cl ALT WA14 .....165 E3
...RAD 66 H4
Marwood Dr WYTH/NTH M22..168 C5
Maryfield Ct OLDTF/WHR * M16 ..141 H4
Mary France St HULME M15 .....126 D2
Maryland Av BOLE BL2 .....50 A2
Marylon Dr WYTH/NTH M22 ...168 D1
Mary St CHD/CHDH SK8 .....182 B6
...CSLFD M3 .....113 F2
...DTN/ASHW * M34 .....116 C4
...DUK SK16 .....118 A5
...FWTH BL4 .....64 D5
...HEY OL10 .....40 D4
...HYDE SK14 .....132 B5

MILN OL16 20 A4
RAMS BL0 16 C3
STKP SK1 13 J2
Masboro St CHH M8 100 A3
Masbury Cl BOL BL1 22 D4
Masefield Av PWCH M25 84 C4
RAD M26 51 H5
Masefield Cl DUK SK16 133 G1
Masefield Crs DROY M43 116 B4
Masefield Dr FWTH BL4 64 C5
HTNM SK4 158 D4
Masefield Gv RDSH SK5 144 D2
Masefield Rd BOLS/LL BL3 51 E5
DROY M43 116 B4
OLD OL1 75 E2
Mason Gdns BOLS/LL BL3 2 C7
Mason St ANC M4 7 H2
AULW OL7 117 G4
BURY BL9 5 G5
EDGW/EG * BL7 22 D2
HEY OL10 40 C4
MILN OL16 10 D7
Massey Av AUL OL6 105 F4
FAIL M35 103 G2
Massey Cft WHIT OL12 18 B1
Massey Rd HALE/TIMP WA15 165 H5
SALE M33 155 F2
Massey St BURY BL9 5 J2
ORD M5 112 B4
STKP SK1 13 G4
WILM/AE SK9 201 B4
Massey Wk WYTH/NTH M22 181 E3
Massie St CHD/CHDH SK8 170 A3
Matham Wk HULME * M15 127 E1
Mather Av ECC M30 109 H3
PWCH M25 99 F1
WHTF M45 68 C2
Mather Cl WHTF M45 68 C3
Mather Fold Rd WALK M28 94 C1
Mather Rd BURY BL9 27 G4
ECC M30 109 H3
Mather St BOLS/LL * BL3 2 D7
FAIL M35 102 C3
FWTH BL4 65 F4
RAD M26 67 F1
Mather Wy SLFD * M6 111 H2
Matisse Wy BRO M7 99 E2
Matley Cl HYDE SK14 133 G3
Matley Gn RDSH SK5 145 H5
Matley La STLY SK15 133 H2
Matlock Av AUL OL6 106 A4
BRO M7 98 D3
DID/WITH M20 142 A5
DTN/ASHW M34 146 D3
URM M41 138 A3
Matlock Cl FWTH BL4 65 F3
SALE M33 154 D2
Matlock Dr BRAM/HZG SK7 185 F4
Matlock Rd CHD/CHDH SK8 181 H5
RDSH SK5 145 F2
STRET M32 124 B5
Matlock St ECC M30 109 F5
Matt Busby Cl SWIN M27 97 G3
Matthew Cl OLDS OL8 91 F3
Matthew Moss La ROCH OL11 42 A2
Matthews Av FWTH BL4 65 G5
Matthews La BNG/LEV M19 144 A1
Matthew's St WGTN/LGST M12 128 C1
Matthew St MPL/ROM SK6 175 F3
Mattison St OP/CLY M11 129 H1
Maudsley St BURY BL9 4 C6
Maud St BOLE BL2 34 D1
WHIT OL12 10 E1
Mauldeth Cl HTNM SK4 158 D3
Mauldeth Rd DID/WITH M20 142 D4
HTNM SK4 158 C2
Mauldeth Rd West CCHDY M21 141 H3
Maunby Gdns LHULT M38 80 D4
Maureen Av CHH M8 100 B2
Maureen St WHIT OL12 11 F1
Maurice Cl DUK SK16 132 D1
Maurice Dr SLFD M6 111 G1
Maurice St SLFD M6 111 G1
Maveen Gv OFTN SK2 172 B5
Mavis Gv MILN OL16 31 H5
Mavis St ROCH OL11 42 B5
Mawdsley Dr CHH M8 100 D2
Mawdsley St BOL BL1 2 E5
Maxwell Av OFTN SK2 172 D4
Maxwell St BOL BL1 33 H2
BURY BL9 5 J3
Max Woosnam Wk
RUSH/FAL M14 127 F5
Mayall St MOSL OL5 106 D1
Mayall St East OLDE * OL4 75 F5
Mayan Av CSLFD M3 6 A2
May Av CHD/CHDH SK8 193 E1
HTNM * SK4 12 A2
Maybank St BOLS/LL BL3 48 C5
Mayberth Av CHH M8 86 B5
Maybreck Cl BOLS/LL BL3 48 B4
Mayburn Cl MDTN M24 88 B2
Maybury St GTN M18 129 H2
Maycroft Av DID/WITH M20 157 H1
May Dr BNG/LEV M19 143 G5
Mayer St OFTN * SK2 172 D2
Mayes Gdns ANC M4 114 A4
Mayes St ANC M4 7 G2
Mayfair Av RAD M26 51 G5
SLFD M6 110 C2
URM M41 138 A1
WHTF * M45 68 C5
Mayfair Cl DUK SK16 119 E5
POY/DIS SK12 195 F2
Mayfair Ct HALE/TIMP * WA15 166 C2
Mayfair Crs FAIL M35 103 G2
Mayfair Dr IRL M44 136 B1
ROY/SHW OL2 74 A2
SALE M33 153 H4
Mayfair Gdns ROCH OL11 42 C1
Mayfair Ms DID/WITH * M20 157 E2
Mayfair Pk DID/WITH * M20 157 E2
Mayfair Rd WYTH/NTH M22 168 D5
Mayfield BOLE BL2 35 E1
Mayfield Av BOLS/LL BL3 64 C1
DTN/ASHW M34 146 D4
FWTH BL4 64 D5
OLDE OL4 76 B5
RDSH SK5 160 A1
SALE M33 155 F2
STRET M32 139 G2
SWIN M27 96 B4
WALK M28 81 E4
Mayfield Cl HALE/TIMP WA15 166 C3
RAMS BL0 26 B1
Mayfield Gv GTN M18 130 A5
RDSH SK5 160 A1
WILM/AE SK9 198 D5
Mayfield Houses RAD * M26 66 D2
Mayfield Rd BRAM/HZG SK7 193 H3
BRO M7 99 E1
HALE/TIMP WA15 166 C3
MPL/ROM SK6 163 G5
OLD OL1 75 E3
OLDTF/WHR M16 126 D5
RAMS BL0 26 B1
Mayfield St DTN/ASHW M34 131 F3
MILN OL16 11 H3
Mayfield Ter MILN OL16 11 H2
Mayflower Av ORD M5 111 H5
Mayford Rd BNG/LEV M19 143 H1
Maygate OLD OL1 74 A4
May Gv BNG/LEV M19 144 A3
Mayhill Dr SLFD M6 110 B1
WALK M28 95 H2
Mayhurst Av CCHDY M21 156 C3
Mayorlowe Av RDSH SK5 160 D2
Mayor's Rd HALE/TIMP WA15 165 H5
Mayor St BOLS/LL BL3 2 B6
TOT/BURYW BL8 37 H3
Mayo St WGTN/LGST M12 114 A5
Maypool Dr RDSH SK5 145 E5
May Rd CHD/CHDH SK8 192 D1
OLDTF/WHR M16 126 C5
SWIN M27 97 G4
May St BOLE BL2 3 H5
ECC M30 109 F1
HEY * OL10 56 B1
NEWH/MOS M40 102 B5
OLDS OL8 89 H3
RAD M26 67 F1
Mayton St OP/CLY M11 114 D5
Mayville Dr DID/WITH M20 157 G1
Maywood Av DID/WITH M20 169 G1
Maze St BOLS/LL BL3 50 A4
McConnell Rd NEWH/MOS M40 101 H3
McCready Dr ORD * M5 112 A5
McDonna St BOL BL1 33 F3
McDonough Cl OLDS OL8 90 D4
McEvoy St BOL BL1 34 A4
McKean St BOLS/LL BL3 49 F5
McKie Cl OLDS OL8 90 D4
McLaren Ct CCHDY M21 140 D2
McLean Dr IRL M44 121 B4
McNaught St MILN OL16 30 C5
Meachin Av CCHDY M21 141 F5
The Mead CCHDY * M21 141 E4
ORD M5 111 F3
The Meade BOLS/LL BL3 63 H2
WILM/AE SK9 199 G2
Meade Cl URM M41 138 B1
Meade Gv BRUN/LGST M13 128 C5
Meade Hill Rd PWCH M25 85 H4
Meadfoot Av PWCH M25 85 F4
Meadfoot Rd GTN M18 129 G2
Meadland Gv BOL BL1 34 A2
The Meadow BOL BL1 47 E2
Meadow Av HALE/TIMP WA15 178 C1
SWIN M27 97 G1
Meadowbank AULW OL7 104 D4
Meadow Bank CCHDY M21 140 D4
HALE/TIMP WA15 166 B2
HTNM SK4 159 E4
MPL/ROM SK6 161 G3
Meadowbank Cl FAIL M35 103 F4
Meadow Bank Cl OLDE * OL4 91 H3
Meadow Bank Ct STRET M32 139 G2
Meadowbank Rd BOLS/LL BL3 63 E2
Meadowbrook Cl BURY BL9 39 F2
Meadow Brook Wy
CHD/CHDH SK8 171 E5
Meadow Brow WILM/AE SK9 201 B3
Meadow Cl BOLS/LL BL3 66 A2
BRAM/HZG SK7 185 F1
DTN/ASHW M34 146 D4
HALE/TIMP WA15 178 C1
HEY OL10 40 D4
MOSL OL5 93 F4
MPL/ROM SK6 161 H1
MPL/ROM SK6 187 E4
STRET M32 140 B2
Meadow Ct CCHDY M21 140 C3
Meadow Cft BRAM/HZG SK7 185 F1
WHTF M45 83 H1
Meadowcroft HYDE SK14 134 C4
RAD M26 52 A4
Meadowcroft La OLD OL1 74 D3
ROCH OL11 28 C5
Meadowfield HOR/BR BL6 46 C2
MILN OL16 43 G3
Meadowfield Ct HYDE SK14 132 C4
Meadowfield Dr WALK M28 94 C4
Meadow Fold UPML OL3 78 B4
Meadowgate URM M41 138 C2
WALK M28 95 G2
Meadowgate Rd SLFD M6 110 D2
Meadow Head Av WHIT OL12 18 C2
Meadow La BOLE BL2 50 D2
DTN/ASHW M34 146 D4
DUK SK16 118 C5
OLDS OL8 90 B5
ROY/SHW OL2 59 H3
WALK M28 95 G5
Meadow Ri ROY/SHW OL2 44 D5
Meadow Rd BRO M7 112 B2
MDTN M24 87 F1
URM M41 138 C2
The Meadows IRL M44 135 C5
MDTN M24 88 A1
MPL/ROM SK6 162 A2
OLDE OL4 92 B1
PWCH M25 85 E3
RAD M26 51 H4
WHIT OL12 14 B4
Meadows UPML OL3 78 A5
Meadowside BRAM/HZG SK7 183 F2
MILN OL16 45 F2
Meadowside Av BOLE BL2 49 H1
IRL M44 136 B1
WALK M28 81 F3
WYTH/NTH M22 168 D5
Meadowside Cl RAD M26 52 B4
Meadowside Gv WALK M28 81 F4
Meadows La BOLE BL2 35 G3
Meadows Rd CHD/CHDH SK8 181 G3
CHD/CHDH SK8 182 C4
HTNM SK4 144 B5
SALE M33 139 H5
Meadow St HYDE SK14 147 H2
OFTN SK2 172 D4
Meadow Vw WHIT OL12 28 D2
Meadow Wk FWTH BL4 64 B5
LIT * OL15 20 C3
Meadow Wy HALE/TIMP WA15 178 C1
NEWH/MOS M40 101 H1
TOT/BURYW BL8 25 H5
The Meads CHAD OL9 89 F1
Meadscroft Dr WILM/AE SK9 201 A4
Meads Gv FWTH BL4 63 G4
Meadway BRAM/HZG SK7 193 H2
BURY BL9 53 G3
CHAD OL9 88 D5
DUK SK16 132 D1
MPL/ROM SK6 187 E4
POY/DIS SK12 194 C2
ROCH OL11 42 A2
SALE M33 153 H4
STLY SK15 134 B2
Meadway Cl SALE M33 153 H3
Meadway Rd CHD/CHDH SK8 183 E1
Mealhouse Brow STKP SK1 13 G3
Mealhouse La BOL BL1 2 E4
Meal St HTNM SK4 159 H3
Meanwood Brow WHIT OL12 29 G2
Meanwood Fold ROCH OL11 29 F3
Measham Ms CMANE M1 127 F1
Meddings Cl WILM/AE SK9 201 B5
Medina Cl CHD/CHDH SK8 171 E5
Medley St WHIT OL12 10 C2
Medlock Cl FWTH BL4 64 C4
Medlock Dr OLDS OL8 104 D1
Medlock Rd FAIL M35 103 F5
Medlock St CMANE M1 127 E1
DROY M43 116 B3
OLD OL1 9 K2
Medlock Valley Wy OLDE OL4 61 F4
Medlock Wy OLDE OL4 91 H1
WHTF M45 69 F4
The Medway HEY OL10 40 C3
Medway Cl OLDS OL8 89 H4
ORD M5 111 E2
WILM/AE SK9 192 A5
Medway Crs ALT WA14 165 F3
Medway Dr FWTH BL4 82 A2
Medway Rd OLDS OL8 89 H4
ROY/SHW OL2 59 H1
WALK M28 94 C2
Medway Wk NEWH/MOS M40 114 A2
Meech St OP/CLY M11 115 F5
Meek St OLD OL1 74 D2
Meerbrook Rd EDGY/DAV SK3 170 D1
Mee's Sq ECC M30 109 G5
Megna Cl CHAD OL9 8 B2
Melandra Crs HYDE SK14 149 F1
Melanie Dr RDSH SK5 145 E3
Melba St OP/CLY M11 115 H5
Melbecks Wk NTHM/RTH M23 155 G4
Melbourne Av CHAD OL9 73 F5
MANAIR M90 179 H4
STRET M32 140 A1
Melbourne Cl ROCH OL11 43 F4
Melbourne Rd BOLS/LL BL3 48 A4
BRAM/HZG SK7 193 H1
ROCH OL11 43 F4
Melbourne St BKLY M9 101 F2
BRO M7 99 G5
CHAD OL9 73 G5
DTN/ASHW M34 146 B1
RDSH SK5 145 E3
STLY SK15 119 F4
SWIN M27 97 G2
Melbourne St North AUL OL6 118 B1
Melbourne St South AUL OL6 118 D2
Melbury Av DID/WITH M20 158 A2
Melbury Dr HOR/BR * BL6 46 A1
Melbury Rd CHD/CHDH SK8 193 E1
Meldon Rd BRUN/LGST M13 143 F1
Meldrum St OLDS OL8 90 C3
Melford Av NEWH/MOS M40 102 D1
Melford Gv OLDE OL4 91 G1
Melford Rd BRAM/HZG SK7 185 G3
Melfort Av STRET M32 140 B2
Meliden Crs BOL * BL1 33 E5
WYTH/NTH M22 180 D2
Melksham Cl ORD M5 112 A3
Mellalieu St MDTN M24 71 F3
ROY/SHW OL2 74 B2
Melland Av CCHDY M21 156 B1
Melland Rd GTN M18 129 F5
Meller Rd BRUN/LGST M13 143 G1
Melling Av CHAD OL9 72 D3
HTNM SK4 144 D5
Melling Rd OLDE OL4 91 F1
Melling St WGTN/LGST M12 128 D4
Mellington Av DID/WITH M20 169 H1
Mellodew Dr OLD OL1 75 G1
Mellor Brow HEY OL10 40 C4
Mellor Cl AUL OL6 118 D3
Mellor Ct OFTN SK2 173 F2
Mellor Dr BURY BL9 53 E2
WALK M28 94 D1
Mellor Gv BOL BL1 33 E5
Mellor Rd AUL OL6 118 D2
CHD/CHDH SK8 183 E3
Mellors Rd TRPK M17 124 C1
Mellor St DROY M43 116 A4
ECC M30 109 G4
FAIL M35 102 C3
NEWH/MOS M40 114 A2
OLDE OL4 91 H1
PWCH M25 84 C3
RAD M26 67 G2
ROCH OL11 29 G4
ROY/SHW OL2 59 E4
STRET M32 125 E4
Mellor Wy CHAD OL9 89 G3
Mellowstone Dr
OLDTF/WHR M16 142 A3
Melloy Pl CHH M8 113 F1
Melon Pl SLFD M6 112 A3
Melrose WHIT OL12 10 B5
Melrose Av BOL BL1 32 D5
DID/WITH M20 157 H3
ECC M30 108 D1
EDGY/DAV * SK3 170 C2
HEY OL10 40 D3
LIT OL15 20 D1
SALE M33 154 C3
TOT/BURYW BL8 37 H3
Melrose Cl WHTF M45 68 C2
Melrose Ct CHAD * OL9 89 F3
Melrose Crs EDGY/DAV SK3 171 G5
HALE/TIMP WA15 178 C3
POY/DIS SK12 196 C2
Melrose Gdns RAD M26 51 H4
Melrose Rd BOLS/LL BL3 65 G1
RAD M26 51 H4
Melrose St BURY BL9 26 C1
NEWH/MOS M40 102 B5
OLD OL1 75 E3
ROCH OL11 29 G4
Melsomby Rd NTHM/RTH M23 155 H4
Meltham Av DID/WITH M20 142 B5
Meltham Cl HTNM SK4 158 B5
Meltham Pl BOLS/LL * BL3 48 B5
Meltham Rd HTNM SK4 158 B5
Melton Av DTN/ASHW M34 130 B5
URM M41 121 D5
Melton Cl HEY OL10 40 C5
WALK M28 80 D5
Melton Dr BURY BL9 53 H4
Melton Rd CHH M8 99 H1
Melton St BKLY M9 101 G1
HEY OL10 40 C5
RAD M26 52 A5
RDSH SK5 160 A2
Melverley Rd BKLY M9 86 B2
Melville Cl OP/CLY M11 129 H1
Melville Rd FWTH BL4 81 G1
IRL M44 150 B1
STRET M32 124 C5
Melville St AUL OL6 118 A1
BOLS/LL BL3 49 F5
CSLFD M3 6 A3
OLDE OL4 91 H2
ROCH OL11 42 C5
Melvin Av WYTH/NTH M22 168 D5
Melyncourt Rd HYDE * SK14 134 B5
Memorial Cottages SWIN * M27 83 E4
Memorial Rd WALK M28 81 E4
Menai Gv CHD/CHDH SK8 170 D3
Menai Rd EDGY/DAV SK3 171 H3
Menai St BOLS/LL * BL3 48 A5
Mendip Av WYTH/NTH M22 169 E5
Mendip Cl BOLE BL2 50 D2
CHAD * OL9 89 F2
CHD/CHDH SK8 181 G5
HTNM SK4 159 H3
ROY/SHW OL2 73 H1
Mendip Crs TOT/BURYW BL8 37 F3
Mendip Dr BOLE BL2 50 D3
MILN OL16 31 H5
Mendip Rd OLDS OL8 90 A4
Mendips Cl ROY/SHW OL2 59 G1
Menston Av NEWH/MOS M40 102 D1
Mentmore Rd MILN OL16 31 E4
Mentone Crs WYTH/NTH M22 168 D5
Mentone Rd HTNM SK4 159 E3
Mentor St BRUN/LGST M13 143 G1
Mercer La ROCH OL11 28 B3
Mercer Rd GTN M18 129 G3
HEY OL10 56 A2
Mercer St BNG/LEV M19 144 A2
DROY M43 116 C3
Merchants Quay SALQ M50 125 H2
Mercian Wy EDGY/DAV SK3 12 D7
Mercia St BOLS/LL BL3 48 B4
Mercury Pk URM * M41 124 A2
Mercury Wy URM M41 124 A3
Mere Av DROY M43 115 H5
MDTN M24 87 H1
SLFD M6 111 F3
Merebank Cl ROCH OL11 28 B3
Mere Cl BURY BL9 54 A4
DTN/ASHW M34 145 G1
SALE M33 155 G3
Mereclough Av WALK M28 95 G1
Meredew Av SWIN M27 96 D4
Meredith St BOLS/LL BL3 64 A1
RUSH/FAL M14 143 E4
Mere Dr DID/WITH M20 157 G2
SWIN M27 83 F5
Merefield Av ROCH OL11 42 D1
Merefield Rd HALE/TIMP WA15 166 D4
Merefield St ROCH OL11 42 D1
Merefield Ter ROCH * OL11 42 D1
Mere Fold WALK M28 80 C4
Mere Gdns BOL BL1 2 C2
Merehall Cl BOL BL1 2 C2
Merehall Dr BOL BL1 2 C2
Merehall St BOL BL1 2 B1
Mereland Av DID/WITH M20 157 H2
Mere La ROCH OL11 43 E1
Meremanor WALK M28 95 G1
Merepool Cl MPL/ROM SK6 174 B2
The Mere AUL OL6 105 H4
CHD/CHDH SK8 170 C5
Mere Side STLY SK15 119 E1
Mereside Cl CHD/CHDH SK8 170 C5
Mereside Gv WALK M28 81 F4
Mere St ROCH OL11 30 A5
Mere Wk BOL BL1 2 C2
Merewood Av WYTH/NTH M22 168 C3
Meriden Cl RAD M26 52 A3
Meriden Gv HOR/BR BL6 47 E3
Meridian Centre OLDS * OL8 9 F5
Meridian Pl DID/WITH M20 157 F2
Merinall Cl MILN OL16 11 K7
Meriton Rd WILM/AE SK9 191 H3
Merlewood Av BNG/LEV M19 144 B4
DTN/ASHW * M34 116 C4
UPML OL3 78 A4
Merlewood Dr SWIN M27 96 B4
Merlin Cl LIT OL15 31 H1
OFTN SK2 173 H3
OLDS OL8 104 D2
Merlin Gv BOL BL1 33 E5
Merlin Rd IRL M44 121 B4
MILN OL16 31 G5
Merlyn Av DID/WITH M20 157 H2
DTN/ASHW M34 146 B1
SALE M33 139 H5
Merrick Av WYTH/NTH M22 168 D5
Merrick St HEY OL10 41 F5
The Merridale HALE/TIMP WA15 178 A4
Merrill St ANC M4 114 A4
Merriman St OLDTF/WHR M16 126 D4
Merrion St FWTH BL4 64 D2
Merrow Wk CMANE * M1 127 G1
Merrybent Cl OFTN SK2 173 E5
Merrybower Rd BRO M7 99 H2
Merrydale Av ECC M30 109 H1
Merryman Hall MILN * OL16 30 C1
Merseybank Av CCHDY M21 156 C2
Mersey Cl WHTF M45 69 E3
Mersey Crs DID/WITH M20 156 C3
Mersey Dr PART M31 151 F2
WHTF M45 69 E3
Mersey Mdw DID/WITH M20 157 E3
Mersey Rd DID/WITH M20 157 E3
HTNM SK4 158 C4
SALE M33 139 G5
Mersey Rd North FAIL M35 103 F1
Mersey Sq STKP SK1 12 E3
Mersey St OP/CLY M11 115 H5
STKP SK1 13 J2
Mersey Vw URM * M41 137 F3
Merseyway STKP SK1 13 F2
Merston Dr DID/WITH M20 169 H2
Merton Av BRAM/HZG SK7 185 G4
MPL/ROM SK6 161 H2
OLDS OL8 90 A4
Merton Cl BOLS/LL * BL3 48 B4
Merton Dr DROY M43 115 H4
Merton Gv CHAD OL9 88 C4
HALE/TIMP WA15 166 C3
Merton Rd EDGY/DAV * SK3 171 E2
POY/DIS SK12 194 C3
PWCH M25 85 F2
SALE M33 154 B1
Merton St TOT/BURYW BL8 4 A2
Merville Av NEWH/MOS M40 101 G1
Mervyn Rd BRO M7 98 D4
Merwell Rd URM M41 137 F2
Merwood Av CHD/CHDH SK8 182 A4
Merwood Gv RUSH/FAL M14 128 B4
Meshaw Cl NTHM/RTH M23 155 F4
Mesnefield Rd BRO M7 98 D2
Mesne Lea Gv WALK * M28 95 F2
Mesne Lea Rd WALK M28 95 F2
Metcalfe Ct LHULT * M38 80 A3
Metfield Pl BOL BL1 48 B1
Methuen St WGTN/LGST M12 129 E5
Methwold St BOLS/LL * BL3 48 B5
The Mews BOL BL1 48 A1
CHD/CHDH SK8 169 G4
NEWH/MOS M40 114 B2
PWCH M25 85 E4
SALE * M33 154 D3
WHTF * M45 68 A4
Meyer St EDGY/DAV * SK3 172 A3
Meyrick Rd SLFD M6 111 H2
Miall St ROCH OL11 30 B5
Micawber Rd POY/DIS SK12 195 F5
Michael St MDTN M24 71 G4
Michigan Av SALQ M50 111 G5
Mickleby Wk NEWH/MOS M40 113 H2
Micklehurst Av DID/WITH M20 156 D2
Micklehurst Gn OFTN SK2 173 F4
Micklehurst Rd MOSL OL5 107 E2
Middlebourne St SLFD M6 111 F3
Middlebrook Dr HOR/BR BL6 46 D3
Middlefield OLDS OL8 104 D2
Middle Fld ROCH OL11 28 B2
Middlefields CHD/CHDH SK8 171 E5
Middlegate NEWH/MOS M40 88 C4
Middle Ga OLDS OL8 90 B5
Middle Gn AUL OL6 118 B1
Middleham St RUSH/FAL M14 142 B1
Middle Hl WHIT OL12 19 E4
Middle Hillgate STKP SK1 13 H4
Middlesex Dr BURY BL9 53 G1
Middlesex Rd BKLY M9 87 E5
RDSH SK5 145 H5
Middlesex Wk CHAD OL9 8 D4
Middlestone Dr BKLY M9 101 E3
Middle St WHIT OL12 14 B4
Middleton Av FAIL M35 103 E3
Middleton Dr BURY BL9 68 C1
Middleton Old Rd BKLY M9 87 E5
Middleton Rd BKLY M9 86 A2
CHAD OL9 8 D3
CHAD OL9 72 C3
CHH M8 86 A5
HEY OL10 56 B2
RDSH SK5 145 E1
ROY/SHW OL2 73 G1
Middleton Rd West CHAD OL9 72 D4
Middleton Wy MDTN M24 71 G4
Middleway OLDE OL4 92 C2
Middlewood Dr HTNM SK4 158 D5
Middlewood Gn CHAD OL9 73 F5
Middle Wood La WHIT OL12 20 B2
Middlewood Rd POY/DIS SK12 186 B5
POY/DIS SK12 195 H3
Midford Av ECC M30 109 E3
Midford Dr BOL BL1 22 D4
Midge Hall Dr ROCH OL11 28 D5
Midgley Av GTN M18 129 H2
Midgley Crs AUL OL6 118 D1
Midgley St SWIN M27 96 C4
Midgrove La UPML OL3 77 G1
Midhurst Av NEWH/MOS * M40 115 E1
Midhurst Cl CHD/CHDH SK8 182 C4
Midhurst St ROCH OL11 43 E1
Midland Rd BRAM/HZG SK7 183 H1
RDSH SK5 145 E1
Midland St WGTN/LGST M12 128 A1
Midland Ter ALT * WA14 177 G2
Midland Wk BRAM/HZG SK7 183 H1
Midlothian St OP/CLY M11 115 E3
Midville Rd OP/CLY M11 115 F2
Midway CHD/CHDH SK8 193 E2
Midway St BNG/LEV M19 143 H1
Milan St BRO M7 99 H4
Milbourne Rd BURY BL9 27 G5
Milburn Av NTHM/RTH M23 156 A4
Milbury Dr LIT OL15 31 H1
Milden Cl DID/WITH * M20 157 H2
Mildred Av OLDE OL4 92 C2
PWCH M25 85 F5
ROY/SHW OL2 74 B2
Mildred St BRO M7 99 F5
Mile End La OFTN SK2 172 C4
Mile La TOT/BURYW BL8 37 E5
Miles St BOL BL1 33 G4
HYDE SK14 148 A1
OLD OL1 75 E4
WGTN/LGST M12 128 D1
Milford Av OLDS OL8 89 H5
Milford Brow OLDE OL4 75 H5
Milford Crs LIT OL15 21 E2
Milford Dr BNG/LEV M19 144 B4
Milford Gv OFTN SK2 172 D2
Milford Rd BOLE BL2 35 G2
BOLS/LL BL3 63 H1
Milford St BKLY M9 86 C4
SLFD M6 111 F4
WHIT OL12 10 C2
Milkstone Pl ROCH * OL11 30 A5

Milkstone Rd ROCH OL11 ....30 A5
Milk St CMANW M2 ....7 F4
  HYDE SK14 ....147 G1
  RAMS * BL0 ....16 C3
  ROCH OL11 ....30 A5
Millwood Gv CTN M18 ......129 G4
Millais St NEWH/MOS M40 ...101 H1
Millard St CHAD OL9 ....73 F5
Mill Bank RAD M26 ....67 G2
Millbank Gdns BOL * BL1 ....33 F5
Millbank St CMANE M1 ....7 G1
Millbank Cl ROY/SHW OL2 ...45 G4
  HEY OL10 ....40 C4
Millbeck Gv BOLS/LL * BL3 ..48 D5
Millbeck Rd MDTN M24 ......71 E2
Millbeck St HULME M15 .....28 A4
Millbrae Gdns ROY/SHW OL2 .59 G2
Millbrook Av DTN/ASHW M34 .129 G4
Millbrook Bank ROCH * OL11 .28 A2
Millbrook Cl ROY/SHW OL2 ...60 C5
Millbrook Fold BRAM/HZG SK7 .185 H5
Millbrook Rd NTHM/RTH M23 .179 H1
Millbrook St STKP SK1 ......13 G3
Mill Brow AUL OL6 ....105 F1
  BKLY M9 ....86 D5
  HYDE * SK14 ....149 H5
  OLD OL1 ....73 F2
  WALK M28 ....95 G4
Millcrest Cl WALK M28 ......94 A5
Mill Cft BOL BL1 ....2 C2
  ROY/SHW OL2 ....60 B3
Milldale Cl HOR/BR BL6 .....46 C2
Miller Meadow Cl HEY * OL10 .60 B1
Millers Brook Cl HEY * OL10 .41 E3
Millers Cl SALE M33 ....155 E4
Millers St ORD M5 ....110 B3
Miliers St SANC M4 ....7 G2
  AUL OL6 ....118 B1
  BOL BL1 ....33 H2
  BURY BL9 ....26 D1
  HEY OL10 ....41 E4
  RAD M26 ....52 A3
Millett St BURY BL9 ....4 E5
  RAMS BL0 ....17 E1
Millfield Ct HALE/TIMP WA15 .177 H1
Millfield Dr WALK M28 ......94 C4
Millfield Gv MILN OL16 .....30 C5
Millfield Rd BOLE BL2 ......50 D2
Millfold WHIT OL12 ....18 B1
Mill Fold Rd MDTN M24 ......71 G5
Millford Av URM M41 ....137 F2
Mill Ga MILN OL16 ....30 C1
  OLDS OL8 ....90 A4
Millgate ANC * M4 ....7 F3
  EDGW/EG BL7 ....8 C1
  STKP SK1 ....13 H2
Millgate La DID/WITH M20 ..157 H5
Mill Green St WGTN/LGST * M12 .114 A5
Millhall Cl HULME M15 ......28 A4
Millham Av NEWH/MOS M40 ..116 D3
Mill Hill BOL * BL1 ....3 H5
  LHULT M38 ....79 H2
Mill Hill Av POY/DIS SK12 ..185 E5
Mill Hill Caravan Pk BOLE BL2 .3 H5
Mill Hill Gv HYDE SK14 ....149 G1
Mill Hill Hollow POY/DIS SK12 .185 E5
Mill Hill St BOL * BL1 ......3 H5
Millhouse Av NTHM/RTH M23 .167 H5
Mill House Cl WHIT OL12 ....10 A4
Milliner Ct OFTN * SK2 .....173 G2
Millington Wk HULME M15 ...28 A4
Mill La AUL OL6 ....118 A3
  BRAM/HZG SK7 ....185 G4
  CHAD OL9 ....89 H3
  CHD/CHDH SK8 ....170 A3
  CHD/CHDH SK8 ....183 E1
  DTN/ASHW M34 ....147 E2
  HALE/TIMP WA15 ....189 F3
  MOSL OL5 ....102 C4
  MPL/ROM SK6 ....161 H1
  OLDE OL4 ....77 E5
  RDSH SK5 ....145 F2
  ROY/SHW OL2 ....58 D5
  TOT/BURYW BL8 ....27 F2
  WYTH/NTH M22 ....156 D5
Millom Av NTHM/RTH M23 ...156 A5
Millom Cl MILN OL16 ....11 J3
Millom Ct HALE/TIMP * WA15 .167 E3
Millom Dr BURY BL9 ....68 A4
Millow Pl CHD/CHDH SK8 ...181 G1
Millow St ANC M4 ....7 F1
Mill Rd BURY BL9 ....199 G3
  WILM/AE SK9 ....199 G3
Mills Farm Cl OLDS OL8 ....104 D1
Mills Hill Rd OLD OL1 ....73 H1
Mills St HEY OL10 ....40 C4
  WHIT OL12 ....14 C4
Millstone Cl POY/DIS SK12 ..195 G2
Millstone Rd BOL BL1 ....32 C5
Millstream La DROY M43 ...115 H2
Mill St ALT WA14 ....165 H4
  BOL BL1 ....3 H5
  BRAM/HZG SK7 ....185 E4
  EDGW/EG BL7 ....23 E5
  FAIL M35 ....102 B3
  FWTH BL4 ....64 D4
  HYDE SK14 ....132 D3
  MOSL OL5 ....106 D3
  OP/CLY M11 ....114 D2
  RAD M26 ....52 C4
  RAMS * BL0 ....16 B4
  ROY/SHW OL2 ....58 D5
  SLFD M6 ....111 H1
  STLY SK15 ....119 H4
  TOT/BURYW BL8 ....37 H2
  UPML OL3 ....78 A4
  WILM/AE SK9 ....199 G3
Milltown St RAD M26 ....68 A2
Millwall Cl OP/CLY M11 ....129 G3
Millway HALE/TIMP WA15 ...178 A5
Millwell La BOL BL1 ....2 D4
Millwood Cl CHD/CHDH SK8 .182 B4
Millwood Ct BURY BL9 ....53 G3
Millwood Ter HYDE SK14 ....147 F1
Millwright St NEWH/MOS M40 .102 A5
Milne St BURY BL9 ....4 E1
Milner Av ALT WA14 ....165 E2
Milner St WYTH/NTH M22 ...168 B5
Milne St WHTF M45 (RAD M26) ..66 D1

SWIN M27 ....97 F2
  WHIT OL12 ....14 B5
Milne St CHAD OL9 ....8 A6
  CHAD OL9 ....73 C5
  OLD OL1 ....74 D2
  OLDE OL4 ....42 B4
  ROY/SHW OL2 ....60 A5
Milngate Ct MILN OL16 ......43 H5
Milnholme BOL BL1 ....33 E3
Milnrow Cl BRUN/LGST M13 ..127 G1
Milnrow Rd LIT OL15 ....31 G1
  MILN OL16 ....11 J7
  ROY/SHW OL2 ....45 F5
Milnthorpe Rd BOLE BL2 .....50 B1
Milnthorpe St SLFD M6 ......98 D5
Milnthorpe Wy
  WGTN/LGST * M12 ....128 B2
Milo St BKLY * M9 ....87 E4
Milsom Av BOLS/LL BL3 ......63 F1
Milton Av BOLS/LL BL3 ......63 E1
  BOLS/LL * BL3 ....63 E1
  DROY M43 ....116 B4
  IRL M44 ....135 D5
  ORD M5 ....111 E3
  STLY SK15 ....120 B1
Milton Cl DUK SK16 ....133 G1
  MPL/ROM SK6 ....175 E5
  STRET M32 ....125 F5
Milton Ct BNG/LEV M19 ....158 D2
Milton Crs CHD/CHDH SK8 ...169 H4
  FWTH BL4 ....80 C1
Milton Dr POY/DIS SK12 .....89 F1
  HALE/TIMP WA15 ....154 E5
  POY/DIS SK12 ....185 F1
  SALE M33 ....139 F5
Milton Pl SLFD M6 ....96 C2
Milton Rd DTN/ASHW M34 ....117 E4
  PWCH M25 ....85 F2
  RAD M26 ....51 G5
  SWIN M27 ....96 D5
Milton St BRO M7 ....112 D1
  DTN/ASHW M34 ....131 F4
  ECC M30 ....109 G3
  HYDE SK14 ....132 C4
  MDTN M24 ....71 E3
  MILN OL16 ....10 D5
  MOSL OL5 ....92 D5
  ROY/SHW OL2 ....59 F4
Milton Vw MILN OL16 ....30 D1
Milverton Av HYDE SK14 ....148 D1
Milverton Cl HOR/BR BL6 ....47 E4
Milverton Dr CHD/CHDH SK8 .193 G4
Milverton Rd RUSH/FAL M14 .142 A1
Milverton Wk HYDE SK14 ....148 D1
Milwain Dr HTNM SK4 ....144 B5
Milwain Rd BNG/LEV M19 ...143 G3
Mimosa Dr SWIN M27 ....97 F2
Mincing St ANC * M4 ....7 H4
Minden Cl DID/WITH M20 ....157 H2
  BURY BL9 ....69 G2
Minden Pde BURY BL9 ....4 F4
Minden St SLFD M6 ....98 B4
Minehead Av DID/WITH M20 .142 A4
  URM M41 ....138 A3
Minerva Rd DUK SK16 ....118 C4
  FWTH BL4 ....64 B3
Minnie St HEY OL10 ....41 E2
Minnie St BOLS/LL * BL3 ....48 A5
  WHIT * OL12 ....14 C3
Minoan Gdns BRO M7 ....99 H2
Minorca Cl ROCH OL11 ....28 D4
Minorca St BOLS/LL BL3 .....48 D5
Minor St FAIL M35 ....103 F1
  OLDS OL8 ....90 B6
  ROCH OL11 ....42 B6
Minshull St CMANE M1 ....7 H5
Minshull St South CMANE M1 .7 H6
Minstead Cl HYDE SK14 .....148 B2
Minster Cl BOLE BL2 ....34 C2
  DUK SK16 ....132 C2
Minster Dr ALT WA14 ....176 B3
  CHD/CHDH SK8 ....170 D4
Minster Rd BKLY M9 ....101 G2
  BOLE BL2 ....34 D4
Minster Wy CHAD OL9 ....73 F3
Minstrel Cl SWIN M27 ....96 C3
Minto St AUL OL6 ....102 B2
  OLDE OL4 ....9 G6
Minto St AULW OL7 ....104 D5
Mirabel St CSLFD M3 ....6 D1
Mirfield Av BKLY M9 ....87 H4
  HTNM SK4 ....159 E4
  OLDS OL8 ....90 B3
Mirfield Dr ECC M30 ....109 G1
  MDTN M24 ....71 G3
  URM M41 ....123 F4
Mirfield Rd BKLY M9 ....87 H4
Miriam St BOLS/LL * BL3 .....48 C5
  NEWH/MOS M40 ....102 C4
Missouri Av ORD M5 ....111 H4
Mistletoe Gv CSLFD * M5 .....6 A1
Mitcham Av BKLY M9 ....87 H4
Mitchell Cl CHD/CHDH * SK8 .169 E3
Mitchell Hey WHIT OL12 .....10 B6
Mitchells Quay FAIL M35 ...102 D3
Mitchell St ECC M30 ....109 F2
  MDTN M24 ....71 G3
  MILN OL16 ....10 D4
  NEWH/MOS M40 ....102 A5
  OLD OL1 ....9 G1
  OP/CLY * M11 ....128 C1
  TOT/BURYW BL8 ....37 H2
  WHIT OL12 ....11 G4
Mitcheson Gdns SLFD M6 ...111 H2
Mitford Rd RUSH/FAL M14 ..142 B3
Mitford St STRET M32 ......139 H1
Mitre Rd BRUN/LGST M13 ...128 A3
Mitre St BOL BL1 ....34 A5
  FAIL M35 ....103 E2
Mitton Cl HEY OL10 ....40 D5
  TOT/BURYW BL8 ....36 D4
Mizzy Rd WHIT OL12 ....14 C1
Moadlock MPL/ROM SK6 .....162 B2
Moat Av WYTH/NTH M22 .....168 B3
Moatfield Gdns BOL BL1 ......2 B2
Moat Gdns WYTH/NTH M22 ..168 B5

Moat Hall Av ECC M30 ......108 D5
Moat Rd WYTH/NTH M22 ....168 B5
Mobberley Cl BNG/LEV M19 .158 B2
Mobberley Rd BOLE BL2 .....50 B1
  WILM/AE SK9 ....198 B1
Mocha Pde BRO M7 ....112 C2
Modbury Cl BRAM/HZG SK7 .184 B5
Mode Hill La WHTF M45 ......69 F4
Model Cottages
  HALE/TIMP * WA15 ......167 E5
Mode Wheel Rd South ORD M5 .111 E4
Modwen Rd ORD * M5 ....126 A2
Moelfre Dr CHD/CHDH SK8 ..183 F5
Moffat Cl BOLE BL2 ....50 C3
Moisant St BOLS/LL BL3 .....63 C1
Mold St BOL BL1 ....34 B4
  OLD OL1 ....74 B4
Molesworth St MILN OL16 ...10 E7
Mollets Wd DTN/ASHW M34 .131 H5
Mollington Rd WYTH/NTH M22 .180 D4
Molyneux Rd BNG/LEV M19 .144 B2
Molyneux St RAD M26 ....12 G3
Mona Av CHD/CHDH SK8 .....182 A3
  STRET M32 ....124 D5
Monaco Dr WYTH/NTH M22 ..180 C4
Monarch Cl IRL M44 ....135 D5
  ROY/SHW OL2 ....74 B2
Monart Rd BKLY M9 ....101 F1
Moncrieffe St BOLS/LL BL3 ...3 F7
Mond Rd IRL M44 ....121 C4
Money Ash Rd
  HALE/TIMP WA15 ....177 G1
Monfa Av EDGY/DAV SK3 ....172 B5
Monica Av CHH M8 ....86 A5
Monica Gv BNG/LEV M19 ....143 G3
Monks Cl MILN OL16 ....31 F5
Monksdale Av URM M41 .....138 A1
Monks Hall Gv ECC M30 .....110 A3
Monks La BOLE BL2 ....35 E4
Monkton Av GTN M18 ....129 F5
Monkwood Dr BKLY * M9 ...101 F3
Monmouth Av BURY BL9 ......38 C1
  SALE M33 ....154 A1
Monmouth Rd CHD/CHDH SK8 .183 E5
Monmouth St CHAD OL9 ....8 D7
  MDTN M24 ....72 B4
  ROCH OL11 ....41 H6
Monroe Cl SLFD M6 ....111 F1
Monsal Av BRO M7 ....98 D5
  OFTN SK2 ....175 E2
Monsall Cl BURY BL9 ....68 D2
Monsall Rd NEWH/MOS M40 .101 F4
Monsall St NEWH/MOS M40 ..101 E5
  OLDS OL8 ....91 H4
Mons Av ROCH OL11 ....29 F3
Montague Rd AUL OL6 ......118 C2
  OLDTF/WHR M16 ....125 H5
  SALE M33 ....154 B3
Montague St BOLS/LL * BL3 ..63 E1
Montagu Rd OFTN SK2 ......173 E2
Montagu St MPL/ROM SK6 ..161 G5
Montana Sq OP/CLY M11 ....129 H1
Montcliffe Crs OLDTF/WHR M16 .142 A2
Monteagle St BKLY M9 ....86 C3
Montford St SALO M50 ......111 G4
Montgomery ROCH * OL11 ...29 H5
Montgomery Dr BURY BL9 ....69 E2
Montgomery Rd
  BRUN/LGST M13 ....143 G1
Montgomery St OLDS OL8 ....91 H5
Montgomery Wy RAD M26 ....51 F4
Montondale ECC M30 ....109 F2
Montonfields Rd ECC M30 ..109 E2
Monton Gn ECC M30 ....109 F1
Monton La ECC M30 ....109 H3
Monton Mill Gdns ECC M30 .109 F2
Monton Rd ECC M30 ....109 F2
  RDSH SK5 ....145 G3
Monton St BOLS/LL BL3 .....65 H1
  RAD M26 ....67 E1
  RUSH/FAL M14 ....127 H5
Montpelier Rd WYTH/NTH M22 .180 A4
Montreal St BNG/LEV M19 ..144 A2
  OLDS OL8 ....90 C3
Montrose Av BOLE BL2 ......34 D5
  DID/WITH M20 ....157 E1
  DUK SK16 ....132 B1
  EDGY/DAV SK3 ....184 B1
  RAMS BL0 ....16 C3
  STRET M32 ....124 D5
Montrose Dr EDGW/EG BL7 ..23 E1
Montrose Gdns ROY/SHW OL2 .57 F1
Montserrat Rd BOL BL1 ......32 B4
Moon Gv RUSH/FAL M14 .....128 A5
Moon St CHAD OL9 ....8 A6
Moor Bank La MILN OL16 .....44 A2
Moorby Av BNG/LEV M19 ....158 B2
Moorby Wk BOLS/LL * BL3 ...48 B4
Moorcl Cl RAD M26 ....51 H4
Moorclose Rd MDTN M24 .....72 B4
Moorcock Av SWIN M27 ......97 G2
Moor Crs UPML OL3 ....78 A1
Moorcroft ROCH OL11 ....43 E3
Moorcroft Dr BNG/LEV M19 .158 A4
Moorcroft Rd NTHM/RTH M23 .155 G5
Moorcroft St DROY M43 .....116 B4
  OLDS OL8 ....89 H5
Moordale Av OLDE OL4 ....77 E4
Moordale St DID/WITH M20 .157 F1
Moordown Cl CHH M8 ....100 D4
Moor Edge Rd STLY SK15 ...107 H5
Mooredge Ter ROY/SHW OL2 .74 B2
Moor End WYTH/NTH M22 ...180 C4
Moor End Av BRO M7 ....99 F2
Moores Ct BOL BL1 ....48 B1
Moore St MILN OL16 ....11 G5
Moorfield DID/WITH M20 ...157 F1
Moorfield Av DTN/ASHW M34 .146 D2
  LIT OL15 ....21 E3
  RUSH/FAL M14 ....142 D1
  STLY SK15 ....121 H2
Moorfield Cha FWTH BL4 .....65 E3
Moorfield Cl IRL * M44 .....121 H1
  SWIN M27 ....98 A4
Moorfield Dr HYDE * SK14 ..132 D3

Moorfield Gv BOLE BL2 ......34 C5
  HTNM SK4 ....158 D1
  SALE M33 ....155 E3
Moorfield Hamlet ROY/SHW OL2 .59 G2
Moorfield Hts MOSL OL5 ...107 F5
Moorfield Ms ROY/SHW * OL2 .59 G2
Moorfield Pl WHIT * OL12 ...10 D2
Moorfield Rd DID/WITH M20 .157 E2
  IRL M44 ....135 E2
  OLDS OL8 ....89 C5
  SLFD M6 ....96 A4
  SWIN M27 ....96 B4
Moorfield St DID/WITH M20 .142 C4
Moor Ga BURY BL9 ....35 E1
  SALE M33 ....155 E3
Moorgate BURY BL9 ....4 E1
  ROCH OL11 ....28 C2
Moorgate Ct BOLE BL2 ....3 K1
Moorgate Dr STLY SK15 ....107 F4
Moorgate Ms MOSL * OL5 ...107 F5
Moorgate Rd MDTN M24 .....55 H1
  STLY SK15 ....107 F3
Moorgate St UPML OL3 ......78 A4
Moorhead St ANC M4 ....7 J1
Moorhey Rd LHULT M38 ......80 A1
Moorhey St OLDE OL4 ....9 K6
Moor HI ROCH OL11 ....28 B2
Moorhouse Farm MILN OL16 .31 H5
Moor House Fold MILN OL16 .31 F5
The Moorings MOSL OL5 .....93 F4
  WALK M28 ....95 H5
Moorings Rd TRPK M17 .....110 C5
Moorland Av CHH M8 ....86 A6
  DROY M43 ....116 C4
  MILN OL16 ....44 C1
  ROCH OL11 ....42 D5
  SALE M33 ....154 D5
  UPML OL3 ....77 G1
  WHIT OL12 ....18 B1
Moorland Crs WHIT OL12 .....18 B1
Moorland Dr CHD/CHDH SK8 .182 C4
  LHULT M38 ....80 B1
Moorland Gv BOL BL1 ....32 C4
Moorland Rd DID/WITH M20 .157 H3
  OFTN SK2 ....172 B5
  STLY SK15 ....120 D5
Moorlands Av URM * M41 ...123 E5
Moorlands Crs MOSL OL5 ...107 E1
Moorlands Dr MOSL OL5 .....93 G1
Moorland St ROY/SHW OL2 ..60 B2
  WHIT OL12 ....10 D2
Moorlands Vw BOLS/LL BL3 ..62 D2
Moorland Ter WHIT OL12 ....18 B2
Moor La BOL BL1 ....33 G5
  BRO M7 ....98 D2
  BRAM/HZG SK7 ....195 G4
  NTHM/RTH M23 ....167 F1
  TOT/BURYW BL8 ....36 C4
  UPML OL3 ....78 B2
  WILM/AE SK9 ....201 E4
Moor Nook SALE M33 ....155 E3
Moor Park Av ROCH OL11 ...42 A4
Moor Park Rd DID/WITH M20 .157 H5
Moor Rd LIT OL15 ....15 H3
  NTHM/RTH M23 ....167 F1
  TOT/BURYW BL8 ....26 C1
Moorsholme Av
  NEWH/MOS M40 ....101 H4
Moorside Av BOL BL1 ....32 D4
  BOLE BL2 ....36 C5
  DROY M43 ....116 C2
  FWTH BL4 ....64 C4
  OLDE OL4 ....75 E5
Moorside Ct DTN/ASHW M34 .131 G4
Moorside Crs DROY M43 ....116 C3
Moorside La DROY M43 .....116 C3
Moor Side Rd NTHM/RTH M23 .155 F1
Moorside Rd BRO M7 ....99 F1
  CHH * M8 ....100 B5
  HTNM SK4 ....158 D1
  MOSL OL5 ....107 F1
  SWIN M27 ....97 E1
  TOT/BURYW BL8 ....36 B1
  URM M41 ....122 D4
Moorside St DROY M43 .....116 C3
Moors La WILM/AE SK9 .....193 H5
Moorside Vw TOT/BURYW BL8 .26 C1
Moorsley Dr BKLY M9 ....87 H1
Moor St BURY BL9 ....5 F2
  ECC M30 ....109 G2
  HEY OL10 ....40 C4
  OLD * OL1 ....75 E5
  ROY/SHW OL2 ....60 B3
  SWIN M27 ....97 H2
Moorsview RAMS BL0 ....16 C2
Moorton Av BNG/LEV M19 ..143 H2
Moorton Pk BNG/LEV M19 ..143 G4
Moortop Cl BKLY M9 ....100 C1
Moor Top Pl HTNM SK4 .....158 D1
Moor View Cl WHIT OL12 ...18 D2
Moorville Rd SLFD M6 ....97 H5
Moorway WYTH/NTH M22 ...180 C4
Moorwood Dr OLDS OL8 ......90 C5
  SALE M33 ....153 H3
Mora Av CHAD OL9 ....73 H1
Moran Cl WILM/AE SK9 .....201 E3
Moran Wk HULME M15 ....127 G2
Morar Dr BOLE BL2 ....35 F4
Morar Rd DUK SK16 ....118 D4
Mora St BKLY M9 ....101 G2
Moravian Cl BKLY M9 ......118 B4
Moravian Fld DROY * M43 ...116 C5
Moray Cl RAMS BL0 ....16 D4
Moray Rd CHAD OL9 ....89 E1
Morbourne Cl WGTN/LGST M12 .128 A2
Morecambe Cl NEWH/MOS M40 .102 A4
Morecroft Pl SALFD
Morely St BURY BL9 ....5 K1
Moresby Dr DID/WITH M20 .169 G1
Moret Cl WHIT OL12 ....29 H5
Moreton Av BKLY M9 ....129 G3
Moreton Cl DUK SK16 ....132 C4
Moreton Dr POY/DIS SK12 ..195 G3
  BURY BL9 ....53 G1
Moreton La OFTN SK2 ......172 D2
Moreton St CHAD OL9 ....8 B3
Morgan Pl RDSH SK5 ....145 E5
Morgan St LIT OL15 ....21 E3
Morillon Rd IRL M44 ....121 B4

Morland Rd OLDTF/WHR M16 .126 B4
Morley Av RUSH/FAL M14 ...142 D2
  SWIN M27 ....96 D4
Morley Green Rd WILM/AE SK9 .198 B1
Morley Rd RAD M26 ....51 G5
Morley St BOLS/LL BL3 ....2 B6
  BURY BL9 ....11 G3
  MILN OL16 ....11 G5
  WHTF M45 ....68 C4
Morna Wk WGTN/LGST M12 .114 A5
Morningside Dr DID/WITH M20 .169 H1
Mornington Av CHD/CHDH SK8 .130 A1
  WHIT * OL12 ....14 A3
Mornington Cl CHD/CHDH SK8 .170 A3
  CHD/CHDH SK8 ....170 A5
Mornington Crs RUSH/FAL M14 .142 B5
Mornington Rd BOL BL1 .....33 F5
  CHD/CHDH SK8 ....170 A5
  ROCH OL11 ....43 E4
  SALE M33 ....155 E1
Morpeth Cl AULW OL7 ......117 F1
  WGTN/LGST M12 ....96 D4
Morpeth St SWIN M27 ......96 D4
Morrell Rd WYTH/NTH M22 .168 D1
Morris Fold Dr HOR/BR BL6 .46 D5
Morris La BOLS/LL BL3 ......63 F2
Morris Green La BOLS/LL BL3 .63 F2
Morris Green St BOLS/LL * BL3 .63 F2
Morris St URM M41 ....137 F5
Morrison St BOLS/LL BL3 ...63 H1
Morris St BOL BL1 ....3 G3
  DID/WITH M20 ....142 C4
  OLDE OL4 ....9 K6
  RAD M26 ....53 F4
Morse Rd NEWH/MOS M40 ...102 A5
Mortar St OLDE OL4 ....75 F5
Mortfield Gdns BOL BL1 .....2 A2
Mortfield La BOL BL1 ....2 A2
Mortimer Av BKLY M9 ....87 F1
Mortimer St OLD OL1 ....74 D3
Mortlake Cl LHULT M38 .....80 A4
Mortlake Dr NEWH/MOS M40 .102 A5
Mort La TYLD M29 ....79 G5
Morton St FAIL M35 ....159 H2
  MDTN M24 ....71 H3
  RDSH SK5 ....67 G2
Mort St FWTH BL4 ....64 B4
Morven Av BRAM/HZG SK7 ..185 G1
Morven Dr NTHM/RTH M23 ..167 H4
Morven Gv BOLE BL2 ....50 C2
Morville Rd CHAD OL9 ......141 G2
Morville St CMANE * M1 .....7 K6
Moscow Rd EDGY/DAV SK3 ..171 G2
Moscow Rd East EDGY/DAV SK3 .171 G2
Mosedale Av NTHM/RTH M23 .167 F3
Mosedale Rd MDTN M24 .....56 B4
Moseldene Rd OFTN SK2 ....173 E4
Moseley Rd CHD/CHDH SK8 .182 C4
  RUSH/FAL M14 ....143 E3
Moseley St EDGY/DAV SK3 ..12 E6
Mosley Av BURY BL9 ....26 C3
  RAMS BL0 ....16 C3
Mosley Cl HALE/TIMP WA15 .166 A2
Mosley Common Rd WALK M28 .166 A2
Mosley Rd HALE/TIMP WA15 .166 A3
  TRPK M17 ....110 D5
Mosley Rd North TRPK M17 .110 D5
Mosley St CMANW M2 ....7 F4
  RAD M26 ....52 A5
The Moss MDTN M24 ....70 D4
Mossack Av WYTH/NTH M22 .180 C5
Moss Av MILN OL16 ....30 D5
Moss Bank CHD/CHDH SK8 ..193 F2
  CHH M8 ....100 B2
Moss Bank Av DROY M43 ...116 D3
Moss Bank Cl BOL BL1 ......33 G2
Moss Bank Gv SWIN M27 ....82 C5
Moss Bank Pk BOL * BL1 ....33 G2
Moss Bank Rd SWIN M27 ....82 C5
Moss Bank Wy BOL BL1 .....32 D4
Mossbray Av BNG/LEV M19 .158 A2
Moss Bridge Rd MILN OL16 .30 C5
Mossbrook Dr LHULT M38 ...81 F1
Moss Cl RAD M26 ....51 G4
Mossclough Ct BKLY M9 ....101 H1
Moss Colliery Rd SWIN M27 .82 C5
Mosscot Wk BRUN/LGST M13 .127 G1
Moss Croft Cl URM M41 .....122 B5
Mossdale Av BOL BL1 ....47 G1
Mossdale Rd NTHM/RTH M23 .155 H5
  SALE M33 ....153 H5
Mossdown Rd ROY/SHW OL2 .74 D1
Mossfield Cl BURY BL9 ....5 K1
  TOT/BURYW BL8 ....159 E4
Mossfield Ct BOL BL1 ....47 G1
Mossfield Rd BKLY M9
  FWTH BL4 ....81 G2
  HALE/TIMP WA15 ....167 E5
  SWIN M27 ....
Moss Gate Rd ROY/SHW OL2 .74 D1
Moss Grange Av
  OLDTF/WHR M16 ....126 C6
Moss Gn PART M31 ....137 G5
Moss Gv ROY/SHW OL2 ......44 B5
Mossgrove Rd
  HALE/TIMP WA15 ....166 A3
Mosshall Cl HULME M15 ....127 H2
Moss Hall Rd BURY BL9 .....53 G3
Moss Hey Dr NTHM/RTH M23 .156 A5
Moss Hey St ROY/SHW OL2 ..60 A3
Moss House La WALK M28 ...93 H5
Moss House Ter BKLY * M9 .100 D1
Moss La AULW OL7 ....117 G3
Mossland Gv BOLS/LL BL3 ...62 A2
Moss La AULW OL7 ....117 G3
  BRAM/HZG SK7 ....185 G4
  FWTH BL4 ....64 D4
  HALE/TIMP WA15 ....165 G3
  HYDE SK14 ....149 G1
  IRL M44 ....150 C1
  LYMM WA13 ....
  MDTN M24 ....
  PART * M31 ....
  ROY/SHW OL2 ....
  SWIN M27 ....96 C4
  URM M41 ....123 G3

WALK M28 .....81 F4
WHTH M45 .....68 C4
WILM/AE SK9 .....190 C2
WILM/AE SK9 .....201 C3
Moss La East OLDTF/WHR M16 .....126 D4
Moss La West HULME M15 .....126 D4
Moss Lea BOL BL1 .....33 G2
Mosslee Av CHH M8 .....86 B2
Mossley Rd AUL OL6 .....106 A5
AUL OL6 .....118 D2
OLDE OL4 .....93 E3
Moss Meadow Rd SLFD * M6 .....110 D1
Mossmere Rd CHD/CHDH SK8 .....170 D5
Moss Mill St URM 43 G1
Moss Park Rd STRET M32 .....139 F1
Moss Pl BURY * BL9 .....53 F1
Moss Rd FWTH BL4 .....65 F5
IRL M44 .....135 A1
PART M31 .....153 E2
STRET M32 .....136 C2
WILM/AE SK9 .....201 D3
Moss Rose WILM/AE SK9 .....201 C3
Moss Ter MILN OL16 .....30 B5
Moss Vale Crs STRET M32 .....124 A4
Moss Vale Rd URM M41 .....138 C1
Moss View Rd BOLE * BL2 .....50 D1
PART M31 .....151 F3
Mossway MDTN M24 .....87 G2
Moss Wy SALE M33 .....153 H3
Mosswood Pk DID/WITH M20 .....169 G1
Mosswood Rd WILM/AE SK9 .....200 D1
Mossylea Cl MDTN M24 .....88 A2
Moston Bank Av BKLY M9 .....101 F3
Moston La BKLY M9 .....101 H1
NEWH/MOS M40 .....101 H1
Moston La East NEWH/MOS M40 .....88 C1
Moston Rd MDTN M24 .....88 C1
Moston St BRO M7 .....100 A3
Mostyn Av BURY BL9 .....38 D1
CHD/CHDH SK8 .....182 B3
RUSH/FAL M14 .....143 F3
Mostyn Rd BRAM/HZG SK7 .....184 D3
Mostyn St DUK SK16 .....119 E5
Motcombe Farm Rd
CHD/CHDH SK8 .....181 F1
Motcombe Gv CHD/CHDH SK8 .....181 F1
Motcombe Rd CHD/CHDH SK8 .....181 F1
Motherwell Av BNG/LEV M19 .....143 H2
Mottashead Av BOLS/LL BL3 .....50 C3
Mottershead Rd
WYTH/NTH M22 .....168 A5
Mottram Av CCHDY M21 .....156 B1
Mottram Cl CHD/CHDH SK8 .....170 C4
Mottram Dr HALE/TIMP WA15 .....166 B4
Mottram Fold STKP SK1 .....13 G5
Mottram Old Rd HYDE SK14 .....149 H4
STLY SK15 .....119 H4
SALE M33 .....155 F3
STLY SK15 .....119 H4
Mottram St STKP SK1 .....13 G5
Mough La CHAD OL9 .....88 C4
Mouldsworth Av
DID/WITH M20 .....142 B4
WHTN M22 .....144 C5
Moulton St CHH M8 .....112 D1
Mouncey St CMANE * M1 .....127 F1
The Mount ALT WA14 .....165 G4
HALE/TIMP WA15 .....166 C4
Mountain Ash WHIT OL12 .....18 A5
Mountain Ash Cl SALE M33 .....153 F1
WHIT OL12 .....18 A5
Mountain Gv WALK M28 .....80 D1
Mountain St MOSL OL5 .....106 D1
NEWH/MOS M40 .....115 G1
STKP SK1 .....13 G2
WALK M28 .....80 D3
Mount Av LIT OL15 .....20 D1
WHIT OL12 .....29 G2
Mountbatten Av DUK SK16 .....133 E1
Mountbatten Cl BURY BL9 .....69 E2
Mountbatten St GTN M18 .....126 B3
Mount Carmel Crs ORD * M5 .....126 A1
Mount Dr MPL/ROM SK6 .....174 A3
URM M41 .....139 E1
Mountfield PWCH M25 .....85 E3
Mountfield Rd BRAM/HZG SK7 .....193 H2
EDGY/DAV SK3 .....171 F2
Mount Fold MDTN M24 .....71 H5
Mountford Av CHH * M8 .....86 A5
Mount Gv WYTH/NTH M22 .....169 E4
Mount La UPML OL3 .....78 D1
Mountmorres CH WHTN BL5 .....62 D2
Mount Pleasant BOLS/LL * BL3 .....49 H4
BRAM/HZG SK7 .....185 E1
LIT * OL15 .....15 H3
MDTN M24 .....70 D4
PWCH M25 .....85 H2
WILM/AE SK9 .....199 G1
Mount Pleasant Rd
DTN/ASHW M34 .....146 C1
FWTH BL4 .....64 A4
Mount Pleasant St AUL OL6 .....118 D2
OLDE * OL4 .....75 E5
Mount Rd GTN M18 .....129 F3
HTNM SK4 .....159 E1
MDTN M24 .....71 H5
PWCH M25 .....85 G5
Mountroyal Cl HYDE SK14 .....133 E4
Mount St Joseph's Rd
BOLS/LL BL3 .....48 A5
Mountside Cl WHIT OL12 .....10 C1
Mountside Crs PWCH M25 .....84 C4
Mount Sion Houses RAD * M26 .....66 C2
Mount Sion Rd RAD M26 .....66 D2

Mount Skip La LHULT M58 .....80 B3
Mount St BOL BL1 .....33 H5
CMANW M2 .....6 E6
CSLFD M3 .....6 A2
ECC M30 .....109 F5
HEY OL10 .....41 E5
HYDE SK14 .....147 H1
RAMS BL0 .....16 C1
ROCH OL11 .....42 B5
ROY/SHW OL2 .....74 B1
WHIT OL12 .....10 A5
Mount View Rd ROY/SHW OL2 .....60 B3
Mount Zion Rd BURY BL9 .....53 G4
Mousell St CHH M8 .....113 F1
Mowbray Av PWCH M25 .....85 F5
SALE M33 .....154 D5
Mowbray St AULW OL7 .....117 G3
BOL * BL1 .....33 E5
OLD OL1 .....9 H4
ROCH OL11 .....42 A3
STKP SK1 .....13 H5
Mow Halls La UPML OL3 .....77 H3
Moxley Rd CHH M8 .....99 H1
Moyse Av TOT/BURYW BL8 .....37 E1
Mozart Cl ANC M4 .....113 H5
Muirfield Av MPL/ROM SK6 .....161 H2
Muirfield Cl BOLS/LL BL3 .....62 C1
NEWH/MOS M40 .....102 B3
WILM/AE SK9 .....200 A2
Mulberry Cl CHD/CHDH SK8 .....181 H5
ROCH OL11 .....42 D1
Mulberry Ct SLFD * M6 .....111 H2
Mulberry Ms HTNM SK4 .....12 E1
Mulberry Mount St
EDGY/DAV SK3 .....13 F6
Mulberry Rd SLFD M6 .....111 H3
Mulberry St AUL * OL6 .....118 B2
Mulberry Wk DROY M43 .....115 H5
SALE M33 .....138 C5
Mule St BOLE BL2 .....3 H1
Mulgrave Rd WALK M28 .....95 H2
Mulgrave St BOLS/LL BL3 .....63 F2
SWIN M27 .....96 C1
Mullacre Rd WYTH/NTH M22 .....168 A4
Mull Av WGTN/LGST M12 .....128 B3
Mulliner St BOL * BL1 .....34 A5
Mullion Cl BOLS/LL BL3 .....144 C1
Mullion Dr HALE/TIMP WA15 .....165 H2
Mullion Wk CHH M8 .....100 D5
Mulmount Cl OLDS OL8 .....89 H4
Munday St ANC M4 .....114 A4
Municipal Cl HEY * OL10 .....41 E4
Munn Rd BKLY M9 .....86 C2
Munro Av WYTH/NTH M22 .....181 E2
Munster St ANC * M4 .....7 F2
Muriel St BRO M7 .....99 G5
HEY OL10 .....41 F4
Murieston Rd HALE/TIMP WA15 .....177 H2
Murrayfield ROCH OL11 .....28 B5
Murray Rd BURY BL9 .....4 E5
Murray St ANC M4 .....7 K3
BRO M7 .....99 G4
Musabbir Sq WHIT * OL12 .....19 F6
Musbury Av CHD/CHDH SK8 .....183 E2
Museum St CMANW M2 .....6 E6
Musgrave Gdns BOL BL1 .....48 B1
Musgrave Rd BOL BL1 .....48 B1
WYTH/NTH M22 .....180 C1
Muslin St ORD M5 .....112 B4
Muter Av WYTH/NTH M22 .....181 E2
Mutual St HEY OL10 .....41 F3
Myerscroft Cl NEWH/MOS M40 .....102 C1
Myrrh St BOL BL1 .....33 H5
Myrtle Bank PWCH M25 .....98 D1
Myrtle Cl OLDS OL8 .....9 F7
Myrtle Gdns BURY BL9 .....53 C1
Myrtle Gv DROY M43 .....116 D2
PWCH M25 .....85 E5
Myrtleleaf Gv ORD * M5 .....111 E3
Myrtle Pl BRO * M7 .....112 B1
Myrtle Rd MDTN M24 .....72 B5
PART M31 .....150 C4
Myrtle St BOL * BL1 .....2 D2
EDGY/DAV SK3 .....171 E1
OLDTF/WHR * M16 .....126 B4
OP/CLY M11 .....114 B5
Myrtle St North BURY BL9 .....5 J5
Myrtle St South BURY BL9 .....5 J5
My St ORD M5 .....111 F4
Mytham Gdns BOLS/LL BL3 .....66 A2
Mytham Rd BOLS/LL BL3 .....66 A1
Mythorne Av IRL M44 .....150 B3
Mytton Rd BOL BL1 .....33 E3
Mytton St HULME M15 .....126 D3

N

Nabbs Fold RAMS BL0 .....16 A5
Nabbs Wy TOT/BURYW BL8 .....26 B2
Naburn Cl RDSH SK5 .....145 H1
Naburn St BRUN/LGST M13 .....128 A4
Nada Rd CHH M8 .....100 A1
Nadine St OLDS OL8 .....90 B4
Nairn Cl NEWH/MOS * M40 .....114 B2
Nall St BNG/LEV M19 .....144 A4
MILN OL16 .....44 B2
Nameplate Cl ECC M30 .....109 E3
Nancy St HULME M15 .....126 C2
Nandywell BOLS/LL BL3 .....66 A1
Nangreave Rd OFTN SK2 .....172 B5
Nan Nook Rd NTHM/RTH M23 .....155 H3
Nansen Av ECC M30 .....109 F2
Nansen Cl STRET M32 .....125 F4
Nansen Rd CHD/CHDH SK8 .....169 F5
Nansen St OP/CLY M11 .....115 F3
SLFD M6 .....111 F3
STRET M32 .....125 G5
Nansmoss La WILM/AE SK9 .....198 C5
Nantwich Av WHIT OL12 .....19 E5
Nantwich Rd RUSH/FAL M14 .....142 B2
Nantwich Wk BOLS/LL * BL3 .....2 D5
Napier Ct HULME * M15 .....126 C2
Napier Gn ORD M5 .....126 A1
Napier Rd CCHDY M21 .....141 E3

ECC M30 .....109 F2
HTNM SK4 .....159 E5
Napier St BRAM/HZG SK7 .....185 E1
HYDE SK14 .....147 H2
ROY/SHW OL2 .....60 A1
SWIN M27 .....96 C5
Napier St East OLDS OL8 .....8 D6
Napier St West OLDS OL8 .....8 D7
Naples Rd EDGY/DAV SK3 .....171 E3
Naples St ANC M4 .....7 H1
Narbonne Av ECC M30 .....110 B1
Narbuth Dr CHH M8 .....100 A5
The Narrows ALT WA14 .....165 F5
Naseby Av BKLY M9 .....87 G5
Naseby Pl PWCH M25 .....85 H3
Naseby Rd RDSH SK5 .....144 D3
Naseby Wk WHTF M45 .....69 F4
Nash Rd TRPK M17 .....109 H5
Nash St HULME M15 .....126 D2
Nasmyth Av DTN/ASHW M34 .....146 B1
Nasmyth Rd ECC M30 .....109 F5
Nasmyth St CHH M8 .....100 B3
Nately Rd OLDTF/WHR * M16 .....140 D1
Nathan Dr CSLFD M3 .....6 B2
Nathans Rd WYTH/NTH M22 .....168 B4
National Dr ORD M5 .....111 H5
Naunton Rd MDTN M24 .....72 A5
Naval St ANC M4 .....7 K3
Nave Ct SLFD M6 .....111 H1
Navenby Av OLDTF/WHR M16 .....126 B4
Navigation Rd ALT WA14 .....165 G2
Naylor St NEWH/MOS M40 .....114 A2
OLD OL1 .....9 J1
Nazeby Wk CHAD OL9 .....8 B7
Naze Ct OLD OL1 .....74 B4
Neal Av AUL OL6 .....118 C2
Near Birches Pde OLDE OL4 .....91 H5
Nearbrook Rd WYTH/NTH M22 .....168 B5
Nearcroft Rd NTHM/RTH M23 .....167 H4
Near Hey Cl RAD M26 .....66 D1
Nearmaker Av WYTH/NTH M22 .....168 B5
Nearmaker Rd WYTH/NTH M22 .....168 B5
Neary Wy URM M41 .....123 F3
Neasden Gv BOLS/LL * BL3 .....48 B4
Neath Av WYTH/NTH M22 .....168 A5
Neath Cl POY/DIS SK12 .....195 E2
WHTF M45 .....69 F5
Neath Fold BOLS/LL BL3 .....63 G1
Neath St CHAD OL9 .....8 D5
Nebo St BOLS/LL BL3 .....63 G1
Nebraska St BOL * BL1 .....33 H5
Neden Cl OP/CLY M11 .....115 E5
Needham Av CCHDY M21 .....141 E3
Needwood Cl NEWH/MOS M40 .....112 B1
Needwood Rd MPL/ROM SK6 .....162 B2
Neenton Sq WGTN/LGST M12 .....128 D1
Neild St CMANE M1 .....7 J7
OLDS OL8 .....8 D5
Neill St BRO M7 .....112 D1
Neilson Ct NTHM M23 .....72 B5
Neil Carrs RAMS BL0 .....17 F4
Nellie St HEY OL10 .....40 C4
Nell La CCHDY M21 .....141 H5
DID/WITH M20 .....142 A4
Nelson Av ECC M30 .....109 G2
POY/DIS SK12 .....195 H4
Nelson Dr DROY M43 .....115 H3
IRL M44 .....135 G5
Nelson Fold SWIN M27 .....97 F1
Nelson Rd BKLY M9 .....87 E2
Nelson Sq BOL BL1 .....3 F5
Nelson St BOLS/LL BL3 .....49 H5
ROLS/LL * BL3 .....65 H1
BRAM/HZG SK7 .....173 G5
BRO * M7 .....99 G5
BRUN/LGST M13 .....127 G3
BURY BL9 .....53 C1
DTN/ASHW M34 .....146 C2
ECC M30 .....109 G3
FWTH BL4 .....64 A5
HEY OL10 .....41 E5
HYDE SK14 .....147 H1
LIT OL15 .....20 C2
MDTN M24 .....72 B5
MILN OL16 .....10 D6
NEWH/MOS M40 .....114 A1
OLDE * OL4 .....9 H2
ORD M5 .....111 F4
STRET M52 .....140 A2
Nelstrop Crs HTNM SK4 .....144 D5
Nelstrop Rd HTNM SK4 .....144 D5
Nelstrop Rd North RDSH SK5 .....144 D4
Nepaul Rd BKLY M9 .....101 F1
Neptune Gdns BRO M7 .....112 B1
Nesbit St BOLE * BL2 .....34 C3
Nesfield Rd NTHM/RTH M23 .....155 G4
Neston Av BOL BL1 .....34 A1
DID/WITH M20 .....157 E3
SALE M33 .....155 F4
Neston Gv EDGY/DAV SK3 .....171 G4
Neston Rd MILN OL16 .....43 H2
TOT/BURYW BL8 .....37 E3
Neston St OP/CLY M11 .....130 A1
Neston Wy WILM/AE SK9 .....192 D4
Netherbury Cl GTN M18 .....129 F5
Nethercote Av NTHM/RTH M34 .....167 H2
Nethercroft ROCH OL11 .....28 B3
Nethercroft Rd
HALE/TIMP WA15 .....166 D4
Netherfield Cl OLDS OL8 .....90 B5
Netherfield Rd BOLS/LL BL3 .....63 G1
Netherfields WILM/AE SK9 .....201 E5
Netherhey La ROY/SHW OL2 .....73 H2
Nether Hey St OLDS OL8 .....9 G7
Netherhouse Rd ROY/SHW OL2 .....59 H2
Netherland St SALO M50 .....111 G4
Netherlees OLDE OL4 .....92 D1
Nether St HYDE SK14 .....148 A4
WGTN/LGST * M12 .....127 H3
Netherton Rd RUSH/FAL M14 .....142 B2
Nethervale Dr BKLY M9 .....101 F3
Netherwood OLDS OL8 .....103 G2
Netherwood Rd
HALE/TIMP WA15 .....166 D4

Nettleton Gv BKLY M9 .....101 G1
Nevada St BOL * BL1 .....33 H5
Nevendon Dr NTHM/RTH M23 .....167 G5
Nevern Cl BOL BL1 .....47 H4
Nevile Rd BRO M7 .....99 E2
Neville Cardus Wk
RUSH/FAL M14 .....142 D1
Neville Cl BOL BL1 .....2 D3
Neville Dr IRL M44 .....121 H4
Neville Rd BRAM/HZG SK7 .....185 E1
Neville St BRAM/HZG SK7 .....185 E1
CHAD OL9 .....74 B2
Nevin Av DTN/ASHW M34 .....146 B5
Nevin Cl BRAM/HZG SK7 .....184 B5
Nevin Rd NEWH/MOS M40 .....102 C1
Nevis Gv BOL BL1 .....33 G1
Nevis St ROCH OL11 .....41 H4
New Allen St NEWH/MOS M40 .....113 H2
Newall Rd NTHM/RTH M23 .....179 G1
Newall St CHAD M40 .....89 C5
LIT OL15 .....21 G2
Newark Av RAD M26 .....51 F4
RUSH/FAL M14 .....127 G5
Newark Park Wy ROY/SHW OL2 .....58 D5
Newark Rd RDSH SK5 .....160 A1
SWIN M27 .....97 G2
WHIT OL12 .....19 E5
Newark Sq WHIT OL12 .....19 E5
New Bailey St CSLFD M3 .....6 B4
Newbank Cha CHAD OL9 .....73 H2
New Bank St WGTN/LGST M12 .....128 B3
Newbank Cl MDTN M24 .....88 A2
New Barn La ROCH OL11 .....42 C1
New Barn Rd OLDS OL8 .....91 H5
New Barns Av CCHDY M21 .....141 F5
New Barn St BOL BL1 .....33 E5
ROCH OL11 .....43 F1
ROY/SHW OL2 .....59 H2
New Barton St SLFD M6 .....97 F5
Newbeck St ANC * M4 .....7 G2
New Beech Rd HTNM SK4 .....158 B4
Newberry Gv EDGY/DAV SK3 .....171 G4
Newbold Moss MILN OL16 .....11 H6
Newbold St BOLE BL2 .....3 K5
TOT/BURYW BL8 .....37 H2
Newboult Rd CHD/CHDH SK8 .....170 B3
Newbourne Cl BRAM/HZG SK7 .....185 E1
Newbreak Cl OLDE OL4 .....75 H5
Newbridge Gdns BOLE BL2 .....35 F2
Newbridge La STKP SK1 .....13 J3
New Bridge St CSLFD M3 .....6 D2
Newbridge Vw MOSL * OL5 .....107 E2
New Briggs Fold EDGW/EG BL7 .....22 D1
New Broad La MILN OL16 .....31 H5
Newbrook Av CCHDY M21 .....156 C3
New Buildings Pl MILN OL16 .....10 C5
Newbury Av SALE M33 .....153 H4
Newbury Av SALE M33 .....153 F2
Newbury Cl CHD/CHDH SK8 .....192 D1
Newbury Ct HALE/TIMP * WA15 .....166 A4
Newbury Dr ECC M30 .....109 E3
URM M41 .....123 F5
Newbury Gv HEY OL10 .....56 A1
Newbury Rd BOLS/LL BL3 .....65 G3
CHD/CHDH SK8 .....181 H5
CHAD OL9 .....8 A2
Newby Dr ALT * WA14 .....165 H5
SALE M33 .....155 E3
MDTN M24 .....88 A4
DTN/ASHW M34 .....146 A1
IRL M44 .....135 G5
Newby Rd BOLE BL2 .....35 F3
BRAM/HZG SK7 .....184 D2
HTNM SK4 .....12 A2
Newchurch OLDS OL8 .....104 D2
New Church Ct WHTF * M45 .....68 C5
New Church Rd BOL BL1 .....52 C4
New Church St RAD M26 .....67 E1
Newchurch St OP/CLY M11 .....114 C5
ROCH OL11 .....42 C1
New City Rd WALK M28 .....94 B2
Newcliffe Rd BKLY M9 .....87 G3
New Coin St ROY/SHW OL2 .....74 A1
New Colliers Rw BOL * BL1 .....32 C5
Newcombe Cl OP/CLY M11 .....114 C4
Newcombe Rd RAMS BL0 .....26 B3
Newcombe St CSLFD * M3 .....113 G2
Newcroft FAIL M35 .....105 G4
Newcroft Crs URM M41 .....139 E2
Newcroft Dr EDGY/DAV SK3 .....171 G5
URM M41 .....139 E2
Newcroft Rd URM M41 .....139 E2
New Cross St SLFD M6 .....110 D3
SWIN M27 .....97 F5
New Earth St MOSL OL5 .....108 C1
OLDE OL4 .....91 F2
New Elizabeth St CHH M8 .....100 B5
New Ellesmere Ap WALK M28 .....80 D5
New Elm Rd CSLFD M3 .....6 B5
New Field Cl MILN OL16 .....44 C2
RAD M26 .....66 D1
Newfield Head La MILN OL16 .....45 H5
Newfield Vw MILN OL16 .....45 H5
New Forest Rd NTHM/RTH M23 .....166 D1
Newgate MILN OL16 .....11 G6
Newgate Cottages WHTN * BL5 .....62 D3
Newgate Dr LHULT M38 .....80 A4
Newgate Rd SALE M33 .....153 E5
WILM/AE SK9 .....198 C3
Newgate St ANC M4 .....7 G4
New George St TOT/BURYW BL8 .....37 H3
Newhall Av BOLE BL2 .....51 E3
New Hall Av BRO M7 .....111 G1
ECC M30 .....122 D1
WYTH/NTH M22 .....181 G5
New Hall Cl SALE M33 .....155 G2
New Hall La BOL BL1 .....47 H1
New Hall Pl BOL BL1 .....47 H1
New Hall Rd BRO M7 .....99 E4
BURY BL9 .....39 F2
SALE * M33 .....155 G2
Newham Dr TOT/BURYW BL8 .....37 G5
New Haven Av OP/CLY M11 .....130 A1
Newhaven Av OP/CLY M11 .....130 A1
Newhaven Cl CHD/CHDH SK8 .....183 F2
TOT/BURYW BL8 .....26 B3
New Herbert St SLFD M6 .....97 H5
Newhey Av WYTH/NTH M22 .....168 C4

New Hey Rd CHD/CHDH SK8 .....170 D5
Newhey Rd MILN OL16 .....44 D2
WYTH/NTH M22 .....168 C5
New Heys Wy BOLE BL2 .....24 A5
New Holder St BOL BL1 .....2 C5
Newholme Gdns LHULT M38 .....80 D4
Newholme Rd DID/WITH M20 .....156 D1
Newhouse Cl WHIT OL12 .....19 H2
Newhouse Crs ROCH OL11 .....28 B3
Newhouse Rd HEY OL10 .....56 A1
New Houses OLDE OL4 .....76 D4
Newington Av CHH M8 .....86 A4
Newington Ct ALT WA14 .....177 E1
Newington Dr BOL * BL1 .....2 E1
TOT/BURYW BL8 .....52 B1
Newington Wk BOL * BL1 .....2 E1
New Islington ANC M4 .....113 H5
New Kings Head Yd CSLFD * M3 .....6 D2
Newland Dr WHTN BL5 .....62 C5
Newlands FAIL M35 .....115 H1
Newlands Av BOLE BL2 .....35 E5
BRAM/HZG SK7 .....183 H4
CHD/CHDH SK8 .....182 D5
ECC M30 .....108 C5
IRL M44 .....121 H2
WHIT OL12 .....19 E5
WHTF * M45 .....68 B5
Newlands Cl CHD/CHDH SK8 .....182 D5
CHAD OL9 .....89 A2
Newlands Dr DID/WITH M20 .....169 H1
PWCH M25 .....84 D2
SWIN M27 .....97 H4
Newlands Rd CHD/CHDH SK8 .....170 A3
ROY/SHW OL2 .....59 H3
Newland St CHH M8 .....100 C1
New La BOLE BL2 .....35 E5
ECC M30 .....109 E3
MDTN M24 .....71 H5
ROY/SHW OL2 .....59 H2
New Lane Ct BOLE * BL2 .....35 F4
New Lawns RDSH SK5 .....145 F2
Newlea Cl BOL BL1 .....33 F4
Newlee St AUL OL6 .....105 G5
New Lester Wy LHULT M38 .....79 D3
Newlyn Av STLY SK15 .....120 A2
Newlyn Dr BRAM/HZG SK7 .....185 E5
SALE M33 .....154 D5
Newlyn St RUSH/FAL M14 .....142 C1
Newman St AUL OL6 .....117 H3
HYDE SK14 .....132 D5
New Market CMANW M2 .....6 E5
Newmarket Cl SALE M33 .....153 E4
Newmarket Gv AULW OL7 .....104 D5
New Market La CMANW M2 .....6 E4
Newmarket Ms BOLS/LL BL3 .....65 H2
New Meadow HOR/BR BL6 .....46 D2
New Mill St LIT OL15 .....20 D3
New Moor La BRAM/HZG SK7 .....184 D2
New Mount St ANC * M4 .....7 G1
Newnham St BOL BL1 .....48 B1
New Park Rd ORD M5 .....126 A1
Newport Av RDSH SK5 .....144 D4
Newport Rd BOLS/LL BL3 .....64 D2
CCHDY M21 .....140 D2
DTN/ASHW M34 .....146 C5
Newport St BOL * BL1 .....2 E6
FWTH BL4 .....65 E5
MDTN M24 .....72 B4
OLDS OL8 .....90 B3
RAD M26 .....67 G2
WHIT OL12 .....14 A5
New Royd Av OLDE OL4 .....76 D4
Newry Rd ECC M30 .....109 H5
Newry St BOL BL1 .....33 G3
Newsham Cl BOLS/LL BL3 .....2 M7
Newsham Rd EDGY/DAV SK3 .....171 H5
Newsholme Cl WHTF M45 .....68 B2
Newsholme St CHH M8 .....100 B4
New Springs BOL * BL1 .....33 E8
Newstead OLDE OL4 .....92 D1
Newstead Av DID/WITH M20 .....157 E2
Newstead Cl POY/DIS SK12 .....195 E2
Newstead Dr BOLS/LL BL3 .....63 F3
Newstead Gv MPL/ROM SK6 .....161 G3
Newstead Rd URM M41 .....138 D1
Newstead Ter
HALE/TIMP WA15 .....166 A2
New St ALT WA14 .....165 F6
BOL BL1 .....1 G2
DROY M43 .....116 B5
ECC M30 .....108 B2
HYDE SK14 .....149 H3
LIT * OL15 .....20 D1
MILN OL16 .....31 G5
NEWH/MOS M40 .....114 B1
OLDE OL4 .....91 H1
RAD M26 .....52 D4
STLY SK15 .....119 G5
SWIN M27 .....97 E4
TOT/BURYW BL8 .....37 G2
UPML OL3 .....78 D3
WHTF M45 .....69 E4
WILM/AE SK9 .....198 D5
New Tempest Rd HOR/BR BL6 .....46 D5
New Ter SK14 .....147 H2
New Thomas St SLFD M6 .....111 H2
Newton Av DID/WITH M20 .....142 B5
WGTN/LGST M12 .....128 C4
Newton Dr TOT/BURYW BL8 .....36 B2
Newton Hall Ct HYDE SK14 .....132 C3
Newton Hall Rd HYDE SK14 .....132 C3
Newton Rd ALT WA14 .....165 H2
FAIL M35 .....102 D5
MDTN M24 .....70 C5
URM M41 .....138 B1

WILM/AE SK9 ....199 F1
Newton St AUL * OL6 ....118 B2
  BOL BL1 ....33 H4
  BURY BL9 ....27 G5
  CMANE M1 ....7 H4
  DROY M43 ....116 D2
  EDGY/DAV SK3 ....1 E6
  FAIL * M35 ....102 B4
  HYDE SK14 ....132 C4
  MILN OL16 ....43 F1
  STLY * SK15 ....119 E3
  STRET M32 ....140 A2
Newton Ter BOL * BL1 ....33 H4
Newton Wk BOL BL1 ....33 H4
Newton Wood Rd DUK SK16 ....132 A2
Newtown Av DTN/ASHW M34 ....146 C1
Newtown Cl OP/CLY M11 ....115 E5
  SWIN M27 ....85 E5
Newtown St PWCH M25 ....85 F3
  ROY/SHW OL2 ....60 A3
New Union St ANC M4 ....7 K3
New Vernon St BURY BL9 ....5 H3
New Viaduct St OP/CLY M11....114 B3
Newville Dr DID/WITH M20 ....158 A1
New Vine St HULME * M15 ....127 E2
New Wakefield St CMANE * M1 ....127 F1
New Way WHIT OL12 ....14 C4
New York BOLS/LL BL3 ....47 G5
New York St HEY OL10 ....40 C4
New Zealand Rd STKP SK1....13 K2
Neyland Cl BOL BL1 ....47 G2
Ney St AULW OL7 ....104 C4
Niagara St OFTN SK2 ....172 B3
Nicholas Cft ANC M4 ....7 H3
Nicholas Owen Cl OP/CLY M11 ....115 H5
Nicholas St BOLE BL2 ....3 H5
  CMANW M2 ....7 F5
Nicholls St SLFD * M6 ....111 H2
Nickleby Rd POY/DIS SK12 ....195 F6
Nicolas Rd CCHDY M21 ....140 D2
Nield Rd DTN/ASHW M34 ....131 G5
Nield's Brow ALT * WA14 ....177 F2
Nield St MOSL OL5 ....92 C5
Nigel Rd BKLY M9 ....101 G3
Nigher Moss Av MILN OL16 ....11 K7
Nightingale Cl WILM/AE SK9 ....199 G1
Nightingale Dr DTN/ASHW M34 ....116 D3
Nightingale Gdns
  NTHM/RTH M23 ....155 H5
Nile St BOLS/LL BL3 ....49 E4
  MILN OL16 ....11 F5
  OLD OL1 ....9 F1
Nile Ter BRO M7 ....99 G5
Nimble Nook CHAD OL9 ....8 B2
Nine Acre Dr NEWH/MOS M40 ....88 B4
Nine Acre Dr ORD M5 ....108 B6
Ninfield Rd NTHM/RTH M23 ....168 A5
Ninth Av OLDS OL8 ....104 A1
Nipper La WHIT M45 ....68 B5
Nisbet Av WYTH/NTH M22 ....180 D1
Niven St WGTN/LGST M12 ....7 J6
Nixon Rd BOLS/LL BL3 ....63 F1
Nixon Rd South BOLS/LL BL3 ....63 F1
Nixon St EDGY/DAV SK3 ....13 E6
  FAIL M35 ....102 D3
No 11 Pas DID/WITH * M20 ....157 E1
Noble Meadow WHIT * OL12 ....30 A4
Noble St BOLS/LL BL3 ....48 C3
  OLDS OL8 ....90 C3
Noel Dr SALE M33 ....155 E2
Noel St BOL BL1 ....2 D4
Nolan St BKLY M9 ....101 F2
Nona St SLFD M6 ....111 F5
The Nook ECC M30 ....108 D2
  URM M41 ....138 C2
Nook Farm Av WHIT OL12 ....19 E5
Nook Flds BOLE BL2 ....35 H4
Nook La AUL OL6 ....105 H3
Noon Sun St UPML OL3 ....93 H3
Noon Sun St WHIT OL12 ....10 C2
Norbet Wk BKLY M9 ....101 F3
Norbreck Av CCHDY M21 ....141 E4
  CHD/CHDH SK8 ....170 B4
Norbreck Gdns BOLE BL2 ....49 H1
Norbreck St BOLE BL2 ....49 H1
Norburn Rd BRUN/LGST M13 ....148 C1
Norbury Av MPL/ROM SK6 ....174 D3
  OLDE OL4 ....92 D1
  SALE M33 ....154 A2
  SLFD M6 ....98 A5
Norbury Cl NEWH/MOS * M40 ....116 C1
Norbury Crs BRAM/HZG SK7 ....185 E2
Norbury Dr MPL/ROM SK6 ....175 E3
Norbury Gv BRO M7 ....99 H2
  BRAM/HZG SK7 ....185 E2
  SWIN M27 ....97 E3
Norbury Hollow Rd
  BRAM/HZG SK7 ....186 A4
Norbury La OLDS OL8 ....91 G4
Norbury Ms MPL/ROM * SK6 ....174 D3
Norbury St BRO M7 ....99 H2
  MILN * OL16 ....43 G2
  STKP SK1 ....13 G4
Norcot Wk HULME * M15 ....126 C2
Norcross Cl OFTN SK2 ....173 E4
Nordale Pk WHIT OL12 ....59 E4
Nordek Cl ROY/SHW OL2 ....59 G4
Nordek Dr ROY/SHW OL2 ....59 G4
Norden Av DID/WITH M20 ....142 B5
Norden Ct BOLS/LL BL3 ....48 D5
Norden Rd HEY OL10 ....41 E1
Nordens Dr CHAD OL9 ....73 G1
Nordens Rd CHAD OL9 ....73 E4
Nordens St CHAD OL9 ....73 G2
Noreen Av PWCH M25 ....85 J2
Norfield Cl DUK SK16 ....118 B5
Norfolk Av DROY M43 ....116 A2
  DTN/ASHW M34 ....130 D5
  GTN * M18 ....131 E2
  HEY OL10 ....40 A4
  STKP SK1 ....13 G4
Norfolk Cl BOLS/LL BL3 ....51 E5
  IRL M44 ....150 A1
  LIT OL15 ....15 H3
  ROY/SHW OL2 ....59 G2

Norfolk Crs FAIL M35 ....102 D4
Norfolk Dr FWTH BL4 ....65 E3
Norfolk Gdns URM M41 ....122 A5
Norfolk Rd CTN M18 ....129 F4
Norfolk St CHAD OL9 ....89 G3
  CMANW M2 ....6 E4
  HYDE SK14 ....147 G1
  ROCH OL11 ....29 H5
  SLFD M6 ....98 D5
  WALK M28 ....81 E1
Norfolk Wy ROY/SHW OL2 ....74 A2
Norford Wy ROCH OL11 ....28 B4
Norgate St DID/WITH M20 ....157 G3
Norlan Av DTN/ASHW M34 ....131 F1
Norleigh Rd WYTH/NTH M22 ....168 C1
Norley Av STRET M32 ....125 G5
Norley Cl OLD OL1 ....75 G2
Norley Dr BNG/LEV M19 ....144 B1
Norman Av BRAM/HZG SK7 ....184 D1
  SALE M33 ....155 F3
Normanby Cha ALT WA14 ....165 E5
Normanby Gv WALK * M28 ....96 D1
Normanby Rd WALK M28 ....94 D1
Normanby St BOLS/LL BL3 ....63 E2
  RUSH/FAL M14 ....127 F4
  SWIN M27 ....96 D1
Norman Cl MDTN * M24 ....72 B3
Normandale Av BOL BL1 ....32 D5
Normandy Crs RAD M26 ....67 E1
Norman Gv RDSH SK5 ....144 D5
  WGTN/LGST * M12 ....128 D4
Norman Rd ALT WA14 ....165 F3
  AUL OL6 ....105 F4
  BRO * M7 ....99 H2
  HTNM SK4 ....159 E3
  ROCH OL11 ....29 G5
  RUSH/FAL M14 ....143 E1
  SALE M33 ....154 C2
  STLY SK15 ....119 E3
Norman Rd West BKLY * M9 ....101 G5
Norman's Pl ALT WA14 ....165 G5
Norman St BURY BL9 ....5 J1
  FAIL M35 ....8 D1
  HYDE SK14 ....147 H1
  MDTN M24 ....72 A3
  WGTN/LGST M12 ....129 E3
Normanton Av BOLS/LL * M5 ....110 D2
Normanton Dr BKLY M9 ....87 G1
Normanton Rd EDGY/DAV SK3 ....170 D2
Norman Weall Ct MDTN * M24 ....71 H2
Normington St OLDE * OL4 ....75 G5
Norreys Av URM M41 ....122 B5
Norreys St MILN OL16 ....10 D5
Norris Av HTNM SK4 ....12 A2
Norris Bank Ter HTNM SK4 ....12 A3
Norris Hill Dr HTNM SK4 ....12 A3
Norris Rd SALE M33 ....154 D4
Norris St BOLS/LL BL3 ....48 D4
  BOLS/LL BL3 ....65 H1
  FWTH BL3 ....64 D5
Northampton Rd
  NEWH/MOS M40 ....101 H4
North Av BNG/LEV M19 ....143 G4
  BURY BL9 ....54 A5
  FWTH BL4 ....66 A4
  STLY SK15 ....119 F2
  TOT/BURYW BL8 ....26 A1
  URM M41 ....123 H4
North Back Rock BURY BL9 ....4 C3
Northbank Gdns BNG/LEV M19 ....143 F5
North Blackfield La BRO M7 ....99 F2
Northbrook Av CHH M8 ....86 A3
North Broughton St CSLFD M3 ....6 D5
North Cir WHIT M45 ....62 D6
North Clifden La BRO M7 ....99 H4
Northcliffe Rd OFTN SK2 ....172 D1
Northcombe Rd EDGY/DAV SK3 ....171 H4
Northcote Rd BRAM/HZG SK7 ....184 A5
North Crs NEWH/MOS M40 ....88 C4
  OP/CLY M11 ....115 G2
North Cft OLDS OL8 ....90 C2
North Dean St SWIN M27 ....97 F1
Northdene Dr ROCH OL11 ....28 C5
North Dr HULME M15 ....126 C2
  SWIN M27 ....97 H3
North Downs Rd
  CHD/CHDH SK8 ....182 C1
Northdowns Rd ROY/SHW OL2 ....59 G1
Northen Gv DID/WITH M20 ....156 D4
  SWIN M27 ....97 G3
Northenden Rd CHD/CHDH SK8 ....169 F3
  SALE M33 ....154 D2
Northend Rd STLY SK15 ....119 G3
Northern Av SWIN M27 ....97 F1
Northern Gv BOL BL1 ....33 F5
Northern Service Rd
  NTHM/RTH * M23 ....167 G4
Northfield Av NEWH/MOS M40 ....89 E3
Northfield Dr WILM/AE SK9 ....200 A2
Northfield Rd BOLS/LL BL3 ....48 B4
Northfleet Rd ECC M30 ....104 A4
North Ga OLDS OL8 ....90 B4
Northgate WHIT OL12 ....18 B1
Northgate La OLD OL1 ....75 H1
Northgate Rd EDGY/DAV SK3 ....12 A5
North George St CSLFD M3 ....6 B2
North Gv BRUN/LGST M13 ....128 A3
  URM M41 ....138 B2
North Harvey St STKP SK1 ....13 H1
North Hill St CSLFD M3 ....6 A1
North La WHIT OL12 ....10 D4
Northlands RAD M26 ....53 E5
Northleach Cl TOT/BURYW BL8 ....37 F3
Northleigh Dr PWCH * M25 ....85 J3
Northleigh Rd OLDTF/WHR M16 ....126 A5
North Lonsdale St STRET M32 ....125 G6
North Nook OLDE OL4 ....76 A4
Northolme Gdns BNG/LEV M19 ....158 B2
Northolt Cl OP/CLY * M11 ....115 E3
Northolt Ct OP/CLY * M11 ....115 E3
Northolt Dr BOLS/LL BL3 ....49 E5
Northolt Rd NTHM/RTH M23 ....155 G5
North Pde CSLFD M3 ....6 D4

MILN OL16 ....45 F2
SALE M33 ....155 F2
North Park Rd BRAM/HZG SK7 ....184 D1
North Phoebe St ORD M5 ....112 A5
North Pl STKP SK1 ....13 G3
Northridge Rd BKLY M9 ....87 E1
North Rd DTN/ASHW M34 ....117 E4
  HALE/TIMP WA15 ....178 B4
  MANAIR M90 ....190 B1
  OP/CLY M11 ....115 F5
  PART M31 ....152 A2
  PWCH M25 ....84 C2
  STRET M32 ....124 C4
Northside Av URM M41 ....137 G2
North Star Dr CSLFD M3 ....6 A4
Northstead Av DTN/ASHW M34 ....147 E1
North St AUL OL6 ....117 H3
  CHH M8 ....100 D5
  HEY OL10 ....40 C4
  MDTN M24 ....71 H2
  RAD M26 ....52 D5
  ROY/SHW OL2 ....74 A1
  WHIT OL12 ....14 B4
Northumberland Av AULW OL7 ....118 A1
Northumberland Cl
  OLDTF/WHR * M16 ....126 B3
Northumberland Crs
  OLDTF/WHR * M16 ....126 B3
Northumberland Rd
  OLDTF/WHR M16 ....126 B3
  PART M31 ....152 B2
  RDSH SK5 ....145 G5
Northumberland St BRO M7 ....99 G3
Northumbria St BOLS/LL BL3 ....48 B4
Northurst Dr CHH M8 ....86 A4
North Vale Rd
  HALE/TIMP WA15 ....166 A3
North Veiw WHIT M45 ....10 E4
North View Rd OLDE OL4 ....92 D2
Northward Rd WILM/AE SK9 ....199 E4
Northway DROY M43 ....116 B5
  HYDE SK14 ....147 H1
  RDSH SK5 ....145 H5
North Western St
  BNG/LEV M19 ....143 J1
  CMANE M1 ....7 K6
  WGTN/LGST M12 ....113 H5
Northwold Dr BKLY M9 ....88 A1
  BOL BL1 ....47 F1
Northwood BOLE BL2 ....35 E2
Northwood Av NEWH/MOS M40 ....89 H2
Northwood Crs BOLS/LL * BL3 ....48 B4
Northwood Gv SALE M33 ....154 C2
North Zetland Dr BOLS/LL BL3 ....63 E2
Norton Av DTN/ASHW M34 ....155 G1
  URM M41 ....123 G4
  WGTN/LGST M12 ....129 E5
Norton Gra PWCH M25 ....85 G4
Norton Rd WHIT OL12 ....19 E5
Norton St BOL BL1 ....34 A3
  BRO M7 ....99 G5
  CMANE M1 ....115 H5
  CSLFD M3 ....6 D2
  NEWH/MOS M40 ....114 B1
Norview Dr DID/WITH M20 ....169 G4
Norville Av NEWH/MOS M40 ....88 C4
Norway Gv RDSH * SK5 ....53 G4
Norway St BOL BL1 ....48 A2
  OP/CLY M11 ....114 D4
  SLFD M6 ....111 F3
  STRET M32 ....125 F5
Norwell Rd WYTH/NTH M22 ....180 C3
Norwich Av CHAD OL9 ....73 F3
  DTN/ASHW M34 ....146 C2
  DUK SK16 ....119 H3
Norwich Dr TOT/BURYW BL8 ....4 C2
Norwich Rd STRET M32 ....124 A3
Norwich St ROCH OL11 ....43 F1
Norwick Cl BOLS/LL BL3 ....47 F5
Norwood PWCH M25 ....85 J3
Norwood Av BRAM/HZG SK7 ....193 F2
  BRO M7 ....99 G2
  DID/WITH M20 ....158 A2
  MPL/ROM SK6 ....186 C5
Norwood Cl ROY/SHW OL2 ....59 H1
  WALK M28 ....95 F2
Norwood Crs ROY/SHW OL2 ....74 B2
Norwood Dr HALE/TIMP WA15 ....178 A4
  SWIN M27 ....96 B5
Norwood Gv BOL * BL1 ....33 H3
Norwood Rd CHD/CHDH SK8 ....169 G3
  OFTN SK2 ....172 C5
  STRET M32 ....140 B2
Nottingham Av RDSH SK5 ....145 H5
Nottingham Cl RDSH SK5 ....145 H5
Nottingham Dr AUL OL6 ....105 J3
  BOL BL1 ....34 A2
  FAIL M35 ....103 G4
  RDSH SK5 ....145 H5
Nowell Rd MDTN M24 ....71 H1
Nudger Cl UPML OL3 ....77 H2
Nudger Gn UPML OL3 ....77 H2
Nuffield Rd WYTH/NTH M22 ....168 D5
Nugent Rd BOLS/LL BL3 ....63 E1
Nugget St OLDE * OL4 ....91 E1
Nuneaton Dr NEWH/MOS M40 ....114 A2
Nuneham Av DID/WITH M20 ....142 D4
Nunfield Cl NEWH/MOS M40 ....88 C3
Nunnery Rd BOLS/LL BL3 ....48 A5
Nunthorpe Dr CHH M8 ....100 B3
Nursery Av HALE/TIMP WA15 ....177 H4
Nursery Cl OFTN SK2 ....172 C3
  SALE M33 ....153 H2
Nursery Dr POY/DIS SK12 ....195 G3
Nursery Gv PART M31 ....151 E2
Nursery La EDGY/DAV SK3 ....170 D2
  WILM/AE SK9 ....199 G5
Nursery Rd CHD/CHDH SK8 ....182 C5
  FAIL M35 ....103 G3
  HTNM SK4 ....158 D1
  PWCH M25 ....84 D1
  SALE M33 ....154 A4
  URM M41 ....123 H5
Nursery St OLDTF/WHR M16 ....127 E5
  SLFD M6 ....111 G1
Nuthatch Av WALK M28 ....95 J2
Nuthurst Rd NEWH/MOS M40 ....88 D1
Nutsford V WGTN/LGST M12 ....128 D2

Nuttall Av BOLS/LL BL3 ....66 B1
  WHTF M45 ....68 C3
Nuttall Cl RAMS BL0 ....16 D5
Nuttall Hall Rd RAMS BL0 ....17 E4
Nuttall Ms WHTF M45 ....68 C4
Nuttall Rd RAMS BL0 ....17 E4
Nuttall St BURY BL9 ....5 G6
  IRL M44 ....135 D5
  OLDS * OL8 ....91 E3
  OLDTF/WHR M16 ....126 B3
  OP/CLY M11 ....128 D1
Nutt La PWCH M25 ....69 H4

O

Oadby Cl WGTN/LGST M12 ....128 D4
Oak Av BOLS/LL BL3 ....66 A1
  CCHDY M21 ....141 E5
  CHD/CHDH SK8 ....170 D4
  GTN M18 ....130 A4
  IRL M44 ....159 E4
  ILK M44 ....150 C1
  MDTN M24 ....71 H5
  MPL/ROM SK6 ....162 B4
  RAMS BL0 ....26 B1
  SALE M33 ....155 G2
  WHTF M45 ....69 E3
  WILM/AE SK9 ....199 H1
Oak Bank BKLY M9 ....101 G2
  PWCH M25 ....98 C1
Oak Bank Av BKLY M9 ....100 C1
Oakbank Av CHAD OL9 ....72 D4
Oak Bank Cl WHTF M45 ....69 E4
Oakbank Dr BOL BL1 ....22 C5
Oakbarton HOR/BR BL6 ....46 A5
Oakcliffe Rd WHIT OL12 ....19 H3
Oak Cl HYDE SK14 ....134 D4
  WHIT OL12 ....14 C1
  WILM/AE SK9 ....199 E4
Oak Coppice BOL BL1 ....47 H2
Oakcroft STLY SK15 ....134 B1
Oakdale BOLE BL2 ....35 E2
Oakdale Cl WHTF M45 ....68 D2
Oakdale Ct UPML OL3 ....77 F1
Oakdale Dr CHD/CHDH SK8 ....181 G2
  DID/WITH M20 ....157 H5
Oakdene SWIN M27 ....96 A4
Oakdene Av CHD/CHDH SK8 ....181 G5
  HTNM SK4 ....159 G3
Oakdene Crs MPL/ROM SK6 ....175 E3
Oakdene Gdns MPL/ROM SK6 ....175 E3
Oakdene Rd HALE/TIMP WA15 ....178 A4
  MPL/ROM SK6 ....175 E3
Oakdene St NEWH/MOS M40 ....101 G2
Oak Dr BRAM/HZG SK7 ....183 F5
  DTN/ASHW M34 ....146 A4
  MPL/ROM SK6 ....174 C3
  RUSH/FAL M14 ....143 E1
Oaken Bank Rd MDTN M24 ....56 C3
Oakenbottom Rd BOLE BL2 ....34 D3
Oaken Clough AULW OL7 ....104 A4
Oakenclough Cl WILM/AE SK9 ....192 A5
Oaken Clough Dr AULW OL7 ....104 A4
Oakenclough Rd WILM/AE SK9 ....192 A5
Oakenden Rd RUSH/FAL * M14 ....127 G5
Oakenshaw Av WHIT OL12 ....18 B2
Oakenshaw Vw WHIT OL12 ....18 B2
Oaker Av DID/WITH M20 ....156 D2
Oakes St FWTH BL4 ....65 H2
Oakfield DUK SK16 ....132 D2
  PWCH M25 ....85 J2
  SALE M33 ....154 B1
Oakfield Av CHD/CHDH SK8 ....170 D3
  DROY M43 ....116 C4
  OLDTF/WHR M16 ....125 J4
  WILM/AE SK9 ....200 A3
Oakfield Cl BRAM/HZG SK7 ....195 H5
  WILM/AE SK9 ....200 A3
Oakfield Dr LHULT M38 ....80 D2
Oakfield Gv FWTH BL4 ....66 A3
  GTN M18 ....129 G4
Oakfield Rd DID/WITH M20 ....157 E4
  EDGY/DAV SK3 ....170 D5
  HALE/TIMP WA15 ....165 H4
  HYDE SK14 ....134 D4
  POY/DIS SK12 ....195 G5
  URM M41 ....138 D2
Oakfield St CHH M8 ....100 C2
  HALE/TIMP WA15 ....165 H4
Oakfield Ter ROCH OL11 ....42 B6
Oakford Av NEWH/MOS M40 ....113 H2
Oakford Wk BOLS/LL * BL3 ....48 B5
Oak Gates EDGW/EG BL7 ....22 D1
Oak Gv AUL OL6 ....107 G3
  CHD/CHDH SK8 ....170 D4
  ECC M30 ....110 A1
  POY/DIS SK12 ....195 G4
  URM M41 ....138 C2
Oaklands WALK M28 ....95 E2
Oaklands Av CHD/CHDH SK8 ....182 D2
  MPL/ROM SK6 ....161 J1
Oaklands Dene HYDE SK14 ....148 B1
Oaklands Dr BRAM/HZG SK7 ....193 F1
  PWCH M25 ....85 F3
  ROCH OL11 ....42 D6
  SWIN M27 ....96 A4
Oaklands Pk OLDE OL4 ....77 F4
Oaklands Rd BRO M7 ....99 E1

  SWIN M27 ....96 B4
Oak La WHTF M45 ....69 E4
  SK9 ....199 E4
Oak Lea Av WILM/AE SK9 ....199 F5
Oaklea Rd SALE M33 ....153 D5
Oakleigh Av BNG/LEV M19 ....143 G4
  BOLS/LL BL3 ....64 B2
Oakleigh Cl HEY OL10 ....166 B2
Oakleigh Rd CHD/CHDH SK8 ....182 B4
Oakleigh Wk NEWH/MOS M40 ....102 B5
  RAD M26 ....67 H4
Oakley Pk BOL BL1 ....47 G5
Oakley St ORD M5 ....111 E4
Oakley Vls HTNM SK4 ....159 E3
Oak Ldg BRAM/HZG * SK7 ....184 A5
Oakmere Av ECC M30 ....109 F1
Oakmere Cl WYTH/NTH SK4 ....168 C5
Oakmere Rd CHD/CHDH SK8 ....170 C5
  WILM/AE SK9 ....192 A2
Oaks Av BOLE BL2 ....34 C2
The Oaks CHD/CHDH SK8 ....181 F2
  HYDE SK14 ....133 F5
Oaks Av BOLE BL2 ....34 C2
Oak Shaw Cl BKLY M9 ....87 F4
Oakshaw Dr WHIT OL12 ....28 D2
Oaks La BOL BL1 ....34 C1
Oak St ANC M4 ....7 G3
  BRAM/HZG SK7 ....185 E1
  DTN/ASHW M34 ....132 C1
  ECC M30 ....109 G4
  EDGY/DAV SK3 ....171 E1
  HEY OL10 ....40 C3
  HYDE SK14 ....132 D4
  LIT OL15 ....21 F1
  MDTN * M24 ....72 C5
  MILN OL16 ....10 C7
  OLD OL1 ....9 G4
  RAMS * BL0 ....16 C5
  ROY/SHW OL2 ....60 B3
  SWIN M27 ....97 F1
Oak Ter LIT OL15 ....5 H3
Oak Tree Cl CHD/CHDH SK8 ....170 A3
Oak Tree Crs STLY SK15 ....133 E1
Oak Tree Dr DUK SK16 ....133 E1
Oakville Dr SLFD M6 ....110 B1
Oakville Ter NEWH/MOS M40 ....101 G1
Oakway DID/WITH M20 ....169 H1
  MDTN M24 ....73 H3
Oakwell Dr BURY BL9 ....69 E1
  CHH M8 ....99 H4
Oakwood WALK M28 ....79 H1
Oakwood Av ALT WA14 ....177 E4
  DROY M43 ....117 J3
  NEWH/MOS M40 ....102 C1
Oakworth Cft OLDE OL4 ....61 G5
Oakworth Dr BOL BL1 ....33 G1
Oakworth St BKLY M9 ....86 D4
Oatlands WILM/AE SK9 ....198 D2
Oatlands Rd WYTH/NTH M22 ....180 D2
Oat St STKP SK1 ....13 J7
Oban Av NEWH/MOS M40 ....115 E1
  OLD OL1 ....75 E3
Oban Crs EDGY/DAV SK3 ....170 B5
Oban Dr SALE M33 ....155 E3
Oban Gv BOL BL1 ....33 G1
Oban St BOL * BL1 ....33 G3
Oberlin St CHAD OL9 ....90 C2
  ROCH OL11 ....42 C1
Occlestone Cl SALE M33 ....155 F1
Occupiers La BRAM/HZG SK7 ....186 A5
Ocean St ALT WA14 ....165 E5
Ockendon Dr BKLY M9 ....101 F3
Octagon Ct BOL * BL1 ....2 E6
Octavia Dr NEWH/MOS M40 ....115 F1
Odell St OP/CLY * M11 ....129 E1
Odessa Av SLFD M6 ....97 G6
Odette St GTN M18 ....129 J3
Offerton Dr OFTN SK2 ....173 E2
Offerton Fold OFTN SK2 ....172 D2
Offerton Gn OFTN SK2 ....173 E3
Offerton La OFTN SK2 ....172 D2
Offerton Rd BRAM/HZG SK7 ....185 H1
  OFTN SK2 ....173 H5
Offerton St STKP SK1 ....160 C4
Off Green St STLY * SK15 ....120 A3
Off Ridge Hill La STLY * SK15 ....120 A3
Off Stamford St STLY * SK15 ....120 A3
Ogbourne Wk BRUN/LGST M13 ....127 H2
Ogden Cl HEY OL10 ....40 D3
Ogden La DUK SK16 ....45 G1
  OP/CLY M11 ....130 B1
Ogden Rd BRAM/HZG * SK7 ....184 D1
  FAIL M35 ....103 G4
Ogden St CHAD OL9 ....90 A3
  DID/WITH M20 ....157 E2
  MDTN * M24 ....72 C5
  OLDE * OL4 ....9 J5
  PWCH M25 ....85 F3
  ROCH OL11 ....43 G4
  SWIN M27 ....97 F1
Ogden Dr PWCH M25 ....85 F3
Ohio Av SALFD M6 ....111 G5
Okehampton Cl RAD M26 ....51 F4
Okehampton Crs SALE M33 ....153 G1

Okeover Rd BRO M7 99 G2
Olaf St BOLE BL2 3 J1
Old Bank Cl MPL/ROM SK6 161 H3
Old Bank St CMANW M2 6 E4
Old Bank Vw OLD OL1 60 B5
Old Barn Pl EDGW/EG BL7 23 F3
Old Barton Rd TRPK M17 123 F1
Old Bent La WHIT OL12 19 F1
Old Birley St HULME M15 127 E3
Old Broadway DID/WITH M20 157 G1
Old Brook Cl ROY/SHW OL2 60 C1
Oldbrook Fold
HALE/TIMP WA15 166 C5
Old Brow MOSL OL5 106 D2
Old Brow La MILN OL16 19 H5
Old Brown Ct MOSL OL5 106 D2
Oldbury Cl HEY OL10 56 A2
NEWH/MOS M40 114 A2
Oldcastle Av DID/WITH M20 142 B4
Old Chapel St EDGY/DAV SK3 12 B7
Old Church Ms DUK SK16 118 D5
Old Church St NEWH/MOS M40 102 A4
OLD OL1 9 H3
Old Clay Dr WHIT OL12 20 A4
Old Clough La WALK M28 95 G2
Old Colliers Rw BOL * BL1 32 B1
Oldcott Cl WALK M28 94 A5
The Old Ctyd WYTH/NTH * M22 169 E4
Old Cft OLDE OL4 92 B1
Old Croft Ms STKP SK1 172 C2
Old Crofts Bank URM M41 123 F4
Old Cross St AUL * OL6 118 B2
Old Dairy Ms HYDE SK14 132 B3
Old Delph Rd ROCH OL11 28 B2
Old Doctors St TOT/BURYW BL8 26 A4
Old Eagley Ms BOL BL1 23 E5
Old Edge La ROY/SHW OL2 74 B2
Old Elm St BRUN/LGST * M13 127 H2
Oldershaw Dr BKLY M9 101 E4
Old Farm Crs DROY M43 116 A5
Old Farm Dr OFTN SK2 173 G3
Oldfield Dr HALE/TIMP WA15 166 A3
Oldfield Gv SALE M33 154 D1
Oldfield Rd ALT WA14 164 D4
ORD M5 126 B1
PWCH M25 69 F5
SALE M33 154 D1
Oldfield St OP/CLY M11 115 E4
The Old Gdn HALE/TIMP WA15 166 C2
Old Gardens St STKP SK1 13 H5
Oldgate Wk HULME * M15 126 C2
Old Gn BOLE BL2 24 B5
Old Ground St RAMS * BL0 16 D2
Old Hall Cl TOT/BURYW BL8 26 C4
Old Hall Clough HOR/BR BL6 46 D2
Old Hall Crs WILM/AE SK9 192 B4
Old Hall Dr GTN M18 129 G4
OFTN SK2 173 F3
Old Hall La BRUN/LGST M13 143 F1
HYDE SK14 134 D3
MPL/ROM SK6 175 H4
PWCH M25 70 A5
WALK M28 95 F3
WHTF M45 83 H1
Old Hall Rd BRO M7 99 G2
CHD/CHDH SK8 169 F3
NEWH/MOS M40 102 A3
SALE M33 155 F2
STRET M32 124 B4
WHTF M45 67 H5
Old Hall St DUK SK16 131 H1
FWTH BL4 65 F5
MDTN M24 71 H4
OP/CLY * M11 129 H1
Old Hall St North BOL BL1 2 E4
Oldham Av STKP SK1 160 C5
Oldham Dr MPL/ROM SK6 161 H2
Oldham Rd ANC M4 7 J2
AULW OL7 104 D4
AULW OL7 117 H2
FAIL M35 102 D3
MDTN M24 71 G4
MILN OL16 10 D7
NEWH/MOS M40 101 G5
NEWH/MOS M40 113 H2
OLDE OL4 77 E3
OLDE OL4 92 B1
OLDE OL4 93 G1
ROCH OL11 58 C1
ROY/SHW OL2 60 A5
UPML OL3 61 F3
Oldhams La BOL BL1 33 G1
Oldham St CMANE M1 7 G4
DROY M43 116 C3
DTN/ASHW M34 145 H1
HYDE SK14 147 G1
ORD M5 112 C4
RDSH * SK5 144 D4
Oldham Wy CHAD OL9 8 D2
MILN OL16 44 C5
OLDE OL4 93 E2
OLDS OL8 8 E5
Old Kiln La BOL BL1 32 A4
OLDE OL4 92 C3
Oldknow Rd MPL/ROM SK6 175 F3
Old La BURY BL9 27 G3
CHAD OL9 89 G3
LHULT M38 80 A1
OLDE OL4 76 A4
OLDE OL4 93 F1
OP/CLY M11 129 G1
UPML OL3 78 A2
Old Lansdowne Rd
DID/WITH M20 157 E2
Old Lees St AUL OL6 105 G5
Old Malt La DID/WITH M20 142 B4
Old Market Pl ALT WA14 165 G4
Old Market St BKLY M9 86 D5
Old Meadow Dr
DTN/ASHW M34 131 G3
Old Meadow La
HALE/TIMP WA15 178 C1
Old Medlock St CSLFD * M3 6 A6
Old Mill Cl SWIN M27 97 G2
Old Mill La BRAM/HZG SK7 185 H4
OLDE OL4 92 B2
Old Mills Hl MDTN M24 72 C3
Old Mill St ANC M4 113 H4
Oldmill St WHIT OL12 10 C4
Old Moat La DID/WITH M20 142 C5
Oldmoor Rd MPL/ROM SK6 161 F1
Old Mount St ANC M4 7 G1
Old Nans La BOLE BL2 35 G4
Old Nursery Fold BOLE BL2 35 F2
The Old Orch HALE/TIMP WA15 166 C1
Old Oak Cl BOLE BL2 51 E4
Old Oak Dr DTN/ASHW M34 131 H5
Old Oake Cl WALK * M28 81 F5
Old Oak St DID/WITH M20 157 G3
Old Orch WILM/AE SK9 199 F3
Old Park La TRPK M17 123 F2
Old Parrin La ECC M30 109 E2
Old Pasture Cl OFTN SK2 173 F2
Old Quarry La EDGW/EG BL7 23 E2
Old Rectory Gdns
CHD/CHDH SK8 170 A4
Old River Cl IRL M44 136 B1
Old Rd AUL OL6 106 A5
BKLY M9 87 E5
BOL BL1 33 H3
CHD/CHDH SK8 170 C3
DUK SK16 118 B5
FAIL M35 102 D3
HTNM SK4 159 H3
HYDE SK14 132 C4
HYDE SK14 134 C3
MILN OL16 20 B4
STLY SK15 119 H5
WILM/AE SK9 192 A4
WILM/AE SK9 199 G2
Old School Dr BKLY * M9 86 D5
Old School Ms DUK * SK16 118 D5
Old Shaw St ORD * M5 111 H5
Old Station St ECC M30 109 F4
Oldstead Gv BOLS/LL BL3 47 G5
Old St AUL OL6 117 H3
HYDE SK14 149 H3
OLDE OL4 91 G2
STLY SK15 119 F3
Old Swan Cl EDGW/EG * BL7 22 D1
Old Towns Cl TOT/BURYW BL8 26 A4
Old Vicarage Gdns WALK M28 81 E4
Old Wellington Rd ECC M30 109 H3
Old Wells Cl LHULT M38 80 B1
Oldwood Rd NTHM/RTH M23 179 H1
Old Wool La CHD/CHDH SK8 170 C5
Old York St HULME M15 126 D2
Olebrook Cl WGTN/LGST M12 128 A2
Oleo Ter IRL M44 121 D5
Olga St BOL BL1 33 G4
Olga Ter BKLY * M9 87 E5
Olivant St BURY BL9 53 F1
Olive Bank TOT/BURYW BL8 37 G2
Oliver Cl LIT OL15 20 C3
Olive Rd HALE/TIMP WA15 166 B1
Oliver St EDGY/DAV SK3 13 G6
OP/CLY * M11 114 C5
Olive Shapley Av
DID/WITH M20 157 G3
Olive St BOLS/LL BL3 48 C5
FAIL M35 102 D2
HEY OL10 41 F4
RAD M26 67 H1
ROCH * OL11 42 B5
TOT/BURYW BL8 4 A4
Olivia Gv RUSH/FAL M14 128 A5
Ollerbarrow Rd
HALE/TIMP WA15 177 H2
Ollerbrook Ct BOL BL1 34 A4
Ollerton WHIT OL12 10 B5
Ollerton Av SALE M33 153 G1
Ollerton Rd WILM/AE SK9 192 A2
Ollerton St BOL BL1 23 E5
Ollier Av WGTN/LGST M12 143 H1
Olney ROCH * OL11 29 H5
Olney Av WYTH/NTH M22 168 C3
Olney St BRUN/LGST M13 128 A4
Olsberg Cl RAD M26 52 D5
Olwen Crs RDSH SK5 145 E3
Olympic Ct SALQ M50 111 G5
Omer Av BRUN/LGST M13 143 G1
Omer Dr BNG/LEV M19 143 F4
Onchan Av OLDE OL4 91 E1
One Ash Cl WHIT OL12 10 C1
One Oak La WILM/AE SK9 200 C3
Onslow Av NEWH/MOS M40 102 D1
Onslow Cl OLD OL1 8 E1
Onslow Rd EDGY/DAV SK3 12 A6
Onslow St ROCH OL11 42 B2
Onward St HYDE SK14 147 G1
Oozewood Rd ROY/SHW OL2 58 B4
Opal Ct RUSH/FAL * M14 143 E3
Opal St BNG/LEV M19 144 A3
Openshaw Fold Rd BURY BL9 53 E2
Openshaw La IRL M44 135 D5
Openshaw Pl FWTH BL4 64 C4
Openshaw St BURY BL9 5 G6
Orama Av SLFD M6 110 B1
Orama Ml WHIT * OL12 14 B5
Oram St BURY BL9 38 D2
Orange Hill Rd PWCH M25 85 F2
Orange St SLFD M6 111 H2
Orbital Wy DTN/ASHW M34 131 E5
The Orchard URM M41 138 B2
Orchard Av BOL BL1 34 A3
GTN M18 129 H4
PART M31 151 E2
WALK M28 94 C3
Orchard Cl CHD/CHDH SK8 183 F5
POY/DIS SK12 195 F4
WILM/AE SK9 199 E5
Orchard Ct OFTN * SK2 173 E3
Orchard Dr HALE/TIMP WA15 178 B1
WILM/AE SK9 192 B4
Orchard Gdns BOLE BL2 35 G3
Orchard Gn WILM/AE SK9 201 C4
Orchard Gv DID/WITH M20 157 E1
ROY/SHW OL2 59 H2
Orchard Pl HALE/TIMP WA15 166 C2
POY/DIS * SK12 195 E3
SALE M33 154 C1
Orchard Ri HYDE SK14 148 A3
Orchard Rd FAIL M35 103 E3
HALE/TIMP WA15 165 H4
MPL/ROM SK6 163 G4
Orchard Rd East
WYTH/NTH M22 156 C4
Orchard Rd West
WYTH/NTH M22 156 C4
Orchard St DID/WITH M20 157 E1
HEY OL10 41 F3
HYDE SK14 147 H1
SLFD M6 98 D5
STKP SK1 13 H3
Orchard V EDGY/DAV SK3 171 F3
Orchid Av FWTH BL4 64 C3
Orchid Cl IRL M44 135 D3
OLD OL1 74 A3
Orchid Dr BURY BL9 53 H1
Orchid St BKLY M9 101 E3
Ordsall Av LHULT M38 80 C3
Ordsall Dr ORD M5 126 A1
Ordsall La ORD M5 112 C5
ORD M5 125 H2
Oregon Av OLD OL1 74 B3
Oregon Cl BRUN/LGST M13 127 H2
Orford Cl MPL/ROM SK6 186 D5
Orford Rd NEWH/MOS M40 102 B5
PWCH M25 84 D2
Oriel Av OLDS OL8 90 B4
Oriel Cl CHAD OL9 89 F3
OFTN SK2 172 C3
Oriel Rd DID/WITH M20 157 F2
Oriel St BOLS/LL BL3 48 B4
ROCH OL11 43 E1
Orient Rd SLFD M6 110 B1
Orient St BRO M7 100 A3
Oriole Cl WALK M28 94 C3
Oriole Dr WALK M28 94 C2
Orion Pl BRO * M7 112 B1
Orkney Cl NTHM/RTH M23 167 H5
RAD M26 52 C5
Orkney Dr URM M41 123 G3
Orlanda Av SLFD M6 110 B1
Orlanda Dr BRO M7 100 A4
Orlando St BOLS/LL BL3 49 F4
Orleans Wy OLD OL1 9 F2
Orley Wk OLD OL1 60 C5
Orme Av MDTN M24 71 H5
SLFD M6 97 H5
Orme Cl OP/CLY M11 114 B4
URM M41 139 E1
Ormerod Av ROY/SHW OL2 74 B1
Ormerod Cl MPL/ROM SK6 161 G5
Ormerod St HEY OL10 41 F5
Orme St OLDE OL4 9 J6
STKP * SK1 160 C4
WILM/AE SK9 201 B4
Ormonde Av SLFD M6 110 C1
Ormonde Ct AUL OL6 118 B1
Ormond St BOLS/LL BL3 50 A4
BURY BL9 5 G3
Ormrod St BOL BL1 2 D6
BOLE BL2 34 D1
BURY BL9 5 H5
FWTH BL4 64 D4
Ormsby Av GTN M18 129 E4
Ormsby Cl EDGY/DAV SK3 171 H5
Ormsgill Cl HULME M15 127 E2
Orms Gill Pl OFTN * SK2 173 F3
Ormsgill St HULME M15 127 E2
Ormskirk Av DID/WITH M20 142 A5
Ormskirk Cl TOT/BURYW BL8 52 A1
Ormskirk Rd RDSH SK5 145 E5
Ornatus St BOL * BL1 34 A1
Orphanage St HTNM SK4 159 H3
Orpington Dr TOT/BURYW BL8 37 G5
Orpington Rd BKLY M9 101 F3
Orrell St OP/CLY * M11 115 G5
TOT/BURYW BL8 37 H3
Orrel St SLFD M6 111 F3
Orrishmere Rd CHD/CHDH SK8 182 C1
Orron St LIT OL15 20 D3
Orsett Cl NEWH/MOS M40 113 H2
Orthes Gv HTNM SK4 159 G1
Orton Av NTHM/RTH M23 155 H5
Orton Rd NTHM/RTH M23 155 H5
Orvietto Av SLFD M6 110 B1
Orville Dr BNG/LEV M19 143 G4
Orwell Av DTN/ASHW M34 130 B5
WYTH/NTH M22 168 C3
Orwell Cl TOT/BURYW BL8 4 B2
WILM/AE SK9 192 A5
Orwell Rd BOL BL1 33 E4
Osborne Cl TOT/BURYW BL8 52 C1
Osborne Dr SWIN M27 97 H3
Osborne Gv BOL BL1 33 F5
CHD/CHDH SK8 181 F1
Osborne Rd BKLY * M9 101 F3
BNG/LEV M19 143 G2
DTN/ASHW M34 131 G4
HALE/TIMP WA15 165 H4
HYDE SK14 147 H2
OFTN SK2 172 A2
OLDS OL8 8 C7
SLFD * M6 110 B2
Osborne St CHAD OL9 8 B1
HEY OL10 41 E5
MPL/ROM SK6 160 D3
NEWH/MOS M40 113 H1
ROCH OL11 42 D1
ROY/SHW OL2 60 A3
SLFD M6 111 G2
Osborne Ter SALE M33 154 C2
Osbourne Cl FWTH BL4 65 E3
WILM/AE SK9 200 A4
Osbourne Pl ALT WA14 165 G5
Osbourne St DID/WITH M20 157 F3
Oscar St BOL * BL1 33 F4
NEWH/MOS M40 101 H3
Oscott Av LHULT M38 80 B2
Oscroft Cl CHH M8 100 A4
Osmond St OLDE OL4 75 F5
Osmund Av BOLE BL2 50 A2
Osprey Cl DUK SK16 132 D1
HULME M15 126 D3
Osprey Dr DROY M43 116 D2
IRL M44 121 B5
WILM/AE SK9 199 H2
Osprey Wk BRUN/LGST * M13 127 H2
Ossory St RUSH/FAL M14 127 G5
Osterley Rd BKLY M9 87 H4
Ostlers Ga DROY M43 117 E3
Ostrich La PWCH M25 85 F4
Oswald Cl SLFD M6 98 D5
Oswald La CCHDY M21 141 E2
Oswald Rd CCHDY M21 141 E1
Oswald St ANC M4 7 F1
BOLS/LL BL3 48 B5
CHAD OL9 74 A4
MILN OL16 11 F4
RDSH SK5 130 A5
ROY/SHW OL2 60 B1
Oswestry Cl TOT/BURYW BL8 25 H3
Otago Rd OLDE OL4 75 F3
Otago St OLDE * OL4 75 F3
Othello Dr ECC M30 109 G3
Otley Av SLFD M6 110 D2
Otley Cl CHAD OL9 89 G1
Otley Gv EDGY/DAV SK3 171 G5
Otmoor Wy ROY/SHW OL2 59 H5
Otranto Av SLFD M6 110 C1
Ottawa Cl NTHM/RTH M23 167 G5
Otterburn Pl OFTN SK2 173 E3
Otterbury Cl TOT/BURYW BL8 37 E4
Otter Dr BURY BL9 54 A5
CHH M8 99 H5
Otterspool Rd MPL/ROM SK6 162 A5
Oulder Hl ROCH OL11 28 D4
Oulder Hill Dr ROCH OL11 29 E4
Oulder Mt ROCH * OL11 29 E4
Ouldfield Cl MILN * OL16 30 C5
Oulton Av SALE M33 155 F1
Oulton St BOL BL1 34 B1
Oulton Wk NEWH/MOS M40 114 A3
Oundle Cl RUSH/FAL M14 127 H5
Ouse St SALQ M50 110 D4
Outram Cl MPL/ROM * SK6 175 E5
Outram Rd DUK SK16 132 A2
Outram Sq DROY * M43 116 B5
Outrington Dr OP/CLY M11 114 D5
Outwood Av SWIN M27 82 C3
Outwood Dr CHD/CHDH SK8 181 F4
Outwood Gv BOL BL1 33 H1
Outwood La MANAIR M90 180 B4
Outwood La West MANAIR M90 180 A4
Outwood Rd CHD/CHDH SK8 181 G4
RAD M26 67 F3
The Oval CHD/CHDH SK8 181 G4
Oval Dr DUK SK16 132 A1
Overbridge Rd BRO M7 112 D1
Overbrook Av NEWH/MOS M40 101 E5
Overbrook Dr PWCH M25 85 E4
Overdale SWIN M27 97 F4
Overdale Cl OLD OL1 74 B3
Overdale Crs URM M41 137 G1
Overdale Dr BOL BL1 47 H2
Overdale Rd MPL/ROM SK6 161 H5
WYTH/NTH M22 168 C4
Overdell Dr WHIT OL12 18 B5
Overdene Cl HOR/BR BL6 46 C3
Overens St OLDE OL4 75 E5
Overfield Wy WHIT OL12 30 A1
Overgreen BOLE BL2 35 F3
Overhill Dr WILM/AE SK9 200 B3
Overhill La WILM/AE SK9 200 B3
Overhill Rd CHAD OL9 73 E4
WILM/AE SK9 200 A3
Overlea Dr BNG/LEV M19 158 B1
Overlinks Dr SLFD M6 97 G5
Overstone Dr CHH M8 100 A3
Overton Av WYTH/NTH M22 168 C4
Overton Crs BRAM/HZG SK7 173 F5
SALE M33 153 G4
Overton Rd WYTH/NTH M22 168 C4
Overt St ROCH OL11 43 E1
Overwood Rd WYTH/NTH M22 168 C1
Owen Fold OLDE OL4 76 A5
Owenington Gv LHULT M38 80 B2
Owens Cl CHAD OL9 72 D4
Owens Farm Dr OFTN SK2 173 F2
Owens Pk RUSH/FAL * M14 143 E2
Owen St ECC M30 109 E4
EDGY/DAV SK3 12 D4
OLD OL1 75 H1
SLFD M6 98 D5
Owlerbarrow Rd
TOT/BURYW BL8 37 F3
Owler La CHAD OL9 88 C4
Owlwood Cl LHULT M38 79 D4
Owlwood Dr LHULT M38 79 D4
Oxbridge Cl SALE M33 153 G3
Oxbrow Wy WHTF M45 68 D4
Oxendale Dr MDTN M24 70 D3
Oxenhurst Gn OFTN SK2 173 F4
Oxford Av DROY M43 116 A2
ROCH OL11 28 D3
SALE M33 153 G2
WHTF M45 68 D4
Oxford Cl FWTH BL4 64 A4
Oxford Ct CMANE * M1 6 E7
OLDTF/WHR * M16 126 C3
Oxford Dr MDTN M24 72 B2
MPL/ROM SK6 162 B2
Oxford Gv BOL BL1 2 A2
IRL M44 135 B5
Oxford Ml AULW * OL7 117 G5
Oxford Pl MILN OL16 43 F1
RUSH/FAL M14 127 H4
Oxford Rd ALT WA14 177 G1
BOLS/LL BL3 65 G1
BRUN/LGST M13 127 G3
DUK SK16 118 C5
HOR/BR BL6 46 A1
SLFD M6 110 B1
Oxford St BOL BL1 2 E4
BURY BL9 5 G6
CHAD OL9 8 A7
CMANW M2 6 E6
ECC M30 109 H4
ROY/SHW OL2 60 A2
STLY SK15 119 H4
Oxford St East AULW OL7 117 G5
Oxford St West AULW OL7 117 G5
Oxford Wy HTNM SK4 159 G3
WHIT OL12 29 H1
Ox Ga BOLE BL2 35 E1
Oxley St OP/CLY M11 114 D3
Oxney Rd RUSH/FAL M14 127 H4
Ox St RAMS BL0 16 C3
Oxton Av WYTH/NTH M22 168 B5
Oxton St OP/CLY M11 130 A1

P

Pacific Rd ALT WA14 164 D3
Pacific Wy SALQ M50 110 D5
Packer St BOL BL1 33 F4
MILN OL16 10 C6
Packwood Cha CHAD OL9 73 E4
Padbury Cl URM M41 122 A5
Padbury Wy BOLE BL2 35 F4
Padden Brook MPL/ROM SK6 162 A4
Paddington Av
NEWH/MOS * M40 102 A5
Paddington Cl SLFD M6 111 H3
Paddison St SWIN M27 96 D3
The Paddock BRAM/HZG SK7 183 G3
CHD/CHDH SK8 170 B4
HALE/TIMP WA15 166 C5
RAMS BL0 16 C1
UPML OL3 93 G3
WALK M28 95 F3
Paddock Cha POY/DIS SK12 195 G1
Paddock La FAIL M35 103 E5
Paddock Rd HYDE * SK14 147 G3
The Paddocks EDGY/DAV SK3 172 B4
Paddock St WGTN/LGST M12 127 H1
Paderborn Ct BOL BL1 2 C6
Padiham Cl BURY BL9 53 E2
Padstow Cl HYDE SK14 134 A5
Padstow Dr BRAM/HZG SK7 184 A5
Padstow St NEWH/MOS * M40 114 B2
Padstow Wk HYDE SK14 134 A5
Pagan St MILN OL16 10 D5
Paget St NEWH/MOS M40 101 E5
Pagnall Ct CHAD * OL9 89 G2
Paignton Av BNG/LEV M19 143 G3
HYDE SK14 148 D1
Paignton Dr SALE M33 153 G1
Paignton Gv HTNM SK4 144 D4
Pailin Dr DROY M43 116 D3
Pailton Cl HOR/BR BL6 47 E3
Painswick Rd WYTH/NTH M22 180 A3
Paisley Pk FWTH BL4 64 D3
Paiton St BOL BL1 48 B2
Palace Gdns ROY/SHW OL2 74 A2
Palace Rd AUL OL6 105 H5
SALE M33 154 B1
Palace St BOL BL1 2 E3
BURY BL9 5 H5
CHAD OL9 8 B3
Palatine Av DID/WITH M20 142 C5
Palatine Cl IRL M44 136 A2
Palatine Crs DID/WITH M20 157 G1
Palatine Dr BURY BL9 27 G3
Palatine Rd DID/WITH M20 157 E3
ROCH OL11 28 D3
WYTH/NTH M22 156 C5
Palatine St BOL BL1 2 E4
DTN/ASHW M34 131 F3
MILN OL16 11 J7
RAMS BL0 16 D2
Paley St BOL BL1 3 F4
Palfrey Pl WGTN/LGST M12 127 H1
Pall Ml CMANW M2 6 E5
Palma Av MANAIR M90 179 H4
Palm Cl SALE M33 153 F1
Palmer Av CHD/CHDH SK8 170 C3
Palmer Cl OLDS OL8 90 C3
Palmerston Av
OLDTF/WHR M16 141 G1
Palmerston Cl DTN/ASHW M34 130 C5
RAMS BL0 16 C5
Palmerston Rd DTN/ASHW M34 130 C5
OFTN SK2 184 B1
Palmerston St WGTN/LGST M12 114 A5
Palmer St BRO M7 99 F5
DUK SK16 118 A4
SALE M33 154 B2
Palm Gv CHAD OL9 73 G4
Palm St BOL BL1 34 A3
BRUN/LGST M13 128 C5
DROY M43 115 G3
OLDE OL4 75 F4
Pandora St DID/WITH M20 157 F1
Panfield Rd WYTH/NTH M22 168 B5
Pangbourne Av URM M41 123 H5
Pangbourne Cl EDGY/DAV SK3 171 F3
Pankhurst Wk RUSH/FAL M14 127 G5
Panmure St OLDS OL8 90 C3
Pansy Rd FWTH BL4 64 B4
Paper Mill Rd EDGW/EG BL7 23 E4
Parade Rd MANAIR M90 180 B5
Paradise St DTN/ASHW M34 131 G1
RAMS BL0 16 D2
Parbold Av DID/WITH M20 142 B4
Pargate Cha ROCH OL11 28 D3
Paris Av ORD M5 126 A1
Parish Vw ORD M5 112 A5
Paris St BOLS/LL BL3 48 A5
The Park OLDE OL4 93 E2
Park 66 BURY * BL9 54 A3
Park Av ALT WA14 165 H1
BNG/LEV M19 143 G2
BOL * BL1 33 H2
BRAM/HZG SK7 193 F2
BRO M7 100 A2
CHAD OL9 73 G3
CHD/CHDH SK8 182 C3
EDGY/DAV SK3 170 C2
FAIL M35 102 C2
HALE/TIMP WA15 178 A3
HYDE SK14 132 C4
MPL/ROM SK6 162 B4
OLDTF/WHR M16 126 B3
POY/DIS SK12 195 F3
PWCH M25 85 E3
RAD M26 53 E5
RAMS BL0 17 E2
SALE M33 139 F5
URM M41 138 B1
WHTF M45 84 A1
WILM/AE SK9 199 H2
Park Bridge Rd AULW OL7 105 E2
Parkbrook Rd NTHM/RTH M23 168 A2
Park Brow Cl CCHDY M21 141 F4
Park Cl ALT WA14 166 A1
CHAD OL9 73 G3
STLY SK15 119 E2
WHTF M45 84 C1
Park Cottages BOL * BL1 33 F3
ROY/SHW OL2 59 G1
Park Court Ms CHD/CHDH * SK8 170 B5
Park Crs AUL OL6 118 D3
CHAD OL9 73 E3
RUSH/FAL M14 127 H5
WILM/AE SK9 199 G1
Parkdale CHAD OL9 73 G3
Parkdale Av DTN/ASHW M34 131 E1
GTN M18 129 F3
Parkdale Rd BOLE BL2 34 D5
Parkdene Cl BOLE BL2 35 E2
Park Dr ECC M30 109 G1
HALE/TIMP WA15 166 B2
HALE/TIMP WA15 178 A3
HTNM SK4 159 E4
HYDE SK14 132 C4
OLDTF/WHR M16 141 F1
Parkend Rd NTHM/RTH M23 167 H4
Parker St BURY BL9 5 G5
CMANE M1 7 G5
Parkfield CHAD OL9 73 F3
ECC * M30 121 D4
ORD M5 111 E3
Parkfield Av FWTH BL4 64 D5
MPL/ROM SK6 175 E3

OLDS OL8 ....89 G5
PWCH M25 ....85 G4
RUSH/FAL M14 ....127 C5
URM M41 ....138 A2
Parkfield Dr MDTN M24 ....71 F4
Parkfield Rd ALT WA14 ....165 F5
BOLS/LL BL5 ....64 A1
CHD/CHDH SK8 ....182 C3
OLDE OL4 ....93 F1
Parkfield Rd North
NEWH/MOS M40 ....88 D5
Parkfield Rd South
DID/WITH M20 ....157 F2
Parkfields STLY SK15 ....120 A2
Parkfield St ROCH OL11 ....43 G4
RUSH/FAL M14 ....127 C5
Parkgate CHAD OL9 ....73 C3
TOT/BURYW BL8 ....36 D1
Park Gate Av CHD/CHDH M20 ....142 C5
Park Gate Cl MPL/ROM SK6 ....161 F1
Parkgate Dr BOL BL1 ....2 A3
OFTN SK2 ....172 C5
SWIN M27 ....97 G5
Park Gates Av CHD/CHDH SK8 ....183 F3
Parkhall STLY SK15 ....120 A2
Parkhill Av NEWH/MOS M40 ....142 C1
Park Gv BNG/LEV M19 ....143 H1
HTNM SK4 ....159 E2
RAD M26 ....52 A5
WALK M28 ....95 E2
Park Hl PWCH * M25 ....85 C5
Parkhill Av CHH M8 ....86 C5
Park Hill Dr WHTF M45 ....68 B4
Park Hill Rd HALE/TIMP WA15 ....178 B3
Parkhills Rd BURY BL9 ....5 F7
Park Hill St BOL BL1 ....2 A3
Park House Bridge Est
SLFD * M6 ....98 C3
Park House Bridge Rd SLFD 98 C4
Parkhouse St OP/CLY M11 ....115 E5
Parkhurst Av NEWH/MOS M40 ....102 D1
Parkin Cl DUK * SK16 ....118 B5
Parkinson St BOLS/LL BL3 ....48 B4
BURY BL9 ....38 C1
Parkin St WGTN/LGST M12 ....128 D5
Parklake Av BRO M7 ....99 G2
The Parklands HTNM SK4 ....159 F2
ROY/SHW OL2 ....58 D3
Parklands Rd NTHM/RTH M23 ....167 G2
Parklands Wy POY/DIS SK12 ....195 F5
Park Lane W *M6 ....99 C2
DUK SK16 ....118 D4
HALE/TIMP WA15 ....178 B3
MILN OL16 ....10 C5
OLDS OL8 ....90 C5
POY/DIS SK12 ....59 E5
ROY/SHW OL2 ....59 E5
SLFD M6 ....97 H5
STKP SK1 ....15 G3
WHTF M45 ....68 B5
Park Lane Ct WHTF * M45 ....68 B5
Park La West SWIN M27 ....98 A3
Parkleigh Dr NEWH/MOS M40 ....88 D5
Park Ldg BNG/LEV M19 ....143 H2
Park Lodge Cl CHD/CHDH SK8 ....170 D3
Park Ms OLDTF/WHR M16 ....141 F1
Parkmount Rd BKLY M9 ....101 F1
Park Pde AULW OL7 ....117 H5
ROY/SHW OL2 ....59 E5
Park Pl ANC M4 ....7 J1
BRO M7 ....158 C4
PWCH M25 ....85 F2
SLFD M6 ....110 B2
Park Range RUSH/FAL M14 ....128 A5
Park Ri MPL/ROM SK6 ....161 E1
Park Rd ALT WA14 ....176 D2
BOL BL1 ....2 A5
BOLS/LL BL3 ....50 C5
BURY BL9 ....4 D1
CHD/CHDH SK8 ....169 E3
CHD/CHDH SK8 ....170 B3
DTN/ASHW M34 ....117 E5
DTN/ASHW M34 ....131 F5
DUK SK16 ....118 C4
ECC M30 ....109 C1
HALE/TIMP WA15 ....178 B3
HALE/TIMP WA15 ....178 A3
HTNM SK4 ....159 E1
HYDE SK14 ....132 C4
MPL/ROM SK6 ....71 G2
OLDS OL8 ....90 C5
PART M31 ....151 F3
POY/DIS SK12 ....197 E1
PWCH M25 ....85 F2
RAMS BL0 ....16 A5
SALE M33 ....139 F5
SLFD M6 ....110 B1
STRET M32 ....126 C4
WALK M28 ....94 D1
WHIT OL12 ....11 F2
WILM/AE SK9 ....199 G3
Park Rd North URM M41 ....123 F5
Park Rd South URM M41 ....123 F5
Park Rw BOL BL1 ....23 E5
HTNM SK4 ....158 C5
Park Seventeen WHTF M45 ....68 C4
Parkside BRO M7 ....99 H4
Parkside Av BRO M7 ....87 F1
FAIL M35 ....102 D5
Park Side Av ROY/SHW OL2 ....60 B1
Parkside Av WALK M28 ....95 E1
Parkside Cl MPL/ROM SK6 ....53 F5
RAD M26 ....53 F5
Parkside La MPL/ROM SK6 ....175 H5
Park Side Rd RUSH/FAL M14 ....142 A1
SALE M33 ....155 E3
Parkside Rd BOLE * BL2 ....34 D5
WGTN/LGST M12 ....127 H1
Parkside Wk BRAM/HZG SK7 ....183 H1
Parkstone Av BURY BL9 ....4 E7
ECC M30 ....124 B3
Parkstone Cl TOT/BURYW BL8 ....37 E4
Parkstone Dr SWIN M27 ....97 G4
Parkstone La WALK M28 ....108 C1

Parkstone Rd IRL M44 ....121 B5
Park St AULW OL7 ....117 H4
BOL BL1 ....2 A3
BRO M7 ....99 F2
CSLFD M3 ....112 C4
DROY M43 ....116 D3
DTN/ASHW M34 ....131 E5
FWTH BL4 ....66 B3
HEY OL10 ....56 B1
MILN OL16 ....30 A5
MOSL OL5 ....106 D2
MPL/ROM SK6 ....161 G3
OLDE OL4 ....8 E6
PWCH M25 ....85 F3
RAD M26 ....52 D5
ROY/SHW OL2 ....59 F5
STKP SK1 ....13 G2
STLY SK15 ....119 G4
SWIN M27 ....97 F3
Parksway BKLY M9 ....86 C1
PWCH M25 ....85 F5
SWIN M27 ....97 H4
Parks Yd BURY BL9 ....4 D5
Park Vw BKLY M9 ....100 D4
CHAD OL9 ....73 F3
DTN/ASHW * M34 ....117 E5
EDGY/DAV SK3 ....170 C2
FWTH BL4 ....65 H3
FWTH BL4 ....66 B3
LIT OL15 ....21 E2
RUSH/FAL * M14 ....143 F4
STKP SK1 ....172 C2
WILM/AE SK9 ....199 H2
Park View Ct PWCH * M25 ....85 C5
Park View Rd BOLS/LL * BL3 ....48 B5
PWCH M25 ....85 C5
Parkville Rd DID/WITH M20 ....157 H1
PWCH M25 ....69 F5
Park Wy STRET M32 ....124 A4
Parkway BRAM/HZG SK7 ....183 H2
CHAD OL9 ....73 F3
DTN/ASHW M34 ....131 G3
EDGY/DAV SK3 ....170 C2
LHULT M38 ....79 D4
ROCH OL11 ....29 E3
WILM/AE SK9 ....199 G4
Parkway Gv LHULT M38 ....79 D5
Parkwood Dr WHTN BL5 ....62 C5
Parkwood Rd NTHM/RTH M23 ....168 B2
Parlane St ANC * M4 ....115 F2
Parliament Pl BURY BL9 ....4 C7
Parliament St BURY BL9 ....4 C7
Parndon Dr OFTN SK2 ....172 D2
Parnell Av WYTH/NTH M22 ....168 C5
Parnham Cl BOLS/LL BL3 ....51 E4
Parrbrook Cl WHTF M45 ....68 C3
Parr Cl FWTH BL4 ....65 E3
Parrenthorn Rd PWCH M25 ....69 F4
Parrfield Rd WALK M28 ....95 E3
Parr Fold BURY BL9 ....69 E2
Parr Fold Av WALK M28 ....94 D1
Parrin La ECC M30 ....109 D2
Parrot St BOLS/LL BL3 ....48 D4
OP/CLY M11 ....115 G4
Parrs Mount Ms HTNM * SK4 ....158 C4
Parr St ECC M30 ....109 G4
OP/CLY * M11 ....115 G4
Parrs Wood Av DID/WITH M20 ....157 H5
Parrs Wood La DID/WITH M20 ....157 H5
Parrs Wood Rd DID/WITH M20 ....157 H5
DID/WITH M20 ....169 G1
Parry Md MPL/ROM SK6 ....161 H2
Parslow Av CHH M8 ....100 D2
Parsonage Cl BURY BL9 ....5 H4
ORD M5 ....112 B5
Parsonage Dr WALK M28 ....80 D5
Parsonage Gdns CSLFD * M3 ....6 D4
MPL/ROM SK6 ....175 C5
Parsonage La CSLFD * M3 ....6 D4
DID/WITH M20 ....142 D4
HTNM SK4 ....159 E2
RAD * M26 ....66 D1
URM M41 ....137 F2
WALK M28 ....80 D5
Parsonage Rd HTNM SK4 ....159 E2
DID/WITH M20 ....142 D4
HULME M15 ....126 D3
HYDE * SK14 ....133 H1
Parsonage Wy CHD/CHDH SK8 ....170 D4
Parsons Dr MDTN M24 ....71 G2
Parsons Fld SLFD * M6 ....98 D5
Parson's La BURY BL9 ....4 E1
Parsons St CHAD OL9 ....8 D3
Parson St HEY OL10 ....39 G5
Partington Ct FWTH BL4 ....64 B4
Partington La SWIN M27 ....96 D3
Partington Pk ROCH OL11 ....57 F1
Partington Pl SALE M33 ....153 F2
Partington St BOLS/LL BL3 ....63 F2
ECC M30 ....103 H3
FAIL M35 ....103 E3
HEY OL10 ....40 B1
NEWH/MOS M40 ....101 C5
OLD * OL1 ....9 J3
ROCH OL11 ....42 A4
SWIN M27 ....96 B2
Partridge Av NTHM/RTH M23 ....168 A3
Partridge Cl ROCH OL11 ....28 C4
Partridge Ri DROY M43 ....117 E2
Partridge St STRET M32 ....125 G5
Partridge Wy CHAD OL9 ....73 G3
Parvet Av DROY M43 ....116 A2
Pascal St BNG/LEV M19 ....144 A1
The Pass MILN OL16 ....11 F5
Passmonds Crs ROCH OL11 ....29 F3
Passmonds Wy ROCH OL11 ....29 F3
Pass St CHAD OL9 ....8 C5
Paston Rd WYTH/NTH M22 ....168 C3
Pasture Cl HEY OL10 ....40 A4
Pasturefield Cl SALE M33 ....155 G3
Pasture Field Rd
WYTH/NTH M22 ....181 E1
Pasturegreen Wy IRL M44 ....121 G5
Pastures La OLDE OL4 ....76 D5
Patch Croft Rd WYTH/NTH M22 ....181 E1
Patchett St WGTN/LGST M12 ....128 C2

Patch La BRAM/HZG SK7 ....193 H2
Patey St WGTN/LGST M12 ....128 D5
Patience St WHIT OL12 ....29 F2
Patmos St RAMS BL0 ....17 E2
Paton Av BOLS/LL BL3 ....65 E3
Paton Ct BRO M7 ....112 B1
Paton St CMANE M1 ....7 H5
WHIT OL12 ....18 C5
Patricia Dr WALK M28 ....81 F5
Patten St DID/WITH M20 ....142 C5
Patterdale Av AULW OL7 ....104 C5
URM M41 ....123 H4
Patterdale Cl OLD OL1 ....74 D3
ROCH OL11 ....42 A5
Patterdale Dr BURY BL9 ....53 F2
MDTN M24 ....71 F2
Patterdale Rd AULW OL7 ....104 C5
BOLE BL2 ....34 D2
MPL/ROM SK6 ....162 A2
OFTN SK2 ....172 C3
PART M31 ....150 D3
WYTH/NTH M22 ....168 D2
Patterson Av CCHDY M21 ....140 D2
Patterson St BOLS/LL BL3 ....47 H5
DTN/ASHW M34 ....131 C4
Patting Cl IRL M44 ....121 D5
Pattishall Cl ANC M4 ....114 A4
Pattison Cl WHIT OL12 ....14 D2
Patton Cl BURY BL9 ....69 E2
Paulden Av NTHM/RTH M23 ....168 A3
OLDE OL4 ....75 H5
Paulden Dr FAIL M35 ....103 F3
Paulette St BOL BL1 ....33 H4
Paulhan Rd DID/WITH M20 ....158 A2
Paulhan St BOLS/LL BL3 ....63 H1
Pauline St WHIT OL12 ....18 D5
Paulin Dr OFTN SK2 ....172 C2
Paulton Dr AUL OL6 ....105 G5
The Pavilions CHD/CHDH SK8 ....170 A5
Pavilion Wk RAD M26 ....52 A5
Pavilion Cl WHIT OL12 ....18 A1
Paythorne Gn OFTN SK2 ....171 F4
Peabody St BOLS/LL BL3 ....48 D5
Peaceful Cl MPL/ROM SK6 ....174 D4
Peace St BOLS/LL BL3 ....48 D4
FAIL * M35 ....103 F1
Peaceville Rd BNG/LEV M19 ....143 G2
Peach Bank MDTN M24 ....71 H4
Peach Rd OLDE OL4 ....75 G3
Peach Tree Cl BRO * M7 ....100 A4
Peach Tree Ct SLFD * M6 ....111 H3
Peacock Av SLFD M6 ....98 B5
Peacock Cl GTN M18 ....129 F2
Peacock Dr CHD/CHDH SK8 ....191 G1
Peacock Gv GTN M18 ....129 G4
Peak Bank MPL/ROM SK6 ....161 H4
Peakdale Av CHD/CHDH SK8 ....181 E1
CHH M8 ....86 A3
Peakdale Rd DROY M43 ....115 H2
MPL/ROM SK6 ....175 F5
Peaknaze Cl SWIN M27 ....97 G2
Peak St BOL BL1 ....33 G4
CHAD OL9 ....8 A6
CMANE M1 ....7 J5
STKP SK1 ....13 J3
Pear Av BURY BL9 ....39 F2
Pear Cl MDTN M24 ....88 A1
Pear Av BRO M7 ....99 H1
Pearl Mill Cl OLDS OL8 ....91 E3
Pearl St BRAM/HZG SK7 ....173 F5
DTN/ASHW M34 ....131 F5
Pearl St DTN/ASHW M34 ....131 E4
Pearn Av BNG/LEV M19 ....158 C1
Pearn Rd BNG/LEV M19 ....158 C1
Pearson Cl MILN OL16 ....31 G4
PART M31 ....151 F3
Pearson Gv OLDE OL4 ....91 H1
Pearson St BURY BL9 ....5 J2
DUK SK16 ....132 B2
MILN OL16 ....11 H5
RDSH SK5 ....160 A3
Peart Av MPL/ROM SK6 ....147 F5
Pear Tree Cl SLFD M6 ....111 H3
Pear Tree Dr STLY SK15 ....119 G3
Peart St DTN/ASHW M34 ....131 E5
Peary St ANC M4 ....115 C2
Peaslake Cl MPL/ROM SK6 ....162 C4
Peatfield Av SWIN M27 ....97 F3
Peatfield Wk HULME * M15 ....127 E3
Pebble Cl STLY SK15 ....119 F1
Peckford Dr NEWH/MOS M40 ....101 G5
Peckforton Cl CHD/CHDH SK8 ....169 E4
WHIT OL12 ....28 C2
Pedder St BOL BL1 ....33 F5
Pedley Wk BRUN/LGST * M13 ....127 G1
HEY OL10 ....40 C3
LHULT M38 ....80 A3
Peel La CHH M8 ....113 H1
Peel Moat Rd HTNM SK4 ....159 E1
Peel Mt RAMS BL0 ....17 E1
SLFD M6 ....98 C5
Peel Park Crs LHULT M38 ....80 A3
Peels Av OLDE OL4 ....76 D5
Peel Rd OLDE OL4 ....76 D5
Peel St AUL OL6 ....119 G3
CHAD OL9 ....73 H5
DROY M43 ....116 A5
DTN/ASHW M34 ....131 B4
DUK SK16 ....118 D4
ECC M30 ....110 A3
FAIL M35 ....102 C4
FWTH BL4 ....66 C4
HYDE SK14 ....148 A1
LIT OL15 ....21 E3
OLDS OL8 ....9 F7
RDSH SK5 ....145 E2
SALE M33 ....154 D4
OFTN SK2 ....172 A3

WALK M28 ....81 G5
WHTF M45 ....69 E5
Penrith Cl PART M31 ....150 D2
Penrith St ROCH OL11 ....43 G3
Penrod Pl SLFD M6 ....112 A1
Penrose Av MDTN M24 ....72 A3
Penrose Gdns MDTN M24 ....72 A3
Penrose St BOLE * BL2 ....49 H2
Peel Wy BURY BL9 ....4 C5
Penroy Av DID/WITH M20 ....156 C3
Penruddock Wk
BRUN/LGST * M13 ....128 C4
Penry Av IRL M44 ....135 G3
Penryn Av ROY/SHW OL2 ....59 E5
SALE M33 ....155 G3
Pensarn Av RUSH/FAL M14 ....143 F3
Pensarn Gv RDSH SK5 ....160 A2
Pensby Cl SWIN M27 ....97 H3
Pensford Ct BOLE BL2 ....24 D5
Pensford Rd NTHM/RTH M23 ....179 C1
Penshurst Rd RDSH SK5 ....145 G3
Penthorpe Dr ROY/SHW OL2 ....74 C1
Pentland Av NEWH/MOS M40 ....87 H1
Pentland Cl BRAM/HZG SK7 ....184 C5
The Pentlands ROY/SHW OL2 ....59 E1
Pentlands Av BRO M7 ....99 G4
Pentland Ter BOL * BL1 ....33 H5
Pentland Wy HYDE SK14 ....133 G2
Pentwyn Gv NTHM/RTH M23 ....168 A2
Penworthem St
NEWH/MOS M40 ....114 C1
Penzance St
NEWH/MOS * M40 ....114 B2
Peover Av SALE M33 ....155 F2
Peover Rd WILM/AE SK9 ....192 B2
Pepler Av NTHM/RTH M23 ....156 A4
Pepperhill Rd OLDTF/WHR M16 ....127 F4
Peppermint Cl MILN OL16 ....45 F2
Pepper Rd BRAM/HZG SK7 ....184 A4
Percival Cl BRO * M7 ....100 A4
Percival Rd DROY M43 ....116 C4
Percy Dr ORD M5 ....124 D1
Percy Rd DTN/ASHW M34 ....146 B1
Percy St BOL * BL1 ....34 A4
BURY BL9 ....5 F5
FWTH * BL4 ....65 F5
HULME M15 ....43 G1
MILN OL16 ....43 G1
OLDE OL4 ....8 D6
RAMS * BL0 ....16 C2
STKP SK1 ....13 G2
STLY * SK15 ....119 G4
Peregrine Crs DROY M43 ....116 D2
Peregrine Dr IRL M44 ....136 A2
Peregrine Rd OFTN SK2 ....173 H5
Peregrine St HULME M15 ....127 E3
Perendale Ri BOL BL1 ....23 E4
Perivale Dr OLDS OL8 ....91 E3
Pernham St OLDE OL4 ....76 D4
Perrin St HYDE SK14 ....147 C1
Perry Av HYDE SK14 ....133 F4
Perry Cl ROCH OL11 ....41 H4
Perrygate Av DID/WITH M20 ....142 C5
Perrymead PWCH M25 ....85 E5
Perry Rd HALE/TIMP WA15 ....166 C5
Pershore WHIT OL12 ....10 B5
Pershore Rd MDTN M24 ....71 H1
Perth Av CHAD OL9 ....73 F4
Perth Cl BRAM/HZG SK7 ....193 H2
Perth St BOLS/LL BL3 ....63 F1
ROY/SHW OL2 ....59 G4
SWIN M27 ....96 C2
Peru St CSLFD M3 ....112 C3
Peterborough Cl AUL OL6 ....105 G4
Peterborough Dr BOL BL1 ....23 E5
Peterborough St GTN M18 ....130 A2
Peterborough Wk BOL * BL1 ....33 H4
Peterhead Cl BOL BL1 ....33 G3
Peterhead Wk ORD * M5 ....111 H4
Peterloo Ct SLFD * M6 ....98 A5
Peter Moss Wy BNG/LEV M19 ....144 B2
Petersburg Rd EDGY/DAV SK3 ....171 E3
Petersfield Dr NTHM/RTH M23 ....167 C2
Petersfield Wk BOL * BL1 ....33 C1
Peter St ALT WA14 ....177 E2
BRAM/HZG SK7 ....185 E1
BURY BL9 ....5 K3
CMANE M1 ....6 E6
DTN/ASHW M34 ....131 H5
ECC M30 ....109 G5
STKP SK1 ....9 G4
Peterswood Cl WYTH/NTH M22 ....180 A3
Petherbridge Dr WYTH/NTH M22 ....180 A3
Petrel Av POY/DIS SK12 ....194 B3
Petrel Cl DROY M43 ....117 E2
EDGY/DAV SK3 ....171 G5
Petrie Ct SLFD M6 ....98 A5
Petrock Wk NEWH/MOS M40 ....102 D1
Petts Crs LIT OL15 ....21 G2
Petworth Cl WYTH/NTH M22 ....168 D4
Petworth Rd CHAD OL9 ....90 B2
Pevensey Ct SLFD M6 ....98 B5
Pevensey Rd SLFD M6 ....98 B5
Peveril Cl WHTF M45 ....69 H1
Peveril Crs CCHDY M21 ....141 E3
Peveril Dr BRAM/HZG SK7 ....185 C4
Peveril Rd ALT WA14 ....165 F2
OLD OL1 ....75 C2
Peveril St BOLS/LL BL3 ....48 C4
Pewsey Rd WYTH/NTH M22 ....181 E1
Pexwood OLD OL1 ....59 G5
Pheasant Cl WALK M28 ....95 E3
Pheasant Dr CCHDY M21 ....140 C4
Pheasant Ri ALT WA14 ....177 G3
Phelan Cl NEWH/MOS M40 ....101 G5
Philip Av DTN/ASHW M34 ....131 C3
Philip Dr SALE M33 ....154 C4
Philips Av FWTH BL4 ....66 B3
Philips Dr WHTF M45 ....69 F1
Philips Park Rd OP/CLY M11 ....114 D3
WHTF M45 ....69 C1
Philip St BOLS/LL BL3 ....48 C4
ECC M30 ....110 C4
OLDE OL4 ....77 C4
ROCH OL11 ....43 C1
Phillimore St OLDE OL4 ....91 H1

Phillips Park Rd WHTF M45 ....84 C1
Phipps St WALK M28 ....80 D3
Phoebe St BOLS/LL * BL3 ....48 B5
  ORD M5 ....111 H5
Phoenix Cl HEY OL10 ....41 C5
Phoenix St OLD BL1 ....5 C2
  BURY BL9 ....4 B4
  CMANW * M2 ....7 E4
  FWTH BL4 ....6 F5
  LIT OL15 ....21 E2
  OLD OL1 ....9 F2
  WHIT OL12 ....29 F2
Phoenix Wy RAD M26 ....40 F2
  URM M41 ....123 H2
Phyllis St MDTN M24 ....72 B5
  WHIT OL12 ....29 E2
Piccadilly CMANE M1 ....7 G4
  CMANE M1 ....7 G4
  STKP SK1 ....13 G4
Piccadilly Plaza CMANE M1 ....7 F4
Piccadilly South CMANE M1 ....7 H6
Piccard Cl ANC M4 ....7 H2
Pickering Cl HALE/TIMP WA15 ..166 B2
  RAD * M26 ....65 H4
  TOT/BURYW BL8 ....37 C1
  URM M41 ....138 A1
Pickford Av BOLS/LL BL3 ....66 A1
Pickford Ct DUK * SK16 ....118 B5
Pickford La DUK * SK16 ....118 B5
Pickford Ms DUK * SK16 ....118 B5
Pickford's Brow STKP SK1 ....13 C5
Pickhill St ANC M4 ....7 J3
Pickhill La UPML OL3 ....78 A4
Pickmere Av DID/WITH M20 ....142 C3
Pickmere Cl DROY M43 ....116 C4
  EDGY/DAV SK3 ....171 F5
  SALE M33 ....155 C4
Pickmere Gdns CHD/CHDH SK8 ..170 C4
Pickmere Ms UPML OL3 ....78 A4
Pickup St MILN OL16 ....10 E7
Pickwick Rd POY/DIS SK12 ....195 E4
Picton Cl CSLFD M3 ....6 A2
Picton Dr WILM/AE SK9 ....192 B5
Picton Sq OLDE OL4 ....9 J5
Picton St AULW OL7 ....104 D4
  CSLFD M3 ....112 C2
Piercy Av BRO M7 ....112 C1
Piercy St ANC M4 ....114 A4
  FAIL * M35 ....102 D3
Pierthorne Cl MILN OL16 ....45 F2
Pigeon St CMANE M1 ....7 H4
Piggott St FWTH BL4 ....64 D5
Pike Av FAIL M35 ....103 H4
Pike Fold La BKLY M9 ....86 D4
Pike Rd BOLS/LL BL3 ....192 A2
Pike St ROCH OL11 ....43 E1
Pike View Cl OLDE OL4 ....91 E2
Pilgrim Dr OP/CLY M11 ....114 C4
Pilkington Dr WHTF M45 ....89 F5
Pilkington Rd BKLY M9 ....87 H5
  FWTH BL4 ....81 C1
  RAD M26 ....52 A4
Pilkington St BOLS/LL BL3 ....48 D4
  MDTN M24 ....73 H1
  RAMS BL0 ....16 C3
Pilkington Wy RAD M26 ....67 F2
Pilling Fld EDGW/EG BL7 ....22 D2
Pilling St DTN/ASHW M34 ....131 G5
  NEWH/MOS M40 ....88 D5
  TOT/BURYW BL8 ....37 H5
  WHIT OL12 ....29 G3
Pilning St BOLS/LL BL3 ....49 F5
Pilot St BURY BL9 ....53 H5
Pilsworth Rd BURY BL9 ....54 C2
  HEY OL10 ....40 C5
Pilsworth Wy BURY BL9 ....53 H5
Pimblett St CSLFD M3 ....113 E2
Pimhole Fold BURY BL9 ....5 H5
Pimhole Rd BURY BL9 ....5 H5
Pimlico Cl BRO * M7 ....99 C4
Pimlott Gv HYDE SK14 ....132 C3
  PWCH M25 ....84 B5
Pimlott Rd BOL BL1 ....34 C3
Pine Av WHTF M45 ....69 F4
Pine Cl DTN/ASHW M34 ....131 F2
  MPL/ROM SK6 ....174 D5
Pine Gv DTN/ASHW M34 ....131 H5
  DUK SK16 ....119 E5
  ECC M30 ....109 H1
  FWTH BL4 ....64 C4
  PWCH M25 ....84 D1
  ROY/SHW OL2 ....59 E3
  RUSH/FAL M14 ....128 B4
  SALE M33 ....155 E4
  SWIN M27 ....96 C5
  WALK M28 ....95 F2
Pinehurst Rd NEWH/MOS M40 ..101 F5
Pine Ldg BRAM/HZG SK7 ....184 A5
Pine Meadow RAD M26 ....20 B3
Pine Rd BRAM/HZG SK7 ....184 A4
  DID/WITH M20 ....157 F2
  DUK SK16 ....118 D5
  POY/DIS SK12 ....195 C4
Pine St AUL OL6 ....118 A1
  BOL BL1 ....34 A4
  BURY BL9 ....5 J4
  CHAD OL9 ....73 H4
  CMANE M1 ....7 H5
  EDGY/DAV SK3 ....12 C5
  HEY OL10 ....41 E4
  HYDE SK14 ....132 C3
  LIT OL15 ....21 E3
  MDTN M24 ....72 B5
  MILN * OL16 ....11 G7
  MILN OL16 ....45 E3
  MPL/ROM SK6 ....162 A1
Pine St North BURY BL9 ....5 J3
Pinetop Cl CCHDY M21 ....141 G4
Pine Tree Rd OLDS OL8 ....104 A4
Pinetree St GTN M18 ....129 F5
Pineway OLDE OL4 ....92 A1
Pinewood ALT WA14 ....165 G5
  CHAD OL9 ....72 D5
  SALE M33 ....153 G2
Pinewood Cl BOL BL1 ....33 H6
  DUK SK16 ....118 B4
Pinewood Ct ALT WA14 ....177 H5
  SALE M33 ....155 E1

Pinewood Rd CCHDY * M21 ....140 D4
  WILM/AE SK9 ....200 B2
The Pinewoods MPL/ROM SK6 ..162 A1
Pinfold Av BKLY M9 ....87 H5
Pinfold Cl HALE/TIMP WA15 ....179 E5
Pinfold Dr CHD/CHDH SK8 ....182 D3
Pinfold La MANAIR M90 ....189 C1
  MPL/ROM SK6 ....162 C2
  WHTF M45 ....68 B4
Pinfold Rd WALK M28 ....94 D1
Pingate Dr CHD/CHDH SK8 ....192 D1
Pingate La CHD/CHDH SK8 ....192 D1
Pingate La South
  CHD/CHDH SK8 ....192 D1
The Pingot IRL M44 ....121 C5
Pingot Av NTHM/RTH M23 ....156 A4
Pink Bank La WGTN/LGST M12 ..128 C4
Pin Mill Brow WGTN/LGST M12 ..114 A5
Pinnacle Dr EDGW/EG BL7 ....22 C1
Pinner Pl BNG/LEV M19 ....143 H5
Pinners Cl RAMS BL0 ....16 D1
Pinnington La STRET * M52 ....140 A2
Pinnington Rd GTN M18 ....129 C2
Pintail Av EDGY/DAV SK3 ....171 C3
Pioneer Rd SWIN M27 ....84 A5
Pioneer St LIT OL15 ....21 E5
  OP/CLY M11 ....115 E2
  ROCH OL11 ....30 B5
Pioneer Vls MILN * OL16 ....45 H1
Piperhill Av WYTH/NTH M22 ....156 C5
Pipers Cl ROCH OL11 ....28 A5
Pipewell Av GTN M18 ....129 F5
Pipit Cl DTN/ASHW M34 ....116 D5
Pitchcombe Rd
  WYTH/NTH M22 ....180 A2
Pitcombe Cl BOL BL1 ....22 C4
Pitfield Gdns WYTH/RTH M23 ..167 G2
Pitfield La BOLE BL2 ....35 C3
Pitfield St BOLE BL2 ....3 J5
Pit La ROY/SHW OL2 ....44 B5
Pitman Cl OP/CLY M11 ....114 D5
Pits Farm Av ROCH OL11 ....43 F2
Pitsford Rd NEWH/MOS M40 ..101 F5
Pitshouse La WHIT * OL12 ....28 B1
Pitt St OP/CLY M11 ....89 C3
  DTN/ASHW M34 ....131 C5
  HEY OL10 ....40 D4
  HYDE SK14 ....132 C5
  OLDE OL4 ....9 K5
  RAD M26 ....66 D1
  WHIT OL12 ....10 D4
Pitt St East OLDE OL4 ....9 K4
Pixmore Av BOL BL1 ....34 C1
Place Rd ALT WA14 ....165 F3
Plain Pit St WHIT OL12 ....132 B3
Plainsfield Cl OLDTF/WHR M16 ..127 E4
Plane Cl SLFD * M6 ....111 H5
Plane Rd FAIL M35 ....103 E5
Plane St OLDE OL4 ....91 E5
Plane Tree Cl MPL/ROM SK6 ..174 C4
Planetree Rd HALE/TIMP WA15 ..178 B2
Plane Tree Rd PART M31 ....150 C3
Planet Wy DTN/ASHW M34 ....131 F3
Plantation Av WALK M28 ....94 D3
Plantation St AUL OL6 ....118 C4
  GTN M18 ....129 H5
Plant Cl SALE M33 ....154 D1
Plant Hill Rd BKLY M9 ....86 D2
Plant St CMANE * M1 ....7 H5
Plant Tar BKLY * M9 ....87 E2
Plate St OLD OL1 ....9 H5
Plato St CHAD OL9 ....8 C5
Platt Av AUL OL6 ....105 F4
Plattbrook Cl RUSH/FAL M14 ..142 C2
Platt Cl MILN OL16 ....44 D1
Platt Hill Av BOLS/LL BL3 ....47 H5
Platting La RUSH/FAL M14 ....42 A2
Platting Rd OLDE OL4 ....91 C4
Platt La RUSH/FAL M14 ....142 A2
  UPML OL3 ....77 F1
Platts Dr IRL M44 ....136 B1
Platt St CHD/CHDH SK8 ....170 B3
  DUK SK16 ....131 H1
Plattwood Wk HULME * M15 ..126 C2
Playfair Cl HEY OL10 ....56 B1
Playfair St BOL BL1 ....23 E5
  RUSH/FAL M14 ....127 G4
Pleachway HTNM SK4 ....158 C4
Pleasant Gdns BOL BL1 ....2 C2
Pleasant Rd ECC M30 ....109 H4
Pleasant St BKLY M9 ....101 E5
  HEY OL10 ....40 D2
  ROCH OL11 ....42 B4
  TOT/BURYW BL8 ....37 E2
Pleasant Wy CHD/CHDH SK8 ..193 F1
Pleasington Dr NEWH/MOS M40 ..88 B5
  TOT/BURYW BL8 ....36 D4
Plevna St BOLE BL2 ....3 K2
Plodder La FWTH BL4 ....63 G4
Ploughbank Dr CCHDY M21 ....141 G4
Plough Cl URM M41 ....136 D2
Plough Flds WALK M28 ....94 A5
Plough St DUK SK16 ....118 C5
Plover Cl ROCH OL11 ....28 B4
Plover Dr ALT WA14 ....165 E1
  BURY BL9 ....4 B2
  IRL M44 ....136 B1
Plowden Av BOLS/LL BL3 ....63 F1
Plowden Rd WYTH/NTH M22 ..180 A3
Plowley Cl DID/WITH M20 ....157 F1
Plucksbridge Rd MPL/ROM SK6..187 F1
Plumbley Dr OLDTF/WHR M16 ..126 B5
Plumbley St OP/CLY * M11 ....129 H1
Plumley Cl EDGY/DAV SK3 ....172 A5
Plumley Rd WILM/AE SK9 ....198 A4
Plummer Av CCHDY M21 ....141 E5
Plumpton Cl ROY/SHW OL2 ....59 H1
Plumpton Dr BURY BL9 ....27 F5
Plumpton Rd ROCH OL11 ....28 B5
Plumtree Wk
  BRUN/LGST * M13 ....128 C4
Plum St OLDS OL8 ....8 D6
Plum Tree Ct SLFD M6 ....111 H5
Pluto Cl SLFD * M6 ....112 D1
Plymouth Av BRUN/LGST M13..128 B3
Plymouth Cl AUL OL6 ....105 F3
Plymouth Dr BRAM/HZG SK7 ..185 H5
  FWTH BL4 ....64 A5
Plymouth Gv BRUN/LGST M13..128 A3
  EDGY/DAV SK3 ....171 E2

RAD M26 ....51 G4
Plymouth Gv West
  BRUN/LGST M13 ....128 A3
Plymouth Rd SALE M33 ....153 C1
Plymouth St OLDS OL8 ....8 D7
Plymouth Vw BRUN/LGST M13..127 H2
Plymtree Cl CHH M8 ....85 H5
Pobgreen La UPML OL3 ....78 C3
Pochard Dr ALT WA14 ....165 E2
  POY/DIS SK12 ....194 B3
Pochin St NEWH/MOS M40 ....114 B2
Pocklington Dr NTHM/RTH M23..167 C2
Podsmead Rd WYTH/NTH M22 ..180 A2
Poise Brook Dr OFTN SK2 ....173 G4
Poise Brook Rd OFTN SK2 ....173 C4
Poise Cl BRAM/HZG SK7 ....185 H1
Poland St ANC M4 ....7 K2
  DTN/ASHW M34 ....117 F5
Poleacre La MPL/ROM SK6 ....175 E1
Polebrook Av WGTN/LGST M12 ..128 A2
Pole Ct BURY * BL9 ....69 F1
Polefield Ap PWCH M25 ....85 E1
Polefield Cir PWCH M25 ....85 E1
Polefield Gdns PWCH M25 ....85 E1
Polefield Gra PWCH M25 ....85 E1
Polefield Gv PWCH M25 ....85 E1
Polefield Hall Rd PWCH M25 ....85 E1
Polefield Rd BKLY M9 ....87 E5
  PWCH M25 ....69 E5
Pole La BURY BL9 ....69 F2
Pole St ANC M4 ....7 J1
Polesworth Cl WGTN/LGST M12 ..128 D2
Police St ALT WA14 ....165 G4
  CMANW M2 ....6 D4
Pollard St ANC M4 ....109 G3
Pollard St East CMANE M1 ....7 K6
Pollen Cl SALE M33 ....154 D4
Pollen Rd ALT WA14 ....165 H5
Pollerts Av RDSH SK5 ....165 H5
Pollitt Cl WGTN/LGST * M12 ....128 C2
Pollitt Cft ECC M30 ....109 G8
Pollitts Ct ECC M30 ....109 C8
Polonia Ct OLDS OL8 ....89 H4
Polperro Cl ROY/SHW OL2 ....59 H5
Poiruan Rd CCHDY M21 ....140 D1
Polworth Rd BKLY M9 ....101 F1
Polygon Av BRUN/LGST M13 ..127 H2
Polygon Rd CHH M8 ....100 A1
Polygon St BRUN/LGST M13 ..127 H1
Pomfret St SLFD * M6 ....97 H5
  WGTN/LGST M12 ....128 D2
Pomona Crs ORD M5 ....126 A1
Pomona Strd HULME M15 ....125 H5
Pomona St ROCH OL11 ....43 E1
Ponds Cl CCHDY * M21 ....141 E2
Pondwater Cl LHULT M38 ....80 A4
Ponsford Av BKLY M9 ....87 H4
Ponsonby Rd STRET M32 ....125 E5
Pontefract Ct SWIN M27 ....97 H2
Pool Av WYTH/NTH M22 ....101 F1
Poolcroft SALE M33 ....155 C3
Poole Cl BRAM/HZG SK7 ....184 A5
Pooley Cl MDTN M24 ....70 C5
Poolfield Cl RAD M26 ....66 D1
Pool Fold FAIL M35 ....103 F4
Pool House Rd POY/DIS SK12 ..196 B2
Pool St BOL BL1 ....3 G3
  OLDS OL8 ....90 C3
Pool Ter BOL BL1 ....32 D4
Poolton Rd BKLY M9 ....86 C3
Poorfield St OLDS OL8 ....8 A5
Poplar Av ALT WA14 ....165 G5
  BNG/LEV M19 ....144 A4
  BOL BL1 ....34 A2
  BURY BL9 ....4 C1
  OLDE OL4 ....92 D3
  OLDS OL8 ....90 A5
  WILM/AE SK9 ....198 D5
Poplar Cl CHD/CHDH SK8 ....169 G4
Poplar Ct DTN/ASHW * M34 ....131 G2
  EDGY/DAV * SK3 ....172 A4
Poplar Gv AUL OL6 ....105 F5
  GTN M18 ....129 G4
  IRL M44 ....135 C5
  OFTN SK2 ....172 D5
  RAMS BL0 ....17 E1
  SALE M33 ....154 B3
  URM M41 ....138 D1
Poplar Rd BRAM/HZG SK7 ....158 A3
  DUK SK16 ....133 E4
  ECC M30 ....109 H1
  STRET M32 ....139 H1
  SWIN M27 ....96 C5
  WALK M28 ....95 H2
The Poplars MOSL OL5 ....107 F1
Poplars Rd STLY SK15 ....120 D3
Poplar St DTN/ASHW M34 ....131 G2
  FAIL M35 ....102 C4
  HTNM SK4 ....158 B4
  OP/CLY M11 ....114 B5
Poplar Wk CHAD * OL9 ....73 H3
Poppyhom La PWCH M25 ....187 F5
Poppy Cl MDTN M24 ....72 C5
Poplin Cl CSLFD M3 ....6 C1
Poppy Cl CHAD * OL9 ....71 H4
Poppyfield Vw ROCH OL11 ....28 B3
Poppythorn La PWCH M25 ....84 D2
Porchester Dr RAD M26 ....51 F4
Porchfield Sq CSLFD M3 ....6 C6
Porlock Av DTN/ASHW M34 ....118 D1
  HYDE SK14 ....148 D1
Porlock Cl STKP SK1 ....172 D1
Porlock Rd NTHM/RTH M23 ..168 A3
  URM M41 ....138 A3
Porritt Cl ROCH OL11 ....28 B5
Porritt St BURY BL9 ....5 K1
Porritt Wy RAMS BL0 ....16 D1
Portal Gv DTN/ASHW M34 ....147 E2
Porter Dr NEWH/MOS M40 ....88 C5
Porter St BURY BL9 ....5 J1
Porthleven Dr NTHM/RTH M23..167 F3
Portinscale Cl TOT/BURYW BL8..37 G1

Portland Cl BRAM/HZG SK7 ....184 C3
Portland Crs BRUN/LGST M13..128 A3
Portland Gv HTNM SK4 ....159 E2
Portland Houses
  MPL/ROM * SK6 ....174 D4
Portland Pl AULW OL7 ....117 H4
  BRUN/LGST M13 ....128 A3
Portland Rd ALT WA14 ....177 F1
  BRUN/LGST M13 ....128 A3
  ECC M30 ....110 A2
  STRET M32 ....125 F4
  SWIN M27 ....97 F3
  WALK M28 ....80 D2
Portland St BOL BL1 ....33 H4
  BURY BL9 ....5 F6
  CMANE M1 ....7 F6
  MILN OL16 ....10 D5
Portland St North AUL OL6 ....117 H2
Portland St South AULW OL7 ..117 H3
Portloe Rd CHD/CHDH SK8 ....181 G5
Portman Cl OLDTF/WHR M16 ..126 D5
Portman St MOSL OL5 ....106 D1
Portrea Cl EDGY/DAV SK3 ....171 E2
Portree Cl ECC M30 ....109 E5
Portrush Rd WYTH/NTH M22 ..180 D2
Portside Cl WALK M28 ....94 C5
Portsmouth Cl BRO M7 ....99 H4
Portsmouth St BRUN/LGST M13..127 H2
Port Soderick Av ORD M5 ....111 H4
Portstone Cl OLDTF/WHR M16 ..126 D4
Portstone St OLDTF/WHR * M16..126 D4
Port St CMANE M1 ....7 J4
  OLDS OL8 ....90 C5
  STKP SK1 ....12 E2
Portugal Rd PWCH M25 ....85 E5
Portugal St ANC M4 ....7 K2
  AULW OL7 ....117 G5
  BOLE BL2 ....3 J5
Portugal St East CMANE M1 ....7 K6
Portville Rd BNG/LEV M19 ....143 H2
Portway WYTH/NTH M22 ....180 A2
Portwood Pl RDSH SK5 ....13 C1
Posnett St EDGY/DAV SK3 ....12 A5
Postal St CMANE M1 ....7 H4
Postbridge Cl BRUN/LGST M13..127 H2
Post Office St ALT WA14 ....165 G5
Potato Whf CSLFD M3 ....6 A7
Pot HI AUL OL6 ....118 B1
Pot Hill Sq AUL * OL6 ....118 B1
Potters La BKLY M9 ....101 F5
Potter St BURY BL9 ....5 K2
  RAD M26 ....53 E5
Pottery La WGTN/LGST M11 ..114 D5
Pottinger St AULW OL7 ....117 G5
Poulton Av BOLE BL2 ....50 B2
Poulton St OP/CLY M11 ....129 H1
Poundswick La WYTH/NTH M22..180 A1
Powell St OLDTF/WHR M16 ..126 A1
  OP/CLY M11 ....115 G3
  TOT/BURYW BL8 ....37 G5
Powicke Dr MPL/ROM SK6 ....161 G5
Powicke Wk MPL/ROM SK6 ....161 G5
Powis Rd URM M41 ....136 D2
Pownall Av BRAM/HZG SK7 ....194 A3
  DID/WITH M20 ....142 B3
Pownall Rd ALT WA14 ....177 C4
  CHD/CHDH SK8 ....182 C5
  WILM/AE SK9 ....199 G5
Pownall St BRAM/HZG SK7 ....185 E1
  HALE/TIMP WA15 ....178 A4
Poynings Dr WYTH/NTH M22 ..180 B3
Poynt Cha WALK M28 ....94 A4
Poynter St NEWH/MOS M40 ..102 B3
Poynton St BURY BL9 ....5 G7
  HULME M15 ....127 E2
Praed Rd TRPK M17 ....124 D3
The Precinct EDGY/DAV * SK3 ..12 E2
  OFTN * SK2 ....173 G3
Preece Cl HYDE SK14 ....133 F4
Preesall Av CHD/CHDH SK8 ....181 G4
Preesall Cl TOT/BURYW BL8 ....52 A4
Premier Rd CHH M8 ....113 E1
Premier St OLDTF/WHR M16 ..126 C4
Prenton Wy TOT/BURYW BL8 ....37 E1
Presall St SLFD * BL2 ....49 H1
Prescot Cl BURY BL9 ....5 G1
Prescot Rd BKLY M9 ....101 E3
  HALE/TIMP WA15 ....178 A2
Prescott Av WILM/AE SK9 ....199 G2
Prescott Rd WILM/AE SK9 ....199 G2
Prescott St BOLS/LL * BL3 ....48 B5
  MILN OL16 ....30 D1
  WALK M28 ....80 C4
Press St OP/CLY M11 ....129 G1
Presswood Ct SLFD * M6 ....97 H4
Prestage St OFTN SK2 ....172 D2
Prestbury Av HALE/TIMP WA15 ..144 A2
Prestbury Cl BOL BL1 ....33 F2
  OFTN SK2 ....173 G3
Prestbury Dr MPL/ROM SK6 ..161 F3
  OFTN SK2 ....173 G3
Prestbury Rd BOL BL1 ....34 A2
  WILM/AE SK9 ....200 B5
Prestfield Rd WHTF M45 ....68 D5
Presto Gdns BOLS/LL * BL3 ....48 A5
Prestolee Rd BOLS/LL BL3 ....66 B3
Preston Av ECC M30 ....110 B2
Preston Cl ECC M30 ....110 B2
Preston Rd BNG/LEV M19 ....144 A1
Preston St BOLS/LL * BL3 ....49 G5
  GTN M18 ....129 F2
  MDTN M24 ....71 H4
  OLDE OL4 ....9 G6
  SLFD M6 ....111 E4
Prestwich Av DTN/ASHW M34 ..131 H4
  URM M41 ....138 A3
Prestwich Hills PWCH M25 ....84 D5
Prestwich Park Rd South
  PWCH M25 ....84 D4
Prestwood Cl BOL BL2 ....33 H5
Prestwood Dr BOL BL2 ....33 H5
Prestwood Rd FWTH BL4 ....64 B5
  SLFD M6 ....110 D1
Pretoria Rd BOLE BL2 ....50 B2
  OLDS OL8 ....90 C4
Pretoria St WHIT * OL12 ....29 F2
Prettywood BURY BL9 ....39 G4
Price St ANC * M4 ....114 A4

  BURY BL9 ....5 G7
  DUK * SK16 ....118 B5
  FWTH BL4 ....65 E3
Prichard St STRET M32 ....140 A1
Prickshaw La WHIT OL12 ....18 A2
Pridmouth Rd DID/WITH M20..142 D5
Priest Av CHD/CHDH SK8 ....169 F5
Priestley Rd WALK M28 ....96 B2
Priestley Wy ROY/SHW OL2 ....60 C2
Priestnall Rd HTNM SK4 ....158 C3
Priest St STKP SK1 ....172 A2
Priestwood Cl OLDE OL4 ....61 E5
Primrose Av FWTH BL4 ....64 B5
  HYDE SK14 ....147 H2
  MPL/ROM SK6 ....174 D3
  UPML OL3 ....79 F3
  URM M41 ....138 C1
  WALK M28 ....81 E5
Primrose Bank ALT WA14 ....177 F5
  OLDS OL8 ....8 E7
  TOT/BURYW BL8 ....37 G1
Primrose Cl BOLE BL2 ....35 H2
  ORD M5 ....111 G3
Primrose Cottages ALT * WA14 ..177 F5
Primrose Crs HYDE SK14 ....147 G3
Primrose Dr BURY BL9 ....39 G2
  DROY M43 ....116 D2
Primrose St ANC M4 ....7 J2
  BOL * BL1 ....34 A2
  FWTH BL4 ....64 B5
  OLDS OL8 ....9 G7
  WHIT OL12 ....29 G5
Primrose Wk OLDS OL8 ....9 G7
Primula St BOL BL1 ....34 A1
Prince Albert Av
  BNG/LEV * M19 ....143 H1
Prince Charlie St OLD OL1 ....75 E4
Princedom St BKLY M9 ....101 F2
Prince Edward Av
  DTN/ASHW M34 ....146 C1
  OLDE OL4 ....91 H5
Prince George St OLD * OL1 ....75 F3
Prince Rd POY/DIS SK12 ....196 B2
Princes Av BOLS/LL BL3 ....51 E5
  DID/WITH M20 ....157 H2
  IRL M44 ....136 B5
  MPL/ROM SK6 ....161 H5
Princes Dr MPL/ROM SK6 ....174 C2
  SALE M33 ....155 E3
Princes Rd ALT WA14 ....163 H5
  HTNM SK4 ....158 D2
  NEWH/MOS M40 ....89 E5
  SALE M33 ....155 E3
Princess Av CHD/CHDH SK8 ..182 D1
  DTN/ASHW M34 ....131 F5
  FWTH BL4 ....81 G2
  PWCH M25 ....99 H4
  WHIT OL12 ....19 H4
Princess Cl DUK SK16 ....118 C5
  HEY OL10 ....41 E5
  MOSL OL5 ....107 F2
Princess Dr MDTN M24 ....71 F4
Princess Gv FWTH BL4 ....65 E4
Princess Pkwy WYTH/NTH M22..156 B5
Princess Pde BURY BL9 ....4 E5
  RUSH/FAL M14 ....142 B2
Princess Pkwy MANAIR M90 ..180 B4
  DID/WITH M20 ....142 B2
  HOR/BR BL6 ....46 C2
  HULME M15 ....31 E4
  MILN OL16 ....31 E4
  PWCH * M25 ....99 H4
  ROY/SHW OL2 ....59 F2
  RUSH/FAL M14 ....142 A3
  URM M41 ....138 A1
  WILM/AE SK9 ....199 F5
Princess Rd ALT WA14 ....165 F1
  AUL OL6 ....118 C1
  BOL BL1 ....3 H5
  CMANW M2 ....6 D5
  ECC M30 ....109 H1
  FAIL M35 ....102 D3
  HYDE SK14 ....147 H1
  NEWH/MOS M40 ....114 B1
  OLDE OL4 ....91 H1
  OP/CLY M11 ....114 D4
  RAD M26 ....66 C1
  SLFD M6 ....112 A1
  SWIN M27 ....97 F3
  URM M41 ....138 A1
  WILM/AE SK9 ....199 F5
Prince's St BOL BL1 ....13 F3
  MILN OL16 ....43 C1
  OLD OL1 ....9 F4
  RAMS BL0 ....17 E2
Princes Wk BRAM/HZG SK7 ..184 B6
Princethorpe Cl HOR/BR BL6 ..47 E3
Princeton Cl SLFD M6 ....112 B1
Prinknash Rd WYTH/NTH M22..180 C3
Printers La BOLE BL2 ....35 H5
Printer St OLD OL1 ....9 H4
  OP/CLY * M11 ....115 G5
Printon Av BKLY M9 ....86 C3
Printworks La BNG/LEV M19 ..144 B2
Printworks Rd STLY SK15 ....119 G2
Prior St OLDS OL8 ....91 E5
The Priory BRO M7 ....99 E3
Priory Av CHD/CHDH SK8 ....169 F5
  CCHDY M21 ....141 E1
Priory Cl DUK SK16 ....132 C2
  OLDS OL8 ....90 A5
  SALE M33 ....140 A5
Priory Ct RDSH SK5 ....144 D4
Priory Gv BRO M7 ....99 F4
  CHAD OL9 ....8 B1
Priory La RDSH SK5 ....145 G3
Priory Pl BOLE BL2 ....34 D3
Priory Rd ANC M4 ....7 J1
  CHD/CHDH SK8 ....169 G4
  SALE M33 ....155 E1
  SWIN M27 ....98 D2
  WILM/AE SK9 ....198 D2
Priory St WHIT * OL12 ....29 F2
  BOLE BL2 ....35 G4
  ROCH OL11 ....42 B5
Proctor St TOT/BURYW BL8 ....37 G5
Progress Av DTN/ASHW M34 ..131 G2
Progress St AUL OL6 ....104 C5
  BOL BL1 ....2 F5
  ROCH OL11 ....43 E5
Promenade St HEY OL10 ....41 F4

Propps Hall Dr FAIL M35 102 C4
Prospect Av FWTH BL4 65 E5
IRL M44 135 D5
Prospect Ct TOT/BURYW BL8 26 A4
Prospect Dr FAIL M35 103 E5
HALE/TIMP WA15 179 E5
Prospect Hl BOLE BL2 35 G2
Prospect Pl AUL OL6 105 G5
FWTH BL4 64 D5
HEY OL10 41 E3
Prospect Rd AUL OL6 105 H5
CHAD OL9 8 A2
DUK SK16 118 C5
IRL M44 135 D5
Prospect St BOL BL1 34 A5
HEY OL10 56 B1
LIT * OL15 21 E3
ROCH OL11 42 D2
Prospect Ter TOT/BURYW BL8 4 A1
Prospect V CHD/CHDH SK8 181 G3
Prospect Vw SWIN M27 97 F3
Prout St WGTN/LGST M12 128 D5
Providence St ANC M4 114 A4
AUL * OL6 118 B1
BOLS/LL BL3 49 E4
DTN/ASHW M34 131 G1
Provident Av BNG/LEV M19 144 B2
Provident St ROY/SHW * OL2 60 A2
Provident Wy HALE/TIMP WA15 166 B2
Provis Rd CCHDY M21 141 E4
Prubella Av DTN/ASHW M34 131 F3
Pryce St BOL BL1 2 B1
Pryme St HULME M15 126 D1
Pudding La HYDE SK14 133 H5
Puffin Av POY/DIS SK12 194 B4
Puffingate Cl STLY SK15 107 F3
Pulborough Cl TOT/BURYW BL8 26 C4
Pulford Av CCHDY M21 156 C2
Pulford Rd SALE M33 154 D4
Pullman Cl BNG/LEV M19 144 A3
Pullman Dr STRET M32 139 E1
Pullman St ROCH OL11 43 E1
Punch La BOLS/LL BL3 62 A2
Punch St BOLS/LL BL3 2 B7
Purbeck Cl WYTH/NTH M22 180 B3
Purbeck Dr HOR/BR BL6 46 A1
TOT/BURYW BL8 26 D5
Purcell Cl BOL BL1 33 G5
Purcell St WGTN/LGST M12 128 D5
Purdon St BURY BL9 27 G5
Purley Av NTHM/RTH M23 156 A5
Purley Dr IRL M44 150 B1
Purple St BOL BL1 3 F4
Purslow Cl WGTN/LGST M12 114 B4
Putney Cl OLD OL1 74 B3
Pymgate Dr CHD/CHDH SK8 181 F2
Pymgate La CHD/CHDH SK8 181 F2
Pym St ECC M30 109 G3
HEY OL10 41 E5
NEWH/MOS * M40 101 G2
Pyramid Ct BRO M7 99 G4
Pyrus Cl ECC M30 108 C5
Pytha Fold Rd DID/WITH M20 158 A1

Q

The Quadrant BKLY M9 87 H4
DROY M43 116 A4
MPL/ROM SK6 161 H4
STKP SK1 160 C5
Quail Dr IRL M44 121 B5
Quail St OLDE OL4 91 F2
Quakers Fld TOT/BURYW BL8 26 A3
Quantock Cl HTNM SK4 12 E1
Quantock St OLDTF/WHR * M16 126 D4
Quarmby Rd GTN M18 130 A4
Quarry Bank Rd WILM/AE SK9 191 E4
Quarry Clough STLY SK15 120 A5
Quarry Hts STLY SK15 119 E5
Quarry Pond Rd WALK M28 80 B4
Quarry Ri MPL/ROM SK6 162 A3
STLY SK15 119 E5
Quarry Rd FWTH BL4 65 H5
MPL/ROM SK6 162 A4
Quarry St MPL/ROM * SK6 162 A1
RAD M26 67 G1
RAMS BL0 17 E2
STLY SK15 119 E4
WHIT OL12 10 B3
Quarry Wk OP/CLY * M11 114 C4
The Quays SALQ M50 125 G1
Quayside Cl WALK M28 94 C5
Quay St CSLFD M3 6 B5
HEY * OL10 41 F5
Quay Vw ORD M5 111 H5
Quebec Pl BOLS/LL BL3 48 B4
Quebec St BOLS/LL BL3 48 C4
CHAD OL9 8 B1
DTN/ASHW M34 131 F3
Queen Alexandra Cl ORD * M5 112 B5
Queen Ann Dr WALK M28 94 B3
Queenhill Dr HYDE SK14 133 E3
Queenhill Rd WYTH/NTH M22 156 D5
Queen's Av EDGW/EG BL7 23 F4
MPL/ROM SK6 161 H3
WHIT OL12 19 H4
Queensbrook BOL BL1 2 C4
Queensbury Cl BOL BL1 33 G1
WILM/AE SK9 200 A2
Queensbury Pde
NEWH/MOS * M40 114 B2
Queens Cl HTNM SK4 158 D4
HYDE * SK14 147 H4
WALK M28 94 A3
Queens Ct NEWH/MOS M40 101 E5
Queens Dr CHD/CHDH SK8 182 D1
HTNM SK4 158 D4
HYDE SK14 148 A4
PWCH M25 85 F5
ROCH OL11 42 D3
Queensferry St
NEWH/MOS M40 102 B4
Queensgate BOL BL1 48 A1
BRAM/HZG SK7 193 H2
Queensgate Dr ROY/SHW OL2 58 D3
Queen's Gv WGTN/LGST M12 128 D4
Queensland Rd GTN M18 129 E3
Queens Pk BOL * BL1 2 A5
Queen's Park Rd HEY OL10 41 E3
Queens Pl BURY BL9 26 D1
Queen's Rd AUL OL6 105 G5
BOLS/LL BL3 48 A5
BRAM/HZG SK7 185 F1
CHAD OL9 73 F5
CHD/CHDH SK8 170 C5
CHH M8 100 C5
HALE/TIMP WA15 177 H1
LIT OL15 21 E3
MPL/ROM SK6 161 H3
NEWH/MOS M40 101 E5
OLDS OL8 9 J6
SALE M33 154 A2
URM M41 138 C2
WILM/AE SK9 199 F4
Queenston Rd DID/WITH M20 157 E2
Queen St AUL OL6 118 C2
BOL BL1 2 D5
BURY BL9 5 G4
CHD/CHDH SK8 170 B3
CMANW M2 6 D5
CSLFD M3 6 C2
DTN/ASHW M34 131 F4
DTN/ASHW M34 131 G2
DUK SK16 118 A4
ECC * M30 110 A4
FAIL M35 102 D3
FWTH BL4 65 E4
HEY OL10 41 E4
HYDE SK14 147 H2
LHULT M38 80 C4
LIT OL15 21 E3
MDTN M24 72 B4
MOSL OL5 106 D1
MPL/ROM SK6 175 E3
OLD OL1 9 H3
OLDE OL4 92 A1
RAD M26 67 H2
RAMS BL0 16 C3
ROY/SHW OL2 59 E5
ROY/SHW OL2 60 A3
SLFD M6 98 A5
STKP SK1 13 K1
STLY * SK15 119 F3
TOT/BURYW BL8 37 F1
WHIT OL12 10 C4
Queen St West DID/WITH M20 142 C4
Queens Vw LIT OL15 20 D5
Queensway BNG/LEV M19 158 A4
CHD/CHDH SK8 181 H4
DUK SK16 133 E1
FWTH BL4 65 E3
IRL M44 136 A1
MOSL OL5 107 E3
PART M31 151 E2
POY/DIS SK12 195 E4
ROCH OL11 42 C3
ROCH OL11 43 F2
SWIN M27 83 F5
URM M41 123 H4
WALK M28 94 C2
Queen Victoria St ECC M30 109 F3
ROCH OL11 43 F2
Quenby St HULME M15 126 C2
Quendon Av BRO M7 112 D1
Quick Edge La OLDE OL4 92 D5
Quickedge Rd MOSL OL5 92 D5
Quick Rd OLDE OL4 92 D3
Quick Vw MOSL OL5 93 F4
Quill Ct IRL M44 135 D5
Quilter Gv BKLY M9 86 D5
Quinney Crs OLDTF/WHR M16 127 E5
Quinn St OP/CLY M11 114 D4
Quinton WHIT OL12 10 B5
Quinton Wk BRUN/LGST M13 127 G2
Quixall St OP/CLY M11 114 D3

R

Raby St OLDTF/WHR M16 126 D4
The Race WILM/AE SK9 192 A5
Racecourse Pk WILM/AE SK9 199 E4
Racecourse Rd WILM/AE SK9 198 D4
Racefield Rd ALT WA14 165 F5
Rachel St WGTN/LGST M12 113 H5
Rackhouse Rd NTHM/RTH M23 156 A5
Radbourne Cl WGTN/LGST M12 128 D2
Radbourne Gv BOLS/LL BL3 47 G5
Radcliffe Moor Rd BOLE BL2 51 E4
Radcliffe New Rd WHTF M45 67 H2
Radcliffe Park Crs SLFD M6 97 H5
Radcliffe Park Rd SLFD M6 97 G5
Radcliffe Rd BOLE BL2 3 J5
BOLS/LL BL3 50 D5
BURY BL9 53 F2
OLDE OL4 75 G2
Radcliffe St OLD OL1 8 E3
OLD OL1 9 G1
OLDE * OL4 92 B1
ROY/SHW OL2 59 F5
Radclyffe St CHAD OL9 73 G4
MDTN M24 71 H2
Radclyffe Ter MDTN M24 71 H2
Radelan Gv RAD M26 51 G5
Radford Cl OFTN SK2 173 E2
Radford Dr BKLY M9 101 F2
IRL M44 121 B5
Radford St BRO M7 99 F2
Radium St ANC M4 7 J2
Radlet Dr HALE/TIMP WA15 166 B1
Radlett Wk BRUN/LGST * M13 127 H3
Radley Cl BOL BL1 32 D5
SALE M33 153 G3
Radley St DROY M43 115 H5
OLDTF/WHR M16 127 E5
Radnor Av DTN/ASHW M34 130 C5
Radnormere Dr CHD/CHDH SK8 170 C5
Radnor St CHAD OL9 8 A6
GTN M18 129 F4
HULME M15 127 E3
STRET M32 140 A1
Radstock Cl BOL BL1 22 D4
RUSH/FAL M14 142 C2
Radstock Rd STRET M32 139 H1
Raeburn Dr MPL/ROM SK6 175 G1
Rae St EDGY/DAV SK3 12 B5
Raglan Av SWIN M27 83 G5
WHTF M45 69 E5
Raglan Dr ALT WA14 165 H1
Raglan Rd SALE M33 154 A3
STRET M32 124 C5
Raglan St BOL BL1 33 G4
HYDE SK14 147 F1
ROCH OL11 42 B5
Raglan Wk HULME * M15 127 E2
Ragley Cl POY/DIS SK12 195 G3
Raikes La BOLS/LL BL3 49 G5
Raikes Rd BOLS/LL BL3 50 A4
Raikes Wy BOLS/LL BL3 50 A4
Railton Av OLDTF/WHR M16 126 C5
Railton Ter BKLY * M9 101 G3
Railway Ap ROCH OL11 42 B4
Railway Brow ROCH OL11 42 B5
Railway Rd CHAD OL9 8 C5
CHAD OL9 89 F5
EDGY/DAV SK3 13 F5
STRET M32 125 G3
URM M41 138 C1
Railway St ALT WA14 165 G5
BURY BL9 26 C1
DUK SK16 118 A5
FWTH BL4 65 F3
GTN M18 129 F2
HEY OL10 41 F5
HTNM SK4 12 D3
LIT OL15 21 E3
MILN OL16 30 B5
MILN OL16 45 F2
RAD M26 67 F2
RAMS BL0 16 D2
Railway Ter TOT/BURYW BL8 37 H5
Railway Vw OLDE OL4 92 A1
ROY/SHW OL2 45 F5
Raimond St BOL BL1 33 F3
Rainbow Cl CCHDY M21 141 E4
Raincliff Av BRUN/LGST M13 143 G1
Raines Crest MILN OL16 31 H5
Rainford Av DID/WITH M20 142 B3
HALE/TIMP WA15 166 B4
Rainford St BOLE BL2 23 H5
Rainforth St BRUN/LGST M13 128 C5
Rainham Dr BOL BL1 2 D1
CHH M8 100 B3
Rainham Wy CHAD OL9 89 G1
RDSH SK5 145 G5
Rainow Av DROY M43 115 H5
Rainow Dr POY/DIS SK12 195 H5
Rainow Rd EDGY/DAV * SK3 171 F3
Rainshaw St BOL BL1 34 A2
OLDE * OL4 75 G4
Rainsough Av PWCH M25 98 C1
Rainsough Brow PWCH M25 98 C1
Rainsough Cl PWCH M25 98 D1
Rainwood CHAD OL9 72 D4
Raja Cl CHH M8 100 C3
Rake ROCH OL11 28 A4
Rake La SWIN M27 83 E4
Rake St BURY BL9 38 C2
Rake Ter LIT OL15 21 F2
Rakewood Dr OLDE OL4 60 D5
Rakewood Rd LIT OL15 21 E5
Raleigh Cl DID/WITH M20 157 F1
OLD OL1 74 C4
Raleigh Gdns LIT OL15 15 B4
Raleigh St RDSH SK5 159 H2
STRET M32 140 A1
Ralli Cts CSLFD M3 6 B4
Ralph Av HYDE SK14 147 H4
Ralph Green St CHAD OL9 89 G4
Ralphs La DUK SK16 132 B1
Ralph St BOL BL1 33 G4
OP/CLY M11 115 G4
WHIT OL12 10 E3
Ralston Cl BRO M7 100 A2
Ralstone Av OLDS OL8 90 C3
Ramage Wk WGTN/LGST M12 114 B4
Ramillies Av CHD/CHDH SK8 183 E3
Ramp Rd East MANAIR M90 180 B5
Ramp Rd South MANAIR M90 180 B5
Ramp Rd West MANAIR M90 180 A5
Ramsay Av FWTH BL4 64 C5
Ramsay Pl MILN OL16 10 E5
Ramsay St BOL BL1 33 H2
MILN OL16 10 E5
Ramsay Ter MILN * OL16 10 E5
Ramsbottom La RAMS BL0 16 D1
Ramsbottom Rd BOLE BL2 24 C1
Ramsbury Dr NEWH/MOS M40 88 C5
Ramsdale Rd BRAM/HZG SK7 183 H4
Ramsdale St CHAD OL9 73 F5
Ramsden Cl OLD OL1 8 E2
Ramsden Crs OLD OL1 8 E2
Ramsden Rd WHIT OL12 19 H1
Ramsden St AUL OL6 118 C1
BOLS/LL BL3 50 A4
OLD OL1 8 E2
Ramsey Av BNG/LEV M19 144 C2
Ramsey Gv TOT/BURYW BL8 37 G4
Ramsey St CHAD OL9 89 G2
NEWH/MOS M40 102 A3
OLD OL1 75 E4
Ramsgate Rd NEWH/MOS M40 115 F1
RDSH SK5 145 E4
Ramsgate St BRO M7 99 H5
Ramsgill Cl NTHM/RTH M23 155 F5
Ramsgreave Cl BURY BL9 53 E2
Ram St LHULT M38 80 A3
Ramwell Gdns BOLS/LL * BL3 48 C4
Ramwells Brow EDGW/EG BL7 23 E3
Ramwells Ct EDGW/EG * BL7 23 G3
Ramwells Ms EDGW/EG * BL7 23 G3
Ranby Av BKLY M9 87 G3
Randale Dr BURY BL9 68 D2
Randal St BOLS/LL BL3 48 B5
Randerson St WGTN/LGST M12 127 H1
Randlesham St PWCH M25 85 F3
Randolph Pl EDGY/DAV SK3 13 F7
Randolph Rd FWTH BL4 65 G5
Randolph St BNG/LEV M19 143 H1
BOLS/LL BL3 48 B3
OLDS OL8 89 H5
Rands Clough Dr WALK M28 94 C4
Rand St OLD OL1 75 G3
Ranelagh Rd SWIN M27 97 H3
Ranelagh St OP/CLY M11 115 E3
Raneley Gv ROCH OL11 43 F4
Ranford Rd BNG/LEV M19 143 H3
Range Dr MPL/ROM SK6 147 F5
Rangemore Av
WYTH/NTH * M22 168 C1
Range Rd DUK SK16 133 G2
EDGY/DAV SK3 171 H3
OLDTF/WHR M16 126 D5
STLY SK15 119 G5
Range St BOLS/LL BL3 48 C5
OP/CLY M11 115 F5
Rankine Ter BOLS/LL * BL3 48 C4
Rannoch Rd BOLE BL2 50 C2
Ransfield Rd CCHDY M21 140 D1
Ranulph Ct SLFD * M6 98 A5
Ranworth Av HTNM SK4 158 C4
Ranworth Cl BOL BL1 23 F5
Raper St OLDE OL4 75 F4
Raphael St BOL BL1 33 G4
Rappax Rd HALE/TIMP WA15 178 B4
Rasbottom St BOLS/LL BL3 2 B7
Raspberry La IRL M44 121 A4
Rassbottom Brow STLY * SK15 119 E3
Rassbottom St STLY SK15 119 E3
Ratcliffe Av IRL M44 136 B1
Ratcliffe St BNG/LEV M19 144 A2
STKP SK1 13 G6
Rathan Rd URM M41 123 F4
Rathbone St MILN OL16 11 J7
Rathbourne Av BKLY M9 87 E4
Rathen Rd DID/WITH M20 157 G1
Rathmel Rd NTHM/RTH M23 155 G4
Rathmore Av NEWH/MOS M40 101 F5
Rathvale Dr WYTH/NTH M22 180 B4
Rathybank Cl BOL BL1 33 E4
Rattenbury Ct SLFD M6 97 H5
Raveden Cl BOL BL1 33 F3
Raveley Av RUSH/FAL M14 143 E3
Ravelston Dr BKLY M9 101 E4
Raven Av CHAD OL9 89 F2
Raven Cl DROY M43 116 D2
Ravendale Cl WHIT OL12 28 D2
Raven Dr IRL M44 121 B5
Ravenfield Gv BOL * BL1 2 B2
Ravenhead Cl RUSH/FAL M14 143 E3
Ravenhead Sq STLY SK15 107 F5
Ravenhurst Dr BOL BL1 47 E3
Ravenna Av NTHM/RTH M23 167 E2
Ravenoak Av BNG/LEV M19 144 A3
Ravenoak Dr FAIL M35 103 F2
Ravenoak Park Rd
CHD/CHDH SK8 183 E4
Ravenoak Rd CHD/CHDH SK8 183 E3
EDGY/DAV SK3 172 B5
Raven Rd BOLS/LL * BL3 47 H5
HALE/TIMP WA15 154 C5
Ravensbury St OP/CLY M11 115 E3
Ravenscar Crs WYTH/NTH M22 180 C4
Ravens Cl PWCH M25 85 H5
Ravenscraig Rd LHULT M38 80 C1
Ravensdale Gdns ECC M30 109 H2
Ravensdale Rd BOL BL1 47 E2
Ravensdale St RUSH/FAL M14 127 H5
Ravens Holme BOL BL1 47 F2
Ravenside Pk CHAD OL9 89 F2
Ravenstonedale Dr
ROY/SHW OL2 59 F4
Ravenstone Dr SALE M33 155 F1
UPML OL3 78 B1
Raven St BURY BL9 5 F1
ROCH OL11 28 A2
WGTN/LGST M12 113 H5
Ravensway PWCH M25 85 G5
Ravens Wd BOL BL1 47 F2
Ravenswood Av HTNM SK4 158 D5
Ravenswood Dr BKLY M9 87 F4
BOL BL1 47 F2
CHD/CHDH SK8 183 E4
Ravenswood Rd STRET M32 125 G3
WILM/AE SK9 201 A1
Raven Wy SLFD M6 111 G2
Ravenwood CHAD OL9 72 C5
Ravenwood Dr DTN/ASHW M34 131 F2
HALE/TIMP WA15 179 E5
Ravine Av BKLY M9 101 F3
Rawcliffe Av BOLE BL2 50 C2
Rawcliffe St RUSH/FAL M14 127 G5
Rawdon Cl BNG/LEV M19 144 A2
Rawkin Cl HULME M15 126 D3
Rawlyn Rd BOL BL1 32 C5
Rawpool Gdns NTHM/RTH M23 167 H2
Rawson Av FWTH BL4 65 F3
Rawson Rd BOL BL1 33 F5
Rawsons Rake TOT/BURYW BL8 16 B2
Rawson St FWTH BL4 65 E3
Rawsthorne St BOL BL1 33 H4
Rawstron St WHIT OL12 14 B4
Rayburn Wy CHH M8 100 B5
Raycroft Av BKLY M9 87 H5
Raydon Av NEWH/MOS * M40 101 E5
Rayleigh Av OP/CLY M11 130 A1
Raymond Av BURY BL9 38 C1
CHAD OL9 89 G3
Raymond Rd NTHM/RTH M23 156 A4
Raymond St SWIN M27 97 E1
Rayner La AULW OL7 117 F3
Rayners Cl STLY SK15 119 E4
Rayner St STKP SK1 172 C1
Raynham Av DID/WITH M20 157 G3
Raynham St AUL OL6 118 B2
Rayson Hill Dr BKLY * M9 86 D5
Rayson St BKLY M9 86 D5
Reabrook Av WGTN/LGST M12 128 C2
The Reach WALK M28 81 F5
Read Cl BURY BL9 53 E2
Reade Av URM M41 137 F2
Reading Cl OP/CLY M11 115 F5
Reading Dr SALE M33 153 G2
Reading St SLFD M6 99 E5
Readitt Wk OP/CLY M11 115 E3
Read St HYDE SK14 132 B5
Read St West HYDE SK14 132 B5
Reaney Wk WGTN/LGST * M12 128 D2
Reather Wk NEWH/MOS M40 113 H2
Rebecca St CHH M8 100 B2
Recreation Rd FAIL M35 103 F1
Recreation St BOLE BL2 35 F1
BOLS/LL BL3 48 D5
PWCH M25 85 F3
Rectory Av CHH M8 100 B1
PWCH M25 85 E3
Rectory Cl DTN/ASHW M34 146 D1
RAD M26 53 E5
Rectory Flds STKP SK1 13 J3
Rectory Gdns PWCH M25 85 E3
Rectory Gn PWCH M25 84 D3
STKP SK1 13 J3
Rectory Gv PWCH M25 85 E4
Rectory Hl BURY BL9 39 G3
Rectory La BURY BL9 39 G2
PWCH M25 84 D3
RAD M26 67 H1
Rectory Rd CHH M8 100 A1
Rectory St MDTN M24 71 G3
Redacre POY/DIS SK12 195 G1
Redacre Rd GTN M18 129 H3
Red Bank ANC M4 113 F2
Red Bank Rd RAD M26 52 A4
Redbarn Cl MPL/ROM SK6 161 G2
Redbourne Dr URM M41 122 C4
Redbrick Ct AULW OL7 117 H4
Redbrook Av NEWH/MOS M40 101 F5
Redbrook Cl FWTH * BL4 65 F3
Redbrook Rd HALE/TIMP WA15 167 E3
PART M31 150 D4
Red Brook St ROCH OL11 29 G4
Redburn Rd NTHM/RTH M23 168 A2
Redby St OP/CLY * M11 129 E1
Redcar Av DID/WITH M20 142 C5
URM M41 122 D4
Redcar Cl BRAM/HZG SK7 185 H3
OLD OL1 75 E3
Redcar Rd BOL BL1 33 E2
BOLS/LL BL3 65 H1
SWIN M27 97 H3
Redcar St WHIT OL12 10 B4
Redclyffe Av RUSH/FAL M14 127 H5
Redclyffe Rd DID/WITH M20 157 F1
URM M41 109 G5
Redcot BOL * BL1 48 A2
Redcote St NEWH/MOS M40 101 H2
Redcourt Av DID/WITH M20 157 G2
Redcroft Gdns BNG/LEV M19 158 B2
Redcroft Rd SALE M33 138 D5
Redcross St WHIT OL12 10 C3
Redcross St North WHIT OL12 10 B3
Reddaway Cl SLFD M6 98 D5
Reddish Cl BOLE BL2 24 B5
Reddish La GTN M18 129 H5
Reddish Rd RDSH SK5 145 E5
Reddish Vale Rd RDSH SK5 145 F4
Reddyshore TOD * OL14 15 B1
Reddyshore Brow LIT OL15 15 C5
Redesmere Cl DROY M43 116 C4
HALE/TIMP WA15 167 E3
Redesmere Dr CHD/CHDH SK8 170 C5
WILM/AE SK9 201 A4
Redesmere Pk URM M41 138 A3
Redesmere Rd WILM/AE SK9 192 A2
Redfearn Wd WHIT OL12 29 E1
Redfern Av SALE M33 155 F3
Redfern St ANC M4 7 F2
Redfern Wy ROCH OL11 28 A2
Redfield Cl OP/CLY M11 114 C4
Redford Dr BRAM/HZG SK7 184 B2
Redford Rd CHH M8 86 A3
Redford St TOT/BURYW BL8 37 H3
Redgate HYDE SK14 147 G3
Redgate La WGTN/LGST M12 128 D3
Redgates Wk CCHDY * M21 141 E2
Redgate Wy FWTH BL4 64 A3
Redgrave Pas OLDE OL4 75 G4
Redgrave St OLDE OL4 75 G4
Red Hall St OLDE OL4 91 F1
Redhill Dr MPL/ROM SK6 161 E3
Redhill Gv BOL BL1 2 C1
Redhill St ANC M4 7 J4
Redhouse La MPL/ROM SK6 161 G2
Redington Cl WALK M28 94 B5
Redisher Cft TOT/BURYW BL8 16 A5
Redland Av RDSH SK5 160 A1
Redland Cl LIT OL15 21 E2
Redland Crs CCHDY M21 141 E5
Red La BOLE BL2 35 E5
POY/DIS SK12 197 G2
WHIT OL12 11 G1
Red Lion St ANC * M4 7 G3
Redmere Dr BURY BL9 53 H1
Redmere Gv RUSH/FAL M14 142 D3
Redmire Ms DUK SK16 133 E1
Redmond Cl DTN/ASHW M34 131 F1
Redmoor Sq CMANE M1 127 G1
Red Pike Wk OLD OL1 74 D4
Redpoll Cl WALK M28 94 C3
Red Rock La RAD M26 82 C1
Red Rose Crs BNG/LEV M19 144 B4
Redruth St RUSH/FAL M14 142 C1
Redshaw Av BOLE BL2 23 G5
Redshaw Cl RUSH/FAL M14 143 E2
Redstart Gv WALK M28 95 E2
Redstone Rd BNG/LEV M19 158 A3
Redthorn Av BNG/LEV M19 143 G4
Redvale Rd BRO M7 99 H4
Redvales Rd BURY BL9 53 F2
Redvers St OLD OL1 8 D1
OP/CLY M11 114 B5
Redwater Cl WALK M28 94 B4
Redwing Rd TOT/BURYW BL8 26 A1
Redwood CHAD OL9 72 C5
SALE M33 153 F2
Redwood Cl WHIT OL12 18 A5
Redwood Dr CHH M8 100 C5
DTN/ASHW M34 131 F2
MPL/ROM SK6 161 G3
Redwood La OLDE OL4 75 H5
Redwood Park Gv MILN OL16 31 E4
Redwood Rd UPML OL3 78 B5
Redwood St SLFD M6 111 H1
Reedbank RAD M26 67 F4
Reed Ct OLD * OL1 74 B4
Reedham Cl BOL BL1 48 B1
Reedham Wk CHAD * OL9 89 H3
NEWH/MOS * M40 114 A1
Reed Hl MILN OL16 10 C5
Reedley Dr WALK M28 94 D2
Reedmace Cl WALK M28 95 F1
Reedshaw Bank OFTN SK2 173 E4
Reedshaw Rd BKLY M9 100 D4
Reed St GTN M18 129 G2
OLD * OL1 9 J3
Reeman Cl MPL/ROM SK6 161 H2
Reeve Cl OFTN SK2 173 G4
Reeves Rd CCHDY M21 141 E4
Reevey Av BRAM/HZG SK7 184 D2
Reform St WHIT OL12 10 C4
Reform Wk OP/CLY M11 115 E5
Refuge St ROY/SHW OL2 60 A3
Regal Cl WHTF M45 69 E4
Regan Av CCHDY M21 141 G4
Regan St BOL BL1 33 G3
RAD M26 67 G2
Regatta Cl CHAD OL9 89 F4
Regatta St SLFD M6 98 C4
Regency Cl NEWH/MOS M40 101 E5
OLDS OL8 90 A3
Regency Ct HALE/TIMP * WA15 178 C3
ROCH OL11 28 C4
Regency Gdns CHD/CHDH SK8 182 B4
Regency Ldg PWCH * M25 84 D4
Regency Pk WILM/AE SK9 199 E5

Regent Av LHULT M38 80 D3
RUSH/FAL M14 142 A1
Regent Cl BRAM/HZG SK7 193 G3
CHD/CHDH SK8 171 F5
WILM/AE SK9 199 E5
Regent Ct HTNM SK4 159 F1
Regent Crs FAIL M35 102 D4
ROY/SHW OL2 74 A2
Regent Dr DTN/ASHW M34 146 A2
HOR/BR BL6 46 C2
Regent Pl RUSH/FAL M14 127 H4
Regent Rd ALT WA14 165 G5
HOR/BR BL6 46 C3
OFTN SK2 172 B3
ORD M5 112 A5
Regents Dr MOSL OL5 107 E3
Regents Hl HOR/BR BL6 46 D3
Regents Pk ORD * M5 112 B5
Regents Sq ORD M5 112 A5
Regent St BURY BL9 4 E1
ECC M30 110 B3
HEY OL10 40 C5
LIT OL15 21 E3
MDTN M24 71 G2
NEWH/MOS M40 102 C5
OLD OL1 9 J3
RAMS BL0 16 B3
WHIT OL12 10 D2
Regent Wk FWTH * BL4 65 E4
Regina Av STLY SK15 119 F3
Reginald St BOLS/LL * BL3 62 D2
ECC M30 108 D5
OP/CLY M11 130 A1
SWIN M27 96 C1
Reid Cl DTN/ASHW M34 146 D3
Reigate Cl TOT/BURYW * BL8 37 G5
Reigate Rd URM M41 137 F3
Reilly St HULME M15 127 E2
Reins Lee Av OLDS OL8 90 D5
Reins Lee Rd AULW OL7 104 D4
Reliance St NEWH/MOS M40 102 B4
Rembrandt Wk OLD OL1 60 C4
Rena Cl HTNM SK4 159 G3
Rendel Cl STRET M32 140 A1
Renfrew Dr BOLS/LL BL3 62 C1
Rennie Cl STRET M32 140 A1
Renshaw Av ECC M30 109 G4
Renshaw Dr BURY BL9 39 F3
Renshaw St ECC M30 109 G4
Renton Rd BOLS/LL BL3 63 E1
STRET M32 140 B1
WYTH/NTH M22 168 C5
Repton Av DROY M43 115 G2
DTN/ASHW M34 130 B5
HYDE SK14 132 D5
NEWH/MOS M40 102 D1
OLDS OL8 90 A4
URM M41 137 E1
Reservoir Rd EDGY/DAV SK3 171 G2
Reservoir St CSLFD M3 6 C1
MILN OL16 11 J4
SLFD M6 111 G3
Retford Av MILN OL16 43 G2
Retford Cl TOT/BURYW BL8 38 B1
Retford St OLDS * OL8 91 E2
Retiro St OLD OL1 9 H3
The Retreat MPL/ROM SK6 162 A5
Reuben St HTNM SK4 159 H2
Revers St TOT/BURYW BL8 4 A3
Reveton Gn BRAM/HZG SK7 184 B2
Reynard Rd CCHDY M21 141 E4
Reynard St HYDE * SK14 132 C5
Reynell Rd BRUN/LGST M13 143 G1
Reyner St AUL OL6 118 D3
CMANE M1 7 F6
Reynolds Dr GTN M18 129 G2
MPL/ROM SK6 175 G1
WHTN BL5 62 C5
Reynolds Ms WILM/AE SK9 200 B2
Reynolds Rd OLDTF/WHR M16 126 B4
Reynold St HYDE SK14 147 G1
Rhine Cl TOT/BURYW BL8 26 A4
Rhine Dr CHH M8 99 H5
Rhiwlas Dr BURY BL9 53 G1
Rhodes Av OLDE OL4 92 A2
UPML OL3 78 B3
Rhodes Bank OLD OL1 9 J4
Rhodes Crs ROCH OL11 43 E3
Rhodes Dr BURY BL9 68 D2
Rhodes Hl OLDE OL4 92 A2
Rhodes St HYDE SK14 132 B5
NEWH/MOS M40 114 B1
OLD OL1 9 J3
WHIT OL12 19 G5
Rhodes St North HYDE SK14 132 B5
Rhode St TOT/BURYW BL8 26 A5
Rhos Av CHD/CHDH SK8 182 C3
MDTN M24 71 H5
RUSH/FAL M14 143 F3
Rhos Dr BRAM/HZG SK7 185 E3
Rhosleigh Av BOL BL1 33 H2
Rialto Gdns BRO * M7 99 H4
Ribble Av BOLE BL2 50 B2
CHAD OL9 73 E3
LIT OL15 20 C2
Ribble Dr BURY BL9 27 G3
FWTH BL4 82 A2
WALK M28 94 A4
WHTF M45 68 D3
Ribble Rd OLDS OL8 89 H4
Ribblesdale Cl HEY * OL10 56 B2
Ribblesdale Dr NEWH/MOS M40 100 D5
Ribblesdale Rd BOLS/LL BL3 48 C5
Ribble St ROCH OL11 42 C2
Ribbleton Cl TOT/BURYW BL8 37 E5
Ribchester Dr BURY BL9 53 E2
Ribchester Gv BOLE BL2 35 F5
Ribston St HULME M15 126 D2
Rice St CSLFD M3 6 B7
Richard Burch St BURY BL9 5 F2
Richards Cl DTN/ASHW M34 131 F1
Richardson Cl WHTF M45 68 C3
Richardson Rd ECC M30 109 H3
Richardson St OP/CLY M11 129 H1
STKP SK1 172 B2
Richard St FAIL M35 103 E3
RAD M26 67 E1
RAMS BL0 17 F1
ROCH OL11 30 B5
STKP SK1 13 H1
Richbell Cl IRL M44 135 D4
Richborough Cl BRO M7 99 H5
Richelieu St BOLS/LL BL3 49 F5
Richmond Av CHAD OL9 89 F3
PWCH M25 99 F1
ROY/SHW OL2 59 E5
URM M41 138 D1
WILM/AE SK9 192 A2
Richmond Cl DUK SK16 132 C2
MILN OL16 43 H3
MOSL OL5 107 F2
ROY/SHW OL2 60 A4
SALE M33 155 G3
STLY SK15 119 F4
TOT/BURYW BL8 26 A5
WHTF M45 68 A5
Richmond Crs MOSL OL5 107 F2
Richmond Dr WALK M28 96 B2
Richmond Gdns BOLS/LL BL3 64 C1
Richmond Gn ALT WA14 177 E2
BRAM/HZG * SK7 194 A1
Richmond Gv BRUN/LGST M13 128 A4
CHD/CHDH SK8 182 C2
FWTH * BL4 64 B3
Richmond Gv East
WGTN/LGST M12 128 B3
Richmond Hill Rd
CHD/CHDH SK8 169 H4
Richmond Rd ALT WA14 165 G4
ALT WA14 177 E2
DTN/ASHW * M34 130 B5
DUK SK16 132 C2
FAIL M35 103 F2
HTNM SK4 158 C4
MPL/ROM SK6 162 B3
RUSH/FAL M14 143 E3
TRPK M17 124 B1
Richmond St AULW OL7 117 G1
BURY BL9 53 F1
CMANE M1 7 G6
CSLFD M3 6 B1
DROY * M43 116 D3
DTN/ASHW M34 131 E2
HYDE SK14 147 H1
STLY SK15 119 G3
Richmond Wk CHAD OL9 8 C4
Ricroft Rd MPL/ROM SK6 163 G3
Ridding Av WYTH/NTH M22 180 D1
Ridding Cl OFTN SK2 173 E3
Riddings Ct HALE/TIMP WA15 166 A1
Riddings Rd HALE/TIMP WA15 166 B1
HALE/TIMP WA15 178 A3
Ridge Av HALE/TIMP WA15 188 D1
MPL/ROM SK6 175 F5
Ridge Cl MPL/ROM SK6 162 D4
Ridge Crs MPL/ROM SK6 187 E1
WHTF M45 69 E4
Ridgecroft AULW OL7 105 E4
The Ridgedales OLD OL1 60 D5
Ridge End Fold MPL/ROM SK6 187 F3
Ridgefield CMANW M2 6 D5
Ridgefield St FAIL M35 102 C3
Ridgegreen WALK * M28 94 B5
Ridge Gv WHTF M45 69 E4
Ridge Hill La STLY SK15 119 E3
Ridgemont Av HTNM SK4 159 E4
Ridge Pk BRAM/HZG SK7 193 G1
Ridge Rd MPL/ROM SK6 175 F5
The Ridgeway POY/DIS SK12 187 H5
Ridgeway BOL * BL1 2 E4
SWIN M27 97 G1
WILM/AE SK9 200 C3
Ridgeway Gates BOL BL1 2 E4
Ridgeway Rd HALE/TIMP WA15 166 D4
Ridgeway St NEWH/MOS M40 114 A4
Ridgewood CHAD OL9 72 D4
Ridgewood Av
NEWH/MOS M40 101 F5
Ridgmont Dr WALK M28 94 A4
Ridgmont Rd BRAM/HZG SK7 193 H3
The Ridgway MPL/ROM SK6 161 H5
Riding Fold DROY M43 117 E2
Riding Fold La WALK M28 95 H5
Riding Ga BOLE BL2 24 B5
Riding Gate Ms BOLE BL2 24 B5
Ridings Ct UPML OL3 77 H2
Ridings St NEWH/MOS M40 101 G5
OP/CLY M11 115 E5
Riding St CSLFD M3 6 B4
Ridings Wy CHAD OL9 8 A5
Ridley Dr ALT WA14 153 H5
Ridley Gv SALE M33 155 G3
Ridley St OLDE OL4 9 K5
Ridley Wk HULME * M15 127 E3
Ridling La HYDE SK14 147 H1
Ridsdale Av DID/WITH M20 142 C5
Ridyard St LHULT M38 80 D3
Riefield BOL BL1 33 E3
Rifle Rd SALE M33 155 G1
Rifle St OLD OL1 9 G1
Riga Rd RUSH/FAL M14 142 D2
Riga St ANC M4 7 G2
Rigby Av RAD M26 52 D4
Rigby Ct BOLS/LL BL3 49 E5
Rigby Gv LHULT M38 79 D3
Rigby La BOLE BL2 23 H5
Rigby St ALT WA14 177 G1
BOLS/LL BL3 49 E5
BRO M7 99 G3
Rigel Pl BRO M7 112 B2
Rigel St ANC M4 113 H2
Rigton Cl WGTN/LGST M12 128 D3
Rildene Wk ROCH OL11 28 A3
Riley Cl SALE M33 153 E5
Riley Ct BOL BL1 34 A5
Riley Wood Cl MPL/ROM * SK6 161 G5
Rimington Fold MDTN M24 56 A5
Rimmer Cl OP/CLY M11 114 B5
Rimmington Cl BKLY M9 87 H5
Rimsdale Cl CHD/CHDH SK8 181 F1
Rimworth Dr NEWH/MOS M40 113 H1
Ringcroft Gdns
NEWH/MOS M40 102 A1
Ringley Cha WHTF M45 68 B4
Ringley Cl WHTF M45 68 A4
Ringley Dr WHTF M45 68 A5
Ringley Gv BOL BL1 33 H1
Ringley Hey WHTF M45 68 A4
Ringley Mdw RAD M26 66 B5
Ringley Old Brow RAD M26 66 B5
Ringley Pk WHTF M45 68 A4
Ringley Rd RAD M26 66 A4
RAD M26 67 G4
Ringley Rd West RAD M26 66 D4
Ringley St BKLY * M9 101 E2
Ringlow Av SWIN M27 96 B3
Ringlow Park Rd SWIN M27 96 B4
Ring Lows La WHIT OL12 19 F4
Ringmer Dr WYTH/NTH M22 180 B3
Ringmere Ct OLD * OL1 74 B4
Ringmore Rd BRAM/HZG SK7 184 B2
Rings Cl FAIL M35 103 E4
Ringstead Cl WILM/AE SK9 200 A1
Ringstead Dr NEWH/MOS M40 113 H2
WILM/AE SK9 200 A1
Ringstone PWCH M25 84 D4
Ringway Gv SALE M33 155 F4
Ringway Rd MANAIR M90 180 B5
Ringway Rd West MANAIR M90 180 B4
Ringwood Av BRAM/HZG SK7 184 C3
DTN/ASHW M34 116 D4
HYDE SK14 148 B2
RAD M26 67 G3
RAMS BL0 16 B4
WGTN/LGST M12 144 A1
Ringwood Wy CHAD OL9 8 A1
Rink St RUSH/FAL M14 143 E4
Ripley Av CHD/CHDH SK8 193 E2
OFTN SK2 172 C5
Ripley Cl ANC * M4 114 A5
BRAM/HZG SK7 185 F4
Ripley Crs URM M41 122 C3
Ripley St BOL BL1 34 C2
Ripon Av BOL BL1 32 C5
WHTF M45 68 C2
Ripon Cl BOLS/LL BL3 65 G1
CHAD OL9 89 G1
HALE/TIMP WA15 178 D3
RAD M26 53 E4
STKP SK1 13 G6
WHTF M45 68 C2
Ripon Crs STRET M32 124 A5
Ripon Dr BOL BL1 32 C5
Ripon Gv SALE M33 139 E5
Ripon Hall Av RAMS BL0 16 C4
Ripon Rd STRET M32 124 A5
Ripon St AUL * OL6 118 B2
OLD OL1 74 A4
Rippenden Av CCHDY M21 140 D1
Rippingham Rd DID/WITH M20 142 C4
Rippleton Rd WYTH/NTH M22 168 D5
Ripponden Rd OLDE OL4 75 G3
Ripponden St OLD OL1 75 F3
The Rise OLDE OL4 76 A5
Rishton Av BOLS/LL BL3 64 A2
Rishton La BOLS/LL BL3 49 E5
Rishworth Cl OFTN SK2 173 E4
Rishworth Dr NEWH/MOS M40 102 D2
Rishworth Ri ROY/SHW OL2 44 C5
Rising La OLDS OL8 90 B5
Risley Av BKLY M9 101 E2
Risley St OLD OL1 74 C4
Rissington Av NTHM/RTH M23 168 A3
Rita Av RUSH/FAL * M14 127 G5
Ritson Cl GTN M18 129 E2
Riva Rd BNG/LEV M19 158 A4
The Riverbank RAD M26 66 D4
Riverbank Dr TOT/BURYW BL8 4 B1
Riverbanks BOLS/LL BL3 49 H4
Riverdale Rd BKLY M9 86 B4
River La PART M31 151 E2
Rivermead MILN OL16 45 E3
Rivermead Av
HALE/TIMP WA15 188 C1
Rivermead Cl DTN/ASHW M34 146 D4
Rivermead Rd DTN/ASHW M34 146 D4
Rivermead Wy WHTF M45 68 D4
Riverpark Rd NEWH/MOS M40 114 D2
River Pl HULME M15 126 D1
MILN * OL16 31 G5
Riversdale Dr OLDS OL8 104 D1
Riversdale Rd CHD/CHDH SK8 169 H4
Riversdale Vw MPL/ROM SK6 161 H1
The Rivers Edge WHIT OL12 14 B5
Rivershill SALE M33 139 F5
Rivershill Dr HEY OL10 40 C5
Rivershill Gdns
HALE/TIMP WA15 188 D1
Riverside BOL BL1 34 A4
BRO M7 112 B2
DUK SK16 118 B3
OLD OL1 72 D3
Riverside Av IRL M44 136 B2
Riverside Ct MPL/ROM * SK6 175 F1
Riverside Dr MILN OL16 11 J1
RAD M26 66 A4
RAMS BL0 16 C5
URM M41 138 A3
Riverside Gdns SALE M33 139 F5
Riverside Rd RAD M26 53 E5
Rivers La URM M41 123 F3
Riversleigh Cl BOL BL1 32 C3
Riversmeade BOLE BL2 23 H4
Riverstone Br LIT OL15 20 D3
Riverstone Dr NTHM/RTH M23 167 E2
River St BOLE BL2 3 G5
HEY OL10 41 E2
HULME M15 127 E1
MILN OL16 10 D6
RAD M26 67 G1
RAMS BL0 16 D2
STKP SK1 160 C3
WGTN/LGST * M12 113 H5
WILM/AE SK9 199 G2
Riverton Rd DID/WITH M20 169 G2
River Vw RDSH SK5 145 F4
River View Cl PWCH M25 84 C5
Riverview Wk BOL * BL1 2 A6
Rivington Av SWIN M27 97 H3
Rivington Dr ROY/SHW OL2 60 C2
TOT/BURYW BL8 37 F5
Rivington Gv DTN/ASHW M34 116 D5
IRL M44 135 C5
Rivington Rd HALE/TIMP WA15 178 A2
OLDE OL4 76 B5
SLFD M6 110 D1
Rivington St OLD OL1 74 C3
WHIT OL12 10 D3
Rivington Wk
WGTN/LGST * M12 128 B3
Rixon St OLDE OL4 75 G3
Rixson St OLDE * OL4 75 G3
Rix St BOL BL1 33 H4
Roach Bank Rd BURY BL9 54 B2
Roaches Ms MOSL OL5 93 E4
Roaches Wy MOSL OL5 93 F4
Roachill Cl ALT WA14 165 E4
Roach Pl MILN OL16 10 E5
Roach St BURY BL9 39 F5
BURY BL9 53 G5
Roach V MILN OL16 30 D1
Roachwood Cl CHAD OL9 72 D5
Roading Brook Rd BOLE BL2 35 H3
Road La WHIT OL12 10 C4
Roads Ford Av MILN OL16 31 G4
Roan Wy WILM/AE SK9 201 C5
Roaring Gate La
HALE/TIMP WA15 179 F1
Robert Hall St ORD M5 112 A5
Robert Lawrence Ct
URM * M41 137 H2
Robert Malcolm Cl
NEWH/MOS M40 101 E5
Robert Owen Gdns
WYTH/NTH * M22 168 C1
Robert Salt Ct ALT * WA14 165 H3
Robertscroft Cl
WYTH/NTH M22 168 B5
Robertshaw Av CCHDY M21 141 E5
Robertson St RAD M26 52 B5
Roberts St ECC M30 109 G4
Robert St BOLE * BL2 35 F1
CSLFD M3 113 E2
DUK SK16 118 A5
FAIL M35 103 F1
HEY OL10 56 B1
HYDE SK14 147 F1
MILN OL16 10 D5
NEWH/MOS M40 101 G5
PWCH M25 85 F3
SALE M33 155 F2
TOT/BURYW BL8 37 H3
Robeson Wy WYTH/NTH M22 169 E3
Robin Cft MPL/ROM SK6 161 E3
Robin Dr IRL M44 121 B5
Robin Hood St CHH M8 100 A2
Robinia Cl ECC M30 108 C5
Robin Rd RAMS BL0 16 C5
Robinsbay Rd WYTH/NTH M22 180 D5
Robins Cl BRAM/HZG SK7 183 H5
DROY M43 116 D2
Robin's La BRAM/HZG SK7 183 H5
Robinson La AULW OL7 117 G2
Robinson St CHAD OL9 89 G1
EDGY/DAV SK3 12 D7
HYDE * SK14 133 E5
MILN OL16 10 E6
OLDS OL8 90 C4
STLY SK15 118 D5
Robin St OLD * OL1 74 B4
Robinsway ALT WA14 177 F3
Robinswood Rd
WYTH/NTH M22 180 C3
Robson Av URM M41 123 H1
Robson St OLD OL1 9 H4
Roby Rd ECC M30 109 F5
Roby St CMANE M1 7 H5
Roch Av HEY OL10 40 B4
Rochbury Cl ROCH OL11 28 C5
Roch Cl WHTF M45 69 E3
Roch Crs WHTF M45 69 E3
Rochdale La HEY OL10 41 E4
ROY/SHW OL2 59 E4
Rochdale Old Rd BURY BL9 39 F3
Rochdale Rd ANC M4 7 H2
BKLY M9 87 E4
BURY BL9 5 F4
HEY OL10 41 F4
MDTN M24 72 A1
MILN OL16 31 E4
MILN OL16 44 B5
OLD OL1 8 E1
ROY/SHW OL2 58 D3
ROY/SHW OL2 59 F1
TOD OL14 15 B1
Rochdale Rd East HEY OL10 41 F4
Roche Gdns CHD/CHDH SK8 193 E1
Rochester Av BOLE BL2 35 F5
CCHDY M21 141 G5
PWCH M25 85 F5
WALK M28 94 D1
Rochester Cl AUL OL6 105 F3
DUK SK16 133 F1
Rochester Dr ALT WA14 153 H5
Rochester Gv BRAM/HZG SK7 185 F1
Rochester Rd URM M41 123 G4
Rochester Wy CHAD OL9 89 G1
Rochford Av WHTF M45 68 A5
WYTH/NTH M22 180 C4
Rochford Rd ECC M30 108 C5
Roch Mills Crs ROCH OL11 42 B1
Roch Mills Gdns ROCH OL11 42 B1
Roch St MILN OL16 11 H2
Roch Valley Wy ROCH OL11 29 F5
Roch Wy WHTF M45 69 E3
The Rock BURY BL9 4 D4
BURY BL9 5 F3
Rockall Wk OP/CLY * M11 114 C4
Rock Av BOL BL1 33 F4
Rock Bank BRO * M7 99 F4
MOSL * OL5 106 D1
Rockdove Av HULME M15 127 E1
Rocket St CSLFD M3 6 A4
Rockfield Dr BKLY * M9 101 F2
Rock Fold EDGW/EG * BL7 23 E2
Rockhampton St GTN M18 129 H3
Rockhouse Cl ECC M30 109 G5
Rockingham Cl ROY/SHW OL2 59 F1
WGTN/LGST M12 128 A2
Rockley Gdns SLFD M6 112 A1
Rocklyn Av NEWH/MOS M40 88 B5
Rocklynes MPL/ROM SK6 162 A4
Rockmead Dr BKLY M9 87 F4
Rock Rd URM M41 139 E1
Rock St AULW OL7 104 D5
BRO M7 99 G4
HEY OL10 41 F5
HYDE SK14 147 H4
OLD OL1 9 H3
OP/CLY M11 129 H1
RAD M26 67 G2
RAMS BL0 17 F1
Rock Ter EDGW/EG BL7 23 E2
MOSL OL5 93 E4
Rocky La ECC M30 109 G1
Roda St BKLY M9 101 G3
Rodborough Rd
NTHM/RTH M23 179 G1
Rodeheath Cl WILM/AE SK9 200 A3
Rodenhurst Dr
NEWH/MOS M40 101 H4
Rodepool Cl WILM/AE SK9 192 A5
Rodmell Av NEWH/MOS * M40 101 E5
Rodmell Cl EDGW/EG BL7 23 E4
Rodmill Ct RUSH/FAL M14 142 D2
Rodmill Dr CHD/CHDH SK8 169 F5
Rodney Ct ANC M4 7 K1
Rodney Dr MPL/ROM SK6 161 H1
Rodney St ANC M4 113 H3
AUL OL6 118 C1
CSLFD M3 112 C4
ROCH OL11 42 A4
Roeacre St HEY OL10 41 F4
Roebuck Gdns SALE * M33 154 B2
Roebuck La OLDE OL4 76 B1
SALE M33 154 B2
Roe Cross Gn HYDE SK14 134 C3
Roe Cross Rd HYDE SK14 134 C3
Roedean Gdns URM M41 137 E1
Roefield Ter ROCH OL11 29 F3
Roe Gn WALK M28 95 H2
Roe Green Av WALK M28 95 H2
Roe La OLDE OL4 91 G2
Roe St ANC M4 7 K1
WHIT OL12 29 F2
Rogate Dr NTHM/RTH M23 167 H4
Roger Cl MPL/ROM SK6 161 G5
Rogerstead BOLS/LL * BL3 48 B3
Roger St ANC M4 113 F2
Rokeby Av STRET M32 140 A2
Roker Av BRUN/LGST M13 143 G1
Roker Park Av DTN/ASHW M34 131 E1
Roland Rd BOLS/LL BL3 48 B4
RDSH SK5 145 E4
Rolla St CSLFD M3 6 C2
Rollesby Cl TOT/BURYW BL8 38 A1
Rolleston Av NEWH/MOS M40 114 A3
Rollins La MPL/ROM SK6 163 F5
Rolls Crs HULME M15 127 E2
Rollswood Dr NEWH/MOS M40 101 H4
Roman Rd FAIL M35 103 F2
HTNM SK4 13 F2
PWCH M25 98 C1
ROY/SHW OL2 74 B1
Roman St RAD M26 66 D1
Romer Av NEWH/MOS * M40 102 D1
Rome Rd NEWH/MOS M40 7 K1
Romer St BOLE BL2 49 H2
Romford Av DTN/ASHW M34 131 H4
Romford Cl OLDS * OL8 9 F7
Romford Rd SALE M33 138 D5
Romiley Crs BOLE BL2 50 A1
Romiley Dr BOLE BL2 50 A1
Romiley St SLFD M6 98 A5
STKP SK1 160 C4
Romley Rd URM M41 123 G4
Romney Av ROCH OL11 42 D4
Romney Rd BOL BL1 32 B4
Romney St AUL OL6 118 B2
NEWH/MOS M40 101 H2
SLFD M6 98 D5
Romney Wk CHAD OL9 89 G1
Romney Wy RDSH SK5 145 G5
Romsey WHIT OL12 10 B5
Romsey Av MDTN M24 71 G1
Romsey Dr CHD/CHDH SK8 193 E1
Romsley Cl WGTN/LGST M12 128 D2
Romsley Dr BOLS/LL BL3 63 F1
Ronaldsay Gdns ORD M5 111 F4
Ronald St OLDE OL4 75 F5
OP/CLY M11 115 G4
ROCH OL11 42 B5
Rondin Cl WGTN/LGST M12 128 B1
Rondin Rd WGTN/LGST M12 128 B1
Roocroft Ct BOL BL1 2 B1
Rookery Av GTN M18 130 A2
Rookery Cl STLY SK15 134 B1
Rookerypool Cl WILM/AE SK9 192 A5
Rooke St ECC M30 108 D5
Rookfield Av SALE M33 154 D1
Rookley Wk RUSH/FAL * M14 127 H5
Rook St HULME M15 126 D3
OLDE OL4 91 F2
RAMS BL0 16 D2
Rookswood Dr ROCH OL11 42 A3
Rookway MDTN M24 71 G5
Rookwood OLD OL1 72 D3
Rookwood Av NTHM/RTH M23 167 G2
Rookwood Hl BRAM/HZG SK7 183 H3
Rooley Moor Rd WHIT OL12 29 E1
Rooley St WHIT OL12 29 F2
Roosevelt Rd FWTH BL4 65 G5
Rooth St HTNM SK4 12 C2
Ropefield Wy WHIT OL12 18 D5
Rope St WHIT OL12 10 C4
Rope Wk CSLFD M3 6 C1
Rosa Gv BRO M7 99 G4
Rosamond Dr CSLFD M3 6 A3
Rosamond St BOLS/LL BL3 48 B5
HULME M15 127 F2
Rosamond St West
HULME M15 127 F2
Rosary Cl OLDS OL8 104 C1
Rosary Rd OLDS OL8 104 D1
Roscoe Rd IRL M44 135 D2
Roscoe St EDGY/DAV SK3 12 D5
OLD OL1 9 H4
Roscow Av BOLE BL2 50 B1
Roscow Rd FWTH BL4 81 H1
Rose Acre WALK M28 94 C3
Roseacre Cl BOLE BL2 49 H1
Roseacre Dr CHD/CHDH SK8 181 H3
Rose Av IRL M44 136 A2
LIT OL15 20 C5
ROCH OL11 28 A1
Rosebank HOR/BR BL6 46 D2
Rosebank Cl BOLE BL2 36 B5
Rosebank Rd IRL M44 150 B3
NEWH/MOS M40 115 E1
Roseberry Cl RAMS BL0 16 D5
Roseberry St BOLS/LL BL3 48 B5
OFTN SK2 173 E5
OLDS * OL8 8 D5
Rosebery St RUSH/FAL M14 127 E5
Rosebury Av OLD OL1 75 E3
Rose Cottage Rd
DID/WITH M20 142 C4
Rose Crs IRL M44 136 A2
Rosecroft Cl EDGY/DAV SK3 171 H5
Rosedale Av BOL BL1 33 H1
Rosedale Cl OLD OL1 75 E3
Rosedale Ct DTN/ASHW * M34 131 F5
Rosedale Rd HTNM SK4 159 G1
RUSH/FAL M14 142 B1
Rosedale Wy DUK SK16 132 B2
Rosefield Cl EDGY/DAV SK3 171 H4
Rosefield Crs MILN OL16 11 H7
Rosegarth Av DID/WITH M20 156 C2
Rose Gv FWTH BL4 65 G5
TOT/BURYW BL8 37 F4

Rosehay Av DTN/ASHW M34 146 C1
Rose Hey La FAIL M35 115 H1
Rose Hl BOLE BL2 49 F4
DTN/ASHW M34 131 E5
DUK SK16 119 E5
UPML OL3 77 G1
Rose Hill Av NEWH/MOS * M40 115 E1
Rose Hill Cl EDGW/EG BL7 23 F4
Rosehill Cl SLFD M6 111 G3
Rose Hill Dr EDGW/EG BL7 23 F4
Rose Hill Rd AUL OL6 106 A5
Rosehill Rd SWIN M27 83 E5
Rose Hill St HEY OL10 40 C4
Roseland Av DID/WITH M20 157 G2
Roseland Dr PWCH M25 85 F1
Roselands Av SALE M33 154 A4
Rose La MPL/ROM SK6 174 D4
Rose Lea BOLE BL2 35 F2
Rosemary Dr HYDE SK14 147 G4
LIT OL15 20 C2
Rosemary Gv BRO M7 99 F5
Rosemary La STKP SK1 13 J4
WHTN BL5 79 A1
Rosemary Rd CHAD OL9 72 D4
Rosemount HYDE SK14 132 C3
Rose Mt MDTN M24 71 G2
Rosemount Crs HYDE SK14 132 C3
Roseneath BRAM/HZG SK7 183 G3
Roseneath Av BNG/LEV M19 144 B2
Roseneath Gv BOLS/LL BL3 63 G1
Roseneath Rd BOLS/LL BL3 63 G1
URM M41 123 F5
Rosen Sq CHAD * OL9 73 G5
Rose St BOLS/LL BL3 49 F4
CHAD OL9 89 F4
MDTN M24 72 B4
RDSH SK5 160 A3
Rose Ter STLY SK15 119 F4
Rosethorns Cl MDTN M24 56 C5
Rose V CHD/CHDH SK8 181 G3
Rosevale Av BNG/LEV M19 158 B1
Roseway BRAM/HZG SK7 184 A2
Rosewell Cl NEWH/MOS M40 114 A1
Rose Wd DTN/ASHW M34 131 E5
Rosewood ROCH OL11 28 B2
Rosewood Av DROY M43 116 C3
HTNM SK4 158 D5
TOT/BURYW BL8 37 F1
Rosewood Cl DUK SK16 132 A1
Rosewood Crs CHAD OL9 73 G3
Rosewood Gdns
CHD/CHDH SK8 169 E3
Rosford Av RUSH/FAL M14 142 C1
Rosgill Cl HTNM SK4 158 B4
Rosina St OP/CLY M11 130 A1
Roslin St OP/CLY M11 115 G3
Roslyn Av URM M41 137 F3
Roslyn Rd EDGY/DAV SK3 171 H4
Rossall Av RAD M26 67 H4
STRET M32 124 D5
Rossall Cl BOLE BL2 49 H1
Rossall Dr BRAM/HZG SK7 194 A1
Rossall Rd BOLE BL2 49 H1
WHIT OL12 10 E1
Rossall St BOLE BL2 49 H1
Rossall Wy SLFD M6 111 H2
Ross Av CHAD OL9 89 E4
EDGY/DAV SK3 171 H4
WHTF M45 84 C1
Ross Dr SWIN M27 82 D3
Rossenclough Rd WILM/AE SK9 200 A1
Rossendale Av BKLY M9 101 G1
Rossendale Cl ROY/SHW OL2 60 C2
Rossendale Rd CHD/CHDH SK8 181 H4
Rossett Av HALE/TIMP WA15 166 B1
WYTH/NTH M22 180 C3
Rossett Dr URM M41 122 C4
Ross Gv URM M41 138 B1
Rosshill Wk HULME * M15 126 C2
Rossington St NEWH/MOS M40 102 C5
Rossini St BOL BL1 33 G3
Rosslare Rd WYTH/NTH M22 180 D2
Ross Lave La DTN/ASHW M34 145 H3
Rosslyn Gv HALE/TIMP WA15 166 B3
Rosslyn Rd CHD/CHDH SK8 182 A3
NEWH/MOS M40 101 H1
OLDTF/WHR M16 140 D1
Rossmere Av ROCH OL11 29 F5
Rossmill La HALE/TIMP WA15 178 D5
Ross St OLDS OL8 8 D6
Rostherne Av MPL/ROM SK6 186 D4
RUSH/FAL M14 142 B2
Rostherne Gdns BOLS/LL BL3 48 A5
Rostherne Rd EDGY/DAV SK3 171 H4
SALE M33 155 G3
WILM/AE SK9 198 D5
Rostherne St ALT WA14 177 G1
SLFD * M6 111 F4
Rosthernmere Rd
CHD/CHDH SK8 170 C5
Rosthwaite Cl MDTN M24 70 D3
Roston Rd BRO M7 99 H2
Rostrevor Rd EDGY/DAV SK3 171 H4
Rostron Av WGTN/LGST M12 128 B2
Rostron Rd RAMS BL0 16 C2
Rostron St BNG/LEV M19 144 A2
Rothay Cl BOLE BL2 35 G5
Rothay Dr MDTN M24 71 F1
RDSH SK5 145 E3
Rothbury Av AULW OL7 104 B5
Rothbury Cl TOT/BURYW BL8 37 E4
Rothbury Ct BOLS/LL BL3 63 E1
Rotherby Rd WYTH/NTH M22 168 D5
Rotherdale Av
HALE/TIMP WA15 167 E4
Rotherwood Av STRET M32 125 F5
Rotherwood Rd WILM/AE SK9 198 C5
Rothesay Av DUK SK16 132 B1
Rothesay Crs SALE M33 153 F4
Rothesay Rd BOLS/LL * BL3 63 E1
CHH M8 85 H5
OLD OL1 75 F3
Rothesay Ter MILN OL16 43 H2
Rothiemay Rd URM M41 137 F2
Rothley Av WYTH/NTH M22 168 C4
Rothman Cl FAIL M35 102 B4
Rothwell Crs LHULT M38 79 D1
Rothwell La LHULT M38 79 D2
Rothwell St BOLS/LL BL3 48 D4
NEWH/MOS M40 102 B4
RAMS BL0 16 C2
ROY/SHW OL2 73 H1
WALK M28 81 G4
WHIT OL12 11 F2
Rottingdene Dr
WYTH/NTH M22 180 B3
Roughey Gdns WYTH/NTH M22 168 B5
Rough Hey Wk MILN OL16 30 C5
Rough Hill La BURY BL9 39 H2
Roughlee Av SWIN M27 96 C3
Roughtown Ct MOSL OL5 93 E5
Roughtown Rd MOSL OL5 93 E5
Roundcroft MPL/ROM SK6 162 C3
Roundhey CHD/CHDH SK8 181 G4
Round Hey MOSL OL5 106 D2
Round Hill Wy BOL BL1 3 F2
Roundhill Wy OLDE OL4 75 H3
Round Thorn Rd MDTN M24 72 A5
Roundthorn Rd
NTHM/RTH M23 167 G3
OLDE OL4 91 F2
Roundway BRAM/HZG SK7 193 G1
Roundwood Rd
WYTH/NTH M22 168 C2
Rousdon Cl NEWH/MOS * M40 101 E5
Rouse St ROCH OL11 42 B2
Rowan Av OLDTF/WHR M16 126 C5
SALE M33 154 D4
URM M41 123 G5
Rowan Cl FAIL M35 103 E5
Rowan Crs DUK SK16 133 E1
Rowan Dr CHD/CHDH SK8 183 F4
Rowanlea PWCH * M25 85 F3
Rowan Pl PWCH M25 85 E4
The Rowans BOL BL1 47 F2
MOSL OL5 107 E1
Rowans Cl STLY SK15 119 H2
Rowanside Dr WILM/AE SK9 200 B2
Rowans St TOT/BURYW BL8 37 H2
Rowan St HYDE SK14 148 A2
Rowanswood Dr HYDE SK14 133 F5
Rowan Tree Dr SALE M33 154 C5
Rowan Tree Rd OLDS OL8 104 A1
Rowanwood CHAD OL9 72 D5
Rowany Cl PWCH M25 84 D5
Rowarth Av DTN/ASHW M34 146 D3
Rowarth Rd NTHM/RTH M23 179 G2
Rowbottom Wk OLDS OL8 9 F7
Rowcon Cl DTN/ASHW M34 131 F3
Rowden Rd OLDE OL4 91 H3
Rowe Gn DTN/ASHW M34 131 G5
Rowena St BOLS/LL BL3 64 D2
Rowendale St CMANE * M1 6 D7
Rowfield Dr NTHM/RTH M23 179 G1
Rowland Av URM M41 123 H5
Rowland Ct MILN * OL16 30 C5
Rowlands Rd BURY BL9 27 F2
Rowland St MILN OL16 30 C5
ORD M5 111 H5
Rowlandsway WYTH/NTH M22 180 C2
Rowland Wy OLDE OL4 75 H5
Rowley Rd BRAM/HZG SK7 185 F4
Rowley St AUL OL6 105 G4
Rowood Av CHH M8 100 C4
RDSH SK5 145 E1
Rowrah Crs MDTN M24 70 C3
Rowsley Av BOL BL1 32 D5
DID/WITH M20 156 D2
Rowsley Gv RDSH SK5 144 D4
Rowsley Rd ECC M30 109 F5
STRET M32 124 B5
Rowsley St OP/CLY M11 114 B3
SLFD M6 95 F5
Rowson Ct SALE * M33 155 E2
Rowson Dr IRL M44 135 C5
Rowton St BOLE BL2 34 C3
Roxalina St BOLS/LL BL3 48 D5
Roxburgh St GTN M18 129 G3
Roxbury Av OLDE OL4 91 G2
Roxby Cl WALK M28 80 C4
Roxholme Wk WYTH/NTH M22 180 B4
Roxton Rd HTNM SK4 144 B5
Royal Av BURY BL9 38 C1
CCHDY M21 140 D4
DROY M43 116 C3
HEY OL10 41 E5
URM M41 138 C1
Royal Court Dr BOL BL1 2 B3
Royal Ex CMANW * M2 6 E4
Royal Exchange Ar CMANW * M2 6 E4
Royal Gdns ALT WA14 176 C2
Royal George St EDGY/DAV SK3 13 F6
Royal Oak Rd NTHM/RTH M23 167 G2
Royal St MILN OL16 30 D1
Royalthorn Dr WYTH/NTH M22 168 B3
Royalthorn Rd WYTH/NTH M22 168 C3
Royce Av HALE/TIMP WA15 165 H4
Royce Rd HULME M15 126 D2
Roydale St NEWH/MOS M40 114 B2
Royden Av BKLY M9 87 E2
IRL M44 136 A3
Roydes St MDTN M24 72 A2
Royds Cl BRUN/LGST M13 128 A3
TOT/BURYW BL8 37 F1
Royds Pl MILN OL16 43 F1
Royds St BURY BL9 39 G2
LIT OL15 21 F3
MILN OL16 43 G1
MILN OL16 44 D1
TOT/BURYW BL8 26 A4
Royds St West MILN OL16 43 F1
Royd St OLDS OL8 89 H3
Royland Av BOLS/LL BL3 64 B1
Royle Barn Rd ROCH OL11 42 B4
Royle Cl OFTN SK2 172 B4
OLDS OL8 90 C4
Royle Green Rd
WYTH/NTH M22 168 D1
Royle Rd ROCH OL11 42 C3
Royle St DTN/ASHW M34 131 G3
OFTN SK2 13 H7
ORD * M5 111 G4
RUSH/FAL M14 143 E4
WALK M28 81 E5
Royley ROY/SHW OL2 73 H1
Royley Crs ROY/SHW OL2 73 H1
Royley Rd OLDS OL8 90 B3
Royon Dr EDGY/DAV SK3 171 E2
Royston Av BOLE BL2 3 K2
DTN/ASHW M34 130 A5
OLDTF/WHR M16 126 D5
Royston Cl TOT/BURYW BL8 26 A2
Royston Rd OLDTF/WHR M16 126 A5
URM M41 123 H5
Roy St BOLS/LL BL3 48 A5
ROY/SHW OL2 59 E5
Royton Av SALE M33 155 F4
Rozel Sq CSLFD M3 6 C6
Ruabon Rd DID/WITH M20 157 H4
Rubens Cl MPL/ROM SK6 175 H1
Ruby St BOL BL1 34 A3
DTN/ASHW M34 131 F5
HULME M15 127 F2
RAMS BL0 16 D5
Rudcroft Cl BRUN/LGST M13 127 G2
Rudding St ROY/SHW OL2 74 D2
Ruddpark Rd WYTH/NTH M22 180 C3
Rudd St NEWH/MOS M40 101 H3
Rudford Gdns BOLS/LL * BL3 49 E5
Rudgwick Dr TOT/BURYW BL8 26 D4
Rudheath Av DID/WITH M20 142 B4
Rudman Dr ORD M5 112 B5
Rudman St WHIT OL12 10 A1
Rudolph St BOLS/LL BL3 64 A1
Rudston Av NEWH/MOS M40 88 A5
Rudyard Av MDTN M24 72 B1
Rudyard Gv HTNM SK4 144 C5
ROCH OL11 43 E4
SALE M33 153 H4
Rudyard Rd SLFD M6 97 H5
Rudyard St BRO M7 99 G4
Rufford Av HYDE SK14 148 A1
ROCH OL11 42 C2
Rufford Cl AUL OL6 105 F3
ROY/SHW OL2 59 G2
WHTF M45 68 D2
Rufford Dr BOLS/LL BL3 63 G2
WHTF M45 68 C2
Rufford Gv BOLS/LL BL3 63 G2
Rufford Pl GTN * M18 130 A4
Rufford Rd OLDTF/WHR M16 126 C5
Rufus St RUSH/FAL M14 143 F4
Rugby Dr SALE M33 154 B4
Rugby Rd SLFD M6 110 B2
WHIT OL12 10 E3
Rugby St BRO M7 112 D1
Rugeley St SLFD M6 99 E5
Ruins La BOLE BL2 35 F2
Ruislip Av NEWH/MOS M40 101 F5
Ruislip Cl OLDS OL8 91 E3
Rumworth Rd HOR/BR BL6 46 D3
Rumworth St BOLS/LL BL3 48 C5
Runger La MANAIR M90 179 G4
Runhall Cl WGTN/LGST M12 128 D2
Running Hill Ga UPML OL3 78 C3
Running Hill La UPML OL3 78 C2
Runnymeade SLFD M6 97 F4
Runnymede Cl EDGY/DAV SK3 171 F2
Runnymede Ct BOLS/LL BL3 48 C4
ROY/SHW OL2 59 F5
Rupert St BOLS/LL BL3 49 E5
NEWH/MOS M40 115 H1
RAD M26 67 G3
RDSH SK5 144 D4
WHIT OL12 29 F2
Ruscombe Fold MDTN M24 71 E1
Rush Acre Cl RAD M26 66 D1
Rush Bank ROY/SHW OL2 59 G1
Rushbrooke Av OP/CLY M11 115 F2
Rushbury Dr ROY/SHW OL2 59 H5
Rushcroft Rd ROY/SHW OL2 59 G1
Rushden Rd BNG/LEV M19 144 A1
Rushen St OP/CLY M11 115 F4
Rushey Cl HALE/TIMP WA15 179 E5
Rushey Fld EDGW/EG BL7 23 E3
Rushey Fold La BOL BL1 33 G4
Rusheylea Cl BOL BL1 33 F4
Rushey Rd WYTH/NTH M22 168 B4
Rushfield Dr BRUN/LGST M13 128 B5
Rushfield Rd CHD/CHDH SK8 192 D1
Rushford Av BNG/LEV M19 143 H1
Rushford Gv BOL BL1 34 A2
Rushford St WGTN/LGST M12 128 D4
Rush Gv UPML OL3 78 A5
Rush Hill Rd UPML OL3 78 A5
Rush Hill Ter UPML OL3 78 A5
Rushlake Dr BOL BL1 33 H5
Rushlake Gdns ROCH OL11 28 B3
Rushley Av BRO M7 99 E3
Rushmere AUL OL6 105 H4
Rushmere Av BNG/LEV M19 144 A2
Rushmere Dr TOT/BURYW BL8 37 H1
Rushmere Wk OLDTF/WHR M16 126 C3
Rushmoor Cl IRL M44 136 B1
Rush Mt ROY/SHW OL2 44 C5
Rusholme Gv RUSH/FAL M14 127 H5
Rusholme Pl RUSH/FAL M14 127 H4
Rushside Rd CHD/CHDH SK8 192 C1
Rush St DUK SK16 119 E5
Rushton Cl MPL/ROM * SK6 175 F4
Rushton Dr BRAM/HZG SK7 183 G1
MPL/ROM SK6 162 B3
MPL/ROM SK6 175 E5
Rushton Gv OLDE OL4 75 H1
OP/CLY M11 129 H1
Rushton Rd BOL BL1 33 E5
CHD/CHDH SK8 192 D1
EDGY/DAV SK3 171 E2
Rushton St DID/WITH M20 157 G4
WALK M28 81 E5
Rushwick Av NEWH/MOS M40 101 F4
Rushworth Ct HTNM SK4 159 F1
Rushycroft HYDE SK14 134 D4
Rushyfield Crs MPL/ROM SK6 162 C3
Rushy Hill Vw WHIT * OL12 29 E2
Ruskin Av CHAD OL9 89 E4
DTN/ASHW M34 130 D1
DTN/ASHW M34 146 B2
FWTH BL4 65 G5
RUSH/FAL M14 127 G4
Ruskin Crs PWCH M25 84 C4
Ruskin Dr SALE M33 153 F2
Ruskin Gdns MPL/ROM SK6 161 H3
Ruskin Gv MPL/ROM SK6 161 H3
Ruskington Dr BKLY M9 101 E3
Ruskin Rd DROY M43 116 B3
OLDTF/WHR M16 126 B5
PWCH M25 84 B4
RDSH SK5 144 D2
ROCH OL11 42 D4
Ruskin St CHAD OL9 8 D1
RAD M26 52 D5
Rusland Ct STKP * SK1 172 C2
Rusland Dr BOLE BL2 35 F4
Russell Av MPL/ROM SK6 186 D5
OLDTF/WHR M16 141 G1
SALE M33 155 E1
Russell Cl BOL BL1 48 B1
Russell Ct FWTH * BL4 65 F4
LHULT M38 80 D4
Russell Dr IRL M44 136 B1
Russell Gdns HTNM SK4 159 E5
Russell Rd OLDTF/WHR M16 126 C5
PART M31 151 F3
SLFD M6 97 G5
Russell St AUL OL6 118 C1
BOL BL1 48 B1
BURY BL9 5 F1
CHAD * OL9 73 G5
CHH M8 113 E1
DTN/ASHW M34 131 G5
DUK SK16 118 B5
ECC M30 109 H3
FWTH BL4 65 E5
HEY OL10 41 F4
LHULT M38 80 D4
MOSL OL5 106 D1
OFTN SK2 172 B3
OLDTF/WHR M16 127 E5
PWCH M25 85 F3
Russet Rd BKLY M9 101 E1
Ruth Av NEWH/MOS M40 102 D1
Ruthen La OLDTF/WHR M16 126 A4
Rutherford Av RUSH/FAL M14 127 G5
Rutherford Cl HYDE SK14 147 G1
Rutherford Dr WHTN BL5 62 C5
Rutherglade Cl
NEWH/MOS M40 100 D4
Rutherglen Dr BOLS/LL BL3 47 F3
Rutherglen Wk
NEWH/MOS M40 101 F5
Ruthin Av BKLY M9 86 D2
CHD/CHDH SK8 182 B2
MDTN M24 87 H1
Ruthin Cl OLDS OL8 89 G5
Ruth St BOL BL1 2 C3
BURY BL9 5 H2
GTN M18 129 G5
OLD OL1 9 H1
WHIT OL12 14 C4
Rutland ROCH * OL11 29 H5
Rutland Av DID/WITH M20 157 F1
OLDTF/WHR M16 125 H5
SWIN M27 83 E5
URM M41 138 D1
Rutland Cl AUL OL6 118 C3
BOLS/LL BL3 51 E5
CHD/CHDH SK8 169 G3
Rutland Crs RDSH SK5 161 E1
Rutland Dr BRO M7 99 F2
BURY BL9 53 H1
Rutland Gv BOL BL1 33 F5
FWTH * BL4 64 D5
Rutland La SALE M33 155 G2
Rutland Rd ALT WA14 165 G3
BRAM/HZG SK7 185 F4
DROY M43 115 H3
ECC M30 110 A2
IRL M44 150 C1
PART M31 150 D4
WALK M28 94 D1
Rutland St AUL OL6 118 C3
BOLS/LL BL3 48 C5
CHAD OL9 8 A7
FAIL * M35 103 E2
GTN M18 129 H2
HEY OL10 41 E3
HYDE SK14 132 C3
SWIN M27 96 D1
Rutland Wy ROY/SHW OL2 60 B1
Rutter's La BRAM/HZG SK7 184 D2
Ryall Av ORD M5 112 A5
Ryall Av South ORD M5 112 A5
Ryan St OP/CLY M11 129 H1
Rydal Av BRAM/HZG SK7 184 D1
CHAD OL9 72 D3
DROY M43 115 H4
ECC M30 109 E1
HYDE SK14 132 B3
MDTN M24 87 G1
MPL/ROM SK6 186 D4
ROY/SHW OL2 58 D1
SALE M33 154 A1
URM M41 137 H3
Rydal Cl BURY BL9 53 F2
CHD/CHDH SK8 181 G1
DTN/ASHW M34 145 G1
Rydal Ct BOL * BL1 32 C5
Rydal Crs SWIN M27 97 E4
WALK M28 95 F1
Rydal Dr HALE/TIMP WA15 179 E4
Rydal Gv AULW OL7 117 G1
FWTH BL4 64 A5
HEY OL10 56 A1
WHTF M45 68 C4
Rydal Rd BOL BL1 32 D5
BOLS/LL BL3 65 H1
STRET M32 125 E5
Ryde Av DTN/ASHW M34 147 E3
HTNM SK4 159 E4
Ryder Av ALT WA14 165 H2
Ryder Brow GTN M18 129 G4
Ryderbrow Rd GTN M18 129 G4
Ryder St BOL BL1 33 F4
HEY * OL10 41 E4
NEWH/MOS M40 114 A1
Ryde St BOLS/LL * BL3 47 H5
Rydings La WHIT OL12 19 F2
Rydings Rd WHIT OL12 19 G4
Rydley St BOLE BL2 3 J6
Ryebank Gv AUL OL6 105 G5
Ryebank Ms CCHDY * M21 140 C2
Ryebank Rd CCHDY M21 140 C2
Rye Bank Rd OLDTF/WHR M16 140 D1
Ryeburn Av WYTH/NTH M22 180 C1
Ryeburn Dr BOLE BL2 34 C1
Ryeburne St OLDE OL4 75 F5
Ryeburn Wk URM M41 122 C4
Rye Cft WHTF M45 67 H5
Rye Croft Av SLFD M6 110 D2
Ryecroft Av HEY OL10 41 F4
TOT/BURYW BL8 26 A5
Ryecroft Cl CHAD OL9 89 E4
Ryecroft Gv NTHM/RTH M23 167 H2
Ryecroft La DTN/ASHW M34 131 F1
WALK M28 108 C1
Ryecroft Rd STRET M32 139 H2
Ryecroft St AULW OL7 117 G4
Ryecroft Vw DTN/ASHW M34 116 D5
Ryedale Av NEWH/MOS M40 101 E5
Ryedale Cl HTNM SK4 159 E3
Ryefield Cl HALE/TIMP WA15 166 D4
Ryefield Rd SALE M33 153 F4
Ryefields ROCH OL11 28 D5
Ryefields Dr UPML OL3 78 A3
Ryefield St BOL BL1 3 G1
Ryeland Cl MILN OL16 43 G2
Rye St HEY OL10 41 F3
Rylance St OP/CLY M11 114 B4
Rylands St GTN * M18 129 H2
Rylane Wk NEWH/MOS M40 101 E5
Ryley Av BOLS/LL BL3 48 A4
Ryleys La WILM/AE SK9 201 A4
Ryley St BOLS/LL * BL3 2 A7
Rylstone Av CCHDY M21 156 C3
Ryther Gv BKLY M9 86 C2
Ryton Av GTN M18 129 F5

S

Sabden Cl BURY BL9 27 G4
HEY OL10 40 B4
NEWH/MOS M40 114 B2
Sabden Rd BOL BL1 32 B4
Sabrina St CHH M8 99 H5
Sackville Cl ROY/SHW OL2 44 D5
Sackville St AUL OL6 118 A2
BOLE * BL2 49 H2
CMANE M1 7 F6
CSLFD M3 6 B3
ROCH OL11 42 B5
Saddleback Cl WALK M28 94 C4
Saddlecote WALK * M28 108 D1
Saddle Gv DROY M43 117 E2
Saddle St BOLE BL2 34 C4
Saddlewood Av BNG/LEV M19 158 A4
Sadie Av STRET M32 124 B4
Sadler Ct HULME M15 126 D3
Sadler St BOLS/LL BL3 49 F5
MDTN M24 71 G3
Saffron Dr OLDE OL4 75 G2
Sagars Rd WILM/AE SK9 191 H3
Sagar St CHH M8 113 E1
St Agnes Rd BRUN/LGST M13 143 G1
St Agnes St RDSH SK5 130 A5
St Aidan's Cl ROCH OL11 42 B1
St Aidan's Gv BRO M7 99 E4
St Albans Av AUL OL6 105 E4
HTNM SK4 159 F1
NEWH/MOS M40 102 A5
St Albans Cl OLDS OL8 90 C3
St Albans Crs ALT WA14 165 F1
St Alban's St MILN OL16 29 H5
St Alban's Ter CHH M8 100 A5
ROCH * OL11 29 H5
St Aldates MPL/ROM SK6 161 G4
St Aldwyn's Rd DID/WITH M20 157 G1
St Ambrose Gdns SLFD * M6 111 G3
St Ambrose Rd OLD OL1 75 F3
St Andrew's Av DROY M43 115 H4
ECC M30 109 H4
HALE/TIMP WA15 165 H2
St Andrews Cl ALT WA14 153 F5
HTNM SK4 159 E2
MPL/ROM SK6 162 A5
RAMS BL0 16 D3
WHIT OL12 20 B4
St Andrews Ct BOL * BL1 2 E5
St Andrew's Dr HEY OL10 41 E5
St Andrews Rd CHD/CHDH SK8 181 H3
HOR/BR BL6 46 B2
HTNM SK4 159 E2
RAD M26 52 A3
STRET M32 139 G1
St Andrew's Sq CMANE M1 113 H5
St Andrew's St CMANE M1 7 K6
St Andrew's Vw RAD M26 52 A3
St Anne's Av ROY/SHW OL2 74 A1
SLFD M6 111 F2
St Anne's Ct DTN/ASHW * M34 131 G2
SALE M33 154 D2
SLFD * M6 111 G1
St Anne's Crs OLDE OL4 92 D2
St Anne's Dr DTN/ASHW M34 131 H4
St Anne's Gdns HEY OL10 41 G4
St Annes Meadow
TOT/BURYW BL8 26 A4
St Annes Rd CCHDY M21 141 E4
DTN/ASHW M34 131 H4
St Annes St BURY * BL9 38 C2
HYDE SK14 149 H3
NEWH/MOS M40 101 G4
St Anns Cl PWCH M25 84 D4
St Anns Pas CMANW M2 6 E4
St Ann's Rd BRAM/HZG SK7 184 D3
MILN OL16 11 K5
PWCH M25 84 C4
St Ann's Rd North
CHD/CHDH SK8 181 G3
St Ann's Rd South
CHD/CHDH SK8 181 H3
St Ann's Sq CHD/CHDH SK8 181 H4
CMANW M2 6 E4
St Ann's St CMANW M2 6 D4
SALE M33 155 G3
SWIN M27 96 D2
St Ann St BOL * BL1 33 H5
St Asaphs Dr AUL OL6 105 E3
St Aubin's Rd BOLE BL2 3 J7
St Augustine's Rd
EDGY/DAV SK3 171 E1
St Augustine St BOL BL1 33 G4
NEWH/MOS M40 101 E5
St Austell Dr CHD/CHDH SK8 181 G4
TOT/BURYW BL8 26 A1
St Austell Rd OLDTF/WHR M16 141 H2
St Austells Dr PWCH M25 85 E2
SWIN M27 97 H4
St Barnabas's Dr LIT OL15 20 D2
St Barnabas Sq OP/CLY M11 115 E5
St Bartholomew's Dr ORD M5 112 B5
St Bartholomew St
BOLS/LL BL3 49 F5
St Bede's Av BOLS/LL BL3 63 E2
St Bees Cl CHD/CHDH SK8 181 G1
RUSH/FAL M14 127 F4
St Bees Rd BOLE BL2 34 D4
St Benedicts Av
WGTN/LGST * M12 128 C2
St Benedict's Sq
WGTN/LGST M12 128 C2
St Bernard's Av SLFD M6 99 F5
St Boniface Rd BRO M7 112 B1
St Brannock's Rd CCHDY M21 141 F2
CHD/CHDH SK8 183 E5
St Brelades Dr BRO M7 100 A2
St Brendan's Rd DID/WITH M20 142 C4

St Brendan's Rd North
DID/WITH M20 142 C4
St Brides Wy OLDTF/WHR M16 126 C3
St Catherines Dr FWTH BL4 64 A4
St Catherine's Rd
DID/WITH M20 142 C4
St Chad's Av MPL/ROM SK6 162 B4
St Chad's Cl MILN OL16 10 D7
St Chads Ct MILN OL16 10 D7
St Chads Crs OLDS OL8 104 A1
UPML OL3 78 B4
St Chad's Gv MPL/ROM SK6 162 B4
St Chad's Rd DID/WITH M20 143 E4
St Chad's St CHH * M8 113 F1
St Christopher's Av AUL OL6 105 H4
St Christophers Cl
DID/WITH M20 142 A5
St Christopher's Dr
MPL/ROM SK6 161 H4
St Christopher's Rd AUL OL6 105 G4
St Clair Rd RAMS * BL0 16 A5
St Clare Ter HOR/BR * BL6 46 A1
St Clements Ct OLDS OL8 9 G6
St Clement's Dr ORD M5 126 A1
St Clements Fold URM * M41 138 D1
St Clement's Rd CCHDY M21 140 D3
St Cuthberts Fold OLDS OL8 104 D1
St Davids Av CHD/CHDH SK8 170 D4
MPL/ROM SK6 162 A4
St David's Cl AUL OL6 105 G3
St David's Rd BRAM/HZG SK7 184 D3
CHD/CHDH SK8 170 D3
St Domingo Pl OLD * OL1 9 F3
St Dominics Ms BOLS/LL BL3 63 F1
St Dominics Wy MDTN M24 71 H5
St Edmund Hall Cl RAMS BL0 16 D4
St Edmund's Rd
NEWH/MOS M40 101 F4
St Edmund St BOL BL1 2 D4
St Elisabeth's Wy RDSH SK5 144 D4
St Elmo Av OFTN SK2 173 E2
St Elmo Pk POY/DIS SK12 196 B3
St Ethelbert's Av BOLS/LL BL3 48 A4
St Gabriel's Cl ROCH OL11 42 C5
St George's Av
HALE/TIMP WA15 166 B1
HULME * M15 126 C1
St George's Ct ALT WA14 165 E2
BOL BL1 2 E3
HYDE * SK14 147 G1
STRET * M32 139 H2
St George's Crs
HALE/TIMP WA15 166 B1
SLFD * M6 110 B2
WALK M28 81 E5
St Georges Dr HYDE SK14 147 G2
NEWH/MOS M40 102 A3
St George's Gdns
DTN/ASHW M34 146 D2
St George's Rd BOL BL1 2 B3
BURY BL9 54 B5
DROY M43 116 A2
PART M31 137 E5
ROCH OL11 28 C3
RUSH/FAL M14 143 F4
STRET M32 139 G1
St Georges Sq BOL BL1 3 F3
CHAD OL9 88 D4
St George's St BOL BL1 2 E3
STLY SK15 119 F2
St George's Wy SLFD * M6 111 H1
SLFD M6 111 H1
St Germain St FWTH BL4 64 D4
St Giles Dr HYDE SK14 148 A1
St Gregorys Cl FWTH BL4 64 D5
St Helena Rd BOL BL1 2 C4
St Helens Cl GOL/RIS/CU WA3 150 A3
St Helens Rd BOLS/LL BL3 48 B5
WHTN BL5 62 C3
St Helier's Dr BRO M7 100 A2
St Heliers St BOLS/LL BL3 48 C5
St Hilda's Dr OLD OL1 74 A4
St Hilda's Rd DTN/ASHW M34 131 F2
OLDTF/WHR M16 126 A3
WYTH/NTH M22 156 C5
St Hilda's Vw DTN/ASHW * M34 131 F3
St Hugh's Cl ALT WA14 165 H1
St Ignatius Wk ORD * M5 112 A5
St Ives Av CHD/CHDH SK8 170 D3
St Ives Crs SALE M33 154 B5
St Ives Rd RUSH/FAL M14 142 C1
St James Av BOLE BL2 50 B1
TOT/BURYW BL8 37 G3
St Jame's Cl MILN OL16 58 D1
St James Ct HALE/TIMP WA15 165 H5
SLFD * M6 110 C2
St James Dr SALE M33 154 B3
WILM/AE SK9 199 F4
St James Rd HTNM SK4 159 E1
St James's Gv ALT WA14 154 A5
St James's Rd BRO M7 99 H4
St James's Sq CMANW * M2 6 E5
St James's St OLD OL1 75 E5
St James's Ter HEY OL10 40 D4
St James St AUL OL6 118 C3
CMANE M1 7 F6
ECC * M30 109 H3
FWTH BL4 64 C5
HEY OL10 40 D4
MILN OL16 35 G5
ROY/SHW OL2 60 A2
St James' Wy CHD/CHDH SK8 192 C1
St John's Av DROY M43 116 C3
St John's Cl BRO * M7 99 G4
DUK SK16 118 D5
MPL/ROM SK6 162 A4
St Johns Ct BRO * M7 99 G4
HOR/BR BL6 46 C5
HYDE SK14 133 E5
MILN * OL16 30 C5
OLDE OL4 76 A5
RAD M26 67 G2
St John's Dr HYDE SK14 133 E5
MILN OL16 30 C5
St John's Gdns MOSL OL5 92 D5
St John's Rd ALT WA14 177 F1
BRAM/HZG SK7 184 C3
BRUN/LGST M13 128 C4
DTN/ASHW M34 131 G3
HTNM SK4 158 B4
OLDTF/WHR M16 126 B4
St John's St BRO M7 99 G4
CHAD OL9 8 B6
FWTH BL4 65 F4
RAD M26 67 G2
St John St CSLFD M3 6 C6
DUK * SK16 118 D5
ECC M30 109 G4
IRL M44 136 B1
OLDE OL4 91 H1
SWIN M27 98 A4
WALK M28 80 D3
St John's Wk CHAD OL9 8 B5
EDGY/DAV * SK3 171 E1
St Johns Wd HOR/BR BL6 46 C5
St Josephs Av WHTF M45 69 E5
St Joseph's Dr MILN OL16 43 G2
ORD M5 112 A5
St Joseph St BOL BL1 33 G4
St Kilda Av FWTH BL4 81 G1
St Kildas Av DROY M43 116 A2
St Lawrence Quay SALQ M50 125 G1
St Lawrence Rd
DTN/ASHW M34 131 G5
St Leonard's Ct SALE M33 154 A2
St Leonards Dr
HALE/TIMP WA15 166 A3
St Leonard's Rd HTNM SK4 159 G1
St Leonard's St MDTN M24 71 H3
St Lesmo Rd EDGY/DAV SK3 12 A7
St Lukes Ct CHAD OL9 73 F5
St Luke's Rd SLFD M6 111 E3
St Luke St ROCH * OL11 43 E1
St Margaret's Av BNG/LEV M19 143 G5
St Margaret's Cl BOL * BL1 48 A1
PWCH M25 85 F1
St Margarets Gdns OLDS * OL8 89 H4
St Margaret's Rd ALT WA14 165 F5
BOL BL1 48 A1
CHD/CHDH SK8 170 D3
NEWH/MOS M40 88 C4
PWCH M25 85 F2
St Mark's Av ALT WA14 164 D4
ROY/SHW OL2 59 H5
St Mark's Cl ROY/SHW OL2 59 H5
St Mark's Crs WALK M28 95 E1
St Mark's La CHH M8 100 A3
St Mark's Sq BURY BL9 5 F1
St Mark's St BNG/LEV M19 144 B2
BOLS/LL BL3 49 E4
MPL/ROM SK6 161 H2
St Mark St DUK SK16 118 A4
St Mark's Vw BOLS/LL * BL3 49 E4
St Marks Wk BOLS/LL BL3 48 D5
St Martin's Av HTNM SK4 12 A2
St Martins Cl DROY M43 116 A2
DROY * M43 116 A2
HYDE * SK14 148 A1
St Martin's Dr BRO M7 100 A2
St Martin's Rd MPL/ROM SK6 175 F3
OLDS OL8 90 D5
SALE M33 138 C5
St Martin's St ROCH OL11 42 B5
St Mary's Av BOLS/LL BL3 47 H4
DTN/ASHW M34 146 D3
St Mary's Cl MILN OL16 43 G2
PWCH M25 84 D3
STKP SK1 13 J3
St Marys Ct NEWH/MOS M40 102 A2
NEWH/MOS * M40 102 A2
OLD * OL1 9 F2
St Mary's Dr CHD/CHDH * SK8 170 C3
RDSH SK5 160 A1
St Marys Est OLD OL1 9 G2
St Mary's Ga CMANE M1 6 E4
ROY/SHW * OL2 60 A2
UPML * OL3 78 A2
WHIT OL12 10 B6
St Mary's Hall Rd CHH M8 100 A1
St Mary's Parsonage CSLFD M3 6 D4
St Mary's Pl BURY BL9 4 C5
St Mary's Rd ALT WA14 177 E2
ECC M30 110 A3
HYDE SK14 132 D3
NEWH/MOS M40 102 A3
PWCH M25 84 D3
SALE M33 154 A1
WALK M28 80 D3
St Mary's St CSLFD M3 6 D4
HULME M15 126 D3
OLD OL1 9 G1
OLDTF/WHR M16 127 E4
St Mary's Wy OLD OL1 9 F2
STKP SK1 13 J6
St Matthews Ct STRET * M32 139 H2
St Matthew's Dr OLD OL1 73 F2
St Matthews Gra BOL * BL1 33 H5
St Matthew's Rd EDGY/DAV SK3 12 D6
St Matthews Ter
EDGY/DAV * SK3 12 D6
St Matthews Wk BOL * BL1 33 H5
St Mawes Ct RAD * M26 51 F4
St Michael's Av BOLS/LL BL3 64 C2
BRAM/HZG SK7 183 H5
St Michaels Cl TOT/BURYW BL8 52 A1
St Michaels Ct SALE M33 138 D5
St Michaels Gdns WHTF M45 69 E3
St Michael's Rd HYDE SK14 148 A1
St Michael's Sq ANC * M4 7 G1
St Modwen Rd STRET M32 124 A3
St Osmund's Dr BOLE BL2 50 B2
St Osmund's Gv BOLE BL2 50 B2
St Oswald's Rd BNG/LEV M19 144 A1
St Pauls Cl STLY SK15 119 H3
St Paul's Ct RAD M26 67 F3
St Paul's Hill Rd HYDE SK14 148 A1
St Paul's Rd BRO M7 99 F1
DID/WITH M20 142 D5
HTNM SK4 159 E2
WALK * M28 81 F5
St Paul's St BURY BL9 5 H3
HYDE SK14 132 D5
RAMS * BL0 16 D2
STKP SK1 160 B3
STLY SK15 119 H3
St Pauls Vls BURY BL9 5 H3
St Peter's Av BOL BL1 32 D4
St Peters Cl AULW OL7 117 G3
St Peters Ct STRET * M32 125 F5
St Peter's Dr HYDE * SK14 148 A1
St Petersgate STKP SK1 13 F4
St Peter's Rd BURY BL9 53 G3
SWIN M27 96 D3
St Peter's Sq CMANW M2 6 E6
STKP SK1 13 F3
St Peter's St AUL OL6 117 H3
MILN OL16 30 C5
St Peter's Ter FWTH BL4 65 E5
St Peter's Wy BOL BL1 3 F3
BOLE BL2 3 H7
BOLS/LL BL3 49 G5
St Philip's Av BOLS/LL BL3 48 C5
St Philip's Pl CSLFD * M3 112 C3
St Philip's Rd GTN M18 129 G4
St Phillip's Dr ROY/SHW OL2 74 B3
St Saviour's Rd OFTN SK2 172 D4
Saintsbridge Rd
WYTH/NTH M22 180 B2
St Simons Cl OFTN SK2 172 D1
St Simon St CSLFD M3 112 C2
St Stephen's Av
DTN/ASHW M34 117 F5
St Stephen's Cl BOLE BL2 49 H4
BRUN/LGST M13 128 A3
St Stephens Ct BKLY * M9 101 E3
St Stephens St OLD OL1 9 J1
St Stephen St CSLFD M3 6 B3
OLD OL1 9 J1
St Stephens Vw DROY M43 116 B3
St Teresa's Rd OLDTF/WHR M16 125 H5
St Thomas Ct BURY BL9 5 H4
St Thomas' Pl CHH * M8 113 F1
St Thomas's Cir OLDS OL8 8 D7
St Thomas's Pl STKP SK1 13 G6
St Thomas St BOL * BL1 33 G4
St Thomas St North OLDS OL8 8 D6
St Thomas St South OLDS OL8 8 D7
St Vincent St ANC M4 113 H3
HALE/TIMP WA15 165 H5
St Werburgh's Rd CCHDY M21 141 F3
St Wilfred's Dr WHIT * OL12 18 C4
St Wilfrids St HULME M15 126 D2
St Williams Av BOLS/LL BL3 63 H1
Salcombe Av BOLE BL2 36 C5
Salcombe Cl SALE M33 153 H1
Salcombe Gv BOLE BL2 50 C3
Salcombe Rd OFTN SK2 172 D1
OP/CLY M11 115 G5
Salcot Wk NEWH/MOS * M40 113 H2
Sale Heys Rd SALE M33 154 A3
Salem Gv OLDE OL4 91 G1
Sale Rd NTHM/RTH M23 155 H4
Sale St LIT OL15 21 E2
Salford Ap CSLFD M3 6 D2
Salford Rd WHTN BL5 62 D4
Salford St BURY BL9 38 D2
OLDE OL4 91 F2
Salik Gdns ROCH OL11 43 E1
Salisbury Av HEY OL10 55 H1
Salisbury Crs AUL OL6 105 G3
Salisbury Dr DUK SK16 133 F1
PWCH M25 85 F5
Salisbury Rd ALT WA14 165 G2
CCHDY M21 141 E2
ECC M30 110 A1
OLDE OL4 91 E1
RAD M26 51 H4
SWIN M27 96 D3
URM M41 123 G4
WHTF M45 68 C4
Salisbury St BOLS/LL BL3 2 B6
MDTN M24 72 A3
RDSH SK5 145 E3
ROY/SHW OL2 59 G1
RUSH/FAL M14 127 F4
Salisbury Ter BOLS/LL BL3 66 B1
Salkeld St ROCH OL11 43 E1
Salmon Flds ROY/SHW OL2 74 C1
Salmon St ANC M4 7 G3
Salmsbury Hall Cl RAMS BL0 16 C4
Salop St BOLE BL2 3 G6
SLFD M6 111 H1
Saltash Cl WYTH/NTH M22 180 C3
Saltdene Rd WYTH/NTH M22 180 B3
Saltergate BOLS/LL BL3 47 G5
Saltergate Ms SLFD * M6 111 H3
Salterton Dr BOLS/LL BL3 62 C2
Salteye Rd ECC M30 108 D4
Saltford Av ANC M4 113 H3
Saltford Ct ANC M4 113 H3
Salthill Av HEY OL10 56 B2
Salthill Dr WYTH/NTH M22 180 D2
Salthouse Cl TOT/BURYW BL8 26 D5
Saltire Gdns BRO M7 99 H2
Saltney Av DID/WITH M20 142 A4
Saltram Cl BOLS/LL BL3 51 F4
Saltrush Rd WYTH/NTH M22 180 C2
Salts Dr LIT OL15 20 D2
Salts St ROY/SHW OL2 60 A2
Saltwood Gv BOL BL1 2 E1
Salutation St HULME M15 127 E2
Sam Cowan Cl RUSH/FAL M14 127 F5
Samian Gdns BRO M7 99 F5
Samlesbury Cl DID/WITH M20 157 E3
ROY/SHW OL2 59 G2
Samouth Cl NEWH/MOS M40 114 A2
Sampson Sq RUSH/FAL M14 127 F4
Samson St MILN OL16 11 K4
Sam Swire St HULME M15 126 D3
Samuel La ROY/SHW OL2 59 F1
Samuel Ogden St CMANE M1 7 G7
Samuel St BNG/LEV M19 144 A3
BURY BL9 5 G2
FAIL M35 103 E2
HEY OL10 40 D4
HTNM SK4 159 G3
ROCH OL11 42 B4
Sanby Av GTN M18 129 F4
Sanby Rd GTN M18 129 F4
The Sanctuary HULME M15 126 D2
Sanctuary Cl BRUN/LGST M13 127 G3
Sandacre Rd NTHM/RTH M23 168 A2
Sandal St NEWH/MOS M40 114 B2
Sandbach Av RUSH/FAL M14 142 A3
Sandbach Rd RDSH * SK5 144 D1
SALE M33 155 G3
Sandbank Gdns WHIT OL12 14 B3
Sand Banks BOL BL1 23 E5
Sandbed La MOSL OL5 92 D5
Sandbrook Pk ROCH * OL11 42 D2
Sandbrook Wy DTN/ASHW M34 131 G3
ROCH OL11 42 D2
Sandby Dr MPL/ROM SK6 175 G1
Sanderling Rd OFTN SK2 173 H4
Sanderson Cl WALK M28 96 A2
Sanderson St BURY BL9 5 H3
NEWH/MOS M40 101 F5
Sanderstead Dr BKLY M9 87 F4
Sandfield Dr HOR/BR BL6 46 D3
Sandfield Rd MILN OL16 43 G1
Sandford Av GTN * M18 129 G2
Sandford Cl BOLE BL2 35 F3
Sandford Rd SALE M33 155 G3
Sandford Station La RDSH SK5 144 C1
Sandford St RAD M26 53 E5
Sandgate Av OP/CLY M11 115 G3
RAD M26 66 A5
Sandgate Dr URM M41 123 F4
Sandgate Rd CHAD OL9 89 G1
WHTF M45 69 E5
Sandham St BOLS/LL BL3 49 E5
Sandham Wk BOLS/LL * BL3 49 E5
Sandheys DTN/ASHW M34 131 G3
Sandheys Gv GTN M18 129 H4
Sandhill Cl BOLS/LL * BL3 49 E5
Sandhill St HYDE SK14 133 E5
Sandhill Wk WYTH/NTH M22 180 A2
Sand Hole La ROCH OL11 41 F1
ROCH OL11 43 E5
Sand Hole Rd FWTH BL4 81 H1
Sandhurst Av DID/WITH M20 142 B5
Sandhurst Cl TOT/BURYW BL8 37 G3
Sandhurst Ct BOLE BL2 50 B3
Sandhurst Dr BOLE BL2 50 B3
WILM/AE SK9 199 H1
Sandhurst Rd DID/WITH M20 157 G4
OFTN SK2 172 C4
Sandhutton Rd BKLY M9 101 E1
Sandilands Rd NTHM/RTH M23 167 E1
Sandileigh Av CHD/CHDH SK8 170 D3
DID/WITH M20 157 G1
HALE/TIMP WA15 178 A1
RDSH SK5 160 C1
Sandileigh Dr HALE/TIMP WA15 178 A1
Sandiway BRAM/HZG SK7 183 H2
HEY OL10 41 F4
IRL M44 136 B1
MPL/ROM SK6 161 G3
Sandiway Cl MPL/ROM SK6 175 E1
Sandiway Dr DID/WITH M20 157 F3
Sandiway Pl ALT WA14 165 G4
Sandiway Rd ALT WA14 165 G3
SALE M33 154 A2
WILM/AE SK9 192 A2
Sandon St BOLS/LL BL3 48 C5
Sandown Av SLFD M6 111 F3
Sandown Cl OLD OL1 74 D3
WILM/AE SK9 200 A2
Sandown Crs BOLS/LL BL3 65 H2
GTN M18 129 G5
Sandown Dr DTN/ASHW M34 147 E3
HALE/TIMP WA15 189 E1
SALE M33 153 H3
Sandown Gdns URM M41 137 H1
Sandown Rd BOLE BL2 35 F3
BRAM/HZG SK7 185 H3
BURY BL9 68 D2
EDGY/DAV SK3 171 E1
Sandown St GTN M18 129 H2
Sandpiper Cl DUK SK16 132 D1
FWTH BL4 64 A5
ROCH OL11 28 C4
Sandpiper Dr EDGY/DAV SK3 171 G3
Sandray Cl BOLS/LL BL3 47 G4
Sandray Gv ORD M5 111 F4
Sandridge Cl FWTH BL4 65 F4
Sandridge Wk WGTN/LGST M12 128 B2
Sandringham Av
DTN/ASHW M34 130 B5
DTN/ASHW M34 131 E2
STLY SK15 119 F2
Sandringham Cl ALT WA14 176 C3
Sandringham Dr DUK SK16 133 E1
HTNM SK4 158 D5
MILN OL16 31 H5
POY/DIS SK12 195 E4
RAMS BL0 26 B2
Sandringham Gra PWCH M25 85 H4
Sandringham Rd
BRAM/HZG SK7 185 G2
CHD/CHDH SK8 182 D1
HYDE SK14 147 H4
MPL/ROM SK6 160 D3
WALK M28 94 B4
Sandringham St GTN M18 129 F4
Sandringham Wy ROY/SHW OL2 58 D3
WILM/AE SK9 199 F4
Sands Av CHAD OL9 72 C4
Sands Cl HYDE SK14 149 E2
Sandsend Cl CHH M8 99 H5
Sandsend Rd URM M41 123 F5
Sandstone Rd MILN OL16 31 G4
Sandstone Wy CCHDY M21 141 G5
Sand St NEWH/MOS M40 113 H1
STLY SK15 119 E5
Sandwell Dr SALE M33 139 G5
Sandwich Rd ECC M30 110 A2
Sandwich St WALK M28 81 E5
Sandwick Crs BOLS/LL BL3 48 C4
Sandwood Av BOLS/LL BL3 47 F4
Sandy Acre MOSL OL5 106 D2
Sandy Bank ROY/SHW OL2 59 G1
Sandy Bank Av HYDE SK14 149 E2
Sandy Bank Rd CHH M8 100 A2
Sandy Bank Wk HYDE * SK14 149 E2
Sandybrook Cl TOT/BURYW BL8 26 A5
Sandy Brow BKLY M9 87 E5
Sandy Cl BURY BL9 68 C1
Sandygate Cl SWIN M27 96 D3
Sandy Gv DUK SK16 118 C5
SLFD M6 111 F2
SWIN M27 97 E2
Sandy Haven Cl HYDE SK14 149 E2
Sandyhill Rd BKLY M9 86 B4
Sandyhills BOLS/LL BL3 48 D5
Sandylands Dr PWCH M25 98 C1
Sandy La CCHDY M21 141 E3
DROY M43 116 D2
DUK SK16 118 C5
IRL M44 121 B5
MDTN M24 72 A5
MPL/ROM SK6 162 B3
NTHM/RTH M23 167 E2
OLDS * OL8 8 D5
PWCH M25 84 D5
RDSH SK5 159 H3
ROCH OL11 29 F4
ROY/SHW OL2 59 E5
SLFD M6 111 F2
STRET M32 139 G2
UPML OL3 78 A2
WILM/AE SK9 198 C2
Sandy Meade PWCH M25 84 D4
Sandyway PWCH * M25 84 D4
Sandywell Cl OP/CLY M11 129 G1
Sandywell St OP/CLY M11 115 G5
Sandy Wd SLFD M6 111 F2
Sanfold La BNG/LEV M19 144 B1
Sangster Ct ORD M5 111 H5
Sankey Gv BKLY M9 86 C4
Sankey St BURY BL9 4 B4
Santiago St RUSH/FAL M14 127 G5
Santley St WGTN/LGST M12 128 D5
Santon Av RUSH/FAL M14 143 F3
Sapling Gv SALE M33 153 G4
Sapling Rd BOLS/LL BL3 63 F2
SWIN M27 96 C5
Sarah Butterworth Ct
MILN OL16 11 H7
Sarah Butterworth St
MILN OL16 30 C5
Sarah St ECC M30 109 E4
MDTN M24 71 G4
OP/CLY M11 114 C5
ROCH OL11 30 A5
ROY/SHW OL2 60 A4
Sargent Dr OLDTF/WHR M16 126 D4
Sargent Rd MPL/ROM SK6 161 E4
Sark Rd CCHDY M21 140 D1
Sarn Av WYTH/NTH M22 168 C5
Saturn Gv SLFD M6 112 B1
Saunton Av BOLE BL2 35 G4
Saunton Rd OP/CLY M11 115 G5
Sautridge Cl MDTN M24 57 G2
Savernake Rd MPL/ROM SK6 162 B1
Savick Av BOLE BL2 50 B2
Saville Rd CHD/CHDH SK8 169 G3
RAD M26 52 A2
Saville St BOLE BL2 3 G5
MDTN M24 72 C5
Saviours Ter BOLS/LL * BL3 48 B4
Savio Wy MDTN M24 71 H5
Savoy Ct WHTF * M45 68 B3
Savoy Dr ROY/SHW OL2 74 A2
Savoy St OLDE OL4 91 E2
ROCH OL11 29 F3
Sawley Av LIT OL15 20 D1
OLDE OL4 91 G3
WHTF M45 68 C2
Sawley Dr CHD/CHDH SK8 193 E1
Sawley Rd NEWH/MOS M40 114 A1
Saw St BOL BL1 33 H4
Sawyer Brow HYDE SK14 133 E4
Sawyer St TOT/BURYW BL8 37 G2
WHIT OL12 10 C3
Saxby Av EDGW/EG BL7 23 E3
Saxby St SLFD M6 97 H5
Saxelby Dr CHH M8 100 C4
Saxfield Dr NTHM/RTH M23 168 B3
Saxon Av CHH M8 86 B5
DUK SK16 118 B5
Saxon Cl TOT/BURYW BL8 37 G4
Saxon Dr CHAD OL9 72 D4
DROY M43 116 B3
DTN/ASHW M34 131 F1
Saxonholme Rd ROCH OL11 57 F1
Saxon St DROY M43 116 C3
DTN/ASHW M34 131 G5
MDTN M24 72 A4
NEWH/MOS M40 114 B2
OLDE OL4 75 F5
RAD M26 67 E1
Saxthorpe Cl SALE M33 153 G1
Saxthorpe Wk WGTN/LGST M12 128 B3
Saxwood Av BKLY M9 101 E1
Saxwood Cl WHIT OL12 28 C2
Scafell Av AULW OL7 117 G1
Scafell Cl MPL/ROM SK6 186 D4
OLD OL1 74 C3
Scale St ORD M5 112 A4
Scarborough St
NEWH/MOS M40 101 H2
Scarcroft Rd WGTN/LGST M12 128 D3
Scardale Av BOL BL1 32 D5
Scarfield Dr ROCH OL11 28 B2
Scargill Cl RUSH/FAL * M14 142 D3
Scargill Rd BOLS/LL BL3 47 H5
Scarisbrick Av DID/WITH M20 158 A3
Scarisbrick Rd BNG/LEV M19 143 G3
Scarr Av RAD M26 67 H2
Scarr Dr WHIT OL12 30 A1
Scarr La ROY/SHW OL2 60 B2
Scarsdale Rd RUSH/FAL M14 128 B4
Scarsdale St SLFD M6 112 A2
Scarthwood Cl BOLE BL2 35 F1
Scawfell Av BOLE BL2 34 C4
Schofield Rd DROY M43 116 C4
ECC M30 108 D4
Schofield St FAIL * M35 103 E2
HEY OL10 41 E5
LIT OL15 15 C3
LIT OL15 21 F2
MILN OL16 44 D1
OLDS OL8 90 B4
OP/CLY M11 115 F3
ROCH OL11 43 F2
ROY/SHW OL2 59 E4
Scholars Dr DID/WITH M20 142 B4
Scholars Wy MDTN M24 71 G3
Scholes Dr NEWH/MOS M40 88 D5
Scholes La PWCH M25 85 F4
Scholes St CHAD OL9 89 F3
FAIL M35 103 F1
OLD OL1 9 J3
ROCH OL11 42 B5
SWIN M27 97 F2
TOT/BURYW BL8 37 H3
Scholes Wk PWCH M25 85 E4
Scholey St BOLE BL2 49 F4
Scholfield Av URM M41 139 E2
School Av AUL OL6 105 G4
STRET * M32 125 G5
School Brow BURY BL9 4 D3
MPL/ROM SK6 161 H4
WALK M28 95 G4
School Cl POY/DIS SK12 195 G4
School Ct ANC M4 7 K3
EDGY/DAV SK3 172 A3
School Crs STLY SK15 119 E2
School Gv DID/WITH M20 142 D5
PWCH M25 84 D5
School Gv West
DID/WITH * M20 142 D5
School Hl BOL BL1 2 D2
School House Flats OLDS * OL8 89 H5
School La ALT WA14 164 A5
BKLY M9 86 D5
BURY BL9 27 F3
CHD/CHDH SK8 182 D4
DID/WITH M20 157 H3

HTNM SK4 ... 159 F1
HYDE SK14 ... 147 H4
IRL M44 ... 24 A1
IRL M44 ... 150 C1
MILN OL16 ... 10 C7
MOSL OL5 ... 107 F3
MPL/ROM SK6 ... 163 C5
MPL/ROM SK6 ... 135 G5
PART M31 ... 157 C4
POY/DIS SK12 ... 195 G4
School Ms MILN * OL16 ... 45 E2
School Rd ECC M30 ... 109 F5
FAIL M35 ... 105 E3
HALE/TIMP WA15 ... 178 A1
OLDS OL8 ... 89 C5
STRET M32 ... 139 H1
WILM/AE SK9 ... 192 A3
Schools HI CHD/CHDH SK8 ... 182 A1
Schoolside CI CHH M8 ... 100 C4
Schoolside La MDTN M24 ... 72 D2
Schools Rd GTN M18 ... 129 H5
School St ANC M4 ... 7 G1
BOLS/LL BL3 ... 66 A1
BRAM/HZG SK7 ... 185 G2
BRO M7 ... 112 D1
BURY BL9 ... 5 H6
ECC M30 ... 109 E2
EDGW/EG BL7 ... 23 E4
HEY OL10 ... 40 D4
LIT OL15 ... 20 B3
OLDE OL4 ... 92 B1
OLDS OL8 ... 8 D6
RAD M26 ... 67 E1
RAMS BL0 ... 16 C3
UPML OL3 ... 78 A4
WHIT OL12 ... 10 C5
School Wk OLDTF/WHR M16 ... 126 C3
Schuter Rd RUSH/FAL M14 ... 128 A5
Schwabe St MDTN M24 ... 70 D4
Scobell St TOT/BURYW BL8 ... 37 E1
Score St OP/CLY M11 ... 114 D4
Scorton Av BOLE BL2 ... 50 C2
Scorton St BOL * BL1 ... 48 A3
Scotforth CI HULME M15 ... 126 D1
Scotland ANC M4 ... 7 H3
Scotland Hall Rd
NEWH/MOS M40 ... 102 A5
Scotland St AUL OL6 ... 118 D3
NEWH/MOS M40 ... 102 B5
Scott Av BURY BL9 ... 53 G3
CCHDY M21 ... 141 E1
ECC M30 ... 109 G5
Scott CI RDSH SK5 ... 160 A2
Scott Dr HALE/TIMP WA15 ... 166 A5
MPL/ROM SK6 ... 175 G1
Scottfield OLDS OL8 ... 9 G7
Scottfield Rd OLDS OL8 ... 9 G7
Scott Ga DTN/ASHW M34 ... 131 F1
Scott Rd DROY M43 ... 116 B4
DTN/ASHW M34 ... 118 C1
PWCH M25 ... 84 C4
Scott St OLDS OL8 ... 9 G7
RAD M26 ... 67 E1
Scout Dr NTHM/RTH M23 ... 167 G5
Scout La MDTN M24 ... 71 H1
Scout Vw TOT/BURYW BL8 ... 26 B5
Scovell St BRO M7 ... 99 G4
Scowcroft La ROY/SHW OL2 ... 59 F5
Scowcroft St BOLE BL2 ... 3 J1
Scroggins La PART M31 ... 151 E2
Scropton St NEWH/MOS M40 ... 101 E5
Seabright Wk OP/CLY * M11 ... 114 C4
Seabrook Crs URM M41 ... 123 G4
Seabrook Rd NEWH/MOS M40 ... 102 B5
Seacombe Av EDGY/DAV SK3 ... 171 E1
Seacombe Gv EDGY/DAV SK3 ... 171 E1
Seaford Rd BOLE BL2 ... 35 E5
SLFD M6 ... 99 E5
Seaford Wk CHAD * OL9 ... 89 C1
Seaforth Rd BOL BL1 ... 33 H1
Seaham Dr TOT/BURYW BL8 ... 26 B5
Seaham Wk RUSH/FAL M14 ... 127 G5
Sealand CI SALE M33 ... 155 F4
Sealand Dr ECC M30 ... 108 D5
Sealand Rd NTHM/RTH M23 ... 155 G4
Sealey Wk NEWH/MOS * M40 ... 114 B1
Seal Rd BRAM/HZG SK7 ... 184 A4
Seamon's Dr ALT WA14 ... 164 D4
Seamon's Rd ALT WA14 ... 164 C5
Searby Rd GTN M18 ... 129 H4
Seares St AULW OL7 ... 117 F1
Seascale Av OP/CLY M11 ... 115 E2
Seathwaite Rd FWTH BL4 ... 64 A5
Seatoller Dr MDTN M24 ... 72 D2
Seaton CI BRAM/HZG SK7 ... 185 E3
Seaton Ms AULW OL7 ... 117 F1
Seaton Rd BOL BL1 ... 33 F4
Sebastian CI MPL/ROM SK6 ... 175 C2
Sebastopol Wk ANC M4 ... 7 F3
Second Av BOL BL1 ... 48 A2
BURY BL9 ... 39 G2
OLDS OL8 ... 89 H5
OP/CLY M11 ... 115 C3
STLY SK15 ... 107 F5
SWIN M27 ... 96 C5
TRPK M17 ... 125 C2
Second St BOL BL1 ... 2 E6
Sedan CI ORD M5 ... 111 H4
Sedburgh CI SALE M33 ... 155 E4
Sedbury CI NTHM/RTH M23 ... 155 C5
Sedbury CI NTHM/RTH M23 ... 155 G5
Seddon Av GTN M18 ... 129 G2
Seddon Gdns RAD M26 ... 52 B5
Seddon La RAD M26 ... 65 H4
Seddon Rd ALT WA14 ... 177 G2
Seddon Av TOT/BURYW BL8 ... 26 A4
Seddon St BNG/LEV M19 ... 144 A1
BOLS/LL * BL3 ... 66 A1
LHULT M38 ... 80 A2
Sedgeborough Rd
OLDTF/WHR M16 ... 126 D5
Sedge CI RDSH SK5 ... 145 F5
Sedgefield CI ORD M5 ... 111 H4
Sedgefield Dr BOL BL1 ... 33 E1
Sedgefield Pk OLDE OL4 ... 91 C1
Sedgefield Rd RAD M26 ... 65 H4
Sedgefield Wk WILM/AE SK9 ... 199 H1

Sedgemoor CI CHD/CHDH SK8 ... 183 E2
Sedgemoor V BOLE BL2 ... 35 G4
Sedgemoor Wy OLD OL1 ... 9 F2
PWCH M25 ... 85 F5
Sedgley CI MDTN M24 ... 85 F5
Sedgley Park Rd PWCH M25 ... 85 F5
Sedgley Rd CHH M8 ... 100 B2
Sedgley St MDTN M24 ... 72 B5
Seedfield Rd BURY BL9 ... 38 C1
Sefton Av LHULT M58 ... 80 C3
Sefton CI BRUN/LGST M13 ... 127 G2
MDTN M24 ... 71 H4
OLD OL1 ... 60 C5
Sefton Crs SALE M33 ... 139 G5
Sefton Dr BURY BL9 ... 27 H5
SWIN M27 ... 96 C4
WALK M28 ... 95 H4
WILM/AE SK9 ... 191 H5
Sefton Rd BOL BL1 ... 33 G4
CCHDY M21 ... 141 E3
RAD M26 ... 71 H4
SALE M33 ... 154 C1
SWIN M27 ... 97 E1
Sefton St BURY BL9 ... 27 G5
CHAD OL9 ... 89 F5
CHH M8 ... 100 B2
HEY OL10 ... 41 E3
RAD M26 ... 67 H3
ROCH OL11 ... 42 D1
WHIT OL12 ... 10 C5
Selborne Rd CCHDY M21 ... 141 E2
Selby Av CHAD OL9 ... 73 E3
WHTF M45 ... 68 C2
Selby CI MILN OL16 ... 31 F5
POY/DIS * SK12 ... 195 E2
RAD M26 ... 53 E4
STRET M32 ... 124 A5
Selby Dr SLFD M6 ... 110 C2
URM M41 ... 122 C3
Selby Gdns CHD/CHDH SK8 ... 193 F1
Selby Rd MDTN M24 ... 71 G1
STRET M32 ... 124 B5
Selby St HTNM SK4 ... 159 C2
MILN OL16 ... 11 H6
OP/CLY M11 ... 114 D5
Selham Wk BRUN/LGST * M13 ... 127 H1
Selhurst Av OP/CLY M11 ... 115 F3
Selkirk Av OLDS OL8 ... 90 A3
Selkirk Dr BKLY M9 ... 87 G4
Selkirk Rd BOL BL1 ... 33 C1
CHAD OL9 ... 89 E3
Sellars Sq DROY M43 ... 116 B5
Sellers Wy CHAD OL9 ... 89 F4
Selsby Av ECC M30 ... 109 E5
Selsey Av CHD/CHDH SK8 ... 170 C2
SALE M33 ... 154 A3
Selside Wk RUSH/FAL M14 ... 142 D3
Selstead Rd WYTH/NTH M22 ... 180 B3
Selston Rd BKLY M9 ... 86 C2
Selworth Av SALE M33 ... 155 F2
Selworth CI HALE/TIMP WA15 ... 165 H5
Selworthy Rd OLDTF/WHR M16 ... 126 C4
Selwyn Av BKLY M9 ... 101 G2
Selwyn CI OLDS * OL8 ... 8 B6
Selwyn Dr CHD/CHDH SK8 ... 183 F5
Selwyn St BOLE BL2 ... 3 H6
Senior Av RUSH/FAL M14 ... 143 F4
Senior St CSLFD M3 ... 6 C1
Senior Vw HYDE * SK14 ... 133 C5
Sepal CI RDSH SK5 ... 145 F2
Sepia Gv MDTN M24 ... 72 A2
Sequoia St BKLY M9 ... 101 F2
Sergeants La WHTF M45 ... 67 H5
Serin CI OFTN SK2 ... 173 C5
Service St HTNM SK4 ... 171 E1
Set St STLY SK15 ... 120 D3
Settle St BOLS/LL BL3 ... 63 H1
BOLS/LL BL3 ... 66 D2
Settstones La UPML OL3 ... 95 G1
Seven Acres La WHIT OL12 ... 28 A1
Seven Acres Rd WHIT OL12 ... 28 B1
Sevenoaks Av HTNM SK4 ... 158 D1
URM M41 ... 123 H5
Sevenoaks Dr BOLS/LL BL3 ... 63 H1
SWIN M27 ... 96 C5
Sevenoaks Rd CHD/CHDH SK8 ... 169 C3
Sevenoaks Wk
BRUN/LGST * M13 ... 127 H3
Seven Stiles Dr MPL/ROM SK6 ... 174 D2
Seventh Av OLDS OL8 ... 105 H1
Seventh CI ALT WA14 ... 165 C3
Severn CI BURY BL9 ... 27 C4
MILN OL16 ... 31 H5
Severn Dr BRAM/HZG SK7 ... 185 F3
Severn Rd CHAD OL9 ... 73 H4
HEY OL10 ... 41 C5
OLDS OL8 ... 105 C1
Severn Wy FWTH BL4 ... 82 A3
RDSH SK5 ... 160 A1
Seville St ROY/SHW OL2 ... 59 H4
ROY/SHW OL2 ... 59 H4
Sewell Wy LHULT M58 ... 80 A4
Sewerby CI OLDTF/WHR M16 ... 127 G3
Sewerby St OLDTF/WHR M16 ... 127 G3
Sexa St OP/CLY M11 ... 115 G4
Sexton St HEY OL10 ... 40 D4
Seymour Av OP/CLY M11 ... 115 C3
Seymour CI OLDTF/WHR M16 ... 126 C1
Seymour Dr BOLE BL2 ... 23 H5
Seymour Gv FWTH BL4 ... 64 C4
HALE/TIMP WA15 ... 166 A3
MILN OL16 ... 43 G3
OLDTF/WHR M16 ... 126 C1
SALE M33 ... 154 C2
Seymour PI OLDTF/WHR * M16 ... 126 C1
Seymour Rd BOL BL1 ... 34 A1
CHH M8 ... 86 D4
OFTN SK2 ... 172 C2
Seymour Rd South
OP/CLY M11 ... 115 G3
Seymour St BOLE BL2 ... 23 H5

DTN/ASHW M34 ... 131 E5
CTN M18 ... 129 G2
HEY OL10 ... 40 D5
RAD M26 ... 67 G1
Shackleton Gv BOL BL1 ... 32 B4
Shackleton St ECC M30 ... 109 F2
Shackliffe St NEWH/MOS M40 ... 88 A5
Shaddock Av ROCH OL11 ... 28 C2
Shade Av OLDS OL8 ... 92 A2
Shadowbrook CI OLD OL1 ... 74 B3
Shadowmoss Rd
WYTH/NTH M22 ... 180 D4
Shadows La MOSL OL5 ... 93 F5
Shadwell St East HEY OL10 ... 41 E3
Shadwell St West HEY OL10 ... 41 E3
Shady La BOLE BL2 ... 35 C5
BURY BL9 ... 27 H3
LIT OL15 ... 31 H1
Shady Oak Rd OFTN SK2 ... 173 C5
Shaftesbury Av CHD/CHDH SK8 ... 183 E3
ECC M30 ... 109 F5
HALE/TIMP WA15 ... 166 C4
HOR/BR BL6 ... 46 A1
LIT OL15 ... 31 H1
Shaftesbury Dr WHIT OL12 ... 20 A2
Shaftesbury Gdns URM M41 ... 136 D1
Shaftesbury Rd CHH M8 ... 100 B3
EDGY/DAV SK3 ... 170 D3
SWIN M27 ... 97 E3
Shaftsbury Dr HEY OL10 ... 55 H1
Sheffield St CMANE M1 ... 7 J6
Sheffield Rd HYDE SK14 ... 133 E5
RAD M26 ... 51 H5
STLY SK15 ... 120 B2
Shakespeare Av BURY BL9 ... 53 G3
DTN/ASHW M34 ... 146 C3
RAD M26 ... 51 H5
Shakespeare CI LIT OL15 ... 15 G4
Shakespeare Crs DROY M43 ... 116 B3
ECC M30 ... 109 G3
Shakespeare Rd
CHAD/CHDH SK8 ... 170 C3
MPL/ROM SK6 ... 161 F3
OLD OL1 ... 75 F2
PWCH M25 ... 84 C4
RDSH SK5 ... 96 C2
Shakespeare Wk
BRUN/LGST * M13 ... 127 H2
Shalbourne Av BKLY M9 ... 87 H4
Shalbourne Rd WALK M28 ... 81 C5
Shaldon Dr NEWH/MOS M40 ... 115 H1
Shalfleet CI BOLE BL2 ... 35 F1
Shalford Dr WYTH/NTH M22 ... 180 C4
Shambles Sq ANC M4 ... 6 E3
Shandon Av WYTH/NTH M22 ... 168 C2
Shanklin Av URM M41 ... 138 B1
Shanklin CI CCHDY M21 ... 140 D2
DTN/ASHW M34 ... 147 E3
Shanklin Wk BOLS/LL BL3 ... 49 H4
Shannon CI HEY OL10 ... 40 D5
Shannon Rd WYTH/NTH M22 ... 180 D1
Shap Av HALE/TIMP WA15 ... 167 G4
Shap Dr WALK M28 ... 81 G5
Sharcott CI CLDTF/WHR M16 ... 127 E4
Shardlow CI NEWH/MOS M40 ... 114 A1
Shargate St SALE M33 ... 153 F4
Sharman St BOLS/LL BL3 ... 49 G4
Sharnford CI BOLE BL2 ... 3 J7
Sharnford Sq
WGTN/LGST * M12 ... 128 C2
Sharon Av OLDE OL4 ... 93 E2
Sharon CI AULW OL7 ... 117 F4
Sharples Av BOL BL1 ... 23 G5
Sharples Dr TOT/BURYW BL8 ... 37 E2
Sharples Hall Dr BOL BL1 ... 23 E5
Sharples Hall Fold BOL BL1 ... 34 A1
Sharples Hall Ms BOL BL1 ... 23 G5
Sharples St OLDE OL4 ... 75 G3
Sharples Pk BOL BL1 ... 33 G2
Sharples St HTNM SK4 ... 159 H5
Sharp St ANC M4 ... 7 H1
MDTN M24 ... 72 C5
PWCH * M25 ... 84 D3
WALK M28 ... 81 H4
Sharrington Dr NTHM/RTH M23 ... 167 F3
Shavington Av CHD/CHDH SK8 ... 182 D3
Shaving La WALK M28 ... 81 E5
Shaw Av HYDE SK14 ... 148 A3
Shawbrook Rd WALK M28 ... 94 C2
Shawbury CI HEY OL10 ... 40 D5
Shawbury Gv SALE M33 ... 154 A4
Shawbury Rd NTHM/RTH M23 ... 168 A5
Shawbury St MDTN M24 ... 72 B5
Shawclough CI WHIT OL12 ... 18 C5
Shawclough Dr WHIT OL12 ... 18 B5
Shawclough Ri WHIT OL12 ... 18 B5
Shawclough Rd WHIT OL12 ... 18 B5
Shawclough Wy WHIT OL12 ... 18 C5
Shawcroft CI POY/SHW OL2 ... 59 H4
Shawcross Fold STKP * SK1 ... 14 D2
Shawcross La WYTH/NTH M22 ... 180 C5
Shawdene Rd WYTH/NTH M22 ... 168 B1
Shawe Hall Av URM M41 ... 137 H3
Shawe Hall Crs URM M41 ... 137 H3
Shawe Rd URM M41 ... 137 H2
Shawe View URM M41 ... 137 H2
Shawfield CI RUSH/FAL M14 ... 142 D3
Shawfield La WHIT OL12 ... 18 B5
Shawfields STLY SK15 ... 120 D2
Shawgreen CI HULME M15 ... 126 D2
Shaw Hall Av HYDE SK14 ... 133 C5
Shaw Hall Bank Rd UPML OL3 ... 93 C2
Shaw Head Dr FAIL M35 ... 103 H4
Shawheath CI HULME M15 ... 126 C2
Shawhill Wk NEWH/MOS M40 ... 114 A1
Shaw La ALT WA14 ... 165 C5
Shaw Moor Av STLY SK15 ... 119 H4
Shaw Rd HTNM SK4 ... 159 H1
NEWH/MOS M40 ... 159 H1
OLDE OL4 ... 75 H5
ROY/SHW OL2 ... 59 F3
RUSH/FAL M14 ... 142 D3
Shaw Rd South EDGY/DAV SK3 ... 171 H4
Shaws Fold OLDE * OL4 ... 76 D3
Shaw's Rd ALT WA14 ... 165 G5
Shaw St AUL OL6 ... 118 C2
BOLS/LL BL3 ... 48 D4
BURY BL9 ... 5 J5

CSLFD M3 ... 6 E1
FWTH * BL4 ... 64 D2
HYDE SK14 ... 134 D4
OLD OL1 ... 9 F2
OLDE OL4 ... 92 B1
ROY/SHW OL2 ... 59 F5
UPML OL3 ... 93 H1
WHIT OL12 ... 11 G1
Shay Av HALE/TIMP WA15 ... 179 E5
Shayfield Av CHAD OL9 ... 72 D4
WYTH/NTH M22 ... 168 B2
Shayfield Dr WYTH/NTH M22 ... 168 C4
Shayfield Rd WYTH/NTH M22 ... 168 C4
Shay La HALE/TIMP WA15 ... 179 F3
Sheader Dr ORD M5 ... 110 C4
Sheard Av AUL OL6 ... 105 G4
Shearer Wy SWIN M27 ... 98 A5
Shearing Av WHIT OL12 ... 28 C2
Shearsby CI HULME M15 ... 126 D2
Shearwater Av DROY M43 ... 116 D3
Shearwater Gdns ECC M30 ... 108 D5
Shearwater Rd OFTN SK2 ... 173 G4
The Sheddings BOLS/LL BL3 ... 49 F5
Shed St WHIT * OL12 ... 11 H4
Sheepfoot La OLD OL1 ... 74 A3
PWCH M25 ... 85 G4
Sheep Gap WHIT * OL12 ... 29 E2
Sheep Gate TOT/BURYW BL8 ... 36 D1
Sheffield Rd HYDE SK14 ... 133 E5
Sheffield St CMANE M1 ... 7 J6
HTNM SK4 ... 159 H3
Shefford CI OP/CLY M11 ... 114 C5
Sheiling Ct ALT WA14 ... 165 F5
Shelbourne Av BOL BL1 ... 33 E4
Shelderton CI NEWH/MOS M40 ... 101 H3
Sheldon CI PART M31 ... 150 D3
Sheldon Ct AULW OL7 ... 105 G5
Sheldon Rd BRAM/HZG SK7 ... 185 E5
POY/DIS SK12 ... 196 B5
Sheldon St OP/CLY M11 ... 115 E3
Sheldrake CI DUK SK16 ... 133 F1
Sheldrake Rd ALT WA14 ... 165 E1
Shelfield CI ROCH OL11 ... 28 C2
Shelfield La ROCH OL11 ... 28 B2
Shelford Av GTN M18 ... 129 E4
Shelley Av DTN/ASHW M34 ... 131 F5
Shelley Gv DROY M43 ... 116 B4
HYDE SK14 ... 132 C4
STLY SK15 ... 120 B1
Shelley Ri DUK SK16 ... 133 C1
Shelley Rd CHAD OL9 ... 90 B1
LHULT * M58 ... 80 B2
OLD OL1 ... 75 F3
PWCH M25 ... 84 D3
SWIN M27 ... 96 C2
Shelley St NEWH/MOS M40 ... 102 B2
Shelley Wk BOL BL1 ... 33 G5
Shelton Av SALE M33 ... 153 G2
Shenfield Wk NEWH/MOS M40 ... 114 A2
Shentonfield Rd
WYTH/NTH M22 ... 168 D5
Shenton St HYDE SK14 ... 147 G1
Shenton Park Av SALE M33 ... 153 F5
Shepherd Cross St BOL BL1 ... 33 F5
Shepherds Ct TOT/BURYW BL8 ... 26 A2
Shepherd St BKLY * M9 ... 101 E1
BURY BL9 ... 5 F6
HEY OL10 ... 40 D4
ROCH OL11 ... 29 H4
ROY/SHW OL2 ... 59 F5
TOT/BURYW BL8 ... 26 A3
Shepherds Wy MILN OL16 ... 44 B1
Shepley Av BOLS/LL BL3 ... 48 B4
Shepley CI BRAM/HZG SK7 ... 185 E4
Shepley Dr BRAM/HZG SK7 ... 185 E4
Shepley La MPL/ROM SK6 ... 175 G5
Shepley Rd DTN/ASHW M34 ... 131 G2
Shepley St CMANE M1 ... 7 H6
DTN/ASHW M34 ... 131 G2
FAIL M35 ... 103 F1
HYDE SK14 ... 147 H1
OLDE * OL4 ... 91 H1
Shepton CI BOL BL1 ... 22 C4
Shepton Dr NTHM/RTH M23 ... 179 G2
Sheraton Rd OLDS OL8 ... 90 B3
Sherborne Rd EDGY/DAV SK3 ... 170 C2
MDTN M24 ... 71 G1
URM M41 ... 123 H5
Sherborne St CHH M8 ... 6 D1
CSLFD M3 ... 113 E1
Sherborne St West CSLFD M3 ... 112 D2
Sherbourne CI CHD/CHDH SK8 ... 193 E1
OLDS OL8 ... 91 F3
RAD M26 ... 52 A5
Sherbourne Rd HEY OL10 ... 40 D3
BOL BL1 ... 48 D5
Sherbrook CI SALE M33 ... 84 D3
Sherbrooke Av UPML OL3 ... 78 B3
Sherdley Ct CHH M8 ... 100 B1
Sherdley Rd CHH M8 ... 100 B1
Sherford CI BRAM/HZG SK7 ... 184 B2
Sheridan Wy CHAD * OL9 ... 72 D4
Sheriff St BOLE BL2 ... 3 K1
MILN OL16 ... 44 D1
ROCH OL11 ... 10 A5
Sheringham Dr HYDE SK14 ... 133 F5
SWIN M27 ... 97 E4
Sheringham PI BOLS/LL BL3 ... 48 C4
Sheringham Rd RUSH/FAL M14 ... 142 C5
Sherlock St RUSH/FAL M14 ... 143 E3
Sherratt St ANC M4 ... 7 J2
Sherrington St
WGTN/LGST * M12 ... 128 D3
Sherway Dr HALE/TIMP WA15 ... 166 D3
Sherwell Rd BKLY M9 ... 87 G3
Sherwin Wy ROCH OL11 ... 42 C5
Sherwood Av BRO M7 ... 99 F1
DROY M43 ... 116 D3
HTNM SK4 ... 158 D5
RAD M26 ... 52 B5
ROY/SHW OL2 ... 59 F3
RUSH/FAL M14 ... 142 D3
SALE M33 ... 154 B4
Sherwood CI AUL OL6 ... 105 F5
MPL/ROM SK6 ... 175 C5
ORD M5 ... 111 H3
TOT/BURYW BL8 ... 26 A4
Sherwood Dr SWIN M27 ... 97 G3

Sherwood Rd DTN/ASHW M34 ... 130 C5
MPL/ROM SK6 ... 162 A1
Sherwood St BOL BL1 ... 34 A1
OLD OL1 ... 74 A4
ROCH OL11 ... 42 C4
RUSH/FAL M14 ... 142 D3
Sherwood Wy ROY/SHW OL2 ... 59 F1
Shetland Rd NEWH/MOS M40 ... 114 A2
Shetland Wy RAD M26 ... 52 B4
URM M41 ... 123 G3
Shevington Gdns
NTHM/RTH M23 ... 156 A5
Shieldborn Dr BKLY M9 ... 101 A5
Shield CI OLDS OL8 ... 8 B6
Shield Dr WALK M28 ... 96 B1
Shiel St EDGY/DAV SK3 ... 81 E4
Shiers CI CHD/CHDH SK8 ... 170 B5
Shiffnall St BOLE BL2 ... 3 J4
Shilford Dr ANC M4 ... 7 J1
Shillingford Rd FWTH BL4 ... 64 D4
Shillingstone CI BOLE BL2 ... 35 G2
Shillington CI LHULT M38 ... 80 A4
Shiloh La OLDE OL4 ... 76 C2
Shilton Gdns BOLS/LL * BL3 ... 48 D4
Shilton St RAMS BL0 ... 16 C3
Shipgate BOL BL1 ... 3 F4
Shipla CI CHAD OL9 ... 8 C5
Shipley Av SLFD M6 ... 110 D2
Shipley Vw URM M41 ... 122 C3
Shipper Bottom La RAMS BL0 ... 17 E5
Shippey St RUSH/FAL M14 ... 143 E5
Shipston CI TOT/BURYW BL8 ... 37 G3
Shipton St BOL BL1 ... 33 E5
Shirburn ROCH * OL11 ... 29 H5
Shirebrook Dr RAD M26 ... 52 A5
Shireburn Av BOLE BL2 ... 49 H1
Shiredale CI CHD/CHDH SK8 ... 171 E5
Shiredale Dr BKLY M9 ... 100 D1
Shiregreen Av NEWH/MOS M40 ... 100 D5
Shirehills PWCH M25 ... 84 D4
Shireoak Rd DID/WITH M20 ... 143 E4
The Shires DROY M43 ... 117 E2
RAD M26 ... 52 D4
Shirley Av BRO M7 ... 98 D3
CHAD OL9 ... 89 G5
CHD/CHDH SK8 ... 191 H1
DTN/ASHW M34 ... 116 D5
ECC M30 ... 109 C5
HYDE SK14 ... 132 C3
STRET M32 ... 125 G5
SWIN M27 ... 97 H3
Shirley CI BRAM/HZG SK7 ... 184 D2
Shirley Gv EDGY/DAV SK3 ... 171 H4
Shirley Rd CHH M8 ... 86 D3
Shirley St ROCH OL11 ... 42 C5
Shoecroft Av DTN/ASHW M34 ... 146 B3
Sholver Hill CI OLD OL1 ... 60 C5
Sholver La OLD OL1 ... 60 C5
Shone Av WYTH/NTH M22 ... 180 D2
Shoreditch CI HTNM SK4 ... 159 E1
Shorefield CI MILN * OL16 ... 11 K4
Shorefield Mt EDGW/EG BL7 ... 22 C2
Shore Fold LIT OL15 ... 20 D2
Shoreham Wk CHAD * OL9 ... 89 F1
Shore HI LIT OL15 ... 21 F2
Shore La Lea LIT OL15 ... 21 F2
Shore Mt LIT OL15 ... 20 D2
Shore Rd LIT OL15 ... 20 D2
Shore St MILN OL15 ... 31 G5
OLD OL1 ... 9 K2
Shoreswood BOL BL1 ... 22 C5
Shorland St SWIN M27 ... 96 B5
Shorrocks St TOT/BURYW BL8 ... 26 A5
Short Av DROY M43 ... 116 A5
Shortcroft St HULME * M15 ... 127 E1
Shortland Crs BNG/LEV M19 ... 158 A3
Shortlands Av BURY BL9 ... 5 F7
Short St ANC M4 ... 7 G4
BRAM/HZG SK7 ... 185 E1
BRO M7 ... 112 D1
HEY OL10 ... 40 C5
HTNM SK4 ... 159 H4
Short St East HTNM SK4 ... 159 H4
Shotton Wk RUSH/FAL * M14 ... 142 C2
Shrewsbury Ct
OLDTF/WHR * M16 ... 126 C3
Shrewsbury Gdns
CHD/CHDH SK8 ... 193 F1
Shrewsbury Rd BOL BL1 ... 33 G4
DROY M43 ... 116 B3
PWCH M25 ... 84 D4
SALE M33 ... 154 B4
Shrewsbury St OLDE OL4 ... 75 C4
OLDTF/WHR M16 ... 126 C3
Shrigley CI WILM/AE SK9 ... 200 A3
Shrigley Rd POY/DIS SK12 ... 196 B5
Shropshire Av RDSH SK5 ... 145 H4
Shropshire Rd FAIL M35 ... 103 F4
Shropshire Sq
WGTN/LGST * M12 ... 128 D2
Shrowbridge Wk
WGTN/LGST * M12 ... 128 D2
Shudehill ANC M4 ... 6 E3
Shurmer St BOLS/LL BL3 ... 48 D5
Shutt La UPML OL3 ... 77 G2
Shuttle St ECC * M30 ... 110 A3

Shuttleworth CI
OLDTF/WHR * M16 ... 141 H1
Shutts La STLY SK15 ... 120 D3
Sibley Rd HTNM SK4 ... 159 H1
Sibley St OP/CLY M11 ... 114 C5
Sibson Rd CCHDY M21 ... 140 D2
SALE M33 ... 154 B2
Sickle St CMANE M1 ... 6 E4
OLDS * OL8 ... 9 H6
Sidbury Rd CCHDY M21 ... 141 E3
Sidcup Rd NTHM/RTH M23 ... 167 G4
Siddall St HEY OL10 ... 40 C4
OLD OL1 ... 9 G3
RAD M26 ... 52 B5
ROY/SHW OL2 ... 60 A2
WGTN/LGST M12 ... 143 H1
Siddington Av DID/WITH M20 ... 142 B3
Siddington Rd POY/DIS SK12 ... 195 G3
MPL/ROM SK6 ... 174 C5
Side Av ALT WA14 ... 177 G2
Sidebotham St MPL/ROM SK6 ... 161 G2

Sidebottom St DROY * M43 116 A4
OLDE OL4 75 H4
STLY SK15 119 F3
Side St OLDS OL8 89 H5
OP/CLY M11 115 E4
Sidford Cl BOLS/LL BL3 50 A4
The Sidings WALK M28 95 H5
Sidley Av BKLY M9 87 G3
Sidley St HYDE SK14 133 E5
Sidmouth Av URM M41 122 B5
Sidmouth Dr BKLY M9 87 E5
Sidmouth Gv CHD/CHDH SK8 182 C5
Sidmouth Rd SALE M33 153 G1
Sidmouth St CHAD OL9 89 G2
DTN/ASHW M34 131 E1
Sidney Rd BKLY M9 101 E1
Sidney St BOLS/LL BL3 49 E4
CMANE M1 127 F1
CSLFD M3 6 A3
CSLFD * M3 6 D5
OLD OL1 74 D3
Sidwell Wk ANC * M4 114 A4
Siebers Bank WHIT * OL12 29 G1
Siemens Rd IRL M44 150 D1
Sienna Cl IRL M44 135 D5
Signal Cl ECC M30 109 E3
Signal Dr NEWH/MOS M40 101 E4
Signet Wk CHH M8 100 C5
Silas St AUL * OL6 105 G5
Silburn Wy MDTN M24 70 D5
Silchester Dr NEWH/MOS M40 101 E4
Silchester Wy BOLE BL2 35 F5
Silfield Cl OP/CLY M11 114 B4
Silkhey Gv WALK M28 95 E1
Silkin Cl BRUN/LGST * M13 127 G1
Silkstone St OP/CLY M11 129 F1
Silk St ANC M4 7 J2
CSLFD M3 112 C2
MDTN M24 71 G4
NEWH/MOS M40 102 B4
ROCH OL11 42 C2
Sillavan Wy CSLFD M3 6 B3
Silsden Av BKLY M9 86 C2
Silton St BKLY M9 101 G1
Silverbirch Cl SALE M33 153 G4
Silver Birches DTN/ASHW M34 147 E2
Silver Birch Gv SWIN M27 97 G4
Silverbirch Wy FAIL M35 103 E3
Silver Cl DUK SK16 132 A1
Silvercroft St HULME M15 126 D1
Silverdale SWIN M27 83 F5
Silverdale Av CHAD OL9 89 F1
DTN/ASHW M34 146 D1
IRL M44 121 C4
PWCH M25 85 H5
Silverdale Cl BURY BL9 53 H1
MPL/ROM SK6 186 D4
Silverdale Dr OLDE OL4 92 A1
WILM/AE SK9 201 B1
Silverdale Rd BOL BL1 48 B2
CCHDY M21 141 F2
CHD/CHDH SK8 169 G5
FWTH BL4 64 B3
HTNM SK4 159 F2
Silverdale St OP/CLY M11 130 A1
Silver Hl MILN OL16 31 G5
Silver Hill Rd HYDE SK14 147 H2
Silver Jubilee Wk ANC M4 7 H3
Silverlea Dr BKLY M9 86 D5
Silvermere AUL OL6 105 H4
Silver Spring HYDE SK14 148 A3
Silverstone Dr NEWH/MOS M40 115 G1
Silver St BURY BL9 4 D5
CMANE M1 7 G5
IRL M44 121 C4
OLD OL1 9 F4
RAMS BL0 16 D2
WHIT * OL12 29 G3
WHTF * M45 68 B3
Silverthorne Cl STLY SK15 119 F4
Silverton Cl HYDE SK14 149 E1
Silverton Gv BOL BL1 34 A2
MDTN M24 56 A5
Silverwell La BOL BL1 3 F5
Silverwell St BOL BL1 3 F5
NEWH/MOS M40 102 C5
Silverwood CHAD OL9 72 D5
Silverwood Av CCHDY M21 141 E3
Simeon St ANC * M4 7 H1
Simister Dr BURY BL9 68 D2
Simister Gn PWCH M25 69 H4
Simister La PWCH M25 69 G4
Simister Rd FAIL M35 103 E3
Simister St BKLY M9 101 F2
Simkin Wy OLDS OL8 104 D1
Simms Cl CSLFD M3 112 C3
Simonbury Cl TOT/BURYW BL8 37 E4
Simon Freeman Cl
BNG/LEV M19 144 B5
Simon La MDTN M24 70 B2
Simons Cl SALE M33 154 B3
Simon St MILN OL16 31 G5
Simonsway NTHM/RTH M23 179 H1
Simpson Av SWIN M27 83 H5
Simpson Gv WALK M28 94 B4
Simpson Hill Cl HEY OL10 41 G3
Simpson Rd WALK M28 94 B4
Simpson St ANC M4 7 G1
CHAD OL9 89 G3
EDGY/DAV * SK3 13 F6
HYDE SK14 132 B5
OP/CLY M11 114 D4
WILM/AE * SK9 199 E4
Sinclair St ROCH OL11 42 C3
Sinderland La ALT WA14 151 H5
Sinderland Rd ALT WA14 165 E1
PART M31 151 H3
Sindsley Gv BOLS/LL BL3 63 H1
Sindsley Rd SWIN M27 82 C5
Singapore Av MANAIR M90 179 H4
Singleton Av BOLE BL2 50 B2
Singleton Cl BRO M7 99 F1
Singleton Rd BRO M7 99 F1
HTNM SK4 159 E2
Singleton St RAD M26 51 G5
Sion St RAD M26 67 E2
Sirdar St OP/CLY * M11 116 A5
Sirius Pl BRO M7 112 C2
Sir Matt Busby Wy
OLDTF/WHR M16 125 G3
Sir Richard Fairey Rd
HTNM SK4 144 A5
Sir Robert Thomas Ct
BKLY * M9 101 E2
Siskin Rd OFTN SK2 173 G4
Sisley Cl BRO M7 99 E2
Sisson St FAIL M35 102 D3
Sisters' St DROY M43 116 B5
Sixpools Gv WALK M28 94 D2
Sixth Av BOL BL1 48 A2
BURY BL9 39 G2
OLDS OL8 103 H1
Sixth St TRPK M17 125 E3
Size St WHIT OL12 14 C4
Skagen Ct BOL BL1 2 D1
Skaife Rd SALE M33 155 F2
Skarratt Cl WGTN/LGST M12 128 C2
Skegness Cl TOT/BURYW BL8 38 A1
Skelton Gv BOLE BL2 50 C1
BRUN/LGST M13 143 G1
Skelton Rd ALT WA14 165 H2
STRET M32 125 E5
Skelwith Av BOLS/LL BL3 64 A2
Skelwith Cl URM M41 122 D4
Skerry Cl BRUN/LGST M13 127 G1
Skerton Rd OLDTF/WHR M16 126 A4
Skip Pl CSLFD M3 113 F2
Skipton Av CHAD OL9 73 E3
NEWH/MOS M40 102 C1
Skipton Cl BRAM/HZG SK7 184 D4
RDSH SK5 144 D3
TOT/BURYW BL8 37 E4
Skipton Dr URM M41 122 C3
Skipton St BOLE BL2 49 H2
OLDS OL8 91 E3
Skipton Wk BOLE * BL2 49 H2
Skye Cl HEY OL10 40 A5
Skye Cft MPL/ROM SK6 162 C3
Skye Rd URM M41 123 G3
Slackcote La UPML OL3 61 H2
Slackey Brow FWTH BL4 82 B2
Slack Fold La FWTH BL4 63 G3
Slack Ga WHIT OL12 14 D5
Slack La BOLE BL2 24 B4
SWIN M27 97 F1
Slack Rd CHH M8 100 D1
Slack St HYDE SK14 133 E4
MILN OL16 10 D6
Slade Gv BRUN/LGST M13 128 C5
Slade Hall Rd WGTN/LGST M12 143 H1
Slade La BNG/LEV M19 143 G2
Slade Mt BNG/LEV * M19 143 G3
Sladen St WHIT OL12 10 C3
Slade St BOLS/LL BL3 65 H1
Slaidburn Av BOLE BL2 50 C3
Slaidburn Cl MILN OL16 44 C1
Slaidburn Dr TOT/BURYW BL8 36 D3
Slaithwaite Dr OP/CLY M11 115 F3
Slateacre Rd HYDE SK14 148 A4
Slate Av ANC M4 113 H4
Slate La DTN/ASHW M34 116 D5
Slaterfield BOLS/LL BL3 48 D4
Slater La BOL BL1 3 G2
Slater St BOL BL1 2 D2
CHAD OL9 8 E5
ECC M30 109 E3
FAIL M35 103 E1
Slate Whf HULME * M15 6 A7
Slawson Wy HEY OL10 41 G3
Sleaford Cl NEWH/MOS M40 114 A2
TOT/BURYW BL8 38 A1
Sleddale Cl OFTN SK2 173 E4
Sledmere Cl BOL BL1 34 A4
OP/CLY M11 114 D4
Sledmoor Rd NTHM/RTH M23 155 G5
Slimbridge Cl BOLE BL2 35 H5
Sloane Av OLDE OL4 75 H4
Sloane St AUL OL6 118 B2
BOLS/LL BL3 63 F1
OP/CLY * M11 114 D3
Smallbridge Cl WALK M28 94 D2
Smallbrook Rd ROY/SHW OL2 45 E4
ROY/SHW OL2 60 B1
Smalldale Av OLDTF/WHR M16 127 E5
Smalley St ROCH OL11 42 B4
Smallfield Dr BKLY M9 101 E2
Smallridge Cl NEWH/MOS M40 114 A2
Smallshaw La AUL OL6 105 F5
Smallwood St NEWH/MOS M40 102 B4
Smart St WGTN/LGST M12 128 D5
Smeaton Cl STRET M32 140 B1
Smeaton St CHH M8 100 D4
Smedley Av BOLS/LL BL3 64 B1
Smedley La CHH M8 100 C4
Smedley Rd CHH M8 100 C4
Smedley St CHH M8 100 B4
Smethurst Hall Rd BURY BL9 39 H2
Smethurst La BOLS/LL BL3 63 E2
Smethurst St BKLY M9 101 E1
HEY OL10 40 C4
MDTN M24 72 C5
TOT/BURYW BL8 37 G2
Smith Farm Cl OLDE OL4 76 A4
Smith Fold La WALK M28 80 B4
Smith Hl MILN OL16 31 G5
Smithies Av MDTN M24 71 H2
Smithies St HEY OL10 41 F4
Smithills Croft Rd BOL BL1 32 D3
Smithills Dean Rd BOL BL1 32 D1
Smithills Dr BOL BL1 33 G3
Smithills Hall Cl RAMS BL0 16 C4
Smith La EDGW/EG BL7 23 E3
Smiths Lawn WILM/AE SK9 199 F5
Smith's Rd BOLS/LL BL3 65 E1
Smith St AULW OL7 117 G4
BURY BL9 5 G2
CHD/CHDH * SK8 170 C3
DTN/ASHW M34 146 C1
HEY OL10 41 E4
HYDE SK14 132 C3
LIT OL15 21 E3
MILN OL16 10 D6
MOSL OL5 92 C5
OLDE OL4 75 H4
OLDTF/WHR M16 126 B2
RAMS BL0 16 C3
WALK M28 81 E4
Smithybridge Rd LIT OL15 20 B4
Smithy Bridge Rd LIT OL15 31 H1
Smithy Cft EDGW/EG BL7 23 E3
Smithy Fold WHIT OL12 29 E2
Smithy Fold Rd HYDE SK14 147 H3
Smithy Gn CHD/CHDH * SK8 182 D4
MPL/ROM SK6 162 A1
Smithy Gv AUL OL6 118 B1
Smithy Hl BOLS/LL BL3 47 H5
Smithy La ALT WA14 176 A1
CSLFD * M3 6 D4
HYDE SK14 147 H2
PART M31 151 E3
UPML OL3 78 A4
Smithy St BRAM/HZG SK7 185 E1
RAMS * BL0 16 D2
Smyrna St HEY OL10 40 D5
OLDE * OL4 91 F2
ORD M5 111 F4
RAD M26 52 A5
Snape St RAD M26 52 A3
Snell St ANC M4 114 A4
Snipe Av ROCH OL11 28 C4
Snipe Cl POY/DIS SK12 194 B4
Snipe Rd OLDS OL8 91 E5
Snipe St BOLS/LL BL3 49 E4
Snipe Wy DTN/ASHW M34 117 E5
Snowden Av URM M41 138 A3
Snowden St BOL BL1 2 C3
HEY OL10 56 B1
OLDS OL8 90 C3
Snowdon Rd ECC M30 110 B2
Snowdon St ROCH OL11 43 F4
Snow Hill Rd BOLS/LL BL3 50 A4
Snydale Wy BOLS/LL BL3 62 A2
Soapstone Wy IRL M44 136 B3
Soap St ANC M4 7 G3
Sofa St BOL BL1 33 E5
Soho St BOL BL1 2 E6
OLDE OL4 75 E5
Solent Av CHH M8 86 B5
Solent Dr BOLS/LL BL3 49 H4
Solness St BURY BL9 27 G5
Solway Cl BOLS/LL BL3 63 G1
OLDS OL8 9 F7
SWIN M27 82 D3
Solway Rd WYTH/NTH M22 168 D5
Somerby Dr WYTH/NTH M22 180 B3
Somerdale Av BOL BL1 47 H1
Somerfield Rd BKLY M9 101 E1
Somerford Av DID/WITH M20 142 B3
Somerford Rd RDSH SK5 145 F1
Somersby Dr EDGW/EG BL7 23 E3
Somersby Wk BOLS/LL * BL3 48 D4
Somerset Av ROY/SHW OL2 59 G2
Somerset Cl IRL M44 135 C5
RDSH SK5 160 D2
Somerset Dr BURY BL9 53 G1
Somerset Gv ROCH OL11 28 D3
Somerset Pl SALE M33 139 G5
Somerset Rd ALT WA14 165 G3
BOL BL1 48 A1
DROY M43 116 B2
ECC M30 110 B1
FAIL M35 102 D4
Somerset St OLDE OL4 91 F1
Somers Rd RDSH SK5 145 E2
Somerton Av SALE M33 154 D3
WYTH/NTH * M22 180 B1
Somerton Rd BOLE BL2 50 C4
Somerville Gdns
HALE/TIMP WA15 166 A2
Somerville Sq BOL BL1 33 F3
Somerville St BOL BL1 33 F3
Somerwood Wk
WGTN/LGST * M12 128 C2
Sonning Dr BOLS/LL BL3 62 D2
Sopwith Dr RUSH/FAL M14 142 B2
Sorbus Cl SLFD M6 112 A3
Sorby Rd IRL M44 136 B4
Sorrel Bank SLFD M6 111 G1
Sorrel Dr LIT OL15 20 C2
Sorrell Bank RDSH SK5 145 F2
Sorrel St HULME M15 126 D2
Sorrel Wy OLDE OL4 75 H2
Sorton St CMANE * M1 127 F1
Soudan Rd OFTN SK2 172 B3
Soudan St MDTN M24 72 B3
Souracre Fold STLY SK15 119 G2
South Acre Dr WILM/AE SK9 192 A4
Southall St CSLFD M3 113 E2
Southampton Cl BRO M7 99 G5
Southam St BRO M7 100 A3
South Av BNG/LEV M19 143 G4
FWTH BL4 81 G1
HEY OL10 40 C4
SWIN M27 96 C5
WHTF M45 68 B3
South Back Rock BURY BL9 4 E4
South Bank Cl WILM/AE * SK9 201 G3
Southbank Rd BNG/LEV M19 158 A1
South Bank Rd BURY BL9 4 C7
Southbourne Av URM M41 139 E1
Southbourne St SLFD M6 111 F3
Southbrook Av CHH M8 86 A4
Southbrook Gv BOLS/LL BL3 64 A1
Southcliffe Rd RDSH SK5 145 E5
South Cliffe St OP/CLY M11 130 A1
South Cl BURY BL9 68 D1
WILM/AE SK9 199 E4
South Crs NEWH/MOS M40 88 C4
OP/CLY M11 115 G3
South Cft OLDS OL8 91 E4
Southcross Rd GTN M18 129 G5
South Cross St BURY BL9 5 F5
South Croston St
OLDTF/WHR M16 126 C4
Southdene Av DID/WITH M20 156 D2
Southdown Cl HTNM SK4 12 D1
ROCH OL11 42 B1
Southdown Crs BKLY M9 87 H5
CHD/CHDH SK8 182 C4
Southdown Dr WALK M28 94 A4
Southdowns Cl ROY/SHW OL2 59 G1
South Downs Dr ALT WA14 177 G4
South Downs Rd ALT WA14 177 F3
South Dr BOLE BL2 35 F3
CCHDY M21 141 E5
CHD/CHDH SK8 169 F5
HALE/TIMP WA15 166 B2
Southend Av HULME M15 126 C2
Southend St BOLS/LL BL3 63 F1
Southern Ap SWIN M27 83 H5
Southernby Cl
BRUN/LGST * M13 128 C4
Southern Cl BRAM/HZG SK7 184 A2
DTN/ASHW M34 146 B3
Southern Crs BRAM/HZG SK7 184 A3
Southern Rd SALE M33 139 F5
Southern St CSLFD M3 6 C7
SLFD M6 111 F3
WALK M28 81 E2
Southey Cl LIT OL15 31 G1
Southfield Av BURY BL9 27 F5
Southfield Cl DUK SK16 132 C2
Southfield Rd RAMS BL0 26 B1
Southfields Dr
HALE/TIMP WA15 166 C2
Southfield St BOLS/LL BL3 49 G5
Southgarth Rd SLFD M6 111 F2
Southgate BOLE BL2 35 F2
CCHDY M21 141 E4
HTNM SK4 159 F1
UPML OL3 77 H2
URM M41 138 A3
WHIT OL12 18 A1
Southgate Av
NEWH/MOS * M40 114 D1
Southgate College Land
CSLFD M3 6 D4
Southgate Rd BURY BL9 68 C1
CHAD OL9 88 D4
Southgate St OLD OL1 9 H4
South Gv BRUN/LGST M13 128 A3
SALE M33 154 C3
WALK M28 80 D5
WILM/AE SK9 201 B4
Southgrove Av BOL BL1 22 D5
South Hl OLDE OL4 92 A2
South Hill St OLDE OL4 9 K5
South King St CMANW M2 6 D4
ECC M30 109 E3
Southlands Av ECC M30 108 C5
South Langworthy Rd ORD M5 111 G4
Southlea Rd DID/WITH M20 158 A1
Southleigh Dr BOLE BL2 50 D3
Southlink OLDE * OL4 9 K4
South Lonsdale St STRET M32 125 F5
South Md POY/DIS SK12 194 C2
South Meade CCHDY M21 141 E4
HALE/TIMP WA15 166 B2
PWCH M25 85 G5
SWIN M27 96 D4
South Meadway MPL/ROM SK6 187 E5
Southmere Cl BKLY M9 88 B5
South Mesnefield Rd BRO M7 98 D3
Southmill St CMANW M2 6 D6
Southmoor Rd NTHM/RTH M23 167 F4
Southmoor Wk BOLS/LL * BL3 48 D4
South Oak La WILM/AE SK9 199 E4
South Pde BRAM/HZG SK7 184 A2
MILN OL16 10 C6
South Park Dr POY/DIS SK12 195 F3
South Park Rd CHD/CHDH SK8 169 G3
South Pine St BURY BL9 5 J5
Southpool Cl BRAM/HZG SK7 184 B2
South Pump St CMANE * M1 7 H6
South Radford St BRO M7 98 D3
South Rdg DTN/ASHW M34 131 G3
South Rd ALT WA14 177 F2
DID/WITH M20 157 G4
STRET M32 124 B4
SWIN M27 84 A5
South Rw PWCH M25 98 C1
South Royd St TOT/BURYW BL8 26 A4
Southsea St OP/CLY M11 129 G1
Southside MPL/ROM SK6 146 B5
WILM/AE * SK9 190 A3
South St AULW OL7 117 F5
BOLS/LL BL3 63 H1
MILN OL16 10 E5
OLDS OL8 89 G5
OP/CLY M11 115 E5
RAMS BL0 17 E2
WGTN/LGST M12 128 B3
WILM/AE SK9 201 B4
South Ter RAD M26 53 E2
South Terrace Ct MILN OL16 43 F1
South Vale Crs
HALE/TIMP WA15 166 A4
South Vw MPL/ROM SK6 147 F5
RDSH SK5 130 A5
ROCH OL11 28 B5
STLY SK15 107 G4
South View Gdns
CHD/CHDH SK8 181 H1
South View Rd MILN OL16 20 B5
South View St BOLE BL2 49 H2
South View Ter MILN OL16 20 B4
Southview Wk OLDE * OL4 75 H3
Southwark Dr DUK SK16 132 C2
Southway ALT WA14 165 H3
AULW OL7 104 D4
DROY M43 116 B5
NEWH/MOS M40 89 E5
South Wy OLDS OL8 90 B5
Southwell Cl BOL BL1 2 C2
MPL/ROM SK6 161 H5
Southwell Ct STRET * M32 139 H2
Southwell Gdns AUL OL6 105 E3
Southwell St BKLY M9 101 F3
Southwick Rd NTHM/RTH M23 155 H4
South William St CSLFD * M3 112 C4
Southwood Cl BOLS/LL BL3 64 A1
Southwood Dr BKLY M9 86 B2
Southwood Rd OFTN SK2 172 C5
Southyard St BNG/LEV * M19 144 A3
Sovereign St SLFD M6 111 H1
Sowerby Cl TOT/BURYW BL8 37 E4
Spa Cl RDSH SK5 144 D3
Spa Crs LHULT M38 80 B1
Spa Gv LHULT M38 80 B1
Spa La LHULT M38 80 B1
OLDE OL4 91 G2
Spalding Dr NTHM/RTH M23 179 H2
Sparkford Av NTHM/RTH M23 155 E5
Sparkle St CMANE M1 7 J5
Spark Rd NTHM/RTH M23 167 G2
Spa Rd BOL BL1 2 B6
Sparrow Cl RDSH SK5 144 D1
Sparrowfield Cl STLY SK15 107 F3
Sparrow Hl MILN OL16 10 B7
Sparrow St ROY/SHW OL2 74 B2
Sparta Av WALK M28 80 D5
Sparta Wk OP/CLY M11 114 D5
Sparth Bottoms Rd ROCH OL11 29 G5
Sparthfield Av ROCH OL11 42 D1
Sparthfield Rd HTNM SK4 159 G3
Sparth La HTNM SK4 159 G3
Sparth Rd NEWH/MOS M40 102 C5
Spa St HULME M15 127 G3
Spath La WILM/AE SK9 192 A2
Spath La East CHD/CHDH SK8 193 E2
Spath Rd DID/WITH M20 157 F3
Spath Wk CHD/CHDH SK8 193 E2
Spaw St CSLFD M3 6 B3
Spear St CMANE M1 7 H4
Spectator St ANC M4 114 A3
Spencer Av BOLS/LL BL3 66 B1
HYDE SK14 132 C3
OLDTF/WHR M16 141 F1
WHTF M45 68 B2
Spencer La ROCH OL11 41 F1
Spencer St CHAD OL9 89 G3
DUK SK16 118 B5
ECC M30 109 F4
MOSL OL5 106 C1
OLD OL1 9 K1
RAD * M26 52 D5
RAMS BL0 16 C3
RDSH SK5 145 E3
TOT/BURYW BL8 37 H3
Spender Av CHH M8 100 B4
Spen Fold LIT OL15 20 D4
TOT/BURYW BL8 52 B1
Spennithorne Rd URM M41 138 A1
Spenser Av DTN/ASHW M34 146 D3
RAD M26 51 H5
Spenwood Rd LIT OL15 20 C3
Spey Cl ALT WA14 165 F3
Speyside Cl WHTF * M45 68 D4
Spindle Av STLY SK15 119 H2
Spindlepoint Dr WALK M28 94 D2
The Spindles MOSL OL5 107 E2
Spindlewood Cl STLY SK15 120 A3
Spiningdale LHULT M38 79 C1
Spinks St OLDE OL4 91 E2
Spinners Gdns WHIT OL12 19 H4
Spinners Gn WHIT OL12 30 A1
Spinners La POY/DIS SK12 194 D3
Spinners Ms BOL BL1 2 D2
Spinners Wy OLDE OL4 61 E5
The Spinney CHD/CHDH SK8 182 B1
EDGW/EG BL7 23 H1
OLDE OL4 76 B4
SWIN * M27 96 B4
URM * M41 137 H1
WHIT OL12 18 C5
WHTF M45 67 H5
Spinney Dr BURY BL9 27 G5
SALE M33 153 G3
Spinney Gv DTN/ASHW M34 131 G3
Spinney Nook BOLE BL2 35 E4
Spinney Rd NTHM/RTH M23 168 A2
Spinningfields BOL * BL1 2 A2
Spinningfield Wy HEY OL10 56 A2
Spinning Jenny Wk ANC * M4 113 H3
Spinning Meadow BOL BL1 2 B2
Spinning Mdw BOL BL1 2 B2
The Spinnings RAMS * BL0 16 D5
Spire Wk WGTN/LGST * M12 114 A5
Spirewood Gdns MPL/ROM SK6 161 H4
Spodden Fold WHIT OL12 14 B5
Spodden St WHIT OL12 29 G3
Spod Rd WHIT OL12 29 F2
Spokeshave Wy MILN OL16 30 D1
Sportside Av WALK M28 81 F3
Sportside Cl WALK M28 81 E3
Sportside Gv WALK M28 81 E3
Sportsmans Dr OLDS OL8 90 D4
Spotland Rd WHIT OL12 29 G3
Spotland Tops WHIT OL12 28 D2
Spreadbury St NEWH/MOS M40 101 H3
Spring Av HYDE SK14 148 A3
WHTF M45 68 B2
Springbank CHAD * OL9 73 F5
Spring Bank STLY SK15 119 G5
Spring Bank Av AUL OL6 105 E5
DTN/ASHW M34 131 E1
Springbank Cl MPL/ROM SK6 147 F5
Spring Bank La ROCH OL11 28 B3
STLY SK15 106 D5
Spring Bank Pl EDGY/DAV * SK3 13 F5
Springbank Rd MPL/ROM SK6 147 F5
Spring Bank St CHAD OL9 89 H3
Spring Bridge Rd
OLDTF/WHR M16 142 A1
Springburn Cl WALK M28 94 B4
Spring Cl OLDE OL4 91 G2
RAMS BL0 16 C2
TOT/BURYW BL8 25 H5
Spring Clough SWIN M27 96 A5
Spring Clough Av WALK M28 81 G5
Spring Clough Dr OLDS OL8 91 E3
WALK M28 81 G5
Springdale Gdns DID/WITH M20 157 F3
Springfield RAD M26 82 B1
Springfield Av BRAM/HZG SK7 185 E1
HTNM SK4 144 D4
LIT OL15 20 D1
MPL/ROM * SK6 175 E3
Springfield Cl FAIL M35 102 D2
Springfield Dr WILM/AE SK9 198 C5
Springfield Gdns FWTH BL4 81 H1
Springfield La CSLFD M3 6 C1
IRL M44 136 A1
MILN OL16 20 A5
ROY/SHW OL2 58 D2
Springfield Rd ALT WA14 165 G4
BOL BL1 22 D4
CHD/CHDH SK8 169 G4
DROY M43 116 A2
FWTH BL4 64 B3
FWTH BL4 81 G1
MDTN M24 71 G2
RAMS BL0 26 B1
SALE M33 154 C2
Springfield St AUL * OL6 105 H5
BOLS/LL BL3 49 F5
DTN/ASHW M34 131 G2
HEY OL10 40 B4
Spring Gdns BOLE BL2 35 G2
BRAM/HZG SK7 185 E1
CMANW M2 7 F4
HALE/TIMP WA15 166 D4
HYDE SK14 132 C4
MDTN M24 71 H2
SLFD M6 111 G2
STKP SK1 13 J4
Spring Hall Ri OLDE OL4 61 E5
Springhead Av DID/WITH M20 142 B4
OLDE OL4 92 A2
Springhill ROY/SHW OL2 59 E5
Spring La OLDE OL4 91 H2
RAD M26 67 G1
Springlawns BOL * BL1 47 G1
Spring Meadow La UPML OL3 78 B4
Spring Mill Wk MILN OL16 30 D1
Spring Pl WHIT OL12 14 C3
Spring Ri ROY/SHW OL2 44 D5
Spring Rd ALT WA14 177 G2
POY/DIS SK12 195 G5
The Springs ALT WA14 177 E2

ROCH OL11 28 B4
Springside HTNM SK4 144 C4
Spring Side WHIT OL12 14 C1
Springside Av WALK M28 81 F4
Springside Cl WALK * M28 81 F4
Springside Gv WALK M28 81 F4
Springside Rd BURY BL9 27 F3
Springside Vw TOT/BURYW BL8 26 D4
Springside Wk HULME * M15 126 C2
Springs La STLY SK15 119 E1
Springs Rd MDTN M24 88 D1
Spring St BOLS/LL BL3 49 E4
BURY BL9 5 F6
FWTH BL4 65 E3
MOSL OL5 92 D5
OLDE OL4 92 A2
RAMS BL0 16 C2
RAMS BL0 17 E1
STLY SK15 119 F3
TOT/BURYW BL8 25 H4
TOT/BURYW * BL8 37 E2
UPML * OL3 78 A4
WGTN/LGST M12 143 H1
WILM/AE SK9 199 F3
Spring Ter CHAD OL9 73 F5
MILN * OL16 45 E3
Spring V BRAM/HZG * SK7 185 F2
MDTN M24 71 H4
PWCH M25 84 D5
Springvale Cl AULW OL7 104 C5
Spring Vale Dr TOT/BURYW BL8 25 H4
Spring Vale St TOT/BURYW BL8 25 H5
Spring Vale Ter LIT OL15 21 E3
Spring Vale Wy ROY/SHW OL2 59 H4
Spring Vw BURY * BL9 39 G1
Springville Av BKLY M9 101 G3
Springwater Av RAMS BL0 16 B5
Springwater Cl BOLE BL2 35 F3
Springwater La WHTF M45 68 B2
Springwell Cl SLFD * M6 111 F3
Springwell Gdns HYDE SK14 149 F2
Springwood Av CHAD OL9 72 D3
SWIN M27 97 G4
Springwood Crs MPL/ROM SK6 162 D4
Springwood Hall Rd OLDS OL8 75 F4
Springwood La MPL/ROM SK6 163 E4
Spring Wood St RAMS BL0 16 C1
Spruce Av BURY BL9 5 K4
Spruce Ct SLFD M6 112 A3
Spruce Crs BURY BL9 27 G4
Spruce St HULME M15 126 D2
MILN * OL16 11 F7
RAMS BL0 16 B4
Sprucewood CHAD OL9 72 C4
The Spur OLDS OL8 90 D5
Spurn La UPML OL3 78 A1
The Square DUK * SK16 133 E1
HALE/TIMP WA15 178 D4
HTNM SK4 159 E3
SWIN M27 96 D5
UPML OL3 77 H2
WHTF * M45 68 B4
Square St RAMS BL0 16 D2
Squire Rd CHH M8 100 A3
Squirrel Dr ALT WA14 165 F1
Squirrel's Jump WILM/AE SK9 201 C4
Stablefold MOSL OL5 106 D2
Stable Fold RAD M26 52 B5
Stablefold WALK M28 95 H5
Stableford Av ECC M30 109 F1
The Stables DROY M43 117 E2
WHIT OL12 14 B4
Stable St CHAD OL9 89 F5
The Stablings WILM/AE SK9 199 F5
Stafford Rd ECC M30 109 H2
FAIL M35 103 F5
SWIN M27 97 E2
WALK M28 94 D1
Stafford St CHAD OL9 89 H3
TOT/BURYW BL8 38 A2
Stag Pasture Rd OLDS OL8 104 A1
Stainburne Rd OFTN SK2 172 D3
Stainburn Rd OP/CLY M11 115 E5
Staindale OLDE OL4 91 G1
Stainer St WGTN/LGST M12 128 D5
Stainforth Cl TOT/BURYW BL8 37 G4
Stainforth St OP/CLY M11 128 C1
Stainmoor Ct OFTN SK2 173 E3
Stainmore Av AUL OL6 105 F3
Stainsbury St BOLS/LL BL3 48 B5
Stainton Av GTN M18 129 H4
Stainton Cl RAD M26 51 H5
Stainton Dr MDTN M24 71 E1
Stainton Rd RAD M26 51 H4
Staithes Rd WYTH/NTH M22 180 C4
Stakeford Dr CHH M8 100 D2
Stakehill La MDTN M24 57 H4
Staley Cl STLY * SK15 119 H3
Staley Hall Crs STLY SK15 119 H2
Staley Hall Rd STLY SK15 119 H3
Staley St OLDE * OL4 91 F1
OLDE OL4 92 A1
Stalham Cl NEWH/MOS M40 114 A2
Stalmine Av CHD/CHDH SK8 181 G4
Stalybridge Rd HYDE SK14 134 D4
Stalyhill Dr STLY SK15 134 B1
Stamford Av ALT WA14 164 D3
STLY SK15 118 D3
Stamford Cl STLY SK15 118 D3
Stamford Dr FAIL M35 103 G5
STLY SK15 118 D3
Stamford Gv STLY SK15 119 E3
Stamford New Rd ALT WA14 165 G5
Stamford Park Rd
HALE/TIMP WA15 177 H1
Stamford Pl SALE M33 154 D2
Stamford Rd ALT WA14 177 F2
BRO M7 99 E4
BRUN/LGST M13 128 C5
DTN/ASHW M34 131 E1
MOSL OL5 92 D5
OLDE OL4 76 A4
PART M31 137 E4
URM M41 138 A1
WILM/AE SK9 199 F1
WILM/AE SK9 201 B4
Stamford Sq AUL OL6 118 C3
Stamford St ALT WA14 165 G4
AUL OL6 118 D3
HEY OL10 41 F5
MILN OL16 30 C5
MOSL OL5 106 C1
OLDE * OL4 91 H1
OLDTF/WHR M16 126 C4
SALE M33 139 F5
STLY SK15 120 A1
SWIN M27 97 F1
Stamford St Central AUL OL6 118 A3
Stamford St East AUL OL6 118 B3
Stamford St West AUL OL6 117 H3
Stamford Wy ALT WA14 165 G4
Stampstone St OLD OL1 75 E5
Stanage Av BKLY * M9 87 G3
Stanbank St HTNM SK4 159 H2
Stanbourne Dr BOL BL1 34 A2
Stanbrook St BNG/LEV M19 144 B2
Stanbury Cl HEY * OL10 39 G5
Stanbury Dr DUK SK16 118 C5
Stanbury Wk NEWH/MOS * M40 114 A2
Stancliffe Rd WYTH/NTH M22 168 D4
Stancross Rd NTHM/RTH M23 154 D5
Stand Av WHTF M45 68 B3
Stand Cl WHTF M45 67 H4
Standedge Rd UPML OL3 78 A1
Standfield Dr WALK M28 94 B3
Standish Rd RUSH/FAL M14 143 E3
Stand La RAD M26 67 G2
Standmoor Ct WHTF * M45 68 A5
Standmoor Rd WHTF M45 68 A5
Standring Av TOT/BURYW BL8 52 B1
Stand Ri RAD M26 67 G4
Stanedge Cl RAMS BL0 16 D4
Stanford Cl RAD * M26 66 B5
Stanford Hall Crs RAMS BL0 16 C4
Stanhope Av DTN/ASHW M34 131 F3
PWCH M25 84 D2
Stanhope Cl WILM/AE SK9 200 A2
Stanhope Ct PWCH M25 84 D1
Stanhope Rd ALT WA14 176 D2
SLFD M6 98 B5
Stanhope St AUL * OL6 118 C1
BNG/LEV M19 144 A2
DTN/ASHW M34 131 F3
MOSL OL5 106 D2
RDSH * SK5 144 D4
ROCH OL11 43 E1
Stanhope Wy FAIL M35 102 D2
Stanhorne Av CHH M8 86 B5
Stanier Av ECC M30 109 G2
Stanier St BKLY M9 101 F2
Stanion Gv DUK SK16 118 B5
Stan Jolly Wk OP/CLY M11 115 F5
Stanley Av BRAM/HZG SK7 185 E1
HYDE SK14 132 D4
MPL/ROM SK6 174 C2
RUSH/FAL M14 127 H5
Stanley Av North PWCH M25 84 D1
Stanley Av South PWCH M25 84 D1
Stanley Cl WHTF M45 68 C3
Stanley Ct BURY BL9 5 F3
OLDTF/WHR M16 126 B3
Stanley Dr CHD/CHDH SK8 192 A1
HALE/TIMP WA15 166 B4
WHTF M45 84 C1
Stanley Gv HTNM SK4 159 E2
URM M41 138 C1
WGTN/LGST M12 128 D4
Stanley Hall La POY/DIS SK12 187 H5
Stanley Ms BOLE BL2 50 A2
Stanley Mt SALE M33 154 B3
Stanley Park Wk BOLE BL2 49 H1
Stanley Pl WHIT OL12 10 B4
Stanley Rd BOL BL1 33 E5
BRO M7 99 H2
CHAD OL9 89 G4
CHD/CHDH SK8 192 A1
DTN/ASHW M34 130 C5
ECC M30 109 F4
FWTH BL4 63 H4
HTNM SK4 159 E2
OLDTF/WHR M16 126 B3
OLDTF/WHR M16 141 H1
RAD M26 51 H3
SWIN M27 97 F2
WALK M28 81 E5
WHTF M45 68 C3
Stanley St BKLY * M9 101 F2
CHAD OL9 73 G5
CHH M8 113 F1
HEY OL10 41 E5
NEWH/MOS M40 101 G5
OLDE OL4 91 H2
OP/CLY M11 129 H1
ORD M5 6 A5
PWCH M25 85 F3
RAMS BL0 16 C3
STKP SK1 13 J2
STLY * SK15 119 E4
WHIT OL12 10 B3
WHTF * M45 68 C3
Stanley St South BOLS/LL BL3 2 C6
Stanmore Av STRET M32 139 G1
Stanmore Dr BOLS/LL BL3 48 B4
Stannard Rd ECC M30 108 C4
Stanneybrook Cl MILN OL16 11 H5
Stanney Cl MILN OL16 44 B1
Stanneylands Cl WILM/AE SK9 191 H5
Stanneylands Dr WILM/AE SK9 191 G5
Stanneylands Rd WILM/AE SK9 191 G3
Stanney Rd MILN OL16 11 H4
Stannybrook Rd FAIL M35 104 A4
Stanrose Cl EDGW/EG BL7 22 D2
Stansbury Pl OFTN SK2 173 F3
Stansby Gdns WGTN/LGST M12 128 B2
Stansfield Cl BOLE * BL2 49 H2
Stansfield Dr ROCH OL11 28 B2
Stansfield Hall LIT OL15 15 B4
Stansfield Rd BOLE BL2 3 J3
FAIL M35 103 F1
HYDE SK14 132 D4
Stansfield St CHAD OL9 89 G2
NEWH/MOS M40 115 G1
OLD OL1 74 B4
OP/CLY M11 115 G5
Stanthorne Av DID/WITH M20 142 B4
Stanton Av BRO M7 99 E4
DID/WITH * M20 156 D2
Stanton Gdns HTNM SK4 159 E5
Stanton St CHAD OL9 89 G4
OP/CLY M11 115 F3
STRET M32 125 E4
Stanway Av BOLS/LL * BL3 2 B7
Stanway Cl BOLS/LL * BL3 2 B7
MDTN M24 88 A1
Stanway Dr HALE/TIMP WA15 178 A1
Stanway Rd WHTF M45 69 E4
Stanway St BKLY M9 101 F2
STRET M32 125 E5
Stanwell Rd NEWH/MOS M40 102 B1
SWIN M27 96 D3
Stanwick Av BKLY M9 86 B3
Stanworth Av BOLE BL2 50 B2
Stanworth Cl OLDTF/WHR M16 126 D5
Stanyard Ct ORD M5 111 H5
Stanycliffe La MDTN M24 72 A1
Stapleford Cl NTHM/RTH M23 167 G5
SALE M33 155 F1
Stapleford Gv TOT/BURYW BL8 37 F4
Staplehurst Rd
NEWH/MOS M40 114 D1
Stapleton Av BOL BL1 47 F1
Stapleton St SLFD M6 97 H5
Starbeck Cl TOT/BURYW BL8 37 E4
Starcliffe St BOLS/LL BL3 65 E2
Starfield Av LIT OL15 31 G1
Star Gv BRO M7 99 H4
Starkey St HEY OL10 41 E3
Starkie Rd BOLE BL2 3 K1
The Starkies BURY * BL9 53 F2
Starkie St WALK M28 95 H2
Starling Cl DROY M43 117 E2
Starling Dr FWTH BL4 64 A5
Starling Rd RAD M26 51 H1
TOT/BURYW BL8 36 D5
Starmoor Dr CHH M8 100 B4
Starmount Cl BOLE BL2 50 D3
Starring La LIT OL15 20 E3
Starring Rd WHIT OL12 20 B3
Starring Wy LIT OL15 20 C3
Stash Gv NTHM/RTH M23 168 A2
Statford Av ECC M30 109 F5
Statham Cl DTN/ASHW M34 131 H5
Statham Fold HYDE SK14 133 F4
Statham St SLFD M6 112 A3
Station Ap CMANE M1 7 H5
Station Cl HYDE SK14 147 F1
Stationers Entry MILN OL16 10 C6
Station La OLDE OL4 92 C2
Station Rd CHD/CHDH SK8 183 E3
CHH M8 100 B1
ECC M30 109 F4
EDGY/DAV SK3 12 E5
FWTH BL4 65 G5
HTNM SK4 158 B5
HYDE SK14 148 C1
IRL M44 135 D4
LIT OL15 21 E3
MILN OL16 44 C1
MOSL OL5 107 E1
MPL/ROM SK6 162 A1
MPL/ROM SK6 175 E3
MPL/ROM SK6 187 H3
OLDE OL4 92 B2
RDSH SK5 144 D1
ROCH OL11 30 A5
STRET M32 125 E5
SWIN M27 97 E1
TOT/BURYW BL8 26 A2
UPML OL3 78 A4
URM M41 138 C2
WHIT OL12 14 C2
WHIT OL12 18 A3
WILM/AE SK9 191 F4
WILM/AE SK9 192 A4
WILM/AE SK9 199 G3
Station St AULW OL7 118 A4
BOLS/LL BL3 3 F7
BRAM/HZG SK7 185 E2
OLDE OL4 92 A1
Station Vw BNG/LEV M19 143 H2
Staton Av BOLE BL2 49 H1
Staton St OP/CLY M11 115 F5
Statter St BURY BL9 53 H5
Staveley Av BOL BL1 22 D5
STLY SK15 119 F2
Staveley Cl ROY/SHW OL2 60 C3
Staverton Cl BRUN/LGST M13 127 H1
Staveton Cl BRAM/HZG SK7 184 A1
Stavordale WHIT OL12 10 B5
Staycott Cl OLDTF/WHR M16 127 E4
Staycott St OLDTF/WHR M16 127 E4
Stayley Dr STLY SK15 119 H3
Stayley Rd MOSL OL5 107 E2
Stead St RAMS BL0 16 D2
Stedman Cl OP/CLY M11 114 B4
Steele Gdns BOLE BL2 50 A4
Steeles Av HYDE SK14 132 D5
Steeple Cl CHH M8 100 A5
Steeple Dr ORD M5 111 H5
Steeple Vw ROY/SHW OL2 59 E5
Stelfox Av HALE/TIMP WA15 166 D2
RUSH/FAL M14 142 B2
Stelfox La DTN/ASHW * M34 131 G1
Stelfox St ECC M30 109 E5
Stella St BKLY M9 86 C3
Stelling St GTN M18 129 G3
Stenbury Cl RUSH/FAL M14 127 H5
Stenner La DID/WITH M20 157 F4
Stephen Cl TOT/BURYW * BL8 37 H4
Stephenson Av DROY M43 116 B4
Stephenson Rd STRET M32 140 A2
Stephenson St FAIL M35 103 F1
OLDE OL4 75 G4
Stephens Rd DID/WITH M20 142 D5
STLY SK15 119 E1
Stephens St BOLE BL2 50 B1
Stephen St CSLFD M3 113 E1
STKP SK1 172 C1
TOT/BURYW BL8 37 H4
URM M41 138 D1
Stephen St South
TOT/BURYW BL8 37 H5
Stephen Wk STKP * SK1 172 C1
Steps Meadow WHIT OL12 19 H4
Stern Av ORD * M5 111 H5
Sterndale Rd EDGY/DAV SK3 171 H4
MPL/ROM SK6 162 A5
WALK M28 94 A4
Sterratt St BOL BL1 35 E5
Stetchworth Dr WALK M28 94 C3
Stevenson Dr OLD OL1 60 D5
Stevenson Pl CMANE * M1 7 H4
Stevenson Rd SWIN M27 96 D2
Stevenson Sq CMANE M1 7 H4
Stevenson St CSLFD * M3 112 C4
WALK M28 80 C4
Stevens St WILM/AE SK9 201 B4
Stewart Av FWTH BL4 64 C5
Stewart St AULW OL7 117 G3
BOL BL1 33 H5
MILN OL16 45 E3
TOT/BURYW BL8 37 G3
Steynton Cl BOL BL1 47 G1
Stile Cl URM M41 136 D1
Stiles Av MPL/ROM SK6 174 D2
Stilton Dr OP/CLY * M11 114 D5
Stirling Av BRAM/HZG SK7 185 E3
DID/WITH M20 142 A3
MPL/ROM SK6 175 E4
Stirling Cl EDGY/DAV SK3 171 F3
Stirling Dr STLY SK15 119 F2
Stirling Gv WHTF M45 68 D4
Stirling Rd BOL BL1 33 H1
CHAD OL9 89 E3
Stirling St CHAD OL9 8 B2
Stirrup Brook Gv WALK M28 94 A5
Stirrup Ga WALK M28 95 H5
Stitch La HTNM SK4 159 G3
Stitch-mi-lane BOLE BL2 35 F4
Stiups La MILN OL16 43 H2
Stobart Av PWCH M25 85 F5
Stockburn Dr FAIL M35 103 G3
Stock Cl WHIT OL12 29 H1
Stockdale Av EDGY/DAV SK3 172 A4
Stockdale Gv BOLE BL2 35 G5
Stockdale Rd BKLY M9 87 F3
Stockfield Mt CHAD OL9 89 G1
Stockfield Rd CHAD OL9 73 G5
Stock Gv MILN OL16 31 G4
Stockholm Rd EDGY/DAV SK3 171 G3
Stockholm St OP/CLY M11 115 E3
Stock La CHAD OL9 73 G5
Stockley Av BOLE BL2 35 F4
Stockley Wk HULME * M15 126 C2
Stockport Rd AULW OL7 117 G5
CHD/CHDH SK8 170 A3
DTN/ASHW M34 146 B2
HALE/TIMP WA15 166 A4
HYDE SK14 147 H2
HYDE SK14 149 F2
MOSL OL5 92 D5
MPL/ROM SK6 162 A4
MPL/ROM SK6 174 B3
MPL/ROM SK6 174 D3
OLDE OL4 92 D2
Stockport Rd East
MPL/ROM SK6 161 G2
Stockport Rd West
MPL/ROM SK6 160 D3
Stockport Village STKP * SK1 13 F3
Stocksfield Dr BKLY M9 87 F4
LHULT M38 80 A2
Stocks Gdns STLY SK15 119 H4
Stocks La STLY SK15 119 G4
Stocks St CHH M8 113 F1
Stocks St East CHH M8 113 F1
Stock St TOT/BURYW BL8 38 B1
Stockton Av EDGY/DAV SK3 171 E1
Stockton Dr TOT/BURYW BL8 37 G1
Stockton Pk OLDE OL4 91 G1
Stockton Rd CCHDY M21 140 D3
FWTH BL4 64 D2
WILM/AE SK9 201 A1
Stockton St LIT OL15 20 D3
SWIN M27 96 D3
Stoke Abbott Cl BRAM/HZG SK7 183 H5
Stokesay Cl BURY BL9 53 G4
ROY/SHW OL2 59 H5
Stokesay Dr BRAM/HZG SK7 184 D3
Stokesay Rd SALE M33 153 H1
Stokes St OP/CLY M11 115 G4
Stoke St MILN OL16 30 C5
Stokoe Av ALT WA14 164 D3
Stonall Av HULME M15 126 C2
Stoneacre HOR/BR BL6 46 A1
Stoneacre Ct SWIN M27 97 E3
Stoneacre Rd WYTH/NTH M22 180 B2
Stonebeck Rd NTHM/RTH M23 167 G4
Stone Breaks Rd OLDE OL4 76 C5
Stonebridge Cl HOR/BR BL6 46 D3
Stonechat Cl DROY * M43 116 D2
WALK M28 94 C2
Stonecliffe Av STLY SK15 119 F3
Stone Cl RAMS BL0 16 B4
Stoneclough Rd FWTH BL4 65 G5
Stonedelph Cl BOLE BL2 36 C5
Stonefield Dr CHH M8 99 H5
Stonefield St MILN OL16 44 C1
Stoneflat Ct WHIT OL12 29 G3
Stonehaven BOLS/LL BL3 62 C1
Stonehead St BKLY * M9 101 G3
Stonehewer St RAD M26 67 G2
Stone Hill La WHIT OL12 28 D1
Stone Hill Rd FWTH BL4 81 F1
Stonehouse EDGW/EG BL7 23 G4
Stonehurst Cl WGTN/LGST M12 128 D2
Stonelands Wy OLDE OL4 92 B3
Stoneleigh Av SALE M33 153 G1
Stoneleigh Dr RAD M26 66 A5
Stoneleigh Rd OLDE OL4 76 B5
Stoneleigh St OLD OL1 75 E3
Stonelow Cl HULME M15 127 E2
Stone Md MPL/ROM SK6 162 D3
Stone Mead Av
HALE/TIMP WA15 178 D5
Stonemead Cl BOLS/LL BL3 49 E5
Stonepail Cl CHD/CHDH SK8 169 E4
Stonepail Cottages
CHD/CHDH * SK8 169 F4
Stonepail Rd CHD/CHDH SK8 169 F4
Stone Pale WHTF M45 68 C5
Stone Pl RUSH/FAL M14 127 H5
Stone Rw MPL/ROM SK6 175 F3
Stonesby Cl OLDTF/WHR * M16 126 C4
Stonesdale Cl ROY/SHW OL2 59 F4
Stonesteads Dr EDGW/EG BL7 23 F3
Stonesteads Wy EDGW/EG BL7 23 F3
Stone St BOLE BL2 3 J1
CSLFD M3 6 C7
Stoneswood Dr MOSL OL5 93 E5
Stoneswood Rd UPML OL3 77 F1
Stoney Bank RAD M26 66 B5
Stoneyfield STLY SK15 119 F1
Stoneyfield Cl OLDTF/WHR M16 142 A1
Stoneygate Wk OP/CLY M11 129 G1
Stoneyhurst Cl HULME M15 127 E2
Stoney La WILM/AE SK9 199 E5
Stoneyroyd WHIT * OL12 14 C3
Stoneyside Av WALK M28 81 F3
Stoneyside Gv WALK M28 81 F4
Stonie Heyes Av WHIT OL12 30 C1
Stonyford Rd SALE M33 155 E2
Stonyhurst Av BOL BL1 33 H1
Stopes Rd BOLS/LL BL3 51 F5
Stopford Av LIT OL15 20 B4
Stopford St EDGY/DAV SK3 12 D6
OP/CLY M11 129 H1
Stores Cottages OLDE * OL4 93 F1
Stores St PWCH M25 85 F3
Store St AULW OL7 104 D5
CMANE M1 7 K5
OFTN SK2 172 D5
OP/CLY * M11 129 E1
RAD M26 53 E5
ROCH OL11 28 B2
ROY/SHW OL2 60 B1
Storeton Cl WYTH/NTH M22 180 D2
Stortford Dr NTHM/RTH M23 156 A4
Stothard Rd STRET M32 139 G2
Stott Dr URM M41 136 D2
Stottfield ROY/SHW OL2 73 G1
Stott La BOLE BL2 34 C5
MDTN M24 56 C4
SLFD M6 110 C2
Stott Milne St CHAD OL9 89 G2
Stott Rd CHAD OL9 88 D4
SWIN M27 96 C4
Stott's La NEWH/MOS M40 102 C4
Stott St MILN OL16 20 A4
MILN OL16 44 C2
NEWH/MOS M40 102 C4
WHIT OL12 10 D3
Stourbridge Av LHULT M38 80 B1
Stour Cl ALT WA14 165 F3
Stourport Cl MPL/ROM SK6 161 H5
Stourport St OLD OL1 74 D3
Stovell Av WGTN/LGST M12 143 H1
Stovell Rd NEWH/MOS M40 101 H2
Stow Cl TOT/BURYW BL8 38 A1
Stowell Ct BOL BL1 33 H5
Stowell St BOL BL1 33 H5
ORD M5 111 F4
Stowfield Cl BKLY M9 86 C3
Stow Gdns DID/WITH M20 142 B5
Stracey St NEWH/MOS * M40 114 B2
Stradbroke Cl GTN M18 129 E3
Strain Av BKLY M9 87 E3
The Strand ROCH OL11 43 E4
Strand Ct STRET M32 139 H3
Strand Wy ROY/SHW OL2 74 A2
Strangford St RAD M26 51 G5
Strang St RAMS BL0 16 D2
Stranton Dr WALK M28 96 B2
Stratfield Av NTHM/RTH M23 155 E5
Stratford Av BOL BL1 33 E5
BURY BL9 27 F3
DID/WITH M20 157 E1
OLDS OL8 90 B4
ROCH OL11 42 D1
Stratford Cl FWTH BL4 64 A3
Stratford Gdns MPL/ROM SK6 161 G3
Stratford Rd MDTN M24 88 A2
Strathblane Cl DID/WITH * M20 142 C4
Strathfield Dr OP/CLY M11 115 E3
Strathmere Av STRET M32 125 E5
Strathmore Av CCHDY M21 141 E1
DTN/ASHW M34 147 E1
Strathmore Cl RAMS BL0 16 D5
Strathmore Rd BOLE BL2 35 F5
Stratton Rd OFTN SK2 172 D1
OLDTF/WHR M16 141 E1
SWIN M27 97 E1
Strawberry Bank SLFD * M6 112 A2
Strawberry Cl ALT WA14 165 E2
Strawberry Hl SLFD M6 112 A2
Strawberry Hill Rd BOLE BL2 49 G4
Strawberry La WILM/AE SK9 198 D4
Strawberry Rd SLFD M6 111 H2
The Stray BOL BL1 34 C2
Stray St OP/CLY M11 115 H5
Streamside Cl HALE/TIMP WA15 166 C5
Stream Ter STKP SK1 160 C5
Streetbridge OLD OL1 73 F2
Street Bridge Rd OLD OL1 73 F2
Streetgate LHULT M38 80 B2
Streethouse La UPML OL3 77 G3
Street Kirklees TOT/BURYW BL8 26 A4
Street La RAD M26 51 H1
Stretford Rd HULME M15 127 E2
OLDTF/WHR M16 126 B3
URM M41 138 C2
Stretton Av DID/WITH M20 157 H3
SALE M33 153 H2
STRET M32 124 B5
Stretton Cl NEWH/MOS M40 101 E5
Stretton Rd BOLS/LL BL3 48 A5
RAMS BL0 26 B1
Striding Edge Wk OLD * OL1 74 D3
Strines Rd MPL/ROM SK6 175 F4
Stringer Av HYDE SK14 149 G1
Stringer Cl HYDE SK14 149 G1
Stringer St STKP SK1 13 K2
Stroma Gdns URM M41 123 F3
Strong St BRO M7 112 D1
Stroud Av ECC M30 109 E2
Stroud Cl MDTN M24 87 H2
Stuart Av IRL M44 136 A1
Stuart Dr MPL/ROM SK6 174 B2
Stuart Rd ALT WA14 165 E2
MPL/ROM SK6 146 A5
STRET M32 125 B4
Stuart St MDTN M24 72 B4
MILN OL16 30 C5
OLDS OL8 8 E7
OP/CLY M11 114 D3
Stuart St East OP/CLY M11 114 D3
Stuart Wk MDTN M24 71 G5
Stubbins Cl NTHM/RTH M23 155 F5
Stubbs Cl BRO M7 99 E2
Stubley Gdns LIT OL15 20 D3
Stubley La LIT OL15 20 C4
Stubley Mill Rd LIT OL15 20 B4
Studforth Wk HULME * M15 127 E3
Studland Rd WYTH/NTH M22 181 E1
Studley Cl ROY/SHW OL2 59 H5
Styal Av RDSH SK5 160 A1
STRET M32 124 B5
Styal Gv CHD/CHDH SK8 181 F1
Styal Rd WILM/AE SK9 199 F1
WYTH/NTH M22 168 D2
Styal Vw WILM/AE SK9 191 G5
Styhead Dr MDTN M24 71 E1
Style St ANC M4 7 G1
Styperson Wy POY/DIS SK12 195 F4
Sudbury Dr CHD/CHDH SK8 181 H5
HOR/BR BL6 46 D3
Sudbury Rd BRAM/HZG SK7 185 F4
Sudden St ROCH OL11 42 B2
Sudell St ANC M4 7 J1
Sudley Rd ROCH OL11 42 B1

Sudlow St MILN OL16 11 H1
Sudren St TOT/BURYW * BL8 37 E3
Suffield St MDTN M24 71 G4
Suffolk Av DROY M43 116 B2
Suffolk Cl BOLS/LL BL3 51 E4
Suffolk Dr RDSH SK5 145 H5
WILM/AE SK9 199 G1
Suffolk Rd ALT WA14 165 E5
Suffolk St CHAD OL9 89 G3
ROCH OL11 30 A5
SLFD M6 98 D5
Sugar La UPML OL3 77 H2
Sugden St AUL OL6 118 C2
Sulby Av STRET M32 140 B1
Sulby St NEWH/MOS M40 101 H2
RAD M26 66 A4
Sulgrave Av POY/DIS SK12 195 G3
Sullivan St WGTN/LGST M12 128 D5
Sultan St BURY BL9 53 G1
Sulway Cl SWIN * M27 97 F3
Sumac St OP/CLY M11 115 G3
Summer Av URM M41 138 D1
Summer Castle MILN OL16 10 D7
Summercroft CHAD OL9 89 G4
Summerdale Dr RAMS BL0 26 C1
Summerfield Av DROY M43 115 H2
Summerfield Dr MDTN M24 72 B2
Summerfield Pl WILM/AE SK9 199 F4
Summerfield Rd BOLS/LL BL3 49 G5
WALK M28 95 H3
WYTH/NTH M22 180 B2
Summerfields Vw OLDS OL8 91 F4
Summer Hl MOSL * OL5 93 E5
Summerlea CHD/CHDH * SK8 183 E4
Summer Pl RUSH/FAL M14 142 D1
Summers Av STLY SK15 119 H3
Summerseat Cl OLDE OL4 76 B5
ORD * M5 111 H5
Summerseat La RAMS BL0 26 B1
Summershades La OLDE OL4 93 E1
Summershades Ri OLDE OL4 93 E1
Summers St CHAD OL9 8 A3
Summer St MILN OL16 10 E7
Summerville Av BKLY M9 101 G3
Summerville Rd SLFD M6 98 B5
Summit Cl BURY BL9 40 A2
Summit St HEY OL10 40 A4
Sumner Av BOLE BL2 36 C5
Sumner Rd SLFD M6 98 A5
Sumner St ROY/SHW OL2 60 A4
Sumner Wy URM M41 138 B1
Sunadale Cl BOLS/LL BL3 48 A4
Sunbank Cl WHIT OL12 29 G1
Sunbank La HALE/TIMP WA15 189 E1
Sunbury Cl DUK SK16 119 E5
WILM/AE SK9 192 B5
Sunbury Dr NEWH/MOS M40 115 G1
Sunderland Av AUL OL6 118 B1
Sundew Pl MDTN M24 72 C5
Sundial Cl HYDE SK14 134 A5
Sundial Rd OFTN SK2 173 E3
Sundridge Cl BOLS/LL BL3 62 D1
Sunfield MPL/ROM SK6 162 A3
Sunfield Av OLDE OL4 75 H1
Sunfield Crs ROY/SHW OL2 74 B1
Sunfield Dr ROY/SHW OL2 74 C1
Sunfield Rd OLD OL1 74 B4
Sunfield Wy OLDE OL4 75 H5
Sunflower Meadow IRL M44 136 C1
Sunhill Cl MILN OL16 43 G4
Sunk La MDTN M24 71 H5
Sunlight Rd BOL BL1 48 B2
Sunningdale Av OP/CLY M11 115 E3
RAD M26 51 G4
SALE M33 155 F3
WHTF M45 67 H5
Sunningdale Cl HYDE SK14 132 D3
TOT/BURYW BL8 52 B1
Sunningdale Dr BRAM/HZG SK7 184 B5
HEY OL10 56 A1
IRL M44 121 A5
PWCH M25 84 D2
SLFD M6 97 F5
Sunningdale Rd CHD/CHDH SK8 182 D5
DTN/ASHW M34 146 D3
URM M41 138 A2
Sunningdale Wk BOLS/LL * BL3 48 B4
Sunning Hill St BOLS/LL BL3 48 C5
Sunny Av BURY BL9 38 C1
Sunny Bank OLDE OL4 91 H2
RAD M26 65 H4
Sunny Bank Av DROY M43 116 A4
Sunnybank Av ECC M30 110 A2
HTNM SK4 158 C2
Sunny Bank Rd ALT WA14 177 F4
BRUN/LGST M13 128 B5
BURY BL9 68 D1
Sunnybank Rd BOL BL1 33 F4
DROY M43 116 A4
Sunny Bower St
TOT/BURYW BL8 25 H5
Sunny Brow Rd GTN M18 129 F3
MDTN M24 71 F4
Sunny Dr PWCH M25 84 C3
Sunnyfield Rd HTNM SK4 158 C3
PWCH M25 69 F5
Sunnylea Av BNG/LEV M19 158 B1
Sunnymead Av BOL BL1 34 A2
Sunnymede V RAMS BL0 16 B5
Sunnyside AULW OL7 104 B5
Sunnyside Av DROY M43 116 A1
Sunnyside Ct DROY * M43 116 A2
Sunnyside Crs AUL * OL6 118 C3
Sunnyside Gv AUL OL6 118 C3
Sunnyside Rd BOL BL1 33 F4
DROY M43 116 B2
Sunnywood Dr TOT/BURYW BL8 26 B5
Sunnywood La TOT/BURYW BL8 26 B5
Sunset Av WYTH/NTH M22 156 C4
Sun St MOSL OL5 106 D1
RAMS BL0 16 C1
Sunwell Ter MPL/ROM SK6 187 E1
Surbiton Rd NEWH/MOS M40 102 A5
Surma Cl CHAD OL9 8 C2
MILN OL16 43 G1
Surrey Av DROY M43 116 A2
ROY/SHW OL2 59 G2
Surrey Cl BOLS/LL BL3 51 E5
Surrey Dr BURY BL9 53 G1
Surrey Park Cl ROY/SHW * OL2 60 A1
Surrey Rd BKLY M9 87 E5
Surrey St AUL OL6 105 G5
BKLY * M9 86 D5
CHAD OL9 8 A7
Surrey Wy RDSH SK5 160 D1
Surtees Rd NTHM/RTH M23 155 H4
Sussex Av DID/WITH M20 157 G2
HEY OL10 39 H5
Sussex Cl CHAD OL9 89 G1
SWIN M27 83 F5
Sussex Dr BURY BL9 53 G1
DROY M43 116 B2
Sussex Pl HYDE SK14 133 E3
Sussex Rd EDGY/DAV SK3 171 E1
IRL M44 135 B5
PART M31 150 D4
Sussex St BRO M7 112 C2
CMANW M2 6 E4
ROCH * OL11 30 A5
Sutcliffe Av WGTN/LGST M12 143 H1
Sutcliffe St AULW OL7 117 G4
BOL BL1 33 H4
LIT OL15 21 E2
MDTN M24 72 B4
OLDS OL8 9 F7
ROY/SHW OL2 74 D1
Sutherland Cl OLDS OL8 104 C1
Sutherland Gv FWTH BL4 64 D4
Sutherland Rd BOL BL1 47 H1
HEY OL10 40 A5
OLDTF/WHR M16 125 H5
Sutherland St AUL OL6 118 D2
ECC M30 109 E2
FWTH BL4 64 D4
SWIN M27 96 D1
Suthers St CHAD OL9 8 A5
RAD M26 67 H3
Sutton Cl TOT/BURYW BL8 52 C1
Sutton Dr DROY M43 115 H2
Sutton Dwellings SLFD M6 111 G2
Sutton Rd BOLS/LL BL3 47 G5
GTN M18 129 F5
HTNM SK4 159 F3
POY/DIS SK12 195 G5
WILM/AE SK9 201 A4
Suttons La MPL/ROM SK6 175 F4
Swailes St OLDE OL4 91 E1
Swaindrod La LIT OL15 21 H1
Swaine St EDGY/DAV SK3 12 E4
Swainsthorpe Dr BKLY M9 101 F2
Swain St WHIT * OL12 10 B2
Swalecliff Av NTHM/RTH M23 155 E5
Swale Cl WILM/AE SK9 192 B5
Swaledale Cl ROY/SHW OL2 59 F4
Swale Dr ALT WA14 165 F3
Swallow Bank Dr ROCH * OL11 42 A3
Swallow Cl STLY SK15 107 G3
Swallow Dr BURY BL9 39 E2
IRL M44 121 B5
ROCH OL11 28 C4
Swallow La STLY SK15 107 G3
Swallow St OLDS OL8 90 A5
OP/CLY M11 114 C4
STKP SK1 13 H7
WGTN/LGST * M12 143 H1
Swanage Av NTHM/RTH M23 155 E5
OFTN SK2 173 E3
Swanage Cl TOT/BURYW BL8 26 D5
Swanage Rd ECC M30 109 E2
Swanbourne Gdns
EDGY/DAV SK3 171 F3
Swan Cl POY/DIS SK12 194 C3
Swan Ct ROY/SHW * OL2 60 A3
Swanhill Cl GTN M18 130 A2
Swan La BOLS/LL BL3 48 A5
Swanley Av NEWH/MOS M40 101 F5
Swann Gv CHD/CHDH SK8 183 E4
Swann La CHD/CHDH SK8 183 E3
Swan Rd HALE/TIMP WA15 154 B5
TOT/BURYW BL8 26 A1
Swansea St OLDS OL8 91 E3
Swan St ANC M4 7 G2
AUL OL6 118 B2
RAD M26 66 D2
WILM/AE SK9 199 G3
Swarbrick Dr PWCH M25 84 C5
Swayfield Av BRUN/LGST M13 128 C5
Swaylands Dr SALE M33 154 C5
Sweetbriar Cl ROY/SHW OL2 60 A2
Sweet Briar Cl WHIT OL12 29 H1
Sweet Briar La WHIT OL12 29 H1
Sweetlove's Gv BOL BL1 33 H1
Sweetlove's La BOL BL1 33 H1
Sweetnam Dr OP/CLY M11 115 E3
Swettenham Rd WILM/AE SK9 192 A2
Swift Cl MPL/ROM SK6 162 B1
Swift Rd OLD OL1 60 A5
ROCH OL11 28 C4
Swift St AUL * OL6 105 G5
Swinbourne Gv DID/WITH M20 142 D4
Swinburne Av DROY M43 116 B2
Swinburne Gn RDSH SK5 144 C2
Swinburn St BKLY M9 101 G1
Swindells St HYDE SK14 132 D3
OP/CLY * M11 129 H1
Swindon Cl GTN M18 129 G3
Swinfield Av CCHDY M21 140 C3
Swinford Gv ROY/SHW OL2 59 H4
Swinley Cha WILM/AE SK9 200 C1
Swinside Cl MDTN M24 70 D2
Swinside Rd BOLE BL2 50 C1
Swinstead Av
NEWH/MOS * M40 101 F5
Swinton Crs BURY BL9 68 D3
Swinton Gv BRUN/LGST M13 127 H3
Swinton Hall Rd SWIN M27 97 F2
Swinton Park Rd SLFD M6 97 G5
Swinton St BOLE BL2 50 B2
OLDE OL4 91 F2
Swiss Hl WILM/AE SK9 201 G4
Swithin Rd WYTH/NTH M22 180 D4
Swythamley Cl EDGY/DAV SK3 170 D1
Swythamley Rd
EDGY/DAV SK3 170 D1
Sybil St LIT OL15 20 D2
Sycamore Av ALT WA14 164 D4
CHAD OL9 89 E4
DTN/ASHW M34 146 C1
HEY OL10 40 D5
MILN OL16 44 D3
OLDE OL4 75 G4
RAD M26 66 C2
Sycamore Cl AUL OL6 118 D3
DID/WITH * M20 142 D4
DUK SK16 119 E5
LIT OL15 20 C3
WILM/AE SK9 191 G5
Sycamore Ct SLFD M6 111 H2
Sycamore Crs AUL OL6 105 F5
Sycamore Dr BURY BL9 27 G5
RAD M26 52 B4
Sycamore Gv FAIL M35 103 G3
Sycamore Ldg BRAM/HZG * SK7 184 A5
Sycamore Pl WHTF M45 84 C1
Sycamore Rd ECC M30 108 D1
MPL/ROM SK6 161 H2
PART M31 150 C4
TOT/BURYW BL8 37 E1
The Sycamores MOSL OL5 107 F1
OLDE OL4 76 A4
RAD M26 82 A1
STLY SK15 119 G5
Sycamore St EDGY/DAV SK3 171 E1
SALE M33 155 F2
Sycamore Wk CHD/CHDH SK8 170 A3
Sydall St DTN/ASHW M34 131 G5
Syddal Cl BRAM/HZG SK7 193 G2
Syddal Crs BRAM/HZG SK7 193 G3
Syddal Gn BRAM/HZG SK7 193 G2
Syddall Av CHD/CHDH SK8 182 A4
Syddall St HYDE SK14 147 G1
Syddal Rd BRAM/HZG SK7 193 G2
Sydenham St OLD OL1 75 E3
Sydney Av ECC M30 109 G3
MANAIR M90 179 H4
Sydney Gdns LIT OL15 15 B4
Sydney Jones Ct
NEWH/MOS M40 102 B1
Sydney Rd BRAM/HZG SK7 194 A2
Sydney St FAIL M35 102 D3
OFTN SK2 172 D2
SLFD M6 111 F3
STRET M32 140 A1
SWIN M27 96 C2
Syke La WHIT OL12 19 E4
Syke Rd WHIT OL12 19 E4
Sykes Av BURY BL9 54 A5
Sykes Ct MILN * OL16 30 C5
Sykes Meadow EDGY/DAV SK3 171 F3
Sykes St BURY BL9 5 G2
MILN OL16 30 C5
MILN OL16 44 D2
RDSH SK5 145 E3
Sylvan Av FAIL M35 102 D5
HALE/TIMP WA15 166 A1
SALE M33 154 D3
URM M41 123 G5
WILM/AE SK9 199 E5
Sylvan Cl MDTN M24 71 E2
Sylvandale Av BNG/LEV M19 143 H2
Sylvan Gv ALT WA14 165 G4
Sylvan St CHAD OL9 8 B2
Sylvester Av STKP SK1 172 C3
Sylvester Cl HYDE SK14 149 F1
Sylvia Gv RDSH SK5 144 D4
Symms St SLFD M6 112 A1
Symond Rd BKLY M9 87 F2
Symons Rd SALE M33 154 C1
Symons St BRO M7 99 H3
Syndall Av WGTN/LGST M12 128 A2
Syndall St WGTN/LGST M12 128 A2

T

Tabley Av RUSH/FAL M14 142 C1
Tabley Gdns MPL/ROM SK6 175 F5
Tabley Gv BRUN/LGST M13 143 G1
HALE/TIMP WA15 166 B1
RDSH SK5 144 D4
Tabley Mere Gdns
CHD/CHDH SK8 182 C1
Tabley Ms ALT WA14 165 G4
Tabley Rd BOLS/LL BL3 48 A5
SALE * M33 155 F4
WILM/AE SK9 192 A2
Tabley St DUK SK16 118 D5
MOSL OL5 107 E2
SLFD M6 99 E5
Tabor St MDTN M24 71 G2
Tackler Cl SWIN M27 97 E3
Tadman Gv ALT WA14 164 D3
Tadmor Cl LHULT M38 80 A3
Tagore Cl BRUN/LGST M13 128 B4
Tahir Cl CHH M8 100 C3
Talavera St BRO M7 99 G5
Talbenny Cl BOL BL1 47 G1
Talbot Cl OLDE OL4 75 F4
Talbot Ct BOL BL1 34 A2
Talbot Gv BURY BL9 27 H5
Talbot Pl OLDTF/WHR M16 126 A3
Talbot Rd ALT WA14 177 E2
HYDE SK14 132 D3
RUSH/FAL M14 143 E1
SALE * M33 155 F2
STRET M32 125 G4
WILM/AE SK9 201 C4
Talbot St AUL OL6 117 H2
BRAM/HZG SK7 173 E5
ECC M30 109 H4
MDTN M24 71 H2
ROCH OL11 30 A5
Talford Gv DID/WITH M20 157 F1
Talgarth Rd NEWH/MOS M40 113 H1
Talkin Dr MDTN M24 71 F1
Talland Wk BRUN/LGST M13 128 A3
Tallarn Cl DID/WITH M20 142 D4
Tallis St WGTN/LGST M12 128 D5
Tallow Wy IRL M44 136 B3
Tall Trees Cl ROY/SHW OL2 58 D5
Tall Trees Pl OFTN SK2 172 D3
Tallyman Wy SWIN M27 98 B3
Talmine Av NEWH/MOS M40 101 F5
Tamar Cl FWTH BL4 82 A2
Tamar Ct HULME M15 126 C2
Tamar Dr NTHM/RTH M23 167 H5
Tamarin Cl SWIN M27 96 B1
Tamebank MOSL OL5 93 E4
Tame Barn Cl MILN * OL16 31 H5
Tame Cl STLY SK15 119 H2
Tame La UPML OL3 61 H2
Tamerton Dr CHH M8 100 B4
Tameside Ct DUK * SK16 132 A1
Tame St ANC M4 114 A4
DTN/ASHW M34 131 G1
DTN/ASHW M34 131 G4
MOSL OL5 93 F4
STLY SK15 118 D4
UPML OL3 78 A4
Tamworth Av ORD M5 112 A5
WHTF M45 69 E5
Tamworth Av West ORD * M5 111 H5
Tamworth Cl BRAM/HZG * SK7 184 D4
HULME M15 126 D3
Tamworth Dr TOT/BURYW BL8 37 H1
Tamworth Gn STKP SK1 160 C4
Tamworth St CHAD OL9 8 A6
STKP SK1 160 C4
Tamworth Wk ORD M5 111 H5
Tandis Ct SLFD * M6 110 B2
Tandle Hill Rd ROY/SHW OL2 58 C3
Tandlewood Ms
NEWH/MOS M40 102 B5
Tandlewood Pk ROY/SHW OL2 58 C3
Tanfield Dr RAD M26 66 A5
Tanfield Rd DID/WITH M20 169 G2
Tangmere Cl NEWH/MOS * M40 88 B4
Tanhill Cl OFTN SK2 173 F3
Tanhill La OLDS OL8 90 D5
Tanhouse Rd URM M41 122 A5
Tanners Cft RAMS BL0 16 C2
Tanners Fold OLDS OL8 90 D5
Tanners Gn SLFD M6 111 G2
Tanners St RAMS BL0 16 C2
Tanner St HYDE * SK14 132 C5
Tannery Wy ALT WA14 165 H2
Tannock Rd BRAM/HZG SK7 185 G3
Tanpits Rd BURY BL9 4 C3
Tansey Gv BRO M7 100 A3
Tansley Rd CHH M8 86 B5
Tanworth Wk BOL * BL1 33 H4
Tan Yard Brow GTN M18 129 H4
Tanyard Dr HALE/TIMP WA15 188 D1
Tanyard Gn RDSH SK5 160 A1
Tanyard La HALE/TIMP WA15 188 A2
Tape St RAMS BL0 16 C2
Tapley Av POY/DIS SK12 195 F5
Taplin Dr GTN M18 129 F3
Taplow Gv CHD/CHDH SK8 182 C2
Taplow Wk RUSH/FAL M14 128 B5
Tarbet Dr BOLE BL2 50 C3
Tarbet Rd DUK SK16 132 B1
Tarbolton Crs HALE/TIMP WA15 178 D1
Tariff St CMANE M1 7 J4
Tarleton Pl BOLS/LL BL3 62 D1
Tarleton Wk BRUN/LGST * M13 127 H2
Tarnbrook Cl WHTF M45 69 F4
Tarnbrook Wk HULME * M15 127 E3
Tarn Dr BURY BL9 53 F3
Tarn Gv WALK M28 95 G1
The Tarns CHD/CHDH SK8 181 G1
Tarnside Cl MILN OL16 19 H5
OFTN SK2 173 G3
Tarporley Av RUSH/FAL M14 142 B3
Tarporley Cl EDGY/DAV SK3 171 F4
Tarran Gv DTN/ASHW M34 147 E2
Tarran Pl ALT WA14 165 H3
Tarrington Cl WGTN/LGST M12 128 D3
Tartan St OP/CLY M11 115 E3
Tarvin Av DID/WITH M20 142 B4
HTNM SK4 144 C4
Tarvin Dr MPL/ROM SK6 161 F2
Tarvington Cl
NEWH/MOS * M40 100 D4
Tarvin Rd CHD/CHDH SK8 170 D5
Tarvin Wk BOL BL1 33 H4
Tasle Aly CMANW M2 6 E5
Tatchbury Rd FAIL M35 103 E3
Tate St OLDS OL8 91 E3
Tatham Cl BRUN/LGST M13 128 C5
Tatham St MILN OL16 10 E7
Tatland Dr WYTH/NTH M22 181 E1
Tattersall Av BOL BL1 32 B4
Tattersall St CHAD OL9 8 C5
Tatton Cl BRAM/HZG SK7 173 G5
CHD/CHDH SK8 170 D5
Tatton Gdns MPL/ROM SK6 162 C1
Tatton Gv DID/WITH M20 142 C5
Tatton Mere Dr DROY M43 116 C4
Tattonmere Gdns
CHD/CHDH SK8 170 D5
Tatton Pl SALE M33 154 C1
Tatton Rd DTN/ASHW M34 146 D2
SALE M33 154 C1
WILM/AE SK9 192 B2
Tatton Rd North HTNM SK4 159 F1
Tatton Rd South HTNM SK4 159 F2
Tatton St HULME M15 126 C2
HYDE SK14 147 H4
ORD M5 112 A5
STKP SK1 13 G3
STLY SK15 119 G3
Taunton Av AULW OL7 117 H1
ECC M30 109 E2
RDSH SK5 160 D1
URM M41 138 A3
Taunton Cl BOL * BL1 33 F5
BRAM/HZG SK7 185 H2
Taunton Dr FWTH BL4 64 A3
Taunton Gn AULW OL7 104 C5
Taunton Gv WHTF M45 84 D1
Taunton Hall Cl AULW OL7 104 C5
Taunton Lawns AULW OL7 117 H1
Taunton Pl AULW * OL7 104 C5
Taunton Platting AULW * OL7 104 C4
Taunton Rd AULW OL7 104 D5
CHAD OL9 73 F3
SALE M33 153 G2
Taunton St ANC M4 114 A4
Taurus St OLDE OL4 75 F4
Tavern Court Av FAIL M35 103 F3
Tavery Cl ANC M4 113 H3
Tavistock Cl HYDE SK14 149 F1
Tavistock Dr CHAD OL9 73 E3
Tavistock Rd BOL BL1 2 A6
ROCH OL11 43 E3
SALE M33 153 G1
Tawton Av HYDE SK14 149 F1
Taxi Rd MANAIR M90 180 A5
Tay Cl OLDS OL8 8 E7
Tayfield Rd WYTH/NTH M22 180 B2
Taylor Av ROCH OL11 28 C3
Taylor Green Wy OLDE OL4 76 A5
Taylor La DTN/ASHW M34 131 E4
Taylor Rd ALT WA14 164 D4
URM M41 123 H1
Taylor's La BOLE BL2 51 E2
Taylorson St ORD M5 126 A1
Taylorson St South ORD M5 125 H2
Taylors Pl WHIT * OL12 10 C3
Taylor's Rd STRET M32 125 F4
Taylor St BOL * BL1 3 F6
BURY BL9 5 G2
CHAD OL9 73 F5
DROY M43 116 B4
DTN/ASHW M34 131 G4
GTN M18 129 F2
HEY OL10 40 D4
HYDE SK14 133 E5
MDTN M24 71 H4
OLD OL1 75 F4
OLDE OL4 91 H1
PWCH M25 85 F3
RAD M26 67 F1
ROY/SHW * OL2 59 E4
RUSH/FAL M14 127 H5
STLY SK15 119 G4
WHIT OL12 10 D2
WHIT OL12 14 C5
Taywood Rd BOLS/LL BL3 62 A2
Teak Dr FWTH BL4 82 C3
Teak St BURY BL9 5 J4
Teal Av POY/DIS SK12 194 B3
Tealby Av OLDTF/WHR M16 126 B4
Tealby Rd GTN M18 129 E4
Teal Cl ALT WA14 165 E1
OFTN SK2 173 G4
Teal Ct ROCH OL11 28 C4
Teal St BOLS/LL BL3 49 E5
Teasdale Cl CHAD OL9 88 D4
Tebbutt St ANC M4 7 J1
Tedder Cl BURY BL9 69 E2
Tedder Dr WYTH/NTH M22 181 E5
Teddington Rd
NEWH/MOS M40 102 B1
Ted Jackson Wk OP/CLY * M11 114 C5
Teer St NEWH/MOS M40 114 A3
Teesdale Av URM M41 122 D4
Teesdale Cl OFTN SK2 173 F3
Tees St MILN * OL16 30 C5
Teignmouth Av
NEWH/MOS * M40 113 H1
Teignmouth St
NEWH/MOS M40 113 H1
Telfer Av BRUN/LGST M13 143 F1
Telfer Rd BRUN/LGST M13 143 F1
Telford Cl DTN/ASHW M34 131 F1
Telford Ms UPML OL3 78 A3
Telford Rd MPL/ROM SK6 175 F5
Telford St CHH M8 100 D5
Telford Wk OLDTF/WHR M16 126 C4
Telford Wy ROCH OL11 43 F4
Tellson Cl SLFD M6 98 A4
Tellson Crs SLFD M6 98 A4
Tell St WHIT OL12 29 G4
Temperance St BOLS/LL BL3 48 C4
HYDE * SK14 149 H3
WGTN/LGST M12 7 K7
Tempest Cha HOR/BR BL6 46 C5
Tempest Ct HOR/BR * BL6 46 D5
Tempest Rd HOR/BR BL6 46 D5
WILM/AE SK9 201 D4
Tempest St BOLS/LL BL3 48 A5
Temple Cl OLDE OL4 75 H4
Templecombe Dr BOL BL1 22 C5
Temple Dr BOL BL1 33 F3
SWIN M27 97 G3
Temple La LIT OL15 15 B4
Temple Rd BOL BL1 33 F3
SALE M33 155 E2
Temple St HEY OL10 41 E4
MDTN M24 72 A3
OLD OL1 75 E5
Templeton Cl ALT WA14 165 E3
Ten Acre Ct WHTF * M45 68 A5
Ten Acre Dr WHTF M45 68 A5
Ten Acres La NEWH/MOS M40 101 H5
Tenax Rd TRPK M17 124 C1
Tenbury Cl SLFD * M6 111 G2
Tenbury Dr MDTN M24 87 H2
Tenby Av BOL BL1 32 D5
DID/WITH M20 142 C5
STRET M32 125 F4
Tenby Ct HULME * M15 126 B2
Tenby Dr CHD/CHDH SK8 183 E3
SLFD M6 98 A5
Tenby Gv WHIT OL12 29 F2
Tenby Rd EDGY/DAV SK3 171 E2
OLDS OL8 89 G5
Tenby St WHIT OL12 29 F2
Tenement La BRAM/HZG SK7 183 G2
Teneriffe St BRO M7 99 G5
Tennis St BOL BL1 33 G4
OLDTF/WHR M16 126 A4
Tennyson Av BURY BL9 53 G3
DTN/ASHW * M34 146 D4
DUK SK16 133 F1
RAD M26 51 H5
Tennyson Cl HTNM SK4 158 D5
Tennyson Gdns PWCH M25 84 C4
Tennyson Rd CHD/CHDH SK8 170 C3
DROY M43 116 B3
FWTH BL4 80 C1
MDTN M24 72 A2
RDSH SK5 144 C2
SWIN M27 96 C2
Tennyson St BOL BL1 33 H5
BRUN/LGST M13 127 H3
OLD OL1 75 F3
ROCH OL11 43 F1
SLFD M6 112 B1
Tensing Av AULW OL7 105 E5
Tensing St OLDS OL8 104 D2
Tentercroft WHIT OL12 10 A6
Tenterden St BURY BL9 4 B5
Tenterhill La WHIT OL12 28 A1
Tenters St BURY BL9 4 B5
Tenth St TRPK M17 125 E2
Terence St NEWH/MOS M40 102 C5
Terminal Rd East MANAIR M90 180 A5
Terminal Rd North
MANAIR M90 180 A5
Terminal Rd South
MANAIR M90 180 A5
Tern Av FWTH BL4 64 A4
Tern Cl ALT WA14 165 E1
DUK SK16 132 D1
ROCH OL11 28 C4
Tern Dr POY/DIS SK12 194 C3
Ternhill Ct FWTH BL4 64 D4
The Terrace PWCH M25 85 E4
Terrace St OLDE OL4 75 E5
Terrington Cl CCHDY M21 141 H4
Tetbury Dr BOLE BL2 50 C1
Tetbury Rd WYTH/NTH M22 180 A3
Tetlow Gv ECC M30 109 F4
Tetlow La BRO M7 99 H2
Tetlow St HYDE * SK14 132 D3

MDTN M24 ....71 H4
NEWH/MOS M40 ....102 B5
OLDS * OL8 ....8 D5
Teviot St BRUN/LGST M13 ....128 D4
Teviot Wy STKP SK1 ....160 A3
Tewkesbury Av AUL OL6 ....105 F5
DROY M43 ....116 B2
HALE/TIMP WA15 ....178 D1
MDTN M24 ....71 G1
URM M41 ....123 G4
Tewkesbury Cl CHD/CHDH SK8 ...193 E1
POY/DIS SK12 ....195 E5
Tewkesbury Dr PWCH M25 ....85 E5
Tewkesbury Rd EDGY/DAV SK3 ...171 F3
NEWH/MOS M40 ....114 A2
Texas St DUK SK16 ....118 B3
Textile St WGTN/LGST M12 ......128 D1
Textilose Rd TRPK M17 ....124 C3
Thackeray Cl CHH M8 ....100 B4
Thackeray Gv DROY M43 ....91 E3
Thackeray Rd OLD OL1 ....75 F3
Thames Cl BURY BL9 ....27 H1
OP/CLY M11 ....115 E5
Thames Ct HULME M15 ....126 C2
Thames Rd MILN OL16 ....31 H5
Thames St MILN OL16 ....30 C5
OLD OL1 ....9 J1
Thanet Cl BRO M7 ....99 H5
Thankerton Av DTN/ASHW M34 ...117 E4
Thatcher Cl ALT WA14 ....177 E5
Thatcher St OLDS OL8 ....90 D4
Thatch Leach CHAD OL9 ....9 G1
Thatch Leach La WHTF M45 ....68 D5
Thaxmead Dr NEWH/MOS M40 ...115 G1
Thaxted Dr OFTN SK2 ....173 H4
Thaxted Pl BOL BL1 ....48 B1
Thbeechwood La STLY SK15 ......119 H1
Theatre St OLD OL1 ....9 H3
Thekla St CHAD OL9 ....8 D1
Thelma St RAMS BL0 ....16 C2
Thelwall Av BOLE BL2 ....50 A1
RUSH/FAL M14 ....142 B3
Thelwall Cl HALE/TIMP WA15 ....165 H3
Thelwall Rd SALE M33 ....155 F1
Theobald Rd ALT WA14 ....177 G3
Theta Cl OP/CLY M11 ....115 E3
Thetford WHIT OL12 ....14 A4
Thetford St TOT/BURYW BL8 ....38 A1
Thetford Dr CHH M8 ....100 C3
Thicketford Brow BOLE BL2 ....35 E5
Thicketford Cl BOLE BL2 ....34 D4
Thicketford Rd BOLE BL2 ....34 D4
Thimble Cl WHIT OL12 ....20 A4
The Thimbles WHIT OL12 ....20 A4
Third Av BOL BL1 ....48 A2
BOLS/LL BL3 ....50 B5
BURY BL9 ....39 G2
OLDS OL8 ....89 H4
OP/CLY M11 ....115 F3
STLY SK15 ....107 F4
TRPK M17 ....125 E3
Third St BOL BL1 ....48 A2
Thirlby Dr WYTH/NTH M22 ....180 C3
Thirlemere Rd STKP SK1 ....172 C2
Thirlemere Av AULW OL7 ....117 G1
STRET M32 ....124 D5
SWIN M27 ....79 F3
Thirlmere Cl WILM/AE SK9 ....201 A4
Thirlmere Dr BURY * BL9 ....53 E2
LHULT M38 ....80 B2
MDTN M24 ....71 H1
Thirlmere Gv FWTH BL4 ....63 H4
ROY/SHW OL2 ....59 E3
Thirlmere Rd PART M31 ....150 D2
ROY/SHW OL2 ....59 E3
URM M41 ....122 B5
WHTN BL5 ....62 C5
WYTH/NTH M22 ....180 A2
Thirlspot Cl BOL BL1 ....23 G5
Thirstone Av OLDE * OL4 ....61 E5
Thirsfield Dr OP/CLY M11 ....115 F3
Thirsk Av CHAD OL9 ....73 E3
SALE M33 ....153 H3
Thirsk Cl TOT/BURYW BL8 ....37 C1
Thirsk Rd BOLS/LL BL3 ....64 C3
Thirsk St WGTN/LGST M12 ....127 H1
Thistle Cl STLY SK15 ....134 B1
Thistledown Cl ECC M30 ....109 F5
Thistle Gn MILN OL16 ....31 F4
Thistle Sq PART M31 ....151 F4
Thistleton Rd BOLS/LL BL3 ....62 C1
Thistle Wy OLDE OL4 ....75 G2
Thistlewood Dr WILM/AE SK9 ....200 A3
Thistleyfields MILN * OL16 ....31 F4
Thomas Cl DTN/ASHW M34 ....131 H4
Thomas Dr BOLS/LL BL3 ....48 A5
Thomas Gibbon Cl STRET * M32 ...159 H2
Thomas Henshaw Ct ROCH OL11 ...42 D2
Thomas Holden St BOL BL1 ....2 B3
Thomas Johnson Cl ECC * M30 ...109 F4
Thomas More Cl FWTH BL4 ....33 H5
Thomasson Cl BOL BL1 ....33 H5
Thomas St ANC M4 ....7 J2
BOLS/LL BL3 ....49 E4
CHH M8 ....100 A4
FWTH BL4 ....65 E5
HALE/TIMP WA15 ....165 H5
MILN OL16 ....10 E4
MPL/ROM SK6 ....161 H5
ROY/SHW OL2 ....58 D3
DROY M43 ....91 H2
RAD M26 ....67 G1
ROY/SHW OL2 ....60 B3
STKP SK1 ....13 G3
STRET M32 ....125 E5
Thomas St West OFTN SK2 ....13 G7
Thomas Telford Basin CMANE M1 ....7 J3
Thompson Av BOLE BL2 ....35 H2
WHTF M45 ....68 D1
Thompson Cl DTN/ASHW M34 ....130 C1
Thompson Ct DTN/ASHW M34 ....130 C1
Thompson Dr BURY BL9 ....39 F3
Thompson Fold STLY SK15 ....119 G3
Thompson La CHAD OL9 ....89 F3
Thompson Rd BOL BL1 ....33 G3
DTN/ASHW M34 ....130 C1
TRPK M17 ....109 H5
Thompson St ANC M4 ....7 J1
BOLS/LL BL3 ....49 E4
MDTN M34 ....54 D3
NEWH/MOS M40 ....101 G5
Thomson Rd GTN M18 ....129 F4

Thomson St BRUN/LGST M13 ....127 H2
EDGY/DAV SK3 ....13 F6
Thoralby Cl WGTN/LGST M12 ....128 D5
Thorburn Dr WHIT OL12 ....18 A1
Thoresby Cl BOLS/LL BL3 ....51 F4
Thoresway Rd BRUN/LGST M13 ...128 D5
WILM/AE SK9 ....199 E5
Thor Gv ORD M5 ....112 B5
Thorley Cl CHAD OL9 ....88 D5
Thorley Dr HALE/TIMP WA15 .....166 C4
Thorley La HALE/TIMP WA15 .....166 C5
HALE/TIMP WA15 ....179 G3
Thorley Ms BRAM/HZG SK7 ......184 A5
Thorley St FAIL M35 ....103 E2
Thornage Dr NEWH/MOS M40 ...113 H1
Thorn Av FAIL M35 ....105 E4
Thornbank BOLS/LL BL3 ....48 B5
Thornbeck Cl HEY OL10 ....56 B2
Thornbeck Dr BOL BL1 ....32 C5
Thornbridge Av CCHDY M21 ....141 E3
Thornbury ROCH * OL11 ....29 H5
Thornbury CI WILM/AE SK9 ....134 B5
Thornbury Cl CHD/CHDH SK8 ....183 F3
Thornbury Rd STRET M32 ....125 F4
Thornbury Wy GTN M18 ....129 F3
Thornbush Wy MILN OL16 ....11 H5
Thorncliffe Av OLDS OL8 ....90 B4
Thorncliffe Av DUK SK16 ....132 B1
ROY/SHW OL2 ....58 D3
Thorncliffe Gv BNG/LEV M19 ......144 B2
Thorncliffe Pk ROY/SHW OL2 ......58 D3
Thorncliffe Rd BOL BL1 ....33 H1
Thorn Cl HEY OL10 ....40 C3
Thorncombe Rd
OLDTF/WHR M16 ....126 D5
Thorn Ct SLFD M6 ....112 A3
Thorndale Cl ROY/SHW OL2 ....59 F4
Thorndale Gv HALE/TIMP WA15 ...166 B4
Thorn Dr WYTH/NTH M22 ....181 F4
Thorne Av URM M41 ....137 H1
Thornes Cl HEY OL10 ....40 C3
Thorneside DTN/ASHW M34 ....131 G3
Thorne St FWTH BL4 ....64 D3
Thorneycroft Av CCHDY M21 .....156 A1
Thorneycroft Rd
HALE/TIMP WA15 ....166 C4
Thorney Dr BRAM/HZG SK7 ......195 F1
Thorney Hill Cl OLDE * OL4 ....9 K5
Thorneyholme Cl HOR/BR BL6 .....46 D3
Thornfield Av AUL OL6 ....118 D2
Thornfield Crs LHULT M38 ....80 A2
Thornfield Dr SWIN M27 ....80 A2
Thornfield Gv CHD/CHDH SK8 ....182 D2
Thornfield Hey WILM/AE SK9 .....200 B2
Thornfield Houses
CHD/CHDH * SK8 ....182 D2
Thornfield Rd BNG/LEV M19 ......158 B1
HTNM SK4 ....158 C4
TOT/BURYW BL8 ....25 G1
Thornfield St ORD M5 ....111 E4
Thorngate Rd CHH M8 ....100 B5
Thorn Gv CHD/CHDH SK8 ....183 E5
HALE/TIMP WA15 ....165 H4
RUSH/FAL M14 ....143 E5
SALE M33 ....154 C2
Thorngrove Av NTHM/RTH M23 ...167 E2
Thorngrove Dr WILM/AE SK9 .....199 H4
Thorngrove Hl WILM/AE SK9 .....199 H4
Thorngrove Rd WILM/AE SK9 .....199 H4
Thornham Cl TOT/BURYW BL8 .....26 D5
Thornham Dr BOL BL1 ....23 G5
Thornham La MDTN M24 ....57 G3
ROY/SHW OL2 ....57 H5
Thornham New Rd ROCH OL11 .....43 H3
Thornham Old Rd ROY/SHW OL2 ...58 B2
Thornham Rd ROY/SHW OL2 ....58 B3
SALE M33 ....155 H4
Thornhill Cl DTN/ASHW M34 ......145 F1
Thornhill Dr WALK M28 ....95 F2
Thornhill Rd BOLE BL2 ....34 C2
HTNM SK4 ....158 D2
RAMS BL0 ....16 C4
Thornholme Cl GTN M18 ....129 E5
Thornholme Rd MPL/ROM SK6 ...175 F2
Thornlea DROY M43 ....117 G4
Thornlea Av OLDS OL8 ....105 G1
Thorn Lea CI BOL BL1 ....47 G2
Thornlea Dr WHIT OL12 ....14 B3
Thornleigh Rd RUSH/FAL M14 ....142 C2
Thornley Av BOL BL1 ....33 G3
Thornley Cl MPL/ROM SK6 ....161 H5
OLDE OL4 ....92 B2
Thornley La MPL/ROM SK6 ....161 H5
Thornley La North RDSH SK5 .....130 A5
Thornley La South RDSH SK5 .....130 A5
Thornley Ms BOL * BL1 ....2 C3
Thornley Park Rd OLDE OL4 ....92 B2
Thornley Rd DTN/ASHW M34 .....131 H4
WHTF M45 ....69 F5
Thornley St HYDE SK14 ....147 H2
MDTN M24 ....54 D3
RAD M26 ....51 E5
Thornmere Cl SWIN M27 ....82 B5
Thorn Rd BRAM/HZG SK7 ....193 H1
OLDS OL8 ....91 H2
SWIN M27 ....96 C4
The Thorns CCHDY M21 ....141 E4
Thorns Av BOL BL1 ....33 G3
Thorns Cl BOL BL1 ....33 G3
Thornsett Cl BKLY * M9 ....101 F2
Thornsgreen Rd
WYTH/NTH M22 ....180 C4
Thorns Rd BOL BL1 ....34 A4
RAMS BL0 ....16 B4
Thorns Villa Gdns WALK M28 ....94 B5
Thornton Av BOL BL1 ....47 H1
DTN/ASHW M34 ....131 E1
URM M41 ....137 H1
Thornton Cl BOLS/LL BL3 ....64 C1
FWTH BL4 ....64 C3
Thornton Crs PWCH M25 ....85 H3
Thornton Dr WILM/AE SK9 ....192 A4
Thornton Ga CHD/CHDH SK8 ....182 D3
Thornton PI HTNM SK4 ....158 C3
Thornton Rd CHD/CHDH SK8 .....181 H5
RUSH/FAL M14 ....142 A3

Thornton St BOLE BL2 ....3 H4
NEWH/MOS M40 ....115 H1
OLDE OL4 ....9 H6
ROCH * OL11 ....43 E1
Thornton St North
NEWH/MOS M40 ....100 D5
Thorntree Cl BKLY M9 ....101 F3
Thorntree PI WHIT OL12 ....29 G5
Thorntree Vw BURY BL9 ....39 F5
Thornway BRAM/HZG SK7 ....183 F4
MPL/ROM SK6 ....175 F2
WALK M28 ....94 B5
Thornwood Av GTN M18 ....129 H4
Thornydyke Av BOL BL1 ....33 H1
Thorold Gv SALE M33 ....155 F2
Thorpe Av RAD M26 ....53 E4
SWIN M27 ....96 D1
Thorpebrook Rd
NEWH/MOS M40 ....101 H4
Thorpe Cl DTN/ASHW M34 ....131 G4
OLDE OL4 ....76 B4
Thorpe Gv HTNM SK4 ....144 C5
Thorpe Hall Gv HYDE SK14 ....133 E2
Thorpe La OLDE OL4 ....76 B4
Thorpeness Sq GTN M18 ....129 G3
Thorpe St BOL BL1 ....33 G4
MDTN M24 ....70 D5
OLDTF/WHR M16 ....126 B4
RAMS * BL0 ....16 C3
MDTN M24 ....81 E3
Thorp Rd NEWH/MOS M40 ....101 H4
ROY/SHW OL2 ....59 H5
Thorp St ECC M30 ....109 E5
WHTF M45 ....69 F5
Thorp Vw ROY/SHW OL2 ....58 D3
Thorsby Av HYDE SK14 ....148 A1
Thorsby Cl EDGW/EG BL7 ....23 E3
Thorsby Rd HALE/TIMP WA15 ....166 B3
Thraxton Av DTN/ASHW M34 ....117 E4
Threadfold Wy EDGW/EG BL7 ......23 E4
Threaphurst La BRAM/HZG SK7 ...186 B2
Threapwood Rd
WYTH/NTH M22 ....180 D3
Three Acre Av ROY/SHW OL2 ......59 H5
Threlkeld Cl MDTN M24 ....70 D3
Threlkeld Rd BOL BL1 ....22 C4
MDTN M24 ....70 D3
Thresher Cl SALE M33 ....155 G3
Threshfield Cl BURY BL9 ....27 G4
Threshfield Dr
HALE/TIMP WA15 ....166 D2
Throstle Bank St HYDE SK14 .....132 B4
Throstle Gv MPL/ROM SK6 ....174 D4
TOT/BURYW BL8 ....37 H1
Throstle Hall Ct MDTN * M24 ......71 G3
Throstles Cl DROY M43 ....116 D2
Throstle Fold WHIT OL12 ....14 A2
Thrum Hall La WHIT OL12 ....18 D5
Thrush Av FWTH BL4 ....64 A4
Thrush Dr BURY BL9 ....5 J1
Thrush St WHIT OL12 ....14 A2
Thruxton Ct OLDTF/WHR M16 ....126 D1
Thurland Rd OLDE OL4 ....91 F1
Thurland St CHAD OL9 ....72 D4
Thurlby Av BKLY M9 ....87 F2
Thurlby St BRUN/LGST M13 ....128 A4
Thurleigh Rd DID/WITH M20 ....157 E3
Thurlestone Av BOLE BL2 ....36 C5
Thurlestone Dr BRAM/HZG SK7 ...184 C2
URM M41 ....123 H5
Thurlestone Rd ALT WA14 ....165 E3
Thurloe St RUSH/FAL M14 ....143 E1
Thurlow St SALQ M50 ....111 G4
Thurlston Crs CHH M8 ....100 C3
Thurlwood Av DID/WITH M20 .....142 D4
Thurnham St BOLS/LL BL3 ....63 F1
Thursfield St SLFD M6 ....99 E5
Thurstane St BOL BL1 ....33 F4
Thurston Cl BURY BL9 ....68 D2
Thurston Clough Rd OLDE OL4 .....77 E3
Thurston Gn WILM/AE SK9 ....201 B4
Thynne St BOLS/LL BL3 ....3 F7
FWTH BL4 ....65 F2
Tiber Av OLDS OL8 ....103 H1
Tib La CMANW M2 ....6 E5
Tib St ANC M4 ....7 G2
DTN/ASHW M34 ....146 C1
RAMS * BL0 ....16 C3
Tideswell Av NEWH/MOS M40 ...114 A2
Tideswell Cl CHD/CHDH SK8 .....182 A4
Tideswell Rd BRAM/HZG SK7 .....185 F4
DROY M43 ....115 H2
Tideway Ct SWIN M27 ....80 C4
Tidworth Av ANC M4 ....114 A3
Tiflis St WHIT OL12 ....10 B4
Tig Fold Rd FWTH BL4 ....63 H4
Tilbury St OLD OL1 ....74 D4
Tilby Cl URM M41 ....137 H1
Tildsley St BOLS/LL BL3 ....48 A5
Tile St BURY BL9 ....4 E2
Tillard Av EDGY/DAV SK3 ....171 E1
Tillbrook Rd WILM/AE SK9 ....180 D2
Tilley Av STRET M32 ....125 H4
Tilshead Wk BRUN/LGST M13 ....127 H2
Tilson Rd NTHM/RTH M23 ....167 G4
Tilton St OLD OL1 ....75 F2
Timberbottom BOLE BL2 ....34 D4
Timberhurst BURY BL9 ....39 G4
Times St MDTN M24 ....72 A4
Timothy Cl SLFD M6 ....110 C2
Timperley Cl OLDS OL8 ....90 D5
Timperley Fold AUL OL6 ....105 E4
Timperley St OP/CLY * M11 ....115 E5
Timsbury Ct BOLE BL2 ....36 A2
Timson St FAIL M35 ....103 E3
Tindall St ECC M30 ....110 A5
RDSH SK5 ....130 A1
Tintagel Ct RAD M26 ....52 A4
Tintern Av BOLE BL2 ....3 J4
DID/WITH M20 ....157 E1
HEY OL10 ....40 D3
OLD OL15 ....21 G4
URM M41 ....137 H3
WHIT OL12 ....29 H1

WHTF M45 ....68 C3
Tintern Cl POY/DIS SK12 ....195 E2
Tintern Dr HALE/TIMP WA15 .....178 D2
Tintern Gv STKP SK1 ....160 C5
Tintern PI HEY OL10 ....40 D2
Tintern St RUSH/FAL M14 ....142 C1
Tipperary St STLY SK15 ....107 F5
Tipping St ALT WA14 ....177 G1
Tipton Cl CHD/CHDH SK8 ....193 E1
RAD M26 ....51 G5
Tipton Dr NTHM/RTH M23 ....155 H4
Tiree Cl BRAM/HZG SK7 ....184 C2
Tirza Av BNG/LEV M19 ....143 G4
Titanian Ri OLD OL1 ....60 C4
Tithe Barn Cl WHIT * OL12 ....20 A4
Tithe Barn Crs BOL BL1 ....33 F2
Tithebarn Rd HALE/TIMP WA15 ...178 D2
The Tithe Barn HTNM SK4 ....158 C2
Tithebarn St BURY BL9 ....4 E4
Titherington Cl RDSH * SK5 ....144 C2
Titterington Av CCHDY M21 ....141 E1
Tiverton Av SALE M33 ....154 A3
Tiverton Cl RAD M26 ....51 G4
WILM/AE SK9 ....200 A1
Tiverton Dr WILM/AE SK9 ....200 A1
Tiverton Rd URM M41 ....123 H4
Tiverton Wk BOL * BL1 ....33 F5
Tiviot Dl STKP SK1 ....13 G2
Tiviot St CSLFD M6 ....6 D1
Tiviot Wy RDSH SK5 ....160 A3
Tivoli St CSLFD M3 ....5 H4
Toad La WHIT OL12 ....10 D3
Tobermory Cl OP/CLY M11 ....115 G4
Tobermory Rd CHD/CHDH SK8 ...181 H2
Todd St BRO M7 ....6 F1
CSLFD M3 ....7 F2
HEY OL10 ....40 B4
MILN OL16 ....11 G5
Todmorden Rd LIT OL15 ....21 F2
Toft Rd GTN M18 ....129 F4
Toledo St OP/CLY M11 ....115 H4
Tolland La HALE/TIMP WA15 ......178 A4
Tollard Av NEWH/MOS M40 ....115 E1
Tollard Cl CHD/CHDH SK8 ....183 E5
Toll Bar St STKP SK1 ....13 H5
Tollemache Rd WHIT OL12 ....14 D3
Tollemache St HYDE SK14 ....134 D3
Tollesbury Cl NEWH/MOS M40 ...114 B1
Toll Gate Cl BRUN/LGST M13 .....128 B4
Tollgate Wy MILN OL16 ....31 J5
Tolworth Dr CHH M8 ....100 C2
Tomcroft La DTN/ASHW M34 .....146 A1
Tomlinson Cl OLDS OL8 ....90 D5
Tomlinson St HULME M15 ....126 D2
NEWH/MOS M40 ....86 C4
ROCH OL11 ....42 B2
Tomlin Sq BOLE BL2 ....34 D2
Tommy Browell Cl
RUSH/FAL M14 ....127 F5
Tommy Johnson Wk
RUSH/FAL M14 ....127 F5
Tommy La BOLE BL2 ....36 B5
Tommy Taylor Cl
NEWH/MOS * M40 ....102 B5
Tom Shepley St HYDE SK14 ....147 H1
Tonacliffe Ter WHIT OL12 ....18 D1
Tonacliffe Wy WHIT OL12 ....18 D1
Tonbridge Cl TOT/BURYW BL8 .....26 D4
Tonbridge Rd BNG/LEV M19 ......144 A3
RDSH SK5 ....145 E3
Tonge Bridge Wy BOLE BL2 ....49 H1
Tonge Cl WHTF M45 ....69 E3
Tonge Fold Rd BOLE BL2 ....49 H2
Tonge Gn STLY * SK15 ....121 E2
Tonge Hall Cl MDTN M24 ....72 A4
Tonge Moor Rd BOLE BL2 ....3 K1
Tonge End WHIT OL12 ....14 B3
Tonge Old Rd BOLE BL2 ....49 H2
Tonge Park Av BOLE BL2 ....34 D5
Tonge Roughs MDTN M24 ....57 H4
Tonge St HEY OL10 ....40 E4
ROCH * OL11 ....30 B5
WGTN/LGST M12 ....128 A2
Tongfields EDGW/EG BL7 ....23 E3
Tong Head Av BOL BL1 ....34 A2
Tong La WHIT OL12 ....19 H2
Tong Rd BOLS/LL BL3 ....50 D5
Tonman St CSLFD M3 ....6 C6
Tonnacliffe Rd WHIT OL12 ....18 B3
Tonne Rd BOLS/LL BL3 ....50 D5
Toon Crs TOT/BURYW BL8 ....26 B3
Tootal Dr SLFD M6 ....110 C3
Tootal Gv SLFD M6 ....110 D3
Tootal Rd SLFD M6 ....110 D3
Topcroft Ct WYTH/NTH M22 ....168 D1
Topfield Rd WYTH/NTH M22 ....180 B2
Topley St NEWH/MOS M40 ....100 D4
Top o' th' Brow BOLE * BL2 ....35 E3
Top O' Th' Gn OLDE OL4 ....89 H1
Top o' th' Lil's BOLS/LL * BL3 ....50 C5
Top o' th' Meadows La
OLDE OL4 ....76 B3
Topping Fold Rd BURY BL9 ....39 H3
The Toppings MPL/ROM SK6 ......161 H5
Topping St EDGW/EG BL7 ....23 E3
Topping St BOL BL1 ....33 G5
BURY BL9 ....5 F2
Topp St FWTH BL4 ....65 F5
Topp Wy BOL BL1 ....2 D2
Top Schwabe St MDTN M24 ....71 F4
OLDE OL4 ....71 F4
Torah St CHH M8 ....6 F1
Torbay Dr OFTN SK2 ....172 C2
Torbay Rd CCHDY M21 ....141 E3
URM M41 ....138 D2
Torcross Rd BKLY M9 ....87 G2
Torkington Av SWIN M27 ....97 E1
Torkington La BRAM/HZG SK7 ...186 C3
Torkington Rd BRAM/HZG SK7 ...185 G4
CHD/CHDH SK8 ....169 G4
WILM/AE SK9 ....199 F1
Torkington St EDGY/DAV SK3 .....12 C7
Torness Wk OP/CLY M11 ....115 G4
Toronto Av MANAIR M90 ....180 A5
Toronto Rd OFTN SK2 ....172 B5
Toronto St BOLE BL2 ....50 B1

Torquay Cl BRUN/LGST M13 ....127 H3
Torquay Gv OFTN SK2 ....172 C5
Torra Barn Cl EDGW/EG BL7 ....22 D1
Torrax Cl SLFD M6 ....96 C4
Torre Cl MDTN M24 ....71 H1
Torrens St SLFD M6 ....98 A5
Torridon Rd BOLE BL2 ....50 C2
Torrin Cl EDGY/DAV SK3 ....172 A4
Torrington Av BKLY M9 ....87 H5
BOL BL1 ....33 H4
Torrington Rd SWIN M27 ....97 G4
Torrington St HEY OL10 ....56 B1
Torrisdale Cl BOLS/LL BL3 ....48 A4
Torside Wy SWIN M27 ....80 C5
Torver Dr BOLE BL2 ....50 B2
MDTN M24 ....71 E2
Torwood Dr CHAD OL9 ....72 D3
Totland Cl WGTN/LGST M12 ......128 D5
Totnes Av BRAM/HZG SK7 ....184 B2
The Tithe Barn HTNM SK4 ....158 C2
SALE M33 ....153 C1
Totnes Rd CCHDY M21 ....141 E3
SALE M33 ....153 C1
Tottenham Dr NTHM/RTH M23 ...167 E4
Tottington Av OLDE OL4 ....76 A5
Tottington La PWCH M25 ....84 B2
Tottington Rd BOLE BL2 ....24 C1
BOL BL1 ....35 E1
TOT/BURYW BL8 ....25 F1
Tottington St OP/CLY M11 ....115 F3
Totton Rd FAIL M35 ....103 E3
Touchet Hall Rd MDTN M24 ....57 C5
Tours Av NTHM/RTH M23 ....167 G4
Towcester Cl ANC M4 ....114 A4
Tower Cl TOT/BURYW * BL8 ....26 A3
Towers Av BOLS/LL BL3 ....47 H5
Towers Ct POY/DIS SK12 ....195 G2
Towers Sq BRUN/LGST * M13 ....127 F3
Towers Rd POY/DIS SK12 ....195 G1
Tower St OLDE OL4 ....75 G3
Tower St DUK SK16 ....118 C4
Tower St MDTN M24 ....54 B5
HEY OL10 ....147 G2
RAD M26 ....53 E5
Towey Cl GTN M18 ....129 G2
Towncliffe Wk HULME * M15 ....126 C2
Towncroft DTN/ASHW M34 ....131 G4
Towncroft La BOL BL1 ....47 F1
Townend St HYDE SK14 ....147 H1
Townfield URM M41 ....138 A1
Townfields Gdns ALT * WA14 .....165 G4
Townfield Rd ALT * WA14 ....165 G4
Town Fields Cl BURY BL9 ....4 E6
Townfield St OLDE OL4 ....9 K5
Town Gate Dr URM M41 ....136 D1
Town Hall La CMANW * M2 ....6 D4
Town House Rd LIT OL15 ....21 F2
Town La DTN/ASHW M34 ....146 A2
DUK SK16 ....118 B3
Townley Fold HYDE SK14 ....133 G2
Townley Rd MILN OL16 ....31 H5
Townley St CHH M8 ....100 A5
MDTN M24 ....71 H5
URM M41 ....114 C5
Townley Ter MPL/ROM * SK6 .....175 F3
Town Mdw MILN OL16 ....10 D5
Town Mill Brow WHIT OL12 ....10 B5
Townscliffe La MPL/ROM SK6 .....175 C5
Townsend Rd SWIN M27 ....97 E1
Townside Row BURY BL9 ....4 E6
Townsley Gv AUL OL6 ....105 G5
Townsley Gv AUL OL6 ....105 G5
Town St MPL/ROM SK6 ....175 C2
Towton St BKLY M9 ....101 F2
Toxteth St OP/CLY M11 ....128 B1
Tracey St CHH M8 ....100 B1
Traders Av URM M41 ....123 H4
Trafalgar Av DTN/ASHW M34 ....130 D1
Trafalgar Ct RUSH/FAL * M14 .....195 H4
Trafalgar Gv BRO * M7 ....99 G5
Trafalgar PI DID/WITH M20 ....157 F2
Trafalgar Rd ALT WA14 ....177 F4
SLFD M6 ....110 C2
Trafalgar Sq AULW OL7 ....117 G4
BRO M7 ....99 H5
OLD OL1 ....9 H1
Trafford Av URM M41 ....123 H4
Trafford Bank Rd
OLDTF/WHR M16 ....126 B3
Trafford Bvd URM M41 ....123 F2
Trafford Dr HALE/TIMP WA15 .....166 C2
LHULT M38 ....80 C2
Trafford Gv FWTH BL4 ....64 D5
STRET M32 ....140 A1
Trafford Park Rd TRPK M17 ....124 D1
Trafford PI HULME M15 ....126 C4
WILM/AE * SK9 ....200 A4
Trafford Rd ECC M30 ....109 G3
ORD M5 ....6 A7
WILM/AE SK9 ....199 F1
Trafford Sq OFTN SK2 ....90 B5
Trafford St CSLFD M3 ....6 C7
FWTH BL4 ....65 F5
ROCH OL11 ....42 D1
Trafford Wharf Rd TRPK M17 .....124 C2
Tragan Cl OFTN SK2 ....173 E5
Tragan Dr OFTN SK2 ....173 E5
Tram St SLFD M6 ....115 F1
Tramway Bri IRL M44 ....150 C5
Tramway Rd DTN/ASHW M34 .....169 G5
Tranmere Cl GTN M18 ....129 E2
Tranmere Dr WILM/AE SK9 ....192 A3
Tranmere Rd EDGY/DAV SK3 .....171 G1
Transvaal St OP/CLY M11 ....115 G4
Travis Brow HTNM SK4 ....12 C3
Travis Ct CMANE M1 ....7 F4
HYDE SK14 ....134 A1
MILN OL16 ....45 E2
Trawden Av BOL BL1 ....33 F4
Trawden Dr BURY BL9 ....27 F3
Trawden Gn OFTN SK2 ....173 E5
Traylen Wy WHIT OL12 ....20 D2
Tree Av DROY M43 ....116 B2

Tree Cl OLDE OL4 75 G4
Tree House Av AULW OL7 104 C4
Treelands Wk ORD M5 126 A2
Tree Tops BOLE BL2 23 H5
Treetops Av RAMS BL0 16 B5
Treetops Cl UPML * OL3 77 G3
Trefoil Wy LIT OL15 20 C2
Tregaer Fold MDTN M24 72 B4
Trenam Pl ORD M5 112 A3
Trenant Rd SLFD M6 98 A5
Trenchard Dr WYTH/NTH M22 181 E5
Trencherbone RAD M26 51 H4
Trengrove St WHIT * OL12 29 F2
Trent Av CHAD OL9 72 D4
HEY OL10 40 B3
MILN OL16 31 H5
Trent Bridge Wk
OLDTF/WHR M16 125 H5
Trent Cl BRAM/HZG SK7 193 F1
RDSH SK5 160 D1
Trent Ct HULME * M15 126 C2
Trent Dr BURY BL9 27 G3
WALK M28 80 C5
Trentham Av FWTH BL4 64 D3
HTNM SK4 158 C3
Trentham Cl FWTH BL4 64 D3
Trentham Gv NEWH/MOS M40 101 H1
Trentham Lawns SLFD M6 111 H1
Trentham Rd OLDTF/WHR M16 125 H5
Trentham St FWTH BL4 64 D3
HULME M15 126 B1
SWIN * M27 96 D1
Trent Rd ROY/SHW OL2 59 H1
Trent St MILN OL16 30 C5
Trent Wk DROY M43 116 C5
Trent Wy FWTH BL4 82 A2
Tresco Av STRET M32 140 B2
Trevelyan St ECC M30 110 B3
Trevor Av SALE M33 154 A4
Trevor Dr NEWH/MOS M40 88 D5
Trevor Gv STKP SK1 13 K5
Trevor Rd ECC M30 109 E2
SWIN M27 96 D4
URM M41 122 C5
Trevor St OP/CLY M11 129 H1
ROCH OL11 42 A3
The Triangle HALE/TIMP WA15 166 C2
Tribune Av ALT WA14 165 E2
Trident Rd ECC M30 122 C1
Trillo Av BOLE BL2 3 K7
Trimdon Cl OP/CLY M11 115 E3
Trimingham Dr
TOT/BURYW BL8 27 E5
Trimley Av NEWH/MOS M40 101 E5
Trinity Av SALE M33 155 E2
Trinity Buildings MOSL * OL5 93 E5
Trinity Cl DUK SK16 118 D5
Trinity Ct AUL OL6 117 H2
Trinity Crs WALK M28 81 F5
Trinity Gdns EDGY/DAV SK3 184 A1
Trinity Gn RAMS BL0 26 C1
Trinity Rd SALE M33 154 D2
Trinity St BOLS/LL BL3 2 D7
BURY BL9 4 E6
MDTN * M24 71 G4
MPL/ROM * SK6 175 E3
OLD OL1 74 B4
STLY SK15 119 F4
Trinity Wy ORD M5 6 A5
Trippier Rd ECC M30 108 C5
Tripps Ms DID/WITH M20 157 E2
Triscombe Wy
OLDTF/WHR M16 126 D5
Tristam Cl BRUN/LGST M13 127 H2
Trojan Gdns BRO M7 99 F5
Troon Cl BOLS/LL BL3 62 C1
BRAM/HZG SK7 184 B5
Troon Dr CHD/CHDH SK8 181 H3
Troon Rd NTHM/RTH M23 167 G3
Trough Ga OLDS OL8 90 A5
Troutbeck Av ANC M4 113 H3
Troutbeck Cl TOT/BURYW BL8 25 E1
Troutbeck Dr RAMS BL0 16 D1
Troutbeck Rd CHD/CHDH SK8 181 G1
HALE/TIMP WA15 167 E4
Troutbeck Wy ROCH OL11 42 A2
Trowbridge Dr
NEWH/MOS M40 102 B1
Trowbridge Rd DTN/ASHW M34 146 D2
Trows La ROCH OL11 42 B5
Trowtree Av WGTN/LGST M12 128 B2
Troydale Dr NEWH/MOS M40 101 H4
Troy Wk ORD * M5 126 A1
Trumpet St CMANE M1 6 D7
Truro Av AUL OL6 105 G3
RDSH SK5 160 D1
STRET M32 140 B1
Truro Cl BRAM/HZG SK7 184 A5
TOT/BURYW BL8 4 B2
Truro Dr SALE M33 153 G2
Truro Rd CHAD OL9 73 F3
Trust Rd GTN M18 129 F5
Tudbury Wy CSLFD M3 6 A2
Tudor Av BKLY M9 101 F1
BOL BL1 48 A2
CHAD OL9 88 C4
FWTH BL4 64 C5
STLY SK15 120 A2
Tudor Cl MOSL OL5 107 F1
RDSH SK5 144 D4
Tudor Ct PWCH M25 85 F4
WHIT OL12 11 G2
Tudor Gn WILM/AE SK9 200 B1
Tudor Gv MDTN M24 71 E1
Tudor Hall St ROCH OL11 42 B4
Tudor Rd ALT WA14 165 E2
WILM/AE SK9 200 B1
Tudor St BOLS/LL * BL3 48 B5
MDTN M24 72 A4
OLDS OL8 8 D6
ROY/SHW OL2 60 A2
Tuffley Rd NTHM/RTH M23 167 H5
Tugford Cl OLDTF/WHR M16 126 D5
Tuley St OP/CLY M11 128 C1
Tulip Av FWTH BL4 64 B3
FWTH BL4 81 G2
Tulip Cl CHAD OL9 72 D5
EDGY/DAV SK3 171 G4
SALE M33 173 E2
Tulip Dr HALE/TIMP WA15 166 A3
Tulip Gv WHIT OL12 18 D5
Tulip Rd PART M31 150 D4
Tully Pl BRO M7 112 D1
Tully St BRO M7 99 H3
Tully St South BRO M7 99 H4
Tulpen Sq CHAD OL9 73 G5
Tulworth Rd POY/DIS SK12 195 E3
Tumblewood Dr
CHD/CHDH SK8 170 B5
Tunbridge Sq ORD M5 111 H3
Tunshill Rd NTHM/RTH M23 155 F5
Tuns Rd OLDS OL8 91 E5
Tunstall Rd OLDE OL4 91 F1
Tunstall St HTNM * SK4 159 H3
OP/CLY * M11 129 H1
Tunstead Av DID/WITH M20 142 A5
Turbary Wk MILN OL16 31 E5
Turf Cl ROY/SHW OL2 74 B1
Turf Hill Rd MILN OL16 43 G2
Turf House Cl LIT * OL15 20 C1
Turfland Av ROY/SHW OL2 74 B1
Turf La CHAD OL9 89 F4
ROY/SHW OL2 74 C1
Turf Lea Rd MPL/ROM SK6 187 G3
Turf Park Rd ROY/SHW OL2 74 B1
Turf Pit La OLDE OL4 75 H1
Turf St RAD M26 67 E1
Turf Ter LIT OL15 20 D2
Turfton Rd ROY/SHW OL2 74 C1
Turks Rd RAD M26 51 G4
Turk St BOL BL1 48 B1
Turley St CHH M8 100 C4
Turnberry BOLS/LL BL3 62 C1
Turnberry Dr WILM/AE SK9 200 A2
Turnberry Rd CHD/CHDH SK8 181 H3
Turnbull Av PWCH M25 69 F5
Turnbull Rd BRUN/LGST M13 143 G1
GTN M18 130 A5
Turnbury Cl SALE M33 139 G5
Turnbury Rd WYTH/NTH M22 168 D4
Turncliff Crs MPL/ROM SK6 174 C2
Turncroft La STKP SK1 13 K4
Turncroft Wy WALK M28 94 A3
Turnell Wy WALK M28 95 H5
Turner Av FAIL M35 102 D4
IRL M44 121 B5
Turner Bridge Rd BOLE BL2 49 H1
Turner Dr URM M41 139 E1
Turnerford Cl EDGW/EG BL7 22 D2
Turner Gdns HYDE SK14 132 D4
Turner La AUL OL6 118 A1
HYDE SK14 133 E4
MPL/ROM SK6 146 C5
Turner Rd MPL/ROM SK6 175 E3
Turner's Pl WHIT OL12 18 D5
Turner St ANC M4 7 G3
AUL OL6 118 A1
BOL BL1 3 H2
BRO M7 99 H3
DTN/ASHW M34 131 G3
GTN M18 129 G3
OLDE OL4 75 H4
OLDTF/WHR M16 126 B2
OP/CLY M11 115 F4
WHIT OL12 10 B2
Turnfield Cl MILN OL16 20 A5
Turnfield Rd CHD/CHDH SK8 181 H1
Turnhill Rd MILN OL16 43 G3
Turn Moss Rd STRET M32 140 C3
Turnough Rd MILN OL16 31 G4
The Turnpike MPL/ROM SK6 174 C2
Turnpike Gn SLFD * M6 111 G2
Turnpike Wk OP/CLY M11 114 C4
Turnstone Rd BOLE BL2 3 G7
OFTN SK2 173 H4
Turn St AUL OL6 118 B1
Turton Cl HEY OL10 40 B4
TOT/BURYW BL8 52 B1
Turton Hts BOLE BL2 23 G5
Turton La PWCH M25 84 C2
Turton Rd BOLE BL2 23 H5
TOT/BURYW BL8 24 D1
TOT/BURYW BL8 25 H3
Turton St BOL BL1 3 F2
OP/CLY * M11 129 G1
Turves Rd CHD/CHDH SK8 182 C3
Tuscan Rd DID/WITH M20 169 G1
Tuscany Vw BRO M7 99 E2
Tutbury St ANC M4 114 A4
Tuxford Wk NEWH/MOS M40 101 E5
Tweedale Av BKLY M9 86 D2
Tweedale St ROCH OL11 42 D1
Tweedale Wy CHAD OL9 89 E5
Tweed Cl ALT WA14 165 F3
OLDS OL8 9 F6
Tweedle Hill Rd BKLY M9 86 C3
Tweenbrook Av
NTHM/RTH M23 179 H1
Tweesdale Cl WHTF M45 69 E3
Twelve Yards Rd ECC M30 122 A1
Twigworth Rd
WYTH/NTH M22 180 B2
Twillbrook Dr CSLFD * M3 6 C1
Twinegate WHIT OL12 18 D5
Twining Brook Rd
CHD/CHDH SK8 183 E1
Twining Rd TRPK M17 109 H5
Twinnies Rd WILM/AE SK9 199 G1
Twin St HEY OL10 41 F5
Twirl Hill Rd AUL OL6 105 H1
Twisse Rd BOLE BL2 50 C2
Twoacre Av WYTH/NTH M22 168 B4
Two Acre Dr ROY/SHW OL2 59 G1
Two Acre La OLDE OL4 76 B2
Two Bridges Rd MILN OL16 45 E3
Two Brooks La TOT/BURYW BL8 25 E1
Two Trees La DTN/ASHW M34 146 D2
Twyford Cl DID/WITH M20 157 E3
Tybyrne Cl WALK M28 94 A3
Tydden St OLDS OL8 90 C4
Tydeman Wk MILN * OL16 44 D1
Tyldesley St RUSH/FAL M14 127 F5
Tyler St WILM/AE SK9 201 B4
Tymm St NEWH/MOS M40 102 B2
Tyndall Av NEWH/MOS M40 101 H1
Tyndall St OLDE OL4 91 F1
Tyne Ct WALK M28 80 D4
Tynedale Cl RDSH SK5 159 H1
Tynesbank WALK M28 80 D5
Tynesbank Cottages
WALK * M28 80 D4
Tyne St OLDE OL4 75 F5
Tynwald St OLDE OL4 75 F5
Tyrol Wk OP/CLY M11 114 C5
Tyrone Cl NTHM/RTH M23 167 E1
Tyrone Dr ROCH OL11 41 G1
Tyro St OLDS * OL8 90 C4
Tyrrell Gv HYDE SK14 148 B2
Tyrrel Rd RDSH SK5 145 E2
Tysoe Gdns CSLFD M3 6 A2
Tyson St CHH M8 100 A2
Tytherington Dr RDSH SK5 144 C2

U

Uganda St BOLS/LL BL3 63 F2
Ukraine Rd BRO M7 98 D4
Uldale Dr MDTN M24 71 F3
Ullesthorpe WHIT OL12 10 B5
Ulleswater Cl BOLS/LL BL3 65 G1
Ullswater St BOL BL1 34 A4
Ullswater Av AULW OL7 117 H1
ROY/SHW OL2 59 E3
WHIT OL12 29 F2
Ullswater Dr BURY * BL9 53 F2
FWTH BL4 63 H5
MDTN M24 71 G1
Ullswater Gv HEY OL10 56 A1
Ullswater Rd STKP SK1 172 C2
URM M41 122 B5
WILM/AE SK9 191 H3
WYTH/NTH M22 180 A2
Ullswater Ter STLY SK15 119 F1
Ulster Av ROCH OL11 42 D1
Ulundi St RAD M26 67 F1
Ulverston Av CHAD OL9 89 F1
DID/WITH M20 142 A4
Umberton Rd WHTN BL5 62 C5
Uncouth Rd MILN OL16 31 F4
Underhill MPL/ROM SK6 162 B4
Underhill Rd OLD OL1 74 B3
Underhill Wk NEWH/MOS M40 115 E1
Under La CHAD OL9 89 G4
OLDE OL4 92 C3
Underwood WHIT OL12 10 B6
Underwood Cl GTN M18 130 A2
Underwood Rd HYDE SK14 134 A5
WILM/AE SK9 201 D4
Underwood St DUK SK16 118 A5
Underwood Wy ROY/SHW OL2 60 C1
Undsworth Ct HEY * OL10 41 E4
Unicorn St ECC M30 109 E5
Union Ar BURY BL9 4 E4
Union Buildings BOL * BL1 3 F6
Union Ct BOL * BL1 34 B4
Union Rd AUL OL6 118 B1
BOL BL1 34 B4
MPL/ROM * SK6 175 E3
WHIT OL12 20 B4
Union St ANC M4 7 G3
AUL OL6 118 A1
BURY BL9 4 E4
CHAD OL9 89 G3
EDGW/EG BL7 22 C1
GTN M18 129 H2
HYDE SK14 147 H1
MDTN M24 71 H3
OLD OL1 9 G4
OLDE OL4 91 H1
RAMS BL0 16 D2
ROY/SHW OL2 59 E5
RUSH/FAL * M14 127 G5
SLFD M6 111 H1
STKP SK1 13 G6
SWIN M27 96 D2
WGTN/LGST M12 127 H1
WHIT OL12 10 C4
WHIT OL12 14 B5
Union St West CHAD OL9 8 E5
Union Ter CHH * M8 100 A2
United Rd OLDTF/WHR M16 125 F3
Unity Cl HEY OL10 40 C5
Unity Crs HEY OL10 40 C5
Unity Dr BRO M7 99 H4
Unity St HEY OL10 40 C5
Unity Wy STKP SK1 13 H6
University Rd SLFD M6 112 A2
University Rd West ORD * M5 112 A3
Unsworth St RAD M26 52 A5
Unsworth Wy OLD OL1 9 F1
Unwin Av GTN M18 129 G4
Upavon Rd WYTH/NTH M22 181 E1
Upland Dr LHULT M38 80 A1
Upland Rd OLDS OL8 90 B3
The Uplands MOSL OL5 107 E1
Uplands MDTN M24 71 H5
Uplands Av RAD M26 67 H2
Uplands Rd HYDE SK14 148 B5
URM M41 137 F3
Upper Brook St
BRUN/LGST M13 127 G2
STKP SK1 13 H4
Upper Camp St BRO M7 99 G5
Upper Chorlton Rd
OLDTF/WHR M16 126 B5
Upper Cleminson St CSLFD M3 112 C3
Upper Cliff Hl ROY/SHW OL2 45 F5
Upper Conran St BKLY M9 101 F2
Upper Cyrus St
NEWH/MOS M40 114 B3
Upper Dover St OP/CLY M11 114 D4
Upper Downs ALT WA14 177 F1
Upper George St WHIT OL12 10 D3
Upper Gloucester St SLFD M6 111 H2
Upper Hayes Cl MILN OL16 11 J5
Upper Helena St
NEWH/MOS M40 114 B3
Upper Hibbert La
MPL/ROM SK6 175 E5
Upper Kent Rd RUSH/FAL M14 128 A5
Upper Kirby St ANC M4 113 H4
Upper Lloyd St RUSH/FAL M14 127 F5
Upper Md EDGW/EG BL7 23 E2
Upper Medlock St HULME M15 127 E2
Uppermill Dr BNG/LEV M19 158 A3
Upper Monsall St
NEWH/MOS M40 101 F4
Upper Moss La HULME M15 126 D2
Upper Park Rd BRO M7 99 G1
RUSH/FAL M14 127 H4
Upper Passmonds Gv
ROCH OL11 29 E3
Upper Stone Dr MILN OL16 31 E5
Upper West Gv
BRUN/LGST M13 128 A3
Upper Wilton St PWCH M25 85 F3
Uppingham Dr RAMS BL0 16 C1
Upton ROCH OL11 29 H5
Upton Av CHD/CHDH SK8 182 D4
HTNM SK4 158 B2
Upton Cl MDTN M24 87 H2
Upton Dr ALT WA14 165 H1
Upton St CMANE M1 7 H6
Upton Wy TOT/BURYW BL8 37 E1
Urban Dr HALE/TIMP WA15 165 H5
Urban Rd HALE/TIMP WA15 165 H5
SALE M33 154 B2
Urmson St OLDS OL8 90 C4
Urmston La STRET M32 139 F2
Urmston Pk URM M41 138 D1
Urwick Rd MPL/ROM SK6 162 A5
Usk Cl WHTF M45 69 F5
Uttley St BOL BL1 33 G4
ROCH OL11 42 B2
Uxbridge St AUL OL6 117 H2

V

Vaal St OLDS OL8 89 H4
Valance Cl WGTN/LGST M12 128 D2
Valdene Cl FWTH BL4 65 E5
Valdene Dr FWTH BL4 65 E5
WALK M28 95 E2
The Vale MOSL OL5 106 C1
Vale Av BURY BL9 53 E2
HYDE SK14 133 F5
RAD M26 66 B5
SALE M33 155 F1
SWIN M27 97 F1
URM M41 137 F2
Vale Cl BRAM/HZG SK7 173 F5
HTNM SK4 158 C4
MPL/ROM SK6 163 E4
Vale Cottages LIT OL15 20 D3
Vale Crs CHD/CHDH SK8 182 C2
Vale Dr CHAD OL9 8 C4
PWCH M25 84 D5
Vale Edge RAD M26 52 B4
Vale Head WILM/AE SK9 192 A5
Vale La FAIL M35 103 F5
Valencia Rd BRO M7 99 E4
Valentia Rd BKLY M9 87 E3
Valentine St FAIL M35 102 D3
OLDE OL4 91 F1
Valerie Wk HULME M15 127 E1
Vale Rd ALT WA14 177 E3
DROY M43 116 C2
HALE/TIMP WA15 166 B4
HTNM SK4 158 C5
MPL/ROM SK6 174 A1
ROY/SHW OL2 60 C3
STLY SK15 107 F4
WILM/AE SK9 198 D2
Vale Side MOSL OL5 106 D1
Vale St AULW OL7 104 D4
BOLE BL2 50 D2
HEY OL10 41 F4
MDTN M24 72 A4
OP/CLY M11 115 F3
Vale Top Av BKLY M9 101 F3
Valetta Cl RUSH/FAL M14 142 C2
Vale Vw ALT * WA14 177 F3
Valewood Av HTNM SK4 158 D5
Valletts La BOL BL1 33 F5
Valley Av TOT/BURYW BL8 37 G2
Valley Cl CHD/CHDH SK8 182 B1
MOSL OL5 92 C5
Valley Dr WILM/AE SK9 191 H4
Valley Gv DTN/ASHW M34 147 E1
Valley Ml EDGW/EG * BL7 23 E3
Valley New Rd ROY/SHW OL2 74 B1
Valley Ri ROY/SHW OL2 44 D5
Valley Rd BRAM/HZG SK7 184 A3
CHD/CHDH SK8 182 B1
HYDE SK14 149 F3
MDTN M24 72 A2
MPL/ROM SK6 161 E2
ROCH OL11 42 D2
ROY/SHW OL2 74 B1
URM M41 122 A4
Valley Rd South URM M41 136 D1
Valley Vw HYDE SK14 133 F4
WHIT OL12 14 C1
Valley Wk OP/CLY M11 114 C4
Valley Wy STLY SK15 119 H4
Valpy Av BOLE BL2 34 C3
Vancouver Quay SALQ M50 125 G1
Vandyke Av SLFD M6 110 C2
Vandyke St ROCH OL11 28 C2
Vane St ECC M30 109 F3
Vannes Gv HYDE SK14 134 C5
Vantomme St BOL BL1 33 H2
Varden Gv EDGY/DAV SK3 171 G4
Varden Rd POY/DIS SK12 195 F4
Vardon Dr WILM/AE SK9 200 A4
Varey St GTN M18 129 G3
Varley Rd BOLS/LL BL3 47 H5
Varley St NEWH/MOS M40 114 A1
Varna St OP/CLY M11 129 G1
Vauban Dr SLFD M6 110 C2
Vaudrey Dr BRAM/HZG SK7 185 F2
CHD/CHDH SK8 182 D1
HALE/TIMP WA15 166 B1
Vaudrey La DTN/ASHW M34 146 D1
Vaudrey Rd MPL/ROM SK6 161 H1
Vaudrey St STLY SK15 119 F4
Vaughan Av NEWH/MOS M40 101 H2
Vaughan Gv OLDE OL4 92 A1
Vaughan Rd CCHDY M21 141 G3
HTNM SK4 159 G3
Vaughan St ECC M30 109 E2
ROY/SHW OL2 74 B1
WGTN/LGST M12 128 C1
Vauxhall St NEWH/MOS M40 113 G1
Vavasour Ct MILN * OL16 30 C5
Vavasour St MILN OL16 30 C5
Vawdrey Dr NTHM/RTH M23 155 G4
Vaynor WHIT OL12 10 B4
Vega St CHH M8 112 D1
Velmere Av BKLY M9 86 B2
Velour Cl BRO M7 112 C2
Vendale Av SWIN M27 96 C4
Venetia St NEWH/MOS * M40 102 B5
Venice St BOLS/LL BL3 48 B5
CMANE * M1 7 G7
Venlow Gdns CHD/CHDH SK8 183 E3
Ventnor Av BNG/LEV M19 144 B3
BOL BL1 34 A3
BURY BL9 68 C1
SALE M33 139 G5
Ventnor Cl DTN/ASHW M34 147 E3
Ventnor Rd DID/WITH M20 157 H3
HTNM SK4 158 D4
Ventnor St BKLY M9 101 E2
ROCH OL11 43 E1
SLFD M6 99 E5
Ventura Cl RUSH/FAL M14 142 B2
Venture Scout Wy BRO M7 100 A4
Venture Wy POY/DIS SK12 195 G4
Venwood Ct PWCH * M25 84 C5
Venwood Rd PWCH M25 84 C5
Verbena Av FWTH BL4 64 B3
Verbena Cl PART M31 151 E3
Verdant La ECC M30 108 C5
Verdant Wy MILN OL16 43 H3
Verdon St ANC M4 7 F1
Verdun Av SLFD M6 110 C2
Verdun Crs ROCH OL11 29 F3
Verdun Rd ECC M30 109 E1
Verdure Av BOL BL1 47 F1
SALE M33 154 D5
Verdure Cl FAIL M35 103 G2
Vere St SALQ M50 111 G4
Verity Cl DID/WITH M20 142 C5
ROY/SHW OL2 74 A2
Vermont St BOL BL1 2 A2
Verne Av SWIN M27 96 D2
Verne Dr OLD OL1 60 D4
Verney Rd ROY/SHW OL2 74 B2
Vernham Wk BOLS/LL BL3 48 D5
Vernon Av ECC * M30 110 A3
STKP SK1 160 C4
STRET M32 140 A2
Vernon Cl CHD/CHDH SK8 182 B3
POY/DIS SK12 195 E5
Vernon Dr MPL/ROM SK6 174 B2
PWCH M25 84 D5
Vernon Gv SALE M33 155 F3
Vernon Pk HALE/TIMP WA15 166 B2
Vernon Rd BRO M7 99 F1
DROY M43 115 H3
MPL/ROM SK6 161 G3
POY/DIS SK12 195 F5
TOT/BURYW BL8 26 A2
Vernon St AUL OL6 118 B1
BKLY M9 101 F3
BOL BL1 2 C3
BRAM/HZG SK7 185 E1
BRO M7 99 G5
BURY BL9 4 E1
FWTH BL4 65 F4
HYDE SK14 147 H1
MOSL * OL5 92 D5
STKP * SK1 13 G2
Vernon Wk BOL BL1 2 D2
Verona Dr NEWH/MOS M40 115 F1
Veronica Rd DID/WITH M20 157 H3
Verrill Av NTHM/RTH M23 156 B5
Vesper St FAIL M35 103 F2
Vesta St ANC M4 113 H4
RAMS BL0 16 C2
Vestris Dr SLFD M6 110 C2
Vetch Cl GOL/RIS/CU WA3 150 A1
Viaduct Rd ALT WA14 165 G2
Viaduct St CSLFD M3 6 C2
EDGY/DAV SK3 12 E4
WGTN/LGST M12 114 B5
Vicarage Av CHD/CHDH SK8 183 E4
Vicarage Cl BURY BL9 27 F3
DUK SK16 118 D5
OLDE OL4 76 A5
SLFD M6 110 C2
Vicarage Crs AUL OL6 105 G5
Vicarage Dr DUK SK16 118 D5
MILN OL16 19 H5
Vicarage Gdns EDGY/DAV * SK3 12 E6
HYDE SK14 147 H1
Vicarage Gv ECC M30 110 A3
Vicarage La ALT WA14 177 F3
MDTN M24 72 C5
POY/DIS SK12 195 F2
Vicarage Rd AULW OL7 105 E5
EDGY/DAV SK3 171 H3
IRL M44 136 B1
SWIN M27 96 D2
URM M41 123 E4
WALK M28 80 D3
Vicarage Rd North ROCH OL11 42 B5
Vicarage Rd South ROCH OL11 42 B5
Vicarage St BOLS/LL BL3 48 C4
OLDS OL8 89 H5
RAD M26 67 F1
ROY/SHW OL2 60 A2
Vicarage Vw ROCH OL11 42 C5
Vicarage Wy ROY/SHW OL2 59 H3
Vicar's Dr MILN OL16 10 C7
Vicar's Ga MILN OL16 10 C7
Vicars Hall Gdns WALK M28 94 A5
Vicars Hall La WALK M28 94 A5
Vicars Rd CCHDY M21 140 D3
Vicars St ECC M30 110 A3
Vicker Cl SWIN M27 83 E5
Vicker Gv DID/WITH M20 157 E1
Vickerman St BOL BL1 33 G4
Vickers Rw FWTH BL4 64 C4
Vickers St BOLS/LL BL3 48 C4
NEWH/MOS M40 114 B2
Victor Av BURY BL9 38 B2
Victoria Av BKLY M9 86 D2
BNG/LEV M19 143 H3
BRAM/HZG * SK7 185 F1
CHD/CHDH SK8 182 D2
DID/WITH M20 157 F3
ECC M30 110 A2
HALE/TIMP WA15 165 H2
MPL/ROM SK6 161 G3
SWIN M27 97 F2
WHTF M45 68 D4
Victoria Av East BKLY M9 87 G3
Victoria Bridge St CSLFD M3 6 D2
Victoria Cl BRAM/HZG SK7 193 G1
EDGY/DAV SK3 13 F7
WALK * M28 94 B4
Victoria Ct AULW OL7 117 H4
FWTH BL4 64 D2
Victoria Crs ECC M30 110 A2
Victoria Dr SALE M33 155 E3
Victoria Gdns HYDE SK14 133 E4
ROY/SHW * OL2 60 A2
Victoria Gv BOL BL1 33 F5
HTNM SK4 159 F1
RUSH/FAL M14 142 D4
Victoria La SWIN M27 96 C2
WHTF M45 68 C5

Victoria Ldg BRO * M7 99 F5
Victoria Ms BURY BL9 69 E2
Victoria Pk STKP * SK1 172 C1
Victoria Pl TRPK M17 125 G3
Victoria Rd ALT WA14 177 G2
BOL BL1 47 E2
DUK SK16 132 B2
ECC M30 109 H2
FWTH BL4 81 H1
HALE/TIMP WA15 166 B3
IRL M44 136 A2
OLDTF/WHR M16 141 G1
RUSH/FAL M14 142 C3
SALE M33 155 E3
STKP SK1 160 C5
STRET M32 140 A1
URM M41 138 A1
WILM/AE SK9 199 F4
WYTH/NTH M22 168 C1
Victoria Sq ANC * M4 7 J2
BOL BL1 2 E5
Victoria Station Ap CSLFD M3 6 E2
Victoria St ALT WA14 165 G4
AULW OL7 117 H4
CHAD OL9 8 A1
CHAD OL9 73 G5
CSLFD M3 6 E2
DTN/ASHW M34 131 F5
DUK SK16 118 C5
FAIL M35 102 C4
FWTH BL4 64 C3
HEY OL10 41 F5
HYDE SK14 133 E4
HYDE SK14 133 G3
LIT OL15 21 E3
MDTN M24 71 H4
OLDE OL4 9 K4
OLDE OL4 91 H1
OLDS * OL8 104 C2
OP/CLY M11 115 F5
RAD M26 67 F1
RAMS BL0 16 C2
ROY/SHW OL2 60 A2
STLY SK15 119 E3
STLY SK15 120 A1
TOT/BURYW BL8 4 A4
TOT/BURYW BL8 25 H4
WALK M28 94 B4
WHIT * OL12 10 C3
WHIT * OL12 14 B5
Victoria St East AULW OL7 117 H4
Victoria Ter ROY/SHW * OL2 59 E4
WGTN/LGST M12 128 C4
Victoria Wk CHAD OL9 73 H3
Victoria Wy BRAM/HZG SK7 193 G1
Victor Mann St OP/CLY M11 130 B1
Victor St CSLFD M3 6 A3
HEY OL10 56 B1
NEWH/MOS M40 113 H1
OLDS OL8 103 G1
Victory Gv DTN/ASHW M34 130 D1
Victory Rd BOLS/LL BL3 50 D5
IRL M44 150 B2
Victory St BOL * BL1 48 B1
RUSH/FAL M14 127 H5
Vienna Rd EDGY/DAV SK3 171 G3
Vienna Rd East EDGY/DAV SK3 171 G3
Viewlands Dr WILM/AE SK9 192 A5
View St BOLS/LL BL3 48 C4
Vigo Av BOLS/LL BL3 63 E1
Vigo St HEY OL10 41 F5
OLDE OL4 91 G2
Viking Cl OP/CLY M11 114 C4
Viking St BOLS/LL BL3 49 F5
ROCH OL11 29 F3
The Village URM M41 137 G3
Village Ct TRPK M17 124 D2
Village St BRO M7 99 F5
Village Wy WILM/AE SK9 200 A1
Village Wy (Ashburton Rd East)
TRPK M17 124 C2
Villa Rd OLDS OL8 90 C3
Villdale Av OFTN SK2 172 D2
Villiers Ct WHTF * M45 84 D1
Villiers Dr OLDS OL8 8 E6
Villiers St AUL OL6 118 C3
BURY BL9 5 H2
HYDE SK14 133 E5
Vinca Gv BRO M7 99 G4
Vincent Av CCHDY M21 140 D2
OLDE OL4 75 F4
Vincent St BOL BL1 2 A6
BRO M7 99 G3
HYDE SK14 148 A2
MDTN M24 71 H2
MILN * OL16 43 F1
OP/CLY M11 115 F5
Vine Av SWIN M27 97 G2
Vine Cl ROY/SHW OL2 60 A2
SALE M33 153 F1
Vine Ct MILN * OL16 11 G7
STRET M32 140 A2
Vine Fold NEWH/MOS M40 103 E1
Vine Gv OFTN SK2 172 D3
Vine Pl ROCH OL11 43 E1
Vinery Gv DTN/ASHW M34 131 F5
Vine St BRAM/HZG SK7 185 F1
BRO M7 99 E2
CHAD OL9 89 G4
ECC M30 109 F4
OP/CLY M11 129 H1
RAMS BL0 16 B4
Vineyard Cl WHIT OL12 19 H1
Vineyard St OLDE OL4 75 E5
Viola St OP/CLY M11 115 G3
Violet Av FWTH BL4 64 B3
Violet St GTN M18 130 A2
OFTN SK2 172 A3
Violet Wy MDTN M24 72 C5
Virgil St HULME M15 126 B2
Virginia Cha CHD/CHDH SK8 182 C4
Virginia Cl NTHM/RTH M23 167 E2
Virginia St BOLS/LL BL3 48 A5
ROCH * OL11 42 D2
Viscount Dr CHD/CHDH SK8 182 A5
MANAIR * M90 179 G5
Viscount St RUSH/FAL M14 127 H5
The Vista IRL M44 150 B2
Vivian St ROCH OL11 42 D1
Vixen Cl CCHDY M21 141 H4
Voltaire Av SLFD M6 110 C2
Vorlich Dr CHAD OL9 73 E4
Vulcan St OLD OL1 75 E3
Vyner Gv SALE M33 139 E5

W

Waddicor Av AUL OL6 105 H4
Waddington Cl TOT/BURYW BL8 36 D4
Waddington Fold MILN OL16 43 H4
Waddington Rd BOL BL1 32 D5
Waddington St CHAD OL9 8 B1
Wadebridge Av
NTHM/RTH M23 167 E2
Wadebridge Dr TOT/BURYW BL8 37 E4
Wadeford Cl ANC M4 7 K1
Wade Hill La OLDE OL4 77 F4
Wade Rw UPML OL3 78 A4
Wadesmill Wk CMANE * M1 127 G1
Wadeson Rd BRUN/LGST M13 127 G1
Wade St BOLS/LL BL3 64 A1
MDTN M24 88 C1
Wade Wk OP/CLY M11 114 D5
Wadham Gdns MPL/ROM SK6 162 B1
Wadham Wy HALE/TIMP WA15 178 A3
Wadhurst Wk
BRUN/LGST * M13 127 H3
Wadlow Cl CSLFD * M3 6 B1
Wadsley St BOL BL1 2 C2
Wadsworth Cl WILM/AE SK9 192 B4
Wadsworth Ms DROY M43 116 A4
Waggoners Ct SWIN M27 97 E3
Waggon Rd BOLE BL2 50 A1
MOSL OL5 106 D2
Wagner St BOL BL1 33 G3
Wagstaffe Dr FAIL M35 103 E3
Wagstaffe St MDTN M24 71 H3
Wagtail Cl WALK M28 95 E2
Waincliffe Av CCHDY M21 156 C2
Waingap Crs WHIT OL12 14 C5
Waingap Ri WHIT OL12 19 E4
Waingap Vw WHIT OL12 18 C1
Wainman St SLFD M6 99 E5
Wainwright Av DTN/ASHW M34 130 A5
Wainwright Cl OFTN SK2 172 B2
OLDE OL4 76 B5
Wainwright Rd ALT WA14 165 E4
Wainwright St DUK SK16 118 C4
OLDS OL8 9 F6
Waithlands Rd MILN OL16 30 C5
Wakefield Crs MPL/ROM SK6 161 H5
Wakefield Dr OLD OL1 73 H3
SWIN M27 82 C3
Wakefield Ms EDGW/EG BL7 23 E4
Wakefield Rd STLY SK15 119 G3
Wakefield St CMANE * M1 127 F1
Wakeling Rd DTN/ASHW M34 146 B3
Walcott Cl BRUN/LGST M13 128 A3
Wald Av RUSH/FAL M14 143 F4
Waldeck St BOL BL1 48 B1
Walden Av OLDE OL4 75 G2
Walden Cl RUSH/FAL M14 142 B3
Walden Crs BRAM/HZG SK7 184 D1
Walderton Av NEWH/MOS M40 101 H4
Waldon Av CHD/CHDH SK8 170 A4
Waldon Cl BOLS/LL BL3 48 B5
Wales St OLD OL1 75 F3
The Walk MILN OL16 10 C6
Walkdene Dr WALK M28 80 C4
Walkden Market Pl WALK * M28 81 E4
Walkden Rd WALK M28 81 E5
WALK M28 95 E1
Walkden St WHIT OL12 10 C3
Walker Av BOLS/LL BL3 64 A1
FAIL * M35 103 G4
STLY SK15 119 H3
WHTF M45 84 D1
Walker Cl FWTH BL4 81 H1
HYDE SK14 148 A1
Walker Fold Rd BOL BL1 32 A1
Walker La HYDE SK14 148 A1
Walker Rd BKLY M9 87 F3
CHAD OL9 89 E5
ECC M30 108 D1
IRL * M44 136 A2
Walkers Cl UPML OL3 78 A4
Walkers Ct FWTH BL4 65 E4
Walker's Cft CSLFD M3 6 E2
Walker's La OLDE OL4 92 B1
Walkers Rd OLDS OL8 89 H5
Walker St BOL BL1 2 B6
BURY BL9 53 F1
DTN/ASHW M34 131 F4
HEY OL10 40 D5
MDTN M24 70 D5
MILN OL16 11 F7
OLDS OL8 8 C5
RAD M26 67 H3
STKP SK1 13 F3
Walkerwood Dr STLY SK15 120 A3
Walkmill UPML OL3 77 G3
Walk Mill Cl WHIT OL12 20 A4
The Walkway BOLS/LL BL3 47 G4
Wallace Av RUSH/FAL M14 128 A5
Wallace St OLDS OL8 90 C3
Wallasey Av RUSH/FAL M14 142 A2
Wallbank Dr WHIT OL12 18 A1
Wallbank Rd BRAM/HZG SK7 184 B3
Wallbrook Crs LHULT M38 80 B1
The Walled Gdn SWIN M27 96 C4
Waller Av RUSH/FAL M14 142 D3
Walley St BOL BL1 33 H3
Wallhead Rd MILN OL16 31 E4
Wall Hill Rd UPML OL3 77 G3
Wallingford Rd URM M41 123 H5
WILM/AE SK9 191 H2
Wallis St CHAD OL9 89 F3
NEWH/MOS * M40 102 B5
Wallness La SLFD M6 112 B2
Wallshaw Pl OLD OL1 9 K3
Wallshaw St OLD OL1 9 J2
Wall St OLDS OL8 9 G6
SLFD M6 111 G3
Wall Wy GTN M18 129 H4
Wallwork Cl ROCH OL11 28 B2
Wallwork St OP/CLY M11 115 H5
RDSH * SK5 145 E1
Wallworth Av GTN M18 129 G3
Wally Sq BRO M7 99 H4
Walmer Dr BRAM/HZG SK7 184 B3
Walmersley Ct MPL/ROM * SK6 175 E3
Walmersley Old Rd BURY BL9 27 G3
Walmersley Rd BURY BL9 5 F2
BURY BL9 27 F2
NEWH/MOS M40 88 D5
Walmer St GTN M18 129 H2
RUSH/FAL M14 127 G5
Walmer St East RUSH/FAL M14 127 H5
Walmley Gv BOLS/LL BL3 63 F1
Walmsley Av LIT OL15 20 C5
Walmsley Gv URM M41 138 B1
Walmsley St RDSH SK5 160 A3
STLY SK15 119 F5
TOT/BURYW BL8 37 G2
Walney Rd WYTH/NTH M22 168 C5
Walnut Av BURY BL9 5 K3
OLDE OL4 75 G4
Walnut Cl HYDE SK14 148 B1
SWIN M27 82 C3
WILM/AE SK9 200 B2
Walnut Rd ECC M30 108 D1
PART M31 150 C3
Walnut St BOL BL1 34 A3
GTN M18 129 G2
Walnut Tree Rd EDGY/DAV SK3 170 D2
Walnut Wk STRET M32 139 H3
Walpole St MILN OL16 11 F7
Walsall St SLFD M6 98 D5
Walsden St OP/CLY M11 115 F3
Walsh Av BKLY M9 86 D5
Walshaw Brook Cl
TOT/BURYW BL8 37 E2
Walshaw Dr SWIN M27 97 E3
Walshaw La TOT/BURYW BL8 37 E2
Walshaw Rd TOT/BURYW BL8 37 E2
Walshe St BURY BL9 4 B5
Walsh St CHAD OL9 89 G1
Walsingham Av DID/WITH M20 157 E2
MDTN M24 87 H2
Walter Scott St OLD OL1 75 E4
Walters Dr OLDS OL8 90 D4
Walter St BKLY M9 101 E2
GTN M18 129 H2
OLD OL1 9 H4
OLDTF/WHR M16 126 B4
PWCH M25 84 C3
RAD M26 52 A2
WALK M28 81 E5
Waltham Dr CHD/CHDH SK8 193 E1
Waltham Rd OLDTF/WHR M16 141 H2
Waltham St OLDS OL8 91 F3
Walton Cl MDTN M24 70 D3
Walton Ct BOLS/LL BL3 49 E5
Walton Dr BURY BL9 27 F5
MPL/ROM SK6 174 C2
Walton Hall Dr RDSH SK5 144 C2
Walton Houses FAIL * M35 103 E2
Walton Pl FWTH BL4 65 F5
Walton Rd ALT WA14 165 E4
BKLY M9 87 E2
SALE M33 154 A5
Walton St AULW OL7 104 C5
HEY OL10 56 A1
MDTN * M24 71 H2
STKP * SK1 13 H7
Walwyn Cl STRET M32 140 B2
Wandsworth Av OP/CLY M11 115 G3
Wansbeck Cl STRET M32 140 B2
Wansfell Wk ANC M4 114 A3
Wansford St RUSH/FAL M14 127 F5
Wanstead Av BKLY M9 87 H4
Wapping St BOL BL1 33 G4
Warbeck Cl RDSH SK5 145 F1
Warbeck Rd NEWH/MOS M40 88 C5
Warbreck Gv SALE M33 155 E3
Warburton Cl HALE/TIMP WA15 189 E1
MPL/ROM SK6 161 H5
Warburton Dr
HALE/TIMP WA15 189 E1
Warburton La PART M31 151 E3
Warburton Rd WILM/AE SK9 192 A3
Warburton St BOL BL1 34 A4
DID/WITH M20 157 G3
ECC M30 109 H4
ORD M5 126 A2
Warburton Wy
HALE/TIMP WA15 166 D2
Warcock Rd OLDE OL4 75 F5
Wardend Cl LHULT * M38 80 B1
Warden St NEWH/MOS M40 102 A4
Warde St HULME M15 126 D2
Wardle Brook Av HYDE SK14 134 A5
Wardle Cl RAD M26 51 H4
STRET M32 140 B1
Wardle Edge WHIT OL12 19 G5
Wardle Fold WHIT OL12 19 H1
Wardle Gdns WHIT OL12 19 H5
Wardle Rd SALE M33 154 C3
WHIT OL12 19 H3
Wardle St BOLE BL2 49 G4
LIT * OL15 20 D2
NEWH/MOS M40 114 B2
OLDE OL4 91 E1
Wardley Av CCHDY M21 141 H3
WALK M28 80 C5
Wardley Hall La WALK M28 95 H2
Wardley Hall Rd WALK M28 96 A1
Wardley St SWIN M27 97 E2
Wardlow St BOLS/LL BL3 48 A5
Ward Rd DID/WITH M20 157 G3
DROY M43 116 C4
Wardsend Wk HULME * M15 126 C2
Ward St BKLY M9 86 D5
CHAD OL9 8 A3
FAIL M35 102 D2
HYDE SK14 147 H1
MPL/ROM SK6 161 G3
NEWH/MOS M40 101 G2
STKP SK1 13 J7
Wareham Gv ECC M30 109 F2
Wareham St CHH * M8 100 C1
Wareings Yd ROCH OL11 43 F2
Wareing Wy BOLS/LL BL3 2 C6
Warford Av POY/DIS SK12 195 H5
Warford St ANC M4 113 G1
Warham St WILM/AE SK9 199 G3
The Warke WALK M28 95 G4
Warley Cl CHD/CHDH SK8 170 B3
Warley Gv DUK SK16 118 B5
Warley Rd OLDTF/WHR M16 125 H5
Warley St LIT OL15 21 E2
Warlingham Cl TOT/BURYW BL8 37 G5
Warlow Crest UPML OL3 93 H3
Warlow Dr UPML OL3 93 H3
Warmbly Gdns OLDS OL8 104 A1
Warmington Dr
WGTN/LGST M12 128 B2
Warmley Rd NTHM/RTH M23 167 E1
Warne Av DROY M43 116 D3
Warnford Cl NEWH/MOS M40 115 G1
War Office Rd ROCH OL11 28 B5
Warren Av CHD/CHDH SK8 170 A4
Warren Bank BKLY M9 86 D4
Warren Bruce Rd TRPK M17 125 E2
Warren Cl BRAM/HZG SK7 183 G2
DTN/ASHW M34 146 A1
POY/DIS SK12 194 C3
Warren Dr HALE/TIMP WA15 179 E5
SWIN M27 96 C5
Warrener St SALE M33 155 E3
Warren Hey WILM/AE SK9 200 B2
Warren La OLDS OL8 91 E3
Warren Lea MPL/ROM SK6 163 G4
POY/DIS SK12 195 F2
Warren Rd CHD/CHDH SK8 182 D2
EDGY/DAV SK3 171 H3
TRPK M17 124 C2
WALK M28 81 F4
Warren St BKLY M9 86 D5
BRO M7 100 A2
STKP SK1 13 G2
TOT/BURYW BL8 37 G5
Warre St AUL OL6 118 A2
Warrington Rd BKLY M9 86 D3
Warrington St AUL OL6 118 A2
OLDE OL4 91 H2
STLY SK15 119 G4
Warsall Rd WYTH/NTH M22 168 D2
Warslow Dr SALE M33 155 F5
Warsop Av WYTH/NTH M22 168 D4
Warstead Wk
BRUN/LGST * M13 127 H3
Warth Fold Rd RAD M26 52 D3
Warth Rd BURY BL9 52 D2
Warton Cl BRAM/HZG SK7 184 B5
TOT/BURYW BL8 37 E5
Warton Dr NTHM/RTH M23 167 H4
Warwick Av DID/WITH M20 157 E2
DTN/ASHW M34 146 C2
SWIN M27 82 C5
WHTF M45 69 E5
Warwick Cl CHD/CHDH SK8 170 D5
DUK SK16 132 B2
HTNM SK4 159 F2
MDTN M24 87 H2
ROY/SHW OL2 59 G2
TOT/BURYW BL8 26 B2
TOT/BURYW BL8 37 G2
WHTF M45 68 D5
Warwick Ct MDTN * M24 71 H4
OLDTF/WHR M16 125 H5
Warwick Dr BRAM/HZG SK7 185 E4
HALE/TIMP WA15 177 H3
SALE M33 155 E2
URM M41 123 E4
Warwick Gdns BOLS/LL BL3 63 E2
Warwick Gv DTN/ASHW M34 116 D5
Warwick Rd AUL OL6 105 F5
CCHDY M21 141 E2
FAIL M35 103 E5
HALE/TIMP WA15 177 H3
HTNM SK4 159 F3
IRL M44 150 C1
MDTN M24 88 A2
MPL/ROM SK6 161 H4
OLDTF/WHR M16 125 G3
RAD M26 52 A3
WALK M28 94 D1
Warwick Rd South
OLDTF/WHR M16 125 H5
Warwick St ANC M4 7 H3
BOL BL1 33 H2
CHAD OL9 8 A7
HULME M15 126 D2
PWCH M25 84 D3
SWIN M27 97 E1
WHIT OL12 11 G1
Wasdale Av BOLE BL2 35 G5
URM M41 123 E5
Wasdale Dr CHD/CHDH SK8 181 G1
MDTN M24 71 F2
Wasdale St ROCH OL11 42 B5
Wasdale Ter STLY SK15 119 F1
Wasdale Wk OLD OL1 9 J1
Wash Brook CHAD OL9 89 G3
Washbrook Av WALK M28 94 C1
Washbrook Dr STRET M32 139 G2
Wash Ford TOT/BURYW BL8 37 G2
Washford Dr NTHM/RTH M23 167 E1
Washington Ct BURY BL9 5 F2
Washington St BOLS/LL BL3 48 B3
CHAD OL9 8 B3
Wash La BURY BL9 5 H3
BURY BL9 5 K5
Wash Lane Ter BURY BL9 5 K4
Wash Ter TOT/BURYW BL8 37 G1
Washway Rd ALT WA14 153 H5
Washwood Cl LHULT * M38 80 C1
Wasnidge Wk HULME * M15 127 E3
Wasp Av ROCH OL11 43 F3
Wastdale Av BURY BL9 68 D1
Wastdale Rd NTHM/RTH M23 167 G5
Waste St OLD * OL1 9 K2
Wastwater St OLD OL1 74 D3
Watchgate Cl MDTN M24 71 E1
Waterbridge WALK M28 95 H5
Watercroft ROCH OL11 28 A2
Waterdale Cl WALK M28 94 C5
Waterdale Dr WHTF M45 68 D4
Waterfield Cl BURY BL9 27 G4
Waterfield Wy FAIL M35 103 F4
Waterfold La BURY BL9 5 K7
Waterfoot Cottages
HYDE SK14 134 D4
Waterford Av DID/WITH M20 156 C3
MPL/ROM SK6 162 D4
Waterfront Quay SALQ M50 125 G1
Watergate DTN/ASHW M34 116 D5
Water Ga UPML OL3 78 A4
Watergate Dr WHTN BL5 63 F5
Watergate La WHTN BL5 63 F5
Water Grove Rd DUK SK16 133 E1
Waterhouse Cl WHIT OL12 19 H3
Waterhouse Rd GTN M18 129 H4
Waterhouse St WHIT OL12 10 B5
Water La DROY M43 115 H4
FWTH BL4 65 F5
MILN OL16 44 D1
WILM/AE SK9 199 F3
Water Lane St RAD M26 67 E1
Waterloo Ct BURY * BL9 53 F1
Waterloo Gdns AUL OL6 105 H5
Waterloo Pl STKP * SK1 13 H4
Waterloo Rd AUL OL6 105 E5
BKLY M9 100 D1
BRAM/HZG SK7 184 A3
CHH M8 112 D1
MPL/ROM SK6 162 D4
POY/DIS SK12 195 H5
STKP SK1 13 H4
STLY SK15 119 F3
Waterloo St AUL OL6 118 C1
BOL BL1 3 F1
CHH M8 100 D2
CMANE M1 7 F6
OLD OL1 9 H4
TOT/BURYW BL8 4 A4
Watermans Cl BKLY M9 101 G2
Waterman Vw MILN OL16 11 J4
Watermead Cl EDGY/DAV SK3 171 H5
Watermeetings La
MPL/ROM SK6 162 D4
Watermill Cl MILN OL16 31 E5
Watermill Ct AULW OL7 104 D5
Watermillock Gdns BOL BL1 34 A3
Waterpark Rd BRO M7 99 H2
Water's Edge FWTH BL4 64 B2
MPL/ROM SK6 175 F1
UPML OL3 93 H2
Watersedge Cl CHD/CHDH SK8 183 E1
Waters Edge Fold OLD OL1 60 B5
Watersfield Cl CHD/CHDH SK8 182 C4
Watersheddings St OLDE OL4 75 G3
Waterside HYDE SK14 149 E1
MPL/ROM SK6 175 E4
TRPK M17 125 G2
Waterside Av MPL/ROM SK6 175 E4
Waterside Cl CCHDY M21 156 C2
HYDE SK14 149 E1
OLD OL1 60 B5
RAD M26 53 E5
Waterside Ct URM * M41 137 E1
Waterside La MILN OL16 11 H5
Waterside Rd BURY BL9 26 D1
Waterslea ECC M30 109 F3
Waterslea Dr BOL BL1 47 G2
Watersmead Cl BOL BL1 34 A4
Watersmead St BOL BL1 34 A4
Watersmeet STRET M32 124 D4
Waters Meeting Rd BOL BL1 34 A3
Waterson Av NEWH/MOS M40 101 H3
Waters Reach POY/DIS SK12 195 G2
TRPK M17 125 G2
Water Sreet RAD M26 67 F1
Water St AUL OL6 118 A2
BKLY M9 101 E2
BOL BL1 3 F4
CSLFD M3 6 A6
DTN/ASHW M34 131 G1
EDGW/EG BL7 22 C1
HYDE SK14 132 C5
MDTN M24 71 G4
MILN OL16 10 D6
ROY/SHW OL2 59 H5
STKP SK1 160 B3
STLY * SK15 119 F3
WHIT OL12 14 A5
Waterton Av MOSL OL5 92 C5
Waterton La MOSL OL5 92 C5
Waterview Cl MILN OL16 45 E3
Waterworks Rd OLDE OL4 75 H3
Watford Av RUSH/FAL M14 142 C1
Watkin Cl BRUN/LGST M13 127 G2
Watkins Dr PWCH M25 85 H4
Watkin St CSLFD * M3 112 C2
HYDE SK14 133 F3
MILN OL16 43 F2
Watling St TOT/BURYW BL8 24 C1
TOT/BURYW BL8 37 E5
Watlington Cl OLD OL1 75 G1
Watson Gdns WHIT OL12 18 C5
Watson Rd FWTH BL4 64 A4
Watson Sq STKP SK1 13 H4
Watson St CMANW M2 6 D7
DTN/ASHW M34 132 A5
ECC M30 109 F3
OLDE OL4 75 F4
RAD M26 52 B5
SWIN M27 97 E1
Watton Cl SWIN * M27 83 E5
Watts St BNG/LEV M19 144 A3
CHAD OL9 73 G5
OLDS OL8 90 A5
WHIT OL12 10 D4
Waugh Av FAIL M35 103 E4
Wavell Dr BURY BL9 68 D3
Wavell Rd WYTH/NTH M22 180 C2
Waveney Dr ALT WA14 165 F3
WILM/AE SK9 192 A5
Waveney Rd ROY/SHW OL2 59 H1
WYTH/NTH M22 168 D5
Waverley WHIT OL12 10 B4
Waverley Av FWTH BL4 81 G1
STRET M32 125 F5
Waverley Crs DROY M43 116 B2
Waverley Dr CHD/CHDH SK8 193 E1
Waverley Rd BKLY M9 101 G3
BOL BL1 33 H3
EDGY/DAV SK3 12 B7
HYDE SK14 147 G3
MDTN M24 71 H1
SALE M33 139 H5
SWIN M27 97 H3
WALK M28 94 C1
Waverley Rd West
NEWH/MOS M40 101 G4
Waverley St OLD OL1 75 E4
ROCH OL11 42 B5
Waverton Av HTNM SK4 144 C4
Waverton Rd RUSH/FAL M14 142 B2
Wavertree Rd BKLY M9 86 D3
Wayfarers Wy SWIN M27 96 D3
Wayland Rd GTN M18 129 G5
Wayland Rd South RDSH SK5 129 G5
Wayne Cl DROY M43 116 D1
Wayne St OP/CLY M11 115 H5
Wayside Dr POY/DIS SK12 194 D3
Wayside Gdns BRAM/HZG SK7 185 H2
Wayside Gv WALK M28 81 F3
Weald Cl BRUN/LGST M13 127 H2
Wealdstone Gv BOL * BL1 34 C4
Weardale Rd BKLY M9 86 C2
Weaste Av LHULT M38 80 C3
Weaste Dr SLFD M6 111 E2
Weaste La ORD M5 111 E3
Weaste Rd ORD M5 111 E4
Weatherall St North BRO M7 100 A3
Weatherley Cl OLDS OL8 104 C1

Weatherley Dr MPL/ROM SK6....174 C3
Weaver Av WALK M28 ....80 B5
Weaver Cl ALT WA14...............177 F3
Weaver Ct HULME * M15 ....126 C2
Weaver Dr BURY BL9.................27 G3
Weaverham Cl BRUN/LGST M13..128 C5
Weavers Ct BOLS/LL BL3............48 D4
  MDTN M24 ....71 G3
Weavers Gn FWTH BL4..............65 E5
Weavers La BRAM/HZG SK7 ......193 G1
Weavers Rd MDTN M24 ....71 G3
Webb Gv FWTH BL4.................149 F2
Webb La STKP SK1.....................13 K4
Webb St TOT/BURYW BL8............4 A3
Webdale Dr NEWH/MOS M40....101 H5
Weber Dr BOLS/LL BL3................49 E4
Webster Gv PWCH M25..............84 C5
Webster St BOLS/LL BL3..............49 G4
  MOSL OL5 ....92 D5
  OLDS OL8 ....9 G6
Wedgewood St
  NEWH/MOS M40 ....114 C1
Wedgwood Rd SWIN M27...........83 C5
Wedhurst St OLDE * OL4 ....75 F5
Weedall Av DID M5...................125 H2
Weedon St MILN OL16................11 G5
Weeton Av BOLE BL2..................50 C2
Weighbridge Ct IRL M44 ....121 F5
Weir Mill Rd MILN OL16..............31 F4
Weir St FAIL M35 ....102 D3
Welbeck Av CHAD OL9 ....88 C4
  LIT OL15...................................20 D2
Welbeck Cl MILN OL16...............31 F5
  WHTF M45 ....68 C2
Welbeck Gv BRO M7 ....99 H3
Welbeck Rd BOL BL1 ....47 H1
  ECC M30 ....109 H1
  HYDE SK14 ....148 A1
  MILN OL16...............................43 G2
  RDSH SK5 ....145 E3
  WALK M28 ....96 A4
Welbeck St GTN M18 ....129 G2
Welbeck St South AUL OL6 ....117 H3
Welburn Av NTHM/RTH M23.....180 C1
Welburn St ROCH OL11...............43 E1
Welbury Rd NTHM/RTH M23.....155 C5
Welby St BRUN/LGST M13 ....128 A4
Welch Rd HYDE SK14 ....133 E4
Welcomb Cl MPL/ROM SK6.......161 G2
Welcomb St OP/CLY M11 ....129 E3
Welcome Pde OLDS OL8.............91 F4
Welcroft St STKP SK1 ....13 H5
Weldon Av BOLS/LL BL3..............62 D2
Weldon Crs EDGY/DAV SK3 ....171 H5
Weldon Dr BKLY M9 ....87 E4
Weldon Rd ALT WA14................165 F3
Weld Rd DID/WITH M20 ....143 E4
Welford Av WALK M28 ....95 F2
Welford Cl BRAM/HZG * SK7 ......193 H5
Welford Gn DUH M8 ....72 D5
Welford Rd SLFD M6 ....112 A1
Welkin Rd MPL/ROM SK6..........160 D3
Wellacre Av URM M41 ....137 E1
Welland Av HEY OL10 ....40 B6
Welland Cl HULME * M15 ....126 C2
Welland Ct HULME M15 ....126 C2
Welland Rd ROY/SHW OL2 ....59 H1
  WILM/AE SK9 ....192 A5
Welland St OP/CLY M11 ....129 G5
  RDSH SK5 ....145 E2
Wellbank PWCH * M25 ....84 C4
Wellbank Cl AUL OL6 ....119 H5
Wellbank Cl BOLS/LL BL3............66 A1
  OLDS OL8 ....90 D3
Wellbank St TOT/BURYW BL8 .....26 A5
Wellbrook Gv WHIT OL12 ....28 C1
Wellbrow Ter WHIT OL12 ....29 G4
Wellens Wy MDTN M24 ....70 D5
Weller Av CCHDY M21 ....141 G4
  POY/DIS SK12 ....195 E5
Weller Cl POY/DIS SK12 ....195 E5
Wellesbourne Dr
  NTHM/RTH M23 ....167 G2
Wellesley Av GTN M18 ....129 G2
Wellfield Cl BURY BL9.................53 F3
Wellfield La HALE/TIMP WA15....166 D5
Wellfield Pl ROCH OL11 ....43 F1
Wellfield Rd BOLS/LL BL3 ....48 B4
  CHH M8 ....86 B2
  NTHM/RTH M23 ....167 H2
  OFTN SK2 ....172 D3
Wellfield St ROCH OL11 ....43 F1
Wellgate Av BNG/LEV M19 ....144 A3
Wellgreen Cl HALE/TIMP WA15...178 D1
Well Green Ldg
  HALE/TIMP * WA15 ....178 D1
Well Gv WHTF M45 ....68 B1
Wellhead Cl HULME M15 ....127 E3
Wellhouse Dr BKLY M9 ....88 B4
Well-i-Hole Rd UPML OL3...........93 G5
Welling St NEWH/MOS M40......102 D2
Welling St BOLE BL2 ....3 J1
Wellington Av OLDTF/WHR M16..141 G1
Wellington Cl SALE M33 ....153 H5
Wellington Clough AULW OL7....104 C4
Wellington Ct OLDS * OL8 ....90 A3
Wellington Crs
  OLDTF/WHR M16...................141 G1
Wellington Gv HULME M15 ....126 C2
  OFTN SK2 ....172 A2
Wellington Pl ALT WA14............177 G1
  MILN OL16...............................11 F5
Wellington Rd AUL OL6 ....119 G4
  BRAM/HZG SK7 ....186 A4
  BURY BL9 ....4 E7
  BURY BL9 ....53 F1
  CHH M8 ....100 C2
  ECC M30 ....109 H3
  HALE/TIMP WA15 ....166 A4
  OLDS OL8 ....89 H3
  OLDTF/WHR M16...................141 G1
  RAD/FAL M14.........................142 D4
  SWIN M27 ....97 E2
  UPML OL3 ....93 H1
Wellington Rd North HTNM SK4..144 A4
Wellington Rd South OFTN SK2 ...13 G7
Wellington Sq TOT/BURYW BL8 .....2 D1
Wellington St AUL OL6 ....118 A3
  BOLS/LL BL3 ....2 B6
  BRAM/HZG SK7 ....185 G1
  CHAD OL9 ....73 G4
  CSLFD M3 ....6 A2

DTN/ASHW M34 ....131 G2
FAIL * M35..............................103 F1
FWTH BL4 ....65 E4
GTN M18 ....130 C3
HYDE SK14 ....132 B5
LIT OL15...................................21 E5
MILN OL16...............................31 H5
OLDE OL4 ....9 G5
RAD M26 ....52 D5
STKP SK1 ....13 G4
STRET M32 ....139 H2
TOT/BURYW BL8 ....4 A4
WHIT OL12 ....10 D3
Wellington St East BRO M7 ....99 G3
Wellington St West BRO M7 ....99 G4
Wellington Ter ORD M5 ....111 E5
Wellington Vls TOT/BURYW BL8 ...37 H5
Well i' Th' La ROCH OL11 ....43 F1
Well La WHTF M45 ....68 C2
Well Md MPL/ROM SK6 ....161 F3
Wellmead Cl CHH M8 ....100 A5
Well Meadow HYDE SK14 ....132 C4
Well Meadow La LHULT M38 ......37 H1
Wellock St NEWH/MOS M40......101 H4
Well Rw HYDE SK14 ....149 H5
Wells Av CHAD OL9 ....73 F5
  PWCH M25 ....85 F5
Wells Ct CHD/CHDH SK8 ....181 H5
  MDTN M24 ....70 D5
  OP/CLY M11 ....116 A5
Wells Dr DUK SK16 ....132 B2
Wells Dr DUK SK16 ....132 B2
  HALE/TIMP WA15 ....166 C2
Wells Rd OLD OL1 ....60 D4
Wells St BURY BL9 ....8 C7
Wellstock La LHULT M38 ....36 A1
Well St BOL BL1 ....2 E4
  BOLE BL2 ....18 B5
  HEY OL10 ....40 D4
  ROCH OL11 ....43 F1
Well St West RAMS * BL0 ....16 C2
Wellwood Dr NEWH/MOS M40 ..101 H5
Wellyhole St OLDE OL4 ....91 G1
Welman Wy HALE/TIMP WA15...166 A5
Welney Rd OLDTF/WHR M16 .....126 A5
Welshpool Cl NTHM/RTH M23 ...156 A4
Welton Av DID/WITH M20 ....157 H4
Welton Cl WILM/AE SK9 ....201 A1
Welwyn Cl URM M41 ....123 F3
Welwyn Dr SLFD M6 ....97 F5
Welwyn Wk NEWH/MOS M40 ...114 A3
Wembley Gv RUSH/FAL M14 ......142 D5
Wembley Rd GTN M18 ....130 D4
Wembury St BKLY * M9 ....101 F3
Wembury St North BKLY M9 ......101 F2
Wemsley Gv BOLE BL2 ....34 C5
Wem St CHAD OL9 ....89 F5
Wemyss Av RDSH SK5 ....145 G2
Wendlebury Gn ROY/SHW OL2 ...59 H4
Wendon Rd NTHM/RTH M23 .....168 A4
Wendover Dr BOLS/LL BL3 ....47 F4
Wendover Rd NTHM/RTH M23 ...166 D2
  URM M41 ....138 B1
Wenfield Dr BKLY M9 ....87 H4
Wenlock Av AUL OL6 ....105 E5
Wenlock Cl OFTN SK2 ....173 H5
Wenlock Rd SALE M33 ....154 B4
Wenlock St SWIN M27 ....96 C2
Wenlock Wy WGTN/LGST M12 ..128 D2
Wenning Cl WHTF M45................69 F5
Wensleydale Av CHD/CHDH SK8..169 H5
Wensleydale Cl BURY BL9 ....27 H1
  NTHM/RTH M23 ....179 C1
  ROY/SHW OL2 ....59 H3
Wensley Dr BRO M7 ....98 D1
  CHD/CHDH SK8 ....169 H3
  RDSH SK5 ....160 A2
Wensley Wy MILN OL16 ....30 C5
Wentbridge Rd BOL BL1 ....2 B5
Wentworth Av FWTH BL4...........129 H5
  GTN M18 ....129 H5
  HALE/TIMP WA15 ....166 B3
  HEY OL10 ....56 A1
  IRL M44 ....121 D5
  SLFD M6 ....110 D2
  TOT/BURYW BL8 ....37 G2
  WHTF M45 ....68 A3
Wentworth Cl MDTN M24 ....71 G4
  MPL/ROM SK6 ....175 E1
  RAD M26 ....51 H5
Wentworth Dr BRAM/HZG SK7 ..184 B5
  SALE M33 ....154 A1
Wentworth Rd ECC M30 ....110 A1
  RDSH SK5 ....145 E2
  SWIN M27 ....96 C4
Wenworth Av URM M41 ....138 A2
Werneth Av HYDE SK14 ....148 A3
  RUSH/FAL M14 ....141 G4
Werneth Cl BRAM/HZG * SK7 .....173 F5
  DTN/ASHW M34 ....131 G5
Werneth Crs OLDS OL8 ....89 H3
Werneth Hall Rd OLDS OL8 ....8 C7
Werneth Hollow MPL/ROM SK6 ..147 E5
Werneth Low Rd
  MPL/ROM SK6 ....162 C2
Werneth Ri HYDE SK14 ....148 A3
Werneth Rd HYDE SK14 ....148 A1
  MPL/ROM SK6 ....161 G3
Werneth St DTN/ASHW M34 ......131 G5
  STKP SK1 ....160 C3
Wesley Cl WHIT OL12 ....30 C1
Wesley Ct WALK * M28 ....81 E5
Wesley Ms BOLE * BL2 ....3 J4
Wesley Sq URM M41 ....137 H1
Wesley St BOLS/LL * BL3 ....48 D4
  BRAM/HZG SK7 ....185 F1
  ECC M30 ....109 E3
  EDGW/EG BL7 ....23 F3
  FAIL M35 ....103 F1
  FWTH BL4 ....65 H3
  HEY OL10 ....40 D4
  MILN OL16...............................10 C5
  OP/CLY M11 ....114 D5
  ROY/SHW OL2 ....74 B1
  STKP SK1 ....13 H4
  STRET M32 ....125 F4
  SWIN M27 ....97 E2

TOT/BURYW BL8 ....25 H4
  WHIT * OL12 ....19 G5
Wessenden Bank East
  OFTN SK2 ....173 E4
Wessenden Bank West
  OFTN SK2 ....173 E4
Wessex Park Cl ROY/SHW OL2 ....60 A1
Westage Gdns NTHM/RTH M23 ..167 H2
West Ashton St SALQ M50 ....111 G5
West Av ALT WA14 ....164 D4
  BNG/LEV M19 ....143 G4
  CHD/CHDH SK8 ....181 H5
  FWTH BL4 ....64 C4
  GTN * M18 ....129 H3
  NEWH/MOS M40 ....102 C1
  STLY SK15 ....119 H1
  WALK M28 ....68 B2
  WHTF M45 ....68 B2
West Bank OP/CLY M11 ....130 B1
  WILM/AE SK9 ....201 B5
Westbank Rd DID/WITH M20 .....158 A1
  HOR/BR BL6 ....47 E3
West Bank St ORD M5 ....112 B5
Westbourne Av BOLS/LL BL3 ....64 B1
  FWTH BL4 ....64 C4
  WHTF M45 ....68 A3
Westbourne Gv BKLY M9 ....101 G2
  DID/WITH M20 ....142 B5
  RDSH SK5 ....145 F5
  SALE M33 ....154 B2
Westbourne Pk URM M41 ....123 G5
Westbourne Range GTN M18 .....130 A5
Westbourne Rd
  DTN/ASHW M34 ....146 B1
  ECC M30 ....109 E1
  RUSH/FAL M14 ....143 E3
  URM M41 ....138 C1
Westbourne St CHAD OL9 ....8 D7
Westbrook Cl BOLE BL2 ....3 G7
  ROCH OL11 ....57 C5
Westbrook Ct BOLE * BL2 ....3 G7
Westbrook Rd SWIN M27 ....97 F5
  TRPK M17 ....124 D1
Westbrook Sq WGTN/LGST M12 ..128 D2
Westbrook St BOLE BL2 ....3 H7
Westbury Av SALE M33 ....153 F5
Westbury Cl TOT/BURYW BL8 ....37 F5
Westbury Dr MPL/ROM SK6 ......174 D5
Westbury Rd CHH M8 ....100 B1
Westbury St AUL OL6 ....118 B2
  HYDE SK14 ....132 B5
Westbury Wy DUK SK16 ....133 C2
Westcombe Dr TOT/BURYW BL8 ...37 H2
Westcott Av DID/WITH M20 ....142 B5
Westcott Cl BOLE BL2 ....3 J7
Westcott Gv ROY/SHW OL2 ....59 H4
Westcourt Rd BOLS/LL BL3 ....63 G1
  SALE M33 ....154 B1
Westcraig Av NEWH/MOS M40 ..102 A1
West Craven St ORD M5 ....126 A1
Westcroft Rd DID/WITH M20 .....158 A2
West Crown Av ORD M5 ....112 A5
Westdale Gdns BNG/LEV M19 ....158 C1
Westdean Crs BNG/LEV M19 ......158 C1
West Dean St SALQ M50 ....112 B4
West Downs Rd CHD/CHDH SK8 ..182 C1
West Dr BKLY M9 ....169 H5
  CHD/CHDH SK8 ....169 H5
  DROY M43 ....116 A4
  SLFD M6 ....98 B4
  SWIN M27 ....97 G3
West Duke St ORD M5 ....112 A5
West Egerton St ORD M5 ....112 A4
West End Av CHD/CHDH SK8 .....169 F3
West End Rd AUL OL6 ....8 C3
Westerdale OLDE OL4 ....91 F1
Westerdale Dr BOLS/LL BL3 ....47 H4
  ROY/SHW OL2 ....72 D4
Westerham Av ORD M5 ....111 H4
Western Av SWIN M27 ....97 C5
Wester Hill Rd OLDS OL8 ....104 D1
Westering Wy
  OLDTF/WHR M16...................126 D5
Western Access Dr
  TRPK * M17 ....110 A5
Western Cir BNG/LEV M19 ....158 A3
Western Rd DTN/ASHW M34 .....143 G5
Western Rd URM M41 ....137 F2
Western St GTN M18 ....129 H2
  SLFD M6 ....111 F2
Westerton Ct BOLS/LL BL3 ....48 B2
Westfield SLFD M6 ....111 F1
Westfield Av MDTN M24 ....71 H5
Westfield Cl ROCH OL11..............28 C2
Westfield Dr MPL/ROM SK6 ....162 A1
Westfield Gv DTN/ASHW M34 ....131 F5
Westfield Rd BOLS/LL BL3 ....63 E2
  CCHDY M21 ....141 E2
  CHD/CHDH SK8 ....182 C4
  DROY M43 ....115 H5
Westfields HALE/TIMP WA15 .....178 A4
Westfield St BRO M7 ....99 G1
  CHAD OL9 ....73 H4
Westgate HALE/TIMP WA15 ......177 H2
  SALE M33 ....154 B2
  URM M41 ....138 A2
  WILM/AE SK9 ....199 F5
Westgate Av BKLY * M9 ....99 E5
  BOL BL1 ....48 B2
  BURY BL9 ....4 C7
  RAMS BL0 ....16 D4
Westgate Cl WHIT OL12 ....18 A1
Westgate Dr SWIN M27 ....97 F3
Westgate Rd SLFD M6 ....110 C2
Westgate St AULW OL7 ....117 H4
West Grove Av BOL BL1 ....22 D5
West High St SMD M6 ....111 H5
West Hill ROCH * OL11 ....42 D5
Westholm Av HTNM SK4 ....144 A4
Westholme Ct WILM/AE SK9 .....198 D7
Westholme Rd DID/WITH M20 ...157 G2
  WHTF M45 ....69 F5

West Hope St ORD M5 ....112 A4
Westhulme Av OLD OL1 ....74 A3
Westhulme St OLD OL1 ....74 A3
Westhulme Wy OLD OL1 ....73 H1
Westinghouse Rd TRPK M17 ......124 C2
West King St CSLFD M3 ....6 E2
Westland Av BOL BL1 ....80 D1
  FWTH BL4 ....80 D1
  STKP * SK1 ....160 C5
Westland Dr BKLY M9 ....87 E3
The Westlands SWIN M27 ....97 G4
Westlands WHTF M45 ....84 C1
West Lea DTN/ASHW M34 ....131 H5
Westlea Dr GTN M18 ....129 G5
Westleigh Dr PWCH M25 ....85 G4
Westleigh St BKLY M9 ....101 F2
Westmarsh Cl BOL BL1 ....2 D1
West Marwood St BRO M7 ....99 H4
Westmead Dr CHH M8 ....99 H5
Westmeade Rd WALK M28 ....80 D2
West Meadow RDSH SK5 ....145 F2
Westmere Dr BKLY M9 ....100 A4
Westminister Av
  AUL OL6 ....105 C5
Westminister Rd
  ROY/SHW OL2 ....60 A1
Westminster Av AUL OL6 ....105 G5
  FWTH BL4 ....64 D4
  HTNM SK4 ....144 D4
  RAD M26 ....51 G5
  WHTF M45 ....68 C4
Westminster Cl ALT WA14 ....117 H1
  DUK SK16 ....118 D5
Westminster Cl RDSH * SK5 ....145 G5
  WHIT OL12 ....20 A2
Westminster Rd
  ECC M30 ....109 H2
  FAIL M35 ....103 G2
  HALE/TIMP WA15 ....179 G1
  URM M41 ....125 G4
  WALK M28 ....81 E5
Westminster St BNG/LEV * M19 ..144 A2
  BURY BL9 ....5 J4
  FWTH BL4 ....64 D4
  OLD OL1 ....75 E4
  ROCH OL11 ....42 C1
  SWIN M27 ....96 C1
Westminster Wy DUK SK16 ....132 C2
Westmoreland Cl ALT WA14 ......177 E4
  BURY BL9 ....53 F3
Westmorland Av AULW OL7 ......117 H1
  DUK SK16 ....118 D5
Westmorland Cl RDSH * SK5 ......145 G5
  WHIT OL12 ....20 A2
Westmorland Dr RDSH SK5 ....145 G5
  WHIT OL12 ....20 A2
Westmorland Rd
  DTN/ASHW M34 ....157 F4
  ECC M30 ....097 F5
  PART M31 ....150 D4
  SALE M33 ....154 D4
  URM M41 ....138 B2
West Mosley St CMANW M2 ....7 H3
Westmount Cl NEWH/MOS M40 ..100 D4
West Oak Pl CHD/CHDH * SK8 ...182 C3
Weston Av MILN OL16 ....43 C2
  NEWH/MOS M40 ....102 D1
  SWIN M27 ....83 E3
  URM M41 ....138 A2
Weston Dr CHD/CHDH SK8 ....171 H5
  DTN/ASHW M34 ....144 B5
  WYTH/NTH M22 ....168 D1
Weston Rd IRL M44 ....122 B6
  WILM/AE SK9 ....200 A4
Weston St BOLS/LL BL3 ....49 C5
  MILN OL16...............................11 F6
  NEWH/MOS * M40 ....114 A3
  RDSH * SK5 ....159 H2
Westover MPL/ROM SK6 ....173 H1
Westover Rd URM M41 ....122 D5
Westover St SWIN M27 ....96 C1
West Pk HYDE SK14 ....147 H4
West Park Rd BRAM/HZG SK7 ...193 G4
  STKP SK1 ....160 C4
West Pl BNG/LEV M19 ....143 G4
Westray Crs SLFD * M6 ....111 G4
Westray Rd BRUN/LGST M13 .....143 F1
West Rd ALT WA14 ....177 F2
  PWCH M25 ....84 C2
  STRET M32 ....124 B4
West Row PWCH M25 ....84 D5
West Starkey St HEY OL10 ....40 D3
West St AUL OL6 ....118 A2
  BOL BL1 ....48 B2
  DUK SK16 ....118 A4
  EDGY/DAV SK3 ....171 G4
  FAIL M35 ....102 D3
  FWTH BL4 ....65 E5
  HEY OL10 ....41 E5
  HYDE SK14 ....132 C3
  LIT OL15...................................21 E5
  MDTN M24 ....71 E3
  MILN OL16...............................31 H5
  OLD OL1 ....9 F3
  OLDE OL4 ....91 G2
  OP/CLY M11 ....115 C5
  STLY SK15 ....119 E3
  WILM/AE SK9 ....201 B4
West View Gv WHTF M45 ....68 C2
West View Rd WYTH/NTH M22 ..168 D1
Westville Gdns BNG/LEV M19 ....158 B1
West Wk EDGW/EG BL7 ....22 D2
Westward Ho MILN OL16 ....31 G5
Westward Rd WILM/AE SK9 ....199 E4
West Wy BOL BL1 ....22 B5
  LHULT M38 ....80 B2
Westway BKLY M9 ....87 F5
  DROY M43 ....130 B1
  OLDE OL4 ....91 H2

ROY/SHW OL2 ....60 A3
Westwood Av BRO M7 ....99 H2
  HALE/TIMP WA15 ....166 A2
  HYDE SK14 ....133 C5
  NEWH/MOS * M40 ....102 D1
  URM M41 ....139 E2
Westwood Cl FWTH BL4 ....65 E4
Westwood Crs ECC M30 ....109 E1
Westwood Dr CHAD OL9 ....8 C3
  SALE M33 ....154 C4
  SWIN M27 ....97 H4
Westwood Rd BOL BL1 ....48 B1
  CHD/CHDH SK8 ....181 G4
  OFTN SK2 ....172 C5
Westwood St RUSH/FAL M14 .....127 E4
Westworth Cl BOL BL1 ....2 B2
Wetheral Dr BOLS/LL BL3 ....63 H1
Wetherall St BNG/LEV M19 ....144 A2
Wetherby Dr BRAM/HZG * SK7 ..185 H4
  ROY/SHW OL2 ....58 D4
Wetherby Cl OP/CLY M11 ....129 E1
Weybourne Av BKLY M9 ....87 H5
Weybourne Dr MPL/ROM SK6 ...161 G2
Weybourne Gv BOLE BL2 ....34 C2
Weybridge Rd ANC M4 ....113 H3
Weybrook Rd HTNM SK4 ....144 A4
Weycroft Cl BOLE BL2 ....35 G2
Wey Gates Dr HALE/TIMP WA15..188 C1
Weyhill Rd NTHM/RTH M23 ....167 H5
Weylands Gv SLFD M6 ....97 C5
Weymouth Rd AUL OL6 ....105 H4
  ECC M30 ....109 E1
Weymouth St BOL BL1 ....33 H4
Weythorne Dr BOL BL1 ....40 A1
  BURY BL9 ....52 A2
Whalley Av BNG/LEV M19 ....144 A2
  BOL BL1 ....2 B2
  CCHDY M21 ....141 E4
  LIT OL15...................................20 D2
  OLDTF/WHR M16...................126 C4
  SALE M33 ....154 D1
  URM M41 ....123 H5
Whalley Cl HALE/TIMP WA15 .....166 A1
  MILN * OL16 ....31 F5
  WHTF M45 ....68 C3
Whalley Dr TOT/BURYW BL8 ....37 F4
Whalley Gdns WHIT OL12 ....29 F2
Whalley Gv AUL OL6 ....105 F5
  OLDTF/WHR M16...................126 C4
Whalley Rd HALE/TIMP WA15 ....178 B2
  HEY OL10 ....40 B4
  MDTN M24 ....71 G2
  OFTN SK2 ....172 D2
  WHIT OL12 ....18 C4
  WHTF M45 ....68 C3
Whalley St NEWH/MOS M40 ......114 A3
Wham Bar Dr HEY OL10 ....40 B4
Wham Bottom La WHIT OL12 ......18 A4
Wham St HEY OL10 ....41 E5
Wharf Cl CMANE M1 ....7 J5
Wharfedale Av
  NEWH/MOS M40 ....101 H1
Wharfedale Rd RDSH SK5 ....144 D3
Wharf End TRPK M17 ....124 D2
Wharf Rd ALT WA14 ....165 G2
  SALE M33 ....154 C4
Wharfside Av ECC M30 ....109 G5
Wharfside Wy (Trafford Park Rd)
  TRPK M17 ....125 F2
Wharf St CHAD OL9 ....89 G4
  DUK SK16 ....118 B4
  HTNM SK4 ....144 B5
Wharmton Ri OLDE OL4 ....93 E1
Wharmton Vw MOSL OL5 ....93 H1
  UPML OL3 ....93 F4
Wharton Av CCHDY M21 ....141 G4
Wharton La LHULT M38 ....79 C3
Wharton Ldg ECC M30 ....109 H2
Wheat Cl BRUN/LGST M13 ....127 H3
Wheater's Crs BRO M7 ....112 B1
Wheater's St BRO M7 ....112 B1
Wheater's Ter BRO M7 ....112 C1
Wheatfield STLY SK15 ....134 B1
Wheatfield Cl BRAM/HZG * SK7 ...27 G4
Wheatfield St BOLE BL2 ....49 G4
  MPL/ROM SK6 ....161 G2
Wheatfields SWIN M27 ....83 C5
Wheatley Wk WGTN/LGST M12 ..128 D2
Wheeldale OLDE OL4 ....74 B1
Wheeldale Cl BOL BL1 ....33 H4
Wheelock Cl WILM/AE SK9 ....200 A4
Wheelton Cl TOT/BURYW BL8 ......37 H2
Wheelwright Cl MPL/ROM SK6 ...175 E1
  ROCH * OL11 ....42 B5
Wheelwright Dr MILN OL16 ....11 H6
Whelan Av BURY BL9 ....53 F2
Wheler St OP/CLY M11 ....115 C5
Whernside Av AUL OL6 ....95 H2
  NEWH/MOS M40 ....101 H1
Wherside Cl HTNM SK4 ....13 H1
Whetstone Hill Cl OLD OL1 ....75 F3
Whetstone Hill La OLD OL1 ....75 F2
Whewell Av RAD M26 ....67 H4
Whickham Ct RUSH/FAL M14 .....127 C5
Whiley St BRUN/LGST M13 ....128 A1
Whimberry Cl ORD M5 ....126 A1
Whimberry Wy OLDE OL4 ....75 H4
Whimbrel Rd OFTN SK2 ....173 H4
Whinberry Rd ALT WA14 ....165 E2
Whinberry Wy OLDE OL4 ....75 H4
Whinchat Cl OFTN SK2 ....173 H5
Whinfell Dr MDTN M24 ....70 C5
Whinfield Cl WALK M28 ....78 D5
Whinmoor Wk BKLY M9 ....87 F1
Whins Av FWTH BL4 ....64 A4
Whins Crest HOR/BR BL6 ....46 D2
Whinslee Dr HOR/BR BL6 ....46 A3
Whinstone Wy OLD OL1 ....72 C5
Whipp St HEY OL10 ....40 C3
Whirley Cl HTNM SK4 ....159 C1
Whiston Dr BOLE BL2 ....49 H5
Whiston Rd CHH M8 ....100 C2
Whitaker St MDTN M24 ....57 G4
Whitbrook Wy MDTN M24 ....56 A3
Whitburn Av BRUN/LGST M13 ...143 F1
Whitburn Cl BOLS/LL BL3 ....48 B3
Whitburn Dr TOT/BURYW BL8 .....37 H1

Whitburn Rd NTHM/RTH M23 167 H5
Whitby Av HEY OL10 40 D3
OLDTF/WHR M16 126 C5
RUSH/FAL M14 143 F3
SLFD M6 110 D2
URM M41 138 D1
Whitby Cl CHD/CHDH SK8 169 H3
POY/DIS SK12 194 D2
TOT/BURYW BL8 37 E4
Whitby Rd OLDS OL8 91 F4
RUSH/FAL M14 143 E3
Whitby St MDTN M24 72 B3
ROCH OL11 43 F1
Whitchurch Dr
OLDTF/WHR M16 126 C3
Whitchurch Gdns BOL BL1 33 H4
Whitchurch Rd DID/WITH M20 142 A4
Whitchurch St BRO M7 112 D2
Whiteacre Rd AUL OL6 118 C1
Whiteacres SWIN M27 96 B3
White Bank Av RDSH SK5 160 D2
White Bank Rd OLDS OL8 104 A1
Whitebarn Rd WILM/AE SK9 201 C5
Whitebeam Cl
HALE/TIMP WA15 167 F4
MILN OL16 44 D3
SLFD M6 111 H2
Whitebeam Ct SLFD * M6 111 H2
White Birk Cl TOT/BURYW BL8 26 A1
White Brook La UPML OL3 78 B4
Whitebrook Rd RUSH/FAL M14 142 C2
Whitecar Av NEWH/MOS M40 102 D1
White Carr La BURY BL9 27 H2
Whitecarr La HALE/TIMP WA15 179 F1
Whitechapel St DID/WITH M20 157 G3
White City Wy OLDTF/WHR M16 125 H3
Whitecliff Cl RUSH/FAL M14 127 H5
Whitecroft Av ROY/SHW OL2 60 C2
Whitecroft Dr TOT/BURYW BL8 37 E4
Whitecroft Gdns BNG/LEV M19 158 B2
Whitecroft Rd BOL BL1 32 D5
MPL/ROM SK6 187 H2
Whitecroft St OLD OL1 75 F3
Whitefield HTNM SK4 159 G3
Whitefield Av ROCH OL11 28 C3
Whitefield Rd BURY BL9 53 E2
MPL/ROM SK6 161 F2
SALE M33 154 A1
Whitegate LIT OL15 20 B4
Whitegate Av CHAD OL9 89 E3
Whitegate Cl NEWH/MOS M40 102 D1
Whitegate Dr BOL BL1 34 A1
ORD M5 111 E2
SWIN M27 83 G5
Whitegate La CHAD OL9 89 E3
Whitegate Pk URM M41 137 F1
Whitegate Rd CHAD OL9 88 C4
Whitegates Cl
HALE/TIMP WA15 166 C4
Whitegates La OLDE OL4 76 C2
Whitegates Rd CHD/CHDH SK8 170 A4
MDTN M24 57 F5
Whitehall Cl WILM/AE SK9 199 F5
Whitehall La BOL BL1 22 C5
OLDE OL4 61 E5
Whitehall Rd DID/WITH M20 157 H3
SALE M33 154 C4
Whitehall St OLD OL1 9 H1
WHIT OL12 10 C3
White Hart Meadow MDTN M24 71 H2
White Hart St HYDE SK14 132 C4
Whitehaven Gdns
DID/WITH M20 157 F4
Whitehaven Rd BRAM/HZG SK7 193 F2
Whitehead Crs RAD M26 66 A5
TOT/BURYW BL8 37 H1
Whitehead Rd CCHDY M21 140 C3
SWIN M27 83 G5
Whitehead St MILN * OL16 31 F5
MILN OL16 45 G2
ROY/SHW OL2 59 G1
WALK M28 81 E3
White Hill Cl WHIT OL12 18 C4
Whitehill Dr NEWH/MOS M40 101 H3
Whitehill St HTNM SK4 159 H2
Whitehill St West HTNM SK4 159 G2
Whiteholme Av CCHDY M21 156 C2
White Horse Gdns SWIN * M27 96 B4
White Horse Mdw MILN * OL16 43 H4
White House Av CHH M8 85 H4
Whitehouse Av OLDE OL4 91 F2
White House Cl HEY OL10 56 A2
Whitehouse Dr
HALE/TIMP WA15 178 C4
NTHM/RTH M23 167 H4
Whitehouse La ALT WA14 164 A2
Whitehurst Rd HTNM SK4 158 C2
Whitekirk Cl BRUN/LGST M13 127 G2
White Lady Cl WALK M28 80 A4
Whitelake Av URM M41 122 C5
Whitelake Vw URM M41 122 B5
Whiteland Av BOLS/LL BL3 48 A4
Whitelands DUK SK16 118 B3
Whitelands Rd AUL OL6 118 B3
Whitelea Dr EDGY/DAV SK3 171 G4
Whitelees Rd LIT OL15 20 D3
Whitelegge St TOT/BURYW BL8 37 G2
Whiteley Dr MDTN M24 72 B5
Whiteley Pl ALT WA14 165 G3
Whiteley St CHAD OL9 89 G3
OP/CLY M11 115 E3
White Lion Brow BOL BL1 2 C4
Whitelow Rd CCHDY M21 140 D3
HTNM SK4 158 D3
RAMS BL0 17 F3
Whitemead St DTN/ASHW M34 131 G1
Whitemoss WHIT * OL12 29 E1
White Moss Av CCHDY M21 141 F3
White Moss Rd BKLY M9 87 F4
Whitemoss Rd East BKLY M9 87 G3
Whiteoak Cl MPL/ROM SK6 174 D2
Whiteoak Rd RUSH/FAL M14 142 D3
Whiteoak Vw BOLS/LL BL3 50 A4
Whites Cft SWIN M27 97 E2
Whiteside Cl ORD M5 111 E3
Whiteside Fold WHIT OL12 28 D2
Whitestone Cl HOR/BR BL6 47 E3
Whitestone Wk
BRUN/LGST * M13 128 A3
White St HULME M15 126 C2
SLFD M6 111 F4
TOT/BURYW BL8 37 G5
White Swallows Rd SWIN M27 97 F4
Whitethorn Av BNG/LEV M19 143 H4
OLDTF/WHR M16 126 C5
Whitethorn Cl MPL/ROM SK6 174 D2
Whitewater Dr BRO M7 98 C3
Whiteway St BKLY M9 101 F3
Whitewell Cl BURY BL9 53 E2
MILN OL16 11 J4
Whitewillow Cl FAIL M35 103 F4
Whitfield Crs MILN OL16 45 E3
Whitfield Dr MILN OL16 44 D4
Whitfield Ri ROY/SHW OL2 44 D5
Whitfield St CSLFD M3 113 F2
Whiting Gv BOLS/LL BL3 47 F3
Whitland Av BOL BL1 47 G1
Whitland Dr OLDS OL8 89 G5
Whit La SLFD M6 98 C4
Whitley Gdns HALE/TIMP WA15 166 C2
Whitley Pl HALE/TIMP WA15 166 C2
Whitley Rd HTNM SK4 159 E3
NEWH/MOS M40 113 H1
Whitley St BOLS/LL BL3 65 E2
Whitlow Av ALT WA14 165 E1
Whitman St BKLY M9 101 G2
Whitmore Rd RUSH/FAL M14 142 C2
Whitnall Cl OLDTF/WHR M16 126 D5
Whitnall St HYDE * SK14 132 C3
Whitsand Rd WYTH/NTH M22 168 D4
Whitsbury Av GTN M18 129 G5
Whitstable Cl CHAD OL9 89 G1
Whitstable Rd
NEWH/MOS * M40 102 B1
Whitsters Hollow BOL BL1 33 E3
Whittaker Dr LIT OL15 31 G1
Whittaker Fold LIT * OL15 21 H3
Whittaker La LIT OL15 21 G4
PWCH M25 85 F3
ROCH OL11 28 A2
Whittaker St CHAD OL9 73 G5
NEWH/MOS M40 101 H2
RAD M26 52 C5
ROCH * OL11 28 B2
WGTN/LGST M12 114 A5
Whittingham Dr RAMS BL0 16 D5
Whittingham Gv OLD OL1 74 A4
Whittington St AULW OL7 117 H4
Whittlebrook Gv HEY OL10 56 B2
Whittle Dr ROY/SHW OL2 60 C1
WALK M28 81 E2
Whittle Gv BOL BL1 33 E5
WALK M28 81 F4
Whittle La HEY OL10 55 F4
Whittles Av DTN/ASHW M34 131 H5
Whittle's Cft CMANE * M1 7 J5
Whittles St WHIT OL12 14 C1
Whittle St ANC * M4 7 H3
LIT OL15 20 C3
SWIN M27 96 D3
TOT/BURYW * BL8 37 H3
WALK M28 81 F4
Whitwell Wy GTN M18 129 F3
Whitworth Cl AUL OL6 118 B1
Whitworth La RUSH/FAL M14 143 E2
Whitworth Rake WHIT OL12 14 C5
Whitworth Rd WHIT OL12 10 C1
Whitworth Sq WHIT OL12 14 C5
Whitworth St CMANE M1 7 G7
MILN * OL16 30 D1
MILN OL16 31 G5
OP/CLY M11 129 F1
Whitworth St East OP/CLY M11 129 F1
Whitworth St West CMANE M1 6 D7
Whixhall Av WGTN/LGST M12 128 B2
Whoolden St FWTH BL4 64 D3
Whowell Fold BOL BL1 33 F3
Whowell St BOLS/LL BL3 2 C7
Wibbersley Pk URM * M41 137 G1
Wichbrook Rd WALK M28 80 A4
Wicheaves Crs WALK M28 80 A4
The Wicheries LHULT M38 80 A4
Wicken Bank HEY OL10 56 B2
Wickenby Dr SALE M33 154 B2
Wicken St OFTN SK2 172 D2
Wickentree Holt WHIT OL12 28 D1
Wickentree La FAIL M35 103 F1
Wicker La HALE/TIMP WA15 178 C4
Wicket Gv SWIN M27 82 D3
Wickliffe Pl ROCH OL11 30 A5
Wickliffe St BOL * BL1 2 D3
Wicklow Av EDGY/DAV SK3 171 E2
Wicklow Dr WYTH/NTH M22 180 D2
Wicklow Gv OLDS OL8 90 B4
Widcombe Dr BOLS/LL BL3 50 C4
Widdop St CHAD OL9 8 C3
Widecombe Cl URM * M41 123 E4
Widgeon Cl POY/DIS SK12 194 C3
RUSH/FAL M14 142 C3
Widgeon Rd ALT WA14 165 E1
Widnes St OP/CLY * M11 129 F1
Wigan Rd BOLS/LL BL3 47 H5
Wiggins Wk RUSH/FAL * M14 127 H5
Wigley St WGTN/LGST M12 128 B1
Wigmore Rd CHH M8 100 C3
Wigmore St AUL OL6 118 C1
Wigsby Av NEWH/MOS M40 102 B1
Wigwam Cl POY/DIS SK12 194 D3
Wike St TOT/BURYW BL8 4 A3
Wilbraham Rd CCHDY M21 141 E3
OLDTF/WHR M16 141 H2
WALK M28 81 E4
Wilburn St ORD M5 112 C5
Wilby Av BOLS/LL BL3 50 D4
Wilby Cl TOT/BURYW * BL8 38 A1
Wilby St CHH M8 100 C4
Wilcock Cl OLDTF/WHR M16 126 D4
Wilcott Dr SALE M33 153 H1
WILM/AE SK9 201 A1
Wilcott Rd CHD/CHDH SK8 169 F4
Wildbank Cha STLY SK15 134 B1
Wildbrook Cl LHULT M38 79 D4
Wildbrook Crs OLDS OL8 90 D4
Wildbrook Gv LHULT M38 79 D4
Wildbrook Rd LHULT M38 79 D3
Wildbrook Ter OLDS * OL8 90 D4
Wild Clough HYDE SK14 148 A2
Wildcroft Av NEWH/MOS M40 101 H1
Wilderswood Cl DID/WITH M20 157 H1
Wilde St DTN/ASHW M34 131 G5
Wildhouse La LIT OL15 31 G2
Wildman La FWTH BL4 64 A4
Wildmoor Av OLDE OL4 91 H4
Wilds Pl RAMS * BL0 16 C3
Wild St BRAM/HZG * SK7 185 E2
DUK SK16 118 C5
HEY OL10 41 F4
MPL/ROM SK6 161 G4
OLD OL1 9 K2
OLDE OL4 91 H1
ROY/SHW OL2 60 B3
Wildwood Cl RAMS BL0 16 B4
Wilford Av SALE M33 154 B4
Wilfred Dr BURY BL9 5 J1
Wilfred Rd ECC M30 108 D5
WALK M28 81 E5
Wilfred St EDGW/EG * BL7 23 F4
NEWH/MOS M40 101 H2
Wilfrid St SWIN M27 97 E2
Wilkes St OLD OL1 75 G1
Wilkin Cft CHD/CHDH SK8 182 B3
Wilkins La WILM/AE SK9 190 D2
Wilkinson Av BOLS/LL BL3 50 D5
Wilkinson Rd BOL BL1 33 G1
HTNM SK4 12 E1
Wilkinson St AUL OL6 117 H2
HTNM SK4 12 E1
MDTN M24 71 G4
SALE M33 155 E1
Wilks Av WYTH/NTH M22 181 E2
Willand Cl BOLE BL2 50 D3
Willand Dr BOLE BL2 50 D4
Willan Rd BKLY M9 86 D3
ECC M30 109 H3
Willard St BRAM/HZG * SK7 185 E1
Willaston Cl CCHDY M21 140 D4
Willbutts La ROCH OL11 29 F2
Willdale Cl OP/CLY M11 114 D3
Willdor Gv EDGY/DAV SK3 171 E3
Willenhall Rd NTHM/RTH M23 156 B4
Willerby Rd BRO M7 99 H5
Willesden Av BRUN/LGST M13 128 B5
Will Griffith Wk OP/CLY M11 114 B5
William Chadwick Cl
NEWH/MOS M40 113 H2
William Cl URM M41 138 B2
William Greenwood Cl HEY OL10 40 D4
William Henry St ROCH OL11 43 F2
William Jessop Ct CMANE M1 7 K5
William Kay Cl HULME M15 126 D4
William Lister Cl
NEWH/MOS * M40 115 G1
Williams Crs CHAD OL9 89 E4
Williamson Av MPL/ROM SK6 161 H2
RAD M26 52 A3
Williamson La DROY M43 116 C5
Williamson St ANC M4 113 G2
AUL OL6 118 A3
RDSH SK5 144 D4
Williamson's Yd OLD * OL1 75 E5
Williams Rd GTN M18 129 F3
NEWH/MOS M40 102 A3
Williams St BOLS/LL BL3 66 A1
GTN M18 129 F4
William St AULW OL7 117 G3
CSLFD M3 6 B3
DID/WITH M20 157 G3
FAIL M35 103 F1
LIT OL15 20 D3
MDTN M24 72 A4
MILN OL16 20 A4
RAD M26 52 C5
ROCH OL11 30 A5
STKP SK1 172 C2
WGTN/LGST M12 114 A5
WHIT OL12 14 B4
Willingdon Cl TOT/BURYW BL8 26 D4
Willingdon Dr PWCH M25 85 E2
Willis Rd EDGY/DAV SK3 171 H3
Willis St BOLS/LL BL3 48 B5
Willock St BRO M7 99 H4
Willoughby Av DID/WITH M20 157 H2
Willoughby Cl SALE M33 154 B1
Willow Av CHD/CHDH SK8 182 C2
MDTN M24 72 B5
RDSH SK5 160 A2
URM M41 138 D1
Willow Bank CHD/CHDH SK8 192 D1
OLDE OL4 75 H4
RUSH/FAL M14 142 D3
Willowbank RAD M26 67 F4
Willowbank Av BOLE BL2 3 K7
Willow Bank Cl OFTN SK2 173 E2
Willowbrook Av
NEWH/MOS M40 101 H3
Willow Cl BOLS/LL BL3 48 A5
DUK SK16 133 E1
POY/DIS SK12 195 F4
Willow Ct MPL/ROM SK6 175 E4
SALE M33 155 F1
Willowdale Av CHD/CHDH SK8 181 G2
Willowdene Cl EDGW/EG BL7 23 E3
NEWH/MOS M40 100 D5
Willow Dr SALE M33 153 H4
WILM/AE SK9 192 A4
Willowfield Rd OLDE OL4 75 G2
Willow Fold DROY M43 116 C5
Willow Gv CHAD * OL9 73 G4
DTN/ASHW M34 131 F5
GTN * M18 129 H4
MPL/ROM SK6 175 E4
Willow Hill Rd CHH M8 86 B5
Willow Lawn CHD/CHDH * SK8 182 D2
Willowmead Wy WHIT OL12 28 D1
Willowmoss Cl WALK M28 95 F1
Willow Ri LIT OL15 20 C5
Willow Rd ECC M30 108 D1
MPL/ROM SK6 187 E5
PART M31 150 D4
PWCH M25 84 D1
UPML OL3 78 B5
The Willows BOLE BL2 50 D4
CCHDY M21 140 D4
MOSL OL5 107 F1
PART M31 151 E3
Willows Dr FAIL M35 116 A1
Willows End STLY SK15 120 A2
Willows La BOLS/LL BL3 48 B5
MILN OL16 31 E5
Willows Rd ORD * M5 111 E3
Willow St BURY BL9 5 K4
CHH M8 112 D1
HEY OL10 41 E4
OLD OL1 9 K2
OP/CLY M11 114 D4
SWIN M27 96 C5
WALK M28 96 B3
Willow Tree Ms CHD/CHDH SK8 181 G3
Willow Tree Rd ALT WA14 177 G2
Willow Wy BRAM/HZG SK7 183 F5
DID/WITH M20 157 H3
Willow Wood Cl AUL OL6 118 D2
Wilma Av BKLY M9 86 D3
Wilmcote Cl HOR/BR BL6 47 E3
Wilmcote Rd NEWH/MOS M40 113 H1
Wilmington Rd STRET * M32 139 G1
Wilmot St BOL BL1 33 F3
Wilmott St HULME M15 127 E1
Wilmslow Av BOL BL1 33 H1
Wilmslow Old Rd
HALE/TIMP WA15 189 G1
Wilmslow Park Rd
WILM/AE SK9 199 H3
Wilmslow Rd CHD/CHDH SK8 170 A5
CHD/CHDH SK8 182 A1
DID/WITH M20 142 C4
DID/WITH M20 157 H5
HALE/TIMP WA15 189 G1
WILM/AE SK9 192 A2
WILM/AE SK9 201 B3
Wilmur Av BRO M7 99 H4
WHTF M45 68 D5
Wilpshire Av WGTN/LGST M12 129 E5
Wilshaw Gv AULW OL7 105 E4
Wilshaw La AULW OL7 104 D5
Wilson Av HEY OL10 40 B4
SWIN M27 83 G5
Wilson Crs AUL OL6 118 D1
Wilson Rd BKLY M9 101 E1
HTNM SK4 159 E2
Wilsons Pk NEWH/MOS * M40 101 F5
Wilson St BOL * BL1 2 E6
BRUN/LGST M13 127 H2
BURY BL9 5 G6
FWTH BL4 65 F4
HYDE SK14 147 H1
OLDS OL8 90 B3
OP/CLY M11 114 D5
RAD M26 52 A5
STRET M32 125 F4
UPML OL3 93 H2
WHIT OL12 10 C4
Wilson Wy OLD OL1 9 G2
Wilsthorpe Cl BNG/LEV M19 144 B5
Wilton Av CHD/CHDH SK8 181 H5
OLDTF/WHR M16 125 H5
PWCH M25 85 G5
SWIN M27 97 H3
Wilton Ct DTN/ASHW M34 130 B4
Wilton Crs WILM/AE SK9 201 A3
Wilton Dr BURY BL9 53 H4
HALE/TIMP WA15 178 D4
Wilton Gdns RAD M26 52 D4
Wilton Gv DTN/ASHW M34 130 B4
HEY OL10 41 E5
Wilton Paddock
DTN/ASHW M34 130 B4
Wilton Pl CSLFD * M3 112 C3
Wilton Rd BOL BL1 33 H1
CCHDY M21 141 E3
CHH M8 86 B5
SLFD M6 110 C1
Wilton St BOL BL1 34 A3
CHAD OL9 89 G4
DTN/ASHW M34 131 F4
HEY OL10 40 D4
MDTN M24 70 C5
PWCH M25 85 F3
RDSH SK5 145 E1
WHTF M45 68 C5
Wilton Ter WHIT OL12 10 A4
Wiltshire Av RDSH SK5 160 D2
Wiltshire Cl BURY BL9 53 H1
Wiltshire Rd CHAD OL9 89 G2
FAIL M35 103 E4
PART M31 150 D4
Wiltshire St BRO M7 99 H4
Wimbledon Dr EDGY/DAV SK3 171 F3
ROCH OL11 42 C1
Wimbledon Rd FAIL M35 103 G2
Wimborne Av URM M41 123 G4
Wimborne Cl CHD/CHDH SK8 171 F5
Wimpole St AUL OL6 118 B2
OLD OL1 74 D4
Wimpory St OP/CLY M11 129 G1
Winbolt St OFTN SK2 172 D5
Wincanton Av NTHM/RTH M23 167 E1
Wincanton Dr BOL BL1 22 C4
Wincanton Pk OLDE OL4 91 G1
Wince Cl MDTN M24 88 B1
Wincham Cl HULME M15 126 C2
Wincham Rd SALE M33 153 H4
Winchester Av AUL OL6 105 G3
CHAD OL9 73 E3
DTN/ASHW M34 146 C2
HEY OL10 55 H1
PWCH M25 85 F5
Winchester Cl ROCH OL11 28 C4
TOT/BURYW BL8 26 D4
WILM/AE SK9 198 D5
Winchester Dr HTNM SK4 159 E4
SALE M33 153 G2
Winchester Pk DID/WITH M20 157 E3
Winchester Rd DUK SK16 133 F1
ECC M30 110 B1
HALE/TIMP WA15 178 D3
RAD M26 51 G4
URM M41 123 G5
Winchester Wy BOLE BL2 35 E5
Wincle Av POY/DIS SK12 195 G5
Wincombe St RUSH/FAL M14 142 C1
Windale WALK M28 80 C4
Windcroft Cl OP/CLY M11 114 C5
Winder Dr ANC M4 113 H4
Windermere Av BOLS/LL BL3 50 D5
DTN/ASHW M34 145 F1
SALE M33 155 E3
SWIN M27 97 F3
Windermere Cl OP/CLY M11 114 D5
PWCH M25 84 B2
STRET M32 124 D5
Windermere Crs AULW * OL7 117 G1
Windermere Dr BURY BL9 53 F2
RAMS BL0 16 D1
WILM/AE SK9 201 A4
Windermere Rd FWTH BL4 63 H5
HYDE SK14 132 B3
MDTN M24 70 D2
MPL/ROM SK6 186 C3
ROY/SHW OL2 59 E2
STKP SK1 172 C2
STLY SK15 119 F2
URM * M41 138 B2
WILM/AE SK9 191 H3
Windermere St BOL BL1 34 A3
Winder St BOL BL1 2 E2
Winders Wy SLFD M6 112 A1
Windfields Cl CHD/CHDH SK8 183 E1
Windgate Ri STLY SK15 107 E5
Windham St MILN OL16 19 H5
Windle Av CHH M8 86 A4
Windle Ct OFTN SK2 173 F4
Windlehurst Dr WALK M28 94 C3
Windlehurst Old Rd
MPL/ROM SK6 187 E2
Windlehurst Rd MPL/ROM SK6 186 C4
Windley St BOLE BL2 3 H2
Windmill Av ORD M5 126 A1
Windmill Cl DTN/ASHW M34 145 G1
WALK M28 80 D2
Windmill Ct MILN * OL16 30 C5
Windmill La RDSH SK5 145 F2
Windmill Rd SALE * M33 155 G3
WALK M28 80 D2
Windmill St CMANW M2 6 D6
MILN OL16 30 C5
Windover Cl WHTN BL5 62 D5
Windover St BOLS/LL BL3 47 H5
The Windrush WHIT OL12 18 B4
Windrush Av RAMS BL0 26 B1
Windrush Dr BKLY M9 101 E3
Windsor Av BOLS/LL BL3 65 H1
CHAD OL9 89 F3
CHD/CHDH SK8 169 E4
FAIL M35 103 G2
HEY OL10 40 C4
HTNM SK4 158 D3
IRL M44 121 C5
LHULT M38 80 C2
SALE M33 139 G5
SWIN M27 83 F5
URM M41 137 G1
WHTF M45 68 D5
WILM/AE SK9 199 E4
Windsor Cl POY/DIS SK12 195 E3
TOT/BURYW BL8 26 B2
Windsor Dr ALT WA14 166 A1
ALT WA14 176 C3
AULW OL7 117 G1
DTN/ASHW M34 117 E4
DUK SK16 133 E1
MPL/ROM SK6 174 D4
STLY SK15 119 F2
TOT/BURYW BL8 52 C1
Windsor Gv AUL OL6 105 F3
BOL BL1 33 F5
CHD/CHDH SK8 182 C4
MPL/ROM SK6 162 D4
RAD M26 66 A5
Windsor Rd BKLY M9 101 F3
BNG/LEV M19 143 G2
BRAM/HZG SK7 185 G2
DROY M43 115 G3
DTN/ASHW M34 130 B5
EDGW/EG BL7 23 F4
HYDE SK14 147 G4
MPL/ROM SK6 160 D3
NEWH/MOS M40 115 H1
OLDS OL8 8 C6
PWCH M25 85 H4
Windsor St FAIL M35 103 F2
GTN M18 129 F4
NEWH/MOS M40 115 H1
OFTN SK2 172 B3
OLD OL1 74 D3
ORD M5 112 A4
ROCH OL11 43 F1
Windsor Ter MILN OL16 11 K6
Windybank BKLY M9 86 D2
Windy Harbour La EDGW/EG BL7 23 G3
Windyhill Dr BOLS/LL BL3 62 D1
Winfell Dr NEWH/MOS M40 114 A2
Winfield Av DID/WITH M20 158 A1
Winfield Dr GTN M18 129 G2
Winfield Gv MPL/ROM SK6 163 G5
Winfield St HYDE SK14 148 A1
Winford St BKLY M9 101 F2
Wingate Av TOT/BURYW BL8 37 G4
Wingate Dr DID/WITH M20 157 H4
HALE/TIMP WA15 166 B4
WHTF M45 68 B3
Wingate Rd HTNM SK4 159 F2
LHULT M38 80 C3
Wingate St ROCH OL11 28 A2
Wingfield Av WILM/AE SK9 198 D4
Wingfield Dr SWIN M27 97 F4
WILM/AE SK9 198 D4
Wingfield St STRET M32 125 E4
Wings Gv HEY OL10 56 A2
Winifred Av BURY BL9 40 A2
Winifred Rd DID/WITH M20 157 G3
FWTH BL4 64 B3
NEWH/MOS M40 102 A3
OFTN SK2 172 B4
URM M41 123 F5
Winifred St ECC M30 109 E4
HYDE SK14 147 H4
RAMS BL0 16 C3
WHIT OL12 29 E2
Winmarith Dr HALE/TIMP WA15 179 E5
Winmarleigh Cl TOT/BURYW BL8 37 E5
Winnie St NEWH/MOS M40 101 H2
Winning Hill Cl GTN M18 129 G4
Winnington Gn OFTN SK2 173 E4
Winnington Rd MPL/ROM SK6 175 E1
Winnipeg Quay SALQ M50 125 G1
The Winnows DTN/ASHW M34 131 E5
Winscombe Dr
NEWH/MOS M40 113 H1
Winser St CMANE M1 7 F7
Winsfield Rd BRAM/HZG SK7 185 E4
Winsford Dr ROCH OL11 41 G1
Winsford Gv BOLS/LL BL3 47 G4
Winsford Rd RUSH/FAL M14 142 B2
Winskill Rd IRL M44 136 B3
Winslade Cl BRAM/HZG SK7 184 B2
OLDE OL4 75 G3
Winslade Ms FWTH BL4 65 E3
Winsley Rd NTHM/RTH M23 155 G4
Winslow Av HYDE SK14 149 G1
Winslow Pl BNG/LEV M19 143 G5
Winslow St OP/CLY M11 114 D5
Winstanley Rd NEWH/MOS M40 114 A2
SALE M33 154 D1
Winster Av BRO M7 99 E4
DID/WITH M20 156 D2
STRET M32 124 B5
Winster Cl BOLE BL2 35 G5
WHTF M45 69 E4
Winster Dr BOLE BL2 35 F5

MDTN M24 71 F2
Winster Gv OFTN SK2 172 B3
Winster Rd ECC M30 109 E5
Winston Av BOLS/LL BL3 66 B1
ROCH OL11 28 B5
Winston Cl MPL/ROM SK6 174 C2
RAD M26 51 H4
Winston Rd BKLY M9 101 G1
SALE M33 154 A1
Winswell Cl OP/CLY M11 115 E3
Winterbottom Gv HYDE SK14 149 G1
Winterbottom St CHAD OL9 8 D3
Winterburn Av BOLE BL2 23 G5
CCHDY M21 156 B2
Winterburn Gn OFTN SK2 173 F4
Winterdyne St BKLY M9 101 F3
Winterfield Dr BOLS/LL BL3 62 D1
Winterford Av BRUN/LGST M13 128 A3
Winterford Rd CHH M8 100 A3
MOSL OL5 107 F1
Wintermans Rd CCHDY M21 141 G5
Winterslow Av NTHM/RTH M23 155 E5
Winter St BOL BL1 33 G3
Winterton Rd RDSH SK5 145 F2
Winthrop Av NEWH/MOS M40 101 E5
Winton Av DTN/ASHW M34 131 E1
NEWH/MOS M40 102 C1
Winton Cl BRAM/HZG SK7 183 F3
Winton Gn HOR/BR BL6 46 A1
Winton Gv BOLS/LL BL3 47 F5
Winton Rd ALT WA14 177 F2
SLFD M6 98 A4
Winton St AUL OL6 118 A2
LIT OL15 21 E3
STLY SK15 119 G4
Winward St BOLS/LL * BL3 47 H5
Winwood Dr MDTN M24 72 A2
Winwood Rd DID/WITH M20 169 H1
Wirral Cl SWIN * M27 83 F5
Wirral Crs EDGY/DAV SK3 170 D1
Wisbech Dr NTHM/RTH M23 155 G5
Wisbeck Rd BOLE BL2 49 H1
Wiseley St OP/CLY M11 114 B5
Wiseman Ter PWCH M25 85 F3
Wishaw Sq CCHDY M21 141 H5
Wisley Cl RDSH SK5 145 E3
Wistaria Rd GTN M18 129 G3
Witham Av WYTH/NTH M22 168 D4
Witham Cl HEY OL10 40 B3
Witham St AUL OL6 118 D1
Withenfield Rd NTHM/RTH M23 167 G1
Withens Gn OFTN SK2 173 F3
Withington Gn MDTN M24 56 D5
Withington Rd CCHDY M21 141 G3
OLDTF/WHR M16 126 C5
Withington St HEY * OL10 56 B1
SLFD M6 112 A3
Withins Av RAD M26 52 D4
Withins Cl BOLE BL2 50 B1
Withins Dr BOLE BL2 50 B1
Withins Gv BOLE BL2 50 B1
Withins La BOLE BL2 35 F5
RAD M26 52 D4
Withins Rd OLDS OL8 89 G5
Withins St RAD M26 52 D5
Withnell Dr TOT/BURYW BL8 37 F5
Withnell Rd DID/WITH M20 158 A3
Withycombe Pl SLFD M6 98 D5
Withy Gv ANC M4 7 F3
Withypool Dr OFTN SK2 172 C4
Withy Tree Gv
DTN/ASHW * M34 146 D1
Witley Dr SALE M33 138 C5
Witley Rd MILN OL16 11 H7
Wittenbury Rd HTNM SK4 159 E4
Witterage Cl WGTN/LGST * M12 128 C2
Woburn Abbey UPML * OL3 77 H3
Woburn Av BOLE BL2 34 D3
Woburn Cl MILN OL16 31 F5
Woburn Dr BURY BL9 53 G4
HALE/TIMP WA15 178 C2
Woburn Rd OLDTF/WHR M16 140 D1
Woburn St OLDTF/WHR M16 127 E5
Woden's Av ORD M5 126 B1
Woking Back Gdns BOL BL1 33 H5
Woking Rd CHD/CHDH SK8 192 D1
Woking Ter BOL * BL1 33 H5
Wolfenden St BOL BL1 33 H4
Wolfenden Ter BOL * BL1 33 H4
Wolfreton Crs SWIN M27 83 F4
Wolseley Pl DID/WITH M20 157 G1
Wolseley Rd SALE M33 139 G5
Wolseley St MILN OL16 45 E2
TOT/BURYW BL8 37 G5
Wolsey Dr ALT WA14 176 D3
Wolsey St HEY OL10 40 D5
RAD M26 67 F1
Wolstenholme Av BURY BL9 27 G5
Wolstenvale Cl MDTN M24 72 A3
Wolver Cl LHULT * M38 80 C1
Wolverton Av OLDS OL8 90 A4
Wolverton Dr WILM/AE SK9 199 H1
Wolvesey ROCH * OL11 29 H5
Woodacre OLDTF/WHR M16 141 H2
Woodacres Ct WILM/AE SK9 199 E4
Woodall Cl SALE M33 155 E2
Woodark Cl OLDE OL4 92 A2
Woodbank BOLE BL2 35 E4
Woodbank Av MPL/ROM SK6 161 F3
STKP SK1 172 C1
Woodbank Ct URM * M41 123 E5
Woodbank Dr TOT/BURYW BL8 37 H2
Wood Bank Rd LIT OL15 20 D5
Woodbine Av IRL M44 150 C2
Woodbine Crs OFTN SK2 172 A2
Woodbine Rd BOLS/LL BL3 63 F1
Woodbine St MILN OL16 43 F1
Woodbine St East MILN OL16 43 G1
Woodbourne Rd HTNM SK4 144 B5
SALE M33 154 B4
Woodbray Av BNG/LEV M19 158 B1
Woodbridge Av
DTN/ASHW M34 131 E1
Woodbridge Gdns WHIT OL12 29 F1
Woodbridge Gv
NTHM/RTH M23 155 H5
Woodbridge Rd URM M41 122 A5
Woodbrook Av OLDE OL4 76 C5
Wood Brook La OLDE OL4 76 C5
Wood Brook Rd OLDE OL4 76 B5
Woodbrook Rd WILM/AE SK9 201 G4
Woodburn Dr BOL BL1 33 E3
Woodburn Rd WYTH/NTH M22 168 C1
Woodbury Crs DUK * SK16 132 A1
Woodbury Rd EDGY/DAV SK3 171 E2
Woodchurch Wk CHAD * OL9 89 G1
Woodcock Cl DROY M43 116 D2
ROCH OL11 28 C4
Woodcote Av BRAM/HZG SK7 183 F3
Woodcote Rd ALT WA14 152 D5
ALT WA14 153 G5
Woodcote Vw WILM/AE SK9 200 C1
Wood Cottage Cl WALK M28 80 A4
Wood Crs OLDE OL4 91 H4
Woodcroft OFTN SK2 173 E3
Woodcroft Av BNG/LEV M19 158 B2
Woodeaton Cl ROY/SHW OL2 59 H5
Wooded Cl BURY BL9 38 C1
Wood Edge Cl BOLS/LL * BL3 64 D1
Wood End BRAM/HZG SK7 183 G2
Woodend ROY/SHW OL2 45 F5
Woodend Dr STLY SK15 134 A2
Woodend La HYDE SK14 147 F2
STLY SK15 134 A1
WHIT OL12 20 A2
Woodend Rd EDGY/DAV SK3 172 A5
WYTH/NTH M22 168 C5
Woodend St OLD OL1 74 B3
OLDE OL4 92 A2
Woodfield WYTH/NTH M22 180 C1
Woodfield Av HYDE SK14 147 G3
MPL/ROM SK6 161 H2
WHIT OL12 10 A1
Woodfield Cl OLDS OL8 89 H3
Woodfield Ct OFTN * SK2 172 B5
Woodfield Crs MPL/ROM SK6 161 G4
Woodfield Dr WALK M28 94 C4
Woodfield Gv ECC M30 109 F4
FWTH BL4 80 D1
SALE M33 139 F5
Woodfield Ms HYDE * SK14 147 G3
Woodfield Rd ALT WA14 165 F3
CHD/CHDH SK8 183 E5
CHH M8 100 B1
MDTN M24 87 F1
SLFD M6 111 E1
Woodfield St BOLS/LL BL3 64 B1
Wood Fold BOLE BL2 23 H5
Woodfold Av BNG/LEV M19 143 H1
Woodfold Rd FAIL M35 103 F2
Woodford Av DTN/ASHW M34 131 H4
ECC M30 109 E5
ROY/SHW OL2 60 C2
Woodford Dr SWIN M27 82 D5
Woodford Gdns DID/WITH M20 157 F4
Woodford Gv BOLS/LL BL3 48 B5
Woodford Rd BRAM/HZG SK7 193 H2
POY/DIS SK12 194 C2
WILM/AE SK9 200 D2
Woodgarth Av
NEWH/MOS M40 102 C5
Woodgarth Dr SWIN M27 96 D4
Woodgarth La WALK M28 95 G5
Woodgate Av BURY BL9 39 G2
ROCH OL11 28 D5
Woodgate Cl MPL/ROM SK6 161 G3
Woodgate Dr PWCH M25 85 F1
Woodgate Hill Rd BURY BL9 39 F3
Woodgate Rd OLDTF/WHR M16 141 H2
Woodgate St BOLS/LL BL3 64 B1
Woodgrange Cl SLFD M6 111 F3
Woodgreen Dr RAD M26 67 F4
Wood Gv DTN/ASHW M34 131 G4
MPL/ROM SK6 161 H1
WHTF M45 68 B1
Woodhall Av DID/WITH M20 142 B4
WHTF M45 84 A1
Woodhall Cl BOLE BL2 34 D3
Woodhall Crs BRAM/HZG SK7 193 G4
TOT/BURYW * BL8 38 A1
Woodhall Crs RDSH SK5 160 B1
Woodhall Rd RDSH SK5 160 B2
Woodhall St FAIL M35 103 E2
Woodhalt Rd CHH M8 100 B2
Woodham Rd NTHM/RTH M23 155 G5
Woodham Wk BOLS/LL BL3 48 C4
Woodhead Cl RAMS BL0 16 D4
Woodhead Dr
HALE/TIMP WA15 178 A3
Woodhead Rd
HALE/TIMP WA15 178 A3
Woodhead St OLDTF/WHR M16 126 D4
Wood Hey Cl RAD M26 66 C1
Wood Hey Gv DTN/ASHW * M34 146 D4
WHIT OL12 19 E4
Woodhey Rd RAMS BL0 16 B5
Woodheys HTNM SK4 158 C3
Woodheys Dr SALE M33 153 G5
Woodheys Rd LIT OL15 31 H1
Woodhill Cl MDTN M24 71 G2
WGTN/LGST M12 129 E4
Woodhill Dr PWCH M25 85 E5
Woodhill Fold TOT/BURYW BL8 4 B2
Woodhill Gv PWCH M25 85 E4
Woodhill Rd TOT/BURYW BL8 4 A2
Woodhill St TOT/BURYW BL8 4 A1
Woodhill V TOT/BURYW BL8 4 A2
Woodhouse La SALE M33 153 E5
SALE M33 153 G4
WYTH/NTH M22 168 C4
WYTH/NTH M22 180 C5
Woodhouse La East
HALE/TIMP WA15 154 C5
Woodhouse Rd ROY/SHW OL2 45 F5
URM M41 122 C4
WYTH/NTH M22 180 C4
Woodhouse St GTN M18 129 G3
NEWH/MOS M40 101 G5
Wooding Cl PART M31 151 F2
Woodlake Av CCHDY M21 156 B2
Woodland Av BOLS/LL BL3 64 C2
BRAM/HZG SK7 185 F3
GTN M18 129 H4
Woodland Crs PWCH M25 85 E5
Woodland Gv EDGW/EG BL7 22 C1
Woodland Pk ROY/SHW OL2 58 C3
Woodland Rd BNG/LEV M19 143 H3
GTN M18 129 H4
HEY OL10 41 F3
WHIT OL12 18 B5
The Woodlands DROY * M43 115 H2
HEY OL10 56 B1
HOR/BR BL6 46 D1
TOT/BURYW BL8 38 A1
Woodlands FAIL M35 115 H1
URM M41 123 F5
Woodlands Av CHD/CHDH SK8 182 D2
ECC M30 108 C5
IRL M44 121 B5
MPL/ROM SK6 161 H1
ROCH OL11 28 D4
STRET M32 140 A1
SWIN M27 96 B4
URM M41 136 D1
WHTF M45 68 B3
Woodlands Cl CHD/CHDH SK8 182 D4
HYDE SK14 149 G2
STLY SK15 134 A1
WALK M28 95 F3
Woodlands Dr MPL/ROM SK6 162 A1
OFTN SK2 172 D1
SALE M33 154 D5
Woodlands Gv HYDE SK14 149 G2
TOT/BURYW BL8 37 G3
Woodlands La
HALE/TIMP WA15 165 H4
Woodlands Park Rd OFTN SK2 173 E1
Woodlands Pkwy
HALE/TIMP WA15 165 H4
Woodlands Rd ALT WA14 165 H4
AUL OL6 105 H4
CHH M8 100 B2
HTNM SK4 158 A4
MILN OL16 44 B1
OLDTF/WHR M16 141 H2
SALE M33 154 D1
STLY SK15 134 A1
WALK M28 95 F3
WILM/AE SK9 192 B4
WILM/AE SK9 198 D1
Woodlands St CHH M8 100 A2
Woodland St HEY OL10 41 E4
WGTN/LGST M12 129 E3
WHIT OL12 30 B1
Woodlands Vw MILN OL16 11 J5
Woodland Vw EDGW/EG BL7 23 G3
Woodland Wy MDTN M24 87 G1
Wood La AULW OL7 105 E5
HALE/TIMP WA15 166 B4
MDTN M24 72 A5
MPL/ROM SK6 174 C4
PART M31 150 D3
Woodlark Cl CSLFD * M3 6 A4
Woodlawn Ct OLDTF/WHR M16 126 B5
Woodlea CHAD OL9 72 C5
Woodlea Av BNG/LEV M19 143 F5
Woodlea Gv WALK M28 95 F2
Woodleigh Dr DROY M43 116 D1
Woodleigh Rd OLDE OL4 76 B5
Woodleigh St BKLY M9 101 G1
Woodley Av RAD M26 67 G3
Woodley Cl OFTN SK2 173 E2
Woodley St BURY BL9 53 G1
Woodman Dr BURY BL9 27 F5
Woodman St STKP SK1 13 F2
Woodmeadow Ct MOSL OL5 92 D5
Woodmere Dr BKLY M9 87 F4
Wood Mt HALE/TIMP WA15 166 C4
Woodmount Cl MPL/ROM SK6 162 D4
Woodnewton Cl GTN M18 129 F4
Woodpark Cl OLDS OL8 90 D4
Woodpecker Pl WALK * M28 95 E2
Woodridge Dr BOLE BL2 34 C5
Wood Rd HALE/TIMP WA15 154 B5
OLDTF/WHR M16 126 B5
Wood Road La BURY BL9 26 C3
Wood Rd North
OLDTF/WHR M16 126 B5
Woodrow Wk WGTN/LGST M12 128 C2
Woodrow Wy IRL M44 136 A3
Woodroyd Cl BRAM/HZG SK7 183 G3
Woodroyd Dr BURY BL9 39 F3
Woodruffe Gdns MPL/ROM SK6 173 H1
Woods Ct BOL BL1 3 F4
Woodseats La GLSP SK13 149 H4
Woodsend Cir URM M41 122 A5
Woodsend Crescent Rd
URM M41 137 E1
Woodsend Rd URM M41 122 B5
Woodsend Rd South URM M41 137 F2
Woods Gv CHD/CHDH SK8 183 E5
Woodshaw Gv WALK M28 94 D2
Woodside MILN OL16 45 F1
ROY/SHW OL2 60 C1
Woodside Av BNG/LEV M19 158 C1
WALK M28 81 G5
Woodside Cl OLDE OL4 91 H1
Woodside Dr HYDE SK14 147 H2
MPL/ROM SK6 186 D5
SLFD M6 110 D2
Woodside La POY/DIS SK12 195 F3
Woodside Rd OLDTF/WHR M16 141 E1
Woodside St STLY SK15 107 F4
Woods La CHD/CHDH SK8 183 E5
UPML OL3 77 H3
Woods Lea BOL BL1 47 G2
Woodsley Rd BOL BL1 32 C4
Woods Moor La EDGY/DAV SK3 172 B5
Woodsmoor Rd SWIN M27 96 C3
Wood Sq DROY M43 116 B5
Woods Rd IRL M44 136 A3
The Woods ALT WA14 165 H3
Woodstock Av CHD/CHDH SK8 182 D5
RDSH SK5 160 A1
Woodstock Cl HEY OL10 41 F4
Woodstock Crs MPL/ROM SK6 161 H1
Woodstock Dr BOL BL1 32 D5
SWIN M27 97 F4
TOT/BURYW BL8 25 G4
WALK M28 95 H4
Woodstock Gn RDSH SK5 160 B1
Woodstock Rd ALT WA14 165 F1
NEWH/MOS M40 102 B1
OLDTF/WHR M16 126 A5
Woodstock St OLDE OL4 9 H6
WHIT OL12 29 F2
Wood St ALT WA14 165 G5
AUL OL6 118 A3
BOL BL1 3 F5
CHD/CHDH SK8 170 A3
CSLFD M3 6 C3
DTN/ASHW M34 131 G4
DUK SK16 132 B2
EDGY/DAV SK3 12 C5
HEY OL10 41 E4
HYDE SK14 147 H1
LIT OL15 21 E3
MDTN M24 71 F2
MILN OL16 45 F2
OLD OL1 75 E4
OP/CLY M11 129 E1
RAD M26 66 D4
RAMS BL0 16 C3
ROCH OL11 30 B5
ROY/SHW OL2 59 F2
STLY SK15 119 E3
TOT/BURYW BL8 37 H3
Wood Ter BOLE BL2 36 C5
Woodthorpe Cl PWCH M25 85 G5
Woodthorpe Dr CHD/CHDH SK8 182 D2
Woodthorpe Gra PWCH M25 85 G5
Wood Top Cl OFTN SK2 173 F2
Woodvale ALT WA14 177 F2
MDTN M24 56 D5
Woodvale Av BOLS/LL BL3 63 G2
Woodvale Dr BOLS/LL BL3 63 G2
Woodvale Gdns BOLS/LL BL3 63 G2
Woodvale Gv BOLS/LL BL3 63 G2
Woodvale Rd RAD M26 67 G3
Woodvale Wk OP/CLY * M11 114 C4
Wood Vw HEY OL10 40 D2
WYTH/NTH M22 156 C5
Woodview Av BNG/LEV M19 158 C1
Woodville Dr MPL/ROM SK6 174 D5
SALE M33 154 B1
STLY SK15 120 A2
Woodville Gv RDSH SK5 145 E5
Woodville Rd ALT WA14 165 F5
SALE M33 154 B1
Woodville Ter NEWH/MOS M40 101 G1
Woodward Cl BURY BL9 38 C1
Woodward Ct ANC * M4 113 H3
Woodward Pl ANC M4 113 H3
Woodward Rd PWCH M25 84 C5
Woodward St ANC M4 113 H3
Woodwise La NTHM/RTH M23 155 F5
Woolden St ECC M30 109 E2
Woollacot St OLD * OL1 9 H4
Woollam Pl CSLFD M3 6 A6
Woolley Av POY/DIS SK12 195 E5
Woolley St CHH M8 113 E1
Woolmore Av OLD OL1 74 B3
Woolpack Gn SLFD * M6 111 G2
Wool Rd UPML OL3 78 A2
Wootton St HYDE SK14 132 C4
Worcester Av DTN/ASHW M34 146 D2
RDSH SK5 160 D1
Worcester Cl AUL OL6 105 G2
BURY BL9 53 H1
MPL/ROM SK6 161 H5
Worcester Rd BOLS/LL BL3 65 G1
CHD/CHDH SK8 170 D5
MDTN M24 87 G2
SALE M33 153 G3
SLFD M6 110 D1
SWIN M27 82 C5
Worcester St BOL * BL1 33 H5
BRO M7 99 H4
CHAD OL9 89 G2
ROCH OL11 42 D2
TOT/BURYW BL8 38 A2
Wordsworth Av BURY * BL9 53 G3
CHH M8 100 B4
DROY M43 116 A3
FWTH BL4 64 C5
RAD M26 51 H5
Wordsworth Cl DUK SK16 133 F1
Wordsworth Crs AULW OL7 104 B5
LIT OL15 31 G1
Wordsworth Gdns PWCH M25 84 C4
Wordsworth Rd
DTN/ASHW M34 146 D4
LHULT M38 80 B2
MDTN M24 72 A2
OLD OL1 75 E3
OLDTF/WHR M16 126 A5
RDSH SK5 144 C2
SWIN M27 96 C1
Wordsworth St BOL * BL1 33 G4
SLFD M6 112 B1
Wordsworth Wy ROCH OL11 28 B5
Workesleigh St
NEWH/MOS M40 102 B5
World Wy MANAIR M90 180 A4
Worrall St EDGY/DAV SK3 12 E7
NEWH/MOS M40 101 H4
ORD M5 126 B1
WHIT OL12 29 G1
Worsbrough Av WALK M28 80 D5
Worsefold St NEWH/MOS * M40 101 H2
Worsel St BOLS/LL BL3 48 B5
Worsley Av NEWH/MOS M40 101 G1
WALK M28 80 B5
Worsley Brow WALK M28 95 F4
Worsley Ct WALK M28 81 E4
Worsley Crs OFTN SK2 172 C2
Worsley Gv BNG/LEV M19 143 H2
WALK M28 80 B5
Worsley Pl ROY/SHW OL2 59 H3
Worsley Rd BOLS/LL BL3 47 H5
ECC M30 109 E3
FWTH BL4 81 E1
WALK M28 95 H5
Worsley Rd North WALK M28 81 E2
Worsley St BOLS/LL * BL3 48 D4
CSLFD M3 6 C4
CSLFD * M3 6 C7
HULME M15 126 C1
MILN OL16 11 G7
OLDS OL8 91 E2
SWIN M27 83 E5
SWIN M27 97 F3
TOT/BURYW BL8 25 H4
Worston Av BOL BL1 32 C4
Worthenbury Wk
RUSH/FAL M14 128 B5
Worthing Cl OFTN SK2 173 E3
Worthing St RUSH/FAL M14 142 C1
Worthington Av HEY OL10 56 B2
PART M31 151 E3
Worthington Cl HYDE * SK14 149 F1
Worthington Dr BRO M7 99 G1
Worthington Rd
DTN/ASHW M34 147 E1
SALE M33 155 F2
Worthington St AULW OL7 104 D5
BOLS/LL BL3 63 F1
NEWH/MOS M40 102 B2
STLY SK15 119 E4
Worth's La DTN/ASHW M34 146 D4
Wortley Av SLFD M6 110 D2
Wortley Gv NEWH/MOS M40 88 A5
Wragby Cl TOT/BURYW BL8 38 A1
Wrath Cl BOLE BL2 23 G5
Wray Pl MILN OL16 30 D5
Wrekin Av NTHM/RTH M23 179 H1
Wren Av SWIN M27 83 G4
Wrenbury Av DID/WITH M20 142 A4
Wrenbury Crs EDGY/DAV SK3 171 F3
Wrenbury Dr BOL BL1 23 E5
CHD/CHDH SK8 170 B3
MILN OL16 43 H2
Wren Cl DTN/ASHW M34 116 D3
FWTH BL4 64 A4
OFTN SK2 173 G4
Wren Dr BURY BL9 39 E2
IRL M44 121 B4
Wren Gdns MDTN M24 71 G3
Wren Gn MILN OL16 30 C5
Wren's Nest Av ROY/SHW OL2 60 B1
Wren St OLDE OL4 91 F1
Wrenswood Dr WALK M28 94 D2
Wrexham Cl OLDS OL8 89 G5
Wrigglesworth Cl
TOT/BURYW BL8 37 E3
Wright Robinson Cl
OP/CLY M11 114 B5
Wrights Bank North OFTN SK2 173 E4
Wrights Bank South OFTN SK2 173 F4
Wright St AUL OL6 118 C1
CHAD OL9 89 G2
DTN/ASHW M34 117 F5
FAIL M35 103 E2
OLD OL1 9 J3
OLDTF/WHR M16 126 B3
RAD M26 67 E1
Wrigley Crs FAIL M35 103 E3
Wrigley Fold MDTN M24 55 H5
Wrigley Head FAIL M35 103 E2
Wrigley Head Crs FAIL * M35 103 E2
Wrigley Pl LIT OL15 20 C5
Wrigley St AUL OL6 118 A1
OLDE OL4 75 E5
OLDE OL4 76 C4
OLDE OL4 92 A1
Wroe St CSLFD M3 112 C4
OLDE OL4 92 A1
SWIN M27 83 E4
Wroe Ter SWIN * M27 83 E4
Wrotham Cl ORD M5 111 H4
Wroxham Av DTN/ASHW M34 130 B5
URM M41 123 E5
Wroxham Cl TOT/BURYW * BL8 38 A1
Wroxham Rd BKLY M9 86 C4
Wuerdle Cl MILN OL16 20 B5
Wuerdle Farm Wy MILN OL16 20 B4
Wuerdle Pl MILN OL16 20 B4
Wuerdle St MILN OL16 20 B4
Wyatt Av ORD * M5 126 B1
Wyatt St DUK SK16 118 B5
HTNM SK4 12 E2
Wybersley Rd MPL/ROM SK6 187 F3
Wychbury St SLFD M6 111 F3
Wychelm Rd PART M31 151 E3
Wycherley Rd WHIT OL12 29 E1
Wych Fold HYDE SK14 147 H4
Wych St AUL * OL6 118 A3
Wychwood ALT WA14 177 E3
Wychwood Cl MDTN M24 72 A5
Wycliffe Av WILM/AE SK9 199 F4
Wycliffe Rd URM M41 138 B1
Wycliffe St ECC M30 109 F3
HTNM SK4 12 D2
Wycombe Av GTN M18 129 H2
Wycombe Cl URM M41 123 F3
Wye Av FAIL * M35 103 E3
Wyecroft Cl MPL/ROM SK6 162 A1
Wye St OLDS OL8 8 D6
Wykeham Gv WHIT OL12 29 E2
Wykeham Ms BOL BL1 47 H2
Wykeham St RUSH/FAL M14 127 F5
Wyke Pk OLDE OL4 91 G1
Wylam Wk WGTN/LGST M12 129 E5
The Wylde BURY BL9 4 D4
Wynchgate Rd BRAM/HZG SK7 185 H1
Wyndale Dr FAIL M35 103 E5
Wyndale Rd OLDS OL8 90 C4
Wyndcliff Dr URM M41 137 F2
Wyndham Av BOLS/LL BL3 62 D2
SWIN M27 83 E5
Wyndham Cl BRAM/HZG SK7 183 H5
Wyne Cl BRAM/HZG SK7 185 H1
Wynfield Av WYTH/NTH M22 181 E5
Wynford Sq SALQ M50 111 G4
Wyngate Rd CHD/CHDH SK8 182 C3
HALE/TIMP WA15 178 A4
Wynne Av SWIN M27 83 E4
Wynne Cl DTN/ASHW M34 146 C2
OP/CLY M11 114 C5
Wynne Gv DTN/ASHW M34 146 B2
Wynne St BOL BL1 33 H4
LHULT M38 80 B3
SLFD M6 112 A1
Wynnstay Gv RUSH/FAL M14 142 D3
Wynnstay Rd SALE M33 154 C1
Wynyard Cl SALE M33 155 E4
Wynyard Rd WYTH/NTH M22 180 B1
Wyre Dr WALK M28 94 C3
Wyresdale Rd BOL BL1 48 B1
Wyre St CMANE M1 7 J7
MOSL OL5 106 C1
Wythall Av LHULT M38 80 C1
Wythburn Av BOL BL1 32 D5
CHH M8 100 D4
URM M41 123 E5
Wythburn Rd MDTN M24 71 F1
STKP SK1 172 C2
Wythburn St SLFD M6 111 F3
Wythenshawe Pk
NTHM/RTH * M23 167 H1
Wythenshawe Rd
NTHM/RTH M23 155 H5
SALE M33 155 F2
Wythens Rd CHD/CHDH SK8 181 G4
Wythop Gdns ORD M5 111 H4
Wyvern Av HTNM SK4 159 H1
Wyverne Rd CCHDY M21 141 G3
Wyville Cl BRAM/HZG SK7 185 H2
Wyville Dr BKLY M9 86 C1
SLFD M6 111 G2
SWIN M27 96 D4

Y

Yarburgh St OLDTF/WHR M16 126 D5

Yardley Av STRET M32 139 F1
Yardley Cl STRET M32 139 F1
Yarmouth Dr NTHM/RTH M23 156 A5
Yarnton Cl ROY/SHW OL2 59 H4
Yarn Wk ANC * M4 113 H4
Yarrow Cl ROCH OL11 43 E1
Yarrow Pl BOL BL1 2 B1
Yarwell WHIT OL12 10 B4
Yarwood Av NTHM/RTH M23 167 G2
Yarwood Cl HEY OL10 41 F3
Yarwoodheath La ALT WA14 176 B4
Yarwood St ALT WA14 177 G1
BURY BL9 5 G4
Yasmin Gdns OLD OL1 74 A4
Yates Dr WALK M28 80 B4
Yates St BOLE BL2 3 H1
MDTN M24 70 D5
OLD OL1 74 D4
STKP SK1 160 C3
Yates Ter TOT/BURYW BL8 38 A1
Yattendon Av NTHM/RTH M23 167 E1
Yea Fold MILN OL16 20 B5
Yealand Av HTNM SK4 159 G3
Yealand Cl ROCH OL11 29 E5
Yeardsley Cl BRAM/HZG SK7 183 H1
Yeb Fold NEWH/MOS * M40 102 A1
Yeoford Dr ALT WA14 165 E3
Yeoman Cl BRAM/HZG * SK7 185 E1
Yeoman's Cl MILN OL16 31 G4
Yeoman Wk OP/CLY M11 114 C4
Yeovil St OLDTF/WHR M16 127 E5
Yewbarrow Rd OLD OL1 74 D4
Yew Cl BOLS/LL BL3 48 A5
Yew Crs OLDE OL4 75 G4
Yewdale SWIN M27 83 G5
Yewdale Av BOLE BL2 35 G4
Yewdale Dr FAIL M35 103 G2
MDTN M24 71 F3
Yewdale Gdns BOLE BL2 35 G4
Yew Dale Gdns ROCH OL11 42 A2
Yewdale Rd OFTN SK2 172 C3
Yewlands Av BKLY M9 87 E2
Yew St BRO M7 99 F4
BURY BL9 39 F3
DTN/ASHW M34 131 G2
HEY OL10 40 C4
HTNM SK4 159 E5
HULME M15 126 D3
Yew Tree Av BNG/LEV M19 143 H2
BRAM/HZG SK7 185 G4
RUSH/FAL M14 127 F5
WYTH/NTH M22 156 C5
Yew Tree Cl AULW OL7 104 D4
MPL/ROM SK6 174 D4
WILM/AE SK9 200 A3
Yew Tree Crs RUSH/FAL M14 142 C2
Yew Tree Dr HOR/BR BL6 46 C3
MDTN M24 72 C5
MPL/ROM SK6 161 E3
PWCH M25 85 E3
SALE M33 155 F2
URM M41 122 C4
WYTH/NTH M22 156 C5
Yew Tree Gv CHD/CHDH SK8 181 F1
Yew Tree La BOL BL1 34 B1
DUK SK16 132 D2
Yewtree La POY/DIS SK12 195 G5
WYTH/NTH M22 156 C5
Yew Tree Park Rd
CHD/CHDH SK8 193 E1
Yew Tree Rd DTN/ASHW M34 146 B2
EDGY/DAV SK3 184 A1
RUSH/FAL M14 142 C1
York Av BOLS/LL BL3 65 H1
OLDS OL8 90 A3
OLDTF/WHR M16 141 F1
PWCH M25 85 G5
ROCH OL11 28 D5
SALE M33 154 C1
SWIN M27 82 C5
York Cl CHD/CHDH SK8 170 D4
York Crs WILM/AE SK9 200 A3
Yorkdale Rd OLDE OL4 75 G5
York Dr ALT WA14 177 G3
BRAM/HZG SK7 185 H2
MANAIR M90 179 G5
RAMS BL0 16 B5
York Pl AULW OL7 117 H3
York Rd ALT WA14 177 F3
CCHDY M21 141 E3
CHAD OL9 73 E4
DROY M43 116 A2
DTN/ASHW M34 131 G4
HTNM SK4 159 E1
HYDE SK14 147 H3
IRL M44 150 C1
SALE M33 154 B1
Yorkshire Rd PART M31 150 D4
Yorkshire St AUL OL6 118 A1
CSLFD M3 6 C3
MILN OL16 10 D5
OLD OL1 9 G3
York St BKLY M9 101 F2
BNG/LEV M19 143 H3
BURY BL9 5 G4
CHAD OL9 8 E4
CMANE M1 7 F7
CMANE M1 127 F1
CMANW M2 7 F4
DID/WITH M20 157 G3
DTN/ASHW M34 117 F5
EDGY/DAV SK3 12 E5
FWTH BL4 65 F4
HALE/TIMP WA15 177 H1
HEY OL10 41 E4
MILN OL16 30 C5
RAD M26 53 F4
WHTF M45 68 C4
York Ter SALE * M33 139 F5
Young St CSLFD M3 6 C5
FWTH BL4 65 E5
RAMS BL0 16 C2
Yulan Dr SALE M33 153 F2
Yule St EDGY/DAV SK3 12 C5

Z

Zama St RAMS * BL0 16 B4
Zealand St OLDE OL4 75 F4
Zebra St BRO M7 100 A3
Zedburgh WHIT OL12 10 B4
Zeta St BKLY M9 101 G3
Zetland Av BOLS/LL BL3 63 E2
Zetland Rd CCHDY M21 141 E3
Zetland St DUK SK16 118 B4
Zinnia Dr IRL M44 135 D3
Zion Crs HULME M15 126 D2
Zion Ter WHIT OL12 28 B1
Zulu St BOLE BL2 3 K4
Zurich Gdns BRAM/HZG SK7 183 H1
Zyburn Ct SLFD * M6 110 B2

Index - featured places

AA Office
CHD/CHDH SK8 170 B3
Abbey Hey Primary School
GTN M18 129 H3
Abbey Tutorial College
CMANW M2 6 E5
Abbotsford Preparatory School
URM M41 137 H1
Abbott Primary School
NEWH/MOS M40 113 H2
Abingdon Primary School
RDSH SK5 145 E4
Abraham Moss Centre
City College Manchester
CHH M8 100 C2
Abraham Moss High School
CHH M8 100 C2
Acacias CP School
BNG/LEV M19 143 G4
Acorn Business Park
EDGY/DAV SK3 12 D4
Acre Hall Primary School
URM M41 137 E1
Adlow Industrial Park
CMANE M1 113 H5
Adswood Clinic
EDGY/DAV SK3 171 H4
Adswood Industrial Estate
EDGY/DAV SK3 171 G4
Adswood Primary School
EDGY/DAV SK3 171 G4
Adult Learning Centre
RUSH/FAL M14 127 F4
Affetside Primary School
TOT/BURYW BL8 25 E3
Agecroft Crematorium
SWIN M27 98 C2
Albany Trading Estate
CCHDY M21 141 E2
Albert Close Trading Estate
WHTF M45 68 D4
Albert Square
CMANW M2 6 D5
Albion Drive Clinic
DROY M43 116 B2
The Albion High School
BRO M7 99 G5
Albion Road Industrial Estate
ROCH OL11 29 G5
Albion Trading Estate
AUL OL6 118 C2
SLFD M6 111 H1
Alder Community High School
HYDE SK14 149 E1
Alderley Edge Cricket Club
WILM/AE SK9 201 C4
Alderley Edge Primary School
WILM/AE SK9 201 A3
Alderley Edge School for Girls
WILM/AE SK9 201 B3
Alderley Hotel
WILM/AE SK9 201 B4
Alderman Kay Special School
MDTN M24 71 H1
Alder Park CP School
ECC M30 109 E1
Aldwyn CP School
DTN/ASHW M34 116 D4
Alexandra Business Centre
UPML OL3 78 A5
The Alexandra Hospital
CHD/CHDH SK8 170 A3
Alexandra Industrial Estate
DTN/ASHW M34 131 H4
Alexandra Park Junior School
OLDS OL8 90 D3
Alexandra Park Primary School
EDGY/DAV SK3 171 F2
Alexandra Retail Park
OLDE OL4 9 H5
Alf Kaufman Special School
ROCH OL11 28 B2
Alice Ingham RC Primary School
MILN OL16 30 D1
Alkrington Clinic Centre
MDTN M24 87 H2
Alkrington Moss Primary School
MDTN M24 88 A2
All Hallows RC High School
SLFD M6 111 E2
Alliston House Medical Centre
URM M41 138 C1
All Saints CE Primary School
FWTH BL4 65 E3
HTNM SK4 159 G2
MPL/ROM SK6 175 F4
NEWH/MOS M40 102 B5
WHIT OL12 10 E1
WHTF M45 68 D2
All Saints Primary School
GTN M18 129 E2
All Saints RC High School
DUK SK16 132 C1
All Souls CE Primary School
HEY OL10 41 G3
Alma Industrial Estate
WHIT OL12 10 E3
Alma Lodge Hotel
OFTN SK2 172 B3
Alma Park Primary School
BNG/LEV M19 143 H3
Alpha Court Industrial Estate
DTN/ASHW M34 130 D5
Alt Primary School
OLDS OL8 91 G4
Altrincham CE Primary School
ALT WA14 165 F4
Altrincham College of Arts
HALE/TIMP WA15 166 B5
Altrincham Crematorium
ALT WA14 164 A1
Altrincham FC
HALE/TIMP WA15 178 A1
Altrincham General Hospital
ALT WA14 165 F5
Altrincham Golf Club
HALE/TIMP WA15 166 A4
Altrincham Grammar
School for Boys
ALT WA14 177 G2
Altrincham Grammar
School for Girls
ALT WA14 177 F1
Altrincham Ice Rink
ALT WA14 165 G3
Altrincham Industrial Centre
ALT WA14 164 D3
Altrincham (Kersal) RFC
HALE/TIMP WA15 166 D2
Altrincham Leisure Centre
HALE/TIMP WA15 165 H4
Altrincham
Preparatory School
ALT WA14 177 F2
Altrincham Priory Hospital
HALE/TIMP WA15 178 B4
Altrincham Retail Park
ALT WA14 165 F2
Alvanley Industrial Estate
MPL/ROM SK6 161 G2
Amalgamated Sports Club
POY/DIS SK12 197 G1
Ancoats Hospital
ANC M4 113 H4
Angel Trading Estate
ANC M4 7 G1
Angouleme Way Retail Park
BURY BL9 5 F5
Ann Street Health Centre
DTN/ASHW M34 131 F5
Anson Medical Centre
RUSH/FAL M14 128 A4
Apollo Theatre
WGTN/LGST M12 127 H1
Aquinas College
OFTN SK2 172 C3
Arcades Shopping Centre
AUL OL6 118 A2
Arcadia Sports Centre
BNG/LEV M19 143 H2
Arden Business Centre
MPL/ROM SK6 146 B5
Arden Primary School
MPL/ROM SK6 161 E3
Armitage CE Primary School
WGTN/LGST M12 128 B2
Arndale Shopping Centre
ANC M4 7 F3
STRET M32 139 H2
Arrow Trading Estate
DTN/ASHW M34 131 E3
Art Gallery
BURY BL9 4 D5
EDGY/DAV SK3 13 F5
Arts & Craft College
BURY BL9 4 D5
Arundale Primary School
HYDE SK14 134 C5
Ashbury Primary School
OP/CLY M11 114 C5
Ashdene Primary School
WILM/AE SK9 199 E5
Ashfield Valley Primary School
ROCH OL11 42 D2
Ash Lea School
ECC M30 109 H2
Ashley CE (Controlled)
Primary School
HALE/TIMP WA15 188 A2
Ashton on Mersey School
SALE M33 154 A2
Ashton Retail Park
AUL OL6 118 A2
Ashton Swimming Pool
AUL OL6 118 A2
Ashton-under-Lyne Golf Club
AUL OL6 105 H3
Ashton Under Lyne RFC
AUL OL6 105 E3
Ashton Under Lyne
Sixth Form College
AUL OL6 118 C1
Ashton Under Lyne
6th Form College
AUL OL6 118 C2
Ashton United FC
AUL OL6 105 G4
Ashton upon Mersey
Cricket and Tennis Club
SALE M33 138 D4
Ashton upon Mersey Golf Club
SALE M33 138 D4
Aspinal Primary School
GTN M18 129 H5
Astley Bridge Cricket Club
BOL BL1 33 G2
Astra Business Park
TRPK M17 110 A5
Astra Industrial Centre
ROCH OL11 42 B3
Atlantic Business Centre
ALT WA14 165 F2
Atlas
TOT/BURYW BL8 37 H4
Atlas Trading
RDSH SK5 144 D4
Audenshaw High School
DTN/ASHW M34 131 F2
Audenshaw Primary School
DTN/ASHW M34 130 D1
Austerlands Cricket Club
OLDE OL4 76 B4
Avenue Medical Centre
BKLY M9 87 F2
Aviation Viewing Park
MANAIR M90 189 H2
Avicenna Grammar School
DID/WITH M20 157 E2
Avondale Health Centre
BOL BL1 33 F5
Avondale High School
EDGY/DAV SK3 12 A7
Avondale Industrial Estate
EDGY/DAV SK3 171 E1
Avondale Recreation Centre
EDGY/DAV SK3 171 E2
Baguley Hall Primary School
NTHM/RTH M23 167 H3
Baillie Street Health Centre
MILN OL16 10 D5
Balderstone
(Community) School
ROCH OL11 43 F3
Bamford Business Park
RDSH SK5 159 H1
Bamford Primary School
ROCH OL11 28 B5
Band on the Wall
ANC M4 7 G2
Bankfield Trading Estate
RDSH SK5 159 H2
Bank Meadow
Primary School
WGTN/LGST M12 114 A5
Banks Lane Primary School
STKP SK1 172 C1
Bare Trees J & I School
CHAD OL9 73 G4
Baring Street Industrial Estate
CMANE M1 7 K7
Barlow Hall Primary School
CCHDY M21 156 B1
Barlow Medical Centre
DID/WITH M20 157 F3
The Barlow RC High School
DID/WITH M20 157 H4
Barrack Hill Primary School
MPL/ROM SK6 161 H4
Barrington Medical Centre
ALT WA14 165 G3
Barton Business Park
ECC M30 109 F4
Barton Clough Primary School
STRET M32 124 A4
Barton Moss Primary School
ECC M30 108 C4
Bayley Industrial Estate
STLY SK15 119 E4
BBC North
CMANE M1 127 F1
Bealey Community Hospital
RAD M26 53 E5
Bealey Industrial Estate
RAD M26 53 E4
Beal Vale Primary School
ROY/SHW OL2 60 A2
Beaumont Hospital
HOR/BR BL6 46 C1
Beaumont Primary School
HOR/BR BL6 47 F4
Beaver Road Primary School
DID/WITH M20 157 G3
Beech House School
ROCH OL11 42 D1
Beever Primary School
OLD OL1 9 J1
Beis Rochel Girls School
CHH M8 100 A1
Belfield Community
Primary School
MILN OL16 11 J4
Belfield Trading Estate
MILN OL16 31 E2
Belfry House Hotel
WILM/AE SK9 192 A1
Belle Vue Regional
Hockey Centre
WGTN/LGST M12 128 D4
Belmore Hotel
SALE M33 154 C4
Benchill Primary School
WYTH/NTH M22 168 B3
Bentfield Industrial Units
CHAD OL9 89 G1
Bentinck Street
Industrial Estate
HULME M15 126 C1
Bethesda School
CHD/CHDH SK8 182 A1
Birches Health Centre
PWCH M25 85 F1
The Birches School
DID/WITH M20 157 E1
Birchfields Primary School
RUSH/FAL M14 143 F2
Birch Industrial Estate
HEY OL10 55 F3
Birchinley Manor Showground
MILN OL16 31 G3
Birtenshaw Hall School
BOL BL1 23 G5
Birtle View Special School
HEY OL10 40 D3
Bishop Bilsborrow RC
Primary School
OLDTF/WHR M16 142 A1
Bishop Bridgeman CE
Primary School
BOLS/LL BL3 48 D5
B & J Leisure Centre
WILM/AE SK9 199 F3
Blackbrook Trading Estate
BNG/LEV M19 144 A3
Blackley Cemetery
BKLY M9 86 B3
Blackley Crematorium
BKLY M9 86 B3
Blackshaw Lane CP School
ROY/SHW OL2 59 H5
Blackshaw Primary School
BOLE BL2 50 D3
Blessed Thomas Holford
Secondary School
HALE/TIMP WA15 165 H5
Blue Chip Business Park
ALT WA14 165 E2
Blue Coat CE School
OLD OL1 9 H2
Bnos Yisroel Schools
BRO M7 99 H3
Boarshaw Industrial Estate
MDTN M24 72 A4
Boarshaw Primary School
MDTN M24 72 A1
Bodmin Road Clinic
SALE M33 153 G1
Boggart Hole Clough Track
BKLY M9 87 G5
Bolholt Country Park Hotel
TOT/BURYW BL8 37 H3
Bollin CP School
ALT WA14 177 E3
Bolshaw Primary School
CHD/CHDH SK8 181 G5
Bolton Business Centre
BOLE BL2 3 G6
Bolton Community College
BOLE BL2 3 G7
Bolton Excel Leisure Centre
BOLE BL2 3 G7
Bolton Gates Retail Park
BOL BL1 3 F2
Bolton Golf Club
HOR/BR BL6 46 B1
Bolton Institute
BOLS/LL BL3 2 C7
Bolton Institute of He
BOLS/LL BL3 2 C7
Bolton Little Theatre
BOL BL1 2 C5
Bolton Old Links Golf Club
BOL BL1 32 A3
Bolton Open Golf Club
BOLE BL2 35 E3
Bolton Parish CE
Primary School
BOLE BL2 3 J4
Bolton Rugby Union FC
BOL BL1 2 A2
Bolton School (Boys Division)
BOL BL1 48 B2
Bolton School Girls Division
BOL BL1 48 A2
Bolton Sixth Form College
North Campus
BOL BL1 33 E2
Bolton Trophy & Sports Centre
BOLE BL2 49 H2
Bond Street Industrial Estate
WGTN/LGST M12 7 K7
Bonholt Industrial Estate
TOT/BURYW BL8 37 F2
Booth Hall Childrens Hospital
BKLY M9 87 G4
Booth House Trading Estate
CHAD OL9 8 B5
Boothstown Methodist School
WALK M28 94 A4
The Borchardt Medical Centre
DID/WITH M20 142 A5
Bornmore Industrial Centre
TOT/BURYW BL8 37 G3
Boundary Industrial Estate
BOLE BL2 50 D2
Boundary Trading Estate
ECC M30 121 D4
Bowdon CE Primary School
ALT WA14 177 F3
Bowdon Cricket Club
ALT WA14 177 F3
Bowdon Preparatory
School for Girls
ALT WA14 177 F2
Bowdon RUFC
HALE/TIMP WA15 166 D5
Bowdon Vale Cricket Club
ALT WA14 177 F4
Bower Hotel
CHAD OL9 89 E5
Bowker Bank Industrial Park
CHH M8 86 C5
Bowker Vale Primary School
BKLY M9 86 A3
Bowling Alley
BURY BL9 54 A3
OLDTF/WHR M16 125 H3
Bowness Primary School
BOLS/LL BL3 65 G1
Brabyns Recreation Centre
MPL/ROM SK6 175 F2
Brabyns School
MPL/ROM SK6 175 F2
Brackley Municipal Golf Club
LHULT M38 79 D1
Bradley Fold Trading Estate
BOLE BL2 51 F3
Bradley Green Primary School
HYDE SK14 133 E2
Bradshaw Cricket Club
BOLE BL2 34 D1
Bradshaw Hall J & I School
CHD/CHDH SK8 182 B3
Bradshaw Trading Estate
MDTN M24 88 C2
Bramall Hall
BRAM/HZG SK7 183 G3
Bramall Park Golf Club
CHD/CHDH SK8 183 F3
Bramall Park Lawn Tennis Club
BRAM/HZG SK7 183 G2

Bramall Park Tennis Club *BRAM/HZG* SK7 183 G4
Bramhall Golf Club *BRAM/HZG* SK7 194 A1
Bramhall Health Centre *BRAM/HZG* SK7 193 H1
Bramhall High School *BRAM/HZG* SK7 184 A4
Bramhall Moor Industrial Estate *BRAM/HZG* SK7 184 C2
Bramhall Park Medical Centre *BRAM/HZG* SK7 183 H2
Bramhall Village Shopping Centre *BRAM/HZG* SK7 193 G1
Brandwood Primary School *BOLS/LL* BL3 48 B5
Branwood Preparatory School *ECC* M30 109 H2
Bredbury Clinic *MPL/ROM* SK6 161 G2
Bredbury Green Primary School *MPL/ROM* SK6 161 G5
Bredbury Hall Hotel & Country Club *MPL/ROM* SK6 161 E4
Breeze Hill Comprehensive School *OLDE* OL4 91 G2
Breightmet FC *BOLE* BL2 50 C2
Breightmet Golf Club *BOLE* BL2 35 H5
Breightmet Industrial Estate *BOLE* BL2 50 C2
Brentwood Special School *ALT* WA14 165 H2
Bretnall Primary School *BRO* M7 99 G3
Bridge College *OFTN* SK2 173 E1
Bridge Hall Primary School *EDGY/DAV* SK3 171 G3
Bridge House Medical Centre *CHD/CHDH* SK8 183 E1
Bridge Mills Business Park *SLFD* M6 98 C5
Bridgeside Business Centre *MPL/ROM* SK6 146 A5
Bridge Trading Estate *TOT/BURYW* BL8 4 A4
Bridgewater Concert Hall *CMANW* M2 6 E7
Bridgewater Primary School *LHULT* M38 80 D3
Bridgewater School *WALK* M28 95 H4
Brighton Road Industrial Estate *HTNM* SK4 159 E5
Brimrod Primary School *ROCH* OL11 42 C1
Brindale Primary School *RDSH* SK5 160 D2
Brindle Heath Industrial Estate *SLFD* M6 111 G1
Brindle House Community Mental Health Centre *HYDE* SK14 147 G1
Brinksway Trading Estate *HTNM* SK4 12 B5
Brinnington Health Centre *RDSH* SK5 160 D1
Briscoe Lane J & I School *NEWH/MOS* M40 102 A5
Britannia Business Park *BOLE* BL2 34 C4
Britannia Mill Industrial Estate *HEY* OL10 40 C4
Broadbent Fold Primary School *DUK* SK16 133 F1
Broadbottom Primary School *HYDE* SK14 149 G3
Broadfield Industrial Estate *HEY* OL10 40 C5
Broadfield Primary School *OLDS* OL8 90 C3
Broadheath Primary School *ALT* WA14 165 F1
Broadhurst Primary School *NEWH/MOS* M40 102 B3
Broadoak Business Park *TRPK* M17 124 A1
Broad Oak High School *BURY* BL9 39 F4
Broadoak High School *PART* M31 150 D4
Broadoak Primary School *AUL* OL6 105 F4
Broad Oak Primary School *DID/WITH* M20 169 G1
Broadoak Primary School *SWIN* M27 96 B4
Broadoak Sports Centre *AUL* OL6 105 G4
Broadstone Hall Primary School *HTNM* SK4 144 C5
Broadwalk Primary School *SLFD* M6 111 H2
Broadway Business Park *CHAD* OL9 73 G4
CHAD OL9 88 C3
Broadway Industrial Estate *HYDE* SK14 132 A3
ORD M5 111 H5
Brookburn Primary School *CCHDY* M21 140 D4
Brookdale Golf Club *FAIL* M35 103 G5
Brooke Dean Community School *WILM/AE* SK9 192 A3
Brookfield Business Park *CHD/CHDH* SK8 170 C4
Brookhead Junior School *CHD/CHDH* SK8 170 C4
Brooklands Primary School *SALE* M33 154 B4
Brooks Bar Medical Centre *OLDTF/WHR* M16 126 C4
Brookside Business Park *MDTN* M24 88 C1
Brookside Primary School *MPL/ROM* SK6 196 D1
Brookway High School *NTHM/RTH* M23 167 F1
Broomwood CP School *HALE/TIMP* WA15 167 E4
Broughton Baths *BRO* M7 99 G4
Broughton Cricket Club *BRO* M7 99 F4
Broughton Jewish Cassel-Fox Primary School *BRO* M7 99 G2
Brownhill Special School *WHIT* OL12 10 B3
Brownlow Business Centre *BOL* BL1 33 G5
Brownlow Fold Primary School *BOL* BL1 33 G5
Brunswick Health Centre *BRUN/LGST* M13 127 G2
Bruntwood Primary School *CHD/CHDH* SK8 182 B2
Buckley Hall Industrial Estate *WHIT* OL12 30 C1
Buckley Road Industrial Estate *WHIT* OL12 30 C1
Buckstones Primary School *ROY/SHW* OL2 60 C1
Buckton Vale Primary School *STLY* SK15 107 G3
Buile Hill High School *SLFD* M6 111 E1
Bullough Moor Primary School *HEY* OL10 40 B5
Burgess Primary School *BKLY* M9 101 F3
Burnage High School For Boys *BNG/LEV* M19 158 C1
Burnage Rugby Club *HTNM* SK4 158 B5
Burnden Industrial Estate *BOLS/LL* BL3 49 G5
Burnley Brow Community School *CHAD* OL9 73 H3
Burrs Country Park *TOT/BURYW* BL8 27 E5
Bury Business Centre *BURY* BL9 5 H1
Bury Catholic Preparatory School *BURY* BL9 53 F1
Bury CE High School *BURY* BL9 53 F1
Bury Cemetery *BURY* BL9 53 G2
Bury College *BURY* BL9 4 D6
Bury County Court *BURY* BL9 4 C5
Bury FC (Gigg Lane) *BURY* BL9 53 G2
Bury Golf Club *BURY* BL9 53 H5
Bury Grammar School for Girls & Boys *BURY* BL9 4 B6
Bury Industrial Estate *BOLE* BL2 50 C1
Bury Market *BURY* BL9 4 E5
Bury Sports Club *BURY* BL9 53 F1
Business & Arts Centre *HTNM* SK4 144 C4
Business Park *UPML* OL3 77 G1
Business & Technology Centre *ECC* M30 109 F3
Butterstile Primary School *PWCH* M25 84 D5
Button Lane School *NTHM/RTH* M23 155 G4
Byron Street Infant Community School *ROY/SHW* OL2 59 F5
Cadishead Junior School *IRL* M44 135 G5
Cadishead Recreation Centre *IRL* M44 150 C1
Caius House School *URM* M41 138 B2
Caldershaw Primary School *WHIT* OL12 28 C2
Cale Green Primary School *EDGY/DAV* SK3 171 H2
Camberwell Park School *BKLY* M9 86 D3
Cambrian Business Park *BOLS/LL* BL3 48 C4
Cambridge Industrial Estate *BRO* M7 112 D1
Cambridge Street Industrial Area *BRO* M7 112 D1
Campanile Hotel *ORD* M5 112 C5
Cams Lane Primary School *RAD* M26 67 E1
Canalside Industrial Estate *MILN* OL16 43 G1
Cannon Street Health Centre *BOLS/LL* BL3 48 C4
Canon Burrows CE Primary School *AULW* OL7 104 C5
Canon Johnson CE Primary School *AULW* OL7 118 A1
Canon Slade School *BOLE* BL2 34 C2
Canon Williamson CE High School *ECC* M30 108 C4
Canterbury Road J & I School *URM* M41 123 G5
Capital Business Centre *BRAM/HZG* SK7 193 G1
Cardinal Langley RC High School *MDTN* M24 57 F5
Cariocca Business Park *NEWH/MOS* M40 114 B2
WGTN/LGST M12 128 A2
Carlton Industrial Centre *BOLE* BL2 3 G6
Carrbrook Industrial Estate *STLY* SK15 107 H4
Carrington Business Park *PART* M31 136 D5
Castlebrook High School *BURY* BL9 69 F1
Castlefield Gallery *CSLFD* M3 6 C7
Castle Hawk Golf Club *ROCH* OL11 41 H5
Castle Hill Primary School *BOL* BL1 34 C4
Castle Hill School *RDSH* SK5 145 H5
Castle Leisure Centre *BURY* BL9 4 C4
Castle Park Industrial Estate *OLD* OL1 75 E5
Castleton Gabriels FC *ROCH* OL11 42 A4
Castleton Primary School *ROCH* OL11 42 C4
Castleton Swimming Pool *ROCH* OL11 42 B3
Cathedral Visitor Centre *CSLFD* M3 6 E3
Cavendish Industrial Estate *AUL* OL6 117 H2
Cavendish Road Primary School *DID/WITH* M20 157 F1
Central Art Gallery *AUL* OL6 118 A3
Central Industrial Estate *BOLS/LL* BL3 49 E4
MDTN M24 71 H4
Central Leisure Centre *MILN* OL16 10 E6
Central Primary School *DTN/ASHW* M34 131 F5
Central Retail Park *ANC* M4 7 K4
Century Mill Industrial Estate *FWTH* BL4 64 C4
Chadderton AFC *CHAD* OL9 73 G4
Chadderton Cemetery *CHAD* OL9 73 F4
Chadderton Hall Junior School *CHAD* OL9 73 F2
Chadderton Industrial Estate *MDTN* M24 88 B2
Chadderton Shopping Precinct *CHAD* OL9 73 G4
Chadderton Sports Centre & Public Baths *CHAD* OL9 73 G5
Chadderton Town Health Centre *CHAD* OL9 73 G5
Chadkirk Industrial Estate *MPL/ROM* SK6 174 A1
Chalfont Primary School *BOL* BL1 34 A4
Chantlers Primary School *TOT/BURYW* BL8 37 F4
Chapelfield Primary School *RAD* M26 67 H3
Chapel Medical Centre *IRL* M44 136 B1
Chapel Street Primary School *BNG/LEV* M19 144 A2
Charleston Industrial Estate *AULW* OL7 118 A1
Charlestown Health Centre *BKLY* M9 87 H5
Charlestown Primary School *BKLY* M9 88 A4
SLFD M6 112 A1
Cheadle Catholic Primary School *CHD/CHDH* SK8 182 B2
Cheadle Cricket Club *CHD/CHDH* SK8 169 H4
Cheadle Golf Club *CHD/CHDH* SK8 170 B5
Cheadle Heath Clinic *EDGY/DAV* SK3 170 D1
Cheadle Heath Primary School *EDGY/DAV* SK3 170 D2
Cheadle Heath Sports Centre *CHD/CHDH* SK8 170 D3
Cheadle Hulme College *CHD/CHDH* SK8 183 E5
Cheadle Hulme Medical Centre *CHD/CHDH* SK8 182 D4
Cheadle Hulme Recreation Centre *CHD/CHDH* SK8 183 E5
Cheadle Hulme School *CHD/CHDH* SK8 182 D4
Cheadle Primary School *CHD/CHDH* SK8 170 A3
Cheadle Royal Hospital *CHD/CHDH* SK8 181 H3
Cheadle Royel Shopping Centre *CHD/CHDH* SK8 182 A2
Cheadle Swimming & Recreation Centre *CHD/CHDH* SK8 170 B5
Cheadle Town FC *CHD/CHDH* SK8 170 B4
Cheetham CE Community School *BRO* M7 100 A3
Cheetham Hill Cricket Club *CHH* M8 99 H1
Cheethwood Community & Sports Centre *CHH* M8 100 A4
Cheetwood Primary School *CHH* M8 112 D1
Cherry Manor Primary School *SALE* M33 153 F4
Cherry Tree Hospital *OFTN* SK2 172 D4
Cherry Tree Primary School *FWTH* BL4 63 H4
Chesham Industrial Estate *BURY* BL9 38 D2
Chesham Primary School *BURY* BL9 38 D1
Chester Court Hotel *STRET* M32 125 G4
Chethams School of Music *CSLFD* M3 6 E2
Chichester Business Centre *MILN* OL16 11 F7
Child Health Clinic *MDTN* M24 71 G3
Chinese Medical Centre *CSLFD* M3 6 C6
Chorlton-cum-Hardy CE Primary School *CCHDY* M21 140 D3
Chorlton-cum-Hardy Cricket Club *CCHDY* M21 141 E5
Chorlton-cum-Hardy Golf Club *CCHDY* M21 156 B1
Chorlton Leisure Centre *CCHDY* M21 141 E2
Chorlton Park Primary School *CCHDY* M21 141 F4
Chorlton Shopping Centre *CCHDY* M21 140 D2
Chorlton Water Park *CCHDY* M21 156 B2
Christchurch CE Primary School *BOLE* BL2 36 B5
Christ Church CE Primary School *CHAD* OL9 89 F1
TOT/BURYW BL8 37 E2
Christie Hospital & Holt Radium Institute *DID/WITH* M20 142 C5
Christie Street Industrial Estate *STKP* SK1 13 J7
Christs Church CE Primary School *BOLE* BL2 35 G4
Christ the King RC Primary School *WALK* M28 81 F5
Church Road Primary School *BOL* BL1 32 D4
Church Street Industrial Estate *MDTN* M24 71 H2
City Centre Campus *CSLFD* M3 6 B4
City College Manchester *DID/WITH* M20 157 E2
NTHM/RTH M23 156 B5
NTHM/RTH M23 167 E1
City Course Trading Estate *OP/CLY* M11 128 D1
City Court Trading Estate *ANC* M4 7 K2
City Park Business Village *OLDTF/WHR* M16 126 A3
Claremont Primary School *RUSH/FAL* M14 127 F5
Clarendon Cottage School *ECC* M30 110 A2
Clarendon County Primary School *BOLS/LL* BL3 48 D4
Clarendon Fields Primary School *DUK* SK16 118 A5
Clarendon Industrial Estate *HYDE* SK14 132 D5
Clarendon Road Primary School *ECC* M30 110 A2
Clarendon Square Shopping Centre *HYDE* SK14 147 G1
Clarke Industrial Estate *STRET* M32 124 B3
Clarksfield Primary School *OLDE* OL4 91 F1
Clayton Health Centre *OP/CLY* M11 115 E3
Clayton Industrial Estate *OP/CLY* M11 129 G1
Cleavley Athletics Track *ECC* M30 108 D2
Cleggs Lane Industrial Site *LHULT* M38 80 C1
Cleveland Preparatory School *BOL* BL1 47 H2
Clifton Country Park *SWIN* M27 82 D2
Clifton Industrial Estate *SWIN* M27 83 H4
Clifton Primary School *SWIN* M27 83 E4
Cloughside School *PWCH* M25 84 C1
The Club Theatre *ALT* WA14 177 G1
Cobden Mill Industrial Estate *FWTH* BL4 64 C3
Coldhurst Community Centre *OLD* OL1 8 E1
Coldhurst Industrial Estate *OLD* OL1 9 F1
Coliseum Theatre *OLD* OL1 9 J3
Collegiate Medical Centre *CHH* M8 100 B3
Comfort Inn *WGTN/LGST* M12 128 D2
Comfort Inn Hotel *WGTN/LGST* M12 128 D2
Commonwealth House *MANAIR* M90 180 A4
Concord Business Park *WYTH/NTH* M22 180 B3
WYTH/NTH M22 180 D3
Coney Green High School *RAD* M26 52 C5
Constellation Trading Estate *RAD* M26 52 A3
Co-operative Museum *WHIT* OL12 10 B5
Copley High School *STLY* SK15 120 A3
Copper Beeches School *SALE* M33 154 A2
Coppice Industrial Estate *OLDS* OL8 8 C6
Coppice J & I School *OLDS* OL8 90 B3
Copthorne Hotel *SALQ* M50 125 H2
Cornbrook Estate *HULME* M15 126 C1
Cornerhouse Cinema *CMANE* M1 7 F7
Cornishway Industrial Estate *WYTH/NTH* M22 180 C4
Cornwall Street Industrial Estate *OP/CLY* M11 129 G1
Corpus Christi RC Primary School *CHAD* OL9 89 G3
Corpus Christi with St Anne RC Primary School *ANC* M4 114 A4
Corrie Primary School *DTN/ASHW* M34 146 C2
Counthill School *OLDE* OL4 75 G2
County End Business Centre *OLDE* OL4 76 A5
County Hotel *BRAM/HZG* SK7 183 H5
Courts of Justice *CSLFD* M3 6 C5
Crab Lane Primary School *BKLY* M9 86 C3
Craft Centre *ANC* M4 7 G3
Craft Shops *BOL* BL1 2 E3
Cravenwood Primary School *CHH* M8 100 A2
Cresta Court Hotel *ALT* WA14 165 G4
Croft Industrial Estate *BURY* BL9 53 H4
Cromer Industrial Estate *MDTN* M24 72 A3
Cromford Business Park *OLD* OL1 75 E4
Crompton Cricket Club *ROY/SHW* OL2 60 A1
Crompton Fold Primary School *BOLE* BL2 50 B2
Crompton Health Centre *ROY/SHW* OL2 60 A3
Crompton House School *ROY/SHW* OL2 59 G2
Crompton & Royton Golf Club *ROY/SHW* OL2 59 G4
Crompton Swimming Pool *ROY/SHW* OL2 60 A3
Cromwell High School & Astley Sports College *DUK* SK16 132 D2
Cromwell House Community Mental Health Centre *ECC* M30 109 G3
Cromwell Special School *DTN/ASHW* M34 145 E1
Crosland Industrial Estate *MPL/ROM* SK6 161 F2
Crossacres J & I School *WYTH/NTH* M22 169 E5
Crossgates Primary School *MILN* OL16 31 H4
Crowcroft Park Primary School *WGTN/LGST* M12 128 D5
Crown Business Centre *FAIL* M35 103 E2
Crowne Plaza *CMANW* M2 6 E6
Crown Industrial Estate *ALT* WA14 165 H2
ANC M4 7 K2
Crown Royal Industrial Park *STKP* SK1 13 H5
Crumpsall Lane Primary School *CHH* M8 100 B1
Culcheth Hall School *ALT* WA14 177 F1
Curzon Ashton FC *AULW* OL7 117 G3
Curzon Cinema *URM* M41 138 A1
Cutgate Shopping Precinct *WHIT* OL12 29 E2
Dagenham Road Industrial Estate *RUSH/FAL* M14 127 H5
Daisy Nook Country Park *OLDS* OL8 104 B3
Dale Grove Primary Centre (Bankside) *HYDE* SK14 148 A2
Dale Grove Special School *AULW* OL7 104 D5
The Dale Primary School *MPL/ROM* SK6 174 C2
Dale Street Industrial Estate *RAD* M26 67 F2
Dancehouse Theatre & Northern Ballet Scool *CMANE* M1 127 F1
Dane Bank Primary School *DTN/ASHW* M34 145 F1
Dane Road Industrial Estate *SALE* M33 154 D1
Darnhill CP School *HEY* OL10 40 A5
Davaar Medical Centre *DUK* SK16 118 B5
Davenport Golf Club *POY/DIS* SK12 196 A3
David Cuthbert Business Centre *OP/CLY* M11 129 F1
David Medical Centre *CCHDY* M21 141 F5
Davyhulme Park Golf Club *URM* M41 122 C4
Deakins Business Park *EDGW/EG* BL7 22 C1
Deane Golf Club *BOLS/LL* BL3 47 H4
Deane leisure Centre *BOLS/LL* BL3 47 G5
The Deane School *BOLS/LL* BL3 47 G5
Dean Lane Medical Centre *BRAM/HZG* SK7 185 E4
Dean Row Community Junior School *WILM/AE* SK9 200 B1
The Deans CP School *SWIN* M27 96 D2
Deans Road Industrial Estate *SWIN* M27 96 C2
Deanway Trading Estate *WILM/AE* SK9 192 A4
Deeplish Primary School *ROCH* OL11 43 F1

Delamere School URM M41 137 E1
De la Salle Centre & Pendleton College SLFD M6 110 D2
Delta Business Park DTN/ASHW M34 131 F1
Demmings Infant School CHD/CHDH SK8 170 C4
Dental Hospital HULME M15 127 F2
Denton Cemetery DTN/ASHW M34 146 C3
Denton Cricket & Sports Club DTN/ASHW M34 131 F3
Denton Golf Club DTN/ASHW M34 130 C4
Denton St Lawrence Cricket Club DTN/ASHW M34 146 C1
Department of Clinical Psychology ROY/SHW OL2 74 B2
Derby High School BURY BL9 53 E1
Derby Shopping Centre BOLS/LL BL3 48 C4
Derwent Street Trading Estate ORD M5 126 B1
The Designer Outlet SALQ M50 125 G1
Devonshire Road Primary School BOL BL1 47 H1
Devonshire Street Industrial Estate WGTN/LGST M12 128 A2
Dial Park Primary School OFTN SK2 173 E5
Didsbury CE Primary School DID/WITH M20 157 G3
Didsbury Cricket Club DID/WITH M20 157 H5
Didsbury Golf Club WYTH/NTH M22 157 E5
Didsbury Medical Centre DID/WITH M20 157 F2
Didsbury Primary School HTNM SK4 158 C4
Disley Golf Club POY/DIS SK12 187 H5
Downing Street Industrial Estate WGTN/LGST M12 127 G1
Dowry Park Industrial Estate OLDE OL4 75 H5
Dowson Primary School HYDE SK14 147 H3
Droylsden AFC DROY M43 116 B4
Droylsden High School for Girls DROY M43 115 H3
Droylsden Sports Centre DROY M43 115 H3
Droylsden Swimming Pool DROY M43 116 B5
Ducie Athletics Ground Running Track GTN M18 129 E4
Ducie High School RUSH/FAL M14 127 F4
Ducie High School For Boys RUSH/FAL M14 127 G4
Ducie Sports Centre RUSH/FAL M14 127 G4
Dukesgate Primary School LHULT M38 80 B2
Dukinfield Crematorium DUK SK16 118 C4
Dukinfield Golf Club DUK SK16 133 F1
Dukinfield Joint Cemetery DUK SK16 118 C4
Dunham Forest Golf & Country Club ALT WA14 164 C5
Dunscar Golf Club EDGW/EG BL7 22 C3
Dunscar Industrial Estate EDGW/EG BL7 22 D4
Dunstan Medical Centre BOLE BL2 49 H2
Durnford Medical Centre MDTN M24 71 G3
Durn Street Industrial Estate LIT OL15 21 F2
Eagley Infant School EDGW/EG BL7 23 F3
Eagley Junior School EDGW/EG BL7 23 G3
East Crompton St Georges CE Primary School ROY/SHW OL2 60 B2
East Crompton St James CE Primary School ROY/SHW OL2 60 A2
East Lancashire Railway BURY BL9 27 E3
HEY OL10 54 D1
East Ward Primary School BURY BL9 5 K4
Eaton Place Business Centre SALE M33 154 B2
Eccles College ECC M30 110 A1
Eccles Crematorium ECC M30 108 C5
Eccles Health Centre ECC M30 110 A3
Eccles Recreation Centre ECC M30 110 A4
Eccleston Avenue RUSH/FAL M14 142 B2
Eccles Town Hall ECC M30 110 A3
Edge Fold Industrial Estate FWTH BL4 63 F3
Egerton & Dunscar Health Centre EDGW/EG BL7 23 E3
Egerton House Hotel EDGW/EG BL7 22 D1
Egerton Park Arts College DTN/ASHW M34 131 F3
Egerton Park Community High School DTN/ASHW M34 131 E4
Elk Mill Central Retail Park OLD OL1 73 G1
Elladene Park CCHDY M21 141 F3
Ellenbrook Primary School WALK M28 94 C3
Ellesmere Bowling & Tennis Club WALK M28 95 E2
Ellesmere Golf Club WALK M28 95 G1
Ellesmere Retail Park WALK M28 80 D4
Ellesmere Shopping Centre LHULT M38 80 D4
Elmridge Primary School HALE/TIMP WA15 178 D4
Elms Medical Centre WHTF M45 68 B3
Elm Wood Primary School MDTN M24 72 B4
Elsinore Business Centre OLDTF/WHR M16 125 H4
The Elton High School TOT/BURYW BL8 37 F3
Elton Primary School TOT/BURYW BL8 37 H3
Emmanuel Christian School WHIT OL12 29 G2
Emmanuel Holcombe Primary School TOT/BURYW BL8 16 B2
Empress Business Centre OLDTF/WHR M16 126 B2
English Martyrs RC Primary School URM M41 138 B1
Enterprise Trading Estate GTN M18 129 H2
TRPK M17 110 B5
Esplanade Arts & Heritage Centre MILN OL16 10 B7
Etchells Primary School CHD/CHDH SK8 181 H3
Eton Hill Industrial Estate RAD M26 52 D4
Etrop Grange Hotel & Restaurant MANAIR M90 180 A3
ETZ Chaim School CHH M8 85 H5
Europa Business Park EDGY/DAV SK3 171 E3
Europa Trading Estate RAD M26 66 A5
Ewing School DID/WITH M20 157 F1
Express by Holiday Inn GTN M18 129 H3
SALQ M50 125 G1
Express Trading Estate FWTH BL4 81 E1
The Eye Clinic CMANW M2 6 E5
Fahay Industrial Estate NEWH/MOS M40 114 B3
Failsworth Health Centre FAIL M35 102 D3
Failsworth Industrial Estate FAIL M35 102 B4
Failsworth School (Upper) FAIL M35 103 F3
Failsworth Shopping Centre FAIL M35 103 E3
Fairfield General Hospital BURY BL9 39 H2
Fairfield Golf & Sailing Club DTN/ASHW M34 130 C1
Fairfield High School for Girls DROY M43 116 A5
Fairfield Primary School BURY BL9 39 G3
Fairfield Road Primary School DROY M43 116 A5
Fairhill Industrial Estate IRL M44 136 A4
Fairview Medical Centre URM M41 138 A1
Fairway Primary School OFTN SK2 173 F2
Falcon Business Centre CHAD OL9 73 H4
Falinge Park High School WHIT OL12 29 G2
Fallowfield Medical Centre RUSH/FAL M14 143 E3
Fallowfield Shopping Centre RUSH/FAL M14 143 F2
Farjo Medical Centre CMANE M1 7 G6
Farnworth Cemetery FWTH BL4 65 F3
Farnworth Little Theatre FWTH BL4 65 E4
Farnworth Park Industrial Estate FWTH BL4 65 E3
Farnworth Social Circle Cricket Club FWTH BL4 64 D5
Farrowdale House School ROY/SHW OL2 60 A3
Fiddlers Lane Primary School IRL M44 121 C5
Fieldhouse Cricket Club ROCH OL11 28 B5
Fieldhouse Industrial Estate WHIT OL12 10 D1
Firbank Primary School ROY/SHW OL2 59 E2
Firgrove Business Park MILN OL16 31 E3
Firs CP School SALE M33 153 G2
Fir Tree Primary School RDSH SK5 144 D1
Firwood Industrial Estate BOLE BL2 34 D4
Firwood Manor Preparatory School CHAD OL9 73 G3
Firwood Special School BOLE BL2 34 D4
Fishbrook Industrial Estate FWTH BL4 65 G5
Fishpool Infant School BURY BL9 53 G1
Fitton Hill Shopping Precinct OLDS OL8 90 C4
Five Fold Industrial Park CHAD OL9 8 D4
Flixton Cricket Club URM M41 122 B5
Flixton FC URM M41 122 A5
Flixton Girls High School URM M41 137 H1
Flixton Health Clinic URM M41 137 E1
Flixton J & I School URM M41 137 G1
Flowery Field Primary School HYDE SK14 132 C4
Forest Gate Community Primary School PART M31 150 C3
Forest Park School SALE M33 154 B2
Forest School HALE/TIMP WA15 166 A3
Forge Industrial Estate OLDE OL4 75 E5
Forum Leisure Centre WYTH/NTH M22 180 B1
Fourways Trading Estate TRPK M17 124 B2
Freehold Community Primary School CHAD OL9 8 A6
Freetown Business Park BURY BL9 5 G1
The Friars Primary School CSLFD M3 6 A1
Friezland Primary School OLDE OL4 93 F2
Fulshaw CE Primary School WILM/AE SK9 199 E4
Furrow Community School MDTN M24 70 D1
Galleon Leisure Centre DID/WITH M20 169 H1
Gallery of Costume RUSH/FAL M14 142 D1
The Gallery HALE/TIMP WA15 177 G1
Garrick Playhouse ALT WA14 165 G3
Garrick Theatre EDGY/DAV SK3 13 F4
Gaskell Primary School BOL BL1 2 B2
The Gates Shopping Centre BOL BL1 2 E4
Gateway Industrial Estate CMANE M1 7 J5
Gatley Golf Club CHD/CHDH SK8 181 G1
Gatley Health Centre CHD/CHDH SK8 169 F3
Gatley Primary School CHD/CHDH SK8 169 F4
Gee Cross Holy Trinity CE Primary School HYDE SK14 148 A3
Gee Cross Social & Sports Club HYDE SK14 147 H3
George H Carnall Leisure Centre URM M41 123 H4
George Tomlinson School FWTH BL4 81 F1
Georgian Health Centre OLD OL1 9 H3
Gilnow Mill Industrial Estate BOL BL1 48 B3
Gilnow Primary School BOL BL1 48 B3
Glebe House School MILN OL16 29 H5
Glen Trading Estate OLDE OL4 91 G1
Globe Industrial Estate RAD M26 67 G1
Globe Lane Industrial Estate DUK SK16 132 A1
Globe Lane Primary School DUK SK16 132 A2
Glodwick Health Centre OLDE OL4 91 E1
Glodwick Infant School OLDE OL4 91 E2
Gloucester House Medical Centre URM M41 138 C1
GMB National College OLDTF/WHR M16 141 F1
GMEX Centre CMANW M2 6 D7
Golden Tulip Hotel TRPK M17 125 G2
Gorrells Industrial Estate ROCH OL11 42 D3
Gorsefield Primary School RAD M26 52 B5
Gorse Hall Primary School STLY SK15 119 E4
Gorse Hill Health Centre STRET M32 125 F5
Gorse Hill Primary School STRET M32 125 F4
Gorsey Bank Primary School WILM/AE SK9 199 E3
Gorton Brook First School WGTN/LGST M12 128 D2
Gorton Industrial Estate GTN M18 129 F2
Gorton Medical Centre GTN M18 129 G3
Gorton Mount Primary School GTN M18 129 F5
Gorton Retail Market GTN M18 129 G3
Goshen Sports Centre BURY BL9 53 H3
Granada Studios CSLFD M3 6 B5
Grange Primary School WILM/AE SK9 191 H3
Grange School CHAD OL9 8 E2
RUSH/FAL M14 128 A5
Grasscroft Independent School OLDE OL4 92 D2
Great Lever & Farnworth Golf Club FWTH BL4 63 G3
Great Moor Clinic OFTN SK2 172 D4
Great Moor Primary School OFTN SK2 172 C5
Greave Primary School MPL/ROM SK6 162 B2
Greenacres Primary School OLDE OL4 75 F5
Greenbank Primary School WHIT OL12 10 D2
Greenbank School CHD/CHDH SK8 182 D3
Greenbrow Infant School NTHM/RTH M23 179 G1
Greencourts Business Park WYTH/NTH M22 181 F5
Green End Junior School BNG/LEV M19 158 B1
Greenfield Primary School HYDE SK14 147 H2
Green Fold Special School FWTH BL4 64 A4
Greengate Industrial Estate MDTN M24 88 B2
Greenheys Business Centre HULME M15 127 F3
Greenhill Primary School OLDE OL4 9 H6
TOT/BURYW BL8 37 E5
Green Lane Industrial Estate HTNM SK4 12 B2
Greenmount Cricket Club TOT/BURYW BL8 26 A2
Greenmount Primary School TOT/BURYW BL8 25 H1
Green Room Theatre CMANE M1 6 E7
Greenside Primary School DROY M43 116 A3
Greenside Trading Centre DROY M43 116 B4
Greenwood Business Centre ORD M5 111 H4
Greenwood Primary School ECC M30 109 H1
Greswell Primary School DTN/ASHW M34 146 B1
Greyhound & Speedway Stadium GTN M18 129 E3
Greyland Medical Centre PWCH M25 85 E1
Griffin Business Centre SLFD M6 99 F5
Grosvenor Business Park MPL/ROM SK6 146 C5
Grosvenor Industrial Estate AULW OL7 117 H4
Grosvenor Road Primary School SWIN M27 97 G4
Guardian Angels RC Primary School TOT/BURYW BL8 37 G3
Guide Bridge Industrial Estate DTN/ASHW M34 117 F5
Guide Bridge Theatre DTN/ASHW M34 117 F5
Guide Bridge Trading Estate DTN/ASHW M34 117 F5
Guinness Road Trading Estate TRPK M17 110 A5
Hale Barns Cricket Club HALE/TIMP WA15 179 F4
Halebarns Cricket Club HALE/TIMP WA15 189 E1
Hale Golf Club HALE/TIMP WA15 178 B5
Hale Preparatory School HALE/TIMP WA15 177 H1
Halfpenny Bridge Industrial Estate MILN OL16 30 B5
Halliwell Industrial Estate BOL BL1 33 G3
Hampson Street Trading Estate ORD M5 112 C4
Handforth Health Centre WILM/AE SK9 192 A4
Hanover Business Park ALT WA14 165 E2
Harcourt Industrial Centre WALK M28 81 E2
Hardman Fold Special School FAIL M35 102 C3
Hardy Mill Primary School BOLE BL2 35 G2
Harper Green School FWTH BL4 64 C3
Harphurey Business Centre BKLY M9 101 E1
Harp Industrial Estate ROCH OL11 42 C4
Harp Trading Estate TRPK M17 110 B5
Harpurhey Health Centre BKLY M9 101 E2
Harpur Mount Primary School BKLY M9 101 E2
Harrop Fold School WALK M28 80 C5
Harrytown Catholic High School MPL/ROM SK6 161 H4
Hartford Industrial Estate CHAD OL9 8 B5
Hartshead High School AUL OL6 105 H3
Harwood Golf Club (Bolton) BOLE BL2 35 H2
Harwood Health Centre BOLE BL2 35 E1
Harwood Meadows Primary School BOLE BL2 35 G3
Harwood Park Primary School HEY OL10 41 E5
Haslam Park Primary School BOLS/LL BL3 48 A4
Hathershaw Technology College OLDS OL8 90 C5
Hat Museum EDGY/DAV SK3 13 F4
Hattersley Health Clinic HYDE SK14 149 F1
Hattersley Industrial Estate HYDE SK14 149 F2
Hawkins Clinic MILN OL16 10 D7
Hawksley Industrial Estate OLDS OL8 89 H4
Hawthorns Special School DTN/ASHW M34 131 E3
Hayward School BOLS/LL BL3 63 G2
Hayward Sports Centre BOLS/LL BL3 63 F2
Hazeldene Medical Centre NEWH/MOS M40 102 D1
Hazel Grove Clinic BRAM/HZG SK7 185 F1
Hazel Grove Golf Club BRAM/HZG SK7 186 A3
Hazel Grove High School BRAM/HZG SK7 184 D3
Hazel Grove Pools & Fitness Centre BRAM/HZG SK7 184 B3
Hazel Grove Primary School BRAM/HZG SK7 185 F1
Hazel Grove Recreation Centre BRAM/HZG SK7 184 D4
Hazlehurst Primary School RAMS BL0 16 B4
Heald Green Medical Centre CHD/CHDH SK8 181 G4
Heald Place Primary School RUSH/FAL M14 127 G5
Healey Primary School WHIT OL12 18 D5
Heap Bridge Primary School BURY BL9 39 G5
Heathfield Primary School BOLS/LL BL3 62 D2
Heaton Cemetery BOL BL1 48 A3
Heaton Cricket Club BOL BL1 32 D4
Heaton Hall PWCH M25 85 H2
Heaton Medical Centre BOL BL1 32 C5
Heaton Moor Golf Club HTNM SK4 158 D1
Heaton Moor Medical Centre HTNM SK4 159 F1
Heaton Moor RUFC HTNM SK4 159 E3
Heaton Norris Health Centre HTNM SK4 159 G3
Heaton Park Golf Centre PWCH M25 85 H1
Heaton Special School HTNM SK4 159 E1
Hempshaw Business Centre STKP SK1 172 C2
Henshaw Society for the Blind OLDTF/WHR M16 125 H4
Hertford Industrial Estate AULW OL7 117 H4
Heybrook Primary School WHIT OL12 11 F3
Heyes Lane J & I School HALE/TIMP WA15 166 C1
The Heys Primary School AUL OL6 118 C2
Hey With Zion Primary School OLDE OL4 75 H5
Heywood Cemetery ROCH OL11 41 G2
Heywood Community High School HEY OL10 40 A5
Heywood Industrial Park HEY OL10 55 F1
Heywood Sports Complex HEY OL10 40 C3
Higginshaw Sports Club OLD OL1 9 J1
Highbank Trading Estate OP/CLY M11 129 G1
Highbarn Junior School ROY/SHW OL2 59 F4
High Birch Special School ROCH OL11 42 A1
Higher Broughton Health Centre BRO M7 99 H4
Higher Lane Primary School WHTF M45 68 B4
Higher Openshaw Community School OP/CLY M11 115 G5
Highfield Cemetery MPL/ROM SK6 161 G4
Highfield Hospital ROCH OL11 42 C1
Highfield Primary School FWTH BL4 64 B4
URM M41 139 E1
Highfield Secondary School WALK M28 94 A4
High Lane Medical Centre MPL/ROM SK6 186 D5
High Lane Primary School MPL/ROM SK6 186 D4
High Lawn Primary School BOL BL1 22 D5
Highlea Secondary School WALK M28 94 A2
High Lea Tuition Service DID/WITH M20 142 D4
High Point Hotel OLDS OL8 8 D5
Hillcrest Grammar School EDGY/DAV SK3 172 A3
Hillgate Business Centre STKP SK1 13 H6
Hill Top Community Primary School ROCH OL11 43 F5
Hill Top Community Special School OLDE OL4 61 F5
Hilton Lane Primary School WALK M28 80 B4
HM Prison CSLFD M3 113 E1
Hodge Clough Infant School OLD OL1 75 G1
Hodge Clough Junior School OLD OL1 75 G1
Holcombe Brook Primary School RAMS BL0 26 B1
Holcombe Brook Sports Club RAMS BL0 16 B5
Holden Clough Primary School AUL OL6 105 G3

Holiday Inn BOLS/LL BL3 47 F5
Hollingworth High School MILN OL16 31 H5
Hollingworth Lake Activity Centre LIT OL15 31 H1
Hollin Primary School MDTN M24 71 H1
Hollins Grundy Primary School BURY BL9 53 H4
Hollinwood Business Centre FAIL M35 103 G2
Hollinwood Cemetery OLDS OL8 103 H1
Hollinwood Cricket Club OLDS OL8 103 H2
Holly Bank Industrial Estate RAD M26 67 E1
Holly Mount RC Primary School TOT/BURYW BL8 25 G2
Hollywood Bowl NEWH/MOS M40 102 C1
Holt Town Industrial Estate NEWH/MOS M40 114 B3
Holy Cross 6th Form College BURY BL9 53 F1
Holy Cross & All Saints RC Primary School ECC M30 109 G5
Holy Family Catholic Primary School SALE M33 155 F2
Holy Family RC Primary School OLDS OL8 104 A2
ROCH OL11 43 F3
Holy Infant RC Primary School BOL BL1 33 H2
Holy Name RC Primary School HULME M15 127 F3
Holy Rosary RC Primary School OLDS OL8 90 C5
Holy Trinity CE Dobcross School UPML OL3 77 G2
Holy Trinity CE Primary School AUL OL6 117 H2
BKLY M9 101 F2
BURY BL9 4 E6
LIT OL15 21 E3
Hong Sing Chinese Medical Centre BRAM/HZG SK7 185 F1
Hooley Bridge Industrial Estate HEY OL10 40 D2
Hope Hospital SLFD M6 110 C3
Hopwood Cottage MDTN M24 57 F3
Hopwood Hall College MDTN M24 57 E4
Hopwood Medical Centre HEY OL10 41 F5
Hopwood Primary School HEY OL10 56 B1
Horton Mill Primary School OLDE OL4 91 E1
Hotel Ibis CMANE M1 7 F6
Hotel Smokies Park OLDS OL8 104 C2
Houldsworth Golf Club RDSH SK5 144 D3
Houldsworth Medical Centre RDSH SK5 145 E4
Hoyle Street Industrial Estate WGTN/LGST M12 127 H1
Hubert House Jewish Boys School BRO M7 99 G2
Hubert Jewish High School for Girls BRO M7 99 F2
Hulme Adult Education Centre HULME M15 126 D2
Hulme Arch HULME M15 127 E2
The Hulme Grammar School for Girls & Boys OLDS OL8 90 A3
Hulme Hall Grammar School CHD/CHDH SK8 182 D3
Hulton Hospital BOLS/LL BL3 62 D1
Hurstfield Industrial Estate HTNM SK4 144 D5
Hursthead Primary School CHD/CHDH SK8 193 F1
Hurst Knoll CE Primary School AUL OL6 118 B1
Hurst Methodist Junior School AUL OL6 105 G3
Hyde Cricket Club HYDE SK14 148 A5
Hyde Leisure Pool HYDE SK14 147 H1
Hyde Technology School HYDE SK14 132 B4
Hyde United FC HYDE SK14 148 A1
IMAX Cinema ANC M4 7 F3
IMEX Business Park BRUN/LGST M13 128 C5
Imperial War Museum North TRPK M17 125 F1
Indoor Tennis Centre OP/CLY M11 114 C3
Inland Revenue Office CSLFD M3 6 C4
Innes Special School WHIT OL12 29 F2
Innkeepers Lodge WILM/AE SK9 201 B1
Inscape House Special School WALK M28 95 F1
Institute of Islamic Higher Education EDGW/EG BL7 23 F3
The Instructor College STKP SK1 13 G4
International Convention Centre CMANW M2 6 D6
Irlam & Cadishead Community High School IRL M44 135 D4
Irlam County Primary School IRL M44 136 A2
Irlam Endowed Primary School IRL M44 136 B1
Irlam Industrial Estate IRL M44 135 D4
Irlam Swimming Pool IRL M44 136 B2
James Brindley Primary School WALK M28 94 D1
Jeff Joseph Sale Moor Technology College SALE M33 155 E4
Jewish Museum CHH M8 113 F1
Jewish Senior Boys School BRO M7 99 G3
John Rylands Library CSLFD M3 6 D5
Johnson Fold Primary School BOL BL1 32 C3
Joseph Adamson Industrial Estate HYDE SK14 147 F1
Jumbles Country Park EDGW/EG BL7 24 A2
Jury's Inn CMANE M1 6 D7
Kaskenmoor Comprehensive School OLDS OL8 103 G1
Kayley Industrial Estate AULW OL7 117 G2
Kearsley West Primary School FWTH BL4 65 F5
Kenmore Medical Centre WILM/AE SK9 199 F4
Kentmere Primary School WHIT OL12 19 G5
Kenyon Business Park BOLS/LL BL3 48 D4
Kershaw Business Centre BOLS/LL BL3 48 C4
Kiely Business Park BURY BL9 5 G1
King David Junior & High School CHH M8 100 A1
Kingfisher Community Special School CHAD OL9 89 E2
Kings Road Primary School OLDTF/WHR M16 125 H5
King Street Remedial Clinic DUK SK16 118 A4
Kingsway CP School URM M41 123 H4
Kingsway Retail Park MILN OL16 31 E4
Kingsway School CHD/CHDH SK8 169 H5
Kingsway Secondary School CHD/CHDH SK8 169 H4
Kingsway West Business Park MILN OL16 43 G1
Knoll Street Industrial Park BRO M7 99 G3
Knowsley Junior School OLDE OL4 76 B5
Kratos Industrial Estate URM M41 124 A3
Lacey Green Primary School WILM/AE SK9 199 F1
Lady Barn House School CHD/CHDH SK8 182 A1
Ladybarn Primary School DID/WITH M20 143 E5
Ladybridge Primary School BOLS/LL BL3 47 G4
CHD/CHDH SK8 171 E5
Ladybrook Primary School BRAM/HZG SK7 184 A5
Ladysmith Shopping Centre AUL OL6 118 A2
Ladywell Hospital Lodge SALQ M50 110 B3
Ladywood Special School BOLS/LL BL3 51 E5
Lancashire CCC (County Ground, Old Trafford) OLDTF/WHR M16 125 G4
Lancasterian School DID/WITH M20 156 D1
Lance Burn Health Centre SLFD M6 111 H3
Lane End Primary School CHD/CHDH SK8 183 F2
Langdon College BRO M7 99 H1
Langley Primary School MDTN M24 71 F1
Language College STRET M32 125 G4
Langworthy Clinic SLFD M6 111 G3
Langworthy Road Primary School SLFD M6 111 G2
Lark Hill Primary School EDGY/DAV SK3 12 B5
Last Drop Hotel EDGW/EG BL7 23 F2
The Last Drop Village EDGW/EG BL7 23 F2
Lavenham Business Centre CHAD OL9 8 B5
Lawn Cemetery ALT WA14 164 A1
Lawnhurst Trading Estate CHD/CHDH SK8 171 E4
Leigh Infant & Primary School HYDE SK14 147 H1
Leigh Street Primary School HYDE SK14 148 A1
Le Meridien Victoria & Albert Hotel ORD M5 6 A5
Lemon Park Industrial Estate HEY OL10 41 F5
Levenshulme Baths BNG/LEV M19 144 A2
Levenshulme Health Centre BNG/LEV M19 144 A2
Levenshulme High School For Girls BNG/LEV M19 143 H4
Levenshulme Trading Estate BNG/LEV M19 144 B1
Lever Edge Primary School BOLS/LL BL3 63 G2
Library, Museum & Art Gallery OLD OL1 9 H4
Light Oaks Primary School SLFD M6 110 C1
Lily Lane J & I School NEWH/MOS M40 101 H2
Limehurst Primary School OLDS OL8 104 A2
Limeside Primary School OLDS OL8 103 H1
Lime Tree Primary School SALE M33 155 F3
Linden Road Primary School DTN/ASHW M34 131 H5
Linguard Business Park MILN OL16 10 E7
Linkway Industrial Estate MDTN M24 72 A1
Linnyshaw Industrial Estate FWTH BL4 81 F1
Lisburne School OFTN SK2 173 F3
Littleborough Cricket Club LIT OL15 21 E2
Littleborough Primary School LIT OL15 21 E1
Little Lever School BOLS/LL BL3 65 G1
Littlemoor Primary School OLDE OL4 75 F4
Littlemoss Business Park DROY M43 116 D2
Littlemoss High School DROY M43 116 D1
Livingstone Primary School MOSL OL5 106 C2
L & M Business Park ALT WA14 165 E3
Lobden Golf Club WHIT OL12 18 D1
Lockside Medical Centre STLY SK15 119 G3
Longdendale Recreation Centre HYDE SK14 134 C5
Longfield Shopping Centre PWCH M25 84 D2
Longford Park Special School STRET M32 140 C1
Longford Trading Estate STRET M32 125 E5
Longsight Cricket Club WGTN/LGST M12 128 D5
Longsight Health Centre BRUN/LGST M13 128 C4
Longsight Industrial Estate WGTN/LGST M12 128 C4
Longsight Shopping Centre WGTN/LGST M12 128 C4
Lords College BOLS/LL BL3 3 G7
Loreto Convent Grammar School ALT WA14 165 F4
Loreto Preparatory School ALT WA14 165 F5
Lostock College STRET M32 124 B5
Lostock Hall Primary School POY/DIS SK12 194 C4
Lostock Primary School HOR/BR BL6 46 D3
Lower Broughton Health Centre BRO M7 112 C1
Lowercroft Primary School TOT/BURYW BL8 36 D4
Lower Kersal Primary School BRO M7 99 E4
Lower Park Primary School POY/DIS SK12 194 D3
Lowerplace Primary School MILN OL16 43 G2
Lowes Park Golf Club BURY BL9 27 H5
The Lowry Hotel CSLFD M3 6 C3
The Lowry SALQ M50 125 F1
Ludworth Primary School MPL/ROM SK6 175 F1
Lum Head Primary School CHD/CHDH SK8 181 G1
The Lyceum Musical Theatre OLD OL1 9 G4
Lyme Park Country Park POY/DIS SK12 197 G5
Lyndhurst Primary School DUK SK16 118 B4
OLDS OL8 90 A4
Lyntown Trading Estate ECC M30 109 G3
Lyon Industrial Estate ALT WA14 165 E2
Lyon Road Industrial Estate FWTH BL4 81 F2
Macdonald Road Medical Centre IRL M44 135 D3
Mackenzie Industrial Estate CHD/CHDH SK8 171 E3
Magda House Medical Centre OFTN SK2 173 E5
Malbern Industrial Estate DTN/ASHW M34 130 D4
The Mall Shopping Centre ECC M30 110 A3
Mancentral Trading Estate ORD M5 6 A4
Manchester Airport World Freight Terminal MANAIR M90 189 H1
Manchester Aquatics Centre BRUN/LGST M13 127 F2
Manchester (Barton) Airfield ECC M30 122 B1
Manchester Business Park MANAIR M90 180 B4
Manchester Business School HULME M15 127 F2
Manchester Cathedral CSLFD M3 6 E2
Manchester Central Library CMANW M2 6 E6
Manchester Centre for the Deaf BRUN/LGST M13 127 F2
Manchester Centre for Vision BRUN/LGST M13 127 G3
Manchester City Art Galleries CMANE M1 7 F5
Manchester City FC (City of Manchester Stadium) OP/CLY M11 114 C4
Manchester College of Arts & Technology CMANE M1 7 H4
OP/CLY M11 129 E1
Manchester Conference Centre & Hotel CMANE M1 7 H7
The Manchester Crematorium CCHDY M21 141 F5
Manchester Golf Club BKLY M9 88 A3
Manchester Grammar School RUSH/FAL M14 143 F1
Manchester High School for Girls RUSH/FAL M14 142 D2
Manchester Industrial Centre CSLFD M3 6 A6
Manchester International Airport MANAIR M90 190 A2
Manchester Islamic High School CCHDY M21 140 D3
Manchester Jewish Grammar School PWCH M25 85 E4
Manchester Junior Girls School BRO M7 99 G1
Manchester Metropolitan University CMANE M1 7 H6
DID/WITH M20 157 E3
DID/WITH M20 157 G4
OLDTF/WHR M16 142 A1
RUSH/FAL M14 127 H4
RUSH/FAL M14 143 E1
Manchester Metropolitan University Institute of Education (Didsbury) DID/WITH M20 157 F4
Manchester Museum BRUN/LGST M13 127 G2
Manchester Preparatory School DID/WITH M20 157 G2
Manchester Road CP School DROY M43 115 H4
Manchester Royal Infirmary BRUN/LGST M13 127 H3
Manchester RUFC CHD/CHDH SK8 192 D1
Manchester School of Management BRUN/LGST M13 127 F2
Manchester Southern Cemetery CCHDY M21 141 G5
Manchester United FC (Old Trafford) OLDTF/WHR M16 125 G3
Manchester United Museum & Tour Centre OLDTF/WHR M16 125 F3
Manchester University BRUN/LGST M13 127 H3
Manchester Youth Theatre HULME M15 127 E3
Mandelay Health Centre BOL BL1 22 D5
Manley Park Infant School OLDTF/WHR M16 141 F1
Manley Park Primary School OLDTF/WHR M16 141 F1
Manor Golf Club FWTH BL4 82 A3
Manor Green Primary School DTN/ASHW M34 146 D3
Manor High School SALE M33 153 F1
Manway Business Park ALT WA14 165 H2
The Maples Medical Centre NTHM/RTH M23 167 G5
Marcliffe Industrial Estate BRAM/HZG SK7 185 G3
Marjory Lees Health Centre OLD OL1 9 H2
Market Place Shopping Centre BOL BL1 2 E4
Market Street Athletics Track BURY BL9 4 E7
Markland Hill Primary School BOL BL1 47 G1
Marland Fold Special School OLDS OL8 104 D1
Marland Hill Primary School ROCH OL11 42 B1
Marple Clinic MPL/ROM SK6 175 E3
Marple Golf Club MPL/ROM SK6 186 D1
Marple Hall School MPL/ROM SK6 174 B2
Marriott Hotel HALE/TIMP WA15 179 F5
Marriott Worsley Park Hotel & Country Club WALK M28 95 F3
Marsland Street Industrial Centre BRAM/HZG SK7 185 E2
Masefield Primary School BOLS/LL BL3 51 E5
Matthew Moss High School ROCH OL11 41 H2
Mauldeth Medical Centre DID/WITH M20 143 E4
Mauldeth Road Primary School DID/WITH M20 143 F4
Mayfield Industrial Park IRL M44 121 D5
Mayfield Primary School OLD OL1 75 E4
Maypole Farm Estate PART M31 137 E5
Meade Hill School BKLY M9 86 A3
Meadow Industrial Estate FAIL M35 102 C4
RDSH SK5 160 A3
The Meadows School BKLY M9 87 G3
Meadway Health Centre SALE M33 153 H4
Meanwood Primary School WHIT OL12 29 F2
Medlock Infant School BRUN/LGST M13 127 G1
Medlock Leisure Centre DROY M43 116 C2
Medlock Valley Community School OLDS OL8 90 D4
Melland High School RDSH SK5 144 C1
MEN Arena CSLFD M3 6 E1
Mental Health Centre BOLE BL2 35 G5
Menzies Avant Hotel OLDS OL8 8 C6
Meridian Clinic BURY BL9 4 C5
Mersey Drive Primary School WHTF M45 69 F2
Mersey Road Industrial Estate FAIL M35 103 G1
Mersey Trading Estate HTNM SK4 158 C5
Mersey Vale Primary School HTNM SK4 158 D5
Merseyway Centre STKP SK1 13 F2
Mesne Lea Primary School WALK M28 95 F1
Methodist Cemetery BOLE BL2 35 F2
Metro Cinema AUL OL6 118 A3
Micklehurst All Saints Primary School MOSL OL5 107 F1
Micklehurst Cricket Club MOSL OL5 107 F1
Middleton Cemetery MDTN M24 72 B2
Middleton Crematorium MDTN M24 72 B2
Middleton Cricket Club MDTN M24 71 G2
Middleton Parish Church School MDTN M24 71 G2
Middleton Public Baths MDTN M24 71 H4
Middleton Shopping Centre MDTN M24 71 G4
Middleton Technology School MDTN M24 72 A4
Milking Green Industrial Estate OLDE OL4 91 H2
Mill 5 Belgrave Industrial Estate OLDS OL8 90 D4
Millbrook Business Centre NTHM/RTH M23 167 F3
Millbrook Industrial Estate NTHM/RTH M23 167 F3
Millbrook Primary School STLY SK15 107 F5
Mill Gate Shopping Centre BURY BL9 4 E5
Mills Hill Primary School CHAD OL9 72 D4
Mill Street Industrial Estate BOL BL1 3 G4
Millwood Primary Special School BURY BL9 53 G3
Milnrow Cricket Club MILN OL16 44 C1
Milnrow Health Centre MILN OL16 44 C1
Milnrow Parish CE Primary School MILN OL16 31 G5
Milo Industrial Park DROY M43 116 C3
Milton St Johns CE Primary School MOSL OL5 92 D5
Minden Medical Centre BURY BL9 5 F4
Moat House School HTNM SK4 159 H3
Monde Trading Estate TRPK M17 124 B2
Montague Business Park OLDTF/WHR M16 125 H4
Monton Bowling Club ECC M30 109 H1
Monton Cricket Club ECC M30 109 H1
Monton Medical Centre ECC M30 109 F1
Moor Allerton School DID/WITH M20 157 E2
Moorfield Community Primary School IRL M44 121 B5
Moorfield Primary School BRAM/HZG SK7 184 D3
Moorgate Primary School BOLE BL2 3 K2
Moorgate Retail Park BURY BL9 5 F3
Moorhey Industrial Estate OLDE OL4 91 E1
Moorhouse Primary School MILN OL16 31 F5
Moorlands Junior School SALE M33 155 F1
Moor Lane Bus Station BOL BL1 2 D5
Moorside High School SWIN M27 96 C3
Moorside Leisure Centre SWIN M27 96 C3
Moorside Primary School SWIN M27 96 C3
Moravian College DROY M43 116 B5
Morris Green Business Park BOLS/LL BL3 48 B5
Moses Gate Country Park FWTH BL4 65 F2
Moss Field Community Primary School HEY OL10 40 D3

Mossfield County Primary School *SWIN* M27 97 E1
Moss Hey Primary School *BRAM/HZG* SK7 193 F2
Moss Industrial Estate *MILN* OL16 43 G1
Moss Lane Industrial Estate *ROY/SHW* OL2 74 D1
Mossley AFC *MOSL* OL5 106 D1
Mossley Health Centre *MOSL* OL5 106 D1
Mossley Hollins High School *MOSL* OL5 107 F1
Moss Park Junior School *STRET* M32 139 G1
Moss Side Health Centre *RUSH/FAL* M14 127 F4
Moss Side Leisure Centre *HULME* M15 127 E3
Moss View Primary School *PART* M31 151 F3
Moston Fields Primary School *NEWH/MOS* M40 101 H1
Moston Indoor Market *NEWH/MOS* M40 101 G2
Moston Lane Primary School *BKLY* M9 101 F2
Mottram CE Primary School *HYDE* SK14 134 D5
Mount Carmel RC Junior School *BKLY* M9 87 E5
Mount Carmel RC Primary School *BKLY* M9 101 E1
Mountheath Industrial Park *PWCH* M25 99 E1
Mount Pleasant Business Centre *OLDE* OL4 75 E5
Mount St Joseph Business & Enterprise College *BOLS/LL* BL3 64 A2
The Museum of Science and Industry in Manches *CSLFD* M3 6 A6
Museum of the Manchester Regiment *AUL* OL6 118 A2
Museum of Trade Union History *CMANE* M1 7 F6
Mytham Primary School *BOLS/LL* BL3 66 A1
Nasmyth Business Centre *ECC* M30 109 F3
National Cycling Centre (Velodrome) *OP/CLY* M11 114 D3
National Industrial Estate *AULW* OL7 117 H3
National Squash Centre *OP/CLY* M11 114 C3
National Trading Estate *BRAM/HZG* SK7 184 D1
Natural History Museum *OLDS* OL8 8 B7
Navigation Primary School *ALT* WA14 165 G3
Navigation Trading Estate *NEWH/MOS* M40 101 H5
Nelson Business Centre *DTN/ASHW* M34 131 G4
Neville Street Industrial Estate *CHAD* OL9 8 A3
Nevill Road J & I School *BRAM/HZG* SK7 183 H2
Newall Green High School *NTHM/RTH* M23 167 G5
Newall Green Primary School *NTHM/RTH* M23 168 A5
New Ardwick Sports Centre *BRUN/LGST* M13 128 A2
New Barn Infant School *ROY/SHW* OL2 59 H3
Newby Road Industrial Estate *BRAM/HZG* SK7 185 E2
New Croft High School *SLFD* M6 111 G2
Newhaven Business Park *ECC* M30 109 H4
Newhey Community Primary School *MILN* OL16 44 D2
New Kingsway Health Centre *DID/WITH* M20 158 A2
Newlands Medical Centre *BOL* BL1 47 H2
New Moston Primary School *NEWH/MOS* M40 88 D5
New Museum *OLD* OL1 9 F1
New North Manchester Golf Club *MDTN* M24 71 E4
Newspaper Offices *BOL* BL1 3 F4
Newton Business Park *HYDE* SK14 133 F3
Newton Moor Industrial Estate *HYDE* SK14 132 D3
Newton Street Police Museum *CMANE* M1 7 H4
Nicholas Varley Community School *NEWH/MOS* M40 114 B1
Nicholls Sixth Form Centre *WGTN/LGST* M12 128 A1
Norbury Hall Primary School *BRAM/HZG* SK7 185 F3
Norden Community Primary School *WHIT* OL12 28 C1
Norden Cricket Club *WHIT* OL12 28 B1
Norris Bank Medical Centre *HTNM* SK4 12 A3
Norris Bank Primary School *HTNM* SK4 159 E3
Nortex Business Centre *BOL* BL1 48 B1
North Area Sixth Form College *HTNM* SK4 144 A5
Northbank Industrial Park *IRL* M44 135 D5
IRL M44 136 B3
North Cestrian Grammar School *ALT* WA14 165 F4
North Chadderton School (Upper) *CHAD* OL9 73 E3
North Cheshire Jewish Primary School *CHD/CHDH* SK8 181 G2
Northenden Golf Club *WYTH/NTH* M22 156 D4
Northenden Primary School *WYTH/NTH* M22 156 C5
Northern A & O Medical Centre *BURY* BL9 4 E4
Northern Cemetery *SWIN* M27 98 C3
Northern Moor Clinic *NTHM/RTH* M23 155 G5
North Grecian Street Primary School *BRO* M7 99 F4
North Heaton Primary School *HTNM* SK4 144 B5
North Manchester Community School for Girls *BKLY* M9 87 H5
North Manchester General Hospital *CHH* M8 100 D1
North Manchester High School for Boys *BKLY* M9 88 A4
North Quays Business Park *ALT* WA14 153 H5
North Reddish Health Centre *RDSH* SK5 144 D2
North Reddish Infant School *RDSH* SK5 145 E2
North Walkden Primary School *WALK* M28 80 D2
Norton Grange Hotel *ROCH* OL11 57 F2
Novotel *WALK* M28 95 F5
Novotel Hotel *CMANE* M1 6 E6
Oakenclough Primary School *WILM/AE* SK9 200 A1
Oakenrod Primary School *ROCH* OL11 29 G4
Oakfield Primary School *HYDE* SK14 132 D3
Oakfield Trading Estate *HALE/TIMP* WA15 165 H4
Oakgrove School *CHD/CHDH* SK8 181 H5
Oakhill Trading Estate *LHULT* M38 80 C2
Oaklands Infant School *WILM/AE* SK9 200 B1
Oakleigh Medical Centre *CHH* M8 100 C1
The Oaks Business Park *NTHM/RTH* M23 167 E2
The Oaks Primary School *BOL* BL1 23 E5
Oakwood High School *CCHDY* M21 141 F4
CCHDY M21 156 A1
SLFD M6 97 H5
Octagon Theatre *BOL* BL1 2 E5
Odeon Cinema *CMANE* M1 6 E6
ROCH OL11 42 D2
Offerton Green Clinic *OFTN* SK2 173 G4
Offerton Hall Primary School *OFTN* SK2 173 F3
Offerton Health Centre *STKP* SK1 172 C1
Offerton High School *OFTN* SK2 173 F2
Offerton Industrial Estate *OFTN* SK2 172 D1
Old Hall Clinic *CHD/CHDH* SK8 169 G3
Old Hall Drive Primary School *GTN* M18 129 G4
Old Hall Primary School *TOT/BURYW* BL8 26 C4
Oldham 6th Form College *CHAD* OL9 8 E5
Oldham Art Gallery *OLD* OL1 9 H4
Oldham Athletic FC (Boundary Park) *ROY/SHW* OL2 74 A2
Oldham Broadway Business Park *CHAD* OL9 72 D4
Oldham Business Centre *OLD* OL1 9 F5
Oldham Central Industrial Park *OLD* OL1 9 K1
Oldham Central Trading Park *OLD* OL1 74 D4
Oldham College *CHAD* OL9 8 D3
Oldham County Court *OLD* OL1 8 E2
Oldham Crematorium *OLDS* OL8 103 H1
Oldham Cricket Club *OLD* OL1 75 F3
Oldham Golf Club *OLDE* OL4 92 A3
Oldham RUFC *OLDS* OL8 104 C2
Oldham Sports Centre *OLD* OL1 9 G3
Oldhams Primary School *BOL* BL1 33 F1
Oldham Theatre Workshop *ROY/SHW* OL2 59 E5
Oldham West Business Centre *CHAD* OL9 73 G5
Old Mill Hotel & Leisure Centre *RAMS* BL0 16 C1
Old Moat J & I School *DID/WITH* M20 142 B4
Old Rectory Hotel *DTN/ASHW* M34 146 D4
Old Trafford Community School *OLDTF/WHR* M16 126 B3
Oldwood Primary School *WYTH/NTH* M22 180 A2
Olympia Trading Estate *HULME* M15 126 D1
Olympic House *MANAIR* M90 180 B5
The Open University *CCHDY* M21 141 E2
Opera House *CSLFD* M3 6 C5
The Operating Theatre *STRET* M32 125 F5
Orchard House Day Hospital *ROY/SHW* OL2 59 F5
Orchard Industrial Estate *SLFD* M6 111 H1
Orchard Trading Estate *SLFD* M6 98 C5
Ordsall Hall Museum *ORD* M5 126 A2
Ordsall Health Centre *ORD* M5 112 A5
Ordsall Recreation Centre *ORD* M5 125 H1
Oriel Bank High School *EDGY/DAV* SK3 172 A4
Oriental Arch *CMANE* M1 7 F5
Orion Business Park *CHD/CHDH* SK8 171 F4
Orion Trading Estate *TRPK* M17 110 B5
Orrishmere Primary School *CHD/CHDH* SK8 182 D1
Ortenbrook School *PART* M31 150 D4
Osborne Trading Estate *CHAD* OL9 8 B1
Oswald Road Primary School *CCHDY* M21 140 D2
Oulder Hill Community School *ROCH* OL11 29 E4
Our Lady of Grace RC Primary School *PWCH* M25 84 D1
Our Lady of Lourdes RC Primary School *FWTH* BL4 64 B4
PART M31 150 D3
TOT/BURYW BL8 26 D5
Our Lady & St Anselms RC Primary School *WHIT* OL12 14 B3
Our Lady & St Pauls RC Primary School *HEY* OL10 40 A5
Our Ladys Catholic Primary School *EDGY/DAV* SK3 12 E6
Our Ladys RC High School *ROY/SHW* OL2 74 A1
Our Ladys RC Primary School *OLDE* OL4 75 H1
OLDTF/WHR M16 126 C5
Our Ladys RC School *BKLY* M9 87 E1
Our Lady & the Lancashire Martyrs RC Primary School *WALK* M28 80 B4
Overdale Crematorium *BOL* BL1 47 H3
Overdale School *MPL/ROM* SK6 161 G5
Overhead Walkway *MANAIR* M90 179 H5
Owl Business Centre *CHAD* OL9 91 G1
Oxford Grove Primary School *BOL* BL1 33 F5
Palace Cinema *STLY* SK15 119 F3
Palace Hotel *CMANE* M1 7 F7
Palace Theatre *CMANE* M1 7 F7
Palm Business Centre *CHAD* OL9 73 G5
Paragon Industrial Estate *LIT* OL15 20 C5
Parish Church CE Junior School *OLD* OL1 9 G1
Park Dean Special School *OLDS* OL8 91 E5
Parker International Estate *DUK* SK16 132 A1
Parkfield Industrial Estate *MDTN* M24 71 F4
Parkfield Primary School *MDTN* M24 71 F3
Parklands High School *WYTH/NTH* M22 180 B1
Park Mill Industrial Estate *MOSL* OL5 93 E3
Park Parade Industrial Estate *AULW* OL7 117 H3
Park Road CP School *ALT* WA14 165 H1
SALE M33 139 F5
Park School *NTHM/RTH* M23 167 G1
Parkside Industrial Estate *ROY/SHW* OL2 59 F5
Parkview Centre *OLDS* OL8 9 H6
Park View Primary School *PWCH* M25 85 E4
Parkway Business Centre *OLDTF/WHR* M16 142 A2
Parkway Four Industrial Estate *TRPK* M17 124 B1
Parkway Trading Estate *STRET* M32 124 B3
Parochial CE Primary School *AUL* OL6 118 B2
Parrenthorn High School *PWCH* M25 69 G4
Partington CP School *PART* M31 151 E3
Partington Health Centre *PART* M31 151 E3
Partington Shopping Centre *PART* M31 151 E3
Partington Sports Centre *PART* M31 151 E4
Patricroft CE School *ECC* M30 109 F3
Peacefield Primary School *MPL/ROM* SK6 174 D4
Peacock County Primary School *GTN* M18 129 F2
Pear New Mill Industrial Estate *MPL/ROM* SK6 160 D4
Peel Brow Primary School *RAMS* BL0 17 E2
The Peel Centre *STKP* SK1 13 J2
Peel Hall County Primary School *LHULT* M38 80 A4
Peel Health Centre *BURY* BL9 4 E6
Peel Moat Recreation Centre *HTNM* SK4 159 E1
Peerglow Industrial Estate *ALT* WA14 165 H1
Pendleton College *SLFD* M6 111 E1
Pendleton Medical Centre *SLFD* M6 111 H3
Pennant Industrial Estate *OLD* OL1 75 E4
Pennine Business Park *HEY* OL10 55 G1
Peterloo Medical Centre *MDTN* M24 71 F4
Philips High School *WHTF* M45 68 B4
Phoenix Industrial Estate *FAIL* M35 103 F2
Phoenix Medical Centre *STKP* SK1 13 H6
Phoenix Park Industrial Estate *HEY* OL10 56 C1
Piccadilly Trading Estate *ANC* M4 113 H5
CMANE M1 7 H5
Pictor Special School *SALE* M33 154 A2
Pike Fold Primary School *BKLY* M9 86 D4
Pikes Lane Primary School *BOLS/LL* BL3 2 A7
Pilot Industrial Estate *BOLS/LL* BL3 49 G5
Pilsworth Industrial Estate *BURY* BL9 54 A3
Pinfold J & I School *HYDE* SK14 149 F2
Pinnacle Business Centre *HTNM* SK4 159 H3
Piper Hill School *NTHM/RTH* M23 156 A4
Plantation Industrial Estate *AUL* OL6 118 B3
Plant Hill High School *BKLY* M9 86 D3
Plasman Industrial Centre *BNG/LEV* M19 143 H2
BNG/LEV M19 144 C2
Playhouse Theatre *ORD* M5 111 H3
Plodder Lane Primary School *FWTH* BL4 64 C3
Plymouth Court Business Centre *BRUN/LGST* M13 127 H3
Plymouth Grove Primary School *BRUN/LGST* M13 128 B3
The Point Retail Park *MILN* OL16 10 E6
Poland Industrial Estate *ANC* M4 7 K2
Portland Basin Museum *AULW* OL7 117 H4
Portland Industrial Estate *BURY* BL9 38 D2
Portwood Trading Estate *STKP* SK1 13 K1
Potters House School *BURY* BL9 27 G5
Pownall Green Primary School *BRAM/HZG* SK7 183 H5
Pownall Hall School *WILM/AE* SK9 199 E2
Poynton Clinic *POY/DIS* SK12 195 F3
Poynton High School *POY/DIS* SK12 195 G4
Poynton Leisure Centre *POY/DIS* SK12 195 G5
Poynton Sports Club *POY/DIS* SK12 195 F3
Premier Lodge *ALT* WA14 153 H5
ALT WA14 165 G3
CMANW M2 6 E6
CSLFD M3 6 D3
HYDE SK14 134 B5
MDTN M24 70 C5
STKP SK1 13 H3
SWIN M27 96 D3
SWIN M27 97 H3
WILM/AE SK9 192 A4
WILM/AE SK9 198 D3
WILM/AE SK9 201 B5
Premier Lodge (City South) *HULME* M15 127 E1
Prestwich Community High School *PWCH* M25 85 E2
Prestwich Golf Club *PWCH* M25 98 D1
Prestwich Health Centre *PWCH* M25 84 D2
Prestwich Hospital *PWCH* M25 84 C2
Prestwich Preparatory School *PWCH* M25 85 F2
Priestnall School *HTNM* SK4 158 C3
Prince of Wales Business Park *OLD* OL1 75 F4
The Printworks Leisure Complex *ANC* M4 7 F2
Priorsleigh Medical Centre *POY/DIS* SK12 195 F3
Propps Hall Primary School *FAIL* M35 102 D4
Prospect Vale Primary School *CHD/CHDH* SK8 181 G3
Pump House People's History Museum *CSLFD* M3 6 B4
Python Industrial Estate *LIT* OL15 21 F2
Quality Hotel *ALT* WA14 177 G2
Quarry Bank Mill & Styal Estate NT *WILM/AE* SK9 190 D5
Queen Elizabeth Hall *OLD* OL1 9 F3
Queen Elizabeths High School *MDTN* M24 56 C5
Queensgate Primary School *BRAM/HZG* SK7 193 H3
Queens Road Primary School *CHD/CHDH* SK8 182 D1
Queen Street Primary School *FWTH* BL4 65 E4
Queensway Primary School *ROCH* OL11 43 E3
Rack House Primary School *NTHM/RTH* M23 155 H5
Radcliffe Borough AFC *RAD* M26 51 H5
Radcliffe Cricket Club *RAD* M26 51 H5
Radcliffe High School *RAD* M26 67 E1
Radcliffe Junior School *RAD* M26 51 H5
Radclyffe Athletics Centre *CHAD* OL9 73 E5
Radclyffe Primary School *ORD* M5 125 H1
The Radclyffe School (Upper) *CHAD* OL9 73 E5
Radisson SAS Hotel *MANAIR* M90 180 A5
Raikes Lane Industrial Estate *BOLS/LL* BL3 49 G5
Railway Street Industrial Estate *GTN* M18 129 F2
Ralph Williams Clinic *WHIT* OL12 19 H5
Ramillies Hall School *CHD/CHDH* SK8 183 F2
Ramsbottom Cemetery *RAMS* BL0 16 B4
Ramsbottom Cottage Hospital *RAMS* BL0 16 D3
Ramsbottom Health Centre *RAMS* BL0 16 C1
Ramsbottom Swimming Pool *RAMS* BL0 16 D1
Rassbottom Industrial Estate *STLY* SK15 119 E3
Ravensbury Primary School *OP/CLY* M11 114 D2
Ravensfield Industrial Estate *DUK* SK16 117 H4
Ravenside Retail Park *BOLS/LL* BL3 3 F7
Reddish Vale Golf Club *RDSH* SK5 145 F5
Reddish Vale School *RDSH* SK5 145 E4
Red Lane Community School *BOLE* BL2 35 G5
Red Rose Retail Centre *ORD* M5 112 A4
Regal Industrial Estate *WGTN/LGST* M12 128 C1
Regent Cinema *MPL/ROM* SK6 175 E3
Regent Park Golf Course *HOR/BR* BL6 46 C2
Regent Trading Estate *ORD* M5 112 C4
The Regimental Museum of XX Lancashire Fusiliers *TOT/BURYW* BL8 37 G5
Reliance Trading Estate *NEWH/MOS* M40 102 B3
Ribble Drive Primary School *WHTF* M45 68 D3
Richmond J & I School *CHAD* OL9 8 D4
Richmond Medical Centre *AUL* OL6 118 B2
Richmond Park Athletics Stadium *AULW* OL7 117 F1
Richmond Park School *WGTN/LGST* M12 128 B3
The Ridge College *MPL/ROM* SK6 174 D4
Ridge Danyers College *CHD/CHDH* SK8 182 B1
Ridge Hill Primary & Infant School *STLY* SK15 119 E2
Ringway Golf Club *HALE/TIMP* WA15 178 D3
Ringway Primary School *WYTH/NTH* M22 180 C4
Ringway Trading Estate *WYTH/NTH* M22 180 D4
Ripon Avenue School *BURY* BL9 68 C1
Riverside Business Park *WILM/AE* SK9 199 G3
Roaches Industrial Estate *MOSL* OL5 93 F3
Rochdale AFC (Spotland Stadium) *ROCH* OL11 29 F3
Rochdale Cemetery *ROCH* OL11 29 E4
Rochdale Crematorium *ROCH* OL11 29 E4
Rochdale Cricket, Lacrosse & Squash Club *ROCH* OL11 29 F4
Rochdale Curtain Theatre *ROCH* OL11 29 H5
Rochdale Golf Club *ROCH* OL11 28 D3
Rochdale Healthcare NHS Trust *LIT* OL15 20 D3
Rochdale Healthcaret *WHIT* OL12 20 B3
Rochdale Industrial Centre *ROCH* OL11 29 G5
Rochdale Infirmary *WHIT* OL12 10 C3
Roe Cross Industrial Park *HYDE* SK14 134 D3
Roker Industrial Estate *OLD* OL1 75 E4

Rolls Crescent Primary School
HULME M15 126 D3
Roman Fort
CSLFD M3 6 B7
Romiley Golf Club
MPL/ROM SK6 162 C3
Romiley Health Centre
MPL/ROM SK6 162 B4
Romiley Primary School
MPL/ROM SK6 162 C4
Roscoe Fold Primary School
BOLE BL2 50 B1
Rosedale Shopping Centre
NEWH/MOS M40 102 B5
Rosehill Methodist Community School
AUL OL6 105 H5
Rose Hill Primary School
MPL/ROM SK6 174 D3
Rossendale School
RAMS BL0 17 H1
Roundthorn Industrial Estate
NTHM/RTH M23 167 F2
NTHM/RTH M23 167 F4
Roundwood School
WYTH/NTH M22 168 B2
Roxy Cinema
OLDS OL8 103 F1
Royal Bolton Hospital
FWTH BL4 64 A3
Royal Exchange Clinic
CMANW M2 6 E4
Royal Exchange Shopping Centre
ANC M4 6 E3
MILN OL16 10 B6
Royal Exchange Theatre Company
CMANW M2 6 E4
Royal Manchester Childrens Hospital
SWIN M27 97 G3
Royal Northern College of Music
HULME M15 127 F2
Royal Oak Industrial Estate
STKP SK1 13 H6
Royal Oak Primary School
NTHM/RTH M23 167 H2
Royal Oldham Hospital
OLD OL1 74 A3
Royal Pennine Trading Estate
ROCH OL11 42 A3
Royce Trading Estate
TRPK M17 124 A1
Royle Pennine Trading Estate
ROCH OL11 42 C3
Royton and Crompton Comprehensive School
ROY/SHW OL2 59 H5
Royton Medical Centre
ROY/SHW OL2 59 E5
Royton Public Baths
ROY/SHW OL2 59 F5
Rugby Road Industrial Estate
WHIT OL12 10 E3
Runworth School
BOLS/LL BL3 47 G4
Rushcroft Primary School
ROY/SHW OL2 60 A1
Russell Scott Primary School
DTN/ASHW M34 131 F4
Rycroft Park Sports Club
CHD/CHDH SK8 182 C3
Rydings Special School
WHIT OL12 19 G4
Ryecroft Business Park
AULW OL7 117 G4
The Ryleys School
WILM/AE SK9 201 A4
Sacred Heart RC Infant School
GTN M18 129 F4
Sacred Heart RC Primary School
MILN OL16 30 D5
NTHM/RTH M23 167 G3
OLD OL1 75 F2
Saddleworth Golf Club
UPML OL3 77 H4
Saddleworth Museum & Art Gallery
UPML OL3 78 A4
Saddleworth Preparatory School
OLDE OL4 76 D4
Saddleworth School
UPML OL3 78 A3
Saddleworth Swimming Pool
UPML OL3 78 A5
St Agnes CE Primary School
BRUN/LGST M13 128 C5
OLDE OL4 92 B2
St Aidans Catholic Primary School
NTHM/RTH M23 156 A5
St Alphonsus RC Primary School
OLDTF/WHR M16 126 C3
St Ambrose Barlow RC High School
SWIN M27 97 E3
St Ambrose College
HALE/TIMP WA15 178 C3
St Ambrose Preparatory School
HALE/TIMP WA15 178 C4
St Ambrose RC Primary School
CCHDY M21 156 C2
EDGY/DAV SK3 171 G4
St Andrew RC Primary School
BOLE BL2 50 B1
St Andrews CE Primary School
BNG/LEV M19 144 A3
RAD M26 51 H3
RAMS BL0 16 C3
WALK M28 94 B5
WHTN BL5 62 D4
St Andrews CE School
ECC M30 109 H4
St Andrews Medical Centre
ECC M30 109 H3
St Andrews Methodist Primary School
WALK M28 80 C4
St Andrew's VC CE Primary School
WHIT OL12 20 B4
St Annes CE (aided) Primary School
SALE M33 154 D2
St Annes CE Primary School
OLDE OL4 92 D1
ROY/SHW OL2 74 B1
St Annes Ear Nose & Throat Hospital
ALT WA14 177 F1
St Annes Primary School
DTN/ASHW M34 131 H4
St Annes RC High School
HTNM SK4 159 G2
St Annes RC Primary School
CHH M8 100 B2
DTN/ASHW M34 130 B1
OLDE OL4 75 F5
St Anns J & I School
STRET M32 140 A1
St Anthonys RC Primary School
WYTH/NTH M22 180 C3
St Antonys RC High School
URM M41 139 E1
St Augustine of Canterbury RC School
OLDS OL8 90 A4
St Augustines CE Primary School
NEWH/MOS M40 101 F5
SWIN M27 97 G2
St Barnabas Primary School
OP/CLY M11 115 E5
St Bartholomews CE Primary School
WHIT OL12 14 B5
St Bede CE Primary School
BOLS/LL BL3 63 F2
St Bedes College
OLDTF/WHR M16 126 D5
St Benedict's Catholic Primary School
WILM/AE SK9 192 B4
St Benedicts RC Primary School
WILM/AE SK9 192 B3
St Bernadettes RC Primary School
RDSH SK5 160 C2
WHTF M45 68 C2
St Bernard RC Primary School
BOLS/LL BL3 47 F4
St Bernards RC Primary School
BNG/LEV M19 143 G5
St Boniface RC Primary School
BRO M7 99 F4
St Brendan RC Primary School
BOLE BL2 35 F1
St Brigids RC Primary School
OP/CLY M11 114 D4
St Catherines Preparatory School
MPL/ROM SK6 175 G2
St Catherines RC Primary School
DID/WITH M20 157 H3
St Chads CE Junior School
BURY BL9 53 G1
St Chads CE Primary School
UPML OL3 78 B3
St Chads RC Primary School
CHH M8 100 B5
St Charles RC Primary School
SWIN M27 96 C2
St Christophers RC Primary School
AUL OL6 105 H4
MPL/ROM SK6 161 H4
St Chrysostoms CE Primary School
BRUN/LGST M13 127 H3
St Clares RC Primary School
BKLY M9 86 D2
St Clement (Egerton) CE Primary School
ORD M5 126 A1
St Clements CE Primary School
OP/CLY M11 129 H1
St Columba RC Primary School
BOLE BL2 34 C2
St Cuthberts RC High School
MILN OL16 43 G5
St Cuthberts RC Primary School
DID/WITH M20 157 H1
St Damians RC High School
AUL OL6 105 H3
St Dunstans RC Primary School
NEWH/MOS M40 101 H2
St Edmunds RC Primary School
LHULT M38 80 C3
NEWH/MOS M40 101 F4
St Edwards CE Primary School
ROCH OL11 42 A4
St Edwards RC Primary School
OLDE OL4 75 H5
RUSH/FAL M14 142 C1
St Elisabeths CE Primary School
RDSH SK5 144 C3
St Elizabeth RC Primary School
WYTH/NTH M22 180 D2
St Ethelbert RC Primary School
BOLS/LL BL3 48 A4
St Gabriels CE Primary School
MDTN M24 72 B5
St Gabriels Medical Centre
PWCH M25 85 G5
St Gabriels RC High School
BURY BL9 4 A6
St Gabriels RC Primary School
ROCH OL11 42 C5
St Georges CE Primary School
MOSL OL5 106 C1
OFTN SK2 172 A3
St Georges CE (aided) Primary School
HYDE SK14 147 G2
St Georges RC Secondary School
WALK M28 80 D5
St Gilberts RC Primary School
ECC M30 108 D3
St Gregory RC Primary School
FWTH BL4 65 F4
St Helens CE Primary School
GOL/RIS/CU WA3 150 A4
St Herberts RC Primary School
CHAD OL9 73 F5
St Hilarys School
WILM/AE SK9 201 B4
St Hildas CE Primary School
OLD OL1 8 E1
OLDTF/WHR M16 126 A5
PWCH M25 85 F3
St Hugh of Lincoln Primary School
STRET M32 124 A5
St Hughs CE Primary School
OLDE OL4 91 G3
St Hughs RC Primary School
HALE/TIMP WA15 166 A2
St James CE Primary School
AUL OL6 118 B2
GTN M18 129 G2
RUSH/FAL M14 143 E1
St James C E Primary School
WHIT OL12 19 H2
St James RC High School
CHD/CHDH SK8 182 C5
St James RC Primary School
HYDE SK14 149 E1
St James Secondary School
FWTH BL4 64 B4
St James's RC School
SLFD M6 111 G2
St John Baptist's VA RC School
ROCH OL11 30 A5
St John Bosco RC Primary School
BKLY M9 87 H3
St John CE Primary School
FWTH BL4 65 F4
St John Fisher & St Thomas More RC Primary School
WYTH/NTH M22 168 C5
St John Fisher RC Primary School
DTN/ASHW M34 147 E2
St John RC Primary School
EDGW/EG BL7 23 E4
St Johns Cathedral
CSLFD M3 112 C3
St Johns CE Infant School
FAIL M35 103 E2
St Johns CE Junior School
FAIL M35 103 F3
St Johns CE Primary School
BURY BL9 38 B2
DUK SK16 118 D5
HTNM SK4 158 B4
MDTN M24 57 H3
RAD M26 67 F3
SLFD M6 97 H4
St Johns Industrial Estate
OLDE OL4 91 H1
St Johns Medical Centre
ALT WA14 177 F1
St Johns Mosley Common CE Primary School
WALK M28 94 A2
St Johns Primary School
IRL M44 121 B5
St Johns RC Primary School
CCHDY M21 140 D2
St John Vianney School
HTNM SK4 159 E4
St John Vianney Upper School
OLDTF/WHR M16 141 E1
St Joseph RC Primary School
BOL BL1 33 F4
St Josephs RC High School
HEY OL10 55 H1
St Josephs RC Primary & Nursery School
RDSH SK5 144 D3
St Josephs RC Primary School
BOL BL1 33 F5
BRUN/LGST M13 128 B4
HEY OL10 40 D5
LHULT M38 80 B2
MOSL OL5 106 D1
ORD M5 112 A5
RAMS BL0 16 C2
ROY/SHW OL2 59 H4
SALE M33 154 C2
STKP SK1 13 G3
St Josephs & St Bedes RC Primary School
BURY BL9 39 E2
St Judes CE Primary School
ANC M4 7 K3
St Kentigerns Catholic School
RUSH/FAL M14 142 B2
St Lukes CE Primary School
CHAD OL9 73 F5
HEY OL10 41 E3
ORD M5 111 E4
WGTN/LGST M12 128 B3
St Lukes RC Primary School
SLFD M6 97 H5
St Malachys RC Primary School
NEWH/MOS M40 100 D5
St Margaret Marys RC School
NEWH/MOS M40 88 C4
St Margarets CE Primary School
HEY OL10 40 B5
OLDS OL8 89 H5
OLDTF/WHR M16 141 G1
PWCH M25 69 F4
St Margarets Ward RC Primary School
SALE M33 153 F4
St Marie's RC Primary School
BURY BL9 4 E6
St Marks CE Primary School
MPL/ROM SK6 161 H2
NEWH/MOS M40 114 A2
WALK M28 95 G4
St Marks RC Primary School
SWIN M27 83 F5
St Martins School
SALE M33 153 H1
St Mary CE Primary School
BOLS/LL BL3 47 G5
St Mary's Catholic Cemetery
WALK M28 96 A2
St Marys CE Primary School
DROY M43 116 C4
St Mary's CE Primary School
IRL M44 135 B5
St Marys CE Primary School
NEWH/MOS M40 102 B1
OLDTF/WHR M16 126 D4
St Mary's CE Primary School
PWCH M25 84 D3
St Marys CE Primary School
RDSH SK5 145 F5
St Mary's CE Primary School
ROCH OL11 43 F2
St Marys CE Primary School
ROY/SHW OL2 59 G1
TOT/BURYW BL8 25 E1
URM M41 123 E4
St Mary's Hospital
BRUN/LGST M13 127 H4
St Marys Medical Centre
OLD OL1 9 H3
St Marys RC Primary School
AUL OL6 118 C1
BNG/LEV M19 143 H3
DTN/ASHW M34 131 F5
DUK SK16 132 D2
St Mary's RC Primary School
ECC M30 109 H4
St Marys RC Primary School
FAIL M35 102 D4
HTNM SK4 12 E1
St Mary's RC Primary School
LIT OL15 20 D3
St Marys RC Primary School
MDTN M24 71 F2
MPL/ROM SK6 175 F2
RAD M26 52 B5
SWIN M27 97 E2
St Matthew CE Primary School
BOL BL1 2 D1
BOL BL1 33 H5
BOLS/LL BL3 65 H1
St Matthews CE Infant School
OLD OL1 73 E2
St Matthews CE Primary School
EDGY/DAV SK3 12 E6
STRET M32 139 H3
St Matthews RC High School
NEWH/MOS M40 88 B5
St Maxentius CE Primary School
BOLE BL2 35 E1
St Michael CE Primary School
BOLS/LL BL3 64 D1
St Michaels CE Primary School
HEY OL10 40 D2
MDTN M24 87 H2
St Michaels CE School
URM M41 137 G2
St Michaels RC Primary School
WHTF M45 69 E4
St Monicas RC High School
PWCH M25 85 F4
St Monicas RC Primary School
URM M41 137 E2
St Osmund RC Primary School
BOLE BL2 50 A2
St Patrick's High School
ECC M30 109 E3
St Patricks RC Primary School
ANC M4 113 H2
OLDS OL8 8 D5
St Patricks VA RC Primary School
WHIT OL12 10 E2
St Paul CE Primary School
BOL BL1 34 A3
St Pauls Catholic High School
NTHM/RTH M23 168 A5
St Pauls Catholic Primary School
POY/DIS SK12 195 F5
St Paul's Cemetery
BOL BL1 33 F4
St Pauls CE Primary School
BRO M7 99 E2
BURY BL9 5 J1
DID/WITH M20 142 C5
RAMS BL0 16 D1
RDSH SK5 160 C2
ROY/SHW OL2 73 H1
STLY SK15 119 H3
WALK M28 81 F5
St Pauls New Windsor CE Primary School
ORD M5 112 A4
St Pauls Peel CE Primary School
LHULT M38 80 A2
St Pauls RC Primary School
HYDE SK14 133 E4
St Pauls Trading Estate
STLY SK15 119 H3
St Peter CE Primary School
FWTH BL4 65 E5
St Peter & Paul RC Primary School
BOLS/LL BL3 48 D4
St Peter & St John Primary School
CSLFD M3 6 A2
St Peters Catholic Primary School
BRAM/HZG SK7 185 E3
STLY SK15 119 G4
St Peters CE Primary School
AULW OL7 117 H5
BURY BL9 53 F3
SWIN M27 96 D2
St Peters Primary School
NTHM/RTH M23 179 H1
St Peters RC High School & Lower School
GTN M18 144 C1
St Peter's RC High School Upper School
DROY M43 115 H5
St Peters RC Primary School
MDTN M24 71 H5
St Peters Smithills Dean CE Primary School
BOL BL1 33 E2
St Peters VC CE Primary School
MILN OL16 43 G1
St Philips RC Primary School
BRO M7 99 F1
OFTN SK2 173 F3
St Philips School
CSLFD M3 112 C4
St Raphaels Catholic Primary School
STLY SK15 107 F5
St Saviour Primary School
RAD M26 66 B5
St Sebastians RC Primary School
SLFD M6 98 D5
St Simon & Jude CE Primary School
BOLS/LL BL3 64 A1
St Simons Catholic Primary School
BRAM/HZG SK7 185 F1
St Stephen & All Martyrs Ce Primary School
BOLE BL2 49 H3
BOLE BL2 49 H3
St Stephen CE Primary School
FWTH BL4 81 H1
St Stephens & All Martyrs Infant School
OLD OL1 9 H1
St Stephens CE Primary School
BRAM/HZG SK7 173 G5
DTN/ASHW M34 117 F5
TOT/BURYW BL8 37 G5
St Stephen's RC School
DROY M43 116 B3
St Teresa RC Primary School
BOLS/LL BL3 65 H1
St Teresas RC Primary School
IRL M44 135 D3
STRET M32 125 H5
St Thomas Aquinas RC High School
CCHDY M21 141 F4
St Thomas CE Primary School
BOL BL1 33 G4
BURY BL9 5 J6
St Thomas C E Primary School
HTNM SK4 144 B5
St Thomas CE Primary School
OLD OL1 60 D5
OLDS OL8 8 E6
STKP SK1 13 H5
St Thomas Hospital
EDGY/DAV SK3 13 F7
St Thomas Leesfield CE Primary School
OLDE OL4 91 H2
St Thomas More RC High School
DTN/ASHW M34 146 C1
St Thomas More RC Primary School
MDTN M24 87 H2
St Thomas of Canterbury Catholic Primary School
BOL BL1 47 H1
St Thomas Primary School
CHH M8 100 D2
St Thomas RC Primary School
BRO M7 99 H4
St Thomas VA CE Primary School
MILN OL16 45 E2
St Vincent RC Infant School
HALE/TIMP WA15 165 H4
St Vincents RC Primary School
WHIT OL12 28 D2
St Wilfrids CE Primary School
NEWH/MOS M40 102 C5
WYTH/NTH M22 168 D1
St Wilfrids RC Primary School
HULME M15 126 D2
St William RC Primary School
BOLS/LL BL3 63 H1
St Willibrords RC Primary School
OP/CLY M11 115 F2
St Winifreds RC Primary School
HTNM SK4 158 D4
Sale Cricket Club
SALE M33 155 E1
Sale Golf Club
SALE M33 155 G1
Sale Grammar School
SALE M33 154 D3
Sale Leisure Centre
SALE M33 154 D1
Salford City Reds RLFC (The Willows)
ORD M5 111 E3
Salford College
ECC M30 108 D3
ORD M5 125 H1
SLFD M6 112 A1
WALK M28 95 E1
Salford County Court
ORD M5 111 H4
Salford Medical Centre
SLFD M6 111 F2
Salford Museum & Art Gallery
ORD M5 112 B3
Salford University Business Park
SLFD M6 112 A1
Samuel Laycock Special School
STLY SK15 119 E1
Sandilands Primary School
NTHM/RTH M23 166 D1
Saviour CE Primary School
NEWH/MOS M40 100 D5
Savoy Cinema
HTNM SK4 158 D3
Saxon Hall Leisure Centre
MILN OL16 11 J5
Saxon Holme Hotel
HTNM SK4 159 G2
School Street Industrial Estate
BRAM/HZG SK7 185 F2
Seaford Industrial Estate
SLFD M6 112 A1
Sedgley Park Primary School
PWCH M25 85 G5
Sedgley Park RUFC
WHTF M45 84 A1
Sedgley Park Trading Estate
PWCH M25 99 E1
Seedley Primary School
SLFD M6 111 F3
Seminar Centre
CMANW M2 6 D6
Severnside Trading Estate
TRPK M17 124 C3

Seymour Park Primary School OLDTF/WHR M16 126 A4
Seymour Road Primary School OP/CLY M11 115 G4
Shandon Clinic (Europe) HULME M15 127 F3
Sharples Primary School BOL BL1 34 B1
Shawclough Primary School WHIT OL12 18 D5
Shawclough Trading Estate WHIT OL12 18 C5
Shawgrove School DID/WITH M20 142 A5
Shaw Heath Health Centre EDGY/DAV SK3 13 F7
Shay Lane Medical Centre HALE/TIMP WA15 178 D3
Shepherd Cross Industrial Estate BOL BL1 33 F4
Shepley North Industrial Estate DTN/ASHW M34 131 H1
Shepley South Industrial Estate DTN/ASHW M34 131 H2
Sherborne Trading Estate CHH M8 100 A5
Sherwood Business Park ROCH OL11 42 C4
Shiv Lodge Medical Centre BRUN/LGST M13 128 C5
The Shopping Centre CHD/CHDH SK8 182 D2
Showcase Cinemas Belle Vue WGTN/LGST M12 129 E3
Siddal Moor Sports College HEY OL10 56 A2
Slough Industrial Estate ORD M5 112 B5
Smallbridge Health Centre WHIT OL12 19 H5
Smallbridge Industrial Park MILN OL16 11 H1
Smedleylane Junior School CHH M8 100 C4
Smithills Museum BOL BL1 33 E2
Smithills School BOL BL1 33 E3
Smithy Bridge Primary School LIT OL15 20 C5
Snipe Retail Park DTN/ASHW M34 117 E5
South Chadderton School CHAD OL9 89 E5
Southern Cross School CCHDY M21 156 B1
South Failsworth Primary School FAIL M35 102 D5
Southfield Industrial Estate TRPK M17 124 D3
Southfields School SALE M33 154 A3
Southgate Industrial Estate HEY OL10 41 G5
Southlink Business Park OLDE OL4 9 K4
South Manchester High School WYTH/NTH M22 180 C1
Southmoor Business Park NTHM/RTH M23 167 F2
Southmoor Industrial Estate NTHM/RTH M23 167 F3
South Oldham Business Park CHAD OL9 73 H4
South Reddish Medical Centre RDSH SK5 160 A2
South Trafford College ALT WA14 165 G1
South West Manchester Cricket Club CCHDY M21 141 F2
Spa Road Industrial Estate BOL BL1 2 B5
Sparrow Hill Community School MILN OL16 10 C7
Spindle Point Primary School FWTH BL4 82 A2
The Spindles Shopping Centre OLD OL1 9 F4
Sport City OP/CLY M11 114 C3
Sports Injury Centre MDTN M24 71 H5
Spotland Bridge Industrial Centre ROCH OL11 29 G3
Spotland Primary School WHIT OL12 29 G2
Spring Brook Special School CHAD OL9 73 E5
Springfield Business Centre CSLFD M3 6 D1
Springfield Hotel MPL/ROM SK6 175 E2
Springfield House Medical Centre OLD OL1 75 F4
Springfield Industrial Estate FAIL M35 102 D2
Springfield Park Golf Club ROCH OL11 41 H1
Springfield Primary School SALE M33 154 C2
Springhead Community Infant & First School OLDE OL4 92 A1
Springhill High School MILN OL16 43 H1
Springside County Primary School BURY BL9 27 F4
Springwood Primary School MPL/ROM SK6 162 D3
Springwood School SWIN M27 97 F4
Spurley Hey High School GTN M18 144 A1
Stag Industrial Estate ALT WA14 165 E3
Stakehill Industrial Estate MDTN M24 57 G5
Stalybridge Celtic AFC STLY SK15 119 H5
Stalybridge Cricket Club DUK SK16 118 D5
Stalybridge Millbrook Cricket Club STLY SK15 120 A1
Stalybridge St Pauls Cricket Club DUK SK16 133 E1
Stalyhill Infants School STLY SK15 134 B1
Stalyhill Junior School STLY SK15 134 A1
Staly Industrial Estate STLY SK15 119 G3
Stamford Golf Club MOSL OL5 107 F3
Stamford High School AUL OL6 118 D1
Stamford Park J & I School HALE/TIMP WA15 177 H1
Stanley Green Industrial Estate
CHD/CHDH SK8 192 B1
CHD/CHDH SK8 192 B3
Stanley Green Retail Park CHD/CHDH SK8 192 C1
Stanley Grove Primary School WGTN/LGST M12 128 C4
Stanley Road Primary School CHAD OL9 89 G3
Stanneylands Hotel WILM/AE SK9 191 G5
Stansfield Hall CE Free Primary School LIT OL15 15 B5
Stansfield Road J & I School FAIL M35 103 F2
Star Industrial Estate OLDS OL8 9 G6
Station Approach Business Estate ROCH OL11 30 A5
Staveleigh Medical Centre STLY SK15 119 F3
Stella Maris School HTNM SK4 158 B4
Stepping Hill Hospital OFTN SK2 172 C5
Stockport Air Raid Shelter STKP SK1 13 F3
Stockport Bus Station EDGY/DAV SK3 12 E4
Stockport College of FE & HE EDGY/DAV SK3 13 F6
Stockport County Court STKP SK1 13 F4
Stockport County FC & Sale Sharks RUFC (Edgeley Park) EDGY/DAV SK3 171 G2
Stockport Crematorium OFTN SK2 172 B2
Stockport Cricket Club EDGY/DAV SK3 172 A3
Stockport Golf Club OFTN SK2 174 A4
Stockport Grammar School OFTN SK2 172 B4
Stockport Mega Bowl EDGY/DAV SK3 13 F5
Stockport RUFC BRAM/HZG SK7 184 A4
Stockport School OFTN SK2 172 C4
Stockport Trading Estate HTNM SK4 171 E1
Stone Hill Industrial Estate FWTH BL4 64 D5
Stoneleigh Primary School OLD OL1 75 E2
The Strand Medical Centre ROCH OL11 43 E4
Stretford Grammar School STRET M32 140 B2
Stretford High School STRET M32 125 G4
Stretford Leisure Centre STRET M32 125 G4
Stretford Memorial Hospital OLDTF/WHR M16 126 A5
St's Aidan & Oswalds RC Primary School ROY/SHW OL2 74 A1
Student Union Building HULME M15 127 F1
Styal Golf Club WILM/AE SK9 191 F2
Styal Primary School WILM/AE SK9 190 D3
Sudden Health Centre ROCH OL11 42 B2
Sudell Street Trading Estate ANC M4 7 J1
Sugden Sports Centre CMANE M1 127 F1
Summerseat Methodist Primary School BURY BL9 27 E1
Summervale Primary School OLDS OL8 8 D5
Summerville Primary School SLFD M6 98 A5
Sunning Hill Primary School BOLS/LL BL3 48 C5
Sunnybank Clinic BURY BL9 68 D1
Sunny Bank Primary School BURY BL9 68 D1
Sunset Business Centre FWTH BL4 82 B2
Swinton Cemetery SWIN M27 82 D5
The Swinton County High School SWIN M27 96 D1
Swinton Cricket Club SWIN M27 97 F3
Swinton Industrial Estate SWIN M27 97 F2
Swinton Leisure Centre SWIN M27 97 E2
Swinton Park Golf Club SWIN M27 97 F4
Tameside Business Development Centre DTN/ASHW M34 130 D5
Tameside Business Park DUK SK16 132 A1
Tameside College HYDE SK14 132 D4
Tameside College of Technology
AUL OL6 118 C2
HYDE SK14 147 G4
Tameside County Court AUL OL6 118 B3
Tameside General Hospital AUL OL6 119 E1
Tame Valley Primary School MPL/ROM SK6 145 H4
Tandle Hill Country Park ROY/SHW OL2 58 B3
Tashbar School BRO M7 99 H1
Tavistock Industrial Estate OP/CLY M11 129 G2
Taylors Sports Club ECC M30 109 H4
Temple Primary School CHH M8 100 C4
Ten Acres Sports Complex NEWH/MOS M40 101 H5
Terminal 1 MANAIR M90 190 A1
Terminal 2 MANAIR M90 179 H4
Terminal 3 MANAIR M90 190 B1
Thames Industrial Estate WGTN/LGST M12 128 A1
Thames Trading Centre IRL M44 136 A4
Thomasson Memorial Special School BOL BL1 48 A2
Thorn Grove Primary School CHD/CHDH SK8 192 D1
Thornham Cricket Club MDTN M24 57 G2
Thornham St James CE Primary School ROY/SHW OL2 59 E1
Thornleigh Salesian College BOL BL1 33 G2
Thorp Primary School ROY/SHW OL2 58 D4
Times Retail Park HEY OL10 40 D4
Timperley Health Centre HALE/TIMP WA15 166 B2
Tithe Barn Primary School HTNM SK4 158 D3
Tonacliffe Primary School WHIT OL12 18 B2
Tonge Bridge Industrial Estate BOLE BL2 3 J3
Tonge Cricket Club BOLE BL2 34 D3
Tonge Fold Health Centre BOLE BL2 49 H2
Tonge Moor Health Centre BOLE BL2 34 D5
Tonge Moor Primary School BOLE BL2 3 K1
Tootal Drive County Primary School SLFD M6 110 D3
Top O'th'brow Primary School BOLE BL2 35 F4
Torkington Primary School BRAM/HZG SK7 185 H2
Tottington Health Centre TOT/BURYW BL8 25 H4
Tottington High School TOT/BURYW BL8 26 A5
Tottington Primary School TOT/BURYW BL8 37 E1
Tower (Remains of) RAD M26 68 A1
Towers Business Park
DID/WITH M20 156 D2
DID/WITH M20 157 G5
Townfield Industrial Estate OLDE OL4 75 E5
Towngate Business Centre LHULT M38 79 D2
Town Hall & Albert Halls BOL BL1 2 E5
Town Square Shopping Centre OLD OL1 9 G3
Trafalgar Business Park BRO M7 112 D1
Trafford Athletics Track STRET M32 140 C2
Trafford Centre TRPK M17 123 G2
Trafford FC URM M41 137 H2
Trafford General Hospital URM M41 122 D5
Trafford Healthcare SALE M33 155 E3
Trafford Retail Park URM M41 123 F3
Trafford Water Sports Centre SALE M33 140 B5
Trans Pennine Trading Estate ROCH OL11 42 C3
Travel Inn
CHAD OL9 88 D5
CHD/CHDH SK8 181 H2
CMANE M1 7 F6
DTN/ASHW M34 130 D5
MILN OL16 44 D2
OFTN SK2 172 B3
PWCH M25 84 D2
SALE M33 138 C5
TRPK M17 123 G2
Travel Inn Hotel SALQ M50 125 H1
Travelodge
CHAD OL9 88 D3
CSLFD M3 6 D3
Trent Industrial Estate ROY/SHW OL2 60 A1
The Triangle ANC M4 6 E3
Trinity CE High School HULME M15 127 F2
Trinity Retail Park BOLE BL2 3 H7
Trinity School STLY SK15 119 E4
Tudor Industrial Estate DUK SK16 131 H1
Tulketh Street I ndustrial Estate NEWH/MOS M40 101 G2
Turton Golf Club EDGW/EG BL7 23 F1
Turton High School EDGW/EG BL7 23 G4
Turton Leisure Centre EDGW/EG BL7 23 F1
Two Trees High School DTN/ASHW M34 147 E2
Tyntesfield CP School SALE M33 153 H5
UCI Cinema TRPK M17 123 G2
UGC Cinema
BOL BL1 34 B3
DID/WITH M20 158 A5
EDGY/DAV SK3 13 F5
UMIST CMANE M1 7 H7
Union Mill Industrial Estate MOSL OL5 93 E4
United Trading Estate OLDTF/WHR M16 125 G3
University College Salford CSLFD M3 112 C3
University of Manchester
BRUN/LGST M13 127 G3
ECC M30 122 A2
RUSH/FAL M14 143 E2
University of Manchester Institute of Science & Technology BRUN/LGST M13 127 G1
University of Salford ORD M5 112 B3
Unsworth Medical Centre BURY BL9 69 F1
Unsworth Primary School BURY BL9 68 D2
Urbis ANC M4 6 E2
Urmston Grammar School URM M41 123 F5
Urmston J & I School URM M41 138 A1
Urmston Leisure Centre URM M41 138 A1
Urmston Town FC URM M41 137 G2
Vaishali Medical Centre CCHDY M21 141 E2
Vale Park Industrial Estate CHH M8 100 D3
The Valley Leisure Centre BOL BL1 34 B3
Valley Special School BRAM/HZG SK7 193 F2
Varley Street Clinic NEWH/MOS M40 114 A1
Varna Street Primary School OP/CLY M11 129 G2
Vaughan Street Industrial Estate WGTN/LGST M12 128 C1
Vauxhall Industrial Estate
RDSH SK5 144 D5
RDSH SK5 160 A2
Vernon Industrial Estate
STKP SK1 13 H2
STKP SK1 13 K1
The Vernon Infant School POY/DIS SK12 195 F4
The Vernon Junior School POY/DIS SK12 195 F4
Vernon Park Museum STKP SK1 160 C4
Vernon Park Primary School STKP SK1 13 J3
Vernon Road Medical Centre TOT/BURYW BL8 26 B2
Victoria Avenue Primary School BKLY M9 87 E2
Victoria Industrial Estate ANC M4 114 A4
Victoria Medical Centre URM M41 138 C1
Victoria Park Infant School STRET M32 140 A1
Victoria Park Junior School STRET M32 140 A1
Victoria Trading Estate CHAD OL9 89 G4
Victory Trading Estate BOLS/LL BL3 49 F4
Village Medical Centre LIT OL15 21 E3
VIP Centre Industrial Estate OLD OL1 75 F3
Wadeson Junior School BRUN/LGST M13 127 H1
Wadsworth Industrial Park BOLS/LL BL3 48 D5
Walkden High School WALK M28 81 F5
Walmsley CE Primary School EDGW/EG BL7 22 D2
Walshaw Sports Club TOT/BURYW BL8 37 E1
Walton Park Leisure Centre SALE M33 154 B4
Wardle High School WHIT OL12 20 A3
Wardley Industrial Estate WALK M28 96 B1
Warner Village SALQ M50 125 G1
Warner Village Cinema BURY BL9 54 A3
Warren Wood Primary School OFTN SK2 173 H4
Warth Park Industrial Estate BURY BL9 52 D2
Washway Road Medical Centre SALE M33 154 B2
The Watergate Clinic MILN OL16 10 D6
Waterloo Industrial Park
BOL BL1 3 G2
STKP SK1 13 H4
Waterloo Primary School AULW OL7 104 C5
The Water Place BOL BL1 2 E6
Waters Edge Business Park ORD M5 126 A2
Watersheddings Primary School OLD OL1 75 F3
The Waterside Hotel DID/WITH M20 169 H1
Waterside Industrial Park BOLS/LL BL3 64 D1
Watersports Centre SALQ M50 125 G1
Waybridge Industrial Estate ORD M5 111 E5
Weaste Trading Estate ORD M5 111 E3
Webster Primary School RUSH/FAL M14 127 F4
Welfare Clinic MDTN M24 71 E2
Welkin Road Industrial Estate STKP SK1 160 C3
Wellacre High School for Boys URM M41 137 E2
Wellfield Junior School SALE M33 139 E5
Wellfield Medical Centre CHH M8 100 A2
Well Green Primary School HALE/TIMP WA15 178 C2
Wellington Road Industrial Estate AUL OL6 117 H2
Wellington School HALE/TIMP WA15 166 A3
Wentworth High School ECC M30 110 A1
Werneth Cricket Bowling & Tennis Club OLDS OL8 8 D7
Werneth Golf Club OLDS OL8 104 B1
Werneth J & I School OLDS OL8 90 A3
Werneth Low Golf Club HYDE SK14 148 C5
Werneth Private Preparatory School OLDS OL8 8 C6
Werneth School MPL/ROM SK6 161 G4
Wesley Methodist Primary School RAD M26 51 H4
Westbrook Trading Estate TRPK M17 125 E1
Westbury Street Industrial Estate HYDE SK14 132 B3
West Croft Industrial Estate MDTN M24 70 D5
West End Medical Centre AULW OL7 117 G4
West End Primary School
AULW OL7 117 G3
DTN/ASHW M34 130 B5
West End Trading Estate SWIN M27 97 E1
Westernlea Clinic DTN/ASHW M34 131 F3
West Gorton Medical Centre WGTN/LGST M12 128 C2
West Hill School STLY SK15 119 E3
Westinghouse Industrial Estate TRPK M17 125 E3
West Liverpool Street Primary School SLFD M6 111 G3
Westmorland Primary School RDSH SK5 145 H5
West One Retail Park SALQ M50 110 B4
Westpoint Medical Centre BNG/LEV M19 143 G2
Westwood Business Centre CHAD OL9 8 C4
Westwood Industrial Estate CHAD OL9 8 B3
Westwood Park Primary School ECC M30 109 E2
Westwood Primary School CHAD OL9 8 C3
Westwood Trading Estate MPL/ROM SK6 174 C4
Whalley Range FC CCHDY M21 141 G2
Whalley Range High School OLDTF/WHR M16 142 A3
Wharfside Business Centre TRPK M17 125 G2
Wharton Primary School LHULT M38 79 D1
Wheatfield Industrial Estate ROY/SHW OL2 74 A1
Wheatsheaf Industrial Estate SWIN M27 97 G1
Wheatsheaf Shopping Centre MILN OL16 10 D5
White City Retail Park OLDTF/WHR M16 125 H3
Whitefield Community Primary School WHTF M45 68 D4
Whitefield Golf Club WHTF M45 68 B5
Whitefield Medical Centre WHTF M45 68 B4
Whitegate End Primary School CHAD OL9 88 D4
Whitehill Industrial Estate HTNM SK4 159 H1
Whitehill Primary School HTNM SK4 159 H2
White Swan Industrial Estate OLD OL1 75 F4
Whitley Road Medical Centre NEWH/MOS M40 113 H1
Whittaker Golf Club LIT OL15 21 G4
Whittaker Moss Primary School ROCH OL11 28 A2
The Whitworth Art Gallery BRUN/LGST M13 127 G4
Whitworth Community High School WHIT OL12 14 B4
Whitworth Football & Cricket Club WHIT OL12 14 B4
Whitworth Park School RUSH/FAL M14 127 F4
Whitworth Swimming Pool WHIT OL12 14 C3

Wilbraham Primary School
  RUSH/FAL M14 .... 142 B2
Wild Bank Community School
  STLY SK15 .... 120 A3
Willan Industrial Estate
  ORD M5 .... 111 G4
William Andrews
  Swimming Baths
  DUK SK16 .... 132 C1
William Hulmes Grammar School
  OLDTF/WHR M16 .... 142 A2
William Roet Flixton Golf Club
  URM M41 .... 137 H3
William Wroe Municipal
  Golf Course
  URM M41 .... 137 H1
Willow Bank Hotel
  RUSH/FAL M14 .... 142 D5
Willow Grove Cemetery
  RDSH SK5 .... 160 B1
The Willows Primary School
  HALE/TIMP WA15 .... 166 A3
  WYTH/NTH M22 .... 180 B2
Wilmslow Albion FC
  WILM/AE SK9 .... 191 F4
Wilmslow Health Centre
  WILM/AE SK9 .... 199 F4

Wilmslow High School
  WILM/AE SK9 .... 199 G4
Wilmslow Leisure Centre
  WILM/AE SK9 .... 199 G4
Wilmslow Preparatory School
  WILM/AE SK9 .... 199 G3
Wilmslow RFC
  WILM/AE SK9 .... 199 E1
Wilmslow Road Medical Centre
  RUSH/FAL M14 .... 127 H5
  WILM/AE SK9 .... 192 A3
Windmill Lane Industrial Estate
  DTN/ASHW M34 .... 145 H1
Withington Bowling Club
  RUSH/FAL M14 .... 142 D4
Withington Girls School
  RUSH/FAL M14 .... 142 C3
Withington Golf Club
  DID/WITH M20 .... 157 E4
Withington Hospital
  DID/WITH M20 .... 142 A5
Withington Swimming Baths
  DID/WITH M20 .... 142 C5
Withins High School
  BOLE BL2 .... 35 F4
Wolfenden Primary School
  BOL BL1 .... 33 H4

Woodbank Cricket Club
  TOT/BURYW BL8 .... 38 A2
Woodbank Park
  Athletics Track
  STKP SK1 .... 160 D5
Woodbank Primary School
  TOT/BURYW BL8 .... 38 A2
Woodend Mills
  Industrial Estate
  OLDE OL4 .... 92 A2
Woodfields Retail Park
  BURY BL9 .... 4 D3
Woodford Cricket Club
  BRAM/HZG SK7 .... 193 G5
Woodhey High School
  RAMS BL0 .... 16 B5
Woodheys Primary School
  SALE M33 .... 153 H4
Woodhouse Primary School
  URM M41 .... 122 D4
Woodhouses Voluntary
  Primary School
  FAIL M35 .... 103 H4
Woodlands Hospital
  WALK M28 .... 80 B3
Woodley Health Centre
  MPL/ROM SK6 .... 161 H1

Woodley Primary School
  MPL/ROM SK6 .... 162 A1
Woodley Sports Centre
  MPL/ROM SK6 .... 146 D5
Woodsend Primary School
  URM M41 .... 121 D5
Woodside School
  WYTH/NTH M22 .... 169 E5
Woolfold Industrial Estate
  TOT/BURYW BL8 .... 37 G2
Woolworths Sports Club
  ROCH OL11 .... 42 B3
Worsley Business Park
  TYLD M29 .... 94 A2
Worsley Golf Club
  ECC M30 .... 109 F1
Worsley Road
  Industrial Estate
  FWTH BL4 .... 80 D1
Worsley Trading Estate
  LHULT M38 .... 79 D2
Worthington Primary School
  SALE M33 .... 155 G2
Worth Primary School
  POY/DIS SK12 .... 195 G4
Wright Robinson Sports College
  GTN M18 .... 130 A2

The Wycliffe Hotel
  EDGY/DAV SK3 .... 12 A7
Wythenshawe Hall
  Country Park
  NTHM/RTH M23 .... 168 A1
Wythenshawe Hospital
  NTHM/RTH M23 .... 167 G5
Wythenshawe Park Track
  NTHM/RTH M23 .... 167 H1
Xaverian Sixth Form College
  RUSH/FAL M14 .... 127 H5
Yeargate Industrial Estate
  BURY BL9 .... 39 G4
Yew Tree J & I School
  CHAD OL9 .... 89 G5
Yew Tree Primary School
  DUK SK16 .... 132 D2
York House Hotel
  AUL OL6 .... 117 H3
Y Sport & Leisure Centre
  CSLFD M3 .... 6 B6

Acknowledgements

The Post Office is a registered trademark of Post Office Ltd. in the UK and other countries.

Schools address data provided by Education Direct.

Petrol station information supplied by Johnsons

One-way street data provided by © Tele Atlas N.V. Tele Atlas

Garden centre information provided by:

Garden Centre Association   Britains best garden centres

Wyevale Garden Centres

Notes

Notes

Street by Street QUESTIONNAIRE

Dear Atlas User
Your comments, opinions and recommendations are very important to us.
So please help us to improve our street atlases by taking a few minutes
to complete this simple questionnaire.

You do NOT need a stamp (unless posted outside the UK). If you do not want to remove this page from your street atlas, then photocopy it or write your answers on a plain sheet of paper.

Send to: The Editor, AA Street by Street, FREEPOST SCE 4598,
Basingstoke RG21 4GY

ABOUT THE ATLAS...

Which city/town/county did you buy?
_____

Are there any features of the atlas or mapping that you find particularly useful?
_____
_____
_____

Is there anything we could have done better?
_____
_____
_____

Why did you choose an AA Street by Street atlas?
_____
_____
_____

Did it meet your expectations?

Exceeded ☐   **Met all** ☐   **Met most** ☐   **Fell below** ☐

Please give your reasons
_____
_____
_____
_____
_____

ML043z

continued overleaf

Where did you buy it?

For what purpose? (please tick all applicable)

To use in your own local area ☐   To use on business or at work ☐

Visiting a strange place ☐   In the car ☐   On foot ☐

Other (please state)

LOCAL KNOWLEDGE...

Local knowledge is invaluable. Whilst every attempt has been made to make the information contained in this atlas as accurate as possible, should you notice any inaccuracies, please detail them below (if necessary, use a blank piece of paper) or e-mail us at *streetbystreet@theAA.com*

ABOUT YOU...

Name (Mr/Mrs/Ms)

Address

                                                    Postcode

Daytime tel no

E-mail address

Which age group are you in?

Under 25 ☐   25-34 ☐   35-44 ☐   45-54 ☐   55-64 ☐   65+ ☐

Are you an AA member?   YES ☐   NO ☐

Do you have Internet access?   YES ☐   NO ☐

Thank you for taking the time to complete this questionnaire. Please send it to us as soon as possible, and remember, you do not need a stamp (unless posted outside the UK).